VALERO

THE
LAW OF CONTRACT

First Edition	.	.	.	.	*July 1945*
Second Edition	.	.	.	.	*June 1949*
Third Edition	.	.	.	.	*August 1952*
Reprinted	.	.	.		*November 1954*
Second Reprint	.	.			*November 1955*
Fourth Edition	.	.	.	.	*March 1956*
Reprinted	.	.	.		*December 1957*
Second Reprint	.	.			*September 1958*
Third Reprint .	.	.	.		*October 1959*
Fifth Edition	.	.	.	.	*April 1960*
Reprinted	.	.	.		*February 1962*
Second Reprint	.	.	.	.	*July 1963*
Sixth Edition	.	.	.	.	*March 1964*
Reprinted	.	.	.		*September 1966*
Second Reprint	.	.	.	.	*June 1967*
Third Reprint .	.	.	.		*February 1968*
Seventh Edition .	.	.	.	.	*April 1969*
Reprinted	.	.	.		*January 1971*
Eighth Edition	.	.	.	.	*September 1972*
Ninth Edition	.	.	.	.	*June 1976*

CHESHIRE AND FIFOOT'S
LAW OF
CONTRACT

NINTH EDITION

BY

M. P. FURMSTON
T.D., B.C.L., M.A.

OF GRAY'S INN, BARRISTER; FELLOW AND TUTOR IN
JURISPRUDENCE OF LINCOLN COLLEGE, OXFORD; LECTURER IN
COMMON LAW TO THE COUNCIL OF LEGAL EDUCATION

HISTORICAL INTRODUCTION
by
A. W. B. SIMPSON, M.A., D.C.L., J.P.

DEAN OF THE FACULTY OF SOCIAL SCIENCES AND PROFESSOR OF LAW IN
THE UNIVERSITY OF KENT AT CANTERBURY

LONDON
BUTTERWORTHS
1976

ENGLAND :	BUTTERWORTH & CO. (PUBLISHERS) LTD. LONDON: 88 Kingsway, WC2B 6AB
AUSTRALIA :	BUTTERWORTH'S PTY. LTD. SYDNEY: 586 Pacific Highway, Chatswood, NSW 2067 Also at MELBOURNE, BRISBANE, ADELAIDE, and PERTH
CANADA :	BUTTERWORTH & CO. (CANADA) LTD. TORONTO: 2265 Midland Avenue, Scarborough M1P 4S1
NEW ZEALAND :	BUTTERWORTHS OF NEW ZEALAND LTD. WELLINGTON: 26/28 Waring Taylor Street, 1
SOUTH AFRICA :	BUTTERWORTH & CO. (SOUTH AFRICA) (PTY.) LTD. DURBAN: 152/154 Gale Street
USA :	BUTTERWORTH & CO. (PUBLISHERS) INC. BOSTON: 19 Cummings Park, Woburn, Mass. 01801

©

G. C. CHESHIRE
ESTATE OF C. H. S. FIFOOT
1976

ISBN—Casebound: 0 406 56529 5
Limp: 0 406 56530 9

PREFACE TO THE NINTH EDITION

IT was one summer evening in Chipping Campden in 1965 that it was first suggested to me that I might like to collaborate in the editing of this work. Fortunately eleven years and two editions passed by before I was called upon to play more than a minor role and this is the first edition to appear without the active participation of the authors. I had originally hoped that Cecil Fifoot would oversee my work but his untimely death in January 1975 made this impossible. I have been greatly fortified, however, by his aid and advice in the past and by the continuing encouragement of Geoffrey Cheshire. Their imprint remains, of course, firmly on the book and its continuing merits are theirs. All errors and infelicities are mine alone.

One who essays to edit another's book has, no doubt, to steer between the Scylla of publishing one's own work under another's name and the Charybdis of excessive respect for the *ipsissima verba* of the original text. Critics may judge to which side the rudder has lent but the moment seemed appropriate for an anxious scrutiny of the whole text. It was soon clear to me that the historical introduction needed extensive revision and even more clear that I was incompetent to undertake it. I was exceptionally fortunate therefore that my former colleague Brian Simpson, now Professor of Law in the University of Kent at Canterbury agreed to undertake this task.

The most obvious change in the work is in the chapter on *The Contents of The Contract* which has been completely recast. Substantial rewriting has also taken place in the chapters on *Agreement, Consideration, Unenforceable Contracts* and *Privity of Contract.* A good deal of new material has been introduced but it has been possible to restrict the increase in the text to six pages by leaving out some of the detailed discussion of implied terms in contracts of sale and hire-purchase and by removing some material now largely of historical interest, especially on the formalities for corporate contracts at common law and on the capacity of married women to contract. I have attempted to state the law as it appeared to me on December 1st, 1975.

The preparation of this edition has left many debts of gratitude: to pupils and colleagues discussion with whom has illuminated many corners of this fascinating but elusive subject and especially to my colleague William Bishop who first introduced me to the mysteries of the competition provisions of the Treaty of Rome; to Mrs. I. P. Allen, Mrs. J. Dandridge,

Mrs. V. Lucas and Mrs. T. Tattersall, all of whom have struggled bravely with my impenetrable script and inarticulate dictation; to the printers for much guidance and encouragement and even more patience; to my five daughters for allowing me to work on many Sundays during the last year and to my wife but for whose encouragement the conclusion of the work would not have been possible.

LINCOLN COLLEGE, OXFORD.

April, 1976.   M.P.F.

PREFACE TO THE FIRST EDITION

PALEY, in the preface to his once celebrated *Principles of Moral and Political Philosophy*, remarks that " when a writer offers a book to the public upon a subject on which the public are already in possession of many others, he is bound by a kind of literary justice to inform his readers, distinctly and specifically, what it is he professes to supply and what he expects to improve." If we are to obey the first of these injunctions, we must say boldly that we profess to examine the principles underlying the English law of Contract, to indicate the difficulties which surround their application, to illustrate them from the accidents of litigation and the practices of life, and, where such a course seems profitable, to justify or excuse their vagaries by a reference to their history. To answer the second and more invidious injunction, we hasten to disown with Paley " any propensity to depreciate the labours of our predecessors, much less to invite a comparison between the merits of their performances and our own "; but we suggest that, even on so well-trodden a road, there is room for a new guide. *Anson on Contract*, for example, has directed the steps, not only of the present authors, but of generations of pupils. But the very success which has demanded the publication of eighteen editions has in some measure impaired its utility, and a mode of treatment, apposite sixty years ago, may be thought out of focus with present needs. *Pollock on Contract*, on the other hand, while it retains through successive editions the inimitable imprint of its distinguished author, does not profess to be comprehensive, and for this reason cannot be offered without support to the student.

Whether we have made out a case for a new book on Contract, still less whether we have succeeded in supplying it, is not for us to say. Once more to quote Paley, " of the execution the reader must judge; but this was the design." But we must be allowed one word of apology. The preparation of our book has been unduly protracted by the alarms and excursions of the last six years. Set aside in the early stages of the war, it was later resumed and had then to be largely rewritten. We are conscious that it has suffered in the process and that signs of over-writing may be apparent. Unexpected delays have aggravated the difficulty, always anxious, of absorbing current developments in Parliament and in the courts, in the business world and in professional literature, and have accentuated the feeling, ever present to authors of text-books, that they may pursue, but can never overtake, the fleeting vision of the law. We may only hope that we have set an established subject in a new perspective, neither disdaining older authorities where they are valuable nor citing new cases merely because they are novelties.

It is customary for authors to lighten their labours and resolve their doubts by importuning friends more learned than themselves. We are conscious that many of our colleagues, well qualified to advise, would have corrected our errors. But in the special circumstances in which the book had to be written, we felt constrained to forego this advantage and to accept, for good or ill, the consequences of isolated judgment. We cannot, however, refrain from acknowledging our debt to Mr. F. H. Lawson, M.A., Fellow of Merton College, Oxford, whose gift of illuminating a dark problem by a quick and penetrating observation has offered us fruitful suggestions which we have gratefully accepted. It is perhaps proper to add that, while each chapter has been separately prepared by one of the authors and then subjected to the criticism of the other, we accept joint and several liability for the whole.

OXFORD,

June, 1945.

G. C. CHESHIRE.

C. H. S. FIFOOT.

TABLE OF CONTENTS

PART I

HISTORICAL INTRODUCTION

PART II

FORMATION OF CONTRACT

PART V

CAPACITY OF PARTIES

PART VI

PRIVITY OF CONTRACT

PART VII

DISCHARGE OF CONTRACT

PART VIII

REMEDIES FOR BREACH OF CONTRACT

PART IX

QUASI-CONTRACT

INDEX

TABLE OF STATUTES

References to "*Statutes*" are to Halsbury's Statutes (Third Edition) showing the volume and page at which the annotated text of the Act will be found.

LIST OF CASES

PART I

HISTORICAL INTRODUCTION

SUMMARY

Historical Introduction

A. THE MEDIAEVAL LAW[1]

ENGLISH contract law as we know it to day developed around a form of action known as the action of *assumpsit*, which came into prominence in the early sixteenth century as a remedy for the breach of informal agreements reached by word of mouth—by " parol ".[2] As a coherent court-centred system the common law itself, the Royal law of the central courts, is much older, a product of the twelfth century. The early common law was largely concerned with serious crime and land tenure, and Glanvill, writing in about 1180, tells us that in his time,

> " . . . it is not the custom of the court of the Lord King to protect private agreements."[3]

Three centuries were to pass before the common law courts acquired a general jurisdiction over both formal and informal contracts. But the limitations upon the scope of the common law of contract at any given time did not mean that there then existed no forum for contractual business, but merely that remedies had to be sought elsewhere. For the common law evolved in a society served by a bewildering diversity of courts outside the common law system, enforcing a variety of bodies of law. Thus there were county courts, borough courts, courts of markets and fairs, courts of universities, courts of the Church, courts of manors, and courts of privileged places such as the Cinque Ports. Many such courts handled contractual business.[4] In addition the Court of Chancery in the fifteenth century developed an extensive contractual jurisdiction. The story of the growth of the common law, in contract law and elsewhere, is the story of the expansion of the common law courts' jurisdiction at the expense of other

---

1. BIBLIOGRAPHICAL NOTE: The principle secondary literature on the history of English contract law comprises: Ames, *Lectures on Legal History and Miscellaneous Legal Essays* (1913); Barbour, " The History of Contract in Early English Equity," Vol. IV, *Oxford Studies in Social and Legal History* (1914); Fifoot, *History and Sources of the Common Law, Tort and Contract* (1949); Holdsworth, *A History of English Law* (1922–66) esp. vols. III and VIII; Kiralfy, *The Action on the Case* (1951); Simpson, *A History of the Common Law of Contract. The Rise of Assumpsit* (1975); Stoljar, *A History of Contract at Common Law* (1975). There is also an extensive periodical literature, and much material is available in the publications of the Selden Society.
2. The account given in this introduction can only pick out certain salient developments, and is kept as free from technical detail as possible. The student can also usefully start by reading Baker, *An Introduction to English Legal History* (1971) esp. Chaps. IX, X and XVI, and Milsom, *Historical Foundations of the Common Law*, esp. Chaps. 10–12.
3. Glanvill, X. 18.
4. For examples see Fifoot, *History and Sources*, Chap. 13, and recently Helmholz, 91 L.Q.R. 406.

jurisdictions, and the consequential development—whether by
invention or reception—of common law with which to regulate
the newly acquired business.

**Contracts
under seal**

Mediaeval law was a formulary system, developed around the
writs which a litigant could obtain from the chancery to initiate
litigation in the Royal courts, and each writ gave rise to a particular manner of proceeding or form of action, with its individual
rules and procedures.[1] It is convenient, in setting out the
elements of mediaeval contract law, to differentiate between
formal and informal contracts;[2] not surprisingly formal contracts
were absorbed into the common law first. Then as now important contracts were made in writing, and it was the practice
to authenticate written documents by sealing them. Contracts
thus entered into soon became generally actionable at common
law by one of two forms of action. The action of covenant,
which came into common use in the thirteenth century, originated
as an action for the specific performance of agreements to do
something, such as to build a house, as opposed to agreements
to pay a definite sum of money; it developed into an action for
damages, assessed by a jury, for the wrong of breaking a covenant.
In the early fourteenth century this action came to be limited
to agreements under seal, and hence the term " covenant,"
originally meaning simply " agreement," came to mean " agreement under seal " as it still does. Where there was a formal
agreement under seal to pay a definite sum of money—that is a
debt—the appropriate form of action was debt " on an obligation." Such agreements were looked upon as grants of debts,
and the term " obligation " or " bond " was used to describe
the sealed document which generated the duty to pay. The
formality involved in sealing a document should not be over-
stressed—the seal might be very elaborate, or a mere blob of wax
impressed with a finger nail, but a sealed instrument was quite
essential.

Penal bonds

In practice, for reasons which are not fully understood, the
action of covenant was little used; instead important agreements
were commonly reduced to agreements whereby the parties
entered into bonds to pay penal sums of money unless they
carried out their side of the bargain. Thus if C wished to lend
D £100, D would execute a bond binding himself to pay C £200
on a certain day; the bond would have a condition that it became
void (a condition of defeasance) if £100 was paid before the day,
and D would hand over this bond as he received the loan of £100.
In, for example, a sale of land at a price of £100 the seller would
execute a bond binding himself to pay a penal sum *unless* he
conveyed the land as agreed, and the buyer similarly would bind
himself to pay a penalty *unless* he paid the price; disputes as to
whether the condition had been performed or not (and the
condition contained the real agreement) were triable by jury.
Such penal bonds with conditional defeasance could be adapted
to cover virtually any transaction, and were widely used as con-

1. Though in some respects now superseded the best introduction is still
Maitland, *The Forms of Action at Common Law* (1954).
2. For a fuller account see Simpson, *History*, Part I.

tractual instruments; they began to pass out of use in the late seventeenth century, when the court of chancery began to give relief against contracts involving penal provisions.[1] Until this development the vast preponderance of the common law of contract concerned bonds and the rules which governed them.

This law was flexible though tough, sometimes to the point of harshness; it was also highly developed in a complex case law. A creditor for example who lost the bond, or allowed the seal to come off, was remediless; a debtor who paid but failed to have the bond defaced remained liable. The debtor who defaulted was very much at the mercy of his creditor, who could, if he wished, have him imprisoned indefinitely for default. The institution, with its topsy-turvy treatment of the underlying agreement, gave rise to much law on conditions, for it was in the condition to the bond that the real agreement lurked. Hence in mediaeval law such matters as illegality and impossibility are largely dealt with in connection with conditions—is an illegal or impossible condition void? Some of this old law was later to be absorbed into the law of assumpsit, and the modern rules out-lawing penal contracts originate in the seventeenth centuries attack on the penal bond.[2]

So far as informal or parol agreements are concerned mediaeval common law was more restrictive.[3] One general limitation was financial; under the Statute of Gloucester (1278) an attempt was made to limit claims in the common law courts to those involving more than forty shillings, then a very large sum. This could be and was evaded; more serious were the restrictions developed by the courts themselves and associated with the relevant forms of action. Covenant, as we have seen, could not be used on parol agreements at all, and hence never grew into a general contractual remedy. Debt, and detinue, could however be brought, the former (known as debt *sur contract*) for claims to specific sums owed by informal transaction, for example the price of goods sold, or money lent, the latter to enforce claims to chattels due, for example a horse sold or lent. These two actions covered a very considerable area of informal contract law—sale of goods, bailment, loans of money. In a money economy a debt is the normal outstanding obligation, and so an action to recover debts will cover a very large field of demand. There were however serious gaps in the law; in particular there was no action for breach of an informal agreement to *do* something, for example build a house. Thus there was no action for failure to convey land, though the price of land sold could be recovered by debt. More generally the method of trial in debt and detinue on informal contracts was not jury trial, but compurgation. The defendant could swear an oath that he owed nothing, and bring eleven others to support his oath, and if they carried out the ritual correctly the action was lost; perjury might imperil the soul, but no temporal remedy existed. In the sixteenth century

Informal contracts

---

1. For a fuller account see Yale in Selden Society, Vol. 79, esp. at pp. 7–30.
2. See *infra*, pp. 607–611.
3. For a fuller account see Simpson, *History* esp. pp. 47–52 and 136–198; and on sale see Milsom, 77 L.Q.R. 257 and Fifoot, *History and Sources* Chap. 10.

compurgation (wager of law) came to be regarded as farcical, and oath swearers could indeed be hired for a modest fee.[1]   There existed other apparent defects in the law of debt and detinue; rules developed by the mediaeval courts came to be attached to these forms of action, and were immune from frontal attack. For example, executors were not liable on informal contracts; the debt died with the debtor.   Informal guarantees, and promises of marriage gifts were not actionable by debt, and the latter situation in particular provoked controversy.

When the common law courts provided no remedy, or one inadequate in some respect, the litigant had to go elsewhere, and in many cases this may not have been an unsatisfactory alternative.   But it is clear that there existed in the fifteenth century a considerable demand for the intervention of royal justice in areas not covered by the common law, in particular in the case of informal contracts, and this encouraged the fifteenth century chancellors to develop equitable remedies to supplement the common law.[2]   This may have been a factor which spurred the common law courts into taking action themselves to remedy the defects of their own system; although the maxim is that equity follows the law the historical process has often been the reverse.

B. THE ORIGIN OF ASSUMPSIT

The mechanism by which the old common law of informal contracts was supplemented, and eventually superseded, was an extremely curious one; it involved the use of a form of action which would not naturally appear to be concerned with contract at all. Back in the fourteenth century the common law courts developed a general jurisdiction over wrongs or torts (then called trespasses) in which the Crown had a special interest, typically those involving breach of the royal peace.[3] Actions of trespass (i.e. tort actions) were commenced by a writ form which was flexible, and writs could be drafted which were adapted to the special circumstances of the case—these were called writs " on the case." The method of trial in such actions was trial by jury, and the remedy damages, which the jury assessed.   Round about 1370 it came to be settled that such tort actions on the case could be brought to remedy purely private wrongs, not involving breach of the royal peace or any special Crown interest. Amongst actions brought about this time there were some where the plaintiff relied in his writ on an allegation that the defendant had entered into an informal arrangement with him, and then by misconduct caused damage in a way not envisaged by the transaction. Thus in a case in 1367, *Skyrne* v. *Butolf*,[4] the plaintiff sued a doctor to whom he had come for cure of the ringworm: he alleged that the defendant,

---

1. For an account see Baker, [1971] C. L.J. at pp. 228–30.
2. Barbour's account of this development has not been superseded, though published as long ago as 1914.
3. Milsom's articles in 74 L.Q.R. 195, 407, 561, have superseded all earlier work on the evolution of trespass and case.
4. Y.B. II Ric. II (Ames Series), 223.   For other examples see Fifoot, *History and Sources*, Chap. 14.

undertook (*assumpsit*), in London, in return for a certain sum of money previously paid into his hand, competently to cure [the plaintiff] of a certain infirmity.

Having set out these special circumstances, he went on to allege that the defendant had so negligently performed his cure as to cause damage. This form of trespass on the case has come to be called the action of assumpsit, the name being derived from the allegation in the latin pleadings that he undertook (*assumpsit*). The early examples all involve negligent misconduct after an undertaking.[1]

Such trespass or tort actions could no doubt be viewed as involving a liability based upon the breach of an informal agreement, and as being (in our terms) contract actions. But as tort actions they did not of course require the production by the plaintiff of any formal evidence under seal, and this could be exploited by lawyers who wished to sue on informal agreements at common law. In 1400 in the case of *Watton* v. *Brinth*[2] an attempt was made to bring such an action against a builder who had undertaken to build a house, but done nothing at all to fulfil his undertaking. This amounted to an attempt to achieve by trespass action what one could not achieve by action of covenant—sue on an agreement to do something without producing an instrument under seal. The court rejected the action; as was said in 1425[3] in a similar case by MARTIN, J.,

Misfeasance and nonfeasance

> " Verily if this action be maintainable on this matter, for every broken covenant in the world a man shall have an action of trespass."

To prevent this a curious compromise was reached: it came to be the basic doctrine of the fifteenth century that assumpsit lay for *misfeasance*, for doing something badly, but not for *nonfeasance*, doing nothing at all. Though attacked and qualified, and indeed at times rejected, the nonfeasance doctrine survived for over a century.

It was abandoned in the early sixteenth century in a series of cases[4] culminating in *Pickering* v. *Thoroughgood* (1533),[5] for reasons which are still not wholly clear, but may owe something to rivalry with chancery. SPILMAN, J., in that case said,

> " And in some books a difference has been taken between nonfeasance and malfeasance; thus on the one an action of covenant lies, and on the other an action on the case lies. This is no distinction in reason, for if a carpenter for £100 covenants with me to make me a house, and does not make it before the day assigned, so that I am deprived of lodging, I shall have an action for this nonfeasance just as well as if he had made it badly . . ."

The action for breach of promise

This was a momentous development, for the common law now had a form of action whereby in principle any undertaking could be sued upon: the action had become an action for breach of

---

1. For a fuller account see Simpson, *History*, Pt. II, Chap. 1.
2. Y.B. 2 Hen. IV, M. f. 3, pl. 9, Fifoot, *History and Sources*, p. 340.
3. Y.B. 3 Hen. VI, H. f. 36, pl. 33, Fifoot, *op. cit.*, p. 341.
4. See in particular *Orwell* v. *Mortoft* or *The Case of the Sale of Barley* (1505) Y.B. 20 Hen. VII M. f. 8 pl. 18, *Anon, Keilwey* f. 69 and 77 (Fifoot, *op. cit.*, p. 351) and the note, properly dated 1498, in Y.B. 21 Hen. VII, M. f. 41, pl. 66 (Fifoot, *op. cit.*, p. 353).
5. *Spilman's Reports*, Brit. Lib. M.S. Hargrave 388 f. 151a. For a text see Simpson, *History*, p. 628. These reports are being edited for the Selden Society.

promise, and the allegation of an undertaking was indeed commonly coupled with one of a promise. The action could now remedy breach of any informal agreement. It was triable by jury and led to the award of compensatory damages. This new departure gave rise to two problems, which preoccupied the courts in the sixteenth century. The first involved the relationship between assumpsit and the older forms of action, particularly debt *sur contract*. The second involved the evolution of a body of doctrine which would define which promises were actionable, and which not, a doctrine to define the scope of promissory liability.

C. ASSUMPSIT AND DEBT

Attempts were soon made to use assumpsit not to fill gaps in the law, but to replace the action of debt *sur contract;* the primary purpose of doing so was to deprive the defendant of his right to wage his law, and force him to submit to trial by jury. *Pickering* v. *Thoroughgood* (1533) is itself such a case, and from the 1520's onward the King's Bench allowed the plaintiff election between the older and newer remedies. The Court of Common Pleas by the 1570's took the same course, but in the late years of the sixteenth century the practice became a matter of acute disagreement between the courts of King's Bench and Common Pleas, the former court allowing assumpsit to supersede debt *sur contract*, whilst the judges of the latter court insisted that this was improper. The history of this dispute is complex[1] and to some extent still controversial; its complexity is increased by the general acceptance in sixteenth century law of a principle, variously formulated, whereby actions on the case ought not to be used simply as alternatives to older forms of actions. Great ingenuity was expended by progressives in reconciling this dogma with allowing election of remedies in practice.

Slade's Case   The dispute was settled in *Slade's Case* (1602),[2] after prolonged argument, and the view which triumphed was that of the King's Bench. The principal significance of this case was that by allowing plaintiffs to use assumpsit in place of debt *sur contract* (which they would always in practice choose to do) it produced a situation in which assumpsit became the general remedy on informal contracts, whether the plaintiff was complaining about a failure to pay a definite sum of money, or a failure to do something else—such as build a house. After *Slade's Case* the law of informal agreements was the law of a single form of action. About the same time another similar dispute between the courts was resolved in *Pinchon's Case* (1611)[3] when it was held that liability to pay debts, now enforceable in assumpsit, passed to the executors of the debtor; this case began the process of making simple contract liability passively transmissible.

---

1. The development has given rise to a considerable literature. See in particular Ames, *Lectures*, pp. 147 *et seq.*; Simpson, 74 L.Q.R. 382; Lücke, 81 L.Q.R. 422, 539; 82 L.Q.R. 81; Baker, [1971] C.L.J. 51, 213, Simpson, *History*, pp. 282 *et seq.*
2. 4 Co. Rep 92a, Yelv. 21, Moo. K.B. 433, 667; Baker gives further texts in [1971] C.L.J. 51.
3. 9 Co. Rep. 86b, 2 Brownl. 137, Cro. Jac. 293.

D. THE DOCTRINE OF CONSIDERATION

The other principal achievement of the sixteenth and early seventeenth centuries was the evolution of a body of doctrine to define the scope of the newly recognised promissory liability. Where assumpsit was merely taking over a long established liability, previously remedied by debt *sur contract*—such as liability to pay the price of goods sold—new doctrine was not urgently required; where innovation in the form of recognition of new contractual liabilities was involved it was. The answer given to the problems posed was the doctrine of consideration,[1] which is found in assumpsit cases around the mid-sixteenth century.[2] A " consideration " meant a motivating reason, and the essence of the doctrine was the idea that the actionability of a parol promise should depend upon an examination of the reason why the promise was made. The reason for the promise became the reason why it should be enforced, or not enforced. In contemporary thought a promise was a declaration of will, and the effect of the doctrine was to deprive a bare declaration of will of legal effect. Only a declaration of will supported by a good reason or motive bound the declarer to performance.

This basic idea was capable of great elaboration in two respects. Firstly, the courts could and did develop, case by case, a vast body of learning as to which reasons were good or sufficient, and which not. Would a promise in consideration of natural love and affection to a kinsman be actionable? Would a promise to pay a debt, in consideration that a debt was owed? Would a promise in consideration of a nominal payment? Here what starts life as a list of good considerations eventually comes to be summed up in terms of a general principle, the first attempt to formulate such a principle being found in Coke's argument in *Stone* v. *Wythipol* (1588),[3]

Consideration analysed

> " every consideration that doth charge the defendant in an assumpsit must be to the benefit of the defendant or charge of the plaintiff, and no case can be put out of this rule."

The reference to a " charge " is an echo of the passage in St. Germain's *Doctor and Student* (1530) where the author, in a critical discussion of contract law, offers the idea of induced reliance as an alternative theory of promissory liability to an analysis in terms of consideration.[4] But by 1588 detriment consideration had uneasily absorbed the idea that a promise should bind if the promisee had been induced to rely upon it.

Secondly, the courts evolved or adapted an analysis in temporal terms of the relationship between promise and consideration,

---

1. The history of consideration is controversial; in addition to the works listed, *ante*, p. 1, n. 1, see Holmes, *The Common Law*, Lect VII; Salmond, *Essays in Jurisprudence and Legal History*, pp. 187 *et. seq.*; Milsom, [1954] C.L.J. 105; Barton, 85 L.Q.R. 372.
2. The earliest assumpsit case in the printed reports to mention consideration *eo nomine* is *Joscelin* v. *Shelton* (1557), 3 Leon. 4, Benloe 57, Moo. K.B. 51: the consideration was a future marriage, and the case concerned a promised marriage gift or dowry.
3. Cro. Eliz. 126; a Leon. 113; Owen 94; Latch 21.
4. Selden Society, vol. 91, at p. 230.

which is first found in *Hunt* v. *Bate* (1568).[1]   A promise might be motivated by something in the past, for example a past favour: such a *past* (or executed) consideration was in general bad. A consideration might be some continuous state of affairs—such as the existence of a marriage—and this was a *continuous* consideration, and good.   A *present* consideration meant an act or promise contemporaneous with the promise, and a *future* (or executory) consideration—something yet to happen, such as a marriage not yet celebrated.   Into this analysis, which in part survives, was fitted the important rule that an actionable counter-promise would rank as a good consideration.

This rule was settled by 1589, when in *Strangeborough* v. *Warner*[2] it was said

Mutual promises

"Note, that a promise against a promise will maintain an action on the case. ...."

and seems to have originated in connection with bets, the earliest case being *West* v. *Stowel* (1577);[3] plainly unless an unperformed counter-promise is a good consideration, a bet can never be enforced.   When the plaintiff's promise was relied upon as a consideration it had to be a present consideration—i.e. contemporaneous with the defendant's promise, and as in the case of other present considerations the plaintiff did not have to perform before he could sue; in the case of a future consideration performance had to be shown, for without performance no consideration yet existed.   Seventeenth century case law settled that one party to such an agreement could not withdraw without the consent of the other, and thus it came to be law that wholly executory contracts were both binding and actionable.

But this was a highly unsatisfactory rule, for often it was not the intention that one party could sue without performing his side of the agreement, and a right of action represents a bird in the bush, as compared with actual performance—a bird in the hand. In time the courts evolved an intricate body of law whereby mutual promises where commonly treated as mutually dependent, the obligation to perform one side being treated as conditional upon performance of the other[4]. The involved old learning on dependent and independent promises was summed up in the notes to *Pordage* v. *Cole* (1669)[5] and *Cutter* v. *Powell* (1795).[6]

Origins of consideration

Whether the doctrine of consideration was an indigenous product, or in part derived from the doctrine of *causa promissionis* of canon or civil law, has long been a matter of controversy, and it cannot be said that its pedigree has yet been explained in a fully satisfactory way.[7]   Those who have seen it as a purely homespun product have sought its origin either in a doctrine associated with debt in mediaeval case law (the doctrine of *quid pro quo*),[8]

---

1. Dyer 272a.   See Simpson, *History*, pp. 452–465.
2. 4 Leon. 3.
3. 2 Leon. 154.
4. See Stoljar, *History*, Chap. 12 and the same author in 2 Sydney L.R. 217.
5. 1 Wms. Saund. 319.
6. 6 T.R. 320.
7. See Simpson, *History*, Pt. II, Chaps. IV–VII for a full account.
8. Notably Holmes.

or in the acceptance by the sixteenth century judges of a notion that only " bargains " (i.e. commercial contracts of exchange) should be enforced,[1] or in a transmutation of the need to show damage in a tort action into detriment suffered as a form of consideration in a contract action.[2]. The opposing view,[3] which the present writer has argued at length elsewhere, relates the early doctrine of consideration in assumpsit to the earlier doctrine of consideration in relation to uses of land (the ancestor of the modern trust) and sees its ultimate source in canon and civil law, though the precise mechanism of the reception remains problematical.

E. THE SEVENTEENTH AND EIGHTEENTH CENTURIES

The structure of informal contract law established in the Elizabethan period was essentially simple; as it was said in *Golding's Case* (1586),[4]

> " In every action upon the case upon a promise there are three things considerable, consideration, promise and breach of promise."

In essence this simple structure was not radically altered until the nineteenth century, when the essentially one sided or *unilateral* concept of an actionable promise was supplanted by the more complex conception of an actionable contract, a bilateral transaction. The seventeenth and eighteenth centuries saw an extensive development of commercial law and reception of the law merchant, but in basic informal contract law what was involved was largely elaboration rather than innovation. There were however certain areas of significant development, particularly in relation to the place of formality in contract law and to the enforcement of duties imposed rather by law than by the consent of the parties.

So far as the first is concerned assumpsit began life as an action on parole, that is to say verbal, promises, and its evolution into a general promissory remedy, limited by the doctrine of consideration, left the old law of formal written contracts under seal, appropriate to commercial and social contracts of real significance, untouched. Such contracts were actionable quite irrespective of consideration, and were normally embodied in penal bonds. Though never wholly superseded the traditional system of using formal contracts under seal for important transactions received a serious blow in the seventeenth century when the Court of Chancery began to grant relief against the penal element in such contracts, and by the eighteenth century the principle had emerged that,

Relief against penalties

> " Equity suffers not advantage to be taken of a penalty or forfeiture, where compensation can be made."[5]

This approach, soon adopted by the common law courts, canonised the compensatory principle in formal contracts, and it had already

---

1. Strenuously argued by Fifoot himself; see also Shatwell, 1 Sydney L.R. 289.
2. In different forms argued by Holdsworth and, recently, by Milsom.
3. In modern times first argued by Salmond.
4. 2 Leon. 72.
5. Francis, *Maxims of Equity* (1728).

been long accepted in assumpsit; hence the penal bond came to be less used. At the same time assumpsit, though in origin an action on verbal promises, could in principle be used where promises were *evidenced* in written documents, such as letters. Such use was no doubt encouraged by the increase in the practice of authenticating documents by signature or mark, and the general increase in the use of writing.

Statute of
Frauds

Against this background was passed the *Statute of Frauds* (1677).[1] The unregulated character of seventeenth century jury trial had made it, in the opinion of some, too easy for plaintiffs in assumpsit to bring actions on verbal promises inadequately proved; if the old system of wager of law had unduly favoured defendants, its supersession by *Slade's Case* unduly favoured plaintiffs. The remedy adopted was to require formality, in the new form of writing under signature, for actions on the more important agreements—for example on agreements to transfer interests in land, and contracts for the sale of goods worth more than ten pounds. The Statute, an essentially reactionary measure, produced a curious list of agreements which needed writing, and was from the start supplemented by the equitable doctrine of part performance; in the eighteenth century it provoked Lord MANSFIELD'S rational, if heretical suggestion, that the general structure of contract law needed revision, the doctrine of consideration being confined to contracts by word of mouth (where it originated), whilst written contracts under signature ought, like contracts authenticated by the more ancient seal, be actionable without proof of consideration. But this approach was emphatically rejected in the opinion of the judges in *Rann* v. *Hughes* (1778),[2]

> " All contracts are by the laws of England distinguished into agreements by specialty [i.e. under seal] and agreements by parol; nor is there any such third class as some of the counsel have endeavoured to maintain, as contracts in writing. If they be merely written and not specialties, they are parol, and a consideration must be proved."

Thus was an opportunity to rationalise the law defeated.

Quasi-contract

The seventeenth century also saw the extension of assumpsit into what came to be called quasi-contract.[3] The pleaders of the late sixteenth century evolved a form of assumpsit which came to be known as *indebitatus assumpsit*, where the plaintiff averred that the defendant was indebted to him (*indebitatus*) in a certain sum, and had promised to pay this sum. This was appropriate when a debtor was sued in the new action, and after *Slade's Case* (1602) sanctioned this use of assumpsit it came to be settled that in *indebitatus assumpsit* the details of the transaction generating the debt need only be set out in a summary form—the defendant would be said to be indebted " for the price of goods sold and delivered," " for money lent," " for work and services performed." These were known as the common *indebitatus* courts, and the promise to pay relied upon was normally implied only,

---

1. 29 Car II, c. 3.
2. 4 Bro. Parl. Cas. 27, 7 Term. Rep. 350n.
3. For fuller discussion see Jackson, *The History of Quasi-Contract in English Law*, in addition to the works cited *supra*, p. 1, n. 1.

and need not be proved. *Indebitatus assumpsit* was contrasted with *special assumpsit*, a form of pleading where the details of the transaction were set out " in detail " (specially). Now the action of debt had lain in the old law in any situation where a precise sum was due by law, whether the obligation arose from agreement, or by operation of law. In such cases the defendant was indebted, and at least from the late seventeenth century onwards *indebitatus assumpsit* could be used, as in *London City Corporation v. Goree* (1676)[1] were the action was for customary wharfage dues. This extended assumpsit to wholly fictitious promises. In addition a standard count was evolved in *indebitatus assumpsit* to recover money " had and received to the plaintiff's use," the earliest successful attempt being *Rooke v. Rooke* (1610).[2] The evolution of *indebitatus assumpsit* provided the courts with a procedure whereby, in the guise of promissory or contractual liability, any obligation to pay money which the law was prepared to recognise might be enforced; it opened the way to the assertion by Lord MANSFIELD in the great case of *Moses v. Macferlan* (1760)[3] that an action of *indebitatus assumpsit* on an implied promise could be brought whenever natural justice and equity required a defendant to return money. The courts also evolved a form of special assumpsit which lay on agreements to pay reasonable prices or remuneration—actions on a *quantum meruit* or *quantum valebat*. In the old law debt did not lie in the absence of any agreement for a definite sum, and this excluded *indebitatus assumpsit* which presupposed a debt; eventually the rule changed, and either special or *indebitatus assumpsit* could be used. Such actions again tended to blur the distinction between genuine promissory liability, and liability on implied or fictional promises, and thus laid the foundation for the extensive use of the concept of an implied promise in English contract law.

F. THE NINETEENTH CENTURY

The nineteenth century is usually regarded as the classical age of English contract law, and this for two reasons. The first is that the century witnessed an extensive development of the principles and structure of contract law into essentially the form which exists today, and this process appears to modern lawyers more significant when linked to the belief (which is perhaps too readily accepted) that until the industrial revolution contract law was somewhat crude and inadequate. The second involves a change in the attitude of thinking lawyers to contract. In previous years lawyers, in so far as they troubled themselves at all, conceived of contract law primarily as an adjunct to property law. In the nineteenth century a powerful school of thought, originating in the work of Adam Smith, saw in the extension of voluntary social co-operation through contract law, and in particular through " freedom of contract," a principal road to social improvement and human happiness, and one distinct from the static

---

1. 2 Lev. 174, 3 Keb. 677, 1 Vent. 298, Freeman 433.
2. Cro. Jac. 245, 1 Rolle 391, Moo. K.B. 854.
3. 2 Burr. 1005.

conditions involved in the possession of private property.   This
line of thought, variously developed, led firstly to an increased and
self-conscious emphasis on a policy summed up in the words of
Sir George Jessel in *Printing and Numerical Registering Co.
v. Sampson* (1875),[1]

> " if there is one thing more than another which public policy
> requires, it is that men of full age and competent understanding
> shall have the utmost liberty in contracting, and that their contracts,
> when entered into freely and voluntarily, shall be held sacred and
> shall be enforced by Courts of Justice."

Secondly, an increase in the moral dignity of contract encouraged
thinking lawyers to feel that contract law was of central significance
in the scheme of civilised legal regulation.   This development
lives on to this day in the presence of contract law, particularly
the law governing the formation of contract, in the core of legal
education.

Although many of the nineteenth century authorities on
contract are familiar as timeless living law, the period has been
relatively little studied from a historical point of view, and the
doctrinal history is, in consequence, still inadequately understood.[2]   It is clear however that the basic structure of the law of
assumpsit, as established in the sixteenth and seventeenth centuries, remained generally unaltered until the nineteenth century,
which saw a shift in emphasis from the essentially unilateral
notion of a promise, to the conception of a contract—a bilateral
conception—which generated rights and duties in the parties.
This process was accompanied by a very remarkable elaboration
in contractual doctrine, and the new doctrine was superimposed
upon the old ideas derived from earlier case law.   To a very
considerable extent the initial impetus for this elaboration came
from the treatise writers on contract, whose existence was a new
phenomenon in the history of English contract law.

For until 1790, when Joseph Powell published his *Essay upon
the Law of Contracts and Agreements*, there existed no systematic
treatise expounding the English law of contract, and no tradition
of writing such works.   Powell set out " to discover the general
rules and principles of natural and civil equity " on which the case
law of contract was founded, and he started a tradition in which
the present treatise stands.   Many contract treatises appear in the
nineteenth century, of which perhaps the most celebrated were
Chitty (1826), Addison (1847), Leake (1867), Pollock (1875) and
Anson (1879).   The new literature, lacking a native tradition,
leant heavily upon contractual writers in the civil (i.e. Roman)
law tradition, and in particular upon the work of R. J. Pothier,
the great eighteenth century French legal scholar whose work, a
product of the natural law tradition, profoundly influenced the
French Civil Code.   Pothier's *Treatise on the Law of Obligations*
was translated and published in England in 1806, after original
publication in 1761–64.   Appearing as it did at a critical period,
the new literature led to a partial reception of ideas derived from

---

1. L.R. 19 Eq. 462.
2. Recent periodical literature includes Nicholas, 48 Tulane L.R. 946; Horwitz,
   87 Harvard L.R. 917; Simpson 91 L.Q.R. 247. See also Fifoot, *Judge and
   Jurist in the Reign of Victoria.*

the civil law of continental Europe, many of which, adapted through the case law, remain as contractual categories, as chapter headings in the books, to-day.

Thus the doctrine of *offer and acceptance* first clearly emerges in the cases in *Adams* v. *Lindsell*[1] in 1818 as a mechanism for settling the moment of contracting in agreement by correspondence; it became a central doctrine, and in 1882[2] Sir William Anson was able to claim that

Offer and acceptance

> " Every expression of a common intention arrived at by the parties is ultimately reducible to question and answer."

The doctrine derives ultimately from a title in Justinian's Digest[3] which distinguishes between " pollicitations " and " promises," the former being promises made and not accepted; it first appears in English Law in Powell's treatise in 1790. Eventually the doctrine was even applied, albeit somewhat unhappily, to unilateral contracts in *Carlill* v. *Carbolic Smoke Ball Co.* in 1893.[4] The relationship between the new doctrine of offer and acceptance and the old requirement of consideration, which was re-emphasized as an essential in *Eastwood* v. *Kenyon* (1840)[5] was and remains difficult simply because two layers of development in contractual thought are involved.

Another new development was the reception of a requirement that there must be *an intention to create legal relations* for there to be a binding contract. The earlier common law scorned such a requirement for,

Intention to contract

"of the intent inward of the heart man's law cannot judge."[6]

The doctrine, in one form or another, was commonplace in continental legal thought, and versions are found in Leake (1867) and in Pollock's influential treatise (1875), the latter version being derived from the German jurist Savigny. It was received in the case law in *Carlill* v. *Carbolic Smoke Ball Co.* (1893) and accepted by the House of Lords in *Heilbut, Symons & Co.* v. *Buckleton* in 1913.[7]

More radically the nineteenth century case law came to emphasize what is variously called the " consensus " or " will " theory of contract. This asserts that contractual obligations are by definition self-imposed: hence any factor showing lack of consent is fatal to the existence of a contract, and conversely the rules governing the formation of contract are all conceived of as designed to differentiate cases of true *consensus*, where two wills become one will, from cases where *consensus* is lacking. In terms of the functions of the court this theory finds expression in the idea that the exclusive task of a court in contract cases is to discover what the parties have agreed, and give effect to it, except in cases of mistake, duress or illegality. This approach was not novel in English law, but it received a new emphasis from the

The will theory

---

1. 1 B. & Ald. 681.
2. Anson, *Principles of the English Law of Contract*, 2nd Edn., p. 15.
3. D. 50. 12. 3.
4. [1892] 2 Q.B. 484; [1893] 1 Q.B. 256.
5. 11 A. & E. 438.
6. St. Germain, *Doctor and Student*, Bk. III, Chap. VI, see sec. V.
7. [1913] A.C. 30.

text-writers, under the influence of foreign models; as Evans wrote in 1806:[1]

> " As every contract derives its effect from the intention of the parties, that intention, as expressed, or inferred, must be the ground of every decision respecting its operation and extent, and the grand object of consideration in every question with regard to its construction."

The ramifications of the will theory were extensive, and still influence both the law and the form in which it is expressed. Perhaps its most striking expression in nineteenth century legal development is to be found in cases dealing with *mistake*, for, given the premise,

Mistake

"Error is the greatest defect that can occur in contract . . ."[2] In consequence a doctrine of mistake follows inevitably. A good example of a case decided under the influence of a full blown *consensus* theory is *Cundy* v. *Lindsay* (1878),[3] the well known case on error as to the person; a more recent conquest may be *Bell* v. *Lever Bros.*[4] in 1932. Another branch of contract law much influenced by the will theory was the assessment of damages, when the landmark is the decision in *Hadley* v. *Baxendale* (1854),[5] which related the damages recoverable on breach of contract to the notional foresight of the contracting party when the contract was made; contract liability was self-imposed, and the contractor's liability was to be related to what he reasonably thought he was taking on. Later nineteenth century case law even required, in the case of unusual or special loss, a contract to bear that loss,[6] a notion close to Holmes' theory that a contract was really an agreement to pay damages in certain eventualities.[7] *Hadley* v. *Baxendale* itself was much influenced by the French Code Civil, and by Pothier, as well as by American literature on damages, and is a particularly good example of the reception of alien ideas.[8]

G. IMPLIED TERMS

The basic philosophy of the will theory confines the function of a court to enforcing the contract which the parties have made; when however a contractual dispute arises for which the express terms of a contract make no advance provision the court has of necessity to employ, in resolving the dispute, material not to be found in the terms of the express contract, and in the common law system the conceptual vehicle employed is the " implied term." In a sense the extensive development of the use of " implied terms " to supplement contracts, and at times to modify them, runs contrary to the credo of the will theory; in another

---

1. In Appendix V to his edition of Pothier's *Treatise on Obligations*, at p. 35.
2. At p. 152 of Vol. I of Evans' edition.
3. (1878) 3 App. Cas. 459. See *infra*, pp. 230–1.
4. [1932] A.C. 161. See *infra*, pp. 213–5.
5. 9 Exch. 341. For discussion see Washington in 48 L.Q.R. 90, and Simpson in 91 L.Q.R. 273–277.
6. *British Columbia Saw Mills Co.* v. *Nettleship* (1868), L.R. 3 C.P. 499.
7. See Holmes, *The Common Law*, Lect. VIII.
8. For recent discussion see Danzig, 4 Journal of Legal Studies 249.

sense it reconciles the will theory with activities of the courts which, in strict theory, ought never to be undertaken.

The use of the concept of an implied promise has a long history in the law of assumpsit; implied promises to pay debts had, for example, been used as a basis of liability in *indebitatus assumpsit*, and there are other early examples of the implication of promises by the courts to produce just results.[1] In eighteenth and nineteenth century law the courts made extensive use of the notion of an implied term to read into particular contracts normal or usual incidents of that type of contract. In doing so, whilst purporting to fill out the understandings of the parties, what might in reality be involved was the imposition *ab extra* of standards derived from continental mercantile law or civil law.[2] Thus in sale of goods the original position was *caveat emptor*. On an *express* warranty, if one had been given, it was possible to sue in tort for deceit; *Stuart* v. *Wilkins* (1778)[3] is the earliest reported case where action was brought on the contract, though the practice began rather earlier around 1750. The development of the notion of an *implied* warranty was a slow process. So far as warranty of title is concerned the law started from the position that there was no implied warranty; from the time of *Medina* v. *Stoughton* (1700)[4] the insistence on an express warranty began to be eroded, and by the time of the decision in *Eicholz* v. *Bannister* (1864)[5] the exception had for all practical purposes eaten up the rule; the development had taken a century and a half. So far as quality is concerned the principle of *caveat emptor* was never wholly abandoned. Although there is some slight evidence in eighteenth century law of an implied warranty of merchantable quality where a proper price was paid,[6] or at least of the imposition of liability where the seller knew of the defect, it was held in 1802 in *Parkinson* v. *Lee*[7] that there was no such implied warranty in the case of a sale by sample, and assumed that in general *caveat emptor* applied in the absence of fraud or an express warranty. But *Laing* v. *Fidgeon* (1815)[8] held that in a sale by description the goods must be merchantable, and *Jones* v. *Bright* (1829)[9] that there was an implied term that goods sold for a particular purpose were suitable for it. In these and following cases the courts built up the complex structure of implied obligations codified by Chalmers in the Sale of Goods Act of 1893. During the same period the courts were also using the concept of an implied term to impose a solution in cases where there had been mistake, and in cases where some drastic change of circumstances had affected a contract, as in the leading case of *Taylor* v. *Caldwell*.[10] In the implied term the courts possessed a conceptual device of great potential, but one which suffered from one major drawback—in

Implied terms in sale

---

1. See Simpson, *History*, pp. 491–493, 503.
2. No full historical study of the evolution of the implied term exists.
3. 1 Doug. K.B. 18.
4. 1 Salk. 210, 1 Ld. Raym. 593.
5. 17 C.B. N.S. 708.
6. See Horwitz, 87 Harvard L.R. 926.
7. 2 East 314.
8. 6 Taunt. 108.
9. 5 Bing. 533.
10. 32. L.J.Q.B. 164.

principle an implied term could never override an express provision, however unjust its operation.   Much of the development
of contract law in this century has been provoked by attempts to
grapple with this difficulty.

For history continues, and although the present century has
not perhaps witnessed so extensive a reformulation of the categories of contract law as the last, it has nevertheless produced a
considerable body of new law.   Thus the doctrine of frustration,
though its roots lie back in the early nineteenth century law on
charterparties, has acquired a prominence it never possessed in
the nineteenth century: again the doctrine of promissory or
equitable estoppel, though again based on nineteenth century
case law, has been put to new uses.   In a historical system of law
change has both to be fitted into the past, and if possible justified
by reference to it, and the manner in which new departures are
presented makes it peculiarly difficult to differentiate radical
innovation from mere elaboration of existing doctrine.   Perhaps
the most general significant change has been a general tendency
to reject the nineteenth century's confidence in the virtues of
freedom of contract and the associated will theory, without the
adoption of any very clearly formulated alternative.   But this is a
judgment we ought, perhaps, to leave to future historians.

PART II
FORMATION OF CONTRACT

SUMMARY

CHAPTER ONE

The Phenomena of Agreement

SECTION I.   INTRODUCTION

THIS book deals only with what are usually called *simple* contracts —agreements made either by word of mouth or in writing.[1] In addition to this normal type of contract, it has long been the tradition of English lawyers to speak of " contracts under seal," where a person undertakes an obligation by expressing his intention on paper or parchment, attaching his seal and delivering it " as his deed."[2] The phrase is misleading. It is true that, in the early law, the obligation engendered by the affixing of a

Scope of book

---

1. It has not been found easy to describe by a single epithet both the oral and the written contract, each of which has to be sharply distinguished from the so-called " contract under seal." In the earlier law the word " parol " was used, see *Rann* v. *Hughes* (1778), 7 Term Rep. 350, n., *infra*, p. 63; but it is scarcely apt to designate written as well as oral agreements, and it has generally been replaced in the vocabulary of the modern English lawyer by the word " simple," here adopted. Williston (*Contracts*, s. 12) and the American Law Institute *Restatement of the Law of Contracts*, s. 11, prefer " informal."

2. The solemnities formerly appropriate to the transaction have disintegrated in practice. The " seal " may be a wafer bought from any stationer, and the " delivery " appears to be only a matter of intention: see *Macedo* v. *Stroud*, [1922] 2 A.C. 330; Yale, [1970] C.L.J. 52. On the other hand, the party's signature is now required as well as his seal: Law of Property Act 1925, s. 73.

seal was regarded as essentially " conventional " or contractual.[1]
It is also true that, in the modern law, the deed plays its part.
On the one hand, it may still be necessary, in a few contracts
made with corporations before 1960, that they should have been
concluded by a document under seal.[2] On the other hand, if an
individual wishes to bind himself by a gratuitous promise, the
rule that all simple contracts require to be supported by the
presence of consideration forbids him to implement his intention
otherwise than by deed. If he complies with this formality, he
will doubtless be made to pay damages should he break his
promise. But he is thus bound, not because he has made a
contract, but because he has chosen to act within the limits of
a prescribed formula. The idea of bargain, fundamental to the
English conception of contract, is absent. So far, indeed, is his
liability removed from the normal notion of agreement that it
has even been held that a deed may create a legal duty in favour
of a beneficiary who is unaware of its existence.[3] The affinity of
the deed is with gift, not with bargain, and it is fair to say that
the so-called " contract under seal " has little in common with
agreement save its name and its history, and that it does not
seem to require detailed examination in a modern book upon the
law of contract.

Analysis of contract

The English law of contract, it has been seen, was evolved
and developed within the framework of assumpsit, and, so long
as that framework endured, it was not necessary to pursue too
fervently the search for principle. But when the forms of action
were abolished this task could no longer be avoided. The
lawyers of the nineteenth century, when they braced themselves
to face it, were influenced by two major factors.

Continental influence in the 19th century

The first was the example of continental jurisprudence. This
was felt primarily through the writings of Pothier, who drew an
idealized picture of contract in eighteenth-century France. In
1806 his *Treatise on the Law of Obligations* was translated into
English; in 1822 BEST, J., declared its authority to be " the
highest that can be had, next to a decision of a court of justice in
this country; "[4] in 1835 it was " strenuously recommended "
as a student's text-book;[5] and in 1845 Blackburn made copious
references to it in his work on Sale. It was not surprising,
therefore, that English judges should have been tempted to accept
his analysis of contract as dependent upon " a concurrence of
intention in two parties, one of whom promises something to
the other, who on his part accepts such promise."[6] More
belated, and directed largely upon academic lawyers, was the

---

1. *Supra*, p. 2.
2. *Infra*, p. 200.
3. See *Fletcher* v. *Fletcher* (1844), 4 Hare, 67; *Xenos* v. *Wickham* (1867),
   L.R. 2 H.L. 296; and *Lady Naas* v. *Westminster Bank, Ltd.*, [1940] A.C. 366;
   [1940] 1 All E.R. 485.
4. *Cox* v. *Troy* (1822), 5 B. & Ald. 474, at p. 480.
5, Samuel Warren, *A Popular and Practical Introduction to Law Studies* (1835),
   at p. 336.
6. *Treatise on Obligations,* Part I, section I, article I; see the English translation by Sir W. D. Evans, at p. 4. As late as 1887, KEKEWICH, J., declared
   that the definitions of contract in text-books " were all founded " on Pothier,
   though he himself preferred the " slightly different version " offered by
   Pollock; see *Foster* v. *Wheeler* (1887), 36 Ch.D. 695, at p. 698.

influence of Savigny. The first edition of Pollock's *Treatise on the General Principles concerning the Validity of Agreements in the Law of England* appeared in 1875, and the first edition of Anson's *Principles of the English Law of Contract* in 1879. The former was dedicated to Lord Lindley, who had first taught the writer " to turn from the formless confusion of text-books and the dry bones of students' manuals to the immortal work of Savigny."[1] The latter was equally ready to acknowledge a similar debt. " We may regard contract as a combination of the two ideas of agreement and obligation. Savigny's analysis of these two legal conceptions may with advantage be considered here with reference to the rules of English law." In the result, " agreement " was " necessarily the outcome of consenting minds." As Lord CAIRNS said in a contemporaneous and famous case, there must be " *consensus* of mind " to lead to contract.[2]

The weight of foreign jurisprudence was reinforced by a second factor, the pressure of insular economics. Sir Frederick Pollock once declared that " the sort of men who became judges towards the middle of the century were imbued with the creed of the ' philosophical Radicals ' who drove the chariot of reform and for whom the authority of the orthodox economists came second only to Bentham's." Their patron saint, he added, was Ricardo.[3] Individualism was both fashionable and successful: liberty and enterprise were taken to be the inevitable and immortal insignia of a civilized society. The State, as it were, delegated to its members the power to legislate. When, voluntarily and with a clear eye to their own interests, they entered into a contract, they made a piece of private law, binding on each other and beneficial alike to themselves and to the community at large. The freedom and the sanctity of contract were the necessary instruments of *laisser faire*, and it was the function of the courts to foster the one and to vindicate the other. Where a man sowed, there he should be able to reap. In the words of that formidable individualist, Sir George JESSEL, " if there is one thing more than another which public policy requires, it is that men of full age and competent understanding shall have the utmost liberty of contracting and that their contracts, when entered into freely and voluntarily, shall be held sacred and shall be enforced by courts of justice."[4] In more detached and less complacent language the sentiment was echoed by Henry Sidgwick in his *Elements of Politics*.[5] " Suppose contracts freely made and effectively sanctioned, and the most elaborate social organisation

Influence of economics

---

1. In the third edition, Pollock relegated Savigny to the decent obscurity of an appendix. Lord Lindley's interest in Continental legal thought was further evidenced by his translation in 1855 of Thibaut's *Jurisprudence*.
2. *Cundy* v. *Lindsay* (1878), 3 App. Cas. 459, at p. 465; *infra*, p. 230.
3. 39 L.Q.R. 163, at p. 165. It is suggestive that the judge chosen by Pollock as typical of the general attitude was Lord BRAMWELL, who sought persistently to champion the cause of " real " consent. See his judgment in *British and American Telegraph Co.* v. *Colson* (1871), L.R. 6 Exch. 108.
4. *Printing and Numerical Registering Co.* v. *Sampson* (1875), L.R. 19 Eq. 462, at p. 465.
5. (1879), p. 82: cited in Kessler and Gilmore, *Contracts, Cases and Materials,* 2nd Edn. (1970), p. 4. See the whole of the Introduction to this book, pp. 1–15.

becomes possible, at least in a society of such human beings as the individualistic theory contemplates—gifted with mature reason and governed by enlightened self-interest."

Nineteenth
century
assumptions
re-examined

Such were the assumptions of the common lawyers of the mid-nineteenth century who devised the doctrines and technique of the modern law of contract. But across the gulf of a hundred years both assumptions need re-examination.[1] That English judges and writers in search of principle should admit the claims of Continental jurisprudence was as natural as that their contemporaries should succumb to the more recondite charms of German philosophy. But the temptation, if intelligible, was dangerous. Pothier may have offered an engaging picture of French contract and Savigny an imaginative reconstruction of Roman law; but their tenets did not necessarily possess universal validity and would not inevitably flourish in alien soil. The common law has long stressed the commercial flavour of its contract. An Englishman is liable, not because he has made a promise, but because he has made a bargain. Behind all forms of contract, no doubt, lies the basic idea of assent. A contracting party, unlike a tortfeasor, is bound because he has agreed to be bound. Agreement, however, is not a mental state but an act, and, as an act, is a matter of inference from conduct. The parties are to be judged, not by what is in their minds, but by what they have said or written or done. While such must be, in some degree, the standpoint of every legal system, the common law, preoccupied with bargain, lays peculiar emphasis upon external appearance. As long ago as 1478 and in the context of sale Chief Justice BRIAN proclaimed " that the intent of a man cannot be tried, for the Devil himself knows not the intent of a man,"[2] and in the early years of the nineteenth century this position was re-asserted by judge and jurist alike. Lord ELDON protested that his task was not " to see that both parties really meant the same thing, but only that both gave their assent to that proposition which, be it what it may, *de facto* arises out of the terms of their correspondence."[3] So, too, Austin, after saying that " when we speak of the intention of contracting parties, we mean the intention of the promisor or the intention of the promisee," added " or rather, the sense in which it is to be inferred from the words used or from the transaction or from both that the one party gave and the other received it."[4] In the common law, therefore, to speak of " the outcome of consenting minds " or, even more mystically, of *consensus ad idem* is to mislead by adopting an alien approach to the problem of agreement. The function of an English judge is not to seek and satisfy some elusive mental element but to ensure, as far as practical experience permits, that the reasonable expectations of honest men are not disappointed. This is often compendiously

---

1. See Shatwell, 1 Sydney L.R. 289.
2. *Anon.* (1478), Y.B. 17 Ed. IV, Pasch. fo. 1, pl. 2.
3. *Kennedy* v. *Lee* (1817), 3 Mer. 441.
4. Austin, Lecture XXI, note 90.

expressed by saying that English Law adopts an objective test of agreement.[1]

Limits of individual-istic theory

The second factor has also to be re-assessed. Even when they wrote them, the words of Jessel and Sidgwick could hardly have been received without reservation. To make a serious promise certainly involves a moral duty to keep it: if it is part of what the law calls a contract the moral will be reinforced by a legal sanction. But the intrusion into the context of the epithet " sacred " is at best incongruous, at worst grotesque. Moreover, when these words are examined, it will be seen that, despite their apparent breadth, they are hedged about with qualifications. The men to be accorded " the utmost liberty of contracting " must be " of full age and competent understanding." They are to approximate as best they may to the heroes of an individualistic mythology and to be " gifted with mature reason and governed by enlightened self-interest." Even in the middle years of the nineteenth century the ideal was one to which few could attain. Society had long recognised the need to protect the young, the deranged, the blind, the illiterate. Common law and equity were moving in different ways and with hesitant steps to rescue the victims of misrepresentation and undue influence. It was accepted that, while private enterprise was the main road to public good, freedom of contract must at times yield to the exigencies of the State and to the ethical assumptions upon which it was based. But in less obvious cases the qualifications demanded by Jessel and Sidgwick of their contracting parties were more difficult to define and to secure. How were the courts to assess the due measures of " competent understanding " or to ensure that contracts were " freely and voluntarily made? "

Twentieth century changes

As the nineteenth century waned it became ever clearer that private enterprise predicated some degree of economic equality if it was to operate without injustice. The very freedom to contract with its corollary, the freedom to compete, was merging into the freedom to combine; and in the last resort competition and combination were incompatible. Individualism was yielding to monopoly, where strange things might well be done in the name of liberty. The twentieth century has seen its progressive erosion on the one hand by opposed theory and on the other by conflicting practice. The background of the law, social, political and economic, has changed. *Laisser faire* as an ideal has been supplanted by " social security "; and social security suggests status rather than contract. The State may thus compel persons to make contracts, as where, by a series of Road Traffic Acts from 1930 to 1972, a motorist must insure against third-party risks; it may, as by the Rent Acts, prevent one party to a contract from enforcing his rights under it;[2] or it may empower a tribunal either to reduce or to increase the rent payable under a lease.[3] In many instances

---

1. For an instructive debate as to how the objective test should be formulated and applied, see Spencer, [1973] C.L.J. 104 and Samek, 52 Can. Bar Rev. 351. An illuminating discussion of whether Anglo-American law was wise so wholeheartedly to accept the objective test will be found in the opinion of FRANK, J., in *Ricketts* v. *Pennsylvania R. Co* 153 F. 2d 757 (1946).
2. The earliest act was that of 1915. The law is currently to be found in the Acts of 1968, 1971 and 1974.
3. See, e.g. Rent Act 1974, s. 7.

a statute prescribes the contents of the contract. The Carriage of Goods by Sea Act 1924, contains six pages of rules to be incorporated in every contract for " the carriage of goods by sea from any port in Great Britain or Northern Ireland to any other port; "[1] the Supply of Goods (Implied Terms) Act 1973 (as amended by the Consumer Credit Act 1974), inserts into contracts of sale and hire-purchase a number of terms which the parties are forbidden to exclude;[2] successive Landlord and Tenant Acts from 1927 to 1954 contain provisions expressed to apply " notwithstanding any agreement to the contrary."[3] The erosion of contract by statute continues briskly.[4]

Mass pro-
duction and
standardized
contracts The process of mass production and distribution, which has largely supplemented if it has not supplanted individual effort, has introduced the mass contract—uniform documents which must be accepted by all who would deal with large-scale organizations. Such documents are not in themselves novelties: the classical lawyer of the mid-Victorian years found himself struggling to adjust his simple conceptions of contract to the demands of such powerful bodies as the railway companies.[5] But in the present century many corporations, public and private, have found it useful to adopt, as the basis of their transactions, a series of standard forms with which their customers have little to do but comply.[6] In the complex structure of current society the device has become prevalent and pervasive. The French, though not the English, lawyers have a name for it.

> " The term *contrat d'adhésion* is employed to denote the type of contract of which the conditions are fixed by one of the parties in advance and are open to acceptance by any one. The contract, which frequently contains many conditions, is presented for acceptance *en bloc* and is not open to discussion."[7]

The only choice left to the individual is to accept or decline the transaction *in toto*. The documents are *à prendre ou à laisser*, to take or to leave.

That the contract of adhesion offers massive organizations the temptation and the means to impose their will on the individual is obvious, and it is optimistic to suggest that the temptation will always be resisted. " Well organised commerce " has too often used it to deny all but the shadow of contractual power to the

---

1. See also the Carriage by Air Act 1961.
2. *Infra*, pp. 168–9.
3. See Landlord and Tenant Act 1927, s. 9, and Landlord and Tenant Act 1954, s. 17. By the Wages Council Act 1959, s. 12 (1), a statutory may replace a contractual term. See also 9 Halsbury's Laws (4th Edn.), para. 417.
4. E.g. Contracts of Employment Act 1972; Counter-Inflation Act 1973. See Kahn-Freund, 30 M.L.R. 635.
5. *Infra*, pp. 148–9.
6. An early standard form of contract is the Baltcon charterparty adopted in 1908 for use in the coal trade between the United Kingdom and the Baltic ports: see Rordam, *Treatise on the Baltcon Charterparty*, 1954. See also Sales, 16 M.L.R. 318, and the standard forms issued by the Institute of London Underwriters and re-printed in Appendix II of Chalmers, *Marine Insurance Act 1906*.
7. Amos and Walton, *Introduction to French Law* 2nd Edn. (1963), p. 152. See Kessler, 43 Col. L.R. 629; Friedmann, *Law in a Chanbing Society* (2nd Edn.), Chap. 4; Atiyah, *Introduction to Law of Contract*, (2nd Edn.), Chap. I; Lord Devlin, *Samples of Law Making*, Chap. 2; Thornely, [1962] C.L.J. 39 at pp. 46–49.

citizen.   Even if a particular customer is alive to the danger, he
will find it difficult or impossible to avoid submission to terms of
business generally adopted.[1]   Standard forms, it is true, need not
be sinister documents; as between parties who meet on tolerably
equal terms they may well be both sensible and convenient.   Yet,
for whatever purpose they are used, it may be doubted if much of
contract survives in them save the name.   They are rather
collections of rules made by an organization and imposed upon all
who belong to it or deal with it; and the judge is tempted to
approach them as though they were a body of bye-laws.   In 1952
a firm of builders undertook to construct a number of houses for a
local authority and the work proceeded on the terms of a " standard form of contract " issued by the Royal Institute of British
Architects and the National Federation of Building Trades
Employers.   A dispute arose between the parties which had to be
resolved by interpreting a single clause in the document.   " This
form," it was said, " is used in a great many building contracts
and, like other standard forms, it has come to resemble a
legislative code."[2]

If standard forms are thus to be regarded as legislative codes
the problems of interpretation are formidable.   Nor do they
become easier when, through indolence, ignorance or indifference,
parties borrow a clause from one form or even a section from a
statute and incorporate it in a contract to whose main purport it is
irrelevant or alien.   In 1962, striving to tame refractory words,
Lord REID said:

> " There is no wholly satisfactory interpretation or explanation of
> the third part of the clause, and one must choose between two almost
> equally unsatisfactory conclusions.   In a case like this, where a
> clause in common use has simply been copied, one cannot try to
> find what the parties intended.   They almost certainly never thought
> about things happening as they did."[3]

All these developments emphasise that to make a contract may
no longer be a purely private act.   It may be controlled or even
dictated by legislative or economic pressure, and it may involve the
courts in feats of construction akin to or borrowed from the
technique of statutory interpretation.   Yet it is possible to exag-
gerate the effect.   In daily life individual contracts exist and even
abound.   Moreover, as has already been said, the current law of
contract is essentially the creation of the nineteenth-century
lawyers, and it is this law which their successors have to apply
even in a new and uncongenial environment.   The tools of the
trade remain the same if they are put to uses that their inventors
neither envisaged nor desired.   What must be emphasized is the

---

1. See *Final Report of the Committee on Consumer Protection* (1962) Cmnd. 1781
   para. 435, and *Lowe* v. *Lombank, Ltd.*, [1960] 1 All E.R. 611; [1960] 1
   W.L.R. 196.
2. *Amalgamated Building Contractors, Ltd.* v. *Waltham Holy Cross U.D.C.*,
   [1952] 2 All E.R. 452.   See also *Atlantic Maritime Co. Inc.* v. *Gibbon*, [1954]
   1 Q.B. 88: [1953] 2 All E.R. 1086.
3. *Compania Naviera Aeolus S.A.* v. *Union of India*, [1962] 3 All E.R. 670,
   at p. 674; [1964] A.C. 868, at p. 882.   The connoisseur of interpretation
   will also savour the fluctuating fortunes of *Anglo-Saxon Petroleum Co., Ltd.*
   v. *Adamastos Shipping Co., Ltd.*, [1957] 1 All E.R. 673; on appeal, [1957]
   2 Q.B. 233; [1957] 2 All E.R. 311; [1959] A.C. 133; [1958] 1 All E.R. 725,
   where the judges strove valiantly to make sense out of nonsense.

external approach to the idea of contract which is so conspicuous a feature of the common law.   It is for this reason that the title of the present chapter is not *Agreement* but *The Phenomena of Agreement*, concerned not with the presence of an inward and mental assent but with its outward and visible signs.

SECTION II.   OFFER AND ACCEPTANCE: OFFER[1]

In order to determine whether, in any given case, it is reasonable to infer the existence of an agreement, it has long been usual to employ the language of offer and acceptance.   In other words, the court examines all the circumstances to see if the one party may be assumed to have made a firm " offer " and if the other may likewise be taken to have " accepted " that offer.   These complementary ideas present a convenient method of analysing a situation, provided that they are not applied too literally and that facts are not sacrificed to phrases.

It must be emphasized however that there are cases where the courts will certainly hold that there is a contract even though it is difficult or impossible to analyse the transaction in terms of offer and acceptance[2] for as Lord WILBERFORCE has recently said,[3]

> " English Law, having committed itself to a rather technical and schematic doctrine of contract, in application takes a practical approach, often at the cost of forcing the facts to fit uneasily into the marked slots of offer, acceptance and consideration."

Offer may be made to the world at large

The first task of the plaintiff is to prove the presence of a definite offer made either to a particular person or, as in advertisements of rewards for services to be rendered, to the public at large.   In the famous case of *Carlill* v. *Carbolic Smoke Ball Co.*[4] it was strenuously argued that an effective offer cannot be made to the public at large.   In that case:

> The defendants, who were the proprietors of a medical preparation called " The Carbolic Smoke Ball," issued an advertisement in which they offered to pay £100 to any person who succumbed to influenza after having used one of their smoke balls in a specified manner and for a specified period.   They added that they had deposited a sum of £1,000 with their bankers " to show their sincerity".   The plaintiff, on the faith of the advertisement, bought and used the ball as prescribed, but succeeded in catching influenza. She sued for the £100.

The defendants displayed the utmost ingenuity in their search for defences.   They argued that the transaction was a bet within

---

1. WINFIELD, 55 L.Q.R. 499; Kahn, 72 S.A.L.J. 246.
2. See e.g. *Clarke* v. *Earl Dunraven*, [1897] A.C. 59, discussed *infra*, p. 58.
3. *New Zealand Shipping Co., Ltd.* v. *A. M. Satterthwaite & Co., Ltd.*, [1975] A.C. 154, at p. 167; [1974] 1 All E R 1015, at p. 1020.
4. [1892] 2 Q.B. 484; affd., [1893] 1 Q.B. 256.   It should be noted that the plaintiff bought the smoke ball not from the defendants but from a chemist. In other cases English law has been reluctant to discover a contract between consumer and manufacturer where the consumer has bought from a retailer in reliance on the manufacturer's advertisements.   See *Borrie & Diamond, The Consumer, Society and the Law*, 3rd Edn., pp. 107–111. Cf. LEGH-JONES, [1969] C.L.J. 54.

the meaning of the Gaming Acts, that it was an illegal policy of insurance, that the advertisement was a mere " puff " never intended to create a binding obligation, that there was no offer to any particular person, and that, even if there were, the plaintiff had failed to notify her acceptance. The Court of Appeal found no difficulty in rejecting these various pleas. BOWEN, L.J., effectively destroyed the argument that an offer cannot be made to the world at large.

> " It was also said that the contract is made with all the world—that is, with everybody, and that you cannot contract with everybody. It is not a contract made with all the world. There is the fallacy of the argument. It is an offer made to all the world; and why should not an offer be made to all the world which is to ripen into a contract with anybody who comes forward and performs the condition? . . . Although the offer is made to the world, the contract is made with that limited portion of the public who come forward and perform the condition on the faith of the advertisement."

An offer, capable of being converted into an agreement by acceptance, must consist of a definite promise to be bound provided that certain specified terms are accepted. The offeror must have completed his share in the formation of a contract by finally declaring his readiness to undertake an obligation upon certain conditions, leaving to the offeree the option of acceptance or refusal. He must not merely have been feeling his way towards an agreement, not merely initiating negotiations from which an agreement might or might not in time result. He must be prepared to implement his promise, if such is the wish of the other party. The distinction is sometimes expressed in judicial language by the contrast of an " offer " with that of an " invitation to treat." Referring to the advertisement in the *Carlill* case, BOWEN, L.J., said: *(Offer distinguished from invitation to treat)*

> " It is not like cases in which you offer to negotiate, or you issue advertisements that you have got a stock of books to sell, or houses to let, in which case there is no offer to be bound by any contract. Such advertisements are offers to negotiate—offers to receive offers—offers to chaffer. . . ."

The application of this distinction has long agitated the courts. It arose first in the law of auctions, where the problem may appear in at least three forms. *(Distinction illustrated from auction sales. A bid is an offer)*

First, is the auctioneer's request for bids a definite offer which will be converted into an agreement with the highest bidder, or is it only an attempt to " set the ball rolling?" The latter view was accepted in *Payne* v. *Cave*.[1] The bid itself constitutes the offer which the auctioneer is free to accept or to reject. In accordance with this principle the Sale of Goods Act 1893, provides that a sale by auction is complete when the auctioneer announces its completion by the fall of the hammer or in other customary manner, and that until such announcement is made any bid may be retracted.[2]

Secondly, does an advertisement that specified goods will be sold by auction on a certain day constitute a promise to potential bidders that the sale will actually be held? A negative answer *(Advertisement of auction is not an offer to hold it)*

---

1. (1789), 3 Term Rep. 148.
2. Sale of Goods Act 1893, s. 58 (2).

was given to this question in *Harris* v. *Nickerson*.[1]   In that case
the plaintiff failed to recover damages for loss suffered in travelling
to the advertised place of an auction sale which was ultimately
cancelled.   His claim was condemned as " an attempt to make a
mere declaration of intention a binding contract."   In the words
of BLACKBURN, J.:

> " This is certainly a startling proposition and would be excessively
> inconvenient if carried out.   It amounts to saying that anyone who
> advertises a sale by publishing an advertisement becomes responsible
> to everybody who attends the sale for his cab hire or travelling
> expenses."

Auction
without
reserve

Thirdly, does an advertisement that the sale will be *without
reserve* constitute a definite offer to sell to the highest bidder?   A
Scottish court has denied that this is so, holding, in accordance
with the general rule, that no agreement is complete unless and
until the auctioneer acknowledges the acceptance of the bid by
the fall of his hammer.[2]   The point has not yet been decided in
England, though it was the subject of *obiter dicta* in *Warlow* v.
Harrison.[3]   The action in that case failed both in the Queen's
Bench and in the Court of Exchequer Chamber because the
plaintiff pleaded his claim upon an obviously incorrect ground.
But three of the judges in the Exchequer Chamber were of
opinion that he would succeed if he brought a fresh action pleading that the auctioneer by his advertisement had implicitly pledged
himself to sell to the highest bidder.   In the view of these judges,
two separate questions must be disentangled.   On the one hand,
had a contract of sale been concluded, and, if so, at what moment
of time?   Since the advertisement was not itself an offer to sell
the goods but only an " invitation to treat," the plaintiff's bid
was not an acceptance and did not constitute a sale.   Was there,
on the other hand, a binding promise that the sale should be
without reserve?   The majority of the Exchequer Chamber
were prepared to discover such a promise.   The auctioneer in
his advertisement had made a definite offer to this effect, and the
plaintiff, by making his bid in reliance upon it, had accepted the
offer.   This constituted a distinct and independent contract, and
for its breach an action would lie.   This view was described by
BLACKBURN, J., in *Harris* v. *Nickerson*[4] as resting upon " very
plausible grounds."   But it is not beyond criticism.   It is indis-
putable that the mere advertisement of an auction, without
further qualification, is an invitation to treat and not an offer.
The auction need not be held, and prospective purchasers have
no legal complaint if they have wasted their time and money in
coming to the sale rooms.   But, if the *dicta* in *Warlow* v. *Harrison*
are correct, the addition to the advertisement of the two words
" without reserve " converts it into an offer, presumably to the
public at large, that the sale will in fact be subject to no reserve
price.   If, in these circumstances, the sale is actually held and a

---

1. (1873), L.R. 8 Q.B. 286.
2. *Fenwick* v. *Macdonald, Fraser & Co.* (1904), 6 F. (Ct. of Sess.) 850.
3. (1859), 1 E. & E. 309; see *Johnston* v. *Boyes*, [1899] 2 Ch. 73, and *Rainbow*
   v. *Howkins & Sons,* [1904] 2 K.B. 322.
4. (1873), L.R. 8 Q.B. 286, at p. 288.

prospective purchaser makes a bid, he accepts the offer of a sale " without reserve," and the auctioneer, if he then puts a reserve price upon any of the lots, is liable to an action for breach of contract. But if the auctioneer were to refuse to hold any sale at all, he would not be breaking any binding promise and could not be sued.[1]

The distinction between an offer and an invitation to treat has been applied in other everyday practices. The issue, for instance, of a circular or catalogue advertising goods for sale is a mere attempt to induce offers, not an offer itself.[2] Lord HERSCHELL has exposed the inconvenience of a contrary interpretation:

Instances of invitation to treat

> " The transmission of such a price-list does not amount to an offer to supply an unlimited quantity of the wine described at the price named, so that as soon as an order is given there is a binding contract to supply that quantity. If it were so, the merchant might find himself involved in any number of contractual obligations to supply wine of a particular description which he would be quite unable to carry out, his stock of wine of that description being necessarily limited."[3]

In *Partridge* v. *Crittenden*[4] the appellant had inserted in a periodical entitled *Cage and Aviary Birds* a notice " Bramblefinch cocks and hens, 25s. each." It appeared under the general heading of " Classified Advertisements " and the words " offer for sale " were not used. He was charged with unlawfully offering for sale a wild live bird contrary to the provisions of the Protection of Birds Act 1954, and was convicted. The divisional court quashed the conviction. There had been no " offer for sale." Lord PARKER said:[5]

> " I think that when one is dealing with advertisements and circulars, unless indeed they come from manufacturers, there is business sense in their being construed as invitations to treat and not offers for sale."

A not dissimilar question long remained undecided. If goods are exhibited in a shop-window or inside a shop with a price attached, does this constitute an offer to sell at that price? PARKE, B., at least felt no doubt about the matter, for, when counsel suggested that: " If a man advertises goods at a certain price, I have a right to go into his shop and demand the article at the price marked," the learned judge peremptorily cut him short with the reply: " No; if you do, he has a right to turn you out."[6] This view was confirmed in *Pharmaceutical Society of Great Britain* v. *Boots Cash Chemists (Southern), Ltd.*[7]

---

1. See Slade, 68 L.Q.R. 238; 69 L.Q.R. 21. Cf. Gower, 68 L.Q.R. 457. Support for the two contract analysis can be found in *Tully* v. *Irish Land Commission* (1961), 97 I.L.T.R. 174.
2. Cf. *Spencer* v. *Harding* (1870), L.R. 5 C.P. 561.
3. *Grainger & Son* v. *Gough*, [1896] A.C. 325, at p. 334. A similar rule has been applied to the notice of a scholarship: *Rooke* v. *Dawson*, [1895] 1 Ch. 480.
4. [1968] 2 All E.R. 421; [1968] 1 W.L.R. 1204.
5. [1968] 2 All E.R. 421, at p. 424; [1968] 1 W.L.R. 1204, at p. 1209.
6. *Timothy* v. *Simpson* (1834), 6 C. & P. 499, at p. 500.
7. [1952] 2 Q.B. 795; [1952] 2 All E.R. 456; affd., [1953] 1 Q.B. 401; [1953] 1 All E.R. 482.

The defendants adapted one of their shops to a " self-service " system.   A customer, on entering, was given a basket and, having selected from the shelves the articles he required, put them in the basket and took them to the cash desk.   Near the desk was a registered pharmacist who was authorized, if necessary, to stop a customer from removing any drug from the shop.

The court had to decide whether the defendants had broken the provisions of s. 18 of the Pharmacy and Poisons Act 1933, which made it unlawful to sell any listed poison " unless the sale is effected under the supervision of a registered pharmacist." The vital question was at what time the " sale " took place, and this depended in turn on whether the display of the goods with prices attached was an offer or an invitation to treat.   According to the plaintiffs, it was an offer, accepted when the customer put an article into his basket, and, if this article was a poison, it was therefore " sold " before the pharmacist could intervene.   According to the defendants, the display was only an invitation to treat. An offer to buy was made when the customer put an article in the basket, and this offer the defendants were free to accept or to reject.   If they accepted, they did so only when the transaction was approved by the pharmacist near the cash-desk.   Lord GODDARD, at first instance, had no hesitation in deciding that the display was only an invitation to treat so that the law had not been broken, and the Court of Appeal upheld his decision and adopted his reasoning.

> " The transaction," he said,[1] " is in no way different from the normal transaction in a shop in which there is no self-service scheme. I am quite satisfied it would be wrong to say that the shopkeeper is making an offer to sell every article in the shop to any person who might come in and that that person can insist on buying any article by saying ' I accept your offer.'   I agree with the illustration put forward during the case of a person who might go into a shop where books are displayed.   In most book-shops customers are invited to go in and pick up books and look at them even if they do not actually buy them.   There is no contract by the shopkeeper to sell until the customer has taken the book to the shopkeeper or his assistant and said ' I want to buy this book ' and the shopkeeper says ' Yes.'   That would not prevent the shopkeeper, seeing the book picked up, saying: ' I am sorry I cannot let you have that book; it is the only copy I have got and I have already promised it to another customer.'   Therefore, in my opinion, the mere fact that a customer picks up a bottle of medicine from the shelves in this case does not amount to an acceptance of an offer to sell.   It is an offer by the customer to buy, and there is no sale effected until the buyer's offer to buy is accepted by the acceptance of the price."

In *Fisher* v. *Bell*[2] Lord PARKER treated the point as beyond dispute.

> " It is clear that, according to the ordinary law of contract, the display of an article with a price on it in a shop window is merely an

---

1. [1952] 2 Q.B. 795, at p. 802; [1952] 2 All E.R. 456, at pp. 458, 459.
2. [1961] 1 Q.B. 394, at p. 399: [1960] 3 All E.R. 731, at p. 733.

invitation to treat.   It is in no sense an offer for sale, the acceptance
of which constitutes a contract."[1]

It is surprising that in other matters of daily life the legal
position remains doubtful.   If a passenger boards a bus, is he
accepting an offer of carriage or is he himself making an offer in
response to an invitation to treat?   In *Wilkie* v. *London Passenger
Transport Board*,[2] Lord GREENE thought that a contract is made
when an intending passenger " puts himself either on the platform
or inside the bus."   The opinion was *obiter*;[3] but if it represents
the law it would seem that the corporation makes an offer of
carriage by running the bus and that the passenger accepts the
offer when he gets properly on board.   The contract would then
be complete even if no fare is yet paid or ticket given.

Negotiations for the sale of land present no difference of
principle.   But they may involve the adjustment of so many
questions of detail that the courts will require cogent evidence of
an intention to be bound before they will find the existence of
an offer capable of acceptance.   Thus in *Harvey* v. *Facey*,[4]

Negotiations for sale of land

> the plaintiffs telegraphed to the defendants, " Will you sell us
> Bumper Hall Pen?   Telegraph lowest cash price."   The defendants
> telegraphed in reply, " Lowest price for Bumper Hall Pen, £900."
> The plaintiffs then telegraphed, " We agree to buy Bumper Hall
> Pen for £900 asked by you.   Please send us your title-deeds."   The
> rest was silence.

It was held by the Judicial Committee of the Privy Council that
there was no contract.   The second telegram was not an offer,
but only an indication of the minimum price if the defendants
ultimately resolved to sell, and the third telegram was therefore
not an acceptance.   So, too, in *Clifton* v. *Palumbo*,[5] the plaintiff
and the defendant were negotiating for the sale of a large, scattered
estate.   The plaintiff wrote to the defendant:

> " I . . . am prepared to offer you or your nominee my Lytham
> estate for £600,000 . . .   I also agree that a reasonable and sufficient
> time shall be granted to you for the examination and consideration
> of all the data and details necessary for the preparation of the
> Schedule of Completion."

The Court of Appeal held that this letter was not a definite offer
to sell, but a preliminary statement as to price, which—especially

---

1. Although the rule is well settled, its application to self service stores has been
   criticised.   See Unger 16 M.L.R. 369; Cf. Montrose 4 Am. J. Comp.
   Law 235.   Display of goods in a self service store was held an offer in
   Lasky v. *Economy Grocery Stores* 319 Mass. 224, 65 N.E. 2d 305 (1946)
   and display of deck chairs on a beach an offer to hire in *Chapelton* v. *Barry
   Urban District Council*, [1940] 1 K.B. 532; [1940] 1 All E.R. 356.   In
   practice the question has usually arisen in the context of a criminal statute
   making it an offence to " offer " goods of a prescribed description for sale.
   Display of goods in a shop window may well fall within the mischief of such a
   statute and a well drafted statute may contain a special wider definition of
   " offer."   See e.g. Trade Descriptions Act 1968, s. 6.   See further on the
   application of offer and acceptance to criminal offences, Smith, [1972 B]
   C.L.J. 197, at pp. 198–201, 204–208.
2. [1947] 1 All E.R. 258.
3. The Court of Appeal held on the facts that the plaintiff had not made a
   contract with the Board, but was only a licensee.   See also *infra*, p. 157.
4. [1893] A.C. 552.
5. [1944] 2 All E.R. 497.

in a transaction of such magnitude—was but one of the many questions to be considered.   In the words of Lord GREENE,[1]

> " There is nothing in the world to prevent an owner of an estate of this kind contracting to sell it to a purchaser, who is prepared to spend so large a sum of money, on terms written out on a half sheet of note paper of the most informal description and even, if he likes, on unfavourable conditions.   But I think it is legitimate, in approaching the construction of a document of this kind, containing phrases and expressions of doubtful significance, to bear in mind that the probability of parties entering into so large a transaction, and finally binding themselves to a contract of this description couched in such terms, is remote.   If they have done it, they have done it, however unwise and however unbusinesslike it may be. The question is, Have they done it? "

Both *Harvey* v. *Facey* and *Clifton* v. *Palumbo* were distinguished in *Bigg* v. *Boyd Gibbins, Ltd.*[2]   The Court of Appeal, on the facts before them, here held that the parties were not still negotiating, but had agreed on a price and made a contract.   After reading the relevant letters, RUSSELL, L.J. said that he could not " escape the view that the parties would regard themselves at the end of the correspondence, quite correctly, as having struck a bargain for the sale and purchase of the property."[3]

SECTION III.   OFFER AND ACCEPTANCE: ACCEPTANCE

Offer and acceptance

Proof of an offer to enter into legal relations upon definite terms must be followed by the production of evidence from which the courts may infer an intention by the offeree to accept that offer.   It must again be emphasized that the phrase " offer and acceptance," though hallowed by a century and a half of judicial usage,[4] is not to be applied as a talisman, revealing, by a species of esoteric art, the presence of a contract.   It would be ludicrous to suppose that business men couch their communications in the form of a catechism or reduce their negotiations to such a species of interrogatory as was , formulated in the Roman *stipulatio*. The rules which the judges have elaborated from the premise of offer and acceptance are neither the rigid deductions of logic nor the inspiration of natural justice.   They are only presumptions, drawn from experience, to be applied in so far as they serve the ultimate object of establishing the phenomena of agreement, and their application may be observed under two heads, (A) the fact of acceptance and (B) the communication of acceptance.

---

1. *Ibid.*, at p. 499.
2. [1971] 2 All E.R. 183, especially at p. 185; [1971] 1 W.L.R. 913. See also *Storer* v. *Manchester City Council*, [1974] 3 All E.R. 824; [1974] 1 W.L.R. 1403.
3. Cf. Prichard, 90 L.Q.R. 55.
4. See *Adams* v. *Lindsell* (1818) 1 B. & Ald. 681; Simpson 91 L.Q.R. 247, at pp. 258–262.

A. THE FACT OF ACCEPTANCE

Whether there has been an acceptance by one party of an offer made to him by the other may be collected from the words or documents that have passed between them or may be inferred from their conduct. The task of inferring an assent and of fixing the precise moment at which it may be said to have emerged is one of obvious difficulty, particularly when the negotiations between the parties have covered a long period of time or are contained in protracted or desultory correspondence.

This may be observed in the case of *Brogden* v. *Metropolitan Rail Co.*[1]

> Brogden had for years supplied the defendant company with coal without a formal agreement. At length the parties decided to regularize their relations. The company's agent sent a draft form of agreement to Brogden, and the latter, having inserted the name of an arbitrator in a space which had been left blank for this purpose, signed it and returned it, marked " approved ". The company's agent put it in his desk and nothing further was done to complete its execution. Both parties acted thereafter on the strength of its terms, supplying and paying for the coal in accordance with its clauses, until a dispute arose between them and Brogden denied that any binding contract existed.

The difficulty was to determine when, if ever, a mutual assent was to be found. It could not be argued that the return of the draft was an acceptance of the company's offer, since Brogden, by inserting the name of an arbitrator, had added a new term, which the company had had no opportunity of approving or rejecting. But assuming that the delivery of the document by Brogden to the company, with the addition of the arbitrator's name, was a final and definite offer to supply coal on the terms contained in it, when was that offer accepted? No further communication passed between the parties, and it was impossible to infer assent from the mere fact that the document remained without remark in the agent's desk. On the other hand, the subsequent conduct of the parties was explicable only on the assumption that they mutually approved the terms of the draft. The House of Lords held that a contract came into existence either when the company ordered its first load of coal from Brogden upon these terms or at least when Brogden supplied it.[2]

Whatever the difficulties, and however elastic their rules, the judges must, either upon oral evidence or by the construction of documents, find some act from which they can infer the offeree's intention to accept, or they must refuse to admit the existence of an agreement. This intention, moreover, must be conclusive. It must not treat the negotiations between the parties as still open to the process of bargaining. The offeree must unreservedly assent to the exact terms proposed by the offeror. If, while purporting to accept the offer as a whole, he introduces a new term which the offeror has not had the chance of examining, he is in fact merely making a counter-offer. The effect of this in

Marginal notes:

Agreement may be inferred from conduct

Counter-offer is a final rejection of original offer

---

1. (1877), 2 App. Cas. 666.
2. See also *Robophone Facilities, Ltd.* v. *Blank*, [1966] 3 All E.R. 128; [1966] 1 W.L.R. 1428.

the eyes of the law is to destroy the original offer. Thus in *Hyde* v. *Wrench*,[1]

> the defendant on June 6th offered to sell an estate to the plaintiff for £1,000. On June 8th, in reply, the plaintiff made an offer of £950, which was refused by the defendant on June 27th. Finally, on June 29th, the plaintiff wrote that he was now prepared to pay £1,000.

It was held that no contract existed. By his letter of June 8th the plaintiff had rejected the original offer and he was no longer able to revive it by changing his mind and tendering a subsequent acceptance.

Distinction between counter-offer and request for informationWhether a communication amounts to a counter-offer or not is sometimes difficult to determine. The offeree, for example, may reply to the offer in terms which leave it uncertain whether he is making a counter-offer or merely seeking further information before making up his mind. A mere request for information obviously does not destroy the offer. A relevant and instructive case is *Stevenson* v. *McLean*.[2]

> The defendant offered on Saturday to sell to the plaintiffs 3,800 tons of iron " at 40s. nett cash per ton, open till Monday." Early on Monday the plaintiffs telegraphed to the defendant: " Please wire whether you would accept 40 for delivery over two months, or if not longest limit you would give." No reply was received, so by a telegram sent at 1.34 p.m. on the same day the plaintiffs accepted the offer to sell at 40s. cash. Meanwhile the defendant sold the iron to a third person and informed the plaintiffs of this in a telegram despatched at 1.25 p.m. The telegrams crossed.

The plaintiffs sued to recover damages for breach of contract. They would be entitled to succeed if the original offer was still open when they sent their telegram at 1.34 p.m., for, as will be seen later, an acceptance is complete and effective at the moment when a letter is posted or a telegram is handed in to the post office. But was the first telegram sent by the plaintiffs a counter-offer which destroyed the offer, or was it an innocuous request for information? It might be regarded either as the proposal of a new term or as an inquiry put forward tentatively in the hope of inducing better terms but without any intention to prejudice the position of the plaintiffs if they ultimately decided to accept the original offer. Either construction was reasonable. In the result LUSH, J., held that the plaintiffs had not made a counter-offer, but had addressed to the defendant " a mere inquiry, which should have been answered and not treated as a rejection of the offer."[3]

Conditional assent is not acceptanceA conditional assent to an offer does not constitute acceptance. A man who, though content with the general details of a proposed transaction, feels that he requires expert guidance before committing himself to a binding obligation, often makes his acceptance conditional upon the advice of some third party, such as a solicitor. The result is that neither party is subject to an obligation. A common example of this in everyday life occurs in the case of a purchase or a lease of land. Here it is the almost invariable

---

1. (1840), 3 Beav. 334; and see *Brogden* v. *Metropolitan Rail Co., supra,* p. 33.
2. (1880), 5. Q.B.D. 346.
3. (1880), 5 Q.B.D., at p. 350.

practice to incorporate the terms, after they have been settled, in a signed document which contains some such incantation as "subject to contract," or "subject to a formal contract to be drawn up by our solicitors." Unless there is cogent evidence of a contrary intention, the courts construe these words so as to postpone the incidence of liability until a formal document has been drafted and signed. As regards enforceability the first document is not worth the paper it is written on. It is merely a proposal to enter into a contract—a transaction which is a legal nullity—and it may be disregarded by either party with impunity. Until the completion of the formal contract both parties enjoy a *locus pœnitentiæ*.[1] In the case of *Branca* v. *Cobarro*[2] the court was presented with a delicate question of construction:

> A vendor agreed to sell the lease and goodwill of a mushroom farm on the terms of a written document which was declared to be "a provisional agreement until a fully legalised agreement, drawn up by a solicitor and embodying all the conditions herewith stated, is signed."

The Court of Appeal held that, by using the word "provisional," the parties had intended the document to be an agreement binding from the outset, though subsequently to be replaced by a more formal contract. Had they used the word "tentative" and not "provisional," or had they repeated the hallowed formula "subject to contract," they would have indicated their intention not to be bound until the completion of a later document. It must therefore be in each case a question of construction whether the parties intended to undertake immediate, if temporary, obligations, or whether they were suspending all liability until the conclusion of formalities. Have they, in other words, made the operation of their contract conditional upon the execution of a further document, in which case their obligations will be suspended, or have they made an immediately binding agreement, though one which is later to be merged into a more formal contract?

The usual English practice of making agreements for the sale of land "subject to contract" normally operates to protect the buyer since it provides time for investigation of title and survey of the premises. During the early 1970's however in a period of rapidly increasing house prices it came to appear unfavourable to buyers since it allowed the seller to "gazump," that is to refuse to sign the formal contract unless the buyer would agree to an increased price. However a Law Commission report concluded that "gazumping" was the product of short term factors and that any change in the law or practice would not in general benefit buyers.[3]

---

1. *Winn* v. *Bull* (1877), 7 Ch.D. 29; *Chillingworth* v. *Esche*, [1924] 1 Ch. 97; *Eccles* v. *Bryant and Pollock*, [1948] Ch. 93; [1947] 2 All E.R. 865. See the similar rule in Roman law, Inst. iii, 23 pr.
2. [1947] K.B. 854; [1947] 2 All E.R. 101.
3. Law Com. 65. The "subject to contract" practice is quite independent of the legal requirement that a contract for the sale of land should be evidenced in writing (see *infra*, pp. 174–199) though the two may interact; see *Tiverton Estates, Ltd.* v. *Wearwell, Ltd.*, [1975] Ch. 146; [1974] 1 All E.R. 209, [1974] 2 W.L.R. 176, discussed *infra*, p. 188.

Agreement
may be
inferred
from obser-
vance of
written
terms

Upon the particular phrase " subject to contract " the pressure of litigation has stamped a precise significance. In other cases it is often difficult to decide if the language used justifies the inference of a complete and final agreement.[1] The task of the courts is to extract the intention of the parties both from the terms of their correspondence and from the circumstances which surround and follow it, and the question of interpretation may thus be stated. Is the preparation of a further document a condition precedent to the creation of a contract or is it an incident in the performance of an already binding obligation? As in all questions of construction, the comparison of decided cases is apt to confuse rather than to illuminate. It would appear, however, that, whenever there is evidence that the parties have acted upon the faith of a written document, the courts will prefer to assume that the document embodies a definite intention to be bound and will strive to implement its terms.[2] Such, at least, will be the instinct of a judge in a commercial transaction, where the parties are engaged in a particular trade and may be taken to have accepted its special and familiar usages as the background of their bargain. Thus in *Hillas & Co.* v. *Arcos, Ltd.*,[3]

Hillas
v.
Arcos

> Hillas & Co. had agreed to buy from Arcos, Ltd., " 22,000 standards of soft-wood goods of fair specification over the season 1930." The written agreement contained an option to buy 100,000 standards in 1931, but without particulars as to the kind or size of timber or the manner of shipment. No difficulties arose on the original purchase for 1930, but, when the buyers sought to exercise the option for 1931, the sellers took the point that the failure to define these various particulars showed that the clause was not intended to bind either party, but merely to provide a basis for future agreement.

The House of Lords held that the language used, interpreted in the light of the previous course of dealing between the parties, showed a sufficient intention to be bound.

> " The problem for a court of construction," said Lord TOMLIN " must always be so to balance matters that, without the violation of essential principle, the dealings of men may as far as possible be treated as effective, and that the law may not incur the reproach of being the destroyer of bargains."[4]

---

1. It would be a mistake to assume that the use of the words " subject to " always indicate an inchoate agreement. So an arrangement to sell land " subject to planning permission " may be a binding agreement, conditional on planning permission being obtained. See e.g. *Batten* v. *White* (*No. 2*) (1960), 12 P. & C.R. 66. Such a condition may impose an obligation on one or both parties to do his best to bring the condition about, e.g. *Martin* v. *Macarthur* [1963] N.Z.L.R. 403 ("subject to satisfactory finance "). Cf. *Lee-Parker* v. *Izzet* (*No. 2*), [1972] 2 All E.R. 800, [1972] 1 W.L.R. 775. See further *infra*, pp. 136–138.
2. *Sweet and Maxwell, Ltd.* v. *Universal News Services, Ltd.*, [1964] 2 Q.B. 699; [1964] 3 All E.R. 30.
3. [1932] All E.R. Rep. 494; 38 Com. Cases, 23.
4. [1932] All E.R. Rep., at p. 499; 38 Com. Cases, at p. 29. The earlier decision of the House of Lords in *May and Butcher* v. *R.*, decided in 1929, but not reported until 1934, [1934] 2 K.B. 17, n., presents some difficulties of reconciliation. But it would appear from the judgments of the Court of Appeal in *Foley* v. *Classique Coaches, Ltd.*, [1934] 2 K.B. 1; [1934] All E.R. Rep. 88, and in *National Coal Board* v. *Galley*, [1958] 1 All E.R. 91; [1958] 1 W.L.R. 16, that the views expressed by the House of Lords in *Hillas* v. *Arcos* offer the better guide in what must always be the difficult task of discovering the intention of the parties. See also *Courtney and Fairbairn, Ltd.* v. *Tolaini Brothers (Hotels), Ltd.*, [1975] 1 All E.R. 716; [1975] 1 W.L.R. 297.

Where, on the other hand, there is no particular trade in question and no familiar business practice to clothe the skeleton of the agreement, the task of spelling out a common intention from meagre words may prove too speculative for the court to undertake. Thus in *Scammell* v. *Ouston*,[1]

Scammell
v.
Ouston

> Ouston wished to acquire from Messrs. Scammell a new motor-van on hire-purchase terms. After a considerable correspondence, Ouston gave a written order for a particular type of van, which included the words—" This order is given on the understanding that the balance of purchase price can be had on hire-purchase terms over a period of two years.". The order was accepted by Messrs. Scammell in general terms, but the hire-purchase terms were never specifically determined. It later appeared in evidence that there was a wide variety of hire-purchase agreements and that there was nothing to indicate which of them the parties favoured.
>
> Messrs. Scammell later refused to provide the van, and Ouston sued for damages for non-delivery. Messrs. Scammell pleaded that no contract had ever been concluded, and the House of Lords accepted this view.

Lord WRIGHT[2] said that there were two grounds on which he must hold that no contract had been made.

> " The first is that the language used was so obscure and so incapable of any definite or precise meaning that the Court is unable to attribute to the parties any particular intention. The object of the Court is to do justice between the parties, and the Court will do its best, if satisfied that there was an ascertainable and determinate intention to contract, to give effect to that intention, looking at substance and not mere form. It will not be deterred by mere difficulties of interpretation. Difficulty is not synonymous with ambiguity so long as any definite meaning can be extracted. But the test of intention is to be found in the words used. If these words, considered however broadly and untechnically and with due regard to all the just implications, fail to evince any definite meaning on which the Court can safely act, the Court has no choice but to say that there is no contract. Such a position is not often found. But I think that it is found in this case.[3] My reason for so thinking is not only based on the actual vagueness and unintelligibility of the words used, but is confirmed by the startling diversity of explanations, tendered by those who think there was a bargain, of what the bargain was. I do not think it would be right to hold the appellants to any particular version. It was all left too vague. . . .
>
> But I think the other reason, which is that the parties never in intention nor even in appearance reached an agreement, is a still sounder reason against enforcing the claim. In truth, in my opinion, their agreement was inchoate and never got beyond negotiations. They did, indeed, accept the position that there should be some form of hire-purchase agreement, but they never went on to complete their agreement by settling between them what the terms of the hire-purchase agreement were to be."

A comparison of these two cases is instructive. In *Hillas* v. *Arcos*, though the document itself left a number of points undetermined, these could be settled by referring to the earlier relations of the parties and to the normal course of the trade. In

Comparison
of the cases

---

1. [1941] A.C. 251; [1941] 1 All E.R. 14. Contrast *Sweet and Maxwell, Ltd.* v. *Universal News Services, Ltd.*, [1964] 2 Q.B. 699; [1964] 3 All E.R. 30.
2. [1941] A.C., at pp. 268–9; [1941] 1 All E.R., at pp. 25–6.
3. See *Jaques* v. *Lloyd D. George & Partners, Ltd.*, [1968] 2 All E.R. 187; [1968] 1 W.L.R. 625.

Scammell v. *Ouston* not only were the *lacunæ* themselves more
serious but there was nothing either in the previous dealings of
the parties or in accepted business practice which might help
to supply them.   Vital questions had originally been left unanswered and no subsequent negotiations ever settled them.   In
these circumstances the judges, with the best will in the world,
could not invent a contract which the parties had been too idle
to make for themselves.   At the same time, as Lord WRIGHT
pointed out, the judges will always seek to implement and not to
defeat reasonable expectations.   They will follow, if this is at
all possible, the example of *Hillas* v. *Arcos* rather than that of
Scammell v. *Ouston*.[1]   In particular they will not be deterred
from proclaiming the existence of a contract merely because one
of the parties, after agreeing in substance to the proposals of the
other, introduces a phrase or clause which, when examined, is
found to be without significance.   If there appears to be agreement on all essential matters, either on the face of the documents
or by praying in aid commercial practice or the previous course
of dealing between the parties, the court will ignore a subsidiary
and meaningless addendum.   The case of *Nicolene, Ltd.* v.
Simmonds[2] illustrates this anxiety of the judges to support the
assumptions of sensible men if this is in any way possible.

> The plaintiffs wrote to the defendant offering to buy from him
> a large quantity of steel bars.   The defendant replied in writing
> that he would be happy to supply them and thanking the plaintiffs
> " for entrusting this contract to me."   He added: " I assume that
> we are in agreement that the usual conditions of acceptance apply".
> The plaintiffs acknowledged this letter and said that they awaited
> the invoice for the goods, but made no reference to the " usual
> conditions of acceptance."   The defendant failed to deliver the
> goods and the plaintiffs sued for breach of contract.

The defendant argued that, as there had been no explicit agreement on the " conditions of acceptance," there was no concluded
contract.   His own letter, at the highest, was only a counter-
offer which had not been accepted.   The Court of Appeal dismissed the argument and gave judgment for the plaintiffs.   It
appeared that there were no " usual conditions of acceptance "
to which either party could refer.   The words were therefore
meaningless and must be ignored.

DENNING, L.J., said:[3]

> " It would be strange indeed if a party could escape from every
> one of his obligations by inserting a meaningless exception from some
> of them. . . . You would find defaulters all scanning their contracts
> to find some meaningless clause on which to ride free."

---

1. See *Smith* v. *Morgan*, [1971] 2 All E.R. 1500, [1971] 1 W.L.R. 803; and
   Brown v. *Gould*, [1972] Ch. 53; [1971] 2 All E.R. 1505; Compare *King's
   Motors (Oxford), Ltd.* v. *Lax*, [1969] 3 All E.R. 665; [1970] 1 W.L.R.
   426.
2. [1953] 1 Q.B. 543; [1953] 1 All E.R. 822.
3. [1953] 1 Q.B. 543; [1953] 1 All E.R. 822, at pp. 551–2, 824–5, respectively.

HODSON, L.J., said:[1]

> " I do not accept the proposition that, because some meaningless words are used in a letter which contains an unqualified acceptance of an offer, those meaningless words must, or can, be relied on by the acceptor as enabling him to obtain a judgment in his favour on the basis that there has been no acceptance at all."

The inclination of judges, whenever possible and especially in commercial transactions, to find the existence of a contract is further evident in their readiness to assume that the acceptance of an offer may have a retrospective effect. It may then serve to clothe with legal force the conduct of parties who have acted on the faith of this assumption. Few such cases, indeed, are to be found in the reports. But there seems no reason to doubt that in law as in common sense an acceptance may thus legitimate the past. The question was discussed by MEGAW, J. in *Trollope & Colls, Ltd.* v. *Atomic Power Constructions, Ltd.*[2]

Acceptance may be retrospective

> " Frequently in large transactions a written contract is expressed to have retrospective effect, sometimes lengthy retrospective effect; and this in cases where the negotiations on some of the terms have continued up to almost, if not quite, the date of the signature of the contract. The parties have meanwhile been conducting their transactions with one another, it may be for many months, on the assumption that a contract would ultimately be agreed on lines known to both the parties, though with the final form of various constituent terms of the proposed contract still under discussion. The parties have assumed that when the contract is made—when all the terms have been agreed in their final form—the contract will apply retrospectively to the preceding transactions. Often, as I say, the ultimate contract expressly so provides. I can see no reason why, if the parties so intend and agree, such a stipulation should be denied legal effect."

In the case under consideration there was no such express stipulation. But the parties had assumed that a contract would in due course be made, they had given orders and carried out work on this assumption and no other explanation of their conduct was feasible. The learned judge therefore imported into the contract, when ultimately made, a term that it should apply retrospectively to all that had been done in anticipation of it.

A final illustration of the difficulty experienced in deciding whether an offer has been accepted is afforded by the series of cases where a " tender " is invited for the periodical supply of goods.

Acceptance in the case of tenders

> Suppose that a corporation invites tenders for the supply of certain specified goods to be delivered over a given period. A trader puts in a tender intimating that he is prepared to supply the goods at a certain price. The corporation, to use the language of the business world, " accepts " the tender. What is the legal result of this " acceptance? "

There is no doubt, of course, that the tender is an offer. The question, however, is whether its " acceptance " by the corporation

---

1. *Ibid.*, at pp. 553, 826, respectively. See also *Michael Richards Properties, Ltd.* v. *Corporation of Wardens of St. Saviour's Parish, Southwark*, [1975] 3 All E.R. 416, where the words " subject to contract " were struck out as being meaningless in the context.
2. [1962] 3 All E.R. 1035, especially at p. 1040: [1963] 1 W.L.R. 333, at p. 339.

is an acceptance in the legal sense so as to produce a binding contract.   This can be answered only by examining the language of the original invitation to tender.   There are at least two possible cases.

Two classes of tenders

First, the corporation may have stated that it will definitely require a specified quantity of goods, no more and no less, as, for instance, where it advertises for 1,000 tons of coal to be supplied during the period January 1st to December 31st.   Here the " acceptance " of the tender is an acceptance in the legal sense, and it creates an obligation.   The trader is bound to deliver, the corporation is bound to accept, 1,000 tons, and the fact that delivery is to be by instalments as and when demanded does not disturb the existence of the obligation.

Secondly, if the corporation advertises that it *may* require articles of a specified description up to a maximum amount, as, for instance, where it invites tenders for the supply during the coming year of coal not exceeding 1,000 tons altogether, deliveries to be made *if and when* demanded, the effect of the so-called " acceptance " of the tender is very different.   The trader has made what is called a standing offer.   Until revocation he stands ready and willing to deliver coal up to 1,000 tons at the agreed price when the corporation from time to time demands a precise quantity.   The " acceptance " of the tender, however, does not convert the offer into a binding contract, for a contract of sale implies that the buyer has agreed to accept the goods.   In the present case the corporation has not agreed to take 1,000 tons, or indeed any quantity of coal.   It has merely stated that it may require supplies up to a maximum limit.

Position where tender is a standing offer

In this latter case the standing offer may be revoked at any time provided that it has not been accepted in the legal sense; and acceptance in the legal sense is complete as soon as a requisition for a definite quantity of goods is made.   Each requisition by the offeree is an individual act of acceptance which creates a separate contract.   If the corporation in the case given telephones for twenty-five tons of coal, there is an acceptance of the offer and both parties are bound to that extent and to that extent only—the one to deliver, the other to accept twenty-five tons.   If, however, the tradesman revokes his offer, he cannot be made liable for further deliveries,[1] although he is bound by requisitions already made.[2]

G.N.R. v. Witham

The nature of a standing offer was considered in *Great Northern Rail Co.* v. *Witham*.[3]   In that case:

> The plaintiffs advertised for tenders for the supply of stores. The defendant made a tender in these words: " I undertake to supply the Company for twelve months with such quantities of [specified articles] as the Company may order from time to time." The Company replied by letter accepting the tender, and subsequently gave various orders which were executed by the defendant. Ultimately the Company gave an order for goods within the schedule, which the defendant refused to supply.

---

1. *Offord* v. *Davies* (1862), 12 C.B.N.S. 748.
2. *Great Northern Rail. Co.* v. *Witham* (1873), L.R. 9 C.P. 16.
3. *Ibid.*   See also *Percival, Ltd.* v. *London County Council Asylums and Mental Deficiency Committee* (1918), 87 L.J.K.B. 677.

The company succeeded in an action for breach of contract. The tender was a standing offer, to be converted into a series of contracts by the subsequent acts of the company. An order prevented *pro tanto* the possibility of revocation, and the defendant, though he might regain his liberty of action for the future, was meanwhile bound to supply the goods actually ordered.

B. THE COMMUNICATION OF ACCEPTANCE

Even if the offeree has made up his mind to a final acceptance, the agreement is not yet complete. There must be an external manifestation of assent, some word spoken or act done by the offeree or by his authorised agent which the law can regard as the communication of the acceptance to the offeror.[1] What constitutes communication varies with the nature of the case and has provoked many difficult problems. A number of observations, however, may be made.

(1) An offeror may not arbitrarily impose contractual liability upon an offeree merely by proclaiming that silence shall be deemed consent. In *Felthouse* v. *Bindley*,[2]

Effect of silence

> the plaintiff, Paul Felthouse, wrote to his nephew, John, on February 2nd, offering to buy his horse for £30 15s., and adding, " If I hear no more about him, I consider the horse mine at that price." The nephew made no reply to this letter, but intimated to the defendant, an auctioneer, who was going to sell his stock, that the horse was to be kept out of the sale. The defendant inadvertently sold the horse to a third party at an auction held on February 25th, and the plaintiff sued him in conversion.

The Court of Common Pleas held that the action must fail as there had been no acceptance of the plaintiff's offer before February 25th, and the plaintiff had therefore, at that date, no title to maintain conversion.

> " It is clear," said WILLES, J., " that the uncle had no right to impose upon the nephew a sale of his horse for £30 15s. unless he chose to comply with the condition of writing to repudiate the offer."

Silence is usually equivocal as to consent and the uncle's letter did not render the nephew's failure to reply unequivocal since failure to reply to letters is a common human weakness. It may be going too far, however, to say the silence can never be unequivocal evidence of consent.[3]

(2) While an offeror may not present an offeree with the alternatives of repudiation or liability, he may, for his own purposes, waive the need to communicate acceptance. He may himself run the risk of incurring an obligation, though he may not impose it upon another. Such waiver may be express or may be inferred from the circumstances. It will normally be assumed in what are

Waiver of communication

---

1. See *Powell* v. *Lee* (1908), 99 L.T. 284, and *Robophone Facilities, Ltd.* v. *Blank*, [1966] 3 All E.R. 128; [1966] 1 W.L.R. 1428.
2. (1862), 11 C.B.N.S. 869. Miller, 35 M.L.R. 489.
3. *Manco, Ltd.* v. *Atlantic Forest Products, Ltd.* [1971], 24 D.L.R. (3d) 194. *Way & Waller, Ltd.* v. *Ryde*, [1944] 1 All E.R. 9, discussed by Murdoch, 91 L.Q.R. 357, at p. 378-9.

sometimes called *unilateral* contracts. In this type of case the offer takes the form of a promise to pay money in return for an act; and the performance of that act will usually be deemed an adequate indication of assent.[1]   In *Carlill* v. *Carbolic Smoke Ball Co.*, the facts of which have already been given,[2] the argument that the plaintiff should have notified her intention to put the defendants' panacea to the test was dismissed as absurd.   BOWEN, L.J., after stating the normal requirement of communication, continued:[3]

> " But there is this clear gloss to be made upon that doctrine, that as notification of acceptance is required for the benefit of the person who makes the offer, the person who makes the offer may dispense with notice to himself if he thinks it desirable to do so; . . . and if the person making the offer expressly or impliedly intimates in his offer that it will be sufficient to act on the proposal without communicating acceptance of it to himself, performance of the condition is a sufficient acceptance without notification. . . . In the advertisement cases it seems to me to follow as an inference to be drawn from the transaction itself that a person is not to notify his acceptance of the offer before he performs the condition. . . . From the point of view of commonsense no other idea could be entertained.   If I advertise to the world that my dog is lost and that anybody who brings the dog to a particular place will be paid some money, are all the police or other people whose business it is to find lost dogs to sit down and write me a note saying that they have accepted my proposal? "

It should follow from this that if the nephew on the facts of *Felthouse* v. *Bindley* had sued the uncle, the latter would have been unable to rely on the non-communication of acceptance.[4] It may further be argued that the true principle is that the offeror cannot by ultimatum impose on the offeree an obligation to state his non-acceptance, but that the contract may nevertheless be concluded if the offeree unequivocally manifests his acceptance.[5] This is important, for instance, in relation to the practice of "inertia" selling, where a tradesman sends unsolicited goods to a customer, accompanied by a letter stating that if the goods are not returned within ten days, it will be assumed that they are bought. At Common Law it would seem clear that the customer is under no obligation to return the goods but that if he clearly

---

1. See BRETT, J. in *Great Northern Rail Co.* v. *Witham* (1873), L.R. 9 C.P. 16, and the *Sixth Interim Report* of the Law Revision Committee (1937), p. 23. *Unilateral* contracts are usually contrasted with *bilateral* contracts.   But in *United Dominions Trust (Commercial), Ltd.* v. *Eagle Aircraft Services, Ltd.*, [1968] 1 All E.R. 104, at p. 108; [1968] 1 W.L.R. 74, DIPLOCK, L.J., preferred *synallagmatic* to *bilateral* because there may be more than two parties involved.
2. *Supra*, p. 26.
3. [1893] 1 Q.B. 256, at pp. 269–70.
4. It may appear paradoxical that one party can assert that there is a contract and not the other but this can be explained on terms of estoppel. See, e.g. *Spiro* v. *Lintern*, [1973] 3 All E.R. 319; [1973] 1 W.L.R. 1002.   Cf. *Fairline Shipping Corporation* v. *Adamson*, [1975] Q.B. 180; [1974] 2 All E.R. 967, where this argument was apparently rejected by Kerr, J., though on the facts there was no evidence of reliance sufficient to support an estoppel.
5. One difficulty with this approach is that it looks as if the nephew had indeed unequivocally accepted.   Two possible escapes from this difficulty have been suggested: (*a*) that statements to one's own agent are not unequivocal or (*b*) that the true *ratio* of the case was that there was not sufficient memorandum of the contract within the Statute of Frauds.

shows his acceptance, e.g. by consuming the goods, he should be bound to pay for them. Under the Unsolicited Goods and Services Act 1971 however a tradesman may, in such circumstances, be treated as making a gift of the goods to the customer.

(3) An offeror may prescribe the method of communicating acceptance. Whether some particular mode has been prescribed depends upon the inference to be drawn from the circumstances.[1] There is authority for the view that an offer by telegram is evidence of a desire for a prompt reply, so that an acceptance sent by post may be treated as nugatory.[2] The observance of the mode prescribed by the offeror obviously suffices to complete the agreement. Whether precise observance is necessary is, however, a matter of some doubt.

Suppose, for instance, that a Glasgow distiller sends a note by his lorry driver to a London merchant, making an offer and asking for a reply to be sent by the lorry on its return. Is an acceptance communicated in any other manner ineffective?

If the offeree posts an acceptance in the belief that it will reach Glasgow before the lorry and if this is not the case, the better opinion is that the offeror may repudiate the acceptance.[3] But suppose that the acceptance is telegraphed or telephoned, so that it reaches the offeror before the return of his lorry. Is it to be regarded as ineffective merely because it was not communicated in the manner prescribed? Such a ruling, which would be repugnant to commonsense, does not appear to represent English law, for, in a case where the offeree was told to " reply by return of post," it was said by the Court of Exchequer Chamber that a reply sent by some other method equally expeditious would constitute a valid acceptance.[4] The result would, of course, be otherwise, if the offeror had insisted that a reply should be sent by the lorry *and by that method only*.[5] It is thought that an offeror will need to use very clear words before a means of communication will be treated as mandatory.[6]

(4) If no particular method is prescribed, the form of communication will depend upon the nature of the offer and the circumstances in which it is made. If the offeror makes an oral offer to the offeree and it is clear that an oral reply is expected, the offeree must ensure that his acceptance is understood by the offeror. Suppose that A shouts an offer to B across a river or a courtyard and that A does not hear the reply because it is drowned by an aircraft flying overhead. No contract is formed at that

Marginal notes:
Mode of communication prescribed by offeror

Where no mode of communication is prescribed; oral offers

1. See *Kennedy v. Thomassen*, [1929] 1 Ch. 426; [1928] All E.R. Rep. 525.
2. *Quenerduaine v. Cole* (1883), 32 W.R. 185.
3. Cf. the American decision in *Eliason v. Henshaw* (1819), 4 Wheaton, 225.
4. *Tinn v. Hoffmann & Co.* (1873), 29 L.T. 271. See also *Manchester Diocesan Council for Education v. Commercial and General Investments, Ltd.*, [1969] 3 All E.R. 1593; [1970] 1 W.L.R. 241.
5. Even here the offeror may waive the necessity of following the exclusive method prescribed and allow a substitute; see the difficult case of *Compagnie de Commerce et Commission S.A.R.L. v. Parkinson Stove Co.*, [1953] 2 Lloyd's Rep. 487, discussed Eckersley 17 M.L.R. 476. See also Winfield, 55 L.Q.R. 499, at pp. 515–6.
6. See *Yates Building Co., Ltd. v. R. J. Pulleyn & Sons (York), Ltd.* (1975), 119 Sol. Jo. 370, reversing (1973), 228 Estates Gazette 1597.

moment, and B must repeat his acceptance so that A can hear it.[1]
This rule—that acceptance is incomplete until received by the
offeror—governs conversations over the telephone no less than
discussions in the physical presence of the parties, and it has now
been applied to the most modern methods of communication.
In *Entores, Ltd.* v. *Miles Far East Corporation*,[2]

> the plaintiffs were a London company and the defendants were an
> American corporation with agents in Amsterdam. Both the
> plaintiffs in London and the defendants' agents in Amsterdam had
> equipment known as "Telex Service" whereby messages could
> be despatched by a teleprinter operated like a typewriter in one
> country and almost instantaneously received and typed in another.
> By this instrument the plaintiffs made an offer to the defendants'
> agents to buy goods from them, and the latter accepted the offer.
> The plaintiffs now alleged that the defendants had broken their
> contract and wished to serve a writ upon them. This they could
> do, although the defendants were an American corporation with no
> branch in England, provided that the contract was made in England.

The defendants contended that they had accepted the offer in
Holland and that the contract had therefore been made in that
country. But it was held by the Court of Appeal that the parties
were in the same position as if they had negotiated in each other's
presence or over the telephone, that there was no binding acceptance until it had been received by the plaintiffs, that this took
place in London and that a writ could therefore be issued.
PARKER, L.J., after reciting circumstances where expediency
might demand another rule,[3] said:

> " Where, however, the parties are in each other's presence or,
> though separated in space, communication between them is in
> effect instantaneous, there is no need for any such rule of con-
> venience. To hold otherwise would leave no room for the operation
> of the general rule that notification of the acceptance must be
> received. An acceptor could say: ' I spoke the words of acceptance
> in your presence, albeit softly, and it matters not that you did not
> hear me '; or ' I telephoned to you and accepted, and it matters
> not that the telephone went dead and you did not get my message.'
> ..., So far as Telex messages are concerned, though the despatch
> and receipt of a message is not completely instantaneous, the parties
> are to all intents and purposes in each other's presence just as if
> they were in telephonic communication, and I can see no reason
> for departing from the general rule that there is no binding contract
> until notice of the acceptance is received by the offeror. That
> being so, and since the offer was made by the plaintiffs in London
> and notification of the acceptance was received by them in London,
> the contract resulting therefrom was made in London."[4]

Communica-
tions through
the post

(5) If no particular method of communication is prescribed
and the parties are not, to all intents and purposes, in each other's
presence, the rule just laid down—that an acceptance speaks only
when it is received by the offeror—may be impracticable or
inconvenient. Such may well be the case where the negotiations
have been conducted through the post.[5] The question as to what

---

1. See the illustration given by DENNING, L.J., in *Entores, Ltd.* v. *Miles Far East Corporation*, [1955] 2 Q.B. 327, at p. 332: [1955] 2 All E.R. 493, at p. 495.
2. [1955] 2 Q.B. 327; [1955] 2 All E.R. 493.
3. See *infra*, as to negotiations conducted through the post.
4. [1955] 2 All E.R., at p. 498: [1955] 2 Q.B., at p. 336.
5. Evans, 15 I.C.L.Q. 553.

in these circumstances is an adequate communication of acceptance arose as early as 1818 in the case of *Adams* v. *Lindsell*.[1]

> The plaintiffs were woollen manufacturers in Bromsgrove,
> Worcestershire. The defendants were wool-dealers at St. Ives in
> Huntingdon. On September 2nd, 1817, the defendants wrote to
> the plaintiffs, offering a quantity of wool on certain terms and
> requiring an answer " in course of post ". The defendants mis-
> directed their letter, which did not reach the plaintiffs until the
> evening of September 5th. That same night the plaintiffs posted a
> letter of acceptance, which was delivered to the defendants on
> September 9th. If the original offer had been properly addressed,
> a reply could have been expected by September 7th, and meanwhile,
> on September 8th, not having received such a reply, the defendants
> had sold the wool to third parties.

The trial judge directed a verdict for the plaintiffs on the ground
that the delay was due to the defendants' negligence, and the
defendants obtained a rule nisi for a new trial. The vital question
was whether a contract of sale had been made between the parties
before September 8th. Two cases only were cited by counsel[2]
and none by the court, and it was treated virtually as a case of
first impression.

As an academic problem, three possible answers were available.
An offer made through the post might be regarded as accepted
in the eyes of the law:

Three possible solutions

   (i) As soon as the letter of acceptance is put into the post;
     or

  (ii) When the letter of acceptance is delivered to the offeror's
      address; or

 (iii) When the letter of acceptance is brought to the actual
      notice of the offeror.

As the law is now understood, the plaintiffs would have succeeded
on any of these theories, since the defendants' offer would not be
revoked by their sale to third parties on September 8th.[3] But
in 1818 there were no developed rules as to revocation of offers
and the court may well have thought it arguable that the sale was
sufficient to revoke[4] so that an effective acceptance would need
to take place before September 8th.

Solution in *Adams* v. *Lindsell*: acceptance complete when posted

It is commonly said that the choice between these three
possible solutions is arbitrary.[5] But the logical application of
the doctrine that acceptance must be communicated would
clearly point to the adoption of either (ii) or (iii) depending on
the meaning to be given to " communication." In fact the
Court of King's Bench in *Adams* v. *Lindsell* preferred the first
solution and decided that the contract was concluded when the
letter of acceptance was posted on September 5th. At first sight
it appears strange that the requirement of communication, which

---

1. (1818), 1 B. & Ald. 681.
2. *Payne* v. *Cave* (1789), 3 Term Rep. 148; and *Cooke* v. *Oxley* (1790), 3
Term Rep. 653.
3. See *infra*, p. 50.
4. This view was current as late as *Dickinson* v. *Dodds* (1876), 2 Ch.D. 463,
discussed *infra*, p. 51.
5. See Winfield, 55 L.Q.R. 499 at pp. 506–7. See also Nussbaum, 36 Col.
L.R. 920.

is largely devoid of practical content in contracts *inter praesentes*, should not be applied to postal contracts, which provide the most important arena for its application.   It is perhaps less surprising if we attend to the history of the matter.   *Adams* v. *Lindsell* was the first genuine offer and acceptance case in English law[1] and, in 1818 there was no rule that acceptance must be communicated.   As so often happens in English law, the exception is historically anterior to the rule.

The decision in *Adams* v. *Lindsell* did not at once command uncritical acceptance.   Although applied by the House of Lords in 1848 in an appeal from Scotland,[2] it was distinguished in two cases[3] where the letter of acceptance did not arrive but it was applied to that situation too by the Court of Appeal in *Household Fire and Carriage Accident Insurance Co.* v. *Grant*.[4] In 1880, in *Byrne* v. *Van Tienhoven*, LINDLEY, J., treated the question as beyond dispute.

> " It may be taken as now settled that, where an offer is made and accepted by letters sent through the post, the contract is completed the moment the letter accepting the offer is posted, even though it never reaches its destination."[5]

Some notes of warning may, however, be sounded.   The solution is to be applied only where no particular mode of communication is prescribed by the offeror;[6] and, as it is itself the creature of expediency, it must yield to manifest inconvenience or absurdity.   As Lord BRAMWELL said in 1871,

> " If a man proposed marriage and the woman was to consult her friends and let him know, would it be enough if she wrote and posted a letter which never reached him? "[7]

Recently LAWTON, L.J., has stated:[8]

> " In my judgment, the factors of inconvenience and absurdity are but illustrations of a wider principle, namely, that the rule does not apply if, having regard to all the circumstances, including the nature of the subject-matter under consideration, the negotiating parties cannot have intended that there should be a binding agreement until the party accepting an offer or exercising an option had in fact communicated the acceptance or exercise to the other."[9]

It would appear further that the rule should apply only to a letter which is properly stamped and addressed.[10]   A number of

---

1. Simpson, 91 L.Q.R. 247, at p. 260.
2. *Dunlop* v. *Higgins* (1848), 1 H.L. Cas. 381.
3. *British and American Telegraph Co.* v. *Colson* (1871), L.R. 6 Exch. 108; *Re Imperial Land Co. of Marseilles, Harris' Case* (1872), 7 Ch. App. 587.
4. (1879), 4 Ex. D. 216.
5. (1880), 5 C.P.D. 344, at p. 348.
6. *Holwell Securities Ltd.* v. *Hughes*, [1974] 1 All E.R. 161; [1974] 1 W.L.R. 155.
7. *British and American Telegraph Co.* v. *Colson* (1871), L.R. 6 Exch. 108.
8. [1974] 1 All E.R. 161; [1974] 1 W.L.R. 155, at pp. 167, 161, respectively.
9. A warning against the assumption that the rule in *Byrne* v. *Van Tienhoven* is to be applied automatically was given by the court in the Australian case of *Tallerman* v. *Nathan's Merchandise, Ltd.* (1957), 98 C.L.R. 93, especially at pp. 111–112.
10. *Re London and Northern Bank, Ex parte Jones*, [1900] 1 Ch. 220; *Gertreide-Import-Gesellschaft M.B.H.* v. *Contimar, S.A. Compania Industrial Commercial y Maritima*, [1953] 2 All E.R. 223; [1953] 1 W.L.R. 793.

questions, however, remain unanswered, and some of these must now be considered.

May acceptance be recalled before it reaches offeror?

May an offeree, perhaps by telephone or telegram, recall his acceptance after he has posted it but before it has reached the offeror? A rigorous application of the rule last laid down would forbid him to do so: the contract is complete from the moment that his letter has been put into the post. There is no English decision upon the point. The Scots case of *Dunmore (Countess)* v. *Alexander*[1] is sometimes cited to support the view that the offeree may be allowed to withdraw. The scope of this decision, however, is not clear. It involved a question of agency, to which perhaps it is exclusively relevant; and the courts were concerned to determine the effect, not of a telegram recalling a letter, but of the simultaneous receipt of two letters. In New Zealand, CHAP-MAN, J., denied the possibility of altering the effect of a letter of acceptance once it has been put into the post[2] and the same view has recently been taken in South Africa.[3] English courts are free to choose between these opinions, and their choice rests upon expediency rather than upon logic. Even upon this basis there is room for differing opinions. It may be argued, on the one hand, that to allow a letter of acceptance to be withdrawn would give the offeree the best of both worlds. By posting an acceptance he would be free either to hold the offeror to it or to recall it by telegram or telephone. On the other hand, the basic principle laid down in *Adams* v. *Lindsell* rests, as a matter of convenience, upon the ground that it is the offeror who has chosen the post as the medium of negotiation and who must accept the hazards of his choice. If he takes " the risks of delay and accident in the post, it would not seem to strain matters to say that he also assumes the risk of a letter being overtaken by a speedier means of communication".[4] He may guard against any of these risks by framing his offer in appropriate terms.

Must acceptor have knowledge of offer?

In the second place, do contractual obligations arise if services are rendered, which in fact fulfil the terms of an offer, but are performed in ignorance that the offer exists? The defendant may have offered a reward to anyone who gives information ensuring the conviction of a criminal. If the plaintiff supplies the information before he knows of the reward can be afterwards claim it? In *Neville* v. *Kelly* in 1862,[5] though the decision rested upon another point, the Court of Common Pleas was inclined to favour such a claim, and in *Gibbons* v. *Proctor* in 1891[6] DAY and LAWRANCE, JJ., sitting as a divisional court, apparently supported it. But they gave no reasons for their opinion, which has been generally condemned by academic laywers.[7] Agreement, it is true, has often to be inferred from the conduct of the parties although it does not exist in fact, but the inference can scarcely

---

1. (1830), 9 Sh. (Ct. of Sess.) 190.
2. *Wenkheim* v. *Arndt*, 1 J.R. 73.
3. *A to Z Bazaars (Pty), Ltd.* v. *Minister of Agriculture* 1974 (4) S.A. 392.
4. Hudson, 82 L.Q.R. 169, at p. 170.
5. (1862), 12 C.B.N.S. 740.
6. (1891), 64 L.T. 594.
7. See the strictures of Pollock, 13th Edn., p. 16, and of Salmond and Williams, at p. 72. Cf. Hudson, 84 L.Q.R. 503.

be drawn from the mere coincidence of two independent acts. The plaintiff, when he acted, intended not to sell his information, but to give it, and there was nothing to justify any reasonable third party in inferring the contrary.

These academic objections were received as valid in the American case of *Fitch* v. *Snedaker*,[1] where WOODRUFF, J., pertinently asked, " How can there be consent or assent to that of which the party has never heard ? " The position was reviewed, and the ruling in *Fitch* v. *Snedaker* taken, perhaps, a little further in the Australian case of *R.* v. *Clarke*.[2]

> The Government of Western Australia offered a reward of £1,000 " for such information as shall lead to the arrest and conviction of " the murderers of two police officers, and added that, if the information should be given by an accomplice, not being himself the murderer, he should receive a free pardon. Clarke saw the offer and some time later gave the necessary information. He claimed the reward from the Crown by Petition of Right. He admitted not only that he had acted solely to save his own skin, but that, at the time when he gave the information, the question of the reward had passed out of his mind.

The High Court of Australia held that his claim must fail. He was, in their opinion, in the same position as if he had never heard of the reward. In the words of HIGGINS, J.,

> " Clarke had seen the offer, indeed, but it was not present to his mind—he had forgotten it and gave no consideration to it in his intense excitement as to his own danger. There cannot be assent without knowledge of the offer; and ignorance of the offer is the same thing, whether it is due to never hearing of it or to forgetting it after hearing."

Chief Justice ISAACS re-inforced his opinion with a hypothetical illustration.

> " An offer of £100 to any person who should swim a hundred yards in the harbour on the first day of the year would not in my opinion be satisfied by a person who was accidentally or maliciously thrown overboard on that date and swam the distance simply to save his life, without any thought of the offer."

The position would be different if the offer of the reward had been present to the plaintiff's mind when he acted, although he may have been predominantly influenced by some other motive. In *Williams* v. *Carwardine*,[3] where a notice had been published in terms similar to those in *R.* v. *Clarke*, the plaintiff had supplied the information with knowledge of the reward but moved rather by remorse for her own misconduct. At the Assizes, PARKE, J., gave judgment in her favour, and the defendant moved to enter a nonsuit on the ground that the suggested contract had been

---

1. (1868), 38 N.Y. 248.
2. (1927), 40 C.L.R. 227. In *Bloom* v. *American Swiss Watch Co.*, (1915), App. D. 100, the Appellate Division of the Supreme Court of South Africa held, disapproving *Gibbons* v. *Proctor*, that, where information had been given without knowledge that a reward had been offered, the informer could not recover the reward.
3. The case was decided in 1833 and was variously reported; 5 C. & P. 566 is the best report and brings out clearly the fact that the plaintiff knew of the reward. Other reports are 4 B. & Ad. 621; 1 Nev. & M. K.B. 418; 2 L.J.K.B. 101.

negatived by the finding of the jury " that the plaintiff gave the information to ease her conscience and not for the sake of the reward." But the judgment was upheld in the King's Bench. Motive was irrelevant, provided that the act was done with knowledge of the reward. Acceptance was then related to offer.[1]

What, in the third place, is the effect of two offers, identical in terms, which cross in the post?

Does agreement result from cross-offers?

> Suppose that A by letter offers to sell his car to B for £100 and that B, by a second letter which crosses the first in the post, offers to buy it for £100. Do these two letters create a contract?

The point was discussed by the Exchequer Chamber in *Tinn* v. *Hoffmann & Co.*,[2] where it was held by five judges against two that on the facts of that case no contract had been concluded. Of the five judges in the majority, ARCHIBALD and KEATING, JJ., proceeded on the ground that the letters in question contained diverse terms so that the parties were not *ad idem*, while BLACKBURN, BRETT and GROVE, JJ., denied that cross-offers could, in the most favourable circumstances, constitute a contract. BLACKBURN, J., said,[3]

> " When a contract is made between two parties, there is a promise by one in consideration of the promise made by the other; there are two assenting minds, the parties agreeing in opinion and one having promised in consideration of the promise made by the other—there is an exchange of promises. But I do not think exchanging offers would, upon principle, be at all the same thing . . . . . The promise or offer being made on each side in ignorance of the promise or offer made on the other side, neither of them can be construed as an acceptance of the other."

The case, however, stands alone in the English common law and the difference of judicial opinion makes it the less impressive. The judgments, moreover, reflect the contemporary preoccupation with *consensus*. The American cases seem equally rare and equally inconclusive, although the Restatement declares categorically that " two manifestations of willingness to make the same bargain do not constitute a contract unless one is made with reference to the other."[4] Authority, therefore, so far as it goes, would seem to deny the efficacy of cross-offers; but it does not go very far. On principle the issue is equally doubtful. It is certainly true that the act of neither party is in direct relation to that of the other and that the strict requirements of offer and acceptance are unsatisfied. But, in contrast with the situation in such cases as *Fitch* v. *Snedaker* and *R.* v. *Clarke*, each party does in truth contemplate legal relations upon an identical basis, and each is prepared to offer his own promise as consideration for the promise of the other. There is not only a coincidence of acts, but, if this is thought to be relevant, a unanimity of mind.

---

1. See also *Taylor* v. *Allon*, [1966] 1 Q.B. 304; [1965] 1 All E.R. 557.
2. (1873), 29 L.T. 271.
3. (1873), 29 L.T., at p. 279.
4. *Restatement of the Law of Contracts* (American Law Institute), s. 23. For the American cases, see *Corbin on Contracts*, § 59.

SECTION IV. TERMINATION OF OFFER

It is now necessary to consider the circumstances in which an offer may be terminated or negatived. It may be revoked, it may lapse, it may be subject to a condition that fails to be satisfied or it may be affected by the death of one of the parties.

A. REVOCATION

It has been established ever since the case of *Payne* v. *Cave* in 1789[1] that revocation is possible and effective at any time before acceptance: up to this moment *ex hypothesi* no legal obligation exists. Nor, as the law stands, is it relevant that the offeror has declared himself ready to keep the offer open for a given period. Such an intimation is but part and parcel of the original offer, which must stand or fall as a whole. The offeror may, of course, bind himself, by a separate and specific contract, to keep the offer open; but the offeree, if such is his allegation, must prove all the elements of a valid contract, including assent and consideration.[2] In *Routledge* v. *Grant*[3] the defendant offered on March 18th to buy the plaintiff's house for a certain sum, " a definite answer to be given within six weeks from date." BEST, C.J., held that the defendant could withdraw at any moment before acceptance, even though the time limit had not expired. The plaintiff could only have held the defendant to his offer throughout the period, if he had bought the option by a separate and binding contract.

Revocation of offer must be communicated

The revocation of an offer is ineffective unless it has been communicated to the offeree. It is not enough for the offeror to change his mind. For some years, it is true, obsessed with the theory of *consensus*, the judges were content with the mere alteration of intention.[4] But business necessity, in this instance no less than in the definition of acceptance, overbore deductions from *a priori* conceptions of contract and required some overt act from which the intention might be inferred. Convenience, indeed, demanded a more stringent rule for revocation than for acceptance. To post a letter was a sufficient act of acceptance, since the offeree was entitled to assume that he thereby satisfied the expectations of the offeror. The offeror, when he decided to

---

1. (1789), 3 Term Rep. 148.
2. It was recommended by the Law Revision Committee in 1937 that the law be altered so as to make binding an agreement to keep an offer open for a definite period of time or until the occurrence of some specified event, even if there is no consideration for the agreement. See *Sixth Interim Report* (1937), p. 31. The Law Commission has recently made a similar recommendation but limited to firm offers made in the " course of business ": Working Paper 60 (1975). There is a statutory exception to the rule in Companies Act 1948, s. 50 (5); see Gower, *Modern Company Law* 3rd Edn., p. 302.
3. (1828), 4 Bing, 653.
4. See *Cooke* v. *Oxley* (1790), 3 Term Rep. 653, and *Head* v. *Diggon* (1828), 3 Man. & Ry. K.B. 97.

revoke, could rely on no such assumption. Thus in *Byrne* v. *Van Tienhoven*:[1]

> The defendants posted a letter in Cardiff on October 1st, addressed to the plaintiffs in New York, offering to sell 1,000 boxes of tinplates. On October 8th they posted a letter revoking the offer. On October 11th the plaintiffs telegraphed their acceptance and confirmed it in a letter posted on October 15th. On October 20th the letter of revocation reached the plaintiffs.

It was held that the revocation was inoperative until October 20th, that the offer, therefore, continued open up to that date, and that it had been accepted by the plaintiffs in the interim. LINDLEY, J., giving judgment for the plaintiffs, pointed out " the extreme injustice and inconvenience which any other conclusion would produce." The decision leaves undefined the precise moment at which communication takes place but it seems reasonable to argue that, at least in the case of a business, a letter which arrives on a normal working day should be treated as a communication even if unopened.[2]

The offeror, therefore, if he relies on a revocation, must prove, not only that he has done some act which manifests his intention, but that the offeree has knowledge of that act. But it would seem that he need not himself have furnished this information. In *Dickinson* v. *Dodds*:[3]

What constitutes communication of revocation?

> The defendant, on June 10th, gave the plaintiff a written offer to sell a house for £800, " to be left over until Friday, June 12th, 9 a.m." On Thursday, June 11th, the defendant sold the house to a third party, Allan, for £800, and that evening the plaintiff was told of the sale by a fourth man, Berry. Before 9 a.m. on June 12th, the plaintiff handed to the defendant a formal letter of acceptance.

The Court of Appeal held that the plaintiff, before attempting to accept, " knew that Dodds was no longer minded to sell the property to him as plainly and clearly as if Dodds had told him in so many words," that the defendant had validly withdrawn his offer and that the plaintiff's purported acceptance was too late. The decision was followed in *Cartwright* v. *Hoogstoel*[4] in 1911, where EVE, J., rested his judgment on the ground that " the defendant had, by conduct brought to the knowledge of the plaintiff, effectually withdrawn the offer before acceptance."

The language of the judgments in *Dickinson* v. *Dodds* reflects the persistence of the *consensus* theory and is not free from practical difficulty. Is the offeree bound by any hint or gossip that he may hear, or must he winnow the truth from the chaff? All that can be said is that it is a question of fact in each case. Was the information such that a reasonable man should have been persuaded of its accuracy?

---

1. (1880), 5 C.P.D. 344. See also *Stevenson* v. *McLean* (1880), 5 Q.B.D. 346, and *Henthorn* v. *Fraser*, [1892] 2 Ch. 27.
2. Cf. Cairns, L.J., in *The Brimnes*, [1974] 3 All E.R. 88, at p. 115; [1974] 3 W.L.R. 613, at p. 642. In *Shuey* v. *U.S.* 92, U.S. 73 (1875) it was held that an offer made by advertisement in a newspaper could be revoked by a similar advertisement even though the second advertisement were not read by some offerees.
3. (1876), 2 Ch.D. 463.
4. (1911), 105 L.T. 628.

A further difficulty is suggested by the nature of " unilateral "
contracts.[1] If the offeror contemplates, not the creation of
mutual promises, but the dependence of his own promise upon
the offeree's performance of an act, may he revoke his offer at
any time before the completion of this act? A reward may have
been advertised for the return of a lost dog to a given address,
a sum of money may have been promised if, at the end of five
years, the offeree can prove that he has abstained from strong
drink throughout the period, or, as in the illustration put by
BRETT, J., in *Great Northern Railway* v. *Witham*,[2] the defendant
may have said to the plaintiff " If you will go to York, I will
give you £100." May the offeror, by giving notice, revoke his
offer when he sees his dog being led through the streets towards
his house, or when the offeree has endured three years of
abstinence, or when, after a laborious journey, he has succeeded
in reaching Doncaster? The application of the ordinary rules
of revocation would suggest an affirmative answer. An offer may
be revoked at any moment before it matures by acceptance into
a contract, and it has generally been assumed that, when a promise
is offered in return for an act, there is no acceptance until the act
has been completely performed.[3]

This solution, has been felt to be hard, and methods of evasion
have been sought.[4] It has been suggested in America that two
separate offers are inherent in the offeror's statement: an express
offer to pay on the performance of the act, and an implied offer
not to revoke if the offeree begins his task within a reasonable
time.[5] On this assumption, the beginning of the task not only
constitutes the acceptance of the implied offer, but also supplies
the consideration which the law requires for its validity, as for
that of every contract not under seal.[6] If the offeror attempts
thereafter to revoke, he may be sued for the breach of this secondary promise. This American suggestion was, indeed, anticipated
by the Supreme Court of New South Wales which, as early as
1860, decided that in the case of a unilateral contract the original
offer may not be withdrawn after the offeree has started to act[7].
In England Sir Frederick Pollock suggested that, a distinction
should be drawn between the acceptance of the offer and the
consideration necessary to support it. The latter, no doubt, is
the completion of the act, and, until this takes place, the offeror
need pay no money. The former may be assumed as soon as
the offeree " has made an unequivocal beginning of the per-

---

1. See *supra,* p. 42.
2. (1873), L.R. 9 C.P. 16. See also *Rogers* v. *Snow* (1572), Dalison 94;
   Simpson, *History*, pp. 426–7.
3. See *supra,* p. 42. An allied but logically distinct difficulty is that in a
   unilateral contract the consideration for the promise is the promissee's
   performance of the stipulated Act. See *infra*, p. 66.
4. It has, however, been argued that too much can be made of the hardship.
   Both parties retain their freedom of volition before acceptance; and if, in
   the hypothetical case suggested above, the abstainer refused to continue his
   course of temperance after two years, he could not be sued. See Wormser,
   26 Yale L.J. 136.
5. See McGovney, 27 Harvard L.R. 644.
6. See *infra,* Chap. 2.
7. *Abbott* v. *Lance*, Legge's New South Wales Reports, 1283. It will be seen
   that this two contract analysis is similar to that propounded in *Warlow* v.
   Harrison, discussed *supra*, p. 28.

formance requested," and proof of this fact makes revocation impossible.[1] The suggestion was adopted in 1937 by the Law Revision Committee.[2]

It may be suggested that neither reason nor justice compels a choice between the stark alternatives of making such offers revocable until performance is complete or irrevocable once performance is commenced.[3] Much must depend on the nature of the offer and it is perhaps unfortunate that discussion has centred upon an apparently frivolous and unexplained walk to York. In some cases the parties may well understand that the offeror reserves a right to revoke at any time until performance is complete, while in others it may be proper to hold that he cannot revoke once the promisee has started performance. There may well be intermediate cases where the promisor can revoke after performance has started but is obliged to compensate the offeree for his trouble.[4]

The two most instructive cases are *Luxor (Eastbourne), Ltd.* v. *Cooper*[5] and *Errington* v. *Errington and Woods*.[6] In the former case an owner of land promised to pay an estate agent a commission of £10,000 if he affected a sale of the land at a price of £175,000. The House of Lords held that the owner could revoke his promise at any time before completion of the sale. At first sight this might appear to support the view that offers of unilateral contracts are freely revocable until performance. But the House of Lords did not rely on any such principle which would have provided a complete and simple answer to the plaintiff's claim. Instead they held that, *in the circumstances of the case*, it would not be proper to imply an undertaking by the owner not to revoke his promise once performance had begun. Clearly this argument assumed that if such an undertaking could be implied, it would be binding.

Luxor (Eastbourne) Ltd. v. *Cooper*

Errington v. *Errington* appears to be just such a case. A father bought a house for his son and daughter-in-law to live in. He paid one third of the purchase price in cash and borrowed the balance on a building society mortgage. He told the son and daughter-in-law that if they paid the weekly instalments, he would convey the house to them when all the instalments were paid. They duly paid the instalments though they never contracted to do so. The Court of Appeal had no doubt that so long as they were paying the instalments, the father's promise was irrevocable. It is easy to see why a promise not to revoke should be implied and binding on such facts[7].

Errington v. *Errington and Woods*

---

1. *Pollock on Contract,* 13th Edn., p. 19.
2. *Sixth Interim Report* (1937), pp. 23–4, 31. A similar solution seems to have been adopted in the *Restatement,* s. 45, though the language used is far from clear. *Corbin on Contracts* § 63.
3. See Atiyah, *Consideration in Contracts*, pp. 21–27. Murdoch 91 L.Q.R. 357 at pp. 369–75.
4. See Viscount HALDANE, L.C., in *Morrison Steamship* v. *R* (1924), 20 LL.L.R. 283, at p. 287.
5. [1941] A.C. 108, [1941] 1 All E.R. 33, discussed *infra*, pp. 486–8. See also the somewhat elusive discussion, *arguendo*, in *Offord* v. *Davies* (1862), 12 C.B.N.S. 748.
6. [1952] 1 K.B. 290, [1952] 1 All E.R. 149.
7. It is true that this case has been doubted by property lawyers but these doubts relate to the proper analysis of the son and daughter-in-law's interest in the land and not to the contractual position. See Cheshire, *Modern Real Property*, 12th Edn., pp. 583–4; Megarry and Wade, Law of Real Property, 4th Edn., p. 783.

Perhaps the most important practical example is that of Bankers' Commercial Credits. These are a device developed to facilitate international trade. Exporters and importers may find themselves dealing with merchants in other countries whose creditworthiness is unknown to them and may in any event be unable to finance the transaction themselves, the buyer being unable to pay for the goods until he has subsold them and the seller unable to obtain or manufacture the goods without a completely reliable assurance of payment.[1]

Bankers
commercial
credits

From the lawyer's point of view, and reduced to its simplest terms, the device involves three separate transactions.

(1) A clause is inserted in the initial contract of sale, whereby the seller requires payment in a particular manner. The buyer is to ask his bank to open a credit in the seller's favour, which shall remain irrevocable for a given time.

(2) The buyer makes an agreement with his bank, whereby the bank undertakes to open such a credit in return for the buyer's promise to reimburse the bank, to pay a small commission, and to give the bank a lien over the shipping documents.

(3) The buyer's bank notifies the seller that it has opened an irrevocable credit in his favour, to be drawn on as soon as the seller presents the shipping documents.

It is upon the third of these transactions that, doubts have arisen. What is the legal position of the seller, should the bank refuse to honour its promise? He could sue the buyer on the original contract of sale, but this would be to abandon the credit scheme.

In earlier editions of this work we have treated this as a problem in privity of contract, that is, as to whether the seller derives rights under the undoubted contract between buyer and bank.[2] In practice however the seller does not seek to enforce the contract between buyer and bank but a direct contract between the banker and himself. Litigation on credits is by no means infrequent but no bank has yet argued that there is no contract between it and the seller. Several dicta support the existence of such a contract[3] and it seems safe to assume that any court would be reluctant to cast doubt on the efficacy of such a valuable commercial tool. Writers on the subject have devoted much care to analysing the theoretical obstacles to such a solution.[4] One such obstacle is the supposed revocability of offers of unilateral contracts. The bank's letter of credit could easily be treated as an offer to pay if the seller presents the prescribed documents but commercial practice treats the bank's offer (where the credit is described as irrevocable) as irrevocable as soon as it is received by the seller.

---

1. Davis, *Law Relating to Commercial Letters of Credit*, 3rd Edn. (1963); Gutteridge and Megrah, *The Law of Bankers' Commercial Credits*, 4th Edn. (1968); Ellinger, *Documentary Letters of Credit* (1970).
2. See e.g. 8th Edn., pp. 432–3.
3. See especially *Hamzeh Malas & Sons* v. *British Imex Industries, Ltd.,* [1958] 2 Q.B. 127; [1958] 1 All E.R. 262; *Urquhart Lindsay & Co. Ltd.* v. *Eastern Bank, Ltd.,* [1922] 1 K.B. 318.
4. Davis, *op. cit.,* Chap. 7; Gutteridge and Megrah, *op. cit.,* Chap. 3; Ellinger, *op. cit.,* pp. 39 *et seq.*

B. LAPSE OF TIME

If an offer states that it is open for acceptance until a certain day, a later acceptance will clearly be ineffective. Even if there is no express time limit an offer is normally open only for a reasonable time. So in *Ramsgate Victoria Hotel Co.* v. *Montefiore*[1]:

> The defendant had applied in June for shares in the plaintiff company and had paid a deposit into the company's bank. He heard nothing more until the end of November, when he was informed that the shares had been allotted to him and that he should pay the balance due upon them.

The Court of Exchequer held that his refusal to take them up was justified. His offer should have been accepted, if at all, within a reasonable time, and the interval between June and November was excessive. The American case of *Loring* v. *City of Boston*[2] offers a further illustration.

> A reward was offered in May, 1837, for the " apprehension and conviction " of incendiaries. The advertisement continued in the papers for a week, but was never followed by any notice of revocation. In January, 1841, the plaintiff secured an arrest and conviction for arson, and sued for the reward.

The offer was held to have lapsed by the passage of time, and the plaintiff failed.

C. FAILURE OF A CONDITION SUBJECT TO WHICH THE OFFER WAS MADE

An offer, no less than an acceptance, may be conditional and not absolute; and if the condition fails to be satisfied, the offer will not be capable of acceptance. The condition may be implied as well as expressed. A striking illustration is afforded by the case of *Financings, Ltd.* v. *Stimson*.[3]

> On March 16th the defendant saw at the premises of X, a dealer, a motor car advertised for £350. He wished to obtain it on hire purchase and signed a form provided by X. The form was that of the plaintiffs, a finance company, and stated: " This ' agreement ' shall be binding on [the plaintiffs] only upon signature on behalf of the plaintiffs ". On March 18th the defendant paid the first instalment of £70 and took away the car. On March 20th, dissatisfied with it, the defendant returned it to X, saying that he was ready to forfeit his £70. On March 24th the car was stolen from X's premises, but was recovered badly damaged. On March 25th, in ignorance of these facts, the plaintiffs signed the " agreement ".

---

1. (1866), L.R. 1 Ex. Ch. 109. See also *Hare* v. *Nicoll*, [1966] 2 Q.B. 130; [1966] 1 All E.R. 285; and *Manchester Diocesan Council for Education* v. *Commercial and General Investments, Ltd.*, [1969] 3 All E.R. 1593; [1970] 1 W.L.R. 241 which contains an instructive examination by BUCKLEY, J., of the rationale of the rule.
2. (1844), 7 Metcalf, 409.
3. [1962] 3 All E.R. 386; [1962] 1 W.L.R. 1184.

When the plaintiffs subsequently discovered what had happened, they sold the car for £240 and sued the defendant for breach of the hire-purchase contract.   The Court of Appeal gave judgment for the defendant.   The so-called " agreement " was in truth an offer by the defendant to make a contract with the plaintiffs.   But it was subject to the implied condition that the car remained, until the moment of acceptance, in substantially the same state as at the moment of offer.   As DONOVAN, L.J., asked:[1]

> " Who would offer to purchase a car on terms that, if it were severely damaged before the offer was accepted, he, the offeror, would pay the bill? . . . The county court judge held that there must be implied a term that, until acceptance, the goods would remain in substantially the same state as at the date of the offer; and I think that this is both good sense and good law."

As the implied condition had been broken before the plaintiffs purported to accept, the offer had ceased to be capable of acceptance and no contract had been concluded.

D. DEATH

Effect of
death of
offeror

The effect of death upon the continuity of an offer is more doubtful.   It is clear that the offeree cannot accept after he has had notice of the offeror's death.[2]   But is the offeror's estate bound if the offeree performs an act of acceptance in ignorance of the death?   In *Dickinson* v. *Dodds*[3] MELLISH, L.J., in an *obiter dictum*, expressed the opinion " that, if a man who makes an offer dies, the offer cannot be accepted after he is dead."   The case of *Bradbury* v. *Morgan*,[4] however, suggests that, in principle at least, this opinion does not represent the law.

> X had written to the plaintiffs, requesting them to give credit to Y and guaranteeing payment up to £100.   The plaintiffs gave credit to Y.   X then died, and the plaintiffs, in ignorance of this fact, continued the credit to Y.   The plaintiffs now sued X's executors on the guarantee.

It was held that the defendants were liable.   In the words of POLLOCK, C.B.:

> " This is a contract, and the question is whether it is put an end to by death of the guarantor.   There is no direct authority to that effect; and I think that all reason and authority, such as there is, are against that proposition ".

CHANNELL, B., was equally emphatic.

> " In the case of a contract death does not in general operate as revocation, but only in exceptional cases, and this is not within them."

---

1. *Ibid,* at p. 390.   Lord DENNING, M.R. and DONOVAN, L.J. (PEARSON, L.J., dissenting) were also prepared to find for the defendant on the ground that, when he returned the car to the dealer, he revoked his offer and that the dealer had ostensible authority to accept the revocation on the plaintiffs' behalf.
2. See *Re Whelan,* [1897] 1 I.R. 575, and *Coulthart* v. *Clementson* (1879), 5 Q.B.D. 42.
3. (1876), 2 Ch.D. 463, at p. 475.   See also *Pollock on Contract,* 13th Edn., p. 30.
4. (1862), 1 H. and C. 249.

The truth would seem to be that the effect of death varies according to the nature of the particular contract. If, as in the case of a guarantee, the offer is of a promise which is independent of the offeror's personality and which can be satisfied out of his estate, death does not, until notified, prevent acceptance. If, as in the case of agency[1] or in an offer to write a book or to perform at a concert, some element personal to the offeror is involved, his death automatically terminates the negotiations.[2]

Upon the converse case of the offeree's death there appears to be no English authority. The question was, indeed, considered *obiter* by Warrington, L.J., in *Reynolds* v. *Atherton*.[3] He was of opinion that an offer ceases, by operation of law, on the death of the offeree, though he regarded the language of revocation in this context as inappropriate.

Effect of death of offeree

> " I think it would be more accurate to say that, the offer having been made to a living person who ceases to be a living person before the offer is accepted, there is no longer an offer at all. The offer is not intended to be made to a dead person or to his executors, and the offer ceases to be an offer capable of acceptance."

The *dictum*, indeed, was coloured by an anachronistic reference to the *consensus* theory, and the point was expressly reserved by Lord Dunedin when the case reached the House of Lords.[4] But it is not unreasonable to suggest that an offer, unless made to the public at large, assumes the continued existence of a particular offeree, and that the destruction of this assumption frustrates the intention to contract. This view has been taken in Canada. In *Re Irvine* it was held by the Appellate Division of the Supreme Court of Ontario that an acceptance, handed by an offeree to his son for posting but not in fact posted until after the offeree's death, was invalid.[5]

SECTION V. CONSTRUCTING A CONTRACT

The rules thus developed by the common law as to the making, acceptance and revocation of offers illustrate the almost self-evident truth that while contract is ultimately based upon the assumption of agreement, the courts, like all human tribunals, cannot peer into the minds of the parties and must be content with external phenomena. The existence of a contract, in many cases, is to be inferred only from conduct. To do justice, however, the courts may have to go beyond the immediate inferences to be drawn from words and acts and may be tempted or driven to construct a contract between persons who would seem, at first sight, not to be in contractual relationship with each other at all.

---

1. *Infra,* p. 490.
2. See Ferson, 10 Minn. L.J. 373.
3. (1921), 125 L.T. 690, at pp. 695–6.
4. (1922), 127 L.T. 189, at p. 191.
5. [1928] 3 D.L.R. 268.

The classical example of this process is the case of *Clarke* v. *Dunraven*.[1]

> The owners of two yachts entered them for the Mudhook Yacht Club Regatta.   The rules of the Club, which each owner undertook in a letter to the Club Secretary to obey, included an obligation to pay " all damages " caused by fouling.   While manœurving for the start, the *Satanita* fouled the *Valkyrie* and sank her.   The owner of the latter sued the owner of the former for damages.

The defendant argued that his only liability was under a statute whereby his responsibility was limited to £8 per ton on the registered tonnage of his yacht.[2]   The plaintiff replied that the fact of entering a competition in accordance with the rules of the Club created a contract between the respective competitors and that by these rules the defendant had bound himself to pay " all damages."   The vital question, therefore, was whether any contract had been made between the two owners: their immediate relations were not with each other but with the Yacht Club. It was held, both by the Court of Appeal and by the House of Lords, that a contract was created between them either when they entered their yachts for the race or, at latest, when they actually sailed.[3]   The competitors had accepted the rules as binding upon each other.

The rôle of the judges in thus constructing a contract was accepted and explained in 1913 by Lord MOULTON.[4]

> " It is evident, both on principle and on authority, that there may be a contract the consideration for which is the making of some other contract. ' If you will make such and such a contract I will give you one hundred pounds,' is in every sense of the word a complete legal contract.   It is collateral to the main contract, but each has an independent existence, and they do not differ in respect of their possessing to the full the character and status of a contract ".

The use of the title " collateral contracts " to designate such creatures is thus sanctioned by high authority and, indeed, had been known to the law for the previous fifty years.[5]

The name is not, perhaps, altogether fortunate.   The word " collateral " suggests something that stands side by side with the main contract, springing out of it and fortifying it.   But, as will be seen from the examples that follow, the purpose of the device usually is to enforce a promise given prior to the main contract and but for which this main contract would not have been made.   It is often, though not always, rather a preliminary than a collateral contract.   But it would be pedantic to quarrel with the name if the invention itself is salutary and successful.   Its

---

1. [1897] A.C. 59, affirming the decision of the Court of Appeal, reported *sub nom. The Satanita*, [1895] P. 248.   See also *Rayfield* v. *Hands*, [1960] Ch. 1; [1958] 2 All E.R. 194.
2. Merchant Shipping (Amendment) Act 1862, s. 54 (1).
3. See the judgments of Lord ESHER, [1895] P., at p. 255, and of Lord HERSCHELL, [1897] A.C., at p. 63.
4. *Heilbut, Symons & Co.* v. *Buckleton*, [1913] A.C. 30, at p. 47.   See Greig, 87 L.Q.R. 179, at pp. 185–190.
5. *Lindley* v. *Lacey* (1864), 17 C.B.N.S. 578;   and *Erskine* v. *Adeane* (1873), 8 Ch. App. 756.   See Wedderburn, [1959] C.L.J. 58.   It may be added that the case of *Collen* v. *Wright* (1857), 8 E. & B. 647, seems to offer an early example of a " collateral contract ": *infra*, pp. 483–4.

value has been attested by a number of cases. Thus in *Shanklin Pier, Ltd.* v. *Detel Products, Ltd.*,[1]

> the plaintiffs had made a contract with X and Co. to repair and repaint their pier. Under this contract the plaintiffs had the right to specify the materials to be used. The defendants induced them to specify the use of a particular paint made by the defendants by giving them assurances as to its quality. The paint was applied by X and Co. with sad effect, and the plaintiffs had to spend £4,000 to put matters right.

The plaintiffs sued the defendants for breach of their undertaking. The defendants argued that there was no contract between the plaintiffs and themselves, because the paint had been bought from the defendants by X and Co. But it was held that in addition to the contract for the sale of the paint, there was a collateral contract between plaintiffs and defendants by which in return for the plaintiffs specifying that the defendants' paint should be used, the defendants guaranteed its suitability.

A series of hire-purchase cases is especially instructive.

Hire-purchase cases

In *Webster* v. *Higgin*:[2]

> The defendant was considering the hire-purchase of a car owned by the plaintiff, a garage proprietor. The plaintiff's agent said to the defendant: " If you buy the Hillman we will guarantee that it is in good condition ". The defendant then signed a hire-purchase agreement containing a clause that " no warranty, condition, description or representation as to the state or quality of the vehicle is given or implied ". The car, in the words of Lord GREENE, " was nothing but a mass of second-hand and dilapidated ironmongery ".

The plaintiff sued for the return of the car and for the balance of the instalments still due. Had the hire-purchase agreement stood alone, the clause quoted might have precluded the defendant from pleading the state of the car.[3] But the Court of Appeal held that not one but two contracts had been made by the parties. The hire-purchase agreement itself had been preceded by a separate contract effected by an exchange of promises. The plaintiff, through his agent, had offered to guarantee the condition of the car in return for the defendant's promise to take it on hire-purchase terms. This separate contract the plaintiff had broken. In the result the parties gave mutual undertakings to the court, the defendant to return the car and the plaintiff to treat the hire-purchase contract as at an end; and the court ordered the plaintiff to refund the deposit and the instalments which the defendant had already paid.

In *Brown* v. *Sheen and Richmond Car Sales, Ltd.*[4]

> The plaintiff wanted to obtain a car. The defendants showed him one, saying that it was " in perfect condition and good for thousands of trouble-free miles." The plaintiff, relying on this statement, decided to take it, but could not pay cash. It was therefore agreed that the transaction should be financed through X

---

1. [1951] 2 K.B. 854; [1951] 2 All E.R. 471.
2. [1948] 2 All E.R. 127.
3. The plaintiff, however, might have been guilty of a fundamental breach: see *infra*, pp. 159–166.
4. [1950] 1 All E.R. 1102.

and Co., a finance company.   In accordance with the usual course of such business, the defendants sold the car to X and Co., and X and Co. made a hire-purchase contract with the plaintiff.   When the car was delivered to the plaintiff, he found that it was not in good condition and had to spend money in putting it in order.

He sued the defendants for breach of their undertaking that the car was " in perfect condition," and the defendants were held liable.

In *Andrews* v. *Hopkinson*:[1]

> The plaintiff wanted to obtain a second-hand car.   The defendant, a car dealer, recommended one, saying: " It's a good little bus. I would stake my life on it."   Hire-purchase arrangements were then made.   The plaintiff paid a deposit of £50 to the defendant; the defendant sold the car to X and Co., a finance company; and X and Co. made a hire-purchase contract with the plaintiff.   X and Co. then delivered the car to the plaintiff, who signed a delivery note stating that he was " satisfied as to its condition."   Up to this moment the plaintiff had not examined the car.   A week later, when the plaintiff was driving it, it suddenly swerved into a lorry. The car was wrecked and the plaintiff was seriously injured.   On examination it became clear that, when the car was delivered, the steering mechanism was badly at fault.

The plaintiff might have been precluded by the delivery note from suing X and Co. on the hire-purchase contract.   But he recovered damages from the defendant for breach of the undertaking given by the latter before the hire-purchase contract had been made.

In each of these cases the defendant had given an undertaking to the plaintiff which induced the plaintiff to make an independent contract.   In each of them the court was able to construct a preliminary or " collateral " contract, " the consideration for which," in Lord MOULTON's words, was " the making of some other contract," and for whose breach an action would lie.   Reciprocal promises could be spelt out of the dealings between the parties.   " If you will promise to specify my paint to be used on your pier or to enter into a contract for the hire-purchase of a car, I will promise that the paint is of good quality, or the car in good condition."[2]   The device, like other judicial inventions, must not be abused.   In 1965, in the case of *Hill* v. *Harris*, DIPLOCK, L.J., said " that, when parties have entered into a lease which has been the subject of negotiations between them over a period of something like six months, [a court] is unlikely to find the terms on which the premises are to be held, or the relevant covenants in relation to the premises, outside the terms of the negotiated lease itself."[3]   On the facts of this particular case the

---

1. [1957] 1 Q.B. 229;   [1956] 3 All E.R. 422.
2. Readers of the judgments in these three cases will observe that the word " warranty " is used to describe the undertaking given by the defendants. As will be seen (*infra*, p. 139), this word, in modern legal language, is used to denote a term of comparatively minor importance included in a contract. It would therefore seem inappropriate in the present context, where the task of the court was to construct an entirely independent contract, one side of which was the undertaking in question.   But, though the language employed may be unhappy, the result of the cases is in line with previous developments, as described by Lord MOULTON.   See Diamond, 21 M.L.R. 177.
3. [1965] 2 All E.R. 358, at p. 362;   [1965] 2 W.L.R. 1331, at p. 1336.

Court of Appeal was not prepared to discover the existence of any agreement other than that contained in the lease. But there is good authority for saying that, where the facts justify the conclusion, a court may properly " construct a collateral contract " from things said or done during the preliminary negotiations.[1] Used with discretion, an instrument has thus been forged which, without offending orthodox views of contract, may enable substantial justice to be done.

---

1. *City and Westminster Properties* (1934), *Ltd.* v. *Mudd,* [1959] Ch. 129; [1958] 2 All E.R. 733. See *infra*, p. 121.

CHAPTER TWO

Consideration

SECTION I. FUNCTION AND DEFINITION

In the previous chapter we saw that agreement, or at least the outward appearance of agreement, was an essential ingredient of a contract. But it is likely that few legal systems treat all agreements as enforceable contracts. In early systems the distinction between unenforceable and enforceable agreements is often one of form and signs of that can be found in English law in the survival of the rule that a promise under seal is legally binding.

In developed English law, that is since the sixteenth century, the crucial factor is the presence or the absence of "consideration." It is natural to assume that the adoption of this test is related to some underlying theory about why agreements are enforced.[1] It has therefore been forcefully argued that " consideration " is a word long rooted in the language of English law and denotes its fundamental attitude to contract and that when, in the middle of the sixteenth century, the lawyers evolved, through the action

---

1. The literature on why contracts are legally enforced is extensive. See e.g. Hughes Parry, *The Sanctity of Contracts in English Law*; Cohen and Cohen, *Readings in Jurisprudence and Legal Philosophy*, pp. 100–195.

of assumpsit, a general contractual remedy, they decided at the same time that it would not avail to redress the breach of any and every promise, whatever its nature. In particular, it has been said that it was decided that assumpsit was not to be used to enforce a gratuitous promise so that the plaintiff must show that the defendant's promise, upon which he was suing, was part of a bargain to which he himself had contributed.[1] So it has been persuasively argued that the doctrine of consideration represents the adoption by English Law of the notion that only bargains should be enforced.[2]

This view has not gone unchallenged. The history of consideration is still not completely clear but it seems inherently unlikely that sixteenth century English judges would ever have asked themselves a highly abstract question such as " Should we enforce bargains or promises? " The pragmatic habits of the English and the absence of institutional writing make it probable that in the sixteenth and seventeenth centuries there was no single *doctrine* of consideration, but a number of considerations which were recognised as adequate to support an action for breach of a promise.[3] So consideration probably meant at this stage the reason for the promise being binding, fulfilling something like the role of *causa* or *cause* in continental systems.[4]

The doctrine of consideration was accepted throughout the seventeenth and in the first half of the eighteenth century as an integral part of the new law of contract. But when Lord MANS-FIELD became Chief Justice of the King's Bench in 1756 its pride of place was challenged. At first Lord MANSFIELD refused to recognise it as the vital criterion of a contract and treated it merely as evidence of the parties' intention to be bound. If such an intention could be ascertained by other means, such as the presence of writing, consideration was unnecessary.[5] This direct assault was repelled with ease. In *Rann* v. *Hughes* in 1778[6] it was proclaimed that

> "all contracts are by the laws of England distinguished into agreements by specialty and agreements by parol; nor is there any such third class . . . as contracts in writing. If they be merely written and not specialties, they are parol, and a consideration must be proved."

Lord MANSFIELD's second approach was more insinuating. Accepting the concept of consideration as essential to English contract, he defined it in terms of moral obligation.

Marginal notes: Consideration and bargains · Lord Mansfield's attack on consideration

---

1. Fifoot. *History and Sources of the Common Law*, pp. 395 *et seq.*
2. See, e.g. Hamson, 54 L.Q.R. 233; Shatwell, 1 Sydney L.R. 289.
3. See Simpson, *History*, Chap. IV–VII.
4. Simpson, 91 L.Q.R. 247, at p. 262. On the relationship between consideration and cause see WINDEYER, J., in *Smith* v. *Jenkins* (1970), 44 A.L.J.R. 78, at p. 83. Atiyah has recently argued in his *Consideration in Contracts* that this is still the function of consideration. The equation of consideration and bargain is also criticised by Pound, 33 Tulane L.R. 455. See also Chloros, 17 I.C.L.Q. 137. On the other hand in the history of ideas what is believed is often more important than what is true. Whatever its historical validity, the equation between consideration and bargain has had a powerful influence on twentieth century writing.
5. *Pillans* v. *Van Mierop* (1756), 3 Burr. 1663. For the varied fortunes of the doctrine of consideration between 1765 and 1840, see Fifoot, *History and Sources of the Common Law*, 406–411.
6. (1778), 7 Term Rep. 350, n.

"Where a man is under a moral obligation, which no Court of law or equity can enforce, and promises, the honesty and rectitude of the thing is a consideration. . . . The ties of conscience upon an upright mind are a sufficient consideration."[1]

According to this view, whenever a man is under a moral duty to pay money and subsequently promises to pay, the pre-existing moral duty furnishes consideration for the promise. The equation of consideration and moral obligation was accepted, though with increasing distrust, for nearly sixty years, and was finally repudiated only in 1840. In *Eastwood* v. *Kenyon*,[2]

> On the death of John Sutcliffe, his infant daughter, Sarah, was left as his sole heiress. The plaintiff, as the girl's guardian, spent money on her education and for the benefit of the estate, and the girl, when she came of age, promised to reimburse him. She then married the defendant, who also promised to pay. The plaintiff sued the defendant on this promise.

Lord Mansfield's views repudiated

Lord DENMAN dismissed the action and condemned the whole principle of moral obligation upon which it was founded. Such a principle was an innovation of Lord MANSFIELD, and to extirpate it would be to restore the pure and original doctrine of the common law. Moreover, as he pointed out, the logical inference from the acceptance of moral duty as the sole test of an actionable promise was the virtual annihilation of consideration. The law required some factor additional to the defendant's promise, whereby the promise became legally binding; but, if no more was needed than the pressure of conscience, this would operate as soon as the defendant voluntarily assumed an undertaking. To give a promise was to accept a moral obligation to perform it.[3]

Attempts to define consideration

As a result of *Eastwood* v. *Kenyon* it was clear that consideration was neither a mere rule of evidence nor a synonym for moral obligation. How then was it to be defined? In the course of the nineteenth century it was frequently said that a plaintiff could establish the presence of consideration in one of two ways. He might prove either that he had conferred a benefit upon the defendant in return for which the defendant's promise was given

---

1. *Hawkes* v. *Saunders* (1782), 1 Cowp. 289.
2. (1840), 11 Ad. & El. 438. Extra-judicial criticism had been offered by the reporters Bosanquet and Puller in 1802 (see the note to *Wennall* v. *Adney* (1802), 3 B. & P. 247), and Lord TENTERDEN had expressed some doubts in 1831 (*Littlefield* v. *Shee* (1831), 2 B. & Ad. 811). But no decisive rejection occurred until 1840.
3. Simpson, *History*, p. 323, argues that far from being an aberration of Lord MANSFIELD, the "moral obligation" consideration lies at the heart of the early history of the doctrine. Some exceptional cases survived *Eastwood* v. *Kenyon*. See e.g. *Flight* v. *Reed* (1863), 1 H. & C. 703, where the plaintiff advanced money to the defendant against promissory notes void under the usury statutes. After the repeal of the statutes and without any further advances, the defendant executed new promissory notes which were held binding, the only consideration being the moral obligation to repay the void loans. This case was not followed in *Sharp* v. *Ellis*, [1972] V.R. 137. See also the cases of past consideration discussed *infra*, pp. 66–9.

or that he himself had incurred a detriment for which the promise was to compensate.[1]

The antithesis of benefit and detriment, though reiterated in the courts, is not altogether happy. The use of the word " detriment," in particular, obscures the vital transformation of *assumpsit* from a species of action on the case to a general remedy in contract. So long as it remained tortious in character, it was necessary to prove that the plaintiff had suffered damage in reliance upon the defendant's undertaking. When it became contractual, the courts concentrated, not on the consequences of the defendant's default, but on the facts present at the time of the agreement and in return for which the defendant's promise was given. " Detriment " is clearly a more appropriate description of the former than of the latter situation. Nor is this criticism of merely antiquarian interest. The typical modern contract is the bargain struck by the exchange of promises. If A orders goods on credit from B both A and B are bound from the moment of agreement, and, if the one subsequently refuses to execute his part of it, the other may sue at once. The consideration for each party's promise is the other party's promise. It is difficult to see that at this stage either party has suffered benefit or detriment unless each party is said to have received the benefit of the other's promise and suffered the detriment of making his own. But such benefit and detriment assumes that the promises are binding, which is precisely what it is sought to prove.[2] A further disadvantage to the use of the word " detriment " is that it has to be understood in a highly technical sense. So a promise to give up smoking is capable of being a detriment in the law of consideration even though smoking is bad for the promisor. This is technically sound but likely to confuse.

A different approach to the problem of consideration may be made through the language of purchase and sale. The plaintiff must show that he has bought the defendant's promise either by doing some act in return for it or by offering a counter-promise. Sir Frederick Pollock summarized the position in words adopted by the House of Lords in 1915:

Antithesis of benefit and detriment not satisfactory

Consideration the price of the promise

---

1. " A consideration of loss or inconvenience sustained by one party at the request of another is as good a consideration in law for a promise by such other as a consideration of profit or convenience to himself."—Lord ELLEN-BOROUGH in *Bunn* v. *Guy* (1803), 4 East, 190.

" Consideration means something which is of value in the eye of the law, moving from the plaintiff: it may be some detriment to the plaintiff or some benefit to the defendant."—PATTESON, J., in *Thomas* v. *Thomas*, [1842] 2 Q.B. 851.

" A valuable consideration in the sense of the law may consist either in some right, interest, profit or benefit accruing to one party, or some forbearance, detriment, loss or responsibility given, suffered or undertaken by the other."—*Currie* v. *Misa* (1875), L.R. 10 Exch. 153.

" The general rule is that an executory agreement, by which the plaintiff agrees to do something on the terms that the defendant agrees to do something else, may be enforced, if what the plaintiff has agreed to do is either for the benefit of the defendant or to the trouble or prejudice of the plaintiff."—*per* Lord BLACKBURN in *Bolton* v. *Madden* (1873), L.R. 9 Q.B. 55.

2. *Harrison* v. *Cage* (1698), 5 Mod. Rep. 411.

"An act or forbearance of one party, or the promise thereof, is the price for which the promise of the other is bought, and the promise thus given for value is enforceable."[1]

This definition of consideration as the price paid by the plaintiff for the defendant's promise is preferable to the nineteenth-century terminology of benefit and detriment. It is easier to understand, it corresponds more happily to the normal exchange of promises and it emphasizes the commercial character of the English contract.

SECTION II.   CONSIDERATION—EXECUTORY, EXECUTED AND PAST

Here and in the next two sections will be examined the technical rules which the judges have evolved for the application of their doctrine of consideration.

Meaning of "executory," "executed." The accepted classification of consideration is into the two categories, *executory* and *executed*. The classification reflects the two different ways in which the plaintiff may buy the defendant's promise. Consideration is called *executory* when the defendant's promise is made in return for a counter-promise from the plaintiff, *executed* when it is made in return for the performance of an act. An agreement between seller and buyer for the sale of goods for future delivery on credit is an example of the former. At the time when the agreement is made, nothing has yet been done to fulfil the mutual promises of which the bargain is composed. The whole transaction remains *in futuro*. Of the latter the best example is the offer of a reward for an act. If A offers £5 to anyone who shall return his lost dog, the return of the dog by B is at once the acceptance of the offer and the performance of the act constituting the required consideration. B has earned the reward by his services, and only the offeror's promise remains outstanding. But whether the plaintiff relies upon an executory or on an executed consideration, he must be able to prove that his promise or act, together with the defendant's promise, constitute one single transaction and are causally related the one to the other.[2]

"Past" consideration If the defendant makes a further promise, subsequent to and independent of the transaction, it must be regarded as a mere expression of gratitude for past favours or as a designated gift, and no contract will arise. It is irrelevant that he may have been induced to give the new promise because of the previous bargain. In such a case the promise is declared, in traditional language, to be made upon *past* consideration; or, more accurately, to be

---

1. *Pollock on Contracts*, 13th Edn., p. 133; *Dunlop v. Selfridge*, [1915] A.C. 847, at p. 855. See also Law Revision Committee, *Sixth Interim Report*, para. 17. The conception of consideration as the price of the promise is similarly stressed by *Williston on Contracts*, 3rd Edn., para. 100, and by the *American Restatement of Contracts*, para. 75. See also Salmond & Williams' *Law of Contract*, p. 101, and Denning, 15 M.L.R. 1.
2. *Wigan v. English and Scottish Law Life Insurance Association*, [1909] 1 Ch. 291.

made without consideration at all. Two illustrations may be offered, one from a classical and one from a modern case. In *Roscorla* v. *Thomas*,[1]

> the declaration stated that, " in consideration that the plaintiff at the request of the defendant, *had* bought of the defendant a certain horse, at and for a certain price, the defendant promised the plaintiff that the said horse was sound and free from vice." The plaintiff sued for breach of this promise.

The court held (1) that the fact of the sale did not itself imply a warranty that the horse was sound and free from vice, and (2) that the express promise was made after the sale was over and was unsupported by fresh consideration. The plaintiff could show nothing but a " past " consideration and must fail. In *Re McArdle*,[2]

> a number of children, by their father's will, were entitled to a house after their mother's death. During the mother's life, one of the children and his wife lived with her in the house. The wife made various improvements to the house, and at a later date all the children signed a document addressed to her, stating that " in consideration of your carrying out certain alterations and improvements to the property, we hereby agree that the executors shall repay to you from the estate, when distributed, the sum of £488 in settlement of the amount spent on such improvements."

The Court of Appeal held that, as all the work on the house had in fact been completed before the document was signed, this was a case of past consideration and that the document could not be supported as a binding contract.

The distinction between executed and past consideration, while comparatively easy to state in the abstract, is often difficult to apply in practice, and a long and subtle line of cases has marked its interpretation in the courts. Both the distinction and the difficulty were appreciated by the judges before the close of the sixteenth century. They were required to consider the position where the plaintiff had performed services for the defendant without any agreement for remuneration and the defendant had subsequently promised to pay for them. They decided that *assumpsit* would lie if, but only if, the services were originally performed at the defendant's request.[3] The law was settled in this sense in 1615 in the case of *Lampleigh* v. *Brathwait*.[4]

Services performed at defendant's request

> Thomas Brathwait had killed Patrick Mahume and had then asked Anthony Lampleigh to do all he could to get a pardon for him from the King. Lampleigh exerted himself to this end, " riding and journeying to and from London and Newmarket " at his own expense, and Brathwait afterwards promised him £100 for his trouble. He failed to pay it and Lampleigh sued in *assumpsit*.

It was argued, *inter alia*, that the consideration was past, but the court gave judgment for the plaintiff on the ground that his services had been procured by the previous request of the defendant.

---

1. [1842] 3 Q.B. 234.
2. [1951] Ch. 669; [1951] 1 All E.R. 905.
3. See *Hunt* v. *Bate* (1586), 3 Dyer, 272a, and *Sidenham and Worlington's Case* (1585), 2 Leonard, 224. See also Simpson, *History*, pp. 452–458.
4. (1615), Hob., 105.

> " It was agreed that a mere voluntary courtesy will not have a consideration to uphold an assumpsit. But if that courtesy were moved by a suit or request of the party that gives the assumpsit, it will bind; for the promise, though it follows, yet it is not naked, but couples itself with the suit before."

The previous request and the subsequent promise were thus to be treated as part of the same transaction.

Distinction between past and executed consideration obscured

This extended definition was applied at the end of the seventeenth century to cases where the defendant promised to pay a debt which was not enforceable at the time of his promise owing to some technical rule of law. Thus in *Ball* v. *Hesketh*[1] the defendant, when an infant, had borrowed money from the plaintiff and, after coming of age, had promised to repay it. In accordance with the general immunity conferred by the law upon infants, he could not have been made liable on the original loan. But it was held that his subsequent promise entitled the plaintiff to sue him in *assumpsit*. So, too, in *Hyleing* v. *Hastings*[2] it was held that a debt, the recovery of which was barred by the Statute of Limitations, was revived by a subsequent promise of payment. At the same time, the influence of commercial practice, felt with increasing urgency, familiarized the courts with the idea that a plaintiff, who sued on a negotiable instrument, need only show that value had once been given for it by some previous holder and was himself absolved from the necessity of proving fresh consideration. All these developments threatened to obliterate the distinction between executed and past consideration. It is not surprising, therefore, that they should have been used by Lord MANSFIELD to support his doctrine of moral obligation.[3]

Modern settlement of question

But when, in the nineteenth century, this doctrine was rejected it became necessary to delimit afresh the boundaries of past and executed consideration. This was achieved by accepting the test of *Lampleigh* v. *Brathwait* that the plaintiff's services must have been rendered at the defendant's request, but emphasizing the further fact that both parties must have assumed throughout their negotiations that the services were ultimately to be paid for.[4] They must have been performed in the way of business, not as an office of friendship. This " revised version " was adopted by the court in *Re Casey's Patents, Stewart* v. *Casey*.[5]

> A and B, the joint owners of certain patent rights, wrote to C as follows: " In consideration of your services as the practical manager in working our patents, we hereby agree to give you one-third share of the patents."

In an action which turned upon the effect of this agreement it was argued for A and B that their promise was made only in return for C's past services as manager and that there was therefore no consideration to support it. BOWEN, L.J., refused to accept this argument and said:

---

1. (1697), Comb. 381.
2. (1699), 1 Ld. Raym., 389.
3. See *supra*, pp. 63–4.
4. This further fact, though it was not expressed by the court in *Lampleigh* v. *Brathwait*, seems on the whole, to be implicit in the language of the judgment.
5. [1892] 1 Ch. 104. See also *Kennedy* v. *Broun* (1863), 13 C.B.N.S. 677.

> " The fact of a past service raises an implication that at the time it was rendered it was to be paid for, and if it was a service which was to be paid for, when you get in the subsequent document a promise to pay, that promise may be treated as an admission which evidences or as a positive bargain which fixes the amount of that reasonable remuneration on the faith of which the service was originally rendered. So that here for past services there is ample justification for the promise to give the third share."[1]

On this reasoning the fact that the promise was subsequent to the performance of the services was irrelevant. The original request was accompanied by a tacit understanding of recompense, and even if no express promise had ensued, the plaintiff might still have recovered reasonable remuneration on a *quantum meruit*. The express promise did little more than relieve the courts of the necessity of valuing the services.

The other exceptional cases discussed above have been removed or confirmed by statute. By section 2 of the Infants Relief Act 1874, no action is allowed upon any promise made after full age to pay a debt contracted during infancy.[2] By the Limitation Act 1939, if the debtor, after the debt has been barred, acknowledges the creditor's claim, the plaintiff may sue on this acknowledgment. No promise, express or implied, is necessary, and no consideration need be sought.[3] The third class of case, where the defendant is sued upon a negotiable instrument, survives as a genuine exception to the ban upon past consideration. It is to be explained as a concession to long-standing commercial custom, and it has been confirmed by section 27 of the Bills of Exchange Act 1882. By this section, " valuable consideration for a bill may be constituted by (a) any consideration sufficient to support a simple contract, (b) an antecedent debt or liability."[4]

Exceptions to rule that past consideration is insufficient

SECTION III. CONSIDERATION MUST MOVE FROM THE PROMISEE

As long as consideration, under Lord MANSFIELD'S influence, could be identified with moral duty, it was possible to support an action by a person for whose benefit a promise had been given even if the consideration had been supplied by someone else.[5] But once this identification was repudiated, the judges insisted that only he could sue on a promise who had paid the price of it. How otherwise could the plaintiff prove his share in the bargain upon which his action was based? Thus in *Price* v. *Easton*[6] the defendant promised X that if X did certain work for him he would pay a sum of money to the plaintiff. X did the work, but the defendant did not pay the money. The court of Queen's Bench

---

1. [1892] 1 Ch., at pp. 115–16.
2. See *infra*, pp. 417–8.
3. See *infra*, pp. 623–5.
4. It has been ruled that the " antecedent debt or liability " must be that of the maker or negotiator of the instrument and not of a stranger: *Oliver* v. *Davis*, [1949] 2 K.B. 727; [1949] 2 All E.R. 353.
5. See *Dutton* v. *Poole* (1678), 2 Lev. 210. See Simpson, *History*, pp. 475-485.
6. (1833), 4 B. & Ad. 433.

held that the plaintiff could not sue the defendant and explained their decision in two different ways. Lord DENMAN said that the plaintiff could not " show any consideration for the promise moving from him to the defendant". LITTLEDALE, J., said that " no privity is shown between the plaintiff and the defendant". In *Tweddle* v. *Atkinson* in 1861[1] the judges, while endorsing the decision in *Price* v. *Easton*, preferred the first of these reasons. " It is now established," said WIGHTMAN, J., " that no stranger to the consideration can take advantage of a contract, although made for his benefit."

Relation of
considera-
tion to the
doctrine of
privity   It has long been a controversial question whether the rule that consideration must move from the promisee and the doctrine of privity of contract are fundamentally distinct or whether they are merely variations on a common theme. Two different factual situations may indeed arise. The plaintiff may be a party to an agreement without furnishing any consideration.

> A, B and C may all be signatories to an agreement whereby C promises A and B to pay A £100 if B will carry out work desired by C.

On the other hand, the person anxious to enforce the promise may not be a party to the agreement at all.

> B and C may make an agreement whereby B promises to write a book for C and C promises to pay £100 to A.

In neither situation, on the existing English cases, may A sue C. But must he be said to fail in the first situation because consideration has not moved from him, and in the second because he is not privy to the contract? The nineteenth-century judges distinguished the two situations in law as well as in fact. So, too, in 1915[2] Viscount HALDANE declared two principles to be " fundamental in the law of England." The first was that " only a person who is a party to a contract can sue on it", and the second that " only a person who has given consideration may enforce a contract not under seal." The distinction was endorsed by the Law Revision Committee in 1937.[3]

This view, however, has been questioned.[4] It has been persuasively argued that there is no basic distinction between the two principles stated by Lord HALDANE: they are but different ways of saying the same thing. The underlying assumption of English law is that a contract is a bargain. If a person furnishes no consideration, he takes no part in a bargain: if he takes no part in a bargain, he takes no part in a contract. In the second of the hypothetical cases stated above it is obvious that A is a stranger to the contract. But he is equally a stranger in the first: he is a party to an agreement, but he is not a party to a contract. It is true that, if the doctrine of consideration were abolished, the problem

---

1. (1861), 1 B. & S. 393.
2. *Dunlop* v. *Selfridge*, [1915] A.C. 847, at p. 853: see *infra*, p. 437.
3. *Sixth Interim Report*, p. 22.
4. See Smith and Thomas, *A Casebook on Contract*, 5th Edn., p. 212; Salmond and Williams, *The Law of Contracts*, 2nd Edn., pp. 99–100; Furmston, 23 M.L.R. 373, at pp. 382–4.

of privity would remain, as it still remains in other legal systems. But so long as consideration is an essential feature of English law it would seem to be immaterial whether a person is forbidden to sue on the ground that he has given no consideration or on the ground that he is a stranger to the contract.

In England this argument—by no means unattractive—has still to be tested in the courts. In Australia it was discussed by the High Court in 1967 in *Coulls v. Bagot's Executor and Trustee Co., Ltd.*[1]

> C agreed to grant to the O'Neil Construction Co., Ltd. the exclusive right to quarry on his land in return for a minimum royalty of £12 a week for a period of ten years. C also " authorised the company " to pay all money arising from this agreement to himself and his wife jointly. The agreement was in writing (not under seal) and was signed by C, by his wife and by O'Neil. Eighteen months later, C died. The O'Neil company in fact paid the royalty to C's wife; and the High Court was now asked, in an action between the wife and C's executors, to decide whether the company was bound or entitled to make such payment to her.

The High Court was divided upon the construction of the agreement.[2] But four of the five judges were of opinion that if, on its true interpretation, the wife was a party to the agreement, she was entitled to receive the royalties payable after her husband's death even though she personally had given no consideration for the company's promise.

The High Court did not define with precision the relationship of privity of contract to the rule that consideration must move from the promisee. BARWICK, C.J., seems to have treated the two rules as separate requirements:

> " It must be accepted," he said,[3] " that, according to our law, a person not a party to a contract may not himself sue upon it so as directly to enforce its obligations. For my part I find no difficulty or embarrassment in this conclusion. Indeed, I would find it odd that a person to whom no promise was made could himself enforce a promise made by another."

WINDEYER, J., on the other hand, asked if there were any " useful distinction between denying a right of action to a person because no promise was made to him, and denying a right of action to a person to whom a promise was made because no consideration for it moved from him."[4]

In the present case, the wife was a party to the agreement; but had consideration moved from her? At first sight it would seem that her husband was the only person who had given consideration for the company's promise. Nevertheless BARWICK, C.J., and WINDEYER, J., found a way round the difficulty. Husband and wife were joint promisees.

[margin note: Consideration and joint promisees]

---

1. [1967] A.L.R. 385.
2. Three judges held that the clause " authorising the company " to pay C's wife was merely a revocable mandate which had been revoked by C's death.
3. [1967] A.L.R., at pp. 394–395.
4. *Ibid.,* at p. 405.

" The promise," said WINDEYER, J.,[1] " is made to them collectively. It must, of course, be supported by consideration, but that does not mean by consideration furnished by them separately. It means a consideration given on behalf of them both, and therefore moving from both of them. In such a case the promise of the promisor is not gratuitous; and, as between him and the joint promisees, it matters not how they were able to provide the price of his promise to them."

The solution is neat and would simply require the rule to be restated so as to insist that consideration must move either from a single promisee or from a number of joint promisees.

It is to be hoped that the English courts may find themselves able to adopt the revised formula, even though it may not always be easy to decide whether the intended beneficiary under the contract is, or is not, a joint promisee with the party who has expressly provided the consideration. There are at least helpful passages in the case of *McEvoy* v. *Belfast Banking Co., Ltd.*[2]:

> A father, who had £10,000 on deposit with the Belfast Bank, transferred it to a deposit account in the names of himself and of his infant son. Soon afterwards he died. The executors were allowed by the Bank to withdraw the money and put it into an account in their own names. The money was in fact lost in attempts to keep the family business alive; and the son sued the bank.

The Bank argued, *inter alia*, that no rights accrued to the son over the deposit account because he had furnished no consideration. The argument was rejected by Lord ATKIN:

> " The contract on the face of it purports to be made with A and B, and I think with them jointly and severally. A purports to make the contract on behalf of B as well as himself, and the consideration supports such a contract."[3]

SECTION IV. SUFFICIENCY OF CONSIDERATION

Not every act or promise amounts to consideration

Consideration has been defined as the act or promise offered by the one party and accepted by the other as the price of that other's promise. The question now arises whether any act and any promise, regardless of their content, will satisfy this definition. Ames, indeed, argued that, with obvious reservations in the interests of morality and public policy, the question must be answered in the affirmative.[4] A survey of decided cases, however, will show that his argument, whatever its logical merits, does not represent the actual position. Certain acts and promises, it

---

1. *Ibid.,* at p. 405.
2. [1935] A.C. 24.
3. *Ibid.,* at p. 43. Lord THANKERTON (at p. 52) said that he would have agreed with this statement if he had thought that the father had designed to make the son a contracting party. See Cullity, 85 L.Q.R. 530, especially at pp. 531–534 and *New Zealand Shipping Co., Ltd.* v. *A. M. Satterthwaite & Co., Ltd.,* [1975] A.C. 154, at p. 180; [1974] 1 All E.R. 1015, at p. 1030, *per* Lord SIMON OF GLAISDALE.
4. See Ames, *Lectures on Legal History,* pp. 323 *et seq.*

will be seen, are deemed incapable in law of supporting an action for breach of contract by the person who has supplied them. But, while most jurists have been forced by the results of litigation to accept this conclusion, there has been great divergence of opinion as to the test of such capacity. Two main lines of divergence may be observed.

There is doubt, in the first place, as to whether the criterion, whatever it may be, is equally applicable to acts and to promises. That such is the case was asserted by Chief Justice HOLT over two centuries ago[1] and re-asserted by Leake in his book on Contracts in the middle of the nineteenth century.

Doubtful whether same test applies to acts and promises

> " It may be observed," said Leake, " that whatever matter, if executed, is sufficient to form a good executed consideration, if promised, is sufficient to form a good executory consideration."[2]

The adoption of a single test would clearly simplify the problem: once determine its character in the case of an act and it could be applied automatically in the case of a promise. Sir Frederick Pollock, however, denied the possibility of a single test and declared that, in certain cases, a promise may, while an actual performance may not, afford a consideration to support a counter-promise.[3]

In the second place, whether the test be single or double, little success has attended the efforts of jurists to express it in language at once definite and comprehensive. Williston, who has devoted particular care to the problem, can only state it in terms of the formula of benefit and detriment current in the nineteenth century, which has already been shown to be unsatisfactory. Executed consideration, according to his view, consists of " a detriment incurred by the promisee or a benefit received by the promisor at the request of the promisor ": executory consideration consists of " mutual promises in each of which the promisor undertakes some act or forbearance that will be, *or apparently may be*, detrimental to the promisor or beneficial to the promisee."[4] This language, it is suggested, restates the problem rather than solves it, and, as will be seen, is to be applied to actual cases only with difficulty and with a certain sense of strain.

Difficulty of defining the precise test

It is, indeed, not without significance that these controversies are, for the most part, carried on outside the courts. The judges have been content to deny the name of consideration to certain acts or promises without attempting to generalize the grounds of their prohibition; and it may well be that the process of judicial thought is purely empirical and does not lend itself to *ex post facto* rationalization. It will be well, at least, to discuss in turn the

The rules adopted by the courts

---

1. " Where the doing a thing will be a good consideration, a promise to do that thing will be so too ": *Thorp* v. *Thorp* (1701), 12 Mod. Rep. 455.
2. *Leake on Contracts*, 1st Edn., p. 314.
3. *Pollock on Contracts*, 13th Edn., pp. 147–50; and see *infra*, pp. 98–100. Williston seems to take a middle view: *Williston on Contracts*, 3rd Edn., para. 103.
4. *Williston on Contracts*, 3rd Edn., paras. 102 and 103. The italics are ours. Williston uses the terms " unilateral " and "bilateral " to express the antithesis " executed " and " executory ". But the latter words have been adopted here as more in consonance with English usage.

individual rules applied by the courts and then to ask if any comprehensive test can be adopted.

These rules may, for the sake of exposition, be grouped into two classes:

    (a) Those rules which forbid the courts to upset a bargain merely because the act or promise supplied by the plaintiff is an inadequate recompense for the defendant's promise;

    (b) Those rules which expressly declare that certain acts or promises do not constitute consideration.

Terminology

Here, as in other aspects of contract, the choice of appropriate terminology to describe a particular legal position is a matter of difficulty. The word " adequacy " has long been associated with the reluctance of the courts lightly to interfere with an agreement which the parties themselves have deemed fair and reasonable, and some other word must be chosen to indicate the cases in which, perhaps as an exceptional measure, the courts reserve the right of interference. For this latter purpose the epithet " sufficient " has been sanctioned, if not hallowed, by more than three centuries of judicial usage. It was adopted by the Elizabethan judges when they established the doctrine of consideration and repeated by their successors in the seventeenth century. It was assumed to be appropriate both by Lord MANSFIELD and by his opponents, and it was accepted by Lord DENMAN in *Eastwood v. Kenyon*[1]. In the present chapter, therefore, though there is a conscious artificiality in contrasting such words as " adequacy " and " sufficiency " which in popular use are regarded as synonyms, consideration will be described as " sufficient " or " insufficient " according as the judges allow or disallow the validity of particular acts or promises.

A. ADEQUACY OF CONSIDERATION

Consideration need not be adequate

It has been settled for well over three hundred years that the courts will not inquire into the " adequacy of consideration." By this is meant that they will not seek to measure the comparative value of the defendant's promise and of the act or promise given by the plaintiff in exchange for it, nor will they denounce an agreement merely because it seems to be unfair. The promise must, indeed, have been procured by the offer of some return capable of expression in terms of value. A parent, who makes a promise " in consideration of natural love and affection " or to induce his son to refrain from boring him with complaints, cannot be sued upon it, since the essential elements of a bargain are

---

1. From examples too numerous for citation in a footnote the following cases may be selected: *Richards and Bartlet's Case* (1584), 1 Leon 19; *Knight v. Rushworth* (1596), Cro. Eliz. 469; *Bret v. J. S.* (1600), Cro. Eliz. 756; *Grisley v. Lother* (1613), Hob. 10; *Davis v. Reyner* (1671), 2 Lev. 3; *Rann v. Hughes* (1778), 7 Term Rep., 350, n.; *Hawkes v. Saunders* (1782), 1 Cowp. 289; *Eastwood v. Kenyon* (1840), 11 Ad. & El. 438. It may also be observed that the phrase " sufficient consideration " is used in this sense by *Williston on Contracts*, 3rd Edn., para. 101; and *see American Restatement of Contracts*, para. 76 *et seq.*

lacking.[1] But if these elements be present the courts will not balance the one side against the other. The parties are presumed to be capable of appreciating their own interests and of reaching their own equilibrium. In 1587 it was said that, " when a thing is to be done by the plaintiff, be it never so small, this is a sufficient consideration to ground an action"[2]; and this rejection of a quantitative test has been constantly reiterated. In *Thomas* v. *Thomas*:[3]

> The plaintiff's husband had expressed the wish that the plaintiff, if she survived him, should have the use of his house. After his death the defendant, his executor, agreed to allow her to occupy the house (a) because of the husband's wishes, (b) on the payment by her of £1 a year.

The court declined to be influenced by the husband's wishes: motive was " not the same thing with consideration." But they accepted the plaintiff's promise to pay the £1 a year as affording consideration for the defendant's promise, and defendant's counsel admitted that he could not rest any argument upon its manifest inadequacy.[4]

The principle may be studied in its application to cases where a person seeks to stay the prosecution of a legal claim with which he is threatened. Such agreements may take a variety of forms. The person against whom the claim is made may admit the claim but ask the claimant to give him more time to pay. Such an agreement is often described as a forbearance. Alternatively he may dispute the claim (or while accepting that there is a claim, dispute the amount) but offer to settle the dispute for less than the amount claimed. Such an agreement is usually described as a compromise. It would appear however that all these situations are subject to the same principles. They will here be discussed as examples of a single category. *[Subject illustrated by a promise not to sue]*

It was originally held that a promise not to pursue a claim which in truth was without legal basis could not be good consideration. If it had been submitted to the arbitrament of the courts the promisor must have failed, and it could not be a " detriment " to be saved from a losing hazard.[5] But in the nineteenth century this position was abandoned, and the compromise of a doubtful claim was upheld by the courts. The change was justified on grounds of convenience. In the words of BOWEN, L.J., *[Compromise of doubtful case is valid]*

> " The reality of the claim which is given up must be measured not by the state of the law as it is ultimately discovered to be, but by the state of the knowledge of the person who at the time has to judge and make the concession. Otherwise you would have to try the whole cause to know if the man had a right to compromise it."[6]

---

1. See *Bret* v. *J. S.* (1600), Cro. Eliz. 756; and *White* v. *Bluett* (1853), 23 L.J. Ex. 36.
2. *Sturlyn* v. *Albany* (1587), Cro. Eliz. 67.
3. (1842), 2 Q.B. 851.
4. A modern illustration is afforded by the case of *Alexander* v. *Rayson*, [1936] 1 K.B. 169; [1935] All E.R. Rep. 185.
5. *Stone* v. *Wythipol* (1588), Cro. Eliz. 126; *Jones* v. *Ashburnham* (1804), 4 East 455. See the useful historical discussion by BEATSON [1974] C.L.J. 97, at pp. 100–103.
6. *Miles* v. *New Zealand Alford Estate Co.* (1886), 32 Ch.D. 266, at p. 291. See also *Callisher* v. *Bischoffsheim* (1870), L.R. 5 Q.B. 449.

In the modern law, the consideration in such cases is said to be the surrender, not of a legal right, which may or may not exist and whose existence, at the time of the compromise, remains untested, but of the *claim* to such a right.

This attitude is sensible.   It is true that if the claim is baseless, the claimant may appear to have got something for nothing or that, contrariwise, if a claimant settles a good claim for less than its true value he may appear to have given up something for nothing but this is to ignore the cost, both monetary and psychic, of litigation.   It is in the public interest to encourage reasonable settlements; indeed the legal system could not operate at all if the vast majority of civil disputes were not settled out of court. The rule has however to be surrounded by certain safeguards. A plaintiff who relies upon the surrender of a claim to support a contract must prove:

   (i) that the claim is reasonable in itself, and not " vexatious or frivolous,"

  (ii) that he himself has an honest belief in the chance of its success, and

 (iii) that he has concealed from the other party no fact which, to his knowledge, might affect its validity.[1]

In *Horton* v. *Horton*:[2]

> The parties were husband and wife. In March, 1954, by a separation agreement under seal, the husband agreed to pay the wife £30 a month. On the true construction of the deed the husband should have deducted income tax before payment, but for nine months he paid the money without deduction. In January, 1955 he signed a document, not under seal, agreeing that, instead of " the monthly sum of £30," he would pay such a monthly sum as " after deduction of income tax should amount to the clear sum of £30". For over three years he paid this clear sum, but then stopped payment. To an action by his wife he pleaded that the later agreement was unsupported by consideration and that the wife could sue only on the earlier deed.

The Court of Appeal held that there was consideration to support the later agreement. It was clear that the original deed did not implement the intention of the parties. The wife, therefore, might have sued to rectify the deed, and the later agreement represented a compromise of this possible action. Whether such an action would have succeeded was irrelevant:[3] it sufficed that it had some prospect of success and that the wife believed in it.

Upon this principle and subject to these safeguards a compromise of a claim and a forbearance to sue will each be upheld,

---

1. Such would seem to be the conclusions to be drawn from the language of the judgments in *Callisher* v. *Bischoffsheim* and *Miles* v. *New Zealand Alford Estate Co.* (*supra*). See also *Owners of Portofino* v. *Berlin Derunaptha* (1934), 39 Com. Cases, 330. In *Miles* v. *New Zealand Alford Estate Co.* (*supra*) at p. 291, BOWEN, L.J., said: " It seems to me that if an intending litigant *bona fide* forbears a right to litigate a question of law or fact which it is not frivolous or vexatious to litigate, he does give up something of value." In an interesting article, in which these words are cited, Kelly points out that the surrender of a defence may furnish consideration no less than the surrender of a claim: 27 M.L.R. 540.
2. [1961] 1 Q.B. 215; [1960] 3 All E.R. 649.
3. Cf. *Whiteside* v. *Whiteside*, [1950] Ch. 65, [1949] 2 All E.R. 913.

and, as has been suggested above, there is no intrinsic difference of principle between them. In the latter case, however, it is irrelevant whether the time of forbearance be long or short or even whether it is for any specified time at all. Nor need there be any actual promise to forbear, if such an understanding can be inferred from the circumstances and is followed by a forbearance in fact.[1]

It is possible that there remain some cases where although the parties believe in good faith that they are compromising a doubtful claim, the court will hold that the claim was manifestly bad and the compromise therefore ineffectual. This can hardly happen where the facts are doubtful, since the court would scarcely investigate the facts in order to strike down a compromise but it might happen where there was ignorance or misapprehension of the law. Even with questions of law, however, it would usually be possible to discover sufficient doubt to support the agreement.[2] In *Magee* v. *Pennine Insurance Co., Ltd.*[3] the majority of the Court of Appeal held that a compromise though valid at common law could be set aside in equity because it was based on a common mistake, since it was clear that the defendants had a complete answer to the plaintiff's claim.

A modern illustration of the premise that it is for the parties to make their own bargain is afforded by the current practice of manufacturers to recommend the sale of their goods by offering, as an inducement to buy, something more than the goods themselves. In *Chappell & Co., Ltd.* v. *Nestlé Co., Ltd.*:[4]

Inducements offered by manufacturers

> The plaintiffs owned the copyright in a dance tune called " Rockin' Shoes". The Hardy Co. made records of the tune which they sold to the Nestlé Co. for 4d. each, and the Nestlé Co. offered them to the public for 1s. 6d. each, but required, in addition to the money, three wrappers of their sixpenny bars of chocolate. When they received the wrappers, they threw them away. Their main object was to advertise their chocolate, but they also made a profit on the sale of the records.

The plaintiffs sued the defendants for infringement of copyright, and the defendants were admittedly liable unless they could rely on s. 8 of the Copyright Act 1956. Under this section a person may make a record of a musical work provided that this is designed for retail sale and provided that he pays to the copyright owner a royalty of $6\frac{1}{4}$ per cent. " of the ordinary retail selling price". The defendants offered the statutory royalty based on the price of 1s. 6d. per record. The plaintiffs refused the offer, contending that the money price was only part of the consideration for the record and that the balance was represented by the three wrappers. The House of Lords by a majority gave judgment for the plaintiffs. It was unrealistic to hold that the wrappers were not part of the consideration. The offer was to supply a record in return, not simply for money, but for the wrappers as well.

---

1. *Alliance Bank* v. *Broom* (1864), 2 Dr. & Sm. 289.
2. See *Haigh* v. *Brooks* (1839), 10 Ad. & El. 309, discussed more fully in the 8th Edn. of this work, pp. 72–73.
3. [1969] 2 Q.B. 507, [1969] 2 All E.R. 891, discussed *infra*, p. 219.
4. [1960] A.C. 87; [1959] 2 All E.R. 701.

"The question", said Lord SOMERVELL,[1] "is whether the three wrappers were part of the consideration. . . . I think that they are part of the consideration. They are so described in the offer. 'They', the wrappers, 'will help you to get smash hit recordings'. . . . It is said that, when received, the wrappers are of no value to the respondents, The Nestlé Co., Ltd. This I would have thought to be irrelevant. A contracting party can stipulate for what consideration he chooses. A peppercorn does not cease to be good consideration if it is established that the promisee does not like pepper and will throw away the corn."

Considera-
tion in
relation to
bailments

The necessity, sometimes assumed, of discovering a consideration to support a bailment presents another aspect of the search for a bargain. A bailment is a delivery of goods on condition that the recipient shall ultimately restore them to the bailor: they may thus be hired or lent or pledged or deposited for safe custody. So natural a transaction must be recognized at an early date by every system of law. In English law it was protected by the writ of detinue long before the evolution of a general contractual remedy, and it was only the pressure of procedural convenience which led to the supersession of this writ by *indebitatus assumpsit*. But, once the rights of the bailor were secured by a form of action normally identified with contract, there was an inevitable temptation to discuss the problems of bailment in terms of contract and to demand the presence of consideration. Thus in *Bainbridge* v. *Firmstone* in 1838:[2]

> The plaintiff, at the defendant's request, had consented to allow the defendant to remove and weigh two boilers, and the defendant had, at the same time, promised to return them in their original sound condition. The plaintiff sued for breach of this promise, and the defendant pleaded lack of consideration.

The Court of Queen's Bench rejected the plea. PATTESON, J., thought that, whether there was a benefit to the defendant or not, there was "at any rate a detriment to the plaintiff from his parting with the possession for even so short a time." Lord DENMAN avoided the language of benefit and detriment.

> "The defendant had some reason for wishing to weigh the boilers; and he could do so only by obtaining permission from the plaintiff, which he did obtain by promising to return them in good condition."

By one or other of these lines of argument it is, of course, possible to find a consideration, though the description of the transaction as a bargain struck by the exchange of a promise on the one side and a permission on the other wears a somewhat artificial appearance. But it is not difficult to suggest cases where such language is wholly inappropriate. If B gratuitously accepts goods which A deposits with him for safe custody, B may undoubtedly be liable if he injures or fails to return them. But there is no benefit to B, and, as the delivery was to secure A's advantage, no detriment to A: nor is there any price paid for B's promise, express or implied, to take care of the goods.

---

1. [1960] A.C., at p. 114; [1959] 2 All E.R., at p. 712. Analogous problems arise where a tradesman gives trading stamps. See *Bulpitt & Sons, Ltd.* v. *S. Bellman* (1962), L.R. 3 R.P. 62.
2. (1838), 8 Ad. & E. 743. See also *Hart* v. *Miles* (1858), 4 C.B.N.S. 371.

The leading case of *Coggs* v. *Bernard*, decided in 1703,[1]
illustrates at once the unique conception of bailment and the
misleading inferences drawn from its fortuitous association with
the writ of assumpsit.

Coggs v.
Bernard

> The plaintiff declared that the defendant had undertaken to
> remove several hogsheads of brandy from one cellar to another, and
> that he had done the work so carelessly that one of the casks was
> staved and a quantity of brandy was spilt. The defendant argued
> that the declaration was bad as disclosing no consideration for the
> undertaking.

Chief Justice HOLT, rejecting the argument, was, indeed, at pains
to find a consideration. " The owner's trusting him with the
goods is a sufficient consideration to oblige him to a careful
management."[2] But that this tribute to the doctrine was mere
lip-service is shown by the ensuing passages in his judgment.

> " If the agreement," he said, " had been executory, to carry these
> brandies from the one place to the other on such a day, the defendant
> had not been bound to carry them. But this is a different case, for
> assumpsit does not only signify a future agreement, but, in such a
> case as this, it signifies an actual entry upon the thing and taking the
> trust upon himself. And if a man will do that and miscarries in the
> performance of his trust, an action will lie against him for that,
> though nobody could have compelled him to do the thing."

The defendant was liable, not because he had agreed to carry the
casks, but only because he had actually started to move them.
The case was not one of contract at all, but turned upon the
peculiar status of the bailee.

At the present day, no doubt, in most instances where goods
are lent or hired or deposited for safe custody or as security for
a debt, the delivery will be the result of a contract. But this
ingredient, though usual, is not essential. An infant may be
liable as a bailee, whereas, had the transaction to be based on
contract, the Infants Relief Act 1874, would protect him: a railway company owes a duty, independently of contract, to an owner
whose goods it has accepted for carriage.[3] Confusion will be
avoided only if it is remembered that bailment is a relationship
sui generis and that, unless it is sought to increase or diminish the
burdens imposed upon the bailee by the very fact of the bailment,
it is not necessary to incorporate it into the law of contract and to
prove a consideration.

Bailment is
a transaction
sui generis

This was clearly stated by Lord DENNING, M.R., in *Building
and Civil Engineering Holidays Scheme Management, Ltd.* v.
Post Office.[4]

---

1. (1703), 2 Ld. Raym. 909.
2. Such " trusting " is clearly not in truth a good consideration. It is not
   the price of any promise: it is not a benefit to the defendant: and, as it was
   designed to effectuate the plaintiff's sole purposes, it was no detriment to him.
3. See *R.* v. *McDonald* (1885), 15 Q.B.D. 323; and *Meux* v. *Great Eastern
   Rail Co.*, [1895] 2 Q.B. 387.
4. [1966] 1 Q.B. 247, at pp. 260–261; [1965] 1 All E.R. 163, at p. 167. See
   also *per* DIPLOCK, L.J., in *Morris* v. *C. W. Martin & Sons*, [1966] 1 Q.B.
   716, at p. 731; [1965] 2 All E.R. 725, at p. 734; and *Chesworth* v. *Farrar*,
   [1967] 1 Q.B. 407; [1966] 2 All E.R. 107. Palmer, 24 I.C.L.Q. 565.

"At common law, bailment is often associated with a contract, but this is not always the case ... An action against a bailee can often be put, not as an action in contract, nor in tort, but as an action on its own, *sui generis*, arising out of the possession had by the bailee of the goods."

Liability
for improper
performance
of gratuitous
service

A somewhat similar position may arise where loss has been caused in the performance of a gratuitous service. The legal consequences of such a situation were discussed in the case of *De la Bere* v. *Pearson.*[1]

> The defendants advertised in their paper that their city editor would answer inquiries from readers desiring financial advice. The plaintiff wrote, asking for the name of a good stockbroker. The editor recommended an " outside broker," who was in fact an undischarged bankrupt. This circumstance was not known to the editor, but could have been discovered by him without difficulty. Relying on the recommendation, the plaintiff sent sums of money to the broker for investment and the broker misappropriated them. The Court of Appeal held the defendants liable in contract.

It is not at first sight easy to see how the facts of this case can be made to satisfy the doctrine of consideration. The plaintiff doubtless paid money for a copy of the paper, but did he pay for the recommendation? The mere act of inquiring the name of a stockbroker can hardly be described with any sense of reality as the price of the editor's reply. It may indeed be urged that the plaintiff paid not only for the physical fact of the paper but for all its contents—news, articles, advertisements and financial advice; and that the payment might thus be regarded as consideration for the whole service offered by the defendants. Colour is lent to this interpretation by the fact that the plaintiff had long been a reader of the paper and knew that one of its features was the provision of financial advice. The case was not, however, argued on this basis nor was the point taken by the Court of Appeal, whose members were content substantially to assume the existence of a contract. While, therefore, it is possible to support the decision on the ground of contract, it is not surprising that Sir Frederick Pollock should have suggested that the cause of action might be better regarded " as arising from default in the performance of a voluntary undertaking independent of contract."[2] The question, in other words, should be approached as a problem in tort, and, viewed from this angle, it would turn upon the scope of the duty of care. To discuss this duty in any detail is outside the ambit of the present book; but, in view of the judgments of the House of Lords in *Hedley Byrne & Co., Ltd.* v. *Heller & Partners, Ltd.,*[3] it is at least possible that, if the facts of *De la Bere* v. *Pearson* were to recur, the plaintiff might succeed in an action of negligence.

Distinction
between gift
and sale not
always
obvious

The refusal of the courts to discuss the adequacy of consideration may make it difficult, on occasion, to distinguish a gift and a sale. If A promises B to give him his new Rolls-Royce car for nothing, there is obviously no consideration and no contract.

---

1. [1908] 1 K.B. 280. See also *Elsee* v. *Gatward* (1793), 5 Term Rep. 143, and *Skelton* v. *London North Western Rail Co.* (1867), L.R. 2 C.P. 631.
2. See *Pollock on Contracts*, 13th Edn., at p. 140.
3. [1964] A.C. 465; [1963] 2 All E.R. 575. See especially *per* Lord DEVLIN, at pp. 527–8, 610, respectively. See *infra*, pp. 258–260.

If A promises B to give him his new Rolls-Royce car, if B will fetch it from the garage, there is still no consideration and no contract. The requirement that B is to fetch the car is not the price of the promise, but the condition precedent to the operation of A's generosity. The transaction is not a sale, but a conditional gift.[1] But, if A promises B to give him his new Rolls-Royce car if B will give him one shilling, there is consideration and there is a contract. Such a conclusion has inspired the comment that the doctrine of consideration corresponds as little with reality and is as much a formality as the rule that a gratuitous promise becomes binding by the mere affixing of a seal.[2] But this view is surely an over-bold generalization upon extreme cases. The fact that the courts will enforce such a transaction as that envisaged in the third hypothesis stated above or in the actual case of *Thomas* v. *Thomas*,[3] though it may appear a legal quibble, is a logical inference from two assumptions, neither of which is unreasonable: that in every parol contract the plaintiff must show that he has bought the defendant's promise, and that the courts will not negative as disproportionate the price which the parties themselves have fixed. If a mere token payment is named, a transaction virtually gratuitous may well be invested with the insignia of contract, but, in the absence of dishonesty, there is no reason why persons should not take advantage of existing legal rules and adapt them to their own requirements. Such adaptations are the commonplace of legal history.[4]

B. INSUFFICIENCY OF CONSIDERATION

It is now necessary to discuss cases where, though a bargain has been struck, the consideration may yet be deemed, in the technical sense already indicated, " insufficient." The judges, when they exercise this power of interference, are applying an extrinsic test which frustrates the expectations of the parties. It does not follow, however, that such a test is necessarily harsh, still less that it is illogical. In some of the cases the law is settled, others are shrouded in controversy; but in all of them the grounds of interference seem to be the same. The plaintiff has procured the defendant's promise by discharging or by promising to discharge a duty already imposed upon him for other reasons. Now consideration need not be adequate and may, on occasion, be extremely tenuous, but it must comprise some element which can be regarded as the price of the defendant's promise; and merely to repeat an existing obligation may well seem to offer nothing at all. The cases in which this argument has been urged may be

---

1. For a case where the judges experienced great difficulty in deciding whether they had to deal with a contract or a conditional gift, see *Wyatt* v. *Kreglinger*, [1933] 1 K.B. 793; [1933] All E.R. Rep. 349. A more recent example is *Dickinson* v. *Abel*, [1969] 1 All E.R. 484; [1969] 1 W.L.R. 295.
2. See Holmes, *The Common Law*, 273; Markby, *Elements of Law,* Chap. XV; Buckland & McNair, *Roman Law and Common Law*, 2nd Edn., 276.
3. *Supra*, p. 75.
4. It is worth observing that the Roman law, untrammelled by a doctrine of consideration, found a similar difficulty in distinguishing gifts and sales. See Digest 18.1.36; 18.1.38.

grouped into four classes. In each of them the essential question is whether the courts can discover the promise or performance of something more than the plaintiff is already bound to do.

1. WHERE A PUBLIC DUTY IS IMPOSED UPON THE PLAINTIFF BY LAW

Discharge of public duty is not consideration

It may readily be appreciated that a person, who by his official status or through the operation of the law is under a public duty to act in a certain way, is not regarded as furnishing consideration merely by promising to discharge that duty. No one, for example, would expect a policeman to bargain with a citizen for the price of his protection. The position was stated in 1831 in *Collins* v. *Godefroy*.[1] The plaintiff had attended on *subpœna* to give evidence on the defendant's behalf in a case in which the defendant was a litigant, and he alleged that the defendant had promised to pay him six guineas for his trouble. Lord TENTERDEN held that there was no consideration for this promise.

> " If it be a duty imposed by law upon a party regularly *subpœnæd* to attend from time to time to give his evidence, then a promise to give him any remuneration for loss of time incurred in such attendance is a promise without consideration."

Acts in excess of the duty constitute consideration

In spite or, perhaps, because of the obvious character of the argument, the cases in which it has been raised are few; and some of them at least disclose a tendency to uphold the agreement by assuming that something more was undertaken than the bare discharge of the duty. Thus in *England* v. *Davidson*,[2] the defendant offered a reward to anyone who should give information leading to the conviction of a felon. The plaintiff, a police constable, gave such evidence. The defendant pleaded, not only that the plaintiff had merely done his duty, but that the contract was against public policy. Lord DENMAN's judgment, rejecting these pleas, consists of two sentences.

> " I think there may be services which the constable is not bound to render and which he may therefore make the ground of a contract. We should not hold a contract to be against the policy of the law, unless the grounds for so deciding were very clear."

Similar arguments were considered and again rejected in the more modern case of *Glasbrook Brothers* v. *Glamorgan County Council*.[3] The question had arisen as to how best to protect a coal mine during a strike. The police authorities thought it enough to provide a mobile force, the colliery manager wanted a stationary guard. It was ultimately agreed to provide the latter at a rate of payment which involved the sum of £2,200. The company refused to pay and, when sued, pleaded the absence of

---

1. (1831), 1 B. & Ad. 950. See also *Morris* v. *Burdett* (1808), 1 Camp. 218, where it was held that, in so far as a High Bailiff or a Sheriff is required by law to do certain acts and incur certain expense in the course of a Parliamentary election, there is no consideration for a promise by the successful candidate to reimburse him.
2. (1840), 11 Ad. & El. 856.
3. [1925] A.C. 270.

consideration. The House of Lords gave judgment for the plaintiffs. The police were bound to afford protection, but they had a discretion as to the form it should take, and an undertaking to provide more protection than in their discretion they deemed necessary was consideration for the promise of reward.

The readiness of the judges thus to find a consideration if this be humanly possible is illustrated by the case of *Ward* v. *Byham*.[1]

> A man and a woman, though not married, lived together from 1949 to 1954. In 1950 a child was born to them. In 1954 the man, the defendant in the case, turned the woman out of his house but kept and looked after the child. Some months later the woman, the plaintiff in the case, asked for the child. The defendant wrote offering to let her have the child and to pay £1 a week for its maintenance provided (a) the plaintiff could " prove that she will be well looked after and happy," and (b) " that she is allowed to decide for herself whether or not she wishes to live with you." The plaintiff then took the child. For seven months the defendant paid the weekly sum as agreed, but the plaintiff then married another man and the defendant stopped payment.

The plaintiff sued for breach of contract and the defendant pleaded the absence of consideration. By s. 42 of the National Assistance Act 1948, the mother of an illegitimate child was bound to maintain it; and it was therefore argued that the mother had done no more than promise to fulfil her statutory duty. But the Court of Appeal gave judgment for the plaintiff. The majority of the court (MORRIS AND PARKER, L.JJ.) held that she had exceeded the duty cast upon her by the Act by promising, in accordance with the terms of the defendant's letter, both to " look after the child well " and satisfy the defendant that it was " happy," and to allow the child to decide which home it preferred. There was thus " sufficient " consideration for the defendant's promise to pay. DENNING, L.J., was prepared to go further and hold that the father's promise was binding even if the mother had done no more than she was already bound to do since " a promise to perform an existing duty, or the performance of it, should be regarded as good consideration, because it is a benefit to the person to whom it is given."[2]

2. WHERE THE PLAINTIFF IS BOUND BY AN EXISTING CONTRACTUAL DUTY TO THE DEFENDANT[3]

The somewhat obvious rule, that there is no consideration if all that the plaintiff does is to perform, or to promise the performance of, an obligation already imposed upon him by a previous contract between him and the defendant, is illustrated by a group of cases in the first half of the nineteenth century. In *Stilk* v. *Myrick*[4] a seaman sued for wages alleged to have been earned on a voyage from London to the Baltic and back. In the course of the voyage

---

1. [1956] 2 All E.R. 318; [1956] 1 W.L.R. 496.
2. *Ibid.*, at pp. 319, 498, respectively. See also *Williams* v. *Williams*, [1957] 1 All E.R. 305; [1957] 1 W.L.R. 148, where DENNING, L.J., repeated this statement but added the qualification, " so long as there is nothing in the transaction which is contrary to the public interest."
3. Reynolds and Treitel, 7 Malaya L.R. 1.
4. (1809), 2 Camp. 317.

two sailors had deserted, and, as the captain could not find any substitutes, he promised the rest of the crew extra wages if they would work the ship home short-handed. In the earlier case of *Harris* v. *Watson*[1] Lord KENYON had rejected a similar claim because it savoured of blackmail; but Lord ELLENBOROUGH in *Stilk* v. *Myrick*, though he agreed that the action would not lie, preferred to base his decision on the absence of consideration. The crew were already bound by their contract to meet the normal emergencies of the voyage and were doing no more than their duty in working the ship home. Had they exceeded their duty, or if the course of events, by making the ship unseaworthy, had relieved them from its performance, the case would have been different. Thus in *Hartley* v. *Ponsonby*[2] the shortage of labour was so great as to make the further prosecution of the voyage exceptionally hazardous, and, by discharging the surviving members of the crew from their original obligation, left them free to enter into a new contract.

Here, as in the case of public duty, the argument, at least in its simplest form, is readily intelligible. A type of case, however, often discussed in this context, offers greater complications.

Can a promise to pay less than amount due be consideration?

> If A owes B a debt and pays or promises to pay part of it in return for B's promise to forgo the balance, can A hold B to this promise?

The problem differs slightly from that propounded in *Stilk* v. *Myrick*. There a person sought fresh remuneration for the performance of an existing contractual duty: here he seeks to avoid the duty.[3] The problem was familiar to the common lawyers before the development of assumpsit as a contractual remedy and therefore before the doctrine of consideration had been envisaged. Its implications were examined within the sphere of debt in 1455 and again in 1495.[4] In the latter year Chief Justice BRIAN stated a rule which, if set in an archaic environment, has still a modern connotation.

> " The action is brought for £20, and the concord is that he shall pay only £10, which appears to be no satisfaction for the £20; for payment of £10 cannot be payment of £20. But if it was of a horse which was to be paid according to the concord, this would be good satisfaction, for it does not appear that the horse be worth more or less than the sum in demand."

The writ of debt rested on the idea not of promise but of duty, and a partial performance could not be received as a discharge of that duty. Even to allow a substituted performance might seem to offend against the principle upon which the writ was based, and was, at any rate, the utmost relaxation which the law could permit.

---

1. (1791), Peake, 102.
2. (1857), 7 E. & B. 872.
3. The agreement to discharge a previous debt is often discussed under the title of *accord and satisfaction*. The *accord* is the agreement to discharge the existing obligation, the *satisfaction* is the consideration required to support it. See *infra*, p. 541.
4. *Anon.* (1455), Y.B. 33 Hy. VI, fo. 48, pl. 32; *Anon.* (1495), Y.B. 10 Hy. VII, fo. 4, pl. 4.

The rule enunciated by Chief Justice BRIAN was adopted in 1602 in *Pinnel's Case.*[1]

Pinnel sued Cole in Debt for £8 10s. due on a bond on November 11th, 1600. Cole's defence was that, at Pinnel's request, he had paid him £5 2s. 6d. on October 1st, and that Pinnel had accepted this payment in full satisfaction of the original debt.

Pinnel's Case

Judgment was given for the plaintiff on a point of pleading, but the court made it clear that, had it not been for a technical flaw, they would have found for the defendant, on the ground that the part payment had been made on an earlier day than that appointed in the bond. The debt could be discharged, not by a merely partial performance of the original obligation, but only through the introduction, at the creditor's request, of some new element— the tender of a different chattel or part payment at a fresh place or on an earlier date.

" Payment of a lesser sum on the day in satisfaction of a greater cannot be any satisfaction for the whole, because it appears to the Judges that by no possibility can a lesser sum be a satisfaction to the plaintiff for a greater sum. But the gift of a horse, hawk or robe, etc. in satisfaction is good. For it shall be intended that a horse, hawk or robe, etc. might be more beneficial to the plaintiff than the money in respect of some circumstance, or otherwise the plaintiff would not have accepted it in satisfaction. . . . The payment and acceptance of parcel before the day in satisfaction of the whole would be a good satisfaction in regard of circumstance of time; for per-adventure parcel of it before the day would be more beneficial to him than the whole at the day, and the value of the satisfaction is not material. So if I am bound in £20 to pay you £10 at West-minster, and you request me to pay you £5 at the day at York, and you will accept it in full satisfaction of the whole £10, it is a good satisfaction for the whole: for the expenses to pay it at York is sufficient satisfaction."

It will be observed that the plaintiff sued in *Pinnel's Case* not in assumpsit but in debt, so that no question of consideration arose. But the problem had already been discussed in the new contractual environment in *Richards* v. *Bartlet* in 1584.[2] A buyer, sued in assumpsit for the price of goods, pleaded a promise by the seller to accept 3s. 4d. in the pound. The plea was held bad on the ground that there was no consideration for this promise. " For no profit but damage comes to the plaintiff by this new agreement, and the defendant is not put to any labour or charge by it." The decision was followed in subsequent cases, and a rule, originating in the peculiar requirements of debt, was thus acclimatized in the alien soil of assumpsit. This trans-ference of thought has been severely criticized.[3] A plaintiff who sued in assumpsit was required to prove consideration for the defendant's undertaking, but there was no logical need to lay a similar burden upon a party who sought to use a promise only by way of defence. The presence of consideration was vital to the formation of a contract, but irrelevant to its discharge. The

Rule introduced into assumpsit

1. (1602), 5 Co. Rep. 117a. Simpson, *History,* pp. 103–107.
2. (1584), 1 Leon. 19. Simpson, *History,* pp. 447–448, 470–475.
3. See Pollock, *Principles of Contract,* 13th Edn., p. 150; Ames, *Lectures on Legal History,* pp. 329 *et seq.*; Corbin, 27 Yale L.J. 535. *Contra, Williston on Contracts,* 3rd Edn., para. 120.

decision in *Richards* v. *Bartlet*, however, while by no means
inevitable and certainly unfortunate in its results, was not
unintelligible. Assumpsit rested on promise as conspicuously as
debt on duty, and the judges not unnaturally reacted by treating
the promise, on which the defendant relied, as binding only on the
same conditions as the original promise on which the plaintiff
sued. But if this argument were once accepted, the defendant
must prove a consideration for the plaintiff's promise to discharge
the contract, and he could hardly satisfy this requirement by
performing or promising to perform no more than a part of what
he was already bound to do.

Foakes v.
Beer

Whatever the merits of these rival arguments, the rule laid
down in *Richards* v. *Bartlet* or, as it is generally if less appropriately
called, the rule in *Pinnel's Case*, was accepted and applied by the
courts. Not, indeed, until 1884 was it challenged in the House of
Lords in the case of *Foakes* v. *Beer*.[1]

> Mrs. Beer had obtained a judgment against Dr. Foakes for £2,090.
> Dr. Foakes asked for time to pay. The parties agreed in writing that,
> if Dr. Foakes paid £500 at once and the balance by instalments, Mrs.
> Beer would not " take any proceedings whatever on the judgment."
> A judgment debt bears interest as from the date of the judgment.
> The agreement made no reference to the question of interest. Dr.
> Foakes ultimately paid the whole amount of the judgment debt itself,
> and Mrs. Beer then claimed the interest. Dr. Foakes refused to pay it
> and Mrs. Beer applied " to be allowed to issue execution or otherwise
> proceed on the judgment in respect of the interest." Dr. Foakes
> pleaded the agreement and Mrs. Beer replied that it was unsupported
> by consideration.

The House of Lords gave judgment in favour of Mrs. Beer for
the amount of the interest. The question, " nakedly raised by the
appeal," was whether the so-called rule in *Pinnel's Case* should be
rejected.

> " The doctrine itself," said Lord SELBORNE, " may have been criti-
> cized as questionable in principle by some persons whose opinions
> are entitled to respect, but it has never been judicially over-ruled;
> on the contrary I think it has always, since the sixteenth century, been
> accepted as law. If so, I cannot think that your Lordships would do
> right if you were now to reverse, as erroneous, a judgment of the
> Court of Appeal, proceeding upon a doctrine which has been ac-
> cepted as part of the law of England for 280 years."

The decision by the House of Lords may be criticised. Lord
BLACKBURN, indeed, had prepared a dissenting judgment, and it
was with reluctance that he ultimately acquiesced in the views of
his colleagues. " All men of business," he pointed out, " everyday recognize and act on the ground that prompt payment of a
part of their demand may be more beneficial to them than it would
be to insist on their rights and enforce payment of the whole "[2]
There is however something to be said on the other side. It
is tempting to think of a creditor as like a villain in a Victorian
melodrama, twiddling his wax moustache at the thought of fore-
closing the mortgage on the heroine's ancestral home. This
vision tends to obscure the fact that in real life, it is often the
debtor who behaves badly, fobbing off the creditor with excuses

---

1. (1884), 9 App. Cas. 605.
2. (1884), 9 App. Cas., at p. 622.

and using every device to avoid repayment so that in the end the creditor is driven to accept less than is due.   The real criticism of *Foakes* v. *Beer* is perhaps that it provides no means by which such cases can be treated differently from genuine bargains.

The decision in *Foakes* v. *Beer* has been criticised but not yet abrogated.[1]   There are however important qualifications to it.   The first is as old as the rule itself.   The rule does not apply where the debtor does something different, for example, where, with the creditor's consent, he delivers a horse in full settlement of the debt.   Just as where A sells a horse to B for £100, the court will not inquire whether the horse is worth more or less than £100, so if A delivers a horse to B in discharge of a debt of £100, the court will again not inquire as to its value.   So an agreed payment of a peppercorn will do and, *a fortiori*, £50 plus a peppercorn will do.   So too early payment of a smaller sum or payment at a different place will do.[2]

Exceptions to the rule

Alternative performance

If any new element in the debtor's promise should be regarded as constituting consideration for the discharge of the original debt, it was tempting to urge that the tender of a promissory note was a sufficient novelty for the purpose.   By accepting the peculiar obligation inherent in a negotiable security, the debtor would be doing something which he was not already bound to do. The point was taken in 1846 in *Sibree* v. *Tripp*.[3]

Introduction of negotiable instrument

The defendant owed the plaintiff £1,000 and was sued for this sum. The action was settled on the terms that the defendant would give the plaintiff promissory notes for £300 in full satisfaction. One of the notes was not met, and the plaintiff then sued (*inter alia*) for the original £1,000.

The Court of Exchequer gave judgment for the defendant. Baron ALDERSON re-examined the whole position.

" It is undoubtedly true that payment of a portion of a liquidated demand, in the same manner as the whole liquidated demand ought to be paid, is payment only in part; because it is not one bargain, but two; namely, payment of part and an agreement, without consideration, to give up the residue. The Courts might very well have held the contrary and have left the matter to the agreement of the parties; but undoubtedly the law is so settled. But if you substitute a piece of paper or a stick of sealing-wax, it is different, and the bargain may be carried out in its full integrity. A man may give, in satisfaction of a debt of £100, a horse of the value of £5, but not £5. Again, if the time or place of payment be different, the one sum may be a satisfaction for the other. Let us, then, apply these principles to the present case. If for money you give a negotiable security, you pay it in a different way. The security may be worth more or less: it is of uncertain value. That is a case falling within the rule of law I have referred to."

---

1. The Law Revision Committee proposed such abrogation in 1937, but the proposal has not so far been implemented.
2. Early payment is always of some value to the creditor. Payment at another place may be simply for the convenience of the debtor, in which case, it would not amount to consideration: *Vanbergen* v. *St. Edmund's Properties, Ltd.*, [1933] 2 K.B. 223.
3. (1846), 15 M. & W. 23, having been previously rejected in *Cumber* v. *Wane* (1721), 1 Stra. 426.

The decision in *Sibree* v. *Tripp* was applied by the divisional court in *Goddard* v. *O'Brien*[1] in 1882 to a payment by cheque, and its rationale was accepted in an *obiter dictum* by Lord SELBORNE in *Foakes* v. *Beer*.[2]　To give negotiable paper was to furnish fresh consideration.

A layman would no doubt be surprised to find that a promissory note for £300 would discharge a debt of a £1,000 whereas payment of £300 in cash would not do.　Granted the premises however the rule was logical enough, since negotiable instruments do have some advantages over cash (e.g. greater ease of portability and transferrability) for which a creditor might be willing to pay. The extension to payment by cheque was another matter since creditors do not usually accept payment by cheque in order to obtain the advantages of a negotiable instrument.　Normally payment by cheque, even of the full sum, affects only a conditional discharge of the debt so that the debt is extinguished only when the cheque is honoured and it would be inconsistent with normal business practice to have different rules for payment by cheque and by cash.　In 1965 in *D. and C. Builders, Ltd.* v. *Rees*[3] the Court of Appeal refused to recognize the distinction.

> The plaintiffs were a small firm.　They did work for the defendant, for which the defendant owed them £482.　For months they pressed for payment.　At length the defendant's wife, acting for her husband and knowing that the plaintiffs were in financial difficulties, offered them £300 in settlement.　If they refused this offer, she said, they would get nothing.　The plaintiffs reluctantly agreed.　They were given a cheque for £300, which was duly honoured.　They then sued for the balance of the original debt.

The Court of Appeal gave judgment for the plaintiffs.　The position was stated in forceful terms by Lord DENNING.[4]

> " It is a daily occurrence that a merchant or tradesman, who is owed a sum of money, is asked to take less.　The debtor says he is in difficulties.　He offers a lesser sum in settlement, cash down.　He says he cannot pay more.　The creditor is considerate.　He accepts the proffered sum and forgives him the rest of the debt.　The question arises: is the settlement binding on the creditor?　The answer is that, in point of law, the creditor is not bound by the settlement.　He can the next day sue the debtor for the balance, and get judgment. . . .　Now suppose that the debtor, instead of paying the lesser sum in cash, pays it by cheque.　He makes out a cheque for the amount.　The creditor accepts the cheque and cashes it.　Is the position any different?　I think not.　No sensible distinction can be taken between payment of a lesser sum by cash and payment of it by cheque.　The cheque, when given, is conditional payment.　When honoured, it is actual payment.　It is then just the same as cash.　If a creditor is not bound when he receives payment by cash, he should not be bound when he receives payment by cheque."

The Court of Appeal thus overruled the decision of the divisional court in *Goddard* v. *O'Brien*. *Sibree* v. *Tripp*, as it had been decided by a tribunal of equal standing with themselves, could not be

---

1. (1882), 9 Q.B.D. 37.
2. (1884), 9 App. Cas. 605.
3. [1966] 2 Q.B. 617; [1965] 3 All E.R. 837.
4. [1966] 2 Q.B., at p. 623; [1965] 3 All E.R., at pp. 839–40.

rejected but was distinguished. In *Sibree* v. *Tripp* the promissory notes were taken not as conditional payment but in absolute discharge of the original debt. Clearly if the notes had been given only as conditional payment, the plaintiff's claim would have succeeded in any event, since one of the notes had not been honoured.[1]

A second exception rests not on the common law but on equity, and was suggested by DENNING, J., as he then was, in *Central London Property Trust, Ltd.* v. *High Trees House, Ltd.*[2]

An equitable exception

> In September, 1939, the plaintiffs leased a block of flats to the defendants at a ground rent of £2,500 *per annum*. In January, 1940, the plaintiffs agreed in writing to reduce the rent to £1,250, plainly because of war conditions, which had caused many vacancies in the flats. No express time limit was set for the operation of this reduction. From 1940 to 1945 the defendants paid the reduced rent. In 1945 the flats were again full, and the receiver of the plaintiff company then claimed the full rent both retrospectively and for the future. He tested his claim by suing for rent at the original rate for the last two quarters of 1945.

DENNING, J., was of opinion that the agreement of January, 1940, was intended as a temporary expedient only and had ceased to operate early in 1945. The rent originally fixed by the contract was therefore payable, and the plaintiffs were entitled to judgment. But he was also of opinion that, had the plaintiffs sued for arrears for the period 1940 to 1945, the agreement made in 1940 would have operated to defeat their claim.

The reasoning of the learned judge is interesting. He agreed that there was no consideration for the plaintiff's promise to reduce the rent. If, therefore, the defendants had themselves sued upon that promise, they must have failed. Their claim would have depended upon a contract of which one of the essential elements was missing. But where the promise was used merely as a defence, why should the presence or absence of consideration be relevant? The defendants were not seeking to enforce a contract and need not prove one. Was there, then, any technical rule of English law whereby the plaintiffs could be prevented from ignoring their promise and insisting upon the full measure of their original rights? At first sight, the doctrine of estoppel would seem to supply the answer. By this doctrine, if one person makes to another a clear and unambiguous representation of fact intending that other to act on it, if the representation turns out to be untrue, and if that other does act upon it to his prejudice, the representor is prevented or " estopped " from denying its truth. He cannot, as it were, give himself the lie and leave the other party to take the consequences. The doctrine would meet admirably the situation in the *High Trees* case but for one difficulty. In 1854 in *Jorden* v. *Money*,[3] a majority of the House of Lords held that estoppel could operate only on a misrepresentation of existing fact. Upon this basis it was improper

The analogy of estoppel

---

1. See Chorley, 29 M.L.R. 317 and in his *Gilbart Lectures on Banking* (1967).
2. [1947] K.B. 130.
3. (1854), 5 H.L. Cas. 185.

to apply it where, as in the *High Trees* case, a party sought to rely on a promise of future conduct.[1]

To avoid this difficulty, DENNING, J., sought to tap a slender stream of authority which had flowed in equity since the judgment of Lord CAIRNS in 1877 in *Hughes* v. *Metropolitan Rail. Co.*[2]

> In October, 1874, a landlord gave his tenant six months' notice to repair the premises. If the tenant failed to comply with it, the lease could be forfeited. In November the landlord started negotiations with the tenant for the sale of the reversion, but these were broken off on December 31st. Meanwhile the tenant had done nothing to repair the premises. On the expiry of six months from the date of the original notice, the landlord claimed to treat the lease as forfeited and brought an action of ejectment.

The House of Lords held that the opening of negotiations amounted to a promise by the landlord that, as long as they continued, he would not enforce the notice, and it was in reliance upon this promise that the tenant had remained quiescent. The six months allowed for repairs were to run, therefore, only from the failure of the negotiations and the consequent withdrawal of the promise, and the tenant was entitled in equity to be relieved against the forfeiture. Lord CAIRNS said:[3]

> " It is the first principle upon which all Courts of Equity proceed, that if parties who have entered into definite and distinct terms involving certain legal results—certain penalties or legal forfeiture—afterwards by their own act or with their own consent enter upon a course of negotiations which has the effect of leading one of the parties to suppose that the strict rights arising under the contract will not be enforced or will be kept in suspense or held in abeyance, the person who otherwise might have enforced those rights will not be allowed to enforce them where it would be inequitable, having regard to the dealings which have thus taken place between the parties."

Taken at their full width and without regard to the facts of the case, these observations might appear in conflict with the decision in *Jorden* v. *Money* but that case was not cited and no mention of estoppel was made in the judgments. It seems unlikely that the House of Lords had forgotten *Jorden* v. *Money* which had been followed with approval only four years before.[4] It is much more probable that the decision was recognized as entirely consistent

---

1. Professor P. S. Atiyah has recently subjected *Jorden* v. *Money* to a searching analysis (*Consideration in Contracts*, Australian National University Press, pp. 50–58). He suggests that, had the judgments in that case been properly interpreted and applied, there would have been no need for the later development of a distinct doctrine of " promissory estoppel." He reluctantly concedes, however, that the doctrine " has now itself grown so strong and vigorous that it may be too late for the courts to recognise what they have actually done." Certainly *Jorden* v. *Money* has been treated in many later cases as authority for the proposition in the text. See, e.g. *Citizens' Bank of Louisiana* v. *First National Bank of New Orleans* (1873), L.R. 6 H.L. 352; *Maddison* v. *Alderson* (1883), 8 App. Cas. 467; Spencer Bower and Turner, *Estoppel by Representation*, 2nd Edn. (1966), pp. 30–34.
2. (1877), 2 App. Cas. 439. This case was followed and applied in *Birmingham and District Land Co.* v. *London and North Western Rail Co.* (1888), 40 Ch.D. 268; *Salisbury* v. *Gilmore*, [1942] 2 K.B. 38; [1942] 1 All E.R. 457.
3. (1877), 2 App. Cas. 439, at p. 448.
4. *Citizens' Bank of Louisiana* v. *First National Bank of New Orleans* (1873), L.R. 6 H.L. 352.

with *Jorden* v. *Money*. Two additional factors, at least, were present. The first was that the landlord sought to enforce a right, that to forfeit the lease, which only arose because the tenant, relying on the landlord, had not repaired. If the decision had gone the other way the landlord's right to have the premises repaired would have been transmuted into a much more valuable right to forfeit the lease. It is easy to see that this would be grossly unfair. The second distinction was that the decision of the House of Lords simply suspended and did not extinguish the landlord's right to have the premises repaired. The tenant was given extra time to repair but not relieved of his obligation to do so.

If we apply the principle of *Hughes* v. *Metropolitan Railway* to the facts of the *High Trees* case it can readily be seen that the landlords, having accepted part of the rent in full settlement one quarter day, could not next day purport to distrain for the balance and that if they decided to claim the balance, they must at least give extra time for payment. But DENNING, J., stated that he would have been prepared to hold the landlord's right to the balance of the rent extinguished and was clearly therefore seeking to take the principle a stage further.

Since 1947 the precise status of the doctrine has been a subject of much speculation[1] and Lord HAILSHAM, L.C., has recently stated[2] that,

" The time may soon come when the whole sequence of cases based on promissory estoppel since the war, beginning with *Central London Property Trust, Ltd.* v. *High Trees House, Ltd.*, may now need to be reviewed and reduced to a coherent body of doctrine by the courts. I do not mean to say that any are to be regarded with suspicion. But, as is common with an expanding doctrine, they do raise problems of coherent exposition which have never been systematically explored."

We will consider first those aspects of the doctrine which appear well settled and then discuss the areas of uncertainty.

(1) There is now substantial judicial support for describing the doctrine, whatever its precise content, as one of "promissory estoppel."[3] In some earlier discussions the title " equitable estoppel " was employed but as MEGARRY, J., has pointed out[4]

Name of doctrine

1. Spencer Bower and Turner, *Estoppel by Representation*, 2nd Edn., Chap. XIV; Denning, 15 M.L.R. 1, 5 J.S.P.T.L. 77; Sheridan, 15 M.L.R. 325; Bennion, 16 M.L.R. 441; Wilson, 67 L.Q.R. 330, [1965] C.L.J. 93; Gordon, [1963] C.L.J. 222; Jackson, 81 L.Q.R. 84, 223; Clarke, [1974] C.L.J. 260; Seddon, 24 I.C.L.Q. 438.
2. *Woodhouse A. C. Israel Cocoa, Ltd., S.A.* v. *Nigerian Produce Marketing Co., Ltd.*, [1972] A.C. 741 at p. 758; [1972] 2 All E.R. 271 at p. 282.
3. See, e.g. Lord HAILSHAM, L.C., *supra*, n. 2; *per* BUCKLEY, J., in *Beesly* v. *Hallwood Estates, Ltd.*, [1961] 2 All E.R. 314, at p. 324; [1960] 1 W.L.R. 549, at p. 560; *per* Lord HODSON in *Emmanuel Ajayi* v. *R. T. Briscoe (Nigeria), Ltd.*, [1964] 3 All E.R. 556, at p. 559; [1964] 1 W.L.R. 1326, at p. 1330; *per* MEGARRY, J., in *Slough Estates, Ltd.* v. *Slough Borough Council* (1967), 19 P. & C.R. 326, at p. 362.
4. *Re Vandervell's Trusts White* v. *Vandervell Trustees, Ltd.*, [1974] Ch. 269, at pp. 300–301; [1974] 1 All E.R. 47, at pp. 74–75; reversed on other grounds, [1974] Ch. 269; [1974] 3 All E.R. 215.

equitable estoppel includes both proprietary estoppel[1] and promissory estoppel.[2]

(2) The doctrine operates only by way of defence and not as a cause of action.

This was made clear by the judgments of the Court of Appeal in *Combe* v. *Combe*.[3]

> A wife started proceedings for divorce and obtained a decree *nisi* against her husband. The husband then promised to allow her £100 per annum free of tax as permanent maintenance. The wife did not in fact apply to the Divorce Court for maintenance, but this forbearance was not at the husband's request. The decree was made absolute. The annual payments were never made and ultimately the wife sued the husband on his promise to make them.

BYRNE, J., gave judgment for the wife. He held, indeed, that there was no consideration for the husband's promise. It had not been induced by any undertaking on the wife's part to forgo maintenance; and, in any case, since it was settled law that maintenance was exclusively a matter for the court's discretion, no such undertaking would have been valid or binding.[4] But he thought that the principle enunciated in the *High Trees* case enabled the wife to succeed, since the husband had made an unequivocal promise to pay the annuity, intending the wife to act upon it, and she had in fact so acted.

*Principle
" a shield not
a sword "*

This decision was clearly an illegitimate extension of a principle which, if it is to be reconciled with orthodox doctrine, must be used only as a defence and not as a cause of action. To allow a plaintiff to sue upon such a promise is simply to ignore the necessity of consideration. The Court of Appeal therefore reversed the decision; and DENNING, L.J., took the opportunity to restate the position.

> " The principle stated in the *High Trees* case . . . does not create new causes of action where none existed before. It only prevents a party from insisting upon his strict legal rights, when it would be unjust to allow him to enforce them, having regard to the dealings which have taken place between the parties. . . . "

The other two judges in the Court of Appeal, BIRKETT and ASQUITH, L.JJ., were clear that the principle must be "used as a shield and not as a sword."[5]   This striking metaphor should not

---

1. That is the line of cases running from *Dillwyn* v. *Llewelyn* (1862), 4 De G.F. & J. 517 to *E. R. Ives Investments, Ltd.* v. *High,* [1967] 2 Q.B. 379; [1967] 1 All E.R. 504. See Spencer Bower and Turner, *Estoppel by Representation,* 2nd Edn., Chap. XII.
2. A different objection is that the name equitable estoppel may obscure the fact that the rule in *Jorden* v. *Money* was in itself an equitable one, the case going on appeal to the House of Lords from the Court of Chancery.
3. [1951] 2 K.B. 215; [1951] All E.R. 767.
4. See *Hyman* v. *Hyman,* [1929] A.C. 601; [1929] All E.R. Rep. 245. The common law position is now modified by statute so that a wife, despite her promise not to sue for maintenance in return for her husband's promise of an allowance, may sue for that allowance, though the husband may not enforce her promise. See Cretney, *Principles of Family Law,* pp. 228–234. This does not overturn the principle in *Hyman* v. *Hyman.*   See *infra,* p. 366.
5. Cf. Jackson, 81 L.Q.R. 84, 223; *Re Wyvern Developments, Ltd.,* [1974] 2 All E.R. 535; [1974] 1 W.L.R. 1097; Atiyah, 38 M.L.R. 67. Promissory estoppel can be a cause of action in the United States: *Restatement of Contracts,* Article 90.

be sloppily mistranslated into a notion that only defendants can rely on the principle. There is no reason whay a plaintiff should not rely on it, provided that he has an independent cause of action. So, if upon the facts of *Hughes* v. *Metropolitan Rail. Co.* the landlord had gone into possession, putting the tenant into the position of plaintiff, the result would surely be the same. On such facts the tenant's cause of action would be the lease and the doctrine would operate to the negative a possible defence by the landlord that he was entitled to forfeit. As Spencer Bower says " Estoppel may be used either as a minesweeper or a minelayer, but never as a capital ship."[1]

(3) Finally it is settled that there must be a promise, either by words or by conduct, and that its effect must be clear and unambiguous.[2] An interesting example of this principle in operation is the decision of the Supreme Court of Canada in *John Burrows, Ltd.* v. *Subsurface Surveys, Ltd.*[3]

> A contract of loan provided for monthly repayments and gave the creditor a right to demand repayment of the whole sum if any instalment were paid more than ten days late. Of the first eighteen payments, eleven were more than ten days late without objection. It was held that this did not disentitle the creditor from exercising his right of acceleration when the nineteenth instalment was late.[4]

We now turn to consider those aspects of the doctrine which remain unsettled.

(1) We have already seen that in *Hughes* v. *Metropolitan Railway* the House of Lords held that the landlord's right to have the premises repaired was suspended and not extinguished. It has been widely thought that the distinction between suspension and extinction is an essential aspect of the doctrine. It is certainly factually present in many of the leading cases including the decision of the House of Lords in *Tool Metal Manufacturing Co., Ltd.* v. *Tungsten Electric Co., Ltd.*[5] Is it suspensory?

> The appellants were the registered proprietors of British letters patent. In April, 1938, they made a contract with the respondents whereby they gave the latter a licence to manufacture " hard metal alloys " in accordance with the inventions which were the subject of the patents. By the contract the respondents agreed to pay " compensation " to the appellants if in any one month they sold more than a stated quantity of the alloys.
> Compensation was duly paid by the respondents until the outbreak of war in 1939, but thereafter none was paid. The appellants agreed to suspend the enforcement of compensation payments pending the making of a new contract. In 1944 negotiations for such new contract were begun but broke down. In 1945 the respondents sued the appellants (*inter alia*) for breach of contract and the appellants counter-claimed for payment of compensation as from June 1st, 1945. The respondents' action was substantially dismissed, and all the arguments then centred on the counter-claim. The Court of Appeal held in the first action[6] that the agreement

---

1. See *per* Luckhoo, J. A., in *Jamaica Telephone Co., Ltd.* v. *Robinson* (1970), 16 W.I.R. 174, at p. 179.
2. *Woodhouse A. C. Israel Cocoa, Ltd., S.A.* v. *Nigerian Produce Marketing Co., Ltd.*, [1972] A.C. 741; [1972] 2 All E.R. 271.
3. (1968), 68 D.L.R. (2d) 354.
4. Cf. *Garlick* v. *Phillips* 1949 (1) S.A. 121, at p. 133, *per* Watermeyer, C.J.
5. [1955] 2 All E.R. 657; [1955] 1 W.L.R. 761.
6. (1950), 69 R.P.C. 108.

operated in equity to prevent the appellants demanding compensation until they had given reasonable notice to the respondents of their intention to resume their strict legal rights and that such notice had not been given.

In September, 1950, the appellants themselves started a second action[1] against the respondents claiming compensation as from January 1st, 1947.   The only question in this second action was whether the appellants' counter-claim in the first action amounted to reasonable notice of their intention to resume their strict legal rights.

At first instance, PEARSON, J., held that the counter-claim in the first action in 1945 amounted to such notice.   The Court of Appeal reversed this decision but the House of Lords disagreed with the Court of Appeal and restored the judgment of PEARSON, J.[2]

It seems to have been regarded as an essential ingredient by the Privy Council in *Emmanuel Ayodeji Ajayi* v. *R. T. Briscoe (Nigeria), Ltd.*[3]

> The defendant had contracted with the plaintiffs for the hire-purchase of eleven lorries. The plaintiffs sued to recover instalments due under the contract and obtained judgment. The defendant appealed to the Federal Supreme Court of Nigeria and for the first time pleaded a promissory estoppel. He alleged that the plaintiffs had voluntarily promised to suspend the payment of the instalments until certain conditions had been fulfilled and that this promise had not been kept.

The Privy Council dismissed the appeal on the ground that the appellant had not proved failure to fulfil the conditions.   But Lord HODSON, in giving the advice of the Judicial Committee stated that the doctrine of promissory estoppel was subject to the following qualifications[4]

> " (a) that the other party has altered his position, (b) that the promissor can resile from his promise on giving reasonable notice, which need not be a formal notice, giving the promisee a reasonable opportunity of resuming his position, (c) the promise only becomes final and irrevocable if the promisee cannot resume his position."

The view that promissory estoppel is only suspensory in operation (except in cases where it is no longer possible to restore the promisee to his original position) is attractive because it provides a ready means of reconciling the decisions in *Jorden* v. *Money, Hughes* v. *Metropolitan Rail. Co.* and *Foakes* v. *Beer*. On the other hand DENNING, J., in the *High Trees* case thought the doctrine operated to extinguish the landlord's right to the balance of the rent[5] and he repeated the view that promissory

---

1. Obviously everything decided by the Court of Appeal in the first action was *res judicata* in the second action.
2. In his judgment, Lord SIMONDS expressed the view that the principle to be found in *Combe* v. *Combe* " may well be far too widely stated ": [1955] 2 All E.R., at p. 660, [1955] 1 W.L.R., at p. 764.
3. [1964] 3 All E.R. 556; [1964] 1 W.L.R. 1326.   See also *Brickwoods, Ltd.* v. *Butler and Walters* (1969), 21 P. & C.R. 256; *Offredy Developments, Ltd.* v. *Steinbock* (1971), 221 Estates Gazette 963.
4. [1964] 3 All E.R. 556; [1964] 1 W.L.R. 1326 at pp. 559, 1330, respectively.
5. In the case the landlord's right to the rent after the war was revived but in DENNING, J.'s analysis this was because the promise was only to last while the flats were not fully occupied.   He does not discuss the question of whether the landlord might have changed his mind in, say, 1943, and claimed the full rent thenceforth.

estoppel can operate to extinguish a debt after part payment in
D. and C. Builders, Ltd. v. Rees.[1] On the face of it, this view
can only be reconciled with *Foakes* v. *Beer* by arguing that that
case was decided on purely common law grounds and that the
House had overlooked its own decision in *Hughes* v. *Metropolitan
Rail. Co.*, decided only seven years earlier.[2]

(2) It is still not clear what conduct by the promisee must
follow the promise before it becomes binding. In the doctrine
of estoppel by representation of fact, the representor is only
estopped if the representee has acted on the representation to his
detriment.[3] . It is not surprising that by analogy it has been argued
that a similar requirement applies to promissory estoppel.

Must
promisee act
to his
detriment?

Such detrimental reliance was factually present in *Hughes* v.
Metropolitan Rail. Co.; indeed the tenant had not only acted to
his detriment but acted to his detriment vis-à-vis the promisor
(the landlord) by omitting to repair. Such action vis-à-vis the
promisor is present in many of the other cases where the doctrine
has been applied.[4] It is perhaps no coincidence that these are
also cases where the doctrine has operated suspensively, since it
will usually be much easier to restore the promisee to his original
position where he has altered it vis-à-vis the promisor than where
he has altered it vis-à-vis a third party.

Action by the promisee to his detriment was regarded as
essential by McVEIGH, J., in *Morrow* v. *Carty.*[5] In *Emmanuel
Ayodeji Ajayi* v. *R. T. Briscoe (Nigeria), Ltd.*,[6] the Privy Council
stated that the promisee must have altered his position and it has
been commonly assumed that this means altered *for the worse*. On
the other hand this has been consistently denied by Lord DENNING,
M.R., who most recently restated his views in *W. J. Alan & Co.,
Ltd.* v. *El Nasr Export and Import Co.*[7] where he said:[8]

> " I know that it has been suggested in some quarters that there
> must be detriment. But I can find no support for it in the authori-
> ties cited by the judge. The nearest approach to it is the statement
> of Viscount SIMONDS in the *Tool Metal* case, that the other must
> have been led to alter his position, which was adopted by Lord
> HODSON in *Emmanuel Ayodeji Ajayi* v. *R. T. Briscoe (Nigeria), Ltd.*
> But that only means that he must have been led to act differently
> from what he otherwise would have done."

However in that case the other two members of the Court of
Appeal left the question open, STEPHENSON, L.J., because he held
the promisee had acted to his detriment[9] and MEGAW, L.J.,

---

1. [1966] 2 Q.B. 617; [1965] 3 All E.R. 837.
2. It is not clear that even such an oversight would render the decision in
   Foakes v. *Beer per incuriam.* See *Cassell & Co.* v. *Broome,* [1972] A.C.
   1027; [1972] 1 All E.R. 801.
3. Spencer Bower and Turner, *Estoppel by Representation,* 2nd Edn.,
   pp. 97–107.
4. E.g. *Birmingham and District Land Co.* v. *London and North Western Railway
   Co.* (1888), 40 Ch.D. 268; *Salisbury* v. *Gilmore,* [1942] 2 K.B. 38; [1942] 1
   All E.R. 457; *Tool Metal Manufacturing Co., Ltd.* v. *Tungsten Electric Co.,
   Ltd.,* [1955] 2 All E.R. 657; [1955] 1 W.L.R. 761.
5. [1957] N.I. 174.
6. *Supra,* p. 94. See also *Jamaica Telephone Co., Ltd.* v. *Robinson* (1970),
   16 W.I.R. 174.
7. [1972] 2 Q.B. 189; [1972] 2 All E.R. 127.
8. *Ibid.,* at pp. 213, 140, respectively.
9. *Ibid.,* at pp. 221, 147, respectively.

because he held that there had been a consensual variation of the contract for consideration.[1]

Another approach was adopted in the New Zealand case of *P. v. P.*[2]

> A husband and wife had separated, and by the deed of separation the husband agreed to pay a monthly sum to the wife. Later the parties were divorced and the court ordered the husband to pay to the wife one shilling a year as maintenance. The wife was insane; and her administrator, the Public Trustee, told the husband (a) that the court order cancelled the provisions of the separation deed, (b) that if he paid the arrears due under the deed he would be under no further liability. The husband accordingly paid the arrears but paid no more instalments. More than four years later the Public Trustee found that he had wrongly interpreted the effect of the court order and sued for the monthly instalments. The husband pleaded the principle set out in the *High Trees* case and in *Combe* v. *Combe*.

McGREGOR, J., gave judgment for the defendant. The latter had been induced by the statement of the Public Trustee not to proceed, as he might have done, to take steps under an Act of 1928 to set aside the separation deed. The Public Trustee, therefore, should not now be allowed to enforce his legal claim.

McGREGOR, J., thought that the governing test was " whether it would be inequitable to allow the party seeking so to do to enforce the strict rights which he had induced the other party to believe will not be enforced." Clearly on the facts of this case, the husband had acted to his detriment and it seems likely that the tests of inequity and detrimental reliance would in practice substantially overlap.

Must promisee act equitably?

(3) A final doubt is whether the promisee must have acted equitably if he is to rely on the doctrine. Such a requirement was stated by Lord DENNING, M.R., in *D. and C. Builders, Ltd.* v. *Rees*[3] the facts of which have already been discussed.[4] This is a case which illustrated perfectly our earlier suggestion that the rule in *Foakes* v. *Beer* was not devoid of virtue since the merits were clearly on the side of the plaintiff creditors.[5] WINN, L.J., simply applied the principle of *Foakes* v. *Beer* and did not consider the application of promissory estoppel but Lord DENNING, M.R., had in earlier cases stated the principle in a form sufficiently wide to cover the defendants. He did not resile from the width of his earlier statements but qualified them by a rider that a promise can only be relied on when it has been given with full consent and not if it has been extracted by threats. If the courts do eventually hold that doctrine of promissory estoppel has outflanked *Foakes* v. *Beer*, it would appear necessary to have some such saving clause. This will clearly involve the gradual working

---

1. *Ibid.,* at pp. 217–8, 143 respectively. STEPHENSON, L.J., agreed that there was a consensual variation. Clarke, [1974] C.L.J. 260, at pp. 278–280, doubts whether there was consideration for such a variation but for present purposes the important point is that two members of the court thought it necessary to find it.
2. [1957] N.Z.L.R. 854; Sheridan, 21 M.L.R. 185. For other New Zealand cases, see the 4th New Zealand edition of this work, pp. 82–84.
3. [1966] 2 Q.B. 617; [1965] 3 All E.R. 837.
4. *Supra,* p. 88.
5. *Supra,* p. 86.

out of what conduct by the promisee should be regarded as inequitable in this context.[1]   In *Adams* v. *R. Hanna & Son, Ltd.*[2] it was suggested that a debtor who seeks to persuade a creditor to accept less than is owed, only acts equitably when he makes full and frank disclosure of his financial position.

3.   COMPOSITIONS WITH CREDITORS

It has long been a common practice for the creditors of an impecunious debtor to make an arrangement with him whereby each agrees to accept a stated percentage of his debt in full satisfaction. The search for a sufficient consideration to support so reasonable an agreement has caused the courts much embarrassment. It would appear at first sight to fall under the ban in *Pinnel's Case*; and such was the view adopted in 1804 by Lord ELLENBOROUGH. " It is impossible to contend that acceptance of £17 10s. is an extinguishment of a debt of £50."[3]   But the inconvenience of such a conclusion was so manifest that it could not be accepted.

Two alternative suggestions have been proffered. The first was the second thought of Lord ELLENBOROUGH himself. There was consideration for the composition, he suggested in 1812, in the fact that each individual creditor agreed to forgo part of his debt on the hypothesis that all the other creditors would do the same.[4] A moment's reflection will expose the weakness of this argument. Such a consideration would, no doubt, suffice to support the agreement as between the creditors themselves. But, if the debtor sought to rely upon it, he would be met by the immediate objection that he himself had furnished no return for the creditors' promises to him, and, as already observed, it is a cardinal rule of the law that the consideration must move from the promisee.[5]   A second solution is to say that no creditor will be allowed to go behind the composition agreement, to the prejudice either of the other creditors or of the debtor himself, because this would be a fraud upon all the parties concerned. This solution was suggested by Lord TENTERDEN in 1818 and supported by WILLES, J., in 1863, and it has since won general approbation.[6] But it is frankly an argument *ab inconvenienti* and evades rather than meets the difficulty.

Similar difficulties arise with a second situation.

Part payment by stranger

> Suppose that A owes B £100 and that C promises B £50 on condition that B will discharge A. If the £50 is paid and B still sues A for the balance, how is A to resist the action?

1. Winder, 82 L.Q.R. 165; Cornish, 29 M.L.R. 428.
2. (1967), 11 W.I.R. 245.
3. *Fitch* v. *Sutton* (1804), 5 East, 230.
4. *Boothbey* v. *Sowden* (1812), 3 Camp. 175. The argument was adopted, though *obiter*, by the court in *Good* v. *Cheesman* (1831), 2 B. & Ad. 328.
5. See *supra*, p. 69.
6. See *Wood* v. *Robarts* (1818), 1 Stark. 417; and *Cook* v. *Lister* (1863), 13 C.B.N.S. 543, at p. 595. See also *Couldery* v. *Bartrum* (1881), 19 Ch.D. 394, where Sir George JESSEL, amid a sustained invective against the rule in *Pinnel's Case*, can say no more than that the law " imports " a consideration. to support the composition agreement; and *Hirachand Punamchand* v. *Temple*, [1911] 2 K.B. 330.

No promise of discharge was given to him, nor, if it had been, would he have supplied any consideration for it. The question arose in 1825 in *Welby* v. *Drake*.[1]

> The defendant had drawn a bill for £18, which had been returned unaccepted and which had come into the hands of the plaintiff. The defendant's father then made an agreement with the plaintiff, whereby he promised to pay him £9 in return for the plaintiff's promise to receive it in full satisfaction of his claim. The money was duly paid, but the plaintiff still sued the defendant.

Lord TENTERDEN directed judgment for the defendant.

> " If," he said, " the father did pay the smaller sum in satisfaction of this debt, it is a bar to the plaintiff's now recovering against the son; because, by suing the son, he commits a fraud on the father, whom he induced to advance his money on the faith of such advance being a discharge of his son from further liability."

The plea of fraud was approved by WILLES, J., in *Cook* v. *Lister*[2] and applied by the Court of Appeal in *Hirachand Punamchand* v. *Temple*,[3] and reliance was placed upon the analogy of composition agreements. Both classes of cases, therefore, may be said to rest upon this basis, and should be treated as exceptions to the general requirement of consideration.

4.   WHERE THE PLAINTIFF IS BOUND BY AN EXISTING CONTRACTUAL DUTY TO A THIRD PARTY

Academic nature of the problem

The next type of case is where the plaintiff performs, or promises to perform, an obligation already imposed upon him by a contract previously made, not between him and the defendant, but between himself and a third party. The question whether such a promise or performance affords sufficient consideration has provoked a voluminous literature—more generous, indeed, than the practical implications would seem to warrant.[4]

The problem stated

The problems involved may thus be stated. If A and B have made a contract under which an obligation remains to be performed by A and A now makes this obligation the basis of a new agreement with C, there are two possibilities. C's promise may have been induced either by A's promise to perform his outstanding obligation under the contract with B, or by A's actual performance of it. In other words, A may seek to support the validity of his agreement with C by reliance either on executory or on executed consideration. There is, as has already been remarked, a divergence of juristic opinion as to the identity of the

---

1. (1825), 1 C. & P. 557.
2. (1863), 13 C.B.N.S. 543, at p. 595.
3. [1911] 2 K.B. 330.   See also *Re L. G. Clarke, Ex parte Debtor* v. *S. Ashton & Son*, [1967] Ch. 1121, [1966] 3 All E.R. 622.   The courts have usually shown greater reluctance to allow A to use a contract between B and C as a defence to an action by B.   See *infra* pp. 154–158.   See also Gold, 19 Can. Bar. Rev. 165.   In *Welby* v. *Drake* the creditor sued for the full amount of the original debt; in *Hirachand Punamchamnd* v. *Temple* only for the balance.
4. Davis, [1937] C.L.J. 203; Barllantine 11 Mich. L.R. 423; Pollock, *Principles of Contract*, 13th Edn., pp. 147–150; Holdsworth, H. E. L. VIII, pp. 40–41; *Williston On Contracts*, 3rd Edn., paras. 131, 131A.

test applicable to determine the sufficiency of the one type of consideration and of the other.[1]

How far is this distinction between executory and executed consideration to be regarded as relevant? Sir Frederick Pollock thought that, in principle at least, it should be decisive.[2] In his opinion the *promise* might be good consideration, for it involved the promisor in two possible actions for breach of contract instead of one, and thus was a detriment within the meaning of the law.[3] The *performance* should not be accepted as good consideration, since, as it discharged the previous contract, it was not a detriment at all. This theory, however, is not altogether convincing. The validity of the promise may be accepted: the insufficiency of the performance is open to criticism. In the first place, it assumes that the only test of consideration is a detriment to the promisee. The assumption may be historically sound: the idea of detriment at least recalls the early association of assumpsit and case. But the complementary idea of benefit was soon introduced into the language of the courts, and has been constantly emphasized by the judges. While, therefore, the performance may not be a detriment to the promisee, it is certainly a benefit to the promisor.[4] In the second place, the distinction involves a practical absurdity. If the mere promise of an act is sufficient consideration to induce a counter-promise, surely the complete performance of that act should be accepted. To hold the contrary, it has been well said, seems to assert " that a bird in the hand is worth less than the same bird in the bush,"[5] Once more, the conflict between principle and technicality comes to the surface, and once more the difficulties inherent in the use of the terms " detriment " and " benefit " would be avoided if the element of bargain were stressed and the language of sale adopted. Promise and performance may equally be regarded as the price of a counter-promise.

Although the question has often been said to be an open one, the cases have with one exception uniformly upheld either promise or performance as sufficient consideration. This seems to be the effect of some seventeenth century cases, though no doubt the court did not there see the problem in modern terms.[6] The one discordant case is *Jones v. Waite*.[7]

> In this case the defendant agreed to pay money to the plaintiff in return for the plaintiff's promise (a) to execute a separation deed and (b) to pay his (the plaintiff's) debts to a third party. The promise to execute the separation deed raised questions of public policy[8] but was held good consideration. The Court of Exchequer Chamber held however that the plaintiff's promise to pay his own debts was no consideration.

Distinction between executory and executed consideration

Jones v. Waite

---

1. See *supra*, p. 73.
2. *Principles of Contract*, 13th Edn., pp. 147–50. Holdsworth appears to agree: H.E.L. VIII, pp. 40–41.
3. To this argument it has sometimes been objected that it assumes what it seeks to prove. The promisor exposes himself to two suits only if he can be sued by the new party. But the new party can sue only if the promisor has given consideration. It seems, however, that Pollock meets the objection fairly by pointing out that this assumption must necessarily be made in the case of all mutual promises.
4. See *Williston on Contracts*, 3rd Edn., paras. 131 and 131A.
5. See Ballantine, 11 Mich. L.R. 423, at p. 427.
6. E.g. *Bagge v. Slade* (1616), 3 Bulst. 162; Simpson, *History*, pp. 451–2.
7. (1839), 5 Bing N.C. 341.
8. See *infra*, p. 367.

Lord Abinger, C.B., said:[1]

" A man is under a moral and legal obligation to pay his just
debts. It cannot therefore be stated as an abstract proposition, that
he suffers any detriment from the discharge of that duty; and the
declaration does not show in what way the defendant could have
derived any advantage from the plaintiff paying his own debts.
The plea therefore shows the insufficiency of that part of the consideration."

This is no doubt a strong authority but it should be noted that
the plaintiff's failure on this point was due, at least in part, to his
failure to allege any benefit to the defendant. This leaves open
the possibility of upholding the contract where a benefit to the
promisor can be shown. In fact the case was not as influential
as might have been expected since it was lost sight of for over a
hundred years, no doubt because when the case was taken to the
House of Lords only the separation agreement point was taken.[2]

Jones v. *Waite* was not therefore cited or discussed in a trilogy
of cases in the 1860's, of which the first is *Shadwell* v. *Shadwell*.[3]

The plaintiff, who was engaged to marry Ellen Nicholl, received
the following letter from his uncle:

" 11th August, 1838, Gray's Inn.

Shadwell v.
Shadwell

My dear Lancey—I am glad to hear of your intended marriage
with Ellen Nicholl; and, as I promised to assist you at starting, I
am happy to tell you that I will pay to you one hundred and fifty
pounds yearly during my life, and until your annual income derived
from your profession of a chancery barrister shall amount to six
hundred guineas, of which your own admission shall be the only
evidence that I shall receive or require.

Your ever affectionate uncle,
Charles Shadwell."

The plaintiff married Ellen Nicholl and never earned as much as
six hundred guineas a year as a barrister. The instalments promised
by the uncle were not all paid during his life, and, after his death,
the plaintiff brought an action to recover the arrears from the
personal representatives.

The defendants pleaded that, as the plaintiff was already bound
to marry Ellen Nicholl before the uncle wrote his letter, there was
no consideration for his promise.

On these facts it might well have been held that there was no
more than a conditional promise of a gift by the uncle and indeed
that was the dissenting view of BYLES, J.[4] The majority of the
court held that the letter was intended contractually and that
there was consideration for it.

ERLE, C.J., giving the opinion of KEATING, J., and himself,
thought that there was both a detriment to the plaintiff and a
benefit to the uncle: a detriment because " the plaintiff may have
made the most material changes in his position and have incurred
pecuniary liabilities resulting in embarrassment, which would be

---

1. 5 Bing N.C. 341 at p. 356
2. (1842), 9 Cl. & F. 99.
3. (1860), 9 C.B.N.S. 159; 30 L.J.C.P. 145.
4. Cf. *Jones* v. *Padavatton*, [1969] 2 All E.R. 166; [1969] 1 W.L.R. 328, discussed infra, pp. 105–6. Though logically it should make no difference,
the Court is perhaps more likely to strain to discover a contract where the
action lies against the executors than against the promisor.

in every sense a loss if the income which had been promised should be withheld," and a benefit, because the marriage was " an object of interest with a near relative."

The facts and the decision in *Chichester* v. *Cobb*[1] were for practical purposes identical and we need only note that BLACKBURN, J., experienced no difficulty in discovering consideration on such facts.

The third case is *Scotson* v. *Pegg*.[2]

Scotson v. Pegg

> The plaintiffs had contracted with a third party, X, to deliver a cargo of coal to X or *to the order of* X. X sold this cargo to the defendant and directed the plaintiffs, in pursuance of their contract, to deliver it to the defendant. The defendant then made an agreement with the plaintiffs in which, " in consideration that the plaintiffs, at the request of the defendant, would deliver to the defendant " the cargo of coal, the defendant promised to unload it at a stated rate.

For breach of this promise the plaintiffs sued, and the defendant once more pleaded lack of consideration. If, it was argued, the plaintiffs were already bound by the contract with X to deliver the coal to the defendant in accordance with X's order, what were they now giving in return for the defendant's promise to unload at a certain rate? However, the two judges present at the hearing, MARTIN and WILDE, BB., both gave judgment for the plaintiffs. MARTIN, B., was content to say that the delivery of the coal was a benefit to the defendant. WILDE, B., thought there was also a detriment to the plaintiffs. It might have suited them, as against X, to break their contract and pay damages, and the delivery to the defendant had prevented this possible course of conduct.[3]

Although these three cases are not entirely satisfactory, they at least all point in the same way and one further along which principle directs us. All doubts on the matter may now be regarded as resolved by the recent decision of the Privy Council in *New Zealand Shipping Co.* v. *A. M. Satterthwaite & Co.*, (*The Eurymedon*).[4] The facts and issues of this case are complex and are discussed more fully later.[5] For present purposes we may say that the essential facts were that the plaintiff made an offer to the defendant that if the defendant would unload the plaintiff's goods from a ship (which the defendant was already bound to do by a contract with a third party), the plaintiff would treat the defendant as exempt from any liability for damage to the goods. The majority of the judicial committee of the Privy Council had no doubt[6] that the defendant's act of unloading the ship was good consideration.[7]

The Eurymedon

1. (1866), 14 L.T. 433.
2. (1861), 6 H. & N. 295; 3 L.T. 753.
3. This argument is only found in 3 L.T.
4. [1975] A.C. 154; [1974] 1 All E.R. 1015. Reynolds, 90 L.Q.R. 301.
5. See *infra*, pp. 157–8.
6. The minority expressed no concluded view for they did not think the transaction could be construed as an offer of this kind.
7. [1975] A.C., at p. 168; [1974] 1 All E.R., at p. 1021.

CHAPTER THREE

Intention to Create Legal Relations

THE question now to be discussed is whether a contract necessarily
results once the court has ruled that the parties must be taken to
have made an agreement and that it is supported by consideration.[1]
This conclusion is commonly denied. The law, it is said, does not
proclaim the existence of a contract merely because of the presence
of mutual promises. Agreements are made every day in domestic
and in social life, where the parties do not intend to invoke the
assistance of the courts should the engagement not be honoured.
To offer a friend a meal is not to invite litigation. Contracts, in
the words of Lord STOWELL,

> " must not be the sports of an idle hour, mere matters of pleasantry
> and badinage, never intended by the parties to have any serious
> effect whatever."[2]

It is therefore contended that, in addition to the phenomena of
agreement and the presence of consideration, a third contractual
element is required—the intention of the parties to create legal
relations.

Views of
Professor
Williston

This view, commonly held in England,[3] has not passed
unchallenged; and the criticism of it made by Professor Williston
demands attention, not only as emanating from a distinguished
American jurist, but as illuminating the whole subject now under
discussion. In his opinion, the separate element of intention is
foreign to the common law, imported from the Continent by
academic influences in the nineteenth century[4] and useful only in
systems which lack the test of consideration to enable them to
determine the boundaries of contract.

> " The common law," he wrote, " does not require any positive
> intention to create a legal obligation as an element of contract. . . .

---

1. It is assumed here that the contract cannot be challenged on the ground that
   it violates public policy or is avoided by statute. Such flaws are discussed,
   infra, Part IV, Chap. 4.
2. *Dalrymple* v. *Dalrymple* (1811), 2 Hag. Con. 54, at p. 105.
3. *E.g. Pollock on Contract*, 13th Edn., p. 3; Law Revision Committee, *Sixth
   Interim Report*, p. 15.
4. Historically this would appear correct. Simpson, 91 L.O.R. 263–265.

A deliberate promise seriously made is enforced irrespective of the promisor's views regarding his legal liability."[1]

His own views may be reduced to three propositions:

(1) If reasonable people would assume that there was no intention in the parties to be bound, there is no contract.

(2) If the parties expressly declare or clearly indicate their rejection of contractual obligations, the law accepts and implements their intention.

(3) Mere social engagements, if accompanied by the requisite technicalities, such as consideration, may be enforced as contracts.

English lawyers may well be prepared to accept the first two of these propositions: decided cases refute the third.[2] But their acceptance does not necessarily justify the complete rejection of intention to create legal relations as an independent element in the formation of contract. It is certainly true, and of great significance, that the very presence of consideration normally implies the existence of such an intention. To make a bargain is to assume liability and to invite the sanction of the courts. Professor Williston performed a valuable service by insisting that the emphasis laid by foreign systems on this element of intention is out of place in the common law, where it follows naturally from the very nature of contract. Consideration, bargain, legal consequences—these are inter-related concepts. But it is possible for this presumption to be rebutted. If A and B agree to lunch together and A promises to pay for the food if B will pay for the drink, it is difficult to deny the presence of consideration and yet equally clear that no legal ties are contemplated or created.[3] It seems necessary, therefore, to regard the intention to create legal relations as a separate element in the English law of contract, though, by the preoccupation of that law with the idea of bargain, one which does not normally obtrude upon the courts.

Standpoint of English law

The cases in which a contract is denied on the ground that there is no intention to involve legal liability may be divided into two classes. On the one hand there are social, family or other domestic agreements, where the presence or absence of an intention to create legal relations depends upon the inference to be drawn by the court from the language used by the parties and the circumstances in which they use it.[4] On the other hand there

---

1. *Williston on Contracts,* 3rd Edn., s. 21. Williston has not lacked support: see Tuck 21 Can. Bar. Rev. 123; Hamson, 54 L.Q.R. 233; Shatwell, 1 Sydney L.R. 289; Unger, 19 M.L.R. 96; Hepple, [1970] C.L.J. 122. Cf. Chloros, 33 Tulane L.R. 607.
2. *E.g. Balfour* v. *Balfour,* [1919] 2 K.B. 571; *infra,* p. 104. See also *Lens* v. *Devonshire Club, Times,* 4th December, 1914, discusses by SCRUTTON, L.J., *Rose and Frank Co.* v. *J. R. Crompton & Brothers, Ltd.,* [1923] 2 K.B. 261.
3. It may be objected that there is only consideration if the promises are given in exchange for each other but some test of intention is needed to discover whether this is so.
4. It is not irrelevant to notice that by s. 1 (1) of the Law Reform (Miscellaneous Provisions) Act 1970, " an agreement between two persons to marry one another shall not under the law of England and Wales have effect as a contract giving rise to legal rights, and no action shall lie in England or Wales for breach of such an agreement, whatever the law applicable to the agreement."

are commercial agreements where this intention is presumed and must be rebutted by the party seeking to deny it.   In either case, of course, intention is to be objectively ascertained.

A. DOMESTIC AGREEMENTS

Agreements
between
husband and
wife

In the course of family life many agreements are made, which could never be supposed to be the subject of litigation.   If a husband arranges to make a monthly allowance to his wife for her personal enjoyment, neither would normally be taken to contemplate legal relations.   On the other hand, the relation of husband and wife by no means precludes the formation of a contract, and the context may indicate a clear intention on either side to be bound.   Whether any given agreement between husband and wife falls on the one side of the borderline or the other is not always easy to determine.   Two contrasting cases may illustrate the position.

In *Merritt* v. *Merritt*,[1]

> the husband left the matrimonial home, which was in the joint names of husband and wife and subject to a building society mortgage, to live with another woman.   The husband and wife met and had a discussion in the husband's car during which the husband agreed to pay the wife £40 a month out of which she must pay the outstanding mortgage payments on the house.   The wife refused to leave the car until the husband recorded the agreement in writing and the husband wrote and signed a piece of paper which stated " in consideration of the fact that you will pay all charges in connection with the house . . . until such time as the mortgage repayment has been completed I will agree to transfer the property in to your sole ownership."   After the wife had paid off the mortgage the husband refused to transfer the house to her.

It was held by the Court of Appeal that the parties had intended to affect their legal relations and that an action for breach of contract could be sustained.

In *Balfour* v. *Balfour*,[2]

> the defendant was a civil servant stationed in Ceylon.   His wife alleged that, while they were both in England on leave and when it had become clear that she could not again accompany him abroad because of her health, he had promised to pay her £30 a month as maintenance during the time that they were thus forced to live apart.   She sued for breach of this agreement.

The Court of Appeal held that no legal relations had been contemplated and that the wife's action must fail.[3]

ATKIN, L.J., had no doubt that, while consideration was present, the evidence showed that the parties had not designed a binding contract.[4]

---

1. [1970] 2 All E.R. 760, [1970] 1 W.L.R. 1211.   See also *McGregor* v. *McGregor* (1888), 21 Q.B.D. 424; *Pearce* v. *Merriman,* [1904] 1 K.B. 80.
2. [1919] 2 K.B. 571.
3. Tuck, op. cit., p. 97, rests the decision in this case on the absence of consideration.   DUKE, L.J., certainly took this view: but the whole tenor both of counsel's arguments and of the judgments of WARRINGTON and ATKIN, L.JJ., shows that the decision turned on the lack of intention to contract.
4. [1919] 2 K.B., at pp. 578–9.

" It is necessary to remember that there are agreements between parties which do not result in contracts within the meaning of that term in our law. The ordinary example is where two parties agree to take a walk together or where there is an offer and an acceptance of hospitality. Nobody would suggest in ordinary circumstances that those agreements result in what we know as a contract, and one of the most usual forms of agreement which does not constitute a contract appears to me to be the arrangements which are made between husband and wife. . . . To my mind those agreements or many of them, do not result in contracts at all . . . even though there may be what as between other parties would constitute consideration. . . . They are not contracts because the parties did not intend that they should be attended by legal consequences."

In the recent case of *Pettitt* v. *Pettitt*,[1] several members of the House of Lords, though accepting the principle enunciated in *Balfour* v. *Balfour*, thought the decision on the facts very close to the line.[2] It was also observed that though many agreements between husband and wife are not intended to be legally binding, performance of such agreements may well give rise to legal consequences.

So Lord DIPLOCK said:[3]

" many of the ordinary domestic arrangements between man and wife do not possess the legal characteristics of a contract. So long as they are executory they do not give rise to any chose in action for neither party intended that non-performance of their mutual promises should be the subject of sanctions in any court (see *Balfour* v. *Balfour*). But this is relevant to non-performance only. If spouses do perform their mutual promises the fact that they could not have been compelled to do so while the promises were executory cannot deprive the acts done by them of all legal consequences on proprietary rights; for these are within the field of the law of property rather than of the law of contract. It would, in my view, be erroneous to extend the presumption accepted in *Balfour* v. *Balfour* that mutual promises between man and wife in relation to their domestic arrangements are prima facie not intended by either to be legally enforceable to a presumption of a common intention of both spouses that no legal consequences should flow from acts done by them in performance of mutual promises with respect to the acquisition, improvement or addition to real or personal property—for this would be to intend what is impossible in law."

Agreements between parent and child may present problems similar to those of husband and wife. An illustration is afforded by the case of *Jones* v. *Padavatton*:[4]

Agreements between parent and child

Mrs. Jones lived in Trinidad. Her daughter had a post in the Indian Embassy in Washington. She had been married and had a young son, but was now divorced. Mrs. Jones wished her to go to England and become a barrister, and offered to make her a monthly allowance while she read for the Bar. The daughter reluctantly

---

1. [1970] A.C. 777; [1969] 2 All E.R. 385.
2. *Per* Lord HODSON, *ibid.*, at pp. 806, 400 respectively; *per* Lord UPJOHN, *ibid.*, at pp. 816, 408, respectively.
3. *Ibid.*, at pp. 822, 413–4, respectively. See also *per* Lord REID, *ibid.*, at pp. 796, 391, respectively: see Lesser, 23 U. of Toronto L.J. 148, at pp. 162–164. That it is easy to lose sight of the distinction between contract and property is shown by the decision in *Spellman* v. *Spellman* [1961] 2 All E.R. 498; [1961] 1 W.L.R. 921, discussed by Diamond, 24 M.L.R. 789.
4. [1969] 2 All E.R. 616; [1969] 1 W.L.R. 328.

accepted the offer and went to England in 1962.   In 1964 Mrs. Jones bought a house in London.   The daughter lived with her child in part of it, and the rest was let to tenants, whose rent covered expenses and the daughter's maintenance.   In 1967, Mrs. Jones and her daughter quarrelled, and Mrs. Jones issued a summons claiming possession of the house.   At the time of the hearing, the daughter had passed only a portion of Part I of the Bar examinations.

Two agreements fell to be considered.   By the first the daughter agreed to leave Washington and read for the Bar in London, and her mother agreed to pay her a fixed monthly sum.   By the second the mother allowed the daughter to live in the house which the mother had bought, and the rent received from the tenants provided for the daughter's maintenance.   In each agreement there was an exchange of promises, but in neither were the terms put into writing, nor was the duration of the agreement precisely defined.   The question was whether in either case the parties had intended to create legal relations.

At the hearing in the county court, the judge dismissed the mother's claim for possession of the house, but his decision was reversed by the Court of Appeal.   DANCKWERTS and FENTON ATKINSON, L.JJ. thought that neither agreement was intended to create legal relations.   " The present case is one of those family arrangements which depend on the good faith of the promises which are made and are not intended to be rigid binding arrangements."[1]   SALMON, L.J. agreed that the appeal should be allowed, but on different grounds.   In his opinion the first agreement was a contract designed to last for a period reasonably sufficient to enable the daughter to pass the Bar examinations.   For this purpose the five years which had elapsed since the date of the agreement was a reasonable time, and the contract had therefore come to an end.   The second agreement, involving the possession of the house, was so imprecise and left so many details unsettled that it was impossible to construe it as a contract.   Nothing in the agreement nor in the available evidence suggested that the mother had intended to renounce her right to dispose of her house as and when she pleased.   The daughter was a mere licensee.[2]

Other domestic arrangements   A further group of cases involve domestic agreements which are made neither between husband and wife nor between parent and child.   In *Simpkins* v. *Pays*,[3]

the defendant owned a house in which she lived with X, her grand-daughter, and the plaintiff, a paying boarder.   The three took part together each week in a competition organized by a Sunday newspaper.   The entries were made in the defendant's name, but there was no regular rule as to the payment of postage and other expenses. One week the entry was successful and the defendant obtained a prize of £750.   The plaintiff claimed a third of this sum, but the defendant refused to pay on the ground that there was no intention to create legal relations but only a friendly adventure.

---

1. [1969] 1 W.L.R., at p. 332; [1969] 2 All E.R., at p. 620.   Both DANCKWERTS and FENTON ATKINSON, L.JJ., cited and applied *Balfour* v. *Balfour*.
2. [1969] 1 W.L.R., at p. 335; [1969] 2 All E.R., at p. 623.
3. [1955] 3 All E.R. 10; [1955] 1 W.L.R. 975.   For a simple case where there was no intention to create legal relations, see *Buckpitt* v. *Oates*, [1968] 1 All E.R. 1145.   See also *Parker* v. *Clark*, [1960] 1 All E.R. 93; [1960] 1 W.L.R. 286.

SELLERS, J., gave judgment for the plaintiff. He agreed that " there are many family associations where some sort of rough and ready statement is made which would not establish a contract." But on the present facts he thought that there was a " mutuality in the arrangements between the parties." It was a joint enterprise to which each contributed in the expectation of sharing any prize that was won.

B. COMMERCIAL AGREEMENTS[1]

In commercial agreements it will be presumed that the parties intended to create legal relations and make a contract. But the presumption may be rebutted.

(1) It is common enough to advertise goods by flamboyant reports of their efficacy and to support these by promises of a more or less vague character if they should fail of their purpose. If a plaintiff, induced to buy on the faith of such reports and promises, finds that they are not borne out by the facts and sues for breach of contract, the defendant may attempt to plead that there was no intention to create legal relations and that only the most gullible customer would think otherwise.

Advertisements

The point arose in the case of *Carlill* v. *Carbolic Smoke Ball Co.*,[2] where the defendants advertised their preparation by offering to pay £100 to any purchaser who used it and yet caught influenza within a given period, and by declaring that they had deposited £1,000 with their bankers " to show their sincerity." The plaintiff bought the preparation, used it and caught influenza. Among the many ingenious defences raised to her action was the plea that no legal relations were ever contemplated. The advertisement, it was said, was " a mere puff," " a mere statement by the defendants of the confidence they reposed in their remedy," " a promise in honour." The Court of Appeal rejected this plea. The fact of the deposit was cogent evidence that the defendants had contemplated legal liability when they issued their advertisement. What would have been the view of the court in the absence of any such deposit is a matter of speculation, and it is not to be concluded that all advertisements are to be treated as serious offers.[3]

In *Carlill* v. *Carbolic Smoke Ball Co.* the plaintiff did not buy the smoke ball from the defendant but from a retailer. The question before the court was therefore whether there was a contract with the defendant. A more common factual situation arises where there is undoubtedly a contract but there is dispute as to whether a statement made by one of the parties before the contract forms part of the contract. This question is discussed

---

1. There can of course be commercial agreements between members of a family, e.g. *Snelling* v. *John E. Snelling, Ltd.*, [1973] 1 Q.B. 87, [1972] 1 All E.R. 79.
2. [1893] 1 Q.B. 256. *Supra*, p. 26.
3. Cf. *supra*, p. 26.

more fully later[1] and it will suffice for the moment to say that here too, the governing test is the parties' intention.[2]

" Honour clauses "

(2) The parties may make an agreement on a matter of business or of some other transaction normally the subject of contract, but may expressly declare that it is not to be binding in law.   If such a declaration is made, it will, like other unambiguous expressions of intention, be accepted by the courts.[3]

Rose & Frank v. Crompton

Perhaps the most remarkable instance of a clause expressly outlawing an agreement is to be found in the case of *Rose and Frank* v. *Crompton*.[4]   The plaintiffs were a New York firm which dealt in tissues for carbonizing papers.   The defendants manufactured such tissues in England.   In July, 1913, the parties made a written agreement whereby the defendants gave the plaintiffs certain rights of selling their tissues in the United States and in Canada for a period of three years with an option to extend the time.   The agreement contained the following clause, described as " the Honourable Pledge Clause :"

> " This arrangement is not entered into nor is this memorandum written, as a formal or legal agreement, and shall not be subject to legal jurisdiction in the law courts either of the United States or England, but it is only a definite expression and record of the purpose and intention of the parties concerned, to which they each honourably pledge themselves."

The agreement was subsequently extended so as to last until March, 1920 ; but in 1919 the defendants terminated it without giving the appropriate notice specified in the agreement, and they further refused to execute orders which had been received and accepted by them before the termination.   The plaintiffs sued for damages for breach of the agreement and for non-delivery of the goods comprised in these orders.   To appreciate the decision reached by the courts, it is necessary to separate these two claims.

Two separate issues raised by the case

The first was for breach of the agreement contained in the written document of July, 1913, whereby the defendants granted selling rights to the plaintiffs.   Here the plaintiffs failed.   The document doubtless contemplated that orders for goods were from time to time to be given by the plaintiffs and fulfilled by the defendants.   But, as the parties had specifically declared that the document was not to impose legal consequences, there was no obligation to give orders or to accept them or to stand by any clause in the agreement.   SCRUTTON, L.J., said in the Court of Appeal :[5]

> " It is quite possible for parties to come to an agreement by accepting a proposal with the result that the agreement does not give rise to legal relations.   The reason of this is that the parties do not intend that their agreement shall give rise to legal relations.   This intention may be implied from the subject-matter of the agreement, but it may also be expressed by the parties.   In social and family relations such an intention is readily implied, while in business

---

1. See *infra*, pp. 116–121.
2. See e.g. *Heilbut Symons & Co.* v. *Buckleton*, [1913] A.C. 30.
3. *Jones* v. *Vernon's Pools Ltd.*, [1938] 2 All E.R. 626; *Appleson* v. *H. Littlewood Ltd.*, [1939] 1 All E.R. 464.
4. [1923] 2 K.B. 261; reversed, [1925] A.C. 445.
5. [1923] 2 K.B., at p. 288.

matters the opposite result would ordinarily follow. But I can see no reason why, even in business matters, the parties should not intend to rely on each other's good faith and honour, and to exclude all idea of settling disputes by any outside intervention, with the accompanying necessity of expressing themselves so precisely that outsiders may have no difficulty in understanding what they mean."

The second claim, on the other hand, was based, not on the promises comprised in the original document, but on the specific orders actually accepted by the defendants before they terminated the agreement. Here the plaintiffs succeeded. As each individual order was given and accepted, this constituted a new and separate contract, inferred by the courts from the conduct of the parties and enforceable without reference to the original memorandum. In the words of Lord PHILLIMORE,[1]

" According to the course of business between the parties which is narrated in the unenforceable agreement, goods were ordered from time to time, shipped, received and paid for, under an established system; but, the agreement being unenforceable, there was no obligation on the American company to order goods or upon the English companies to accept an order. Any actual transaction between the parties, however, gave rise to the ordinary legal rights; for the fact that it was not an obligation to do the transaction did not divest the transaction, when done, of its ordinary legal significance."

Words inserted by one party in an agreement and devised, or subsequently used, to exclude legal relations may be ambiguous. In such a case the onus of proving this intention lies heavily upon the party who asserts it. A helpful example is to be found in *Edwards* v. *Skyways, Ltd.*[2]

Ambiguous words

The plaintiff was employed by the defendants as an aircraft pilot. In January, 1962, the defendants told him that they must reduce their staff and gave him three months' notice to terminate his employment. By his contract he was a member of the defendants' contributory pension fund and was thereby entitled, on leaving their service, to choose one of two options: (a) to withdraw his own total contributions to the fund, (b) to take the right to a paid-up pension payable at the age of fifty. He was a member of the British Air Line Pilots Association. Their officials had a meeting with the defendants, and it was agreed that, if the plaintiff chose option (a), the defendants would make him an " *ex gratia* " payment equivalent or approximating to the defendants' contributions to the pension fund. The plaintiff, relying on this agreement, chose option (a). The defendants paid him the amount of his own contributions but refused to make the " *ex gratia* " payment.

The plaintiff sued the defendants for breach of contract. It was admitted that the Association had acted as the plaintiff's agents and that there was consideration for the defendants' promise. But the defendants argued that the use of the words " *ex gratia* " showed that there was no intention to create legal relations. MEGAW, J., gave judgment for the plaintiff. As this was a business and not a domestic agreement, the burden of rebutting the presumption of legal relations lay upon the defendants: it was

---

1. [1925] A.C., at p. 455.
2. [1964] 1 All E.R. 494; [1964] 1 W.L.R. 349.

a heavy burden and they had not discharged it. He continued:[1]

> " The words ' *ex gratia* ' do not, in my judgment, carry a
> necessary, or even a probable, implication that the agreement is to be
> without legal effect. It is, I think, common experience among
> practitioners of the law that litigation or threatened litigation is
> frequently compromised on the terms that one party shall make to
> the other a payment described in express terms as ' *ex gratia* ' or
> ' without admission of liability.' The two phrases are, I think,
> synonymous. No one would imagine that a settlement, so made, is
> unenforceable at law. The words ' *ex gratia* ' or 'without admission
> of liability ' are used simply to indicate—it may be as a matter of
> *amour propre* or it may be to avoid a precedent in subsequent cases—
> that the party agreeing to pay does not admit any pre-existing
> liability on his part; but he is certainly not seeking to preclude the
> legal enforceability of the settlement itself. . . . I see nothing in the
> mere use of the words ' *ex gratia*,' unless in the circumstances some
> very special meaning has to be given to them, to warrant the con-
> clusion that this promise, duly made and accepted for valid con-
> sideration, was not intended by the parties to be enforceable in
> law."

Trade
Unions

Agreements between industrial corporations and trade unions
have raised the question of intention to create legal relations.
Thus in *Ford Motor Co., Ltd.* v. *Amalgamated Union of Engineering
and Foundry Workers*,[2]

> an agreement was made in 1955 between the Ford Motor Co. on the
> one side and nineteen trade unions on the other side. The agree-
> ment was in writing and was drafted with careful precision. It
> contained a term providing that " at each stage of the procedure set
> out in this agreement every attempt will be made to resolve issues
> raised, and until such procedure has been carried through there shall
> be no stoppage of work or other unconstitutional action." In 1969,
> despite this provision, some unions which were parties to the
> agreement issued notices declaring a strike. The Ford Motor Co.
> applied for interlocutory injunctions to restrain the calling of such a
> strike.

Offer, acceptance and consideration were present. Was there also
an intention to create legal relations? GEOFFREY LANE, J. thought
that there was not. He relied mainly on " the climate of opinion
voiced and evidenced by the extra-judicial authorities."

> " Agreements such as these, composed largely of optimistic
> aspirations, presenting grave practical problems of enforcement and
> reached against a background of opinion adverse to enforceability,
> are in my judgment not contracts in the legal sense and are not
> enforceable at law. Without clear and express provisions making
> them amenable to legal action, they remain in the realm of under-
> takings binding in honour."[3]

This decision was obviously of great importance in Labour
law, where, however, it has been overtaken by statute. The

---

1. *Ibid.*, at pp. 500 and 357, respectively. Cf. the use of the word " understanding " in *J. H. Milner & Son* v. *Percy Bilton, Ltd.*, [1966] 2 All E.R. 894;
[1966] 1 W.L.R. 1582; and of the phrase " without prejudice " in *Tomlin*
v. *Standard Telephones and Cables, Ltd.*, [1969] 3 All E.R. 201; [1969]
1 W.L.R. 1378. The court of appeal appear to have gone very far in discovering a contract in *Gore* v. *Van Der Lann*, [1967] 2 Q.B. 31; [1967] 1 All
E.R. 360, discussed *infra*, p. 157 and cogently criticised by Odgers, 86
L.Q.R. 69 and Harris, 30 M.L.R. 584.
2. [1969] 2 All E.R. 481; [1969] 1 W.L.R. 339.
3. [1969] 2 All E.R., at p. 496; [1969] 1 W.L.R., at p. 356.

Industrial Relations Act 1971, s. 34 (1) (introduced by the Conservative government) provided that collective agreements in writing should be presumed to have been intended to be legally enforceable. It is believed that this provision had little practical effect, since the vast majority of collective agreements were expressly stated not to be intended to be legally enforceable, and it has now in its turn been reversed by the Trade Union and Labour Relations Act 1974, s. 18, which enacts a contrary presumption.

The decision remains of interest to contract lawyers since at first sight collective agreements fall into the category of commercial agreements[1] and one might expect them to be legally binding. Further it is agreed that provisions of collective agreements may be incorporated into individual contracts of employment where they will be legally binding.[2] GEOFFREY LANE, J. relied substantially on evidence that experts in industrial relations regarded collective agreements as not intended to create legal relations.[3] This view has been criticised[4] but on balance it appears correct[5] and substantially validated by practical experience between 1971 and 1974.

---

1. Isadore Katz described a collective agreement as "at once a business compact, a code of relations and a treaty of peace," quoted by Wedderburn, *The Worker and the Law,* 2nd Edn., 1971, p. 177.
2. E.g. *National Coal Board* v. *Galley,* [1958] 1 All E.R. 91; [1958] 1 W.L.R. 16; Wedderburn, *The Worker and the Law,* 2nd Edn., pp. 188–197.
3. See especially Kahn-Freund in *The System of Industrial Relations in Great Britain,* edited by Flanders & Clegg, 1954, and Report of the Royal Commission on Trade Unions (the Donovan Report) (1968 Cmnd. 3623), Chap. VII, especially paras. 465–474. Cf. McCartney in *Labour Relations and the Law,* edited by Kahn-Freund, 1965.
4. Selwyn, 32 M.L.R. 377; Hepple, [1970] C.L.J. 122.
5. See Wedderburn, *The Worker and the Law,* 2nd edn., Chap. 4; Clark, 33 M.L.R. 117.

CHAPTER FOUR

The Contents of the Contract

Scope of this
chapter

ALTHOUGH it may be clear that a valid contract has been made,
it will still be necessary to determine the extent of the obligations
that it creates. Its map must be drawn, its features delineated
and its boundaries ascertained. It must first be discovered what
terms the parties have expressly included in their contract.

The contents of the contract are not necessarily confined to
those that appear on its face. The parties may have negotiated
against a background of commercial or local usage whose implications they have tacitly assumed, and to concentrate solely upon
their express language may be to minimize or to distort the extent
of their liabilities. Evidence of custom may thus have to be
admitted. Additional consequences, moreover, may have been
annexed by statute to particular contracts, which will operate
despite the parties' ignorance or even contrary to their intention.
Finally, the courts may read into a contract some further term
which alone makes it effective and which the parties must be
taken to have omitted by pure inadvertence. All these implications, customary, statutory or judicial, may be as important as the
terms expressly adopted by the parties.

Even when the terms have been established, it does not follow
that they are all of equal importance. One undertaking may be
regarded as of major importance, the breach of it entitling the
injured party to end the contract; the breach of another, though
demanding compensation, may leave the contract intact. Rules
of valuation have therefore to be elaborated.

Finally it will be necessary to consider the important and difficult problems which arise when the contract contains provisions which purport to exclude or limit the liability of one of the parties in certain events.

SECTION I. EXPRESS TERMS

A. WHAT DID THE PARTIES SAY OR WRITE?

If the extent of the agreement is in dispute, the court must first decide what statements were in fact made by the parties either orally or in writing. In exceptional circumstances English law demands a degree of formality either as a substantive or as a procedural requirement of contract. As a general rule, however, no formality is needed.[1] A contract may be made wholly by word of mouth, or wholly in writing, or partly by word of mouth and partly in writing.

If the contract is wholly by word of mouth, its contents are a matter of evidence normally submitted to a judge sitting as a jury. It must be found as a fact exactly what it was that the parties said, as, for example, in *Smith* v. *Hughes*[2] where the question was whether the subject-matter of a contract of sale was described by the vendor as " good oats " or as " good old oats." *(Oral contract)*

If the contract is wholly in writing, the discovery of what was written normally presents no difficulty, and its interpretation is a matter exclusively within the jurisdiction of the judge.[3] But on this hypothesis the courts have long insisted that the parties are to be confined within the four corners of the document in which they have chosen to enshrine their agreement. Neither of them may adduce evidence to show that his intention has been mis-stated in the document. *(Written contract)*

> " It is firmly established as a rule of law that parol evidence cannot be admitted to add to, vary or contradict a deed or other written instrument. Accordingly it has been held that . . . parol evidence will not be admitted to prove that some particular term, which had been verbally agreed upon, had been omitted (by design or otherwise) from a written instrument constituting a valid and operative contract between the parties."[4]

So in *Hawrish* v. *Bank of Montreal.*[5]

> A solicitor, acting for a company, signed a form profered by the company's bank, by which he personally gave a " continuing guarantee " up to $6,000 " of all present and future debts " of the company. He wished to give evidence that the guarantee was intended to be only of a then current overdraft of $6,000.

---

1. *Infra*, pp. 174–201.
2. (1871), L.R. 6 Q.B. 597.
3. See BOWEN, L.J., in *Bentsen* v. *Taylor, Sons & Co. (No. 2)*, [1893] 2 Q.B. 274. So the court is not bound by concessions made by a party as to the meaning of the contract: *Bahamas International Trust Co. Ltd.* v. *Threadgold*, [1974] 3 All E.R. 881; [1974] 1 W.L.R. 1514.
4. *Jacobs* v. *Batavia and General Plantations Trust*, [1924] 1 Ch. 287, *per* P.O. LAWRENCE, J., at p. 295. See *Cross on Evidence*, 4th Edn. (1974), pp. 532–540.
5. (1969), 2 D.L.R. (3d) 600.

The Supreme Court of Canada held that such evidence was inadmissible.

This rule, which is often called the " parol evidence " rule (though the evidence excluded by it is not merely oral), is a general rule applicable to all written instruments and not merely to contracts, but it can, within its proper limitations, be regarded as an expression of the objective theory of contract, that is, that the court is usually concerned not with the parties' actual intentions but with their manifested intention.   In a complex commercial situation, it will often happen that the documents to which the parties eventually put their hands will not fully realise the hopes and aspirations of either party but that should not make the contract any less binding.   So evidence of the parties' negotiations before the contract is excluded[1] and similarly evidence of the parties, post contractual behaviour is not admissible to show their intention,[2] though it might be to show a variation of the contract or to found an estoppel.

Limits of the
parol
evidence
rule

The exclusion of oral evidence to " add to, vary or contradict " a written document has often been pronounced in peremptory language but in practice its operation is subject to a number of exceptions.   In the first place, the evidence may be admitted to prove a custom or trade usage and thus to " add " terms which do not appear on the face of the document and which alone give it the meaning which the parties wished it to possess.[3]   In the second place, there is no reason why oral evidence should not be offered to show that, while on its face the document purports to record a valid and immediately enforceable contract, it had been previously agreed to suspend its operation until the occurrence of some event, such as the approval of a third party, and that this event had not yet taken place.   The effect of such evidence is not to " add to, vary or contradict " the terms of a written contract, but to make it clear that no contract has yet become effective.[4]   Thirdly, there is a limited equitable jurisdiction to rectify a written document where it can be shown that it was executed by both parties under a common mistake.   This will be discussed more fully later.[5]

Contracts
partly
written,
partly
oral

Finally, the exclusion of oral evidence is clearly inappropriate where the document is designed to contain only part of the terms —where, in other words, the parties have made their contract partly in writing and partly by word of mouth.   This situation is so comparatively frequent as in effect to deprive the ban on oral evidence of the strict character of a " rule of law " which has been attributed to it.   It will be presumed, " that a document

---

1. *Prenn* v. *Simmonds,* [1971] 3 All E.R. 237; [1971] 1 W.L.R. 1381.   Cf. *London County Council* v. *Henry Boot & Sons,* [1959] 3 All E.R. 636; [1959] 1 W.L.R. 1069.   In some circumstances it may be permissible to show that the parties have struck out part of a standard form of contract. See, e.g. *Louis Dreyfus et cie.* v. *Parnaso Cia. Naviera S.A.,* [1960] 2 Q.B. 49; [1960] 1 All E.R. 759.
2. *Schuler A.G.* v. *Wickman Machine Tool Sales,* [1974] A.C. 235; [1973] 2 All E.R. 39.
3. *Infra,* p. 121.
4. *Pym* v. *Campbell* (1856), 6 E. & B. 370.
5. *Infra,* pp. 221-3.

which *looks* like a contract is to be treated as the *whole* contract."[1]
But this presumption, though strong, is not irrebuttable.   In
each case the court must decide whether the parties have or have
not reduced their agreement to the precise terms of an all-
embracing written formula.   If they have, oral evidence will not
be admitted to vary or to contradict it; if they have not, the writing
is but part of the contract and must be set side by side with the
complementary oral terms.   The question is at bottom one of
intention and, like all such questions, elusive and conjectural.
It would seem, however, that the more recent tendency is to infer,
if the inference is at all possible, that the parties did not intend
the writing to be exclusive but wished it to be read in conjunction
with their oral statements.[2]

Thus in *Walker Property Investments (Brighton), Ltd.* v. *Walker,*[3]

> the defendant in 1938, then in treaty for the lease of a flat in a house
> belonging to the plaintiffs, stipulated that, if he took the flat, he was
> to have the use of two basement rooms for the storage of his surplus
> furniture and also the use of the garden.   Subsequently, a written
> agreement was drawn up for the lease of the flat, which made no
> reference either to the storage rooms or to the garden.

The Court of Appeal held that the oral agreement should be read
with the written instrument so as to form one comprehensive
contract.

So, too, in *Couchman* v. *Hill,*[4]

> the defendant's heifer was put up for auction.   The sale catalogue
> described it as " unserved," but added that the sale was " subject
> to the auctioneers' usual conditions " and that the auctioneers
> would not be responsible for any error in the catalogue.   The
> " usual conditions " were exhibited at the auction and contained a
> clause that " the lots were sold with all faults, imperfections and
> errors of description."   The plaintiff, before he bid, asked both
> the auctioneer and the defendant if they could confirm that the
> heifer was " unserved," and they both said " Yes."   On this under-
> standing he bid for and secured the heifer.   It was later found that
> the heifer was in calf, and it died as a result of carrying its calf at
> too young an age.

On these facts the Court of Appeal held that the plaintiff was
entitled to recover damages for breach of contract.   The documents in the case, in their opinion, formed not the whole but
part only of the contract, and the oral assurance could be laid
side by side with them so as to constitute a single and binding
transaction.
      Yet another illustration is offered by the case of the *S.S.
Ardennes (Cargo Owners)* v. *Ardennes (Owners).*[5]

---

1. Wedderburn, [1959] C.L.J. 58, especially at pp. 59–64, citing Lord RUSSELL
   OF KILLOWEN, C.J., in *Gillespie Brothers* v. *Cheney, Eggar & Co.,* [1896]
   2 Q.B. 59, at p. 62.
2. But see *Hutton* v. *Watling*, [1948] Ch. 398; [1948] 1 All E.R. 803.
3. (1947), 177 L.T. 204.   Cf. *Henderson* v. *Arthur,* [1907] 1 K.B. 10.
4. [1947] K.B. 554; [1947] 1 All E.R. 103.
5. [1951] 1 K.B. 55; [1950] 2 All E.R. 517.

The plaintiffs were growers of oranges in Spain and the defendants were shipowners.   The plaintiffs wished to export their oranges to England and shipped them on the defendants' vessel on the faith of an oral promise by the defendants' agent that the vessel would sail straight to London.   In fact she went first to Antwerp, so that the oranges arrived late in London and the plaintiffs lost a favourable market.   When the plaintiffs claimed damages for breach of contract, the defendants relied on the bill of lading which expressly allowed them to proceed " by any route and whether directly or indirectly " to London.

Judgment was given for the plaintiffs.   The bill of lading, while it was evidence of the contract between shipper and shipowner,[1] was not in the present case exclusive evidence.   The oral promise made on behalf of the defendants was equally part of the contract and was binding upon them.

B.   ARE THE STATEMENTS OF THE PARTIES TERMS OF THE CONTRACT?

What the parties said or wrote may be clearly established; but it does not necessarily follow that all their words have become part of the contract.   Their statements may be classified either as terms of the contract or as " mere representations."   The distinction was long of great practical importance, but new developments have reduced its effect without lessening its conceptual significance.

Mere representations

If a statement is a term of the contract, it creates a legal obligation for whose breach an appropriate action lies at common law.   If it is a " mere representation," the position is more complicated.[2]   It is clear that, if a party has been induced to make a contract by a fraudulent misrepresentation, he may sue in tort for deceit and may also treat the contract as voidable. But until recently it was believed to be a principle of the common law that there should be " no damages for innocent misrepresentation," and that, in this context, " innocent " meant any misrepresentation which was not fraudulent.[3]   In the nineteenth century, equity indeed allowed the right of rescission to a party who had been induced to make a contract by such an " innocent " misrepresentation, but this remedy was limited in a number of ways.[4]   In 1963 in *Hedley Byrne & Co., Ltd.* v. *Heller & Partners, Ltd.*,[5] the House of Lords held that in some circumstances damages could be obtained for negligent mis-statement. The precise effect of this decision on the law of contract is not clear;[6] but, by the Misrepresentation Act 1967, representees acquired a remedy which in most cases will be preferable to an

---

1. It should be noted that situations such as this can be analysed either as one contract, partly oral, partly in writing, or as two contracts, one in writing, the second an oral collateral contract.   Both analyses are to be found in the cases.   See *infra*, pp. 120–1.
2. The effect of misrepresentation is discussed fully in Part IV, Chap. 2, *infra*.
3. See *per* Lord MOULTON in *Heilbut Symons & Co.* v. *Buckleton*, [1913] A.C. 30, at p. 48.
4. *Infra*, pp. 268–273.
5. [1964] A.C. 465; [1963] 2 All E.R. 575.
6. *Infra*, pp. 258–260.

action of negligence. Section 2 (1) of this Act in effect gives a right to damages to anyone induced to enter a contract by a negligent misrepresentation, and casts upon the representor the burden of disproving negligence.[1] But, where a statement is made neither fraudulently nor negligently, the injured party can still obtain damages only by showing that it forms part of his contract. Contractual cartography thus remains important.

To draw the map of the contract, at least where it is not wholly committed to writing, has proved as difficult as it is important. In the copious litigation which the problem has provoked, three subsidiary tests have been suggested as possible aids to its solution.

Drawing the map of the contract

(a) At what stage of the transaction was the crucial statement made?

It must, in the opinion of the court, have been designed as a term of the contract and not merely be an incident in the preliminary negotiations. Two cases may be contrasted.

In *Bannerman* v. *White* :[2]

Bannerman v. White

> A prospective buyer, in the course of negotiating for the purchase of hops, asked the seller if any sulphur had been used in their treatment, adding that, if it had, he would not even trouble to ask the price. The seller answered that no sulphur had been used. The negotiations thereupon proceeded and resulted in a contract of sale. It was later discovered that sulphur had been used in the cultivation of a portion of the hops—5 acres out of 300—and the buyer, when sued for the price, claimed that he was justified in refusing to observe the contract.

The buyer's claim could not be upheld unless the statement as to the absence of sulphur was intended to be part of the contract, for the jury found that there was no fraud on the part of the seller. The buyer contended that the whole interview was one transaction, that he had declared the importance he attached to his inquiry, and that the seller must have known that if sulphur had been used there could be no further question of a purchase of the hops. The seller, on the other hand, contended that the conversation was merely preliminary to, and in no sense a part of, the contract. The jury found that the seller's statement was understood and intended by both parties to be part of the contract, and their finding was unanimously confirmed by the Court of Common Pleas.

In *Routledge* v. *McKay* :[3]

Routledge v. McKay

> The plaintiff and defendant were discussing the possible purchase and sale of the defendant's motor-cycle. Both parties were private persons. The defendant, taking the information from the registration book, said on October 23rd that the cycle was a 1942 model. On October 30th a written contract of sale was made, which did not refer to the date of the model. The actual date was later found to be 1930. The buyer's claim for damages failed in the Court of Appeal.

In this case, the interval between the negotiations and the contract was well-marked. But the facts are not always so accommodating; and the courts, in their anxiety to reach a result which may

---

1. *Infra*, pp. 260–1 and 273–9.
2. (1861), 10 C.B.N.S. 844.
3. [1954] 1 All E.R. 855; [1954] 1 W.L.R. 615.

reasonably reflect the presumed intention of the parties, have more than once treated the making of the contract as a protracted process. An instance is offered by *Schawel* v. *Reade*, an Irish case which came on appeal to the House of Lords in 1913.[1]

> The plaintiff, who wanted a stallion for stud purposes, started to examine a horse advertised for sale by the defendant. The defendant interrupted him, saying " You need not look for anything: the horse is perfectly sound." The plaintiff therefore stopped his examination. A few days later the price was agreed, and three weeks later still the sale was concluded. The horse in fact was unfit for stud purposes.

The trial judge asked the jury two questions: (1) " Did the defendant, at the time of the sale, represent to the plaintiff that it was fit for stud purposes? " (2) " Did the plaintiff act on that representation in the purchase of the horse? " The vital factor was whether the representation had been made " at the time of the sale." The jury found that it had, and the House of Lords held that the defendant's statement was a term of the contract.

Is there a later document?

(b) Was the oral statement followed by a reduction of the terms to writing?

If it was so followed, the court must decide whether it was the intention of the parties that the contract should be comprised wholly in their document or whether the contract was to be partly written and partly oral.[2] The exclusion of an oral statement from the document may suggest that it was not intended to be a contractual term. The facts of *Routledge* v. *McKay* tend to support such a construction.[3] But in other cases the courts have not shrunk from reading together an earlier oral statement and a later document so as to unite them in a single comprehensive contract. In *Birch* v. *Paramount Estates, Ltd.*:[4]

> The defendants, who were developing an estate, offered a house they were then building to the plaintiff, saying " it would be as good as the show house." The plaintiff later agreed to buy the house, and the written contract of sale contained no reference to this particular representation. The house was not as good as the show house.

The Court of Appeal treated the defendants' statement as part of the concluded contract and allowed the plaintiff's claim for damages.

One party's superior skill or knowledge

(c) Had the person who made the statement special knowledge or skill as compared with the other party?

If this is the case, the court may be more willing to infer an intention to make the statement a term in the contract. Such was the position in *Birch* v. *Paramount Estates, Ltd.* and in *Schawel* v. *Reade*;[5] and such was at least a contributory factor in the decision of the Court of Appeal in *Harling* v. *Eddy*.[6]

---

1. [1913] 2 I.R. 81.   Cf. *Hopkins* v. *Tanqurray* (1854), 15 C.B. 130.
2. *Supra*, p. 113.
3. *Supra*, p. 117.
4. (1956), 16 Estates Gazette 396, cited in *Oscar Chess, Ltd.* v. *Williams*, [1957] 1 All E.R. 325, at p. 329.   Cf. *Heilbut Symons & Co.* v. *Buckleton*, [1913] A.C. 30, critically analysed by Greig in 87 L.Q.R. 179, at pp. 185–190.
5. *Supra*, n. 1.
6. [1951] 2 K.B. 739; [1951] 2 All E.R. 212.   See also *Coffey* v. *Dickson*, [1960] N.Z.L.R. 1135.

The defendant offered his heifer for sale by auction. The auction catalogue contained a clause that " no animal is . . . sold with a warranty unless specially mentioned at the time of offering, and no warranty so given shall have any legal force or effect unless the terms thereof appear on the purchaser's account." The heifer had an " unpromising appearance " and buyers held aloof until the defendant said that there was " nothing wrong with her " and that he would " absolutely guarantee her in every respect." The plaintiff then bid for her and bought her. She was in fact tubercular and she died.

The defendant's guarantee was, in the language of the catalogue, " specially mentioned at the time of offering," but it did not " appear on the purchaser's account." But the defendant had exclusive means of knowing the heifer's condition, and the Court of Appeal allowed the plaintiff to recover damages.

This third test may perhaps offer a less dubious guide to the intention of the parties than either of the two previous tests. But none of them is to be regarded as decisive. In the words of Lord MOULTON,[1]

" they may be criteria of value in guiding a jury in coming to a decision whether or not a warranty was intended; but they cannot be said to furnish decisive tests because it cannot be said as a matter of law that the presence or absence of these features is conclusive of the intention of the parties. [This] can only be deduced from the totality of the evidence, and no secondary principles of such a kind can be universally true."

These three criteria must therefore be received only as possible aids to the interpretation of the facts. Their impact upon the members of a court is vividly illustrated by the case of *Oscar Chess, Ltd.* v. *Williams*.[2]

Oscar Chess, Ltd. v. *Williams*

The plaintiffs were car dealers, and the defendant wished to obtain from them on hire-purchase a new Hillman Minx and to offer a second-hand Morris car in part exchange. The sum available for the Morris depended on its age. According to the registration book its date was 1948; the defendant in good faith confirmed this, and the plaintiffs believed him. On this assumption the sum to be allowed for it was £290. The parties then orally agreed that the plaintiffs would arrange for the hire-purchase of the new Hillman, would take the Morris and allow £290 for it. This agreement was carried out. Eight months later the plaintiffs found that the date of the Morris was not 1948 but 1939, the trade-in price for which year was only £175. The registration book had presumably been altered by a previous holder before reaching the defendant's hands. The plaintiffs now sued the defendant for the difference between the two allowances, *i.e.*, £115.

The county court judge held that the statement as to the age of the car was a term in the contract and gave judgment for the plaintiffs. This decision was reversed by a majority in the Court of Appeal (DENNING and HODSON, L.JJ.). MORRIS, L.J., dissented. It is instructive to apply each of the suggested tests to the facts. There was no apparent or substantial interval between the statement as to the age of the car and the agreement of hire-purchase. The first and chronological test should therefore have helped the plaintiffs. As MORRIS, L.J., said, " there

1. *Heilbut Symons & Co.* v. *Buckleton*, [1913] A.C. 30, at pp. 50–51.
2. [1957] 1 All E.R. 325; [1957] 1 W.L.R. 370.

was a statement made at the time of the transaction." The second test was also in the plaintiffs' favour.   Nothing had been reduced to writing and no point could therefore have been made of the superior claims of a document over mere word of mouth.   HODSON, L.J., was driven to say that " the distinction is a fine one, and one which I shall be reluctant to draw unless compelled to do so "; and DENNING, L.J., emphasized the undoubted truth that there is no basic difference between a written and an oral contract. The third test, on the other hand, so far as it was applicable to the facts, told in the defendant's favour.   It was not he, the maker of the statement, but the plaintiffs, as car dealers, who possessed special knowledge and skill and who, if anyone, could have discovered in time the true age of the car.

Dick Bentley, Ltd. v. Harold Smith, Ltd.

In this case it may seem unfortunate that a serious statement of manifest importance to the parties was not held to be a term of the contract.   Some such impression is left by many of the decisions; and the anxiety of the judges to escape from a perennial dilemma may be illustrated by the subsequent case of *Dick Bentley Productions, Ltd.* v. *Harold Smith (Motors), Ltd.*[1]

> The plaintiffs told the defendants that they were looking for a " well-vetted " Bentley car.   The defendants said that they had such a car.   One morning Mr. Bentley went to see it, and the defendants told him that it had done only 20,000 miles since fitted with a replacement engine and gearbox.   In the afternoon Mr. Bentley took the car for a short run and bought it.   The plaintiffs later found that the car was unsatisfactory and that the statement as to mileage was untrue.   They sued for damages.

The Court of Appeal held that the defendants' statement was a term of the contract and that the plaintiffs were entitled to damages.   This decision may readily be accepted; but it was necessary to distinguish *Oscar Chess, Ltd.* v. *Williams.*   Lord DENNING, who was a member of the court in both cases, found the distinction in the presence or absence of negligence.   In *Oscar Chess, Ltd.* v. *Williams* the defendant had not been negligent.   In *Dick Bentley, Ltd.* v. *Harold Smith, Ltd.* negligence was present: the defendants " ought to have known better."

It is difficult to understand why a statement should be a term of the contract if it is negligent and a " mere representation " if it is not.[2]   It might have been safer to have based the decision upon the existence of a " collateral " contract.   This approach seems to have been envisaged by SALMON, L.J.

Dilemma avoidable by use of collateral contracts

> " In effect, Mr. Smith said: ' If you will enter into a contract to buy this motor car from me for £1,850, I undertake that you will be getting a motor car which has done no more than twenty thousand miles since it was fitted with a new engine and a new gearbox.' "[3]

There is ample authority for the use of a " collateral " contract to avoid the dilemma of " term " or " representation."

---

1. [1965] 2 All E.R. 65; [1965] 1 W.L.R. 623.   Sealy, [1965] C.L.J. 178.   See also *Beale* v. *Taylor*, [1967] 3 All E.R. 253; [1967] 1 W.L.R. 1193, where the vintage of the car was held to be part of its description within s. 13 of Sale of Goods Act, 1893.
2. The presence of negligence may, of course, be significant both in opening the possibility of an action in tort and in proceedings under the Misrepresentation Act 1967; *supra*, p. 116, and *infra*, pp. 258–262.
3. [1965] 2 All E.R., at p. 68; [1965] 1 W.L.R., at p. 629.

A significant case is that of *City and Westminster Properties,* (1934) *Ltd.* v. *Mudd*.[1]

> The defendant had been for six years the tenant of the plaintiffs' shop, to which a small room was annexed and in which, as they knew, he was accustomed to sleep. In 1947 he was negotiating for a new lease, and the plaintiffs inserted a clause restricting the use of the premises to " showrooms, workrooms and offices only." The plaintiffs' agent orally assured the defendant that, if he accepted the lease with this clause intact, he would still be allowed to sleep on the premises. On this understanding he signed the lease. The plaintiffs now brought an action against him for forfeiture of the lease on the ground that he had broken the covenant restricting the use of the premises.

HARMAN, J., held that the defendant had indeed broken this covenant but that, in answer to the breach, he could plead the collateral contract made before the lease was signed. This, he said, is

> " a case of a promise made to him before the execution of the lease, that, if he would execute it in the form put before him, the landlords would not seek to enforce against him personally the covenant about using the property as a shop only. The tenant says that it was in reliance on this promise that he executed the lease and entered on the onerous obligations contained in it. He says, moreover, that but for the promise made he would not have executed the lease, but would have moved to other premises available to him at the time. If these be the facts, there was a clear contract acted on by the tenant to his detriment and from which the landlords cannot be allowed to resile."[2]

The contract protecting the defendant was clearly separate from the tenancy agreement and may thus be stated: " if you will promise me not to enforce this particular clause in the lease I will promise to execute it."

SECTION II. IMPLIED TERMS

The normal contract is not an isolated act, but an incident in the conduct of business or in the framework of some more general relation such as that of landlord and tenant. It will frequently be set against a background of usage, familiar to all who engage in similar negotiations and which may be supposed to govern the language of a particular agreement. In addition, therefore, to the terms which the parties have expressly adopted, there may be others imported into the contract from its context. These implications may be derived from custom or they may rest upon statute or they may be inferred by the judges to reinforce the language of the parties and realize their manifest intention.

Contract may be subject to terms not expressly included

A. TERMS IMPLIED BY CUSTOM

It is a well-established rule that a contract may be subject to terms that are sanctioned by custom, whether commercial or otherwise, although they have not been expressly mentioned by

Landlord and tenant

---

1. [1959] Ch. 129; [1958] 2 All E.R. 733.   For collateral contracts, see *supra,* pp. 58–61.
2. [1959] Ch., at p. 145–6; [1958] 2 All E.R., at p. 742–3.

the parties.   In *Hutton* v. *Warren* in 1836[1] it was proved that, by a local custom, a tenant was bound to farm according to a certain course of husbandry and that, at quitting his tenancy, he was entitled to a fair allowance for seed and labour on the arable land. The Court of Exchequer held that the lease made by the parties must be construed in the light of this custom.   The judgment of Baron PARKE is illuminating both on the possibility of importing terms into a contract and on the underlying rationale.

> " It has long been settled that in commercial transactions extrinsic evidence of custom and usage is admissible to annex incidents to written contracts in matters with respect to which they are silent.   The same rule has also been applied to contracts in other transactions of life in which known usages have been established and prevailed;   and this has been done upon the principle of presumption that, in such transactions, the parties did not mean to express in writing the whole of the contract by which they intended to be bound, but to contract with reference to those known usages. Whether such a relaxation of the strictness of the common law was wisely applied, where formal instruments have been entered into, and particularly leases under seal, may well be doubted.   But the contrary has been established by such authority, and the relations between landlord and tenant have been so long regulated upon the supposition that all customary obligations, not altered by the contract, are to remain in force, that it is too late to pursue a contrary course;   and it would be productive of much inconvenience, if this practice were now to be disturbed.   The common law, indeed, does so little to prescribe the relative duties of landlord and tenant, since it leaves the latter at liberty to pursue any course of management he pleases, provided he is not guilty of waste, that it is by no means surprising that the courts should have been favourably inclined to the introduction of those regulations in the mode of cultivation which custom and usage have established in each district to be the most beneficial to all parties."

Trade customs

A later illustration of the place of custom in contracts is offered by *Produce Brokers Co., Ltd.* v. *Olympia Oil and Cake Co., Ltd.*, in 1916.[2]

> A written agreement for the sale of goods provided that " all disputes *arising out of this contract* shall be referred to arbitration." A dispute was submitted to arbitrators who in their award insisted on taking into consideration a particular custom of the trade.

The House of Lords held that they were right to do so.   Lord SUMNER said:[3]

> " The real question . . . is the definition of the limits as expressed in the submission [to arbitration].   If ' *this contract* ' in the arbitration clause means the real bargain between the parties expressed in the written and printed terms, though, where trade customs exist and apply, not entirely so expressed, then the jurisdiction [of the arbitrators] is complete.   The custom, if any, is part of the bargain. . . .   If the bargain is partly expressed in ink and partly implied by the tacit incorporation of trade customs, the first function of the arbitrators is to find out what it is: to read the language, to ascertain the custom, to interpret them both and to give effect to the whole. . . .   The dispute which arose in fact, and which raised a question of custom, did not arise out of the contract

---

1. (1836), 1 M. & W. 466, especially at pp. 475–6.
2. [1916] 1 A.C. 314.   See also *Cunliffe-Owen* v. *Teather and Greenwood*, [1967] 3 All E.R. 561; [1967] 1 W.L.R. 1421.
3. [1916] 1 A.C., at pp. 330–1.

and something else; it arose *out of the contract itself* and involved the contract by raising the custom, and so it was within the submission."

The importation of usage, as it rests on the assumption that it represents the wishes of the parties, must be excluded if the express language of the contract discloses a contrary intention. The parties must then be supposed, while appreciating the general practice, to have chosen to depart from it. *Expressum facit cessare tacitum.* The position, which, indeed, might be considered self-evident, was vigorously stated by Lord BIRKENHEAD in *Les Affréteurs Réunis Société Anonyme* v. *Walford*.[1]

Custom not imported if contrary to intention

> Walford, as broker, had negotiated a charter-party between the owners of the s.s. " Flore " and the Lubricating and Fuel Oils Co., Ltd. By a clause in the charter-party the owners promised the charterers to pay Walford, *on signing the charter*, a commission of 3 per cent. on the estimated gross amount of hire. The owners, defending an action brought by Walford for this commission, pleaded, *inter alia*, a custom of the trade that commission was payable only when hire had actually been earned. The " Flore " had been requisitioned by the French Government before the charter-party could be operated and no hire had in fact been earned.

Despite the incompatibility of any such custom with the clause in the contract requiring payment as soon as the parties signed, BAILHACHE, J., accepted the plea and gave judgment for the defendants. Lord BIRKENHEAD, reversing the decision, castigated an unhappy error.[2]

> " The learned judge . . . has in effect declared that a custom may be given effect to in commercial matters which is entirely inconsistent with the plain words of an agreement into which commercial men, certainly acquainted with so well-known a custom, have nevertheless thought proper to enter."

Custom thus comes not to destroy but to fulfil the law. It must not contradict the express terms of a contract but must serve rather to reinforce them and assist their general purpose and policy. Lord JENKINS has emphasized both the negative and the positive test to be applied before it is to be admitted.

> " An alleged custom can be incorporated into a contract only if there is nothing in the express or necessarily implied terms of the contract to prevent such inclusion and, further, a custom will only be imported into a contract where it can be so imported consistently with the tenor of the document as a whole."[3]

If, however, a custom satisfies these tests, its operation may be far-reaching. This has certainly been the case in the past. It is not too much to say that the greater part of modern commercial law, and, as Baron PARKE stated in *Hutton* v. *Warren*, no small portion of the law governing landlord and tenant, have been constructed upon its basis. The development of the law exhibits a fairly constant process. A particular practice is shown to exist and the parties to a contract are proved to have relied upon it.

Commercial customs

---

1. [1919] A.C. 801; affirming [1918] 2 K.B. 498. See *infra*, p. 440 as to the right of the broker to sue upon a contract to which he was not a party.
2. [1919] A.C., at p. 809.
3. *London Export Corporation, Ltd.* v. *Jubilee Coffee Roasting Co.*, [1958] 2 All E.R. 411, at p. 420; [1958] 1 W.L.R. 661, at p. 675. See also *Kum* v. *Wah Tat Bank, Ltd.*, [1971] 1 Lloyd's Rep. 439.

In course of time it is assumed by the courts to be so prevalent in a trade or locality as to form the foundation of all contracts made within that trade or locality, unless expressly excluded. Finally, it is often adopted by the legislature as the standard rule for the conduct of the business in question. The law in such cases is not so much imposed *ab extra* by judges or Parliament as developed by the pressure of commercial convenience or local idiosyncrasy.

Terms implied in contracts of marine insurance

This process of development can be traced in many branches of the commercial law. As soon as the common law courts busied themselves with the problems of marine insurance, they accepted the necessity of construing the words of a policy in the light of the surrounding circumstances. In *Pelly* v. *Royal Exchange Assurance*[1] in 1757:

> The plaintiff had insured his ship and tackle during the whole voyage from London to China and back again to London. On arrival in the River Canton, the tackle, according to the usage of the ship-masters, was removed and put into a warehouse where it was accidentally burnt.

To a claim on the policy it was objected that, as the loss had occurred on shore at the end of the outward journey, it was not within the compass of the voyage and fell outside the insured risks. Lord MANSFIELD refused the contention.

> " What is usually done by such a ship, with such a cargo, in such a voyage, is understood to be referred to by every policy and to make a part of it as much as if it was expressed."

Various terms came to be implied as a matter of course in all policies, some vital and some subsidiary; though, with the inveterate tendency, both of business men and of lawyers, to confuse the issues by careless phraseology, the word " warranty " was obstinately established in the law of marine insurance where, at least in modern speech, " condition " was more appropriate. Thus, to give only one example, it was regarded as vital that an insured ship should be sea-worthy, and the courts therefore implied a " warranty " to this effect in every policy. In the words of Baron PARKE,[2]

> " In the case of an insurance for a certain voyage, it is clearly established that there is an implied warranty that the vessel shall be sea-worthy, by which it is meant that she shall be in a fit state as to repairs, equipment and crew, and in all other respects, to encounter the ordinary perils of the voyage insured at the time of sailing upon it."

This and other terms are now implied in policies by ss. 33 to 41 of the Marine Insurance Act 1906, which incidentally perpetuates the terminological confusion by providing that " a warranty is a condition which must be exactly complied with, whether it be material to the risk or not," and that its breach discharges the insurer as from the moment of its occurrence.[3] The contractual basis of the liability is sustained by the proviso that the

---

1. 1 Burr. 341; and see *Salvador* v. *Hopkins* (1765), 3 Burr., 1707.
2. In *Dixon* v. *Sadler* (1839), 5 M. & W. 405, at p. 414.
3. Marine Insurance Act 1906, s. 33 (3).

" warranty " shall be excluded by an express term, if the two are inconsistent.[1]

B.   TERMS IMPLIED BY STATUTE

The provisions of the Marine Insurance Act offer an obvious example of terms implied by statute as the culmination of a long process of development. But the translation of usage into agreement and of agreement into statutory language is most evident in the history of contracts for the sale of goods. Buyers and sellers frequently fail to express themselves with regard to matters that may later provoke a dispute. Two illustrations may be given.

Implied terms in contract for sale of goods

> Suppose that the seller is in fact not the owner of the goods which he has purported to sell. Must he be taken to have tacitly guaranteed the fact of his ownership?
> Suppose that the goods are useless for the purpose for which the buyer requires them.   Is it a tacit term of the contract that they shall be suitable for that purpose?

At first the common law judges refused to recognize any term which had not been expressly inserted in the contract. Thus, in the second hypothesis propounded above, the foundation of the common law, as of Roman law,[2] was the maxim *caveat emptor*. In the absence of fraud, and provided that the goods were open to inspection, the buyer could not complain of defects in the article bought. He should have used his own judgment and not have expected the seller to depreciate his own wares, for he was always free to protect himself by exacting an express warranty.

The original rule, however, was gradually modified by the usage of the market, which recognized that there were several cases in which a contract of sale was subject to a tacit undertaking by the seller; and, during the first half of the nineteenth century, these modifications were recognized by the courts and adopted as normal implications in such contracts. Thus, in a sale *by sample*, it was an implied term of the contract that the bulk should correspond with the sample and that the buyer should, by examination, be able to satisfy himself of such correspondence.[3] In a sale *by description*, the goods must not only answer the description but must be of " merchantable quality."[4] If, moreover, a buyer explained that he required goods for a particular purpose and that he relied on the seller's skill and judgment to provide such goods, then the seller, unless he expressly guarded himself, was taken to have accepted this additional responsibility.[5] There was more hesitation in deciding whether, upon the sale of goods, the seller impliedly undertook to transfer a good title. The implication was denied by Baron PARKE as

Customary terms recognized by courts

---

1. Marine Insurance Act 1906, s. 35 (3).
2. Mackintosh, *Roman Law of Sale*, note D.
3. *Parker* v. *Palmer* (1821), 4 B. & Ald. 387; *Lorymer* v. *Smith* (1822), 1 B. & C. 1.
4. *Gardiner* v. *Gray* (1815), 4 Camp. 144.
5. *Jones* v. *Bright* (1829), 5 Bing. 533.

late as 1849,[1] but in 1864 ERLE, C.J., asserted its existence, and his view prevailed.[2]

By 1868, when Benjamin published the first edition of his *Treatise on the Sale of Personal Property*, he was able to assume that the courts had completed their absorption of commercial practice. By that date the list of tacit undertakings to be read into a contract for the sale of goods was virtually closed. The time was ripe for codification, and the various implications which the judges had gradually accepted were ultimately adopted as normal terms of the contract by the Sale of Goods Act 1893, wherever the parties had not evinced a contrary intention.

The Sale of Goods Act 1893, was substantially a codification of the common law of sale as the draftsman, Sir Mackenzie Chalmers, perceived it.[3] It consists for a large part, of rules which are to be applied unless the parties provide otherwise. As far as the seller's obligations as to title and as to the quality of the goods are concerned, the relevant sections are ss. 12–15,[4] which operate by implying terms into the contract. These terms could however be excluded by contrary intention[5] and it became not unusual for sellers to seek to exclude the undertakings which would otherwise be implied.[6]

The example provided by the Sale of Goods Act 1893 was developed by legislation dealing with the related contract of hire-purchase.

It is over a hundred years since manufacturers and traders first sought to reach potential customers who could not afford at once to pay the price of their goods.[7] They began to make contracts whereby the price was payable in instalments and the possession of the goods passed at once to the customer, but the supplier retained the ownership until the last instalment had been paid. By this means they hoped to protect themselves even if the customer, before completing payment, improperly sold the goods to an honest buyer. But by s. 9 of the Factors Act 1889, substantially reproduced in s. 25 (2) of the Sale of Goods Act 1893, a person who has agreed to buy goods and who has obtained possession of them with the seller's consent may, by delivering

1. *Morley* v. *Attenborough* (1849), 3 Exch. 500.
2. *Eicholz* v. *Bannister* (1864), 17 C.B.N.S. 708.
3. Later writers have sometimes doubted whether his perception of the common law was correct. See e.g. the difficulties over s. 6, discussed *infra*, pp. 211–2. The Act is by no means identical with Chalmers' draft bill: see the first (1890) and the second (1894) editions of Chalmers, *Sale of Goods*.
4. Earlier editions of this work contained a much fuller account of this topic but although of great interest and importance, it is more appropriately discussed in works on sale. See *Benjamin's Sale of Goods* (1974), Chap. 11; Atiyah, *The Sale of Goods*, 4th Edn. (1971), Chaps. 8–12.
5. There was a dispute as to whether the seller could exclude his implied undertakings as to title under s. 12, but this now of purely historical interest.
6. Such attempts were perhaps less frequent than sometimes suggested. A seller would be most likely to seek to exclude his implied obligations in a consumer transaction. But most consumer sales are made without a written contract, the usual vehicle for exclusion clauses. For this reason exclusion clauses were much more common in hire-purchase transactions, where there is always a written contract.
7. See Thornely, [1962] C.L.J. 39. The major works are Goode, *Hire-Purchase Law and Practice* (2nd Edn. 1970) and Guest, *The Law of Hire-Purchase* (1966). A valuable introduction is Diamond, *Introduction to Hire-Purchase Law* (2nd Edn. 1970).

them to a *bona fide* purchaser or pledgee, pass a good title. In
Lee v. *Butler*,[1]

> the plaintiff let furniture on a " hire and purchase agreement " to
> X. X was to pay £1 at once and the balance of £96 in monthly
> instalments from May to August. The furniture was to become
> X's property only when the last instalment was paid. Before this
> condition was satisfied X sold and delivered the furniture to the
> defendant.

The Court of Appeal held that, on the proper construction of the
agreement, X was under an absolute obligation to pay all the
instalments and that he had therefore " agreed to buy " the furniture. He had accordingly passed a good title to the defendant,
who could not be sued by the plaintiff.

To avoid this result a new device was adopted and was tested
in *Helby* v. *Matthews*.[2]

> The plaintiff, a dealer, agreed to hire a piano to X at a monthly
> rent. If the rent was duly paid for 36 months the ownership would
> pass to X; but X was entitled to terminate the hiring whenever he
> pleased. After paying four instalments X improperly pledged the
> piano to the defendant.

The House of Lords held that, as X could determine the hiring
at any time, he was not under any obligation to buy the piano but
had only an option of purchase. He had therefore not " agreed
to buy it " it, neither s. 9 of the Factors Act nor s. 25 (2) of the Sale
of Goods Act applied, and no title passed to the defendant.
Henceforth manufacturers and dealers preferred to adopt not the
first but the second form of contract—a bailment coupled with
an option of purchase. " Hire-Purchase " was not yet a term of
art, but it was a potent commercial instrument.

The present century has seen an enormous extension of this
type of business, covering an ever-widening range of goods.
The diversity of transactions has demanded a corresponding
diversity of legal machinery; and, with the growth not only of
the total volume of hire-purchase but of the cost of the individual
articles involved, the monetary resources of dealers have had to
be reinforced by the formation of finance companies. In addition
to the earlier and simpler " hire-purchase contract " between
supplier and customer there has been evolved a complex arrangement between supplier, customer and finance company. Thus,
if a customer wishes to obtain a car from a dealer on hire-purchase
terms, the dealer will not as a rule make the hire-purchase contract
directly with the customer. He will sell the car to a finance
company, and the finance company will let it on hire-purchase
to the customer. Three contracts are thus involved: a " collateral " or " preliminary " contract between the dealer and the
customer, a contract of sale between the dealer and the finance
company, and a contract of hire-purchase between the finance
company and the customer. The extent to which economic
reality has thus been divorced from legal mechanics has more

---

1. [1893] 2 Q.B. 318.
2. [1895] A.C. 471.

than once been exposed by the courts. In *Yeoman Credit, Ltd.*
v. *Apps*, Lord Justice HARMAN, said:[1]

> " The difficulty and the artificiality about hire-purchase cases
> arise from the fact that the member of the public involved imagines
> himself to be buying the article by instalments from the dealer,
> whereas he is in law the hirer of the article from a finance company
> with whom he has been brought willy-nilly into contact, of whom
> he knows nothing and which, on its part, has never seen the goods
> which are the subject-matter of the hire."

In *Bridge* v. *Campbell Discount Co., Ltd.*,[2] Lord DENNING translated the facts into legal forms or fictions.

> " If you were able to strip off the legal trappings in which [the
> present transaction] has been dressed and see it in its native sim-
> plicity, you would discover that the appellant had agreed to buy a
> car from a dealer for £405, but could only find £105 towards it.
> So he borrowed the other £300 from a finance house and got them
> to pay it to the dealer, and he gave the finance house a charge on
> the car as security for repayment. But if you tried to express the
> transaction in those simple terms, you would soon fall into troubles
> of all sorts under the Bills of Sale Acts, the Sale of Goods Act and
> the Moneylenders Acts. In order to avoid these legal obstacles, the
> finance house has to discard the rôle of a lender of money on security
> and it has to become an owner of goods who let them out on hire.
> So it buys the goods from the dealer and lets them out on hire to
> the appellant. The appellant has to discard the rôle of a man who
> has agreed to buy goods, and he has to become a man who takes
> them on hire with only an option of purchase. And when these
> new rôles have been assumed, the finance house is not a money-
> lender but a hire-purchase company free of the trammels of the
> Moneylenders Acts."

The dominant party in this transaction is the finance company;
and the comparative weakness of the customer, combined with
the insidious temptation to improvidence, has forced Parliament
to come to the customer's aid. The first Hire-Purchase Act was
passed in 1938.

It was followed by further Acts in 1954, 1964, and 1965.
None of these Acts applied to all contracts of hire-purchase but
only to those where the " hire-purchase price "[3] was below a
certain figure. There were therefore two sets of rules applicable
to contracts of hire-purchase; a statutory set for those within the
financial ambit of the relevant Statute and a common law set for
those falling outside. The relative importance of common law
and statute varied as inflation eroded the real value of the current
limit. In particular many hire-purchase transactions concerning
cars fell outside the statute during the 1950's and early 1960's
when the limit was still the £300 settled in 1938.

Whether a hire-purchase contract fell under statute or common
law, terms would normally be implied in it. The courts in
implying terms into common law hire-purchase transactions

---

1. [1962] 2 Q.B. 508, at p. 522; [1961] 2 All E.R. 281, at p. 291.
2. [1962] A.C. 600, at p. 627; [1962] 1 All E.R. 385, at p. 398.
3. I.e. " the total sum payable by the hirer under a hire-purchase agreement in
   order to complete the purchase of goods to which the agreement relates,
   exclusive of any sum payable as a penalty or as compensation or damages for
   a breach of the agreement ": Hire Purchase Act 1965, s. 58 (1).

relied on the helpful analogies provided by the Sale of Goods Act 1893 while the draftsman of the various Hire-Purchase Acts also built upon the models provided by the earlier act. The terms implied at common law or under the statute were therefore similar but not identical. So for instance both followed s. 12 of the Sale of Goods Act in holding that the owner (seller) had implied obligations as to title but while under the Hire-Purchase Act 1965[1] the term implied was that the owner shall have " a right to sell the goods *at the time when property is to pass*," at common law the courts implied a term that the owner should have a right to sell the goods *both at the time when the hiring commences and at the time when the property is to pass*.[2]

There was however a most important difference between the position at common law and under the Hire-Purchase Acts. At common law the implied terms, like those in the Sale of Goods Act 1893, could in principle be excluded by contrary agreement[3] but under the Hire Purchase Acts the owner was either prohibited from contracting out of his implied obligation[4] or allowed to do so only in certain strictly defined conditions.[5]

The position in regard to both Sale and Hire-Purchase has been carried a stage further by the Supply of Goods (Implied Terms) Act 1973.[6] This Act makes a number of very important changes. First, it amends the implied terms contained in ss. 12, 13, 14 of the Sale of Goods Act 1893. The new implied terms are very much in historical prolongation of the old, but the opportunity has been taken to fill gaps and remedy deficiencies which eighty years of experience had revealed.

Secondly, the new implied terms (and also s. 15 of the Sale of Goods Act 1893, dealing with sales by sample which was not amended by the 1973 Act) have been extended to all contracts of hire-purchase, irrespective of the ambit of the Hire-Purchase Act.[7]

Finally, the Act contains comprehensive provisions, prohibiting or limiting the power of the seller (owner) to exclude these implied obligations. These will be discussed more fully later.[8]

---

1. S. 17 (1).
2. *Karflex, Ltd.* v. *Poole*, [1933] 2 K.B. 251.
3. Subject to the various common law rules as to such exclusions. Discussed *infra*, pp. 144–167.
4. E.g. Hire Purchase Act 1965, ss. 17 (1), 18 (3), 19 (2) and 29 (3) (Implied Terms as to title and description).
5. E.g. Hire Purchase Act 1965, ss. 17 (2) (3) (4), 18 (1) (2) (3) (implied terms as to merchantability and fitness for purchase).
6. This gives effect, subject to some modifications, to the first report of the Law Commission on exemption clauses in contracts (Law Com. No. 24, 1969) See Carr, 36 M.L.R. 519; Turpin [1973] C.L.J. 203.
7. These sections have now been replaced by new sections contained in the Consumer Credit Act 1974, Sch. 4. But this involves only changes in terminology. The Consumer Credit Act itself involves a massive conceptual revolution in the structuring of consumer credit arrangements to bring form into line with reality. See Goode, [1975] C.L.J. 79.
8. *Infra*, pp. 168–9.

C.   TERMS IMPLIED BY THE COURTS[1]

The example set by the Sale of Goods Act has been followed not only by the legislature but by the judges.   Thus in *Samuels* v. *Davis*,[2]

> the plaintiff was a dentist who agreed with the defendant to make a set of false teeth for the defendant's wife.   The teeth were made and delivered, but the defendant refused to pay for them on the ground that they were so unsatisfactory that his wife could not use them.

There was controversy as to whether the contract was for the sale of goods or for work and materials, but the Court of Appeal held that, in the circumstances of the case, the question was irrelevant. If it were the former, the provisions of the Sale of Goods Act applied; if the latter, they would import into the contract, on the analogy of the Act, a term that the teeth should be reasonably fit for their purpose.

Contracts to lease furnished house or to build house   Other terms have been judicially implied in a number of transactions.   For well over a hundred years there has thus been imported into a contract for the lease of a furnished house a term that it shall be reasonably fit for habitation at the date fixed for the beginning of the tenancy.   So if the house is infested with bugs or if the drainage is defective or if a recent occupant suffered from tuberculosis, the tenant will be entitled to repudiate the contract and to recover damages.[3]   A similar term is implied if a person contracts to sell land and to build, or to complete the building of, a house upon the land.[4]   But the term may be excluded, in accordance with the general principle of the common law, either by clear and unambiguous language or if its implication would be inconsistent with an express term of the contract.   Thus in *Lynch* v. *Thorne*,[5]

> the defendant contracted to sell to the plaintiff a plot of land on which was a partially erected house and to complete its construction. The contract provided that the walls were to be of nine-inch brick. The defendant built the house in accordance with this specification, but it was in fact unfit for human habitation because the walls would not keep out the rain.

The Court of Appeal gave judgment for the defendant.   They could not imply a term which would " create an inconsistency with the express language of the bargain".

---

1. Burrows, 31 M.L.R. 390.
2. [1943] K.B. 526; [1943] 2 All E.R. 3.   The House of Lords discussed the extent and nature of the terms which may be implied in contracts for work and materials in *Young and Marten, Ltd.* v. *McManus Childs, Ltd.*, [1969] 1 A.C. 454; [1968] 2 All E.R. 1169; and *Gloucestershire County Council* v. *Richardson*, [1969] 1 A.C. 480; [1968] 2 All E.R. 1181.
3. *Smith* v. *Marrable* (1843), 11 M. & W. 5: *Wilson* v. *Finch-Hatton* (1877), 2 Ex. D. 336: *Collins* v. *Hopkins*, [1923] 2 K.B. 617; [1923] All E.R. Rep. 225.
4. *Perry* v. *Sharon Development Co., Ltd.*, [1937] 4 All E.R. 390: see also *Hancock* v. *B. W. Brazier (Anerley), Ltd.*, [1966] 2 All E.R. 901; [1966] 1 W.L.R. 1317.   There is no such implication on the sale of a completed house: *Hoskins* v. *Woodhams*, [1938] 1 All E.R. 692.   But see now Defective Premises Act 1972, discussed Spencer, [1974] C.L.J. 307, [1975] C.L.J. 48.
5. [1956] 1 All E.R. 744; [1956] 1 W.L.R. 303.

In contracts for the building of a house or for the lease of a furnished house the law, if barely adequate, is tolerably clear. In contracts for the hire of goods the possible implications, though these have long exercised the courts, cannot yet be said to be settled. Such contracts vary so widely in content and in context that it is difficult to evolve or to apply uniform rules.[1] But the courts will normally imply a term that the goods must be as fit for the purpose for which they are hired as reasonable skill and care can make them. In 1881 Lord LINDLEY cast this duty upon a jobmaster who hired out horses and carriages.[2] In *Reed* v. *Dean* in 1949,[3]

Hire of goods

> the plaintiff hired the defendant's motor launch for a holiday on the Thames. Two hours after he had set out the launch caught fire. The fire-fighting equipment was out of order, and the plaintiff suffered personal injuries and lost all his belongings on board.

The defendant was held liable for his failure to make the launch as fit for the purpose of the hiring as reasonable care could make it.

A fruitful source of controversy is to be found in the relationship of master and servant, where express contractual terms are often absent or prescribe inadequately the reciprocal rights and duties of the parties. The position here was examined by the House of Lords in *Lister* v. *Romford Ice and Cold Storage Co., Ltd.*[4]

Master and servant

> The appellant Lister was employed by the respondents as a lorry driver. His father was his mate. While backing his lorry, he drove negligently and injured his father. The father sued the respondents, who were held vicariously liable for the son's negligence. The respondents now sued the son, *inter alia*, for breach of contract.

They urged the implication in his contract of service of a term that he would use reasonable care and skill in driving the lorry. The son replied with a battery of implications: that the respondents, as employers, should not require him to do anything unlawful, that they should insure him against any personal liability he might incur in the course of his employment, that they should indemnify him " against all claims or proceedings brought against him for any act done in the course of employment."

The House of Lords, by a majority, gave judgment for the respondents. There was authority for implying in the master's favour that the servant would " serve him with good faith and fidelity "[5] and that he would use reasonable care and skill in the performance of his duties.[6] This latter undertaking the son in the present case had clearly broken. There were certainly reciprocal terms to be implied in the servant's favour. The master for his part must use due care in respect of the premises where the work was to be done, the way in which it should be

---

1. See the cases examined by PEARSON, L.J., in *Astley Industrial Trust, Ltd.* v. *Grimley*, [1963] 2 All E.R. 33, at pp. 41–43; [1963] 1 W.L.R. 584, at p. 590–4.
2. *Hyman* v. *Nye* (1881), 6 Q.B.D. 685.
3. [1949] 1 K.B. 188.
4. [1957] A.C. 555; [1957] 1 All E.R. 125.
5. *Robb* v. *Green*, [1895] 2 Q.B. 315; *Hivac, Ltd.* v. *Park Royal Scientific Instruments, Ltd.*, [1946] Ch. 169; [1946] 1 All E.R. 350.
6. *Harmer* v. *Cornelius* (1858), 5 C.B.N.S. 236.

done and the plant involved; and he must not require the servant to do an unlawful act.[1]   But the respondents had not broken any of these terms, and the further obligations suggested by the appellant were not warranted.

In all these cases the court is really deciding what should be the content of a paradigm contract of hire, of employment, etc. The process of decision is quite independent of the intention of the parties except that they are normally free, by using express words, to exclude the terms which would otherwise be implied. So the court is in effect imposing on the parties a term which is reasonable in the circumstances.[2]

In addition to terms thus imported into particular types of contract, the courts may, in any class of contract, imply a term in order to repair an intrinsic failure of expression.   The document which the parties have prepared may leave no doubt as to the general ambit of their obligations; but they may have omitted, through inadvertence or clumsy draftsmanship, to cover an incidental contingency, and this omission, unless remedied, may negative their design.   In such a case the judge may himself supply a further term, which will implement their presumed intention and, in a hallowed phrase, give " business efficacy " to the contract.   In doing this he purports at least to do merely what the parties would have done themselves had they thought of the matter.   The existence of this judicial power was asserted and justified in the case of *The Moorcock*.[3]

The Moorcock

> The defendants were wharfingers who had agreed, in consideration of charges for landing and stowing the cargo, to allow the plaintiff, a shipowner, to discharge his vessel at their jetty.   The jetty extended into the Thames, and, as both parties realized, the vessel must ground at low water.   While she was unloading, the tide ebbed and she settled on a ridge of hard ground beneath the mud.   The plaintiff sued for the resultant damage.

The defendants had not guaranteed the safety of the anchorage, nor was the bed of the river adjoining the jetty vested in them but in the Thames Conservators.   But the Court of Appeal implied an undertaking by the defendants that the river bottom was, so far as reasonable care could provide, in such a condition as not to endanger the vessel.   BOWEN, L.J., explained the nature of the implication.[4]

> " I believe if one were to take all the cases, and there are many, of implied warranties or covenants in law, it will be found that in all of them the law is raising an implication from the presumed intention of the parties, with the object of giving to the transaction such efficacy as both parties must have intended that at all events it should have.   In business transactions such as this, what the law desires to

---

1. See *Matthews* v. *Kuwait Bechtel Corporation* [1959] 2 Q.B. 57; [1959] 2 All E.R. 345, and *Gregory* v. *Ford*, [1951] 1 All E.R. 121.   In the latter case it was held that the master had committed an unlawful act in requiring the servant to drive an uninsured vehicle contrary to s. 35 (1) of the Road Traffic Act 1930.   In *Lister* v. *Romford Ice and Cold Storage Co., Ltd.*, the appellant argued that the respondents had again broken this section; but the House of Lords held that there had been no such breach.
2. *Per* Lord DENNING, M.R., in *Greaves & Co. (Contractors), Ltd.* v. *Baynham Meikle & Partners*, [1975] 3 All E.R. 99, at p. 103.
3. (1889), 14 P.D. 64.
4. (1889), 14 P.D., at pp. 68 and 70.

effect by the implication is to give such business efficacy to the transaction as must have been intended at all events by both parties who are business men. . . . The question is what inference is to be drawn where the parties are dealing with each other on the assumption that the negotiations are to have some fruit, and where they say nothing about the burden of this unseen peril, leaving the law to raise such inferences as are reasonable from the very nature of the transaction."

Since this case was decided in 1889, its authority has often been invoked; and the principle upon which it rests has been amplified.

"A term can only be implied," said SCRUTTON, L.J., in 1918, " if it is necessary in the business sense to give efficacy to the contract, *i.e.*, if it is such a term that it can confidently be said that if at the time the contract was being negotiated some one had said to the parties: ' What will happen in such a case?' they would both have replied: ' Of course so and so will happen; we did not trouble to say that; it is too clear.' "[1]

" *Prima facie*," said MACKINNON, L.J., in 1939, " that which in any contract is left to be implied and need not be expressed is something so obvious that it goes without saying; so that, if while the parties were making their bargain an officious bystander were to suggest some express provision for it in their agreement, they would testily suppress him with a common, ' Oh, of course.' "[2]

" An unexpressed term can be implied," said Lord PEARSON in 1973, " if and only if the court finds that the parties must have intended that term to form part of their contract: It is not enough for the court to find that such a term would have been adopted by the parties as reasonable men if it had been suggested to them: it must have been a term that went without saying, a term necessary to give business efficacy to the contract, a term which although tacit, formed part of the contract which the parties made for themselves."[3]

Thus explained, *The Moorcock* is still full of life. In *Gardner v. Coutts & Co.*,[4]

X, in 1948, sold freehold property to Y. By a written contract with Y made on the day following the sale, X agreed that Y and her successors should have the option of buying the adjoining property, which X retained, if X at any time during his life wished to sell it. In 1958 the plaintiff was the successor in title to Y. In 1963 X conveyed the adjoining property to his sister by way of gift without giving the plaintiff the option of purchase. In 1965 X died; and the plaintiff now sued his executors for breach of contract.

The written contract between X and Y contained no term providing expressly for the event of X giving, as opposed to selling, the property to a third party. CROSS, J., implied in the contract a term that X's promise should cover a gift as well as a sale.

" If I apply the test laid down by SCRUTTON, L.J., and MACKINNON, L.J., I am confident that at the time, whatever views [X] may have formed later, if somebody had said to him, ' You have not expressly catered for the possibility of your wanting to give

---

1. *Reigate* v. *Union Manufacturing Co. (Ramsbottom)*, [1918] 1 K.B. 592, at p. 605.
2. *Shirlaw* v. *Southern Foundries (1926), Ltd.*, [1939] 2 K.B. 206, at p. 227; [1939] 2 All E.R. 113, at p. 124.
3. *Trollope and Colls. Ltd.* v. *North West Metropolitan Regional Hospital Board*, [1973] 2 All E.R. 260, at p. 268, [1973] 1 W.L.R. 641, at p. 609.
4. [1967] 3 All E.R. 1064; [1968] 1 W.L.R. 173.

away the property,' he would have said, as undoubtedly [Y] would have said, ' Oh, of course that is implied. What goes for a contemplated sale must go for a contemplated gift.' "[1]

The Moorcock to be used with discretion

This power of judicial implication is a convenient means of repairing an obvious oversight. But it may easily be overworked, and it has more than once received the doubtful compliment of citation by counsel as a last desperate expedient in a tenuous case. In a passage immediately preceding the words of Lord Justice MACKINNON, quoted above, the learned judge gave a warning against the abuse of the power, and especially against the temptation to invoke indiscriminately the relevant sentences of BOWEN, L.J., in *The Moorcock*.

> " They are sentences from an *extempore* judgment as sound and sensible as all the utterances of that great judge; but I fancy that he would have been rather surprised if he could have foreseen that these general remarks of his would come to be a favourite citation of a supposed principle of law, and I even think that he might sympathize with the occasional impatience of his successors when *The Moorcock* is so often flushed for them in that guise."[2]

That this warning was needed is shown by two cases decided since it was given. In *Spring* v. *National Amalgamated Stevedores and Dockers Society* :[3]

> The defendants and the Transport and General Workers Union agreed at the Trade Union Congress at Bridlington in 1939 certain rules for the transfer of members from one union to another. This was called the " Bridlington Agreement." In 1955 the defendants, in breach of this agreement, admitted the plaintiff to their Society. He knew nothing of the agreement nor was it expressly included in the defendants' rules. The breach of the agreement was submitted to the Disputes Committee of the Trade Union Congress which ordered the defendants to expel the plaintiff from their Society. When the defendants sought to do so, the plaintiff sued them for breach of contract, claimed a declaration that the expulsion was *ultra vires* and asked for an injunction to prevent it.

The defendants suggested that a term should be implied in their contract with the plaintiff that they should comply with the " Bridlington Agreement " and take any appropriate steps to fulfil it. But the Vice-Chancellor of the County Palatine Court of Lancaster rejected the suggestion and granted the declaration and injunction for which the plaintiff had asked. He referred to the test suggested by MACKINNON, L.J., and said:

> " If that test were to be applied to the facts of the present case and the bystander had asked the plaintiff at the time he signed the acceptance form, ' Won't you put into it some reference to the Bridlington Agreement? ', I have no doubt the plaintiff would have answered, ' What's that? ' "

---

1. *Ibid.*, at p. 1069 and p. 179, respectively. For a recent application of *The Moorcock* see *British School of Motoring, Ltd.* v. *Simms*, [1971] 1 All E.R. 317, where TALBOT, J. was ready to imply a term that any car provided by the school for driving lessons would be covered by insurance. See also *per* MEGARRY, J., in *Coco* v. *A. N. Clark (Engineers) Ltd.*, [1968] F.S.R. 415, at p. 424.
2. *Shirlaw* v. *Southern Foundries* (1926), *Ltd.*, [1939] 2 K.B. 206, at p. 227; [1939] 2 All E.R. 113, at p. 124.
3. [1956] 2 All E.R. 221; [1956] 1 W.L.R. 585. See also *Gallagher* v. *Post Office*, [1970] 3 All E.R. 712.

In *Sethia (1944), Ltd.* v. *Partabmull Rameshwar* :[1]

the plaintiffs carried on business in London and the defendants were Calcutta merchants. In 1947 the plaintiffs bought from the defendants certain quantities of jute which the defendants were to ship to Genoa. As both parties knew, no jute could be exported from India save by licence of the Government of India, and in 1947 the Government adopted a " quota system " whereby a shipper must chose as his " basic year " any one year from 1937 to 1946 and was allotted a quota in regard to the countries to which he had made shipments in that year. The defendants chose 1946 as their basic year, but, as in that year they had shipped nothing to Italy, they were not entitled to any licence for Genoa. Subsequently, however, they were allowed to ship rather less than a third of the contract quantity of jute. The plaintiffs sued for breach of contract. The defendants admitted that the contract did not expressly provide that shipments should be " subject to quota," but argued that such a term must be implied to give it " business efficacy."

The Court of Appeal refused to imply the term. In the first place, it was proved that in the jute trade contracts were sometimes made expressly " subject to quota " and sometimes with no such phrase. The defendants, therefore, by omitting the phrase, must be supposed to have accepted an absolute obligation to deliver the jute. In the second place, to imply the term would be to commit the buyers to consequences dependent upon facts exclusively within the sellers' knowledge. The buyers certainly knew of the quota system; but the sellers chose the basic year and they alone knew to what countries they had previously exported in that year.

SECTION III. THE RELATIVE IMPORTANCE OF CONTRACTUAL TERMS

Common sense suggests and the law has long recognized that the obligations created by a contract are not all of equal importance. It is primarily for the parties to set their own value on the terms that they impose upon each other. But it is rare for them to express with any precision what, if anything, they have in their minds; and the resultant task of inferring and interpreting their intention is, as always, a matter of great difficulty. In the present context it has been further complicated by the phraseology adopted by the judges both to limit the operation of a contract and to value its component parts. Two words in particular, *conditions* and *warranties*, have been employed with such persistence and with so little discrimination that some preliminary attempt must be made to fix their meaning.

To lawyers familiar with the Roman jurisprudence and trained in modern Continental systems the use of the word *condition* in this context must appear a solecism. By them a condition is sharply distinguished from the actual terms of a

Condition: orthodox meaning

---

1. [1950] 1 All E.R. 51.

contract, and is taken to mean, not part of the obligation itself, but an external fact upon which the existence of the obligation depends.[1] The operation of a contract may thus be postponed until some event takes place, or the occurrence of this event may cancel a contract which has already started to function. A purchaser may agree to buy a car only if it satisfies a certain test, or he may conclude the sale, reserving the right in certain circumstances to re-open the whole transaction.

The orthodox application of the word is by no means unknown to English lawyers[2]. Agreements are often made which are expressed to be " subject to " some future event, performance or the like. Such agreements may produce a variety of different effects.

Condition
precedentFirst, there may be no contract at all. This may be either, as in agreements " subject to contract," because the parties have agreed not to be bound until some future event (e.g. the execution of a formal contract) which cannot take place without the concurrance of both parties or because the condition is uncertain. So in *Lee-Parker* v. *Izzet* (*No.* 2)[3] it was held that an agreement " subject to the purchaser obtaining a satisfactory mortgage " was void for uncertainty.[4]

Secondly, the whole existence of the contract may be suspended until the happening of a stated event, or as it is said in the common law, be subject to a *condition precedent*. In *Pym* v. *Campbell*.[5]

> The defendants agreed in writing to buy from the plaintiff a share in an invention. When the plaintiff sued for a breach of this agreement, the defendants were allowed to give oral evidence that it was not to operate until a third party had approved the invention and that this approval had never been expressed.

" The evidence showed," said ERLE, J., " that in fact there was never any agreement at all." A more recent example is offered by the case of *Aberfoyle Plantations, Ltd.* v. *Cheng*,[6] which came before the Judicial Committee of the Privy Council from Malaya.

> In 1955 the parties agreed to sell and to buy a plantation part of which consisted of 182 acres comprised in seven leases that had expired in 1950. In the intervening years the vendor had tried but failed to obtain a renewal of the leases. Clause 4 of the agreement

---

1. See Buckland and McNair, *Roman Law and Common Law*, 2nd Edn., pp. 247–56. For French law, see .the Code Civil, art. 1168. Scots law has substantially adopted the Continental position, though some complaints have been made of confusion arising from a flirtation with the English terminology: see Gow, *The Mercantile and Industrial Law. of. Scotland*, pp. 201–214.
2. See Montrose, 15 Can. Bar Rev. 309; Stoljar, 15 M.L.R. 425; 16 M.L.R. 174.
3. [1972] 2 All E.R. 800, [1972] 1 W.L.R. 775.
4. Similar conditions had been held sufficiently certain in a number of New Zealand cases, e.g. *Barber* v. *Crickett*, [1958] N.Z.L.R. 1057; *Martin* v. *Macarthur*, [1963] N.Z.L.R. 403; *Scott* v. *Rania*, [1966] N.Z.L.R. 527. Much of the learning on uncertain conditions is to be found in cases on conditional gifts. No doubt similar principles may apply to contracts but probably the threshold of uncertainty should be higher in a commercial setting.
5. (1856), 6 E. & B. 370.
6. [1960] A.C. 115; [1959] 3 All E.R. 910.

therefore provided that "the purchase is conditional on the vendor obtaining a renewal " of the leases. If he proved " unable to fulfil this condition this agreement shall become null and void ".

The vendor failed to obtain the renewal, and the Judicial Committee held that the purchaser could recover the deposit that he had paid. Lord JENKINS said:

> " At the very outset of the agreement the vendor's obligation to sell and the purchaser's obligation to buy were, by clause 1, expressed to be subject to the condition contained in clause 4. It was thus made plain beyond argument that the condition was a condition precedent on the fulfilment of which the formation of a binding contract of sale was made to depend."

Thirdly, a condition may operate, not to negative the very existence of a contract, but to suspend, until it is satisfied, some right or duty or consequence which would otherwise spring from the contract. Thus in *Marten v. Whale*,[1]

> the plaintiff agreed with X to buy a plot of land from him subject to the approval by the plaintiff's solicitor " of title and restrictions." At the same time the plaintiff agreed to sell his motor-car to X—this second agreement to be in consideration of the first agreement and to be completed simultaneously with it. The plaintiff allowed X to take possession of the car, and X sold it at once to the defendant who took it without notice of the plaintiff's rights. The plaintiff's solicitor then refused to approve the restrictions binding the land. The plaintiff sued the defendant to recover the car and for damages.

The Court of Appeal held that he must fail. The solicitor's approval was a condition precedent, not to the creation of the contract for the sale of the car, but only to the passing of property under it. It was—though not a sale—an agreement to sell, and the defendant obtained a title under s. 25 (2) of the Sale of Goods Act.

It will not always be easy to decide whether the failure of a condition precedent prevents the formation of a contract or only suspends the obligations created by it. Particular difficulties seem to be raised by the case of *Bentworth Finance, Ltd.* v. *Lubert*.[2]

> The plaintiffs, under a hire-purchase agreement, let a second-hand car to the defendant, who was to pay 24 monthly instalments. The car was delivered to the defendant but without a log-book. The defendant neither licensed nor used it and refused to pay the instalments. The plaintiffs retook possession of the car and sued for the instalments.

The Court of Appeal held that the plaintiffs could not sue the defendant. The delivery of the log-book was a condition precedent upon which the liability to pay the instalments depended. The decision itself may readily be supported. But it is hard to accept the court's view that, until the log-book was supplied, there was no contract at all.

Where there is a contract but the obligations of one or both parties are subject to conditions a number of subsidiary problems arise. So there may be a question of whether one of the parties has undertaken to bring the condition about. In *Bentworth*

---

1. [1917] 2 K.B. 480.
2. [1968] 1 Q.B. 680; [1967] 2 All E.R. 810. See Carnegie 31 M.L.R. 78.

Finance, Ltd. v. *Lubert* it could have been plausibly argued that the plaintiff had promised to deliver the log book.   There is a clear distinction between a promise, for breach of which an action lies and a condition, upon which an obligation is dependent. But the same event may be both promised and conditional, when it may be called a promissory condition.[1]   A common form of contract is one where land is sold " subject to planning permission."   In such a contract one could hardly imply a promise to obtain planning permission, since this would be outwith the control of the parties but the courts have frequently applied a promise by the purchaser to use his best endeavours to obtain planning permission.[2]   Another question is whether the condition may be waived.   It would appear that where the condition is solely for the benefit of one party, he can waive the condition and make the contract unconditional.[3]

There is yet a fourth possibility, that one party may be able unilaterally to bring a contract into existence.   The most common example is an option to buy land.   The holder of the option is under no obligation to exercise it but if he does, a bilateral contract of sale between him and the owner will come into existence. In a unilateral contract, the obligation of the promisor may be conditional.   So in *Carlill* v. *Carbolic Smoke Ball Co.,*[4] there was a binding contract once the plaintiff had bought the smoke ball and used it as prescribed, but the defendant's obligation to pay was conditional on the plaintiff catching influenza.   It appears that where one party has the power unilaterally to bring a contract into existence on certain conditions, strict compliance with those conditions will be required.[5]

Condition subsequent   If a contract has come into existence but is to terminate upon the occurrence of some event, it is said to be subject to a *condition subsequent*.   An example often cited is the case of *Head* v. *Tattersall.*[6]

> The plaintiff bought from the defendant a horse, guaranteed " to have been hunted with the Bicester hounds," with the understanding that he could return it up to the following Wednesday, if it did not answer the description.   While in the plaintiff's possession, but without fault on his part, the horse was injured, and was then found never in fact to have been hunted with the Bicester hounds.   The plaintiff returned it within the time limit and sued for the price he had paid.

---

1. See *Bashir* v. *Commissioner of Lands*, [1960] A.C. 44; [1960] 1 All E.R. 117. Montrose, 23 M.L.R. 350.   See also *per* SACHS, L.J., in *Property and Bloodstock, Ltd.* v. *Emerton*, [1968] Ch. 94, at pp. 120–1; [1967] 3 All E.R. 321, at pp. 330–1.
2. See *Re Longlands Farm, Long Common, Botley, Hants., Alford* v. *Superior Developments*, [1968] 3 All E.R. 552; *Hargreaves Transport, Ltd.* v. *Lynch*, [1969] 1 All E.R. 455; [1969] 1 W.L.R. 215.   See also *Smallman* v. *Smallman*, [1972] Fam. 25; [1971] 3 All E.R. 717 (" subject to the approval of the court " imposes an obligation to apply to the court for approval).
3. See *Wood Preservation* v. *Prior*, [1969] 1 All E.R. 364; [1969] 1 W.L.R. 1077. The judgment of GOFF, J., [1968] 2 All E.R. 849 also repays careful study. Cf. *Heron Garage Properties, Ltd.* v. *Moss*, [1974] 1 All E.R. 421; [1974] 1 W.L.R. 148, discussed Smith, [1974] C.L.J. 211.
4. [1892] 2 Q.B. 484, discussed *supra*, p. 26.
5. See e.g. *Hare* v. *Nicholl*, [1966] 2 Q.B. 130; [1966] 1 All E.R. 285.   See also the difficult but important case of *United Dominions Trust (Commercial), Ltd.* v. *Eagle Aircraft Services, Ltd.*, [1968] 1 All E.R. 104; [1968] 1 W.L.R. 74; criticised Atiyah, 31 M.L.R. 332.
6. (1871), L.R. 7 Ex. Ch. 7.   Cf. Stoljar, 69 L.Q.R. 485, at pp. 506–511; Sealy, [1972B] C.L.J. 225.

It was held that a contract of sale had come into existence, but that the option to return the horse operated as a condition subsequent of which the plaintiff could take advantage. He was entitled to cancel the contract, return the horse despite the injuries it had suffered, and recover the price.

But, while familiar with its orthodox meaning, English lawyers have more often used *condition* with less propriety to denote, not an external event by which the obligation is suspended or cancelled, but a term in the contract which may be enforced against one or other of the parties. The distinction insisted upon by the civilians is thus obliterated. Confusion is worse confounded by the fact that *warranty* is also used to indicate a term in the contract and by the failure over many years to define either word with precision. BULLER, J., thus said in 1789:[1]

" It was rightly held by HOLT, C.J., and has been uniformly adopted ever since, that an affirmation at the time of a sale is a warranty, provided it appear on evidence to have been so intended."

Condition and warranty as contractual terms

The importance of the linguistic problem justifies a slight excursus upon nineteenth-century terminology.[2] In 1885 JAMES, L.J., attempted in the ambit of the land law to distinguish the different uses of the word *condition*.

Nineteenth century terminology

" Conditions may be either precedent, subsequent or inherent. A condition is *precedent* when, unless it is complied with, the estate does not arise. It is *subsequent* when, if it is broken, the estate is defeated. It is *inherent* when the estate is qualified, restrained or charged by it."[3]

Had this analysis been generally accepted, a term in a contract would presumably have been called an " inherent condition." But the Lord Justice was as one crying in the wilderness; and most of his contemporaries continued to use *condition* and *warranty* without discrimination.

It was by the Sale of Goods Act 1893 that some measure of order was imposed upon the language of the law. By s. 11 (1) (b) a condition is defined as a stipulation in a contract of sale, " the breach of which may give rise to a right to treat the contract as repudiated," and a warranty as a stipulation "the breach of which may give rise to a claim for damages but not to a right to reject the goods and treat the contract as repudiated." By s. 62 it is added that a warranty is " collateral to the main purpose of the contract," but no further light is shed upon the nature of a condition.

Sale of Goods Act

The terminology applicable to the sale of goods was thus standardised. It has been borrowed for the purposes of the Hire-Purchase Acts,[4] and it may be said that the dichotomy

---

1. *Pasley* v. *Freeman* (1789), 3 Term Rep. 51.
2. The story begins with the much older distinction between *dependent* and *independent* covenants: see the notes to *Pordage* v. *Cole*, 1 Wms. Saunders, 319. But this is a long and difficult passage in the law and its exploration would be fortunately irrelevant to the present purpose.
3. *Re Lees, ex parte Collins* (1875), 10 Ch. App., at p. 372.
4. *Supra*, pp. 127–9.

of condition and warranty has become a general, but not a universal, feature of the English law of contract.[1]   Its choice and extended application have not been altogether happy: it perpetuates the ambiguity of the word " condition."   Nevertheless it is surely convenient to have generally recognised language to distinguish terms whose breach entitles the injured party to treat a contract as discharged from those which entitle him only to damages; and, while the dichotomy is ideally and historically open to objection, it has been used for almost eighty years. Employed with discretion, it has still its part to play.[2]

Contrasting cases

Whatever the difficulties of terminology, the courts are faced with the practical task of deciding what breach entitles the injured party, in addition to claiming damages, to terminate the contract.   In retrospect the choice has ultimately depended upon judicial impression.   Two cases offer an effective contrast.   In *Poussard* v. *Spiers and Pond*:[3]

> An actress was engaged to play the leading part in a French operetta as from the beginning of its run.   Owing to illness she was unable to take up her role until a week after the season had started. The producers, who had been forced to engage a substitute, then refused her services.

It was held that her promise to perform as from the first night amounted to a condition and that its breach entitled the producers to treat the contract as discharged.   In *Bettini* v. *Gye*,[4] on the other hand:

> A singer, who was engaged for the whole of the season both in theatres and at concerts, undertook to appear six days in advance for the purpose of rehearsals.   He arrived only three days in advance, and the defendant sought on this ground to terminate the contract.

It was held that the rehearsal clause was subsidiary to the main purpose of the engagement and that the defendant, while he might claim compensation for any loss he had incurred, could not lawfully treat the contract as at an end.

The *Hong Kong* case: effect of breach

It must be admitted that there is no sure criterion by which terms and their consequences may be assessed.   But it is legitimate to look for guiding-lines; and two possibilities have been discussed by the Court of Appeal in recent years.

(1) The courts may concentrate on the effect of the breach rather than on the quality of the term broken.   On this assumption, the question should not be whether the term as drafted is itself more or less serious, but whether its breach produces more or less serious results.   In *Hong Kong Fir Shipping Co., Ltd.* v. *Kawasaki Kisen Kaisha, Ltd.,*[5]

---

1. In Scots law the dichotomy has not been accepted: Sale of Goods Act 1893, s. 11 (2).
2. See *Decro-Wall International S.A.* v. *Practitioners in Marketing, Ltd.,* per SACHS, L.J., [1971] 2 All E.R. 216, at p. 227 ; [1971] 1 W.L.R. 361, at p. 374.
3. (1876), 1 Q.B.D. 410.
4. (1876), 1 Q.B.D. 183.
5. [1962] 2 Q.B. 26; [1962] 1 All E.R. 474.

the plaintiffs owned a ship which they chartered to the defendants for a period of 24 months from her delivery at Liverpool in February, 1957. When delivered, her engine-room staff were too few and too incompetent to cope with her antiquated machinery. It was admitted that the plaintiffs had thus broken a term in the contract to provide a ship " in every way fitted for ordinary cargo service " and that the ship was unseaworthy. On her voyage to Osaka she was delayed for 5 weeks owing to engine trouble, and at Osaka 15 more weeks were lost because, through the incompetence of the staff, the engines had become even more dilapidated. Not until September was the ship made seaworthy. In June the defendants had repudiated the charter. The plaintiffs sued for breach of contract and claimed damages for wrongful repudiation.

It was held both by SALMON, J. and by the Court of Appeal that the breach of contract of which the plaintiffs had admittedly been guilty did not entitle the defendants to treat the contract as discharged but only to claim damages, and the plaintiffs won their action. In orthodox language the plaintiffs had broken a warranty and not a condition. The Court of Appeal, however, was reluctant to perpetuate a dichotomy which required each term of a contract to be pressed, at whatever cost, into one of two categories. Lord Justice DIPLOCK acknowledged that it was apposite to simple contractual undertakings. But there were, he thought, other clauses too complicated to respond to such treatment.[1] Thus, in the case before the court, the obligation of seaworthiness was embodied in a clause, adopted in many charter-parties, which —partly through judicial interpretation—had become one of formidable complexity. It comprised, as UPJOHN, L.J., pointed out, a variety of undertakings, some serious and some trivial.

> " If a nail is missing from one of the timbers of a wooden vessel, or if proper medical supplies or two anchors are not on board at the time of sailing, the owners are in breach of the seaworthiness stipulation. It is contrary to common sense to suppose that, in such circumstances, the parties contemplated that the charterer should at once be entitled to treat the contract as at an end for such trifling breaches."[2]

To so heterogeneous a clause the dichotomy of condition and warranty was, in the opinion of the court, inapplicable. It might perhaps have been helpful to regard the undertaking of " seaworthiness," not as a single term, but as a bundle of obligations of varying importance. But even on this construction the task of the court, as envisaged in the *Hong Kong case*, was not to evaluate the term as it stood in the contract, but to wait and see what happened as a result of the breach. Thus if the breach of a term, itself of apparently minor significance, caused severe loss or damage, the injured party might be able to treat the contract as discharged.

(2) A second approach to the problem is to examine the contract as at the time of its making and thence to infer the

Quality of term broken

1. [1962] 2 Q.B., at p. 70; [1962] 1 All E.R., at p. 487. So, too, UPJOHN, L.J., in [1962] 2 Q.B., at p. 64; [1962] 1 All E.R., at p. 484. UPJOHN, L.J. repeated his views in *Astley Industrial Trust, Ltd.* v. *Grimley,* [1963] 2 All E.R. 33, at pp. 46–7; [1963] 1 W.L.R. 584, at pp. 598–599. See Reynolds, 79 L.Q.R. 534; FURMSTON, 25 M.L.R. 584.
2. [1962] 2 Q.B., at pp. 62–63; [1962] 1 All E.R., at p. 483.

probable intention of the parties. That a distinction must be made between major and minor terms, rather than between the more or less serious effect of a breach, was certainly assumed by some judges in the second half of the nineteenth century. They also said that, to draw this distinction, they must place themselves at the date of the contract and not await the chances of the future. In 1863 in *Behn* v. *Burness*, the court had to evaluate a statement in a charter-party that a ship was " now in the port of Amsterdam." The statement was inaccurate: the ship only arrived at Amsterdam four days after the date of the charter. Williams, J. said:

> " The court must be influenced in the construction of the contract not only by the language of the instrument, but also by the circumstances under which, and the purposes for which, the charter-party was entered into. A statement is more or less important in proportion as the object of the contract more or less depends upon it. For most charters . . . the time of a ship's arrival to load is an essential fact for the interest of the charterer. In the ordinary course of charters it would be so: the evidence of the defendant shows it to be actually so in this case. Then, if the statement of the place of the ship is a substantive part of the contract, it seems to us that we ought to hold it to be a condition."[1]

In *Bettini* v. *Gye*, Blackburn, J. declared that the classification of a term as major or minor " depends on the true construction of the contract taken as a whole." He cited Parke, B. in *Graves* v. *Legg*:

> " The court must ascertain the intention of the parties, to be collected from the instrument and the circumstances legally admissible in evidence with reference to which it is to be construed."[2]

In these cases the court insisted that the test is to be found, not in the greater or less degree of loss or damage caused by the breach of contract, but in examination of the contract itself at the time and in the circumstances in which it was made.

The Mihalis Angelos

In 1970 the Court of Appeal had to reconsider the whole question in *The Mihalis Angelos*.[3]

> On 25th May, 1965, the owners of a vessel let it to charterers for a voyage from Haiphong in North Vietnam to Hamburg. In clause 1 of the charter the owners said that the vessel was ' expected ready to load under this charter about 1st July, 1965.' On the date of the charter she was in the Pacific on her way to Hong Kong, where she had to discharge the cargo which she was then carrying and have a special survey lasting two days. It would take her a further two days to reach Haiphong. She did not in fact complete discharge at Hong Kong until 23rd July. It was found as a fact that the owners, when the contract was made, had no reasonable ground for expecting that she would be ready to load under the charter ' about 1st July.'

The members of the Court of Appeal were not unnaturally pressed with the arguments adopted in the *Hong Kong* case. But they were of opinion that the distinction between " con-

---

1. *Behn* v. *Burness* (1863), 3 B. & S. 751, at pp. 757, 759.
2. *Bettini* v. *Gye* (1876), 1 Q.B.D. 183; *Graves* v. *Legg* (1854), 9 Exch. 709. See also *Bentsen* v. *Taylor, Sons & Co.*, [1893] 2 Q.B. 274, at p. 281, *infra*, p. 572.
3. [1971] 1 Q.B. 164; [1970] 3 All E.R. 125. Greig, 89 L.Q.R. 93.

ditions " and " warranties," though not of universal application, was still valuable, apart from statute, in many classes of contract and notably in charter-parties.[1] On the facts before them, the court held that the " expected readiness " clause was a condition.[2] In reaching this conclusion, the court had to choose between the aims of certainty and elasticity, each of which has its part to play in the administration and development of the law. The relative importance of these aims depends upon the type of transaction involved. In a charter-party, where shipowner and charterer meet on equal terms, they, or their lawyers, seek a firm foundation of principle and authority on which they may build and yet make such variations as the law allows and the particular requirements demand. EDMUND DAVIES, L.J., said:

> " Notwithstanding the observations in the *Hong Kong Fir Shipping Co.* case, if the fact is that a provision in a charter-party such as that contained in clause 1 in the present case has generally been regarded as a condition, giving the charterer the option to cancel on proof that the representation was made either untruthfully or without reasonable grounds, it would be regrettable at this stage to disturb an established interpretation. The standard text-books unequivocally state that such a clause as we are here concerned with is to be regarded as a condition."[3]

MEGAW, L.J., said:[4]

> " One of the important elements of the law is predictability. At any rate in commercial law there are obvious and substantial advantages in having, where possible, a firm and definite rule for a particular class of legal relationships. . . . It is surely much better both for shipowners and charterers (and incidentally for their advisers) when a contractual obligation of this nature is under consideration—and still more when they are faced with the necessity of an urgent decision as to the effects of a suspected breach of it—to be able to say categorically: ' If a breach is proved, then the charterer can put an end to the contract.' "

The alternative was to leave the parties to speculate on the ultimate reaction of the courts if litigation ensued.

These two decisions of the Court of Appeal are readily reconcilable on the facts but they do disclose differences of approach and emphasis. Complete understanding must await a decision of the House of Lords but we may meanwhile essay some tentative conclusions.

Present state of law

(1) It is certainly open to the parties to indicate expressly the consequences to be attached to any particular breach. It will not necessarily be sufficient for this purpose to describe the term as " a condition," for as we have seen the word condition has many meanings and the court may decide that in a given contract it does not mean that the term is one any breach of which entitles the injured party to treat the contract as at an end.[5]

---

1. See *Behn* v. *Burness, supra,* p. 142.
2. All three members of the court agreed on this ruling : Lord DENNING dissented on other questions before the court but not in the result.
3. [1971] 1 Q.B. 164, at p. 199; [1970] 3 All E.R. 125, at pp. 133–134.
4. [1971] 1 Q.B., at p. 205; [1970] 3 All E.R., at p. 138.
5. *Schuler A.G.* v *Wickman Machine Tool Sales, Ltd.,* [1974] A.C. 235; [1973] 2 All E.R. 39. The judgments of the Court of Appeal in this case, [1972] 2 All E.R. 1173; [1972] 1 W.L.R. 840 also contain much interesting learning on the use of the word " condition."

(2) What the parties may do expressly, may be done for them by implication or imputation. So the Sale of Goods Act 1893 provides that certain of the seller's implied obligations are conditions and clearly custom might produce the same result. Similarly, if a term is commonly found in contracts of a particular class and such a term has in the past been held to be a condition, this provides strong support for a finding that the parties intended it to be a condition.[2]

(3) In the above situations it is possible, with some confidence, to say at the time of the contract that a term is a condition. In most other situations the question only assumes any significance when the contract is broken. Then as Lord DEVLIN has observed[3] " both term and breach can be considered together. . . . It is . . . by considering the nature of the term in the light of the breach alleged that the judge will have to make up his mind."

(4) In making his decision the judge will sometimes find it helpful to concentrate primarily on the broken term, in others primarily on the extent of the breach.[4] In some contracts, such as sale it has historically been normal to use the first approach, while, in others, such as building contracts, it has been common to use the second[5] but even in a contract of sale it is open to a court to hold that an obligation which has not been stamped either by statute or previous decisions as a " condition," is an intermediate obligation, the effect of whose breach depends on whether it goes to the root of the contract. So in *Cehave N.V.* v. *Bremer Handelgesellschaft m.b.h.*[6] the Court of Appeal held that breach of a term in a cif contract that the goods were " shipped in good condition " did not entitle the buyer to reject the goods unless there was a serious and substantial breach.

SECTION IV. EXCLUDING AND LIMITING TERMS

The common law has long been familiar with the attempt of one party to a contract to insert terms excluding or limiting liabilities which would otherwise be his. The situation frequently arises where a document purporting to express the terms of the contract is delivered to one of the parties and is not read by him.

---

2. *The Mihalis Angelos, supra.*
3. [1966] C.L.J. 192, at pp. 199–200.
4. The words " extent of the breach " themselves conceal an ambiguity since they may refer either to the extent to which the contract is broken or to the effects of that breach. It is not impossible for a small breach to have devastating consequences.
5. See *infra*, pp. 527–9.
6. [1975] 3 All E.R. 739; [1975] 3 W.L.R. 447.

A passenger receives a ticket, stating the terms, or referring to terms set out elsewhere, on which British Railways are prepared to carry him or take charge of his luggage. A buyer or hirer signs a document, containing clauses designed for the seller's or owner's protection. Are these terms or clauses part of the contract so as to bind the passenger, the buyer or the hirer, despite his ignorance of their character or even of their existence?[1]

The problems caused by exclusion clauses overlap with those caused by two other emergent themes of modern contract law, the increased use of standard form contracts[2] and the development of special rules for the protection of consumers.[3] Exclusion clauses are usually, though not necessarily, contained in standard form contracts but they are by no means the only problem which such contracts present for the courts. To a large extent whole areas of English commercial practice are governed by the prevalent standard forms, which exist in a symbiotic relationship with the courts, so that an historical analysis of the development of a particular form would show that a clause represented a response to a decision in the past.[4]

Lord DIPLOCK has recently pointed out that standard form contracts are of two kinds.[5]

Standard forms of contracts are of two kinds. The first, of very ancient origin, are those which set out the terms on which mercantile transactions of common occurrence are to be carried out. Examples are bills of lading, charterparties, policies of insurance, contracts of sale in the commodity markets. The standard clauses in these contracts have been settled over the years by negotiation by representatives of the commercial interests involved and have been widely adopted because experience has shown that they facilitate the conduct of trade. Contracts of these kinds affect not only the actual parties to them but also others who may have a commercial interest in the transactions to which they relate, as buyers or sellers, charterers or shipowners, insurers or bankers. If fairness or reasonableness were relevant to their enforceability the fact that they are widely used by parties whose bargaining power is fairly matched would raise a strong presumption that their terms are fair and reasonable.

The same presumption, however, does not apply to the other kind of standard form of contract. This is of comparatively modern origin. It is the result of the concentration of particular kinds of business in relatively few hands. The ticket cases in the 19th century provide what are probably the first examples. The terms of this kind of standard form of contract have not been the subject of negotiation between the parties to it, or approved by any organisation representing the interests of the weaker party. They have

Standard form contracts

---

1. The theoretical problems raised by the operation of exception clauses are considered by Coote, *Exception Clauses* (1964), an invaluable work.
2. Prausnitz, *The Standardisation of Commercial Contracts in English and Continental Law* (1937).
3. Borrie and Diamond, *The Consumer, Society and the Law* (3rd Edn.), gives a full account of how English law has developed to protect the consumer. See also Jolowicz, 32 M.L.R. 1. The regulation of exemption clauses is of course by no means the only area in which the consumer needs protection. See also e.g. Consumer Credit Act 1974 and Fair Trading Act 1973.
4. See e.g. the building industry where nearly all substantial contracts are made on one or the other of the RIBA or ICE forms. See Duncan Wallace, *Building and Engineering Standard Forms* (reviewed Atiyah, 85 L.Q.R. 564). See also Duncan Wallace, 89 L.Q.R. 36 and *Gilbert-Ash (Northern)* v. *Modern Engineering (Bristol)*, [1974] A.C. 689; [1973] 3 All E.R. 195.
5. *Schroder Music Publishing Co., Ltd.* v. *Macaulay*, [1974] 3 All E.R. 616, at p. 624; [1974] 1 W.L.R. 1308, at p. 1316.

been dictated by that party whose bargaining power, either exercised alone or in conjunction with others providing similar goods or services, enables him to say: " If you want these goods or services at all, these are the only terms on which they are available. Take it or leave it."

Exclusion clauses are to be found in both types of contract. There are strong arguments for treating them differently and as we shall see Parliament has recently done so[1] but the common law has found it very difficult to develop doctrines that can be applied equally appropriately to both commercial and consumer transactions. This failure (in what may well be an impossible task) is responsible for much of the complexity in the account which follows.[2]

Effect of
exclusion
clauses

Before we turn to consider the particular rules which English law has developed, we should notice that there are divergent views as to what exclusion clauses do.[3] One view is that such clauses go to define the promisor's obligation. According to this view one should read the contract as a whole and decide what it is that the promisor has agreed to do. There is no doubt that this is what the courts sometimes do. So in *G. H. Renton & Co., Ltd.* v. *Palmyra Trading Corporation of Panama :*[4]

> The respondent issued bills of lading, subject to the Hague Rules, covering the shipment of timber from ports in British Columbia to London. The bills of lading contained a clause permitting the master, in the event of industrial disputes at the port of delivery, to discharge at the port of loading or any other convenient port. In the event a strike broke out among dock workers in the Port of London and the master discharged the cargo at Hamburg. The appellants argued that the discharge at Hamburg was a breach of contract and that the strike clause did not provide an effective defence since it sought to provide a relief of liability contrary to the Hague Rules.[5] The House of Lords held that the respondents had not broken the contract since the strike clause did not provide a defence in the event of misperformance but went to define what it was that the carrier had agreed to do.[6]

However, in other cases, exclusion clauses have been regarded as mere defences. According to this view one should first construe the contract without regard to the exemption clauses in order to discover the promisor's obligation and only then consider whether the clauses provide a defence to breach of those obligations.[7]

It is clear that this difference is not merely theoretical but likely to provide significantly different results in many cases. Both approaches are to be found in the cases though the second is probably the more common. It is possible that both approaches

---

1. *Infra*, pp. 168–9.
2. See Coote *op. cit.*
3. See *per* Lord REID in *Suisse Atlantique d'Armement Maritime S.A.* v. *N.V. Rotterdamsche Kolen Centrale*, [1967] 1 A.C. 361, at p. 406; [1966] 2 All E.R. 61, at p. 76.
4. [1957] A.C. 149; [1956] 3 All E.R. 957.
5. Art. III, r. 8.
6. See also *East Ham Corporation* v. *Bernard Sunley & Sons*, [1966] A.C. 406; [1965] 3 All E.R. 619. Cf. the construction given to a different strike clause by RUSSELL, L.J., in *Torquay Hotel Co.* v. *Cousins*, [1969] 2 Ch. 106, at p. 143; [1969] 1 All E.R. 522, at p. 534.
7. See, e.g. DENNING, L.J., in *Karsales (Harrow), Ltd.* v. *Wallis*, [1956] 2 All E.R. 866, at p. 869; [1956] 1 W.L.R. 936, at p. 940.

are correct and that the real question is to choose which to apply to a particular clause. Certainly some clauses, e.g. clauses limiting the amount of damages that can be recovered, look like defences[1] while others are more naturally regarded as defining the obligation.

The problems raised by the attempt of one party to a contract to exclude or to limit the liability which would otherwise be his has produced prolific and persistent litigation as a result of which it is possible to hazard certain conclusions.

(1) At the outset of its inquiry the court must be satisfied that the particular document relied on as containing notice of the excluding or limiting term is in truth an integral part of the contract.[2] It must have been intended as a contractual document and not as a mere acknowledgment of payment. To hold a party bound by the terms of a document which reasonable persons would assume to be no more than a receipt is an affront to common sense. An illustration of the point is afforded by the case of *Chapelton* v. *Barry U.D.C.*[3]

> The plaintiff wished to hire two deck-chairs from a pile kept by the defendant Council on their beach. The chairs were stacked near a notice which read . . . " Hire of Chairs 2d. per session of 3 hours" . . . , and which requested the public to obtain tickets from the chair attendant and retain them for inspection. The plaintiff took the chairs and obtained two tickets from the attendant, which he put in his pocket without reading. When he sat on one of the chairs, it collapsed and he was injured. He sued the Council, who relied on a provision printed on the tickets excluding liability for any damage arising from the hire of a chair.

The Court of Appeal held the defendants liable. No reasonable man would assume that the ticket was anything but a receipt for the money. The notice on the beach constituted the offer, which the plaintiff accepted when he took the chair, and the notice contained no statement limiting the liability of the Council. The defendants had failed to satisfy the preliminary requirement of identifying the ticket as a contractual document, and it was superfluous, therefore, to ask if it contained a due announcement of any conditions.

The case of *McCutcheon* v. *David MacBrayne, Ltd.*[4] affords a second illustration.

> The defendants owned steamers operating between the Scottish mainland and the islands. The plaintiff asked a Mr. McSporran to arrange for the plaintiff's car to be shipped to the mainland. Mr. McSporran called at the defendants' office and made an oral contract on the plaintiff's behalf for the carriage of the car. On the voyage, through the defendants' negligence, both ship and car were sunk. The plaintiff sued the defendants for the value of the car.

Marginal note: The writing must be a contractual document

---

1. Though this is denied by BARWICK, C.J., in *State Government Insurance Office of Queensland* v. *Brisbane Stevedoring Pty., Ltd.* (1969), 43 A.L.J.R. 456, at p. 461.
2. Approved by Lord DENNING, M.R., in *White* v. *Blackmore*, [1972] 2 Q.B. 651, at p. 666, [1972] 3 All E.R. 158, at. p. 167.
3. [1940] 1 K.B. 532; [1940] 1 All E.R. 356. See also *Henson* v. *London North Eastern Rail Co. and Coote and Warren, Ltd.*, [1946] 1 All E.R. 653.
4. [1964] 1 All E.R. 430; [1964] 1 W.L.R. 125. See also *Burnett* v. *Westminister Bank, Ltd.*, *infra*, p. 149.

The defendants pleaded terms, excluding liability for negligence, contained in twenty-seven paragraphs of small print displayed both outside and inside their office.   The terms were also printed on a " risk note " which customers, were usually asked to sign.   On this occasion the defendants omitted to ask Mr. McSporran to sign the risk note.   All they did was to give him, when he had paid in advance the cost of carriage, a receipt stating that " all goods were carried subject to the conditions set out in the notices."   The House of Lords gave judgment for the plaintiff.   Neither he nor Mr. McSporran had read the words on the notices or on the receipt;   and there was in truth no contractual document at all. The risk note was not presented to Mr. McSporran, and the receipt was given only after the oral contract had been concluded.

Unsigned documents: question of notice

(2) If the document is to be regarded as an integral part of the contract, it must next be seen if it has, or has not, been signed by the party against whom the excluding or limiting term is pleaded.   If it is unsigned, the question will be whether reasonable notice of the term has been given.   That this was the crucial test was pronounced by MELLISH, L.J., in 1877 in the case of *Parker* v. *South Eastern Rail. Co.*, where the defendants claimed that a passenger was bound by terms stated on a cloakroom ticket of which he was ignorant.[1]   Had the defendants done what was sufficient to give notice of the term to the person or class of persons to which the plaintiff belonged?   The question is one of fact, and the court must examine the circumstances of each case.[2]

Notice to be given in time

The time when the notice is alleged to have been given is of great importance.   No excluding or limiting term will avail the party seeking its protection unless it has been brought adequately to the attention of the other party before the contract is made.   A belated notice is valueless.   Thus in *Olley* v. *Marlborough Court, Ltd.*:[3]

> A husband and wife arrived at a hotel as guests and paid for a week's board and residence in advance.   They went up to the bedroom allotted to them, and on one of its walls was a notice that " the proprietors will not hold themselves responsible for articles lost or stolen unless handed to the manageress for safe custody." The wife then closed the self-locking door of the bedroom, went downstairs and hung the key on the board in the reception office. In her absence the key was wrongfully taken by a third party, who opened the bedroom door and stole her furs.

---

1. (1877), 2 C.P.D. 416, especially at pp. 422–3.   The test was approved by the House of Lords in *Richardson* v. *Rowntree*, [1894] A.C. 217.   See also *Thornton* v. *Shoe Lane Parking, Ltd.*, [1971] 2 Q.B. 163; [1971] 1 All E.R. 686; *infra*, p. 150.
2. There are a vast number of nineteenth and early twentieth century cases on railway and steamship tickets.   These " ticket cases " are more fully discussed in the 4th edition of this work at pp. 104–107.   English judges have tended to take a restricted view of what need be done to give reasonable notice.   See, e.g. *Thompson* v. *London Midland and Scottish Rail. Co.*, [1930] 1 K.B. 41.   American judges starting from the same test have been more demanding, e.g. rejecting tickets in very small print which is difficult to read, e.g. *Lisi* v. *Alitalia Lines Aerea Italiane S.p.A.*, [1968] 1 Lloyds Rep. 505, affirming [1967] 1 Lloyds Rep. 140; *Silvestri* v. *Italia Societa per Azioni di Navigazione*, [1968] 1 Lloyds Rep. 263.
3. [1949] 1 K.B. 532; [1949] 1 All E.R. 127.   In *Chapelton* v. *Barry U.D.C.* (*supra*, p. 147), the ticket, even had it been a contractual document, was given to the plaintiff after he had accepted the offer to hire a chair.

The defendants sought to incorporate the notice in the contract. But the Court of Appeal held that the contract was completed before the guests went up to their room and that no subsequent notice could affect their rights.

A striking if unusual illustration of the time factor is offered by *Burnett* v. *Westminster Bank, Ltd.*[1]

> The plaintiff had for some years accounts at two of the defendants' branches—branch A and branch B. A new cheque book was issued to him by branch A, on the front cover of which was a notice that " the cheques in this book will be applied to the account for which they have been prepared." These cheques were in fact designed for use in a computer system, operated by branch A, and " magnetized ink " was used which the computer could " read." The plaintiff knew that there were words on the cover of the cheque book, but had not read them. He drew a cheque for £2,300, but crossed out branch A and substituted branch B. The computer could not " read " the plaintiff's ink. He later wished to stop the cheque and told branch B. Meanwhile the computer had debited his account at branch A. He sued the defendants for breach of contract, and they pleaded the limiting words on the cover of the cheque book.

MOCATTA, J., gave judgment for the plaintiff. The cheque book was not a document which could reasonably be assumed to contain terms of the contract; and the defendants had not in fact given adequate notice of the restriction to the plaintiff. They were, in effect, seeking, without his assent, to alter the terms of the contract.

A further point must be made. The court may infer notice **Course of** from previous dealings between the parties. In *Olley* v. *Marl-* **dealing** *borough Court, Ltd.*,[2] had the plaintiff and her husband been habitués of the hotel, they would presumably have been acquainted with its ways and would have had sufficient opportunity to see and digest the notice before making a fresh contract for board and residence. The effect of such familiarity was demonstrated in the case of *Spurling* v. *Bradshaw*.[3]

> The defendant had dealt for many years with the plaintiffs, who were warehousemen. He delivered to them for storage eight barrels of orange juice. A few days later he received from them a document acknowledging the receipt of the barrels and referring on its face to clauses printed on the back. One such clause exempted the plaintiffs " from any loss or damage occasioned by the negligence, wrongful act or default " of themselves or their servants. When ultimately the defendant came to collect the barrels, they were found to be empty.

The defendant refused to pay the storage charges, and the plaintiffs sued him. He counter-claimed for negligence and, in answer to this counter-claim, the plaintiffs pleaded the exempting clause. The defendant sought to argue that, as the document containing it was sent to him only after the conclusion of the contract, it was too late to affect his rights. But he admitted that in previous dealings he had often received a similar document, though he had never bothered to read it, and he was now held to be bound by it.

---

1. [1966] 1 Q.B. 742; [1965] 3 All E.R. 81.
2. *Supra*, p. 147.
3. [1956] 2 All E.R. 121; [1956] 1 W.L.R. 461. See Hoggett, 33 M.L.R. 518.

The phrase " course of dealing," on which the inference of notice may rest, is not easily defined.   But it is clear that it must be a consistent course.   In *McCutcheon* v. *David MacBrayne, Ltd.*[1] the plaintiff's agent had dealt with the defendants on a number of occasions.   Sometimes he had signed a " risk note " and sometimes he had not.

> " The respondents," said Lord PEARCE,[2] " rely on the course of dealing.   But they are seeking to establish an oral contract by a course of dealing which always insisted on a written contract. It is the consistency of a course of conduct which gives rise to the implication that in similar circumstances a similar contractual result will follow.   When the conduct is not consistent, there is no reason why it should still produce an invariable contractual result.   The respondents, having previously offered a written contract, on this occasion offered an oral one.   The appellant's agent duly paid the freight for which he was asked and accepted the oral contract thus offered.   This raises no implication that the conditions of the oral contract must be the same as the conditions of the written contract would have been had the respondents proffered one."

Thornton v. *Shoe Lane Parking, Ltd.*

A recent discussion of familiar problems in a novel setting is to be found in *Thornton* v. *Shoe Lane Parking, Ltd.*[3]

> The plaintiff wished to park his car in the defendants' automatic car park.   He had not been there before.   Outside the park was a notice, stating the charges and adding the words " All cars parked at owners' risk."   As the plaintiff drove into the park a light turned from red to green, and a ticket was pushed out from a machine.   Nobody was in attendance.   The plaintiff took the ticket and saw the time on it.   He also saw that it contained other words, but put it into his pocket without reading them.   The words in fact stated that the ticket was issued subject to conditions displayed on the premises.   To find these conditions the plaintiff would have had to walk round the park until he reached a panel on which they were displayed.   The plaintiff never thought to look for them.   One condition purported to exempt the defendants from liability not only for damage to the cars parked but also for injury to customers, however caused.   When the plaintiff returned to collect his car, there was an accident in which he was injured. The defendants pleaded the exempting term.

The Court of Appeal gave judgment for the plaintiff.   The first question raised was the moment at which the contract was made.[4] It was not easy to apply the long line of " ticket cases," reaching

---

1. *Supra*, p. 147, for the facts of this case.   In this case Lord DEVLIN suggested that a term could be introduced by a course of dealings only if there was actual knowledge of its content (as opposed to its existence).   This statement was unnecessary for the decision and clearly goes too far in view of *Henry Kendall & Sons* v. *William Lillico & Sons*, [1969] 2 A.C. 31; [1968] 2 All E.R. 444.   It appears relatively easy to show that terms are included in a contract by a course of dealings in a commercial context.   See *British Crane Hire Corporation, Ltd.* v. *Ipswich Plant Hire, Ltd.*, [1975] Q.B. 303; [1974] 1 All E.R. 1059.   It is more difficult in consumer transactions: see *Mendelssohn* v. *Normand, Ltd.*, [1970] 1 Q.B. 177; [1969] 2 All E.R. 1215; *Hollier* v. *Rambler Motors (A.M.C.), Ltd.*, [1972] 2 Q.B. 71; [1972] 1 All E.R. 399, though these cases can also be explained on the ground that there was not sufficient consistency or continuity of dealing.
2. [1964] 1 All E.R. 430, at pp. 439–440; [1964] 1 W.L.R. 125, at p. 138.
3. [1971] 2 Q.B. 163; [1971] 1 All E.R. 686.
4. MEGAW, L.J., while he concurred in the decision, reserved his opinion as to the precise moment when the contract was made.

back for a hundred years, to the mechanism of an automatic machine. Lord DENNING said :[1]

> " The customer pays his money and gets a ticket. He cannot refuse it. He cannot get his money back. He may protest to the machine, even swear at it; but it will remain unmoved. He is committed beyond recall. He was committed at the very moment when he put his money into the machine: the contract was concluded at that time. It can be translated into offer and acceptance in this way. The offer is made when the proprietor of the machine holds it out as being ready to receive the money. The acceptance takes place when the customer puts his money into the slot. The terms of the offer are contained in the notice placed on or near the machine, stating what is offered for the money. The customer is bound by these terms as long as they are sufficiently brought to his notice beforehand, but not otherwise. He is not bound by the terms printed on the ticket, if they differ from the notice, because the ticket comes too late. The contract has already been made."

Even if the automatic machine was regarded as a booking clerk in disguise and the older ticket cases applied, the plaintiff would still succeed. In the leading case of *Parker* v. *South Eastern Rail. Co.*,[2] three questions were posed. (a) Did the plaintiff know that there was printing on the ticket? In the instant case he did. (b) Did he know that the ticket contained or referred to conditions? In the instant case he did not know. (c) Had the defendants done what was sufficient to draw the plaintiff's attention to the relevant condition? In the instant case the condition was designed to exempt the defendants from liability for personal injury caused to the customer. So wide an exception was, in the context, unusual and required an unusually explicit warning. Such warning the defendants had not given, and they could not escape liability for the plaintiff's injury.

A problem which has not so far received much attention from the courts is the so-called " battle of the forms."[3] This occurs where one party sends a form stating that the contract is on his terms and the other party responds by returning a form stating that the contract is on his terms! At least four solutions seem possible, viz. that there is a contract on the first party's terms, a contract on the second party's terms, a contract on the terms that common law would normally imply in such circumstances or no contract at all. In theory there is much to be said for the last solution since there is neither agreement nor apparent agreement on the terms of the contract. In practice however it is thought that the courts will try to give effect to the intention of the parties to make some contract. It has been suggested that each succeeding form should be treated as a counter-offer so that the last form should be regarded as accepted by the receiver's silence. This is a plausible view though not perhaps easy to reconcile with the conventional view of *Felthouse* v. *Bindley*.[4]

"Battle of the forms"

(3) If the document is signed it will normally be impossible or at least difficult, to deny its contractual character, and evidence

Signed documents

1. [1971] 2 Q.B., at p. 169; [1971] 1 All E.R., at p. 689.
2. (1877), 2 C.P.D. 416: see *supra*, p. 148.
3. See Hoggett, 33 M.L.R. 518.
4. *Supra*, pp. 41–43. See also *British Road Services, Ltd.* v. *Arthur Crutchley & Co., Ltd.*, [1968] 1 All E.R. 811: *Transmotors, Ltd.* v. *Robertson, Buckley & Co., Ltd.*, [1970] 1 Lloyds Rep. 224.

of notice, actual or constructive, is irrelevant.   In the absence of fraud or misrepresentation, a person is bound by a writing to which he has put his signature, whether he has read its contents or has chosen to leave them unread.[1]   The distinction between the signed and the unsigned document was taken by Lord Justice MELLISH in *Parker* v. *South East Rail. Co.*, and was emphasized and illustrated in *L'Estrange* v. *Graucob*.[2]   The plaintiff bought an automatic machine from the defendants on terms contained in a document, described as a " Sales Agreement," and including a number of clauses in " legible, but regrettably small print," which she signed but did not read.   The Divisional Court held that she was bound by these terms and that no question of notice arose.   In the words of SCRUTTON, L.J.[3]

> " In cases in which the contract is contained in a railway ticket or other unsigned document, it is necessary to prove that an alleged party was aware, or ought to have been aware, of its terms and conditions.   These cases have no application when the document has been signed.   When a document containing contractual terms is signed, then, in the absence of fraud, or, I will add, misrepresentation, the party signing it is bound, and it is wholly immaterial whether he has read the document or not."

The qualification imposed upon the absolute character of signed documents by the last sentence quoted from this judgment will be readily understood.   It was applied in the case of *Curtis* v. *Chemical Cleaning and Dyeing Co.*[4]

> The plaintiff took to the defendants' shop for cleaning a white satin wedding dress trimmed with beads and sequins.   The shop asisstant gave her a document headed " Receipt " and requested her to sign it.   With unusual prudence, the plaintiff asked its purport, and the assistant replied that it exempted the defendants from certain risks and, in the present instance, from the risk of damage to the beads and sequins on the dress.   The plaintiff then signed the document, which in fact contained a clause " that the company is not liable for any damage, however caused."   When the dress was returned, it was stained and, in an action by the plaintiff for damages, the defendants relied on this clause.

The Court of Appeal held that the defence must fail.   The assistant, however innocently, had misrepresented the effect of the document, and the defendants were thus prevented from insisting upon the drastic terms of the exemption.   The plaintiff was entitled to assume, as the assistant had assured her, that she was running the risk only of damage to the beads and sequins.

Ambiguities construed against the party inserting the term   (4) If there is any doubt as to the meaning and scope of the excluding or limiting term, the ambiguity will be resolved against the party who has inserted it and who is now relying on it.   As he seeks to protect himself against liability to which he would otherwise be subject, it is for him to prove that his words clearly

---

1. For the possibility of pleading mistake, see *infra*, pp. 237–244.   But even here there are no decided cases where the plea of mistake has availed in the absence of fraud.
2. [1934] 2 K.B. 394; [1934] All E.R. Rep. 16.   For the *dictum* of MELLISH, L.J., see (1877), 2 C.P.D. 416, at p. 421.   See Spencer, [1973] C.L.J. 104.
3. [1934] 2 K.B. 394, at p. 403; [1934] All E.R. Rep. 16, at p. 19.
4. [1951] 1 K.B. 805; [1951] 1 All E.R. 631.   See *Jaques* v. *Lloyd D. George & Partners, Ltd.*, [1968] 2 All E.R. 187.   It may also, in any future case, be necessary to consider the effect of the Misrepresentation Act 1967, s. 3: *infra*, pp. 272–9.

and aptly describe the contingency that has in fact arisen.[1]   Thus it may happen that, apart from the contract, he may find himself in a situation where the law casts upon him not only a duty of care but also some form of strict liability.   In such a case, unless the language of the contract manifestly covers both types of obligation, he will be taken to have excluded only the latter.

The position may be illustrated by reference to the common carrier of goods, who holds himself out as prepared to carry goods for any person whatever.   In addition to his liability for negligence such a person, by virtue of his calling, is strictly responsible for the safety of the goods entrusted to him, save for damage caused by an act of God, the Queen's enemies, an inherent defect in the goods themselves, or the fault of the consignor.   If, therefore, a clause which purports to exclude his liability does not clearly refer to negligence, it will be construed by the courts as limited in its effect to the peculiarly arduous duties cast upon him by his status.[2]

Ambiguities will be construed in a similar way when a party is *prima facie* liable both in tort and in contract.   Thus in *White* v. *John Warrick & Co., Ltd.,*[3]

> the plaintiff hired a tradesman's cycle from the defendants.   While he was riding it, the saddle tilted forward and he was injured.   The contract of hire stated that " nothing in this agreement shall render the owners liable for any personal injury."

If this term had not been inserted in the agreement, the defendants might have been liable on two grounds: in tort for negligence and in contract (even without negligence) for supplying a defective cycle.   As the term was ambiguous, it availed only to exclude the defendants' contractual duty.   They might still be liable for the tort of negligence.

The severity with which the courts will hold a party to the proof of his intentions is shown by the case of *Hollier* v. *Rambler Motors (A.M.C.), Ltd.*[4]

> The plaintiff agreed with the manager of the defendants' garage that his car should be towed to the garage for repair.   While at the garage the car was substantially damaged by a fire as a result of the defendants' negligence.   The defendants contended (in the event unsuccessfully) that the contract was subject to a course of dealings, which incorporated their usual terms.   These terms included a condition that " the company is not responsible for damage caused by fire to customer's cars on the premises."

---

1. See the statements of SCRUTTON, L.J., in *Rutter* v. *Palmer*, [1922] 2 K.B. 87, at p. 92, and in *Szymonowski & Co.* v. *Beck & Co.*, [1923] 1 K.B. 457, at p. 466.
2. See Lord GREENE, M.R., in *Alderslade* v. *Hendon Laundry, Ltd.*, [1945] K.B. 189; [1945] 1 All E.R. 244.   On the facts of the case itself the Court of Appeal held that the defendants had adequately excluded liability for negligence.
3. [1953] 2 All E.R. 1021; [1953] 1 W.L.R. 1285.
4. [1972] 2 Q.B. 71, [1972] 1 All E.R. 399.   See also *Akerib* v. *Booth*, [1961] 1 All E.R. 380; [1961] 1 W.L.R. 367; *Morris* v. *C. W. Martin & Sons*, [1966] 1 Q.B. 716; [1965] 2 All E.R. 725; *Hawkes Bay & East Coast Aero Club*, [1972] N.Z.L.R. 289, Coote, [1972A] C.L.J. 53; *Cf. White (Contractors), Ltd.* v. *Tarmac Civil Engineering. Ltd.*, [1967] 3 All E.R. 586; [1967] 1 W.L.R. 1508; *Adams* v. *Richardson and Starling, Ltd.*, [1969] 2 All E.R. 1221; [1969] 1 W.L.R. 1645.

The Court of Appeal held that even if this clause formed part of the contract, it would not serve to protect the defendants.   Since the defendants could only be responsible for damage by fire if they were negligent, the clause might appear at first sight unambiguous but the Court held that it could be read by a reasonable customer as a warning that the defendants would not be responsible for a fire caused without negligence and was not therefore sufficiently unambiguous to exclude the defendants' liability.[1]

Position of third parties

(5) Even if the excluding or limiting term is an integral part of the contract and even if its language is apt to meet the situation that has in fact occurred, questions may arise as to whether the term can operate to protect a person who is not a party to the contract.[2]   This often happens, for example, under contracts of carriage where the carrier has excluded or limited his own liability and an injured passenger or consignor of goods seeks to sue the servant or agent whose negligence has caused him damage. Thus in *Adler* v. *Dickson*,[3]

> the plaintiff was a passenger in the Peninsular and Oriental Steam Navigation Co.'s vessel *Himalaya*, and was travelling on a first class ticket.   The " ticket " was a lengthy printed document containing terms exempting the company from liability.   There was a general clause that " passengers are carried at passengers' entire risk " and a particular clause that " the company will not be responsible for any injury whatsoever to the person of any passenger arising from or occasioned by the negligence of the company's servants." While the plaintiff was mounting a gangway, it moved and fell and she was thrown on to the wharf from a height of sixteen feet and sustained serious injuries.   She brought an action for negligence, not against the company, but against the master and boatswain of the ship.

The Court of Appeal held that, while the clauses protected the company from liability, they could avail no one else.   The *ratio decivendi* of the court was that the ticket did not, on its true construction, purport to exempt the master or boatswain.   The Court of Appeal also considered, *obiter*, what the position would have been if the ticket had said that the master and boatswain were not to be liable.   On this question there were divergent views. JENKINS, L.J., said, " even if these provisions had contained words purporting to exclude the liability of the company's servants, *non constat* that the company's servants could successfully rely on that exclusion . . . for the company's servants are not parties to the contract."[4]   MORRIS, L.J., agreed but DENNING, L.J., took the opposite view.

Scruttons, Ltd. v. Midland Silicones, Ltd.

In *Scruttons, Ltd.* v. *Midland Silicones, Ltd.*,[5]

> a drum containing chemicals was shipped in New York by X on a ship owned by the United States Lines and consigned to the order of the plaintiffs.   The bill of lading contained a clause

---

1. The case is criticised by Barendt, 35 M.L.R. 644.   Cf. Coote, [1973] C.L.J. 14.
2. See Coote, *Exception Clauses*, Chap. 9: Treitel, 18 M.L.R. 172; Furmston, 23 M.L.R. 373, at pp. 385–397; Atiyah, 46 A.L.J. 212; Rose, 4 Anglo-American L.R. 7.
3. [1955] 1 Q.B. 158; [1954] 3 All E.R. 397.
4. [1955] 1 Q.B. 158, at p. 186; [1954] 3 All E.R. 397, at p. 403.
5. [1962] A.C. 446; [1962] 2 All E.R. 1.

limiting the liability of the shipowners, as carriers, to 500 dollars (£179). The defendants were stevedores who had contracted with the United States Lines to act for them in London on the terms that the defendants were to have the benefit of the limiting clause in the bill of lading. The plaintiffs were ignorant of the contract between the defendants and the United States Lines. Owing to the defendants' negligence the drum of chemicals was damaged to the extent of £593. The plaintiffs sued the defendants in negligence and the defendants pleaded the limiting clause in the bill of lading.

DIPLOCK, J., found for the plaintiffs, and his judgment was upheld both by the Court of Appeal and by the House of Lords.[1] Their Lordships (Lord DENNING dissenting) took the view that privity of contract was a fatal objection to the defendant's claim. The defendants were not parties to the Bill of Lading and could derive no rights under it. This rule appears simple but it is not without difficulties.

(a) The House of Lords relied on the fact that the United States Supreme Court had recently reached the same decision in *Krawill Machinery Corporation*[2] v. *R. C. Herd & Co. Inc.* but that decision owed nothing to the doctrine of privity of contract which does not exist in its English form in the United States. It was rested simply, as *Scrutton* v. *Midland Silicones* could have been, on the basis that nothing in the bill of lading expressly or impliedly excluded the liability of the stevedore. Later American cases have shown that a suitably worded clause can extend immunity to non-parties.[3]

(b) The House of Lords also relied on the decision of the High Court of Australia in *Wilson* v. *Darling Island Stevedoring Co., Ltd.*[4] Stevedores here pleaded an exemption clause in a contract, evidenced by a bill of lading and made between the owner of goods and a carrier. The plea failed. It is true that FULLAGAR, J., said,

" the obvious answer is that the defendant company is not a party to the contract, that it can neither sue nor be sued on that contract, and that nothing in a contract between two other parties can relieve it from the consequences of any tortious act committed by it against the plaintiff."

DIXON, C.J., agreed with FULLAGAR, J., but the remainder of the court took different views and it is clear that the result would have been different if the bill of lading had stated clearly that the stevedores were not to be liable.

(c) The decision of the House is not easy to reconcile with its earlier decision in *Elder Dempster & Co.* v. *Patterson Zochonis & Co.*[5] In that case, SCRUTTON, L.J., and a unanimous House of Lords including Lord SUMNER had assumed that a non-party could in some circumstances shelter behind an exemption clause contained in a contract between two other parties. In *Scruttons*

---

1. [1962] A.C. 446; [1962] 2 All E.R. 1.
2. 359 U.S. 297; [1959] 1 Lloyds Rep 305.
3. E.g. *Carle and Montanari Inc.* v. *American Export Isbrandtsen Lines Inc.*, [1968] 1 Lloyds Rep 260; affirmed 386 F. 2d. 839: cert. denied 390 U.S. 1013 (1968).
4. [1956] 1 Lloyds Rep. 346; 95 C.L.R. 43.
5. [1924] A.C. 522. For fuller discussion of this difficult case see *supra*, p. 154, n. 2.

v. *Midland Silicones* the House of Lords put the *Elder Dempster* case on one side on the ground that its precise ratio was obscure.[1] It may perhaps be thought that in commercial matters what Lord SUMNER and SCRUTTON, L.J., thought self-evidently correct is not often self-evidently wrong.

(d) The House appeared to assume that only a contract between plaintiff and defendant would do to exclude the defendant's liability.   But it is very doubtful whether this is the law. Thus we have seen that a debt owed by A to B may be rendered unenforceable by B's acceptance of part-payment by C.[2]   Further the liability of the stevedores was tortious and not contractual and tortious liability may be excluded by consent, which need not be contractual.[3]

An interesting, if inconclusive case is that of *Morris* v. *C. W. Martin & Sons, Ltd.*[4]

> The plaintiff sent her mink stole to a furrier to be cleaned. The furrier told her that he himself did no cleaning but that he could arrange for this to be done by the defendants.   The plaintiff approved this proposal.   The furrier accordingly, acting as principal and not as agent, made a contract with the defendants, a well-known firm, to clean the plaintiff's fur.   While in the possession of the defendants, the fur was stolen by their servant.   The plaintiff sued the defendants, who pleaded exemption clauses contained in their contract with the furrier.

The Court of Appeal held the defendants liable.   The three members of the court agreed (a) that, when the defendants received the fur in order to clean it, they became bailees for reward: (b) that, as such bailees, they owed a common law duty to the plaintiff; (c) that the clauses on which they relied were not adequate to meet the facts of the case.[5]   It was unnecessary, therefore, to answer the question whether, if the clauses had been unambiguous and comprehensive, they would have protected the defendants as against the plaintiff, who was not a party to the contract.   Lord DENNING thought that the plaintiff might have been bound by these clauses because she had impliedly agreed that the furrier should contract for the cleaning of the fur on terms usual in the trade.   DIPLOCK and SALMON, L.JJ., preferred to keep the question open.

(e) It seems possible that the House of Lords may have taken a somewhat simplistic view of the merits, viz. that exemption clauses are bad and their operation accordingly to be confined as narrowly as possible.   This is understandable if applied to the carriage of passengers as in *Adler* v. *Dickson* but it makes less sense in relation to carriage of goods.[6]   Here the exemption clauses—the Hague rules—have been approved by Parliament and are in many circumstances mandatory.   The parties will (or

---

1. On the relevance of this case to the doctrine of precedent, see Dworkin, 25 M.L.R. 163, at pp. 171–174.
2. See *supra*, pp. 97–98.
3. See KITTO, J., in *Wilson* v. *Darling Island Stevedoring Co., Ltd.* (1955), 95 C.L.R. 43, at p. 81.
4. [1966] 1 Q.B. 716; [1965] 2 All E.R. 725.
5. See *supra*, pp. 152–3.
6. See *per* Lord DENNING, M.R., in *Gillespie Brothers & Co., Ltd.* v. *Roy Bowles Transport, Ltd.*, [1973] 1 Q.B. 400, at p. 412; [1973] 1 All E.R. 193, at pp. 197–198.

at least should) have insured on the basis that liability is as laid down by the rules. It certainly makes no sense to allow their loss to be transferred on to the carrier's servants, who are the least likely to be insured or financially equipped to bear it. (Stevedores are perhaps in a different position since they are normally substantial and/or likely to carry insurance though even here it is not clear why loss should be transferred from the cargo owner's insurer to the stevedore's). These arguments have been substantially accepted by the revised Hague Rules. The Carriage of Goods by Sea Act 1971, if and when brought into force by Order in Council, will give the benefit of limiting terms in the carrier's contract to his servants or agents, but not to independent contractors. Similar provisions are to be found in a number of international transport conventions.[1]

In view of these difficulties, it is perhaps not surprising that ways have been sought to avoid the effect of *Scruttons* v. *Midland Silocones*. One possible course is for the contracting party to intervene in the action and apply to stay it. This possibility was inconclusively tested in *Gore* v. *Van der Lann* (*Liverpool Corporation intervening*).[2] In that case the plaintiff was an old age pensioner who applied for and received a free pass on the Liverpool Corporation's buses. The pass purported to be a licence to travel on the corporation's buses on condition that neither the corporation nor its servants would be liable for injury, etc., however caused. The plaintiff was injured and brought an action against the driver alleging negligence. The corporation sought to intervene to stay the action. In the event the Court of Appeal held that the pass constituted not a licence but a contract,[3] and that the exclusion of liability was therefore void under s. 151 of the Road Traffic Act 1960. The court considered the application for a stay, *obiter*, and suggested that a stay might be obtained either if there were an express promise not to sue the servant or if the employer were under a legal (and not simply a moral) obligation to reimburse the servant for any damages he might be held liable to pay. The former possibility was applied, in a different setting, by ORMROD, J., in *Snelling* v. *John G. Snelling, Ltd.*[4]

A second possibility is to seek to create a direct contract between potential plaintiff and potential defendant. An elaborate attempt to do this was upheld by the majority of the Judicial Committee of the Privy Council in *New Zealand Shipping Co., Ltd.* v. *A. M. Satterthwaite & Co., Ltd.*[5]

New Zealand Shipping Co., Ltd. v. *A. M. Satterthwaite & Co., Ltd.*

> The consignor loaded goods on a ship for carriage to the plaintiff consignee in New Zealand. The carriage was subject to a bill of lading issued by the carrier's Agent, which contained the following clause " it is hereby expressly agreed that no servant or Agent of the carrier (including every independent contractor from time to time employed by the carrier) shall in any circumstances whatsoever be

1. See Giles, 24 I.C.L.Q. 379, at p. 390.
2. [1967] 2 Q.B. 31; [1967] 1 All E.R. 360. Odgers, 86 L.Q.R. 69. See also *Genys* v. *Mathews*, [1965] 3 All E.R. 24; [1966] 1 W.L.R. 758.
3. This decision has been forcefully criticised by Odgers, *op. cit.*, on the ground that it is difficult to reconcile with *Wilkie* v. *London Passenger Transport Board*, [1947] 1 All E.R. 258. See *supra*, p. 31.
4. [1973] 1 Q.B. 87; [1972] 1 All E.R. 79. See *infra*, p. 444.
5. [1975] A.C. 154; [1974] 1 All E.R. 1015. Coote, 37 M.L.R. 453; Reynolds, 90 L.Q.R. 301.

under any liability whatsoever to the shipper, consignee or owner of the goods or to any holder of the bill of lading for any loss or damage or delay of whatsoever kind arising or resulting directly or indirectly from any neglect or default on his part while acting in the course of or in connection with his employment and, without prejudice to the generality of the foregoing provisions in this clause, every exemption, limitation, condition and liberty herein contained, and every right, exemption from liability, defence and immunity of whatsoever nature applicable to the carrier or to which the carrier is entitled hereunder shall also be available and shall extend to protect every such Servant or Agent of the carrier acting as aforesaid and for the purpose of all the foregoing provisions of this clause the carrier is or shall be deemed to be acting as Agent or Trustee on behalf of and for the benefit of all persons who are or might be his servants or Agents from time to time (including independent contractors as aforesaid) and all such persons shall to this extent be or be deemed to be parties to the contract in or evidenced by this bill of lading."[1] After the plaintiff had become the holder of the bill of lading, the cargo was damaged as a result of the negligence of the defendants, the stevedores, employed by the carriers to unload the cargo in New Zealand. The plaintiff sued for damages and the defendant relied on the clause above.

The majority of the Judicial Committee of the Privy Council (Viscount DILHORNE and Lord SIMON OF GLAISDALE dissenting) held for the defendant. They held that the clause, although it looked like an attempt to make the stevedores (and others) parties to the contract of carriage could be treated as an offer by the consignor of a unilateral contract, viz. that if those involved in performance of the main contract would play their part (e.g. in the case of the stevedore, unload the goods) the consignor would hold them free from liability. The stevedore was held to have accepted the offer by unloading the goods and the plaintiff consignee by presenting the bill of lading to have contracted on bill of lading terms.[2]

No doubt both the correctness and the ambit of this decision will be the subject of debate. Critics can plausibly argue that the clause was not aptly worded to produce this result and that it might have been more beneficial to reject the clause and compel the draftsman to try again. They can also point to technical difficulties presented by the majority analysis, e.g. would the result have been different if the stevedore had injured the goods before they had unloaded them or before the consignees took up the bill of lading.[3] Defenders of the decision may well reply with force that it shows a robust awareness of the commercial realities of the situation.

---

1. This clause is popularly known as the " Himalaya Clause", being named after the ship in *Adler* v. *Dickson, supra,* p. 154. That the clause was not revised after *Scruttons, Ltd.* v. *Midland Silicones, Ltd.* is perhaps evidence of the conservatism of both the legal and shipping professions.
2. Cf. *Brandt* v. *Liverpool, Brazil and River Plate Steam Navigation Co.,* [1924] 1 K.B. 575.
3. It is assumed that the burden of an exemption clause cannot be imposed on a non-party without his consent. This seems correct in principle though there are three decisions at first instance which can be read to the contrary— *Fosbrooke-Hobbes* v. *Airwork, Ltd. and British American Air Services, Ltd.* [1937] 1 All E.R. 108; *Pyrene Co.* v. *Scindia Navigation Co.,* [1954] 2 Q.B. 402; [1954] 2 All E.R. 158; *Cockerton* v. *Naviera Aznar S.A.,* [1960] 2 Lloyds Rep. 450.

(6) If a person contracts to deliver or do one thing and he delivers or does another, he has failed to perform his contractual duty. The proposition is self-evident. As long ago as 1838, Lord ABINGER sought to contrast the breach of a term in a contract for the sale of goods with the complete non-performance of the contract.

Sale of goods: non-performance

> " If a man offers to buy peas of another, and he sends him beans, he does not perform his contract. But that is not a warranty; there is no warranty that he should sell him peas; the contract is to sell peas, and if he sends him anything else in their stead, it is a non-performance of it."[1]

So, too, in *Nichol v. Godts*,[2]

> a seller contracted to sell to a buyer " foreign refined rape oil, warranted only equal to sample." The oil delivered corresponded with the sample, but was found not to be " foreign refined rape oil " at all.

The seller was held not to be protected by the term he had inserted; and POLLOCK, C.B., remarked that " if a man contracts to buy a thing, he ought not to have something else delivered to him."

Looking back in 1966 upon these and similar cases, Lord WILBERFORCE said:[3]

> " Since the contracting parties could hardly have been supposed to contemplate such a mis-performance or to have provided against it without destroying the whole contractual substratum, there is no difficulty here in holding exception clauses to be inapplicable."

In the present century the reasoning thus adopted in contracts for the sale of goods has been applied to contracts of hire-purchase. In *Karsales (Harrow), Ltd. v. Wallis*,[4]

> the defendant inspected a car owned by X, found it in good order and wished to take it on hire-purchase. X therefore sold it to the plaintiffs, and they re-sold it to a hire-purchase company. The defendant made a contract with this company. The contract contained a term that " no condition or warranty that the vehicle is road-worthy or as to its condition or fitness for any purpose is given by the owner or implied therein." One night a " car " was left outside the defendant's premises. It looked like the car in question. But it was a mere shell; the cylinder head was broken; all the valves were burnt; two pistons were broken, and it was incapable of self-propulsion.

The defendant refused to accept it or to pay the hire-purchase instalments; and, when sued for these, pleaded the state of the so-called car. In reply to this plea, the plaintiffs relied on the excluding term. The Court of Appeal held that the thing delivered was not the thing contracted for. The excluding term therefore did

---

1. *Chanter v. Hopkins* (1838), 4 M. & W. 399, at p. 404.
2. (1854), 10 Exch. 191. See also *Wieler v. Schilizzi* (1856), 17 C.B. 619.
3. *Suisse Atlantique Société D'Armement Maritime S.A.* v. *N.V. Rotterdamsche Kolen Centrale*, [1967] 1 A.C. 361, at p. 434; [1966] 2 All E.R. 61, at pp. 92–93.
4. [1956] 2 All E.R. 866; [1956] 1 W.L.R. 936.

not avail the plaintiffs, and judgment was given for the defendant.[1]

A parallel but distinct development has long been a feature of the law governing the carriage of goods by sea.   It is implied in every voyage charter-party and in all bills of lading that the ship will not depart from the route laid down in the contract, or, if none is there prescribed, from the normal trade route.   If, without lawful excuse, she does so depart, she is guilty of a deviation.   In *Joseph Thorley, Ltd.* v. *Orchis Steamship Co.*,[2]

Deviation
cases

> a cargo was shipped on a vessel described as " now lying in the port of Limassol and bound for London."   Instead of proceeding direct to London, the ship went first to a port in Asia Minor, then to a port in Palestine and then to Malta.   When she reached London, the cargo was damaged through the negligence of the stevedores.   The shipowners pleaded a term in the bill of lading exempting them from such liability.

It was held that the deviation, though it was not the direct cause of the damage, precluded the shipowners from relying on this term.   FLETCHER MOULTON, L.J., said:[3]

> " The cases show that, for a long series of years, the courts have held that a deviation is such a serious matter and changes the character of the contemplated voyage so essentially that a shipowner who has been guilty of a deviation cannot be considered as having performed his part of the bill of lading contract but something fundamentally different, and therefore he cannot claim the benefit of stipulations in his favour contained in the bill of lading."

The result of the " deviation " cases has been summarized by Lord WILBERFORCE.[4]

> " A shipowner, who deviates from an agreed voyage, steps out of the contract, so that clauses in the contract (such as exception or limitation clauses) which are designed to apply to the contracted voyage are held to have no application to the deviating voyage."

Bailments

From the carriage of goods by sea the courts turned to the carriage of goods by land, and thence to bailment in general.   In *Lilley* v. *Doubleday*,[5] the defendant agreed to store in his repository, goods owned by the plaintiff.   In fact he stored some of them in another warehouse.   These latter goods were destroyed by fire, though without the defendant's negligence.   The plaintiff was held to be entitled to recover their value.   By depositing them elsewhere than in his repository the defendant, had " stepped out of his contract," and he thus lost the benefit of any exemption clauses.   Such cases, based on the analogy of carriage of goods by sea and

---

1. In this case the car was spectacularly defective since (a) it was in very different condition when delivered than it had been when inspected and (b) in some platonic sense it was not a " car " at all, since it was incapable of self-propulsion.   But the principle was quickly extended to a situation where neither of these factors was present but simply a congeries of defects *Yeoman Credit* v. *Apps*, [1962] 2 Q.B. 508, [1961] 2 All E.R. 281.

    See also *Astley Industrial Trust* v. *Grimley*, [1963] 2 All E.R. 33; [1963] 1 W.L.R. 584 and *Charterhouse Credit Co.* v. *Tolly*, [1963] 2 Q.B. 683; [1963] 2 All E.R. 432.

2. [1907] 1 K.B. 660.   " Lawful excuse " covers, e.g. saving life or the ship itself.

3. [1907] 1 K.B., at p. 669.

4. *Suisse Atlantique, etc.* v. *N.V. Rotterdamsche, etc.*, [1967] 1 A.C. 361, at pp. 433–4; [1966] 2 All E.R. 61, at p. 93.

5. (1881), 7 Q.B.D. 510.   See also *Gibaud* v. *Great Eastern Rail. Co.*, [1921] 2 K.B. 426, at p. 435.

attended by similar consequences, are often described as instances of " quasi-deviation."

A later example of such quasi-deviation is given by *Alexander v. Railway Executive* :[1]

> The plaintiff was a stage performer. Together with an assistant, X, he had been on tour and he now deposited in the parcels office at Launceston Railway Station three trunks containing properties for what he called an " escape illusion." He paid 5d. for each trunk, obtained for each a ticket and promised to send instructions for their despatch. Some weeks later, and before such instructions were sent, X persuaded the parcels clerk by telling a series of lies to allow him to open the trunks and remove several articles. X was subsequently convicted of larceny. The plaintiff now sued the defendants for breach of contract and the defendants pleaded the following term: " Not liable for loss, misdelivery or damage to any articles which exceed the value of £5 unless at the time of deposit the true value and nature thereof have been declared by the depositor [and an extra charge paid]." There had been no such declaration or payment.

DEVLIN, J. gave judgment for the plaintiff. Sufficient notice, it is true, had been given of the term, but it did not cover the facts of the case: the word " misdelivery " was not apt to describe a deliberate delivery to the wrong person. Nor, if it did meet the facts, could it avail the defendants. They had been guilty of a " fundamental breach of contract " in allowing X to open the trunks and remove their contents.

The phrase " fundamental breach of contract," used in this case by DEVLIN, J., had been adopted fifteen years earlier by Lord WRIGHT, when he analysed the nature and effect of a contract for the carriage of goods by sea. *[Fundamental breach]*

> " An unjustified deviation is a fundamental breach of a contract of affreightment. . . . The adventure has been changed. A contract, entered into on the basis of the original adventure, is inapplicable to the new adventure."[2]

Whether a party has been guilty of such a fundamental breach is not an easy question to answer: each case must be examined in its context.[3] In border-line cases, much may turn upon the onus of proof. If the defendant pleads an excluding or limiting term and the plaintiff in reply alleges a fundamental breach, is it for the plaintiff to prove such a breach or for the defendant to disprove it?

The question was discussed in *Hunt and Winterbotham (West of England), Ltd. v. B.R.S. (Parcels), Ltd.*[4] *[Onus of proof in fundamental obligation cases]*

---

1. [1951] 2 K.B. 882; [1951] 2 All E.R. 442.
2. *Hain Steamship Co.* v. *Tate and Lyle, Ltd.*, [1936] 2 All E.R. 597, at pp. 607–608.
3. Compare *Hollins* v. *J. Davy, Ltd.*, [1963] 1 Q.B. 844; [1963] 1 All E.R. 370, and *Mendelssohn* v. *Normand, Ltd.*, [1970] 1 Q.B. 177; [1969] 2 All E.R. 1215. The criteria for deciding what is " fundamental " may very well vary between different types of contract. So courts have tended to regard the distinction between deliberate and careless breaches as relevant in bailment cases, but this seems to play no part in sale or hire-purchase. See *A. F. Colverd & Co., Ltd.* v. *Anglo Overseas Transport Co., Ltd.*, [1961] 2 Lloyds Rep. 352, and *John Carter* v. *Hanson Haulage (Leeds), Ltd.*, [1965] 2 Q.B. 495; [1965] 1 All E.R. 113.
4. [1962] 1 Q.B. 617; [1962] 1 All E.R. 111. See Wedderburn, [1962] C.L.J. 17; Aikin, 26 M.L.R. 98.

The defendants contracted with the plaintiffs to carry 15 parcels of woollen goods to Manchester. Only 12 parcels arrived. The plaintiffs sued the defendants for damages equal to the value of the 3 lost parcels, and the defendants pleaded a term of the contract limiting the amount which might be claimed for any such loss "however sustained." The plaintiffs alleged negligence but did not in their pleadings allege a fundamental breach. The defendants offered no evidence to explain why or where the parcels had been lost.

The Court of Appeal gave judgment for the defendants. On the assumption that the defendants had in fact been guilty of negligence, the term protected them unless they had committed a fundamental breach of contract. The vital question was to determine the onus of proof. The court held that the burden lay upon the plaintiffs and that they had not discharged it. Lord EVERSHED admitted that this conclusion was severe: the plaintiffs had no means of knowing how their goods had been lost, and the defendants could not or would not offer any explanation. But, hard as it may seem, it is not illogical. He who makes an allegation must prove it. It is for the plaintiff to make out a *prima facie* case against the defendant. If he succeeds in this task, it is for the defendant to plead and to prove some special plea such as an excluding or limiting term. The burden must then pass back to the plaintiff who must show some reason why the term is to be disregarded.

Rule of construction or rule of law

The courts have thus developed over a period of years two sets of rules. The failure to distinguish them has helped to blur the choice between two propositions: (1) that by a rule of law no excluding or limiting term may operate to protect a party who is in fundamental breach of his contract; and (2) that the question is not one of substantive law but depends upon the interpretation of the individual contract before the court. This distinction between a rule of law and a rule of construction permeates English law as a whole and in its long life has generated many curious subtleties and provoked many petty quarrels.[1] A rule of law is to be applied whether or not it defeats the intention of the parties. A rule of construction exists to give effect to that intention. Within the sphere of contract the doctrine of public policy operates as a rule of law: a contract which offends it is void despite the wishes of the parties. The effect of mutual mistake, on the other hand, is assessed by applying a rule of construction: it must be asked what, if anything, a reasonable person would think was " the sense of the promise."[2]

If there were a rule of law that no exemption clause however clear could exclude liability for fundamental breach, the nature of the exemption clause would be of vital significance. Where the clause went to define the extent of the promisor's obligation, the possibility of fundamental breach would be *pro tanto* excluded since nothing can be a fundamental breach which is not first a breach.[3] There was much academic discussion of the nature of

---

1. The rule in *Shelley's Case*, abrogated in 1925 after three centuries of controversy, is the classical example of this dichotomy. Its memory is happily embalmed in a judgment of sustained irony delivered by Lord MACNAGHTEN in *Van Grutten* v. *Foxwell*, [1897] A.C. 658, at pp. 670–6.
2. *Infra*, p. 225.
3. *The Angelia*, [1973] 2 All E.R. 144; [1973] 1 W.L.R. 210.

the doctrine[1] and puzzlement as to its content. Were there two distinct doctrines—breach of a fundamental term and fundamental breach or were they simply alternative formulations of the same doctrine? What was the relationship between fundamental terms and conditions? Could the doctrine be side-stepped by " shrinking the core of the contract," i.e. by the promisor accepting a small obligation from the beginning instead of accepting a larger obligation and trying to cut it down by exemption clauses?[2]

Before 1964 the tendency of the courts was to prefer the first of these alternatives and to rely upon a rule of law.[3] But in that year, PEARSON, L.J., chose the second alternative.

> " As to the question of fundamental breach," he said, " I think there is a rule of construction that normally an exception or exclusive clause or similar provision in a contract should be construed as not applying to a situation created by a fundamental breach of contract. This is not an independent rule of law imposed by the court on the parties willy-nilly in disregard of their contractual intention. On the contrary it is a rule of construction based on the presumed intention of the parties."[4]

Two years later the House of Lords was given the opportunity to indicate its preference in the case of *Suisse Atlantique Société D'Armement Maritime S.A.* v. *N.V. Rotterdamsche Kolen Centrale.*[5]

> The plaintiffs owned a ship which in December, 1956, they chartered to the defendants for the carriage of coal from the United States to Europe. The charter was to remain in force for two years' consecutive voyages. The defendants agreed to load and discharge cargoes at specified rates; and, if there was any delay, they were to pay a thousand dollars a day as demurrage. In September, 1957, the plaintiffs claimed that they were entitled to treat the contract as repudiated by the defendants' delays in loading and discharging cargoes. The defendants rejected this contention. In October, 1957, the parties agreed (without prejudice to their dispute) to continue with the contract. The defendants subsequently made eight round voyages. The plaintiffs then claimed all the money which they had lost through the delays. The defendants argued that the claim must be limited to the agreed demurrage for the actual days in question. The plaintiffs replied that the delays were such as to entitle them to treat the contract as repudiated: the demurrage clause therefore did not apply, and they could recover their full loss.

Rationale of fundamental breach: Suisse Atlantique case

Mr. Justice MOCATTA, the Court of Appeal and the House of Lords all held that the plaintiffs must fail. They had elected to

---

1. See, e.g. Montrose, 15 Can. Bar Rev. 760; Unger, 4 Business L.R. 30; Melville, 19 M.L.R. 26; Guest, 77, L.Q.R. 98; Reynolds, 79 L.Q.R. 534; Montrose, [1964] C.L.J. 60, 254; Devlin, [1966] C.L.J. 192.
2. See Wedderburn, [1957] C.L.J. 12; [1960] C.L.J. 11. No doubt a shrunken core would be less attractive to a potential promissee than an apparently whole apple. See also Barton, 87 L.Q.R. 20 on possible use of a deed as a method of exemption.
3. See *Alexander* v. *Railway Executive*, [1951] 2 K.B. 882; [1951] 2 All E.R. 442, *supra*, p. 161; *Karsales (Harrow), Ltd.* v. *Wallis*, [1956] 2 All E.R. 866; [1956] 1 W.L.R. 936, *supra*, p. 159; *Yeoman Credit, Ltd.* v. *Apps*, [1962] 2 Q.B. 508; [1961] 2 All E.R. 281.
4. *U.G.S. Finance, Ltd.* v. *National Mortgage Bank of Greece, S.A.*, [1964] 1 Lloyd's Rep. 446, at p. 453. See also the valuable judgments of the High Court of Australia in *Sydney City Council* v. *West* (1965) 114 C.L.R. 481, and *Thomas National Transport (Melbourne) Pty., Ltd.* v. *May and Baker (Australia) Pty., Ltd.*, [1966] 2 Lloyd's Rep. 347.
5. [1967] 1 A.C. 361; [1966] 2 All E.R. 61. Treitel, 29 M.L.R. 546; Drake, 30 M.L.R. 531; Jenkins, [1969] C.L.J. 257.

affirm the contract, and the demurrage clause applied.   But in the House of Lords, and for the first time, the plaintiffs argued that the defendants had been guilty of a fundamental breach of contract which prevented them from relying on a " limiting term." The House of Lords rejected this argument.   There was, on the facts, no fundamental breach, nor was the provision for demurrage a " limiting term ": it was a statement of agreed damages in the event of delay.   In the result it was unnecessary for the House of Lords to discuss the meaning and effect of fundamental breach.   But the arguments offered to them by the plaintiffs raised issues of general contractual importance which they felt they must examine.   Their opinions, though not technically binding on the courts, represent views which cannot be disregarded.

Rules of construction for exception clauses

The five members of the House of Lords who heard the *Suisse Atlantique* case approved, with some doubts but no dissent, the approach to the problem of fundamental breach which PEARSON, L.J., had preferred in 1964.   The rules to be applied should be regarded as rules of construction and not as rules of law.[1]   The inferences to be drawn from their judgments were surveyed in 1970 by Professor Coote in his article, *The Effect of Discharge by Breach on Exception Clauses*.[2]   " There is already in existence," he wrote, " an impressive array of interpretative devices for containing exception clauses." He described seven such instruments of discipline.

" (a) Every exception clause is to be interpreted, in case of ambiguity, *contra proferentem*.
(b) Only in the clearest circumstances will general words of exclusion be interpreted to cover important terms or liability for serious breaches.   The more important the term or the breach, the clearer those circumstances must be.
(c) Exception clauses are to be interpreted consistently with the main object of the contract; and, under this head, the literal meaning can be modified substantially.
(d) In case of genuine inconsistency with the positive parts of the contract, exception clauses can be modified or ignored altogether on grounds of repugnancy.
(e) Exception clauses have no application to acts falling beyond the contemplated ambit of the contract.
(f) General words of exclusion have no application to negligence unless negligence is the only liability to which they could apply.
(g) In bailment contracts, exception clauses have no application once the bailee exceeds any limitation on his authority."

Rules discussed

Of these " devices," (a), (b) and (f) are variations on the theme of ambiguity already discussed.[3]   A party to a contract, who inserts a term designed for his protection, must make his meaning clear; and, if he fails to do so, his words will be read against him.

---

1. It is noteworthy however that their Lordships did not think any of the earlier cases in which the rule was treated as one of law were incorrect in the result.   Both Lord REID and Lord WILBERFORCE appeared to reserve the possibility that there might be super-fundamental breaches liability for which could not be excluded.
2. [1970] C.L.J. 221.   The article offers a valuable approach to a complex and controversial problem, and the present writers are greatly indebted to it.
3. *Supra,* pp. 152–4.

This is a readily intelligible canon of construction, without as well as within the law, and requires neither to be excused nor classified. Devices (c) and (d) suppose a conflict between the exception clause and the main purpose of the contract. The clause must then be read in the light of the contract as a whole and, if necessary, subordinated to that purpose. It is not improper to describe these two devices as rules of construction, though Lord WILBERFORCE had lingering doubts.

> " One may safely say that the parties cannot, in a contract, have contemplated that the [exceptions] clause should have so wide an ambit as in effect to deprive one party's stipulations of all contractual force; to do so would be to reduce the contract to a mere declaration of intent. To this extent it may be correct to say that there is a rule of law against the application of an exceptions clause to a particular type of breach. But short of this, it must be a question of contractual intention whether a particular breach is covered or not."[1]

Stronger doubts may be felt on the nature of devices (e) and (g). The rules governing the effect of a departure from the contemplated ambit of the contract, if they are not rules of law, bear a singular resemblance to them. In view of Professor Coote's well-founded insistence that deviation cases are *sui generis*, it might have been better to segregate them from the rest of the devices. Fashioned at a time when the hazards of the sea were many and the means of communication few, the rules laid down in these cases were bound to be peremptory. When the same rules were extended by analogy to the carriage of goods by land, they might more happily have been brought under the general head of bailment—itself an independent concept.[2] In truth it is not easy to classify any particular judicial weapon as substantive law or as canon of interpretation.

A serious problem in the interpretation of the *Suisse Atlantique* case is that their Lordships attached substantial significance to the fact that the plaintiffs had affirmed the contract. This suggests that the result would have been different if the plaintiffs had terminated the contract, e.g. by sailing away.[3] It has been suggested that this was a reference to the position after sailing away. This would make good sense but it is difficult to see how questions could arise about delays in loading and unloading once the ship had sailed away. It seems more probable therefore that their Lordships meant that the exemption clauses might be disregarded in deciding whether there had been a sufficient breach to entitle the promisor to terminate the contract and that if he did so the excluding or limiting clauses could be treated as ineffective. If this is correct, fundamental breach would continue to this extent to be a rule of law.

Effect of affirmation

It is perhaps unfortunate for the harmonious development of the law in this area that the leading modern authority should have had atypical facts. As a result the Court of Appeal in two later

---

1. *Suisse Atlantique* case: [1967] A.C. 361, at p. 432; [1966] 2 All E.R. 61, at p. 92.
2. *Supra*, pp. 78–80, and p. 153.
3. Cf. *Charterhouse Credit Co.* v. *Tolly*, [1963] 2 Q.B. 683; [1963] 2 All E.R. 432.

cases has come very close to restating the rule as one of law.[1]   In *Kenyon, Son & Craven, Ltd.* v. *Baxter Hoare & Co., Ltd.*[2] DONALDSON, J., made a valiant attempt to achieve a synthesis between the *Suisse Atlantique* case and its successors.[3].

> The defendant warehousemen took delivery of some 5,000 bags of shelled groundnuts for eventual delivery to the plaintiffs.   The nuts were put in a warehouse which was structurally sound but, because of a gap at the bottom of the doors when closed, not rat proof.   The contract included a clause excluding the defendant's liability for loss or damage to the goods " unless such loss or damage is due to the wilful neglect or default of the defendants or their servants."   There were manifest signs of rat infestation over a period of 18 months but the defendants' servants took no effective steps to repel the rats or to secure the groundnuts against them. When the groundnuts were eventually delivered the bags were found to be substantially damaged and the contents contaminated.

DONALDSON, J., thought that the defendants' conduct would, absent an exemption clause, have been negligent, but that it did not amount to " wilful neglect or default " since there was no element of deliberation in it.   The plaintiffs argued however that the exemption clause should be disregarded on grounds of fundamental breach.   DONALDSON, J., rejected this argument. He relied on Lord WILBERFORCE's statement in *Suisse Atlantique* that a fundamental breach is either:[4]

> " (i) a performance totally different from that which the contract contemplates [or] (ii) a breach of contract more serious than one which would entitle the other party merely to damages and which (at least) would entitle him to refuse performance or further performance under the contract."

He thought that in respect of the second class, fundamental breach was no more than a rule of construction but that in the first class (which can be treated as consisting of cases of deviation or quasi-deviation) it might continue after *Suisse Atlantique* to be a rule of law.   The two earlier decisions of the Court of Appeal could be regarded as in the first class but the present case was in the second class and as a matter of construction the defendants has used words clear enough to exclude their liability.   This is an attractive reconciliation though it is not perhaps easy to find express support for Lord WILBERFORCE's classification in the other speeches in *Suisse Atlantique*.[5]

Over the years Parliament has come to intervene more and more extensively in this area.   This intervention has so far been piecemeal, that is, it has operated by the prohibition or regulation

---

1. *Harbutt's Plasticine, Ltd.* v. *Wayne Tank and Pump Co., Ltd.*, [1970] 1 Q.B. 447; [1970] 1 All E.R. 255; *Farnworth Finance Facilities Ltd.* v. *Attryde*, [1970] 2 All E.R. 774; [1970] 1 W.L.R. 1053.   These cases, especially the former, have been subjected to powerful criticism.   See Weir, [1970] C.L.J. 189; Baker, 33 M.L.R. 441.   See also Legh-Jones and Pickering, 86 L.Q.R. 513, 87 L.Q.R. 515; Dawson, 91 L.Q.R. 380; Fridman, 7 Alberta L.R. 281.
2. [1971] 2 All E.R. 708; [1971] 1 W.L.R. 519.
3. See also the valuable judgment of KERR, J., in *The Angelia*, [1973] 2 All E.R. 144; [1973] 1 W.L.R. 210.
4. [1967] 1 A.C., at p. 431; [1966] 2 All E.R., at p. 91.
5. Nor is it perhaps totally clear that *Harbutt's Plasticine, Ltd.* v. *Wayne Tank & Pump Co., Ltd.* and *Farnworth Finance Facilities* v. *Attryde* would properly fall into the first class rather than the second.

of exemption clauses in particular types of contract rather than by the enactment of rules applicable to all contracts. The intervention has been largely but by no means exclusively in the field of consumer protection and in this area Part II of the Fair Trading Act 1973 has now given the Secretary of State a discretion to make orders, on the recommendation of the Consumer Protection Advisory Committee, regulating unfair consumer trade practices.[1] Such an order might forbid the use of particular types of exemption clause in particular situations and it would then be a criminal offence to insert such a term in such a contract. This is a radical new departure from the usual legislative technique of declaring the clause void.[2]

We cannot give an exhaustive list of such provisions here but a number of examples may be given.[3]

Statutory
provisions

(1) The Road Traffic Act 1960, s. 151, provides that

" A contract for the conveyance of a passenger in a public service vehicle shall, so far as it purports to negative or restrict the liability of a person in respect of a claim which may be made against him in respect of the death of, or bodily injury to, the passenger while being carried in, entering or alighting from the vehicle, or purports to impose any conditions with respect to the enforcement of such liability, be void."[4]

(2) A similar, but not identical, provision is contained in the Transport Act 1962. By s. 43 (7) it is enacted that

" The Boards[5] shall not carry passengers by rail on terms or conditions which (a) purport, whether directly or indirectly, to exclude or limit their liability in respect of the death, or bodily injury to, any passenger other than a passenger travelling on a free pass; or (b) purport, whether directly or indirectly, to prescribe the time within which, or the manner in which, any such liability may be enforced."

Any such terms or conditions " shall be void and of no effect."

(3) It is provided by s. 3 of the Misrepresentation Act 1967, that

" If any agreement (whether made before or after the commencement of this Act) contains a provision which would exclude or restrict—

(a) any liability to which a party to a contract may be subject by reason of any misrepresentation made by him before the contract was made; or

(b) any remedy available to another party to the contract by reason of such a misrepresentation;

that provision shall be of no effect except to the extent (if any) that, in any proceedings arising out of the contract, the court or arbitrator may allow reliance on it as being fair and reasonable in the circumstances of the case."

---

1. For a full account, see Cunningham, *The Fair Trading Act 1973: Consumer Protection and Competition Law*, Chap. 3, pp. 30–41.
2. Where a clause is simply declared void, a tradesman may continue to insert it in his contracts and it will give him effective protection against those who do not know the law or do not take legal advice—a very large proportion of the population!
3. See also Grunfeld, 24 M.L.R. 62, at p. 64–5; Patents Act 1949, s. 57.
4. This section was discussed by the Court of Appeal in *Gore* v. *Van der Lann* (*Liverpool Corporation Intervening*), [1967] 2 Q.B. 31; [1967] 1 All E.R. 360. See *supra*, p. 153. See also Motor Vehicles (Passenger Insurance) Act 1971.
5. Four Boards were created by the Transport Act 1962, including the British Railways Board. The Transport Act 1968, has drastically changed the organisation.

The section is discussed more fully elsewhere.[1]

(3) For the general law of contract, the most significant statute is the Supply of Goods (Implied Terms) Act 1973.[2] We have already seen that the act makes a number of changes in the terms to be implied in contracts of sale and hire-purchase.[3] It also makes a number of very important changes in the ability of the seller[4] to exclude the obligations which would otherwise be implied.[5]

(a) There is an absolute prohibition on the seller excluding the implied condition that he has a right to sell the goods.[6] The only qualification is that a transaction is permitted where the " seller " contracts to sell only such interests as he has, but in such a transaction the " seller " impliedly covenants that he has disclosed all incumbrances known to him and that the " buyer " will enjoy quiet possession.[7]

(b) In a consumer sale, any attempt to exclude the terms as to the quality of the goods, contained in ss. 13, 14, 15 of the Sale of Goods Act is void.[8] A " consumer sale " is defined as

> " a sale of goods (other than a sale by auction or by competitive tender) by a seller in the course of a business where the goods—
> (a) are of a type ordinarily bought for private use or consumption; and
> (b) are sold to a person who does not buy or hold himself out as buying them in the course of a business."

(c) In other sales a test of reasonableness is applied. An exemption clause shall " not be enforceable to the extent that it is shown that it would not be fair or reasonable to allow reliance on the term." The Court is given guidance on what is reasonable and directed to pay particular attention to the following matters:

> " (a) the strength of the bargaining positions of the seller and buyer relative to each other, taking into account, among other things, the availability of suitable alternative products and sources of supply;
> (b) Whether the buyer received an inducement to agree to the term or in accepting it had an opportunity of buying the goods or suitable alternatives without it from any source of supply;
> (c) Whether the buyer knew or ought reasonably to have known of the existence and extent of the term (having regard, among other things, to any custom of the trade and any previous course of dealing between the parties);

---

1. See *infra*, pp. 277–9.
2. Amended as to terminology only by **Consumer** Credit Act 1974, Sch. 4. The Act is substantially based on the **Law** Commission's first report on exemption clauses (1969). The second report, published October 1975, proposes analogous legislation for **the** provision of services.
3. See *supra*, p. 129.
4. In the account which follows, we shall **talk** for the simplicity of sellers and contracts of sale; there are **parallel provisions** for owners and contracts of hire purchase, which will be cited **in** the notes.
5. For a fuller account see Benjamin's *Sale of Goods* (1974), paras. 969–991. Despite its title the Act does not apply to all contracts for the supply of goods. So it may, e.g. be necessary to determine whether a contract is one of sale or for work and materials.
6. Ss. 4, 12.
7. Ss. 1, 8.
8. Ss. 4, 12.

(d) where the term exempts from all or any of the provisions of section 13, 14 or 15 of this Act if some condition is not complied with, whether it was reasonable at the time of the contract to expect that compliance with that condition would be practicable;

(e) whether the goods were manufactured, processed, or adapted to the special order of the buyer.[1]

It should be noted that the act does not here displace the common law rules so that a term which is reasonable under the above tests, might, be held ineffective to exclude liability under the doctrine of fundamental breach.

It should perhaps be mentioned in conclusion that Parliament may not only invalidate or regulate exemption clauses but may also impose them. The classic example is the Hague Rules, which by the Carriage of Goods by Sea Act 1924,[2] are mandatory in Bills of Lading covering cargo carrying voyages from U.K. ports.[3] These rules provide for the limitation of the carrier's liability. Such rules are commonly to be found in international conventions on carriage.[4]

---

1. Ss. 4, 12.
2. As amended by the Carriage of Goods by Sea Act 1971 when it comes into force.
3. The rules are incorporated by agreement or imposed by the legislation of other countries in many other cases.
4. See, e.g. the Warsaw Convention on carriage by air incorporated into English Law by the Carriage by Air Act 1932.

PART III
UNENFORCEABLE CONTRACTS

SUMMARY

THE elements required to form a contract have now been considered. Where they are all present, the parties are entitled to assume that the expectations reasonably raised by their conduct will be sanctioned by the courts. It will be necessary hereafter to examine the circumstances in which this assumption may be defeated in greater or in less degree by the presence of other factors—by mistake, for example, which at common law may make the contract " void," or by misrepresentation, which may make it " voidable." But the English law has not been content to classify contracts as " valid " on the one hand and as " void " or " voidable " on the other. It has allowed an intermediate position, where a contract, though valid, may yet be " unenforceable " by an action at law unless and until certain technical requirements are satisfied. The " unenforceable contract " is clearly a creature of procedural rather than of substantive law; and the origin of so peculiar a position is to be found in the passage, as long ago as 1677, of the Statute of Frauds. It is necessary, therefore, to examine the history of this statute and to observe its surviving effects in the modern law.

CHAPTER ONE

History and Policy of the
Statute of Frauds

Statute of
Frauds,
ss. 4 and 17
OF the twenty-five sections of this Statute, two have been important
in the history of contract, s. 4 and s. 17.

Section 4:

"No action shall be brought whereby to charge any executor or
administrator upon any special promise to answer damages out of
his own estate; or whereby to charge the defendant upon any
special promise to answer for the debt, default or miscarriage of
another person; or to charge any person upon any agreement made
upon consideration of marriage; or upon any contract or sale of
lands, tenements or hereditaments, or any interest in or concerning
them; or upon any agreement that is not to be performed within
the space of one year from the making thereof; unless the agreement upon which such action shall be brought, or some memorandum or note thereof, shall be in writing and signed by the party to
be charged therewith or some other person thereunto by him lawfully authorised."

Section 17:

"No contract for the sale of goods, wares or merchandizes for
the price of £10 sterling or upwards shall be allowed to be good
except the buyer shall accept part of the goods so sold and actually
receive the same, or give something in earnest to bind the bargain
or in part payment, or that some note or memorandum in writing
of the said bargain be made and signed by the parties to be charged
by such contract or their agents thereunto lawfully authorised."

The *raison
d'être* of the
Statute
The *raison d'être* of the Statute is to be found partly in the
conditions of seventeenth-century litigation and partly in the
background of social and political uncertainty against which it
must be focused. On the one hand, the difficulty of finding
the facts in a common law action was considerable. Not only
were juries entitled to decide from their own knowledge and
apart from the evidence, but no proper control could be exercised
over their verdicts. Moreover, until the middle of the nineteenth
century, a ludicrous rule of the common law forbade a person
to testify in any proceedings in which he was interested, and the
parties to a contract might have to suffer in silence the ignorant
or wanton misconstruction of facts which they alone could have

set in a proper light.[1] The mischief had been aggravated by the acceptance in the sixteenth century of the validity of mutual promises unaccompanied by formality or by the proof of a *quid pro quo*, or, in other words, by the adoption of the principle of purely consensual contracts. On the other hand, the confusion attending the rapid succession of Civil War, Cromwellian dictatorship and Restoration had encouraged unscrupulous litigants to pursue false or groundless claims with the help of manufactured evidence. The statute, therefore, avowed as its object " prevention of many fraudulent practices which are commonly endeavoured to be upheld by perjury and subornation of perjury."

Contemporary conditions, while they suggest the necessity for some Parliamentary intervention, do not explain the particular form which it took. To modern eyes the choice of contracts in ss. 4 and 17 appears quite arbitrary. It has to be remembered, however, that these form but a small part of the statute, the bulk of which is devoted to the protection of proprietary interests in general. Writing was thus required to support the conveyance of land, the creation of leases, the proof of wills and declarations of trust;[2] and, in 1677, the adolescent law of contract was itself regarded as but a species of the law of property.[3] On this assumption it might be supposed that all contracts would have been included within the scope of the statute, and such, indeed, was apparently the original intention.[4] The reasons for the rejection of this draft and the substitution of specified types of contract remain a matter of speculation. Of the six selected, the close association with the conveyance of property doubtless explains the presence of contracts for the sale of goods, for the sale of interests in land, and, perhaps, with the growing importance of settlements, of agreements in consideration of marriage. A naïve reluctance to rely upon belated recollection apparently prompted the inclusion of agreements not to be performed within a year. Of guarantees and promises by representatives to meet debts out of their own pockets it is only possible to say that, as the language of the section suggests, they were regarded by contemporary lawyers as of a " special " character, either because they appeared strangely disinterested or offered peculiar opportunities to the perjurer. It is interesting, and perhaps significant, that these insular reasons for legislative intervention found a counterpart in parallel action on the Continent, where the acceptance of liability based on promise raised similar difficulties. It has, indeed, been suggested that a French Ordonnance of 1566, and possibly a later Ordonnance of 1667, offered the model or supplied the impetus to the English Statute of 1677.[5]

Upon the foundations thus darkly laid a vast structure of

Only six classes of contracts affected

Defective drafting of the Statute

1. Readers of Pickwick Papers will remember that, in the case of *Bardell* v. *Pickwick*, neither the plaintiff nor the defendant entered the witness-box; Chap. 34. On the history of the Statute, see Holdsworth, *History of English Law*, VI, 379–97; Simpson, *History*, Chap. XIII.
2. Sections 1–3, 5–9.
3. Thus Blackstone described the Statute as " a great and necessary security to private property." Comm. iv., p. 432.
4. See the original draft set out in Holdsworth, *History of English Law*, VI, Appendix I.
5. See Rabel, 63 L.Q.R. 174.

case law has been erected.   Its extent may be gauged from the space accorded to it in standard text-books, not only in England but in America, where the provisions of the statute have been generally accepted.[1]   Through this maze of litigation it is difficult to trace any guiding principle.   But it is possible to suggest some clues to the underlying, and sometimes unconscious, aspirations of the judges.   In the first place, the language of the statute was more than usually obscure.   This fault has been judicially emphasized for at least two hundred years and is not confined to any one section.   Of ss. 5 and 6, relating to wills, Lord MANSFIELD declared the draftsmanship to be " very bad."   He could not believe Lord HALE to be its author " any further than perhaps leaving some loose notes behind him which were afterwards unskilfully digested."[2]   Sir James Stephen, in his analysis of s. 17, concluded that the draftsman failed to understand the words he used and had but an imperfect appreciation of his own intentions.[3]   Lord WRIGHT in 1939 summarized the cases on ss. 4 and 17 as " all devoted to construing badly-drawn and ill-planned sections of a statute, which was an extemporaneous excrescence on the common law."[4]

Statute not
literally
interpretedIn the second place, the literal application of so imperfect a statute was likely to defeat its cardinal aim and to convert it into a potent instrument of fraud.   The honest man disdained, the rogue coveted, its assistance.   Lord MANSFIELD said that " the very title and the ground on which the statute was made have been the reason of many exceptions against its letter,"[5] and his colleague, WILMOT, J., declared that, " had it always been carried into execution according to the letter, it would have done ten times more mischief than it has done good, by protecting, rather than preventing, frauds."[6]   A hundred years later Sir James Stephen expressed himself even more strongly.   " The special peculiarity of the 17th section of the Statute of Frauds is that it is in the nature of things impossible that it ever should have any operation, except that of enabling a man to escape from the discussion of the question whether he has or has not been guilty of a deliberate fraud in breaking his word."[7]   In the third place, the statute, it has been seen, was the product of a particular social and professional environment, and, when conditions changed, the statute itself lost its *raison d'être*.   After the Evidence Act 1851 had permitted litigants to offer oral evidence in courts of common law, it became a conspicuous anachronism.   Once more to quote

---

1. Thus, of the 344 pages which comprise the first edition of *Blackburn on Sale,* published in 1845, 117 are devoted to the interpretation of section 17, and even in the eighth edition of *Benjamin on Sale* (1950) 140 pages are required to deal with the same section.   In *Williston on Contracts,* 3rd Edn., the discussion of sections 4 and 17 occupies six chapters and over eight hundred pages.
2. *Wyndham* v. *Chetwynd* (1757), 1 Wm. Bl. 95.
3. 1 L.Q.R. 1 (1885).
4. *Legal Essays and Addresses,* at p. 226.   The uniform tenor of judicial criticism is interrupted by the lone voice of Lord KENYON, who declared the Statute to be " very beneficial " and to be " one of the wisest laws in our Statute Book."   See *Chater* v. *Beckett* (1797), 7 Term Rep., at p. 204, and *Chaplin* v. *Rogers* (1800), 1 East, 192, at p. 194.   The approval of Lord NOTTINGHAM, as a part-author of the Statute, may be dismissed as *ex parte.*
5. *Anon.* (1773), Lofft, 330.
6. *Simon* v. *Motovis* (1766), 1 Wm. Bl. 599, at p. 601.
7. 1 L.Q.R. 1.

Sir James Stephen, " it is a relic of times when the best evidence on such subjects was excluded on a principle now exploded."[1]

It is not surprising that the judges, impelled by these considerations, should have attempted to avoid the worst effects of the statute by a strained construction of its language. But the process, while often serving justice, more often made confusion worse confounded; and, by the end of the nineteenth century, practitioner and student alike had to pick their way through a tangle of case law behind which the original words of the statute were barely perceptible. In 1893, s. 17 was repealed and replaced by s. 4 of the Sale of Goods Act. Sir M. D. Chalmers, when he drafted this section, did so with obvious reluctance, observing wistfully that the Statute of Frauds had " never applied to Scotland and Scotsmen never appear to have felt the want of it ";[2] but it could not well have been omitted in an Act designed as a measure of codification. In 1925 the provision in s. 4 of the Statute of Frauds governing contracts for the sale of interests in land was repealed and re-enacted with slight modifications by s. 40 of the Law of Property Act 1925; and this re-enactment may be justified by the relative complexity of the land law and the consequent need to secure ample time for investigation and reflection.

Tendency of
judges to
evade the
Statute

While these portions of the Statute of Frauds were being re-produced in modern legislation, criticism of the statute itself became ever more prevalent and ever more vocal. It was condemned by Sir Frederick Pollock in 1913[3] and by Sir William Holdsworth in 1924,[4] and in 1932 Professor Williams ended his study of s. 4 with the words " the case for the repeal of the Statute seems unanswerable."[5] The Law Revision Committee recommended in 1937 that both s. 4 of the Statute of Frauds and s. 4 of the Sale of Goods Act should be repealed. But their report was not accepted, and in 1952 the question was remitted to the Law Reform Committee. They also recommended repeal, but with one modification. Contracts of guarantee, in their opinion, were traps for the unwary and required special treatment. " Inexperienced people might be led into undertaking obligations which they did not fully understand," and unscrupulous persons might " assert that credit had been given on the faith of a guarantee which in fact the alleged surety had no intention of giving."[6] They thought, therefore, that this particular class of contract should retain the protection which it had long enjoyed. The proposals of the Committee were this time accepted. By the Law Reform (Enforcement of Contracts) Act 1954, s. 4 of the Sale of Goods Act was repealed and all s. 4 of the Statute of Frauds save in so far as it concerned " any special promise to answer for the debt, default or miscarriage of another person." The Statute has been an unconscionable time dying and even now is not quite dead. To the surviving aspects of its long and dismal story it is now necessary to turn.

Law
Revision
Committee

---

1. 1 L.Q.R. 1.
2. See Chalmers, *Sale of Goods Act*, 12th Edn. (1945), p. 26.
3. 29 L.Q.R. 247.
4. Holdsworth, *History of English Law*, VI, 396.
5. Williams, *The Statute of Frauds, Section IV*, p. 283.
6. See Law Reform Committee First Report, Cmd. 8809. A minority of the earlier Committee in 1937 had felt an equal solicitude for the victims of spurious guarantees, but had suggested a different remedy; *infra*, p. 178.

CHAPTER TWO

The Statute of Frauds, Section 4, and the Law of Property Act 1925, Section 40

IT is necessary to discuss in turn the two types of contract which may still be unenforceable under these Acts and their interpretation by the courts, the manner in which their technical requirements may be satisfied, and the effect of non-compliance.

A. THE TWO TYPES OF CONTRACT AND THEIR INTERPRETATION

Contract of guarantee

1. SPECIAL PROMISE TO ANSWER FOR THE DEBT, DEFAULT OR MISCARRIAGE OF ANOTHER PERSON

When the Law Revision Committee first reported in 1937, a minority thought that contracts of guarantee should be *void* unless the terms were embodied in a written document. The later Committee, while sharing the view that such contracts offered peculiar perils to the unsophisticated, preferred to retain the old, if scarcely hallowed, language familiar to generations of lawyers, and with it the special quality of " unenforceability." The words quoted above were therefore saved from the general wreck of s. 4 of the Statute of Frauds, and they have still to be applied, encrusted as they are with nearly three centuries of judicial interpretation.

It seems tolerably clear that the Parliament of 1677 designed by these words to cover promises by one person to guarantee the liability of another. But the determination of their exact scope has proved an arduous and complicated task. An obvious difficulty is the significance of the three terms, " debt, default or miscarriage," unless, indeed, they are synonymous. The question was raised in 1819 in *Kirkham* v. *Marter*.[1]

The defendant's son had, without the plaintiff's permission, ridden the plaintiff's horse and killed him, and he was therefore guilty of a tort against the plaintiff. The plaintiff threatened to sue him, and, in consequence of this threat, the defendant orally promised the plaintiff to pay to him the agreed value of the horse if the plaintiff would forbear his suit.

The defendant, when sued on this promise, pleaded the Statute of Frauds, and the plaintiff argued that the statute applied only where the liability guaranteed arose out of a pre-existent debt. The argument was rejected.

" The word ' miscarriage,' " said Chief Justice ABBOTT, " has not the same meaning as the words ' debt ' or ' default.' It seems to me to comprehend that species of wrongful act for the consequences of which the law would make the party civilly responsible."

The words of the statute were not confined to cases of contract; and, as the son had been guilty of a tort for which he might be sued, the father's undertaking was a " promise to answer for the miscarriage of another person." It would seem, therefore, that the guarantee in the case of a contractual liability is covered by the word " debt " and, perhaps, by that of " default," and the guarantee of a tortious liability by the word " miscarriage."

This conclusion may be accepted as a reasonable interpretation of terms which had no precise legal meaning. It is more difficult to justify the construction placed by the judges on the requirement that the liability guaranteed must be that " of another person." They decided that the legislature intended by these words to confine the statute to cases where the defendant had made a direct promise to the plaintiff to guarantee him against the default of some third party. It was thus held in *Eastwood* v. *Kenyon*[2] that, if the promise was made, not to the creditor, but to the debtor himself, the statute did not apply.

Margin notes:
Meaning of " debt, default, miscarriage "

Liability guaranteed must be that of a third party

---

1. (1819), 2 B. & Ald. 613.
2. (1840), 11 Ad. & El. 438, at p. 446.

" The facts were " said Lord DENMAN " that the plaintiff was liable to a Mr. Blackburn on a promissory note; and the defendant, for a consideration, . . . promised the plaintiff to pay and discharge the note to Blackburn.   If the promise had been made to Blackburn, doubtless the Statute would have applied: it would then have been strictly a promise to answer for the debt of another; and the argument on the part of the defendant is that it is not less the debt of another, because the promise is made to that other, viz. the debtor, and not to the creditor, the statute not having in terms stated to whom the promise, contemplated by it, is to be made.   But upon consideration we are of opinion that the Statute applies only to promises made to the person to whom another is answerable."

Third party must continue to be liable

By a more comprehensive process of interpretation it has also been ruled that the use of the words " of another person " assumes the continued existence of some primary liability owed by a third party to the plaintiff, to which the defendant's guarantee is subsidiary and collateral.   A distinction has thus been taken between an arrangement whereby the original debtor continues liable and one in which he is discharged.   In other words, a contract is not a guarantee within the statute unless there are three parties—the creditor, the principal debtor and the secondary debtor or guarantor.   The essence of the contract is that the guarantor agrees, not to discharge the liability in any event, but to do so only if the principal debtor fails in his duty.   There are thus two cases in which a contract is excluded from the statute on the ground that the promisor is not in fact answering " for another person."

If third party eliminated, Statute does not apply

The first case is where the result of a contract is to eliminate a former debtor and to substitute a new debtor in his place.   Here it is idle to speak of guaranteeing the debt of another since that other has been released from all liability.   As was said in an early case, if two come to a shop and one buys, and the other says to the seller:—

" ' Let him have the goods, I will be your paymaster,' or ' I will see you paid,' this is an undertaking as for himself, and he shall be intended to be the very buyer and the other to act but as his servant."[1]

These words, though striking and often quoted, must be taken, not as an infallible test for the operation of the statute, but as an indication of the parties' intention.   Whatever the language used, the question must be whether they intended that the promisor should assume sole or subsidiary liability.   Even the stark phrase, " Let him have the goods, I will see you paid," when thus read in the light of the context, may mean no more than, " If he does not pay, I will."

Again, suppose that a seller is unwilling to accept further orders from a buyer unless payment is made or security given for goods already supplied.   If there is an oral agreement by which the creditor agrees to supply further goods to the debtor in consideration that X will assume sole responsibility for the existing debt, the statute does not apply.   X's undertaking releases the original debtor from the liabilities so far incurred, and it is

---

1. *Birkmyr* v. *Darnell* (1704), 1 Salkeld 27.

thus absolute and not in any way conditional upon non-payment by a third party.[1]

Secondly, a contract is not within the statute if there has never at any time been another person who can properly be described as the principal debtor. This is well illustrated by *Mountstephen* v. *Lakeman*.[2]

If no third party debtor, Statute does not apply

> The defendant was chairman of the Brixham Local Board of Health. The surveyor to the board proposed to the plaintiff, a builder, that he should construct the connections between the drains of certain houses and the main sewer. The plaintiff desired to know how he was to be paid, and the following conversation took place:
> Defendant: " What objection have you to making the con-
>   nections?"
> Plaintiff: " I have none, if you or the board will order the work or become responsible for the payment."
> Defendant: " Go on, Mountstephen, and do the work, and I will see you paid."
> The plaintiff did the work and debited the board, which disclaimed liability on the ground that they had never directly or indirectly made any agreement with him. The plaintiff then sued the defendant, who pleaded the statute.

The court had to consider the purpose and effect of the conversation between the parties. Did it mean that the defendant guaranteed a liability that primarily rested upon the board, or that he himself assumed an original and sole liability? Only in the former case could there be a contract to answer for the debt " of another person." Since the board had not ordered the work to be done and therefore was not a debtor in any sense of the word, it was held that the defendant was himself the only debtor and that his promise was outside the statute.

The court in this case sought to emphasize the distinction by suggesting appropriate nomenclature. If the undertaking was collateral and within the statute, it was to be described as a " guarantee ", if original and outside it, as an " indemnity."[3] Such terminology is doubtless of service in clarifying the issues to be faced. But contracting parties cannot be expected to use words as legal terms of art, and it remains for the court to interpret the sense of their agreement rather than to accept their language at its face value. If its purpose is to support the primary liability of a third party, it is caught by the statute, whatever the words by which this intention is expressed. If there is no third party primarily liable, the statute does not apply.[4]

Guarantee and indemnity

These variations upon the theme " of another person," if

---

1. *Goodman* v. *Chase* (1818), 1 B. & Ald. 297.
2. (1871), L.R. 7 Q.B. 196; affd. (1874), L.R. 7 H.L. 17.
3. See Blair, 29 M.L.R. 522; Stein 90 L.Q.R. 246.
4. See *Guild & Co.* v. *Conrad*, [1894] 2 Q.B. 885, and compare the language of Vaughan Williams, L.J., in *Harburg India Rubber Comb Co.* v. *Martin*, [1902] 1 K.B. 778, at pp. 784–5. The distinction between guarantee and indemnity has passed from the Statute of Frauds into the general conceptual equipment of the English lawyer. See its application in the field of infants' contracts in *Yeoman Credit, Ltd.* v. *Latter*, [1961] 2 All E.R. 294, [1961] 1 W.L.R. 828, Furmston, 24 M.L.R. 648; *Stadium Finance Co., Ltd.* v. *Helm* (1965), 109 Sol. Jo. 471, Stein, 90 L.Q.R. 246, at pp. 251–254; and in the field of recourse agreements between finance companies and dealers *Unity Finance, Ltd.* v. *Woodcock*, [1963] 2 All E.R. 270; [1964] 1 W.L.R. 945; *Goulston Discount Co., Ltd.* v. *Clark*, [1967] 2 Q.B. 493; [1967] 1 All E.R. 61. See also *Western Credit, Ltd.* v. *Alberry*, [1964] 2 All E.R. 938; [1964] 1 W.L.R. 945.

somewhat artificial, may be allowed to rest upon the inherent
ambiguity of the language.   A further distinction can be regarded
only as a deliberate evasion of the statute.[1]   Even though the
defendant's promise is undoubtedly a " guarantee " and not an
" indemnity," it will still be outside the statute, if it is merely
an incident in a larger transaction.   To come within the statute
the guarantee must be the main object of the transaction of which
it forms a part.   The courts have adopted this argument in two
types of case.

The first is where the defendant has given a guarantee in his
capacity as a *del credere* agent.   A *del credere* agent is one who,
for an extra commission, undertakes responsibility for the due
performance of their contracts by persons whom he introduces to
his principal.   Thus in *Couturier* v. *Hastie*[2] the plaintiffs orally
employed the defendants as *del credere* agents to sell a cargo of
corn.   The defendants sold it to a Mr. Callander in ignorance
of the fact that, at the time of the sale, it had ceased to exist as
a commercial entity.   Mr. Callander, when he learned the truth,
repudiated liability and the plaintiffs sued the defendants on their
implied guarantee.   The defendants pleaded, *inter alia*,[3] the
Statute of Frauds, and the court rejected the plea.   A higher
reward had been paid to them, said PARKE, B.,[4] in consideration

> " of their assuming a greater share of responsibility than ordinary
> agents, namely, responsibility for the solvency and performance of
> their contracts by their vendees.   This is the main object of the
> reward being given to them; and, though it may terminate in a
> liability to pay the debt of another, that is not the immediate object
> for which the consideration is given."

This language was adopted and applied by the Court of Appeal
in *Sutton & Co.* v. *Grey*.[5]   The defendants had undertaken to
introduce clients to a firm of stockbrokers.   It was orally agreed
that the defendants should receive half the commission earned
from the resulting transactions and that they should be liable for
half the losses caused by the default of the clients.   It was held
that this last liability, though in essence a guarantee, was but
part of a wider agreement and outside the statute.

The second type of case is where the defendant enjoys legal
rights over property which is subject to an outstanding liability due
to a third party.   If, in order to relieve the property from the
incumbrance, he guarantees the discharge of the liability, his
promise is excluded from the statute and is binding even though
made orally.   In *Fitzgerald* v. *Dressler* :[6]

> A sold linseed to B, who re-sold it at a higher price to C.   A, as
> the seller, was entitled to a lien over the goods; he was free, that
> is to say, to keep them in his possession until he had received pay-
> ment from B.   C was anxious to obtain immediate possession, and
> A agreed to make delivery to C before he had been paid by B, in
> return for C's oral promise to accept liability for this payment.

Marginal notes:

Guarantee
not within
the Statute
if part only
of a larger
contract

Promise by
del credere
agent not
within the
Statute

Guarantee
for protection
of his
property
given by
owner not
within the
Statute

---

1. See the remarks of Lord WRIGHT in *Legal Essays and Addresses*, at
   pp. 226–230.
2. (1852), 8 Exch. 40.
3. The case also raised vital questions upon the effect of mistake.   See *infra*,
   p. 208.
4. 8 Exch. 40, at p. 55.
5. [1894] 1 Q.B. 285.
6. (1859), 7 C.B.N.S. 374.

It was argued that this promise was a guarantee within the meaning of the statute on the ground that, since B remained liable to A, C had in effect promised to discharge B's liability only if B himself failed to do so. The court rejected the argument and held C bound by his promise.

> "At the time the promise was made, the defendant was substantially the owner of the linseed in question, which was subject to the lien of the original vendors for the contract price. The effect of the promise was neither more nor less than this, to get rid of the incumbrance, or, in other words, to buy off the plaintiff's lien. That being so, it seems to me that the authorities clearly establish that such a case is not within the statute."[1]

The result of such cases, however convenient, is so manifest a gloss upon the statute as, in more recent years, to disturb the judicial conscience. It has therefore been ruled that their reasoning will apply only where the defendant was the substantial owner of the property for the protection of which the guarantee was given. If he has no more than a personal interest in its security, he will be within the ambit of the statute. Thus in *Harburg India Rubber Comb Co.* v. *Martin*:[2]

Harburg India Rubber Comb Co. v. Martin

> The defendant was the director of and a shareholder in the Crowdus Accumulator Syndicate, Ltd., which he had in fact financed. The plaintiffs were judgment creditors of the syndicate and had sought by a writ of *fieri facias* to levy execution upon its property. The defendant orally promised the plaintiffs that he would indorse bills for the amount of the debt, if they would withdraw their writ.

The Court of Appeal held that the promise was a guarantee, not an indemnity, and that it did not fall within either of the exceptions discussed above. The defendant was not a debenture-holder but a shareholder, and he had no property in the goods upon which the plaintiffs sought to levy execution. His interest, therefore, was personal rather than proprietary. VAUGHAN WILLIAMS, L.J., sought to rationalize and to delimit the scope of the exceptions.

> "Whether you look at the 'property cases' or at the '*del credere* cases,' it seems to me that in each of them the conclusion arrived at really was that the contract in question did not fall within the section because of the object of the contract. In each of these cases there was in truth a main contract—a larger contract—and the obligation to pay the debt of another was merely an incident of the larger contract. . . . If the subject-matter of the contract was the purchase of property, the relief of property from a liability, the getting rid of incumbrances, the securing greater diligence in the performance of the duty of a factor, or the introduction of business into a stockbroker's office—in all those cases there was a larger matter which was the object of the contract. That being the object of the contract, the mere fact that as an incident to it—not as the immediate object, but indirectly—the debt of another to a third person will be paid, does not bring the case within the section. This definition or rule for ascertaining the kind of cases outside the section covers both 'property cases' and '*del credere* cases.' "

---

1. At p. 394. See also *Williams* v. *Leper* (1766), 3 Burr. 1886.
2. [1902] 1 K.B. 778. See also *Davys* v. *Buswell*, [1913] 2 K.B. 47.

The courts, in applying this part of the section, may thus be confronted with two separate questions. Is the contract a guarantee or an indemnity, and, even if an undoubted guarantee, was it the main object of the parties' solicitude or a mere incident in a larger transaction? The answers given by generations of judges to these questions produce a result which would have astonished the draftsmen of the statute. It also suggests serious doubts as to the wisdom of retaining the old language and its unwieldy accumulation of case law. If it must be assumed that contracts of guarantee require special treatment, it would surely have been better to adopt the minority view of 1937 and declare such contracts void unless their terms were embodied in a written document. The slate would at least have been wiped clean and the judges enabled to approach their problems afresh unhampered by the subtleties and evasions of the past.

2. ANY CONTRACT FOR THE SALE OR OTHER DISPOSITION OF LAND OR ANY INTEREST IN LAND

Law of Property Act 1925

These words, now to be found in s. 40 (1) of the Law of Property Act 1925, replace the old wording of s. 4 of the Statute of Frauds, " any contract or sale of lands, tenements or hereditaments or any interest in or concerning them." The differences are purely linguistic: no substantial alteration in the law seems to have been intended or effected, and the old decisions still apply.

Is the produce of the soil goods or land?

The words " any interest in land " are comprehensive and cover leases as well as sales. They have thus been held to comprise agreements to take or let furnished lodgings or to shoot over land or to take water from a well.[1] A contract will fall within s. 40 (1) if it has as one term a sale or other disposition of land, even though there are many other terms.[2]

The main difficulty, however, has been concerned with the classification of the produce of the soil. Are such products to be regarded as interests in land or as interests in goods? The latter were originally governed, not by s. 4, but by s. 17 of the Statute of Frauds, and afterwards by s. 4 of the Sale of Goods Act 1893. If the products of the soil are interests in land, s. 40 (1) of the Law of Property Act 1925, contemplates a written memorandum as the sole method of satisfying the procedural requirements, while, if they are goods, the Sale of Goods Act admitted other possibilities. Now that s. 4 of the Sale of Goods Act has been repealed, they either fall within s. 40 (1) of the Law of Property Act 1925, or they are exempt from any special statutory form.

Fructus industriales and fructus naturales

The problem has in the past provoked the courts to a display of learning which may be described, according to taste, as nice or pedantic and most of which, fortunately, may now be discarded.

---

1. *Inman* v. *Stamp* (1815), 1 Stark., 12; *Webber* v. *Lee* (1882), 9 Q.B.D. 315; *Tyler* v. *Bennett* (1836), 5 Ad. & El. 377.   See also *Lavery* v. *Pursell* (1888), 39 Ch.D. 508, where it was held that the sale of a house which provided that the house was to be demolished and the materials removed was the sale of an interest in land.   For a more comprehensive discussion, see Farrand, *Contract and Conveyance*, 2nd Edn., pp. 29–33.
2. *Steadman* v. *Steadman*, [1974] Q.B. 161; [1973] 3 All E.R. 977 (C.A.). This point was not argued in the House of Lords, [1974] 2 All E.R. 977; [1974] 3 W.L.R. 56.

The primary distinction at common law was between *fructus industriales* and *fructus naturales*. *Fructus industriales* have been defined as " corn and other growths of the earth produced not spontaneously, but by labour and industry "; *fructus naturales* as the spontaneous product of the soil, such as grass and even planted trees, where " the labour employed in their planting bears so small a proportion to their natural growth."[1] The antithesis, it must be confessed, is somewhat unreal: the cultivation of fruit trees requires as much skill and industry as the cultivation of wheat and barley. But the idea underlying the distinction would seem to be the contrast between seeds that require to be planted afresh each year and the perennial produce of the soil, even if, as in the case of fruit trees, the parent stock has been originally planted by the hand of man.

Fructus industriales have always been regarded as goods. The classification of *fructus naturales* has caused more difficulty. At common law it appeared to depend upon the moment contemplated in the contract of sale for their severance from the soil. If they were to remain unsevered for so long a time that the buyer would derive a substantial benefit from their continued attachment to the soil, the sale was of an interest in land; if no such benefit was contemplated, it was a sale of goods.[2]

Position at common law

But the word " goods " was defined afresh by s. 62 of the Sale of Goods Act 1893.

Statutory definition

> " Goods . . . include emblements and things attached to or forming part of the land, which are agreed to be severed before sale or under the contract of sale."

" Emblements " in turn have been defined as " such vegetable products as are the annual result of agricultural labour,"[3] and are to be identified with *fructus industriales*. These, as has already been stated, have always been regarded as goods, and the rest of the statutory definition may thus be taken to include *fructus naturales*. But as a purchaser, save in the most unlikely case, buys the produce of the soil with a view to its ultimate severance, and as severance, at whatever date it is effected, must be effected " under the contract of sale," the apparent result of the statutory definition is to make every sale of *fructus naturales* a sale of goods. It has been suggested, however, that the definition is confined to the purposes of the Sale of Goods Act and that outside the ambit of this Act the older learning may still prevail. On this assumption an agreement to sell *fructus naturales* may be (a) a contract for the sale of goods within the Sale of Goods Act and (b) a contract for the sale of an interest in land within the Law of Property Act. If it is thus living a double life, the requirements of s. 40 of the latter Act must still be met.[4] Support for this view may be found in *dicta* of the Court of Appeal in *Saunders*

---

1. *Per* Lord COLERIDGE, C.J., in *Marshall* v. *Green* (1875), 1 C.P.D. 35, at pp. 39 and 40.
2. *Marshall* v. *Green* (1875), 1 C.P.D. 35.
3. See Chalmers *Sale of Goods Act 1893*, 14th Edn., pp. 181–2.
4. Megarry and Wade, *The Law of Real Prioerty*, 4th Edn., pp. 548–9. The definition of " land " in s. 205 (ix) of the Law of Property Act 1925, is undoubtedly wide.

v. *Pilcher*.[1] In this case a fruit grower had bought a cherry orchard " inclusive of this year's fruit crop." The decision itself turned upon the meaning and application of the Income Tax Act 1918; but counsel for the taxpayer had pressed the Court with the definition of " goods " in the Sale of Goods Act. The court declined to consider it. " The short answer, " said SINGLETON, L.J., " is that the Act has no application to a sale of land."[2] The statement was admittedly *obiter*, and the point seems still open to argument.[3]

B. THE STATUTORY REQUIREMENTS

". . . The agreement upon which such action shall be brought, or some memorandum or note thereof, shall be in writing and signed by the party to be charged therewith or some other person thereunto by him lawfully authorized."

Such was the language applied by s. 4 of the Statute o f Frauds to all the contracts within its scope and which still applies to the " special promise to answer for the debt, default or miscarriage of another person." It is substantially repeated by s. 40 (1) of the Law of Property Act 1925, and may be assumed to govern both contracts of guarantee and contracts affecting interests in land. The efforts of the courts to interpret these words have provoked a wilderness of cases through which it is possible only to indicate the hazardous and inconsequent paths trodden by the unwilling feet of litigants.[4]

1. THE CONTENTS OF THE "NOTE OR MEMORANDUM"

Nature of the memorandum

The agreement itself need not be in writing. A " note or memorandum " of it is sufficient, provided that it contains all the material terms of the contract. Such facts as the names or adequate identification of the parties,[5] the description of the subject-matter,[6] the nature of the consideration,[7] comprise what may be called the minimum requirements. But the circumstances of each case need to be examined to discover if any individual term has been deemed material by the parties; and, if so, it must be included in the memorandum.[8]

There are however a number of qualifications to this principle. First, it appears that a term which will in any case be implied need not be expressed. So if the parties have agreed that vacant

---

1. [1949] 2 All E.R. 1091.
2. *Ibid.*, at p. 1103.
3. See Hudson, 22 Conv. (N.S.) 137; Benjamin's *Sale of Goods*, (1974), pp. 55–59.
4. Many problems were necessarily worked out on the parts of the Statute now repealed; but these cases will still apply, *pari passu*, to the surviving fragments.
5. Compare *Potter* v. *Duffield* (1874), L.R. 18 Eq. 4, and *Rossiter* v. *Miller* (1878), 3 App. Cas. 1124, *per* Lord CAIRNS, at pp. 1140–1.
6. Compare *Caddick* v. *Skidmore* (1857), 2 De G. & J. 52, and *Plant* v. *Bourne*, [1897] 2 Ch. 281.
7. As a special statutory exception, the consideration need not be stated in a document offered in support of an agreement " to answer for the debt, default or miscarriage of another person." Mercantile Law Amendment Act 1856, s. 3.
8. *Tweddell* v. *Henderson*, [1975] 2 All E.R. 1096; [1975] 1 W.L.R. 1496.

possession should be given on completion, the memorandum will not be defective if it omits this term, since it would in any case be implied. Secondly, if the omitted term is entirely for his favour, a plaintiff may enforce the contract as evidenced by the memorandum and waive the benefit of the omitted term.[1] Conversely, it has been argued that if an omitted term is entirely for the defendant's benefit, a plaintiff should be entitled to submit to the term, that is, to enforce the contract as evidenced in the memorandum plus the omitted term. This exception was applied in *Martin* v. *Pycroft*,[2] denied in *Burgess* v. *Cox*[3] and is now apparently reinstated by *Scott* v. *Bradley*.[4]

Provided, however, that the document relied on by the plaintiff does contain all the material terms, it need not have been deliberately prepared as a memorandum. The courts have accepted as sufficient a telegram, a recital in a will, a letter written to a third party,[5] a written offer,[6] and even a letter written by the defendant with the object of repudiating his liabilities.[7] All that is required is that the " memorandum " should have come into existence before the commencement of the action brought to enforce the contract. Thus in *Farr, Smith & Co.* v. *Messers, Ltd.*[8] an action was started against the defendants in the name of certain plaintiffs, and a statement of defence was filed which set out the terms of the agreement in question. Leave was then given to amend the writ and statement of claim by striking out the original plaintiffs and substituting the plaintiff company. It was held that this new step was in effect the commencement of a new action, and that the original statement of defence, signed by counsel as the defendant's agent, could therefore be regarded as a sufficient memorandum to satisfy the statute.

Document need not have been prepared as memorandum

A document which denies that there is a contract cannot in general be a sufficient memorandum.[9] There is one clear exception to this rule. A written offer will suffice even though it shows on its face that at the time it was written there was no contract.[10] In a recent group of cases the Court of Appeal has been concerned with a second possible exception. In *Griffiths* v. *Young*[11] the agreement was originally " subject to contract " and the memorandum so stated.[12] Subsequently the parties

---

1. *North* v. *Loomes*, [1919] 1 Ch. 378. In *Hawkins* v. *Price*, [1947] Ch. 645; [1947] 1 All E.R. 689, EVERSHED, J., said *obiter* that a plaintiff could not waive a " material " term but it is not clear why not if it is entirely for his benefit. No doubt most " material " terms will usually be for the benefit of both parties and therefore outside the exception.
2. (1852), 2 De. G.M. & G. 785.
3. [1951] Ch. 383; [1950] 2 All E.R. 1212, criticised Megarry, 67 L.Q.R. 299.
4. [1971] 1 Ch. 850; [1971] 1 All E.R. 583.
5. See *Godwin* v. *Francis* (1870), L.R. 5 C.P. 295: *Re Hoyle, Hoyle* v. *Hoyle*, [1893] 1 Ch. 84; *Gibson* v. *Holland* (1865), L.R. 1 C.P. 1.
6. *Parker* v. *Clark*, [1960] 1 All E.R. 93; [1960] 1 W.L.R. 286.
7. *Buxton* v. *Rust* (1872), L.R. 7 Exch. 279.
8. [1928] 1 K.B. 397. See also *Grindell* v. *Bass*, [1920] 2 Ch. 487.
9. *Thirkell* v. *Cambi*, [1919] 2 K.B. 590.
10. *Warner* v. *Willington* (1856), 3 Drew 523, at p. 532; *Reuss* v. *Picksley* (1866), L.R. 1 Exch. 342, at p. 350.
11. [1970] Ch. 675; [1970] 3 All E.R. 601. The many difficulties in this case are exposed by Prichard, 90 L.Q.R. 55.
12. Made up by the combination of letters exchanged by the parties' solicitors, joined together under the rules discussed; *infra*, pp. 189–191.

agreed that the agreement should become binding at once.   It was held that the memorandum was sufficient even though it appeared to state that there was no contract on the ground that the phrase " subject to contract " was a suspensive condition, which had been lifted.   In *Law* v. *Jones*[1] the Court of Appeal (RUSSELL, L.J., dissenting) took this decision a stage further. In this case the parties made an unconditional oral contract for the sale of land but the solicitors' letters which constituted the only possible memorandum were all marked " subject to contract." The majority accepted that a document which denied the existence of a contract would not do but thought that a document marked " subject to contract " did not so much deny the existence of a contract as contemplate that a contract would in the future come into existence.   The validity of this distinction was denied by a differently constituted Court of Appeal in *Tiverton Estates, Ltd.* v. *Wearwell, Ltd.*,[2] where on substantially similar facts it was held that there was no sufficient memorandum.   This decision seems both technically correct and practically convenient, since it had been widely thought that the decision in *Law* v. *Jones* would inhibit the progression of normal " subject to contract " correspondence between conveyancing solicitors.[3]

2. THE SIGNATURE

Only the person whom it is sought to hold liable on the agreement, or his agent, need sign the memorandum.   A plaintiff who has not signed can sue a defendant who has.[4]

" Signature " loosely interpreted

The word " signature " has been very loosely interpreted. In the first place, it need not be a subscription; that is to say, it need not be at the foot of the memorandum, but may appear in any part of it, from the beginning to the end.   In the second place, it need not, in the popular sense of the word, be a " signature " at all.   A printed slip may suffice, if it contains the name of the defendant.   This relaxation of the statutory language was well established a hundred years ago and offers a striking instance of the way in which legislation may be overlaid by judicial precedent.

> " If the matter were *res integra* ", said BLACKBURN, J., in 1862,[5]
> " I should doubt whether a name printed or written at the head of a bill of parcels was such a signature as the statute contemplated; but it is now too late to discuss that question.   If the name of the party to be charged is printed or written on a document intended to be a memorandum of the contract, either by himself or his authorized agent, it is his signature, whether it is at the beginning or middle or foot of the document."

1. [1974] Ch. 112; [1973] 2 All E.R. 437.
2. [1974] 1 All E.R. 209; [1974] 2 W.L.R. 176.   The Court of Appeal held that it was not bound by the decision in *Law* v. *Jones* since that decision was inconsistent with the earlier decision of the Court of Appeal in *Thirkell* v. *Cambi*, [1919] 2 K.B. 590.   Cf. Emery, [1974] C.L.J. 42.   The Court of Appeal also thought the *ratio decidendi* of *Griffiths* v. *Young* incorrect, though the case might be correctly decided because of further facts not set out in the text above.
3. Since it would open the door to allegations that there was an oral contract.
4. *Laythoarp* v. *Bryant* (1836), 2 Bing. N.C. 735.
5. *Durrell* v. *Evans* (1862), 1 H. & C. 174, at p. 191.

A more modern example of generous interpretation is offered by the case of *Leeman* v. *Stocks.*[1]

> The defendant instructed an auctioneer to offer his house for sale. Before the sale the auctioneer partially filled in a printed form of agreement of sale by inserting the defendant's name as vendor and the date fixed for completion.   The plaintiff was the highest bidder, and after the sale the auctioneer inserted in the form the plaintiff's name as purchaser, the price and a description of the premises. The plaintiff signed the form.   The defendant then refused to carry out the contract, and the plaintiff sued for specific performance. The defendant pleaded failure to satisfy s. 40 (1) of the Law of Property Act 1925, and in particular that he had never signed any document.

It was held that there was a sufficient memorandum to satisfy the statute and that the defendant was liable.   It was true that he had not " signed " it in the ordinary sense of the word.   But his agent, acting with his authority, had inserted his name as vendor into the printed form, and this form was clearly designed to constitute the final written record of the contract made between the parties.[2]

In whatever position the " signature " is found, however, it must be intended to authenticate the whole of the document. If it refers only to certain parties or is a mere incidental or isolated phenomenon, it cannot be relied on by the plaintiff.   So in *Caton* v. *Caton*:[3]

> Mr. Caton proposed to marry Mrs. Henley.   He wrote out a document, beginning: " In the event of a marriage between the under-mentioned parties, the following conditions as a basis for a marriage settlement are mutually agreed on."   Then followed several sentences, each in this fashion: " Caton to do so and so, Henley to have so and so."   Neither party signed the paper, either personally or through agents, nor was a settlement ever executed.

It was held that the mere fact that the names appeared in various parts of the document did not make them signatures within the meaning of the statute, for in no single instance did it appear that they were intended to cover the whole of the document.

Where the memorandum is alleged to be signed by an agent, it must be shown that the agent has actual or ostensible authority to sign a memorandum.   So, for instance, an estate agent, although undoubtedly for some purposes an agent of the vendor, does not necessarily have authority to sign a memorandum on his behalf.[4]

3. THE JOINDER OF SEVERAL DOCUMENTS

The framers of the Statute of Frauds clearly contemplated the inclusion of all the contractual terms in a single document.   But here again the judges, in their anxiety to protect honest intentions from the undue pressure of technicality, have departed widely

---

1. [1951] 1 Ch. 941; [1951] 1 All E.R. 1043.
2. Perhaps illogically a more stringent test has been adopted where a signed memorandum has been altered after signature: *New Hart Builders, Ltd.* v. *Brindley*, [1975] 1 All E.R. 1007; [1975] 2 W.L.R. 595.
3. (1867), L.R. 2 H.L. 127.
4. *Gavaghan* v. *Edwards*, [1961] 2 Q.B. 220; [1961] 2 All E.R. 477 (criticised Albery, 78 L.Q.R. 178); *Davies* v. *Sweet* [1962] 2 Q.B. 300; [1962] 1 All E.R. 92.

from the original severity of the statute.   The reports reveal a progressive laxity of interpretation.

Express reference by signed document to another document

It was already settled by the beginning of the nineteenth century that the plaintiff might rely on two or more documents to prove his case.   But at this period it was still necessary that the one document should specifically, and on its face, refer to the other.   To introduce oral evidence so as to form a connecting link between them would be to permit the very process which the statute sought to exclude.   Thus in *Boydell* v. *Drummond*[1] the defendant had agreed to take a number of Shakespearian engravings, to be published over a course of years.   The terms of the agreement were contained in a prospectus which was exhibited in the plaintiff's shop and which the defendant had seen.   The defendant, however, had signed only a book, entitled " Shakespeare Subscribers, their Signatures," which did not refer to the prospectus and which contained no terms at all. The court refused to allow the plaintiff to prove by oral evidence that the book was intended to be read with the prospectus and so to satisfy the statute.

> " If ", said LE BLANC, J.,[2] " there had been anything in that book which had referred to the particular prospectus, that would have been sufficient.   If the title to the book had been the same with that of the prospectus, it might perhaps have done.   But as the signature now stands, without reference of any sort to the prospectus, there was nothing to prevent the plaintiff from substituting any prospectus and saying that it was the prospectus exhibited in his shop at the time, to which the signature related. The case therefore falls directly within this branch of the Statute of Frauds."

Implicit reference by one document to another document

By insisting upon an internal and express reference in one document to the other, the courts, while abandoning the letter, might claim to be promoting the spirit of the statute.   But in the latter half of the nineteenth century they took a more uncompromising step.   They still excluded oral evidence designed to introduce a second document to which no reference at all was made in the first.   But if, without any express reference, the language or form of the document signed by the defendant indicated another document as relevant to the contract, oral evidence was allowed to identify that other.   Thus in *Pearce* v. *Gardner*[3] an envelope and a letter, shown by oral evidence to have been enclosed in it, were allowed to form a joint memorandum within the meaning of the statute.   So, too, in *Long* v. *Millar*[4] the plaintiff was allowed to couple a written agreement to buy land, which he had signed, with a receipt for the deposit, which the defendant had signed.   The present state of the law is illustrated by the case of *Timmins* v. *Moreland Street Property, Ltd.*[5]

> At a meeting between the parties the defendants agreed to buy the plaintiff's freehold property for £39,000.   At this meeting the defendants gave to the plaintiff a cheque for £3,900 as deposit on the price.   The cheque was made out to X and Co., the plaintiff's

---

1. (1809), 11 East, 142.
2. 11 East, 142, at p. 158.
3. [1897] 1 Q.B. 688.
4. (1879), 4 C.P.D. 450.   See also *Stokes* v. *Whicher,* [1920] 1 Ch. 411.
5. [1958] Ch. 110; [1957] 3 All E.R. 265.

solicitors. The plaintiff then gave to the defendants a receipt, which he signed, in which he described the sum of £3,900 as " deposit for the purchase of [named premises] which I agree to sell at £39,000." Later the defendants stopped the cheque and repudiated the contract. The plaintiff sued for breach of contract. The defendants pleaded s. 40 of the Law of Property Act 1925. The plaintiff sought to read together the cheque which the defendants had signed and the receipt which he himself had signed so as to form a complete memorandum.

The Court of Appeal, with some reluctance, gave judgment for the defendants. The law was thus stated by Jenkins, L.J.:[1]

" It is still indispensably necessary, in order to justify the reading of documents together for this purpose, that there should be a document signed by the party to be charged, which, while not containing in itself all the necessary ingredients of the required memorandum, does contain some reference, express or implied, to some other document or transaction. Where any such reference can be spelt out of a document so signed, then parol evidence may be given to identify the other document referred to, or, as the case may be, to explain the other transaction, and to identify any document relating to it. If by this process a document is brought to light which contains in writing all the terms of the bargain so far as not contained in the document signed by the party to be charged, then the two documents can be read together so as to constitute a sufficient memorandum for the purposes of section 40."

A plaintiff, therefore, who wishes to use this means of escape from the strict letter of the statute, must prove:

(1) the existence of a document signed by the defendant;
(2) a sufficient reference, express or implied, in that document to a second document;
(3) a sufficiently complete memorandum formed by the two when read together.

In the present case there was a cheque signed by the defendants, and, if this could be read with the receipt, the two documents might have furnished the required memorandum. But the cheque was made payable, not to the plaintiff, but to a firm of solicitors, and there was nothing on it which served to connect it with the property in question. The plaintiff accordingly failed to satisfy the second of the three conditions stated above, and could not overcome the statutory defence.

C. THE EFFECT OF NON-COMPLIANCE WITH THE STATUTORY REQUIREMENTS

It is declared in s. 4 of the Statute of Frauds, and substantially repeated in s. 40 (1) of the Law of Property Act, that " no action shall be brought " upon the agreements involved unless the necessary memorandum is forthcoming. The value to be placed upon these words has varied at different periods and has been diversely assessed at common law and in equity.

---

1. [1958] Ch., at p. 120; [1957] 3 All E.R., at p. 276.

I. AT COMMON LAW

At first
contract held
to be void

It was at first considered by the common law judges that the effect of non-compliance with the Statute of Frauds was to avoid the contract. Thus Blackstone said that, in the five cases covered by s. 4, " a mere verbal *assumpsit* is void ";[1] and this doctrine was applied with logical severity in 1837 in the case of *Carrington* v. *Roots*.[2] The plaintiff had made an oral agreement to buy a growing crop of grass, with liberty to enter the land and to cut and remove it. He accordingly brought a horse and cart on to the field. The seller removed the horse and cart and the plaintiff sued him in trespass. The Court held that the agreement was caught by the statute, and that the plaintiff could not sue, even in trespass, on any matter arising out of it, as this would be to " charge " the defendant upon it. In the words of Lord ABINGER,

> " The meaning of the statute is, not that the contract shall stand for all purposes except that of being enforced by action, but it means that the contract shall be altogether void."[3]

Contract
now held to
be merely
unenforceable
by action

Even at this date, however, doubts were expressed at so rigorous an interpretation,[4] and in 1852, the year after the passage of the Evidence Act, it was abandoned in favour of a more liberal view. In *Leroux* v. *Brown*:[5]

> An oral agreement was made in France whereby the defendant, resident in England, agreed to employ the plaintiff, a British subject resident in France, for a period exceeding one year. The plaintiff sued in England for a breach of the contract.

The action, as it concerned a foreign contract, was subject to the rules of Private International law. By the operation of these rules upon this particular case, questions affecting the validity of the contract were governed by French law, questions of procedure by English law. By French law the contract, though oral, was valid. If, therefore, the effect of the Statute of Frauds was to invalidate the oral contracts enumerated in s. 4, the plaintiff would succeed; French law would govern and the statute would be irrelevant. But if the statute affected procedure only, it would govern the case and the plaintiff would fail. The court preferred the latter view and gave judgment for the defendant.

> " I am of opinion," said JERVIS, C.J.,[6] " that the fourth section applies, not to the solemnities of the contract, but to the procedure, and therefore that the contract in question cannot be sued upon here. The contract may be capable of being enforced in the country where it was made, but not in England. . . . The statute, in this part of it, does not say that, unless those requirements are complied with, the contract shall be void, but merely that no action shall be brought upon it. . . . This may be a very good agreement, though, for want of a compliance with the requisites of the statute, not enforceable in an English court of justice."

---

1. Comm. iii, 157–8.
2. (1837), 2 M. & W. 248.
3. At p. 255.
4. See BOSANQUET, J., in *Laythoarp* v. *Bryant* (1836), 2 Bing. N.C. 735, at p. 255.
5. (1852), 12 C.B. 801.
6. 12 C.B. 801, at p. 824.

The principle of *Leroux* v. *Brown* was affirmed by the House of Lords in *Maddison* v. *Alderson* in 1883.[1]

> " It is now finally settled," said Lord BLACKBURN, " that the true construction of the Statute of Frauds, both the 4th and the 17th sections, is not to render the contracts within them void, still less illegal, but is to render the kind of evidence required indispensable when it is sought to enforce the contract."

Failure to satisfy the requirements of the Statute of Frauds or of s. 40 (1) of the Law of Property Act does not, therefore, affect the validity but only the enforceability of the contract. It should be observed, however, that a plaintiff will be caught by the statutory provisions whenever he is forced to rely upon the contract for success in a common law action, even if he does not directly claim damages for its breach. Thus in *Delaney* v. *T. P. Smith, Ltd.*,[2]

> the plaintiff in April, 1944, made an oral agreement with the defendants' agent to become tenant of the defendants' house as soon as it had been repaired. After the agreement, and before the repairs were completed, the defendants notified the plaintiff that they had decided to sell the house to a third party. The plaintiff then " made a clandestine entry " into the house and a week later was forcibly ejected by the defendants. He sued them in trespass.

The Court of Appeal held that his action must fail. As the defendants were the owners of the house, the plaintiff had no *locus standi* against them unless he could prove a tenancy agreement. But this he could not do in the absence of a written memorandum. He was in effect " bringing an action on a contract for the disposition of an interest in land," and he must, in the words of WYNN-PARRY, J.,

> " satisfy s. 40 of the [Law of Property] Act or prove such part performance as will take the case out of the section. If this were not so, then it would follow that a person in the plaintiff's position, who has nothing more than an oral agreement to grant a tenancy, upon which therefore he cannot bring an action either for specific performance or damages, may, if he is able to effect a clandestine entry, on eviction successfully bring trespass . . . So to hold would be in my view to defeat the section."

From the premise that the effect of non-compliance with the statutory requirements is procedural and not substantive three inferences have been drawn. *Results of this rule*

In the first place, it is possible to justify the conclusion, already observed,[3] that the memorandum required need not be contemporaneous with the formation of the agreement—a conclusion difficult to sustain if the agreement were void *ab initio*. *(i) Memorandum may be subsequent to the contract*

It follows, in the second place, that the defendant may treat the statutory requirements as designed to confer a privilege upon him, which he may waive if he so pleases. The rules of court, *(ii) Defendant may waive the Statute*

---

1. (1883), 8 App. Cas. 467, at p. 488.
2. [1946] K.B. 393; [1946] 2 All E.R. 23. The case, it will be seen, is similar in result to *Carrington* v. *Roots, supra*, p. 192, though non-compliance with the statute no longer makes a contract void.
3. *Supra*, p. 187.

indeed, have gone further, and have declared that, if he wishes to avail himself of the privilege, he must expressly plead it.[1]

(iii) The contract may be used as a defence

In the third place, a contract, which fails to satisfy the statutory requirements, while it may not be sued upon at common law, may yet be used in certain circumstances as a defence.   If money has been paid or if property has passed in pursuance of such a contract, the transferor will not be allowed to sue for its recovery.   As the contract, though unenforceable, is nevertheless valid, the transferee has obtained a good title.   Thus in *Thomas* v. *Brown*[2] the parties made an oral contract for the sale of land, under which the purchaser paid a deposit to the vendor.   The purchaser then decided not to go on with the transaction and brought an action to recover the deposit.   The action failed.   The seller, while he could not have sued on the contract, could use it to justify the retention of the deposit.

2. IN EQUITY

The doctrine of part performance

When the majority of common law judges so patently disapproved of the Statute of Frauds and stigmatized it as a potential instrument of fraud, it is not surprising that Equity should take the same view.   Within ten years of its enactment successive Chancellors were prepared to interfere where it worked manifest injustice.   They could not, indeed, grant damages and defy the common law, but they could and did apply their peculiar remedy of specific performance.   As early as 1685 such a decree was made to enforce the observance of an unsigned agreement for the sale of land.[3]   This equitable intervention was developed in the course of the next two centuries, and has come to be known as the doctrine of part performance.   Through its operation a modern litigant, though he is unable to claim damages for breach of a contract which is caught by s. 40 of the Law of Property Act and which fails to satisfy its provisions, may yet obtain from the Chancery Division a decree of specific performance.   It is necessary to consider in turn the underlying basis of the equitable doctrine, the type of contract to which it applies and the conditions required for its operation.

(i) Underlying basis of equitable doctrine

Origin was prevention of fraud

Equity judges have had considerable difficulty in justifying their intervention, not, indeed, in common sense, but as a matter of legal principle.   They were content at first to interfere in obvious cases of fraud without examining too closely the implications of their action; but even so they were conscious of some embarrassment in reconciling the grant of decrees with the language of the

---

1. R.S.C., Order 18, r. 8.
2. (1876), 1 Q.B.D. 714, at p. 723.   The limits within which the oral contract may be used as a defence are discussed by Williams in 50 L.Q.R. 532. See also *Wauchope* v. *Maida* (1971), 22 D.L.R. (2d) 142. An unenforceable contract will operate to sever an equitable joint tenancy: *Burgess* v. *Rawnsley*, [1975] 3 All E.R. 142; [1975] 3 W.L.R. 99.
3. *Butcher* v. *Stapely* (1685), 1 Vern. 363, Simpson History, pp. 613–616. It has been plausibly suggested that the statute was only intended to apply at common law but there is no clear evidence for this view. See Yale 73 S.S. at ciii.

statute.   In 1715 Lord COWPER referred to the earlier case of
Halfpenny v. *Ballet* and " said he remembered very well that the
cause was heard before the Master of the Rolls, and the plaintiff
had a decree; but he said, this was on the point of fraud, which
was proved in the cause, and Halfpenny walked backwards and
forwards in the court and bid the Master of the Rolls observe
the statute, which he humorously said, *I do, I do.*"[1]   The task
of reconciliation was somewhat eased when non-compliance with
the statute was understood to render agreements unenforceable
and not void.   In the words of COTTON, L.J., in *Britain* v. *Rossiter*,

> " To hold that this enactment makes void verbal contracts falling
> within its provisions would be inconsistent with the doctrine of the
> court of equity with regard to part performance in suits concerning
> land.   If such contracts had been rendered void by the legislature,
> courts of equity would not have enforced them; but their doctrine
> was that the statute did not render the contracts void, but required
> written evidence to be given of them; and courts of equity were
> accustomed to dispense with that evidence in certain instances."[2]

The view that equity simply fulfils the underlying purpose
of the statute by replacing one type of evidence by another equally
cogent is perhaps as convenient an explanation as it is possible to
find; but it has not been accepted without question.   Sir
Frederick Pollock preferred to rest the equitable intervention on
the basis of estoppel and to assume that a defendant, who plainly
intimated by his conduct the existence of a contract, could not be
allowed to shelter behind the statute.[3]   Lord SELBORNE sought to
evade the difficulties by denying that equity, when it applied its
doctrine of part performance, was enforcing the contract at all; it
was regularizing the situation created by acts of the parties outside
the contract.

*[margin note: Modern jus-
tifications of
the doctrine]*

> " In a suit founded on such part performance, the defendant is
> really ' charged ' upon the equities resulting from the acts done
> in execution of the contract, and not (within the meaning of the
> statute) upon the contract itself.   If such equities were excluded
> injustice of a kind which the Statute cannot be thought to have had in
> contemplation would follow."[4]

Lord BLACKBURN, on the other hand, abandoned the hope of
reconciling the doctrine with the statute and accepted it as a
convenient *fait accompli*.[5]

In a sense this doctrinal dispute has been rendered academic
by s. 40 (2) of the Law of Property Act 1925 which provides
" This section . . . does not affect the law relating to part performance . . ."   However though this gives statutory recognition to
the doctrine, interpretation of the doctrine and its scope may still
be dependent on views as to its correct historical basis, as to which
the statute is wisely silent.

---

1. *Halfpenny* v. *Ballet* is reported in (1699), 2 Vernon, 373, and Lord COWPER's
   remarks are to be found in *Bawdes* v. *Amhurst* (1715), Prec. Ch. 402.
2. (1879), 11 Q.B.D. 123, at p. 130.
3. *Pollock on Contract*, 13th Edn., at p. 521.
4. In *Maddison* v. *Alderson* (1883), 8 App. Cas. 467, at p. 475.
5. *Ibid.*, at p. 489.   The various views are set out and discussed by ROMER, J.,
   in *Rawlinson* v. *Ames*, [1925] Ch. 96, at pp. 109–13.

(ii) The scope of the doctrine

Doctrine applied to contracts concerning land

The opinion was expressed in *Britain* v. *Rossiter*[1] that the doctrine was applicable only to cases concerning land, and the statement was repeated by Lord SELBORNE in *Maddison* v. *Alderson*.[2] This restrictive view has not always passed without question. In the words of KAY, J.,

> " The doctrine of part performance of a parol agreement . . . though principally applied in the case of contracts for the sale or purchase of land or for the acquisition of an interest in land, has not been confined to these cases.   Probably it would be more accurate to say it applies to all cases in which a court of equity would entertain a suit for specific performance, if the alleged contract had been in writing."[3]

This distinction was potentially important before 1954 since the doctrine might have been applied, for instance, where a court would grant specific performance of a contract for the sale of goods.   Since 1954 the two tests lead to the same result since . . . a contract of guarantee is not one " in which a court of equity would entertain a suit for specific performance."

(iii) The nature of the acts required by the doctrine

It is clear that it is not every act of part performance of the contract which will suffice[4] but even after nearly three hundred years it is far from easy to state the appropriate test.   Discussion has been dominated, and perhaps bedevilled, by the tests adumbrated by Sir Edward Fry in his classic work on *Specific Performance*.[5]   Unfortunately he propounded at least two different tests.   Thus at one place he states:[6]

> " The acts of part performance must be such as not only to be referable to a contract such as that alleged, but to be referable to no other title."

While two pages later he says:[7]

> " The true principle of the operation of acts of part performance seems only to require that the acts in question be such as must be referred to some contract, and may be referred to the alleged one; that they prove the existence of some contract and are consistent with the contract alleged."

Both tests require the act of part performance to point to the existence of the oral contract, thus arising naturally out of the theory that the purpose of part performance is to act as an alternative method of proof but clearly the first formulation is much more demanding than the second.

The House of Lords seemed to look with favour on the first test in *Maddison* v. *Alderson*.[8]

---

1. (1879), 11 Q.B.D. 123.
2. (1883), 8 App. Cas. 467, at p. 480.
3. *McManus* v. *Cooke* (1887), 35 Ch.D. 681, at p. 697.
4. See e.g. *New Hart Builders, Ltd.* v. *Brindley*, [1975] 1 All E.R. 1007; [1975] 2 W.L.R. 595.
5. 1st Edn. (1858); 6th Edn. (1921).
6. 6th Edn. p. 276; the same definition occurs in the 1st Edn. p. 174.
7. 6th Edn., p. 278; the same definition occurs in the 1st Edn., p. 175.
8. (1883), 8 App, Cas. 467. See Williams, *Statute of Frauds, Section 4*, pp. 250–261.

Elizabeth Maddison had been the housekeeper of Thomas Alderson for ten years without being paid the wages due to her. She then told him that she wished to leave and get married. According to her evidence, he promised that if she would stay with him he would devise to her in his will a life interest in his farm. She did in fact remain with him without payment until his death. He left a will designed to fulfil his promise, but it was unattested and void.

She sought specific performance of the alleged oral agreement, but failed. Three of their Lordships said that the acts must be unequivocally referable to some such contract as that alleged[1] but it may well be that the same result would be reached on the second test for as was said *per curiam* when the case was before the Court of Appeal, " it cannot with any show of reason be contended that such continuance in his service was referable only to an agreement that he would leave her a life estate in his property, or indeed that it was referable to any agreement at all."[2]

In practice however the courts have adopted the more relaxed test and indeed if the first test were strictly applied it would exclude almost all cases since though, no doubt, there are many acts which point to the existence of some contract, there are few which would not be consistent with two different contracts. So most acts of part performance of a contract to sell a freehold interest in land would be equally consistent with an agreement to give a long lease. It is clear that this degree of equivocation is not fatal.

So in *Kingswood Estate Co. Ltd. v. Anderson.*[3]

the plaintiffs were the landlords of a house within the Rent Restriction Acts. The tenant was a widow with whom lived her invalid son. To get possession of the house the plaintiffs had to satisfy a court that there was suitable alternative accommodation for her. A flat was found, and it was orally agreed that, if she would leave the house and become the tenant of the flat, that tenancy should continue so long as she and her son lived. Accordingly she moved with her son to the flat. Soon afterwards the plaintiffs gave her four weeks' notice to quit and then sued for possession.

The plaintiffs argued, *inter alia,* that there was no sufficient act of part performance since the entry into possession, though it might refer to some contract, was equivocal: it was consistent either with a life tenancy or with a weekly tenancy. The Court of Appeal rejected the argument. UPJOHN, L.J., described the case as " a complete text-book case of part performance."

Another example is *Wakeham v. Mackenzie.*[4]

X's wife died when he was seventy-two years old. The plaintiff, a widow aged sixty-seven, lived near him in a council flat and had long been a friend of both X and his wife. In November, 1964, X agreed orally with the plaintiff that if she would move into his house, look after it and him and pay for her share of food and coal, he would in his will leave her the house and its contents. The plaintiff thereupon gave up her flat and moved into X's house. She looked after X

---

1. *Per* Lord SELBOURNE, L.C., who quoted Fry's first definition with approval: 8 App. Cas. at 479; *per* Lord O'HAGAN, at p. 485 and *per* Lord FITZGERALD, at 491. Lord BLACKBURN, at p. 490, would have restricted the doctrine to changes in the possession of land.
2. (1881) 7 Q.B.D. 174 at 179.
3. [1963] 2 Q.B. 169; [1962] 3 All E.R. 593.
4. [1968] 2 All E.R. 783; [1968] 1 W.L.R. 1175. See also *Rawlinson v. Ames,* [1925] Ch. 96.

and the house and paid her share of food and coal until X died in 1966. X left her nothing in his will. She asked for specific performance of the oral contract.

At first sight these facts bear a resemblance to those in *Maddison* v. *Alderson*. But the evidence offered by the plaintiff in *Wakeham* v. *Mackenzie* was more compelling. " The acts of part performance in this case—the giving up of the plaintiff's home, the moving into a new home, the acts which the plaintiff performed in looking after the deceased and looking after that home, and putting £2 a week into the common pot—clearly raise an equity in her."[1] They were explicable only by reference to some contract and were consistent with the particular contract which the plaintiff alleged. The plaintiff was therefore entitled to a decree of specific performance. The case is no doubt distinguishable from *Maddison* v. *Alderson* but it is probably better regarded as evidence of a more relaxed view.

If there is one proposition on which all the books and cases have agreed it is that the payment of money is not by itself a sufficient act of part performance. Two reasons have been given for this: First, that payment of money is completely equivocal both as to whether there is a contract and as to its nature and secondly that the money would be recoverable if the contract was not performed. So Lord SELBORNE said in *Maddison* v. *Alderson*:[2]

> " It may be taken as now settled that part payment of purchase money is not enough; and judges of high authority have said the same even of payment in full."

Steadman
v. Steadman

This has now been revealed as too simple a view by the decision of the House of Lords in *Steadman* v. *Steadman*.[3]

> The husband and wife were joint owners of a house which had been the family home. The wife left the husband and obtained maintenance orders in favour of herself and the child of the marriage. The husband fell into arrears in paying the wife's maintenance. An oral agreement was reached by which the wife was to transfer her interest in the house to the husband for £1,500; the wife would agree to the discharge of the maintenance made in her favour; the husband would pay £100 of the arrears and the wife would consent to the discharge of the balance. The agreement was revealed to the justices and the relevant parts of it approved by them. The husband duly paid the £100 and his solicitors sent a draft form of transfer to the wife's solicitors but the wife refused to proceed.

The House of Lords held (Lord MORRIS OF BORTH-Y-GEST dissenting) that there were sufficient acts of part performance to render the contract enforceable. The precise combination of circumstances in the case was unusual and we must ask what general principles can be derived from it. Unfortunately divergencies of opinion within the majority make this question difficult to answer with confidence. The one proposition that seems clearly established is negative, viz. it can no longer be stated that mere payment of money is never a sufficient act of part per-

---

1. [1968] 2 All E.R., at pp. 787–8; [1968] 1 W.L.R., at p. 1181.
2. (1883), 8 App. Cas. 467, at p. 479.
3. [1974] 2 All E.R. 977; [1974] 3 W.L.R. 56; Wade, 90 L.Q.R. 433; Emery, [1974] C.L.J. 205; Wallace, 25 N.I.L.Q. 453.

formance,[1] but the case certainly does not state the converse, so that the position of a purchaser's deposit or part payment is unclear. Probably the payment of money will continue to be regarded as usually equivocal but as capable of being rendered persuasive by the surrounding circumstances. Both Lord REID[2] and Lord SALMON[3] suggest that the vendor's inability to repay the money, e.g. because of bankruptcy, may be relevant.[4]

On other questions that there were important differences of opinion. Lord REID[5] and Viscount DILHORNE[6] thought it sufficient that the acts of part performance should on the balance of probabilities establish that there was some contract between the parties but Lord SALMON thought the acts must establish that there was a contract concerning land.[7] Lord SIMON reserved his position on this question.[8] Viscount DILHORNE[9] and Lord SIMON[10] thought the oral recital of the agreement before the magistrates an act of part performance but Lord REID was very doubtful of this.[11] Lord REID,[12] Viscount DILHORNE[13] and Lord SIMON[14] all thought the sending of the draft deed of transfer an act of part performance while Lord SALMON regarded both the statement to the magistrates and the sending of the deed of transfer as part of the surrounding circumstances which explained the payment of the £100.[15] It is no doubt a mistake however to take too schematic a view of the pronouncements on individual acts since it is the complete combination of circumstances which forms the true basis of the decision.

---

1. *Per* Lord REID, [1974] 2 All E.R. 977, at p. 981; [1974] 3 W.L.R. 56, at p. 60; *per* Lord SIMON, at pp. 1002, 83, respectively; *per* Lord SALMON, at pp. 1006, 88, respectively.
2. *Ibid.*, at pp. 981, 60, respectively.
3. *Ibid.*, at pp. 1007, 88, respectively.
4. This would seem to flow from the second reason given for the payment rule, *supra*, p. 198, rather than the first.
5. [1974] 2 All E.R. 977, at p. 981; [1974] 3 W.L.R. 56, at p. 60–61.
6. *Ibid.*, at pp. 992, 72–73, respectively.
7. *Ibid.*, at pp. 1005, 86, respectively.
8. *Ibid.*, at pp. 1000, 80–81, respectively.
9. *Ibid.*, at pp. 992, 72, respectively.
1. *Ibid.*, at pp. 1000, 81, respectively.
2. *Ibid.*, at pp. 980, 60, respectively.
3. *Ibid.*, at pp. 980, 60, respectively.
4. *Ibid.*, at pp. 992, 72, respectively.
5. *Ibid.*, at pp. 1000, 81, respectively.
6. *Ibid.*, at pp. 1007, 89, respectively; cf. pp. 1008, 90.

CHAPTER THREE

Other Rules About Form

It may well be that the most widely held lay misapprehension about English Law is that a contract needs to be in writing and signed. In fact since the sixteenth century the common law has been signally free of any rules requiring contracts to be made or evidenced in a particular way. The only common law exception was that contracts made by corporations had to be made under seal but that rule was first eroded by exceptions and finally abolished by the Corporate Bodies' Contracts Act 1960.[1]

There are however a considerable number of statutory rules about particular types of contract, requiring them to be made or evidenced in a particular way. A detailed account would be out of place here but we may notice that these cases fell into a number of groups.

(1) *The contract must be under seal.* All leases for three years or more must be under seal.[2] A contract to grant such a lease, however, need only be evidenced in writing[3] and will for many purposes create the same rights between the parties.

(2) *The contract must be in writing.* A Bill of Exchange must be in writing[4] but this is perhaps not a true case since an oral agreement to the same effect would still be a contract but would not be a Bill of Exchange. In recent years Parliament has come to regard prescription of formal requirements as a useful tool for consumer protection.[5] The most important example is now the Consumer Credit Act 1974. Under s. 61 (1) a regulated consumer credit agreement must be in the prescribed form and under s. 60 the Secretary of State is required to make regulations as to the form and content of documents.[6] Under s. 65 an improperly executed regulated agreement can be enforced against the debtor only on

1. The common law rules continue to apply to contracts made before July 29th, 1960. A statement of them may be found in the 8th Edn. of this work at pp. 414–417.
2. Law of Property Act 1925, ss. 52, 54 (2).
3. Under Law of Property Act 1925, s. 40 (1) discussed *supra*.
4. Bills of Exchange Act 1882, s. 3 (1). As to whether it should be written on paper see *Board of Inland Revenue* v. *Haddock*. Herbert, *Uncommon Law* (2nd Edn. 1936), p. 201.
5. Particularly under the Hire Purchase Acts of 1938, 1964 and 1965.
6. Similar powers under the Hire Purchase Acts have been used to require particularly important information to be put in prominent boxes or special colours. See further Goode, [1975] C.L.J. 79 at 98–99.

the order of the court but the court is given a wide discretion under s. 127 as to enforcement.

(3) *The contract must be evidenced in writing.* The provisions deriving from the Statute of Frauds are the main examples but another is provided by contracts of marine insurance. Here a written policy is normally issued and the Marine Insurance Act 1906[1] renders a policy " inadmissible in evidence " unless it is embodied in a policy signed by the insurer but the policy is not normally the contract, which is completed when the slip which the broker presents to the insurer is initialled by the latter.[2]

(4) *There are fiscal or criminal sanctions if the contract is not put into writing.* All policies of life insurance are in practice in writing but there is no legal requirement that they should be. However, any insurer who does not issue a stamped policy within a month of receiving the first premium is liable to a fine.[3]

---

1. See ss. 21, 22, 23 and 24.
2. See *per* BLACKBURN J. in *Ionides* v. *Pacific Fire and Marine Insurance Co.* (1871), L.R. 6 Q.B. 674, at p. 685.
3. Stamp Act 1891, as amended by Finance Act 1970, s. 32.

PART IV

CONTRACTS THAT CONTAIN A VITIATING ELEMENT

SUMMARY

CHAPTER ONE

Mistake

SECTION I. INTRODUCTION[1]

THE first fact to appreciate in this somewhat elusive branch of
the law is that the word " mistake " bears a more restricted
meaning in professional than in popular speech. A layman
might well believe that no force whatever should be allowed to
an agreement based on an obvious misunderstanding. The law,
however, does not take the simple line of ruling that a contract
is void merely because one or both of the parties would not have
made it had the true facts been realized. Many examples might
be given of situations where a mistake in the popular sense is
denied legal significance and where a remedy, if available at all,

*Mistake in
the popular
sense not
always
relevant in
law*

---

1. The literature on mistakes is extensive. See, e.g. Stoljar, *Mistake and
Misrepresentation: A study in Contractual Principles* (1968); Slade, 70
L.Q.R. 385; Atiyah, 73 L.Q.R. 340; Wilson, 17 M.L.R. 515; Unger,
18 M.L.R. 259; Smith and Thomas, 20 M.L.R. 38; Atiyah and Bennion,
24 M.L.R. 421; Shatwell, 33 Can., Bar Rev 164; Atiyah, 2 Ottowa
L.R. 337.

is granted upon some other ground.   If, for instance, A agrees
to buy from B a roadside garage abutting on a public highway
and, unknown to A but known to B, a bypass road is about to
be constructed which will divert the traffic from the garage, A
cannot escape from the contract on the ground of mistake.[1]   If
he has been misled by the statement of B, he may be able to
obtain the rescission of the contract, but this will be on the
ground, not of mistake, but of a false representation.   In the
popular sense of the term, indeed, all cases of misrepresentation
involve a misunderstanding; but they by no means all raise the
legal doctrine of mistake.

Different
attitudes of
common law
and equity   The narrow scope allowed to mistake in the English legal
system is a fact to be not only noticed but welcomed.   In the
few cases in which it operates the effect, at least at common law,
is said to be that the whole transaction is void from the very
beginning.   This drastic result may be unobjectionable as far
as the parties themselves are concerned, but the reaction upon
third parties may be deplorable.   From a complete nullity no
rights can be derived.   Goods may have been sold and delivered
on credit by A to B under an apparent contract, and may then
be *bona fide* bought and paid for by C.   If the original contract
between A and B is now declared void for mistake, B has obtained
no title to the goods and can pass none.   C, though he has
acted innocently and in the ordinary course of business, will in
principle be liable to A for the full value of the goods.[2]   If,
indeed, the case can be dealt with not at common law but in
equity, so unfortunate a result may be averted.   The courts, in
the exercise of their equitable jurisdiction to grant a decree *in
personam*, may grant specific relief against the consequences of
mistake without declaring the contract a nullity.   In this way
they may protect not only the innocent stranger who has become
involved in the sequence of events, but also one of the original
parties if the demands of substantial justice are to be satisfied.
It follows, therefore, that in any discussion of mistake it will often
be found necessary to distinguish its treatment at common law
and in equity, with the hope that the jurisdiction of the latter
will develop at the expense of the former.

Classification
of mistake   The classification adopted in this chapter must now be
explained.   If attention is fixed merely on the factual situations,
there are three possible types of mistake: common, mutual and
unilateral.

(i) Common
mistake   In common mistake, both parties make the same mistake.
Each knows the intention of the other and accepts it, but each is
mistaken about some underlying and fundamental fact.   The
parties, for example, are unaware that the subject-matter of their
contract has already perished.

(ii) Mutual
mistake   In mutual mistake, the parties misunderstand each other and
are at cross-purposes.   A, for example, intends to offer his Ford

---

1. Example given by Lord ATKIN in *Bell v. Lever Brothers, Ltd.*, [1932] A.C.
   161, at p. 224.
2. There are, of course, exceptions to the application of the doctrine *nemo
   dat quod hon habet*; see *Benjamin's Sale of Goods*, paras. 461–569.

Cortina car for sale, but B believes that the offer relates to the Ford Zephyr also owned by A.[1]

In unilateral mistake, one only of the parties is mistaken. The other knows, or must be taken to know, of his mistake. Suppose, for instance, that A agrees to buy from B a specific picture which A believes to be a genuine Constable but which in fact is a copy. If B is ignorant of A's erroneous belief, the case is one of mutual mistake, but, if he knows of it, of unilateral mistake.

(iii) Uni-lateral mistake

When, however, the cases provoked by these factual situations are analysed, they will be seen to fall, not into three, but only into two distinct legal categories. Has an agreement been reached or not? Where common mistake is pleaded, the presence of agreement is admitted. The rules of offer and acceptance are satisfied and the parties are of one mind. What is urged is that, owing to a common error as to some fundamental fact, the agreement is robbed of all efficacy. Where either mutual or unilateral mistake is pleaded, the very existence of the agreement is denied. The argument is that, despite appearances, there is no real correspondence of offer and acceptance and that therefore the transaction must necessarily be void.[2]

In effect, two legal categories

One type of problem is thus presented by common mistake, and a second by mutual or unilateral mistake. But the distinction between these two latter forms of mistake is still important. Though the problem they pose is the same, the method of approach to it differs. If mutual mistake is pleaded, the judicial approach, as is normally the case in contractual problems, is objective; the court, looking at the evidence from the standpoint of a reasonable third party, will decide whether any, and if so what, agreement must be taken to have been reached. If unilateral mistake is pleaded, the approach is subjective; the innocent party is allowed to show the effect upon *his* mind of the error in the hope of avoiding its consequences.

Significance of difference between mutual and unilateral mistake

It remains to observe that the discussion in the present chapter is confined to a mistake of fact as distinguished from one of law. The distinction, as will be seen later, is frequently blurred and is difficult to define, but the principle is well established that a mistake of law is no ground for relief from a transaction.[3]

Mistake of fact alone relevant

---

1. The distinction between the epithets " common " and " mutual," though surprisingly often confused both in and out of the reports, is clearly stated in the O.E.D. " Common " is there defined as " possessed or shared alike by both or all the persons or things in question. " " Mutual " was, indeed, at one period used as a synonym for " common "; but according to the O.E.D., this is " now regarded as incorrect " and properly means " possessed or entertained by each of two persons towards or with regard to the other. " See the more caustic words of Fowler in *Modern English Usage* under " mutual".

2. Although the two problems are different in principle, the difference has often been forgotten, especially by those pioneer English writers on contract, Pollock and Anson, who strove to include all types of mistake under the general rubric of *consensus*. It will be seen that the word " mistake " is being used in two different senses. In common mistake and unilateral mistake, mistake means error, but in mutual mistake, mistake means " misunderstanding." The parties are at cross purposes but there is not necessarily an error which can be corrected.

3. *Infra*, pp. 641 *et seq.*

SECTION II.   THE TWO CATEGORIES OF CASES

A.   WHERE AGREEMENT HAS BEEN REACHED, BUT UPON THE BASIS OF A COMMON MISTAKE

No lack
of
agreement

IN this category there is no question of lack of agreement.   The exact offer made by A has been accepted by B.   It is clear, for instance, that B has accepted A's offer to sell a specific picture for £1,000.   It is admitted, however, that both parties wrongly believed the artist to have been Constable.   B now contends that owing to this common mistake the agreement cannot be allowed to stand, since the fundamental assumption upon which its very being is based has proved to be false.

Common law
and equity
require
separate
treatment

The task here is to ascertain what attitude the courts have adopted towards an agreement that neither party would have made had they realized the untruth of what they both honestly believed to be true, and not only true but essential to the making of the bargain.   Equity has partly followed the common law in this matter, but has diverged from it in important respects.

1.   AGREEMENTS THAT ARE VOID BOTH AT COMMON LAW AND IN EQUITY.

Contract not
void unless
it lacks its
intended
subject-
matter

The exact significance of the principle laid down at common law and shared by equity is no doubt somewhat controversial, but if what the judges have said is interpreted in the light of what they have done it would appear that a common mistake has no effect whatsoever at common law unless it is such as to eliminate the very subject-matter of the agreement; in other words, unless it empties the agreement of all content.

Cases of
*res
extincta*

This principle has clearly been applied in a number of decisions dealing with what may conveniently and shortly be called cases of *res extincta*.   It is well established that if, unknown to the parties, the specific subject-matter of the agreement is in fact non-existent, no contract whatever ensues.   In the leading case of *Couturier* v. *Hastie*,[1] the question concerned the sale of a cargo of corn supposed at the time of the contract to be in transit from Salonica to the United Kingdom, but which unknown to the parties had become fermented and had already been sold by the master of the ship to a purchaser at Tunis.   It was held that the buyer was not liable for the price of the cargo.   The case was heard by the Court of Exchequer, the Court of Exchequer Chamber and finally, after a consultation with nine of the judges, by the House of Lords.   It was the unanimous view of each court that everything depended upon the construction of the contract.   Had the purchaser agreed to buy specific goods or had he agreed to buy an adventure—namely the benefit of the

---

1. (1852), 8 Exch. 40; reversed, (1853), 9 Exch. 102; reversal affirmed, (1856), 5 H.L. Cas. 673.   See Nicholas, 48 Tulane L.R. 946, pp. 966–972.

insurance that had been effected to cover the possible failure of the goods to arrive? The former construction was ultimately preferred. Once this had been decided, it followed as a matter of course that the contract was void, for in the nature of things a contract to sell and deliver specific goods presupposes the existence of goods capable of delivery. Both parties contemplated an existing something to be bought and sold. It was not the mistake *per se* that prevented the formation of a contract in *Couturier* v. *Hastie*, and, indeed, the word " mistake " was never mentioned in any of the judgments. The crucial fact was the absence of the contemplated subject-matter, which necessarily emptied the contract of all content.

> " Looking to the contract itself alone," said Lord CRANWORTH, " it appears to me clearly that what the parties contemplated, those who bought and those who sold was that there was an existing something to be sold and bought. . . . The contract plainly imports that there was something which was to be sold at the time of the contract and something to be purchased. No such thing existing, there must be judgment for the defendants."[1]

The view adopted in *Couturier* v. *Hastie* had already been taken in the earlier case of *Strickland* v. *Turner*,[2] where:

Strickland v. *Turner*

> X had bought and paid for an annuity upon the life of a person who, unknown to the buyer and seller, was already dead.

It was held that X had got nothing for his money and that the total failure of consideration entitled him to recovery in full.

Six years after *Couturier* v. *Hastie*, the court in *Pritchard* v. *Merchants' and Tradesman's Mutual Life Assurance Society*,[3] again dealt with the case of *res extincta*.

> The beneficiary of a life insurance policy, which had lapsed owing to the non-payment of the premium, paid to the insurers a renewal premium which was sufficient to revive the policy. The parties, however, were ignorant that the assured had died before the payment was made.

The beneficiary failed to recover the amount due under the policy, since

> " the premium was paid and accepted upon an implied understanding on both sides that the party insured was then alive. Both parties were labouring under a mistake and consequently the transaction was altogether void."[4]

It is true that the presence of a mistake was mentioned in the judgment, but it was the special character of that mistake—the erroneous assumption of the assured's continued existence— that enabled the court to pronounce the contract void.

In *Galloway* v. *Galloway*[5] a separation deed between a man and woman was declared a nullity, because it was made on the

Galloway v. *Galloway*

---

1. (1856), 5 H.L. Cas. 673, at pp. 681–2.
2. (1852), 7 Exch. 208. See also the somewhat analogous case of *Scott* v. *Coulson*, [1903] 2 Ch. 249.
3. (1858), 3 C.B.N.S. 622.
4. *Ibid.*, at p. 640, *per* WILLIAMS, J. As BYLES, J., pointed out at p. 645, the premium could have been recovered as having been paid and received under a mistake of fact.
5. (1914), 30 T.L.R. 531; followed in *Law* v. *Harragin* (1917), 33 T.L.R. 381.

mistaken and common assumption that they were in fact married to each other.   The supposition upon which the parties had proceeded was that the subject-matter of the contract, the marriage, was in existence.

Equity follows the law

Equity was approaching the problem of *res extincta* in much the same way and at the same time as the common law.   In one case where A had bought a remainder in fee expectant upon an estate tail and had given a bond for the money, both parties being ignorant that the entail had been barred and the remainder destroyed, RICHARDS, C.B., said:

> " If contracting parties have treated while under a mistake, that will be sufficient ground for the interference of a court of equity, but in this case there is much more.   Suppose I sell an estate innocently, which at the time is actually swept away by a flood without my knowledge of the fact; am I to receive £5,000 and interest because the conveyance is executed and a bond given for that sum, when in point of fact I had not an inch of that land, so sold, to sell? "[1]

The Chief Baron ordered the refunding of all interest paid and the cancellation and re-delivery of the bond.

Cases of *res sua*

The principle applicable to the *res extincta* has been extended, at any rate in equity, to the analogous case of what may be called the *res sua*, *i.e.* if A agrees to buy or take a lease from B of property which both parties believe to belong to B but which in fact belongs to A.[2]   The contract is of necessity a nullity, since B has nothing to sell or convey.[3]   As KNIGHT BRUCE, L.J., said in one of the cases: " It would be contrary to all the rules of equity and common law to give effect to such an agreement."[4] This is so however only when the *res sua* comprises the whole of the land sold or let.[5]

Basis of the decisions on cases of *res extincta* and *res sua*

If we pause here for a moment, it seems clear that the reason why a contract relating to a *res extincta* or to a *res sua* cannot be recognized is not so much the fact of the common mistake as the absence of any contractual subject-matter.   If a contract may be discharged by subsequent impossibility of performance,[6] then *a fortiori* its very genesis is precluded by a present impossibility. In the case both of the *res sua* and the *res extincta*,

> " the parties intended to effectuate a transfer of ownership; such a transfer is impossible; the stipulation is *naturali ratione inutilis*."[7]

McRae's case

A different view of *res extincta* was taken by the High Court of Australia in *McRae* v. *Commonwealth Disposals Commission*[8] upon the following facts.

> The Commission invited tenders " for the purchase of an oil tanker lying on Journmaund Reef, which is approximately 100 miles

1. *Hitchcock* v. *Giddings* (1817), 4 Price, 135, at p. 141.
2. *Bingham* v. *Bingham* (1748), 1 Ves. Sen. 126; *Cochrane* v. *Willis* (1865), 1 Ch. App. 58.
3. *Debenham* v. *Sawbridge*, [1901] 2 Ch. 98, at p. 109, *per* BYRNE, J.
4. *Cochrane* v. *Willis*, *supra*, at p. 63.
5. *Bligh* v. *Martin*, [1968] 1 All E.R. 1157; [1968] 1 W.L.R. 804.
6. *Infra*, pp. 544 *et seq.*
7. *Bell* v. *Lever Brothers, Ltd.*, [1932] A.C. 161, at p. 218; [1931] All E.R. Rep. 1, at p. 27, *per* Lord ATKIN.
8. (1951), 84 C.L.R. 377; Smith and Thomas, *A Casebook on Contract* 5th Edn., p. 374; Cowen, 68 L.Q.R. 30; Fleming, 15 M.L.R. 229.

north of Samarai." The plaintiff submitted a tender which was accepted. In fact there was no tanker lying anywhere near the latitude or longitude stated by the Commission and no place known as Jourmaund Reef, but the plaintiff did not discover this until he had incurred considerable expense in fitting out a salvage expedition. Though not fraudulent, the employees of the Commission were clearly careless and had no adequate reason for believing that the tanker existed.

The High Court of Australia awarded damages to the plaintiff on the ground that the Commission had implicitly warranted the existence of the tanker.

The first question that arises is whether this decision, though it certainly meets the needs of justice, can be supported on the ground stated by the court. The criticism has been made that it conflicts with the principle derived from a line of cases, of which *Couturier* v. *Hastie*[1] is the most important, that there can be no contract about a non-existent subject matter. The court met this argument by denying that *Couturier* v. *Hastie* established any such principle. It is true that in that case the plaintiff was the seller, and therefore there was no need to rely on the concept of *res extincta* or on the doctrine of mistake to reach the conclusion that a seller who fails to deliver the goods cannot recover the price. The plaintiff could have recovered the price only by showing that the contract was not an ordinary contract of sale of goods, but the sale either of the shipping documents or of the chance that the goods still existed. This he failed to do. It does not necessarily follow that the buyer could not have sued for non-delivery.

On the other hand it would seem that the legislature accepted the conventional view of *Couturier* v. *Hastie* when it enacted that:

> " Where there is a contract for the sale of specific goods and the goods without the knowledge of the seller have perished at the time when the contract is made, the contract is void."[2]

It has, indeed, been argued that this section enacts no rigid rule, but only a rule of construction which can be excluded by evidence of a contrary intention,[3] but there are no words in the section to show that it can be displaced in this way. Even if it be assumed that the section lays down a rigid rule of law, it is still possible to suggest that it is not a complete statement of the common law, and that its scope must therefore be limited to goods which, in its own words, " have perished at the time when the contract was made." On this assumption, *McRae's* case[4] is outside the language of the section. It seems, however, to be a manifest inelegance to distinguish goods which were once *in esse* but have since perished, and goods which have never existed at all; though the inelegance is not altogether surprising in a statutory provision which in terms applies only to part of a problem. But at least, the section, on its literal interpretation, contains nothing to prevent a court from holding that it applies only to " perished

(i) Can the decision be supported on its own ground?

---

1. *Supra*, p. 248.
2. Sale of Goods Act 1893, s. 6.
3. Atiyah, 73 L.Q.R. 340.
4. *McRae* v. *Commonwealth Disposals Commission* (1951), 84 C.L.R. 377.

goods." It is still open to argument that in all other cases it is a question of construction whether (a) the contract is void, or (b) the seller has contracted that the goods are in existence, or (c) the buyer has bought a chance.[1] On the whole, however, it would seem more likely that an English court would regard section 6 of the Sale of Goods Act as a correct statement of the common law and hold that a contract for the sale of non-existent goods is void.

(ii) Can the decision be supported on other grounds?

The second question is whether the decision in *McRae's* case can be supported on other grounds according to the law as administered in England.

In a previous edition of this book, it was suggested that the plaintiff could recover on a collateral contract.[2] The defendants, when they invited tenders from the public, promised that the ship existed, and in reliance on that promise the plaintiff offered to buy it. In effect, what the defendants said in their advertisement to the public was: " In return for any offer you may make we promise that the tanker exists." The difficulty with this suggestion, however, is that the consideration for a collateral contract is usually the entering into the main contract. If the main contract is void, it might be ruled that the consideration is illusory. As against this, however, a collateral contract was discovered in *Strongman (1945), Ltd.* v. *Sincock*,[3] where the main contract was illegal and therefore void.

There are two further grounds upon which the plaintiff might succeed. He might be able to maintain an action for damages either under the Misrepresentation Act 1967, or under the doctrine laid down by the House of Lords in *Hedley Byrne & Co., Ltd.* v. *Heller & Partners, Ltd.* These two possibilities are canvassed at a later stage in this book.[4]

Is there an independent doctrine of common mistake?

If the problems that have arisen in practice were confined to cases of *res extincta* and *res sua*, it would be superfluous to suggest the existence of an independent doctrine of common mistake. It would be unnecessary to attribute the failure of the contract to the mistake *per se*. The supposed contract would be a nullity in English, as it was in Roman law, simply because there was nothing to contract about. It has, however, been suggested that these cases of *res extincta* and *res sua* are only examples of a wider class based upon a wider principle—that, whenever the parties are both mistaken about some fundamental fact, their mistake will be fatal to the existence of the contract. If this view is supported by authority, then it must be admitted that the common law recognizes an independent doctrine of common mistake.

Some judicial statements certainly incline to this view. For instance, Lord WRIGHT, after remarking that in general the test of intention in the formation of contracts is objective, said:

---

1. Atiyah, 73 L.Q.R. 340; Atiyah and Bennion, 24 M.L.R. 421; and Atiyah 2 Ottawa L.R. 337, where he relies heavily on deductions from the decision in *Financings* v. *Stimson*, [1962] 3 All E.R. 386; [1962] 1 W.L.R. 1184.
2. For collateral contracts, see *supra*, pp. 58–61.
3. [1955] 2 Q.B. 525; [1955] 3 All E.R. 90; *infra*, p. 362.
4. *Infra*, pp. 261–2.

" But proof of mistake affirmatively excludes intention. It is,
however, essential that the mistake relied on should be of such a
nature that it can properly be described as a mistake in respect of
the underlying assumption of the contract or transaction or as being
fundamental or basic."[1]

This statement, however, was made *obiter*, and it is necessary to
see if it is supported by actual authority.

The problem was exhaustively discussed by the House of
Lords in *Bell* v. *Lever Brothers, Ltd.*,[2] where the facts were
these:

> Lever Brothers, who had a controlling interest in the Niger
> Company, appointed Bell managing director of the latter company
> for five years at an annual salary of £8,000. After three years the
> services of Bell became redundant owing to the amalgamation of
> the Niger Company with a third company, and Lever Brothers
> agreed to pay him £30,000 as compensation for the loss of his
> employment. After they had paid this money, they discovered for
> the first time that Bell had committed several breaches of duty
> during his directorship which would have justified his dismissal
> without compensation. They therefore sued for the recovery of
> £30,000 on the ground *inter alia* of common mistake, but failed.

The facts did not raise a case of unilateral mistake, for the jury
found that Bell's mind was not directed to his breaches of duty
at the time when he made the compensation agreement. According to the argument of Lever Brothers, that agreement was based
upon the underlying and fundamental assumption that the parties
were bargaining about a service contract which could only be
terminated with compensation; but the truth, unknown to both
of them at the time, was that the contract might in fact have been
terminated without compensation. The parties were dealing with
a terminable contract, but they thought that they were dealing
with one that was non-terminable. Was this sufficient to annul
the contract? The Law Lords assumed that some species of
common mistake is capable of making a contract void. The
difficulty, however, is to ascertain from their speeches what the
character of the mistake must be in order to have this nullifying
effect. The language of their Lordships is open to two interpretations.

First, there are certain passages which suggest that a contract
is void if the parties have proceeded on a false and fundamental
assumption, irrespective of the character of the fact assumed to
be true. Lord WARRINGTON, for example, referred to the judgment of WRIGHT, J., in the court below in these words:

> " The learned judge thus describes the mistake invoked in this
> case as sufficient to justify a court in saying that there was no true
> consent—namely,' ' Some mistake or misapprehension as to some
> facts . . . which by the common intention of the parties, whether
> expressed or more generally implied, constitute the underlying
> assumption without which the parties would not have made the
> contract they did.' That a mistake of this nature common to both
> parties is, if proved, sufficient to render a contract void is, I think,
> established law."[3]

Bell v. *Lever
Brothers,
Ltd.*

Two possible
interpreta-
tions of
Bell v. *Lever
Bros. Ltd.*

(i) Contract
void if both
parties act
on a false
and funda-
mental
assumption

---

1. *Norwich Union Fire Insurance Society, Ltd.* v. *Price*, [1934] A.C. 455, at
    p. 463; [1934] All E.R. Rep. 352, at p. 356.
2. [1932] A.C. 161; [1931] All E.R. Rep. 1.
3. [1932] A.C., at p. 206; [1931] All E.R. Rep., at p. 206.

Lord WARRINGTON then cited *Strickland* v. *Turner*[1] and *Scott* v. *Coulson*[2] in support of the proposition.

Lord THANKERTON was more precise and cautious in describing the expression " underlying assumption," but his description was wide enough to embrace cases other than the non-existence of the subject-matter.   He said:

> " In my opinion it can only properly relate to something which both [parties] must necessarily have accepted in their minds as an essential and integral element of the subject-matter."[3]

He, too, illustrated the proposition by *Strickland* v. *Turner* and *Scott* v. *Coulson* with the addition of *Couturier* v. *Hastie*.

Lord ATKIN, after referring to the cases of *res extincta*, continued as follows:

> " Mistake as to quality of the thing contracted for raises more difficult questions.   In such a case a mistake will not affect assent unless it is the mistake of both parties and is as to the existence of some quality which makes the thing without the quality essentially different from the thing as it was believed to be."[4]

(ii) Common mistake restricted to case of *res extincta*

The second possible interpretation of the speeches, or at least of the decision, is that the only false assumption sufficiently fundamental to rank as operative mistake is the assumption that the very subject-matter of the contract is in existence.   Thus Lord ATKIN, having expressed himself, as we have just seen, in wide terms, offered in a later passage a more restricted view of the case.   The test, he now declared, was merely this:

> " Does the state of the new facts destroy the identity of the subject-matter as it was in the original state of facts? "[5]

It will also be recalled that Lord WARRINGTON and Lord THANKERTON, in illustrating what they had in mind by a fundamental assumption sufficient, if untrue, to nullify a contract, cited only the decisions concerned with *res extincta*.

Semble, second interpretation correct

How then is *Bell* v. *Lever Brothers, Ltd.*, to be interpreted? Despite the wide language of the speeches, the decision, it is submitted, is no authority for any general doctrine of common mistake, and the second of the two possible interpretations is to be preferred.   This submission is supported by the significant fact that, by a majority of three to two, the House of Lords held that the circumstances of the case itself disclosed no operative mistake.   If, however, a false and fundamental assumption by the two parties excludes consent, and if an assumption bears this character when, to quote Lord ATKIN, " the new state of facts makes the contract something different in kind from the contract in the original state of facts,"[6] or again when " it relates to the existence of some quality which makes the thing without the quality essentially different from the thing as it was believed to

---

1. *Supra,* p. 209.
2. [1903] 2 Ch. 249; where a contract for the sale of a life policy was made under the mistaken belief shared by both parties that the assured was alive. The contract was set aside by the court.
3. [1932] A.C., at p. 235; [1931] All E.R. Rep., at p. 36.
4. *Ibid.,* at pp. 218 and 28 respectively.
5. [1932] A.C., at p. 227; [1931] All E.R. Rep., at p. 32.
6. *Ibid.,* at pp. 226 and 32 respectively.

be,"[1] how can it reasonably be denied that the test was satisfied in *Bell* v. *Lever Brothers, Ltd.*? If not satisfied there, it is difficult to see how it can ever be satisfied.[2] The contemplated subject-matter of the bargain was a service contract of great value to Bell, the actual subject-matter was worthless. It was extravagantly different in kind from what the parties originally contemplated, unless the words " in kind " are to be construed in the narrowest sense.

This submission is fortified by later decisions. *Solle* v. *Butcher*,[3] for instance, shows that, in the view of the Court of Appeal, a common mistake, though clearly fundamental, does not as a general principle nullify a contract at common law, and it therefore favours the narrow interpretation of *Bell* v. *Lever Brothers, Ltd.* The facts were these:

Solle v. *Butcher*

> A had agreed to let a flat to X at a yearly rental of £250. Both parties had acted on the assumption that the flat, having been so drastically reconstructed as to be virtually a new flat, was no longer controlled by the Rent Restriction Acts. They were mistaken in this respect. The maximum permissible rent was therefore only £140, for after the execution of the lease it was too late for A to serve the statutory notice under which the sum might have been increased to about £250. The tenant, X, after being in possession for some two years, sought to recover the rent that he had overpaid.

Presuming that the mistake was one of fact, not of law,[4] this was surely a case where the parties had wrongly assumed a fact of fundamental importance. To recall Lord THANKERTON's statement in *Bell* v. *Lever Brothers, Ltd.*,[5] their assumption related " to something which both must necessarily have accepted in their minds as an essential and integral element of the subject-matter." There are few things more essential in modern conditions than the applicability or non-applicability of the Rent Restriction Acts. A controlled flat carrying a rent of £140 is an essentially different thing from a flat that commands the highest rent procurable in the open market. If, therefore, *Bell* v. *Lever Brothers, Ltd.*, is interpreted as deciding that a contract based on a false and fundamental assumption common to the parties is void, the tenant in *Solle* v. *Butcher* should have been entitled at common law to recover the overpaid rent and, indeed, had he so claimed, the whole rent paid, as being money paid without consideration. Yet it was held that the contract was not void *ab initio*. The same conclusion was reached by GOFF, J., in *Grist* v. *Bailey*.[6]

Another significant pointer in the same direction is *Leaf* v. *International Galleries*,[7] where the plaintiff bought from the defendants a picture which they both mistakenly believed had been painted by Constable. Thus the picture without this quality

Leaf v. *International Galleries*

1. [1932] A.C., at p. 218; [1931] All E.R. Rep., at p. 28.
2. The decision of the Privy Council in *Sheikh Brothers, Ltd.* v. *Ochsner*, [1957] A.C. 136, turned solely upon the interpretation of the Indian Contract Act 1872.
3. [1950] 1 K.B. 671; [1949] 2 All E.R. 1107.
4. JENKINS, L.J., took the view that it was a mistake of law and therefore to be disregarded; see as to this *infra*, pp. 641 *et seq*.
5. [1932] A.C., at p. 235; [1931] All E.R. Rep., at p. 36; *supra*, p. 213.
6. [1967] Ch. 532; [1966] 2 All E.R. 875; *infra*, p. 219.
7. [1950] 2 K.B. 86; [1950] 1 All E.R. 693.

was essentially different from what the parties believed it to be. The plaintiff rested his claim for the recovery of the purchase price not upon mistake but upon misrepresentation, and the Court of Appeal, as a whole, agreed that it could not have been based upon mistake. The mistake, though " in one sense essential or fundamental,"[1] did not avoid the contract.

The views expressed in *Solle* v. *Butcher* and *Leaf* v. *International Galleries* were repeated in two later cases.

Harrison and Jones, Ltd. v. *Bunten and Lancaster, Ltd.*

In *Harrison and Jones, Ltd.* v. *Bunten and Lancaster, Ltd.*,[2] the buyers agreed in writing to buy from the sellers " 100 bales of Calcutta kapok, Sree brand," equal to standard sample. The seller delivered goods which in all respects answered this description and which were equal to sample. It appeared, however, that both parties had made the contract in the belief that " Calcutta kapok, Sree brand " was pure kapok and consisted of tree cotton, though the truth was that it contained a mixture of bush cotton and was commercially a quite different and inferior category of goods.

The buyers contended that this common mistake made the contract void, but the contention was rejected by PILCHER, J.

" When goods, whether specific or unascertained, are sold under a known trade description without misrepresentation, innocent or guilty, and without breach of warranty, the fact that both parties are unaware that goods of that known trade description lack any particular quality is, in my view, completely irrelevant. The parties are bound by their contract, and there is no room for the doctrine that the contract can be treated as a nullity on the ground of mutual[3] mistake, even though the mistake from the point of view of the purchaser may turn out to be of a fundamental character."

Rose v. *Pim*

In *Frederick E. Rose (London), Ltd.* v. *William H. Pim, Jnr. & Co., Ltd.*:[4]

The plaintiffs in London received an order from their house in Egypt for " Moroccan horsebeans described here as *feveroles*." The plaintiffs, not knowing what " feveroles " were, enquired of the defendants, who said that the word was a mere synonym for horsebeans, which they were in a position to supply. The plaintiffs thereupon made an oral contract with the defendants for the purchase of " horsebeans " and the contract, in these terms, was later put into writing. The defendants delivered the horsebeans to the plaintiffs, who in turn sold and delivered them to an Egyptian firm. When they reached Egypt, the Egyptian buyers found that, though horsebeans, they were not " feveroles " and claimed damages as on a breach of warranty.

The plaintiffs wished in turn to claim damages from the defendants, but were faced with the initial difficulty that their written contract spoke only of " horsebeans " and these had been duly supplied. They therefore asked for rectification of the contract so as to make it read " feveroles," and intended, if successful, to claim damages for the defendants' failure to supply this mysterious article. Here it is to be observed that one of the arguments raised by the defendants' counsel was that the contract

---

1. [1950] 2 K.B. 86, at p. 89; [1950] 1 All E.R. 693, at p. 694.
2. [1953] 1 Q.B. 646; [1953] 1 All E.R. 903. See also *Diamond* v. *British Columbia Thoroughbred Breeders' Society and Boyd* (1965), 52 D.L.R. (2d) 146.
3. The facts disclosed what in this chapter is denominated common mistake.
4. [1953] 2 Q.B. 450; [1953] 2 All E.R. 739.

was void for mistake. That the parties made their contract under the influence of a common mistake was clear: they thought that " feveroles " was just another name for " horsebeans." But the Court of Appeal refused to hold the contract void.

> " What is the effect in law of this common mistake on the contract between the plaintiffs and defendants? " asked DENNING, L.J. " I am clearly of opinion," he answered, " that the contract was not a nullity. It is true that both parties were under a mistake and that the mistake was of a fundamental character with regard to the subject-matter. The goods contracted for—horsebeans—were essentially different from what they were believed to be—' feveroles.' Nevertheless, the parties to all outward appearances were agreed. They had agreed with quite sufficient certainty on a contract for the sale of goods by description, namely, horsebeans. Once they had done that, nothing in their minds could make the contract a nullity from the beginning, though it might, to be sure, be a ground in some circumstances for setting the contract aside in equity."[1]

It would seem, therefore, that at common law a contract is not void merely because the parties have made the same mistake, however fundamental; in other words, that the common law recognizes no doctrine of common mistake as such. A contract will be void only if there is nothing to contract about, either because the subject-matter does not exist at the time of the agreement or because the object of a purported sale already belongs to the buyer; and the ground of such a nullity is not the mistake but the absence of a *res*. The agreement is void of all content. — Conclusion

2. AGREEMENTS IN RESPECT OF WHICH EQUITY WILL GIVE RELIEF

The fact that a contract founded on common mistake is not a complete nullity does not necessarily mean that English law refuses all relief to the parties. In fulfilment of the principles of equity, the court interferes in two respects. — Summary of jurisdiction in equity

First, it will, if it thinks fit, set aside the contract on such terms as are just whether it is void at common law or not.

Secondly, it rectifies a written contract or deed that does not accurately record the agreement made by the parties.

(i) Agreements that may be set aside

In general, as we have seen, equity follows the law in the case of the *res extincta* and the *res sua* and regards the contract as a nullity. It either refuses specific performance or sets the contract aside notwithstanding that it has been executed.[2] But in exercising this jurisdiction, the court in its desire to do full justice may impose terms upon either party. — Equity generally follows the law

---

1. On this, see *infra*, pp. 217–221.
2. *Colyer v. Clay* (1843), 7 Beav. 188; *Cochrane v. Willis* (1865), 1 Ch. App. 58.

Thus, in *Cooper* v. *Phibbs*:[1]

> X agreed to take a lease of a fishery from Y, although, unknown to both parties, it already belonged to X himself. X filed a petition in Chancery for delivery up of the agreement and for such relief "as the nature of the case would admit of and to the court might seem fit."

The House of Lords set the agreement aside, but only on the terms that Y should have a lien on the fishery for such money as he had expended on its improvement. Lord WESTBURY stated the principle in these words:

> "If parties contract under a mutual [*sic*], mistake and misapprehension as to their relative and respective rights, the result is that the agreement is liable to be set aside as having proceeded upon a common mistake."[2]

This principle is clearly wide enough to embrace any contract based on a common and material mistake, even though there is no question of a *res extincta* or a *res sua*. Such, indeed, is the effect of the authorities.[3] *Huddersfield Banking Co., Ltd.* v. *Henry Lister and Son, Ltd.*[4] affords an illustration:

> In 1889 Lister had mortgaged his mills and the fixtures therein to a bank. In 1890 he converted himself into a limited company which in 1892 went into liquidation. The bank, as mortgagees, claimed to be entitled as against the liquidator to 35 looms in the mills. The question was whether they were fixtures within the terms of the mortgage deed. The agents of the bank and of the liquidator inspected the premises and agreed that the looms were not attached to the mills and were therefore not fixtures; and, on that assumption, they concurred in an order made by the court for their sale by the liquidator. It later appeared that the looms were affixed to the mills at the time when the mortgage was made, and had subsequently been wrongfully separated by some unauthorized person.

The bank now applied to the court to set aside the order on the ground that it represented an agreement based on a common mistake, and the court did set it aside. In the words of KAY, L.J.:[5]

> "It seems to me that, both on principle and on authority, when once the court finds that an agreement has been come to between parties who were under a common mistake of a material fact, the court may set it aside, and the court has ample jurisdiction to set aside the order founded upon that agreement. Of course, if . . .

---

1. (1867), L.R. 2 H.L. 149; followed in *Jones* v. *Clifford* (1876), 3 Ch.D. 779; *Allcard* v. *Walker*, [1896] 2 Ch. 369.
2. *Cooper* v. *Phibbs* (1867), L.R. 2 H.L. 149, at p. 170. In the next sentence, however, he said that the agreement "cannot stand." It was pointed out in *Bell* v. *Lever Brothers, Ltd.* that in the passage cited in the text, the word "void" should be substituted for "liable to be set aside"; [1931] 1 K.B., at p. 585, *per* SCRUTTON, L.J.; at p. 591, *per* LAWRENCE, L.J.; [1932] A.C., at p. 218, *per* Lord ATKIN.
3. Even such an early writer as Story had no doubt on the matter; see his book on *Equity*, paras. 140, 141.
4. [1895] 2 Ch. 273.
5. *Ibid.*, at p. 284.

third parties' interests had intervened and so on, difficulties might arise; but nothing of that kind occurs here."[1]

In *Solle* v. *Butcher*,[2] the Court of Appeal, as we have seen, denied that the contract was void at law. In the exercise of its equitable jurisdiction, however, it held that the lease must be set aside. To set it aside *simpliciter* would have been inequitable to the tenant since this would require his immediate dispossession, and therefore he was put on terms. He was given the choice of surrendering the lease entirely or of remaining in possession at the full rent that would have been permissible under the Acts had the landlord served the statutory notice upon him within the proper time limit. DENNING, L.J., restated the governing principle in words closely corresponding to those used by Lord WESTBURY.[3]

In the later case of *Grist* v. *Bailey*:[4]

> The plaintiff agreed to buy the defendant's house subject to an existing tenancy. The value of the house with vacant possession was about £2,250, but the purchase price was fixed at £850 since both parties believed that the tenancy was protected by the Rent Acts. This belief was wrong. In fact, the tenant left without claiming protection.
>
> In an action for specific performance brought by the plaintiff, the defendant counterclaimed that the contract be set aside on the ground of common mistake.

GOFF, J., held that, though the mistake did not suffice to nullify the contract at law, it was material enough to attract the intervention of equity. In the circumstances, however, the learned judge felt that it would be improper merely to refuse a decree of specific performance. Instead, he dismissed the plaintiff's action, but only on the terms that the defendant would enter into a fresh contract to sell the house at its appropriate vacant possession price.

In *Magee* v. *Pennine Insurance Co., Ltd.*,[5] the Court of Appeal followed these authorities, but imposed no terms upon the mistaken party. The facts were as follows:

> The plaintiff acquired a car on hire-purchase terms through a garage and signed a proposal form for its insurance by the defendants for an amount not exceeding £600. The form, which was filled in by the salesman at the garage, contained several innocent misrepresentations. The defendants accepted the proposal and issued a

---

1. It has been objected by Slade (70 L.Q.R. 385, at p. 405) that an agreement cannot be set aside in equity for common mistake and that the *Huddersfield* case is not relevant since it was " a special case where parties were seeking to set aside a consent order." But the judges, especially VAUGHAN WILLIAMS, J., at p. 276, and KAY, L.J., at p. 284, were at pains to insist that the order was only the fulfilment of the agreement and that neither on principle nor on authority could the liability of the agreement to be set aside be affected by its translation into a consent order. This was later stressed by the Court of Appeal in *Wilding* v. *Sanderson*, [1897] 2 Ch. 534. Further, to deny the general proposition that a contract can be set aside for common mistake is to overlook *Scott* v. *Coulson*, [1903] 2 Ch. 249; and a multitude of statements by Chancery judges.
2. [1950] 1 K.B. 671; [1949] 2 All E.R. 1107, *supra*, p. 215.
3. [1950] 1 K.B., at p. 693. See also critical notes by A.L.G. 66 L.Q.R. 169; and by Atiyah and Bennion, 24 M.L.R. 421, at pp. 440-2.
4. [1967] Ch. 532; [1966] 2 All E.R. 875.
5. [1969] 2 Q.B. 507; [1969] 2 All E.R. 891. Harris, 32 M.L.R. 688.

policy which was later renewed for another car acquired by the plaintiff. This car was seriously damaged in an accident. In reply to the plaintiff's claim for £600, the defendants offered by way of compromise to pay him £375. The plaintiff accepted this offer, but the defendants then discovered the existence of the misrepresentations.

In an action brought to recover the £375, the Court of Appeal by a majority held that the compromise agreement, though not void at law, was founded on a common mistake.

It is clear that both parties were mistaken in the sense that, as a result of the misrepresentations, they considered the plaintiff's rights under the policy to be more valuable than they were in fact. On the other hand there was no mistake as to the subject-matter of the compromise. Each party correctly understood that the purpose of their agreement was to settle the amount to which the plaintiff was entitled. It would, therefore, seem that on the authority of *Bell* v. *Lever Brothers, Ltd.*, the compromise was not void at common law. But the majority of the Court of Appeal held that the mistake under which the parties laboured was sufficiently fundamental to enable the agreement to be set aside in equity. WINN, L.J., dissented. He found it impossible to distinguish the facts from those in *Bell* v. *Lever Brothers, Ltd.*

There is much force in this dissenting judgment unless it can be said that in *Bell* v. *Lever Brothers, Ltd.* the House of Lords confined their attention to the doctrines of the common law.[1] This was certainly not the view of Lord BLANESBURGH who expressed his satisfaction that it had been possible to take a view of " equity and procedure " which shielded the appellants from liability to repay the money received under the compensation agreements.[2] Several equity authorities had been cited by counsel, and Lord WARRINGTON in his dissenting speech stated that the rules on the matter were identical both at law and in equity.[3] Nevertheless, it would be unfortunate if the courts were to lack the power to grant specific relief against the consequences of a common mistake if this is warranted by the requirements of substantial justice, especially where the interest of third parties are affected. It is a particular virtue of such discretion that it enables protection to be given to a stranger, who *bona fide* and for value acquires an interest in the subject-matter from one of the original parties. Equity will not interfere to defeat his interest, if he acquires it before its intervention is sought.[4] At common law, on the other hand, if a contract is declared void, a third party, however honest and whatever money he has paid, obtains no rights.[5] It will thus be readily understood that a court may be anxious to keep a case outside the scope of the

---

1. Atiyah and Bennion 24 M.L.R. 421, at pp. 439–42; 85 L.Q.R. 454–6. See also the discussion of compromises of worthless claims, *supra*, pp. 75–7.
2. [1932] A.C., at p. 200.
3. [1932] A.C. 161, at p. 210.
4. *Huddersfield Banking Co., Ltd.* v. *Henry Lister and Son, Ltd.,* [1895] 2 Ch. 273, at pp. 285–6.
5. *Cundy* v. *Lindsay* (1878), 3 App. Cas. 459, *infra*, p. 230.

common law and to deal with it in equity. It remains for the House of Lords to resolve the dilemma.[1]

(ii) Rectification of written agreements

Equity, in the exercise of its exclusive jurisdiction, has satisfactorily dealt with cases where, though the consent is undoubted and real, it has by mistake been inaccurately expressed in a later instrument. Suppose that A orally agrees to sell a house, exclusive of its adjoining yard, to B. Owing to a mistake the later formal and written instrument includes the yard as part of the property to be sold, and, what is worse, the subsequent conveyance actually conveys the yard to B.[2] Can A have the written agreement and the deed rectified, or will he be successfully met by the plea that what has been written and signed must stand?

It may be answered at once that in cases of this type, where it is proved that owing to a mistake the written contract does not substantially represent the real intention of the parties, the court has jurisdiction, not only to rectify the written agreement, but also to order specific performance of it as rectified.[3]

Court has jurisdiction to rectify later contract

> " The essence of rectification is to bring the document which was expressed and intended to be in pursuance of a prior agreement into harmony with that prior agreement."[4]

It is, however, not the contract itself which is rectified, but the incorrect manner in which the common intention of the parties has been expressed in a later document.

> " What you have got to find out is what intention was communicated by one side to the other and with what common intention and common agreement they made their bargain."[5]

It has long been settled that oral evidence is admissible to prove that the intention of the parties expressed in the antecedent agreement, whether written or not, does not represent their true intention. Thus, rectification forms an exception, but a justifiable exception, to the cardinal principle that parol evidence cannot be received to contradict or to vary a written agreement. The basis of that principle is that the writing affords better evidence of the intention of the parties than any parol proof can supply; but to allow it to operate in a case of genuine mistake would, as Story has said,

Rectification admitted even on parol evidence

> " be to allow an act originating in innocence to operate ultimately as a fraud, by enabling the party who receives the benefit of the mistake to resist the claims of justice under the shelter of a rule framed to promote it. In a practical view, there would be as much mischief done by refusing relief in such cases, as there would be introduced by allowing parol evidence in all cases to vary written contracts."[6]

---

1. See also the instructive judgment of the High Court of Australia in *Svanosio v. McNamara* (1956), 96 C.L.R. 186. The High Court, without denying the equitable jurisdiction, took a narrow view of when it should be exercised.
2. *Craddock Brothers, Ltd. v. Hunt*, [1923] 2 Ch. 136. See also *United States v. Motor Trucks, Ltd.*, [1924] A.C. 196.
3. *United States v. Motor Trucks, Ltd.*, [1924] A.C. 196. *Shipley U.D.C. v. Bradford Corporation*, [1936] Ch. 375, at pp. 394-5.
4. *Lovell and Christmas, Ltd. v. Wall* (1911), 104 L.T. 85. *per* COZENS-HARDY, M.R.
5. *Lovell and Christmas, Ltd. v. Wall, supra*, at p. 93, *per* BUCKLEY, L.J.
6. Story, *Equity Jurisprudence*, s. 155.

Irrelevant
that the
common
intention not
embodied in
a binding
contract

A question that has long agitated the courts and upon which conflicting *dicta* are to be found is whether the common intention of the parties must have crystallized into a legally enforceable contract prior to the written document whose rectification is sought.   This controversy was not resolved until the decision of the Court of Appeal in *Joscelyne* v. *Nissen*[1] where the facts were these :

> The plaintiff, who shared a house with the defendant, his daughter, proposed to her that she should take over his car-hire business.   At an early stage in the ensuing conversations, it was made clear that if the proposal were accepted, she should pay all the household expenses, including the electricity, gas and coal bills due in respect of the part of the house occupied by her father.   This oral bargain no doubt disclosed the common intention of the parties, but it could not be described as a finally binding contract.   The discussions culminated in a written contract which, on its true construction, placed no liability upon the daughter to pay the household expenses. After honouring the bargain for a time, she ultimately refused to pay the electricity, gas and coal bills, though she continued to take the profits of the business.

In an action brought by the father, it was ordered that the written document be rectified so as specifically to include the daughter's liability for these bills.   Her argument that the liability had not been imposed upon her by an antecedent contract was rejected. The court endorsed the view of SIMONDS, J., expressed in *Crane* v. *Hegeman-Harris Co. Inc.*,[2] that

> " it is sufficient to find a common continuing intention in regard to a particular provision or aspect of the agreement.   If one finds that in regard to a particular point, the parties were in agreement up to the moment when they executed their formal instrument, and the formal instrument does not conform with that common agreement, then this court has jurisdiction to rectify, although it may be that there was, until the formal instrument was executed, no concluded and binding contract between the parties."[3]

An antecedent agreement, for instance, is rectifiable notwithstanding that it is unenforceable because of its failure to comply with some statutory provision requiring it to be in writing or to be supported by written evidence.[4]   Thus, the result is that " you do not need a prior contract, but a prior common intention."[5]

Burden and
standard of
proof

The burden of proving this common and continuing intention lies upon the party who claims that the written contract should be

---

1. [1970] 2 Q.B. 86.   Baker, 86 L.Q.R. 303; Bromley, 87 L.Q.R. 532.
2. [1971] 1 W.L.R. 1390, at p. 1391, adopting the view of CLAUSON, J., in *Shipley Urban District Council* v. *Bradford Corporation.*, [1936] 1 Ch. 375. *Crane* v. *Hegeman-Harris Co. Inc.* was decided in 1939 and reported in [1939] 1 All E.R. 662, but this report omits several pages of the judgement.
3. [1939] 1 All E.R., at p. 664.   For inconsistent *dicta*, see *Mackenzie* v. *Coulson* (1869), L.R. 8 Eq. 368, at p. 375, *per* JAMES, V.-C.; *Faraday* v. *Tamworth Union* (1916), 86 L.J. Ch. 436, at p. 438, *per* YOUNGER, J.; *Lovell and Christmas, Ltd.* v. *Wall* (1911), 104 L.T. 85, at p. 88, *per* COZENS-HARDY, M.R.; W. *Higgins, Ltd.* v. *Northampton Corporation*, [1927] 1 Ch. 128, at p. 136, *per* ROMER, J.; *Frederick E. Rose* v. *Wm. H. Pim, Ltd.*, [1953] 2 Q.B. 53, at p. 461, *per* DENNING, L.J.
4. *United States* v. *Motor Trucks, Ltd.*, [1924] A.C. 196.   A decision dealing with the now repealed s. 4 of the Sale of Goods Act 1893.
5. *Earl* v. *Hector Whaling, Ltd.*, [1961] 1 Lloyd's Rep. 459, at p. 464, *per* HARMAN, L.J.   Hudson, 24 M.L.R. 800.

rectified.[1] As regards the standard of proof required, all that can be said is that the claim will fail unless the common intention upon which it is based is proved by *convincing* evidence. It is not necessary that the evidence should be " irrefragable " as Lord Thurlow once suggested, or that it should settle the question " beyond all reasonable doubt " as is demanded by the criminal law.[2] If the negotiations leading up to the execution of the written instrument were vague and inconclusive, so that it is impossible to ascertain what the parties really meant, then the writing represents the only agreement that has been concluded, and there is no antecedent and common intention upon which notification can be based.

Moreover, it must be shown that the alleged common intention, though once undoubtedly reached, continued unchanged down to the time when the instrument was reached. Proof that the parties varied their original intention and that the instrument represents what they finally agreed is fatal to a suit for rectification.[3]

Finally, it must be emphasized that the issue relates not to the individual intention of the parties, but to their common intention. If the defendant can satisfy the court that he understood the agreement to be exactly what was stated in the written instrument, rectification will be excluded.[4]

The issue relates to the common intention

B. WHERE AN APPARENT AGREEMENT IS ALLEGED TO BE VITIATED BY MUTUAL OR UNILATERAL MISTAKE

The second category of case is where to outward appearances a contract has been concluded, but one of the parties alleges that his mind was affected by a fundamental mistake of fact and that he never intended to make that precise contract. Here, unlike the case of common mistake, the question of consent is directly raised. It is alleged that despite appearances there is no genuine agreement since there is no corresponding offer and acceptance. X, who admittedly accepted Y's offer to sell certain pearls, now alleges that he thought that he was being offered real pearls, not imitation as in fact they are.

Question is one of offer and acceptance

Before considering the manner in which the law deals with such an allegation it is necessary to emphasize that at common

The general principles

1. *Tucker* v. *Bennett* (1887), 38 Ch.D. 1, at p. 9, *per* Cotton, L.J.
2. *Joscelyne* v. *Nissen*, [1970] 2 Q.B. 86, at p. 98, *per curiam*. For Lord Thurlow's remark, see *Shelburne* v. *Inchiquin* (1784), 1 Bro. C.C. 338, at p. 341.
3. *Marquess of Breadalbane* v. *Marquess of Chandos* (1837), 2 My & CR. 711, (rectification of a marriage settlement).
4. *Lloyd* v. *Stanbury*, [1971] 2 All E.R. 267; [1971] 1 W.L.R. 535. There are some old cases in which a mistake by one party has by itself been relied on by the Court to justify offering the other party the choice between submitting to rectification or having the whole contract rescinded but these were overruled by the Court of Appeal in *Riverlate Properties, Ltd.*, v. *Paul*, [1975] Ch. 133; [1974] 2 All E.R. 656. A mistake by one party, which is known to the other party will suffice to justify rectification however, at least where the knowledge of the other party is tantamount to sharp practice.

law only fundamental mistake is material. This principle was stated by BLACKBURN, J., in a passage that has always been regarded as an authoritative statement of the law.[1] A mistake is wholly immaterial at common law unless it results in a complete difference in substance between what the mistaken party bargained for and what in fact he will obtain if the contract is fulfilled; as for example where the buyer intends to buy real pearls and the seller intends to sell imitation pearls. Translated into the familiar rubric of offer and acceptance, this means that the only type of mistake which is ever capable of excluding offer and acceptance is one that prevents the mistaken party from appreciating the fundamental character of the offer or the acceptance. The formation of agreement depends upon the correspondence of offer and acceptance, and if the offer is made in one sense but accepted in another, as in the example of the real and imitation pearls, there is at least ground for arguing that there is no consent and therefore no genuine agreement. The mistaken party can at any rate say—for what it is worth—that he personally did not intend to make the contract which he appears to have made.

But once it is admitted that he accepted and intended to accept the precise offer made to him, he obviously cannot deny the existence of the resulting agreement merely by proving that his acceptance was due to a mistake. The evidence may show, for instance, that in a contract for the sale of land the purchaser intended to purchase *that* land from *that* vendor at *that* price, but that his reason for doing so was his mistaken idea that the land was rich in minerals. In other words, he would not have concluded the bargain had he appreciated the true position. Nevertheless, there was no fundamental mistake. He understood the true character of the offer, he intended to accept the exact terms proposed by the vendor and therefore it is vain for him to deny the existence of a common intention. This is so even though his inflated view of the value of the land was known to the vendor. In this case, equitable relief may conceivably be available to him[2] but he may not plead that the contract is a nullity. No doubt the motive or reason that persuaded him to conclude the agreement was utterly false, but an agreement intentionally made does not cease to be an agreement merely because it has been actuated by a mistaken motive. This truism was copiously illustrated by Lord ATKIN in the following passage.

> " A buys B's horse; he thinks the horse is sound and he pays the price of a sound horse; he would certainly not have bought the horse if he had known, as the fact is, that the horse is unsound. If B has made no representation as to soundness and has not contracted that the horse is sound, A is bound and cannot recover back the price. . . . A agrees to take on lease or to buy from B an unfurnished dwelling house. The house is in fact uninhabitable. A would never have entered into the bargain if he had known the fact. A has no remedy, and the position is the same whether B knew the facts or not, so long as he made no representation or gave no warranty. A buys a roadside garage business from B abutting on a public thoroughfare; unknown to A but known to B, it has

At common law, only fundamental mistake material

Mistaken motive immaterial

---

1. *Kennedy* v. *Panama Royal Mail Co.* (1867), L.R. 2 Q.B. 580, at p. 587.
2. *Infra*, p. 235 *et seq.*

already been decided to construct a bypass road which will divert substantially the whole of the traffic from passing A's garage. Again A has no remedy. All these cases involve hardship on A and benefit to B, as most people would say unjustly. They can be supported on the ground that it is of paramount importance that contracts should be observed, and that if parties honestly comply with the essentials of the formation of contracts—*i.e., agree in the same terms on the same subject-matter*—they are bound, and must rely on the stipulations of the contract for protection from the effect of facts unknown to them."[1]

It should also be emphasized that the burden of persuading the court to disturb what to outward appearances is a binding contract falls on the party who alleges the mistake. Moreover, the burden is not light, for the result of holding that there is no contract may seriously prejudice a third party who has in good faith made a bargain relating to the subject-matter of the apparent agreement.

Burden of proof

1. EFFECT OF MUTUAL AND UNILATERAL MISTAKE AT COMMON LAW

(i) Mutual mistake

Let us first examine the case of mutual mistake, where each party is mistaken as to the other's intention, though neither realizes that the respective promises have been misunderstood. This situation would arise, for instance, if B were to offer to sell his Ford Cortina car to A and A were to accept in the belief that the offer related to a Ford Zephyr. In such a case, no doubt, if the minds of the parties could be probed, genuine consent would be found wanting. But, the question is not what the parties had in their minds, but what reasonable third parties would infer from their words or conduct.

Mutual mistake does not per se nullify the contract

Applying itself to this task, the court has to determine what Austin called " the sense of the promise."[2] In other words, it decides whether a sensible third party would take the agreement to mean what A understood it to mean or what B understood it to mean, or whether indeed any meaning can be attributed to it at all. The promisor may have made his promise in one sense, the promisee may have accepted it in another. There may have been mistake of a fundamental character which caused the one to put a wrong interpretation upon the promise of the other. But it is for the court to decide what, if any, is the interpretation to be put on what the parties have said or done.

" The sense of the promise "

In a leading case, BLACKBURN, J., explained the attitude of the law. He said:

> " If whatever a man's real intention may be, he so conducts himself that a reasonable man would believe that he was assenting to the terms proposed by the other party, and that other party upon that belief enters into the contract with him, the man thus conducting himself would be equally bound as if he had intended to agree to the other party's terms."[3]

---

1. *Bell* v. *Lever Brothers, Ltd.,* [1932] A.C. 161, at p. 224; [1931] All E.R. Rep. 1, at p. 30, *per* Lord ATKIN. The case of *Smith* v. *Hughes* (1871), L.R. 6 Q.B. 597, illustrates how difficult it may be to decide whether the parties agreed in the same terms on the same subject-matter.
2. *Lectures on Jurisprudence,* Lecture 21, note 89.
3. *Smith* v. *Hughes* (1871), L.R. 6 Q.B. 597, at p. 607.

Again in another case, POLLOCK, C.B., said:

> " If any person, by a course of conduct or by actual expressions,
> so conducts himself that another may reasonably infer the existence
> of an agreement . . . whether the party intends that he should do so
> or not, it has the effect that the party using that language or who has
> so conducted himself, cannot afterwards gainsay the reasonable
> inference to be drawn from his words or conduct."[1]

The result is that if, from the whole of the evidence, a reasonable
man would infer the existence of a contract in a given sense, the
court, notwithstanding a material mistake, will hold that a contract
in that sense is binding upon both parties.   The apparent contract
will stand.   Two decisions may be cited by way of illustrations.
     In *Wood* v. *Scarth*[2]:

> The defendant offered in writing to let a public house to the plaintiff
> for £63 a year, and the plaintiff, after an interview with the defen-
> dant's clerk, accepted the offer by letter.   The defendant intended
> that a premium of £500 should be payable in addition to the rent
> and he believed that the clerk had made this clear to the plaintiff.
> The latter, however, believed that his only financial obligation was
> the payment of rent.

It was held at *nisi prius* that the apparent contract must stand.
The mistake of the defendant could not at law gainsay what would
obviously be inferred from the acceptance of his exact offer.
     In *Scott* v. *Littledale*[3]:

> The defendants sold by sample to the plaintiff a hundred chests
> of tea then lying in bond " *ex* the ship ' Star of the East,' " but later
> discovered that they had submitted a sample of a totally different
> tea lower in quality than that contained in the chests.

In an action for non-delivery of the hundred chests, the common
law court, though it conceded that the sellers might be entitled
to partial relief in equity, refused to declare the contract void.
The sellers had no doubt submitted a wrong sample by mistake,
but they were precluded by their own conduct from disputing the
natural inference that would be drawn from the facts.

May be
impossible
to infer any
agreement

     Cases may occur, of course, in which it is impossible to
impute any definite agreement to the parties.   If the evidence is
so conflicting that there is nothing sufficiently solid from which
to infer a contract in any final form without indulging in mere
speculation, the court must of necessity declare that no contract
whatsoever has been created.
     An illustration of this situation is *Scriven Brothers & Co.* v.
Hindley & Co.[4]:

> This was an action to recover the price of some Russian tow
> alleged to have been sold at an auction by the plaintiffs to the
> defendants.   The auctioneer was employed to sell both hemp and
> tow, and his catalogue specified two separate lots, one comprising
> 47, the other 176 bales.   The catalogue failed to state that the latter
> contained tow, not hemp.   The same shipping mark, indicating

---

1. *Cornish* v. *Abington* (1859), 4 H. & N. 549, at p. 556.
2. (1858), 1 F. & F. 293.   The full facts cannot be appreciated unless the
   earlier case in equity between the same parties, (1855), s K. & J. 33, is also
   considered.
3. (1858), 8 E. & B. 815.
4. [1913] 3 K.B. 564.   Cf. *Tamplin* v. *James, infra*, p. 235.

what ship had brought the goods to England, was entered against each lot. Samples of each lot were on view, but the defendants did not inspect these as they had already seen samples of the hemp at the plaintiff's show rooms. The defendants, believing that both lots contained hemp, successfuly bid an extravagant price for the 176 bales of tow. Witnesses from both sides admitted that in their experience Russian tow and Russian hemp had never been landed from the same ship under the same shipping mark.

Here the plaintiffs intended to sell tow, the defendants intended to buy hemp. The plaintiffs were unaware of the intention to bid for hemp only, for though the auctioneer realized that the defendants had shown a lack of judgment he thought that this merely reflected their ignorance of the market value of tow. Though clearly there was no genuine agreement between the parties, the question was whether the judge should presume the existence of a contract for the sale of tow. This he declined to do. The sense of the promise could not be determined. Owing to the ambiguity of the circumstances it could not be affirmed with reasonable certitude which commodity was the subject of the contract. There was therefore no binding contract.

In the leading case of *Raffles* v. *Wichelhaus*[1] the facts were these:

Raffles v. *Wichelhaus*

> A agreed to buy and B agreed to sell a consignment of cotton which was to arrive " *ex Peerless* from Bombay." In actual fact two ships called *Peerless* sailed from Bombay, one in October, the other in December. It was held that the buyer was not liable for refusal to accept cotton despatched by the December ship.

For procedural reasons the court never decided whether there was a contract or not. All that was actually decided was that it was open to the defendant to show that the contract was ambiguous and that he intended the October ship. If the case had gone to trial it would then have been open to the jury to hold either that there was no contract or to hold that there was a contract either for the October ship or the December ship. In modern terms this would turn on whether a reasonable man would deduce an agreement from the behaviour of the parties though in 1864 it might well have been thought to turn on whether the parties actually intended the same ship.

(ii) Unilateral Mistake

We must now consider the attitude of common law to unilateral mistake, the distinguishing feature of which, as we have seen, is that the mistake of X is known to the other party, Y. It must be stressed that, in this context, a man is taken to have known what would have been obvious to a reasonable person in the light of the surrounding circumstances. Thus in *Hartog* v. *Colin and Shields*[2]:

Unilateral mistake

> An offer was accepted to sell certain Argentine hareskins at a certain price *per* pound. The preliminary negotiations, however, had proceeded on the clear understanding that the skins would be sold at so much *per* piece, not *per* pound, and at the trial expert evidence proved the existence of a trade custom to fix the price by reference to a piece. The value of a piece was approximately one-third of that of a pound.

---

1. (1864), 2 H. & C. 906. See Simpson, 91 L.Q.R. 247, at p. 268.
2. [1939] 3 All E.R. 566.

It was held that the buyer must be taken to have known the mistake made by the sellers in the formulation of their offer.

Mistake of identity

The majority of cases in which the question of unilateral mistake has arisen have been cases of mistaken identity, and their examination will serve to show the way in which the courts approach the problem.[1]

Suppose that A, pretending to be X, makes an offer to B which B accepts in the belief that A is in fact X. In subsequent proceedings arising out of this transaction, B alleges that he would have withheld his acceptance had he not mistaken A's identity. If this allegation is proved and if B's intention was known to A at the time of the acceptance, there is, as a matter of pure logic, no correspondence between offer and acceptance and therefore there should be no contract. Nevertheless, outward appearances cannot be neglected, and the *prima facie* presumption applicable to this type of case is that, despite the mistake, a contract has been concluded between the parties. The onus of rebutting this presumption lies upon the party who pleads mistake.[2]

Prerequisites for mistake to be operative

To discharge this burden, he must prove (i) that he intended to deal with some person other than the person with whom he has apparently made a contract; (ii) that the latter was aware of this intention; (iii) that at the time of negotiating the agreement, he regarded the identity of the other contracting party as a matter of crucial importance; and (iv) that he took reasonable steps to verify the identity of that party.

(i) Intention to contract with X not with A

(i) The first of these requirements pre-supposes a confusion between two distinct entities. If this is not the case there is no operative mistake. Two cases illustrate this point. In *Sowler v. Potter*:[3]

> In May, 1938, the defendant, who was then known as Ann Robinson, was convicted of permitting disorderly conduct at a café in Great Swan Alley, E.C. In July of the same year she assumed the name of Ann Potter and negotiating under that name obtained a lease of Mrs. Sowler's premises in Coleman St., E.C. The agent who had conducted the negotiations on behalf of Mrs. Sowler stated in evidence that he remembered the conviction of Ann Robinson. "Therefore," said the trial judge, "he thought when he entered into this contract with the defendant that he was entering into a contract with some person other than the Mrs. Ann Robinson who had been convicted."

On this interpretation of the facts TUCKER, J., held the lease to be void *ab initio*, since the plaintiff was mistaken with regard to the identity of the tenant.

It may be questioned, with respect, whether this decision was correct. At the time when the agent concluded the bargain, the possibility that the defendant might be Ann Robinson was not within his contemplation, and therefore he could scarcely deny that he intended to grant the lease to the person with whom he had dealt. It is no doubt true that he would not have formed this

---

1. See Williams, 23 Can. Bar Rev. 271, 380.
2. I.e. upon the offeree in the hypothetical case given above but if the offeror is the mistaken person the onus lies upon him.
3. [1940] 1 K.B. 271. For a fuller report, see [1939] 4 All E.R. 478. For a criticism of the decision, see Goodhart, 57 L.Q.R. 228.

intention had he appreciated what manner of person the tenant was, but once it was clear that he had that intention in fact the mistaken reason or motive that induced it was not enough to nullify the lease. To apply the words of A. L. SMITH, L.J., in an earlier case, there was only one entity—the woman known at one moment as Ann Robinson, at another as Ann Potter—and it was with this one entity that the landlord intended to contract.[1] On the other hand the lease was clearly voidable on the ground of fraudulent misrepresentation, for in answer to a request for a reference, the defendant submitted the name of a certain Mr. Hopfenkopf, an obvious accomplice in her crafty scheme. This gentleman, according to the finding of the judge, " deliberately wrote what he knew perfectly well to be untrue for the purpose of deceiving the plaintiff."[2] The lease was therefore voidable and there was no reason to invoke the law of mistake.[3]

In *King's Norton Metal Co., Ltd.* v. *Edridge, Merrett & Co., Ltd.*,[4]

> A man named Wallis, for the purpose of cheating, set up in business as Hallam & Co. He prepared writing paper at the head of which was a faked illustration of a large factory and a statement that Hallam & Co. had depots at Belfast, Lille and Ghent. Writing on this paper, he ordered and obtained goods from the plaintiffs which were later bought from him in good faith by the defendants. The plaintiffs had previously sold goods to Wallis and had been paid by a cheque signed " Hallam & Co." In an action against the defendants for the value of the goods, the plaintiffs contended that their apparent contract with Hallam & Co. was void, since they mistakenly believed that such a firm existed, and that therefore the property in the goods still resided in them.

The contention failed. The plaintiffs, since they could not have relied on the credit of a non-existent person, must have intended to contract with the writer of the letter, though of course they would not have formed this intention had they known that he was masquerading under an *alias*. They were unable to show that they meant to contract with Hallam & Co., not with Wallis, for there was no other entity in question. The contract was no doubt voidable for fraud, but as it had not been avoided at the time of the sale by Wallis to the defendants, the title of the latter prevailed over that of the plaintiffs.

(ii) To satisfy the second requirement, the mistaken party must prove that the other party was aware of the mistake. This requirement seldom causes difficulty, since in the majority of cases the mistake has been induced by the fraud of that party. In *Boulton* v. *Jones*,[5] however, the matter was by no means clear.

(ii) B's intention known to A

---

1. *King's Norton Metal Co., Ltd.* v. *Edridge, Merrett & Co., Ltd.* (1897), 14 T.L.R. 98, at p. 99.
2. This aspect of the case is reported only in [1939] 4 All E.R. 478.
3. Disapproval of·the decision was expressed by the Court of Appeal in *Gallie* v. *Lee*, [1969] 2 Ch. 17, at p. 33, *per* Lord DENNING; at p. 41, *per* RUSSELL, L.J.; at p. 45, *per* SALMON, L.J.
4. *Supra*, footnote 1. See also *Porter* v. *Latec Finance (Queensland) Pty., Ltd.* (1964), 111 C.L.R. 177.
5. (1857), 2 H. & N. 564; 27 L.J. Ex. 117. It should be noted that the report of this case given in Hurlstone and Norman is incomplete, and that for a proper understanding of the judgment, reference should be made to the other reports, especially to the Law Journal.

Jones, who had been accustomed to deal with Brocklehurst, sent him a written order for fifty feet of leather hose on the very day that Brocklehurst had transferred his business to his foreman, the plaintiff.   The plaintiff executed the order, but Jones accepted and used the goods in the belief that they had been supplied by Brocklehurst.   He refused to pay the price, alleging that he had intended to contract with Brocklehurst personally, since he had a set-off which he wished to enforce against him.

It was held that Jones was not liable for the price, but it is not clear whether the mistake was regarded by the court as unilateral or mutual.   If the court was convinced that the plaintiff knew of the set-off and therefore that the offer was not intended for him, the contract was clearly vitiated by unilateral mistake and was rightly held void.[1]   But on the facts as a whole it is perhaps more reasonable to treat the mistake as mutual.   On this interpretation the sense of the promise fell to be determined, and the decision is more difficult to support.   A disinterested spectator, knowing nothing of the set-off and looking at the circumstances objectively, would naturally assume the identity of the supplier to be a matter of indifference to the purchaser of such an ordinary commodity as hose piping.

Most of the identity cases, however, have been obvious examples of unilateral mistake and in most the mistake has been due to the fraud of one of the parties.   A clear instance is *Hardman v. Booth*[2] where the facts were these:

> X, one of the plaintiffs, called at the place of business of Gandell & Co.   This firm consisted of Thomas Gandell only, though the business was managed by a clerk called Edward Gandell.   X, being fraudulently persuaded by Edward that the latter was a member of the firm, sold and delivered goods to the place of business of Gandell & Co. but invoiced them to " Edward Gandell & Co."   Edward, who carried on a separate business with one Todd, pledged the goods with the defendant for advances *bona fide* made to Gandell & Todd.   The plaintiffs now sued the defendant for conversion.

Here no contract of sale ever came into existence, since X's offer was made to Thomas only, and Edward, though he knew this fact, purported to accept it for himself.   Edward thus acquired no title to the goods capable of transfer to the innocent defendant, and the latter was liable for conversion.

(iii) Identity of his co-contractor of crucial importance to B

(iii) Controversy is most frequently provoked by the need to satisfy the third of the requirements—that, at the time of negotiating the agreement, the person labouring under the mistake regarded the identity of the other contracting party as a matter of crucial importance, and that this was apparent from his conduct during the negotiations.   The problem arose in an acute form in the case of *Cundy* v. *Lindsay*[3]:

---

1. BRAMWELL, B., seems to have taken this view of the facts, for he said: " It is an admitted fact that the defendant supposed he was dealing with Brocklehurst, and the plaintiff misled him by executing the order unknown to him ": (1857), 27 L.J. Ex., at p. 119.
2. (1863), 1 H. & C. 803.
3. (1878), 3 App. Cas. 459.

Cundy v. *Lindsay*

A fraudulent person named Blenkarn, writing from " 37 Wood St., Cheapside," offered to buy goods from the plaintiffs, and he signed his letter in such a way that his name appeared to be " Blenkiron & Co." The latter were a respectable firm carrying on business at 123 Wood St. Blenkarn occupied a room which he called 37 Wood St., but in fact its entrance was from an adjoining street. The plaintiffs, who were aware of the high reputation of Blenkiron & Co., though they neither knew nor troubled to ascertain the number of the street where they did business, purported to accept the offer and despatched the goods to " Messrs. Blenkiron & Co., 37 Wood St., Cheapside." These were received by the rogue Blenkarn, and he in turn sold them to the defendants, who took them in all good faith. The plaintiffs now sued the defendants for conversion.

The case is difficult, for the facts admitted of two different inferences.

First, it might be inferred that, just as in *Hardman* v. *Booth*, the plaintiffs intended to sell to Blenkiron & Co., but that Blenkarn fraudulently assumed the position of buyer. If this represented the true position, an offer to sell to Blenkiron & Co. was knowingly " accepted " by Blenkarn and therefore no contract would ensue.

Secondly, unlike *Hardman* v. *Booth*, it might be inferred that the plaintiffs, though deceived by the fraud of Blenkarn, intended or were at least content to sell to the person who traded at 37 Wood St., from which address the offer to buy had come and to which the goods were sent. If this were the true position, there was a contract with Blenkarn of 37 Wood St., though one that was voidable against him for his fraud.

The second inference was drawn unanimously by three judges in the Queen's Bench Division,[1] but the Court of Appeal and the House of Lords, with equal unanimity, preferred the first view.

Such a conclusion prejudices third parties who later deal in good faith with the fraudulent person. On the view of the facts taken by the House of Lords, the defendants in *Cundy* v. *Lindsay* were of course liable, for there had never been a contract of sale between the plaintiffs and Blenkarn, and Blenkarn therefore possessed no title which he could pass to a third person. On the other hand, had the view of the facts taken by the Queen's Bench Division prevailed, while the contract between the plaintiffs and Blenkarn would have been voidable for the latter's fraud, the defendants would nevertheless have been secure, since they had innocently acquired this voidable title to the goods before it had in fact been avoided by the plaintiffs.

Third parties prejudiced

The problem whether this third requirement has been satisfied has proved even more troublesome where the contract has been made *inter praesentes*, not through the post as in *Cundy* v. *Lindsay*. Three cases concerned with this aspect of the problem invite comparison: *Phillips* v. *Brooks*, *Ltd.*, *Ingram* v. *Little* and *Lewis* v. *Averay*.

Cases where contract made inter praesentes

---

1. *Cundy* v. *Lindsay* (1876), 1 Q.B.D. 348, *per* BLACKBURN, MELLOR and LUSH, JJ.

The facts of *Phillips* v. *Brooks, Ltd.*[1] were as follows:

> A man called North entered the plaintiff's shop and selected pearls
> of the value of £2,550 and a ring worth £450. He then wrote out
> a cheque for £3,000 saying, as he did so, " You see who I am, I am
> Sir George Bullough," and then gave an address in St. James'
> Square. The plaintiff had heard of Bullough and upon consulting
> a directory found that he lived at the address given. He then said:
> " Would you like to take the articles with you?" North replied:
> " You had better have the cheque cleared first, but I should like to
> take the ring, as it is my wife's birthday tomorrow." The plaintiff
> let him do so. North pledged the ring for £350 to the defendant,
> who had no notice of the fraud.

These facts, as in *Cundy* v. *Lindsay*, admitted of two possible
answers. The plaintiff either intended to sell the ring to the
person present in the shop, whoever he was, or he intended to
sell to Bullough and to nobody else. If the first solution was
correct, then a contract of sale had been concluded, though one
that was voidable for the fraudulent representation of North that
the means of payment would be furnished by Bullough. Being
voidable, *i.e.*, valid until disaffirmed, a good title to the ring would
be acquired by the defendant. If, however, the second solution
was correct, then the plaintiff's mistake prevented a contract from
arising. Not even a voidable title would pass to North, and the
defendant could acquire no right of property whatsoever.

HORRIDGE, J., adopted the first solution. He drew the
inference that the jeweller, doubtless gratified that he had secured
Bullough as a customer, intended, come what might, to sell to
the person present in the shop. It is submitted, with respect,
that this was the correct inference. The jeweller could succeed
only upon proof that he intended to contract with Bullough and
with nobody else, but in fact the evidence that he tendered
scarcely supported this view. Beyond looking up Bullough's
address in a directory, he had taken no steps to verify his customer's story and it would seem that he deliberately took the risk
of the story being true.

The facts in *Ingram* v. *Little*[2] were these:

> A swindler, falsely calling himself Hutchinson, went to the
> residence of the plaintiffs and negotiated for the purchase of their
> car. They agreed to sell it to him for £717, but, on hearing his
> proposal to pay by cheque, called the bargain off. He therefore
> told them that he was P. G. M. Hutchinson having business interests
> in Guildford and that he lived at Stanstead House, Caterham.
> Upon hearing this, one of the plaintiffs slipped out of the room,
> consulted the telephone directory at a nearby post office and verified
> that P. G. M. Hutchinson lived at the Caterham address. Feeling
> reassured, the plaintiffs, though they had never previously heard of
> P. G. M. Hutchinson, agreed to sell the car to the swindler. He
> later sold it to the defendant who acted in good faith.

These facts raised similar problems to those which confronted

---

1. [1919] 2 K.B. 243. The only case concerning mistake *inter praesentes* to
reach the House of Lords is *Lake* v. *Simmons*, [1927] A.C. 487 but that case
can be regarded as doing no more than decide the meaning of the word
" customer " in an insurance policy. See also *Dennant* v. *Skinner and
Collom*, [1948] 2 K.B. 164; [1948] 2 All E.R. 29.
2. [1961] 1 Q.B. 31; [1960] 3 All E.R. 332. See Hall, [1961] C.L.J. 86.

HORRIDGE, J., in *Phillips* v. *Brooks, Ltd.*[1] but, unlike that learned judge, the majority of the Court of Appeal held that the offer of the plaintiffs to sell the car was to be interpreted as made solely to P. G. M. Hutchinson and that the swindler was incapable of accepting it. The plaintiffs, therefore succeeded in their claim against the defendant for the return of the car or alternatively for damages.

The facts of *Lewis* v. *Averay*,[2] the most recent decision on the subject, were these:

Lewis v. *Averay*

> A rogue, posing as Richard Greene the well-known film actor, called upon the plaintiff and offered to buy his car which was advertised for sale at £450. The plaintiff accepted the offer, and was given a cheque, signed R. A. Green, for £450. Afraid that the cheque might be worthless, he resisted a proposal that the car should be removed at once. The rogue, by way of showing that he was Richard Greene, produced a special pass of admission to Pinewood Studios bearing an official stamp. Satisfied with this, the plaintiff handed over the log book and allowed the car to be taken away. The cheque had been stolen and was worthless. The rogue, now passing as Lewis, sold the car to the defendant and handed over the log book to him.

The present action of conversion by the plaintiff for the recovery of the car or its value failed. The Court of Appeal followed *Phillips* v. *Brooks, Ltd.*, expressed disagreement with *Ingram* v. *Little*, and held that despite his mistake, the plaintiff had concluded a contract with the rogue. He had failed to rebut the *prima facie* presumption that he had made a contract with the rogue when he allowed the car to be taken away. The contract was no doubt voidable for fraud, but it could not be avoided now that the car had come into the hands of an innocent purchaser for value.

Between these three cases it is not easy to differentiate; and the task has been complicated by the suggestion now current in judicial and academic circles, though vigorously rejected by Lord DENNING, M.R., that a distinction must be drawn between the identity and the attributes of a person. It is said that a mistake as to attributes, as opposed to identity, will not suffice to enable the contract to be treated as void *ab initio*. This distinction reflects, as in a glass darkly, the views of Aristotle,[4] but whatever its significance in philosophy it is not a safe guide through the crude problems of litigation. If A seeks to escape from his apparent contract with B, he must satisfy the court that he mistakenly identified B with X. He will fail unless he shows that by his behaviour during the process of negotiating the contract he made it abundantly clear that such identification was a matter of crucial importance to him. This he will usually seek to do by showing that his mind was directed to some particular attribute possessed by X but wanting in B. This attribute will vary with the circumstances. In one case it may be credit-worthiness or

Alleged distinction between identity and attributes

---

1. [1919] 2 K.B. 243.
2. [1972] 1 Q.B. 198; [1971] 3 All E.R. 907.
3. *Lewis* v. *Averay*, [1971] 3 W.L.R. 603, at p. 609.
4. See Bertrand Russell, *History of Western Philosophy* (2nd impression, 1947), p. 185.

social standing; in another it may be skill in some vocation. A hypothetical example of the latter was suggested by Pearce, L.J., in *Ingram* v. *Little*.[1]

> " If a man orally commissions a portrait from some unknown artist who had deliberately passed himself off, whether by disguise or merely by verbal cosmetics, as a famous painter, the imposter could not accept the offer. For though the offer was made to him physically, it is obviously, as he knows, addressed to the famous painter. The mistake in identity on such facts is clear and the nature of the contract makes it obvious that the identity was of vital importance to the offeror."

In short, it is submitted that for legal purposes, " identity " is not opposed to " attributes ". Rather, it is made manifest by them. It is tempting, indeed, to suggest that a person's identity is but an amalgam of his various attributes.

(iv) Innocent party must take steps to verify identity of co-contractor

(iv) It is not enough for the plaintiff to show that he had made known the importance which he attached to the identity of the other party. In all cases, whether the contract is made *inter praesentes* or *inter absentes*, he must go further and establish that he took all reasonable steps to verify the identity of the person with whom he was invited to deal. This, perhaps, is the heart of the matter. In *Phillips* v. *Brooks, Ltd.* and *Lewis* v. *Averay* the respective plaintiffs failed because their attempts to test the truth of what they had been told were inadequate. What is surprising is that the same conclusion was not reached in *Ingram* v. *Little*.

The true distinction between contract *inter praesentes* and *inter absentes*

It is sometimes said that the distinction between a contract made *inter praesentes* and one made *inter absentes* is one of law. The distinction, however, is merely one of fact. It may, no doubt, be more difficult to rebut the *prima facie* presumption in favour of the contract where the offer is made to, and accepted by, the person to whom it is orally addressed. But the task of the person labouring under the mistake is different not in kind, but in degree. If in *Cundy* v. *Lindsay* the rogue had appeared in person armed with forged references purporting to come from the respectable Blenkiron & Co. the decision would scarcely have gone against the plaintiffs.

State of the authorities on contracts *inter praesentes*

The three cases—*Phillips* v. *Brooks, Ltd., Ingram* v. *Little* and *Lewis* v. *Averay*—are substantially indistinguishable on the facts.[2] In *Lewis* v. *Averay*, the Court of Appeal applied *Phillips* v. *Brooks, Ltd.* They doubted the decision in *Ingram* v. *Little* and it would now be dangerous to rely upon it. *Cundy* v. *Lindsay*, as a decision of the House of Lords is, at common law, unassailable, though it is permissible to regret the inference which their Lordships drew from the facts. The cases as a whole pose the familiar dilemma: which of two innocent parties is to bear a loss caused by the fraud of a third. The common law does not countenance the idea of apportionment. But this idea has already been accepted and applied by the legislature in the doctrine of frustration. By the Law Reform (Frustrated Contracts) Act 1943, the

---

1. [1961] 1 Q.B. 31, at p. 57.
2. In *Phillips* v. *Brooks, Ltd.,* the shopkeeper knew of the existence of Sir George Bullough: In *Ingram* v. *Little,* the plaintiffs had never heard of Mr. P. G. M. Hutchinson. But if this difference is one of importance, it would seem to tell against the plaintiffs and to throw doubt on the decision.

courts are given, within stated limits, the discretion to divide the loss between two innocent parties.[1]   This example might well be followed in a further statute and applied to cases of unilateral mistake.[2]

2. EFFECT OF MUTUAL AND UNILATERAL MISTAKE IN EQUITY

(i) Mutual mistake

Equity follows the law in holding that a mutual mistake does not as a matter of principle nullify a contract.[3]   In the nature of things, indeed, there is no room for equitable relief, since the court, after considering the mistake and every other relevant fact, itself determines the sense of the promise.   In general, therefore, a party is not allowed to obtain rectification or rescission of a contract or to resist its specific performance on the ground that he understood it in a sense different from that determined by the court.

Mutual mistake: equity generally follows the law

The position is illustrated by the case of *Tamplin* v. *James*.[4]

Tamplin v. *James*

> James, who had been the highest bidder at an auction sale of a public house, resisted a suit for specific performance on the ground that he had made a mistake.   At the time when he made his bid he believed that a certain field, which had long been occupied by the publican, was part of the lot offered for sale, though in fact it was held under a separate lease from a third party.   There was no misdescription or ambiguity in the particulars of sale.

On these facts specific performance of the contract in the sense understood by the auctioneer was decreed.

> " Where there has been no misrepresentation," said BAGGALAY, L.J.,[5] " and where there is no ambiguity in the terms of the contract, the defendant cannot be allowed to evade the performance of it by the simple statement that he has made a mistake.   Were such to be the law, the performance of a contract could seldom be enforced upon an unwilling party who was also unscrupulous."

Again, where a lessor's agent had agreed to grant a lease for seven or fourteen years, which the lessor mistakenly understood to mean a lease determinable at *his* option at the end of seven years instead of at the tenant's option, it was held that specific performance must be decreed against the lessor according to the ordinary and accepted meaning of the words used.[6]

Powell v. *Smith*

Nevertheless, the particular remedy of specific performance, since it is exceptional in nature, is one that lies very much within the discretion of the courts, and there certainly are cases in which it has not been forced upon a party who has mistaken the admitted sense of a contract.   The remedy will not, indeed, be withheld

Specific performance not always forced on mistaken party

---

1. *Infra*, p. 561 *et. seq.*
2. This suggestion was made by Lawson in *The Rational Strength of English Law* (1951), at pp. 69–70.   It was supported by DEVLIN, L.J., in *Ingram* v. *Little* but rejected by the Law Reform Committee in its Twelfth Report (Cmnd. 2958) (1966).
3. *Preston* v. *Luck* (1884), 27 Ch.D. 497.
4. (1880), 15 Ch.D. 215; followed in *Van Praagh* v. *Everidge*, [1902] 2 Ch. 266.
5. *Tamplin* v. *James* (1880), 15 Ch.D. 215, at pp. 217–8.
6. *Powell* v. *Smith* (1872), L.R. 14 Eq. 85.

" merely upon a vague idea as to the true effect of the contract not having been known,"[1] but as BACON, V.-C., said in one case:

> " It cannot be disputed that courts of equity have at all times relieved against honest mistakes in contracts, when the literal effect and the specific performance of them would be to impose a burden not contemplated and which it would be against all reason and justice to fix upon the person who, without the imputation of fraud, has inadvertently committed an accidental mistake; and also where not to correct the mistake would be to give an unconscionable advantage to either party."[2]

In the case of mutual mistake, therefore, while equity generally follows the law, it may be prepared, if the occasion warrants, to refuse to grant a decree of specific performance of the contract against the mistaken party.[3]   It is not possible, however, to specify the cases in which this remedy will be withheld, for the exercise of any discretionary jurisdiction must inevitably be governed by the particular circumstances of each case.   But the guiding principle was stated by Lord ROMILLY in an instructive case where a freehold estate that was subject to an existing tenancy had been bought by the defendant at an auction under the honest, but mistaken, belief that the rent stated in the particulars of sale referred not to the whole, but only to half of the land. Had he read the particulars carefully he could have discovered the truth.[4]   Lord ROMILLY, M.R., said:

> " If it appears upon the evidence that there was, in the description of the property, a matter on which a person might *bona fide* make a mistake, and he swears positively that he did make such mistake, and his evidence is not disproved, this court cannot enforce specific performance against him.   If there appear on the particulars no ground for the mistake, if no man with his senses about him could have misapprehended the character of the parcels, then I do not think it is sufficient for the purchaser to swear that he made a mistake or that he did not understand what he was about."[5]

In the result, the Master of the Rolls dismissed the bill for specific performance.

In *Paget* v. *Marshall*[6] BACON, V.C., went further and held that in some circumstances a plaintiff's uncommunicated mistake as to the sense of the contract might be so serious that the defendant could properly be put to his election either to submit to rectification or allow rescision of the whole contract.   This case has long been considered of doubtful authority,[7] and since the decision of the Court of Appeal in *Riverlate Properties, Ltd.* v. *Paul*[8] such a course can only be supported on the ground that the defendant knew of the plaintiff's mistake.[9]

---

1. *Watson* v. *Marston* (1853), 4 De G.M. & G. 230, at p. 238 *per* TURNER, L.J.
2. *Burrow* v. *Scammell* (1881), 19 Ch.D. 175, at p. 182.
3. Compare, for instance, the treatment of *Wood* v *Scarth, supra,* p. 226, by a common law court: (1858), 1 F. & F. 293 and by the Court of Chancery: (1855), 2 K. & J. 33.   For a discussion of equitable relief, see Stoljar, 28 M.L.R. 265, at pp. 269–72.
4. *Swaisland* v. *Dearsley* (1861), 29 Beav. 430.
5. *Ibid.,* at pp. 433–4.
6. (1884), 28 Ch.D. 255.
7. See *May* v. *Platt*, [1900] 1 Ch. 616, at p. 623, *per* FARWELL, J.
8. [1975] Ch. 133; [1974] 2 All E.R. 656.
9. See *supra,* p. 223 and *infra* p. 237.

(ii) Unilateral mistake

In the case of unilateral mistake it is clear that if one party to the knowledge of the other is mistaken as to the fundamental character of the offer—if he did not intend, as the other well knew, to make the apparent contract—the apparent contract is a nullity and there is no need, indeed no room, for any equitable relief. However, although equity follows the law in this respect and admits that the contract is a nullity, it is prepared to clinch the matter by formally setting the contract aside or by refusing a decree for its specific performance.[1] In *Webster* v. *Cecil*,[2] for instance:

Cecil, who had already refused to sell his land to Webster for £2,000, wrote a letter to him in which he offered to sell for £1,250. Webster accepted by return of post, whereupon Cecil, realizing that he had mistakenly written £1,250 for £2,250, immediately gave notice to Webster of the error.

This was operative mistake at common law. Knowledge of the mistake was clearly to be imputed to Webster and in the result Lord ROMILLY refused a decree of specific performance.[3]

A contract may also be rectified on the ground of unilateral mistake, if the plaintiff proves beyond reasonable doubt that it was intended to contain a certain term beneficial to himself, but that the defendant allowed it to be concluded without that term, knowing that the plaintiff was ignorant of its omission. For instance:

A tender by the plaintiffs for the erection of a school for the defendants provided that the work should be completed in eighteen months. The defendants, however, prepared a contract which provided for completion in thirty months, and the plaintiffs executed this contract without noticing the alteration. Before execution by the defendants, one of their officers discovered that the plaintiffs were ignorant of the alteration but they took no steps to disabuse him. The price for the work would have been higher had the tender been based on a period of thirty months.[4]

On these facts, rectification on the ground of common mistake was ruled out, since the parties held different views of what was intended to be inserted in the contract. Nevertheless, the court ordered the contract to be rectified on the ground of unilateral mistake by the substitution of the shorter for the longer period.[5]

SECTION III. DOCUMENTS MISTAKENLY SIGNED

A group of cases must now be considered which have long been treated as forming a separate category at common law and which may be regarded as an appendix to the general discussion

Marginal notes: Unilateral mistake: equity generally follows the law — Rectification on ground of mistake — Signature to a document procured by fraud

---

1. *Wilding* v. *Sanderson*, [1897], 2 Ch. 534; *Re International Society of Auctioneers and Valuers, Baillie's Case*, [1898] 1 Ch. 110.
2. (1861), 30 Beav. 62.
3. In *Garrard* v. *Frankel* (1862), 30 Beav. 445 and *Harris* v. *Pepperell* (1867), L.R. 5 Eq. 1, the party aware of the mistake was given the option of having the contract set aside or of submitting to it with the mistake rectified.
4. *A. Roberts & Co., Ltd.* v. *Leicestershire County Council*, [1961] Ch. 555; [1961] 2 All E.R. 545.
5. See Megarry, 77 L.Q.R. 313.

of mistake.   These cases occur where a person is induced by the false statement[1] of another, to sign a written document containing a contract that is fundamentally different in character from that which he contemplated.   The fraudulent person may be the other party to the apparent contract but more often he is a stranger. The following is a typical illustration of the situation:

Lewis v.
Clay

> Lord William Neville produces to Clay some documents entirely covered with blotting paper except for four blank spaces that have been cut in it.   He says that the hidden documents concern a private family matter and that his own signature requires a witness. Thereupon Clay signs his name in the blank spaces.   The truth is that the documents are promissory notes to the value of £11,113 signed by Clay in favour of Lewis.   On the faith of these notes Lewis advances money to Lord William Neville.[2]

Signer mistaken as to category of document

Such a case as this is affected by mistake in the sense that the first victim of the fraud, the person who signs the document, appears to have made a contract or a disposition of property, though his intention was to append his signature to a transaction of an entirely different character.   The category of document actually signed is not what he thought it was.   But nevertheless can he rely upon this fact as a defence if he is later sued upon the apparent contract by the second victim of the fraud, as for instance by the man who has given value in good faith for a promissory note?

Primary rule

The rule applicable to such a case has come to be that the mistaken party will escape liability if he satisfies the court that the signed instrument is radically different from that which he intended to sign and that his mistake was not due to his carelessness.

Origin of the plea *non est factum*

The origin of this rule is to be found in the mediaeval common law relating to deeds.[3]   At least as early as the thirteenth century, a deed was regarded as being of so solemn a nature that it remained binding upon the obligor until it had been cancelled and returned to him.   It was immaterial that this might cause injustice.   In one case, for instance, in 1313, an absolute deed by which the defendant granted £100 to the plaintiffs was accompanied by a contemporaneous deed which relieved him of this obligation if he satisfied a certain condition.   The condition was satisfied, but the absolute deed survived, and upon its production the payment of the £100 was enforced.[4]   The only defence open to the defendant in such circumstances was to plead that the deed as executed was not his deed in the sense that it did not represent his intention and was not what he had in mind to do.   He did not in truth consent to what he had done.   In the language of the age, *scriptum predictum non est factum suum.*

Extension of the plea for the benefit of illiterates

In the course of its development, this plea of *non est factum* was made available to a defendant who could not read, whether owing to illiteracy or blindness, so as to enable him to escape

---

1. *Hasham* v. *Zenab,* [1960] A.C. 316, at p. 335.
2. *Lewis* v. *Clay* (1897), 67 L.J.Q.B. 224.
3. Fifoot, *History and Sources of the Common Law,* pp. 231–3; 248–9.
4. *Ibid.,* pp. 232; 244–6; *Esthalle* v. *Esthalle,* Y.B. 6 & 7 Ed. II Eyre of Kent. vol. II (S.S. vol. 27, p. 21).

liability upon proof that the written terms of the deed did not correspond with its effect as explained to him before he put his seal to it. In 1582, for instance, in *Thoroughgood's Case*:[1]

> William Chicken, being in arrears with his rent, tendered to his landlord, Thoroughgood, a deed by which he was relieved from " all demands whatsoever " which Thoroughgood had against him. Thus the dispensation on its face comprised not only arrears of rent, but also the right to recover the land. Thoroughgood was illiterate, but a bystander, affecting to be helpful, seized the deed and said: " The effect of it is this, that you do release to William Chicken all the arrears of rent that he doth owe you and no otherwise, and thus you shall have your land back again." After replying, " If it be no otherwise, I am content," Thoroughgood sealed the deed. Chicken subsequently sold the land to an innocent purchaser.

Thoroughgood sued in trespass *quare clausum fregit* and recovered his land. It was said by the Court of Common Pleas to be " the usual course of pleading " that the defendant was a layman and without learning, and that he had been deceived by a distorted recital of the contents of the deed.

The plea, as its language showed, was confined to cases where the defendant was sued on a deed, and at a time when illiteracy was frequent enough to demand special protection, it was unexceptionable. It might have been wiser, therefore, to have discarded it altogether when society became more sophisticated; but in the course of the nineteenth century the courts extended it with little reflection and without warrant to cases of simple contracts, and abandoned the requirement of illiteracy. The justification for these extensions was now said to be want of consent. On this view the contract was a complete nullity. Thus in 1869, in *Foster* v. *Mackinnon*,[2] the following passage occurs in the judgment of a strong court delivered by BYLES, J.:

The plea extended to simple contracts, and based upon lack of consent

> " It seems plain on principle and on authority that if a blind man, or a man who cannot read or who for some reason (not implying negligence) forbears to read, has a written contract falsely read over to him, the reader misreading to such a degree that the written contract is of a nature altogether different from the contract pretended to be read from the paper which the blind or illiterate man afterwards signs; then, at least if there be no negligence, the signature so obtained is of no force. And it is invalid not merely on the ground of fraud, where fraud exists, but on the ground that the mind of the signer did not accompany the signature; in other words that he never intended to sign, and therefore in contemplation of law never did sign, the contract to which his name is appended."[3]

Thus the intention of the mistaken party is the vital factor. In the words of Lord WILBERFORCE: " It is the lack of consent that matters, not the means by which this result was brought about."[4] The document is a nullity just as if a rogue had forged the signer's signature.[5] But fraud that does not induce lack of consent merely renders the contract voidable.

---

1. (1582), 2 Co. Rep. 9a.
2. (1869), L.R. 4 C.P. 704. Present, BOVILL, C.J., BYLES, KEETING & MONTAGUE SMITH, JJ. For the facts, see *infra*, p. 242.
3. *Ibid.*, at p. 711.
4. *Saunders* v. *Anglia Building Society*, [1971] A.C. 1004, at p. 1026; [1970] 3 All E.R. 961, at p. 972.
5. *Ibid. affirming, sub nom. Gallie* v. *Lee*, [1969] 2 Ch. 17, at p. 30 (C.A.); [1969] 1 All E.R. 1062, at p. 1066, *per* Lord DENNING, M.R.

Nature of
the mistake
that evinces
lack of consent

It will be observed that the judgment of BYLES, J., which has now been approved by the House of Lords in *Saunders* v. *Anglia Building Society*[1] (known in the lower courts as *Gallie* v. *Lee*), expanded the scope of the plea *non est factum* in two respects; it extended it to unsealed contracts and to the situation where an educated man, to whom no negligence is attributable, has failed to scrutinize what he has signed.[2]   Nevertheless, the judiciary is now agreed that, if the confidence of third parties who normally rely upon the authenticity of signatures is not to be eroded, the plea must be confined within narrow limits.   A heavy burden of proof lies upon the party by whom it is invoked.   The main difficulty is to define the degree of difference that must exist between the signed contract and that which the mistaken party intended to sign before it can be said that the consent of the signatory was totally lacking.   A definitive formula of universal application is scarcely possible.   Everything depends upon the circumstances of each case.   It will be recalled that the court in *Foster* v. *Mackinnon* required the written contract to be " of a nature altogether different " from that which the mistaken party believed it to be.   In *Saunders* v. *Anglia Building Society* the Law Lords suggested a variety of alternative expressions, such as " radically," " fundamentally," " basically," " totally " or " essentially " different in character or substance from the contract intended; but it is doubtful whether these add much to what was said by BYLES, J.   In the comparatively few cases in which the plea has succeeded, the degree of difference between the intention and the act of the signatory has been wide enough to satisfy the most exacting of arbiters.   The contract, for instance, has been held void where the signatory's intention was directed to a power of attorney, not to a mortgage;[3] to a guarantee, not to a bill of exchange;[4] to a testification to the fraudulent person's signature, not to a promissory note for £11,113;[5] to a proposal for insurance, not to a guarantee of the fraudulent person's overdraft.[6]

Saunders v.
Anglia
Building
Society

The difficulty that confronts a party who pleads that a contract signed by him is altogether different from what was in his mind is well illustrated by *Saunders* v. *Anglia Building Society*[7] where the facts were as follows:

> The plaintiff, a widow 78 years of age, gave the deeds of her leasehold house to her nephew in order that he might raise money on it.   She made it a condition that she should remain in occupation of it until she died.   She knew that the defendant, a friend of her nephew, would help him to arrange a loan.
>
> A document was prepared by a dishonest managing clerk which assigned the leasehold not by way of gift to the nephew, but by way

---

1. [1971] A.C. 1004.
2. As to the meaning of negligence in this context, see *infra*, p. 242.
3. *Bagot* v. *Chapman*, [1907] 2 Ch. 222.
4. *Foster* v. *Mackinnon* (1869), L.R. 4 C.P. 704.   But the bill was not to be void if, at a new trial, the signatory was found to have been negligent; *infra*, p. 242.
5. *Lewis* v. *Clay* (1897), 67 L.J.Q.B. 224.
6. *Carlisle and Cumberland Banking Co.* v. *Bragg*, [1911] 1 K.B. 489; *infra*, p. 243.   In *Muskham Finance Co.* v. *Howard*, [1963] 1 Q.B. 904; [1963] 1 All E.R. 81, the difference between the intention and the act of the signatory was far less pronounced than in the three cases cited above.
7. [1971] A.C. 1004; [1970] 3 All E.R. 961.   Stone, 88 L.Q.R. 190.

of sale to the equally dishonest defendant. Some days later the defendant took this document to the plaintiff and asked her to sign it. She had broken her glasses and was unable to read, but in reply to her request the defendant told her that the document was a deed of gift to her nephew. She therefore executed it. The defendant, who paid no money either to the plaintiff or to her nephew, mortgaged the house to a building society for £2,000, but failed to pay the instalments due under the transaction.

The plaintiff, at the instigation of her nephew, sued the defendant and the building society for a declaration that the assignment was void. She invoked the doctrine *non est factum*, claiming that what she had intended was a gift of the property to her nephew, not its outright sale to the defendant.

The House of Lords, affirming the decision of the Court of Appeal, rejected this claim. The distinction stressed by the plaintiff was no doubt impressive at first sight, but when considered in the light of the evidence it did not establish that the assignment to the defendant was totally different in character and nature from what she had in mind. Three of the Law Lords adopted the view of RUSSELL, L.J., in the Court of Appeal that the paramount consideration was the " object of the exercise."[1] According to the evidence, the object of the plaintiff was to enable the assignee to raise a loan on the security of the property for the benefit of her nephew—an object that would have been attained under the signed document, had the defendant acted in an honest manner.[2]

A question that was canvassed by the House of Lords in this case was whether the distinction between the character and the contents of a document, which had gradually won the recognition of the courts, should be discarded. The effect of this distinction was that if a party appreciated the character and nature of the contract that he had signed, he could not escape liability merely because he was mistaken as to its details or its contents. In *Howatson* v. *Webb*,[3] for instance:

Former distinction between character and contents of document rejected

The defendant held certain property at Edmonton as the trustee and nominee of a solicitor by whom he was employed as managing clerk. After obtaining new employment, he executed certain deeds which, in answer to his request, were described by the solicitor as being " just deeds transferring that property." In fact one of the deeds was a mortgage by the solicitor to X as security for a loan of £1,000. The mortgage was transferred by X to the plaintiff, who now sued the defendant under the personal covenant in the deed for the repayment of the sum together with interest.

The defendant pleaded *non est factum*. What he had in mind was an absolute conveyance to a new nominee, not a conveyance to a third party under which he assumed personal obligations. WARRINGTON, J., however, held that the mistake affected only the contents of the deed and that therefore the plea failed. " He was

---

1. [1969] 2 Ch., at pp. 40–1, adopted by Viscount DILHORNE, Lord WILBERFORCE and Lord PEARSON. See also, *Mercantile Credit Co., Ltd.* v. *Hamblin*, [1965] 2 Q.B. 242; [1964] 3 All E.R. 592.
2. This approach, however, ignored the overriding condition that nothing was to interfere with the plaintiff's right to remain in occupation of the house.
3. [1907] 1 Ch. 537; affirmed, [1908] 1 Ch. 1.

told that they were deeds relating to the property to which they did in fact relate. His mind was therefore applied to the question of dealing with that property. The deeds did deal with that property . . . He knew he was dealing with the class of deed with which in fact he was dealing, but did not ascertain its contents."[1] A Court of Appeal later explained this decision on the ground that " the character and class of document was that of a conveyance of property, and Webb knew this."[2]

In *Gallie* v. *Lee*, Lord DENNING, M.R., rejected this distinction in forcible and convincing terms. Among other objections he found it irrational; a mistake as to contents may be no less fundamental or radical than one relating to the character of a contract. The distinction would mean, for instance, that the plea of *non est factum* will not avail a man who signs a bill of exchange for £10,000 having been told that it is for £100, since he fully appreciates the character of the document. Why should the result be different if he believes the document to be a bill of exchange for £1,000, though in truth it is a guarantee for the same sum?[3] SALMON, L.J., agreed that the liability of a signatory should not be allowed to turn upon " a relatively academic distinction," but he was content to retain it as affording at least some restraint upon a plea that had become " a dangerous anachronism in modern times."[4] In the House of Lords, Lord REID expressed his dissatisfaction with the distinction,[5] Lord WILBERFORCE described it as " terminologically confusing and in substance illogical,"[6] while Viscount DILHORNE accepted the criticisms of Lord DENNING.[7] The inference is that it has received its quietus.

A careless signatory cannot plead his mistake

The final question is whether the plea of *non est factum* will be withheld from a party if the mistake was due to his own negligence. In *Foster* v. *Mackinnon*,[8] the Court of Common Pleas stated in unambiguous terms that a signatory is barred by his negligence from pleading his mistake against an innocent third party who has acted to his loss upon the faith of the document.

> The action before the court was against the defendant, described as " a gentleman far advanced in years," as indorser of a bill of exchange. It appeared that one Callow took the bill to him and asked him to sign it, telling him that it was a guarantee. The defendant, in the belief that he was signing a guarantee similar to one which he had given before, signed the bill on the back. He looked only at the back of the paper, but it was in the ordinary shape of a bill of exchange, and it bore a stamp the impress of which was visible through the paper. The bill was later negotiated to the plaintiff who took it without notice of the fraud.

1. [1907] 1 Ch., at p. 549. See also *Bagot* v. *Chapman*, [1907] 2 Ch. 222, at p. 227, *per* SWINFEN EADY, J. In affirming the decision of WARRINGTON, J., in *Howatson* v. *Webb*, [1908] 1 Ch. 1, the Court of Appeal regarded it as so obviously correct as not to merit considered judgments, and COZENS-HARDY, M.R., remarked that " it would be a waste of time if I were to do more than say that I accept and approve of every word of his judgment."
2. *Muskham Finance, Ltd.* v. *Howard*, [1963] 1 Q.B. 904, at p. 912; [1963] 1 All E.R. 81, at p. 83; *per curiam*.
3. [1969] 2 Ch., at pp. 31–2; [1969] 1 All E.R., at p. 1066. See also SALMON, L.J., at pp. 43–4, and 1078, respectively.
4. *Ibid.*, at p. 44.
5. [1971] A.C., at p. 1017; [1970] 3 All E.R. 961, at p. 964.
6. *Ibid.*, at pp. 1034–5 and 971, respectively.
7. *Ibid.*, at pp. 1022 and 967 respectively.
8. (1869), L.R. 4 C.P. 704.

The action was first tried by the Lord Chief Justice, who told the jury that if the defendant signed the paper without knowing that it was a bill and under the belief that it was a guarantee, and if he was not guilty of any negligence in so signing the paper, then he was entitled to their verdict. The jury found that the defendant had not been negligent and returned a verdict in his favour. On appeal, the Court of Common Pleas endorsed the direction given by the trial judge, but ordered a fresh trial on the ground that the issue of negligence had not been fully and satisfactorily considered. In the result, therefore, the right of the defendant to sustain the plea of *non est factum* was to depend upon whether he was eventually found to have been guilty of negligence.

Unfortunately, this ruling that negligence is material was thrown into confusion by the decision of a later Court of Appeal in *Carlisle and Cumberland Banking Co.* v. *Bragg*[1] on the following facts:

> A man called Rigg produced a document to Bragg and told him that it was a copy of a paper concerning an insurance matter which Bragg had signed some days previously and which had since got wet and blurred in the rain. Bragg signed without reading the paper. The document was in fact a continuing guarantee of Rigg's current account with the plaintiff bank. The jury found that Bragg had been negligent.

Despite this finding, the Court of Appeal affirmed the decision of PICKFORD, J., and held that Bragg was not estopped by his negligence from pleading *non est factum* since *Foster* v. *Mackinnon* was inapplicable in the instant circumstances. This departure from the principle laid down by BYLES, J., in *Foster* v. *Mackinnon* was based upon at least two erroneous grounds.

First, the construction put upon the judgment of BYLES, J., was that negligence is material only where the signed document is a negotiable instrument. What in fact the learned judge clearly indicated was that the signer of a negotiable instrument would be liable, negligence or no negligence; and that negligence was relevant in relation to documents other than negotiable instruments: for example (as in the actual case before him) to a guarantee.

Secondly, it was said that, even if negligence were relevant, it would not be material unless the defendant owed a duty of care to the plaintiff. This reasoning was demolished by the House of Lords in *Saunders* v. *Anglia Building Society*. No doubt a duty of care is an essential element in a plaintiff's cause of action when he sues in tort for negligence, but it has no place where a defendant is sued on a contract. In that context it has no technical significance, and it just means carelessness. In *Foster* v. *Mackinnon*, for instance, the trial judge rejected the plea of *non est factum* not because the defendant had violated a duty of care owed to his neighbour, but on the simple ground that he had failed to act as a reasonable man. In the words of Lord WILBERFORCE:

> " In my opinion, the correct rule, and that which prevailed until *Bragg's* case, is that, leaving aside negotiable instruments to which special rules may apply, a person who signs a document, and parts

---

1. [1911] 1 K.B. 489.

with it so that it may come into other hands, has a responsibility, that of the normal man of prudence, to take care what he signs. . . . I would add that the onus of proof in this matter rests on him, i.e. to prove that he acted carefully, and not in the third party to prove the contrary.   I consider, therefore, that *Carlisle and Cumberland Banking Co.* v. *Bragg* was wrong, both in the principle it states and in its decision, and that it should no longer be cited for any purpose."[1]

---

1. [1971] A.C., at p. 1027; [1970] 3 All E.R., at pp. 972–3.   Similar statements were made by the other Law Lords.   Thus Lord REID said: " The plea [of *non est factum*] cannot be available to anyone who was content to sign without taking the trouble to find out at least the general effect of the document. . . .   It is for the person who seeks the remedy to show that he should have it."   See [1971] A.C., at p. 1016; [1970] 3 All E.R., at pp. 963–4.

CHAPTER TWO

Misrepresentation, Duress and Undue Influence

SECTION I. MISREPRESENTATION[1]

A. INTRODUCTION

MISREPRESENTATION straddles many legal boundaries. More than other topics in the law of contract, it is an amalgam of common law and equity. Equity has, for instance, acted to fill *lacunae* created by the narrow common law definition of fraud and to supplement the inadequate common law remedies for misrepresentation. Again misrepresentation has roots both in contract and in tort, and it is impossible to give a coherent account of the subject without discussing both contract and tort together, though the present account will naturally concentrate on the contractual aspect.

Even within the law of contract, the rules relating to misrepresentation cannot be viewed in isolation. They are part of a web of rules (which includes also the rules as to terms of a contract[2] and as to mistake[3]) affecting the nature and extent of contractual undertakings. Although it is convenient for purposes of exposition to discuss these topics in isolation, practical problems often require their simultaneous application.

The basic problem in misrepresentation is the effect of pre-contractual statements. Suppose that A agrees to sell a second-hand car to B for £500 and in the course of the pre-contractual negotiations he states that it is a 1969 model which has run for only 20,000 miles. After B has bought the car, he discovers that these statements are untrue. What remedies, if any, are available? The initial common law approach to this problem is based on the principle that promissory statements should be ineffective unless they form part of the contract. So the first question to be asked in our hypothetical case is whether A has not merely stated that the car is a 1969 model and has covered only 20,000 miles, but has *contracted* that this is so.[4]

To approach the matter in this way is logical enough, but the result has not been satisfactory. Dissatisfaction might properly

Margin notes:
Mixture of common law and equity

Part contract, part tort

Misrepresentation closely connected with mistake and terms of contract

Nature of problem

Terms of a contract

---

1. Stoljar, *Mistake ahd Misrepresentation* (1968); Spencer Bower and Turner, The Law of Actionable Misrepresentation, 3rd Edn. (1974); Greig, 87 L.Q.R. 179.
2. *Supra*, pp. 113–169.
3. *Supra*, pp. 205–244.
4. This approach can be seen to fit in with the rules about consideration (see e.g. *Roscorla* v. *Thomas*, (1842) 3 Q.B. 234, *supra*, p. 61) and indeed with the view that the English law of contract is concerned with the enforcement of bargains, since clearly it is more expensive to sell warranted cars than unwarranted cars. See Hepple, [1970] C.L.J. 122, at 131–132.

have been directed either at the rules determining when a statement is to be treated as forming part of the contract[1] or at the sometimes strange reluctance of the courts to hold apparently serious undertakings to be terms of the contract.[2]   But in practice, it has been felt that the solution should take the form of devising remedies, which do not depend on holding such statements to be terms of the contract.

Hence arose the concept of a " mere representation "—a statement of fact which had induced the representee to enter into the contract but which did not form part of the contract.   The common law came to give rescission for fraudulent misrepresentation and to grant damages in the tortious action of deceit. During the nineteenth century, equity also developed a general remedy of rescission for all misrepresentations inducing contracts. The right to rescind, however, was subject to the operation of certain " bars,"[3] and equity could not grant financial compensation for consequential loss except in the restricted form of an " indemnity ".

Until 1963, however, it was held to be a fundamental principle that there could be " no damages for innocent misrepresentation."[4] It was well established that an action for damages based on a pre-contractual statement must show either that the statement was fraudulent or that it was a term of the contract.   In 1963, it was decided by the House of Lords in *Hedley Byrne & Co., Ltd.* v. *Heller & Partners, Ltd.*[5] that the principle " no damages for innocent misrepresentation " had never been fundamental or, at least, was no longer fundamental. In law, however, it is impossible to expunge the heresies (or outworn orthodoxies) of the past and all cases decided before 1963 have to be re-examined in the light thus shed on them.

The decision of the House of Lords in *Hedley Byrne & Co., Ltd.* v. *Heller & Partners, Ltd.*[6] was a decision in tort and its impact on the law of contract is difficult to assess.   Before the courts had had time to solve the problems thus created, Parliament intervened by passing the Misrepresentation Act 1967.   This act did not attempt a radical restatement of the law.   It made important changes in the law but at all points it assumes a knowledge of the existing law.   This is a dangerous assumption since, in some respects, the pre-Act law was far from clear.   The draughtsman did not avoid the hazards thus created but compounded them by curious drafting.   In the result, though the Misrepresentation Act undoubtedly improves the position of representees as a class, it makes the exposition of the law even more complex.

Side notes: Misrepresentation at common law — In equity — No damages for innocent misrepresentation? — Important recent changes

---

1. *Supra*, pp. 116–121.   Both because the rules make results unpredictable and because some of them, especially the parol evidence rule, hinder decisions that an oral statement forms part of the contract.
2. E.g., *Oscar Chess* v. *Williams*, [1957] 1 All E.R. 325; [1957] 1 W.L.R. 370. Cf., *Dick Bentley Productions, Ltd.* v. *Harold Smith (Motors), Ltd.*, [1965] 2 All E.R. 65; [1965] 1 W.L.R. 623, and *Beale* v. *Taylor* [1967] 3 All E.R. 253, [1967] 1 W.L.R. 1193.
3. *Infra*, pp. 268–273.
4. *Heilbut, Symons & Co.* v. *Buckleton*, [1913] A.C. 30, at p. 49, *per* Lord MOULTON.   Innocent at this stage meant simply non-fraudulent.
5. [1964] A.C. 465; [1963] 2 All E.R. 575.
6. [1964] A.C. 465; [1963] 2 All E.R. 575.

We shall start our discussion by examining more fully precisely what is meant by misrepresentation and considering the types of misrepresentation.   This will be followed by an account of the remedies for misrepresentation and a summary of the effects of the Misrepresentation Act 1967.   Finally we shall examine those exceptional cases where the law imposes liability for non-disclosure, and the relationship between misrepresentation and estoppel.

B.   THE NATURE OF
MISREPRESENTATION

A representation is a statement of fact made by one party to the contract (the representor) to the other (the representee) which, while not forming a term of the contract, is yet one of the reasons that induces the representee to enter into the contract.   A misrepresentation is simply a representation that is untrue.   The representor's state of mind and degree of carefulness are not relevant to classifying a representation as a misrepresentation but only to determining the type of misrepresentation, if any.[1]

It has already been observed[2] that while terms of a contract may be of a promissory nature, the concept of a representation is limited to statements of facts.   But precedent has given a sophisticated meaning to the notion of a statement of fact and it is therefore necessary to consider in some detail the meaning of representation and also of inducement.

I.   THE MEANING OF REPRESENTATION

A representation means a statement of *fact* not a statement of intention or of opinion or of law.

A representation, as we have seen, relates to some existing fact or some past event.   It implies a *factum*, not a *faciendum*,[3] and since it contains no element of futurity it must be distinguished from a statement of intention.   An affirmation of the truth of a fact is different from a promise to do something *in futuro*, and produces different legal consequences.[4]   The distinction is of practical importance.   If a person alters his position on the faith of a representation, the mere fact of its falsehood entitles him to certain remedies.[5]   If, on the other hand, he sues upon what is in truth a promise, he must show that this promise forms part of a valid contract.   The distinction is well illustrated by *Maddison* v. *Alderson*,[6] where the plaintiff, who was prevented by the Statute of Frauds from enforcing an oral promise to devise a house, contended that the promise to make a will in her favour

---

1. See *infra*, pp. 256–262.
2. See *supra*, p. 247.
3. Spencer Bower and Turner, *Actionable Misrepresentation*, 3rd Edn., p. 42.
4. *Beattie* v. *Lord Ebury* (1872), 7 Ch. App. 777, at p. 804, *per* MELLISH, L.J.
5. *Infra*, pp. 262–276.
6. (1883), 8 App. Cas. 467; *supra*, p. 196.

should be treated as a representation which would operate by way of estoppel. The contention, however, was dismissed, for:

> " The doctrine of estoppel by representation is applicable only to representations as to some state of facts alleged to be at the time actually in existence, and not to promises *de futuro*, which, if binding at all, must be binding as contracts."[1]

Despite the antithesis, however, between a representation of fact which is untrue and an unfulfilled promise to do something *in futuro*, it by no means follows that a statement of intention can never be a representation of fact. It at least implies that the alleged intention does indeed exist, and if this is not true there is a clear misrepresentation of an existing fact. The state of mind is not what it is represented to be, and as BOWEN, L.J., observed in *Edgington* v. *Fitzmaurice*:[2]

Representation of intention may represent a fact

> " The state of a man's mind is as much a fact as the state of his digestion. It is true that it is very difficult to prove what the state of a man's mind at a particular time is, but, if it can be ascertained, it is as much a fact as anything else. A misrepresentation as to the state of a man's mind is, therefore, a misstatement of fact."

In this case, a company issued a prospectus which invited a loan from the public and stated that the money would be employed in the improvement of the buildings and the extension of the business. This was untrue, since the intention from the first had been to expend the loan upon the discharge of certain existing liabilities. It was held that the prospectus was a fraudulent misrepresentation of a fact. The company had not made a promise which they might or might not be able to fulfil; they had simply told a lie. It will be perceived that both the requirement that the representation be a statement of fact and its qualification in *Edgington* v. *Fitzmaurice* owe much to an origin in fraud. It is difficult to misrepresent the state of one's mind other than dishonestly.

The expression of an opinion properly so called, i.e. the statement of a belief based on grounds incapable of actual proof, as where the vendor of a business estimates the prospective profits at so much a year, is not a representation of fact, and, in the absence of fraud, its falsity does not afford a title to relief. Thus in *Bisset* v. *Wilkinson*,[3] the vendor of a holding in New Zealand, which had not previously been used as a sheep farm, told a prospective purchaser that in his judgment the carrying capacity of the land was two thousand sheep. It was held that this was an honest statement of opinion of the capacity of the farm, not a representation of its actual capacity.

Opinion distinguished from fact

It has never been doubted, however, that an expression of opinion may in certain circumstances constitute a representation of fact, as for instance where it is proved that the opinion was not actually held, or that it was expressed upon a matter upon which the speaker was entirely ignorant.

A statement of opinion may be a statement of fact

---

1. *Ibid.*, at p. 473. The judgment of STEPHEN, J., in the court of first instance ((1880), 5 Ex.D. 293) should be closely studied.
2. (1885), 29 Ch.D. 459, at p. 483; and see *Angus* v. *Clifford*, [1891] 2 Ch. 449, at p. 470, *per* BOWEN, L.J.
3. [1927] A.C. 177.

" It is often fallaciously assumed that a statement of opinion cannot involve the statement of a fact. In a case where the facts are equally well known to both parties, what one of them says to the other is frequently nothing but an expression of opinion . . . But if the facts are not equally well known to both sides, then a statement of opinion by the one who knows the facts best involves very often a statement of a material fact, for he impliedly states that he knows facts which justify his opinion."[1]

Thus, if it can be proved that the speaker did not hold the opinion or that a reasonable man possessing his knowledge could not honestly have held it, or that he alone was in a position to know the facts upon which the opinion must have been based,[2] there is a misrepresentation of fact for which a remedy lies. In *Smith v. Land and House Property Corporation*,[3] a vendor described his property in August as being " let to Mr. Frederick Fleck (a most desirable tenant) at a rental of £400 a year (clear of rates, taxes, insurance, etc.) for an unexpired term of 27½ years, thus offering a first-class investment." In fact the Lady Day rent had been paid by instalments under pressure and no part of the Midsummer rent had been paid. It was held that the description of Fleck as ' a most desirable tenant' was not a mere expression of opinion. It was an untrue assertion that nothing had occurred which could be regarded as rendering him an undesirable tenant.

Again, if what is really an opinion is stated as a fact, as for instance where company promoters, desiring to magnify the future earning capacity of a mine, publish the forecasts of experts as if they were positive facts,[4] there is a representation in the true sense of the term.

Simplex commendatio non obligat

Somewhat akin to the distinction between opinion and fact is the general rule that *simplex commendatio non obligat*. Eulogistic commendation of the *res vendita* is the age-old device of the successful salesman. Thus to describe land as " uncommonly rich water meadow "[5] or as " fertile and improvable,"[6] is not to make a representation of fact. Nevertheless, a statement which purports to be supported by facts and figures, as for instance that timber trees are of an average size approaching a given number of feet,[7] does not cease to be a representation of fact merely because it is expressed in a laudatory vein. The Trade Descriptions Act 1968 extends the criminal liability for false descriptions; but, by s. 35, a contract for the supply of goods is not to be " unenforceable " by reason only of a contravention of the Act.

Representations of law

It is clear that a representation of law cannot found an action merely because it is wrong. But a representation of law is basically a statement of the representor's opinion as to what the law is and it follows that if the representor does not in fact hold this opinion he misrepresents his state of mind and liability should

1. *Smith* v. *Land and House Property Corporation* (1884), 28 Ch.D. 7, at p. 15, *per* BOWEN, L.J.
2. *Brown* v. *Raphael*, [1958] Ch. 636; [1958] 2 All E.R. 79.
3. (1884), 28 Ch.D. 7.
4. *Reese River Silver Mining Co., Ltd.* v. *Smith* (1869), L.R. 4 H.L. 64.
5. *Scott* v. *Hanson* (1829), 1 Russ. & M. 128.
6. *Dimmock* v. *Hallett* (1866), 2 Ch. App. 21.
7. *Lord Brooke* v. *Rounthwaite* (1846), 5 Hare. 298.

accrue under the principle in *Edgington* v. *Fitzmaurice*.[1] It might further be argued that, as with other statements of opinion, there will be cases where the representor implicitly represents that he has reasonable grounds for his belief. In any case it is difficult to distinguish between representations of fact and of law. A representation, for instance, that the drains of a house are sanitary is obviously a statement of fact. It is equally obvious that to state an abstract proposition of law, as for instance that an oral contract of guarantee is not enforceable by action, is a representation of law.[2] The distinction, however, becomes intractable when a statement of fact is coupled, expressly or implicitly, with a proposition of law. It is evident that in practice contracts are much more likely to be induced by mixed statements of this kind than by abstract propositions of law. Suppose that, as in *Solle* v. *Butcher*,[3] a man states that a flat is not an old but a new flat and is therefore outside the Rent Restrictions Act, is this to be regarded as a statement of fact or of law? This particular aspect of the distinction is discussed later.[4]

A representation, whether expressed as a positive assertion of fact or inferred from conduct, normally assumes an active form, but an important question is whether it can ever be implied from silence. To put the enquiry in another form: when, if ever, is it the duty of a contracting party to disclose facts that are within his own knowledge?

Can silence constitute misrepresentation?

The general rule is that mere silence is not misrepresentation.[5] " The failure to disclose a material fact which might influence the mind of a prudent contractor does not give the right to avoid the contract "[6] even though it is obvious that the contractor has a wrong impression that would be removed by disclosure.[7] Tacit acquiescence in the self-deception of another creates no legal liability, unless it is due to active misrepresentation or to misleading conduct. Thus, to take one important example, there is no general duty of disclosure in the case of a contract of sale, whether of goods or of land.

> " There being no fiduciary relation between vendor and purchaser in the negotiation, the purchaser is not bound to disclose any fact exclusively within his knowledge which might reasonably be expected to influence the price of the subject to be sold. Simple reticence does not amount to legal fraud, however it may be viewed by moralists. But a single word, or (I may add) a nod or a wink, or a shake of the head, or a smile from the purchaser intended to induce

---

1. (1885), 29 Ch.D. 459; Hudson (1958), S.L.T. 16.
2. *Beattie* v. *Lord Ebury* (1872), 7 Ch. App. 777, at p. 802; *Beesly* v. *Hallwood Estates, Ltd.,* [1960] 2 All E.R. 314, at p. 323; [1960] 1 W.L.R. 549, at p. 560. Similarly, a common *mistake* of law has no effect, e.g., where the parties to a contract each believe that the other is bound to make it, when as a matter of fact neither is so bound: *British Homophone, Ltd.* v. *Kunz and Crystallate Gramophone Record Manufacturing Co., Ltd.* (1935), 152 L.T. 589; [1935] All E.R. Rep. 627. Winfield, 59 L.Q.R. 327; and *infra*, pp. 641–5.
3. [1950] 1 K.B. 671; [1949] 2 All E.R. 1107; *supra*, p. 215.
4. *Infra*, p. 641.
5. *Fox* v. *Mackreth* (1788), 2 Cox, Eq. Cas. 320 at pp. 320 and 321, *per* Lord THURLOW.
6. *Bell* v. *Lever Brothers, Ltd.,* [1932] A.C. 161, at p. 227; [1931] All E.R. Rep. 1, at p. 32, *per* Lord ATKIN.
7. *Smith* v. *Hughes* (1871), L.R. 6 Q.B. 597.

the vendor to believe the existence of a non-existing fact, which might influence the price of the subject to be sold, would be sufficient ground for a Court of Equity to refuse a decree for a specific performance of the agreement."[1]

This general rule, of course, is not confined to contracts of sale. In *Turner* v. *Green*,[2] for instance:

> Shortly before two solicitors effected a compromise on behalf of their respective clients, the plaintiff's solicitor was informed of certain legal proceedings which made the compromise a prejudicial transaction for the defendant. He kept the information to himself.

It was held that the solicitor's silence was not sufficient ground for withholding a decree of specific performance.

Silence constitutes mis-representation in three cases

There are, however, at least three sets of circumstances in which silence or non-disclosure affords a ground for relief. These are, firstly, where the silence distorts a positive representation; secondly, where the contract requires *uberrima fides*; thirdly, where a fiduciary relation exists between the contracting parties. Only the first of these will be discussed at this stage.[3]

A half truth may be a mis-representation

Silence upon some of the relevant factors may obviously distort a positive assertion. A party to a contract may be legally justified in remaining silent about some material fact, but if he ventures to make a representation upon the matter it must be a full and frank statement, and not such a partial and fragmentary account that what is withheld makes that which is said absolutely false.[4] A half truth may be in fact false because of what it leaves unsaid, and, although what a man actually says may be true in every detail, he is guilty of misrepresentation unless he tells the whole truth. If a vendor of land states that the farms are let, he must not omit the further fact that the tenants have given notice to quit.[5] If a tradesman accepts a dress for cleaning and asks the client to sign a document, telling him that it exempts him from liability for damage to beads and sequins, though in fact the exemption extends to " any damage howsoever arising ", he has conveyed a false impression which amounts to a misrepresentation.[6]

Changes affecting accuracy of representation must be disclosed

Moreover, a party who makes a false statement in the belief that it is true comes under an obligation to disclose the truth should he subsequently discover that he was mistaken.[7] Similarly if he makes a statement which is true at the time, but which is

---

1. *Walters* v. *Morgan* (1861), 3 De G.F. & J. 718, at p. 723, *per* Lord Campbell.
2. [1895] 2 Ch. 205.
3. See *infra*, p. 279 *et seq*.
4. *Oakes* v. *Turquand and Harding* (1867), L.R. 2 H.L. 325, at pp. 342–3. In *Jaques* v. *Lloyd D. George & Partners, Ltd.*, [1968] 2 All E.R. 187, at pp. 190–191; [1968] 1 W.L.R. 625, at p. 630, Lord Denning, M.R., suggested that an estate agent who tendered a contract to a client for signature, impliedly represented that it contained the usual provision for payment, viz. on completion of the sale only, and that failure to reveal that the contract contained a provision for payment more favourable to the estate agent might, without more, amount to a misrepresentation. These remarks were *obiter* and should be treated with some reserve. Wilkinson, 31 M.L.R. 700.
5. *Dimmock* v. *Hallett* (1866), 2 Ch. App. 21.
6. *Curtis* v. *Chemical Cleaning and Dyeing Co.*, [1951] 1 K.B. 805; [1951] 1 All E.R. 631, *supra*, p. 129. See also *Ames* v. *Milward* (1818), 8 Taunt. 637.
7. *Davies* v. *London and Provincial Marine Insurance Co.* (1878), 8 Ch.D. 469, at p. 475, *per* Fry, J.; *With* v. *O'Flanagan*, [1936] Ch. 575; [1936] 1 All E.R. 727.

found to be untrue in the course of the subsequent negotiations, he is equally under an obligation to disclose the change of circumstances. This latter issue was raised in *Davies* v. *London and Provincial Marine Insurance Co.*[1]

> A company ordered the arrest of their agent in the belief that he had committed a felony under the Larceny Act 1861. Certain friends of the agent, in order to prevent his arrest, offered to deposit a sum of money as security for any deficiency for which he might be liable. While this offer was under consideration the company, having been advised by counsel that no felony had been committed, withdrew the instructions for arrest. Later in the same day the offer was renewed and it was accepted by the company without disclosing that there could no longer be any question of arrest.

It was held that the contract must be rescinded.

2. THE MEANING OF INDUCEMENT

A representation does not render a contract voidable unless it was intended to cause and has in fact caused the representee to make the contract. It must have produced a misunderstanding in his mind, and that misunderstanding must have been one of the reasons which induced him to make the contract. A false statement, whether innocent or fraudulent, does not *per se* give rise to a cause of action.

A misrepresentation is no ground for relief unless it induces the contract

It follows from this that a misrepresentation is legally harmless if the plaintiff:

    (a) never knew of its existence; or
    (b) did not allow it to affect his judgment; or
    (c) was aware of its untruth.

Let us take these hypotheses *seriatim*.

    (a) A plaintiff must always be prepared to prove that an alleged misrepresentation had an effect upon his mind, a task which he certainly cannot fulfil if he was never aware that it had been made. Thus in one case a shareholder who pleaded that he had been induced to acquire shares by a misrepresentation, failed in his action for rescission, since, though false reports concerning the financial state of the company had previously been published, he was unable to prove that he had read one syllable of the reports or that anyone had told him of their contents.[2] Perhaps the most remarkable case on the subject is *Horsfall* v. *Thomas*,[3] where the facts were these:

Ignorance of misrepresentation bars the right to relief

> A gun containing a defect was delivered to a buyer, and after being fired for six rounds, flew to pieces. It is not quite clear what exact form the defect took, for the case was withdrawn from the jury. The buyer alleged that " the breach end of the chamber was all soft and spongy, and that a metal plug had been driven into the breach over this soft part."[4] BRAMWELL, B., said that the seller or his workmen " had done something to the gun which concealed the

Horsfall v. *Thomas*

---

1. (1878), 8 Ch.D. 469.
2. *Re Northumberland and Durham District Banking Co., Ex parte Bigge* (1858), 28 L.J. Ch. 50.
3. (1862), 1 H. & C. 90.
4. *Ibid.*, at pp. 94–5.

defect in it." But one fact which was quite clear was that the buyer had never examined the gun.

To an action brought upon a bill of exchange which the buyer had accepted by way of payment, it was pleaded that the acceptance had been induced by the fraud and misrepresentation of the seller. The Court of Exchequer Chamber unanimously held, however, that even if all the allegations of the buyer could be proved, his plea could not succeed, for since he had never examined the gun, the attempt to conceal the defect had produced no effect upon his mind.[1]

Misrepresentation no ground for relief if it is ignored by the plaintiff

(b) A representee who does not allow the representation to affect his judgment, although it was designed to that end, cannot make it a ground for relief. He may, for instance, have regarded it as unimportant, as in *Smith* v. *Chadwick*,[2] where:

> A prospectus contained a false statement that a certain important person was on the board of directors, but the plaintiff frankly admitted in cross-examination that he had been in no degree influenced by this fact.

He may on the other hand have preferred to rely upon his own acumen or business sense or upon an independent report which he specially obtained. Thus in *Attwood* v. *Small*:[3]

> A vendor accompanied an offer to sell a mine with statements as to its earning capacities which were exaggerated and unreliable. The buyers agreed to accept the offer if the vendor could verify his statements and they appointed experienced agents to investigate the matter. The agents, who visited the mine and were given every facility for forming a judgment, reported that the statements were true, and ultimately the contract was completed.

It was held by the House of Lords that an action to rescind the contract for misrepresentation must fail, since the purchasers did not rely on the vendor's statements, but tested their accuracy by independent investigations and declared themselves satisfied with the result.

But the misrepresentation need not be the sole inducement

It is clear, however, that the right to relief would be endangered if a defendant were free to evade liability by proof that there were contributory causes, other than his misrepresentation, which induced the plaintiff to make the contract, and that his representation was not the decisive cause.

> " Who," asked KNIGHT BRUCE, L.J., " can say that the untrue statement may not have been precisely that which turned the scale in the mind of the party to whom it was addressed?"[4]

---

1. This decision, although a simple illustration of the doctrine that an intention to mislead must be followed by success in order to justify rescission, is not altogether satisfactory on other grounds. BRAMWELL, B., in delivering the judgment of the court, indicated that the manufacturing seller of an article is bound to disclose any latent defect of which he is aware, but if this is the rule, it is a little difficult to see why the facts alleged by the buyer, presuming them to be true, did not make it applicable. It is doubtful, however, whether any such duty is imposed on the seller; see the remarks of COCKBURN, C.J., in *Smith* v. *Hughes* (1871), L.R. 6 Q.B. 597, at p. 605, where he dissented from *Horsfall* v. *Thomas*.
2. (1884), 9 App. Cas 187, at p. 194.
3. (1838), 6 Cl. & Fin. 232.
4. *Reynell* v. *Sprye* (1852), 1 De G.M. & G. 660, at p. 708.

The courts, therefore, although denying relief to a plaintiff who entirely disregards the misrepresentation, have consistently held that the misrepresentation need not be his sole reason for making the contract. If it was clearly one inducing cause it is immaterial that it was not the only inducing cause.[1] In *Edgington* v. *Fitzmaurice*,[2] for instance:

> The plaintiff was induced to take debentures in a company, partly because of a misstatement in the prospectus and partly because of his own erroneous belief that debenture holders would have a charge upon the property of the company.

Thus he had two inducements, one the false representation, the other his own mistake, and on this ground it was pleaded, but unsuccessfully pleaded, that he was disentitled to rescission.

The attitude thus adopted by the courts is the real explanation of the statement, sometimes put as if it were a separate requirement, that a representation must be material. This statement is ambiguous. If it means that a representation creates no liability unless it induces consent, it is correct but redundant, since it merely repeats in somewhat obscure language what we have already seen—that a representation which does not actually mislead the plaintiff affords no ground for relief. If it means that a representation creates no liability unless it was the decisive cause that induced the plaintiff to make the contract, it is scarcely accurate. Once it is shown that a representation was calculated to influence the judgement of a reasonable man, the presumption is that the representee was so influenced; this presumption is not rebutted by showing that there were other contributory causes which played a substantial part, perhaps even a more notable part, in the formation of his intention. The court allows no *post-mortem* examination into the relative importance of the contributory causes.[3] *(margin: Meaning of statement that misrepresentation must be material)*

(c) Knowledge of the untruth of a representation is a complete bar to relief, since the plaintiff cannot assert that he has been misled by the statement,[4] even if the misstatement was made fraudulently. In such a case, " the misrepresentation and the concealment go for just absolutely nothing, because it is not *dolus qui dat locum contractui*."[5] *(margin: Knowledge that representation is untrue bars relief)*

It must be carefully noticed, however, that relief will not be withheld on this ground except upon clear proof that the plaintiff possessed actual and complete knowledge of the true facts—actual not constructive, complete not fragmentary. The onus is on the defendant to prove that the plaintiff had unequivocal notice of the truth. In particular, the mere fact that a party has been afforded an opportunity to investigate and verify a representation does not deprive him of his right to resist specific performance or to sue for rescission.[6] As Lord DUNEDIN once said: *(margin: It must be actual not constructive knowledge)*

1. Approved in *Barton* v. *Armstrong*, [1975] 2 All E.R. 465, at p. 475; [1975] 2 W.L.R. 1050, p. 1061.
2. (1885), 29 Ch.D. 459.
3. *Smith* v. *Chadwick* (1882), 20 Ch.D. 27, at pp. 44–5, *per* JESSEL, M.R.
4. *Jennings* v. *Broughton* (1854), 5 De G.M. & G. 126; *Begbie* v. *Phosphate Sewage Co.* (1875), L.R. 10 Q.B. 491.
5. *Irvine* v. *Kirkpatrick* (1850), 7 Bell. Sc. App. 186, at p. 237, *per* Lord BROUGHAM.
6. *Redgrave* v. *Hurd* (1881), 20 Ch.D. 1.

" No one is entitled to make a statement which on the face of it conveys a false impression and then excuse himself on the ground that the person to whom he made it had available the means of correction."[1]

If, for instance,

a prospectus mis-describes the contracts made by the promoters on behalf of the company; or
a vendor of land makes a false statement about the contents of a certain lease; or
a vendor of a law partnership misstates the average earnings of the business during the last three years,

it is no answer to a suit for relief to say that inspection of the contracts or of the lease or of the bills of costs was expressly invited but was not accepted.[2]

C. TYPES OF MISREPRESENTATION

I. FRAUDULENT MISREPRESENTATION

Fraud implies absence of honest belief

Fraud in common parlance is a somewhat comprehensive word that embraces a multitude of delinquencies differing widely in turpitude, but the types of conduct that give rise to an action of deceit at common law have been narrowed down to rigid limits. In the view of the common law, " a charge of fraud is such a terrible thing to bring against a man that it cannot be maintained in any court unless it is shown that he had a wicked mind."[3] Influenced by this consideration, the House of Lords has established in the leading case of *Derry* v. *Peek*[4] that an absence of honest belief is essential to constitute fraud. If a representor honestly believes his statement to be true, he cannot be liable in deceit, no matter how ill-advised, stupid, credulous or even negligent he may have been. Lord HERSCHELL, indeed, gave a more elaborate definition of fraud in *Derry* v. *Peek*,[5] saying that it means a false statement " made (1) knowingly, or (2) without belief in its truth, or (3) recklessly, careless whether it be true or false," but, as the learned judge himself admitted, the rule is accurately and comprehensively contained in the short formula that a fraudulent misrepresentation is a false statement which, when made, the representor did not honestly believe to be true.

Negligence is not fraud

The important feature of this decision is the insistence of the House of Lords that the distinction between negligence and fraud must never be blurred. Fraud is dishonesty, and it is not necessarily dishonest, though it may be negligent, to express a belief upon grounds that would not convince a reasonable man.

---

1. *Nocton* v. *Lord Ashburton*, [1914] A.C. 932, at p. 962.
2. The first two instances are given by JESSEL, M.R., in *Redgrave* v. *Hurd, supra,* at p. 14; the last represents the facts in the case itself. See also *Central Rail. Co. of Venezuela (Directors, etc.)* v. *Kisch* (1867), L.R. 2 H.L. 99, at p. 120.
3. *Le Lievre* v. *Gould*, [1893] 1 Q.B. 491, at p. 498, *per* Lord ESHER.
4. (1889), 14 App. Cas. 337.
5. *Derry* v. *Peek* (1889), 14 App. Cas. 337, at p. 374.

The facts of *Derry* v. *Peek* were these:

> A company, after submitting its plans to the Board of Trade, applied for a special Act of Parliament authorizing it to run trams in Plymouth by steam power. The Act which was ultimately passed provided that the trams might be moved by animal power, or, if the consent of the Board of Trade were obtained, by steam or mechanical power. The directors, believing that this consent would be given as a matter of course, since the plans had already been submitted to the Board of Trade without encountering objection, thereupon issued a prospectus saying that the company had the right to use steam power instead of horses. The respondent took shares upon the faith of this statement. The Board of Trade refused their consent, and the company was ultimately wound up.

It was held by the House of Lords, reversing the decision of the Court of Appeal, that an action of deceit against the directors claiming damages for fraudulent misrepresentation must fail.

> " The prospectus," said Lord HERSCHELL, " was inaccurate. But that is not the question. If they [the directors] believed that the consent of the Board of Trade was practically concluded by the passing of the Act, has the plaintiff made out, which it was for him to do, that they have been guilty of a fraudulent misrepresentation? I think not. I cannot hold it proved as to any one of them that he knowingly made a false statement, or one which he did not believe to be true, or was careless whether what he stated was true or false. In short I think they honestly believed that what they asserted was true."[1]

In testing the honesty of the representor's belief, his statement must not be considered according to its ordinary meaning, but according to its meaning as understood by him.[2] Carelessness is not dishonesty; but, of course, if a man is reckless, a court may well be justified in concluding that he could not have been honest. " There may be such an absence of reasonable ground for his belief as, in spite of his assertion, to carry conviction to the mind that he had not really the belief which he alleges."[3]

Again, if a representor deliberately shuts his eyes to the facts or purposely abstains from their investigation, his belief is not honest and he is just as liable as if he had knowingly stated a falsehood.[4]

Motive is irrelevant in an action of deceit. Once it has been proved that the plaintiff has acted upon a false representation which the defendant did not believe to be true, liability ensues, although the defendant may not have been actuated by any bad motive.[5]

---

1. *Derry* v. *Peek* (1889), 14 App. Cas., at p. 379. It should be noted that the decision of the House of Lords was based on the trial judge's finding that the defendants believed their statements to be true. He might well have held that they merely hoped and believed that they would soon become true. Such a finding would have led to judgement for the plaintiffs. See Pollock, 5 L.Q.R. 410; Anson, 6 L.Q.R. 72.
2. *Akerhielm* v. *De Mare*, [1959] A.C. 789; [1959] 3 All E.R. 485; *Gross* v. *Lewis Hillman, Ltd.*, [1970] 1 Ch. 445; [1969] 3 All E.R. 1476; *McGrath Motors (Canberra), Pty., Ltd.* v. *Applebee* (1964), 110 C.L.R. 656.
3. *Derry* v. *Peek*, *supra*, at p. 369, *per* Lord HERSCHELL.
4. *Ibid.*, at p. 376, *per* Lord HERSCHELL.
5. *Foster* v. *Charles* (1830), 6 Bing. 396; affirmed, 7 Bing. 105.

2. NEGLIGENT MISSTATEMENT AT COMMON LAW

Effect of
Derry v. *Peek*

The plaintiffs in *Derry* v. *Peek*[1] formulated their claim as an action in the tort of deceit. But it was assumed at the time, and for seventy years afterwards[2], that the House of Lords in this case decided that no action would lie for negligent words, at least where reliance on them produced purely financial loss, as opposed to physical damage. All non-fraudulent misrepresentations should be classed together as innocent misrepresentations.

Equitable
exception

There was, however, an important equitable exception in that, by an application of the general doctrine of " constructive fraud," which is discussed below,[3] an action would lie for negligent misrepresentation if there was a fiduciary relationship between the parties. So in *Nocton* v. *Lord Ashburton*[4] this principle was applied by the House of Lords to negligent advice given by a solicitor to his client.[5]

*Hedley Byrne
& Co., Ltd.
v. Heller &
Partners, Ltd.*

In 1963 the House of Lords delivered its famous judgment in *Hedley Byrne & Co., Ltd.* v. *Heller & Partners, Ltd.*[6] in which it held that in some circumstances an action would lie in tort for negligent misstatement. In this case the plaintiffs entered into advertising contracts on behalf of Easipower on terms under which they would themselves be liable if Easipower defaulted. Wishing to check on Easipower's credit, they asked their bank to inquire of the defendants, who were Easipower's bankers. Relying on the replies, they continued to place orders and suffered substantial loss when Easipower went into liquidation. The House of Lords held that the plaintiffs' action failed since the defendants' replies had been given " without responsibility "; but they also stated that, but for this disclaimer, an action for negligence could lie in such circumstances. Their Lordships did not however attempt to define with precision the circumstances in which such an action would lie. Detailed consideration of the resultant problems must be left to works on the law of torts[7] but a few observations must be made since it is now possible to argue that a negligent pre-contractual misrepresentation made by one party to the contract to the other may give rise to an action for damages in tort.

It is clear that the House of Lords did not simply assimilate negligent statements to negligent acts. Liability for negligent

---

1. (1889), 14 App. Cas. 337.
2. *Le Lievre* v. *Gould*, [1893] 1 Q.B. 491; *Candler* v. *Crane, Christmas & Co.*, [1951] 2 K.B. 164; [1951] 1 All E.R. 426.
3. See *infra*, pp. 283–9.
4. [1914] A.C. 932. On the difficult question of the relationship between fraud at common law and fraud in equity, see Sheridan, *Fraud in Equity*, 12–37.
5. Negligent advice given by a solicitor to his client would normally amount to a breach of an implied term of the contract between them. In *Nocton* v. *Lord Ashburton* the plaintiff did not formulate his claim in contract because of problems of limitation. Before 1873, a plaintiff could not have recovered damages for a claim of this kind but only specifically equitable remedies such as account. Damages were awarded in *Woods* v. *Martins Bank*, [1959] 1 Q.B. 55; [1958] 3 All E.R. 166.
6. [1964] A.C. 465; [1963] 2 All E.R. 575.
7. There are many articles discussing the effect of the case on the law both of tort and of contract. These include Honoré, 8 J.S.P.T.L. 284; Stevens, 27 M.L.R. 121; Weir, [1963] C.L.J. 216; Gordon, 38 A.L.J. 39, 79; Coote, 2 N.Z.U.L.R. 263.

statements depends upon the existence of a " special relationship " between plaintiff and defendant. Such a relationship does not necessarily involve direct contact between the parties. In *Hedley Byrne & Co., Ltd.* v. *Heller & Partners, Ltd.* itself, the advice was passed through the plaintiff's bank and neither party knew the identity of the other. The defendant knew, however, that the information would be passed to a customer of the inquiring bank and that it was required so that the customer could decide whether to extend credit to Easipower. It would seem probable that the advisor must know in general terms the purpose for which the advice is sought. But where advice is given before entering into a contract between the person giving advice and the person receiving it, this is not likely to be a practical difficulty.

It has been suggested that the duty to take care in giving advice is imposed only on professional men and perhaps only on those professional men whose profession it is to give advice. If such a limitation exists, it would gravely restrict the application of this rule to pre-contractual statements. Though the possibility was extensively discussed by the Privy Council in *Mutual Life and Citizen's Assurance Co., Ltd.* v. *Evatt*,[1] the position is far from clear.

It is important to note that there is nothing in the judgement in *Hedley Byrne & Co., Ltd.* v. *Heller & Partners, Ltd.* to suggest that liability can attach only to statements of fact as defined above.[2] It can extend beyond this to other forms of negligent advice, such as the expression of an opinion about the law.

Early decisions after 1963 did little to clarify whether, and if so when, the doctrine in *Hedley Byrne & Co., Ltd.* v. *Heller & Partners, Ltd.* might be used to impose liability for negligent pre-contractual statements. It was held that actions would not lie in tort against an architect[3] or a solicitor[4] for negligent advice which was in breach of contract on the theory that a single duty cannot give rise to actions both in contract and tort. This theory has been criticized[5], and is certainly hard to reconcile with numerous decisions allowing actions by servants against masters or by passengers against carriers to be brought indifferently in contract or tort.[6] Even if correct, the decisions do not exclude imposition of a duty in tort to govern statements made during the

---

1. [1971] A.C. 793; [1971] 1 All E.R. 150; Rickford, 34 M.L.R. 328. The decision should probably be regarded as turning primarily on what a plaintiff must allege in his pleadings under the unreformed New South Wales procedure. Furthermore, since of the three Lords who sat in both *Hedley Byrne & Co.* v. *Heller* and *Mutual Life* v. *Evatt*, two were in the minority in the latter case, it cannot be regarded as clear that *Mutual Life* v. *Evatt*, whatever it decided, is law in England. In *W. B. Anderson & Sons, Ltd.* v. *Rhodes (Liverpool), Ltd.*, [1967] 2 All E.R. 850, liability was imposed in a purely commercial context.
2. *Supra*, pp. 243 *et seq.*
3. *Bagot* v. *Stevens, Scanlan & Co.*, [1966] 1 Q.B. 197; [1964] 3 All E.R. 577.
4. *Clark* v. *Kirby-Smith*, [1964] Ch. 506; [1964] 2 All E.R. 835.
5. Poulton, 82 L.Q.R. 346, and see *Reid* v. *Traders General Insurance Co., Dares Motors and Myers* (1963), 41 D.L.R. (2d) 148, at p. 154, *per* ILSLEY, C.J.
6. See e.g., *Matthews* v. *Kuwait Bechtel Corporation*, [1959] 2 Q.B. 57; [1959] 2 All E.R. 345.

pre-contractual negotiations and which do not form part of the contract.[1]

These doubts have been substantially resolved by *Esso Petroleum Co., Ltd.* v. *Mardon.*[2]

> In this case the plaintiffs had let a petrol filling station to the defendant for three years. The station was on a newly developed site and during the negotiations for the lease one L, a dealer sales representative employed by the plaintiffs, with over forty years' experience, had told the defendant that he thought the potential " throughput " of the station in the third year would be of the order of 200,000 gallons. The defendant suggested that 100,000 gallons might be a more realistic figure but his doubts were quelled by L's expertise and great experience. In the event the throughput in the third year was only 86,502 gallons. At this level the station was uneconomic and the defendant gave up the tenancy. The plaintiffs sued for arrears of rent and the defendant counterclaimed for damages for negligence.

LAWSON, J., held for the defendant.[3]   In making statements about the station's prospects during the pre-contractual negotiations, the plaintiffs owed the defendant a duty of care since they had a financial interest in the advice they were giving and knew that the defendant was relying on their knowledge and expertise. Further they were in breach of the duty of care, since L's forecast, although honestly made, failed to take into account the actual configuration of the site as developed.

It does not of course follow from this decision that parties in pre-contractual negotiations always owe each other a duty of care, but it appears that we can now confidently state that if all the ingredients of a duty of care are present, the duty is not excluded by the fact that the parties are in a pre-contractual situation.

3.   NEGLIGENT MISREPRESENTATION UNDER THE MISREPRESENTATION ACT 1967

In 1962 the Law Reform Committee in its 10th Report recommended that damages should be given for negligent misrepresentation.[4]   This recommendation was, of course, based on the law as it was assumed to be before *Hedley Byrne & Co., Ltd.* v. *Heller & Partners, Ltd.*, and it may well be that it would have been wise to reconsider it in the light of that decision. Instead it was enacted by the Misrepresentation Act 1967,[5] Section 2 (1) of which provides that:

> " Where a person has entered into a contract after a misrepresentation has been made to him by another party thereto and as a result thereof he has suffered loss, then, if the person making the misrepresentation would be liable to damages in respect thereof had the

---

1. This is how *Woods* v. *Martins Bank,* [1959] 1 Q.B. 55; [1958] 3 All E.R. 166, should now be explained. The possibility might have been raised in *Dick Bentley Productions* v. *Harold Smith (Motors),* [1965] 2 All E.R. 65; [1965] 1 W.L.R. 623, but the case went on other grounds.
2. [1975] 1 All E.R. 203; [1975] 2 W.L.R. 147. See also *Dillingham Construction Pty., Ltd.* v. *Downs,* [1972] 2 N.S.W.R. 49.
3. The facts took place before 1967 and there was therefore no claim under the Misrepresentation Act 1967. See *infra,* pp. 260–2.
4. Cmnd. 1762, paras. 17 and 18.
5. 1967, s. 7.

misrepresentation been made fraudulently, that person shall be so liable notwithstanding that the misrepresentation was not made fraudulently, unless he proves that he had reasonable ground to believe and did believe up to the time the contract was made that the facts represented were true."

It is clear that the object of this subsection is to impose liability in damages for negligent misrepresentation and to reverse the normal burden of proof by requiring the representor to disprove his negligence, but a singularly oblique technique was adopted for this purpose[1] since the draftsman elected to proceed by reference to the common law rules on fraud. This has led some commentators to talk of a " fiction of fraud."[2] Though it would be quixotic to defend the drafting of the section, it is suggested that there is no such " fiction of fraud " since the section does not say that a negligent misrepresentor shall be treated for all purposes as if he were fraudulent. No doubt the wording seeks to incorporate by reference some of the rules relating to fraud but, for instance, nothing in the wording of the subsection requires the measure of damages for deceit to be applied to the statutory action.[3]

Since in an action based on the Act the representor will have to bear the burden of disproving his negligence, it would seem that a plaintiff will usually formulate his claim under the Act rather than sue at common law for fraud or negligence. But in some cases an action at common law may still be preferred.

Advantages of action at common law

Firstly, a plaintiff who relies upon the doctrine in *Hedley Byrne & Co., Ltd.* v. *Heller & Partners, Ltd.*, need not establish that a misrepresentation *stricto sensu* has been made.[4]

Secondly, it may well be that different rules as to remoteness and measure of damages apply to the three forms of action open to the plaintiff.[5] The prospect of recovering heavier damages might spur him to assume the greater burden of proving fraud or negligence.

Thirdly, the statutory action only applies " where a person has entered into a contract." If, as will sometimes happen, the effect of the representor's statements is to make the contract void *ab initio* for mistake, it would seem that there would be no action under the statute for there would be no contract. This may be illustrated by considering the case of *McRae* v. *Commonwealth Disposals Commission.*[6] It will be remembered that in this case the defendants sold the plaintiffs a non-existent ship and later argued that they were not liable for loss incurred by the plaintiffs in searching for the ship since there was no contract for lack of subject matter. We have already suggested[7] that an English court might prove unwilling to follow the High Court of Australia's view that there was a contract that the ship existed. If an English court were to hold the contract void in such a situation, it would

---

1. Atiyah & Treitel, 30 M.L.R. 369, at pp. 372 and 375; Fairest, [1967] C.L.J. 239, at pp. 244–245.
2. Atiyah & Trietel, *op. cit.*
3. See *infra*, p. 275.
4. See *supra*, pp. 258–260.
5. See *infra*, pp. 275–6.
6. (1951), 84 C.L.R. 377.
7. *Supra*, pp. 210–2.

seem that no action could be brought under the Act. But the plaintiff could still recover in tort at common law by proving that the defendant was either fraudulent or negligent in stating that the ship existed, since it is not a requirement of these actions that the representee shall have entered into a contract but simply that he shall have suffered loss in reliance on the statement. Since the defendants in *McRae* v. *Commonwealth Disposals Commission* were clearly negligent it would seem that the decision in that case can now best be explained by reliance on *Hedley Byrne & Co., Ltd.* v. *Heller & Partners, Ltd.*

4. INNOCENT MISREPRESENTATION

Before 1963, the phrase " innocent misrepresentation " was used to describe all misrepresentations which were not fraudulent. Now that two classes of negligent misrepresentation have appeared, the appellation " innocent " should clearly be restricted to misrepresentations that are made without fault.

D. REMEDIES FOR MISREPRESENTATION

1. RELATIONSHIP BETWEEN REMEDIES FOR BREACH OF CONTRACT AND REMEDIES FOR MISREPRESENTATION

As we have already seen,[1] classical doctrine drew a firm distinction between those statements which formed terms of a contract and those which constituted mere representations. The practical effect of this distinction has been diminished by the Misrepresentation Act 1967 but it remains conceptually significant. Before the Act, however, it was not clear whether the same statement could simultaneously be both a term of the contract and a mere representation.

In discussing this possibility we must consider two separate types of case. The first is where a statement is made during pre-contractual negotiations and the same statement later appears as a term of the (written) contract. In this case one might think that the representee could exercise his remedies for misrepresentation in respect of the first statement and his remedies for breach of contract in respect of the second, but there was some authority for the view that the representation " merged " with the term so that no remedies would be available for the misrepresentation.[2] All doubts on this question are now resolved by section 1 of the Misrepresentation Act 1967, which provides:

> " Where a person has entered into a contract after a misrepresentation has been made to him and—
>
> (a) the misrepresentation has become a term of the contract; . . .
> then, if otherwise he would be entitled to rescind the contract

---

1. *Supra*, p. 246.
2. *Pennsylvania Shipping Co.* v. *Compagnie Nationale de Navigation*, [1936] 2 All E.R. 1167.   Cf., *Compagnie Française des Chemins de Fer Paris-Orleans* v. *Leeston Shipping Co.* (1919), 1 Ll. L. Rep. 235.   Fairest, [1967] C.L.J. 239, at pp. 241–2.

without alleging fraud, he shall be so entitled . . . notwithstanding the matters mentioned in paragraph (a) . . ." of this section

This obscurely worded provision means that a misrepresentee may rescind for a misrepresentation, even though the same undertaking has later become a term of the contract.

The second type of case arises where it is possible to argue that a statement, which occurs only once in the history of a transaction may be classified either as a term of the contract or as a representation. If it is classified as a representation, there would be no question of granting the remedies appropriate to a contractual term and if it is classified as a term, there would be no question of granting the remedies for " mere representations ". In practice, the classification has always been made where the plaintiff claims damages on the ground that the statement is a term of the contract. But in the converse case where the plaintiff claims rescission for misrepresentation, it does not appear ever to have been argued that the remedy should be refused because the statement was properly classified as a term.

A good example is *Leaf* v. *International Galleries*[1] where the plaintiff bought a picture from the defendant, which the latter stated incorrectly to have been painted by Constable. Clearly this statement might well have been held to be a term of the contract if the plaintiff had sought damages, but he wished to return the picture, and therefore sued for rescission for innocent misrepresentation. Though the Court of Appeal was clearly somewhat embarrassed at the possibility of a plaintiff being able to rescind for innocent misrepresentation when the right to reject for breach of condition was lost,[2] the case was decided on the basis that the defendant's statement was a " mere " representation but that the right to rescind was lost by lapse of time.[3] In other cases, also, the same assumption has been allowed to go unchallenged.[4] Nevertheless it is suggested that in principle the categories of terms and representations are mutually exclusive and that a plaintiff cannot elect to treat a term as a representation. If this is so, it would follow that section 1 of the Misrepresentation Act 1967 had no application to such a case, since it is not one in which a misrepresentation has become a term, but one in which a statement has always been a term.[5]

2. RESCISSION

It is a fundamental principle that the effect of a misrepresentation is to make the contract voidable and not void.[6] This means that the contract is valid unless and until it is set aside by the repre-

---

1. [1950] 2 K.B. 86; [1950] 1 All E.R. 693; *supra*, p. 215.
2. [1950] 2 K.B., at p. 91; [1950] 1 All E.R., at p. 695.
3. See *infra*, p. 269.
4. E.g., *Long* v. *Lloyd*, [1958] 2 All E.R. 402; [1958] 1 W.L.R. 753. See Atiyah, 22 M.L.R. 76, where the argument in the text is forcefully put.
5. The thesis in this section is also important in connection with the provisions of the Misrepresentation Act as to exemption clauses—see *infra*, pp. 277-9.
6. In exceptional cases, as in that of mistaken identity [*supra*, p. 228] a misrepresentation may cause a mistake which may entitle the misrepresentee to treat the contract as void. But this is the result of the mistake and not of the misrepresentation.

sentee.[1] On discovering the misrepresentation the representee may elect to affirm or to rescind the contract.

Affirmation of the contract

A contract is affirmed if the representee declares his intention to proceed with the contract or does some act from which such an intention may reasonably be inferred.[2]

Rescission of the contract

A contract is rescinded if the representee makes it clear that he refuses to be bound by its provisions. The effect then is that the contract is terminated *ab initio* as if it had never existed. In the words of Lord ATKINSON:

> " Where one party to a contract expresses by word or act in an unequivocal manner that by reason of fraud or essential error of a material kind inducing him to enter into the contract he has resolved to rescind it, and refuses to be bound by it, the expression of his election, if justified by the facts, terminates the contract, puts the parties *in statu quo ante* and restores things, as between them, to the position in which they stood before the contract was entered into."[3]

An election, once it has been unequivocally made, whether in favour of affirmation or of rescission, is determined for ever.[4] It cannot be revived. If the representee elects to rescind the contract, the general rule is that within a reasonable time he must

Finality of election

communicate his decision to the representor, for the latter is entitled to treat the contractual *nexus* as continuing until he is informed of its termination.[5] This general rule, however, is subject to two exceptions.

Firstly, if the result of the misrepresentation is that possession of property is delivered to the representor, the recaption of the property by the representee is itself a communication of the rescission.[6]

Secondly, if the representor disappears so effectively that it is impossible to find him, the requirement of communication will be satisfied if the representee records his intention to rescind the contract by some overt act that is reasonable in the circumstances. This was recognised for the first time in *Car and Universal Finance Co., Ltd.* v. *Caldwell*[7] on the following facts:

> The defendant sold and delivered a car to X in return for a cheque that was dishonoured the next day, by which time both the car and X had disappeared. The defendant immediately notified the police and the Automobile Association and requested them to find the car. While the search was proceeding, X sold the car to

1. *Newbigging* v. *Adam* (1886), 34 Ch.D. 582, at p. 592.
2. See *infra*, p. 268.
3. *Abram Steamship Co.* v. *Westville Steamship Co.,* [1923] A.C. 773, at p. 781. Unfortunately the word " rescission " is also o(ten used to describe the position where a party elects to treat a contract as discharged because of a breach of one of the essential terms (*infra*, p. 576). But there the contract is not rendered void *ab initio*: *Mussen* v. *Van Diemen's Land Co.,* [1938] 1 Ch. 253, at p. 260; [1938] 1 All E.R. 210 at p. 215, *per* FARWELL, L.J. The *further* liability of either party to perform the outstanding contractual obligations is terminated, but causes of action that have already arisen by virtue of the breach remain remediable by an action for damages. See *R. V. Ward* v. *Bignall,* [1967] 1 Q.B. 534, at p. 548; [1967] 2 All E.R. 449, at p. 455 *per* DIPLOCK, L.J. It would clearly add greatly to clarity if the word rescission were confined to the present remedy.
4. *Clough* v. *London and North Western Rail. Co.* (1871), L.R. 7 Exch. 26, at p. 35, *per curiam.*
5. *Car and Universal Finance Co., Ltd.* v. *Caldwell,* [1965] 1 Q.B. 525; [1964] 1 All E.R. 290.
6. *Ibid.*
7. *Supra,* footnote 5.

M, Ltd. motor dealers, who had notice of X's defective title. Ultimately, M, Ltd. sold the car to the plaintiffs who bought it in good faith.

It was held that the defendant, by setting the police and the Automobile Association in motion, had sufficiently evinced his intention to rescind the contract. As soon as he made this clear, the ownership of the car reverted to him, and therefore the later sale by M, Ltd. vested no title in the plaintiffs, the innocent purchasers.[1]

Rescission, even though enforced by a court, is always the act of the defrauded party in the sense that it is his election which effectively destroys the contractual *nexus* between him and the other party.[2] It follows that rescission is effective from the date it is communicated to the representor and not from the date of any judgement in subsequent litigation. Nevertheless, the representee may fortify his position by bringing an action for rescission in equity, a step that is desirable if the fraudulent party ignores the cancellation of the contract and if there is a possibility that innocent third parties may act on the assumption that it still exists.

Rescission is essentially the act of the representee

As we have seen, the effect of rescission is to nullify the contract *ab initio*. An essential requirement of this remedy, where the contract has been partly or wholly performed, is therefore the restoration of the parties to their original positions. In the language of the law, *restitutio in integrum* is essential.[3]

Rescission requires restitutio in integrum

Common law, unlike equity, provides no action for rescission. But it has always recognized that a contract is automatically terminated if the representee elects to rescind rather than to affirm it, provided that the restoration of the *status quo ante* is feasible. In this latter respect, however, common law is at a disadvantage as compared with equity. The remedial procedure

Restitutio in integrum at common law

---

1. In this case the car was not sold by the rogue X directly to the innocent purchaser. It was first sold by him to M, Ltd. who had notice of his defective title, and later sold to the innocent purchaser. In *Newtons of Wembley, Ltd.* v. *Williams*, [1965] 1 Q.B. 560; [1964] 3 All E.R. 532, the facts were similar except that there was a direct sale by the rogue to the innocent buyer, and it was held that the latter acquired a good title by virtue of the Factors Act 1889, s. 9.

This distinction between the effect of a direct and an indirect sale after the contract between the rogue and the true owner has been rescinded is a reproach to the law (see Cornish, 27 M.L.R. 477). The Law Reform Committee, however, has recommended in its 12th Report that until notice of rescission of a contract is communicated to the other contracting party (i.e. in the instant example, to the rogue) an innocent purchaser from the latter shall be able to acquire a good title (Cmnd. 2958 (1966)). If statutory effect is given to this recommendation, the distinction between a direct and an indirect sale will virtually disappear, for it will usually be impossible for the true owner to communicate with the rogue before the sale to the innocent purchaser.

It would seem that the exception to the general rule recognized in *Caldwell's* case concerning communication of rescission, applies equally to a case of innocent misrepresentation, though it is difficult to envisage circumstances in which the problem would arise, since an innocent person, unlike the rogue in *Caldwell's* case, would have no occasion to abscond; [1965] 1 Q.B. at pp. 551–2, *per* SELLERS, L.J. UPJOHN, L.J., left the question open: *ibid.*, at p. 555. In *McLeod* v. *Kerr*, [1965] S.C. 253, the Court of Session took the opposite view to *Car and Universal Finance Co., Ltd.* v. *Caldwell*.

2. *Abram Steamship Co.* v. *Westville Shipping Co.*, [1923] A.C. 773, at p. 781.
3. See *infra*, pp. 265–270.

at its command is not sufficiently flexible and comprehensive to enable the process of restoration to be effected according to the exigencies of each particular case. The court is restricted to saying that there can be no rescission unless the parties can be restored to the exact positions that they formerly occupied.[1]

The courts of equity, however, soon developed a suit for rescission, and since their remedial procedure was far more elastic than that of the common law, they were able to take a more realistic view of *restitutio in integrum*. In the words of Lord BLACKBURN, the court, in the exercise of its equitable jurisdiction, " can take accounts of profits and make allowance for deterioration. And I think the practice has always been for a court of equity to give this relief whenever, by the exercise of its powers, it can do what is practically just, though it cannot restore the parties precisely to the state they were in before the contract."[2] Therefore, if satisfied that the misrepresentation has been made, it annuls the contract and then makes such consequential orders as may be necessary in the particular circumstances to restore as far as possible the *status quo ante* of both parties.

At one time equity followed the common law in limiting relief to cases of fraudulent misrepresentation but this was seen to be too harsh a view. The rule gradually established was that where a party was induced to enter into a contract by the innocent misrepresentation of the other party, he was entitled to escape from his obligations by electing to rescind the contract. To render this election effective, he must make his intention clear by word or act to the other party, or institute a suit for rescission, or plead the misrepresentation as a defence to a suit for a specific performance.[3] It was early decided that an innocent misrepresentation was a good ground for refusal of specific performance, but for a considerable period the view prevailed that a greater degree of misrepresentation, in fact fraudulent misrepresentation, was necessary to justify a suit for rescission.[4] This illogical distinction was later abandoned, and it was established by the middle of the nineteenth century that, whether the misrepresentation was fraudulent or not, the representee was entitled to rescind the contract, and if it was written to have it delivered up for cancellation.[5]

The result of this development was that, by the middle of the nineteenth century, rescission had become a general remedy for misrepresentation though damages were available only for fraudulent misrepresentation. Rescission might often be a completely effective remedy, but this would not always be the case. If a farmer bought a cow, represented, incorrectly, to be free from tuberculin, and it infected the rest of his herd, it would comfort him little to be able to return the cow. If the representation was

---

1. *Clarke* v. *Dickson* (1858), E.B. & E. 148, at p. 155. *Erlanger* v. *New Sombrero Phosphate Co.* (1878), 3 App. Cas. 1218, at p. 1278.
2. 3 App. Cas., at pp. 1278–9. See also *Spence* v. *Crawford*, [1939] 3 All E.R. 271.
3. *Rawlins* v. *Wickham* (1858), 3 De G. & J. 304; *Torrance* v. *Bolton* (1872), 8 Ch. App. 118.
4. *Cadman* v. *Horner* (1810), 18 Ves. 10.
5. *Cooper* v. *Joel* (1859), 1 De G.F. & J. 240; *Re Liverpool Borough Bank, Duranty's Case* (1858), 26 Beav. 268; *Torrance* v. *Bolton* (1872), 8 Ch. App. 118; *Wauton* v. *Coppard*, [1899] 1 Ch. 92.

fraudulent there was no problem since an action for damages could be brought. If it were not fraudulent, the question arose whether the right to rescind could be manipulated so as to restore the representee entirely to the *status quo ante*. It was held that to do this *in toto* would be to give damages; but the courts drew a subtle distinction between an award of damages and the grant of an indemnity and held that the representee must be indemnified against obligations incurred as a result of the representation.

Distinction between indemnity and damages

To what obligations, then, does the indemnity relate? The answer is that the plaintiff must be indemnified, not against all obligations even though they may be correctly described as having arisen under, or out of or as a result of the contract but only against those necessarily *created by* the contract.[1] The burden must be one that has passed to the representee as a necessary and inevitable result of the position which he assumed upon completion of the contract.

To what obligations indemnity extends

If, for example, A procures the dissolution of his partnership with B and C on the ground of innocent misrepresentation, he nevertheless remains personally liable for partnership debts contracted while he was a member of the firm. His position as partner was created by the contract and it is the inevitable and automatic result of having occupied this position that he is now burdened with liability for debts. Hence they are a proper subject for indemnity.

The distinction between what is true indemnity and what is equivalent to damages is neatly illustrated by *Whittington* v. *Seale-Hayne*:[2]

> The plaintiffs, who were breeders of prize poultry, were induced to take a lease of certain property belonging to the defendants by an oral representation that the premises were in a thoroughly sanitary condition. This representation was not contained in the lease that was later executed, and so was not a term of the contract. The premises were in fact insanitary. The water supply was poisoned, and in consequence the manager of the poultry farm became seriously ill, and the poultry either died or became valueless. Moreover the Urban District Council declared that the house and premises were unfit for habitation and required the plaintiffs to renew the drains.

In their action for rescission the plaintiffs, while admitting that owing to the absence of fraud they could not recover damages, contended that they were entitled to an indemnity against the consequences of having entered into the contract. These consequences were serious, since they included the following losses: value of stock lost, £750; loss of profit on sales, £100; loss of breeding season, £500; rent and removal of stores, £75; medical expenses, £100. It was held that the claim for the plaintiffs in respect of these losses was in effect a claim for damages, and that their right to an indemnity was limited to what they had expended upon rates and to the cost of effecting the repairs

---

1. *Newbigging* v. *Adam* (1886), 34 Ch.D. 582, at p. 594, *per* BOWEN, L.J.; the other judges, COTTON and FRY, L.JJ., gave a wider scope to indemnity, but it is believed that the narrower test stated by BOWEN, L.J., is correct. Such was the view of FARWELL, J., in *Whittington* v. *Seale-Hayne* (1900), 82 L.T. 49.
2. (1900), 82 L.T. 49.

ordered by the Council.   The obligation to pay rates and to effect the repairs were obligations which the plaintiffs were required to assume by the contract; but the contract created no obligation to erect sheds, to appoint a manager or to stock the premises with poultry.

Diminished importance of distinction between indemnity and damages

The practical importance of the distinction between indemnity and damages has been reduced by recent developments which have extended the right to damages.[1]   Further, as we shall see,[2] the Misrepresentation Act 1967, s. 2 (2), gives the court a general power to grant damages in lieu of rescission.   But there will remain cases in which the representee has no *right* to damages and in which the court will decide not to use its *power* to grant damages.   In such cases the distinction will still be operative.

LIMITS TO THE RIGHT OF RESCISSION

It is a paradoxical result of the history of this branch of the law that rescission should be regarded as the second best alternative to damages.   In fact, it is in many ways a much more drastic remedy and it is natural therefore that restrictions have been placed upon its availability.   The right to rescind is lost (i) if the representee has affirmed the contract; (ii) if *restitutio in integrum* is no longer possible, or (iii) if rescission would deprive a third party of a right in the subject matter of the contract which he has acquired in good faith and for value.   We shall now consider these limits *seriatim* and then discuss the changes made by the Misrepresentation Act 1967.

(i) Affirmation of the contract

Express or implicit affirmation

Affirmation is complete and binding when the representee, with full knowledge of the facts and of the misrepresentation, either declares his intention to proceed with the contract or does some act from which such an intention may reasonably be inferred.[3]   The Reports contain many examples of implicit affirmation by shareholders.   A person who applies for and obtains shares upon the faith of a prospectus containing misrepresentation is entitled to rescind the allotment and to recover the price paid; but if after learning of the misrepresentation he attempts to sell the shares or pays money due upon the allotment or retains dividends paid to him, he loses his right of rescission, since these acts show an intention to treat the contract as subsisting.[4]   They are acts of

---

1. Under *Hedley Byrne & Co., Ltd.* v. *Heller & Partners, Ltd.* and Misrepresentation Act 1967, s. 2 (1).
2. *Infra*, p. 273.
3. *Clough* v. *London and North Western Rail. Co.* (1871), L.R. 7 Exch. 26, at p. 34.   *Seddon* v. *North Eastern Salt Co., Ltd.*, [1905] 1 Ch. 326, at p. 334; *Car and Universal Finance Co., Ltd.* v. *Caldwell*, [1965] 1 Q.B. 525, at p. 550; [1964] 1 All E.R. 290, at p. 293.   The difficult case of *Long* v. *Lloyd*, [1958] 2 All E.R. 402; [1958] 1 W.L.R. 753, would seem to have been decided on the ground that the plaintiff's conduct amounted to an affirmation of the contract: see especially, [1958] 1 W.L.R. at 761.   The *ratio decidendi*, however, is not clear; see Atiyah, 22 M.L.R. 76; Odgers, [1958] C.L.J. 166.
4. *Re Hop and Malt Exchange and Warehouse Co., Ex parte Briggs* (1866), L.R. 1 Eq. 483; *Scholey* v. *Central Rail. Co. of Venezuela* (1868), L.R. 9 Eq. 266, note.

ownership over the shares wholly inconsistent with an intention to repudiate the allotment.

Lapse of time without any step towards repudiation being taken does not in itself constitute affirmation, but it may be treated as evidence of affirmation, and it was said in a leading case that when the lapse of time is great " it probably would in practice be treated as conclusive evidence " of an election to recognize the contract.[1] Everything depends upon the facts of the case and the nature of the contract. In particular it is material to consider whether the representor has altered his position in the reasonable belief that rescission will not be enforced, or whether third parties have been misled by the inactivity of the representee.[2]

In principle, lapse of time can only be evidence of affirmation if it comes after the representee has discovered that he is entitled to rescind. But in *Leaf* v. *International Galleries*,[3] it was held that a contract for the sale of goods could not be rescinded on the basis of a non-fraudulent misrepresentation when five years had elapsed between the sale and the discovery of the truth. It was said that " it behoves the purchaser either to verify or, as the case may be, to disprove the representation within a reasonable time, or else stand or fall by it."[4] It may be doubted whether this reasoning would apply to a fraudulent representation.

Lapse of time may be evidence of affirmation

(ii) Restitutio in integrum impossible

Part of the consequential relief to which a representee is entitled upon rescission is the recovery of anything that he may have paid or delivered under the contract. It is, however, a necessary corollary of this right that he should make a similar restoration of anything obtained by him under the contract. Otherwise the main object of rescission, which is that the parties should both be remitted to their former position, would not be attained. A buyer, for instance, who avoided a contract for misrepresentation, would be able to recover the price in full while retaining the goods. This would be inequitable as well as inconsistent with the object of rescission.

Rescission must be total, not partial

> " Though the defendant has been fraudulent, he must not be robbed, nor must the plaintiff be unjustly enriched, as he would be if he both got back what he had parted with and kept what he had received in return. The purpose of relief is not punishment but compensation."[5]

The rule is, therefore, that rescission cannot be enforced if events which have occurred since the contract and in which the representee has participated make it impossible to restore the parties substantially to their original position. The representee must be, not only willing, but also able, to make *restitutio in integrum*.

---

1. *Clough* v. *London and North Western Rail. Co.* (1871), L.R. 7 Exch. 26, at p. 35.
2. *Lindsay Petroleum Co.* v. *Hurd* (1874), L.R. 5 P.C. 221, at 240; *Aaron's Reef* v. *Twiss*, [1896] A.C. 273, at p. 294.
3. [1950] 2 K.B. 86; [1950] 1 All E.R. 693.
4. [1950] 2 K.B., at p. 92; [1950] 1 All E.R., at p. 696, *per* JENKINS, L.J.
5. *Spence* v. *Crawford*, [1939] 3 All E.R. 271, at pp. 288–9, *per* Lord WRIGHT.

Property
must be
restored in
its original
condition

This doctrine finds its most common application when the things delivered to the representee under the contract have been radically changed in extent or character by him or with his consent. Thus if a partnership in which the representee was induced to take shares is converted into a limited liability company, rescission is excluded, since the existing shares are wholly different in nature and status from those originally received.[1] Rescission is equally impossible if the subject-matter of the contract is a mine that has been worked out[2] or operated for a substantial time,[3] or if it comprises goods that have been consumed or altered by the buyer.[4]

The rule requiring restoration is not, however, enforced to the letter if the result will be unfair. Thus property transferred by the defendant may have deteriorated in the hands of the plaintiff, so that it cannot be restored in its original state. Nevertheless, provided that its substantial identity remains, its restoration will be ordered on the terms that the plaintiff pay compensation for its deterioration. It is considered fairer on equitable principles that the defendant should be compelled to accept compensation than to keep the full profit of his wrongdoing.[5]

(iii) Injury to third parties

No rescission
if third
parties
acquire
right under
the contract

The right of the representee to elect whether he will affirm or disaffirm a contract procured by misrepresentation is subject to this limitation, that, if before he reaches a decision an innocent third party acquires for value an interest in the subject-matter of the contract, the right of rescission is defeated.[6]

Sale under a
voidable
title
illustrates
the rule

The most frequent instance of this limitation is where goods have been obtained from their owner by fraud. If the fraud makes the contract void at common law on the grounds already discussed in the chapter on Mistake,[7] no title passes to the fraudulent person and the latter can pass none to any third party, however innocent this third party may be. If, however, the contract is voidable only, then the title so obtained by the fraudulent person is valid until it has been avoided, and any transfer of it made before avoidance to an innocent third party for valuable consideration cannot be defeated by the owner.[8] An apt illustration of the rule is *White* v. *Garden*[9] where the facts were these:

---

1. *Clarke* v. *Dickson* (1858), E.B. & E. 148; *Western Bank of Scotland* v. *Addie* (1867), L.R. 1 Sc. & Div. 145.
2. *Vigers* v. *Pike* (1842), 8 Cl. & Fin. 562.
3. *Attwood* v. *Small* (1838), 6 Cl. & Fin. 232; *Clarke* v. *Dickson*, footnote 1, *supra*.
4. *Clarke* v. *Dickson, supra, per* CROMPTON, J., at p. 155.
5. *Lagunas Nitrate Co.* v. *Lagunas Syndicate*, [1899] 2 Ch. 392, at p. 457, *per* RIGBY, L.J.; adopted in *Spence* v. *Crawford*, [1939] 3 All E.R. 271, at pp. 279–80. See also *Newbigging* v. *Adam* (1886), 34 Ch.D. 582; *Adam* v. *Newbigging* (1888), 13 App. Cas. 308.
6. *Clough* v. *London and North Western Rail. Co.* (1871), L.R. 7 Exch. 26, at p. 35.
7. *Supra*, pp. 221–231.
8. *White* v. *Garden* (1851), 10 C.B. 919; *Babcock* v. *Lawson* (1879), 4 Q.B.D. 394, affirmed (1880), 5 Q.B.D. 284; *Phillips* v. *Brooks, Ltd.,* [1919] 2 K.B. 243; *Stevenson* v. *Newnham* (1853), 13 C.B. 285, at p. 302, *per* PARKE, B.
9. (1851), 10 C.B. 919.

Parker bought fifty tons of iron from Garden by persuading him to take in payment a bill of exchange which had apparently been accepted by one Thomas of Rochester. Parker re-sold the iron to White, who acted in good faith, and Garden made delivery in one of his barges at White's wharf. Garden, upon discovering that the bill of exchange was worthless since there was no such person as Thomas of Rochester, seized and removed part of the iron that was still in the barge.

Garden was held liable in trover. The title to the iron had passed to Parker under a contract that was temporarily valid and, while still undisturbed, had been passed to an innocent purchaser. It was not a case of operative mistake, since Garden intended to contract with Parker. It must be added that a third party, if he is to acquire an indefeasible title under a voidable contract, must not only act *bona fide*, but also give consideration.[1] In one case for instance:

Third party must be bona fide and must give consideration

> A debtor and his surety persuaded the creditor to accept from the debtor a transfer of a mortgage which the debtor knew to be imaginary but which the surety believed to be valid. Later, at the solicitation of the surety and in reliance on the transfer which he believed to be genuine, the creditor released the surety from further obligation.[2]

It was held that the creditor was entitled to rescind the release and to be restored to his rights against the surety, since the latter, though honest, had given no consideration for his release.

Another type of case where the remedy of rescission is affected by the existence of third party rights, concerns the winding-up of companies. A person who is induced to become a shareholder by reason of a false representation is entitled to rescind the contract as against the company, which means that he can divest himself of the shares and recover what he has paid. But this right is lost if its exercise will prejudice the creditors of the company. The established rule is, therefore, that the commencement of winding-up proceedings completely bars the right of a shareholder to avoid the contract under which he obtained his shares.[3]

Right to rescind purchase of shares barred by winding-up proceedings

(iv) Effect of Misrepresentation Act 1967

The law relating to limits to the right of rescission was substantially amended by section 1 of the Misrepresentation Act 1967 which provides:

> " Where a person has entered into a contract after a misrepresentation has been made to him, and—
>
> (a) the misrepresentation has become a term of the contract; or
> (b) the contract has been performed;
>
> or both, then, if otherwise he would be entitled to rescind the contract without alleging fraud, he shall be so entitled, subject to the provisions of this Act, notwithstanding the matters mentioned in paragraphs (a) and (b) of this section."

---

1. *Scholefield* v. *Templer* (1859), 4 De G. & J. 429, at pp. 433-4, *per* Lord CAMPBELL.
2. *Ibid.*
3. *Oakes* v. *Turquand and Harding* (1867), L.R. 2 H.L. 325.

Purpose of section

The effect of this provision is that the only limits to the right of rescission are now the three already mentioned.   The purpose of the section can only be understood by examining the pre-existing law.   We have already discussed paragraph (a).[1]   Paragraph (b) was designed to abolish two previous rules, or perhaps more accurately, one rule and one supposed rule, *viz.*: the rule in *Wilde* v. *Gibson* and the rule in *Seddon* v. *North Eastern Salt Co., Ltd.*

Rule in *Wilde* v. *Gibson*

In *Wilde* v. *Gibson*,[2] the House of Lords held that a conveyance of land could not be avoided after completion on the basis of an innocent misrepresentation by the vendor about a defect in title, *viz.* the existence of a right of way.   Lord CAMPBELL said that " where the conveyance has been executed . . . a court of equity will set aside the conveyance only on the ground of actual fraud."[3] It can be seen that there is much to be said for this rule, since it is the normal practice of purchasers to employ solicitors who carry out a full investigation of title.   These considerations would not apply so strongly to physical defects in the property though the employment of surveyors is becoming more common and would have little weight in the case of sale of goods or shares or the performance of other contracts.

Rule in *Seddon* v. *North Eastern Salt Co., Ltd.*

Despite these considerations, JOYCE, J., in *Seddon* v. *North Eastern Salt Co., Ltd.*[4] treating Lord CAMPBELL's statement in *Wilde* v. *Gibson* as one of general application, purported to lay down a rule that " the court will not grant rescission of an executed contract for the sale of a chattel or chose in action on the ground of an innocent misrepresentation."[5]   This rule was clearly based on a misunderstanding of the rationale of *Wilde* v. *Gibson*; it ignored contrary earlier authority[6] and it was not even necessary for the decision in *Seddon's* case itself, since the representee had affirmed the contract.   Yet it succeeded in muddying the waters for the next sixty years.   It was applied in *Angel* v. *Jay*[7] to an executed lease induced by an innocent misrepresentation that the drains were not defective and it was re-stated by McCARDIE, J., in *Armstrong* v. *Jackson*.[8]   In three cases in the 1950s[9] the Court of Appeal had an opportunity to confirm or overrule *Seddon's* case but in each case the opportunity was spurned and the decision went on other grounds, though in the first two of the cases DENNING, L.J., declared that the rule did not exist.

Recommendations of Law Reform Committee

If the authority of the rule in *Seddon's* case was doubted, its injustice was almost universally accepted.   In its 10th Report,[10] the Law Reform Committee agreed with this verdict and recommended the abolition of the rule in *Seddon's* case.   The Committee thought however that the rule in *Wilde* v. *Gibson* should be retained in the interests of finality and that it should apply both to

---

1. *Supra*, pp. 262–3.
2. (1848), 1 H.L. Cas. 605.
3. *Ibid.*, at pp. 632–3.
4. [1905] 1 Ch. 326.
5. Reporter's headnote.   See [1905] 1 Ch. 332–3.
6. See Hammelmann, 55 L.Q.R. 90.   But cf. Howard, 26 M.L.R. 272.
7. [1911] 1 K.B. 666.
8. [1917] 2 K.B. 822, at p. 825.
9. *Solle* v. *Butcher*, [1950] 1 K.B. 671; [1949] 2 All E.R. 1107; *Leaf* v. *International Galleries*, [1950] 2 K.B. 86; [1950] 1 All E.R. 693; *Long* v. *Lloyd*, [1958] 2 All E.R. 402; [1958] 1 W.L.R. 753.
10. Cmnd. 1782, paras. 3 to 13 (1962).

defects in title and to physical defects and to sales and long leases of land.[1]

It will be seen that Parliament has abolished both rules so that it is now possible for a representee to seek rescission of any type of contract including one for the sale of land even though it has been performed. It would seem that this change has created the possibility of considerable hardship to an owner-occupier who sells his house and uses the purchase money to buy another. Such a vendor will normally only be able to repay the purchase price by selling his new house and rearranging a mortgage on his old house. It is clear that justice does not always require these heavy burdens to be imposed on an innocent representor-vendor and it is important therefore in considering the practical effect of section 1 (b) of the Act to bear in mind that under section 2 (2) the court now has a general power to give damages in lieu of rescission.[2] It would seem that this type of case might well be one where the court would choose to exercise this power.

Misrepresentation Act goes further

3. DAMAGES

We have seen that as the law has finally developed, any misrepresentation gives rise to a right in the representee to rescind. The right to damages, on the other hand, is not universal but depends on showing that the representor's statement is either fraudulent or negligent in the senses set out above.[3] However the Misrepresentation Act 1967 made a further important change by conferring on the court a general power to grant damages in lieu of rescission. By section 2 (2) of the Act it is provided that:

Damages in lieu of rescission

" Where a person has entered into a contract after a misrepresentation has been made to him otherwise than fraudulently, and he would be entitled by reason of the misrepresentation to rescind the contract, then, if it is claimed in any of the proceedings arising out of the contract that the contract ought to be or has been rescinded, the court or arbitrator may declare the contract subsisting and award damages in lieu of rescission, if of the opinion that it would be equitable to do so, having regard to the nature of the misrepresentation and the loss that would be caused by it if the contract were upheld, as well as to the loss that rescission would cause to the other party."

Thus, the victim of an innocent misrepresentation may be awarded damages instead of, but not in addition to, rescission if the court in its discretion considers it equitable to do so.

For subsection 2 (2) of the Act to operate, the facts must be such that the representee " would be entitled, by reason of the misrepresentation, to rescind the contract." These words presumably mean that the remedy of rescission must be still available to him at the time of the action. Under the general law, as we have seen,[4] the facts may be such that this remedy, though

Award of damages dependent upon right to rescission

---

1. The Committee recommended drawing a line between long and short leases by using the test provided by section 54 (2) of the Law of Property Act 1925.
2. See *supra*, p. 268.
3. See *supra*, pp. 256–262.
4. See *supra*, pp. 268–273.

once available to him, has been lost; as for example, because *restitutio in integrum* is no longer possible or because an innocent third party has acquired an interest in the subject-matter of the contract. In these circumstances, therefore, there is no room for the operation of section 2 (2) of the Act, or for the exercise of the judicial discretion which it gives.

Under section 2 (2) of the Act, rescission and damages are alternatives; but if the representee has a right to damages because of the representor's fraud or negligence, he may sue for damages either instead of or as well as rescinding. In these cases rescission and damages are in no sense mutually exclusive though clearly the amount of damages to which the representee will be entitled will be affected by whether or not he has successfully rescinded. In some cases rescission will repair all the loss the representee has suffered but in other cases he will have suffered consequential loss.[1]

In any case, wherever the representee seeks damages, it will be necessary to decide upon what principles damages are to be assessed. It appears not improbable that different rules apply to each of the possible heads of claim and it is therefore necessary to consider them *seriatim*. But before doing so a basic distinction must be drawn between damages in contract and damages in tort. This distinction is important for two reasons. First, the purpose of damages is different in contract and in tort. In contract the object of damages is to put the injured party as nearly as maybe in the position he would have enjoyed if the contract had been performed; in tort it is to restore the injured party to the position he occupied before the tort was committed. This difference in approach will mean that sometimes a greater sum can be obtained in contract than in tort and sometimes a greater sum in tort than in contract though in other cases it may make no difference.[2] Secondly, the test of remoteness of damage in tort is generally foreseeability at the moment of breach of duty; in contract it appears that some higher degree of probability than is embraced by the word "foreseeable" is required and it is clear that the relevant moment is that of the making of the contract.[3]

We will now consider each of the possible claims for damages in turn.

General principles governing damages

---

1. See, e.g., the example of the infected cow, *supra*, p. 266. In these cases the plaintiff is resciding the contract and pursuing a claim in tort. A plaintiff cannot normally rescind the contract for initial invalidity and at the same time seek damages for breach of that contract. See *Horsler* v. *Zorro*, [1975] 1 All E.R. 584; [1975] 2 W.L.R. 183; Albery, 91 L.Q.R. 337.
2. Suppose for instance that X buys and pays for a set of dining room chairs represented incorrectly to be Chippendale and that he is unable to rescind. Then if A is the actual price, B the value of a genuine set of Chippendale chairs of this type and C the actual value of the chairs bought then *prima facie* the amount recoverable in contract would be B–C and in tort A–C. Only if A and B are the same will the amount recoverable in tort and contract be the same. If A is greater than B, the plaintiff should try to formulate his claim in tort. If B is greater than A he should try to formulate it in contract. In either case there may also be claims for consequential loss, which will be governed by the rules of remoteness stated in the text.
3. For fuller discussion of these problems in contract, see *infra*, pp. 588–604, and for tort, see Salmond, *The Law of Torts*, 15th Edn., pp. 713–749; Winfield & Jolowicz, *Tort*, 10th Edn., pp. 84–106 and 552–584; Street, *The Law of Torts*, 6th Edn., pp. 142–151.

(i) For fraudulent misrepresentation

It is clear that the claim for damages for fraudulent misrepresentation is a claim in tort. So the general governing rule is that the plaintiff should be restored to the position he would have been in if the representation had not been made.[1] There is authority however for the view that in considering what consequential loss can be recovered, the test of remoteness is not the normal one of foreseeability. In *Doyle* v. *Olby (Ironmongers)*,[2] the Court of Appeal held that " the defendant is bound to make reparation for all the actual damages directly flowing from the fraudulent inducement . . . it does not lie in the mouth of the fraudulent person to say that [the damage] could not reasonably have been foreseen."[3]

Fraudulent misrepresentation

(ii) For negligent misstatement at common law

Here again it is clear that the claim is one in tort and so the tortious rules apply. Furthermore, since the action lies in negligence, there can be no doubt that any problems of remoteness are to be resolved by applying the foreseeability test.

Negligent misstatement

(iii) Under the Misrepresentation Act 1967

Neither section 2 (1) nor section 2 (2) of the Misrepresentation Act 1967 contains any statement of the test to be applied in assessing damages under them. The only dim clue is provided by section 2 (3) which states:

Misrepresentation Act 1967

" Damages may be awarded against a person under subsection (2) of this section whether or not he is liable to damages under subsection (1) thereof, but where he is so liable any award under the said subsection (2) shall be taken into account in assessing his liability under the said subsection (1)."

This perhaps suggests that less may be recovered under section 2 (2) than under section 2 (1) and this would not be irrational since the defendant needs to be at fault for the action to succeed under section 2 (1) but not under section 2 (2). It still leaves unresolved the tests to be applied.

It has been suggested[4] that damages under section 2 (1) should be calculated on the same principles as govern the tort of deceit. This suggestion is based on a theory that section 2 (1) is based on a " fiction of fraud." We have already suggested that

Section 2 (1)

---

1. Mayne & McGregor, *Damages,* 12th Edn., paras. 955–957. Winfield & Jolowicz, *Tort,* 10th Edn., p. 220.
2. [1969] 2 Q.B. 158; [1969] 2 All E.R. 119.
3. [1969] 2 Q.B., at p. 167; [1969] 2 All E.R., at p. 122. The Court of Appeal relied on the discussion in Mayne & McGregor, *Damages,* 12th Edn., *op. cit.* Cf. the critical discussion by Treitel, 32 M.L.R. 556. At one time it was not clear whether exemplary damages might be recovered in deceit, *Mafo* v. *Adams,* [1970] 1 Q.B. 548; [1969] 3 All E.R. 1404; *Denison* v. *Fawcett* (1958), 12 D.L.R. (2d) 537, but there were clear statements that they could not in *Cassell & Co., Ltd.* v. *Broome,* [1972] A.C. 1027; [1972] 1 All E.R. 801, *per* Lord HAILSHAM, L.C., at pp. 1076, 828, respectively, and *per* Lord DIPLOCK, at pp. 1131, 874, respectively.
4. Atiyah and Treitel, 30 M.L.R., at pp. 373–4. But cf. Treitel, *The Law of Contract,* 4th Edn., p. 237.

this theory is misconceived.[1] On the other hand the action created by section 2 (1) does look much more like an action in tort than one in contract and it is suggested that the rules for negligence are the natural ones to apply.

However, although it is thought that this approach is correct in principle, it must be admitted that such authority as exists is against it. In *Jarvis* v. *Swans Tours, Ltd.*[2] Lord DENNING, M.R., said[3] " it is not necessary to decide whether they were representations or warranties; because, since the Misrepresentation Act 1967, there is a remedy in damages for misrepresentation as well as for breach of warranty," and in *Watts* v. *Spence*[4] GRAHAM, J., gave damages for loss of bargain under s. 2 (1) of the Misrepresentation Act 1967. In neither case however does the difference between damages in contract and in tort appear to have been in the forefront of the argument.

Section 2 (2)

As far as section 2 (2) is concerned, it is pertinent to stress that damages under this subsection are given in lieu of rescission. It seems probable, therefore, that in the case of innocent misrepresentation, the Act does not disturb the rule that financial relief for consequential loss should be limited to an indemnity. It is suggested therefore that in assessing damages under section 2 (2), the guiding rule is to produce, as nearly as maybe, the same effect as could be obtained by rescission plus indemnity and not to recoup consequential loss which would fall outside this limited relief. Thus on facts such as those in *Whittington* v. *Seale-Hayne*[5] it would seem that a plaintiff whose claim to damages rested solely on section 2 (2) would not be compensated for such items as the value of stock lost.

E. REVIEW OF EFFECTS OF
MISREPRESENTATION ACT 1967[6]

Our discussion has involved very frequent references to the Misrepresentation Act 1967 but it is perhaps worthwhile now to attempt to look at the Act as a whole.

Some general criticisms

Although there can be little doubt that the general effect of the Act will be to improve the lot of representees as a class, this has been achieved at the cost of making an already complex branch of the law still more complicated. At least three factors have contributed to this. The first was the general policy decision to proceed by a limited number of statutory amendments to the common law. This means that the Act can only be understood if the previous law has been mastered and since the previous law was often far from clear the Act has been erected on an uncertain base. Secondly, the Act was based on the view of the common law taken by the Law Reform Committee in 1962, which was overtaken by

1. *Supra*, p. 261.
2. [1973] 1 Q.B. 233; [1973] 1 All E.R. 71.
3. *Ibid.*, at pp. 237, 73, respectively.
4. [1975] 2 All E.R. 528; [1975] 2 W.L.R. 1039, criticised Baker, 91 L.Q.R. 307.
5. (1900), 82 L.T. 49. See *supra*, p. 267.
6. Atiyah and Treitel, 30 M.L.R. 369; Fairest, [1967] C.L.J. 239.

the decision in *Hedley Byrne & Co., Ltd.* v. *Heller & Partners*.[1] This has meant the creation of two different kinds of negligent misrepresentation with different rules and an uncertain relationship. Thirdly, these defects in approach were compounded by drafting which is frequently obscure and sometimes defective.[2]

An important example of the type of problem created by the Act is the meaning of the phrases " after a misrepresentation has been made to him " (which occurs three times in sections 1 and 2) and " any misrepresentation made by him " (which occurs in section 3). The Act does not define " misrepresentation " and the question has been raised whether these words are apt to extend to situations where the law imposes a duty of disclosure.[3] It would seem reasonably clear that the Act extends to those cases where silence is treated as assertive conduct, as where it distorts a positive assertion made by the representor or where the representor fails to reveal that an earlier statement made by him is no longer true.[4] It is much more debatable whether the word " misrepresentation " is wide enough to cover cases of non-disclosure *stricto sensu*,[5] such as contracts *uberrimae fidei*, but even here, it might be argued that failure to disclose the existence of a material fact is equivalent to affirmation of its non-existence. Similar difficulties may arise from the failure to define the meaning of " rescission " in the Act.[6]

[margin note: Scope of misrepresentation in Act]

We have already dealt at length with the effects of sections 1 and 2 of the Act. Both are concerned to improve the representee's remedies for misrepresentation, section 1 by removing possible limits to the right of rescission and section 2 by widening the possibility of obtaining damages. Apart from section 5, which deals with problems of retrospectivity, the other enacting sections of the Act are sections 3 and 4. Section 4 makes some changes in the Sale of Goods Act designed to render the buyer's right to reject for breach of condition less liable to defeasance. Section 3 calls for further discussion.

1. MISREPRESENTATION AND EXEMPTION CLAUSES

Section 3 provides:

> " If any agreement (whether made before or after the commencement of this Act) contains a provision which would exclude or restrict—
>
> (a) any liability to which a party to a contract may be subject by reason of any misrepresentation made by him before the contract was made; or
> (b) any remedy available to another party to the contract by reason of such a misrepresentation;
>
> that provision shall be of no effect except to the extent (if any) that, in any proceeding arising out of the contract, the court or arbitrator may allow reliance on it as being fair and reasonable in the circumstances of the case."

1. [1964] A.C. 465; [1963] 2 All E.R. 575.
2. See Atiyah and Treitel, *op. cit.* and the critical remarks of the New Zealand Contracts and Commercial Law Reform Committee in their Report on Misrepresentation and Breach of Contract (1967).
3. Atiyah and Treitel, 30 M.L.R. 369–370; Hudson, 85 L.Q.R. 524.
4. *Supra*, pp. 252–3.
5. See *infra*, pp. 278–284.
6. Atiyah and Treitel, 30 M.L.R. 370–371.

This section again goes beyond the Law Reform Committee's recommendations which would simply have barred the exclusion of liability for fraudulent and negligent misrepresentation.[1]   The section does not go well with the rules relating to clauses excluding liability for breach of contractual terms since, as we have seen,[2] there is no general power in the court to strike down such clauses. It seems probable that in the fullness of time there may be legislation to deal with such clauses but meanwhile the position is inelegant and indeed irrational.   Even worse, this approach has aroused doubts as to what in fact the law is.   Thus it may be argued[3] that section 3 invalidates *in toto* a clause which purports to exclude liability for both misrepresentation and breach of a contractual term.   Furthermore it is often arguable whether a statement is properly classified as a term or a representation and, as we have seen,[4] there is no clear decision as to whether it is open to a plaintiff to treat a contractual term as a representation.   If this is permissible, a plaintiff may by formulating his claim in misrepresentation, deprive of effect a clause which would have excluded liability for breach of contract.

If there should be legislation dealing with the general problem of exemption clauses, section 3 offers a model to be avoided.[5] Although it is clearly aimed both at clauses which exclude liability and at those which restrict remedies, it contains no definition of its ambit in either area.   Yet it is well known that the line between clauses excluding and defining liability is very fine and such common commercial occurrences as non-cancellation or arbitration clauses would seem to fall within the literal scope of (b).   These difficulties are well illustrated by *Overbrooke Estates, Ltd.* v. *Glencombe Properties, Ltd.*[6]

> The plaintiffs instructed auctioneers to sell a property.   The particulars of sale stated that " neither the auctioneers nor any person in the employment of the auctioneers has any authority to make or give any representation or warranty."   The defendants, who were the highest bidders at the auction, alleged that three days before the auction, they had asked the auctioneers questions about the development plans of the local authorities, to which they had received inaccurate answers.

BRIGHTMAN, J., held that even if the defendants could prove these allegations, they would constitute no defence.   It was clear that the defendants had the particulars of sale and therefore knew or ought to have known that nothing told them by the auctioneers could bind the plaintiffs.   Section 3 of the Misrepresentation Act 1967 was irrelevant since the provision in the particulars of sale did not constitute an exemption clause, but was a limitation on the apparent authority of the auctioneers.   This decision appears impeccable but one may suspect that if the draftsman had foreseen it, he would have proceeded differently.

Perhaps the most serious criticism should be directed however

---

1. Cmnd. 1782, paras. 23–24.
2. *Supra*, pp. 144–169.
3. Atiyah and Treitel, 30 M.L.R. 383.
4. *Supra*, pp. 262–3.
5. Atiyah and Treitel, 30 M.L.R. 379–385. Cf. Supply of Goods (Implied Terms) Act 1973, discussed, *supra*, pp. 168–9.
6. [1974] 3 All E.R. 511; [1974] 1 W.L.R. 1335.   Coote, [1975] C.L.J. 17.

at the very wide discretion which is conferred on the judge since no guidance is given on its exercise. It may often be difficult for the court to decide whether a particular clause is reasonable since this may depend on evidence relating to the public interest which will not have been given.

F. NON-DISCLOSURE

We have already seen that English law draws a clear distinction between misrepresentation and non-disclosure.[1] Apart from exceptional cases where silence amounts to assertive conduct,[2] there is no general duty to disclose information that would be likely to affect the other party's decision to conclude the contract. To this rule there are two important exceptions.

I. CONTRACTS *UBERRIMAE FIDEI*

In certain contracts where, from the very necessity of the case, one party alone possesses full knowledge of all the material facts, the law requires him to show *uberrima fides*. He must make full disclosure of all the material facts known to him, otherwise the contract may be rescinded.[3] It is impracticable to give an exact list of these contracts, nor can it be said that the extent of the duty of disclosure is constant in each case. We will deal somewhat fully with the contract of insurance and then more briefly with contracts for the purchase of shares and with family arrangements.

Contracts uberrimae fidei

    Contracts of insurance provide the outstanding example.[4] These are generally sub-divided into two classes according as they are designed to meet a marine or a non-marine risk, for the law with regard to the former has been codified by the Marine Insurance Act 1906. It has been established, however, since at least the eighteenth century, that every contract of insurance, irrespective of its subject-matter, involves *uberrima fides* and requires full disclosure of such material facts as are known to the assured. As Lord MANSFIELD demonstrated in *Carter* v. *Boehm*,[5] insurance is a contract upon speculation where the special facts upon which the contingent chance is to be computed lie generally in the knowledge of the assured only, so that good faith requires that he should not keep back anything which might influence the insurer in deciding whether to accept or reject the risk. A fact is material if it is one that would affect the mind of a prudent man, even though its materiality is not appreciated by the assured.[6] In the words of BAYLEY, J.:

Contract of insurance

Assured's opinion of materiality is irrelevant

---

1. *Supra*, p. 257.
2. *Supra*, p. 252–3.
3. Where there is a duty to disclose, non-disclosure makes the contract voidable and not void. *Mackender* v. *Feldia A.G.*, [1967] 2 Q.B. 590; [1966] 3 All E.R. 847.
4. Hasson, 32 M.L.R. 615.
5. (1766), 3 Burr. 1905, at p. 1909. Exceptionally a contract of guarantee, e.g. a fidelity guarantee, may rank as a contract of insurance: *London General Omnibus, Ltd.* v. *Holloway*, [1912] 2 K.B. 72. Blair, 29 M.L.R. 522, at pp. 524–536.
6. *London Assurance* v. *Mansel* (1879), 11 Ch.D. 363.

" I think that in all cases of insurance, whether on ships, houses or lives, the underwriter should be informed of every material circumstance within the knowledge of the assured; and that the proper question is, whether any particular circumstance was in fact material, and not whether the party believed it to be so. The contrary doctrine would lead to frequent suppression of information, and it would often be extremely difficult to show that the party neglecting to give the information thought it material. But if it be held that all material facts must be disclosed, it will be in the interest of the assured to make a full and fair disclosure of all the information within their reach."[1]

Duty of disclosure in marine insurance

The duty of disclosure in the case of marine insurance is prescribed as follows in the Marine Insurance Act:

Subject to the provisions of this section, the assured must disclose to the insurer, before the contract is concluded, every material circumstance which is known to the assured, and the assured is deemed to know every circumstance which, in the ordinary course of business, ought to be known by him. If the assured fails to make such disclosure, the insurer may avoid the contract.[2]

Every circumstance is material which would influence the judgment of a prudent insurer in fixing the premium, or determining whether he will take the risk.[3]

Thus, for example, the assured must inform the underwriter that the ship is overdue[4] or has put into an intermediate port for repair;[5] that the insured goods are to be carried on deck, a place where it is not usual to stack them;[6] or that the cargo is to be taken on board at a particular port where loading is a hazardous operation.[7]

Irrelevant that non-disclosure causes no loss

The question in each case is whether the fact would have been material in influencing the mind of a prudent insurer, not whether loss has resulted from the undisclosed fact. Thus, where the assured concealed a report that the ship when last seen was in a position of danger, though as a matter of fact she survived on this occasion only to be captured later by the Spaniards, it was held that the policy could be avoided for non-disclosure.[8]

Disclosure in non-marine insurances

A similar duty of disclosure exists in the case of non-marine insurances. Whether the policy is taken out for a life, fire, burglary, fidelity or accidental risk, it is the duty of the assured to give full information of every material fact; and it has been held by the Court of Appeal that the definition of " material " contained in the Marine Insurance Act 1906, namely every circumstance " which would influence the judgment of a prudent insurer in fixing the premium, or determining whether he will take the risk,"

---

1. *Lindenau* v. *Desborough* (1828), 8 B. & C. 586, at p. 592.
2. Marine Insurance Act 1906, s. 18 (1).
3. *Ibid.*, s. 18 (2).
4. *Kirby* v. *Smith* (1818), 1 B. & Ald. 672.
5. *Uzielli* v. *Commercial Union Insurance Co.* (1865), 12 L.T. 399.
6. *Hood* v. *West End Motor Car Packing Co.*, [1917] 2 K.B. 38.
7. *Harrower* v. *Hutchinson* (1870), L.R. 5 Q.B. 584.
8. *Seaman* v. *Fonereau* (1743), 2 Stra. 1183. In its 5th Report, the Law Reform Committee suggested that it would be practicable to frame a new statutory definition of " material " on the following lines: " For the purposes of any contract of insurance no fact shall be deemed material unless it would have been considered material by a reasonable insured ": Cmnd. 62 (1957), p. 7.

is applicable to all forms of insurance.[1] It has thus been held in each of the following cases that the policy was vitiated for non-disclosure:

> In a proposal for fire insurance, the assured stated that no proposal by him had previously been declined by any other company; in fact, another company had previously refused to issue a policy in respect of his motor vehicle.[2]
>
> In applying for a fire insurance policy, the proposer omitted to mention that a fire had broken out next door upon the day of the proposal.[3]
>
> In a proposal for a policy insuring the repayment of a loan, the proposer failed to divulge that, owing to the financial debility of the borrower, the interest had been fixed at 40 per cent.[4]

The duty of disclosure thus imposed by law is confined to facts which the assured knows or ought to know. " The duty," said FLETCHER-MOULTON, L.J., " is a duty to disclose, and you cannot disclose what you do not know."[5] Thus if the question— " Have you any disease?"—is put to an applicant for a life assurance policy, and he answers in the negative, fully believing his health to be sound, the resulting contract cannot be rescinded upon proof that at the time of his answer he was suffering from malignant cancer. The duty, however, may be enlarged by the express terms of the contract, and in fact insurers have taken extensive, perhaps indeed unfair, advantage of this contractual freedom. In practice they almost invariably require the assured to agree that the *accuracy* of the information provided by him shall be a condition of the validity of the policy. To this end it is common to insert a term in the proposal form providing that the declarations of the assured shall form the basis of the contract. The legal effect of this term is that if his answer to a direct question is inaccurate, or if he fails to disclose some material fact long forgotten or even some fact that was never within his knowledge, the contract may be avoided despite his integrity and honesty of purpose. Nay more, his incorrect statement about a matter that is nothing more than a matter of opinion is sufficient to avoid the policy. Thus, for instance, one of the commonest questions put to a person who applies for a life insurance is " Have you any disease?", a matter which, even for a doctor, is often a subject of mere speculation or opinion.

Duty confined to known facts

The contract may make innocent non-disclosure fatal

> " But the policies issued by many companies are framed so as to be invalid unless this and many other like questions are correctly— not merely truthfully—answered, though the insurers are well aware that it is impossible for anyone to arrive at anything more certain than an opinion about them. I wish I could adequately warn the public against such practices on the part of insurance offices."[6]

---

1. *Locker and Woolf, Ltd.* v. *Western Australian Insurance Co., Ltd.,* [1936] 1 K.B. 408. As to the burden of proof, see *Slattery* v. *Mance,* [1962] 1 Q.B. 676; [1962] 1 All E.R. 525.
2. *Locker and Woolf, Ltd.* v. *Western Australian Insurance Co., Ltd., supra.*
3. *Bufe* v. *Turner* (1815), 6 Taunt. 338.
4. *Seaton* v. *Heath,* [1899] 1 Q.B. 782.
5. *Joel* v. *Law Union and Crown Insurance Co.,* [1908] 2 K.B. 863, at p. 884, *per* FLETCHER-MOULTON, L.J.
6. *Joel* v. *Law Union and Crown Insurance Co.,* [1908] 2 K.B., at 885, *per* FLETCHER-MOULTON, L.J. See Hasson, 34 M.L.R. 29.

The courts view this practice with distaste and they do what they can to mitigate its severity by imposing a strict burden of proof upon insurers.[1]

Contracts to take shares in companies

A contract to take shares in a company is often made on the faith of the prospectus issued by the promoters.   It has long been recognized that the document is a fruitful source of deception, for persons who desire to foist an undertaking upon the public are not usually remarkable either for the accuracy of their representations or for the industry with which they search for facts that might usefully be disclosed.   There are a number of statutes which have

Prospectus must give full information

provisions affecting liability in this respect[2] and the Companies Act 1948, section 38, contains a list of matters that every prospectus must contain.   The result of the statutory provisions, especially when taken together with the extra legal controls operated by the Stock Exchange, is that a contract to take shares has become closely akin to one which is *uberrimae fidei*.[3]

The expression " family arrangement " covers a multitude of agreements made between relatives and designed to preserve the

Family arrangements

harmony, to protect the property or to save the honour of the family.[4]   It comprises such diverse transactions as the following: a re-settlement of land made between the father as tenant for life and the son as tenant in tail in remainder; an agreement to abide by the terms of a will that has not been properly executed, or to vary the terms of a valid will; the release of devised property from a condition subsequently imposed by the testator; or an agreement by a younger legitimate son to transfer family property to an illegitimate elder son.

Equity, though always anxious to sustain family arrangements, insists that there should be the fullest disclosure of all material facts known to each party, even though no inquiry about them may have been made.   The parties must be on an equal footing.

Thus, in *Gordon* v. *Gordon*,[5] a division of property, based upon the probability that the elder son was illegitimate, was set aside nineteen years afterwards upon proof that the younger son had concealed his knowledge of a private ceremony of marriage solemnized between his parents before the birth of his brother; and in *Greenwood* v. *Greenwood*[6] an agreement to divide the property of a deceased relative was avoided on the ground that one of the parties failed to disclose information which he alone possessed concerning the amount of the estate.

---

1. *Bond Air Services, Ltd.* v. *Hill*, [1955] 2 Q.B. 417; [1955] 2 All E.R. 476; *West* v. *National Motor and Accident Insurance Union, Ltd.*, [1955] 1 All E.R. 800.   For other respects in which the scales are weighted against the insured, see the 5th Report of the Law Reform Committee (1957), Cmnd. 62.
2. Companies Act 1948, especially ss. 38 and 43; Prevention of Fraud (Investments) Act 1958; Protection of Depositors Act 1963; Gower, *Modern Company Law*, 3rd Edn., pp. 315–340.
3. There was authority for a duty of disclosure at common law.   *Central Rail. Co. of Venezuela (Directors, Etc.)* v. *Kisch* (1867), L.R. 2 H.L. 99, at p. 113. Cf. *Aaron's Reefs, Ltd.* v. *Twiss*, [1896] A.C. 273, at p. 287.
4. See generally, White & Tudor's *Leading Cases in Equity*, vol. I, p. 198 *et seq.*
5. (1821), 3 Swan, 400.
6. (1863), 2 De G.J. and Sm. 28.

2. CONSTRUCTIVE FRAUD

In cases where the representor had no honest belief in the truth of his statement, equity has long had a concurrent jurisdiction with the common law. The court to which a plaintiff would resort before the Judicature Act would depend upon whether the remedy he sought was on one hand the recovery of damages for deceit or on the other rescission and an account of profits. Equity, however, in the exercise of its exclusive jurisdiction has from early days given a more extended meaning to the word " fraud " than has the common law, and has developed a doctrine of *constructive fraud*.

The doctrine of constructive fraud

> " But in addition to this concurrent jurisdiction," said Lord HALDANE in a leading case, " the Court of Chancery exercised an exclusive jurisdiction in cases which, although classified in that court as cases of fraud, yet did not necessarily import the element of *dolus malus*. The court took upon itself to prevent a man from acting against the dictates of conscience as defined by the court, and to grant injunctions in anticipation of injury, as well as relief where injury had been done."[1]

It is not unnatural that a principle of jurisdiction defined in such expansive terms should have been gradually applied to a wide field of human activities and to what at first sight appear to be a welter of unrelated items;[2] but one important example pertinent to the present discussion is where, owing to the special relationship between the parties, a transaction may be voidable in equity for non-disclosure. " Under certain circumstances a duty may arise to disclose a material fact, and its non-disclosure may have the same effect as a representation of its non-existence."[3] Whenever the relation between the parties to a contract is of a confidential or fiduciary nature, the person in whom the confidence is reposed and who thus possesses influence over the other cannot hold that other to the contract unless he satisfies the court that it is advantageous to the other party and that he has disclosed all material facts within his knowledge.[4]

Such a confidential relationship is deemed to exist between persons connected by certain recognized ties, such as parent and child, principal and agent,[5] solicitor and client, religious superior and inferior, and trustee and beneficiary. But the courts have always refused to confine this equitable jurisdiction to such familiar relations. They are prepared to interfere in a contract wherever one party deliberately and voluntarily places himself in such a position that it becomes his duty to act fairly and to have due regard to the interests of the other party. In a leading case, Lord CHELMSFORD stated the general principle in these words:

1. *Nocton* v. *Lord Ashburton*, [1914] A.C. 932, at p. 952.
2. See for instance the extended meaning of fraud given by Lord Hardwicke in *Earl of Chesterfield* v. *Janssen* (1751), 2 Ves. Sen. 125, at p. 155.
3. Ashburner, *Principles of Equity*, 2nd Edn., 283. For a classification of relationships, see Sealy, [1962] C.L.J. 69; [1963] C.L.J. 119.
4. *Moody* v. *Cox and Hatt*, [1917] 2 Ch. 71, at p. 88, *per* SCRUTTON, L.J.
5. *Regal (Hastings), Ltd.* v. *Gulliver*, [1967] 2 A.C. 134; [1942] 1 All E.R. 378.

" Wherever two persons stand in such a relation that, while it continues, confidence is necessarily reposed by one, and the influence which naturally grows out of that confidence is possessed by the other, and this confidence is abused, or the influence is exerted to obtain an advantage at the expense of the confiding party, the person so availing himself of his position will not be permitted to retain the advantage, although the transaction could not have been impeached if no such confidential relation had existed."[1]

These words were spoken in a case where X, an extravagant undergraduate much pressed by his Oxford creditors and anxious to extricate himself from his financial embarrassment, sought the advice of Y. Having recommended the sale of the undergraduate's Staffordshire estate, Y offered to buy it himself for £7,000 without disclosing that, owing to the existence of subjacent minerals, X's interest was worth at least double that amount. The offer was accepted and the conveyance executed, but some years later the sale was set aside by the court at the insistence of X's heir. Y was constructively fraudulent in the sense that he wrongfully exploited to his own advantage the commanding position in which he stood.

G. RELATIONSHIP BETWEEN MISREPRESENTATION AND ESTOPPEL[2]

It not infrequently happens that A enters into a contract with B on the faith of a misrepresentation made by X. Here, unless X is the agent of B, there can be no question of a remedy against B and since there will normally be no contract between A and X,[3] many of the remedies discussed in this chapter will be unobtainable. One cannot rescind a contract that does not exist and actions under the Misrepresentation Act 1967 only lie where the representation "has been made . . . by another party " to the contract. X can certainly be sued in tort if he is fraudulent and in some cases an action may now lie for negligence under *Hedley Byrne & Co., Ltd.* v. *Heller & Partners.*[4]

In some such cases, assistance may be obtained from the doctrine of estoppel by representation. This was stated by Lord MACNAGHTEN as follows:

" It is . . . a principle of universal application, that if a person makes a false representation to another and that other acts upon that false representation, the person who has made it shall not afterwards be allowed to set up that what he said was false and to assert the real truth in place of the falsehood which has so misled the other."[5]

It would appear that the constituents of a representation for estoppel by misrepresentation are the same as for actionable misrepresentation.[6] The main obstacle to a wide use of this

1. *Tate* v. *Williamson* (1866), 2 Ch. App. 55, at p. 61.
2. Spencer Bower and Turner: *The Law Relating to Estoppel by Representation*, 2nd Edn. (1966); Ewart on *Estoppel*; Atiyah, 9 Alberta L.R. 347; Jackson, 81 L.Q.R. 84, 223.
3. Unless the court discovers a " collateral " contract with X.
4. [1964] A.C. 465; [1963] 2 All E.R. 575.
5. *Balkis Consolidated Co.* v. *Tomkinson*, [1893] A.C. 396, at p. 410, citing Lord CRANWORTH in *Jorden* v. *Money* (1854), 5 H.L.C. 185, at pp. 210, 212.
6. Spencer Bower and Turner: *The Law Relating to Estoppel by Representation*, 2nd Edn. (1966), p. 27 *et seq.*

principle is that it is said that estoppel is not in itself a cause of action.[1]   If this is right, it follows that the plaintiff who wishes to employ the principle of estoppel must formulate some independent cause of action which would have succeeded had the estoppel statement been true.   He may then rely on estoppel to defeat a defence which would otherwise be available to the defendant, since evidence to prove the untruth of the statement will be inadmissible.

Estoppel not
a cause of
action

This possibility is neatly illustrated by *Burrowes* v. *Lock*.[2] The facts were these:

> X was entitled to a sum of £288 held on his behalf by a trustee, A. He assigned part of this to Y by way of security, notice of the assignment being given to A. Ten years later he purported to assign the whole of the £288 to Z in return for valuable consideration. Before completing this transaction, Z consulted A, who having forgotten the previous assignment to Y, represented that X was still entitled to the full sum of £288.

Z later filed a bill against A, who was held liable for so much of the trust fund as had previously been assigned to Y.   Here Z had an independent cause of action, for had the representation of the trustee been correct he would have been entitled to the whole sum of £288 against the trustee, for the effect of the assignment would have been that the trustee held the £288 on behalf of Z.   In fact the trustee held part of the fund on trust for Y, but he was estopped from setting this up to defeat the claim of Z.

The possibility of formulating an action for damages for negligent misstatement will have reduced but not removed the importance of this more devious route to damages.   In addition it should be noted that cases may arise where estoppel will operate as a defence and here of course there will be no need to formulate an independent cause of action.

SECTION II.   DURESS AND UNDUE INFLUENCE[3]

Since agreement depends on consent, it should follow that agreement obtained by threats or undue persuasion is insufficient. Both common law with a limited doctrine of duress and equity with a much wider doctrine of undue influence have acted in this area.   It is clear that in equity the effect of undue influence is to make the contract voidable, but it is disputed whether the effect of duress at common law is to make the contract void or voidable. The question would be important if questions of affirmation or third party rights were involved but there is no satisfactory modern authority.   The majority of writers state that duress

Effect of
duress and
undue
influence

---

1. This is certainly the orthodox view.   See especially *Low* v. *Bouverie*, [1891] 3 Ch. 82.   Cf. the views of Atiyah and Jackson, *supra*, p. 284 footnote 2.
2. (1805), 10 Ves. 470.   Sheridan, *Fraud in Equity*, pp. 31–36.
3. Winder, 56 L.Q.R. 97; 3 M.L.R. 97; 4 Conv. (N.S.) 274; Winfield, 60 L.Q.R. 341.

makes the contract voidable[1] but this has been vigorously con-
troverted.[2]   There are a number of modern cases which discuss
whether duress renders a marriage void or voidable and it is
sometimes assumed that the rule is the same for marriage and for
contract.[3]   But even if this assumption is correct, it does not
provide a clear answer since the cases do not agree[4] and in none
of them was it necessary to decide the question.

Both common law and equity agree that a party cannot be held
to a contract unless he is a free agent, but the contribution made
by common law to this part of the subject has been scanty.   It is
Duress at   confined to the avoidance of contracts obtained by duress, a word
common law   to which a very limited meaning has been attached.   Duress at
common law, or what is sometimes called *legal duress*, means actual
violence or threats of violence to the person, i.e. threats calculated
to produce fear of loss of life or bodily harm.[5]   It is a part of the
law which nowadays seldom raises an issue.

That a contract should be procured by actual violence is
difficult to conceive, and a more probable means of inducement is a
threat of violence.   The rule here is that the threat must be illegal
in the sense that it must be a threat to commit a crime or a tort.[6]
Thus to threaten an imprisonment that would be unlawful if
Threats, if   enforced constitutes duress, but not if the imprisonment would be
illegal,   lawful.[7]   Again a contract procured by a threat to prosecute for a
constitute   crime that has actually been committed,[8] or to sue for a civil
duress   wrong,[9] or to put the member of a trade association on a stop-
list,[10] is not as a general rule voidable for duress.   But it may be
void as being contrary to public policy, as for example where it is in
effect an agreement tending to pervert the course of justice.[11]
It must be established that the threats were a reason for entering
into the contract but it need not be shown that they were the only
or even the main reason.   Once it has been proved that unlawful
threats were made, it is for the threatener to show that they were
not a reason for the other party contracting.[12]

---

1. See, *e.g.* Pollock, *Principles of Contract*, 13th Edn., 179, citing the second rule
   in *Whelpdale's Case* (1604), 5 Co. Rep. 119a.
2. Lanham, 29 M.L.R. 615.
3. *Parojcic* v. *Parojcic*, [1958] 1 W.L.R. 1280, at p. 1283.
4. See, e.g. *Parojcic* v. *Parojcic, supra*; *Buckland* v. *Buckland*, [1968] P. 296;
   [1967] 2 All E.R. 300. (Manchester, 29 M.L.R. 622); *Singh* v. *Singh*,
   [1971] 2 All E.R. 828, at p. 830.   An elaborate historical survey by Tolstoy,
   27 M.L.R. 385, shows that the rule was originally that the marriage was
   void.   For marriage the question has been resolved by the Nullity of
   Marriage Act 1971, s. 2 (c), whereby the effect of duress is to render the
   marriage voidable.   In *Lynch* v. *Director of Public Prosecutions for Northern
   Ireland*, [1975] 1 All E.R. 913, at p. 938, [1975] 2 W.L.R. 641, at p. 669,
   Lord SIMON OF GLAISDALE stated that duress made contracts voidable
   though this was clearly *obiter*.   The whole of this case repays study for its
   analysis of the operation of duress.
5. Co. Litt. 253b.   For a modern example see *Friedeberg-Seeley* v. *Klass*
   (1957), *The Times*, February 19th; 101 Sol. Jo. 275.
6. Cf. *Ware and De Freville, Ltd.* v. *Motor Trade Association*, [1921] 3 K.B. 40.
7. *Cumming* v. *Ince* (1847), 11 Q.B. 112; *Biffin* v. *Bignell* (1862), 7 H. & N. 877;
   Smith v. *Monteith* (1844), 13 M & W 427.
8. *Fisher & Co.* v. *Appolinaris Co.* (1875), 10 Ch. App. 297.
9. *Powell* v. *Hoyland* (1851), 6 Exch. 67.
10. *Thorne* v. *Motor Trade Association*, [1937] A.C. 797; [1937] 3 All E.R. 157.
11. *Infra*, pp. 338–341.
12. *Barton* v. *Armstrong*, [1975] 2 All E.R. 465; [1975] 2 W.L.R. 1050.

For duress to afford a ground of relief, it must be duress of a man's person, not of his goods.[1]   In *Skeate* v. *Beale*,[2] for instance, a tenant agreed that if his landlord would withdraw a distress for £19 10s. in respect of rent, he would pay £3 7s. 6d. immediately and the remainder, £16 2s. 6d., within one month.   To an action to recover £16 2s. 6d. the tenant pleaded that the distress was wrongful, since only £3 7s. 6d. was due, and that the landlord threatened to sell the goods at once unless agreement was made. This plea was disallowed.   But it has been held that money paid under duress of goods may be recovered.[3]   Clearly these two rules are difficult to reconcile.[4]

Equity had concurrent jurisdiction with the courts of common law with regard to duress, but by an application of its comprehensive doctrine of constructive fraud,[5] it exercised a separate and wider jurisdiction over contracts made without free consent. It developed a doctrine of undue influence.[6]   This doctrine is accurately stated by Ashburner:[7]

> " In a court of equity if A obtains any benefit from B, whether under a contract or as a gift, by exerting an influence over B which, in the opinion of the court, prevents B from exercising an independent judgment in the matter in question, B can set aside the contract or recover the gift.   Moreover in certain cases the relation between A and B may be such that A has peculiar opportunities of exercising influence over B.   If under such circumstances A enters into a contract with B, or receives a gift from B, a court of equity imposes upon A the burden, if he wishes to maintain the contract or gift, of proving that in fact he exerted no influence for the purpose of obtaining it."

The only rider to make to this statement is that an intention by A to benefit himself personally is not essential to justify rescission of a contract.   It is enough that in the exercise of his influence he has not made the welfare of B, to the exclusion of all other persons, his paramount consideration.[8]

Historically this area of equity has embraced not only the present doctrine of undue influence and the special rules about disclosure, discussed above,[9] but also rules about unconscionable bargains.[10]   As is so often the case however, the term " unconscionable bargains " bears a much narrower meaning in equity than

---

1. *Atlee* v. *Backhouse* (1838), 3 M. & W. 633, at p. 650, *per* PARKE, B.
2. (1840), 11 Ad. & El. 983.
3. *Astley* v. *Reynolds* (1731), 2 Stra. 915;   *T. D. Keegan, Ltd.* v. *Palmer*, [1961] 2 Lloyds Rep. 449.
4. Goff & Jones, *The Law of Restitution*, pp. 148–151.   Beatson, [1974] C.L.J. 97, shows that the duress of goods doctrine owes its existence to a factual overlap with the rule that a compromise of a doubtful claim is valid.
5. *Supra*, p. 283.
6. See especially White and Tudor, *Leading Cases in Equity*, vol. 1, pp. 203 *et seq.* Hanbury, *Modern Equity*, 9th Edn., pp. 651–654.   Sheridan, *Fraud in Equity*, pp. 87–106.
7. *Ashburner on Equity*, 2nd Edn., p. 299; see also *Allcard* v. *Skinner* (1887), 36 Ch.D. 145, at pp. 181 and 183, *per* LINDLEY, L.J.
8. *Bullock* v. *Lloyds Bank, Ltd.*, [1955] Ch. 317; [1954] 3 All E.R. 726.
9. *Supra*, pp. 283–4.
10. See Sheridan, *Fraud in Equity*, pp. 125–145;   Goff & Jones, *The Law of Restitution*, pp. 169–172.   The special statutory rules about money lending contained in the Money-Lenders Acts 1900 and 1927 were substantially a strengthening of equitable doctrine in a particularly vulnerable area.   They have now been replaced and extended by the Consumer Credit Act 1974. See especially ss. 137–140.

Unconscion-
able bargains

in lay usage. The typical transaction, assumed by the older
authorities, involved an improvident arrangement by an expectant
heir to anticipate his inheritance—a situation unlikely to occur
often today with the virtual disappearance of strict settlements.
Though there are old cases under this rubric which turn on the
infirmity of one of the parties,[1] it has been doubted whether an
English court would now set aside a transaction merely because
one of the parties was poor, ignorant or weak-minded.[2] A
Northern Ireland court did so however in *Buckley* v. *Irwin*[3] and
there are several Canadian decisions to the same effect.[4]

In the past English law, unlike American law,[5] has not used
these fertile doctrines to deal with the general problem of inequality
of bargaining power. This battle has been fought on other
fronts.[6] A prophetic exception however may be found in the
judgment of Lord DENNING, M.R., in *D & C Builders, Ltd.*

An English
doctrine of
economic
duress?

v. *Rees,*[7] where he held that the plaintiffs' consent to acceptance of
part payment in full satisfaction of a debt " was no true accord.
The debtor's wife held the creditor to ransom. The creditor was
in need of money to meet his own commitments and she knew it."[8]
This case involved not the creation of a contract through improper
pressure, but its discharge.[9]

In the eighth edition of this work we suggested that it was
possible that one day a bold court might use this statement as a
springboard for a new development. This prophecy has been
fulfilled, with perhaps surprising speed, by the judgment of
Lord DENNING, M.R., in *Lloyds Bank, Ltd.* v. *Bundy.*[10]

> The defendant was an elderly farmer, whose home and only
> asset was a farmhouse, which had belonged to the family for genera-
> tions. The defendant, his son and a company of which the son
> was in control all banked at the same branch of the plaintiff bank.
> The company ran into difficulties and the defendant guaranteed its
> overdraft up to £1,500 and charged his house to the bank for that
> sum. Later he executed a further guarantee for £5,000 and a
> further charge for £6,000. As the farmhouse was worth only
> £10,000 he was advised by his solicitor that that was the most he
> should commit to the son's business. However the company's

1. *E.g. Evans* v. *Llewellin* (1787), 1 Cox Eq. Cas. 333.
2. Treitel, *Law of Contract*, 3rd Edn., p. 351. Cf. 4th Edn., p. 276.
3. [1960] N.I. 98.
4. See, e.g., *Knupp* v. *Bell* (1968), 67 D.L.R. (2) 256; *Marshall* v. *Canada Permanent Trust Co.* (1968), 69 D.L.R. (2d) 260, *Mundinger* v. *Mundinger* (1968), 3 D.L.R. (3d) 338.
5. See the masterly survey by J. P. Dawson, 45 Michigan L.R. 253.
6. See *supra*, pp. 144–169. English law has been in some danger of treating exemption clauses as the only manifestation of unequal bargaining power.
7. [1966] 2 Q.B. 617; [1965] 3 All E.R. 837. Discussed *supra*, pp. 88–9. See Winder, 82 L.Q.R. 165; Cornish, 29 M.L.R. 428.
8. [1966] 2 Q.B., at p. 625; [1965] 3 All E.R., at p. 841.
9. See Reynolds & Treitel, 7 Malaya L.R. 1, at pp. 21–23.
10. [1975] Q.B. 326; [1974] 3 All E.R. 757. See also *per* Lord DIPLOCK in *Schroeder Music Publishing Co., Ltd.* v. *Macaulay*, [1974] 3 All E.R. 616, at p. 623; [1974] 1 W.L.R. 1308, at p. 1315; *Clifford Davis Management, Ltd.* v. *W.E.A. Records, Ltd.*, [1975] 1 All E.R. 227; [1975] 1 W.L.R. 61. Though these two latter cases concern the application of the restraint of trade doctrine (*infra*, pp. 368 *et seq.*) they contain observations of general application. See too the dictum of BRIGHTMAN, J., in *Mountford* v. *Scott*, [1974] 1 All E.R. 248, at p. 252 (not reported in [1975] Ch. 258); affirmed on other grounds, [1975] Ch. 258; [1975] 1 All E.R. 198. " The Court would not permit [an] educated person to take advantage of the illiteracy of the other."

difficulties persisted and in December 1969 a newly appointed assistant manager of the branch told the son that further steps must be taken. The son said that his father would help. The assistant manager went to see the father at his farmhouse taking with him completed forms for a further guarantee and charge up to a figure of £11,000. He told the father that the bank could only continue to support the company if he executed the guarantee and charge and the father did so. In May 1970 a Receiver was appointed of the company and the bank took steps to enforce the guarantee and charge.

The Court of Appeal set aside the guarantee and charge. The father looked to the bank for financial advice and placed confidence in it. Since it was in the bank's interest that the father should execute the new guarantee, the bank could not discharge the burden of giving independent advice itself. It was incumbent on the bank therefore to see that the father received independent advice on the transaction and in particular on the affairs of the company. This they had failed to do.

This reasoning was well within the scope of the traditional statements of the doctrine and CAIRNS, L.J., and Sir Eric SACHS so decided the case. Lord DENNING, M.R., however, conducted a broad review of the existing law and concluded:[1]

> " Gathering all together, I would suggest that through all these instances there runs a single thread. They rest on inequality of bargaining power. By virtue of it, the English law gives relief to one who, without independent advice, enters into a contract on terms which are very unfair or transfers property for a consideration which is grossly inadequate, when his bargaining power is grieviously impaired by reason of his own needs or desires, or by his own ignorance or infirmity, coupled with undue influences or pressures brought to bear on him by or for the benefit of the other. When I use the word ' undue ' I do not mean to suggest that the principle depends on proof of any wrongdoing. The one who stipulates for an unfair advantage may be moved solely by his own self-interest, unconscious of the distress he is bringing to the other. I have also avoided any reference to the will of the one being ' dominated ' or ' overcome ' by the other. One who is in extreme need may knowingly consent to a most improvident bargain, solely to relieve the straits in which he finds himself. Again, I do not mean to suggest that every transaction is saved by independent advice. But the absence of it may be fatal. With these explanations, I hope this principle will be found to reconcile the cases."

This statement was neither approved nor disapproved by the other members of the Court and therefore does not technically form part of the *ratio decidendi* of the case. The same could no doubt be said of many historic pronouncements in English law, such as Lord ATKIN'S speech in *Donoghue* v. *Stevenson*.[2] Although a general reception of notions of inequality of bargaining power into English law would probably generate a need for sub-rules and qualifications, it is submitted that it would on balance be a fruitful source for future development of the law.[3]

Contracts which may be rescinded for undue influence fall into two categories: Firstly, those where there is no special relationship

---

1. [1975] Q.B., at p. 339; [1974] 3 All E.R., at p. 765.
2. [1932] A.C. 562. See Pollock's *Law of Torts*, 15th Edn., pp. 326–333.
3. Cf. Sealy, [1975] C.L.J. 21; Carr, 38 M.L.R. 463.

between the parties.   Secondly, those where a special relationship exists.

In the first case, undue influence must be proved as a fact, in the second it is presumed to exist.   In litigation the two classes are not mutually exclusive and a plaintiff may allege both that undue influence should be presumed and that it existed in fact.   It is by no means unknown for both allegations to be successful.[1]

Two classes of undue influence

(i) No special relationship between the contracting parties

Undue influence must be proved as a fact

Here it must be affirmatively proved that one party in fact exerted influence over the other and thus procured a contract that would otherwise not have been made.   The courts have never attempted to define undue influence with precision, but it has been described as " some unfair and improper conduct, some coercion from outside, some overreaching, some form of cheating and generally, though not always, some personal advantage obtained by "[2] the guilty party.   Examples are: coercing the mind of a person of weak intellect by a claim to possess supernatural powers;[3] taking advantage of a lady who suffers from religious delusions[4] or who is convinced of the truth of messages from the dead transmitted through a spiritualistic medium,[5] playing on the fears of a son concerning the state of his father's health.[6]

Williams v. Bayley

A leading case on the subject is *Williams* v. *Bayley*[7] where the facts were these:

> A son gave to his bank several promissory notes upon which he had forged the endorsements of his father.   At a meeting between the three parties, the banker made it reasonably evident that if some arrangement were not reached the son would be prosecuted.   This impression was conveyed in such expressions as: " We have only one course to pursue; we cannot be parties to compounding a felony ": " This is a serious matter, a case of transportation for life."   The effect of these expressions upon the father is shown by his somewhat despairing words: " What be I to do?   How can I help myself? You see these men will have their money."   In the result the father agreed in writing to make an equitable mortgage to the bank in consideration of the return of the promissory notes.

This agreement was held to be invalid on the ground that undue pressure had been exerted.   The bankers had clearly exploited the fears of the father for the safety of his son, and had thus brought themselves within the equitable principle that, where there is inequality between parties and one of them by taking an unfair advantage of the situation of the other forces an agreement upon him, the transaction will be set aside.[8]

---

1. *Re Craig, Meneces* v. *Middleton*, [1971] Ch. 95; [1970] 2 All E.R. 390.
2. *Allcard* v. *Skinner* (1887), 36 Ch.D. 145, at p. 181, *per* LINDLEY, L.J.
3. *Nottidge* v. *Prince* (1860), 2 Giff. 246.
4. *Norton* v. *Relly* (1764), 2 Eden. 286.
5. *Lyon* v. *Home* (1868), L.R. 6 Eq. 655.
6. *Mutual Finance, Ltd.* v. *John Wetton & Sons, Ltd.*, [1937] 2 K.B. 389; [1937] 2 All E.R. 657.
7. (1866), L.R. 1 H.L. 200.
8. (1866), L.R. 1 H.L. 200, *per* Lord CHELMSFORD, at p. 216.

(ii) Where a confidential relationship exists between the parties

In this second class of case the equitable view is that undue influence must be presumed, for the fact that confidence is reposed in one party either endows him with exceptional authority over the other or imposes upon him the duty to give disinterested advice. The possibility that he may put his own interest uppermost is so obvious that he comes under a duty to prove that he has not abused his position.[1] Whether a confidential relationship exists or not, the question is always the same—was undue influence used to procure the contract or gift? But the burden of proof is different. If B seeks to avoid a contract with A, then in the absence of any confidential relationship, the entire onus is on B to prove undue influence, but if he proves the existence of such a relationship, the onus is on A to prove that undue influence was not used. A must rebut the presumption of undue pressure.

Undue influence is presumed

The onus is on the party in whom confidence is reposed to show that the party to whom he owed the duty in fact acted voluntarily, in the sense that he was free to make an independent and informed estimate of the expediency of the contract or other transaction.[2] It has been said in several cases that the only way in which the presumption can be rebutted is proof that the person to whom the duty of confidence was owed received independent advice before completion of the contract, and one judge at least has stated that the giving of advice does not suffice unless it has actually been followed.[3] On the other hand, the Privy Council has emphasised that if evidence is given of circumstances sufficient to show that the contract was the act of a free and independent mind, the transaction will be valid even though no external advice was given.[4]

How presumption of undue influence is rebutted

Importance of independent advice

> " Their Lordships are not prepared to accept the view that independent legal advice is the only way in which the presumption can be rebutted; nor are they prepared to affirm that independent legal advice, when given, does not rebut the presumption, unless it be shown that the advice was taken. It is necessary for the donee to prove that the gift was the result of the free exercise of independent will. The most obvious way to prove this is by establishing that the gift was made after the nature and effect of the transaction had been fully explained to the donor by some independent and qualified person so completely as to satisfy the court that the donor was acting independently of any influence from the donee and with the full appreciation of what he was doing; and in cases where there are no other circumstances this may be the only means by which the donee can rebut the presumption."[5]

---

1. *Allcard* v. *Skinner* (1887), 36 Ch.D. 145, at p. 181.
2. *Ibid.*, at p. 171.
3. *Powell* v. *Powell*, [1900] 1 Ch. 243, at p. 246, *per* FARWELL, J.
4. *Inche Noriah* v. *Shaik Allie Bin Omar*, [1929] A.C. 127; [1928] All E.R. Rep. 189; approved by LAWRENCE, L.J., in *Lancashire Loans, Ltd.* v. *Black*, [1934] 1 K.B. 380, at p. 413.
5. [1929] A.C., at p. 135; [1928] All E.R. Rep., at p. 193. The case concerned a gift, which in the present connection is on the same footing as a contract. An aged and wholly illiterate woman made a gift of land to her nephew who managed her affairs. A lawyer gave her independent and honest advice prior to the execution of the deed, but he did not know that the gift included practically all her property and he did not explain that a will would be a wiser method of benefiting the nephew. The gift was set aside.

Their Lordships then added, however, that facts which indicate that the donor was a free agent cannot be disregarded " merely because they do not include independent advice from a lawyer."

Fiduciary
relations
which raise
the
presumption

It is not every fiduciary relation that raises the equitable presumption of undue influence. As FLETCHER-MOULTON, L.J., once observed, fiduciary relations are many and various, including even the case of an errand boy who is bound to bring back change to his master, and to say that every kind of fiduciary relation justifies the interference of equity is absurd. " The nature of the fiduciary relation must be such that it justifies the interference."[1] On the other hand equity has not closed the list of persons against whom the presumption is raised. There are certain special relations where undue influence is invariably presumed, but they do not cover all the possible cases, for the basis of the doctrine is that " the relief stands upon a general principle, applying to all the variety of relations in which dominion may be exercised by one person over another."[2]

Certain
definite
relations
raise the
presumption

The special relationships that raise a presumption in favour of undue influence include those of solicitor and client,[3] doctor and patient,[4] trustee and *cestui que trust*,[5] guardian and ward,[6] parent and child,[7] religious adviser and disciple;[8] but do not include husband and wife.[9] Whether they include parties engaged to be married does not admit of a simple answer since the decision of the Court of Appeal in *Zamet v. Hyman*.[10] The *ratio decidendi* of that case is far from clear, but perhaps a fair interpretation of the judgements is that the presumption will not arise unless the transaction is patently and strikingly unfavourable to the party who seeks its avoidance.[11] We will now illustrate the operation of the principle by considering the case of religious adviser and disciple.

Religious
adviser and
disciple

It may well be that the origin of the strict law relating to undue influence is the hostility which the courts have always shown towards spiritual tyranny, for as LINDLEY, L.J., said in a leading case: " The influence of one mind over another is very subtle, and of all influences religious influence is the most dangerous and the most powerful, and to counteract it courts of equity have gone very far."[12] The facts of *Allcard v. Skinner*, the case from which these words are taken, bear this out.

---

1. *Re Coomber, Coomber v. Coomber*, [1911] 1 Ch. 723, at pp. 728–9.
2. *Huguenin v. Baseley* (1807), 14 Ves. 273, at 286, *per* Sir S. ROMILLY, *arguendo*, adopted by Lord COTTENHAM; *Dent v. Bennett* (1839), 4 My. & Cr. 269, at p. 277. Examples are: *Tate v. Williamson* (1866), 2 Ch. App. 55; *Inche Noriah v. Shaik Allie Bin Omar*, [1929] A.C. 127; [1928] All E.R. Rep. 189; *Tufton v. Sperni*, [1952] 2 T.L.R. 516.
3. See White and Tudor's *Leading Cases in Equity*, vol. 1, pp. 232–4.
4. *Radcliffe v. Price* (1902), 18 T.L.R. 466; *Re C.M.G.*, [1970] Ch. 574; [1970] 2 All E.R. 740.
5. *Ellis v. Barker* (1871), 7 Ch. App. 104.
6. *Hylton v. Hylton* (1754), 2 Ves. Sen. 547.
7. *Lancashire Loans, Ltd. v. Black*, [1934] 1 K.B. 380; [1933] All E.R. Rep. 201.
8. *Infra*, pp. 286–7.
9. *Bank of Montreal v. Stuart*, [1911] A.C. 120, at p. 126. *Domenco v. Domenco and Ignat* (1963), 41 D.L.R. (2d) 267.
10. [1961] 3 All E.R. 933; [1961] 1 W.L.R. 1442. See Megarry, 78 L.Q.R. 24.
11. The court did not appear to agree with the stricter view of MAUGHAM, J., in *Re Lloyd's Bank, Ltd.*, [1931] 1 Ch. 289.
12. *Allcard v. Skinner* (1887), 36 Ch.D. 145, at p. 183.

In 1868 the plaintiff, a woman about 35 years of age, was introduced by her spiritual adviser, one Nihill, to the defendant, who was the lady superior of a Protestant institution known as " The Sisters of the Poor." Nihill was the spiritual director and confessor of this sisterhood. Three years later the plaintiff became a sister and took the vows of poverty, chastity and obedience. The vow of poverty was strict, since it required the absolute surrender for ever of all individual property. The plaintiff remained a sister for eight years until 1879 during which time she gave property to the value of about £7,000 to the defendant. She left the sisterhood in 1879 by which time all but £1,671 of the money given had been spent by the defendant upon the purposes of the institution. The plaintiff took no action until 1885, but in that year she sued for the recovery of the £1,671 on the ground that it had been procured by the undue influence of the defendant.

The Court of Appeal found as a fact that no personal pressure had been exerted on the plaintiff and no unfair advantage taken of her position, but that the sole explanation of the gift was her own willing submission to the vow of poverty. Notwithstanding this, however, the court held that her gifts were in fact made under a pressure that she could not resist and that, so far as they had not been spent with her consent on the purposes of the institution, they were recoverable in principle when the pressure was removed by her resignation from the sisterhood.[1] Not only had there been no independent advice, but there was no opportunity of obtaining it, for one of the rules of the sisterhood said: " Let no Sister seek advice of any extern without the Superior's leave."

Nevertheless the plaintiff did not recover, for it was held that her claim was barred by her laches[2] and her acquiescence after she had left the sisterhood. Admittedly the claim was not one to which the Statutes of Limitation applied, and no doubt the general principle of equity is that delay alone is not a bar to relief. Nevertheless it has always been held that for a person to remain inactive for a long period with a full appreciation of what his rights are, materially affects the question whether he ought to obtain relief. Moreover in the present case there was evidence of acquiescence by the plaintiff. She had been surrounded by advisers for the last five years, she had taken care to revoke a will previously made in favour of the sisterhood, she had ceased to be a Protestant and had joined the Church of Rome, and the reasonable inference was that having considered the question of claiming relief she had determined not to challenge the validity of her gifts. *[marginal note: Effect of delay in claiming relief]*

In contrast with *Allcard* v. *Skinner* may be mentioned *Morley* v. *Loughnan*,[3] where an action, brought six months after the donor's death to recover £140,000 extorted from an epileptic by a Plymouth Brother, was successful.

A contract procured by undue influence cannot be rescinded after affirmation, express or implied, as is seen from *Allcard* v. *Skinner*, nor against persons who acquire rights under it for value and without notice of the facts,[4] but it may be avoided against *[marginal note: Persons against whom contract is voidable]*

---

1. *Allcard* v. *Skinner* (1887), 36 Ch.D. 145, at p. 186.
2. Laches is the neglect of a person to assert his rights. See *infra*, pp. 626–7.
3. [1893] 1 Ch. 736.
4. *Bainbrigge* v. *Browne* (1881), 18 Ch.D. 188.

purchasers for value with notice[1] and also against volunteers, i.e. persons who give no consideration, though they may be unaware of the undue influence.   In the lofty words of WILMOT, C.J.:

> " Whoever receives [the gift] must take it tainted and infected with the undue influence and imposition of the person procuring the gift; his partitioning and cantoning it out amongst his relations and friends will not purify the gift, and protect it against the equity of the person imposed upon.   Let the hand receiving it be ever so chaste, yet, if it comes through a corrupt polluted channel, the obligation of restitution will follow it."[2]

---

1. *Maitland* v. *Irving* (1846), 15 Sim. 437; *Lancashire Loans, Ltd.* v. *Black*, [1934] 1 K.B. 380.
2. *Bridgeman* v. *Green* (1757), Wilm. 58, at p. 65.

CHAPTER THREE

Contracts Rendered Void by Statute

Of the various contracts rendered void by statute, there are only three which seem to require discussion in a general book upon contract. These are, firstly, wagering contracts; secondly, restrictive trading agreements; thirdly, arrangements for the maintenance of resale prices. These three classes will now be considered in turn.[1]

A. WAGERING CONTRACTS

1. THE DEFINITION OF A WAGERING CONTRACT

The primary meaning of " wagering " is staking something of value upon the result of some future uncertain event, such as a horse race, or upon the ascertainment of the truth concerning some past or present event, such as the population of London, with regard to which the wagering parties express opposite views. In *Carlill* v. *Carbolic Smoke Ball Co.*,[2] HAWKINS, J., gave the following definition of a wagering contract which later received the unqualified approval of the Court of Appeal[3]:

Definition
of wagering
contract

---

1. Certain contracts by infants are also declared void by the Infants Relief Act, but as these raise difficult questions of construction they are dealt with specially in the chapter on Capacity, *infra*, pp. 413 *et seq*.
2. [1892] 2 Q.B. 484, at p. 490.
3. *Ellesmere* v. *Wallace*, [1929] 2 Ch. 1, at pp. 24, 36, 48–9.

" A wagering contract is one by which two persons, professing to hold opposite views touching the issue of a future uncertain event, mutually agree that, dependent upon the determination of that event, one shall win from the other, and that other shall pay or hand over to him, a sum of money or other stake; neither of the contracting parties having any other interest in that contract than the sum or stake he will so win or lose, there being no other real consideration for the making of such contract by either of the parties."

There are several aspects of this definition which require to be stressed.

Wager may relate to past, present or future event

In the first place, its limitation to a future uncertain event is incorrect, for a wager is none the less a wager though it concerns a past or present fact or event.

Each party must stand to win or lose

Secondly, an essential feature of a wagering contract is that one party is to win and the other to lose upon the determination of the event.[1]   Each party must stand either to win or lose under the terms of the contract.   It is not a wagering contract if one party may win but cannot lose, or if he may lose but cannot win, or if he can neither win nor lose.   For instance, in *Ellesmere* v. *Wallace*:[2]

> Edgar Wallace nominated a horse for a race, the advertised con-
> ditions of which were that £5 or £2 had to be paid to the Jockey
> Club according as a nominated horse started or did not start in the
> race.   Another condition was that the owner of the winning horse
> should receive £200 provided by the Jockey Club and also the
> entrance moneys paid by the various nominators less a sum of £30.
> Wallace's horse did not run, and when sued for the recovery of £2
> he pleaded that the contract between him and the Jockey Club was
> void as being a wagering contract.

The Court of Appeal held that the money was recoverable.   The argument that the contract was a wager, since if the horse was successful Wallace would win £200 plus a further amount and if it failed he would lose £5, was fallacious, for the Jockey Club did not stand to win or lose anything as a result of the nomination. They did not lose under the contract merely because that particular horse succeeded, for their liability was to pay £200 to the successful owner no matter who he might be.   Their liability would be no greater or less whether Wallace nominated or did not nominate a horse.   Moreover they did not win anything if Wallace's horse failed in the race, since the nomination fee did not accrue to them but was earmarked for the successful owner.

Only two parties, or two groups of parties, to a wager

Thus, a bet placed with the Horseracing Totalisator Board is not a wagering contract within the meaning of the Gaming Act 1845, since the board can neither win nor lose on the transaction. Its function is merely to divide the aggregate amount received, less expenses, among the successful contributors.[3].   The same is true of the " treble chance " on the football pools.   It will be seen therefore that many betting transactions are not legally wagers.

Thirdly, if an essential feature of a wager is that there must

1. *Thacker* v. *Hardy* (1878), 4 Q.B.D. 685; *Lockwood* v. *Cooper*, [1903] 2 K.B. 428.
2. [1929] 2 Ch. 1.
3. *Tote Investors, Ltd.* v. *Smoker*, [1968] 1 Q.B. 509; [1967] 3 All E.R. 242.

be two persons either of whom is capable of winning or losing,
it follows that there must be no more than two parties or two
groups of parties to the contract.   It was argued, for instance, in
Ellesmere v. *Wallace* that there was a multipartite wagering
contract between Wallace and each of the other nominators, but,
as RUSSELL, L.J., demonstrated, it was impossible to express in
terms of wagers the effect of several persons nominating horses
for the race.   It could not be shown that Wallace made a bet
with each nominator.   If his horse lost the race then he himself
would lose the alleged bet, *i.e.* what he had paid as entrance fee,
but the other party to the supposed wager would not necessarily
win anything.   He would win only if his horse won the race.[1]

> " The truth is that you cannot have more than two parties or
> two sides to a bet.   You may have a multipartite agreement to con-
> tribute to a sweepstake (which may be illegal as a lottery if the
> winner is determined by chance, but not if the winner is determined
> by skill), but you cannot have a multipartite agreement for a bet
> unless the numerous parties are divided into two sides, of which
> one wins or the other loses, according to whether an uncertain event
> does or does not happen."[2]

The last essential feature of a wager is that the stake must
be the only interest which the parties have in the contract.[3]   If
A lays B ten to one in sovereigns against a particular horse for
the St. Leger, B stands to win £10, A stands to win £1, but
neither of them has any other interest whatsoever in the contract.
On the other hand if either party to a contract, under which
money is payable upon the determination of an uncertain event,
possesses an interest in the subject matter of the contract that will
be affected in value according to the determination of the event,
the contract is not void as being a wager.   Thus in one sense
every contract of insurance is a bet on the outcome of a future
uncertain event and therefore literally speaking a wager.   A
wife, for instance, who insures her husband's life for £10,000 in
return for an annual premium of £200, stands to gain or lose
according to the eventual length of the life assured.   To apply
this rigorous reasoning, however, would not be practical politics
and it has long been established that whether a contract of insurance is a wager depends upon whether the assured has what is
called an insurable interest in the event upon which the insurance
money becomes payable.   If A ships cargo on B's vessel bound
for a foreign port, the contract by which he insures the safe arrival
of the ship is not a wager since his own property is at risk during
the voyage, though in effect it means that the insurer will pay £*x*
in one event but nothing in another.   But if A has no cargo on
board, the contract by which he insures the safe arrival of the
vessel is a wager, for his only interest in the fate of the vessel is
that if she is lost he recovers £*x*, while if she reaches her destination he loses the amount of his premium.[4]   The modern practice
of insuring against bad weather provides another example.   If a

Marginal note: Not a wager if one party has a proprietary interest in the event

---

1. [1929] 2 Ch. 1, at pp. 50–1.
2. *Ellesmere* v. *Wallace*, [1929] 2 Ch. 1, at p. 52, *per* RUSSELL, L.J.   See also
   Tote Investors, Ltd. v. *Smoker, supra.*
3. *Carlill* v. *Carbolic Smoke Ball Co.*, [1892] 2 Q.B. 484.
4. Cf. *Kent* v. *Bird* (1777), 2 Cowp. 583.

cricketer insures against the fall of more than one-eighth of an inch of rain during the first three days of the Canterbury cricket week, the contract is valid if he is financially interested in the match, as for instance if it is being played for his benefit, but void if he has no such interest.

Whether a
contract is
a wager
depends
upon its
substance
The question whether the parties are interested in something more than the mere winning or losing of a stake depends upon the substance of the agreement, not upon its outward form.

> " In construing a contract with a view to determining whether it is a wagering one or not, the court will receive evidence in order to arrive at the substance of it, and will not confine its attention to the mere words in which it is expressed, for a wagering contract may be sometimes concealed under the guise of language which, on the face of it, if words were only to be considered, might constitute a legally enforceable contract."[1]

Thus in *Brogden* v. *Marriott*,[2] A agreed to buy a horse from B, the price to be £200 if it trotted within a month at eighteen miles an hour, but a shilling if it failed to attain this speed. The horse having failed in its attempt, A claimed it at the nominal price of a shilling, but the agreement was held to be a wager, not a *bona fide* conditional contract. A rather more subtle case is *Rourke* v. *Short*[3] where the facts were these:

> The parties to a proposed contract for the sale of rags disagreed about the price that had been paid upon the occasion of a former sale. They ultimately agreed that if the seller's memory proved to be accurate the price of the present sale should be six shillings *per cwt.*, otherwise it should be three shillings *per cwt.* The seller proved to be correct.

The buyer refused to accept the rags, and an action by the seller to recover the price failed. Lord CAMPBELL expressed the view that:

> " The previous price was the point on which the wager was to turn and the stake was the difference of the price to be now paid. . . . It makes no difference that there was a real intention to part with the goods."

Another type of case in which it becomes necessary to ascertain the real nature of an agreement is where a client instructs a stockbroker to buy or sell shares. A contract of this nature may be a wager, and it is so where it takes the form of what is called a contract for differences, *i.e.* where the parties agree merely to pay or receive the difference between the price of certain shares on one day and their price on another day.[4] For instance:

> A instructs B, a stockbroker, to procure a thousand ordinary shares in a certain company at £80 a share, the transaction to be completed at the next Stock Exchange settling day, a fortnight hence.

If in this case it is found as a fact that neither party contemplated the delivery of shares, but intended that if the market price rose above £80 at the next settling day, B should pay the difference

---

1. *Carlill* v. *Carbolic Smoke Ball Co.*, [1892] 2 Q.B. 484, at pp. 491–2, *per* HAWKINS, J. Cf. *Universal Stock Exchange* v. *Strachan*, [1896] A.C. 166, at p. 173.
2. (1836), 3 Bing. N.C. 88.
3. (1856), 5 E. & B. 904.
4. *Grizewood* v. *Blane* (1852), 11 C.B. 538.

between that price and £80 to A, while if it fell A should pay the difference to B, then the contract is void as a wager. If on the other hand the intention is that the shares shall actually be purchased by B, the contract is not a wager. This is so even though A, to the knowledge of B, is not prepared to take the shares up but intends to re-sell them before the settling day and thus to gain or lose according as the price since the day of their purchase rises or falls.[1] Where such is the intention of the parties, B is clearly authorized to enter into contracts for the purchase of shares from jobbers, and is entitled to be indemnified by A against the obligations that he thereby incurs.[2] Thus contracts for the purchase of shares are not wagers unless the agreement is that the purchaser has no right to claim delivery and the seller has no right to insist upon it.[3] As CAVE, J., said in his direction to the jury in *Universal Stock Exchange, Ltd.* v. *Strachan*:[4]

" In order to be a gambling transaction such as the law points at it must be a gambling transaction in the intention of both the parties to it."

2. THE EFFECT OF A WAGERING CONTRACT

(i) The effect as between the parties

The Gaming Act 1845 in the following section renders all wagering contracts void.

A wagering contract is void

" All contracts or agreements, whether by parole or in writing, by way of gaming or wagering, shall be null and void; and no suit shall be brought or maintained in any court of law or equity for recovering any sum of money or valuable thing alleged to be won upon any wager, or which shall have been deposited in the hands of any person to abide the event on which any wager shall have been made.

Provided always that this enactment shall not be deemed to apply to any subscription or contribution or agreement to subscribe or contribute for or towards any plate, prize or sum of money to be awarded to the winner or winners of any lawful game, sport, pastime or exercise."[5]

It is convenient for purposes of exposition to deal separately with the four branches of this section.

The first is as follows:

All contracts or agreements, whether by parole or in writing, by way of gaming or wagering shall be null and void.

First branch of the section

The effect of these words is that a wagering contract is " struck with invalidity at the outset, i.e. before the event contemplated by the wager has occurred."[6] It is void, though not illegal. It confers no rights upon either party. If the loser fails to pay,

---

1. *Thacker* v. *Hardy* (1878), 4 Q.B.D. 685; *Weddle, Beck & Co.* v. *Hackett*, [1929] 1 K.B. 321; *Woodward* v. *Wolfe*, [1936] 3 All E.R. 529.
2. *Thacker* v. *Hardy, supra.*
3. *Ironmonger & Co.* v. *Dyne* (1928), 44 T.L.R. 497, at p. 499, *per* SCRUTTON, L.J.
4. [1896] A.C. 166, at pp. 167-8.
5. Section 18.
6. *Hill* v. *William Hill (Park Lane), Ltd.*, [1949] A.C. 530, at p. 552; [1949] 2 All E.R. 452, at p. 464, *per* Lord GREENE.

recovery cannot be enforced by action, whether brought for the amount of the bet or on an account stated.[1]   If he stops a cheque which he has given for the amount, he cannot be sued.   If he pays the winner in cash or gives him a cheque which is honoured, it might be expected that, as the contract is void and the payment therefore made without consideration, he should be entitled to recover the money.   The law does not take this view.   The Act is apparently treated as conferring a privilege which the loser may waive if he pleases, and payment constitutes waiver.   In the words of BOWEN, L.J., the loser merely " waives a benefit which the statute has given to him and confers a good title to the money upon the person to whom he pays it."[2]

The second branch is as follows:

Second branch of the section

> No suit shall be brought or maintained in any court of law or equity for recovering any sum of money or valuable thing alleged to be won upon any wager.

More extensive than the first

The interpretation put upon these words by the House of Lords in *Hill* v. *William Hill (Park Lane), Ltd.*,[3] is that they do not merely repeat what is enacted in the first branch, but that they strike at fresh agreements made by the parties subsequently to the original wagering contract itself.

The earlier doctrine of *Hyams* v. *Stuart King*

The result of this interpretation is to overrule a number of decisions dating back at least to 1870.   These had distinguished the original wager from a later and distinct contract under which the loser, for a fresh consideration, promises to pay the amount of the bet.   In several cases of this type the courts had enforced the later contract.   What generally happens is that the winner puts pressure upon the loser by a threat to do something to his detriment if he continues to be recalcitrant.   He may thus threaten to expose the loser's dishonourable conduct to his club[4] or to his bank manager[5] or, if he happens to be a bookmaker or an owner of race horses, to report him to Tattersalls[6] or to the Jockey Club.[7]   The loser then makes a fresh promise to pay in consideration that the winner will forbear to implement his threat.   Thus, in *Hyams* v. *Stuart King*:[8]

> Two bookmakers, A and B, had betting transactions which resulted in a sum becoming due from A to B.   A failed to pay, but ultimately agreed to do so in consideration that B would refrain from declaring him a defaulter to the injury of his business with his customers.

Although the agreement was in substance no more than a repetition of the void wagering contract, the majority of the Court of Appeal held it to be enforceable.   They took the view that it was free from vice.   In the opinion of FARWELL, L.J., it was unaffected by the Act of 1845 since it was not a wager but merely a contract

---

1. *Alberg* v. *Chandler* (1948), 64 T.L.R. 394.
2. *Bridger* v. *Savage* (1885), 15 Q.B.D. 363, at p. 367.
3. [1949] A.C. 530; [1949] 2 All E.R. 452.
4. *Re Browne, Ex parte Martingell*, [1904] 2 K.B. 133.
5. *Poteliakhoff* v. *Teakle*, [1938] 2 K.B. 816; [1938] 3 All E.R. 686.
6. *Goodson* v. *Baker* (1908), 98 L.T. 415.   Such a threat does not constitute blackmail: *Burden* v. *Harris*, [1937] 4 All E.R. 559.
7. *Bubb* v. *Yelverton* (1870), L.R. 9 Eq. 471.
8. [1908] 2 K.B. 696.

designed to avoid the consequences of having made a wager. Again, it was not illegal *per se*, since it is not illegal to tell the members of the betting fraternity that a bookmaker is prone to default; nor was it tainted with illegality merely because it sprang from a wager, for a wager, though void, is not illegal. FLETCHER MOULTON, L.J., dissented. He could not regard the contract as other than a contract to pay money alleged to have been won upon a wager and therefore directly within the language of the second limb of the statute. The sole object of this colourable agreement was that the bet should be paid.

The controversy aroused by this decision was finally laid to rest forty years later by the decision of the House of Lords in *Hill* v. *William Hill (Park Lane), Ltd.*[1] The facts were these:

Hyams v. *Stuart King* overruled by *Hill* v. *William Hill (Park Lane), Ltd.*

> On July 22nd, 1946, the committee of Tattersalls made an order that the appellant, an owner of race horses, should discharge the amount of his unpaid bets of £3,635 12s. 6d. due to the respondents by paying £635 12s. 6d. within fourteen days and thereafter by paying monthly instalments of £100.
>
> In August, 1946, the appellant, having failed to comply with the order, gave the respondents a cheque for £635 12s. 6d. post-dated to October 10th and promised to begin the monthly instalments in November in consideration that the respondents would refrain from enforcing the order. Enforcement of the order would involve his being posted as a defaulter and warned off Newmarket Heath. The appellant failed to pay the instalments and the respondents sued to recover their amount.

By a majority of four to three, the House of Lords held that this contract, though unaffected by the first branch of the statute since it was clearly not a contract " by way of gaming or wagering," was nevertheless void under the second branch.

The minority were of opinion that the second branch was neither intended nor apt to invalidate a contract that was not itself a wager. In their view, it was a mere procedural provision designed to fortify the preceding words. " The second or procedural part," said Lord RADCLIFFE, " is introduced by the word *and*; the words *alleged to be won* are used to describe the sum of money of which recovery by legal action is forbidden."[2] Lord GREENE expressed his disagreement with this argument in the following words:

> " The language of the first branch is entirely different from the language of the second branch. Under the first branch the agreement is a nullity before the race is run. The second branch assumes the race to have been run and the bet to have been lost. It is true that the language of the second branch would prohibit the bringing of an action upon a wager which had been won. To that extent I agree that it covers ground already adequately covered by the first branch. But this is no justification for limiting the words of the second branch as suggested. They are quite general and when read in their ordinary meaning they extend to any action to recover money alleged to be won on a wager."[3]

---

1. [1949] A.C. 530; [1949] 2 All E.R. 452.
2. [1949] A.C., at p. 579; and see p. 541, *per* Lord JOWITT.
3. *Hill* v. *William Hill (Park Lane), Ltd.*, [1949] A.C. 530, at p. 552; [1949] 2 All E.R. 452, at p. 465; see also Lord MACDERMOTT at pp. 577 and 480, respectively.

The same conclusion was reached by the majority of the Law Lords. The respondents' action was brought to " recover a sum of money alleged to be won upon a wager " and was therefore rendered void by the statute.

Whether
new contract
is void is a
question of
intention

The single question of fact, therefore, that always falls to be determined in this type of case is not whether there was a fresh bargain but whether, according to the true nature and substance of the contract, the money sought to be recovered is money alleged, either by plaintiff or defendant, to be won upon a wager.[1] This question is, in essence, one of intention. In each case " the court must look to the reality of the transaction and come to a finding as to what the true intention was."[2]   Thus in *Hill* v. *William Hill (Park Lane), Ltd.*, there could be no doubt that the subject-matter of the fresh contract was the very sum of money won on the wager. The contract referred specifically and solely to the sum fixed in the order of Tattersall's committee, and this sum was identical in amount and character with the wagering debt.[3]   Again, if, as in *Coral* v. *Kleyman*,[4] A fails to pay a lost bet to B and his father promises to pay the amount due in consideration that B will not report the failure to Tattersalls, an action brought on this promise must fail; the transaction is but a transparent device to avoid the second branch of the statute. The position, however, may be more doubtful. Suppose, for instance, that the loser promises to transfer his motor-car to the winner in return for the latter's promise that the non-payment of the wager shall be concealed from the loser's friends. Is the subject-matter of this promise " a valuable thing alleged to be won on a wager " within the meaning of the statute? If the words of the statute are to be read literally, the promise is not caught by them; it cannot be said that the motor-car was " alleged to be won on the wager." But the courts are hardly likely to suffer so obvious an evasion. The view emphasized in *Hill* v. *William Hill (Park Lane), Ltd.*, is that one object of the second branch of section 18 is " to preclude resort to an obvious way round the earlier provision,"[5] and a promise by the loser to transfer to the winner a car substantially equal to the amount of the bet is only a slightly less transparent device to avoid the statute than a new promise to pay the money itself. But the loser's promise may wear, at least on the surface, a more innocent aspect. Suppose he agrees to sell to the winner for £2,000 a horse worth £3,000, and, when sued for breach of contract, pleads that the agreement was made in consideration that his failure to pay the lost bet should not be published by the winner. Such a case may well provoke prolonged argument, and human ingenuity may yet

---

1. *Ibid.*, at pp. 578 and 481 respectively, *per* Lord MACDERMOTT.
2. *Ibid.*, at pp. 574 and 478 respectively, *per* Lord MACDERMOTT. At pp. 559 and 468 respectively, Lord GREENE says: " I must not be understood as suggesting that there can never be a case where a promise by a defaulting backer given in consideration of a promise by the winner of a bet not to report the defaulter may be enforced."
3. *Ibid.*, at pp. 564 and 472 respectively, *per* Lord NORMAND; at pp. 546 and 461 respectively, *per* Lord SIMON.
4. [1951] 1 All E.R. 518.
5. [1949] A.C. 530; [1949] 2 All E.R. 452, at pp. 577 and 480 respectively, *per* Lord MACDERMOTT.

devise more subtle methods of evasion. The principle, however, remains the same, however difficult to apply. No fresh contract is valid if, in the opinion of the court, it discloses in substance an intention that the wager shall be paid.[1]

The third branch of section 18 may be rendered as follows: Third branch of the section

> No suit shall be brought or maintained in any court of law or equity for recovering any sum of money or valuable thing which shall have been deposited in the hands of any person to abide the event on which any wager shall have been made.

The construction put upon these words is that they merely prevent recovery by the winner of the money deposited with the stake-holder by his opponent.[2] They do not prevent either party from recovering his own stake before it has been paid away by the stakeholder.[3]

The last branch of the section consists of the proviso and is expressed in these words: Fourth branch

> Provided always that the enactment shall not be deemed to apply to any subscription or contribution or agreement to subscribe or contribute for or towards any plate, prize or sum of money to be awarded to the winner or winners of any lawful game, sport, pastime or exercise.

The object of this is that lawful prizes shall be recoverable. It does not, however, save any transaction which is substantially a wager. If the so-called prize is in truth nothing more than a stake put up by wagering parties and merely masquerading as a prize, it is not recoverable.[4] This was the position in *Diggle* v. *Higgs*,[5] where:

> A and B agreed to walk a match for £200 a side and each deposited this amount with X to be paid to the winner.

It was held that the winner was not entitled to recover the loser's deposit from X, since the money was deposited by way of wager. It was held in *Ellesmere* v. *Wallace*,[6] as we have already seen,[7] that there cannot be a multipartite wagering contract. It would seem to follow, therefore, that the winner of a lawful game in which there are several competitors can recover the agreed prize, even though it consists wholly of money deposited by the competitors themselves, always presuming, of course, that they are not divided into two sides.

At common law games of mere skill, *i.e.* those in which the element of chance is negligible, such as football, cricket, billiards, horse and foot racing, are lawful. Formerly, certain games in Unlawful gaming

---

1. The attitude of the courts is indicated by the case of *R.* v. *Weisz*, [1951] 2 K.B. 611; [1951] 2 All E.R. 408. A client alleged that a firm of book makers owed him £373 upon bets placed with them, and, to induce them to pay, he instructed his solicitors to issue a writ. The writ was endorsed as a claim for money due on an account stated, though the endorsement was completely fictitious. It was held that an attempt to deceive the court by disguising the true nature of the claim and putting forward a feigned issue was a contempt of court and could be punished as such.
2. *Varney* v. *Hickman* (1847), 5 C.B. 271; *Diggle* v. *Higgs* (1877), 2 Ex.D. 422.
3. *Infra*, p. 305.
4. *Diggle* v. *Higgs* (1877), 2 Ex.D. 422; *Trimble* v. *Hill* (1879), 5 App. Cas. 342.
5. (1877), 2 Ex.D. 422.
6. [1929] 2 Ch. 1.
7. *Supra*, pp. 296–7.

which success depended upon chance, such as pharaoh, passage, roulette and all games played with dice, except backgammon, were declared illegal by statute.[1] Now no game is *per se* illegal, but " gaming " will be illegal if it contravenes the Gaming Act 1968. To attempt any detailed analysis of this Act in the present book would be out of place, but two points may be made.

Firstly, " gaming " for the purposes of the Act is defined by section 52 as

> " the playing of a game of chance for winnings in money or money's worth, whether any person playing the game is at risk of losing any money or money's worth or not."[2]

By the same section " game of chance " excludes any " athletic game or sport," but with that exception includes " a game of chance and skill combined and a pretended game of chance and skill combined."

Secondly, Part I of the Act deals with gaming elsewhere than on premises licensed or registered under Part II; Part II deals with gaming on premises which are so licensed or registered; and Part III deals with gaming by means of machines. Under Part I, which is alone relevant to this book, gaming is prohibited if:

(i) the game involves playing or staking against a bank, whether the bank is held by one of the players or not; or

(ii) the chances in the game are not equally favourable to all the players; or

(iii) the chances in the game lie between the player and some other person, or (if there are two or more players) lie wholly or partly between the players and some other person, and those chances are not as favourable to the player or players as they are to that other person.[3]

Moreover, no charge, whether in money or money's worth, may be made " in respect of the gaming," and no levy may be charged, directly or indirectly, on any of the stakes or winnings of the players.[4] In streets and public places gaming, subject to an exception for certain games played on licensed premises, is completely prohibited.[5] The Act lays down penalties for contraventions of any of these prohibitions.[6]

(ii) The effect as between principal and agent

Two types of agency

The relationship of principal and agent may arise under a wagering contract in two distinct cases.

Firstly, where the stakes are deposited with an agent as a stakeholder.

---

1. Gaming Act 1738, s. 2; Gaming Acts 1739 and 1744. These statutes were repealed by the Betting and Gaming Act 1960, Schedule 6.
2. Contrast the definition of a " wagering contract " given above at p. 296. If one party is not at risk, there is no wagering contract within the meaning of that definition; but the statutory definition of " gaming " is satisfied.
3. Gaming Act 1968, section 2 (1). By section 2 (2), this prohibition does not apply to gaming on a domestic occasion in a private dwelling, or to gaming in a hostel, hall of residence, etc., by the residents or inmates thereof. As to gaming at entertainments not held for private gain, see section 41.
4. Sections 3 and 4. See however s. 40 as to special charges for playing at certain clubs and institutes.
5. Sections 5 and 6. See also section 7 for special provisions as to persons under eighteen.
6. Section 8. See also s. 46 as to forfeiture of anything relating to the offence.

Secondly, where a principal instructs an agent to effect wagering transactions on his behalf.

Where the two wagering parties, A and B, each deposit a stake with X to abide the event, the legal position of X is that he is the agent of A with regard to A's stake and the agent of B with regard to B's stake. In each case his authority is the same, namely, to pay the money to the winner. The rule of agency law relevant to this case is that if an agent acts within the scope and during the continuance of his lawful authority the principal is bound, but that if he exercises the authority after it has been revoked he is liable to his principal for the consequences.

(i) Stake deposited with stakeholder as agent

The effect of this upon a wagering contract in which stakes are deposited is that, notwithstanding the determination of the event upon which the wager turns, either party may require the repayment of his stake before it has been paid away in accordance with his former instructions. If the loser makes no demand until his stake has been paid to the winner, his right of recovery is gone, for the stakeholder has merely exercised the authority actually conferred upon him.[1] If, on the other hand, the loser demands the return of his money before it has been paid to the winner, the stakeholder is personally liable if he disregards the revocation of his authority and hands the stake to the winner.[2] In *Diggle* v. *Higgs*, the facts of which have already been given,[3] the stakeholder paid both stakes to the winner in spite of a written order to the contrary from the loser, and he resisted an action for its recovery by relying upon the words of the Gaming Act 1845 that " no suit shall be brought to recover any sum of money . . . deposited in the hands of any person to abide the event."[4] But, as we have seen, the meaning attributed to these words by the Court of Appeal was that the winner cannot recover his *opponent's* stake from the stakeholder, not that a depositor is disentitled to recover his own stake.[5]

Where an agent is instructed to effect a wagering transaction on behalf of his principal, litigation may arise in two ways: the agent may claim relief against the consequences of having acted within the scope of his authority, or the principal may sue the agent for failure to carry out the authority.

(ii) Agent instructed to effect a wagering transaction

In considering the first of these problems it is necessary to notice the general rule of law that an agent is entitled to be indemnified by his principal against liability incurred by him in executing his instructions, unless the instructions are unlawful.[6] The rule has been neatly summarized by HAWKINS, J., in these words:

At common law agent indemnifiable against the consequences

" If one man employs another to do a legal act, which in the ordinary course of things will involve the agent in obligations

---

1. *Varney* v. *Hickman* (1847), 5 C.B. 271.
2. *Hampden* v. *Walsh* (1876), 1 Q.B.D. 189.
3. *Supra*, p. 303.
4. *Supra*, p. 299.
5. It has also been decided that the recovery of a party's own stake is not prevented by the Gaming Act 1892 (*infra*, p. 306), since the word " paid " there means " paid out and out ": *O'Sullivan* v. *Thomas*, [1895] 1 Q.B. 698.
6. *Thacker* v. *Hardy* (1878), 4 Q.B.D. 685, at p. 687, *per* LINDLEY, J.

pecuniary or otherwise, a contract on the part of the employer to indemnify his agent is implied by law."[1]

*Read v.
Anderson:*
betting
agent
entitled to
indemnity

The question whether this doctrine applies where an agent is employed to effect a wager arose in *Read* v. *Anderson*:[2]

> The defendant instructed the plaintiff, a turf commission agent and a member of Tattersalls, to back certain horses at the Ascot meeting.   The plaintiff did so, and in the result a sum of £175 became due to him from the defendant in respect of the bets that had been lost.   A turf commission agent always backs a horse in his own name and becomes solely responsible to the person with whom the bet is made.   If he is declared a " defaulter " owing to his failure to pay a lost bet, he becomes subject to certain disqualifications which have a serious effect upon his business.

It was held that the plaintiff, having paid £175 out of his own pocket to the person with whom he had made the bet, was entitled to recover the amount from the defendant.

*Read v.
Anderson*
reversed
by Gaming
Act 1892

The decision in *Read* v. *Anderson* provoked so many actions of a similar nature that eight years later the Legislature intervened and stopped the practice by the Gaming Act 1892.   This provides as follows:

> Any promise, express or implied, to pay any person any sum of money paid by him under or in respect of any contract or agreement rendered null and void by the Gaming Act 1845, or to pay any sum of money by way of commission, fee, reward or otherwise in respect of any such contract, or of any services in relation thereto, or in connexion therewith, shall be null and void, and no action shall be brought or maintained to recover any such sum of money.[3]

In short, any promise, express or implied, to pay to X any money which has been *paid by him under or in respect of* a wagering contract is void.   Thus, although the rule that a principal must indemnify his agent against the consequences of exercising a lawful authority is still a leading doctrine of English law, it has no application where the consequences result from steps taken in furtherance of a wagering contract.   The agent has no cause of action either on an account stated[4] or for money paid at the request of his principal.

Rights of
principal
against
agent

With regard to the other aspect of agency, i.e. to claims made by the principal against the agent, two rules have been established.

Agent not
liable for
failure to
exercise his
authority

Firstly, the principal cannot sue the agent for a failure to carry out instructions.   In *Cohen* v. *Kittell*:[5]

> The defendant, who had been employed by the plaintiff to bet on commission, failed to place bets upon certain horses which he had been instructed to back.   The plaintiff therefore sued him for breach of the contract of agency, and claimed as damages the money that he would have received had the bets been made.

It was held that the action failed, since an agent can incur no legal liability for failure to make a contract which, even if it had been made, would have been void.

---

1. *Read* v. *Anderson* (1882), 10 Q.B.D. 100, at p. 108.
2. (1882), 10 Q.B.D. 100; affirmed (1884), 13 Q.B.D. 779.
3. Section 1.
4. *Law* v. *Dearnley*, [1950] 1 K.B. 400; [1950] 1 All E.R. 124.
5. (1889), 22 Q.B.D. 680.

Secondly, it is well established as a general rule of law that where a person has received money on behalf of another he cannot resist an action for its recovery by the plea that he received it in respect of a void transaction.[1] In accordance with this rule it has been held that a principal can successfully maintain an action for money had and received against an agent who has made bets on his behalf and who refuses to hand over winnings received from the loser.[2]

> " If one agrees to receive money for the use of another upon consideration executed, however frivolous or void the consideration might have been in respect of the person paying the money, if indeed it were not absolutely immoral or illegal, the person so receiving it cannot be permitted to gainsay his having received it for the use of that other."[3]

The result is that if A backs a horse with B and wins, the Gaming Act 1845 prevents him from recovering his winnings from B. But if he employs C to make the bet with B, he can recover any winnings that are actually paid by B to C. In this last case C, if he is unscrupulous, may plead that he did not in fact place the bet as agent but accepted it himself as a principal. If, however, C holds himself out as a betting agent he may, at any rate in the absence of clear evidence to the contrary, be estopped from denying that he acted as agent.[4]

Agent liable to pay winnings to principal

(iii) Securities given in respect of wagering contracts

The type of question that requires consideration here is this: suppose that a cheque or other security, given by A to B in payment of money due under a wagering contract, is transferred by B to X, is it enforceable in the hands of X or some subsequent transferee from him? In order to answer this question it is necessary to distinguish two classes of wagers, namely those on games and those on events other than games, for the Gaming Acts of 1710 and 1835 have dealt specially with securities given for gaming wagers.

Scope of inquiry

Two classes of wagers

The first section of the Gaming Act 1710, may be summarized as follows:

(i) Securities given in respect of wagers on games. Gaming Act 1710

> All securities given for money won by playing at any game whatsoever, or by betting on games, or for the repayment of money knowingly lent for the purpose of gaming or betting as aforesaid shall be utterly void, frustrate and of no effect.

This stringent enactment might well cause disaster to an innocent person, for a cheque or other negotiable instrument given in any of the circumstances specified by the statute would be worthless in the hands of a subsequent transferee, notwithstanding that he had given value for it in ignorance of its origin.

---

1. *Cheshire & Co.* v. *Vaughan Brothers & Co.*, [1920] 3 K.B. 240, at p. 255, *per* SCRUTTON, L.J.
2. *Bridger* v. *Savage* (1885), 15 Q.B.D. 363; *De Mattos* v. *Benjamin* (1894), 63 L.J.Q.B. 248.
3. *Griffith* v. *Young* (1810), 12 East. 513, at p. 514, *per* Lord ELLENBOROUGH.
4. *Moore* v. *Peachey* (1891), 7 T.L.R. 748; *Potter* v. *Codrington* (1892), 9 T.L.R. 54; *Grimerd* v. *Wiltshire* (1894), 10 T.L.R. 505.

Gaming
Act 1835

This injustice was therefore nullified by section one of the Gaming Act 1835, which provides that every security rendered void by the Act of 1710 shall no longer be void but shall be deemed to have been given for an illegal consideration.

> To illustrate the operation of this section, let us suppose that A, having lost a bet to B on a horse race, gives B a cheque for the amount. Let us suppose further that the cheque in the ordinary course of business passes through several hands and that the present holder, X, sues A to recover the amount for which it is drawn.

Security is
enforceable
by a *bona fide*
holder for
value

Now here X holds a cheque which at the time when it was given suffered from two defects: firstly, it was unsupported by consideration, since it was given in respect of a void wagering contract; secondly, it was tainted by illegality, since it came within the terms of the Act of 1835. X, however, can cure these defects by proof that he is a " holder in due course," an expression which describes the holder of a bill of exchange, cheque or promissory note, complete and regular on the face of it, who takes it in good faith and for value without notice of any defect of title in the person who negotiated it to him.[1] Normally every holder is presumed to be a holder in due course; but where the instrument is tainted in its origin by illegality, as it is in the hypothetical case under discussion, the burden is on the holder to prove affirmatively that " subsequent to the . . . illegality value has in good faith been given."[2]

The result, therefore, is that X can recover on the cheque provided that he proves two facts, namely, that he or some previous holder gave value for it and that he had no notice of the illegal consideration. When the action is heard, the defendant, A, will give evidence that the cheque was drawn in payment of a gaming debt, and then X must prove that when he took the cheque he was unaware of the circumstances in which it was given.[3] In short, the effect of the Act of 1835 is to throw the burden of proving value and good faith upon the holder of the bill or note.

The position with regard to a cheque which is drawn to enable a person to game on licensed premises is considered later.[4]

(ii) Securities
given in
respect of a
non-gaming
wager

A cheque or other security given for money lost under a non-gaming wager is given without consideration, since the wager itself is void, but there is no rule either at common law or by statute which taints it with illegality. Its one defect is want of consideration, and this is cured by its subsequent transfer

Security is
enforceable
if value is
later given
for it

for value. If, for instance, a cheque is given by A to B in payment of a bet on the date of the next war, and is later indorsed by B to X in settlement of an account for goods delivered, it is enforceable at the suit of X. It is quite immaterial that at the time of taking the cheque he was aware of the circumstances in which it was given by A to B.

Value is
presumed
to have been
given by
the holder

Further, in a case such as this, where the consideration for the original drawing of the cheque is void but not illegal, there is a presumption that the holder, *i.e.* X in the above example, has

---

1. Bills of Exchange Act 1882, section 29 (1) (a) and (b).
2. *Ibid.*, section 30.
3. *Hay* v. *Ayling* (1851), 16 Q.B. 423; *Woolf* v. *Hamilton*, [1898] 2 Q.B. 337.
4. *Infra*, p. 310.

given consideration. In other words the burden is on the defendant to prove that consideration has not been given.[1] Thus in *Fitch* v. *Jones*:[2]

> Jones made a bet with B concerning the amount of the hop duty in 1854. Having lost, he gave B a promissory note for £40 in payment. B indorsed the note to Fitch. When sued on the note, Jones pleaded that a duty lay on Fitch to prove that consideration had been given.

The plea failed and judgment was given for the plaintiff.

What has been said in this section applies only to subsequent transfers of a security. An original party to a wagering contract cannot sue upon a security given in respect of the wager, no matter whether it is given for a void or for an illegal consideration.[3]

Position as between the parties to the security

(iv) The effect as between lender and borrower

The law which regulates the right of a lender to recover loans made for wagering purposes is both confused and illogical, and precludes a scientific analysis. It may be considered under five heads.

It was held in 1838 that money lent for playing at or betting on an illegal game is irrecoverable.[4] Now no game is *per se* illegal, but the right of recovery will still be excluded if the gaming is conducted illegally, i.e. in contravention of the provisions of the Gaming Act 1968.[5]

(i) Loan for illegal gaming

The second question is whether a loan is recoverable if made for the purpose of gaming that will be lawfully conducted. In *Carlton Hall Club* v. *Laurence*,[6] the divisional court invoked the Gaming Acts of 1710 and 1835[7] and denied any right of recovery. The first of these statutes, as we have seen, provided that all securities given for the repayment of money knowingly lent for the purpose of playing at or betting upon any game whatsoever should be utterly void. The second enacted that such a security should not be void but should be deemed to have been given for an illegal consideration. Neither statute, it will be noticed, provided in terms that a loan for gaming as distinct from a security given by the borrower should be void, and the question was whether the contract of loan itself was also statutorily affected. The facts were these:

(ii) Loan for lawful gaming

Carlton Hall Club v. *Laurence*

> The plaintiffs, proprietors of a club in Maida Vale, were accustomed to sell chips representing a money value to members who wished to play games for money. They supplied the defendant with chips to the value of £28 7s. 3d. for the express purpose of playing poker and snooker, and accepted his cheque for this amount. The cheque was dishonoured.

It was clear that the plaintiffs could not recover on the cheque, since it constituted a security within the meaning of the statutes.

---

1. *Fitch* v. *Jones* (1855), 5 E. & B. 238; *Lilley* v. *Rankin* (1886), 56 L.J.Q.B. 248.
2. (1855), 5 E. & B. 238.
3. *William Hill (Park Lane), Ltd.* v. *Hofman*, [1950] 1 All E.R. 1013.
4. *M'Kinnell* v. *Robinson* (1838), 3 M. & W. 434.
5. Certain games were declared illegal by various statutes, but these have now been repealed; *supra*, p. 304.
6. [1929] 2 K.B. 153; [1929] All E.R. Rep. 605.
7. *Supra*, pp. 307–8.

Instead, they sued on the contract of loan, arguing that the statutes did not invalidate the contract and its consideration but only the cheque, and they were able to cite several authorities prior to 1835 in which it had been held that a loan of money for the purpose of gaming, as distinct from a security given in respect of the loan, was valid and enforceable. There is considerable force in this argument. Neither statute deals with the loan itself, but only with the right of a person to enforce a security given in respect of the loan. Moreover, the later statute, so far from prejudicing the rights of lenders, is merely designed to afford some measure of protection to third parties. The court, however, followed a *dictum* of the Court of Exchequer in 1842,[1] and found for the defendant, holding that the combined effect of the Acts of 1710 and 1835 is to avoid all loans where the contractual undertaking is that the money shall be used in playing at or betting upon games.

In *C. H. T., Ltd.* v. *Ward*, the Court of Appeal doubted *Carlton Hall Club* v. *Laurence* and expressed the view *obiter* that a loan for lawful gaming is recoverable,[2] but found that in the instant circumstances the lender was precluded from recovery by the Gaming Act 1892.[3]

> The plaintiffs, proprietors of a club, issued chips on credit to the defendant which she used for the purpose of gaming. They sued her to recover the amount by which her losses had exceeded her winnings.

The plaintiffs contended that the issue of chips was equivalent to a loan for lawful gaming and as such was recoverable; but the fatal flaw in this argument was that they had in fact paid the gaming losses of the defendant, since their practice was to pay cash to the winners at the end of each session. Therefore the promise of the defendant was rendered void by the Gaming Act 1892, as being a promise to pay a sum paid by the club in respect of her gaming contracts.

Loans for gaming on licensed premises

Special provision, however, has now been made for loans connected with gaming that is lawfully conducted on licensed premises. The Gaming Act 1968 provides that where gaming takes place upon premises licensed for this purpose, neither the licensee nor his agent shall make any loan or allow any credit (a) for enabling any person to take part in the game, or (b) in respect of any losses incurred by any person in the gaming.[4] To contravene this provision is an offence under the Act.[5]

Cheques drawn in respect of loans on licensed premises

But a cheque drawn to enable a person to take part in gaming on licensed premises is enforceable if it satisfies certain conditions. It is enacted that neither the licensee nor his agent shall accept such a cheque and give in exchange cash or tokens, unless—

(a) it is not a post-dated cheque;
(b) it is exchanged for the equivalent amount of cash or tokens;

---

1. *Applegarth* v. *Colley* (1842), 10 M. & W. 723, at p. 732.
2. [1965] 2 Q.B. 63, at p. 86; [1963] 3 All E.R. 835, at pp. 842–3, *per curiam*. See also *MacDonald* v. *Green*, [1951] 1 K.B. 594, at p. 600, *per* COHEN, L.J.
3. *Supra*, p. 306.
4. Gaming Act 1968, section 16 (1).
5. *Ibid.*, section 23.

(c) it is delivered to a bank within two " banking days " for payment or collection.[1]

It is expressly provided that nothing in the Gaming Acts of 1710, 1835, 1845 or 1892 shall affect the validity of, or any remedy in respect of, any cheque which is accepted in exchange for cash or tokens to be used by a player on premises licensed or registered under Part II of the Act of 1968.[2]

The third proposition concerns loans made for the purpose of gaming in foreign countries and later sued upon in England. It is now well established that money lent for the purpose of play abroad can be recovered in England, provided that it is recoverable in the country where the gaming takes place.[3] Moreover, a lender who accepts an English cheque or other security in payment of the amount, though he is precluded by the Acts of 1710 and 1835 from enforcing the security, may disregard the cheque and successfully maintain an action in England upon the original contract of loan.[4]

(iii) Loans for gaming abroad

Fourthly, a lender who pays the amount of the loan, not to the borrower, but directly to the person to whom the borrower has lost money under a wagering contract, whether it be a wager upon a game or some other event, has no right of recovery.[5] Further it was held in *MacDonald* v. *Green*[6] that there is no right of recovery if the money is paid directly to the borrower, provided that it is lent subject to an undertaking that it shall be passed to the winner in discharge of the bet. The reason in these cases is that the money has been paid " under or in respect of " a wagering contract, and is therefore rendered irrecoverable by the Gaming Act 1892. For the same reason the amount of a loan is irrecoverable if, at the request of the borrower, it is paid to a stakeholder to abide the event of a wager made by the borrower with a third party.[7]

(iv) Money paid by lender to or for winner

Fifthly, money lent to a borrower and used by him to pay bets which he has already lost is recoverable,[8] provided that it does not impose any obligation upon him to employ the money in this particular manner. The contract of loan in this case is unobjectionable. It is not void under the Gaming Act 1845 since it is not a wagering contract; it is not caught by the Gaming Acts 1710 and 1835 which, so far as regards loans, are confined to money lent for the purpose of gaming or betting on games, and do not extend to loans in respect of games or bets already completed; and it is not void under the Gaming Act 1892 for

(v) Money put at free disposal of borrower, but used to pay bets

---

1. *Ibid.*, section 16 (2) and (3). The expression " banking days " means a day which is a business day under section 92 of the Bills of Exchange Act 1882; Gaming Act 1968, section 16 (5).
2. Gaming Act 1968, section 16 (4), in conjunction with section 9.
3. *Quarrier* v. *Colston* (1842), Ph. 147; *Saxby* v. *Fulton*, [1909] 2 K.B. 208.
4. *Société Anonyme des Grands Etablissements du Touquet Paris-Plage* v. *Baumgart* (1927), 96 L.J.K.B. 789.
5. *Tatam* v. *Reeve*, [1893] 1 Q.B. 44; *Woolf* v. *Freeman*, [1937] 1 All E.R. 178; *Saffery* v. *Mayer*, [1901] 1 K.B. 11. *C. H. T., Ltd.* v. *Ward, supra.*
6. [1951] 1 K.B. 594; [1950] 2 All E.R. 1240; *Hill* v. *Fox* (1859), 4 H. & N. 359.
7. *Carney* v. *Plimmer*, [1897] 1 Q.B. 634.
8. *Re O'Shea, Ex parte Lancaster*, [1911] 2 K.B. 981.

the money is at the free disposal of the borrower and therefore, in the view of the Court of Appeal, it has not been paid to him " under or in respect of " a wagering contract.

> " The distinction is clear enough: a loan which leaves the borrower at liberty to apply the money as he wishes, is not invalidated by the Gaming Act 1892, even though it is contemplated by both parties that he will probably pay betting debts with it; but when a loan is hampered by a stipulation that the money is to be used for payment of a betting debt, then no matter whether the stipulation is express or implied or to be inferred from the circumstances, the loan is a payment in respect of the betting debt and is hit by the Act."[1]

The Court of Appeal construed a contract in the first of these two senses, in the case of *Re O'Shea*,[2] where one Lancaster guaranteed the overdraft of a debtor to the extent of £500 which in fact enabled him to pay lost bets. The debt that thus became due to Lancaster was held to be valid and enforceable. KENNEDY, L.J., described the position in these words:

> " What was done here was that the debtor went to Lancaster and said ' I have incurred a debt. Will you increase the guarantee to the bank in order to enable me to pay it? ' I cannot without forcing the words treat that as a transaction in which there was a payment by Lancaster to the creditor. There has been no payment by him ' in respect of any contract or engagement ' and unless there has been such a payment the statute does not apply."[3]

Thus what should be observed with some care is that a loan is not irrecoverable under the Gaming Act 1892 unless there is a definite agreement, express or implied, that the money is to be used for gaming or for paying lost bets. The mere probability that it will be so used is no bar to recovery. In the *Carlton Hall* case there was perhaps some justification for inferring an agreement in that sense, since apparently the poker chips were useless for any other purpose; in *MacDonald* v. *Green* the Court of Appeal was satisfied that the understanding to apply the money to the payment of betting losses was a true term of the contract; but in *Re O'Shea* the evidence disclosed no obligation binding the borrower to employ the money for any particular purpose.

Loan for purpose of non-gaming wager

Lastly, the question whether money lent for the purpose of making a bet, or paying a lost bet, on a non-gaming wager, which has not yet called for a judicial decision, presumably depends upon the same considerations. The money will be recoverable unless it is lent subject to a binding obligation, express or implied, that it is to be used solely for the purpose of betting.

1. *Macdonald* v. *Green*, [1951] 1 K.B. 594, at pp. 605–6; [1950] 2 All E.R. 1240, at pp. 1244–5, *per* DENNING, L.J.
2. [1911] 2 K.B. 981.
3. [1911] 2 K.B., at p. 988.

B. RESTRICTIVE TRADING AGREEMENTS

Part I of the Restrictive Trade Practices Act 1956[1] provides for the registration and judicial investigation of certain kinds of restrictive trading agreements. Stated in bare outline, this part of the Act defines the particular agreements to which it applies, and provides for their registration with the Registrar of Restrictive Trading Agreements[2] and for their reference by him to the Restrictive Practices Court. The court has then to determine whether or not the restrictions accepted under the agreements are " contrary to the public interest." If the court finds this to be the case, the agreement is rendered void in respect of the offending restrictions. Once an agreement has become subject to the Act, it remains registrable and therefore justiciable by the court, notwithstanding that the parties later terminate it altogether or remove its restrictive content.[3] The court is enabled to restrain the parties from making another registrable agreement to the like effect;[4] but, whereas before 1968 the Registrar was under a statutory duty to refer all registered agreements to the court, he now has a discretion whether or not to refer an agreement which the parties have terminated either as a whole or in respect of its restrictive terms.[5]

The statutory definition of registrable agreements is too long to give in a general work on contract;[6] but it is plainly a very wide one. Broadly it includes any agreement or arrangement,[7] whether or not intended to be enforceable by legal proceedings, between persons carrying on business in the United Kingdom in the production, supply or processing of goods, by which restrictions are accepted by two or more persons as to (a) the prices to be charged, quoted or paid for goods;[8] (b) the conditions of sale; (c) the quantities or descriptions of goods to be produced, supplied or acquired; and (d) the persons to or from whom, or the areas or places in or from which, goods are to be supplied or acquired. Since 1973 the Secretary of State has power, exercisable by statutory instrument, to extend the Act to restrictive agreements relating to services.[9] Also made registrable is an arrangement,

[margin note:] Restrictive Trade Practices Act 1956, Part I

[margin note:] Agreements to which the Act applies

---

1. As amended by the Restrictive Trade Practices Act 1968 and the Fair Trading Act 1973.
2. Fair Trading Act 1973, s. 94 transfers the functions of the Registrar to the Director-General of Fair Trading.
3. *Re Newspaper Proprietors' Agreement* (1963), L.R. 4 R.P. 361; [1964] 1 All E.R. 55.
4. Restrictive Trade Practices Act 1956, s. 20 (3).
5. Restrictive Trade Practices Act 1968, s. 9 (1).
6. For the agreements to which Part I of the Act applies, see ss. 6 to 8 of the 1956 Act, and their interpretation in *Registrar of Restrictive Trading Agreements* v. *Schweppes, Ltd.* (*No.* 2), [1971] 1 W.L.R. 1148. For a full discussion of the 1956 Act, see Wilberforce, Campbell and Elles, *Restrictive Trade Practices and Monopolies.*
7. For the meaning of " arrangement " see *Re British Basic Slag, Ltd.'s Agreements* (1963), L.R. 4 R.P. 116; [1963] 2 All E.R. 807; and *Re Mileage Conference Group of the Tyre Manufacturers' Agreement* (1966), L.R. 6 R.P. 49; [1966] 2 All E.R. 849.
8. See *Re Yarn Spinners' Agreement* (1959), L.R. 1 R.P. 118; [1959] 1 All E.R. 299; where an agreement to observe a minimum price scheme was declared to be contrary to the public interest.
9. Fair Trading Act 1973, Part X.

though not meant to be legally enforceable, which as a result of communication between the parties, intentionally arouses in each an expectation that the other will act in a certain manner.[1]   By the Restrictive Trade Practices Act 1968, section 5, the scope of the 1956 Act was widened so as to provide for the registration of " information agreements."   The importance of this extension is that it brings within the definition of a registrable agreement, arrangements for the exchange of information about prices which could be used so as to have the same effect as price fixing agreements.   But, although most information agreements inhibit competition, it is known that some of them are actually beneficial and so they have not been made automatically registrable.   It will therefore normally be necessary only to register those classes of agreement which are regarded as potentially damaging to the public interest.[2]

Certain agreements are wholly exempt from registration under Part I of the 1956 Act; but generally the Act applies to all agreements, whether made in writing or not.   Specific recommendations made by a trade association to its members must also be registered if they concern the action to be taken or not to be taken in relation to any particular class of goods or process of manufacture in respect of prices and other matters which, if contained, in an agreement, would make the agreement registrable.[3]

By section 6 of the 1968 Act, particulars of a registrable agreement must be furnished by the parties to the Registrar before the restrictions in it take effect or within three months of the making of the agreement, whichever is the earlier.   The purpose of this section and of the following section 7, whereby any registrable agreement which is not registered within the time limits prescribed by the 1968 Act is rendered void and its operation unlawful as respects the restrictions, is to facilitate the enforcement of the 1956 Act by providing a substantial deterrent against failure to register.   Furthermore, under the 1968 Act the Registrar may now ask for an injunction to restrain the parties to such an agreement from enforcing or carrying out the restrictions (or from enforcing or carrying out other registrable agreements which have not been duly registered), and any person who has been injured by the operation of such an agreement is given a remedy in damages.[4]

After registration every agreement (other than agreements too insignificant for reference) is referred to the court which then decides whether the restrictions contained in the agreement are contrary to the public interest.[5]

---

1. *Re British Basic Slag, Ltd.'s Agreements, supra.*
2. The Restrictive Trade Practices (Information Agreements) Order 1969 (S.I. No. 1842) requires the registration (and subsequent judicial examination) of information agreements relating to prices and conditions of supply.
3. Restrictive Trade Practices Act 1956, s. 6 (7).   For an important case on the interpretation of this subsection, see *Re National Federation of Retail Newsagents, Booksellers and Stationers,* [1969] 3 All E.R. 97.
4. Restrictive Trade Practices Act 1968, s. 7 (2).
5. Restrictive Trade Practices Act 1956, s. 20 (1) and (2): Restrictive Trade Practices Act 1968, s. 9 (2).   For a further reference to the Act, see *infra*, pp. 387–9.

Since the United Kingdom joined the European Economic Community[1] it has been necessary to consider also the competition rules of that community. The central rule is contained in art. 85 (1) of the Treaty of Rome which provides:

> The following shall be prohibited as incompatible with the common market: all agreements between undertakings, decisions by associations of undertakings and concerted practices which may affect trade between Member States and which have as their object or effect the prevention, restriction or distortion of competition within the common market, and in particular those which:
>
> (a) directly or indirectly fix purchase or selling prices or any other trading conditions;
> (b) limit or control production, markets, technical development, or investment;
> (c) share markets or sources of supply;
> (d) apply dissimilar conditions to equivalent transactions with other trading parties, thereby placing them at a competitive disadvantage;
> (e) make the conclusion of contracts subject to acceptance by the other parties of supplementary obligations which, by their nature or according to commercial usage, have no connection with the subject of such contracts.

This article and its supporting structure has produced a complex body of law into which it would be inappropriate to venture here[2] but we may make a few observations:

(a) Article 85 (1) only applies to agreements which affect trade between member states and so many domestic English transactions will not fall within its scope. It is certainly not limited however to agreements between companies or persons in different member states and so some agreements whose apparent effect is limited to one county will be held to affect trade between member states.[3]

(b) Questions of community law can be raised and decided in the English courts. In such proceedings the Court may have to decide whether to refer the questions to the European Court.[4] Such a reference may offer attractive possibilities of delay to one party. English judges have so far tended to take a robust attitude to requests for such references and to the disposition of EEC questions in the course of litigation.[5]

(c) The pattern of the EEC legislation and its interpretation by the European Court is noticeably different from that of the English Law. Thus the EEC test is more frankly economic than that in the Restrictive Trade Practices Act and its application may therefore be harder for lawyers to predict.[6] The EEC

---

1. European Communities Act 1972. The effective date of joining the Community was January 1st, 1973.
2. See Bellamy and Child, *Common Market Law of Competition* (1973).
3. See Bellamy and Child, *op. cit.*, paras. 235–236 and 342–344.
4. See Jacobs, 90 L.Q.R. 486.
5. See *Minnesota Mining and Manufacturing Co.* v. *Geerpres Europe*, [1973] C.M.L.R. 259; *Lerose* v. *Hawick Jersey International*, [1973] C.M.L.R. 83; *Esso Petroleum Co.* v. *Kingswood Motors (Addlestone)*, [1974] Q.B. 142; [1973] 3 All E.R. 1057.
6. This raises the whole question, which has been much discussed in England, of " justiciability "—that is, whether the questions which are asked of the courts in the area of a kind that they are equipped to answer by the usual legal techniques. See Stevens and Yamey, *The Restrictive Practices Court.*

legislation provides for fines imposed by the commission for infringement of the treaty provisions but there is no such provision in English law.[1]

(d) There are clearly potential problems of overlap between the two systems.[2]   No problem arises with an agreement which does not effect trade between member states since this is subject only to English law.   But an agreement which does so affect trade may be attacked as invalid both under EEC law and under English law.   The European Communities Act 1972, s. 10 contains provisions to deal with this eventuality, principally the granting to the Director General of Fair Trading of discretion to refrain from taking proceedings and to the Court to delay or decline the taking of jurisdiction in such circumstances.   This provision does not however appear to cover the situation where the agreement is attacked as being contrary to art. 85 (1) of the Treaty of Rome and is said also to be contrary to the common law rules about restraint of trade.[3]   It would seem that the test of validity must be cumulative, that is that an agreement is invalid unless it is valid both under Community law and English law.   If both systems treat the agreement as invalid, murky problems would then be involved as to which system should determine the *effects* of that invalidity but it is thought probable that community rules should prevail.[4]

C. ARRANGEMENTS FOR THE MAINTENANCE OF RESALE PRICES[5]

Object of
Resale
Prices Act
1964

The purpose of the Resale Prices Act 1964 is to prevent manufacturers and other suppliers of any goods which do not qualify for exemption under the Act from imposing conditions for maintaining minimum prices at which those goods may be resold, and to prohibit the enforcement of such prices by the withholding of supplies from dealers who do not observe them.   The effect of the Act is to give individual traders freedom to reduce prices at their own discretion.   Provision is made for the exemption by the Restrictive Practices Court of a resale price arrangement where there is evidence to show that the injury to the public which is presumed to exist in maintained prices is outweighed by

---

1. There is also the EEC doctrine of provision validity, which promises to give rise to some fine scholastic arguments.   See Bellamy and Child, *op. cit.*, paras. 410–422; Dashwood, [1974] C.L.J. 116.
2. See Korah, *Competition Law of Britain and the Common Market*, pp. 227–230.
3. See *infra*, pp. 368–389.
4. See Bellamy and Child, *op. cit.*, paras. 404 and 405.
5. This subject is dealt with in the present chapter because the relevant statute— the Resale Prices Act 1964—renders void certain terms for establishment of minimum prices contained in a contract.   The Act, indeed, makes the inclusion of such a term in a contract of sale an unlawful act on the part of the supplier, but this does not make the contract illegal.

other specific detriments.[1]   It is to be noted, however, that it is any arrangement for the maintainance of *minimum* resale prices against which the Act is directed and that a supplier still has the right to maintain and enforce *maximum* prices in the rare instances in which he may wish to exercise it.

Avoidance of condition for maintaining resale prices

Subject to the exemption procedure, any term or condition of a contract for the sale of goods by a supplier[2] to a dealer, or of any agreement[3] between a supplier and a dealer relating to such a sale, is made *void* by the Act in so far as it provides for the establishment of minimum prices to be charged on the resale of the goods.   Moreover, it is *unlawful* for any supplier of goods to include or require the inclusion of any such provision in any contract of sale or agreement relating to the sale of goods, or to notify to dealers or otherwise to publish resale prices.   There is nothing, however, to prevent a supplier from recommending or suggesting minimum resale prices.[4]

Withholding of supplies unlawful

But, although before the Act, minimum resale price conditions could be enforced by legal proceedings, there could also be, and in practice there very often was, enforcement by the withholding of supplies, or the threat to withhold supplies, from those who had not observed the resale price.   Consequently, the Act makes it *unlawful* for any supplier to withhold supplies of goods from a dealer seeking to obtain them for resale on the ground that he has sold or is likely to sell the goods at less than the resale price.[5]   Any supplier who refuses or fails to supply goods to the dealer; or who refuses to supply goods to the dealer save at prices or on terms or conditions as to credit, discount or other matters significantly less favourable than those at or on which he normally supplies those goods to other dealers carrying on business in similar circumstances; or who treats the dealer in a manner significantly less favourable than that in which he normally treats other such dealers in respect of times or methods of delivery or other matters, is treated, for the purposes of the Act, as withholding supplies of goods from a dealer.[6]   On the other hand, a supplier is not to be treated as withholding supplies of goods on any of these grounds if he had other valid grounds for withholding supplies.[7]   Thus

---

1. Resale Prices Act 1964, section 5 (2).   An arrangement for minimum resale prices may be allowed if, in the opinion of the court, its invalidation would mean that:
   - (a) the quantity or variety of the goods available for sale would be substantially reduced;
   - (b) the number of retail establishments would be substantially reduced;
   - (c) the retail prices of the goods would in general and in the long run be increased;
   - (d) the goods would be sold by retail under conditions likely to cause damage to health in consequence of their misuse by consumers;
   - (e) the provision of after-sale services would be substantially reduced.
2. A supplier is defined as any person carrying on a business of selling goods other than a business in which goods are sold only by retail: Resale Prices Act 1964, section 11 (1).
3. Agreements expressly authorized by any enactment or by any scheme, order or other instrument made under any enactment are exempt; Resale Prices Act 1964, section 13.
4. Resale Prices Act 1964, section 1 (1); section 1 (4).
5. *Ibid.*, s. 2 (1).
6. *Ibid.*, s. 2 (3).
7. *Ibid.*, s. 2 (4).

manufacturers who do not supply prospective price cutters because they do not have suitable establishments for the sale of their products or because they do not provide a proper service are not acting in breach of the Act.[1]   A supplier is also entitled to withhold supplies of any goods from a dealer who has within the past twelve months been using as " loss leaders " any goods of the same or a similar description.[2]

Any contravention of the foregoing provisions is enforceable by civil proceedings for an injunction or other appropriate relief brought on behalf of the Crown; and any individual affected has a remedy against the supplier by way of action for breach of statutory duty.[3]

Power of court to exempt classes of goods

Reference has already been made to the power of the Restrictive Practices Court by order to direct that particular classes of goods shall be exempted goods for the purposes of the Act. Before any such Order can be made by the court, however, it is necessary for the supplier to show that, in default of a system of maintained minimum resale prices applicable to those goods, the public (as consumers or users of those goods) would suffer detriment on any one or more of the five grounds of exemption specified in the Act and, in addition, that any such detriment would outweigh the injury to the public resulting from the maintenance of minimum resale prices in respect of the goods.[4]   A modern case in which the registered suppliers applied for exemption from the general ban on resale price maintenance on four of the five statutory grounds is *Re Chocolate and Sugar Confectionery Resale Price Reference*.[5] The grounds there relied on by the suppliers were that without fixed resale prices there would, as a result of price cutting, be such a substantial shift of trade from those confectionery shops which stocked a wide variety of confectionery to the supermarkets and self-service grocers as would result in a substantial reduction of (i) variety, (ii) retail establishments, and (iii) necessary services provided in connection with or after the sale of confectionery. It was also contended that without fixed resale prices manufacturers would have to increase trade margins to save confectionery shops from extinction, and that these increased margins would be reflected in higher retail prices. On none of these grounds did the suppliers succeed, however, in making out their case for exemption.

Registration of goods for exemption

Suppliers practising minimum resale price maintenance were allowed a period of three months beginning one month after the passing of the Act, *i.e.* July 16th, 1964, in which to give notice to the Registrar in respect of goods of any description supplied by them for which they claimed exemption. The Registrar was required to keep a register of goods in respect of which notices had been given to him and to make references to the court in

---

. *.e Footwear Reference (No. 2)*, [1968] 3 All E.R. 129; [1968] 1 W.L.R.
-555; where the withholding of goods by a supplier from a supermarket on the ground that it did not provide a proper fitting service for its customers was held not to be unlawful.
2. Resale Prices Act 1964, section 1 (1); section 3.
3. *Ibid.*, section 4 (2) and (3).
4. *Ibid.*, section 5 (2).
5. (1967), L.R. 6 R.P. 338; [1967] 3 All E.R. 261. See *supra*, p. 317.

respect of all such goods.[1] Once a notice had been given by a supplier in respect of any goods, all goods of that description were then treated as exempted goods pending the court's decision on the reference.

It should be observed that section 25 of the Restrictive Trade Practices Act 1956 is not repealed by the Resale Prices Act. Subsection (1) of this section, which it is also necessary to consider below in the chapter on privity of contract,[2] gives suppliers the right to enforce price conditions against third parties, provided that the latter have acquired the goods with notice of the condition. Although, apart from exempted goods, conditions for maintaining minimum resale prices are made void by the Resale Prices Act, the subsection may still be required, for the individual enforcement of conditions fixing a *maximum* price; or for the enforcement by a supplier of a condition fixing the *minimum* price at which exempted goods may be re-sold. Only two exemption orders have been made by the court[3] and orders have been refused in respect of all the other classes of registered goods. Thus the subsection, while it may still be invoked in certain circumstances, is in reality now almost obsolete.

---

1. Resale Prices Act 1964, s. 6 (1) and (2).
2. It is important to note the distinction between collective and individual enforcement; *infra*, p. 325. See also *infra*, pp. 450–2.
3. The first order made in 1968 was in respect of books and related goods and the second, made in 1970, was in respect of medicaments and related goods. These are, therefore, the only goods in respect of which resale price maintenance is now permissible.

CHAPTER FOUR

Contracts Illegal by Statute or at Common Law

SECTION I. CONTRACTS PROHIBITED BY STATUTE

A CONTRACT that is expressly or implicitly prohibited by statute is illegal. In this context, " statute " includes the orders, rules and regulations that ministers of the Crown and other officials are so frequently authorized by Parliament to make.

If the contract in fact made by the parties is expressly for-bidden by the statute, its illegality is undoubted. Express statutory prohibition of contracts is by no means uncommon. So Parlia-ment may provide in pursuance of a policy of controlling credit, that no contract of hire-purchase shall be entered into, unless at least 25 % of the cash price is paid by way of an initial payment.[1] Where it is alleged that the prohibition is implied, the court is presented with a problem the solution of which depends upon the construction of the statute. What must be ascertained is whether the object of the legislature is to forbid the contract. In pursuing this enquiry a variety of tests have been applied. For instance, if the sole object of the statute is to increase the national revenue, as for instance by requiring a trader to take out a licence; or to punish the contracting party who fails to furnish certain par-ticulars, the contract that he may have made is not itself pro-hibited and is in no sense tainted with illegality.[2] On the other hand, if even one of the objects is the protection of the public or the furtherance of some other aspect of public policy, a contract that fails to comply with the statute is implicitly prohibited.[3] But no one test is decisive, for in every case the purpose of the legislature must be considered in the light of all the relevant facts and circumstances.[4]

It has recently been persuasively argued that the decisive question ought to be whether the statute necessarily contemplates that the prohibited acts will be done in performance of a contract.[5] The distinction can be simply illustrated. Let us suppose that a Road Traffic Act makes it an offence (a) to sell a car in unroad-worthy condition and (b) to drive on certain roads at more than 30 mph.[6] It can readily be seen that breach of provision (a) will always involve the making of a contract, while breach of pro-vision (b) will only in exceptional circumstances do so. It is plausible therefore to argue that the statute impliedly prohibits contracts to sell unroadworthy cars but does not impliedly prohibit contracts to drive cars in excess of the speed limit.[7]

Prohibition may be implied

---

1. See, *e.g. Stoneleigh Finance, Ltd.* v. *Phillips,* [1965] 2 Q.B. 537; [1965] 1 All E.R. 513; *Kingsley* v. *Sterling Industrial Securities, Ltd.,* [1967] 2 Q.B. 747; [1966] 2 All E.R. 414.
2. *Learoyd* v. *Bracken,* [1894] 1 Q.B. 114.
3. *Victorian Daylesford Syndicate* v. *Dott,* [1905] 2 Ch. 624, at p. 630.
4. *St. John Shipping Corporation* v. *Joseph Rank, Ltd.,* [1957] 1 Q.B. 267, at pp. 285–7; [1956] 3 All E.R. 683, at p. 690, *per* DEVLIN, J.; *infra,* p. 324.
5. Buckley, 38 M.L.R. 535.
6. See Road Traffic Act 1934, s. 8 (1), reversed Road Traffic Act 1972, s. 60 (5) and *Vinall* v. *Howard,* [1953] 2 All E.R. 515; [1953] 1 W.L.R. 987 (reversed on other grounds, [1954] 1 Q.B. 375; [1954] 1 All E.R. 458).
7. Such a contract may still be illegal on common law principles, as being a contract to commit a crime. See *infra,* pp. 333.

An example of a revenue statute is afforded by *Smith* v. *Mawhood*,[1] where a tobacconist was allowed to recover the price of tobacco delivered, notwithstanding his failure to take out a licence and to have his name painted on his place of business as he was statutorily required to do under a penalty of £200. PARKE, B., said:

> " I think the object of the legislation was not to prohibit a contract of sale by dealers who have not taken out a licence pursuant to the Act of Parliament. If it was, they certainly could not recover, although the prohibition was merely for the purpose of revenue. But looking to the Act of Parliament, I think its object was not to vitiate the contract itself, but only to impose a penalty upon the party offending for the purposes of the revenue."[2]

Again, a stockbroker who has bought or sold shares for his principal is not prevented from recovering his commission by his failure in breach of the Stamp Act 1891, to issue a stamped contract note containing details of the transaction.[3]

The more numerous statutes, however, are those directed either to the protection of the public or to the fulfilment of some object of general policy. This is especially true at the present day when State intervention in individual activity is more pronounced than formerly and where even revenue statutes are used in part at least as instruments of policy.

The approach of the courts to this problem of implied prohibition may be illustrated by contrasting the two cases of *Cope* v. *Rowlands*[4] and *Archbolds (Freightage), Ltd.* v. *S. Spanglett, Ltd.*[5]

In the former, a statute provided that any person who acted as broker in the City of London without first obtaining a licence should forfeit and pay to the City the sum of £25 for every such offence. The plaintiff, who was unlicensed, sued the defendant for work that he had done in buying and selling stock. In delivering judgment for the defendant, PARKE, B., said:

> " The legislature had in view, as one object, the benefit and security of the public in those important transactions which are negotiated by brokers. The clause, therefore, which imposes a penalty, must be taken . . . to imply a prohibition of all unadmitted persons to act as brokers, and consequently to prohibit by necessary inference all contracts which such persons make for compensation to themselves for so acting."[6]

The facts of *Archbolds (Freightage), Ltd.* v. *S. Spanglett, Ltd.*[7] were as follows:

> The Road and Rail Traffic Act 1933 provided that no person should *use* a vehicle for the carriage of goods unless he held an 'A' or a 'C' licence. The former entitled him to carry the goods of others for reward; the latter to carry his own goods but not the goods of others.
> The defendants, who held a 'C' licence, agreed with the plaintiffs to carry 200 crates of whisky belonging to third parties from

---

1. (1845), 14 M. & W. 452.
2. *Ibid.*, at p. 463.
3. *Learoyd* v. *Bracken*, [1894] 1 Q.B. 114.
4. (1836), 2 M. & W. 149.
5. [1961] 1 Q.B. 374; [1961] 1 All E.R. 417.
6. (1836), 2 M. & W., at p. 159.
7. [1961] 1 Q.B. 374; [1961] 1 All E.R. 417; see Furmston, 24 M.L.R. 394.

Leeds to London. The plaintiffs were unaware that the defendants held no 'A' licence. The whisky was stolen *en route* and the plaintiffs claimed damages for its loss.

One question that arose in the action,[1] was whether the contract for carriage was prohibited by the Act, either expressly or implicitly.

It was not expressly prohibited, for the Act did not in terms strike at a contract to carry goods, but at the use of an unlicensed vehicle on the road. It was not as if the plaintiffs had contracted for the use of an unlicensed vehicle and had used it themselves. It was argued, however, that contracts for the carriage of goods made with unlicensed carriers were implicitly forbidden by the Act. This depended upon the construction of the Act. What was its fundamental purpose?[2] The Court of Appeal was satisfied that the instant contract did not fall within the ambit of the legislation and that there was no implied prohibition. In the words of PEARCE, L.J.:

> " The object of the Road and Rail Traffic Act 1933, was not (in this connection) to interfere with the owner of goods or his facilities for transport, but to control those who provided the transport, with a view to promoting its efficiency. Transport of goods was not made illegal, but the various licence holders were prohibited from encroaching on one another's territory, the intention of the Act being to provide an orderly and comprehensive service."[3]

A distinction which has an important bearing upon the consequences of illegality is that the disregard of a statutory prohibition may render the contract either illegal as formed or illegal as performed.[4] *(margin: Illegality may infect either formation or performance of contract)*

A contract is illegal as formed if its very creation is prohibited, as for example where one of the parties has neglected to take out a licence as required by statute.[5] In such a case it is void *ab initio*. It is a complete nullity under which neither party can acquire rights whether there is an intention to break the law or not. *(margin: Contract illegal as formed)*

A contract is illegal as performed if, though lawful in its formation, it is performed by one of the parties in a manner prohibited by statute. In *Anderson, Ltd.* v. *Daniel*,[6] for instance: *(margin: Contract illegal as performed)*

> A statute required that every seller of artificial fertilizers should give to the buyer an invoice stating the percentages of certain chemical substances contained in the goods. In the instant case, the sellers had delivered ten tons of artificial manure without complying with the statutory requirement. The sellers brought an action for the price of the goods.

In such circumstances as these, where the contract is lawful in its inception but is executed illegally, the position of the party responsible for the infraction of the statute is clear. All contractual

---

1. For the further question, see *infra*, p. 324.
2. See *St. John Shipping Corporation* v. *Joseph Rank,* [1957] 1 Q.B. 267, at pp. 285–7; [1956] 3 All E.R. 683, at pp. 688–690: *infra*, p. 324.
3. [1961] 1 Q.B., at p. 386; [1961] 1 All E.R., at p. 423.
4. See especially the judgment of DEVLIN, J., in *St. John Shipping Corporation* v. *Joseph Rank Ltd.,* [1957] 1 Q.B. 267, at pp. 283–7.
5. *Cope* v. *Rowlands* (1836), 2 M. & W. 149, *supra*, p. 322; *Re Mahmoud and Ispahani,* [1921] 2 K.B. 716, *infra*, p. 346; *Bostel Brothers, Ltd.* v. *Hurlock,* [1949] 1 K.B. 74; [1948] 2 All E.R. 312.
6. [1924] 1 K.B. 138.

rights and remedies are withheld from him. Thus the sellers in *Anderson, Ltd.* v. *Daniel* lost their action. They had failed to perform the contract in the only way in which the statute allowed it to be performed. On the other hand, as will be seen later,[1] the appropriate remedies are available to the other party provided that he can establish his innocence. If, however, he has been privy to or has condoned the illegality, he will be in the same position as if the contract had been illegal in its formation and he will therefore be remediless.[2]

Whether a contract is illegal as performed raises a question of construction But it must be emphasized that a contract is not automatically rendered illegal as performed merely because some statutory requirement has been violated in the course of its completion.[3] Whether this is the result raises a question of construction similar to that which was considered in *Archbolds (Freightage), Ltd.* v. *S. Spanglett, Ltd.*[4] What has to be determined here is whether it was the express or implied intention of the legislature that such a violation as that which the guilty party has committed should deprive him of all remedies. Was the observance of the particular enactment regarded as a necessary pre-requisite of his right to enforce the contract? That such is the intention, though clear enough in *Anderson, Ltd.* v. *Daniel*[5] is not lightly to be implied. Commercial life is nowadays hedged in by so many statutory regulations, that it would scarcely promote the interests of justice to drive a plaintiff from the seat of judgment merely because he has committed a minor transgression.[6]

If the contract as performed is not expressly prohibited by statute, its alleged illegality must be based upon public policy, and in a passage that has frequently been approved, Lord WRIGHT once remarked that public policy is often " better served by refusing to nullify a bargain save on serious and sufficient grounds."[7] The attitude of the courts where some statutory requirement has been infringed during the performance of a contract, may be illustrated by two leading cases.

In *St. John Shipping Corporation* v. *Joseph Rank, Ltd.*,[8] the facts were as follows:

> The Merchant Shipping Act 1932 forbids the loading of a ship to such an extent that the loadline becomes submerged. A penalty is imposed for breach of the statute.
> The master of the plaintiff's ship, which had been chartered to an English firm for the carriage of grain from a port in Alabama to England, put into a port in the course of the voyage and took on bunkers, the effect of which was to submerge the loadline contrary

---

1. *Infra*, pp. 343–5.
2. *B. & B. Viennese Fashions* v. *Lesane*, [1952] 1 All E.R. 909; *Ashmore, Benson, Pease & Co., Ltd.* v. *Dawson, Ltd.*, [1973] 2 All E.R. 856; [1973] 1 W.L.R. 828; criticized Hamson, [1973] C.L.J. 199. Cf. Buckley, 25 N.I.L.Q. 421.
3. See the rhetorical question of SACHS, L.J., in *Shaw* v. *Groom*, [1970] 2 Q.B. 504, at p. 522.
4. *Supra*, p. 322.
5. *Supra*, p. 323.
6. *St. John's Shipping Corporation* v. *Joseph Rank, Ltd.*, [1957] 1 Q.B. 267, at p. 522, *per* DEVLIN, J.; approved by SACHS, L.J., in *Shaw* v. *Groom*, [1970] 2 Q.B. 504, at p. 522.
7. *Vita Food Products* v. *Unus Shipping Co., Ltd.*, [1939] A.C. 277, at pp. 293; [1939] 1 All E.R. 513, at p. 523.
8. [1957] 1 Q.B. 267; [1956] 3 All E.R. 683.

to the Act. The master was prosecuted in England for the offence and was fined £1,200.

The defendants, to whom the ownership of part of the goods had passed, withheld part of the freight due, contending that the plaintiffs could not enforce a contract which they had performed in an illegal manner.

DEVLIN, J., rejected the contention. The illegal loading was merely an incident in the course of performance that did not affect the core of the contract.

> " In the statutes to which the principle has been applied, what was prohibited was a contract which had at its centre—indeed often filling the whole space within its circumference—the prohibited act; contracts for the sale of prohibited goods, contracts for the sale of goods without accompanying documents where the statute specifically said there must be accompanying documents; contracts for work and labour done by persons who were prohibited from doing all the work and labour for which they demanded recompense." [1]

Again, in *Shaw* v. *Groom*: [2]

> A landlord sued his tenant for arrears of rent amounting to £103 due in respect of a weekly tenancy. The tenant contended that the action must fail, since the rent book issued to him by the plaintiff did not contain all the information required by the Landlord and Tenant Act 1962. Such a default was punishable by a fine not exceeding £50.

The Court of Appeal dismissed this contention. The contract was not to be stigmatized as illegal in its performance. The intention of the legislature was that non-compliance with the statutory requirement should render the landlord liable to a fine, not that it should deny him access to the courts. Unless this limited construction was placed upon the Act, the result might well be that the landlord would forfeit a sum far in excess of the maximum fine. In the words of SACHS, L.J.:

> " It seems to me appropriate, accordingly, to allow this appeal on the broad basis that, even if the provision of a rent book is an essential act as between landlords and weekly tenants, yet the legislature did not by . . . the Act of 1962 intend to preclude the landlord from recovering any rent due or impose any forfeiture on him beyond the prescribed penalty." [3]

It would be inappropriate in a book of this nature to deal in detail with statutes that prohibit contracts, [4] but, as a modern example of importance, a short account is offered of Part II of the Restrictive Trade Practices Act 1956. It has already been seen in a former chapter that, by Part I of this Act, certain restrictive trading agreements may be declared *void* by the Restrictive Practices Court. [5] But by Part II one particular type of agreement, namely an agreement for the collective enforcement

Prohibited contract illustrated by Restrictive Trade Practices Act, Part II

---

1. *Ibid,,* [1957] 1 Q.B., at p. 289; [1956] 3 All E.R., at p. 691.
2. [1970] 2 Q.B. 504; [1970] 1 All E.R. 702.
3. [1970] 2 Q.B., at p. 526. HARMAN, L.J., also found for the plaintiff, but based his decision on the ground that the provision of a correctly completed rent book was not an essential part of the lawful performance of the contract; *ibid.,* at p. 516.
4. Two examples are the Truck Acts 1831–1940, as amended by the Payment of Wages Act 1960; and the Betting, Gaming and Lotteries Act 1963, as amended by the Gaming Act 1968.
5. *Supra,* pp. 313 *et seq.*

of conditions regulating the price at which goods may be re-sold, is prohibited and made *unlawful*.

It has long been a common practice for manufacturers to include in a contract of sale a term that the goods shall not be re-sold at less than a fixed price. At common law such a term was binding upon the contracting parties, but, in accordance with the doctrine of privity of contract, it could not be enforced against persons who bought from the original purchaser.[1] The method adopted by industry to avoid this legal difficulty has. been to bring economic pressure to bear upon dealers, as for example by members of a trade association agreeing between themselves that they will not supply traders who have been put on a stop list for cutting prices, or that they will supply only traders whose names are included in an approved list. This threat has sometimes been qualified by the setting up of a domestic tribunal before which an erring trader may attempt to justify what he has done and thus to avoid, perhaps upon payment of a fine, the sanction of a withdrawal of supplies.

At common law there is nothing necessarily unlawful in these forms of economic pressure. To place the name of a trader on a stop list is not defamatory,[2] a combined operation to withhold supplies from him is not a conspiracy,[3] and, though the combination may possibly be unreasonable in the interest of the parties themselves and may therefore be regarded as a contract in restraint of trade, it will not normally be regarded as contrary to the public interest.

The position has been radically altered by Part II of the Restrictive Trade Practices Act 1956. By this part of the Act an agreement between two or more persons carrying on business in the United Kingdom for the collective enforcement of such price restrictions is made unlawful. It must be observed at once that it is only the *collective* enforcement of restrictions that is condemned. *Individual* enforcement is expressly sanctioned by section 25 of the Restrictive Trade Practices Act 1956, which, as we have seen, must be read subject to the Resale Prices Act 1964.[4] The nature and extent of the right of enforcement is considered in its due place as an innovation upon the doctrine of privity.[5] The statutory provisions controlling *collective* enforcement are directed against two classes of persons—suppliers of goods and dealers who re-sell goods—their general theme being to prohibit any agreement designed to penalize or boycott a person who refuses to observe a scheme for the maintenance of fixed prices.

Thus any agreement or even any arrangement between two or more persons carrying on business in the United Kingdom as suppliers of goods is unlawful,

> if it provides that goods shall be withheld from dealers who have infringed a condition as to fixed prices,[6] or from any person, even

---

1. *Infra*, p. 450.
2. *Ware and De Freville* v. *Motor Trade Association*, [1921] 3 K.B. 40.
3. *Ibid*.
4. *Supra*, p. 316–9.
5. *Infra*, p. 451–2.
6. Restrictive Trade Practices Act 1956, s. 24 (1) (*a*).

though not himself a dealer, who refuses to undertake to withhold supplies from offending dealers;[1] or if it provides that terms less favourable than those usually given, as for example the cancellation of a trade discount,[2] shall be imposed upon offending dealers.[3]

Moreover, any agreement or arrangement authorizing the recovery of penalties or the setting-up of a domestic tribunal is also unlawful.[4]

It will be noticed that the only contracts prohibited are those which provide for the enforcement of certain defined sanctions, namely the withholding of supplies (which includes placing a dealer's name on a stop list), the recovery of penalties and the grant of terms less favourable than those normally given. It follows, therefore, than an agreement to visit a contumacious dealer with some other form of retribution, such as his expulsion from a trade association, is not *per se* unlawful,[5] though if the agreement also contains restrictions which make it subject to Part I of the Act, it may, of course, be declared void by the Restrictive Practices Court.[6]

Much the same provisions are applied to dealers who agree to boycott any supplier unwilling to observe a price maintenance scheme. An agreement or arrangement made between two or more dealers is unlawful if it provides that orders shall be withheld from or discrimination practised against suppliers who fail to observe or enforce conditions regulating the selling prices of goods.[7] As in the case of suppliers, an agreement for the exaction of penalties or for the setting up of a domestic tribunal is also rendered unlawful.[8]

Agreements between dealers

No criminal proceedings lie in respect of an agreement rendered unlawful by the Act, but the Crown may institute civil proceedings in the High Court for " an injunction or other appropriate relief."[9] The remedies available to a person other than the Crown, which are expressly saved by the Act, will vary with the particular circumstances of each case; but presumably they include the right to apply for an injunction and to recover damages for breach of contract or for inducing a breach of contract and, indeed, for conspiracy, since in most cases two or more persons will have conspired to do an unlawful act, *i.e.*, to make an agreement prohibited by statute.[10]

Remedial proceedings

---

1. *Ibid.*, s. 24 (1) (*c*).
2. *Ibid.*, s. 26 (1).
3. *Ibid.*, s. 24 (1) (*b*).
4. Restrictive Trade Practices Act 1956, s. 24 (1).
5. Wilberforce, Campbell and Elles, *Restrictive Trade Practices and Monopolies,* para. 913 (b).
6. Restrictive Trade Practices Act 1956, s. 20 (3); *supra,* pp. 316–9.
7. *Ibid.*, s. 24 (2).
8. *Ibid.*
9. *Ibid.*, s. 24 (7).
10. Wilberforce, Campbell and Elles, *op. cit.,* para. 923; Albery and Fletcher-Cooke, *Monopolies and Restrictive Trade Practices,* p. 104.

SECTION II.　CONTRACTS ILLEGAL AT COMMON LAW ON GROUNDS OF PUBLIC POLICY

A.　INTRODUCTION

Illegality
at common
law based
upon public
policy

Certain types of contract are forbidden at common law and are therefore *prima facie* illegal. The first essential to an understanding of this head of the law, which has been clouded by much confusion of thought, is to discover if possible the principle upon which the stigma of illegality is based. The present law is the result of a development that stretches back to at least Elizabethan times,[1] but its foundations were not effectively laid until the eighteenth century. What the judges of that period were at pains to emphasize was that they would not tolerate any contract that in their view was injurious to society.[2] Injury to society, however, is incapable of precise definition, and it is not surprising that the particular contracts found distasteful on this ground were described in somewhat vague and indeterminate language. To give a few examples, nobody would be allowed " to stipulate for iniquity,"[3] no contract would be enforced that was " contrary to the general policy of the law,"[4] or " injurious to and against the public good,"[5] or *contra bonos mores*[6] or which had arisen *ex turpi causa*.[7]

It seems justifiable to infer from such expressions as these that the judges were determined to establish and sustain a concept of public policy. Contractual freedom must be fostered, but any contract that tended to prejudice the social or economic interest of the community must be forbidden.

Contracts
contrary to
public
policy vary
in their
degree of
impropriety

Not unnaturally a principle stated in such sweeping terms as these has its disadvantages. It is imprecise, since judicial views will inevitably differ upon whether a particular contract is immoral or subversive of the common good; there is no necessary continuity in the general policy of the law, for what is anathema to one generation seems harmless to another; and the public good affects so many walks of life that the causes of action that can be said to arise *ex turpi causa* must in the nature of things vary greatly in their degree of harm to the community.

It is this variation in the degree of harm done that requires emphasis, for the word " illegal " has been, and still is, used to cover a multitude of sins and even cases where little, if any, sin can be discovered. The list of "illegal " contracts includes *inter alia* agreements to commit a crime or a tort, to defraud the revenue, to lend money to an alien enemy, to import liquor into a country where prohibition is in force, to procure a wife for X in return

---

1. Pollock, *Principles of Contract,* 13th Edn., p. 291, note by Winfield.
2. Fifoot, *Lord Mansfield,* pp. 122–5.
3. *Collins v. Blantern* (1767), 2 Wils. 341, at p. 350, *per* WILMOT, L.C.J.
4. *Lowe v. Peers* (1768), 4 Burr. 2225, at p. 2233, *per* ASTON, J.
5. *Collins v. Blantern, supra,* at p. 238.
6. *Girardy v. Richardson* (1793), 1 Esp. 13, *per* Lord KENYON.
7. *Holman v. Johnson* (1775), 1 Cowp. 341, at p. 343, *per* Lord MANSFIELD.

for a reward, to provide for a wife if she should ever separate from her husband and finally an agreement in restraint of trade between master and servant or between the seller and buyer of a business, such as that by which a servant promises not to work in the future for a trade rival of his present employer. If these contracts are scrutinized in the order given, it will be seen that the improbity which they reveal is a constantly diminishing factor and that it is entirely absent from the agreement in restraint of trade. There is nothing disgraceful in a master and servant coming to such an agreement, and the only complaint that their conduct invokes is the possible economic inexpedience of allowing a workman to restrict his freedom to exploit his skill as and where he will.

Commonsense suggests that the consequences at law of entering into one of these so-called illegal contracts should vary in severity according to the degree of impropriety that the conduct of the parties discloses. It is obvious that an agreement to commit a crime cannot be put on the same footing as an undertaking by a servant that he will not later enter the employment of a rival trader. The former is so transparently reprehensible judged by any standard of morals that it must be dismissed as illegal, with the result that both parties must be excluded from access to the courts and denied all remedies; but the latter should certainly not attract the full rigour of the maxim *ex turpi causa non oritur actio*, with its implication that it can originate no rights or liabilities whatsoever. The parties have done nothing disgraceful, they have not conspired against the proprieties and, although they cannot be allowed to enforce such part of the contract as is tainted, it would be unjustifiable to regard them as outcasts of the law unable to enforce even the innocent part of their bargain. To describe their contract as illegal as a whole is an abuse of language. Speaking of the contract in restraint of trade, for instance, FARWELL, L.J., said, " it is not unlawful in the sense that it is criminal or would give any cause of action to a third person injured by its operation, but it is unlawful in the sense that the law will not enforce it."[1] In the eighteenth century, when the principle of public policy was taking root and the instances of unsavoury bargains were comparatively simple, it was perhaps not strange that the judges should have used somewhat exaggerated language in rejecting contracts that revealed wickedness, but in the complex conditions of today the indiscriminate use of the term " illegal " is, to say the least, confusing.

Modern judges have in fact taken a more realistic view of this part of the law and have concluded that the so-called illegal contracts fall into two separate groups according to the degree

So-called illegal contracts fall into two classes according to degree of impropriety

---

1. *North Western Salt Co.* v. *Electrolytic Alkali Co.* (1912), 107 L.T. 439, at p. 444. See also *Mogul Steamship Co.* v. *McGregor, Gow & Co.,* [1892] A.C. 25, at p. 39, *per* Lord HALSBURY. In the court below (1889), 23 Q.B.D. 598, at p. 619, LINDLEY, L.J., said " The term ' illegal ' here is a misleading one. Contracts . . . in restraint of trade are not in my opinion illegal in any sense, except that the law will not enforce them." See also *A.-G. Commonwealth of Australia* v. *Adelaide Steamship Co., Ltd.,* [1913] A.C. 781, at p. 797, *per* Lord PARKER.

of mischief that they involve.[1] Some agreements are so obviously inimical to the interest of the community that they offend almost any concept of public policy; others violate no basic feelings of morality, but run counter only to social or economic expedience. The significance of their separation into two classes, as we shall see, lies in the different consequences that they involve.

That the various contracts traditionally called illegal do not involve similar consequences was stressed by SOMERVELL, L.J., in the following passage :[2]

> " In *Bennett* v. *Bennett*,[2] it was pointed out that there are two kinds of illegality of differing effect. The first is where the illegality is criminal or *contra bonos mores,* and in those cases, which I will not attempt to enumerate or further classify, such a provision [*sic*], if an ingredient in the contract, will invalidate the whole, although there may be many other provisions in it. There is a second kind of illegality which has no such taint; the other terms in the contract stand if the illegal portion can be severed, the illegal portion being a provision which the court, on ground of public policy, will not enforce. The simplest and most common example of the latter class of illegality is a contract for the sale of a business which contains a provision restricting the vendor from competing in or engaging in trade for a certain period or within a certain area. There are many cases in the books where, without in any way impugning the contract of sale, some provision restricting competition has been regarded as in restraint of trade and contrary to public policy. There are many cases where not only has the main contract to purchase been left standing, but part of the clause restricting competition has been allowed to stand."[3]

(i) Illegal contracts

Assuming, then, that contracts vitiated by some improper element must be divided into two classes, how are the more serious example of " illegality " at common law to be distinguished from the less serious? Which of the contracts that have been frowned upon by the courts are so patently reprehensible—so obviously contrary to public policy—that they must be peremptorily styled illegal? Judicial authority is lacking, but it is submitted that the epithet " illegal " may aptly and correctly be applied to the following six types of contract:

A contract to commit a crime, a tort or a fraud on a third party.
A contract that is sexually immoral.
A contract to the prejudice of the public safety.
A contract prejudicial to the administration of justice.
A contract that tends to corruption in public life.
A contract to defraud the revenue.

(ii) Void contracts

There remain three types of contract which offend " public policy," but which are inexpedient rather than unprincipled.

---

1. *Bennett* v. *Bennett*, [1952] 1 K.B. 249, at pp. 260–1; [1952] 1 All E.R. 413, at p. 421, *per* DENNING, L.J.; *Goodinson* v. *Goodinson,* [1954] 2 Q.B. 118, at pp. 120–1; [1954] 2 All E.R. 255, at p. 256, *per* SOMERVELL, L.J. The actual decision in *Bennett* v. *Bennett* was reversed by the Maintenance Agreements Act 1957; now the Matrimonial Causes Act 1973, s. 34.
2. [1952] 1 K.B. 249; [1952] 1 All E.R. 413.
3. *Goodinson* v. *Goodinson, supra,* footnote 2. It should be noticed that the concluding sentence of this citation refers to two forms of severance that are in fact distinguishable; see *infra*, pp. 393 *et seq.*

A contract to oust the jurisdiction of the courts.
A contract that tends to prejudice the status of marriage.
A contract in restraint of trade.

If the word " illegal " is to be reserved for the more reprehensible type of contract, another title must be chosen to designate those which fall within the second degree of public policy, and which for that reason have been treated with comparative leniency by the courts. The most appropriate title seems to be " void," since these contracts are in practice treated by the courts as void either as a whole or at least in part. In *Bennett* v. *Bennett*[1] DENNING, L.J., described covenants in restraint of trade as " void not illegal."

> " They are not ' illegal ' in the sense that a contract to do a prohibited or immoral act is illegal. They are not ' unenforceable ' in the sense that a contract within the Statute of Frauds is unenforceable for want of writing. These covenants lie somewhere in between. They are invalid and unenforceable."

The word " void " used as a descriptive title certainly has its disadvantages. It is already applied to a number of disparate contracts and is not applied to them in any uniform sense or with uniform results. At common law it has long been used to indicate the consequences of mistake; by statute it has been used with dubious results in wagering transactions and in contracts made by infants. But linguistic precision cannot survive the complexity of life. A continental jurist has said that, unlike the physical sciences where there is no interim stage between effect and no-effect, in legal science the effects of disobeying a legal rule may be graded to suit the individual situation.

Justification of the word " void "

> " Thus, the difference between an act that is valid and an act that is void is unlike the difference between ' yes ' and ' no,' between effect and no-effect. It is a difference of grade and quantity. Some effects are produced, while others are not."[2]

For better or for worse, then, it has been decided for the purposes of this book to describe the three less serious types of " illegal " contracts as *contracts void at common law on grounds of public policy*.

Some general observations must be added upon the doctrine of public policy in the current law.[3]

Current doctrine of public policy

Since public policy reflects the mores and fundamental assumptions of the community, the content of the rules should vary from country to country and from era to era. There is high authority for the view that in matters of public policy the courts should adopt a broader approach than they usually do to the use of precedents.[4]

Such flexibility may manifest itself in two ways: by the closing down of existing heads of public policy and by the opening of new heads. There is no doubt that an existing head of public

---

1. [1952] 1 K.B. 249, at p. 260; [1952] 1 All E.R. 413, at p. 421.
2. Baumgarten, cited by Cohn, 64 L.Q.R. 326.
3. See Lloyd, *Public Policy* (1953); Winfield, 42 Harvard L.R. 76; Gellhorn, 35 Columbia L.R. 679; Shand, [1972A] C.L.J. 144.
4. See *Nordenfelt* v. *Maxim Nordenfelt Guns and Ammunition Co.*, [1894] A.C. 535, *per* Lord WATSON, at p. 553.

policy may be declared redundant.   So in the nineteenth century
it was stated that Christianity was part of the law of England and
that accordingly a contract to hire a hall for a meeting to promote
atheism was contrary to public policy[1] but fifty years later this
view was decisively rejected.[2]

More controversy surrounds the question of whether the courts
still retain freedom to recognise new heads of public policy.   It
has been denied that any such freedom exists and Lord THANKER-
TON said that the task of the judge in this area was " to expound and
not to expand," the law.[4]   It may be thought surprising however
that in this of all areas, the courts should abrogate their
function of developing the common law.   To some extent the
discussion is artificial since much development may take place
within the existing heads but it is difficult to assert that new
circumstances cannot arise which do not fall readily into any of
the recognised heads.   Courts have responded to this challenge
in the past by the development of new heads[5] and it is thought
that they will, in exceptional circumstances, do so again.

This question would be relevant, for instance, if it were argued
that contracts involving racial, religious or sexual discrimination
were contrary to public policy.   It is arguable that the Court of
Appeal's decision in *Nagle* v. *Feilden*[6] represents recognition
of such a possibility and there is some Australian authority too.[7]
Undoubtedly any such argument would raise important questions,
in particular whether the existence of legislation in this area[8]
should be regarded as relevant either as (a) delimiting precisely
the area of reprehensible discriminatory conduct or (b) (preferably)
as a legislative signal that discrimination is against the public
interest.[9]   It is thought however that the least satisfactory
answer would be that the Law is totally petrified.

A final observation may be made as to the way in which the
courts determine the content of public policy.   Apart from reliance
on previous precedents, this is done by *a priori* deduction from
broad general principles.   It is not the practice in English courts for
the parties to lead sociological or economic evidence as to whether
particular practices are harmful and it is doubtful to what extent
such evidence would be regarded as relevant if it were adduced.[10]

---

1. *Cowan* v. *Milbourn* (1867), L.R. 2 Ex.Ch. 230.
2. *Bowman* v. *Secular Society*, [1917] A.C. 406.
3. See *Janson* v. *Driefontein Consolidated Mines*, [1902] A.C. 484, at p. 491.
4. *Fender* v. *St. John Mildmay*, [1938] A.C. 1, at p. 23; [1937] 3 All E.R. 402,
   at p. 407.   Cf. the illuminating judgment of WINDEYER, J., in *Brooks* v.
   Burns Philp Trustee Co., Ltd., [1969] A.L.R. 321, at pp. 331–349.
5. See, e.g. *Neville* v. *Dominion of Canada News Co., Ltd.*, [1915] 3 K.B.
   556; Furmston, 16 U. of Toronto L.J. 267, at pp. 293–7.
6. [1966] 2 Q.B. 633; [1966] 1 All E.R. 689.
7. *Newcastle Diocese (Church Property Trustees)* v. *Ebbeck* (1960), 34 A.L.J.R.
   413.
8. E.g. Race Relations Act 1968; Equal Pay Act 1970.
9. See further Lester and Bindman, *Race and Law* Hepple, *Race. Jobs and the
   Law in Britain;* Garner, 34 M.L.R. 478.
10. See, e.g. *Texaco, Ltd.* v. *Mulberry Filling Station*, [1972] 1 All E.R. 513,
    [1972] 1 W.L.R. 814.   Cf. the use of the Monopolies Commission Report
    in *Esso Petroleum Co., Ltd.* v. *Harpers Garage (Stourport), Ltd.*, [1968]
    A.C. 269; [1967] 1 All E.R. 699.   Cf. the use of the " Brandeis Brief " in
    American law: *Muller* v. *Oregon* 208 U.S. 412 (1908).

B. THE CONTRACTS DESCRIBED[1]

It is now necessary to describe and discuss the six contracts that are properly to be termed illegal at common law on the ground of public policy.

(i) A contract to commit a crime, a tort or a fraud on a third party

There is no need to stress the obvious fact that an agreement is illegal and void if its object, direct or indirect, is the commission of a crime or a tort. The rule has been applied to many cases, as for instance where the design was to obtain goods by false pretences;[2] to defraud prospective shareholders;[3] to disseminate obscene prints;[4] to publish a libel;[5] to assault a third party;[6] or to rig the market, i.e., artificially to enhance the true value of shares by entering into a contract to purchase them at a fictitious premium.[7]

An agreement made with the object of defrauding or deceiving[8] a third party is illegal, and a familiar illustration of this is where A agrees to recommend B for a post, whether public or private, in consideration that B, if appointed, will pay part of the emoluments or a secret commission to A.[9]

In this context it is appropriate to remember that the ambit of the crime of conspiracy is wide[10] and that any agreement which amounts to a criminal conspiracy will also be an illegal contract.

An allied rule of public policy is that no person shall be allowed to benefit from his own crime.[11] This is a doctrine of general application. So it is important not only in the law of contract but also, for example, in the law of succession. In one case, for instance, a wife, who had killed her husband by a single blow with a domestic chamber pot, was convicted of manslaughter by reason of her diminished responsibility and was sentenced to be detained without limit of time in Broadmoor hospital. Such a " hospital order " is remedial in nature, and it implies that the convicted person is not deserving of punishment. It was, therefore, argued that the wife was not precluded from taking a benefit under her deceased husband's will. The argument was rejected.

The fruits of a crime are irrecoverable

---

1. See Furmston, 16 U. of Toronto Law Journal 267.
2. *Berg* v. *Sadler and Moore,* [1937] 2 K.B. 158; [1937] 1 All E.R. 637. But for a criticism of this difficult case, see Furmston, 16 U. of Toronto Law Journal 267, at pp. 290–1. See Theft Act 1968, ss. 15 and 16.
3. *Begbie* v. *Phosphate Sewage Co.* (1875), L.R. 10 Q.B. 491.
4. *Fores* v. *Johnes* (1802), 4 Esp. 97.
5. *Apthorp* v. *Neville & Co.* (1907), 23 T.L.R. 575.
6. *Allen* v. *Rescous* (1676), 2 Lev. 174.
7. *Scott* v. *Brown, Doering, McNab & Co.,* [1892] 2 Q.B. 724.
8. *Brown Jenkinson & Co., Ltd.* v. *Percy Dalton (London), Ltd.,* [1957] 2 Q.B. 621; [1957] 2 All E.R. 844.
9. *Waldo* v. *Martin* (1825), 4 B. & C. 319. See also *Harrington* v. *Victoria Graving Dock Co.* (1878), 3 Q.B.D. 549.
10. See e.g. *Kanara* v. *Director of Public Prosecutions,* [1974] A.C. 104; [1973] 2 All E.R. 1242.
11. *Cleaver* v. *Mutual Reserve Fund Life Association,* [1892] 1 Q.B. 147, at p. 156, *per* FRY, L.J.; *In the estate of Crippen,* [1911] P. 108, at p. 112, *per* Sir Samuel EVANS, P. Youdan, 89 L.Q.R. 235; Goval and Smith [1973] C.L.J. 81.

Having been justly convicted of a crime, the degree of her moral guilt was irrelevant.[1]

The rule that the court will not assist a person to recover the fruits of his crime applies equally to his representatives. This is well illustrated by *Beresford* v. *Royal Insurance Co., Ltd.*[2]

> X, who had insured his life with the defendant company for £50,000, shot himself two or three minutes before the policy would have been invalidated by non-payment of the premium. He was sane at the time of his death. As the law then stood, suicide was a crime.[3] On the true construction of the contract, the company had agreed to pay the money to X's representatives even though he should die by his own hand and whether he should then be sane or insane.

An action in which X's executor claimed payment of the £50,000 failed. In the words of Lord MACMILLAN:

> " To enforce payment in favour of the assured's representative would be to give him a benefit, albeit in a sense a post-mortem benefit; the benefit, namely, of having by his last and criminal act provided for his relatives or creditors."[4]

Neither the House of Lords nor the Court of Appeal stigmatized the contract of insurance itself as illegal. It was not void *in toto*. Lord ATKIN and Lord THANKERTON were therefore of opinion that if, for example, X had assigned his policy as security for a loan, the lender would have been entitled to recover the amount of the loan from the insurance company.[5]

In *Gray* v. *Barr*,[6] this rule was applied again.

> The defendant involuntarily killed X in the course of making an unlawful and violent attack upon him with a loaded gun. This amounted to manslaughter. Judgment was given against him in a civil action for the payment of £6,668 by way of compensation to X's widow. He admitted liability, but claimed an indemnity against this sum under an insurance policy which indemnified him against all sums that he might become liable to pay as damages in respect of bodily injury caused by an accident.

His claim failed. Having intentionally attacked the deceased in a violent and unlawful manner, it was contrary to public policy that he should be indemnified against the consequences, however unintentional the killing of his victim might have been. At first sight this decision appears inevitable but it has been forcefully criticised.[7] It has been pointed out that since the policy was one of liability insurance, the defendant would have no claim against the insurance company unless he were liable to the plaintiff and

---

1. *Re Giles, Giles* v. *Giles*, [1972] Ch. 544; [1971] 3 All E.R. 1141.
2. [1937] 2 K.B. 197; [1937] 2 All E.R. 243; affirmed, [1938] A.C. 586; [1938] 2 All E.R. 602.
3. This is no longer so; Suicide Act 1961, s. 1.
4. [1938] A.C., at p. 605.
5. [1938] A.C., at p. 600, *per* Lord ATKIN, with whom Lord THANKERTON agreed. Lord MACMILLAN reserved his opinion on the question: *ibid.*, at p. 605; *Hardy* v. *Motor Insurers Bureau*, [1964] 2 Q.B. 745, at p. 760, *per* Lord DENNING, M.R. For further illustrations, see Furmston, 16 U. of Toronto Law Journal 267, at pp. 269–272.
6. [1970] 2 Q.B. 626; [1970] 2 All E.R. 702; affirmed, [1971] 2 Q.B. 554; [1971] 2 All E.R. 949.
7. Fleming, 34 M.L.R. 176. Cf. *Fire and All Risks* v. *Powell*, [1966] V.R. 513.

it would be the plaintiff who suffered from the decision unless the defendant were sufficiently wealthy to pay the damages from his own resources.[1]

Such considerations, though not adopted in *Gray* v. *Barr* have prevailed in the case of motor car insurance. A motorist, who is insured against liability for damages payable to third persons injured as a result of his negligent driving, is entitled to an indemnity under the policy even though the negligence has been so gross as to amount to manslaughter.[2] This right, however, does not avail him if the injury has been deliberately caused in cold blood. Even in this case, however, the victim of the assault, if he receives no compensation from the guilty party, has a right of recovery against the assurers in accordance with the compulsory insurance regulations laid down by modern legislation.[3]

The exceptional case of motor car insurance

The principle that no benefit can accrue to a criminal from his crime, however, must obviously not be pushed too far. Nowadays there are many statutory offences, some of them involving no great degree of turpitude, which rank as crimes, and it has several times been doubted whether they are all indiscriminately affected by the rule of which *Beresford*'s case is an example.[4]

(ii) A contract that is sexually immoral

Although Lord MANSFIELD laid it down that a contract *contra bonos mores* is illegal,[5] the law in this connexion gives no extended meaning to morality, but concerns itself only with what is sexually reprehensible. For a man to live in sin with a woman is not a crime, but an agreement intended to bring about such illicit intercourse is illegal and therefore void, even if made under seal.[6] This principle, however, affects only agreements for future cohabitation. If a man promises to pay money to a woman as recompense for past cohabitation, no further immorality is contemplated, and, though the promise is void, this is due not to any danger of illegality, but to the absence of consideration.[7] Past consideration is no consideration. Such a promise is therefore enforceable if made under seal.[8]

---

1. There is no evidence in the report as to the defendant's wealth nor is it easy to see how a rule could apply which involved a means test on the defendant. It is clear however that in most tort actions defendants are not worth suing unless they carry liability insurance: Atiyah, *Accidents, Compensation and The Law*, Chaps. 9 and 10.
2. The Court of Appeal, disagreeing with the trial judge on this point, held that in any event the death of the victim was not due to an " accident."
3. *Tinline* v. *White Cross Insurance Association, Ltd.,* [1921] 3 K.B. 327; *James* v. *British General Insurance Co., Ltd.,* [1927] 2 K.B. 311. *Hardy* v. *Motor Insurers Bureau,* [1964] 2 Q.B. 745, at p. 761, *per* Lord DENNING, M.R. citing Road Traffic Act 1960, s. 207.
4. *Beresford* v. *Royal Insurance Co., Ltd.,* [1937] 2 K.B. 197, at p. 220, *per* Lord WRIGHT, M.R.; *Marles* v. *Philip Trant & Sons, Ltd.,* [1954] 1 Q.B. 29, at p. 37, *per* DENNING, L.J.; *St. John Shipping Corporation* v. *Joseph Rank, Ltd.,* [1957] 1 Q.B. 267, at p. 292; [1956] 3 All E.R. 683, at p. 687, *per* DEVLIN, J., and see now *Osman* v. *J. Ralph Moss, Ltd.,* [1970] 1 Lloyd's Rep. 313.
5. *Jones* v. *Randall* (1774), 1 Cowp. 37.
6. *Benyon* v. *Nettlefold* (1850), 3 Mac. & G. 94; *Ayerst* v. *Jenkins* (1873), L.R. 16 Eq. 275.
7. *R.* v. *Bernhard,* [1938] 2 K.B. 264, at p. 271; [1938] 2 All E.R. 140, at p. 144.
8. *Nye* v. *Moseley* (1826), 6 B. & C. 133.

(iii) A contract prejudicial to the public safety

In an early case Lord ALVANLEY said:

> " We are all of opinion that . . . it is not competent to any subject to enter into a contract to do anything which may be detrimental to the interests of his own country, and that such a contract is as much prohibited as if it had been expressly forbidden by Act of Parliament."[1]

Two classes of agreement

Detrimental contracts within the meaning of this statement are those which tend either to benefit an enemy country or to disturb the good relations of England with a friendly country.

(i) Contract with an alien enemy

Contracts made in time of war afford the outstanding example of the first class. A state of war between Great Britain and another country must clearly react upon a contract made with an alien enemy by a British subject or a person owing obedience to the Crown, since it may result in injury to the Commonwealth or advantage to the enemy.[2]

Meaning of " alien enemy "

The expression " alien enemy " is not necessarily restricted to its popular meaning. It denotes a status that depends not upon the nationality of the contracting party, but upon whether he is voluntarily resident in or carrying on a business in the enemy's country or in a country within the effective control of the enemy.[3] Thus a British subject or a neutral who is resident in enemy territory is treated as an alien enemy in the present context. An enemy national who happens to be present in England during the war may be sued in the Queen's courts, but he cannot himself bring any action.[4] On the other hand, if he is resident here with the licence of the Crown, as for instance where he is registered under the Aliens Restriction Acts, the courts are open to him and a contract may be enforced by him even during the continuance of hostilities.[5]

Effect of such contract

It goes without saying that a contract made during war with an alien enemy is illegal. If it is made during peace with a person who later becomes an alien enemy owing to the outbreak of war and if it involves intercourse with the enemy country or is in other respects obnoxious from the standpoint of public policy, then it is immediately abrogated *in so far as it is still executory*.[6] It is not merely suspended during hostilities, but is cut short *eo instanti* upon the commencement of the war. It can give rise to no further rights and obligations, for the object of the law is to provide certainty at a time when everything else

---

1. *Furtado* v. *Rogers* (1802), 3 Bos. & P. 191, at p. 198. See in general McNair, *Legal Effects of War*, especially Chap. 4.
2. The following account is confined to the position at common law. In time of war, many of the matters that arise are governed by special legislation.
3. *Porter* v. *Freudenberg*, [1915] 1 K.B. 857; *Sovracht (V/O)* v. *Van Udens Scheepvaart en Agentuur Maatschappij (N. V. Gebr.)*, [1943] A.C. 203; [1943] 1 All E.R. 76. For the purposes of the Trading with the Enemy Act 1939, which penalizes persons having intercourse with the enemy, *de facto* residence, though not voluntary, is sufficient; *Vamvakas* v. *Custodian of Enemy Property*, [1952] 2 Q.B. 183; [1952] 1 All E.R. 629.
4. *Porter* v. *Freudenberg*, [1915] 1 K.B. 857; *Halsey* v. *Lowenfeld*, [1916] 2 K.B. 707.
5. *Schaffenhius* v. *Goldberg*, [1916] 1 K.B. 284.
6. *Ertel Bieber & Co.* v. *Rio Tinto Co.*, [1918] A.C. 260, at pp. 267–8, 274, *per* Lord DUNEDIN.

is uncertain and to enable the parties to engage in another adventure without waiting to see whether hostilities cease soon enough to render fulfilment of the contract possible.[1] If, for instance, an Englishman agrees to charter a ship to a German company for a period of ten years, the effect of an outbreak of war between Great Britain and Germany is to absolve the parties at once from their future obligations, notwithstanding that peace may be restored before the expiration of ten years. This rule applies not only to contracts with an enemy alien, but also to those made between British subjects and neutrals or even between British subjects themselves if benefit may thereby accrue to the enemy country.[2]

The doctrine of abrogation, then, affects the contract so far as it is still executory. It does not affect it so far as performance has already been completed.[3] Accrued rights, though not immediately enforceable, are not destroyed. Common law, it must be stressed, does not countenance the confiscation of enemy property and, subject to what may be arranged in the ultimate peace treaty and to any statutory provisions for the administration of enemy property found in this country, it is well established that contractual rights already accrued in favour of an alien enemy at the outbreak of war remain intact, though of course the right to enforce them is suspended until hostilities cease.[4]

Suspension of accrued rights

No attempt has ever been made to give an exhaustive definition of " accrued rights," but it is clear that the right to the payment of a liquidated sum of money already due under a contract falls within this category and therefore survives the outbreak of war.[5] Such a sum is regarded as a debt incurred before the creditor was infected with enemy status, and since nothing remains outstanding except its payment and since confiscation of his property is ruled out, he is entitled to enforce payment when hostilities cease. Thus he may ultimately recover the bank balance that was standing to his credit at the outbreak of war.[6] Even future instalments of a debt that have fallen due after the outbreak of war are regarded as liquidated sums within the meaning of the rule, so that the right to recover them is merely postponed.[7]

Example of accrued rights

---

1. *Esposito* v. *Bowden* (1857), 7 E. & B. 763, at p. 792, *per* WILLES, J.
2. *Schering, Ltd.* v. *Stockholms Enskilda Bank Aktiebolag,* [1946] A.C. 219, at p. 257; [1946] 1 All E.R. 36, at p. 40; *Kuenigl* v. *Donnersmarck,* [1955] 1 Q.B. 515; [1955] 1 All E.R. 46.
3. *Ottoman Bank* v. *Jebara,* [1928] A.C. 269, at p. 276; *Schering, Ltd.* v. *Stockholms Enskilda Bank Aktiebolag, supra,* at pp. 241, 258 and 41, and 55 respectively.
4. *Daimler Co., Ltd.* v. *Continental Tyre and Rubber Co. (Gt. Britain), Ltd.,* [1916] 2 A.C. 307, at p. 347, *per* Lord PARKER.
5. McNair, *Legal Effects of War,* 2nd Edn., p. 93, approved in *Schering, Ltd.* v. *Stockholms Enskilda Bank Aktiebolag,* [1946] A.C. 219, at p. 240; [1946] 1 All E.R. 36, at p. 40, *per* Lord THANKERTON; and in *Arab Bank, Ltd.* v. *Barclays Bank, Ltd.,* [1954] A.C. 495, at p. 537; [1954] 2 All E.R. 226, at p. 239, *per* Lord ASQUITH.
6. *Arab Bank, Ltd.* v. *Barclays Bank,* [1954] A.C. 495; [1954] 2 All E.R. 226.
7. *Schering, Ltd.* v. *Stockholms Enskilda Bank Aktiebolag,* [1946] A.C. 219; [1946] 1 All E.R. 36. Though well established, this rule is in fact illogical, since the creditor might, for instance, assign the debt for immediate payment and thus increase the resources of the enemy, *per* Lord GODDARD, at p. 269.

Suspension
of certain
proprietary
rights

A further exception to the principle of abrogation, as described by Lord DUNEDIN, is that those contracts " which are really the concomitants of property " are suspended, not destroyed, even though they are still executory.[1] These, as in the case of accrued rights, have never been precisely defined, but they are generally taken to mean contracts connected with land, such as restrictive covenants and covenants running with the land at common law or by statute.[2]

There is, therefore, no general rule that all executory contracts with an alien enemy are abrogated. " The executory contract which is abrogated must either involve intercourse, or its continued existence must be in some other way against public policy as that has been laid down in decided cases."[3] The judges have refused to formulate what contracts escape abrogation as being innocuous from the point of view of public policy, but one example at least is a separation agreement under which a husband has agreed to make periodic payments to his wife. If in such a case the wife becomes an alien enemy, the husband none the less remains liable to pay the sums falling due under the contract.[4]

(ii) Agreement
inimical
to a
friendly
country

A contract which contemplates the performance in a foreign and friendly country of some act which is inimical to the public welfare of that country is a breach of international comity, and is regarded as illegal by the English courts.[5] Thus it is unlawful to make an agreement in England to raise money in support of a revolt against a friendly Government,[6] to enter into a partnership for the purpose of importing liquor into a country contrary to its prohibition laws,[7] or to do something in a foreign country which will violate the local law.[8]

(iv) A contract prejudicial to the administration of justice

Contract
prejudicial to
administra-
tion of
justice

" It is admitted that any contract or engagement having a tendency, however slight, to affect the administration of justice, is illegal and void."[9] There are many examples of this rule, as for instance, an agreement not to appear at the public examination of a bankrupt nor to oppose his discharge,[10] an agreement not to plead the Gaming Acts as a defence to an action on a cheque given for lost bets,[11] and an agreement to withdraw divorce proceedings;[12] but perhaps the most familiar example is an agreement to stifle a prosecution.

---

1. *Ertel Bieber & Co.* v. *Rio Tinto Co., Ltd.,* [1918] A.C. 260, at p. 269.
2. *Schering* v. *Stockholms Enskilda Bank Aktiebolag,* [1946] A.C., at p. 252; [1946] 1 All E.R., at p. 47, *per* Lord RUSSELL' OF KILLOWEN.
3. *Ertel Bieber & Co.* v. *Rio Tinto Co., Ltd.,* [1918] A.C. 260, at p. 269, *per* Lord DUNEDIN.
4. *Bevan* v. *Bevan,* [1955] 2 Q.B. 227; [1955] 2 All E.R. 206.
5. *Foster* v. *Driscoll,* [1929] 1 K.B. 470, at pp. 510, 520–522.
6. *De Wutz* v. *Hendricks* (1824), 2 Bing. 314.
7. *Foster* v. *Driscoll,* [1929] 1 K.B. 470.
8. *Regazzoni* v. *K. C. Sethia* (1944), *Ltd.,* [1958] A.C. 301; [1957] 3 All E.R. 286.   This is a principle of considerable width.   See Mann, 21 M.L.R. 130; cf. A.L.G. 73 L.Q.R. 32. See also *Fielding and Platt* v. *Selin Najjar,* [1969] 2 All E.R. 150; [1969] 1 W.L.R. 357; *National Westminster Bank, Ltd.* v. *Barclays Bank International, Ltd.,* [1975] Q.B. 654; [1974] 3 All E.R. 834.
9. *Egerton* v. *Brownlow* (1853), 4 H.L. Cas. 1, at p. 163, *per* Lord LYNDHURST.
10. *Kearley* v. *Thomson* (1890), 24 Q.B.D. 742.
11. *Cooper* v. *Willis* (1906), 22 T.L.R. 582.
12. *Gipps* v. *Hume* (1861), 2 John. & H. 517.

It is in the interests of the public that the suppression of a prosecution should not be made the matter of a private bargain.[1] Whether a man ought to be prosecuted or not depends upon considerations that vary in each case, but the person with whom the decision rests is under a social duty in the discharge of which he must be free from the influence of indirect motives.[2] It is therefore well established that the courts will neither enforce nor recognize any agreement which has the effect of withdrawing from the ordinary course of justice a prosecution for a public offence.[3] An agreement to stifle a prosecution, *i.e.* to prevent proceedings already instituted from running their normal course, or to compromise a prosecution, is illegal and void, even though the prosecutor derives no gain, financial or otherwise, and even though the agreement secures the very object for which the proceedings were taken.[4]

> Contract to stifle a prosecution is void

This rule, however, applies only where the offence for which the defendant is prosecuted is a matter of public concern, *i.e.* one which pre-eminently affects the interests of the public. If the offence is not of this nature, but is one in which the injured person has a choice between a civil and a criminal remedy, as for instance in the case of a libel or an assault, a compromise is lawful and enforceable. The question whether the offence was of public concern arose in the leading case of *Keir* v. *Leeman*.[5]

> Void only if prosecution is for a public offence

> A commenced a prosecution for riot and assault against seven defendants who had assaulted and ejected a sheriff's officer and his assistants while they were levying an execution in respect of a judgment debt due to A. Before the trial began, X and Y agreed to pay to A the amount of the debt, together with costs, in consideration that A would not proceed with the prosecution. A accordingly gave no evidence against the defendants and he consented with the leave of the judge to a verdict of " not guilty " being entered. X and Y, when sued upon the agreement, pleaded that it was an unlawful compromise and therefore void. This plea prevailed.

DENMAN, C.J., after remarking that some indictments for misdemeanour might be compromised, said:

> " We shall probably be safe in laying it down that the law will permit a compromise of all offences, though made the subject of criminal prosecution, for which the injured party might sue and recover damages in an action. It is often the only manner in which he can obtain redress. But if the offence is of a public nature, no agreement can be valid that is founded on the consideration of stifling a prosecution for it. . . . In the present instance the offence is not confined to personal injury, but is accompanied with riot and obstruction of a public officer in the execution of his duty. These are matters of public concern and therefore not legally the subject of a compromise."

Other instances of public offences in respect of which no compromise is permitted are perjury,[6] obtaining money or credit by

---

1. *Clubb* v. *Hutson* (1865), 18 C.B.N.S. 414, at p. 417, *per* ERLE, C.J.
2. *Jones* v. *Merionethshire Permanent Benefit Building Society*, [1892] 1 Ch. 173, at p. 183, *per* BOWEN, L.J.
3. *Windhill Local Board of Health* v. *Vint* (1890), 45 Ch.D. 351, at p. 363, *per* COTTON, L.J.
4. *Keir* v. *Leeman* (1846), 9 Q.B. 371; *Windhill Local Board of Health* v. *Vint, supra.*
5. *Supra.*
6. *Collins* v. *Blantern* (1767), 2 Wils. 341.

false pretences,[1] forgery,[2] interference with and obstruction of a public highway.[3]

A private offence may be the subject of a compromise

An example of the rule, that an offence for which either a civil or a criminal remedy is available may be the subject of a lawful compromise, is *Fisher & Co.* v. *Apollinaris Co.*[4] where the facts were these:

> The Apollinaris Co. prosecuted Fisher under the Trade Marks Act for selling his mineral water in bottles that bore their trade mark. It was then agreed that, in consideration of the abandonment of the prosecution, Fisher would give a letter of apology to the company and would authorize them to make what use of it they considered appropriate. After the abandonment, the company proceeded to publish continuously the letter of apology in the daily press. Fisher sued to restrain this publication on the ground that the apology had been obtained by an improper use of criminal proceedings.

It was held that the agreement was valid, since there was nothing unlawful in the withdrawal of a prosecution for an offence of that particular kind.

The account given above is based on the law as it was before the Criminal Law Act 1967. That act made a number of changes in the criminal law. Section 1 abolished the distinction between felonies and misdemeanours and s. 5 (1) introduced a new offence of concealing an arrestable offence, which replaced the wider offences of misprision of felony and compounding a felony. The act makes no mention of the law of contract but it is arguable that it alters it indirectly.[5] Before the act any agreement to conceal a felony was itself a criminal offence and therefore necessarily an illegal contract. So the public-private dichotomy which previously applied only to misdemeanours might in theory be applied to all offences. In the same way since an agreement to conceal an arrestable offence is no longer a criminal offence if the only consideration for it is the making good of the loss or injury caused by the offence, it can be argued that such an agreement should now be enforceable. On balance, however, it is thought that to take an agreement out of the ambit of the criminal law does not by itself indicate that it should be enforced.

Maintenance and champerty

A further example of contracts that tend to pervert the due course of justice are those which savour of maintenance or champerty. " Maintenance may nowadays be defined as improperly stirring up litigation and strife by giving aid to one party to bring or defend a claim without just cause or excuse.[6] Champerty is where there is a further agreement that the person who gives the aid shall receive a share of what may be recovered in the action."

Formerly, maintenance was a misdemeanour, and also a tort for which damages were recoverable by the other party to the action. This is no longer the case. The Criminal Law Act 1967

---

1. *Clubb* v. *Hutson* (1865), 18 C.B.N.S. 414; *Jones* v. *Merionethshire Permanent Benefit Building Society*, [1892] 1 Ch. 173. See Theft Act 1968, ss. 15 and 16.
2. *Brook* v. *Hook* (1871), L.R. 6 Exch. 89.
3. *Windhill Local Board of Health* v. *Vint* (1890), 45 Ch.D. 351.
4. (1875), 10 Ch. App. 297.
5. For a fuller account, see Buckley, 3 Anglo-American L.R. 472.
6. *Re Trepca Mines, Ltd.* (*No. 2*), [1963] Ch. 199, at p. 219; [1962] 3 All E.R. 351, at p. 355E, *per* Lord DENNING.

provides that maintenance, including champerty, shall no longer be punishable as a crime or actionable as a tort.[1] It is further provided, however, that this abolition of criminal and civil liability " shall not affect any such rule of law as to the cases in which a contract is to be treated as contrary to public policy or otherwise illegal."[2] Therefore, the long established rule still stands that an agreement tainted by maintenance or champerty is void as being contrary to public policy.[3]

(v) A contract liable to corrupt public life

It has long been the rule that any contract is illegal which tends to corruption in the administration of the affairs of the nation. A familiar example of a transaction offensive to this principle is a contract for the buying, selling or procuring of public offices.[4]

Sale of public office

> " It is obvious," says Story, " that all such contracts must have a material influence to diminish the respectability, responsibility and purity of public officers, and to introduce a system of official patronage, corruption and deceit wholly at war with the public interests."[5]

Thus in one case:

> A agreed that if by the influence of B he were appointed Customs Officer of a port, he would appoint such deputies as B should nominate and would hold the profits of the office in trust for B. It was held, after A had secured the post, that no action lay against him for breach of this agreement.[6]

Similarly a contract to procure a title for a man in consideration of a money payment is illegal at common law.[7]

On the same principle an agreement to assign or mortgage future instalments of the salary of a public office is void, since the law presumes that the object of the salary is to maintain the dignity of the office and to enable the holder to perform his duties in a proper manner.[8] This restriction was applied in the eighteenth century to officers in the Army,[9] and the common assumption is that it extends to judges[10] and to civil servants generally, such as clerks of the peace[11] and parliamentary counsel to the Treasury,[12] but whether the extension is justified either by the

---

1. Sections 13 (1) and 14 (1).
2. Section 14 (2).
3. *Rees* v. *De Bernardy*, [1896] 2 Ch. 437. As to whether any exceptions may exist to this rule, see now the differing views in *Wallersteiner* v. *Moir* (No. 2), [1975] Q.B. 373; [1975] 1 All E.R. 849.
4. *Blachford* v. *Preston* (1799), 8 Term. Rep. 89.
5. *Equity Jurisdiction*, s. 295.
6. *Garforth* v. *Fearon* (1787), 1 Hy. Bl. 328.
7. *Parkinson* v. *College of Ambulance, Ltd., and Harrison*, [1925] 2 K.B. 1. See now the Honours (Prevention of Abuses) Act 1925, which makes the parties to such a contract guilty of a misdemeanour.
8. *Liverpool Corporation* v. *Wright* (1859), John. 359.
9. *Flarty* v. *Odlum* (1790), 3 Term Rep. 681; *Barwick* v. *Reade* (1791), 1 Hy. Bl. 627.
10. *Arbuthnot* v. *Norton* (1846), 5 Moo. P.C.C. 219.
11. *Palmer* v. *Bate* (1821), 2 Brod. & Bing. 673.
12. *Cooper* v. *Reilly* (1829), 2 Sim. 560. For the view that this decision and those cited in the two preceding notes are not conclusive, see Logan, 61 L.Q.R. 241, at pp. 247–8.

authorities themselves or by the change that has gradually occurred in the status of the civil service is doubtful.[1]

Meaning of
" public
office "

To attract the doctrine the office must be public in the strict sense of that word, and the holder of an office whose emoluments do not derive from national funds, such as a clergyman of the Church of England, is not subject to the restriction.[2]

(vi) A contract to defraud the revenue

Fraud on
the national
revenue

There is a clear infringement of the doctrine of public policy if it is apparent, either directly from the terms of a contract or indirectly from other circumstances, that the design of one or both of the parties is to defraud the revenue, whether national[3] or local.[4] In *Miller* v. *Karlinski*, for instance,[5]

> the terms of a contract of employment were that the employee should receive a salary of £10 weekly and repayment of his expenses, but that he should be entitled to include in his expenses account the amount of income tax due in respect of his weekly salary.

In an action brought by him to recover ten weeks' arrears of salary and £21 2s. 8d. for expenses it was divulged that about £17 of this latter sum represented his liability for income tax. It was held that the contract was illegal, since it constituted a fraud upon the revenue. No action lay to recover even arrears of salary, for in such a case the illegal stipulation is not severable from the lawful agreement to pay the salary.[6]

Fraud on the
local
revenue

It is doubtful whether the well-known case of *Alexander* v. *Rayson*[7] exemplifies this principle. The facts were these:

> The plaintiff agreed to let a service flat to the defendant at an annual rent of £1,200. This transaction was expressed in two documents, one a lease of the premises at a rent of £450 a year, the other an agreement by the plaintiff to render certain specified services for an annual sum of £750. It was alleged that his object was to produce only the lease to the Westminster Assessment Committee, and by persuading this body that the premises were worth only £450 a year, to obtain a reduction of their rateable value. The defendant was ignorant of this alleged purpose. The plaintiff ultimately failed to accomplish his fraudulent object. He sued the defendant for the recovery of £300, being a quarter's instalment due under both documents.

The Court of Appeal held that, if the alleged fraud was not disproved by the plaintiff when the trial was resumed in the court of first instance, he could recover neither on the lease nor on the contract.

It is clear that both the agreement and the lease were harmless in themselves and might well have been performed without any

---

1. The authorities are closely and critically reviewed by Logan, 61 L.Q.R. 241.
2. *Re Mirams*, [1891] 1 Q.B. 594.
3. *Miller* v. *Karlinski* (1945), 62 T.L.R. 85; *Napier* v. *National Business Agency, Ltd.*, [1951] 2 All E.R. 264; 67 L.Q.R. 449–51.
4. *Alexander* v. *Rayson*, [1936] 1 K.B. 169; [1935] All E.R. Rep. 185; applied in *Edler* v. *Auerbach*, [1950] 1 K.B. 359; [1949] 2 All E.R. 692.
5. *Supra.*
6. *Napier* v. *National Business Agency, Ltd.*, *supra*; *Warburton* v. *Birkenhead & Co., Ltd.* (1951), 102 L. Jo. 52.
7. [1936] 1 K.B. 169; [1935] All E.R. Rep. 185.

fraud on the part of the lessor. In the words of one critic: " The contract was not one to do an act contrary to the policy of the law (defrauding the revenue); but one to do an act in itself legal but intended by one of the parties to provide a setting for an act contrary to the policy of the law (defrauding the revenue)."[1] The case exemplifies the general principle that a contract *ex facie* lawful will be unenforceable by the plaintiff if his intention is to exploit it for an illegal purpose.[2]

SECTION III. THE CONSEQUENCE OF ILLEGALITY

A. INTRODUCTION: THE RELEVANCE OF THE STATE OF MIND OF THE PARTIES

Whether the parties are influenced by a guilty intention is inevitably material in estimating the consequences of an illegal contract. Its materiality may be stated in three propositions.

Materiality of guilty intention

First, if the contract is illegal in its inception, neither party can assert that he did not intend to break the law. Both parties have expressly and clearly agreed to do something that in fact st prohibited at common law, as for example, where a British subjeci agrees to insure an alien enemy against certain risks. The position is the same if the parties have agreed to do something that is expressly or implicitly forbidden by statute.[3] In both these cases, the contract is intrinsically and inevitably illegal, and, so far as consequences are concerned, no allowance is made for innocence. The British subject, for instance, may well be ignorant that it is unlawful to contract with an alien enemy, but none the less he will be precluded by the maxim *ignorantia juris haud excusat* from relying upon his ignorance.[4] The very contract is unlawful in its formation.

(i) Contract illegal in its inception

Secondly, if the contract is *ex facie* lawful, but both parties intend to exploit it for an illegal purpose, it is illegal in its inception despite its innocuous appearance. Both parties intend to accomplish an unlawful end and both are remediless. This is true, for instance, of an agreement to let a flat if there is a common intention to use it for immoral purposes.

(ii) Contract lawful in its inception: common guilty intention

Thirdly, if the contract is lawful in its formation, but one party alone intends to exploit it for an illegal purpose, the law not unnaturally takes the view that the innocent party need not be adversely affected by the guilty intention of the other.[5] This has been frequently stressed by the judges. In one case in 1810, for

(iii) Contract lawful in its inception: one party innocent

1. Furmston, 16 U. of Toronto L.J. 267, at p. 287.
2. *Infra*, pp. 359 *et seq.*
3. *Re Mahmoud and Ispahani*, [1921] 2 K.B. 716.
4. *Waugh* v. *Morris* (1873), L.R. 8 Q.B. 202, at p. 208, *per curiam*, as explained in *J. M. Allan (Merchandising)* v. *Cloke*, [1963] 2 Q.B. 340; [1963] 2 All E.R. 258.
5. See for example, *Oom* v. *Bruce* (1810), 12 East 225; *Clay* v. *Yates* (1856), 1 H. & N. 73, at p. 80; *Pearce* v. *Brooks* (1866), L.R. 1 Exch. 213, at pp. 217, 221; *Alexander* v. *Rayson*, [1936] 1 K.B. 169, at p. 182; *Re Trepca Mines, Ltd.* (*No.* 2), [1963] Ch. 199, at pp. 220-1; [1962] 3 All E.R. 351.

instance, the plaintiffs, acting on behalf of a Russian owner, had insured goods on a vessel already en route from St. Petersburgh and had paid the premium. The contract was made after war had broken out between Russia and England, but the fact was not known, and could not have been known to the plaintiffs. The ship was seized by the Russians and taken back to St. Petersburgh. The plaintiffs succeeded in an action for the recovery of the premium.[1] Lord Ellenborough, after remarking that the insurance would have been illegal in its inception had the plaintiffs known of the outbreak of war, said:—

> " But here the plaintiffs had no knowledge of the commencement of hostilities by Russia when they effected this insurance; and therefore no fault is imputable to them for entering into the contract; and there is no reason why they should not recover back the premiums which they have paid for an insurance from which, without any fault imputable to themselves, they could never have derived any benefit."[2]

Whether a party is innocent or guilty in this respect depends upon whether " he is himself implicated in the illegality,"[3] or more precisely whether he has participated in the furtherance of the illegal intention.[4] If, for instance, A lets a flat to B, a woman whom he knows to be a prostitute, the very contract will be unlawful if he knows that B's object is to use the premises for immoral purposes,[5] or if he expects the rent to be paid by the man whose mistress she is.[6] But this will not be the case if all that he is aware of is B's mode of life, for a reasonable person would not necessarily infer that the purpose of the letting was to further immorality.[7] Even a prostitute must have a home.

Pearce v. *Brooks*

Perhaps the best known case on this subject so far as illegality at common law is concerned, is *Pearce* v. *Brooks*,[8] where the facts were as follows:

> The plaintiffs agreed to supply the defendant with a new miniature brougham on hire until the purchase money should be paid by instalments during a period that was not to exceed twelve months. The defendant was a prostitute and she undoubtedly intended to use the carriage, which was of a somewhat intriguing nature, as a lure to hesitant clients. One of the two plaintiffs was aware of her mode of life, but there was no direct evidence that either of them knew of the use to which she intended to put the carriage. The jury, however, found that the purpose of the woman was to use the carriage as part of her display to attract men and that the plaintiffs were aware of her design. On this finding, Bramwell, B., gave judgment for the defendant in an action brought against her to recover a sum due under the contract.

It was held on appeal that there was sufficient evidence to support the finding of the jury. The Court of Exchequer Chamber was

---

1. *Oom* v. *Bruce* (1810), 12 East. 225.
2. *Ibid.*, at p. 226.
3. *Scott* v. *Brown, Doering, McNab & Co., Ltd.*, [1892] 2 Q.B. 724, at p. 728, *per* Lindley, L.J.
4. *In Re Trepca Mines, Ltd.* (*No.* 2), [1963] Ch. 199; [1962] 3 All E.R. 351. *J. M. Allan* (*Merchandising*), *Ltd.* v. *Cloke*, [1963] 2 Q.B. 340, at p. 348.
5. *Girardy* v. *Richardson* (1793), 1 Esp. 13.
6. *Upfill* v. *Wright*, [1911] 1 K.B. 506.
7. *Crisp* v. *Churchill* (1794), cited in 1 Bos. & P. at p. 340.
8. (1866), L.R. 1 Exch. 213.

satisfied on the evidence that the plaintiffs were not only aware of the defendant's intention, but were even guilty of some complicity in her provocative scheme.

In order to emphasize the distinction between innocence and guilt that affects this branch of the law, the precise consequences of an illegal contract will now be detailed under two separate heads, namely:

The consequence where a contract is illegal in its inception.

The consequence where a contract lawful in its inception is later exploited illegally or is illegally performed.

B. THE CONSEQUENCE WHERE THE CONTRACT IS ILLEGAL IN ITS INCEPTION

The general principle, founded on public policy, is that any transaction that is tainted by illegality in which both parties are equally involved is beyond the pale of the law. No person can claim any right or remedy whatsoever under an illegal transaction in which he has participated.[1] *Ex turpi causa non oritur actio.* The court is bound to veto the enforcement of a contract once it knows that it is illegal, whether the knowledge comes from the statement of the guilty party or from outside sources.[2] Even the defendant can successfully plead the *turpis causa,* and though this " defence is very dishonest "[3] and " seems only worthy of the Pharisee who shook himself free of his natural obligations by saying Corban,"[4] it is allowed for the reasons given by Lord MANSFIELD in *Holman* v. *Johnson*:

> " The objection that the contract is immoral or illegal as between plaintiff and defendant sounds at all times very ill in the mouth of the defendant. It is not for his sake, however, that the objection is ever allowed; but it is founded in general principles of policy, which the defendant has the advantage of, contrary to the real justice, as between him and the plaintiff, by accident, if I may say so. The principle of public policy is this: *ex dolo malo non oritur actio.* No court will lend its aid to a man who founds his cause of action upon an immoral or an illegal act. If from the plaintiff's own stating or otherwise, the cause of action appears to arise *ex turpi causa,* or the transgression of a positive law of this country, then the court says he has no right to be assisted. It is upon that ground the court goes; not for the sake of the defendant, but because they will not lend their aid to such a plaintiff. So if the plaintiff and defendant were to change sides, and the defendant was to bring his action against the plaintiff, the latter would then have the advantage of it, for where both are equally in fault *potior est conditio defendentis.*"[5]

The practical application of this general principle must now be stated in some detail.

The general principle: ex turpi causa non oritur actio

---

1. *Gordon* v. *Metropolitan Commr.,* [1910] 2 K.B. 1080, at p. 1098, *per* BUCKLEY, L.J.
2. *Re Mahmoud and Ispahani,* [1921] 2 K.B. 716, at p. 729, *per* SCRUTTON, L.J.
3. *Thomson* v. *Thomson* (1802), 7 Ves. 470, at p. 473, *per* Sir William GRANT, M.R.
4. The words of Lord DUNEDIN in *Sinclair* v. *Brougham,* [1914] A.C. 398, at p. 436, adapted to the present context by Street, *Law of Gaming,* p. 464.
5. (1775), 1 Cowp. 341, at p. 343.

(i) The contract is void

Contract
enforceable by
neither
party

A contract that is illegal as formed and is therefore void *ab initio* is treated by the law as if it had not been made at all.[1] It is totally void, and no remedy is available to either party. No action lies for damages, for an account of profits or for a share of expenses. Thus, in the case of an illegal contract for the sale of goods, the buyer, even though he has paid the price, cannot sue for non-delivery; the seller who has made delivery cannot recover the price. A servant cannot recover arrears of salary under an illegal contract of employment.[2] In the case of an illegal lease, the landlord cannot recover the rent or damages for the breach of any other covenant.[3] The position is the same not only where a contract is prohibited at common law on grounds of public policy, but also where its very formation is prohibited by statute. An apt illustration is afforded by *Re Mahmoud and Ispahani*[4] where the facts were these:

> The plaintiff agreed to sell linseed oil to the defendant, who refused to take delivery and was sued for non-acceptance of the goods. A statutory order provided that no person should buy or sell certain specified articles, including linseed, unless he was licensed to do so. Before the conclusion of the contract, the defendant untruthfully alleged that he held a licence and the plaintiff, who himself was licensed, believed the allegation.

Once it was established that each party was forbidden by statute to enter into the contract, the court had no option but to enforce the prohibition even though the defendant relied upon his own illegality. The honest belief of the plaintiff that the defendant held a licence was irrelevant.[5]

Again, an award made by an arbitrator in respect of a prohibited contract will be set aside by the court.[6] A builder who does work at a cost exceeding the sum authorized by statute cannot recover the excess,[7] and if, having done both authorized and unauthorized work, he receives payment under the contract generally, he cannot appropriate the sum to the unlawful work.[8]

In all cases where a contract is illegal in its formation, neither party can circumvent the rule—*ex turpi causa non oritur actio*—by pleading ignorance of the law.[9]

Can owner-
ship be
transferred
under
illegal
contract?

Although a contract is illegal in its formation and therefore void, the Court of Appeal has now held that the ownership of goods may pass to the buyer under an illegal contract of sale even

---

1. *Mogul Steamship Co.* v. *McGregor, Gow & Co.*, [1892] A.C. 25, at p. 39, *per* Lord HALSBURY.
2. *Miller* v. *Karlinski* (1945), 62 T.L.R. 85.
3. *Alexander* v. *Rayson*, [1936] 1 K.B. 69; [1935] All E.R. Rep. 185.
4. [1921] 2 K.B. 716.
5. Distinguish the case when a contract *lawful* in its formation is performed in an illegal manner by one of the parties; *infra*, pp. 359 *et seq.*
6. *David Taylor & Son, Ltd.* v. *Barnett Trading Co.*, [1953] 1 All E.R. 843; [1953] 1 W.L.R. 562.
7. *Bostel Brothers, Ltd.* v. *Hurlock*, [1949] 1 K.B. 74; [1948] 2 All E.R. 312; *Dennis & Co., Ltd.* v. *Nunn*, [1949] 2 K.B. 327; [1949] 1 All E.R. 616.
8. *A. Smith & Son (Bognor Regis), Ltd.* v. *Walker*, [1952] 2 Q.B. 319; [1952] 1 All E.R. 1008.
9. *J. M. Allan (Merchandise), Ltd.* v. *Cloke*, [1963] 2 Q.B. 340; [1963] 2 All E.R. 258. See also Higgins, 25 M.L.R. 149.

if both parties are *in pari delicto*.[1] This decision requires to be examined with some particularity.

A preliminary necessity is to observe the distinction, emphasised in the English cases of the early nineteenth century, between " general property " and " special property." In these cases the phrase " general property " denotes the ownership of movables; " special property " denotes the limited interest which may be enjoyed by a bailee of chattels. Where, for instance, a borrower delivers a chattel to a lender as security for repayment of a loan, the lender, *qua* pledgee, may acquire a right to dispose of the chattel in order to realize his security; but he does not become the owner of the chattel.

> " The very expression ' special property ' seems to exclude the notion of that general property which is the badge of ownership. If the pledgee sells, he does so by virtue and to the extent of the pledgor's ownership, and not with a new title of his own."[2]

The phrase " special property " is misleading, and Chalmers, when he drafted the Sale of Goods Act 1893, had expressly to define " property " for the purposes of the Act, as " general " and not " special " property.[3] The question under discussion, therefore, is whether *general*, not *special* property can pass under an illegal contract: it is the *ownership* of movables with which we are concerned.

Since an illegal contract is totally void, the inescapable conclusion would seem to be that the ownership of movables cannot pass by virtue of the contract itself if this arises *ex turpi causa* and if both parties to it are *in pari delicto*. *Nil posse creari de nilo*.[4]

If, therefore, the ownership is to pass at all, this must be effected by some independent rule of law extraneous to the so-called but abortive contract. It is true that in the case of a gift the ownership of goods may be transferred by delivery, provided that this is what the parties intend. But since this intention is one of the decisive elements of the transaction, it would seem logical to insist that it must be disregarded if it is tainted by illegality.[5] In 1960, however, Lord DENNING, giving the opinion of the Privy Council in *Singh* v. *Ali*[6] expressed a view which it is respectfully suggested goes beyond previous statements of the law.

> " There are many cases which show that when two persons agree together in a conspiracy to effect a fraudulent or illegal purpose —and one of them transfers property to the other in pursuance of the conspiracy—then, so soon as the contract is executed and the fraudulent or illegal purpose is achieved, the property (be it absolute or special) which has been transferred by the other remains vested

Marginal notes:
Distinction between general property and special property

Transfer cannot be effected by the contract itself

Controversy whether transfer effected by delivery of goods

View of the Privy Council considered

1. *Belvoir Finance Co., Ltd.* v. *Stapleton*, [1971] 1 Q.B. 210; [1970] 3 All E.R. 664.
2. *The Odessa*, [1916] 1 A.C. 145, at p. 159, *per* Lord MERSEY.
3. Section 62 (1); and see the notes to the word property in this subsection in the book by Chalmers on the Act.
4. Lucretius, *De Rerum Natura*, i. 155.
5. See, however, an *obiter dictum* by PARKE, B., in *Simpson* v. *Nicholls* (1838), 3 M. & W. 244, as revised, (1839), 5 M. & W. 702, where he was commenting upon the earlier case of *William* v. *Paul* (1830), 6 Bing. 653.
6. [1960] A.C. 167.

in the transferee, notwithstanding its illegal origin . . . The reason is because the transferor, having fully achieved his unworthy end, cannot be allowed to turn round and repudiate the means by which he did it—he cannot throw over the transfer."[1]

This statement invites three comments.

Firstly, the transfer of ownership is here said to depend not upon delivery, but upon the execution of the contract. A contract is executed as soon as one party has fully performed his side of the bargain, even if it still remains in whole or in part to be performed by the other party. A contract of sale, therefore, is executed by the seller when he delivers the goods to the buyer; and in this context at least delivery and execution are synonymous.

Secondly, Lord DENNING cited, as authority for his statement, an *obiter dictum* of PARKE, B., in *Scarfe* v. *Morgan*.[2] In that case the court was concerned with the validity of a bailee's lien which, it had been argued, was illegal and void. The lien was in fact held to be untainted by illegality. But PARKE, B., said that even if it had been illegal, it would still exist " because the contract was executed and the special property had passed by the delivery of the chattel to the defendant. The maxim would apply—*in pari delicto potior est conditio possidentis*." It will be seen that this *dictum* of Baron PARKE was confined to the case of a " special property " in the chattel, but that in *Singh* v. *Ali* it was extended to include the " general property." Thus the vital distinction between ownership and the limited interest which a bailee might enjoy in the chattel was obscured.

The question
of transfer
as it affects
parties

Thirdly, as between the parties themselves, the question whether the property has passed is academic, for if the contract is illegal and if the parties are *in pari delicto* neither can establish a cause of action against the other without disclosing his own wrongdoing. But if an innocent third party becomes involved in the cycle of events, it is vital to determine which of the original parties is the owner of the contractual subject-matter. This is well illustrated by *Belvoir Finance Co., Ltd.* v. *Stapleton*,[3] the facts of which were as follows:

> The plaintiffs bought three cars from dealers, paid for them and let them on hire-purchase terms to the Belgravia Car Co., who kept a fleet of cars for letting out on hire to the public. The plaintiffs never took delivery of the three cars in question, which went directly from the dealers to the Belgravia Car Co. Both the contract of sale between the dealers and the plaintiffs and the hire-purchase contracts between the plaintiffs and the Belgravia Co. were illegal to the knowledge of all three parties as contravening statutory regulations. The Belgravia Co., fraudulently and in breach of the hire-purchase contracts, sold the three cars to innocent purchasers. One of these sales was effected by the defendant, the assistant manager of the Belgravia Co., and the plaintiffs now sued him personally in conversion.

To succeed in this action the plaintiffs had to show that the ownership of the car was vested in them at the time of the conversion. They had therefore to prove that despite the illegality

---

1. [1960] A.C., at p. 176; [1960] 1 All E.R., at p. 272.
2. (1838), 4 M. & W. 270.
3. [1971] 1 Q.B. 210; [1970] 3 All E.R. 664.

of the original contract of sale, they had acquired and still enjoyed the " general property " in the car. The Court of Appeal decided this issue in their favour. Lord DENNING, M.R., cited his statement in *Singh* v. *Ali*[1] and continued:

> " Although the plaintiffs obtained the car under a contract which was illegal, nevertheless, in as much as the contract was executed and the property passed, the car belonged to them and they can claim it.''

It is submitted with respect that this decision, based upon the failure to distinguish " general " and " special " property, is contrary to the established principles which determine the effect of illegality. It will be observed, moreover, that in the instant case the car had never been delivered to the plaintiffs. The court endeavoured to counter this formidable objection by falling back upon the rules for the passing of property contained in sections 17 and 18 of the Sale of Goods Act 1893. These rules are based essentially upon the intention of the parties as disclosed by their conduct, the terms of the contract and the circumstances of the case. But they clearly envisage the existence of a valid contract and can scarcely operate where the parties have deliberately sought to implement an agreement that is vitiated by illegality.

The Lords Justices expressed the opinion that, were the finance company to be precluded by the illegality of the contract from maintaining the action, any stranger would be free to seize the car with impunity since there would be nobody able to establish a legal title against him. This would be to recognize a right of confiscation. It is submitted with respect, however, that the suggestion is not well founded. The person who happens to be in possession of the car after and as a result of the illegal contract, (as in the instant case the Belgravia Co. or the ultimate purchaser), would be able to maintain trespass against a wrongful intruder. In an action of trespass, the existing possession of the plaintiff, even though held without title, is conclusive evidence of his right to possession against a wrongdoer. The latter cannot set up the better title of a third person, unless he shows that he acted with the authority of that third person.[2] The position is the same in trover and detinue, unless the wrongdoer shows that he acted with the authority of a third person who has a better right to possession than the plaintiff.[3]

(ii) Money paid and chattels or land transferred are irrecoverable

No restitution if disclosure of illegality essential to cause of action

Neither party can recover what he has given to the other under an illegal contract if in order to substantiate his claim he is driven to disclose the illegality.[4] The maxim *in pari delicto*

---

1. *Supra*, p. 347.
2. *Jeffries* v. *The Great Western Rail. Co.* (1856), 5 E. & B. 802.
3. *Ibid.*
4. *Scott* v. *Brown, Doering, McNab & Co.*, [1892] 2 Q.B. 724, at p. 734, *per* A. L. SMITH, L.J.; *Chettiar* v. *Chettiar*, [1962] A.C. 294; [1962] All E.R. 494.

potior est conditio defendentis applies and the defendant may keep what he has been given. If, for instance, a seller sues for the recovery of goods sold and delivered under an illegal contract he will fail, for to justify his claim he must necessarily disclose his own iniquity. Thus in *Taylor* v. *Chester*:[1]

> The plaintiff deposited with the defendant the half of a £50 note as a pledge to secure the payment of money due for a debauch held by the plaintiff and divers prostitutes at the defendant's brothel.

An action of detinue, based upon a refusal by the defendant to redeliver the note, was dismissed, for the plaintiff could not impugn the validity of the pledge without revealing the immoral character of the contract.

Gains and losses remain intact

The result is that gains and losses remain where they have accrued or fallen. If, for instance, a scheme to defraud X, concocted by A and B, succeeds, and the money is obtained by B, no action for an account or recovery lies at the suit of A,[2] as was once solemnly adjudged in a case where one highwayman sued another for an account of their plunder.[3] The general position is well illustrated by *Parkinson* v. *College of Ambulance, Ltd., and Harrison*,[4] where the facts were these:

> The secretary of the defendant charity fraudulently represented to the plaintiff that the charity was in a position to divert the fountain of honour in his direction and to procure him at least a knighthood, if he would make an adequate donation. After a certain amount of bargaining, the plaintiff paid £3,000 to the charity and undertook to do more when the knighthood was forthcoming. He did not, however, receive any honour and he sued for the return of the money as had and received to his use.

It was held by LUSH, J., that the action must fail. The transaction was manifestly illegal to the knowledge of the plaintiff. He could sue neither for money had and received nor for the recovery of damages, nor could he repudiate the contract and regain his money on the plea that the transaction was executory.

Property recoverable if disclosure of illegality not essential to cause of action

A plaintiff, however, may recover money, chattels or land transferred under an illegal contract to the defendant, if he can frame a cause of action entirely independent of the contract, for in these circumstances he is not compelled to disclose the illegality. " Any rights which he may have irrespective of his illegal interest will, of course, be recognized and enforced."[5]

Suppose, for instance, that a lease for ten years is made by A to B for a purpose known by both parties to be illegal. A cannot sue for the recovery of rent, since to substantiate his claim he must necessarily rely upon the illegal transaction.[6] Nor, it is

---

1. (1869), L.R. 4 Q.B. 309. The numerous authorities to the same effect are given by Goff and Jones, *The Law of Restitution*, p. 289.
2. *Sykes* v. *Beadon* (1879), 11 Ch.D. 170; *Berg* v. *Sadler and Moore*, [1937] 2 K.B. 158.
3. *Everet* v. *Williams* (1725), cited in Lindley, *The Law of Partnership*, 13th Edn., p. 130, n.; *Sykes* v. *Beadon, supra*, at pp. 195–6, *per* JESSEL, M.R.; 9 L.Q.R. 197.
4. [1925] 2 K.B. 1.
5. *Scott* v. *Brown, Doering, McNab & Co.*, [1892] 2 Q.B. 724, at p. 729, *per* LINDLEY, L.J. Gooderson, [1958] C.L.J. 199.
6. *Gas Light and Coke Co.* v. *Turner*, (1840), 6 Bing. N.C. 324.

apprehended, can he recover possession of the land before expiry of the agreed term. If he attempted to do so, B would allege possession by virtue of the lease, the illegality of which would preclude A from enforcing the covenant for the payment of rent.[1] But once the term of ten years has expired, A has an independent cause of action by virtue of his ownership. Though he cannot be allowed to recover what he has transferred in pursuance of the illegal transaction, yet he cannot be denied the right of ownership which he has not transferred.[2] Once the illegal, but temporary, title has ceased, he can rely upon his prior and lawful title.

The principle, that a plaintiff can recover what he has transferred under an illegal contract if he can found his action upon some independent and lawful ground, was applied by the Privy Council in *Amar Singh* v. *Kulubya*[3] on the following facts:

> A statutory ordinance in Uganda prohibited the sale or lease of " Mailo " land by an African to a non-African except with the written consent of the Governor. Without obtaining this consent, the plaintiff, an African, agreed to lease such land of which he was the registered owner to the defendant, an Indian, for one year and thereafter on a yearly basis. The agreement, therefore, was void for illegality, and no leasehold interest vested in the defendant. After the defendant had been in possession for several years, the plaintiff gave him seven weeks' notice to quit and ultimately sued him for recovery of the land.

He succeeded. His claim to possession was based not upon the agreement, to the illegality of which on his own admission he had been a party, but on the independent and untainted ground of his registered ownership. He was not forced to have recourse to the agreement.[4]

This decision illustrates the familiar statement of DU PARCQ, L.J., in an earlier case when delivering the judgment of the court:

> " *Prima facie,* a man is entitled to his own property, and it is not a general principle of our law (as was suggested) that when one man's goods have got into another's possession in consequence of some unlawful dealings between them, the true owner can never be allowed to recover those goods. The necessity of such a principle to the interests and advancement of public policy is certainly not obvious."[5]

A similar, though perhaps more dubious decision was given in *Bowmakers, Ltd.* v. *Barnet Instruments, Ltd.* upon the following facts:[6]

The *Bowmaker* case discussed

---

1. *Alexander* v. *Rayson*, [1936] 1 K.B. 169, at pp. 196–7, *per curiam*; [1935] All E.R. 185, at p. 193. See Salmond & Williams, *Principles of the Law of Contracts*, p. 347, note *d*.
2. *Jajbhay* v. *Cassim*, [1939] App. D. 537, at p. 557.
3. [1964] A.C. 142; [1963] 3 All E.R. 499. Criticized Cornish, 27 M.L.R. 225.
4. The Privy Council considered that the notice of seven weeks to quit the land, which was insufficient to determine a yearly tenancy was not referable to the illegal agreement: [1964] A.C. 142; at p. 150.
5. *Bowmakers, Ltd.* v. *Barnet Instruments, Ltd.*, [1945] K.B. 65, at p. 70.
6. [1945] K.B. 65; [1944] 2 All E.R. 579. See Hamson, 10 C.L.J. 249; Coote, 35 M.L.R. 38.

One Smith sold machine tools to the plaintiffs. This sale was illegal, since it contravened an Order made by the Minister of Supply under the Defence of the Realm Regulations. The plaintiffs delivered the tools to the defendants under three separate hire-purchase agreements which were assumed by the Court of Appeal to be themselves illegal. The defendants, after paying only a few of the instalments due under the contracts, sold the tools delivered under the first and third agreements and refused the demand of the plaintiffs to re-deliver those that were the subject-matter of the second agreement.

Judgment was given for the plaintiffs in their action to recover damages for the conversion of the tools.

In considering this decision it is necessary to distinguish the first and third agreements where the defendants had wrongfully sold the goods, from the second where they had retained them contrary to the demand of the plaintiffs.

The significant feature of the wrongful sales was that they constituted an act of conversion which *ipso facto* terminated the bailment.[1] The plaintiffs might therefore argue that there was no longer any existing contract upon which the defendants could found a possessory right. The right to immediate possession had automatically revested in the plaintiffs. Could it not thus be said that owing to the termination of the bailment the plaintiffs had an independent cause of action in virtue of their admitted ownership? The defendants, on the other hand, might argue that they had acquired effective possession under the bailment and that the plaintiffs were driven to rely upon that illegal transaction in order to show that the sale was a breach of the contractual terms, just as a lessor who alleged the termination of a lease for condition broken would be required to prove the existence of a proviso for re-entry.

The Court of Appeal preferred the first line of reasoning. It was completely irrelevant that the chattels had originally come into the possession of the defendants by virtue of the illegal contract. That contract was now defunct. It formed no part of the cause of action. Thus, with the disappearance of the only transaction that could restrict their rights, the plaintiffs could base their claim to possession solely upon their ownership of the chattels.

While few would dispute this conclusion and the limitation thus put upon the application of the maxim *ex turpi causa non oritur actio*, it is a little difficult to agree that the second agreement was susceptible of the same *ratio decidendi*. In the case of this agreement the cause of action was the refusal of the defendants to comply with the demand for the return of the goods. Since the effective possession had passed to them by virtue of its delivery, the sole justification for this demand was their failure to pay the agreed instalments. The plaintiffs, therefore, were inevitably driven back to the contract in order to prove the amounts of the instalments, the dates at which they were due and the agreed effect of their non-payment. This part of the decision, therefore, seems open to question.

---

1. *North Central Wagon and Finance Co., Ltd.* v. *Graham,* [1950] 2 K.B. 7; [1950] 1 All E.R. 780.

There are two exceptions to the general rule that a party cannot recover what he has given to the other party under an illegal contract. These are (a) where the parties are not *in pari delicto*, and (b) where the plaintiff repents before the contract has been performed.

If the parties to an illegal contract are not *in pari delicto*, the court in certain circumstances will allow the less blameworthy to recover what he may have transferred to the other. This relief is granted to the plaintiff upon proof that he has been the victim of fraud, duress or oppression at the hands of the defendant, or that the latter stood in a fiduciary position towards him and abused it.[1] Where, for instance, the plaintiff has effected an insurance which in fact is illegal but which was represented to him by the insurer as lawful, he will be entitled to recover the premiums which he has paid if the representation was fraudulent,[2] but not if it was not.[3] A common illustration of want of delictual parity is oppression. " It can never be predicated as *par delictum* where one holds the rod and the other bows to it."[4] For instance, in *Smith* v. *Cuff*,[5] the defendant, a creditor of the plaintiff, agreed with the other creditors to accept a composition of ten shillings in the pound, but he consented to this only after he had secretly arranged that the plaintiff should give him a promissory note for the remainder of his debt. The note was given, negotiated to a third party and its amount paid by the plaintiff. It was held that, since there had been oppression on one side and submission on the other, the plaintiff was entitled to recover the amount from the defendant. In a later case where the facts were similar, COCKBURN, C.J., said: " It is true that both are *in delicto*, because the act is a fraud upon the other creditors, but it is not *par delictum*, because the one has the power to dictate, the other no alternative but to submit."[6]

Another type of case where the parties are not regarded as equally delictual is where the contract is rendered illegal by a statute, the object of which is to protect one class of persons from the machinations of another class, as for example where it forbids a landlord to take a premium from a prospective tenant. Here, the duty of observing the law is placed squarely upon the shoulders of the landlord, and the protected person, the tenant, may recover an illegal premium in an action for money had and received, even if the statute omits to afford him this remedy either expressly or by implication.[7] In the words of Lord MANSFIELD:

" Where contracts or transactions are prohibited by positive statutes, for the sake of protecting one set of men from another set of men; the one from their situation and condition being liable to be

---

1. *Harse* v. *Pearl Life Assurance Co.*, [1904] 1 K.B. 558, at p. 563.
2. *Hughes* v. *Liverpool Victoria Legal Friendly Society*, [1916] 2 K.B. 482.
3. *Harse* v. *Pearl Life Assurance Co.*, *supra*.
4. *Smith* v. *Cuff* (1817), 6 M. & S. 160, at p. 165, *per* Lord ELLENBOROUGH.
5. (1817), 6 M. & S. 160.
6. *Atkinson* v. *Denby* (1862), 7 H. & N. 934, at p. 936.
7. *Kiriri Cotton Co., Ltd.* v. *Dewani*, [1960] A.C. 192; [1960] 1 All E.R. 177, where there was no express provision in the statute that the premium should be recoverable. If there is such a provision, as in *Gray* v. *Southouse*, [1949] All E.R. 1019, the fact that the tenant is *particeps criminis* does not affect his right of recovery.

oppressed and imposed upon by the other; there the parties are not *in pari delicto*; and in furtherance of these statutes, the person injured after the transaction is finished and completed, may bring his action and defeat the contract."[1]

(b) Where party to executory contract repents before performance

The second exception to the ban on restitution recognizes the virtue of repentance in the case of a contract which is still executory. A party to such a contract, despite its illegality, is allowed a *locus poenitentiae*, and he may recover what he has transferred to his co-contractor, provided that he takes proceedings before the illegal purpose has been substantially performed. If he repents in time, he will be assisted by the court, but in the present state of the authorities it is not clear at what point his repentance is to be regarded as overdue.

What constitutes performance in this context?

The leading case on the subject is *Kearley* v. *Thomson*,[2] where the defendants, who were the solicitors of the petitioning creditor in certain bankruptcy proceedings, agreed neither to appear at the public examination of the bankrupt nor to oppose his discharge in consideration of a sum of money paid to them by the plaintiff. They did not appear at the examination, and before any application had been made for the discharge of the bankrupt they were sued by the plaintiff for the return of the money. The contract was illegal as tending to pervert the course of justice, and it was held that the non-appearance at the examination was a sufficient execution of the illegal purpose to defeat the plaintiff's right to recovery.

> " I hold, therefore," said FRY, L.J., " that where there has been a partial carrying into effect of an illegal purpose in a substantial manner, it is impossible, though there remains something not performed, that the money paid under that illegal contract can be recovered back."[3]

Taylor v. *Bowers*

The word " partial " in this statement must be regarded as qualified by the later word " substantial," for otherwise it is difficult to reconcile the earlier case of *Taylor* v. *Bowers*.[4] In that case:

> T, being financially embarrassed and desiring to avoid the seizure of his stock by his creditors, made a fictitious assignment of it to A, and received sham bills of exchange in return. The stock, having been removed, was later mortgaged by A to the defendant without the knowledge of T. The defendant was aware of the unlawful assignment.

It was held that T was entitled to recover his goods. It is clear that the illegal purpose had been *partially* effected, for the creditors, realizing that the greater part of T's visible wealth had disappeared with the removal of his stock, would probably abandon any attempt to exact payment by process of law. In the unanimous opinion of seven judges, however, nothing had been done to carry out the illegal purpose beyond the removal

---

1. *Browning* v. *Morris* (1778), 2 Cowp, 790, at p. 792. See *Barclay* v. *Pearson*, [1893] 2 Ch. 154, at pp. 166–8.
2. (1890), 24 Q.B.D. 742. See *Re National Benefit Assurance Co., Ltd.*, [1931] 1 Ch. 46; *Harry Parker, Ltd.* v. *Mason,* [1940] 2 K.B. 590; [1940] 4 All E.R. 199. Beatson, 91 L.Q.R. 313.
3. (1890), 24 Q.B.D., at p. 747.
4. (1876), 1 Q.B.D. 291.

of the stock and this was insufficient to defeat the plaintiff. In *Kearley* v. *Thomson*, on the other hand, the fraudulent injury to the creditors had been *substantially* accomplished, for the general body of creditors would be influenced by the abstention of the petitioning creditor from the cross-examination of the debtor.[1]

In *Taylor* v. *Bowers*, MELLISH, L.J., made a statement that is transparently too wide if it is divorced from the facts. He said:

> " If money is paid or goods delivered for an illegal purpose, the person who has so paid the money or delivered the goods may recover them back before the illegal purpose is carried out."[2]

If this were correct, it would frequently happen that the mere frustration of his illegal scheme owing to circumstances beyond his control would entitle such a person to recover his property. *Bigos* v. *Bousted*,[3] concerned with statutory illegality, is a case in point.

> A, in contravention of the Exchange Control Act 1947, agreed to supply B with the equivalent of £150 in Italian currency. B, as security for his promise to repay the loan, deposited a share certificate with A. A failed to supply any Italian currency and B sued him for recovery of the certificate.

The statement of MELLISH, L.J., literally construed, would justify recovery, since the illegal purpose had not been carried out. B had in fact received no more Italian money than was permissible by law. He therefore pleaded that he had repented in time. His so-called repentance, however, was " but want of power to sin," for it is clear that he would gladly have accepted the promised lire had his illegal design not been foiled by A's breach of faith. PRITCHARD, J., therefore held that the case was on all fours with *Alexander* v. *Rayson*[4] and that B's change of heart after his scheme had failed did not bring him within the exception.

Another type of case in which recovery can be had despite a partial performance of the illegal purpose is where money has been deposited with a stakeholder under an illegal contract, as for example where competitors in a lottery, such as a missing-word competition, pay entrance fees to the organizer. Here the money is recoverable, not merely before the result has been ascertained, but even after this event, provided that payment has not been made to the winner.[5] In such a case the illegal purpose has obviously been performed by the holding of the lottery, yet it is said that " the contract is not completely executed until the money has been paid over, and therefore the party may retract at any time before that has been done."[6]

Money deposited with stakeholder under illegal contract

---

1. In *George* v. *Greater Adelaide Land Development Co., Ltd.,* (1929), 43 C.L.R. 91, a decision of the High Court of Australia, KNOX, C.J., at p. 100, regarded *Taylor* v. *Bowers* as a case of property deposited with a stakeholder, as to which see *infra* footnote 5
2. *Taylor* v. *Bowers* (1876), 1 Q.B.D., at p. 300.
3. [1951] 1 All E.R. 92.
4. [1936] 1 K.B. 169; [1935] All E.R. 185; *supra*, p. 342.
5. *Barclay* v. *Pearson*, [1893] 2 Ch. 154; *Greenberg* v. *Cooperstein*, [1926] Ch. 657, at p. 665.
6. *Hastelow* v. *Jackson* (1828), 8 B. & C. 221, at pp. 226–7 *per* LITTLEDALE, J.

The truth is that it is difficult to extract from these authorities the precise meaning in the present context of an " executory " contract. Over seventy years ago, FRY, L.J., observed that the principle which forbids the recovery of property delivered under an illegal contract requires reconsideration by the House of Lords.[1] Such reconsideration is still awaited.

Later
transactions
springing
from illegal
contract
void

(iii) A subsequent or collateral contract, which is founded on or springs from an illegal transaction, is illegal and void[2]

It would be singular if the law were otherwise.[3] It is irrelevant that the new contract is in itself innocuous, or that it formed no part of the original bargain, or that it is executed under seal,[4] or that the illegal transaction out of which it springs has been completed. If money is due from A to B under an illegal transaction and A gives B a bond[5] or a promissory note[6] for the amount owing, neither of these instruments is enforceable by B.

The leading authority is *Fisher* v. *Bridges*,[7] where A agreed to sell to B certain land which was to be used for the purposes of a lottery that was illegal because forbidden by statute. The land was conveyed to B and the price except for £630 was paid. Later, B executed a deed by which he covenanted to pay £630 to A. In an action to enforce this covenant, it was pleaded that the action must fail, since the agreement to sell was made " to the intent and in order, and for the purpose, as the defendant well knew," that the land when conveyed should be sold by way of an illegal lottery.[8] The Exchequer Chamber, reversing the Court of Queen's Bench, held the plea to be good and dismissed the action.

> " It is clear that the covenant was given for the payment of the purchase money. It springs from and is the creature of the illegal agreement, and as the law would not enforce the original illegal contract, so neither will it allow the parties to enforce a security for the purchase money, which by the original bargain was tainted with illegality."[9]

---

1. *Kearley* v. *Thomson* (1890), 24 Q.B.D. 742, at p. 746. For a critical appraisal of the present state of the law, see Grodecki, 74 L.Q.R. 254.
2. *Simpson* v. *Bloss* (1816), 7 Taunt. 246; *Redmond* v. *Smith* (1844), 7 Man & G. 457, *Geere* v. *Mare* (1863), 2 H. & C. 339; *Clay* v. *Ray* (1864), 17 C.B. N.S. 188.
3. *Redmond* v. *Smith, supra,* at p. 494, *per* TINDAL, J.
4. *Fisher* v. *Bridges* (1854), 3 E. & B. 642.
5. *Ibid.*
6. *Jennings* v. *Hammond* (1882), 9 Q.B.D. 225.
7. (1854), 3 E. & B. 642.
8. See the report of the case in the court of first instance: (1853), 2 E. & B. 118.
9. (1854), 3 E. & B. 642, *per curiam* at p. 649. It is respectfully submitted that in *Belvoir Finance* v. *Cole, Ltd.,* [1969] 2 All E.R. 904; [1969] 1 W.L.R. 1877, DONALDSON, J., was scarcely justified in holding that the original purchase of the two Triumph cars was not tainted by the illegality of the subsequent hire-purchase transaction. As in *Fisher* v. *Bridges,* the contract of sale was made to the intent and in order that the cars should be bailed by way of hire purchase transactions which both parties knew were to be effected in a manner contrary to a statutory order. It is a little difficult to subscribe to the view of the learned judge that the two pairs of contracts, though commercially connected, were not legally connected.

In *Fisher* v. *Bridges* the parties to the illegal transaction and to the subsequent contract were the same persons. The question arises, therefore, whether a contract made by a third party in furtherance of the illegal purpose is itself tainted. This was the issue in *Cannan* v. *Bryce*[1] where the court made the solution of this problem turn upon the knowledge of the third party. Did he know that the original contract was illegal? Position of third parties

> X had entered into a stock-jobbing contract by which he agreed to pay differences according to the rise and fall of the stock.[2] A statute of 1734 prohibited the practice of stock-jobbing.[3] He borrowed money from Y in order to pay the losses that he ultimately incurred, and by way of security he assigned to Y the proceeds of certain cargoes which he had shipped abroad. X then became bankrupt and his trustee claimed that the cargoes still formed part of the bankrupt estate, since the assignment to Y was illegal.

It was held that the trustee was entitled to judgment. In the words of ABBOTT, L.J., " if it be unlawful for one man to pay, how can it be lawful for another to furnish him with the means of payment?" But the Chief Justice was careful to emphasize that his statement was confined to a case where the third party had full knowledge of the object to which the loan was to be applied.[4]

A similar question arose in the recent case of *Spector* v. *Ageda*[5] on the following facts.

> A memorandum dated September 8th, 1967, stated that a Mrs. Maxwell, a moneylender, had lent £1,040 to the borrower, to be paid on November 8th with interest at two *per cent.* a month. In fact only £1,000 was lent, since interest for two months, amounting to £40, had been added to the principal sum. Such a provision for the payment of compound interest is illegal under the Moneylenders Act 1927.[6] The illegal loan was not repaid on November 8th, and Mrs. Maxwell sued the borrower in the following February for the recovery of £1,180, the amount then due.
>
> At that point the plaintiff entered upon the scene. She was the sister and the solicitor of Mrs. Maxwell, but she was now also acting as the solicitor of the borrower. She agreed to advance to the latter £1,180 with interest at 12 *per cent. per annum.* She honoured this agreement and the Maxwell loan was repaid.

In the present action, the question was whether the plaintiff could recover from the borrower £1,180 with interest at 12 *per cent.* In the view of MEGARRY, J., *Cannan* v. *Bryce* did not wholly support the contention that the agreement to make the advance was illegal, but he had no doubt that it was warranted by *Fisher* v. *Bridges.* " In that case, the subsequent contract was between the original parties: but a third party who takes part in the subsequent transaction with knowledge of the prior illegality can, in general, be in no better position."[7] In the instant case, it was clear that the plaintiff had concurred in the making of the

---

1. (1819), 3 B. & Ald. 179.
2. As to contracts for differences, see *supra*, p. 298.
3. 7 Geo. 2 c. 8; repealed by the Gaming Act 1845.
4. (1819), 3 B. & Ald., at p. 185.
5. [1971] 3 All E.R. 417, at p. 427; [1971] 3 W.L.R. 498. See also *Portland Holdings, Ltd.* v. *Cameo Motors, Ltd.,* [1966] N.Z.L.R. 571.
6. Section 7.
7. [1971] 3 All E.R. 417, at p. 427; [1971] 3 W.L.R., at p. 509.

Maxwell loan and had been fully aware of the illegal provision for the payment of compound interest. Therefore her action failed.

Foreign
contract

(iv) A foreign contract, if contrary to English public policy, is unenforceable

An action is frequently brought in England upon a foreign contract. By a foreign contract is meant one which is more closely connected with a foreign country than with England, as, for instance, when it is made in France by an Englishman and a Frenchman and is performable only in France. In such a case the rule is that the substance of the obligation—the essential validity of the contract—must be governed by what is called the " proper law," i.e. in effect the law of the country with which the transaction is most closely connected. The English doctrine of consideration, for instance, could not be invoked in an action for breach of the contract given above. Nevertheless, the rights of the parties as fixed by the proper law, if put in suit in England, are subject in general to the English doctrine of public policy. If the contract, though valid by the foreign law, is repugnant to what has been called the " stringent domestic policy " of England,[1] it cannot be enforced in England. This, however, does not mean that each individual rule comprised in the comprehensive doctrine of public policy applies to a foreign contract. That doctrine strikes at acts which vary greatly in their degree of turpitude. Certain of its prohibitory rules exemplify principles which in the English view it is of paramount importance to maintain in English courts; others, such as that directed against a fraud on the revenue, are presumably designed to protect purely English interests. It is the former rules only, those upon which there can be no compromise, that apply to an action on a foreign contract.

Scope of the
rule

Which of the rules are sufficiently important to be applied without exception is a somewhat controversial question that cannot be adequately discussed in a book on the elements of contract.[2] The decisions, however, at least warrant the statement that most of the contracts already described in this chapter as being repugnant to public policy and illegal, would not be enforced in an English action, whatever view might be taken of their validity by their proper law.[3] This is clearly so, for instance, in the case of a French contract to commit a crime or a tort, or to promote sexual immorality, or to prejudice the public safety of England. It might be thought that an agreement to stifle a foreign prosecution would scarcely arouse the moral indignation of an English court, but no such indifference to what is normal in certain countries was shown by the Court of Appeal in *Kaufman* v. *Gerson*.[4] In that case:

---

1. Westlake, *Private International Law,* 7th Edn., p. 51.
2. See, e.g. Dicey and Morris, *The Conflict of Laws,* 9th Edn., pp. 748–762; Cheshire's *Private International Law,* 9th Edn., pp. 148–159; Kahn-Freund, 39 *Grotius Society* 39.
3. *Robinson* v. *Bland* (1760), 2 Burr. 1077, at p. 1084; *Dynamit Act* v. *Rio Tinto Co.,* [1918] A.C. 260.
4. [1904] 1 K.B. 591.

A Frenchman coerced a Frenchwoman into signing a contract in France by the threat that if she refused to sign he would prosecute her husband for a crime of which he was accused.

The contract was valid by French law, but an action brought for its breach in England was dismissed on the ground that to enforce it " would contravene what by the law of this country is deemed an essential moral interest."[1] Presumably, therefore, an English court would apply the rule that has been laid down in the United States of America and would refuse to enforce any contract which tended to promote corruption in the public affairs of a foreign country, however irreproachable such conduct might be in the view of the foreign·law.[2]

C. THE CONSEQUENCE WHERE A CONTRACT LAWFUL IN ITS INCEPTION IS LATER ILLEGALLY EXPLOITED OR PERFORMED

The situation envisaged here is that a contract is lawful *ex facie* and is not disfigured by a common intention to break the law, but that one of the parties, without the knowledge of the other, in fact exploits it for some unlawful purpose. In these circumstances, the guilty party suffers the full impact of the maxim *ex turpi causa non oritur actio* and all remedies are denied to him.[3] " Any party to the agreement who had the unlawful intention is precluded from suing upon it . . . The action does not lie because the court will not lend its help to such a plaintiff."[4]

(margin: No remedies available to guilty party)

On the other hand, the rights of the innocent party are unaffected, except in respect of anything done by him after he has learned of the illegal purpose. In *Cowan* v. *Milbourn*,[5] for instance, the defendant agreed to let a room to the plaintiff on January 20th, but chancing to hear that the premises were to be used for an unlawful purpose, he notified the plaintiff that the agreement would not be fulfilled. An action brought against him for breach of contract failed. But if, after the intended purpose had come to his knowledge, he had let the defendant into possession in accordance with the contract, BRAMWELL, B., observed that he could not have recovered the agreed price.[6]

(margin: Rights of innocent party unaffected)

Apart from this exceptional case of acquired knowledge, however, all the normal contractual remedies are available to the innocent party. He may enforce the contract;[7] he may sue on a *quantum meruit* or *quantum valebant* for the value of work or

---

1. *Ibid.*, at pp. 599–600.
2. *Oscanyan* v. *Arms Co.*, 103 U.S. 261, at p. 277.
3. *Cowan* v. *Milbourn* (1867), L.R. 2 Exch. 230; *Alexander* v. *Rayson*, [1936] 1 K.B. 169.
4. *Alexander* v. *Rayson, supra*, at p. 182, *per curiam*.
5. *Supra*.
6. This had been made clear in *Jennings* v. *Throgmorton* (1825), Ry. & Mood. 251.
7. *Lloyd* v. *Johnson* (1798), 1 Bos. & Pul. 340; *Mason* v. *Clarke*, [1955] A.C. 778, at pp. 793, 805; [1955] 1 All E.R. 914, at pp. 920, 927; *Fielding & Platt, Ltd.* v. *Najjar*, [1969] 2 All E.R. 150; [1969] 1 W.L.R. 357.

goods supplied before discovery of the unlawful intention;[1] and he may recover property that he has transferred to the guilty party.[2]

It must be noticed that this right to recover property does not conflict with the decision of the Exchequer Chamber in *Feret* v. *Hill*, where:[3]

> The plaintiff induced the defendant to grant him a lease of premises in Jermyn Street by falsely representing that he intended to carry on therein the business of a perfumier. His intention, however, was to use them for immoral purposes, and, having obtained possession he converted them into a common brothel. He refused to quit and was forcibly ejected by the defendant. He brought an action of ejectment to recover possession and was successful.

This decision of a common law court must not be misunderstood. The elemental facts are simple: the lease had been executed, the tenant had been let into possession, and therefore in the eyes of the law a legal estate, together with the right to possession, had become vested in him. The court did not decide that the landlord was precluded from recovering possession. It merely decided that the tenant was not prevented by his antecedent fraud from acquiring a right to possession and that his right was not automatically forfeited either by his fraud or by his subsequent immoral use of the premises.[4] The landlord was ill-advised. He was not entitled to take the law into his own hands, to treat the lease as a nullity and to extrude the tenant from a possession recognized, at any rate for the time being, as lawful. But he would have been entitled, as indeed was assumed by the members of the court,[5] to take proceedings in equity for the rescission of the lease.

The rule is that if X transfers an interest in land or goods to Y, being induced to do so by a fraudulent misrepresentation similar to that made in *Feret* v. *Hill*, he can, subject to any rights that may have been obtained for value by innocent third parties, take proceedings in any division of the High Court to secure the rescission of the contract and the recovery of his property.[6]

Contract illegal as performed

The superior position of the innocent party is equally apparent where a contract, though lawful as formed, is performed by his co-contractor in a manner prohibited by statute.[7] In such a case, the party responsible for the illegal performance is remediless. So far as he alone is concerned, he is in exactly the same position as if the contract had been illegal and void *ab initio*.[8] But the innocent party is little affected, for in the words of Pollock:

> " The fact that unlawful means are used in performing an agreement which is *prima facie* lawful and capable of being lawfully performed does not of itself make an agreement unlawful."[9]

---

1. *Clay* v. *Yates* (1856), 1 H. & N. 73; *Bowry* v. *Bennett* (1808), 1 Camp. 348.
2. *Oom* v. *Bruce* (1810), 12 East 225; *supra*, p. 343.
3. (1854), 15 C.B. 207.
4. See the remarks of MAULE, J. (one of the judges in *Feret* v. *Hill*) in *Canham* v. *Barry* (1855), 15 C.B. 597, at pp. 611–12.
5. *Feret* v. *Hill*, *supra*, at p. 226, *per* MAULE, J.
6. *Alexander* v. *Rayson*, *supra*, at p. 192, *per curiam*.
7. *Supra*, pp. 321 *et seq.*
8. *Anderson, Ltd.* v. *Daniel*, [1924] 1 K.B. 138, at p. 145, *per* PARKER, L.J.
9. *Principles of Contract*, 13th Edn., p. 346.

If, indeed, the innocent party knows or ought to know that the contract can only be performed illegally or that the party responsible intends to perform it illegally, he is precluded from enforcing it either directly or indirectly.[1] Otherwise the normal remedies are open to him.

Thus he may recover damages for breach of contract.[2] It is not open to the defendant to plead that, because he himself adopted an illegal mode of performance, the apparent contract is no contract.

Damages for breach of contract recoverable

> Suppose that B has agreed to sell goods to A and that upon making delivery he is required by statute to furnish A with an invoice stating certain prescribed particulars. B in fact delivers goods that fall short of the standard fixed by the contract, and also fails to furnish the statutory invoice.

A, as the innocent party, must surely be able to sue B for breach of contract. Otherwise the absurd result would follow that if B delivered no goods at all he would be liable in damages, since there would have been no performance and no illegality; but that if he broke his contract by delivering inferior goods without the requisite invoice, this illegal mode of performance would free him from liability. Escape from a lawful obligation can scarcely be gained by a self-induced act of illegality.

That the sensible is also the judicial solution was adumbrated in 1924 in *Anderson* v. *Daniel*,[3] where the Court of Appeal stressed that in such a case as that supposed above it is only the guilty party who is remediless, a conclusion which has now been confirmed by *Marles* v. *Philip Trant & Sons, Ltd. (No. 2)*:[4]

> X agreed to sell to the defendants seed described as spring wheat. He delivered winter wheat and thereby broke his contract, but no illegality had as yet been committed either in the formation or the performance of the contract. The defendants innocently re-sold the wheat as spring wheat to the plaintiff, a farmer. This contract was still lawful as formed. It was, however, illegal as performed, since the defendants failed to comply with a statute which required an invoice to be delivered with the goods.

The farmer, upon discovering the seed to be winter wheat, sued the defendants for breach of contract. Despite the illegality of performance, he was allowed, as the innocent party, to recover damages. It was also held that the defendant's illegal performance of his contract with the plaintiff did not debar him from recovery against X for X's breach of their contract.

It is also reasonably clear in principle that the innocent party is entitled to take legal action to recover money or other property transferred by him under the contract.[5] Since he has taken no part in the unlawful performance, he can be in no worse position than a party to a contract illegal in its formation, who is

Property transferred recoverable

---

1. *Archbolds (Freightage), Ltd.* v. *S. Spanglett, Ltd.,* [1961] 1 Q.B. 374, at p. 374; [1961] 1 All E.R. 417, at p. 422, *per* PEARCE, L.J.
2. *Neilson* v. *James* (1882), 9 Q.B.D. 546.
3. [1924] 1 K.B. 138, at p. 145, *per* BANKES, L.J.; at p. 147, *per* SCRUTTON, L.J.; at p. 149, *per* ATKIN, L.J.
4. [1954] 1 Q.B. 29; [1953] 1 All E.R. 651.
5. *Siffken* v. *Allnutt* (1813), 1 M. & S. 39.

allowed at common law to recover what he has parted with if he is not *in pari delicto* with the other party.[1]

A separate
promise for
lawful
performance
is enforceable Where a contract will become illegal unless performed in the manner required by statute, one party, as a condition of entering into it, may exact a promise from the other agreeing to keep performance free from the taint of illegality. If so, this exchange of promises creates a distinct promise separate from the main contract and in the event of its breach the guilty party is liable in damages. Such a case was *Strongman (1945), Ltd.* v. *Sincock.*[2]

> The plaintiffs, a building firm, agreed to modernize certain houses belonging to the defendant, an architect. In view of certain statutory regulations, it was illegal to carry out the work without the licence of the Ministry of Works. Before the contract was made, the defendant orally promised that he would make himself responsible for obtaining the necessary licences. The plaintiffs did work to the value of £6,359, but since licences for only £2,150 had been obtained, the defendant, who had paid them £2,900, refused to pay the balance of £3,459 on the ground that the work had been illegally performed.

The plaintiffs' claim to enforce the main contract for the recovery of the balance failed. They could not evade the consequences of their contravention of the law by passing to the defendant the responsibility for legalizing the work. But in the sense that they had trusted him to take the necessary steps, the Court of Appeal were prepared to regard them as so far " innocent " as to allow them an independent cause of action based on the defendant's promise to obtain the requisite licences. This promise was given before the work started and in consideration of the undertaking by the plaintiffs to do the work. There was thus constituted a " collateral " or " preliminary " contract valid in itself and distinct from the main contract.

It was stressed by the Court of Appeal, however, that only exceptionally will a collateral contract relieve the promisee from his obligation to observe a statutory regulation.[3] The circumstances must justify his belief that the obligation is no longer his. There was adequate justification in the instant circumstances, for the defendant said in evidence: " I agree that where there is an architect it is the universal practice for the architect and not the builder to get licences."

---

1. *Supra*, p. 353.
2. [1955] 2 Q.B. 525; [1955] 3 All E.R. 90.
3. See especially *per* BIRKETT, L.J., at p. 540. In a case where the defendant represented that he already held a licence, the Supreme Court of New South Wales held that the plaintiff, upon learning the truth and upon disaffirming the contract, could sue the defendant in fraud for damages to the amount of the work done and materials supplied; *Hatcher* v. *White* (1953), 53 S.R. (N.S.W.) 285.

SECTION IV.   PROOF OF ILLEGALITY

The rules of evidence that govern the proof of illegality, whether the contract is illegal by statute or at common law, may be summarized as follows:

Firstly, where the contract is *ex facie* illegal, the court takes judicial notice of the fact and refuses to enforce the contract, even though its illegality has not been pleaded by the defendant.

Secondly, where the contract is *ex facie* lawful, evidence of external circumstances showing that it is in fact illegal will not be admitted, unless those circumstances have been pleaded.

Thirdly, when the contract is *ex facie* lawful, but facts come to light in the course of the trial tending to show that it has an illegal purpose, the court takes judicial notice of the illegality notwithstanding that these facts have not been pleaded. But it must be clear that all the relevant circumstances are before the court.[1]

---

1. *North Western Salt Co., Ltd.* v. *Electrolytic Alkali Co., Ltd.,* [1914] A.C. 461; *Edler* v. *Auerbach,* [1950] 1 K.B. 359, especially at p. 371; [1949] 2 All E.R. 692; *Chettiar* v. *Chettiar,* [1962] A.C. 294; [1962] 1 All E.R. 494; *Snell* v. *Unity Finance Co., Ltd.,* [1964] 2 Q.B. 203; [1963] 3 All E.R. 50.

CHAPTER FIVE

Contracts Void at Common Law on Grounds of Public Policy

IT is now necessary to describe the three types of contract which, though they offend public policy, are treated by the courts not as illegal but as void, and to discuss their consequences.

SECTION I. THE CONTRACTS DESCRIBED

1. CONTRACTS TO OUST THE JURISDICTION OF THE COURTS

Contract to prevent access to the courts

It has long been established that a contract which purports to destroy the right of one or both of the parties to submit questions of law to the courts is contrary to public policy and is *pro tanto void.*[1] Speaking of the common practice of referring disputes to domestic tribunals, Lord DENNING said:

> " Parties cannot by contract oust the ordinary courts from their jurisdiction. They can, of course, agree to leave questions of law, as well as questions of fact, to the decision of the domestic tribunal. They can, indeed, make the tribunal the final arbiter on questions of fact, but they cannot make it the final arbiter on questions of law. They cannot prevent its decisions being examined by the courts. If parties should seek, by agreement, to take the law out of the hands of the courts and put it into the hands of a private tribunal, without any recourse at all to the courts in cases of error of law, then the agreement is to that extent contrary to public policy and void."[2]

In *Baker* v. *Jones*,[3] for instance, an association was formed to promote the sport of weightlifting in the United Kingdom, and control of its affairs was vested in a central council. It was provided that this council should be the sole interpreter of the rules of the association and that its decisions should in all cases and in all circumstances be final. It was held that to give the council the sole right of interpretation was void and that the court had jurisdiction to consider whether the interpretation adopted by the council in a given case was correct in law.

It should be observed, however, that an arbitration agreement, by which contracting parties provide that, before legal proceedings are taken, questions of law and fact shall be decided by a private tribunal, is not *per se* a contract to oust the jurisdiction of the courts, but is valid and enforceable. If, in breach of its terms, one of the parties commences legal proceedings against the other party, the latter may apply to the court for an order staying those proceedings.[4] Such an order will only rarely be refused. The onus lies upon the opposing party to advance some convincing reason why the agreement for arbitration should not be carried out.[5] {*Arbitration agreement*}

But, as the House of Lords recognized over a hundred years ago in *Scott* v. *Avery*,[6] though it is lawful to make the award of an arbitrator on a question of law a condition precedent to the institution of legal proceedings, it is contrary to public policy to agree that the submission of such a question to the court shall be prohibited. The Arbitration Act 1950 now provides that an arbitrator may, and must if so directed by the High Court, state {*" Scott* v. *Avery"* clause}

---

1. *Thompson* v. *Charnock* (1799), 8 Term Rep. 139. An agreement to oust the jurisdiction of the courts must be distinguished from the case where the parties do not intend that their legal relations shall be affected by their agreement (*supra*, pp. 102 *et seq.*). Parties are at liberty to declare that they do not wish to make a legally binding contract, but only a " gentleman's agreement." But having decided to make and having in fact made a binding contract, they are not allowed to exclude it from the supervision of the courts.
2. *Lee* v. *The Showmen's Guild of Great Britain*, [1952] 2 Q.B. 329, at p. 342; [1952] 1 All E.R. 1175, at p. 1181.
3. [1954] 2 All E.R. 553; [1954] 1 W.L.R. 1005. *In Re Davstone Estates, Ltd.'s Leases, Manprop* v. *O'Dell*, [1969] 2 Ch. 378; [1969] 2 All E.R. 849.
4. Arbitration Act 1950, section 4 (1).
5. *Metropolitan Tunnel and Public Works* v. *London Electric Rail. Co.*, [1926] Ch. 371, at p. 385. A term in the arbitration agreement that no application for a stay of proceedings shall be made is void: *Czarnikow* v. *Roth, Schmidt & Co.*, [1922] 2 K.B. 478.
6. (1856), 5 H.L. Cas 811. *Czarnikow* v. *Roth, Schmidt & Co.*, [1922] 2 K.B. 478.

in the form of a special case for the opinion of the court any question of law that has arisen.[1]

Another example of this principle is an agreement by a wife not to apply to the court for maintenance. It is clear that there is a public interest against such promises since if the husband does not maintain the wife, her support may become a charge on public funds[2] but where such a promise by the wife is given in exchange for a promise by the husband to pay maintenance, it may appear unmeritorious to allow the husband to escape performance of his promise. After producing much litigation[3] such situations are now governed by legislation.[4] An agreement may also be invalid[5] insofar as it attempts to exclude mandatory rules of law. So for instance a perfectly valid agreement between two companies as to how accounts between them are to be settled may become inoperative if one goes into liquidation because it runs contrary to the provisions of the insolvency legislation.[6]

2. CONTRACTS PREJUDICIAL TO THE STATUS OF MARRIAGE

Sanctity of marriage a matter of public interest

The status of marriage is a matter of public interest in all civilized countries and it is important that nothing should be allowed to impair the sanctity of its solemn obligations or to weaken the loyalty that one spouse owes to the other. The general view of English law is that any contract is void which unduly restricts or hampers the freedom of persons to marry whom they will, or which after marriage tends to encourage in one or both of the parties an immoral mode of life incompatible with their mutual obligations.

Contracts in restraint of marriage void

Marriage ought to be free, and therefore a contract which restrains a person from marrying anybody, or from marrying anybody except a particular person without imposing a similar and reciprocal restriction on that person, is void as being contrary to the social welfare of the State.[7] Thus in *Lowe* v. *Peers*[8] a contract made by a man under seal to the following effect was held to be contrary to public policy:

---

1. Section 21 (1).
2. *Hyman* v. *Hyman*, [1929] A.C. 601.
3. See eg. *Bennett* v. *Bennett*, [1952] 1 K.B. 249; [1952] 1 All E.R. 413; *Brooks* v. *Burns Philp Trustee Co.*, [1969] A.L.R. 321.
4. Matrimonial Causes Act 1973, s. 34.
5. Does a clause providing that disputes under a contract are to be litigated in a foreign forum infringe the principle? This question has been much discussed in the United States. See Nadelman, 21 Am. Jo. Comp. Law 124; Denning, 2 Jo. Maritime Law and Commerce 17, Mendelssohn, *ibid* 661; Delaume, 4 Journal of Maritime Law and Commerce 275. But see now *Bremen* v. *Zapata* 407 U.S.1. (1972); [1972] 2 Lloyds Rep. 315.
6. *British Eagle International Airlines, Ltd.* v. *Compagnie Nationale Air France*, [1975] 2 All E.R. 390; [1975] 1 W.L.R. 758. Similarly an agreement between master and servant to release the master from a statutory duty to provide safe working conditions is invalid: *Baddeley* v. *Earl Granville* (1887), 19 Q.B.D. 423. But cf. *Imperial Chemical Industries* v. *Shatwell*, [1965] A.C. 656; [1964] 2 All E.R. 999. See Dias, [1966] C.L.J. 75.
7. Story, *Equity Jurisprudence*, s. 274.
8. (1768), 4 Burr. 2225. See also *Re Michelhan's Will Trusts* [1964] Ch. 550; [1963] 2 All E.R. 188.

> I do truly promise Mrs. Catherine Lowe that I will not marry
> with any person besides herself: if I do, I agree to pay to the said
> Catherine Lowe £2,000 within three months next after I shall
> marry anybody else.

Again, it is in the interests of society that reckless or unsuitable marriages should be prevented, but this desirable state of affairs is not likely to be attained if third parties are free to reap financial profit by bringing about matrimonial unions. It has therefore been ruled that what is called a marriage brokage contract, i.e. a contract by which A undertakes in consideration of a money payment to procure a marriage for B, is void.[1] This is so whether the contract is to procure B's marriage with one particular person or with one out of a whole class of persons.[2] *(margin: Marriage brokage contract void)*

Considerations of public policy, which, as we have just seen, apply to contracts made prior to marriage, also affect those made after marriage. The difficulty is to state the governing principle with precision, and we probably cannot venture further than this: that any contract which during cohabitation tends to encourage infidelity in one or both of the spouses or to provide an inducement for immoral conduct is void as being contrary to public policy. It is sometimes claimed that any contract whatsoever, that tends to induce a course of conduct inconsistent with the maintenance of the marriage tie, is void, but the authorities show that this is to state the rule too widely. Two lines of decisions illustrate the subject: those relating to separation agreements and those concerned with a promise made by a married person to marry a third person at some future time. *(margin: Contracts prejudicing an existing marriage)*

It has been established for over a hundred years that a contract providing for immediate separation of the spouses is valid and enforceable if followed by immediate separation, notwithstanding that this breaks the *consortium vitae* and is therefore to that extent inconsistent with the primary and fundamental obligation of the marriage tie.[3] On the other hand, a contract for a possible future separation, *e.g.* a promise by a husband that he will make provision for his wife if she should ever live apart from him, is contrary to public policy and void as being opposed to elementary considerations of morality.[4] The distinction between the two classes of agreement is obvious. Once the melancholy fact is apparent that the parties cannot live together in amity, it is desirable that the separation which has become inevitable should be concluded upon reasonable terms; but a promise for the benefit of one of the parties in the event of a possible future separation, if it does not put a premium on immorality, at least weakens the resolve of the promisee to maintain with loyalty and fidelity the obligations of the marriage tie. *(margin: Separation agreements)*

> " If a separation has actually occurred or become inevitable, the
> law allows the matter to be dealt with according to realities and not

---

1. *Hermann* v. *Charlesworth*, [1905] 2 K.B. 123, *infra*, p. 391. See Powell, 1953 Current Legal Problems 254.
2. *Hermann* v. *Charlesworth*, [1905] 2 K.B. 123.
3. *Wilson* v. *Wilson* (1848), 1 H.L. Cas. 538; subsequent proceedings (1854), 5 H.L. Cas. 40.
4. *H.* v. *W.* (1857), 3 K. & J. 382: *Brodie* v. *Brodie*, [1917] P. 271.

according to a fiction. But the law will not permit an agreement which contemplates the future possibility of so undesirable a state of affairs."[1]

The one exception to the rule that a contract for future separation is void occurs where parties, who have been separated already, make a reconciliation agreement and resume cohabitation. In this case the agreement is valid although it may make provision for a renewed separation.[2]

Contract by a married person to marry a third person The second line of cases is concerned with a contract by A, who is already married to B, to marry X at some future date. In *Spiers* v. *Hunt*[3] and *Wilson* v. *Carnley*,[4] PHILLIMORE, J., in the former, and the Court of Appeal in the latter, case, held that a promise of marriage made by a man, who to the knowledge of the promisee was at the time married to another woman, was void on grounds of public policy, and that it could not be enforced after the death of the wife. In *Fender* v. *St. John-Mildmay*[5] the House of Lords held, by a majority, that these decisions did not extend to a promise of marriage made by a married man whose marriage was so moribund that it had already been the subject of a decree nisi of divorce.[6] The practical situation in these cases can no longer be the subject of litigation since the abolition of actions for breach of promise of marriage[7] but they are still of interest as illustrating the public policy in respect of marriage.

3. CONTRACTS IN RESTRAINT OF TRADE[8]

Description of contract in restraint of trade A contract in restraint of trade is one by which a party restricts his future liberty to carry on his trade, business or profession in such manner and with such persons as he chooses. A contract of this class is *prima facie* void, but it becomes binding upon proof that the restriction is justifiable in the circumstances as being reasonable from the point of view of the parties themselves and also of the community.

Such has long been the legal effect of two familiar types of contract. First, one by which an employee agrees that after

---

1. *Fender* v. *St. John-Mildmay*, [1938] A.C. 1, at p. 44; [1937] 3 All E.R. 402, at p. 429, *per* Lord WRIGHT.
2. *Harrison* v. *Harrison*, [1910] 1 K.B. 35. See also *Re Johnson's Will Trusts, National Provincial Bank* v. *Jeffrey*, [1967] Ch. 387; [1967] 1 All E.R. 553.
3. [1908] 1 K.B. 720.
4. [1908] 1 K.B. 729; *Siveyer* v. *Allison*, [1935] 2 K.B. 403.
5. [1938] A.C. 1; [1937] 3 All E.R. 402. See especially the judgment of Lord ATKIN.
6. This reasoning could be argued to cover the case of a marriage factually dead but not yet the subject of legal proceedings. See Furmston, 16 U. of Toronto L.J. 267, at pp. 300–302. Cf. *Dobersek* v. *Petrizza*, [1968] N.Z.L.R. 211.
7. By Law Reform (Miscellaneous Provisions) Act 1970. Under the previous law a woman who accepted a proposal of marriage from a married man in ignorance of his status could enforce the contract. *Shaw* v. *Shaw*, [1954] 2 Q.B. 429; [1954] 2 All E.R. 638. This was a valuable remedy where, as in that case, the parties went through a ceremony of marriage and lived together for years. The action for breach of contract would provide a substitute for the succession rights which the " wife " would have had if the " marriage " had been valid. As to the present law, see s. 6 of the 1970 Act; Thomson, 87 L.Q.R. 158; Gower, 87 L.Q.R. 314.
8. Heydon, *The Restraint of Trade Doctrine*.

leaving his present employment he will not compete against his employer, either by setting up business on his own account or by entering the service of a rival trader. Secondly, an agreement by the vendor of the goodwill of a business not to carry on a similar business in competition with the purchaser.

This doctrine of restraint of trade is based upon public policy, and its application has been peculiarly influenced by changing views of what is desirable in the public interest.[1] This is inevitable. "Public policy is not a constant," and it necessarily alters as economic conditions alter.[2] In Elizabethan days all restraints of trade, whether general or partial, were regarded as totally void because of their tendency to create monopolies. This view, however, did not prevail, for it was gradually realized that a restriction of trading activities was in certain circumstances justifiable in the interests both of the public and of the parties themselves. It was clear, for instance, that the purchaser of a business was at the mercy of the vendor, if the latter were free to carry on his former trade in the same place; and that a master was equally at the mercy of his servants and apprentices if they were free to exploit to their own gain the knowledge that they had acquired of his personal customers or his trade secrets. Moreover, the evil was not limited to one side, for if all contracts against future competition were to be regarded as unlawful, the aim of employers, it was feared, might be to reduce the number of their servants to a minimum and so to increase unemployment. The law was therefore relaxed, though only gradually, and in 1711 in *Mitchel v. Reynolds*,[3] a case which is the foundation of the modern law, Lord MACCLESFIELD stated what he understood to be the current position. He said: Gradual development of the law

> "Wherever a sufficient consideration appears to make it a proper and useful contract, and such as cannot be set aside without injury to a fair contractor, it ought to be maintained; but with this constant diversity—namely where the restraint is general (not to exercise a trade throughout the kingdom), and where it is limited to a particular place, for the former of these must be void, being of no benefit to either party and only oppressive." Statement of the rule in 1711

The true significance of this passage, no doubt, was that everything must turn upon whether the contract was reasonable and fair. Lord MACCLESFIELD, in speaking of the "diversity," presumably did not intend to create a rigid distinction between a general and a limited restraint, the former void, the latter valid if reasonable. He was merely illustrating what, in the conditions of transport and communications prevailing in 1711, obviously could not be reasonable. "What does it signify," he said in a later passage, "to a tradesman in London what another does in Newcastle?" But no doubt he would have been the first to admit that, as conditions changed and communications improved, any rigid demarcation between general and limited restraints would be

---

1. *Attwood v. Lamont*, [1920] 3 K.B. 571, at p. 581, *per* YOUNGER, L.J. See Holdsworth, *History of English Law*, vol. 8, pp. 56–62.
2. *Vancouver Malt and Sake Brewing Co., Ltd.* v. *Vancouver Breweries, Ltd.*, [1934] A.C. 181, at p. 189; [1934] All E.R. Rep. 38, at p. 41, *per* Lord MACMILLAN.
3. (1711), 1 P. Wms. 181.

inconsistent with commercial realities.   Indeed a time was to come
when it might signify a great deal to the purchaser of a business
in London what the vendor did in Newcastle.   A long line of
authority, however, interpreting Lord MACCLESFIELD's words
literally, established, and maintained until the close of the nineteenth century, that a contract, whether made between a master
and servant or between a vendor and purchaser of a business which
imposed a general restraint, was necessarily and without exception
void; but that a partial restraint was *prima facie* valid, and if
reasonable was enforceable.   In summing up these authorities,
BOWEN, L.J., said:

> " Partial restraints, or in other words, restraints which involve
> only a limit of places at which, or persons with whom, or of modes
> in which the trade is to be carried on, are valid when made for a
> good consideration, and when they do not extend further than is
> necessary for the reasonable protection of the covenantee."[1]

The first inroad on this rule came in 1894 in the *Nordenfelt*
case,[2] when Nordenfelt, a manufacturer of quick-firing guns and
other implements of war, sold his business to a company for
£287,500 and entered into a contract restraining his future
activities.   Two years later the company was amalgamated with
another company which agreed to employ Nordenfelt as managing
director at a salary of £2,000 a year.   The deed of employment
continued, indeed amplified, the contract in restraint of trade
made by him two years earlier.   He covenanted that he would

> " not for twenty-five years, if the company so long continued to
> carry on business, engage, except on behalf of the company, either
> directly or indirectly, in the trade or business of a manufacturer of
> guns, gun mountings or carriages, gunpowder explosives or ammu-
> nition, or in *any business competing or liable to compete in any way
> with that for the time being carried on by the company*."

This restraint was general in the most absolute sense, since the
business of the company extended to all parts of the world.
Nevertheless, the House of Lords held that, except for the part
which has been italicized above, it was in the particular circumstances valid.   The actual decision marked a break with the past.
It came to this—that a contract in general restraint of trade,
made between a vendor and purchaser of a business, was not
necessarily void, but only *prima facie* void, and that it was valid
if it was reasonable in the interests of the parties and in the
interests of the public.   It was reasonable in the interests of the
parties to restrain Nordenfelt from trading in guns, gun mountings
or carriages, gunpowder explosives or ammunition, since the
business that he had sold for a large sum of money consisted in
the manufacture of those very things.   This part of the covenant
was also reasonable in the interests of the public, since it secured
to England the business and inventions of a foreigner and thus
increased the trade of the country.   On the other hand, to
restrain Nordenfelt from engaging in " any business competing
or liable to compete in any way with that for the time being

*Former
distinction
between
general and
partial
restraints*

*General
restraint
later
allowed*

---

1. *Maxim Nordenfelt Guns and Ammunition Co.* v. *Nordenfelt*, [1893] 1 Ch. 630,
   at p. 662.
2. *Nordenfelt* v. *Maxim Nordenfelt Guns and Ammunition Co.*, [1894] A.C. 535.

carried on by the company " was unreasonable, since it was
wider than was reasonably necessary to protect the proprietary
interest that the company had bought. That part of the covenant
must therefore be severed from the rest and declared void.

So much then for the actual decision. But the case is equally
important for the further break with tradition made by Lord
MACNAGHTEN, when he denied that general and partial restraints
fell into distinct categories. A partial restraint, in his opinion,
was not *prima facie* valid. It was on the same footing as a general
restraint, *i.e. prima facie* void, but valid if reasonable. The
relevant part of his speech is this:

> " All interferences with individual liberty of action in trading,
> and all restraints of trade of themselves, if there is nothing more,
> are contrary to public policy and therefore void. That is the general
> rule. But there are exceptions: restraints of trade . . . may be
> justified by the special circumstances of a particular case. It is a
> sufficient justification, and indeed it is the only justification, if the
> restriction is reasonable—reasonable, that is, in reference to the in-
> terests of the parties concerned and reasonable in reference to the
> interests of the public, so framed and so guarded as to afford adequate
> protection to the party in whose favour it is imposed, while at the
> same time it is in no way injurious to the public.''[1]

In a later passage he summarized the law in these words:

> " My Lords, I think the only true test in all cases, whether of
> partial or general restraint, is the test proposed by TINDAL, C.J.:
> What is a reasonable restraint with reference to the particular
> case? ''[2]

Lord MACNAGHTEN's view, so far as it related to partial
restraints, did not meet with the approval of all the Law Lords,
and indeed it was irrelevant, since the issue in the *Nordenfelt*
case was confined to the validity of a general restraint. Until
1913 his view was not adopted by the lower courts, which consistently acted on the assumption that partial restraints were
prima facie valid,[3] but in that year the House of Lords in *Mason* v.
Provident Clothing and Supply Co., Ltd.,[4] held that Lord
MACNAGHTEN's proposition was a correct statement of the modern
law. The House of Lords in this case developed the law in two
respects:

First, it held that all covenants in restraint of trade, partial as
well as general, are *prima facie* void and that they cannot be
enforced unless the test of reasonableness as propounded by
Lord MACNAGHTEN is satisfied.

Secondly, it made a sharp distinction, stressed as long ago as
1869 by JAMES, L.J.,[5] between contracts of service and contracts
for the sale of a business. It confirmed that a restraint may be
imposed more readily and more widely upon the vendor of a
business in the interests of the purchaser, than upon a servant

*Develop-
ment of the
law in 1913*

*All restraints
now void
unless
reasonable*

*Restraints
on vendors
more
favoured
than those
on servants*

---

1. [1894] A.C. 535, at p. 565.
2. *Ibid.*, at p. 574. The words of TINDAL, C.J., appear in *Horner* v. *Graves*
   (1831), 7 Bing. 735.
3. *Attwood* v. *Lamont*, [1920] 3 K.B. 571, at pp. 585–6, *per* YOUNGER, L.J.:
   the whole judgment is worthy of the closest attention.
4. [1913] A.C. 724.
5. *Leather Cloth Co.* v. *Lorsont* (1869), L.R. 9 Eq. 345. An agreement between
   professional partners is for this purpose equated to the sale of a business:
   Whitehill v. *Bradford*, [1952] Ch. 236; [1952] 1 All E.R. 115.

in the interests of the master.   In the former case, not only are
the parties dealing at arm's length, but the purchaser has paid
the full market value for the acquisition of a proprietary interest,
and it is obvious that this will lose much of its value if the vendor
is free to continue his trade with his old customers.   Indeed,
public policy demands that the covenantor should be allowed to
restrict his future activities, for otherwise he will find it impossible
to sell to the best advantage what he has created by his skill and
labour.[1]   Different considerations affect a contract of service.
For one thing the parties are not in an equally strong bargaining
position, and the servant will often find it difficult to resist the
imposition of terms favourable to the master and unfavourable
to himself.[2]   He may even find his freedom to request higher
wages seriously impeded, for should he be unsuccessful his
choice of fresh employment will be considerably narrowed if the
restraint is binding.[3]   Again, the master cannot as a rule show
any proprietary interest of a permanent nature that requires
protection, since the servant's skill and knowledge, even though
acquired in the service, are not bought for his life, but only for
the duration of the employment.[4]   The possibility that the
servant may be a competitor in the future is not a danger against
which the master is entitled to safeguard himself.   On the
contrary, it accords with public policy that a servant shall not
be at liberty to deprive himself or the State of his labour, skill
or talent.[5]   Decisive effect was given to these considerations in
Herbert Morris, Ltd. v. *Saxelby*,[6] where the House of Lords held
that a covenant which restrains a servant from competition is
always void as being unreasonable, unless there is some exceptional
proprietary interest owned by the master that requires protection.
In the course of his speech Lord PARKER said:

> " The reason, and the only reason, for upholding such a restraint
> on the part of an employee is that the employer has some proprietary
> right, whether in the nature of trade connection or in the nature
> of trade secrets, for the protection of which such a restraint is—
> having regard to the duties of the employee—reasonably necessary.
> Such a restraint has, so far as I know, never been upheld, if directed
> only to the prevention of competition or against the use of the
> personal skill and knowledge acquired by the employee in his
> employer's business."[7]

Importance
of the
Esso case

 The most recent landmark in the history of the subject is the
decision of the House of Lords in *Esso Petroleum Co., Ltd.* v.
Harper's Garage (Stourport), Ltd.[8]   This is of general importance

---

1. *Mason* v. *Provident Clothing and Supply Co., Ltd.*, [1913] A.C. 724, at
   p. 734, *per* Lord HALDANE;   *Ronbar Enterprises, Ltd.* v. *Green*, [1954] 1
   W.L.R. 815;   [1954] 2 All E.R. 266, *per* JENKINS, L.J., at pp. 270 and 820
   respectively.   If no provision is made upon the sale of goodwill for the
   prevention of competition, the vendor may set up a rival business, but he
   may not canvass his former customers: *Trego* v. *Hunt*, [1896] A.C. 7.
2. *Leather Cloth Co.* v. *Lorsont* (1869), L.R. 9 Eq. 345, at p. 354.   This might
   appear less true with the development of powerful trade unions but most
   restraints affect " white-collar " workers, who are much less unionised.
3. *M. & S. Drapers (A Firm)* v. *Reynolds*, [1956] 3 All E.R. 814, at p. 820;
   [1957] 1 W.L.R. 9, at p. 18, *per* DENNING, L.J.
4. *Attwood* v. *Lamont*, [1920] 3 K.B. 571, at p. 589.
5. *Leather Cloth Co.* v. *Lorsont* (1869), L.R. 9 Eq. 345, at p. 353, *per* JAMES, L.J.
6. [1916] 1 A.C. 688.
7. *Ibid.*, at p. 710.
8. [1968] A.C. 269;   [1967] 1 All E.R. 699.   Heydon, 85 L.Q.R. 229.

on several counts. The speeches show how the issues that arise in a contested case should be segregated; they show that the broad generalizations which figure so frequently in the reports are misleading guides; they reaffirm the true role of public policy in this context; and they contain much of value upon the categories of contract that attract the doctrine of restraint of trade.

In the first place, their Lordships stress the importance of segregating the two independent questions that require an answer where the doctrine is invoked. The first is whether the contract under review is so restrictive of the promisor's liberty to trade with others that it must be treated as *prima facie* void. If such is the finding of the court, the second question is whether the restrictive clause can be justified as being reasonable. If so the contract is valid. {Doctrine of restraint of trade raises two separate questions}

To neglect this segregation is to court confusion, for the facts relevant to the second question are not necessarily relevant to the first. If, for instance, the first is under investigation, it is a matter of indifference that the contract is contained in a mortgage; but in estimating the reasonableness of the restriction, the harshness or moderation of the mortgage terms may be the decisive element.[1] Where a judge combines the two questions, it is often impossible to discern to which of the two issues his remarks are directed.

It is in connexion with the first question that some confusion has been caused by judicial generalizations. The reports abound with statements of the most sweeping nature, such as that of Lord MACNAGHTEN quoted above,[2] in which he dismissed as contrary to public policy " all interferences with individual liberty of action in trading and all restraints of trade themselves, if there is nothing more." But, as was pointed out in the *Esso* case, such statements are not to be taken literally.[3] They were not intended to indicate that " any contract which in whatever way restricts a man's liberty to trade was (either historically under the common law or at the time of which they were speaking) *prima facie* unenforceable and must be shown to be reasonable."[4] Moreover, the changing face of commerce must always be borne in mind.[5] Restrictions which in an earlier age were classified as restraints of trade may, in the different circumstances of today, have become " part of the accepted pattern or structure of trade " as encouraging rather than limiting trade.[6] {Generalized definitions of the doctrine misleading}

Where, then, is the line to be drawn between restrictions that require justification and those that are innocuous? What at any rate is clear beyond doubt is that two categories of contract are *prima facie* void as being in restraint of trade: those which restrict competition by an employee against his employer or by the vendor of a business against the purchaser. {Two categories of contract that are subject to the doctrine}

---

1. *Ibid.*, *per* Lord PEARCE, at p. 326 and p. 725 respectively.
2. *Supra*, p. 369.
3. [1968] A.C. 269; [1967] 1 All E.R. 699; *per* Lord REID, at pp. 293–5 and at p. 705 respectively; *per* Lord MORRIS OF BORTH-Y-GEST, at pp. 307 and 713 respectively.
4. *Ibid.*, *per* Lord WILBERFORCE, at p. 333 and p. 730 respectively. Strictly speaking, the word " unenforceable " used in this passage should be replaced by " void."
5. *Ibid.*, *per* Lord PEARCE, at p. 324 and p. 724 respectively.
6. *Ibid.*, *per* Lord WILBERFORCE, at p. 335 and p. 731 respectively.

Certain
categories
exempt from
the doctrine
On the other hand, it may be said with reasonable confidence
that certain restrictive agreements have now " passed into the
accepted and normal currency of commercial or contractual or
conveyancing relations,"[1] and are therefore no longer suspect.   If,
for instance, a manufacturer agrees that X shall be the sole agent
for the sale of his output, the scope of his liberty of disposition is
no doubt fettered, but the object of the arrangement is to increase
his trade, and it has become a normal incident of commercial
practice.[2]   Again, it has been established for well over a hundred
years that an agreement by the lessee of a public house that he
will sell no beer on the premises except that brewed by his lessor
is outside the doctrine of restraint of trade.[3]

The same reasoning applies to the negative covenants, so
familiar in practice, by which a lessee or purchaser of land agrees
to surrender his common law right to use the premises for trading
purposes.   These have long been an accepted, indeed an essential,
feature of conveyancing practice and for that reason are excluded
from the doctrine of restraint of trade.[4]

In other
cases no
rigid classi-
fication
possible
So much is reasonably clear.   Two categories of contract are
subject to the doctrine of restraint; certain other categories are
exempt.   Where a contract which falls within none of these
categories places some degree of restriction upon a party's trading
activities, the court may feel obliged to consider whether in the
light of its terms and of the attendant circumstances it must be
construed as *prima facie* void.   This may be an enquiry of some
delicacy, for it involves the adjustment of two freedoms, both
based on public policy—the one the freedom to contract, the other
the freedom to trade[5]—or as Lord SHAW once put it, "the right
to bargain and the right to work."[6]   The perplexing problem is to
identify the type of restrictive contract that requires the intervention of the court.   Is there any rigid test that serves to distinguish the impeachable from the unimpeachable restriction?   It
may be answered at once that such a simple solution is unattain-
able.   Any attempt to classify the categories of contract that are
prima facie void is hazardous in the extreme.   There is no accurate

---

1. [1968] A.C., at pp. 332–3; [1967] 1 All E.R., at p. 729, *per* Lord WILBER-
FORCE; see also at p. 327 and p. 724 respectively, *per* Lord PEARCE.
2. *Ibid.*, at pp. 328–9 and 726 respectively, *per* Lord PEARCE; at p. 336 and
731 respectively, *per* Lord WILBERFORCE.   See *Servais Bouchard* v. *Princes
Hall Restaurant, Ltd.* (1904), 20 T.L.R. 574; *infra*, p. 375.
3. *Esso Petroleum Co., Ltd.* v. *Harper's Garage (Stourport), Ltd.*, [1968] A.C.
269, at p. 325; [1967] 1 All E.R., at p. 725, *per* Lord PEARCE; *per* Lord
WILBERFORCE, at pp. 333–4, and pp. 730–1 respectively.   " Tied houses "
became common while partial restraints were thought *prima facia* valid.
4. [1968] A.C., at pp. 334–5; [1967] 1 All E.R., at p. 731, *per* Lord WILBER-
FORCE.   The reason for this exclusion given by the other Law Lords was that
the covenantor surrenders no freedom that he formerly possessed, since prior
to the contract he had no right to trade on the land.   This, however, would
not explain the exclusion where the owner of two properties sells one and
covenants not to trade on the other that he retains.   This reason was relied
on however in *Cleveland Petroleum Co. Ltd.* v. *Dartstone, Ltd.*, [1969],
1 All E.R. 201; [1969] 1 W.L.R. 116.   See *infra*, p. 386.
5. [1968] A.C., at p. 306; [1967] 1 All E.R., at p. 712, *per* Lord MORRIS OF
BORTH-Y-GEST.
6. *Mason* v. *Provident Clothing and Supply Co., Ltd.*, [1913] A.C. 724, at
p. 738.

rubric under which they can be brought. " The classification must remain fluid and the categories can never be closed."[1]

The manner in which the courts approach the problem is illustrated by the decision of the House of Lords in the *Esso* case,[2] where the respondent company had tied its two garages to the appellant company under what is called the " *solus* system."[3] Separate contracts were entered into in respect of each garage, but each contained the following main provisions.

> The respondent company agreed to buy its total requirements of motor fuel from Esso; and to operate the garages in accord with the Esso co-operation plan under which it was obligatory to keep the garages open at all reasonable hours and not to sell them without ensuring that the purchaser entered into a similar sale agreement with Esso. The appellant agreed to allow a rebate of 1d. a gallon on all fuels bought. The agreements were to operate for four years five months in the case of one of the garages, but for twenty-one years in respect of the other. In addition, the latter was mortgaged to Esso in return for an advance of £7,000 which was to be repaid by instalments lasting for twenty-one years and not at any earlier date. In other words, the mortgage was not redeemable before the end of that period.

It was held unanimously that both agreements fell within the category of contracts in restraint of trade. They were not mere contracts of exclusion as in the case of a sole agency, for they restricted the manner in which the respondent company was to carry on its trade during a fixed period that could not be terminated before it had run its full course. Nor could it be said that the solus system had become a normal and established incident of the motor trade, since it was of far too recent an origin. Moreover, there was no substance in the appellant's main argument that the restrictions against trading were imposed not upon the respondent company personally, but upon its use of the land, and that therefore, as in the case where a tenant covenants not to use the demised land for the purposes of trade, they were excluded from the doctrine of restraint of trade. Lord WILBERFORCE stigmatized this argument as artificial and unreal,[4] while Lord PEARCE said that the practical effect of the contract was to create a personal restraint since it imposed a positive obligation upon the respondent to carry on the business in the manner prescribed in the co-operation plan.[5] The further argument that the restriction in respect of the second garage, since it was contained in a mortgage, was exempt from the doctrine of restraint was dismissed as unsound in principle.

---

1. *Esso Petroleum Co., Ltd.* v. *Harper's Garage (Stourport), Ltd.*, [1968] A.C., at p. 337; [1967] 1 All E.R., at p. 732, *per* Lord WILBERFORCE.
2. [1968] A.C. 269; [1967] 1 All E.R. 699.
3. A *solus* agreement normally contains a " tying covenant " by which the garage owner agrees, in return for a rebate on the price, to sell only the supplier's brand of petrol; a " compulsory trading covenant ", which obliges him to keep the garage open at reasonable hours and to provide the public with an efficient service; and a " continuity covenant " which requires him, if he sells his business, to procure the acceptance of the agreement by the purchaser. As a further incentive, the supplier frequently makes a loan to the garage owner on favourable terms: see generally Whiteman, 29 M.L.R. 507; Graupner, 18 I.C.C.Q. 879.
4. [1968] A.C., at p. 338; [1967] 1 All E.R., at p. 733.
5. [1968] A.C., at p. 327; [1967] 1 All E.R., at p. 726.

Thus, both contracts were *prima facie* void and required to be justified according to the test of reasonableness.[1]

Summary of the law

An attempt will now be made to summarize the main rules applicable to contracts in restraint of trade, especially those that relate to the test of reasonableness.

Contract *prima facie* void unless restraint reasonable

The basic rule is that, if the contract is so restrictive of the promisor's liberty to trade as to require review by the court, it is *prima facie* void and cannot become binding unless it is reasonable in the interest of both parties and also in the interest of the public.

The view that the interest of the public should be consulted was current in the nineteenth century, but for many years the courts have usually concentrated their attention on the interests of the parties.   In the *Esso* case, however, three of the Law Lords deprecated this dismemberment of the principle of public policy on which the doctrine of restraint of trade is based.   In every case " there is one broad question: Is it in the interests of the community that this restraint should be held to be reasonable and enforceable? "[2] This is a revival of the view expressed by the Court of Exchequer as long ago as 1843: " The test appears to be whether the contract be prejudicial or not to the public interest, for it is on grounds of public policy alone that these contracts are supported or avoided."[3]

Scope of " public interest."

The concept of public interest admits of no precise definition, and it is not surprising that at times it has been allowed a latitude which it is difficult to defend.   An instance of this in the context of restraint of trade is the decision of the Court of Appeal in *Wyatt* v. *Kreglinger and Fernau*,[4] where the facts were as follows:

> In June, 1923, the defendants wrote to the plaintiff, who had been in their service for many years, intimating that upon his retirement they proposed to give him an annual pension of £200 subject to the condition that he did not compete against them in the wool trade.   The plaintiff's reply was lost, but he retired in the following September and received the pension until June, 1932, when the defendants refused to make further payments.   The plaintiff sued them for breach of contract.   The defendants denied that any contract existed, and also pleaded that if a contract did exist it was void as being in restraint of trade.

The Court of Appeal gave judgment for the defendants, but there was no unanimity with regard to the *ratio decidendi*.   SCRUTTON, L.J., held that the defendants had not bound themselves contractually but had merely made a gratuitous promise.   The other two Lords Justices inclined to a contrary view on this point, but

---

1. The decision on this aspect of the case is discussed *infra*, pp. 385–6.
2. [1968] A.C., at p. 324; [1967] 1 All E.R., at p. 724, *per* Lord PEARCE.   See also [1968] A.C., at p. 319; [1967] 1 All E.R., at p. 720, *per* Lord HODSON; [1968] A.C., at pp. 340–1; [1967] 1 All E.R., at pp. 733–5, *per* Lord WILBERFORCE.   See also *Herbert Morris* v. *Saxelby*, [1916] 1 A.C., at p. 716, *per* Lord SHAW; *Bull* v. *Pitney-Bowes, Ltd.*, [1966] 3 All E.R. 384; [1967] 1 W.L.R. 273, at p. 282, *per* THESIGER, J.
3. *Mallan* v. *May* (1843), 11 M. & W. 653, at p. 665, *per* PARKE, B., delivering the judgment of the court.   The onus of proving that the restraint is reasonable in the interests of the parties lies upon the party who seeks to enforce the agreement; whether it is reasonable in the public interest lies upon the party so alleging.   As to these rules, see the *Esso* case, [1968] A.C., at pp. 319 and 323–4; [1967] 1 All E.R., at pp. 720–1 and 724.
4. [1933] 1 K.B. 793; [1933] All E.R. Rep. 349; followed by THESIGER, J., in *Bull* v. *Pitney-Bowes, Ltd.*, [1966] 3 All E.R. 384; [1967] 1 W.L.R. 273; *infra*, p. 382.

all three held that if the contract existed it was void, since it imposed a restraint that was too wide.   It also appeared to them that the contract was injurious to the interests of the public, for to restrain the plaintiff from engaging in the wool trade was to deprive the community of services from which it might derive advantage.   This is a somewhat extravagant suggestion.   It is a little difficult to appreciate what injury was caused to the public by the retirement of a man who, in common with a very considerable number of his fellow citizens, occupied but a comparatively humble position in the trade.   Reason and justice would seem to prescribe that an agreement, reasonable between the parties, should not be upset for some fancied and problematical injury to the public welfare.

In applying the test of public policy, the first task of the court is to construe the contract in the light of the circumstances existing at the time when it was made in order to determine the nature and extent of the restraint contemplated by the parties. The decisive factor is not the mere wording of the contract, but the object that the parties had in view.   In one case, for instance, a contract with a milk roundsman contained the following clause: *[marginal note: Intended scope of a restraint a matter of construction]*

> The employee expressly agrees not at any time during one year after the determination of his employment, . . . either on his own account or as representative or agent of any person or company, to serve or sell milk or dairy produce to . . . any person or company who at any time during the last six months of his employment shall have been a customer of the employer and served by the employee in the course of his employment.[1]

The expression " dairy produce " manifestly includes butter and cheese and therefore the agreement, literally construed, would preclude the roundsman from entering the employment of a grocer who dealt in those commodities.   The Court of Appeal, however, held that so stringent a restraint was not contemplated by the parties.   The clear object of the contract was to protect the employers *qua* purveyors of milk which was the only commodity in which they dealt.   Since this was the rational construction of the contract, it was held that the restraint was valid.

Once the intention of the parties has been disclosed, the validity of the contract falls to be determined.   This is a question of law.   Evidence is indeed admissible to prove the special circumstances which are alleged to justify the restriction.   The promisee may, for instance, produce evidence to show what is customary in the particular trade, what particular dangers require precautions, what steps are necessary in order to protect him against competition by the promisor, and what is usual among business men as to the terms of employment.[2]   But evidence that a witness considers the restraint to be reasonable is inadmissible, for that is the very question which the court alone can decide.[3] *[marginal note: Validity of the contract a question of law]*

---

1. *Home Counties Dairies, Ltd.* v. *Skilton,* [1970] 1 All E.R. 1227; [1970] 1 W.L.R. 526.
2. *Haynes* v. *Dorman,* [1899] 2 Ch. 13, at p. 24, *per* LINDLEY, M.R.
3. *Ibid.; Leng & Co., Ltd.* v. *Andrews,* [1909] 1 Ch. 763, at pp. 770–1, *per* FLETCHER MOULTON, L.J.   And as to the admissibility of general economic evidence, see *Texaco, Ltd.* v. *Mulberry Filling Station, Ltd.,* [1972] 1 All E.R. 513; [1972] 1 W.L.R. 814.

The onus of proving such special circumstances as are alleged to justify a restraint fall upon the promisee. " When once they are proved, it is a question of law for the decision of the judge whether they do or do not justify the restraint. There is no question of onus one way or the other."[1]

Facts
existing at
date of
contract
alone
relevant

In considering the issue of justification, the court must scrutinize the restraint as at the date when the contract was made in the light of the circumstances then existing and also in the light of what at that date might possibly happen in the future. The temptation to consider what in fact has happened by the time of the trial must be resisted, for a contract containing a restraint alleged to be excessive must be either invalid *ab initio* or valid *ab initio*. There cannot come a moment at which it passes from the class of invalid into that of valid covenants.[2]

A restraint to be permissible must be no wider than is reasonably necessary to protect the relevant interest of the promisee.[3] The existence of some proprietary or other legitimate interest such as his right to work,[4] must first be proved, and then it must be shown to the satisfaction of the court that the restraint as regards its area, its period of operation and the activities against which it is directed, is not excessive.

We will now consider the question of reasonableness with reference to the different categories of contracts in restraint of trade. But, as we have seen, any attempt to classify these categories would be a hazardous, if not an impossible, undertaking. The doctrine of restraint is by no means static. Moreover it extends beyond the confines of contract. It has been extended, for instance, to the refusal of the Jockey Club to grant a training licence to a woman merely on the ground of her sex;[5] to the " retain and transfer " system of the Football League, Ltd., by which a player, " retained " by his club at the end of his year's engagement, is debarred from joining another club unless he obtains the consent of that by which he has been retained;[6] and to restrictions imposed by a professional body, such as the Pharmaceutical Society, upon the trading activities of its members.[7]

In the present book it seems better to limit the discussion to contractual restrictions and to group these under four headings, namely (i) restraints accepted by an employee; (ii) restraints accepted by the vendor of a business; (iii) restraints arising from combinations for the regulations of trade relations; (iv) restraints accepted by distributors of merchandise.

---

1. *Herbert Morris, Ltd.* v. *Saxelby*, [1916] A.C. 688, at p. 707, *per* Lord PARKER.
2. *Gledow Autoparts, Ltd.* v. *Delaney*, [1965] 1 W.L.R. 1366, at p. 1377; [1965] 3 All E.R. 288, at p. 295, *per* DIPLOCK, L.J.   See also *Putsman* v. *Taylor*, [1927] 1 K.B. 637, at p. 643, *per* SALTER, J.
3. *E. Underwood & Son, Ltd.* v. *Barker*, [1899] 1 Ch. 300, at p. 305, *per* LINDLEY, M.R.; *Herbert Morris, Ltd.* v. *Saxelby*, [1916] 1 A.C. 688, at p. 710, *per* Lord PARKER.
4. *Nagle* v. *Feilden*, [1966] 2 Q.B. 633, at p. 646, *per* Lord DENNING, M.R. " A man's right to work at his trade or profession is just as important to him, perhaps more important than, his rights of property."
5. *Nagle* v. *Feilden*, *supra*.
6. *Eastham* v. *Newcastle Football Club*, [1964] Ch. 413; [1963] 3 All E.R. 139.
7. *Pharmaceutical Society of Great Britain* v. *Dickson*, [1970] A.C. 403; [1968] 2 All E.R. 686.

(i) Restraints accepted by employees

It has already been seen that a restraint imposed upon a servant is never reasonable, unless there is some proprietary interest owned by the master which requires protection. The only matters in respect to which he can be said to possess such an interest are his trade secrets, if any, and his business connexion.[1]

It is obvious that a restraint against competition is justifiable if its object is to prevent the exploitation of trade secrets learned by the servant in the course of his employment.[2] An instance of this occurred in *Forster & Sons, Ltd.* v. *Suggett* :[3]

Servant may be restrained from misuse of trade secrets

> The works manager of the plaintiffs, who were chiefly engaged in making glass and glass bottles, was instructed in certain confidential methods concerning, *inter alia*, the correct mixture of gas and air in the furnaces. He agreed that during the five years following the determination of his employment he would not carry on in the United Kingdom, or be interested in, glass bottle manufacture or any other business connected with glass making as conducted by the plaintiffs.

It was held that the plaintiffs were entitled to protection in this respect, and that the restraint was reasonable. In such a case the employer must prove definitely that the servant has acquired substantial knowledge of some secret process or mode of manufacture used in the course of his business. Even the general knowledge, derived from secret information, which has taught an employee how best to solve particular problems as they arise may be a proper subject-matter of protection.[4] But, if as was the case in *Herbert Morris, Ltd.* v. *Saxelby*,[5] the so-called secret is nothing more than a special method of organization adopted in the business, or if only part of the secret is known to the servant so that its successful exploitation by him is impossible, there can be no valid restraint.

An employer is also entitled to protect his trade connexion, *i.e.* to prevent his customers from being enticed away from him by a servant who was formerly in his employ. Protection is required against the unfair invasion of his connexion by a servant who has had special opportunities of becoming acquainted with his clientele, and if the protection is no more than adequate for this purpose it is permitted by the law.[6] The difficulty, however, is to specify the kind of business or the class of servant in respect to which this protection is legitimate. What servants acquire such an intimate knowledge of customers as to make the misuse of their knowledge a potential source of danger to their masters? The answer must depend upon the nature of the business and the nature of the employment entrusted to the servant. In one

Servant may be restrained from exploiting his master's customers

---

1. It was held in *Eastham* v. *Newcastle United Football Club*, [1964] Ch. 413; [1963] 3 All E.R. 139, that the rules of the Football Association and the Football League relating to the retention and transfer of professional footballers were not justified by any interest capable of protection.
2. *Hagg* v. *Darley* (1878), 47 L.J. Ch. 567; *Caribonum Co., Ltd.* v. *Le Couch* (1913), 109 L.T. 587; *Haynes* v. *Doman*, [1899] 2 Ch. 13.
3. (1918), 35 T.L.R. 87.
4. *Commercial Plastics, Ltd.* v. *Vincent*, [1965] 1 Q.B. 623; [1964] 3 All E.R. 546.
5. [1916] 1 A.C. 688.
6. *Dewes* v. *Fitch*, [1920] 2 Ch. 159, at pp. 181–2, *per* WARRINGTON, L.J.

case ROMER, L.J., proposed a test that would seem to be too wide.   He said:

> "It is in my opinion established that when an employee is being offered employment which will probably result in his coming into direct contact with his employer's customers, or which will enable him to obtain knowledge of the names of his employer's customers, then the covenant against solicitation is reasonably necessary for the protection of the employer."[1]

This, however, is surely too sweeping, for most shop assistants come into direct contact with customers, and even where this is not so they frequently have access to lists of clients.   In *Herbert Morris, Ltd.* v. *Saxelby*, Lord PARKER stressed that, before any restraint is justifiable, the servant must be one who will acquire, not merely knowledge of customers, but in addition influence over them.[2]   It seems a reasonable and workable criterion. A restraint is not valid unless the nature of the employment is such that customers will either learn to rely upon the skill or judgment of the servant or will deal with him directly and personally to the virtual exclusion of the master, with the result that he will probably gain their custom if he sets up business on his his own account.

Restraints against the invasion of trade connexion have been upheld in the case of a solicitor's clerk,[3] a tailor's cutter-fitter,[4] a milk roundsman,[5] a stockbroker's clerk,[6] the manager of a brewery[7] and an estate agent's clerk.[8]   On the other hand, they have been disallowed in the case of a 'grocer's assistant;[9] in the case of a bookmaker's " manager who had no personal contact with his employer's " clients, since the business was conducted mostly by telephone;[10] and in a case where the restriction against future competition, imposed upon the traveller of a firm supplying accessories to the lighting system of motor cars, extended to retailers in the prescribed area even though he might never visit them during his employment.[11]

Factors upon which reasonableness of restraint depends   A restraint is permissible if it is designed to prevent a misuse of trade secrets or business connexion, but it will be invalid if it affords any more than adequate protection to the covenantee. In deciding this question the court considers, *inter alia*, the nature and extent of the trade and of the servant's employment therein, but it pays special attention to the two factors of time and area.[12]

---

1. *Gilford Motor Co.* v. *Horne*, [1933] Ch. 935, at p. 966; [1933] All E.R. Rep. 109.
2. [1916] 1 A.C. 688, at p. 709.
3. *Fitch* v. *Dewes*, [1921] 2 A.C. 158.
4. *Nicoll* v. *Beere* (1885), 53 L.T. 659; Cf. *Attwood* v. *Lamont*, [1920] 3 K.B. 571, *infra*, p. 385, where the restraint might have been valid had it been less widely framed.
5. *Cornwall* v. *Hawkins* (1872), 41 L.J. Ch. 435.
6. *Lyddon* v. *Thomas* (1901), 17 T.L.R. 450.
7. *White, Tomkins and Courage* v. *Wilson* (1907), 23 T.L.R. 469.
8. *Scorer* v. *Seymour Jones*, [1966] 3 All E.R. 347; [1966] 1 W.L.R. 1419, distinguishing *Bowler* v. *Lovegrove*, [1921] 1 Ch. 642.
9. *Pearks, Ltd.* v. *Cullen* (1912), 28 T.L.R. 371.
10. *S. W. Strange, Ltd.* v. *Mann*, [1965] 1 All E.R. 1069; [1965] 1 W.L.R. 629.
11. *Gledhow Autoparts, Ltd.* v. *Delaney*, [1965] 3 All E.R. 288; [1965] 1 W.L.R. 1366.
12. *Badische Anilin und Soda Fabrik* v. *Schott, Segner & Co.*, [1892] 3 Ch. 447, at p. 451, *per* CHITTY, J.

" As the time of restriction lengthens or the space of its operation grows, the weight of the onus on the covenantee to justify it grows too."[1]

There are many instances of a restraint being invalidated by the excessive area of its sphere of intended operation. Thus contracts have been held void where an agent employed to canvass for orders in Islington was restricted from trading within twenty-five miles of London;[2] where a junior reporter of the *Sheffield Daily Telegraph* agreed that he would not be connected with any other newspaper business carried on within twenty miles of Sheffield;[3] where a traveller for a firm of brewers was restrained, without limit of area, from being concerned in the sale of ale or porter brewed at Burton;[4] where the manager of a butcher's shop at Cambridge agreed not to carry on a similar business within a radius of five miles from the shop;[5] and where an assistant to a dentist carrying on business in London agreed that he would not practise in any of the other towns in England or Scotland where the covenantee might happen to practise before the end of the covenantor's employment.[6] Nevertheless, everything depends upon the circumstances, and these may well justify a far wider restraint than those repudiated in the above examples. A restriction extending throughout the United Kingdom has been allowed,[7] and in one case the Eastern Hemisphere was regarded as a reasonable area.[8] It is not necessary for the covenantee to prove that the business, for the protection of which the restraint was imposed, has in fact been carried on in every part of the area specified in the contract.[9]

(i) Area of restraint

A restraint may be invalid on the ground that its duration is excessive.[10] The burden on the covenantee to prove the reasonableness of the covenant is increased by the absence of a time limit, but it by no means follows that a restraint for life is void. In *Fitch* v. *Dewes*,[11] for instance, a contract was enforced by which a solicitor's clerk at Tamworth agreed that, after leaving his employer, he would never practise within seven miles of Tamworth Town Hall.

(ii) Duration of restraint

There are, indeed, many cases in which restraints have been upheld notwithstanding that they have been unlimited as regards both area and time, but all decisions prior to *Mason's* case in

---

1. *Attwood* v. *Lamont*, [1920] 3 K.B. 571, at p. 589, *per* YOUNGER, L.J.
2. *Mason* v. *Provident Clothing and Supply Co., Ltd.*, [1913] A.C. 724.
3. *Leng & Co., Ltd.* v. *Andrews*, [1909] 1 Ch. 763.
4. *Allsopp* v. *Wheatcroft* (1872), L.R. 15 Eq. 59.
5. *Empire Meat Co., Ltd.* v. *Patrick*, [1939] 2 All E.R. 85.
6. *Mallan* v. *May* (1843), 11 M. & W. 653.
7. *E. Underwood & Son, Ltd.* v. *Barker*, [1899] 1 Ch. 300.
8. *Lamson Pneumatic Tube Co.* v. *Phillips* (1904), 91 L.T. 363. (Pneumatic tube system for use in shops was invented in Western Hemisphere and practically unknown in the Eastern Hemisphere.)
9. *Connors Brothers, Ltd.* v. *Connors*, [1940] 4 All E.R. 179.
10. *Eastes* v. *Russ*, [1914] 1 Ch. 468 (a lifetime's restraint imposed upon an assistant to a pathologist); *Wyatt* v. *Kreglinger and Fernau*, [1933] 1 K.B. 793; *M. & S. Drapers (A Firm)* v. *Reynolds*, [1956] 3 All E.R. 814; [1957] 1 W.L.R. 9; *Stenhouse Australia, Ltd.* v. *Phillips*, [1974] A.C. 391; [1974] 1 All E.R. 117.
11. [1921] 2 A.C. 158.

1913,[1] which as we have seen revolutionized the law by adopting Lord MACNAGHTEN'S test, should be viewed with suspicion. As YOUNGER, L.J., remarked in 1920:

> " Restrictive covenants imposed upon an employee which a few years ago would not have seemed open to question would now, I think, with equal certainty be treated as invalid."[2]

Indirect evasion of the law unavailing

The courts are astute to prevent an employer from obtaining by indirect means a protection against competition that would not be available to him by an express contract with his employee.   In *Bull* v. *Pitney-Bowes, Ltd.*,[3] for instance:

> The plaintiff was employed by the defendants, manufacturers of postal franking machines, and it was a condition of his employment that he should become a member of a non-contributory pension scheme.   Rule 16 of this scheme provided that a retired member should be liable to forfeit his pension rights if he engaged in any activity or occupation which was in competition with or detrimental to the interests of the defendants.
>
> After twenty-six years service the plaintiff voluntarily retired and joined another company carrying on a business similar to that of the defendants.   On being warned that he might lose his pension unless he left his new employment, he sued for a declaration that rule 16 was an unreasonable restraint of trade and therefore void.

If the rule fell to be classified as a restraint of trade, it was manifestly void, since *inter alia* it was unlimited in duration and area of operation, but the defendants contended that it merely defined the beneficiaries of the pension fund.   THESIGER, J., following the earlier case of *Wyatt* v. *Kreglinger and Fernau*,[4] rejected this contention.   He held that the provisions of the pension fund, including rule 16, were part of the terms of the plaintiff's employment, and that on grounds of public policy this rule was to be treated as equivalent to a covenant in restraint of trade.   It was contrary to public policy that the community should be deprived of the services of a man skilled in a particular trade or technique.[5]

Another case which bears on this problem of indirect evasion is *Kores Manufacturing Co., Ltd.* v. *Kolok Manufacturing Co., Ltd.*[6] where two companies, manufacturers of similar products, agreed that neither would employ any servant who had been employed by the other during the last five years.   The defendants broke their promise, and in the resulting action the arguments and the decision turned solely upon whether the agreement was unreasonable as between the parties.   The Court of Appeal held

---

1. *Mason* v. *Provident Clothing and Supply Co., Ltd.*, [1913] A.C. 724; *supra*, p. 371.
2. *Dewes* v. *Fitch*, [1920] 2 Ch. 159, at p. 185.
3. [1966] 3 All E.R. 384; [1967] 1 W.L.R. 273.
4. [1933] 1 K.B. 793; *supra*, p. 376.
5. THESIGER, J., accepted the reasoning in *Wyatt* v. *Kreglinger and Fernau*, but reached a contrary result.   In *Wyatt's* case the plaintiff lost his pension, in *Bull's* case he won it.   The reason is clear.   In the former case, assuming that there was a contract at all, the covenant in restraint of trade was the only consideration for the promise to give him a pension; in *Bull's* case the covenant formed part of a general agreement for which, apart from the void covenant, there was sufficient consideration.   It was held, therefore, that the covenant could and should be severed, with the result that the promise to give the pension was untainted and enforceable; as to severance, see *infra*, pp. 393 *et seq.*
6. [1959] Ch. 108; [1958] 2 All E.R. 65.

it to be unreasonable in this respect, since it imposed upon the parties a restraint grossly in excess of what was adequate to prevent a misuse of their trade secrets and confidential information.

But Lord REID and Lord HODSON have since observed that it would have been more correct to have stigmatized the agreement as contrary to the public interest.[1] It is respectfully submitted that this is a just criticism. The agreement was clearly designed to prevent employees from moving from one firm to the other in search of higher wages, but had the defendants attempted to do this by taking covenants against competition from individual employees the attempt would have failed. It is against the interests of the State that a man should be allowed to contract out of his right to work for whom he will. It would surely make a mockery of public policy if this liberty could be effectively restricted by a contract between third parties.[2]

(ii) Restraints accepted by the vendor of a business

Although this type of restraint is more readily upheld than one imposed upon a servant, it will not be enforced unless it is connected with some proprietary interest in need of protection.[3] This requirement has at least two repercussions in the present class of contract.

First, there must be a genuine, not merely a colourable, sale of a business by the covenantor to the covenantee. This essential is well illustrated by *Vancouver Malt and Sake Brewing Co., Ltd.* v. *Vancouver Breweries, Ltd.*[4] where the facts were these:

> The appellants held a brewer's licence in respect of their premises under which they were at liberty to brew beer. In fact, however, they brewed only sake, a concoction much appreciated by Japanese. The respondents held a similar licence and did in fact brew beer. The appellants purported to sell the goodwill of their brewer's licence, except so far as sake was concerned, and agreed not to manufacture beer for fifteen years.

Since the appellants were not in fact brewers of beer, the contract transferred to the respondents no proprietary interest in respect of which any restraint was justifiable. The covenant was a naked covenant not to brew beer, and as such it was void.

Secondly, it is only the actual business sold by the covenantor that is entitled to protection. In *British Concrete Co.* v. *Schelff*,[5] for instance:

> The plaintiffs carried on a large business for the manufacture and sale of 'B.R.C.' road reinforcements; the defendant carried on a small business for the sale of 'Loop' road reinforcements. The defendant sold his business to the plaintiffs and agreed not to compete with them in the manufacture or sale of road reinforcements.

The covenant was void. All that the defendant transferred was the business of selling the reinforcements called 'Loop.' It was,

Restraint void unless required for protection of a proprietary interest

---

1. *Esso Petroleum Co., Ltd.* v. *Harper's Garage (Stourport), Ltd.*, [1968] A.C. 269, at pp. 300 and 319. This was the view taken by LLOYD JACOB, J., in the court of first instance in *Kores Manufacturing Co., Ltd.* v. *Kolok Manufacturing Co.*, [1957] 3 All E.R. 158; [1957] 1 W.L.R. 1012.
2. The question of indirect evasion was mentioned by the Court of Appeal in the *Kores* case but was left open.
3. *Supra*, p. 378.
4. [1934] A.C. 181; [1934] All E.R. Rep. 38.
5. [1921] 2 Ch. 563.

therefore, only with regard to that particular variety that it was justifiable to curb his future activities.

An express covenant by a vendor not to carry on a business similar to that which he has sold may, therefore, be valid, but only if it is no wider than is necessary for the adequate protection of the proprietary interest acquired by the purchaser. In considering this question, the court, as in the case of an employee's contract, pays special attention to the two factors of time and area. If there is no limit of time[1] or no reasonable limit of area[2] a restraint may be invalidated. Nevertheless, everything depends upon the circumstances, and a covenant which extends over the whole of the United Kingdom[3] or throughout the Dominion of Canada[4] or over the whole world,[5] or which restricts the covenantor for the remainder of his life,[6] may be valid in appropriate circumstances.

(iii) Restraints arising from combinations for the regulation of trade relations

It frequently happens that manufacturers or traders form an association with the object of restricting the output or maintaining the selling price of certain commodities. At common law, a combination of this nature may be void as being in excessive restraint of trade. Whether it is so or not is determined according to the principles described above. The restriction is *prima facie* void, and it cannot be enforced unless it is reasonable between the parties and consistent with the interests of the public.[7]

In applying these principles, however, the courts have in the past borne in mind the difference of environment in the various types of contract in restraint of trade. While they have looked jealously at a restraint imposed upon a servant, they have been unsympathetic to a trader who, having voluntarily entered into a restrictive arrangement with other traders, attempts to escape from his obligation by the plea that he has imposed an unreasonable burden upon himself.[8] In commercial agreements of this kind, the parties themselves are the best judges of their own interests.[9] This disfavour, indeed distaste, for a plea that sounds peculiarly ill in the mouth of a man of business who has negotiated on an equal footing with the other members of the combination is well illustrated by *English Hop Growers* v. *Dering*,[10] where the defendant had agreed to deliver to the plaintiff association, of

---

1. *Pellow* v. *Ivey* (1933), 49 T.L.R. 422.
2. *Goldsoll* v. *Goldman*, [1915] 1 Ch. 292.
3. *Leather Cloth Co.* v. *Lorsont* (1869), L.R. 9 Eq. 345.
4. *Connors Brothers, Ltd.* v. *Connors*, [1940] 4 All E.R. 179.
5. *Nordenfelt* v. *Maxim Nordenfelt Guns and Ammunition Co.*, [1894] A.C. 535; *supra*, pp. 370–372.
6. *Elves* v. *Crofts* (1850), 10 C.B. 241.
7. *McEllistrim* v. *Ballymacelligott Co-operative Agricultural and Dairy Society*, [1919] A.C. 548, at p. 562, *per* Lord BIRKENHEAD.
8. *English Hop Growers* v. *Dering*, [1928] 2 K.B. 174, at p. 181; [1928] All E.R. Rep. 396, at p. 400, *per* SCRUTTON, L.J.
9. *North Western Salt Co., Ltd.* v. *Electrolytic Alkali Co., Ltd.*, [1914] A.C. 461, at p. 471, *per* Lord HALDANE.
10. [1928] 2 K.B. 174; [1928] All E.R. Rep. 396. See also *Birtley and District Co-operative Society, Ltd.* v. *Windy Nook and District Industrial Co-operative Society, Ltd.* (*No. 2*), [1960] 2 Q.B. 1; [1959] 1 All E.R. 623.

which he was a member, all hops grown on his land in 1926. Short shrift was given by the court to his contention that this restriction upon his power of disposal was unreasonable. Growers were faced with ruin owing to excessive stocks of hops accumulated during Government control in the 1914–1918 war, and the association had been formed in order to ensure that in any year when there was a surplus the inevitable loss to members should be reduced to a minimum and should be equitably distributed among them. In the words of SCRUTTON, L.J.:

> " There was nothing unreasonable in hop growers combining to secure a steady and profitable price, by eliminating competition amongst themselves, and putting the marketing in the hands of one agent, with full power to fix prices and hold up supplies, the benefit and loss being divided amongst the members."[1]

Everything, however, depends upon the circumstances, and a different decision was reached by the House of Lords in *McEllistrim* v. *Ballymacelligott Co-operative Agricultural and Dairy Society*:[2]

Restraint must be reasonable between the parties

> The respondent society manufactured cheese and butter from milk supplied by its members. The rules of the society provided that no member should sell milk to any other person without the consent of a committee; that no member should be entitled to withdraw from the society unless his shares were transferred or cancelled; and that the consent of the committee, which might be refused without giving reasons, should be essential to the effectiveness of such a transfer or cancellation.

It is not surprising that this arrangement was held to be unreasonable between the parties. The society, no doubt, was entitled to such a degree of protection as would ensure stability in the supply of milk. It was not entitled to impose a life-long embargo upon the trading freedom of its members. The obligation of a member to allocate all his milk to the society was to endure for his life, unless he was fortunate enough to obtain the sanction of the committee to a transfer of his shares. Therefore, as Lord BIRKENHEAD remarked, a member, if he joined the society young enough and lived long enough, would be precluded for a period of sixty years or more from selling his milk in the free market.[3] The arrangement was an attempt to eliminate competition altogether and was void.

(iv) Restrictions accepted by distributors of merchandise

The solus system illustrates this type of restriction

It not infrequently happens that a manufacturer or a wholesaler refuses to make merchandise available for distribution to the public unless the distributor accepts certain conditions that restrict his liberty of trading. The object may be, for instance, to prevent him from selling similar goods supplied by competitors of the manufacturer. Such was the main purpose of the *solus* agreements that were discussed in *Esso Petroleum Co., Ltd.* v. *Harper's Garage (Stourport), Ltd.*[4]

---

1. [1928] 2 K.B. 174, at p. 181; [1928] All E.R. 396, at p. 400.
2. [1919] A.C. 548.
3. [1919] A.C., at p. 564.
4. [1968] A.C. 269; [1967] 1 All E.R. 699. For the facts, see *supra*, p. 375.

The primary question that arose in this case was whether the agreements were caught by the doctrine of restraint of trade. Nothing need be added to the account already given of this aspect of the dispute.[1]   But, having decided that the doctrine applied to the facts, the House of Lords then considered the second question, namely, whether the restrictions were nevertheless justifiable and enforceable on the ground that they were reasonable and not in conflict with the requirements of public policy.   On this aspect of the case, it was held that there was nothing unreasonable in the adoption by the parties of the *solus* system.   They both benefited. The Esso firm were able to organize a more efficient and economical system of distribution; the distributor not only gained a rebate on the wholesale price of petrol, but if short of funds he could rely on the financial backing of a powerful corporation. Nevertheless, tying agreements of this nature, though reasonable in general, will become unreasonable if made to endure for an excessive period.   In the instant circumstances, four and a half years was reasonable, twenty-one years was unreasonable. Therefore the first contract was valid, the second was void.[2]

Importance of the date at which the covenantor obtains possession of the premises

The majority of their Lordships emphasized that, since a restraint of trade implies that the covenantor agrees to surrender some freedom which otherwise he would enjoy, a distinction must be drawn between a covenantor who is already in possession of the garage site when he enters into a *solus* agreement with an oil company, and one who obtains possession from the company after the agreement has been made.   In the latter case, the fact that he surrenders no freedom previously enjoyed by him must have a significant bearing upon the question whether the restraint is reasonable.[3]   In the later case of *Cleveland Petroleum Co., Ltd. v. Dartstone, Ltd.*,[4] the Court of Appeal stressed the merit of this distinction and laid down the rule that where a person takes possession of premises under a *solus* agreement, not having been in possession previously, the restrictions placed upon his trading activities are *prima facie* binding upon him.   But the presumption in favour of their validity will be rebutted, it would seem, if the inference from the relevant circumstances is that their enforcement will manifestly be detrimental to the interests of the public. If this were not so, it would be possible to avoid a rule of public policy by a mere conveyancing device.   That the question is one of substance and not of form is clearly shown by the decision of the Privy Council in *Amoco Australia, Pty., Ltd. v. Rocca Brothers Motor Engineering Co., Pty., Ltd.*[5].

An analogy to the restriction placed upon the distributor in these cases is furnished by that type of exclusive agreement by

---

1. *Supra*, pp. 363–4.
2. Distinguishing *Petrofina (Great Britain), Ltd.* v. *Martin*, [1966] Ch. 146; [1966] 1 All E.R. 126.
3. *Esso Petroleum Co., Ltd.* v. *Harper's Garage (Stourport), Ltd.*, [1968] A.C. 269, at p. 298 (Lord REID); at p. 309 (Lord MORRIS OF BORTH-Y-GEST); at pp. 316–7 (Lord HODSON); at p. 325 (Lord PEARCE). Lord PEARCE, indeed, citing the analogy of the tie between a publican and brewer expressed the view that if a man takes a lease of land subject to a tie, thereby obtaining favourable terms, he cannot repudiate the tie and retain the benefits.   The doctrine of restraint of trade is altogether excluded.
4. [1969] 1 All E.R. 201; [1969] 1 W.L.R. 116.
5. [1975] 1 All E.R. 968; [1975] 2 W.L.R. 779.

which a trader promises to take all the goods of a particular kind required in his business from one supplier. Such was the case in *Servais Bouchard* v. *Princes Hall Restaurant, Ltd.*[1] where the plaintiff was given the exclusive right for an indefinite period of supplying burgundy to a restaurant keeper. In the Court of Appeal two views were expressed upon the question whether this agreement was subject to the doctrine of restraint of trade. The majority view, which would seem to be preferable, was that it was *prima facie* void and therefore in need of justification; but HENN COLLINS, M.R., considered that it was not caught by the doctrine. In the result, however, it was unanimously held that in the instant circumstances the restraint was justifiable as being reasonable.

Similar considerations apply to a contract for exclusive services. So in *A. Schroeder Music Publishing Co., Ltd.* v. *Macaulay.*[2]

> The plaintiff, a young and unknown song writer, entered into a contract with the defendants, a music publishing company, on their standard terms. Under the contract the plaintiff assigned the world copyright in any musical composition produced by him solely or jointly. The defendants did not undertake to exploit all or any of the compositions though they agreed to pay royalties on those in fact exploited. The agreement was to run for five years but to be automatically extended for a further five years if the royalties reached a total of £5,000. The defendants could terminate the agreement at any time by giving a month's notice, but there was no similar provision in favour of the plaintiff.

The House of Lords had no difficulty in holding that such an agreement was within the ambit of restraint of trade and that this particular agreement was unreasonable since the terms combined a total commitment by the plaintiff with a striking lack of obligation on the defendant.

These rules of the common law which have brought within the doctrine of restraint of trade restrictions, designed by manufacturers or distributors of goods to stifle competition, have lost much of their value. Their practical importance has been greatly reduced as a result of legislative changes effected during the last quarter of a century. A detailed account of the relevant legislation would be out of place in a book on the general law of contract, but a brief description of it may serve to put the common law rules in their modern context.

Those rules suffered from two major defects as a means of promoting competition. First, though the formal rules embodied a requirement of the public interest, in practice, virtually all cases were decided on the basis of reasonableness between the parties. Secondly, no agreement would come before the court at all unless one of the parties refused to carry it out, and third parties could not complain of the performance of an invalid agreement in restraint of trade.[3] Since those agreements which

Effect of legislation on the common law of restraint of trade

Defects of common law

---

1. (1904), 20 T.L.R. 574.
2. [1974] 3 All E.R. 616; [1974] 1 W.L.R. 1308. See also *Clifford Davis Management, Ltd.* v. *W.E.A. Records, Ltd.*, [1975] 1 All E.R. 237; [1975] 1 W.L.R. 61.
3. So the House of Lords held in *Mogul Steamship Co.* v. *McGregor, Gow & Co.*, [1892] A.C. 25, that a non-party injured by the activities of a price-cutting cartel could not sue in the tort of conspiracy on the basis that the cartel was an invalid restraint of trade.

the parties were happy to perform, whether binding or not, were precisely those best calculated to damage non-parties and the interests of the public in general, these were serious defects.[1]

Monopolies Commission

In 1948, Parliament passed the Monopolies and Restrictive Practices (Inquiry and Control) Act which created the Monopolies and Restrictive Practices Commission.   This body, subsequently renamed first the Monopolies Commission,[2] and now the Monopolies and Mergers Commission[3] is required to investigate matters referred to it by the Board of Trade[4] which may involve either monopolies[5] or mergers.[6]   The Commission has no power to initiate its own enquiries nor does it have any decision-making function.   It reports to the Government, which takes a political decision whether to take action or not.

Restrictive practices legislation

As its original name suggests, the Monopolies Commission was also intended to investigate restrictive practices.   But in 1956, Part I of the Restrictive Trade Practices Act transferred this function to the Restrictive Practices Court, a very different body.   We have already seen that under the Act, a wide range of agreements or arrangements which are likely to restrict competition must be registered with the Registrar of Restrictive Trading Agreements,[7] who is then required to refer them to the court.   The function of the court which is a judicial body having full decision-making powers,[8] is to determine whether or not the restrictions accepted by the parties under their agreement are " contrary to the public interest."   If this is found to be the case, the agreement is rendered void " in respect of " the offending restrictions.[9]

A restriction which falls within the statutory definition is presumed to be contrary to the public interest, and the onus lies upon the parties to the agreement to rebut this presumption. This is no light task.   First, it must be shown that the restriction satisfies one or more of the eight specific tests of validity, generally called the " gateways," laid down by the Act.[10]   But even if this hurdle is surmounted, the benefits, thus shown to be reasonable

---

1. It is possible to detect some recent changes.   Much greater weight was given to the public interest in *Esso Petroleum Co., Ltd.* v. *Harper's Garage (Stourport), Ltd.*, [1968] A.C. 269; [1967] 1 All E.R. 699, discussed *supra*, p. 365.   A non-party was granted a declaration that an agreement was in restraint of trade in *Eastham* v. *Newcastle United Football Club*, [1964] Ch. 413; [1963] 1 All E.R. 137; and in *Nagle* v. *Feilden*, [1966] 2 Q.B. 633; [1966] 1 All E.R. 689; the Court of Appeal thought that in some circumstances, a non-party might be granted an injunction.
2. By Restrictive Trade Practices Act 1956.
3. By the Fair Trading Act 1973, s. 4.
4. Now the Department of Trade and Industry.
5. Broadly situations in which at least one third of the market is controlled by a single firm.
6. By the Monopolies and Mergers Act 1965.
7. The Fair Trading Act 1973 transferrers the functions of the Registrar to the Director-General of Fair Trading.
8. There is an appeal to the Court of Appeal on points of law.   The standard account of the relevant legislation is Wilberforce, Campbell and Elles, *Restrictive Trade Practices and Monopolies*.   An excellent introduction to the subject is Korah, *Competition Law of Britain and the Common Market* (1975).
9. Restrictive Practices Act 1956, s. 20 (3); *supra*, p. 313.
10. Section 21 (1).   As, for example that the removal of the restriction would be likely to have a serious and adverse effect on the general level of employment or would be likely to cause a reduction in the volume of the export trade.

as between the contracting parties, must be set against any detriment that will be caused to the public or to third parties who are purchasers, consumers or users of the goods, or persons engaged in their sale; and the court must then be satisfied that on balance the restriction is still not unreasonable. In short, the restriction will be void if its economic or social disadvantages outweigh its advantages to the parties.

Thus the Act seeks to avoid the two weaknesses of the common law referred to above.[1] The practical result of this legislation is that the common law, though not repealed, is effectively replaced by the statutory provisions so far as registrable agreements are concerned, since it is most unlikely that an agreement which satisfied the stringent tests laid down by the Act would fail to pass the far more lenient tests applied at common law. There remains, however, a substantial body of agreements which are not registrable and which remain subject to the common law rules,[2] while those which are registrable remain subject to scrutiny at common law until they have been declared void by the Restrictive Practices Court. Moreover, the concept of public interest which it is the task of that court to protect, differs widely from the concept of public policy as understood at common law. Therefore, a trade combination declared to be innocuous under the statutory provisions, may still be found to be contrary to public policy at common law.[3] Sometimes, however, a court applying the common law rules may be influenced by the views of the Monopolies Commission. Thus in *Esso Petroleum Co., Ltd.* v. *Harper's Garage (Stourport), Ltd.* which has already been discussed,[4] the House of Lords took account of a report in which the Commission expressed its views on the whole system of marketing petrol in the United Kingdom.[5]

Scope of the common law doctrine greatly reduced

SECTION II. THE LEGAL CONSEQUENCES

1. THE CONTRACT IS VOID IN SO FAR AS IT CONTRAVENES PUBLIC POLICY

Contracts that tend to oust the jurisdiction of the courts or to prejudice the status of marriage and contracts in restraint of trade, though contrary to public policy, are by no means totally void. Suppose, for instance, that as part of a contract of employment a servant enters into a contract in restraint of trade which is in fact excessively wide and therefore void. Is it to be said that this invalidity affects the whole contract and precludes the servant from suing for wrongful dismissal or the master from

The contract is not void in toto

1. The jurisdiction of the court was extended to Resale Price Maintenance by the Resale Prices Act 1964; see *supra*, p. 316; some important *lacunae* in the 1956 Act were filled by the Restrictive Practices Act 1968 and further amendments were made by the Fair Trading Act 1973, Part IX.
2. See, for example, *Kores Manufacturing Co., Ltd.* v. *Kolok Manufacturing Co., Ltd., supra*, p. 382.
3. Wilberforce, Campbell & Elles, *Restrictive Trade Practices and Monopolies*, para. 276.
4. *Supra*, pp. 372–5; pp. 385–6.
5. Report on distribution of petrol by retail in the United Kingdom; Commons Paper no. 264 of 1965.

recovering damages if the servant leaves without due notice? It is clear that the law does not go to these lengths.[1] The truth of this was recognized as far back as 1837 by Lord ABINGER in *Wallis* v. *Day*.[2] In that case the plaintiff had sold his business of a carrier to the defendant and had agreed, in return for a weekly salary of £2 3s. 10d., to serve the defendant as assistant for life. He further agreed that, except as such assistant, he would not for the rest of his life exercise the trade of a carrier. In an action brought by the plaintiff to recover eighteen weeks' arrears of salary, the defendant demurred on the ground that the agreement, being in restraint of trade, was void and that no part of it was enforceable. It became unnecessary to decide this point, since the court held the restraint to be reasonable, but Lord ABINGER dealt with the demurrer as follows:

> " The defendant demurred on the ground that the covenant being in restraint of trade, was illegal, and that therefore the whole contract was void. I cannot, however, accede to that conclusion, If a party enters into several covenants, one of which cannot be enforced against him, he is not therefore released from performing the others. And in the present case the defendant might have maintained an action against the plaintiff for not rendering them the services he covenanted to perform, there being nothing illegal in that part of the contract."[3]

The same reasoning was adopted in a later case,[4] where pensions were payable under a trust which, in one of its clauses, imposed an excessive restraint upon the pensioners. EVE, J., directed that the trust might lawfully be carried out, since it was not invalidated merely because the restraint might be declared void in future litigation. It was impossible, he said, to regard the trust as destroyed by the invalidity of one of its clauses. Any doubt that might still have survived was finally dispelled in two modern cases where the Court of Appeal held that the invalidity of a promise which is contrary to public policy does not nullify the whole contract, but that the valid promises, if severable, remain fully enforceable.[5]

In short, the invalidity of the class of contract now being considered goes no further than is necessary to satisfy the requirements of public policy. Unless the offending clause is in question in the actual litigation, it has no effect upon the validity of the contract.

Infringement of public policy not necessarily a bar to recovery

2. MONEY PAID OR PROPERTY TRANSFERRED BY ONE PARTY TO THE OTHER IS RECOVERABLE

Suppose that the vendor of a business agrees not to compete with the purchaser and that as security for this undertaking he deposits a sum of money with the purchaser. If this restraint

---

1. *Bennett* v. *Bennett*, [1952] 1 K.B. 249, at p. 260; [1952] 1 All E.R. 413, at p. 421; see also Salmond & Williams, *The Law of Contract*, p. 375.
2. (1837), 2 M. & W. 273.
3. *Ibid.*, at pp. 280–1.
4. *Re Prudential Assurance Co.'s Trust Deed*, [1934] Ch. 338; [1933] All E.R. Rep. 839.
5. *Bennett* v. *Bennett*, [1952] 1 K.B. 249; [1952] 1 All E.R. 413; *Goodinson* v. *Goodinson*, [1954] 2 Q.B. 118; [1954] 2 All E.R. 255. As to when the promises may be severed, see *infra*, pp. 393 *et seq.*

against competition is held to be excessive and void, is the vendor precluded from recovering the deposit? It would seem on principle that the right of recovery is unaffected. The contract is not improper in itself, and it would be extravagant to suggest that the whole transaction is so objectionable as to be caught by the maxim *ex turpi causa non oritur actio*. The decisions are too few to be conclusive one way or the other, but there is authority for the view that equity at least does not always regard an infringement of public policy as a bar to relief.[1] Thus Lord ELDON went so far as to say:

> " It is settled that if a transaction be objectionable on grounds of public policy, the parties to it may be relieved; the relief not being given for their sake, but for the sake of the public."[2]

It may be that this statement is too wide in view of the more expanded meaning that has been given to the term " public policy " since Lord ELDON's day, or it may be that relief will be granted only where one party has been less guilty than the other,[3] but at any rate it is well established that money paid under a marriage brokage contract is recoverable both at common law and in equity. This was decided in *Hermann* v. *Charlesworth*,[4] where the facts were as follows:

Money paid
under
marriage
brokage
contract is
recoverable

> Charlesworth agreed that he would introduce gentlemen to Miss Hermann with a view to matrimony, in consideration of an immediate payment of £52 and a payment of £250 on the day of the marriage. He introduced her to several gentlemen and corresponded with others on her behalf, but his efforts were fruitless. Miss Hermann sued for the return of the £52 and was successful.

Her right at common law rested on the principle that money deposited to abide the result of an event is recoverable if the event does not happen. No marriage had taken place and there had been a total failure of consideration. But quite apart from this she was entitled to exploit the wider form of relief granted by equity. Sir Richard HENN COLLINS, citing the old case of *Goldsmith* v. *Bruning*[5] amongst other authorities, showed that equity did not apply the rigid test of total failure of consideration, but so disliked contracts of this type that it was prepared to grant relief even after the marriage had been solemnized.

It is difficult to believe that the court would nowadays apply a more stringent test than this to a contract in restraint of trade. If money paid under a marriage brokage contract is recoverable, on what sensible ground can recovery of payments made under a contract in restraint of trade be refused?

3. SUBSEQUENT TRANSACTIONS ARE NOT NECESSARILY VOID

Subsequent
contract
valid unless
intended to
further the
improper
purpose

It has already been seen that if a contract as formed is illegal at common law, then any transaction which is founded on and

---

1. Ashburner, *Principles of Equity*, 2nd Edn., p. 471.
2. *Vauxhall Bridge Co.* v. *Earl Spencer* (1821), Jac. 64, at p. 66.
3. *Reynell* v. *Sprye* (1852), 1 De G.M. & G. 660, at pp. 678–9, *per* KNIGHT BRUCE, L.J.
4. [1905] 2 K.B. 123.
5. (1700), 1 Eq. Cas. Abr. 89, *pl.* 4.

springs from it is void.[1]   This is not the case with the contracts
under discussion.   They are not illegal nor, indeed, are they void
in toto.   It follows that subsequent contracts are void only so far
as they are related to that part of the original contract that is
itself void.   Suppose, for instance, that the vendor of a business
agrees, in terms which are unreasonably wide, not to compete
with the purchaser, and that after committing a breach of this
void undertaking he executes a bond agreeing to pay £1,000 to
the purchaser by way of reparation.   It goes without saying that
no action will lie on the bond.   It is impossible to divorce the
apparently valid promise of payment from the void restraint.   If,
on the other hand, the title to part of the premises conveyed with
the business turned out to be defective, and the vendor agreed to
compensate the purchaser with the payment of £1,000, there
would be no obstacle to the recovery of this sum.

A contract
governed by
foreign law is
unaffected by
English pub-
lic policy

4. THE CONTRACT, IF SUBJECT TO A FOREIGN LAW BY WHICH IT IS VALID, IS ENFORCEABLE IN ENGLAND

We have seen that a foreign contract which contravenes what
is regarded in England as an essential moral interest is not enforceable by action in this country, notwithstanding that it is valid by
its proper law.[2]   Such is the case where the principle of morality
infringed by the contract is in the English view of so compelling a
nature that it must be maintained at all costs and in all circumstances.   In other words, certain of the specific rules derived
from the doctrine of public policy are of universal, not merely
domestic, application.   It would be an exaggeration, however,
to assert that the three types of contract now being considered
offend any principle of so commanding a nature.   The reason
why these particular contracts are frowned upon by the law is not
that they are essentially reprehensible, but that they conflict
with the accepted standards of English life.   If, for instance, the
employee of a Parisian tradesman were to be sued in England for
breach of an undertaking never to enter a similar employment
anywhere in France, it would be an affectation of superior virtue
for the English court to invoke the doctrine of public policy and
to dismiss the action, always assuming, of course, that such an
undertaking is valid by French law.   The position might no
doubt be different in the exceptional case where a French contract imposed an unreasonable restraint on competition *in England*.

After certain indeterminate decisions,[3] this view has now
prevailed, and it has been held in *Addison* v. *Brown*[4] that a foreign
contract of the present class is unaffected by the English doctrine.

> An American citizen, domiciled in California, agreed to pay his
> wife a weekly sum by way of maintenance, and it was further agreed
> that neither party should apply to the Californian court for a varia-
> tion of the agreement and that if in subsequent divorce proceedings

1. *Supra,* pp. 356-8.   *Fisher* v. *Bridges* (1854), 3 E. & B. 642.
2. *Supra,* pp. 358-9
3. *Rousillon* v. *Rousillon* (1880), 14 Ch.D. 351; *Hope* v. *Hope* (1857), 8 De
   G.M. & G. 731.   These are inconclusive because, certainly in the first
   case and probably in the second, the proper law was English.
4. [1954] 2 All E.R. 213; [1954] 1 W.L.R. 779.   Compare *Bennett* v. *Bennett*,
   [1952] 1 K.B. 249; [1952] 1 All E.R. 413.

the court should provide for maintenance " the provisions hereof shall control notwithstanding the terms of any such judgment." Some years later the Californian court granted a decree of divorce at the instance of the husband and incorporated the agreement as part of the divorce.

To an action brought by the wife in England for the recovery of arrears of maintenance, it was objected that her claim was not sustainable, since the agreement was designed to oust the jurisdiction of the Californian court and was therefore contrary to the English doctrine of public policy. The objection failed. It is not the function of the doctrine to dictate to a foreign law whether an agreement of this kind shall be enforceable.

5. LAWFUL PROMISES MAY BE SEVERABLE AND ENFORCEABLE[1]

Severance means the rejection from a contract of objectionable promises or the objectionable elements of a particular promise, and the retention of those promises or of those parts of a particular promise that are valid.

Meaning of severance

It should be noticed at once that this is not allowed in the case of the contracts discussed in the previous section and which are illegal at common law as being contrary to public policy.

Contracts illegal at common law not severable

" If one of the promises to do an act which is either in itself a criminal offence or *contra bonos mores* the court will regard the whole contract as void."[2]

On principle the same is true of contracts prohibited by statute, and there is clear authority to that effect;[3] but in at least one case, *Kearney* v. *Whitehaven Colliery Co.*[4] the principle seems to have been ignored.

On the other hand, severance may be allowed if the contract is one that is void at common law on grounds of public policy or if it is void by statute, provided in this latter case that the statute, when properly construed, admits the possibility.[5] Most, but by no means all of the relevant decisions have been concerned with agreements in restraint of trade.

Contracts void at common law or by statute are severable

The doctrine of severance in the case of a void contract is used with two meanings to serve two purposes. First, it may be

Two forms of severance

---

1. The history of this branch of the law has been long and tortuous and many of the older decisions and judicial generalizations are no longer acceptable. Its development is fully traced by Marsh, 64 L.Q.R. 230, at p. 347; 69 L.Q.R. 111.
2. *Bennett* v. *Bennett*, [1952] 1 K.B. 249, at pp. 253-4; *Goodinson* v. *Goodinson*, [1954] 2 Q.B. 118, at pp. 120-1. See, for example, *Lound* v. *Grimwade* (1888), 39 Ch.D. 605; *Alexander* v. *Rayson*, [1936] 1 K.B. 169; [1935] All E.R. Rep. 185; *Napier* v. *National Business Agency, Ltd.*, [1951] 2 All E.R. 264; *Kuenigl* v. *Donnersmarck*, [1955] 1 Q.B. 515, at p. 537. In *Fielding and Platt, Ltd.* v. *Selim Najjar, Ltd.*, [1969] 2 All E.R. 150, at p. 153; [1969] 1 W.L.R. 357, at p. 362, Lord DENNING, M.R., suggested that an illegal term might be severed from a contract leaving the test intact. But his statement was clearly an *obiter dictum*, and it is respectfully submitted that it was made *per incuriam*. The contract before the court was lawful, not illegal, though one party without the knowledge of the other had exploited it illegally. Therefore the innocent could enforce it, and no question of severance arose.
3. *Hopkins* v. *Prescott* (1847), 4 C.B. 578; *Ritchie* v. *Smith* (1848), 6 C.B. 462.
4. [1893] 1 Q.B. 700.
5. See, for example, the Race Relations Act 1968, s. 23.

invoked to cut out altogether an objectionable promise from a contract leaving the rest of the contract valid and enforceable, as, for example, where a promise is void as being designed to oust the jurisdiction of the court.   In such a case the offending promise is eliminated from the contract.   Secondly, severance may operate to cut down an objectionable promise in extent, but not to cut it out of the contract altogether, as, for example, where an agreement in restraint of trade which is void as being unreasonably wide is converted into a valid promise by the elimination of its unreasonable features.   In such a case, the promise remains in the contract shorn of its offending parts and so reduced in extent.

To distinguish these two ways in which the doctrine of severance may operate is not mere pedantry, for the test of severability is not the same in each case.   Whether an entire promise may be eliminated from a contract is tested by the rule laid down in *Goodinson* v. *Goodinson*;[1] whether a particular promise may be reduced in extent is governed by the different principle of divisibility laid down in a series of decisions culminating in *Attwood* v. *Lamont*.[2]

(1) Elimination of a promise

Whether an entire promise may be eliminated from a contract depends upon whether it forms the whole or only part of the consideration.   If it is substantially the only return given for the promise of the other party, severance is ruled out and the contract fails *in toto*.   If, on the other hand, it goes only to part of the consideration—if it is merely subsidiary to the main purpose of the contract—severance is permissible.   This distinction was laid down and applied by the Court of Appeal in *Goodinson* v. *Goodinson*.[3]

> A contract made between husband and wife, who had already separated, provided, according to the interpretation put upon it by the court, that the husband would pay his wife a weekly sum by way of maintenance in consideration that she would indemnify him against all debts incurred by her, would not pledge his credit and would not take any matrimonial proceedings against him in respect of maintenance.

The last promise thus made by the wife was void since its object was to oust the jurisdiction of the courts, but it was held that this did not vitiate the rest of the contract.   It was not the only, and in the view of the court not the main, consideration furnished by the wife.   She had also promised to indemnify the husband against her debts and not to pledge his credit.   With the exception of the objectionable promise, therefore, the contract stood and the wife was entitled to recover arrears of maintenance.[4]

---

1. *Infra*, footnote 3.
2. *Infra*, p. 396.
3. [1954] 2 Q.B. 118; [1954] 2 All E.R. 255.   See also *Brooks* v. *Burns Philp Trustee Co., Ltd.*, [1969] A.L.R. 321 and *Stenhouse Australia, Ltd.* v. *Phillips*, [1974] A.C. 391; [1974] 1 All E.R. 117.
4. The Matrimonial Causes Act 1973, s. 7, now provides that the court may approve any agreement made between husband and wife prior to a divorce suit.   This provision, however, in no way affects the rule that any agreement whose object is to oust the jurisdiction of the court is void: *Wright* v. *Wright*, [1970] 3 All E.R. 209, at p. 213; [1970] 1 W.L.R. 1219, at p. 1223, *per* Sir Gordon WILLMER.   See *Hyman* v. *Hyman*, [1929] A.C. 601. See also Matrimonial Causes Act 1973, s. 34.

The second question is whether the scope of an individual promise may be reduced without eliminating it *in toto*.

The predominant principle here is that the court will not rewrite the promise as expressed by the parties. It will not add or alter words and thus frame a promise that the promisor might well have made, but did not make,[1] for that would be to destroy the " main purport and substance " of what has been agreed.[2] The parties themselves must have sown the seeds of severability in the sense that it is possible to construe the promise drafted by them as divisible into a number of separate and independent parts. If this is the correct construction, then one or more of the parts may be struck out and yet leave a promise that is substantially the same in character as that framed by the parties, though it will be diminished in extent by the reduction of its sphere of operation.[3]

In a modern case, it was argued that a clause in a lease was void as purporting to oust the jurisdiction of the court on a question of law.[4] UNGOED THOMAS, J., held that the contract, when properly construed, did not have this object in view. Had such been its purpose, it would have been void. But the learned judge also considered what the situation would have been had he found that the clause did purport to exclude the court's jurisdiction. Might it then have been severed from the contract as a whole ? Its severability would have been *prima facie* possible, since there was no question of illegality and the offending words were subsidiary to the main purpose of the contract. The stumbling-block, however, would have been that the clause had not been so drafted as to enable these words to be deleted without altering the general character of the contract. The removal of the objectionable clause would have required the contract to be remodelled; and this was not within the province of the court.

The possibility of reducing the scope of a promise without eliminating it *in toto* has often arisen in cases of restraint of trade. If a promise not to compete against an employer or against the purchaser of a business is void as being unreasonably wide, the promisee may argue that it may and should be reduced to reasonable dimensions and thus be rendered enforceable.

A clear example of a promise that, according to the language used by the parties, was divisible in the above sense was *Price* v. *Green*[5] where the seller of a perfumery business, apparently carried on in London, agreed with the purchaser that he would not carry on a similar business " within the cities of London or Westminster or within the distance of 600 miles from the same respectively." The promise was held to be valid so far as it related to London and Westminster, but void as to the distance of 600 miles. The substantial character of the promise remained

---

1. *Putsman* v. *Taylor*, [1927] 1 K.B. 637, at pp. 639–40.
2. *Mason* v. *Provident Clothing and Supply Co., Ltd.*, [1913] A.C. 724, at p. 745, *per* Lord MOULTON.
3. *Attwood* v. *Lamont*, [1920] 3 K.B. 571.
4. *Re Davstone Estates, Ltd.'s Leases, Manprop, Ltd.* v. *O'Dell*, [1969] 2 Ch. 378; [1969] 2 All E.R. 849.
5. (1847), 16 M. & W. 346. See also *Scorer* v. *Seymour Jones*, [1966] 3 All E.R. 347; [1966] 1 W.L.R. 1419 (restraint imposed on employee); *Macfarlane* v. *Kent*, [1965] 2 All E.R. 376; [1965] 1 W.L.R. 1019 (restraint imposed on expelled partner); *Bull* v. *Pitney-Bowes*, [1966] 3 All E.R. 384; [1967] 1 W.L.R. 273.

unimpaired, despite the loss of one of its parts.   Again, in *Nordenfelt* v. *Maxim Nordenfelt Guns and Ammunition Co.*,[1] as we have already seen, the House of Lords allowed the severance of a covenant against competition that was clearly divisible into two parts, one reasonable the other not.

Example of indivisible promise

On the other hand, where the promise is indivisible, where it cannot be construed as falling into distinct parts, severance is ruled out, for to attempt it would inevitably result in an agreement different in nature from that made by the parties.   In *Baker* v. *Hedgecock*,[2] for instance :

> A foreman cutter entered the service of the plaintiff, a tailor carrying on business at 61 High Holborn, and agreed that for a period of two years after leaving the employment he would not carry on, either on his own account or otherwise, *any business whatsoever* within a distance of one mile from 61 High Holborn.   After his dismissal he set up as a tailor within 100 yards of that address.

The plaintiff admitted that the agreement, since it extended to any business whatsoever, was so wide as to be unreasonable, but he asked the court " to treat the covenant as divisible and to enforce it to the extent to which it is reasonable, while declining to enforce such part of it as is unreasonable."[3]   In refusing this request, CHITTY, J., illustrated the fallacy of the plaintiff's argument in these words :

> " Thus, if the covenant were, *e.g.*, not to carry on a business in any part of the whole world, the court would be asked to uphold it by construing it as a covenant not to carry on the business within, say, a limit of two miles, which would in effect be making a new covenant, not that to which the parties agreed.   In *Price* v. *Green* there were in fact two covenants or one covenant which was capable of being construed divisibly."[4]

Discussion of *Attwood* v. *Lamont*

A comparison of the two leading cases of *Attwood* v. *Lamont* and *Goldsoll* v. *Goldman* may illustrate the nice problems of discrimination that may arise in this branch of the law.   In *Attwood* v. *Lamont* :[5]

> A carried on business as a draper, tailor and general outfitter in a shop at Kidderminster which was organized in several different departments each with a manager.   X, who was head cutter and manager of the tailoring department but who had nothing to do with the other departments, agreed that he would not at any time either on his own account or on behalf of anybody else carry on the trades of a tailor, dressmaker, general draper, milliner, hatter, haberdasher, gentlemen's, ladies' or children's outfitter at any place within ten miles of Kidderminster.

The question was whether any part of the agreement could be enforced.   It would have been legitimate to restrain the improper use by X of the knowledge of customers acquired by him in his capacity as manager of the tailoring department.   But the restraint as drafted, since it affected trade in other departments where he

---

1. *Supra*, pp. 370–1.   See also *Nicholls* v. *Stretton* (1847), 10 Q.B. 346; *Goldsoll* v. *Goldman*, [1915] 1 Ch. 292; *Putsman* v. *Taylor*, [1927] 1 K.B. 637.
2. (1888), 39 Ch.D. 520.
3. *Ibid.*, *per* counsel, at p. 521.
4. *Ibid.*, at pp. 522–3, see also *Continental Tyre and Rubber (Great Britain) Co., Ltd.* v. *Heath* (1913), 29 T.L.R. 308.
5. [1920] 3 K.B. 571.

would not meet customers, admittedly gave A more than adequate protection. It was argued, however, that the agreement ought to be severed and limited to the business of a tailor.

The divisional court allowed this severance. It took the view that the agreement constituted " a series of distinct obligations in separate and clearly defined divisions,"[1] and that it was possible to run a blue pencil through all the trades except that of tailoring without altering the main " purport and substance "[2] of what the parties had written. The Court of Appeal unanimously reversed this decision. It took the view that the parties had made a single indivisible agreement the substantial object of which was to protect the entire business carried on by the employer. YOUNGER, L.J., summarized this view as follows:

> " The learned judges of the divisional court, I think, took the view that such severance always was permissible when it could be effectively accomplished by the action of a blue pencil. I do not agree. The doctrine of severance has not, I think, gone further than to make it permissible in a case where the covenant is not really a single covenant but is in effect a combination of several distinct covenants. In that case and where the severance can be carried out without the addition or alteration of a word, it is permissible. But in that case only. Now here, I think, there is in truth but one covenant for the protection of the respondent's entire business, and not several covenants for the protection of his several businesses. The respondent is, on the evidence, not carrying on several businesses but one business, and in my opinion this covenant must stand or fall in its unaltered form."[3]

In *Goldsoll* v. *Goldman*:[4]

Discussion of Goldsoll v. Goldman

The defendant, who carried on a business in London for the sale of imitation jewellery, sold his business to the plaintiff and agreed that for a period of two years he would not, either solely or jointly, deal in real or imitation jewellery in any part of the United Kingdom or in France, U.S.A., Russia or Spain, or within twenty-five miles of Potsdammerstrasse, Berlin, or St. Stefans Kirche, Vienna.

The extension of the restraint to the whole of the United Kingdom was reasonable, for the plaintiff, who had for a considerable time carried on a similar business in London, gained most of his customers from advertisements in the illustrated papers which circulated throughout the country. It was held that the contract could and must be severed in two respects: first, the area outside the United Kingdom must be removed from it; secondly, the prohibition against dealing in real jewellery must also be removed.

The question is whether this decision can be reconciled with that in *Attwood* v. *Lamont*. The crux of the matter seems to be whether in each of these cases the contract as framed by the parties was divisible into a number of separate promises, for if so, and only if so, the elimination of one or more of the objectionable promises would still leave the substantial character of the contract unchanged. It may perhaps fairly be said that this basic element of divisibility, while present in *Goldsoll* v. *Goldman*, was absent in *Attwood* v. *Lamont*, for in the latter case the enumeration of the

---

1. [1920] 2 K.B. 146, at p. 159.
2. *Ibid.*, at p. 156.
3. [1920] 2 K.B., at p. 593.
4. [1915] 1 Ch. 292.

various trades was only a laborious description of the entire business carried on by the employer. Since the contract was essentially indivisible, it had to stand or fall as originally drafted.

Distinction between a service contract and one for the sale of a business

It has been thought, however, that the reconciliation of these two decisions is to be found in the fact that the one concerned a service contract, the other a contract for the sale of a business, for it is now generally accepted that the latter merits a less rigorous treatment than the former. It is only common justice that the purchaser shall be able to reap the benefit of what he has bought, and therefore the courts are more astute than they would be in the case of a service contract to construe an agreement by the seller not to compete as a combination of several distinct promises. This distinction was viewed with apparent approval by the Court of Appeal in *Ronbar Enterprises, Ltd.* v. *Green*,[1] (a case of vendor and purchaser) but it was disapproved in *T. Lucas & Co., Ltd.* v. *Mitchell*[2] (a case of master and servant).

---

1. [1954] 2 All E.R. 266; [1954] 1 W.L.R. 815, where the court merely expunged two words from what appears to have been an indivisible covenant. See also Lord MOULTON in *Mason* v. *Provident Clothing and Supply Co., Ltd.*, [1913] A.C. 724, at p. 745; [1911–13] All E.R. Rep. 400, at p. 411.
2. [1974] Ch. 129; [1972] 3 All E.R. 689.

PART V
CAPACITY OF PARTIES

SUMMARY

CHAPTER ONE

Infants

SECTION I. THE EFFECT OF CONTRACTS MADE BY INFANTS

CONTRACTS made by infants, i.e. persons under eighteen years of age,[1] are governed by the rules of common law as altered by the Infants Relief Act 1874.

The general rule at common law was that a contract made by an infant was voidable at his option. The word " voidable," however, was used in two different senses. Certain contracts were voidable in the sense that they were valid and binding upon him unless he repudiated them before, or within a reasonable time after, the attainment of his majority. Other contracts were voidable in a different sense, *i.e.* they were not binding upon the infant unless ratified by him when he reached 21 years of age.

Two types of transactions, namely beneficial contracts of service and contracts for necessaries, were treated as exceptional.

Summary of the law

Prior to Infants Relief Act 1874

---

1. Family Law Reform Act 1969, s. 1. At common law, the age of majority was twenty-one. The Act provides that persons over eighteen but under twenty-one years of age on January 1st, 1970, shall be regarded as having attained full age on that date. The Act also provides that infants may be called " minors ": s. 12. For a comparative survey of the law, see Hartwig, 15 I.C.L.Q. 780; Thomas, 1972 Acta Juridica 151. The Act of 1969 was based on the report of the Committee on the Age of Majority (Cmnd. 3342). That committee also make extensive proposals for changes in the law of infants' contracts but these were not enacted.

The former were regarded as valid.   The latter imposed liability upon the infant, though whether this was of a contractual nature or not was a matter of controversy.

Effect of the Act

These common law rules were affected in two important particulars by the Infants' Relief Act 1874.

First, the statute provided that three particular kinds of contract should be " absolutely void," namely, contracts of loan, contracts for goods (other than necessaries) and accounts stated.

Secondly, it enacted that it should no longer be possible to ratify at 21 those contracts which formerly were not binding on the infant unless ratified.

Postition at the present day

It will be convenient to discuss the different types of transactions in the following order:

1. Contracts for necessaries.
2. Beneficial contracts of service.
3. Voidable contracts.
4. Contracts within the Infants' Relief Act 1874.

A.   CONTRACTS FOR NECESSARIES

Meaning of " necessaries "

It has been recognized from the earliest times that an infant is obliged to pay for necessaries that have been supplied to him. The word *necessaries* is not confined to articles necessary to the support of life, but includes articles and services fit to maintain the particular person in the station of life in which he moves.[1] So far as concerns goods it has been statutorily defined as meaning " goods suitable to the condition in life of such infant and to his actual requirements at the time of the sale and delivery."[2] Perhaps the best statement of the law, at least as applied to nineteenth-century conditions, is that given by ALDERSON, B.

> " Things necessary are those without which an individual cannot reasonably exist.   In the first place, food, raiment, lodging and the like.   About these there is no doubt.   Again, as the proper cultivation of the mind is as expedient as the support of the body, instruction in art or trade, or intellectual, moral and religious information may be a necessary also.   Again, as man lives in society, the assistance and attendance of others may be a necessary to his well-being.   Hence attendance may be the subject of an infant's contract.   Then the classes being established, the subject-matter and extent of the contract may vary according to the state and condition of the infant himself.   His clothes may be fine or coarse according to his rank; his education may vary according to the station he is to fill; and the medicines will depend on the illness with which he is afflicted, and the extent of his probable means when of full age.   So again, the nature and extent of the attendance will depend on his position in society. . . . But in all these cases it must first be made out that the class itself is one in which the things furnished are essential to the existence and reasonable advantage and comfort of the infant contractor.   Thus, articles of *mere* luxury are

1. *Peters* v. *Fleming* (1840), 6 M. & W. 42, at pp. 46–7, *per* PARKE, B.
2. Sale of Goods Act 1893, s. 2.   Winfield, 58 L.Q.R. 82.

always excluded,[1] though luxurious articles of utility are in some cases allowed."[2]

Necessaries for the members of a married infant's family are on the same footing as necessaries for himself, and it is well established that he is liable on a contract for the burial of his wife or children.[3]

To render an infant liable for necessaries it must be proved, not only that the goods are suitable to his station in life, but also that they are suitable to his actual requirements at the time of their delivery. If he is already sufficiently provided with goods of the kind in question, then, even though this fact is not known to the plaintiff, the price is irrecoverable.[4]

Goods not necessaries if infant's existing supply sufficient

> Thus in a case in 1908, where a Savile Row tailor sought to recover £122 19s. 6d. for clothes (including eleven fancy waistcoats at two guineas each), supplied to an infant undergraduate at Cambridge, it was held that the action must fail, since the evidence showed that the defendant was already amply supplied with clothing suitable to his position.[5]

Whether articles are necessaries is a question of mixed law and fact.[6] The preliminary question of law for the court is whether in the circumstances the article is capable of being a necessary. The onus of establishing this lies on the plaintiff, who must prove that the goods are of a description reasonably suitable to a person in the station in life of the infant defendant. If he fails, the court rules that there is no evidence on which it can properly find for him, and judgment is declared in favour of the defendant.

Mixed law and fact

> Thus in one case it was held that a pair of jewelled solitaires worth £25 and an antique goblet worth fifteen guineas could not possibly be regarded as necessaries for an infant possessing an income of £500 a year.[7] There was no case to be submitted to the jury.

If, however, the court decides that the articles are clearly capable of being necessaries, as, for instance, clothes or food, it is a question of fact whether they are necessaries in the particular circumstances. The actual requirements of the infant must be assessed, and it must be decided whether he was adequately supplied with articles of the kind in question at the time of their delivery.[8] Again, if the article is one which may or may not be necessary, such as a watch, an exceptionally expensive coat or a

---

1. " Suppose the son of the richest man in the kingdom to have been supplied with diamonds and racehorses, the judge ought to tell the jury that such articles cannot possibly be necessaries," *Wharton* v. *Mackenzie* (1844), 5 Q.B. 606, at p. 612, *per* COLERIDGE, J. In that case it was held that fruits, ices and confectionery supplied to an Oxford undergraduate for private dinner parties could not without further explanation be treated as necessaries.
2. *Chapple* v. *Cooper* (1844), 13 M. & W. 252, at p. 258. It would appear that in the affluent and permissive society of today many articles that would have ranked as luxurious in the learned baron's time would now be regarded as " things essential to the existence and reasonable advantage and comfort of the infant contractor."
3. *Chapple* v. *Cooper, supra.*
4. *Barnes & Co.* v. *Toye* (1884), 13 Q.B.D. 410; *Nash* v. *Inman*, [1908] 2 K.B. 1.
5. *Nash* v. *Inman*, [1908] 2 K.B. 1.
6. *Ryder* v. *Wombwell* (1868), L.R. 4 Exch. 32, at p. 38.
7. *Ryder* v. *Wombwell, supra.*
8. *Nash* v. *Inman*, [1908] 2 K.B. 1.

pair of binoculars, it must be decided whether it is so in fact
having regard *inter alia* to the social standing, profession and
duties of the infant.

> So in *Peters* v. *Fleming*[1] the court decided that *prima facie* it
> was not unreasonable for an infant undergraduate to have a watch
> and consequently a watch-chain, but they left it to the jury to find
> whether the gold chain supplied to him on credit was of a kind
> reasonably suitable for his requirements.

Examples of necessaries

In addition to food, clothing and lodging, the following
amongst other things, have been held to be necessaries: uniforms
for a member of one of the fighting forces[2]; means of conveyance
required by an infant for the exercise of his calling[3]; and legal
advice.[4]

Onerous terms must not be imposed upon infant

A contract for the supply even of goods or services that are
clearly suitable to the requirements of an infant is void if it
contains terms that are harsh and onerous to him.[5]   In one case,
for instance, a contract by which an infant hired a car for the
transport of his luggage was held to be void, since it stipulated
that he should be absolutely liable for injury to the car whether
caused by his neglect or not.[6]   In other words, a contract for
necessaries will not be binding unless it is substantially for the
benefit of the infant.   This rule, however, is not confined to the
supply of necessaries.   It is only a facet of the wider principle that
no contract is binding upon an infant if it is prejudicial to his
interests, even one which is normally valid.[7]

What is basis of infant's liability?

A question that is by no means of purely academic interest
is—what is the basis of an infant's liability for necessaries?
Two conflicting theories have been advocated.

Does it arise consensu?

First, he is liable *ex contractu* just as a contracting party of
full capacity is liable. " The plaintiff," said Buckley, L.J.,
" when he sues the defendant for goods supplied during infancy,
is suing him in contract on the footing that the contract was such
as the infant, notwithstanding infancy, could make."[8]

Does it arise re?

Secondly, the infant is liable *re*, not *consensu*.   In other words
his liability is based, not on contract, but on quasi-contract.   He
is bound, not because he has agreed, but because he has been
supplied.[9]

> " The old course of pleading was a count for goods sold and
> delivered, a plea of infancy, and a replication that the goods were

---

1. (1840), 6 M. & W. 42.
2. *Coates* v. *Wilson* (1804), 5 Esp. 152.
3. *Barber* v. *Vincent* (1680), Freem. (K.B.) 531 (horse); *Clyde Cycle Co.*
   v. *Hargreaves* (1898), 78 L.T. 296.
4. *Helps* v. *Clayton* (1864), 17 C.B.N.S. 553.
5. *Roberts* v. *Gray*, [1913] 1 K.B. 520, at p. 528.
6. *Fawcett* v. *Smethurst* (1914), 84 L.J.K.B. 473.
7. See, for example *Shears* v. *Mendiloff* (1914), 30 T.L.R. 342 (appointment of a
   manager by an infant boxer); *Chaplin* v. *Leslie Frewin (Publishers), Ltd.*,
   [1966] Ch. 71, at p. 88.   See also beneficial contracts of service, *infra*,
   p. 406.
8. *Nash* v. *Inman*, [1908] 2 K.B. 1, at p. 12.
9. *Re J.*, [1909] 1 Ch. 574, at p. 577, *per* Fletcher-Moulton, L.J.; *Nash*
   v. *Inman*, *supra*, at p. 8, *per* Fletcher-Moulton, L.J.; see *infra*, pp. 662-3.

necessaries; and then the plaintiff did not necessarily recover the price alleged, he recovered a reasonable price for the necessaries. That does not imply a consensual contract."[1]

The question whether an infant is liable on an executory contract for necessaries depends upon which of these two theories is correct. If his obligation arises *re* and is non-existent in the absence of delivery, he clearly cannot be liable for goods not actually supplied, and presumably his refusal of them when tendered is justifiable. A learned writer on the subject failed to find a single case where liability has been established in the absence of delivery,[2] and it is probably safe to assume that in the case of goods the second theory is correct and that an executory contract is unenforceable.

Executory contract for supply of goods unenforceable

A further point must be noted. Even if the goods have been actually supplied there is an express enactment that he shall pay a reasonable, not necessarily the contract, price;[3] and those judges who have advocated the contractual basis of an infant's liability have said that he is still liable only for a reasonable sum.[4] This is a curious admission, for if the basis of liability is truly contractual, it is odd that the infant should not be bound by the price that he has agreed to pay, whether reasonable or not.

Only a reasonable price payable for necessary goods

It is more difficult to determine the basis of liability where the subject-matter is not goods, as for instance in a contract for the hire of lodgings or for education. A case in point is *Roberts* v. *Gray*[5] where the facts were these:

Executory contract for education has been held enforceable

> The defendant, an infant, who desired to become a professional billiard player, made a contract with Roberts, a leading professional, by which the parties agreed to accompany each other on a world tour and to play matches together in the principal countries. Roberts expended much time and trouble and incurred certain liabilities in the course of making the necessary preparations. A dispute arose between the parties and before the tour began Gray repudiated the contract.

Roberts sued for breach of contract and was awarded £1,500 by the court of first instance. The Court of Appeal, in affirming this decision, treated the contract as being one for necessaries. The doctrine of necessaries, said COZENS-HARDY, M.R., applies not merely to bread and cheese and clothes, but also to education, a word which in this connection extends to any form of instruction that is suitable for the particular infant. It had been argued, however, that though the defendant would have been liable to pay on a *quantum meruit* for services rendered had he actually received the plaintiff's instruction, yet, since he had repudiated the contract while it was still to a large extent executory, he was immune from liability. The court would have none of this.

> "I am unable to appreciate," said HAMILTON, L.J., "why a contract which is in itself binding, because it is a contract for necessaries not qualified by unreasonable terms, can cease to be

1. *Pontypridd Union* v. *Drew*, [1927] 1 K.B. 214, at p. 220, *per* SCRUTTON, L.J.
2. Miles, 43 L.Q.R. 389.
3. Sale of Goods Act 1893, s. 2.
4. See *e.g. Nash* v. *Inman*, [1908] 2 K.B. 1, at p. 12.
5. [1913] 1 K.B. 520.

binding merely because it is executory. . . . If the contract is binding at all, it must be binding for all such remedies as are appropriate to the breach of it."[1]

Unless this decision can be discounted on the ground that the contract had been partly executed, it would seem to create a difficult distinction between goods and other types of necessaries such as instruction. In the first case the infant is not liable unless he has actually received the goods, in the second the fact that no instruction has yet been imparted does not release him from his obligation. Perhaps the solution lies in separating the contract for education from the category of necessaries. It is true that Coke included it in the category and that his words have been echoed by modern judges. But there is another and independent type of valid contract, namely the beneficial contract of service, which is wide enough, and certainly more appropriate, to include education and other forms of instruction. As we shall see in the following section such a contract is binding even though it has not been completely executed. It is significant that all the authorities relied upon by the court in *Roberts* v. *Gray* concerned beneficial contracts of service.

B. BENEFICIAL CONTRACTS OF SERVICE

It has been held from a very early date that an infant may bind himself by a contract of apprenticeship or of service, since it is to his advantage that he should acquire the means of earning his livelihood. Such a contract, however, when construed as a whole, must be substantially for his advantage, if he is not to be free to repudiate it.[2] *Prima facie* it is valid, but in the event of a dispute it is the province of the court[3] to decide whether the agreement when carefully examined in all its terms was, at the time when it was entered into[4], for his benefit. The mere fact that one or more of the stipulations are prejudicial to him is not decisive, for some terms not directly beneficial to the servant must be expected in all service agreements. The court must look at the whole contract, must weigh the onerous against the beneficial terms, and then decide whether the balance is in favour of the infant.

" It must be shown that the contract which he entered into with the plaintiff company was not merely a contract under which he improved himself in his business and under which he got a salary which I presume to have been adequate and reasonable, but it must be shown by the plaintiff that it was a contract which contained clauses, and only clauses, that are usual and customary in an employment of this nature."[5]

---

1. [1913] 1 K.B., at p. 530. Yet in *Walter* v. *Everard*, [1891] 2 Q.B. 369, at p. 374, Lord ESHER said: " The person who sues the infant on his covenant must show that he did in fact supply him with the necessary education."
2. *De Francesco* v. *Barnum* (1890), 45 Ch.D. 430; *Clements* v. *London and North Western Rail. Co.*, [1894] 2 Q.B. 482.
3. *Flower* v. *London and North Western Rail. Co.*, [1894] 2 Q.B. 65.
4. *Chaplin* v. *Leslie Frewin (Publishers), Ltd.*, [1966] Ch. 71, at p. 95; [1965] 3 All E.R. 764, *per* DANCKWERTS, L.J.; *Mackinlay* v. *Bathurst* (1919), 36 T.L.R. 31, at p. 33.
5. *Leng & Co., Ltd.* v. *Andrews*, [1909] 1 Ch. 763, at p. 769, *per* COZENS-HARDY, M.R.

Two cases may be contrasted.[1]
In *De Francesco* v. *Barnum*:[1]

> A girl, fourteen years old, bound herself by an apprenticeship deed to the plaintiff for seven years to be taught stage dancing. She agreed *inter alia* that she would not marry during the apprenticeship, and would not accept professional engagements without the plaintiff's permission. The plaintiff did not bind himself to provide the infant with engagements or to maintain her while unemployed, and the pay that he agreed to give in the event of her employment was the reverse of generous. It was 9d. per night and 6d. for each matinee during the first three years, and after that period 1s. per night and 6d. for each matinee. He was entitled to engage her in performances abroad, and in this event was bound to pay her 5s. a week with board and lodging. He could terminate the contract if, after a fair trial, the infant was found unfit for stage dancing.

Example of void contract

It was held by FRY, J., that the provisions of the deed were unreasonable and unenforceable. The learned judge came to the conclusion that the child was at the absolute disposal of the plaintiff. She was to receive no pay and no maintenance except when employed, there was no correlative obligation on the plaintiff to find employment for her, and it was left to him to terminate the contract and thus to destroy her chances of success.

In *Clements* v. *London and North Western Rail. Co.*:[2]

> An infant, upon entering the service of a railway company as a porter, agreed to join the company's own insurance scheme and to relinquish his right of suing for personal injury under the Employers' Liability Act 1880. The scheme was more favourable to him than the Act since it covered more accidents for which compensation was payable, though on the other hand it fixed a lower scale of compensation.

Example of valid contract

It was held that the agreement as a whole was manifestly to the advantage of the infant and was binding.

Benefit to the infant, as we see then, is the keynote to the validity of this type of contract. At the same time there is no general principle that any agreement is binding upon an infant merely because it is for his benefit.[3] For instance, it has been established for over 200 years that a trading contract is not binding upon him however much it may be for his benefit.[4] So in *Cowern* v. *Nield*[5] it was held that an infant hay and straw dealer was not liable to repay the price of a consignment of hay that he had failed to deliver, and in a later case that a haulage contractor aged twenty was not liable for instalments due under a hire-purchase agreement by which a lorry had been hired to him for use

No general principle that any contract beneficial to infant is binding

---

1. (1890), 45 Ch.D. 430.
2. [1894] 2 Q.B. 482; followed in *Slade* v. *Metrodent, Ltd.*, [1953] 2 Q.B. 112; [1953] 2 All E.R. 336 (infant held bound by an arbitration clause contained in an apprenticeship deed).
3. *Martin* v. *Gale* (1876), 4 Ch.D. 428, at p. 431, *per* JESSEL, M.R.; *Clements* v. *London and North Western Rail. Co.*, *supra*, at p. 493, *per* KAY, L.J.; *Doyle* v. *White City Stadium, Ltd.*, [1935] 1 K.B. 110, at p. 131; [1934] All E.R. Rep. 252, at p. 262, *per* SLESSER, L.J.
4. *Whywall* v. *Champion* (1738), 2 Stra. 1083. The remark of MCNAIR, J. in *Slade* v. *Metrodent, Ltd.*, [1953] 2 Q.B. 112, at p. 115; [1953] 2 All E.R. 336, at p. 337, is presumably confined to the case of a service contract.
5. [1912] 2 K.B. 419.

in his business.[1]   The essential fact to appreciate is that, for a beneficial agreement to be valid, it must either be a service or apprenticeship contract properly so called or at least analogous to such a contract.[2].   In recent years, however, the court have taken a progressively wider view of what is a contract of service.   So in *Doyle* v. *White City Stadium, Ltd.*,[3] for instance, it was held that a contract between an infant boxer and the British Boxing Board of Control, under which the infant received a licence to box that enabled him to gain proficiency in his profession, was so closely connected with a contract of service as to be binding.

C. VOIDABLE CONTRACTS

Contracts
valid unless
avoided

We now have to deal with contracts that are voidable in the sense that they are valid and binding upon an infant unless he repudiates them during infancy or within a reasonable time after the attainment of his majority.   They are confined to contracts by which the infant acquires an interest in some subject-matter of a permanent nature, i.e. a subject-matter to which continuous or recurring obligations are incident.   The principle is that if an infant undertakes such a contractual obligation, it " remains until he thinks proper to put an end to it."[4]

Purchase
of land

The most obvious example is a contract made by an infant for a lease.   An infant is precluded by legislation from acquiring a legal estate in land,[5] but a lease which purports to convey to him a term of years absolute gives him an equitable interest for the agreed period.[6]   This is voidable at his option, but while in possession he is subject to the liabilities imposed by the contract and may for instance be successfully sued for the non-payment of rent.[7]   The same principle applies to the acquisition of shares.

Purchase
of shares

An infant purchaser of shares acquires an interest in a subject-matter of a permanent nature carrying with it certain obligations that he is bound to discharge until he repudiates the transaction.[8] Thus a plea of infancy will not relieve him from liability to pay a call, i.e. a demand to pay to the company what is still due on the shares, if it is made before repudiation,[9] but as soon as he repudiates, or as it is often termed " rescinds," the transaction, the

1. *Mercantile Union Guarantee Corporation, Ltd.* v. *Ball,* [1937] 2 K.B. 498; [1937] 3 All E.R. 1.
2. *Cowern* v. *Nield,* [1912] 2 K.B. 419, at p. 422.
3. [1935] 1 K.B. 110; [1934] All E.R. Rep. 252; applied in *Chaplin* v. *Leslie Frewin (Publishers), Ltd.,* [1966] Ch. 71; *infra,* p. 400, where the Court of Appeal extended the analogy to a contract by a publisher to publish the auto-biography of an infant.   Similarly a contract by an infant " pop group " to appoint a manager is valid if beneficial: *Denmark Productions, Ltd.* v. *Boscombe Productions, Ltd.,* [1967] C.L.Y. 1999 (decided on other grounds [1969] 1 Q.B. 699; [1968] 3 All E.R. 513).   See also *Inland Revenue Commissioners* v. *Mills,* [1974] 1 All E.R. 722; [1974] 2 W.L.R. 325.
4. *Goode* v. *Harrison* (1821), 5 B. and Ald. 147, at p. 169, *per* BEST, J.
5. Law of Property Act 1925, s. 1 (6); Settled Land Act 1925, s. 27 (1).
6. *Davies* v. *Beynon-Harris* (1931), 47 T.L.R. 424; Settled Land Act 1925, s. 27 (2).
7. *Davies* v. *Beynon-Harris, supra.*
8. *North Western Rail. Co.* v. *McMichael* (1850), 5 Exch. 114, at pp. 123 and 124.
9. *Cork and Bandon Rail. Co.* v. *Cazenove* (1847), 10 Q.B. 935.

interest acquired by him is at an end, and with it his liability
for future calls.

Much the same principle applies to a partnership. An infant
partner in a firm is not liable for partnership debts contracted
during his infancy,[1] though he has no right to prevent their
discharge out of the common assets. On reaching his majority
he may repudiate the partnership contract altogether, but if
he fails to do so and thus holds himself out as a continuing
partner, he remains responsible for all debts contracted since he
came of age.[2]

Contract of partnership

A contract of the class that we are now considering, in order
to become permanently binding upon an infant, does not require
ratification by him when he attains his majority. It remains binding upon him unless he repudiates it within a reasonable time after
he comes of age.[3]

Repudiation must be within a reasonable time

" If he chooses to be inactive, his opportunity passes away; if he
chooses to be active the law comes to his assistance."[4]

What is a reasonable time depends of course upon the particular
circumstances of each case. In *Edwards* v. *Carter*,[5] for instance:

Edwards v. Carter

A marriage settlement was executed by which the father of the
intended husband agreed to pay £1500 a year to the trustees, who
were to pay it to the husband for life and then to the wife and issue
of the marriage. The intended husband, an infant at the time of
the settlement, executed a deed binding him to vest in the trustees
all property that he might acquire under the will of his father. A
month later he came of age and three and a half years later he
became entitled to an interest under his father's will. More than a
year after his father's death, *i.e.* about four and a half years after he
came of age, he repudiated his agreement.

It was argued that the repudiation was in time, since the infant,
when he signed the agreement, did not realize the extent of his
obligation, and could not decide upon his best course of action
until he knew the extent of his interest under the will. It was held
however, that his repudiation was too late and was ineffective.

It is clear that an infant who repudiates a voidable contract is
no longer liable to honour future obligations. What is not
authoritatively settled, however, is whether he is freed from those
that have accrued due at the time of his repudiation. If, for
example, he repudiates a lease of land, is he none the less liable for
rent *already* due? This is a question upon which there are
conflicting *dicta* and no direct authority in modern times. Two
views have been advanced.

Effect of repudiation

The first is that repudiation is the equivalent of rescission,
which, as we have already seen, is retrospective in its operation.
It " terminates the contract, puts the parties *in statu quo ante* and
restores things, as between them, to the position in which they
stood before the contract was entered into."[6] In *North Western*

The view that it cancels accrued debts

---

1. *Lovell and Christmas* v. *Beauchamp*, [1894] A.C. 607, at p. 611.
2. *Goode* v. *Harrison* (1821), 5 B. & Ald. 147.
3. *Carter* v. *Silber*, [1892] 2 Ch. 278, at p. 284, *per* LINDLEY, L.J.
4. *Edwards* v. *Carter*, [1893] A.C. 360, at p. 366, *per* Lord Watson.
5. *Supra.*
6. *Abram Steamship Co.* v. *Westville Steamship Co.*, [1923] A.C. 773, at p. 781,
per Lord ATKINSON; *supra*, p. 264.

Rail. Co. v. *McMichael*,[1] for instance, an action was brought against an infant to recover a call on certain railway shares that he had bought. The defendant merely pleaded that he had never ratified the purchase and had not received any benefit from it. PARKE, B., however, who delivered the judgment of the court, stated what the position would have been had repudiation been pleaded and substantiated.

> " Our opinion is that an infant is not absolutely bound, but is in the same situation as an infant acquiring real estate or any other permanent interest: he is not deprived of the right which the law gives every infant of waiving and disagreeing to a purchase which he has made; and if he waives it the estate acquired by the purchaser is at an end and with it his liability to pay calls, *though the avoidance may not have taken place till the call was due.*"[2]

The court relied upon a case decided in 1613 which is reported under a variety of names in different reports.[3] In this case, it was indeed affirmed that a voidable lease would be rendered void if disclaimed by an infant; and that if the disclaimer had been made *before* the rent fell due, the tenant's liability in this respect would be cancelled. No mention was made of rent already due.[4] Yet YOUNGER, L.J., once said that an infant shareholder " is no longer liable to pay the instalments [due under a call] which she has not paid."[5]

The view that accrued debts still payable

The principle stated by PARKE, B., however, that the repudiation of his contract by an infant has a retrospective effect, has not been universally accepted. Thus, an Irish judge has reached the opposite conclusion. This was in *Blake* v. *Concannon*,[6] where an infant tenant, after occupying the premises for nearly a year, quitted possession and on attaining full age repudiated the tenancy. Nevertheless, he was held liable for half a year's rent which had accrued due while he was in possession. His liability was based upon his use and occupation of the land.[7] In *Steinberg* v. *Scala (Leeds), Ltd.*,[8] there is a *dictum* of WARRINGTON, L.J., that an infant shareholder who rescinds his purchase is relieved of liability for future calls, no mention being made of calls already due. Moreover, the views of text-book writers are not unanimous on the question, though their general conclusion is that liability for an accrued debt survives a repudiation of the contract.[9]

In view of this disarray of opinions it would be misleading to say that the authorities have reached a definite conclusion upon

---

1. (1850), 5 Exch. 114.
2. (1850), 5 Exch. 114, at p. 125; italics supplied.
3. *Ketsey's Case* (1613), Cro. Jac. 320; *Ketely's Case*, 1 Brownlow 120; *Kirton* v. *Eliott*, Roll. Abr. 731. See Simpson, *History*, pp. 540–544.
4. See JESSEL, M.R., *Re Jones, Ex parte Jones* (1881), 18 Ch.D. 109, at p. 117.
5. *Steinberg* v. *Scala (Leeds), Ltd.*, [1923] 2 Ch. 452, at p. 463.
6. (1870), I.R. 4 C.L. 323.
7. The citation of this case in an English action provoked JESSEL, M.R., to say: " That is founded on an implied contract. How can a court imply a contract against a person who is incapable of contracting?": *Re Jones, Ex parte Jones* (1881), 18 Ch.D., at p. 118.
8. [1923] 2 Ch. 451, at p. 461.
9. Those who take this view include *Sutton and Shannn on Contracts*, 8th Edn., p. 220; Salmond and Winfield, *Principles of the Law of Contracts*, p. 461. The opposite view is expressed by Salmond and Williams, *Principles of the Law of Contracts*, p. 300.

the matter. It is submitted, however, that it is preferable to accept the logic of the retrospective principle as explained by PARKE, B., in *McMichael's* case.

An entirely different question in the present context is whether an infant, on repudiation of a contract, can recover money which he has paid or property which he has delivered to the other party. The rule here is that if, for instance, he has paid money to the defendant, he cannot recover it at common law as being money had and received unless he can show that he has suffered a total failure of consideration.

To succeed, he must prove that he has received no part of what he was promised. This he was able to do in *Corpe v. Overton*.[1]

> An infant agreed to enter into a partnership with the defendant in three months' time and to pay him £1,000 when the partnership deed was executed. He also made an immediate payment of £100 as security for the fulfilment of his promise. He rescinded the contract as soon as he came of age and sued for the recovery of the £100.

The money was held to be recoverable since there had been a total failure of consideration. The money had been deposited by the plaintiff to secure the due performance of the partnership contract, but at the time when that contract was effectively rescinded he had received no consideration for what he had paid.[2]

In *Holmes* v. *Blogg*,[3] however, the test of total failure of consideration was not satisfied. An infant paid a sum of money to a lessor as part of the consideration for a lease of premises in which he and a partner proposed to carry on their trade. He occupied the premises for twelve weeks, but the day after he came of age he dissolved the partnership, repudiated the lease and left the premises. He failed in his attempt to recover what he had paid. There was no total failure of consideration, since he had received the very thing he had been promised and for which he had made the payment.

To the same effect is *Steinberg* v. *Scala (Leeds), Ltd.*[4]

> The plaintiff, an infant, applied for shares in a company and paid the amounts due on allotment and on the first call. She neither received any dividends nor attended any meetings of the company, and the shares appear always to have stood at a discount. Eighteen months after allotment, while still an infant, she rescinded the contract and claimed to recover what she had paid.

Her claim failed. The company, by allotting the shares, had done all that it had bargained to do by way of consideration for her payment.

Some of the expressions used by the judges in the relevant cases on this matter appear at first sight to make the right of recovery turn upon whether or not the infant has derived *any* substantial benefit from the contract. This is misleading. In the

---

1. (1833), 10 Bing. 252.
2. *Steinberg* v. *Scala (Leeds), Ltd.*, [1923] 2 Ch. 452, at p. 461, *per* Lord STERNDALE, M.R.
3. (1818), 8 R. Taunt. 508.
4. [1923] 2 Ch. 452; overruling *Hamilton* v. *Vaughan-Sherrin Electrical Engineering Co.*, [1894] 3 Ch. 589.

words of YOUNGER, L.J.: " The question is not: Has the infant
derived any real advantage?   But the question is: Has the consideration wholly failed?"[1]   Thus in *Steinberg's* case, since the
infant had obtained the very consideration for which she had
bargained, it was irrelevant that what she had obtained might
be valueless.

Recovery of
property,
other than
money
already
transferred

Cases such as *Edwards* v. *Carter*[2] show that a disposition by an
infant of any form of property, whether realty or personalty, is not
finally and conclusively binding upon him.   " There is a total
absolute disability in an infant that by no manner of conveyance
can he dispose of his inheritance."[3]   He may either confirm or
rescind it on the attainment of his majority.   If he exercises his
right of rescission, his disposition, hitherto valid until avoided,
now becomes retrospectively void *ab initio*.   In principle this
requires the restoration of the *status quo ante*—a giving back and a
taking back on both sides—and it has long been understood that
the infant is entitled to recover the property that he has
transferred.

This general principle, which allows an infant to recover what
he has transferred by a completed disposition, has been somewhat
clouded by the decision of the Court of Appeal in *Chaplin* v.
Leslie Frewin (Publishers), Ltd.[4] where the facts were as follows:

> The plaintiffs, an infant and his adult wife, entered into a contract
> with the defendants by which the latter agreed to publish the auto-
> biography of the infant which was to be written by two journalists
> based on information furnished by the plaintiffs.   The plaintiffs
> approved the final page proofs on July 21st, and the legal right to the
> copyright was assigned in writing to the defendants.   Advance
> royalties of £600 were paid to the plaintiffs, who also knew that the
> defendants had contracted with third parties for the foreign publica-
> tion of the work.
>
> On August 26th the plaintiffs repudiated the contract on the
> ground that the book contained libellous matter and attributed to the
> infant views that he did not hold.   They commenced an action for an
> injunction restraining the publication of the book, and for an order
> restoring the copyright to them.   They conceded that, as part of this
> equitable relief, they were obliged to repay the money they had
> received.   Pending the trial of the action, they moved for an inter-
> locutory injunction to prevent publication.

The Court of Appeal was unanimous in holding that the contract
was analogous to a service contract, which, as has been seen,[5] is
valid if it is substantially for the infant's benefit.   The majority,
(Lord DENNING, M.R., dissenting) held that the test of substantial benefit was satisfied, since the contract, viewed at the time
of its making, would enable the infant to make a start in life as an
author.   The contract was valid and there was no room for the
grant of equitable relief.

---

1. *Steinberg* v. *Scala (Leeds), Ltd.*, [1923] 2 Ch. 452, at p. 465.
2. *Supra*, p. 409.
3. *Hearle* v. *Greenbank* (1749), 3 Atk. 695, at p. 712, *per* Lord HARDWICKE.
   See also *Re D'Angibau, Andrews* v. *Andrews* (1880), 15 Ch.D. 228, at p. 241,
   per COTTON, L.J.; *Burnaby* v. *Equitable Reversionary Interest Society* (1885),
   28 Ch.D. 416, at p. 424, *per* PEARSON, J.
4. [1966] Ch. 71; [1965] 3 All E.R. 764. See Mummery, 82 L.Q.R. 471; Yale,
   [1966] C.L.J. 17.
5. *Supra*, p. 406.

This finding was sufficient to dispose of the case and it was unnecessary to consider whether the assignment of the copyright precluded its recovery by the infant. The court, however, canvassed the matter, and again there was a difference of opinion. DANCKWERTS and WINN, L.JJ., held that, even had the contract been voidable, its rescission by the infant could not divest the copyright that had been vested in the publishers. It is submitted with respect that the opposite view expressed by Lord DENNING, M.R., is to be preferred.[1] The infant's claim was not at common law for money had and received, but a claim for equitable relief which, since he who seeks equity must do equity, would be granted only on the footing that any advantages already received by him would be returned to the publishers. The majority did not examine the established principles relating to an infant's right of restitution, but were content to accept the authorities cited by counsel for the publishers, namely *Valentini* v. *Canali*,[2] *Pearce* v. *Brain*[3] and *Steinberg* v. *Scala* (*Leeds*), *Ltd.*[4] The coupling of the first two of these cases with the last is a further instance of the confusion which surrounds the law of infancy. The first two were cases of void contracts, but in *Steinberg* v. *Scala* (*Leeds*), *Ltd.* the contract was voidable. It was assumed by counsel and the Court that if the contract was not valid, it was voidable. It has been plausibly suggested however that the contract if not valid, was void[5] but even if the *contract* were void, it would not necessarily follow that the *assignment* was void.

It is suggested that if this part of the decision in the *Chaplin* case is to be supported it must be based upon the impossibility of *restitutio in integrum*. The infant was prepared to restore the royalty payments, but he could not undo the contracts which to his knowledge the defendants had made with foreign publishers.[6]

D. CONTRACTS WITHIN THE INFANTS' RELIEF ACT 1874[7]

(i) Contracts declared absolutely void by the Act

The first section of the Act provides as follows:

> All contracts, whether by specialty or by simple contract, henceforth entered into by infants for the repayment of money lent or to be lent, or for goods supplied or to be supplied (other than necessaries), and all accounts stated with infants, shall be absolutely void.

Three contracts declared void by Act of 1874

Under this section, all loans of money made to an infant are irrecoverable; and any mortgage of land or goods executed by him as security for the repayment of money lent is absolutely

Loans

---

1. [1966] Ch., at p. 90; [1965] 3 All E.R., at p. 770.
2. (1889), 24 Q.B.D. 166; *infra*, p. 415.
3. [1929] 2 K.B. 310; *infra*, p. 415.
4. [1923] 2 Ch. 452; *supra*, p. 411.
5. Reynolds, 10 J.S.P.T.L. 294, at p. 295. See *infra*, p. 417.
6. Leave to appeal to the House of Lords was granted, but the action was settled. The infant withdrew his repudiation of the contract, and it was agreed that the book should be rewritten.
7. Treitel, 73 L.Q.R. 194; Atiyah, 74 L.Q.R. 97, Treitel, 74 L.Q.R. 104.

void.[1]   A loan is irrecoverable even though its object is to enable the infant to purchase necessaries.   If, however, the money lent for this purpose is actually spent upon the purchase of the necessaries the lender is subrogated to the rights of the seller and is allowed in equity the same right of recovery that the seller would have possessed had he not been paid.[2]   Moreover it has been the rule since at least 1691[3] that an infant is not liable upon a negotiable instrument in any circumstances.   An infant, for instance, who has accepted a bill of exchange in favour of a tradesman in payment for necessaries supplied, cannot be sued upon it either by the tradesman or by an indorsee of the bill.[4]   " This is no hardship upon the person who supplies necessaries to an infant, for he is entitled to sue the infant upon the original contract."[5]

Betting and
Loans Act
1892

The Betting and Loans (Infants) Act 1892 extends the protection enjoyed by infant borrowers.   It provides that an agreement by a person of full age to repay money lent to him during his infancy, together with any negotiable instrument given for the purpose of rendering the agreement effective, shall be absolutely void.[6]

Sale and
exchange of
goods
Accounts
stated

The expression " contract for goods supplied " includes, not only the sale, but also the exchange, of goods.[7]

An account stated is an admission by A that a sum certain is due from him to B.   Such an admission was at one time regarded as raising an implied promise to pay the amount stated, but it was always the rule at common law that an infant could not thereby bind himself,[8] even though the items of account consisted of necessaries.[9]   In the modern law, however, an account stated is only *prima facie* evidence of a debt which may be rebutted by contrary evidence, and therefore its inclusion in the contracts declared by the Act to be void is almost superfluous.[10]

Contracts,
though
declared
void, are not
destitute of
effect

The Act, it will be noticed, provides that the three kinds of contracts mentioned shall be " absolutely void ", from which it might be inferred that they are complete nullities giving rise neither to rights nor to liabilities in either party.   There are, however, two grounds upon which we may say that these so-called " absolutely void " contracts are by no means destitute of effect.[11] We will take as an example a contract for the supply of non-necessary goods.

---

1. *Thurstan* v. *Nottingham Permanent Benefit Building Society*, [1902] 1 Ch. 1; affirmed *sub nom. Nottingham Permanent Benefit Building Society* v. *Thurstan*, [1903] A.C. 6.
2. *Re National Permanent Benefit Building Society* (1869), 5 Ch. App. 309, at p. 313; *Lewis* v. *Alleyne* (1888), 4 T.L.R. 560.
3. *Williams* v. *Harrison* (1691), Carth. 160.
4. *Re Soltykoff, Ex parte Margrett*, [1891] 1 Q.B. 413.
5. *Ibid.*, at p. 416, *per* LOPES, L.J.
6. Section 5.   The Consumer Credit Act 1974, s. 50, makes it an offence to send a document to an infant inviting him to borrow money or obtain goods or services on credit.
7. *Pearce* v. *Brain*, [1929] 2 K.B. 310.
8. *Trueman* v. *Hurst* (1785), 1 T.R. 40.
9. *Williams* v. *Moor* (1843), 11 M. & W. 256, at p. 266.
10. *Siqueira* v. *Noronha*, [1934] A.C. 332; *infra*, pp. 654–5.
11. It should be noted that an infant trader may be adjudicated bankrupt for failure to pay income tax: *R.* v. *Newmarket Income Tax Commissioners, Ex parte Huxley*, [1916] 1 K.B. 788; or purchase tax: *Re A Debtor (No. 564 of 1949), Ex parte Customs and Excise Commissioners* v. *The Debtor,* [1950] Ch. 282; [1950] 1 All E.R. 308.

Firstly, since " infancy is a personal privilege of which no one can take advantage but the infant himself,"[1] it was always held at common law that the other contracting party was bound.[2] Despite the wording of the Act, it has long been the opinion of the profession that the position has not been altered.[3] Further, it is not without significance that the intention of the legislature was to relieve infants, not tradesmen. An infant cannot, however, maintain an action for specific performance, since this remedy cannot be granted against him.[4]

Infant may sue

Secondly, it would seem logical that money paid for goods by an infant under an absolutely void contract ought to be recoverable by him as being money had and received to his use. Property received under a void transaction cannot as a rule be retained. This is not so, however, in the case of an infant's contract. The rule is that money or goods delivered by an infant to the other party to a void contract is recoverable only if there has been a total failure of consideration.

Money paid by infant irrecoverable unless consideration fails

Thus in *Valentini* v. *Canali*:[5]

> An infant took a lease of a house and agreed to buy the furniture for £102. He paid £68 on account, but after occupying the house and enjoying the use of the furniture for some months he repudiated the contract and claimed to recover the £68.

It was held that, though he was not liable on his executory promise to pay the balance of the sum due, the fact that he had received part of the consideration precluded him from recovering the £68. The same principle was applied in *Pearce* v. *Brain*[6] to a contract for the exchange of chattels. An infant exchanged his motor-cycle for a second-hand car belonging to the defendant, both vehicles being valued at £80. The car broke down after being driven for seventy miles. The contract was void under the first section of the Act, but the infant was not allowed to enforce the return of the cycle. He could not show a complete failure of consideration. It will be seen that the practical effect of these decisions is to take virtually all cash sales of non-necessary goods outside the Act.

On the other hand, we should note the decision of OLIVER, J., in *Coutts & Co.* v. *Browne-Lecky*[7]. In that case it was held that, since a loan made to an infant by way of overdraft is void, a guarantee of the loan must also be void. The essence of a guarantee is that there should be a debt due from the principal debtor,

Guarantee of infant's contract is void

---

1. Bacon's Ab. " *Infancy*," 1, 4.
2. *Warwick* v. *Bruce* (1813), 2 M. & S. 205.
3. See Treitel, 73 L.Q.R. 194, at pp. 200–2; cf. Atiyah, 74 L.Q.R. 97, at pp. 99–101.
4. *Flight* v. *Bolland* (1828), 4 Russ. 298; *infra*, p. 613.
5. (1889), 24 Q.B.D. 166. See Treitel, 73 L.Q.R. 194, at pp. 202–5; Atiyah, 74 L.Q.R. 97, at pp. 101–3.
6. [1929] 2 K.B. 310; [1929] All E.R. Rep. 627.
7. [1947] K.B. 104; [1946] 2 All E.R. 207. See Furmston, 24 M.L.R. 648.

and, to quote the words of the learned judge, " there is no debt here, for the Act of 1874 says so."[1]

The question whether the words " absolutely void " are to be taken literally is thus far from settled.   It is a question that can be tested in a practical form by asking whether the delivery on credit by a tradesman to an infant buyer of goods that are not necessaries passes the property to the infant.   If the contract of sale is absolutely void, the logical inference is that the ownership remains unchanged, and that the tradesman should therefore be able to recover the value of the goods in an action of trover or detinue.   It is usually assumed that as between the infant and tradesman the doubt can not be resolved, since there is an independent rule that an infant is not answerable *ex delicto* for a tort such as trover if it is directly connected with a contract declared to be void.[2]   But the question might well arise if the infant were to resell the goods to a third party.   If in such a case the tradesman were to bring trover or detinue against the third party, his success would normally depend upon proof that the property in the goods had not passed to the infant, a task which does not appear difficult when the language of the Act is considered.   LUSH, J., however, was of opinion that the action would fail.

> " I thought at the time that there might be some foundation for this suggestion, and that, as at common law an infant who when of full age avoided the contract would have divested himself of the property, so now it might be contended that the whole transaction was avoided by the Act and that the property had not passed at all.   I am satisfied that that view is wrong and that the property passed by the delivery."[3]

A possible explanation of this view is that the property passes not by virtue of the void contract, but because, as in the case of gifts, the tradesman has delivered the goods with the intention of passing the ownership of them to the infant.   This suggestion, however, has a difficulty of its own, for, though it is doubtless true as a general principle that delivery accompanied by such an intention is an independent method of transferring the ownership of chattels, yet a seller who delivers goods to an infant intends to pass the property only on the hypothesis that the sale is valid.   If the hypothesis is false the intention based upon it would seem to be nullified.   The opinion of LUSH, J., was purely obiter and the controversy remains undecided.

It would seem, therefore, that the phrase " absolutely void " is unfortunate and misleading.   It is at least clear that the results

---

1. It would seem, however, that rightly construed the contract was one of indemnity, not of guarantee.   Since the parties knew that the borrower was an infant and that the lenders had no enforceable right against him, their intention must surely have been that the lenders should be saved harmless in any event: *Guild & Co.* v. *Conrad*, [1894] 2 Q.B. 885.   Had it been an indemnity, it would have been enforceable: *Yeoman Credit, Ltd.* v. *Latter*, [1961] 2 All E.R. 294; [1961] 1 W.L.R. 828.   On the distinction between guarantee and indemnity, see *supra*, pp. 181–2. See also Steyn, 90 L.Q.R. 246 and Consumer Credit Act 1974, s. 113 (7).
2. *Infra*, p. 419.   And similarly that there cannot be recovery of the goods in quasi-contract.   See *Cowern* v. *Nield*, [1912] 2 K.B. 419.   Cf. *Nelson Guarantee Corporation* v. *Farrell*, [1955] N.Z.L.R. 405.
3. *Stocks* v. *Wilson*, [1913] 2 K.B. 235, at p. 246.

normally associated with " void " contracts do not follow in this context, and there is much to be said for the view that the legislature, in its anxiety to protect infants, used technical words without appreciating their technical implications. The law as a result is still in a condition of doubt which, failing legislation, only fresh decisions can ultimately resolve.

(ii) Contracts within the Infants' Relief Act, section 2

An infant, as we have already seen, was bound at common law for necessaries supplied, upon beneficial contracts of service, and upon contracts under which he took a permanent interest in property, unless in this last case he repudiated in time. In all other cases, such as an agreement to buy non-necessary goods, the contract was voidable in the sense that no action could be brought upon it against the infant during his infancy, nor indeed after he came of age unless he elected to confirm it by ratification. On the other hand the contract was not void, for as soon as the infant attained his majority he was free to confirm it and so to bind himself.

Contracts capable of ratification at common law

The Infants' Relief Act 1874 has provided that the ratification of these contracts shall no longer render them enforceable by action. The second section enacts as follows:

Ratification now impossible

> No action shall be brought whereby to charge any person upon any promise made after full age to pay any debt contracted during infancy, or upon any ratification made after full age of any promise or contract made during infancy, whether there shall or shall not be any new consideration for such promise or ratification after full age.

This section applies to all contracts made by an infant except contracts for necessaries, for beneficial service and for the acquisition of some interest in property of a permanent character. It was argued in *Coxhead* v. *Mullis*[1] that the section applied only to the ratification of the three contracts specifically declared void by the first section, but the court repudiated the suggestion and held that a promise to marry was incapable of ratification.[2]

The distinction drawn in the section between a promise to pay any debt and a ratification of any promise or contract is perplexing, and it has been suggested that the draftsman was influenced by the old system of pleading under which a " debt " was enforced by *indebitatus assumpsit* but a contract by *assumpsit*, and thus it would be inappropriate to speak of ratifying a debt.[3] Another and perhaps more likely explanation is that the word " such " was inadvertently omitted before the words " promise or contract," and colour is lent to this by the speech of Viscount MIDDLETON during the second reading of the bill in the House of Lords. He explained that the object of the section was to stop the practice by which moneylenders made a loan to an infant at an exorbitant rate of interest, put no pressure upon him until he attained his majority, but then tempted him by some small

Ratification distinguished from new promise

---

1. (1878), 3 C.P.D. 439.
2. An agreement by two persons to marry one another is no longer actionable: Law Reform (Miscellaneous Provisions) Act 1970.
3. Treitel, 73 L.Q.R. 194, at pp. 209–10.

additional advance to make himself responsible for principal and interest that had accrued during infancy.   Viscount MIDDLETON then said:

> " The second clause of this bill would prevent a man from being sued at law upon any promise made after full age to pay any debt contracted during infancy, or upon any ratification of any *such* contract, whether there should or should not have been any new consideration for such ratification."[1]

However, the section as it now stands enacts two things:

First, that a fresh promise made after full age shall not render actionable a *debt* contracted during infancy.[2]

Secondly, that no ratification after full age of *any* contract made during infancy shall be a ground of action.[3]

It follows, therefore, and has been decided, that a new promise supported by a fresh consideration, made by an infant after his majority to the same effect as one that he made during infancy, is invalid if it relates to a debt but is valid if it concerns a promise to perform any other obligation.[4]   An example is a promise to marry.   This leads to a somewhat subtle distinction between ratification and a fresh and independent promise.   " Ratification " is not the same as " promise."[5]   A ratification refers to the past, and is merely an intentional recognition and confirmation of a previous promise;[6] but a fresh promise is something more than a resuscitation of the past—something more than mere repetition. This is illustrated by the manner in which the courts treated an action for breach of promise of marriage brought before January 1st, 1971, the date at which the statutory abolition of such actions became effective.   If, for instance, an infant made a promise to marry and after coming of age continued to treat himself as an engaged person, his conduct was regarded at the most as a ratification of his promise and did not render him liable;[7] but if he engaged himself afresh, as by asking his fiancée to fix the wedding-day,[8] or by saying to her " now I may and will marry you as soon as possible, as I have obtained my father's consent,"[9] there was, in the view of the courts, sufficient evidence from which a new and independent promise might be inferred.

Infant may
sue

It will be seen from the wording of this section that its interpretation, like that of the first section, is not without difficulty. What at least seems clear, however, is that its effect is not to make a contract falling within its scope void in the sense which lawyers attribute to that word.   Thus, the general view is that an infant, though he may not be sued in any contingency, is entitled, as he was at common law,[10] to sue the other party.[11]

1. *Hansard*, vol. 219 (3rd series), col. 1668.
2. See also Betting and Loans (Infants) Act 1892; *supra*, p. 414.
3. *Ditcham* v. *Worrall* (1880), 5 C.P.D. 410, *per* Lord COLERIDGE, at pp. 418–19.
4. *Ditcham* v. *Worrall* (1880), 5 C.P.D. 410.
5. *Mawson* v. *Blane* (1854), 10 Exch. 206, *per* PARKE, B., at p. 210.
6. *Ditcham* v. *Worrall, supra, per* LINDLEY, J., at pp. 412–13.
7. *Coxhead* v. *Mullis* (1878), 3 C.P.D. 439.
8. *Ditcham* v. *Worrall* (1880), 5 C.P.D. 410.
9. *Northcote* v. *Doughty* (1879), 4 C.P.D. 385.
10. *Warwick* v. *Bruce* (1813), 2 M. & S. 205.
11. But see Treitel, 73 L.Q.R. 194, at pp. 200–2.

SECTION II. DELICTUAL LIABILITY OF INFANTS

Although an infant is generally liable in tort, as, for instance, for defamation, trespass or conversion, he is not answerable for a tort directly connected with any contract upon which no action will lie against him.   It is impossible indirectly to enforce such a contract by changing the form of action to one *ex delicto*.[1]   Thus an action of deceit does not lie against an infant who, by falsely representing himself to be of full age, has fraudulently induced another to contract with him, for " it was thought necessary to safeguard the weakness of infants at large, even though here and there a juvenile knave slipped through."[2]   A fraudulent representation does not estop an infant from relying upon the Infants' Relief Act.[3]   Although perhaps this is to put a premium on knavery, it is clear that to enable a plaintiff to convert a breach of contract into a tort would destroy the protection that the law affords to infants.[4]

(margin note: Infant not liable for a tort connected with a contract)

The only, but a real, difficulty is to determine in each case whether the tort is so directly connected with a contract as to render the infant immune even from delictual liability.   It was held, for instance, in *Jennings* v. *Rundall*[5] that if an infant hires a mare for riding and injures her by excessive and improper riding, he is not liable in tort for negligence;   but in *Burnard* v. *Haggis*[6] that if, contrary to the express instructions of the owner accepted by himself, he jumps and consequently injures her, he can be successfully sued in tort.   At first sight it is not easy to appreciate the exact distinction between these two cases.   In each of them the wrongful act of the infant arose out of and was connected with a contract in the sense that it could not have been committed had no contract been made.   Why was the wrongful jumping in a different legal category from the wrongful riding?   What is the test which determines whether the conduct of the infant is a tort independent of the contract and therefore actionable?   The answer would appear to be that an infant is liable in tort only if the wrongful act that he has done is one of a kind not contemplated by the contract.[7]   If he hires a horse for riding, the act contemplated by the contract is riding, and he cannot be liable however immoderately he may ride;   but on the other hand, the hire of a horse only for riding does not contemplate the act of jumping. The same test serves to distinguish two more recent cases.   In

(margin note: What is meant by a tort connected with a contract)

---

1. *Burnard* v. *Haggis* (1863), 14 C.B.N.S. 45, *per* BYLES, J.
2. *R. Leslie, Ltd.* v. *Sheill*, [1914] 3 K.B. 607, at p. 612, *per* Lord SUMNER.
3. *Levene* v. *Brougham* (1909), 25 T.L.R. 265.
4. *Jennings* v. *Rundall* (1799), 8 Term Rep. 335, at p. 336, *per* Lord KENYON.
5. *Supra.*
6. (1863), 14 C.B.N.S. 45.
7. This was the view of Pollock (*Contracts*, 12th Edn., p. 63).   It was adopted by KENNEDY, L.J., in *R. Leslie, Ltd.* v. *Sheill*, [1914] 3 K.B. 607, at p. 620, and confirmed by ATKIN, J., in *Fawcett* v. *Smethurst* (1914), 84 L.J.K.B. 473; and by the Court of Appeal in *Ballett* v. *Mingay*, [1943] K.B. 281; [1943] 1 All E.R. 143.

Fawcett v. *Smethurst*[1] an infant hired a car for the specific purpose of fetching his luggage from Cairn Ryan Station, and when he got to the latter place he drove further away to Ballantrae. It was held that he was not liable in tort for an accident that occurred during the further drive. In the words of ATKIN, J.:

> " Nothing that was done on that further journey made the defendant an independent tortfeasor. . . . The extended journey was of the same nature as the original one, and the defendant did no more than drive the car further than was intended."

But in *Ballett* v. *Mingay*,[2] an action of detinue succeeded against an infant for the return of certain articles which he had borrowed from the respondent and which he had without authority lent to a friend.

> " On looking at the evidence," said Lord GREENE, M.R., " it seems to me that, when properly construed, the terms of the bailment of these articles to the infant appellant did not permit him to part with their possession at all. If it was the bargain that he might part with them, it was for the infant to establish that fact, and it seems to me that he has failed to do so. On that basis the action of the appellant in parting with the goods was one which fell outside the contract altogether and that fact brings the case within the case . . . of *Burnard* v. *Haggis*."

Whether the act that the infant has done must be taken to be within the contemplation of the parties may perhaps depend upon the nature of the subject-matter. In *Ballett* v. *Mingay* this consisted of an amplifier and a microphone, articles that a lender would naturally expect a borrower to retain in his own possession, but the decision might have been different had the infant parted temporarily with a bicycle that he had hired from the plaintiff.

SECTION III. THE EQUITABLE DOCTRINE OF RESTITUTION

Fraudulent infant must restore ill-gotten gains

We have just seen that at common law an infant is not liable in deceit if he induces another to contract with him by making some false representation, as for example that he has reached the age of majority. If, for instance, he obtains money or non-necessary goods from another by such a misrepresentation, he cannot be sued either on the express contract, or for money had and received, or, since the the fraud is connected with the contract, in tort.[3] But since it should be obvious that " infants are no more entitled than adults to gain benefits to themselves by fraud,"[4] equity has developed a principle which requires benefits to be disgorged, if they are still in the possession of the fraudulent infant.

---

1. (1914), 84 L.J.K.B. 473.
2. [1943] K.B. 281; [1943] 1 All E.R. 143.
3. *R. Leslie, Ltd.* v. *Sheill*, [1914] 3 K.B. 607, *per* Lord SUMNER, at pp. 612–13.
4. *Nelson* v. *Stocker* (1859), 4 De G. & J. 458, *per* TURNER, L.J., at p. 464. Atiyah has suggested that an extended meaning should be given to the word " fraud " in this context; 22 M.L.R. 273.

The limits of this doctrine of restitution are somewhat ill-defined. There are three types of case to which it may be relevant.

Firstly, the infant obtains goods by fraud and remains in possession of them. Here there is no doubt that the doctrine applies and that an order for restitution will be made.[1]

Secondly, the infant obtains goods by fraud but ceases to possess them. If the doctrine is limited to the restitution of the very goods obtained, it follows that it cannot be invoked in this case, for to make the infant liable to repay the value of the goods, or even to restore another article for which they have been exchanged, would in effect be to enforce a contract declared void by statute. The authorities would seem to establish that the doctrine is so limited. As A. T. LAWRENCE, J., said in *R. Leslie, Ltd.* v. *Sheill*,[2] " if when the action is brought both the property and the proceeds are gone, I can see no ground upon which a court of equity could have founded its jurisdiction." In the same case Lord SUMNER stated the position as follows:[3]

> " I think that the whole current of decisions down to 1913, apart from *dicta* which are inconclusive, went to show that when an infant obtained an advantage by falsely representing himself to be of full age equity required him to restore his ill-gotten gains, or to release the party deceived from obligations or acts in law induced by the fraud,[4] but scrupulously stopped short of enforcing against him a contractual obligation entered into while he was an infant, even by means of a fraud. . . . Restitution stopped where repayment began."

The reason why Lord SUMNER confined this review of the law to the discussions prior to 1913 was that in that year LUSH, J., held, in *Stocks* v. *Wilson*,[5] that an infant who had obtained goods by misrepresenting his age and had later sold them was accountable for the proceeds of sale. It is extremely difficult to reconcile this decision either with the principles laid down by the Court of Appeal in *R. Leslie, Ltd.* v. *Sheill* or with what was decided in that case.[6] LUSH, J., relied chiefly upon a decision in 1858 where the Lords Justices held, though with reluctance, that a loan obtained by an infant who had misrepresented his age was provable as a debt in his subsequent bankruptcy.[7] It is now admitted, however, that this decision merely expresses a rule of bankruptcy law, not a principle of general application relevant to such facts as arose in *Stocks* v. *Wilson*.[8] Moreover, the question in the 1858 case was

Doctrine of
restitution
applicable
only where
the very
goods
obtained are
still possessed
by the
infant

---

1. *Clarke* v. *Cobley* (1789), 2 Cox. Eq. Cas. 173; *Lemprière* v. *Lange* (1879), 12 Ch.D. 675.
2. [1914] 3 K.B. 607, at p. 627.
3. *Ibid.*, at p. 618.
4. If, for example, an infant, by fraudulently misrepresenting his age, induces his trustees to pay a sum of money to him and thus to commit a breach of trust, he cannot after he is of full age compel them to rectify the breach by paying the money over again: *Cory* v. *Gertcken* (1816), 2 Madd. 40.
5. [1913] 2 K.B. 235.
6. But see Goff and Jones, *The Law of Restitution*, pp. 319–20. In *R. Leslie, Ltd.* v. *Sheill* the Court of Appeal refrained from expressing a definite opinion upon the decision of LUSH, J., though Lord SUMNER remarked that it was " open to challenge ": [1914] 3 K.B., at p. 619.
7. *Re King, Ex parte Unity Joint Stock Mutual Banking Association* (1858), 3 De G. & J. 63.
8. *R. Leslie, Ltd.* v. *Sheill*, [1914] 3 K.B. 607, at pp. 624, 628.

not whether the lender had a personal claim against the infant, but whether, in competition with other creditors, he could claim a share of the assets that had been surrendered to the trustee in bankruptcy.[1]

Thirdly, the infant obtains a loan of money by fraud. The contrast stressed by Lord SUMNER between restitution and repayment necessarily excludes the doctrine in this case, for the very essence of a loan of money is that the borrower shall repay the equivalent amount, not that he shall restore the identical coins. Thus it was held in *Leslie* v. *Sheill*[2] that an infant could not be compelled to restore a loan of £400 which he had obtained by a fraudulent misstatement of his age, for to do so would constitute in effect an enforcement of the contract, not an application of the doctrine of restitution. If, of course, the very coins or notes obtained by the infant were identifiable and if they were still in his possession, a highly improbable case, the doctrine could no doubt be invoked.

1. *Ibid.*, at p. 616.
2. *Supra.*

CHAPTER TWO

Corporations

THE DOCTRINE OF *ULTRA VIRES*

It is essential, of course, that a contracting party should be a person recognized as such by the law. Persons in law, however, are not confined to individual men and women. If two or more persons form themselves into an association for the purpose of some concerted enterprise, as happens, for example, upon the formation of a club, a trade union, a partnership or a trading company, the association is in some cases regarded by the law as an independent person, *i.e.* as a legal entity called a " corporation," separate from the men and women of whom it consists, but in other cases it is denied a separate personality and is called an unincorporated association. Whether an association falls into one class or the other depends upon whether it has been incorporated by the State.

> " Independent juristic personality can only be conferred upon an association, according to English law, by some act on the part of the State, represented either by the Crown in the exercise of its prerogative rights, or by the sovereign power of Parliament."[1]

An unincorporated association, such as a club, is not a competent contracting party. If a contract is made on its behalf no individual member can be sued upon it except the person who actually made it and any other members who authorized him to do so.[2]

The main classification of corporations is into aggregate and sole. A corporation aggregate is a body of several persons united together into one society which, since it may be maintained by a constant succession of members, has the capacity of perpetual existence. Examples are the mayor and corporation of a city and a trading company incorporated under the Companies Act 1948. A corporation sole consists of a single person occupying a particular office and each and several of the persons in perpetuity who succeed him in that office, such as a bishop or the vicar of a parish.

Marginal notes: Corporations and unincorporated associations

Corporations sole and aggregate

---

1. Stephen's Commentaries, 21st Edn., Vol. II, p. 558. See also Pickering, 31 M.L.R. 481.
2. *Bradley Egg Farm, Ltd.* v. *Clifford*, [1943] 2 All E.R. 378. For a critique of the law, see Keeler, 34 M.L.R. 61.

" The law therefore has wisely ordained that the parson, *quatenus* parson, shall never die, by making him and his successors a corporation.   By which means all the original rights of the parsonage are preserved entire to the successor;   for the present incumbent and his predecessor who lived seven centuries ago are in law one and the same person;   and what was given to the one was given to the other also."[1]

Crown's consent to incorporation may be express or implied

The consent of the Crown, thus necessary to the creation of a corporation, may either be express or implied.   It is express in the case of chartered and statutory corporations.   The Crown has a prerogative right to incorporate any number of persons by charter, and it is to this method that some of the older trading companies such as the Hudson's Bay Company and the P. & O. Steam Navigation Company, owe their existence.   Incorporation by statute may take two forms.   The members of an association, whether united for trade or for some other purpose, may form themselves into a corporation by obtaining a special Act of Parliament;   or alternatively, if united for trading purposes and if not less than seven in number, they may comply with the general conditions laid down in the Companies Act 1948, and obtain registration as a limited liability company.   The consent of the Crown to incorporation is implied in the case both of common law and of prescriptive corporations.   An example of the former is an ecclesiastical corporation sole such as a bishop or a parson.   A prescriptive corporation is a body of persons which has been treated as a corporation from time immemorial but which cannot produce a charter of incorporation.   The existence of a charter is presumed by the law, and such a body enjoys the same rights as a chartered company.

The doctrine of *ultra vires*

The doctrine of *ultra vires* ordains that a statutory corporation can exercise only those powers which are expressly or implicitly conferred by the statute itself.   It does not apply to corporations created by charter.   In the words of BOWEN, L.J.:

" At common law a corporation created by the King's charter has *prima facie* the power to do with its property all such acts as an ordinary person can do, and to bind itself to such contracts as an ordinary person can bind himself to."[2]

But in the case of statutory corporations the position is different. Here, as the same learned judge insists:

" What you have to do is to find out what this statutory creature is and what it is meant to do;   and to find out what this statutory creature is you must look at the statute only, because there, and there only, is found the definition of this new creature."[3]

A trading company, for instance, incorporated under the Companies Act is required to have articles of association (which regulate matters of internal administration), and also a memorandum of association.   The memorandum is the charter which defines the statutory creature by stating the objects of its existence,

---

1. Blackstone's Commentaries, vol. 1, p. 470.
2. *Baroness Wenlock* v. *River Dee Co.* (1877), 36 Ch.D. 674, note at p. 685. *Institution of Mechanical Engineers* v. *Cane and Westminster Corporation*, [1961] A.C. 696, at pp. 724–5;   [1960] 3 All E.R. 715, at pp. 728–9, *per* Lord DENNING;   Hudson, 28 Solicitor 7.
3. *Ibid.*

the scope of its operations and the extent of its powers. A company so created can pursue only those objects set out in the memorandum. Its area of corporate activity is thereby restricted, so that if, for instance, it is authorized to run tramways, it is not entitled to run omnibuses. It may exercise and only exercise the powers set out in the memorandum and such powers as are reasonably incidental to or consequential upon the operations that it is authorized to perform. Everything else is *ultra vires* and void.[1] Thus a contract which relates to some object not defined either expressly or by implication in the memorandum is void, and there are no possible means by which it can be validated, not even by the unanimous vote of all the corporators. A nullity is incapable of ratification. A judgment, for instance, given against the company with its consent for the amount due under the contract is of no avail, for " it cannot be of more validity than the invalid contract upon which it was founded."[2] The *locus classicus* in this matter is *Ashbury Railway Carriage Co.* v. *Riche* :[3]

> The objects of the appellant company, as stated in the memorandum of association, were " to make, sell or lend on hire, railway carriages and waggons, and all kinds of railway plant, fittings, machinery and rolling stock; to carry on the business of mechanical engineers and general contractors; to purchase, lease and sell mines, minerals, land and buildings; to purchase and sell as merchants, timber, coal, metals or other materials, and to buy and sell any such materials on commission ôr as agents."
>
> The directors agreed to assign to a Belgian company a concession which they had bought for the construction of a railway in Belgium.

Ashbury Railway Carriage Co. v. Riche

It was held that this agreement, since it related to the construction of a railway, a subject-matter not included in the memorandum, was *ultra vires*, and that not even the subsequent assent of the whole body of shareholders could make it binding. Therefore, an action brought by the Belgian company to recover damages for breach of the contract necessarily failed.

This doctrine, however, has been debilitated almost to the point of extinction by the decision of the Court of Appeal in *Bell Houses, Ltd.* v. *City Wall Properties, Ltd.*[4] In that case, the company was authorized *inter alia* to carry on any other trade or business which *in the opinion of the directors* might be carried on advantageously in connexion with or ancillary to its main business of developing housing estates. The court held that to make the opinion of the directors the criterion of whether a new business was *intra vires* was legitimate, provided that it was reached in good faith.

Diminished importance of the doctrine

A transaction which clearly falls within the objects set out in the memorandum of association is *intra vires*, notwithstanding that

State of mind of parties irrelevant

---

1. *A.-G.* v. *Great Eastern Rail. Co.* (1880), 5 App Cas. 473, at p. 478. For a fuller account, see Gower, *Modern Company Law*, 3rd Edn., pp. 83–101. Under s. 5 of Companies Act 1948 there is a limited power to change the objects. See Davies, 90 L.Q.R. 79.
2. *Great North-West Central Rail. Co.* v. *Charlebois*, [1899] A.C. 114, at p. 124; adopted in *Re Jon Beauforte (London), Ltd.*, [1953] Ch. 131; [1953] 1 All E.R. 634.
3. (1875), L.R. 7 H.L. 653. As to the right of a company to make gratuitous payments, see *Parke* v. *Daily News, Ltd.*, [1962] Ch. 927; [1962] 2 All E.R. 929.
4. [1966] 2 Q.B. 656; [1966] 2 All E.R. 674; see Baker, 82 L.Q.R. 463; Wedderburn, 29 M.L.R. 673; Baxt, 20 I.C.L.Q. 301.

the persons responsible for it failed to consider whether it was calculated to benefit the corporation.   In applying the objective test of *ultra vires*, the state of mind of the parties is irrelevant.[1]

Although it has thus long been held that a corporation can plead the defence of *ultra vires* when sued for breach of contract, opinions differ as to whether the defence is open to the other party to the contract if he is defendant to the action.   It would seem on principle that it should be available to him, for " since the effect of the *ultra vires* doctrine is to render the contract void and not merely voidable or unenforceable, and since this is insisted on to the extent that neither judgment by consent nor ratification by all the shareholders can render it valid, it should follow that neither party is able to enforce the contract."[2]

The *ultra vires* doctrine has long been criticised.   Although in theory it operates to protect share-holders against use of the company's funds for unauthorised purposes, this protection is largely illusory because of the common practice of drafting the objects clause in very broad and general terms.   On the other hand the doctrine can operate as a trap for those who do business with the company since it is quite unrealistic to expect them to read the memorandum of association to discover the company's authorised purposes.   It is not surprising therefore that both the Cohen Committee in 1945[3] and the Jenkins Committee in 1962[4] recommended substantial amendment of the doctrine.   The

European Communities Act 1972, s. 9 (1) has now made substantial changes in the doctrine.[5]

The sub-section provides:

> " In favour of a person dealing with a company in good faith, any transaction decided on by the directors shall be deemed to be one which it is within the capacity of the company to enter into, and the power of the directors to bind the company shall be deemed to be free of any limitation under the memorandum or articles of association; and a party to a transaction so decided on shall not be bound to enquire as to the capacity of the company to enter into it

---

1. *Charterbridge Corporation, Ltd.* v. *Lloyds Bank, Ltd.*, [1970] Ch. 62; [1969] 2 All E.R. 1185; Leigh, 33 M.L.R. 81; Collier, [1970] C.L.J. 37. In *Re Introductions, Ltd.* v. *National Provincial Bank*, [1970] Ch. 199; [1969] 1 All E.R. 877, the Court of Appeal drew a distinction between objects and powers.   So it was held that a power to borrow money was not unlimited but could only be exercised if the money was borrowed to promote one of the objects. This decision gives rise to many difficulties. The effect of holding that the loan was *ultra vires* was that the money could not be recovered.   This will mean that a bank which lends money to a company will not be able to recover it if the company intends to spend the money on an unauthorised object.   In *Re Introductions, Ltd.* the Court attached weight to the bank's knowledge of the company's purpose but in all previous cases the question whether a transaction was *ultra vires* has been quite independent of the knowledge of the other party.   See Baxter, [1970] C.L.J. 280; Wedderburn, 32 M.L.R. 563.
2. In *Bell Houses, Ltd.* v. *City Wall Properties, Ltd.*, [1966] 2 Q.B. 656; [1966] 2 All E.R. 674, the Court of Appeal did not have to consider the question, since they held the contract to be *intra vires*, reversing in this respect the decision of MOCATTA, J.   The latter examined the authorities and held that a defendant can avail himself of the plea of *ultra vires*: see Furmston, 24 M.L.R. 715, at p. 718, from which the words quoted above are taken. See also *Re Staines Urban District Council's Agreement*, [1969] 1 Ch. 10, [1968] 2 All E.R. 1.
3. Cmd. 6659, para. 12; Horrwitz, 62 L.Q.R. 66.
4. Cmnd. 1249, paras. 35–42.
5. Prentice, 89 L.Q.R. 518: Farrar and Powles, 36 M.L.R. 270.

or as to any such limitation on the powers of the directors, and shall be presumed to have acted in good faith unless the contrary is proved."

It will be seen that this leaves the doctrine intact as between directors and share-holders[1] and that the doctrine can be raised *against* the company. The company can no longer rely on the doctrine against someone who has dealt with it in good faith. This covers the substantial majority of cases where the doctrine has in fact been invoked in the past. It should be noted that the Act contains no definition of " good faith." It is thought that good faith could only be disproved by showing knowledge that the transaction is in fact *ultra vires* so that one who knows the terms of the objects clause but wrongly thinks that the contract falls within it acts in good faith.

---

1. See, e.g. *Parke* v. *Daily News, Ltd.*, [1962] Ch. 927; [1962] 2 All E.R. 929.

CHAPTER THREE

Persons Mentally Disordered, and Drunkards

A. MENTAL DISORDER[1]

Mental
disorder THE word " lunatic " has been used since at least the sixteenth century to describe a person who becomes insane after birth, but it was discarded by the legislature in 1930 in favour of " person of unsound mind,"[2] a term that was not statutorily defined. This in turn has been replaced by " person mentally disordered " or more shortly " mental patient," and mental disorder is exhaustively defined.[3] This definition relates to the treatment and care of mental patients and to the administration of their property, but it does not affect the question of their contractual capacity. This remains subject to the rules formulated by the courts.

If a genuine consent were necessary to the formation of every agreement it would follow that a mental patient could not make a valid contract. Here as elsewhere, however, the necessity of interpreting conduct by its effect upon reasonable persons has forbidden so simple a proposition. The law on the subject has varied, but the modern rules are clear.

The first question in all cases is whether the party at the time of contracting was suffering from such a degree of mental disability that he was incapable of understanding the nature of the contract.[4] If so, the contract is not void but voidable at the mental patient's option, provided that his mental disability was known or ought to have been known by the other contracting party[5]. The burden of proving this knowledge lies upon the

---

1. Fridman, 79 L.Q.R. 502, at pp. 509–516.
2. Mental Treatment Act 1930.
3. Mental Health Act 1959, section 4.
4. *Boughton* v. *Knight* (1873), L.R. 3 P.D. 64, at p. 72.
5. *Molton* v. *Camroux* (1848), 2 Exch. 487; affirmed, (1849), 4 Exch. 17; *Imperial Loan Co.* v. *Stone*, [1892] 1 Q.B. 599. *York Glass Co., Ltd.* v. *Jubb* (1925), 134 L.T. 36.

person mentally disordered.[1]   If, however, the contract was made by him during a lucid interval, it is binding upon him notwithstanding that his disability was known to the other party.[2]

Again, it is immaterial that the mental disability is known to the other party, if necessaries are supplied to a person mentally disordered or to his wife, suitable to the position in life in which he moves, for in this case an implied obligation arises to pay for them out of his property.[3]   The obligation does not arise unless it was the intention of the person supplying the necessaries that he should be repaid.   He must intend, not to play the role of a benefactor, but to constitute himself a creditor.[4]

Necessaries supplied to insane person

As regards the supply of necessary goods, this obligation to pay is converted by the Sale of Goods Act 1893 into a statutory obligation to pay a reasonable price.   Section 2 provides that:

> Where necessaries are sold and delivered to a person who by reason of mental incapacity or drunkenness is incompetent to contract, he must pay a reasonable price therefor.

Jurisdiction to manage the property and affairs of a mental patient is now conferred by Part VIII of the Mental Health Act 1959 upon " the judge," *i.e.* certain nominated judges of the Chancery Division and also the master and deputy master of the Court of Protection.   The jurisdiction is exercisable when the judge is satisfied that a person is incapable by reason of mental disability of managing his property and affairs,[5] and it is of the widest nature.   It includes the power to make contracts for the benefit of the patient and also to carry out a contract already made by him.[6]

Power of the judge to make contracts for mental patients

B.   DRUNKENNESS

It is generally said, both by judges[7] and by textbook writers, that the contractual capacity of a drunken person is the same as that of one who is mentally afflicted, but the decisions are few and not too satisfactory.   The effect of *Gore* v. *Gibson*,[8] as qualified by *Matthews* v. *Baxter*,[9] would seem to be that if A, when he contracts with B, is in such a state of drunkenness as not to know what he is doing, and if this fact is appreciated by B, then the contract is voidable at the instance of A.   It may, for instance, be ratified by him when he regains sobriety.   It would appear, therefore, that a contract with a person so seriously

Drunkenness

1. *Ibid.*
2. *Hall* v. *Warren* (1804), 9 Ves. 605.   *Selby* v. *Jackson* (1844), 6 Beav. 192.
3. *Re Rhodes* (1890), 44 Ch.D. 94;   *Read* v. *Legard* (1851), 6 Exch. 636.
4. *Re Rhodes, supra.*
5. The former procedure under which after a formal inquiry (" inquisition "), a person could be declared to be of unsound mind (" lunatic so found "), and a person appointed (the " committee ") to manage his person and property has been abolished; Mental Health Act 1959, section 149 (2).
6. *Ibid.*, s. 103 (1) (g); cf. *Baldwyn* v. *Smith*, [1900] 1 Ch. 588.
7. *Molton* v. *Camroux* (1848), 2 Exch. 487.
8. (1845), 13 M. & W. 623.
9. (1873), L.R. 8 Exch. 132.

afflicted must always be voidable, for unlike the case of insanity it is almost inconceivable that the extent of his intoxication can be unknown to the other party.

Necessaries supplied to drunkard

Necessaries supplied to drunkard

A drunken person to whom necessaries are sold and delivered is under the same liability to pay a reasonable price for them as is an infant or an insane person.[1]

---

1. Sale of Goods Act 1893, s. 2.

PART VI
PRIVITY OF CONTRACT

SUMMARY

THE parties to a valid contract obtain and incur reciprocal rights and obligations. Are these rights and obligations confined to the contracting parties or may they be extended to persons who took no share in the formation of the contract? Several hypotheses require consideration. Thus the parties may wish, at the very inception of their contract and by the inherent pressure of its terms, to confer benefits or to impose restrictions upon strangers. Or by virtue of the doctrine of agency, third parties may be able to sue or to be sued upon the contract. Or the parties may wish, at some date after the formation of the contract, to transfer to others rights and liabilities originally operating as between themselves. Again, the question arises whether the rights and obligations are transferable by operation of law, as for instance where one of the parties dies before the contract is discharged.

Questions to be considered

CHAPTER ONE

The Scope of the Original Contract

SECTION I. THE DOCTRINE OF PRIVITY OF CONTRACT

Contract affects only the parties

IN the middle of the nineteenth century the common law judges reached a decisive conclusion upon the scope of a contract. No one, they declared, may be entitled to or bound by the terms of a contract to which he is not an original party.[1] The principle is still the determining factor in the common law, but it must be received with reservations.

Law unsettled until 19th century

In the first place, the principle was not accepted as universally true in the earlier common law. In the Middle Ages the actions of debt and account had been available to third parties who wished to reap the benefit of an arrangement made by others on their behalf, and, after the evolution of assumpsit, it was for a long time unclear whether a similar view would be taken.[2]

Agency provides an exception

In the second place, an exception to this rule, admitted in the first half of the eighteenth century, when the rule itself was obscure, has since maintained its ground. If A has made a contract with B, C may intervene and take A's place if he can show that A was acting throughout as his agent, and it is irrelevant that B entered into the contract in ignorance of this fact. This right of intervention, known usually as the doctrine of the undisclosed principal, has, indeed, been attacked on the very ground that it offends the common law doctrine of privity. But criticism

---

1. *Price* v. *Easton* (1833), 4 B. & Ad. 433; *Tweddle* v. *Atkinson* (1861), 1 B. & S. 393.
2. See Simpson, *History,* pp. 475–485; *Dutton* v. *Poole* (1678), 2 Lev. 210; *Bourne* v. *Mason* (1669), 1 Vent 6; E.J.P. 70 L.Q.R. 467. See also the review of the history by WINDEYER, J., in *Coulls* v. *Bagot's Executor and Trustee Co., Ltd.,* [1967] A.L.R. 385, at pp. 407–9.

has been fruitless, and the undisclosed principal is a well-established character in the modern law of agency.[1]

In the third place, the rule is strictly a creature of the common law. Equity, as may well be imagined, tends to take a less rigid view of the boundaries of contract and has sometimes sought to transcend them though its approach has been unusually timid.

Modification of the general rule in equity

Fourthly, the doctrine of privity, while a natural inference from a strict theory of contract, has clashed with the needs and concepts of the law of property. A lease, for instance, is a contract, but it creates rights of property that cannot be kept within contractual bounds. If A lets land to B, the lease will contain mutual rights and duties—to pay the rent, to keep the premises in repair and many other obligations. As between the parties themselves there is privity of contract; but if either transfers his interest to a stranger, convenience demands that he in his turn shall take the benefit and the burden of the original covenants. The need was felt and a partial remedy devised as long ago as the sixteenth century, and the modern position is the result of the combined efforts of common law and statute.[2] Similar problems are raised when a freeholder sells his land and wishes to restrict its use not only by the purchaser but by anyone to whom it may be transferred.[3] Another illustration is offered by the modern case of *Smith and Snipes Hall Farm, Ltd.* v. *River Douglas Catchment Board*.[4]

Impact of the law of property

> By a contract under seal made in 1938 the defendants agreed with eleven owners of land adjoining a certain stream to improve its banks and to " maintain for all time the work when completed." The landowners agreed to pay a proportion of the cost. In 1940 one of the landowners conveyed her land to Smith, the first plaintiff, and in 1944 Smith leased it to Snipes Hall Farm, Ltd., the second plaintiff. In 1946, owing to the defendants' negligence, the banks burst and the land was flooded.

Both plaintiffs were strangers to the contract. But the Court of Appeal held that the covenants undertaken by the defendants affected the use and value of the land, that they were intended from the outset to benefit anyone to whom the land might be transferred and that the defendants were liable. Even in this area however the principle of privity of contract is not rendered irrelevant but rather greatly diminished in importance. If it is sought to enforce a covenant over land either by or against a non-party, the factual situation must be brought within one of the rules which common law, equity and statute have developed. These rules cover much but not all of the ground.

Finally, we should note that the doctrine of privity of contract means only that a non-party cannot bring *an action on the*

---

1. See *infra*, pp. 472–5. The criticism will be found in Ames, *Lectures in Legal History*, pp. 453–463.
2. *Spencer's Case* (1583), 5 Co. Rep. 16a. On the whole subject, see Cheshire, *Modern Law of Real Property*, 12th Edn., pp. 449–461.
3. *Infra*, p. 445, and Cheshire, *Modern Real Property*, 12th Edn., pp. 597 *et seq.*
4. [1949] 2 K.B. 500; [1949] 2 All E.R. 179. This resulted from a combination of a common law exception and the extension of it by s. 78 (1) of Law of Property Act 1925. See Cheshire, *Modern Real Property*, 12th Edn., pp. 593–6.

contract.[1] This does not exclude the possibility that he may have some other cause of action.   Thus if A buys a car from B and gives it to his wife, she will have no rights under the contract against B but she could have an action in tort if she suffered personal injuries because of B's negligent pre-delivery inspection.[2] Similarly if A threatens to break his contract with B unless B dismisses his servant C, C may be able to sue A in the tort of intimidation.[3]

Despite these reservations the doctrine of privity, though often criticized and sometimes modified, is still received as a fundamental assumption of the common law.   Its consequences must now be examined under two heads: the attempt to confer benefits upon strangers and the attempt to impose liabilities upon them.

SECTION II.   ATTEMPTS TO AVOID THE DOCTRINE

A. ATTEMPTS TO CONFER BENEFITS UPON STRANGERS[4]

A promises
B to dis-
charge a
debt due
from B to X

SUCH attempts may be made for two rather different purposes It may be desired, on the one hand, that a debt due to a third person from one of the contracting parties shall be discharged by the other party.   Thus, if B owes money to X he may make a contract with A, whereby A agrees, for good consideration, to discharge this debt.   Can X sue A for a failure to keep his promise?   The possibility of such an action was tested in the common law courts in the case of *Crow* v. *Rogers* as early as 1724,[5] and the judges refused to sanction it.

> Hardy owed Crow £70.   By an agreement between Hardy and Rogers, Rogers promised to discharge this debt in return for Hardy's undertaking to convey a house to him.   Crow sued Rogers on this promise and failed.

The result is inconvenient rather than unjust.   If, in the hypothetical case suggested, A does not keep his promise, X retains

---

1. As to whether a contract can operate to afford a non-party a defence, see *supra.*
2. *Donoghue* v. *Stevenson*, [1932] A.C. 562, where the contrary theory was put to rest.   This is not to say that the present complex of rules is satisfactory since the standards of liability in sale and negligence are very different and legally the wife's position would be much better if A gave her the money to buy the car herself.   Jolowicz, 32 M.L.R. 1; Pasley, 32 M.L.R. 241; Legh-Jones, [1969] C.L.J. 54.
3. *Rookes* v. *Barnard*, [1964] A.C. 1129; [1964] 1 All E.R. 367; Hoffman, 81 L.Q.R. 116.
4. See Dowrick, 19 M.L.R. 374; Furmston, 23 M.L.R. 373; Simpson, 15 I.C.L.Q. 835; Millner, 16 I.C.L.Q. 446; Scammell, 1955 current Legal problems 131; substantial reform of the doctrine was proposed by the Law Revision Committee as long ago as 1937 in its Sixth Interim Report, para. 50 (a), but this has not been implemented.
5. (1724), 1 Stra. 592.

his original remedy against B; and, if B is sued by X, B may, in turn, sue A. The rule of the common law merely involves the expense of double litigation.

On the other hand, it may be desired to confer a benefit upon a third party, towards whom no antecedent liability exists. A may promise B, for good consideration, to pay X £100. The decisive case was *Tweddle* v. *Atkinson* in 1861.[1]

A promises B to confer a benefit on X

> In consideration of an intended marriage between the plaintiff and the daughter of William Guy, a contract was made between Guy and the plaintiff's father, whereby each promised to pay the plaintiff a sum of money. Guy failed to do so, and the plaintiff sued his executors.

The action was dismissed.

> " Some of the old decisions," said WIGHTMAN, J.,[2] " appear to support the proposition that a stranger to the consideration of a contract may maintain an action upon it, if he stands in such a near relationship to the party from whom the consideration proceeds, that he may be considered a party to the consideration. . . . But there is no modern case in which the proposition has been supported. On the contrary, it is now established that no stranger to the consideration can take advantage of a contract, although made for his benefit."

The learned judge, by basing his decision on the rule that consideration must move from the promisee, emphasised the English identification of contract and bargain. But it has already been observed that this rule is itself an insular reflection of the general assumption that contract, as a juristic concept, is the intimate if not the exclusive relationship between the parties who have made it.[3] Thus Roman law, innocent of consideration, declared that a third party could neither be liable nor entitled under a contract. In France the Civil Code formulated the doctrine of " relativity ": " contracts have effect only between the contracting parties." It is, however, easier to proclaim a principle than to maintain it. Even Roman law was forced to admit exceptions, and French law, by developing another article of the Code which allowed certain " stipulations *pour autrui*," has torn a wide breach in its doctrine.[4]

Doctrine of privity

In England the doctrine of privity, proclaimed in the nineteenth century, was re-affirmed by the House of Lords in 1915. In *Dunlop* v. *Selfridge*,[5]

Dunlop v. *Selfridge*

> The plaintiffs sold a number of their tyres to Dew & Co., described as " motor accessory factors," on the terms that Dew & Co. would not re-sell them below certain scheduled prices and that, in the event of a sale to trade customers, they would extract from the latter a similar undertaking. Dew & Co. sold the tyres to Selfridge,

---

1. (1861), 1 B. & S. 393.
2. 1 B. & S., at p. 397.
3. *Supra*, p. 70; and see *Price* v. *Easton* (1833), 4 B. & Ad. 433.
4. See Buckland and McNair, *Roman Law and Common Law*, 2nd Edn., pp. 214–17, and Amos and Walton, *Introduction to French Law*, 2nd Edn., pp. 175–177. On the present position in France, Lawson remarks in *A Common Lawyer looks at the Civil Law* (1955), p. 56, " the French courts have so disturbed the balance between articles 1119 and 1120 of the code as to make the recognition of third party rights in contract normal instead of exceptional, as was assuredly the intention of the compilers."
5. [1915] A.C. 847. *Supra*, p. 70.

who agreed to observe the restrictions and to pay to Messrs. Dunlop
the sum of £5 for each tyre sold in breach of this agreement.
Selfridge in fact supplied tyres to two of their own customers
below the listed price.

As between Dew and Selfridge this act was undoubtedly a breach
of contract for which damages could have been recovered.   But
the action was brought, not by Dew, but by Messrs. Dunlop, who
sued to recover two sums of £5 each as liquidated damages and
asked for an injunction to restrain further breaches of agreement.
They were met by the objection that they were not parties to the
contract and had furnished no consideration for the defendants'
promise.   The objection, indeed, was obvious, and plaintiffs'
counsel, not daring to contest it, sought to evade its application
by pleading that their clients were in the position of undisclosed
principals.   The House of Lords not unnaturally considered such
a suggestion difficult to reconcile with the facts of the case, and
gave judgment for the defendants.

In *Dunlop* v. *Selfridge*, the House of Lords drew the logical
inference from the common law premises.   But the result may
be inconvenient or even unjust.   Thus it is quite common for
insurances to be taken out by one person on behalf of another—a
husband for his wife, or a parent for his child.   Yet, even if the
policy expressly confers benefits on the third party, the latter has
no claim at common law.[1]   A result, so inconsistent with the
needs of the modern world, would seem to invite the intervention
of Parliament, and from time to time Acts have been passed to
redress a particular grievance.   Husband and wife have thus, in
reversal of the common law rule, been enabled to take out life
insurance policies in favour of each other or of their children;
third parties have been allowed, in certain circumstances, to sue
on marine or fire insurance policies, or on the policies covering
road accidents required by the provisions of the Road Traffic Act
1972.[2]   But these statutes are only so many isolated exceptions to
the general rule of the common law, rendering its operation
uncertain, but not impairing its ultimate validity; and, as social
or economic necessity invites some new extension of the principle
of insurance, so the rule may once more disappoint the reasonable
expectation of the parties.

Commercial
innovations

Thus the doctrine of privity, while not an irrational inference
from the nature of contract in general and of English contract in
particular, has in its incidence worked injustice and proved
inadequate to modern needs.   Parliament, when it has intervened, has offered only spasmodic and occasional relief.   In
these circumstances it is not surprising that many and various
attempts have been made to induce the courts to sanction evasions
of the doctrine.   These have, indeed, met with a considerable
measure of success.   It has already been observed that the
undisclosed principal emerged in the eighteenth century as one

1. See the remarks of Lord ESHER, in *Cleaver* v. *Mutual Reserve Fund Life
    Association,* [1892] 1 Q.B. 147, at p. 152.
2. See s. 11 of the Married Women's Property Act 1882 (extended to illegiti-
    mate children by Family Law Reform Act 1969, s. 19); s. 14 (2) of the
    Marine Insurance Act 1906; s. 47 (1) of the Law of Property Act 1925;
    s. 148 (4) of the Road Traffic Act 1972.

who could sue on a contract made by other,[1] and in the sphere of insurance there are several situations where a policy may avail for the benefit of persons who have not themselves effected it.[2] By the rules governing negotiable instruments, moreover, it has long been established—first by the custom of the Law Merchant, then by judicial decision and finally by statute[3]—that a third party may sue on a bill of exchange or a cheque. The usages of trade and commerce have thus done something to modify the rigour of the common law doctrine. Nor is their force exhausted. It is still true that, if it is clear in any particular case that a commercial practice exists in favour of third party rights and that all concerned in the litigation have based their relations upon it, the court will do what it can to support and sanction it.[4]

Outside the law of property and the commercial world few, if any, exceptions have been allowed at common law. Litigants have therefore invoked the assistance of equity. As early as 1753 Lord HARDWICKE indicated the possibilities of the trust. He was prepared, in a case where A promised B to pay money to C, to regard B as trustee for C of the benefit of the contract.[5] In 1817 Sir William GRANT affirmed the suggestion in the case of *Gregory and Parker* v. *Williams*.[6]

Rule modified by equitable doctrine of constructive trust

> Parker owed money both to Gregory and to Williams. He agreed with Williams to assign to him the whole of his property, if Williams would pay the debt due to Gregory. The property was duly assigned, but Williams failed to implement his promise.

Gregory and Parker filed a bill in equity to compel performance of the promise, and succeeded. Sir William GRANT held that Parker must be regarded as trustee for Gregory, and that the latter " derived an equitable right through the mediation of Parker's agreement." After the Judicature Act 1873, the propriety of this device was affirmed and its use sanctioned in any division of the High Court. In the words of LUSH, L.J., in *Lloyd's* v. *Harper*,[7]

> " It is an established rule that, where a contract is made with A for the benefit of B, A can sue on the contract for the benefit of B and recover all that B could have recovered if the contract had been made with B himself."

Implicit in this statement is the conclusion that if A fails in his duty, B, the beneficiary under the implied trust, may successfully

---

1. *Supra*, p. 434, and *infra*, p. 472–5.
2. See, e.g. Married Women's Property Act 1882, s. 11, as amended by Family Law Reform Act 1969 s. 19; Marine Insurance Act 1906, s. 14 (2); Law of Property Act 1925, s. 47 (1); Third Parties (Rights Against Insurers) Act 1930; Road Traffic Act 1972, s. 148 (4); *P. Samuel & Co.* v. *Dumas*, [1923] 1 K.B. 592; affirmed [1924] A.C. 431; *Tomlinson (Hauliers)* v. *Hepburn*, [1966] A.C. 451; [1966] 1 All E.R. 418; *MacGillivray and Parkington, Insurance Law*, 6th Edn., paras. 143–174.
3. See Bills of Exchange Act 1882, s. 29, and *infra*, pp. 508–512.
4. *United Dominions Trust, Ltd.* v. *Kirkwood*, [1966] 2 Q.B. 431 at pp. 454–5; [1966] 1 All E.R. 968, at p. 980, per Lord DENNING, M.R. This may provide a rationale for the enforcement of bankers' commercial credits, discussed *supra*, pp. 54.
5. *Tomlinson* v. *Gill* (1756), Amb. 330. See Corbin, 46 L.Q.R. 12, Williams, 7 M.L.R. 123.
6. (1817), 3 Mer. 582.
7. (1880), 16 Ch.D. 290. See also *Re Flavell, Murray* v. *Flavell* (1883), 25 Ch.D. 89; *Royal Exchange Assurance* v. *Hope*, [1928] Ch. 179; [1927] All E.R. Rep. 67.

maintain an action to which A and the other contracting party are joint defendants.

One particular application of this equitable doctrine was recognized as effective by the House of Lords in *Walford's* case in 1919.[1]

> Walford, as broker, had negotiated a charter-party between the owners of the *S.S. Flore* and the Lubricating and Fuel Oils Co., Ltd. By a clause in the charter-party the oerners promised the charterers to pay Walford a commission of 3 per cent. on the estimated gross amount of hire. Walford brought an action against the owners to obtain this commission.

The charterers were not made parties to the action, but, when Walford applied to join them as such, the owners agreed to raise no objection, and the action proceeded as if they had in fact been joined. The House of Lords affirmed judgment in Walford's favour. Lord BIRKENHEAD cited the previous decisions and declared that

> " in such cases charterers can sue as trustees on behalf of the broker."

Such decisions indicate the possibilities of the trust in evading the rigidity of the common law rule. At first sight it appears to be an effective means of evasion. It is useful to re-call MAITLAND's definition:

> " Where a person has rights which he is bound to exercise on behalf of another or for the accomplishment of some particular purpose, he is said to have those rights in trust for another or for that purpose, and he is called a trustee."[2]

It is true that the subject-matter of a trust is normally some tangible property, such as land or goods, or a definite sum of money, and that, if the conception is to be applied in the present context, it is necessary to speak of the " trust of a promise." But MAITLAND's definition is wide enough to include such a phrase, and, on the assumption that the judges are resolved to avoid the limitations of the common law, the machinery would seem to be simple and adequate. The third party may ask the contracting party to sue as trustee, and, in the event of a refusal, may himself sue and join the " trustee " as co-defendant.[3]

But, despite its promising appearance and the positive terms in which it has occasionally been acclaimed, the device has in practice proved a disappointing and unreliable instrument.

In *Re Schebsman, Official Receiver v. Cargo Superintendents (London), Ltd. and Schebsman*,[4]

---

1. *Les Affréteurs Réunis Société Anonyme v. Walford*, [1919] A.C. 801.
2. Maitland, *Equity*, p. 44.
3. It is strange that the device was not exploited by the plaintiffs in *Dunlop v. Selfridge, supra*, p. 437. Lord HALDANE had recognized its existence, and the facts in the case would seem to suggest the possibility of a trust at least as clearly as those in *Walford's* case. *Dunlop v. Selfridge*, however, was fought and decided exclusively on common law principles.
4. [1944] Ch. 83; [1943] 2 All E.R. 768. See also *Gandy v. Gandy* (1885), 30 Ch.D. 57; *Vandepitte v. Preferred Accident Insurance Corporation of New York*, [1933] A.C. 70; [1932] All E.R. Rep. 527 *Re Stapleton-Bretherton, Weld-Blundell v. Stapleton-Bretherton*, [1941] Ch. 482; [1941] 3 All E.R.5; and *Re Miller's Agreement, Uniacke v. A.-G.*, [1947] Ch. 615; [1947] 2 All E.R. 78.

S was employed by two companies. By a contract made between him and them, one of the companies agreed in certain eventualities to pay £5,500 to his widow and daughter.

It was held that the contract did not create a trust in favour of the widow and daughter. Du Parcq, L.J., said:[1]

" It is true that, by the use possibly of unguarded language, a person may create a trust, as Monsieur Jourdain talked prose, without knowing it, but unless an intention to create a trust is clearly to be collected from the language used and the circumstances of the case, I think that the court ought not to be astute to discover indications of such an intention. I have little doubt that in the present case both parties (and certainly the debtor) intended to keep alive their common law right to vary consensually the terms of the obligation undertaken by the company, and if circumstances had changed in the debtor's lifetime injustice might have been done by holding that a trust had been created and that those terms were accordingly unalterable."

A later example of the reluctance of the courts to discover a trust is offered by the case of *Green* v. *Russell*.[2]

The plaintiff's son, Alfred Green, was employed by the defendant's husband, Arthur Russell. Both son and husband died in a fire at their office. Mr. Russell had made a contract with an insurance company in which he himself was described as " the insured " and by which the company undertook to pay £1,000 if certain of Mr. Russell's employees, including Mr. Green, died as a result of bodily injuries. Nothing in the contract of employment between Mr. Green and Mr. Russell required such a policy to be taken out, nor did its terms confer any right or impose any obligation on Mr. Green in respect of the policy. The insurance company paid the £1,000 to Mrs. Russell, as her husband's administratrix, and she paid it over to the plaintiff.

The plaintiff, as the son's administratrix, sued the defendant, as the husband's administratrix, under the Fatal Accidents Acts 1846 to 1908. The defendant admitted liability in principle but claimed that the £1,000 she had paid over to the plaintiff should be deducted from the damages. The issue turned on the wording of section 1 of the Act of 1908, that " there shall not be taken into account any sum paid or payable on the death of the deceased under any contract of assurance or insurance."[3]

At first sight these words were conclusive. The money had certainly been paid on the death of Mr. Green under a contract of insurance. But the defendant argued that the words applied only to sums to which the deceased had either a legal or an equitable right and that no such right existed. There was none at common law since the deceased was a stranger to the insurance contract, and none in equity since no trust could be inferred in his favour. The Court of Appeal held that the words were clear in themselves and that there was no reason to restrict them on the grounds suggested. This conclusion disposed of the case.

---

1. [1944] Ch., at p. 104.
2. [1959] 2 All E.R. 525; [1959] 2 Q.B. 226. Furmston, 23 M.L.R. 373, at pp. 377–385.
3. Section 1 of the Act of 1908 has now been repealed and replaced by s. 2 (1) of the Fatal Accidents Act 1959; " There shall not be taken into account any insurance money, benefit, pension or gratuity which has been or will or may be paid as a result of the death."

But the court agreed that, had it been necessary to decide the question, they would have ruled that the policy conferred no right on the deceased and therefore none on the plaintiff.   " An intention to provide benefits for someone else and to pay for them," said ROMER, L.J., " does not in itself give rise to a trusteeship "; and he stressed the incompatability of this status with the contractual liberty enjoyed by the insured to terminate the policy without the concurrence of his employees.   " There was nothing to prevent Mr. Russell at any time, had he chosen to do so, from surrendering the policy and receiving back a proportionate part of the premium which he had paid."[1]

At one time it looked as if the trust concept might provide a convenient equitable means to circumvent the common law rule. Over the last fifty years however, without locking the door the courts have consistently failed to open it.   A trust will not now be inferred simply because A and B make a contract with the intention of benefitting C; in the few cases where trusts have been discovered, there have been much stronger indicia.[2]   A variety of reasons have combined to produce this result: a feeling that the trust was a " cumbrous fiction:"[3] an insistence that intention to create a trust be affirmatively proved and a concern lest the irrevocable nature of a trust should prevent the contracting parties from changing their minds.[4]

Section 56 of the Law of Property Act 1925

Since the retreat of equity a further attempt to cut if not to unloose the technical knots has been made by a bold essay in statutory interpretation.   By section 56 (1) of the Law of Property Act 1925, it is declared that:

> " a person may take an immediate or other interest in land or other property, or the benefit of any condition, right of entry, covenant or agreement over or respecting land or other property, although he may not be named as a party to the conveyance or other instrument."

This section replaced section 5 of the Real Property Act 1845, which itself abolished a common law rule that no person could take advantage of a covenant in a deed unless he was a party to that deed; but, in replacing it, it widened its terms, especially by adding the words " or other property " and " or agreement." It must also be noticed that by section 205 (1) of the Law of Property Act, " unless the context otherwise requires . . . ' Property ' includes anything in action and any interest in real or personal property."   In a number of cases Lord DENNING suggested that the section should be read as abrogating the doctrine of privity in the case of contracts in writing affecting

---

1. [1959] 2 Q.B., at p. 241; [1959] 2 All E.R., at p. 531.
2. See *Re Webb, Barclays Bank, Ltd.* v. *Webb,* [1941] Ch. 225; [1941] 1 All E.R. 321.   Re *Foster Clark's Indenture Trusts, Loveland* v. *Horscroft* [1966] 1 All E.R. 43; [1966] 1 W.L.R. 125.
3. See *per* Lord WRIGHT, 55 L.Q.R. 189, at p. 208.
4. Cf. *per* FULLAGAR, J., on *Wilson* v. *Darling Island Stevedoring and Lighterage Co.* (1956), 95 C.L.R. 43, at p. 67.   See also *Olsson* v. *Dyson* (1969), 43 A.L.J.R. 77.

property.[1] This view has now been rejected by the House of
Lords in the case of *Beswick* v. *Beswick*.[2]

> Peter Beswick was a coal merchant. In March, 1962, he con-
> tracted to sell the business to his nephew John in consideration (1)
> that for the rest of Peter's life John should pay him £6 10s. a week,
> (2) that if Peter's wife survived him John should pay her an annuity
> of £5 a week. John took over the business and paid Peter the agreed
> sum until Peter died in November, 1963. He then paid Peter's
> widow £5 for one week and refused to pay any more. The widow
> brought an action against John in which she claimed £175 as arrears
> of the annuity and asked for specific performance of the contract.
> She sued (a) as administratrix of Peter's estate, (b) in her personal
> capacity.

The Court of Appeal held unanimously that she was entitled, as
administratrix, to an order for specific performance. Lord
DENNING and Lord Justice DANCKWERTS also held that she could
succeed in her personal capacity under section 56 (1) of the Law
of Property Act 1925.[3] The defendant appealed to the House of
Lords. The House held that, as administratrix, the widow could
obtain an order for specific performance which would enforce the
provision in the contract for the benefit of herself;[4] but that in
her personal capacity she could derive no right of action from the
statute.

Their lordships admitted that, if section 56 (1) was to be
literally construed, its language was wide enough to support the
conclusions of Lord DENNING and Lord Justice DANCKWERTS.
But they were reluctant to believe that the legislature, in an act
devoted to real property, had inadvertently and irrelevantly revolutionized the law of contract. The avowed purpose of the Act of
1925, according to its title, was " to consolidate the enactments
relating to conveyancing and the law of property in England and
Wales." It must therefore be presumed that the legislature designed no drastic changes in such enactments; and this presumption was to be rebutted only by plain words. The words of
section 56 (1) were not plain. By section 205 (1), moreover, it was
provided that the definitions which it contained were to apply
" unless the context otherwise requires." In so far as the Law of
Property Act 1925 was an essay in consolidation, the context
required the word " property " to be restrictively construed, and it
should not be allowed to spill over into contract. Whatever the
force of this argument, the House of Lords has decisively rejected

---

1. *Smith and Snipes Hall Farm, Ltd.* v. *River Douglas Catchment Board,*
   [1949] 2 K.B. 500, at p. 517; [1949] 2 All E.R. 179, at p. 189; *Drive Yourself
   Hire Co. (London), Ltd.* v. *Strutt,* [1954] 1 Q.B. 250, at p. 274; [1953] 2 All
   E.R. 1475, at p. 1483. Cf. *Re Foster* (1938), 159 L.T. 279, at p. 282; *Re
   Miller's Agreement,* [1947] Ch. 615; [1947] 2 All E.R. 78; *Stromdale and
   Ball, Ltd.* v. *Burden,* [1952] Ch. 223; [1952] 1 All E.R. 59. See Elliott,
   20 Conv (N.S.) 43, 114; Andrews, 23 Conv (N.S.) 179; Furmston, 23
   M.L.R. 373, at pp. 380–385; Ellinger, 26 M.L.R. 396.
2. [1968] A.C. 58; [1967] 2 All E.R. 1197. For the judgments in the Court
   of Appeal, see [1966] Ch. 538; [1966] 3 All E.R. 1.
3. SALMON, L.J., was not prepared to accept this interpretation of the section.
   All three members of the Court of Appeal agreed that no trust could be
   found in the plaintiff's favour.
4. On the order for specific performance see *infra,* p. 612.

the attempt to use section 56 (1) so as to enable third parties to sue upon a contract.[1]

At first sight the decision in *Beswick* v. *Beswick* appears to be a sanguinary defeat for those who would hope to see the doctrine of privity curbed, if not abolished.   It is noteworthy however that the nephew was compelled to perform his promise and this shows that at least in some cases a satisfactory result can be achieved if an action is brought not by the third party beneficiary but by the original promisee.   This possibility is further illuminated by the decision in *Snelling* v. *John G. Snelling, Ltd.*[2]

> The plaintiff and his two brothers were all directors of the defendant company.   The company was financed by substantial loans from all three brothers.   As part of an arrangement to borrow money from a finance company, the three brothers made a contract, to which the company was not a party, not to demand repayment of their loans during the currency of the loan from the finance company.   The agreement further provided that if any of the brothers should voluntarily resign his directorship, he should forfeit the money owing on the loan.   A few months later the plaintiff resigned his directorship and sued the company for repayment of his loan.

The plaintiff argued that as the company was not a party to the agreement with his brothers, that agreement did not affect his rights against the company.   The brothers applied to be joined as co-defendants to the action and ORMROD, J., held that although the company was not entitled to rely directly on the agreement, the co-defendant brothers were entitled to a stay of proceedings and that indeed since all the parties were before the court and the reality of the situation was that the plaintiff's claim had failed, the action should be dismissed.

It seems therefore that what cannot be obtained directly by the third party can, in appropriate circumstances, be obtained on his behalf by the promisee by specific performance, stay of proceedings or (presumably) injunction.   In many circumstances, however, the only satisfactory remedy is an action for damages. It has been widely believed, however, that in an action for damages, the promisee could recover only for the damage he himself suffered (often only nominal) and not the damage suffered by the third party.   This seems to have been assumed by the majority of the House of Lords, though not by Lord PEARCE, in *Beswick* v. *Beswick*.

The principle that a plaintiff can only recover for his own loss is certainly subject to exceptions.   So, for instance, a carrier of goods may insure the full value of the goods and recover it from an insurance company, even though he himself has but a limited interest in the goods.[3]   Similarly, a consignor of goods for carriage by sea can recover the full value of the goods if the contract is broken even though, by the date of breach, he is no

---

1.   It is far from clear what the House of Lords decided that s. 56 (1) did mean. See Treitel, 30 M.L.R. 681.   Fortunately this is now a problem for property lawyers and not for contract lawyers.
2.   [1973] 1 Q.B. 87; [1972] 1 All E.R. 79; Wilkie 36 M.L.R. 214.   See also *Gurtner* v. *Circuit*, [1968] 2 Q.B. 587; [1968] 1 All E.R. 328.
3.   *A. Tomlinson (Hauliers), Ltd.* v. *Hepburn,* [1966] A.C. 451; [1966] 1 All E.R. 418.

longer owner of the goods.[1] It will be remembered, too, that LUSH, L.J., stated the contrary in *Lloyd's* v. *Harper*.[2] It has been widely thought that LUSH, L.J., was talking only of situations of trust[3] but this was firmly denied by Lord DENNING, M.R., in *Jackson* v. *Horizon Holidays, Ltd.*[4]

> The plaintiff made a contract with the defendant for a holiday for himself, his wife and two children in Ceylon. The holiday was a disaster and the defendants accepted that they were in breach of contract.

The Court of Appeal held that the plaintiff could recover damages not only for the discomfort and disappointment he suffered himself but also for that experienced by his wife and children. This could, perhaps, have been put on the (relatively) narrow ground that the plaintiff was recovering for his own disappointment that his family's holiday was spoilt but Lord DENNING, M.R., stated clearly that the words of LUSH, L.J., were of general application. Clearly if this is the law the doctrine of privity will be substantially neutralized in any case where the promisee can be persuaded to sue.[5]

B. ATTEMPTS TO IMPOSE LIABILITIES UPON STRANGERS

The doctrine of privity, while in principle at least it prevents a third party beneficiary from suing on a contract, operates with equal logic to forbid the contracting parties to enforce obligations against a stranger. It has long been an axiom of the common law that a contract between A and B cannot impose a liability upon C.

Contract between A and B cannot impose a liability on C

This rule, however, was found to be so inconvenient in the case of contracts concerning land that counter-measures had to be devised to meet it. It has already been seen that, where a lease was concerned, such measures originated at an early date in the common law itself and were subsequently extended by statute.[6] A second modification is due entirely to equity, and it did not emerge until 1848, when the case of *Tulk* v. *Moxhay*[7] was decided. The problem in that case was this: will a restrictive covenant, voluntarily accepted by the purchaser of land as part of the contract of sale, bind persons who later acquire the land? The facts of the case itself afford a simple illustration.

Restrictive covenants in the land law

---

1. *The Albazero,* [1975] 3 All E.R. 21; [1975] 3 W.L.R. 516.
2. (1880) 16 Ch.D. 290, *supra,* p. 439.
3. See, e.g. *per* WINDEYER, J., in *Coulls* v. *Bagot's Executor and Trustee Co.,* [1967] A.L.R. 385, at pp. 409–411, though in his illuminating judgment WINDEYER, J., did not agree that the promisee could get only nominal damages.
4. [1975] 3 All E.R. 92; [1975] 1 W.L.R. 1468.
5. Clearly if the promisee does recover substantial damages, the question will arise as to whether he must account to the beneficiary but any obligation to do so will not usually sound in contract.
6. *Supra,* p. 435.
7. (1848), 2 Ph. 774.

The plaintiff, the owner of several plots of land in Leicester Square, sold the garden in the centre to one Elms, who agreed not to build upon it but to preserve it in its existing condition. After a number of conveyances the garden was sold to the defendant Moxhay, who, though he knew of the restriction, proposed to build. The plaintiff, accepting his inability at common law to recover damages from one who was not a party to the contract, sought an injunction against the erection of the proposed buildings.

The injunction was granted. The decisive factor in the view of the court was the knowledge by the defendant of the existence of the covenant. A court of equity, being a court of conscience, could not permit him to disregard a contractual obligation affecting the land of which he had notice at the time of his purchase.

Thus was established the doctrine that a restrictive covenant, binding a purchaser not to perform certain acts of ownership upon the land bought, may be enforced, not only against him as the contracting party, but also against third parties who later acquire the land. It is undesirable in a general book on contracts to specify the conditions upon which enforcement depends, but it is essential to observe that the liability of the third party soon ceased to be based exclusively on notice. There has been a radical development in the doctrine initiated by *Tulk* v. *Moxhay*, and it has been established since the latter years of the nineteenth century that something more than mere notice by the third party of the existence of the covenant is necessary to render him liable. In particular it is essential that the covenantee, *i.e.* the original vendor, should have retained other land in the neighbourhood for the benefit and protection of which the restrictive covenant was taken. If an owner sells only a portion of his property, the selling value of what he retains will often depreciate unless restrictions are placed upon the enjoyment of the part sold, and it is only where the covenantee has retained land capable of being benefited in this way that equity will enforce a restrictive covenant against a third party.[1]

Can this equitable doctrine extend to other contracts? The question now arises whether this equitable doctrine may be applied where the subject-matter of the contract is property other than land. The relevant cases and statutes suggest that there are two different situations which require, or at least have received, different treatment.[2]

(1) Attempts to enforce against third parties restrictions upon the use of goods.

(2) Attempts to enforce against third parties restrictions upon the price at which goods may be re-sold.

These situations will be considered separately.

I. RESTRICTIONS UPON USE

It was a restriction upon use that the court enforced in the parent case of *Tulk* v. *Moxhay*; and within a few years of this decision

---

1. See *Formby* v. *Barker,* [1903] 2 Ch. 539, and *London County Council* v. *Allen,* [1914] 3 K.B. 642.
2. This distinction was taken by Wade, 44 L.Q.R. 51.

the propriety of a similar restriction was canvassed in the case of a ship. In *De Mattos* v. *Gibson* in 1858,[1]

> A chartered a ship from X. During the currency of the charter-party X mortgaged the ship to B, who knew at the time that this charter-party existed. A alleged that B now threatened, as mortgagee, to sell the ship in disregard of his contract rights and he applied for an interlocutory injunction to restrain B from doing so.

As applied to ships: *De Mattos* v. *Gibson*

The application was refused by Vice-Chancellor WOOD, but allowed on appeal by KNIGHT BRUCE and TURNER, L.JJ. KNIGHT BRUCE, L.J., observed:[2]

> " Reason and justice seem to prescribe that, at least as a general rule, where a man by gift or purchase acquires property from another, with knowledge of a previous contract lawfully and for valuable consideration made by him with a third person to use and employ the property for a particular purpose in a specified manner, the acquirer shall not, to the material damage of the third person, in opposition to the contract and inconsistently with it, use and employ the property in a manner not allowable to the giver or seller."

TURNER, L.J., was careful not to be involved in so comprehensive a principle. He would not go further than to grant an interlocutory injunction " until the hearing of the cause " because of the " difficult and important questions to be tried at the hearing." The case then went back to WOOD, V.-C., for the cause to be heard; and he ruled that, on the facts before him, no injunction should be granted. This ruling was upheld by the Lord Chancellor, Lord CHELMSFORD, and the plaintiff's application thus finally failed. Lord CHELMSFORD emphasized, however, that his decision was based on the finding that the defendant had not in fact interfered with the performance of the charter-party. Had he done so, an injunction might well have been granted.

Five years later the same court was faced with similar facts in *Messageries Imperiales Co.* v. *Baines*.[3]

> The plaintiff had chartered a ship from X. During the currency of the charter, X sold the ship to the defendant who knew at the time of the existence of the charter but declined to allow the ship to fulfil the charter obligations.

WOOD, V.-C., now felt constrained by the observations of his brothers in the superior courts and granted the injunction for which the plaintiff asked.

For the next fifty years the sweeping assertion of Lord Justice KNIGHT BRUCE was cited from time to time by counsel at a loss for more precise authority. But in 1914 the Court of Appeal refused to accept it as offering a catholic principle upon which it was safe to depend.

---

1. 4 De G. & J. 276.
2. *Ibid.*, at p. 282.
3. (1863), 7 L.T. 763.

" Notwithstanding what was said by Knight Bruce, L.J., in *De Mattos* v. *Gibson,* it is not true as a general proposition that a purchaser of property with notice of a restrictive covenant affecting the property is bound by the covenant."[1]

The *Strathcona* case

In 1926 the case of the *Lord Strathcona Steamship Co.* v. *Dominion Coal Co.* came before the Judicial Committee of the Pricy Council.[2]

B, the owner of the steamer *Lord Strathcona,* chartered her to A on the terms that, for a period of years, A should be free to use her on the St. Lawrence river for the summer season and should surrender her to B in November of each year. During the currency of the charter-party, but while the ship was in B's possession, B sold and delivered her to C, who in turn re-sold her to D. D, though he knew of the charter-party, refused to deliver the ship to A for the summer season.

A obtained an injunction against D in the courts of Nova Scotia restraining him from using the ship in any way inconsistent with the charter-party, and D's appeal to the Privy Council was dismissed. The Privy Council quoted with approval the familiar words of Knight Bruce, L.J., and, adopting them, decided in effect that the defendant in the case before them was caught by the rule in *Tulk* v. *Moxhay.* He had bought a ship with notice that she was affected by a restrictive covenant in favour of the plaintiff and he was therefore, in their view, in the same position as if he had bought an estate in land with notice of a similar restriction. It must be remembered, however, that in the years that had elapsed since the case of *De Mattos* v. *Gibson* the rule in *Tulk* v. *Moxhay* had been radically developed by the courts and had ceased to be based solely upon notice. A restrictive covenant imposed on land could no longer be enforced against later purchasers unless the original covenantee had retained a proprietary interest in other land for the benefit of which the covenant was taken. Where was the proprietary interest in the *Strathcona* case? The Privy Council recognized the necessity for its existence, but they can scarcely be said to have found it in the facts before them. They could only assert that A enjoyed an interest in the ship for the period covered by the charter-party. But this interest was no more than that conferred by the very contract which A sought to enforce against the third party: it was certainly not the independent proprietary interest which equity requires. Moreover, it is well established that a charter-party creates no right of property in a ship.[3] The Privy Council in truth paid lip service to the modern doctrine of *Tulk* v. *Moxhay,* but applied it as it existed in an earlier environment.

Even if the decision in the *Strathcona* case be accepted as valid and worthy to command the assent of English courts, there are no cases in which it has been allowed general application,

1. *London County Council* v. *Allen,* [1914] 3 K.B. 642, at p. 658. See also *Barker* v. *Stickney,* [1919] 1 K.B. 121.
2. [1926] A.C. 108.
3. See Bailhache, J., in *Federated Coal and Shipping Co.* v. *R.,* [1922] 2 K.B. 42, at p. 46, and cases there cited. Except in the case of a charter party by demise, *Baumwoll Manufactur Von Carl Scheibler* v. *Furness,* [1893] A.C. 8.

and in 1936 the Court of Appeal thought that it must in any event be confined " to the very special case of a ship under a charter-party."[1] But the decision itself was challenged in *Port Line, Ltd. v. Ben Line Steamers, Ltd.*[2]

In March, 1955, the plaintiffs chartered a ship from X the owner, for a period of 30 months. The ship was to remain in X's possession but to be at the complete disposal of the plaintiffs.

In February, 1956, X sold the ship to the defendants. The defendants at once chartered it back to X so that it never ceased to be in X's possession. The plaintiffs knew of the sale and acquiesced in it since the ship was to remain available under their own charter. The charter between X and the defendants contained a clause that " if the ship is requisitioned, the charter shall thereupon cease." No such clause existed in the plaintiffs' charter. The defendants, when they bought the ship, knew of the existence of the plaintiffs' charter but not of its terms.

In August, 1956, the Ministry of Transport requisitioned the ship and paid compensation to the defendants as owners. In November, 1956, the requisition ended.

The plaintiffs now sued the defendants to obtain this compensation money and relied, *inter alia*, on the *Strathcona* case and the *dictum* in *De Mattos v. Gibson.*

DIPLOCK, J., gave judgment for the defendants. He thought, in the first place, that the *Strathcona* case was not good law.

> " The difficulty I have found in ascertaining its *ratio decidendi*, the impossibility which I find of reconciling the actual decision with well-established principles of law, the unsolved and, to me, insoluble problems which that decision raises combine to satisfy me that it was wrongly decided."

He stressed, in particular, the necessity, in the twentieth century, of finding some proprietary interest to support a claim based on *Tulk v. Moxhay* and the absence of any such interest in the *Strathcona* case. In the second place, he was of opinion that, even assuming it possible to support the *Strathcona* case in principle, the facts before him did not fall within its scope. The defendants, when they bought the ship, had no actual knowledge of the plaintiffs' rights: though they knew that a charter existed, they did not know its terms. Nor were they in breach of any duty. It was not by their act but by the act of the Crown that the ship had been used inconsistently with the plaintiffs' charter. Finally, the only remedy possible under the doctrine of *Tulk v. Moxhay* and therefore under the *Strathcona* case was the grant of an injunction. No damages or money compensation could be obtained.

Of the different reasons offered by the learned judge to avoid the application of the *Strathcona* case, even assuming it to be good law, the absence of actual knowledge of the plaintiffs' rights would hardly seem conclusive. It is true that in commercial matters the doctrine of constructive notice is not welcomed. But it is surely a facet of the equity upon which *Tulk v. Moxhay* depends and therefore relevant in the present context. The other reasons, however, are more than adequate to ensure the

---

1. *Clore* v. *Theatrical Properties, Ltd.*, [1936] 3 All E.R. 483.
2. [1958] 2 Q.B. 146; [1958] 1 All E.R. 787.

defeat of the plaintiffs' claim.   In the result, the propriety of the *Strathcona* case, though not authoritatively denied, has been severely shaken :

It is perhaps unfortunate that discussion of the application of real property analogies to personal property has concentrated on restrictive covenants to the exclusion of other interests, perhaps more readily applicable to chattels. Thus it is clear that an option to purchase land creates an equitable interest in the land capable of being enforced against a purchaser of the land[1] and there is authority for the application of the same principle to options to purchase chattels[2] and choses in action, such as copyrights.[3]

A question, potentially of great practical importance, is whether a contract under which possession of a chattel is transferred for a fixed term creates property rights analogous to a lease.[4]   Such contracts, e.g. for the rental of television sets or for hire or hire purchase[5] of motor vehicles, are extremely common and it is difficult to see any good reason why the owner of the goods should be able to convert the hirer's right to possession into a right to damages by selling the goods over his head. Holdsworth saw the position with his usual clarity over forty years ago when he said :[6]

> " It is obvious that if A has let or pledged his chattel to B and has transferred its possession to B and if he then sells it to C, C can only take it subject to B's legal rights, and since they are legal rights whether C has notice of those rights or not."[7]

It should also be noted that in some cases in this area, the plaintiff may be able to formulate a claim in tort for inducing breach of contract.[8]

2. RESTRICTIONS UPON PRICE

An attempt to enforce a price restriction against a third party was made in 1904 in the case of *Taddy* v. *Sterious*.[9]

> The plaintiffs, who were manufacturers of " Myrtle Grove " tobacco, sought to prevent retailers from selling it below a minimum price.   They attached to each packet a printed sheet, stating that

---

1. See, e.g. *London and South Western Rail. Co.* v. *Gomm* (1882), 20 Ch. D. 562.
2. *Falcke* v. *Gray* (1859), 4 Drew. 651.
3. *MacDonald* v. *Eyles*, [1921] 1 Ch. 631. *Quaere* whether this depends on the contract being specifically enforceable.
4. This was not the case in *The Strathcona* since the charterer does not ordinarily get possession of the chartered ship but merely a contractual right to control its use. In the special case of a charter party by demise, the charterer does get possession and in the leading authority on such charterparties, *Baumwoll Manufactur Von Carl Scheibler* v. *Furness*, [1893] A.C. 8, extensive use was made of analogies from the law of leases.
5. A hire purchase contract also contains an option to purchase, see supra, p. 127
6. 49 L.Q.R. 576, at p. 579; see also Gutteridge, 51 L.Q.R. 91, at p. 98; Thornely, 13 J.S.P.T.L. 150, at p. 151; Lawson, *The Law of Property*, pp. 71–73.
7. In practice C will very often have notice since A will not have possession.
8. See, e.g. *Winfield and Jolowicz on Tort*, 10th Edn., pp. 445–453. The decision of the Court of Appeal in *Sefton* v. *Tophams* [1965] Ch. 1140; [1965] 3 All E.R. 1 (reversed on other grounds, [1967] 1 A.C. 50; [1966] 1 All E.R. 1039) is particularly instructive.
9. [1904] 1 Ch. 354.

the tobacco was sold " on the express condition that retail dealers do not sell it below the prices above set forth " and adding that " acceptance of the goods will be deemed a contract between the purchaser and Messrs. Taddy & Co. that he will observe these stipulations. In the case of a purchase by a retail dealer through a wholesale dealer, the latter shall be deemed to be the agent of Taddy & Co." The plaintiffs sold tobacco under these conditions to Messrs. Nutter, wholesale dealers, who re-sold it to the defendants, retail tobacconists. The defendants, though they had notice of the conditions, re-sold below the minimum price.

The plaintiffs sued in the Chancery Division for a declaration that the defendants were bound by the conditions. They put their case on two grounds. First, they maintained that the printed sheet constituted a contract between themselves and the defendants and that Messrs. Nutter were their agents. The court dismissed this attempt to create a contract by ultimatum. There was in truth no contract between Taddy and Sterious, Messrs. Nutter were not Taddy's agents, and no unilateral declaration, however peremptory, could alter the legal position. Secondly, the plaintiffs invited the court to extend to them the protection of the rule in *Tulk* v. *Moxhay*. The invitation was summarily rejected. In the words of SWINFEN EADY, J.:

> Price restrictions " do not run with goods "

" Conditions of this kind do not run with goods and cannot be imposed upon them. Subsequent purchasers, therefore, do not take subject to any conditions which the court can enforce."

Another attempt to enforce a price restriction against a third party, made later in the same year, was met by the Court of Appeal with the same uncompromising refusal.[1]

The legal position remained unchanged for half a century, but then became the subject of somewhat irresolute legislation. By section 24 of the Restrictive Trade Practices Act 1956, agreements for the *collective* enforcement of stipulations as to re-sale prices were declared unlawful. But this declaration was balanced by a new sanction given to the *individual* enforcement of such stipulations.[2] By section 25 (1) of the Act,

> Restrictive Trade Practices Act 1956

" Where goods are sold by a supplier subject to a condition as to the price at which those goods may be re-sold, either generally or by or to a specified class or person, that condition may, subject to the provisions of this section, be enforced by the supplier against any person not party to the sale who subsequently acquires the goods with notice of the condition as if he had been party thereto."

Upon the language of this sub-section some observations must be made.[3] The word "condition," with its technical connotations, seems unfortunately chosen, and possible complications would have been avoided had the more colourless word " term " been used. The subsection is confined to stipulations as to the price of re-sale and does not cover terms regulating such matters as the use or display of goods. It is, moreover, to be read subject to the further provisions of the section, and in particular to those con-

---

1. *McGruther* v. *Pitcher,* [1904] 2 Ch. 306.
2. *Supra,* p. 326.
3. See Korah, 24 M.L.R. 219.

tained in section 25 (2) (a). It is here stated that the " condition " is not to be enforceable

> " in respect of the resale of any goods by a person who acquires those goods otherwise than for the purpose of resale in the course of business or by any person who acquires them, whether immediately or not, from such a person."

Once, therefore, the goods come into the hands of a person who does not propose to re-sell them, the right to sue third parties ceases and may not be revived. The word " notice," as used in section 25 (1), is ambiguous. Does it mean actual or constructive notice, or has it some esoteric meaning of its own? The question was considered in 1958 in *Goodyear Tyre Co.* v. *Lancashire Batteries, Ltd.*[1] The Court of Appeal were of opinion that, in the context of the Act, " notice " involved something less than " knowledge " but was not to be equated with the " constructive notice " familiar in the application of *Tulk* v. *Moxhay*. It meant, said Lord EVERSHED, " that the thing of which a man must have notice must be brought clearly to his attention." A plaintiff must prove that he had taken reasonable steps to give " sufficient " notice to the defendant. By a nice discrimination " sufficient " is to be distinguished from " constructive."

Resale Prices Act 1964

The Restrictive Trade Practices Act 1956 must now be read in the light of the Resale Prices Act 1964. By section 1 (1) of this latter Act,

> " any term or condition of a contract for the sale of goods by a supplier to a dealer, or of any agreement between a supplier and a dealer relating to such a sale, shall be void in so far as it purports to establish or provide for the establishment of minimum prices to be charged on the resale of the goods in the United Kingdom."

As such a term is thus declared to be void, it is obvious that it cannot be enforced by the supplier either against his own dealer or against any third party to the contract: there is, indeed, nothing to enforce. But section 1 (1) of the Resale Prices Act does not apply either in the unlikely event of a term providing for a maximum price, or where, under section 5 of this Act, the Restrictive Practices Court exempts from the operation of section 1 any particular class of goods. The scope of section 25 (1) of the Restrictive Trade Practices Act 1956 is therefore now confined to these two exceptional instances.[2]

---

1. [1958] 3 All E.R. 7; [1958] 1 W.L.R. 655, at p. 657; Wedderburn, [1958] C.L.J. 163.
2. See *supra*, p. 319.

CHAPTER TWO

Privity of Contract under the Law of Agency

SECTION I.   THE PLACE OF AGENCY IN ENGLISH LAW

Wide mean-
ing of
" agency "

" AGENCY " is a comprehensive word which is used to describe the relationship that arises where one man is appointed to act as the representative of another. The act to be done may vary widely in nature. It may for example be the making of a contract, the institution of an action, the conveyance of land or, in the case of a power of attorney, the exercise of any proprietary right available to the employer himself. The following account, however, is solely concerned with the case where the agent purports to enter into a contract on behalf of his principal.

The two
aspects
of agency

Regarded from this aspect, an agency agreement is one by which the agent is authorized to establish privity of contract between his employer, called the principal, and a third party.[1] It produces effects of two quite different kinds.

(i) As a
special
contract

First, it creates an obligation between the principal and the agent, under which each acquires in regard to the other certain rights and liabilities. In this respect agency takes its place as one of the special contracts of English law, such as the contract for the sale of goods or for the hire of a chattel.

(ii) As
leading to
privity
between
principal
and third
party

Secondly, when acted upon by the agent, it leads to the creation of privity of contract between the principal and the third party. A contract made with a third party by the agent in the exercise of his authority is enforceable both by and against the principal. Thus the English doctrine is that an agent may make a contract for his principal which has the same consequences as if the latter had made it himself. In other words the general rule is not only that the principal acquires rights and liabilities, but also that the agent drops out and ceases to be a party to the contract. To this extent, therefore, the fundamental rule that a person cannot be affected, either beneficially or adversely, by a contract to which he is not a party, is considerably diminished in its area of operation. The significance of this doctrine is apparent if it is compared with the rule of Roman law upon the subject.[2]

Agent and
independent
contractor
distin-
guished

The question sometimes arises whether a man has acted as an agent or as an independent contractor in his own interest.[3] The latter is a person who is his own master in the sense that he is employed to bring about a given result in his own manner and not according to orders given to him from time to time by his employer. Thus it is obvious that a retailer A, who in response to an order from a customer B, buys goods from a wholesaler C and then re-sells them to B, is acting as an independent contractor. He is a middleman, not the agent of B.

---

1. " The essential characteristic of an agent is that he is invested with a legal power to alter his principal's legal relations with third parties; the principal is under a correlative liability to have his legal relations altered ": Dowrick, 17 M.L.R. 36.
2. Nicholas, *Introduction to Roman Law,* pp. 201–204.
3. Fridman, 84 L.Q.R. 224.

But in other situations it may be a difficult matter to decide whether a person is acting as agent or as independent contractor. What, for example is the position in the case of a hire-purchase transaction where a dealer sells goods to a finance company which then lets them out on hire to the hire-purchaser? Is the dealer the agent of the finance company? Parliament has provided that he shall be deemed the agent of the company (a) as regards any representations concerning the goods made by him in the course of negotiations with the hirer to induce or promote the agreement; (b) for the purpose of receiving notice that the offer to enter the agreement is withdrawn; (c) for the purpose of receiving notice that the agreement is rescinded.[1] But the question whether the dealer is to be regarded in general as the agent of the finance company remains unsettled. Two views have been expressed. On the one hand, PEARSON, L.J., in his judgment in *Financings, Ltd.* v. *Stimson*[2] denied that any general rule could be laid down, and repeated the denial in *Mercantile Credit Co., Ltd.* v. *Hamblin.*[3]

Position of dealer in a hire-purchase contract

> " There is no rule of law that in a hire-purchase transaction the dealer never is, or always is, acting as agent for the finance company or as agent for the customer. In a typical hire-purchase transaction the dealer is a party in his own right, selling his car to the finance company, and he is acting primarily on his own behalf and not as general agent for either of the other two parties. There is no need to attribute to him an agency in order to account for his participation in the transaction. Nevertheless the dealer is to some extent an intermediary between the customer and the finance company, and he may well have in a particular case some *ad hoc* agencies to do particular things on behalf of one or the other or it may be both of these two parties."

On the other hand, Lord DENNING and Lord Justice DONOVAN in *Financings, Ltd.* v. *Stimson* considered the dealer in fact and in law to be the agent for many purposes of the finance company.[4]

In *Branwhite* v. *Worcester Works Finance*[5] the House of Lords discussed the general position of the dealer. The discussion was not strictly necessary to the decision of the case, and divergent views were expressed. Lord MORRIS, Lord GUEST and Lord UPJOHN[6] approved the opinion give by Lord Justice PEARSON in *Mercantile Credit Co., Ltd.* v. *Hamblin.* Lord WILBERFORCE, with the concurrence of Lord REID, supported the opposing opinion of Lord DENNING and Lord Justice DONOVAN in *Financings, Ltd.* v. *Stimson*, and set the question against the mercantile background of hire-purchase transactions.[7]

> " Such questions as arise of the vicarious responsibility of finance companies for acts or defaults of dealers cannot be resolved without reference to the general mercantile structure within which they arise,

---

1. Hire-Purchase Act 1964, sections 10 and 11; Hire-Purchase Act 1965, sections 12 (2) and (3) and see now Consumer Credit Act 1974, ss. 56 (2), 57 (3), 69 (6), 102 (1), 175.
2. [1962] 3 All E.R. 386; [1962] 1 W.L.R. 1184.
3. [1965] 2 Q.B. 242, at p. 269; [1964] 3 All E.R. 592, at pp. 600–1.
4. [1962] 3 All E.R. 386; [1962] 1 W.L.R. 1184.
5. [1969] 1 A.C. 552; [1968] 3 All E.R. 104.
6. [1969] 1 A.C., at pp. 573, 574, 576; [1968] 3 All E.R. 104, at pp. 113 and 115.
7. *Ibid.*, at pp. 586–7 and 121–2 respectively.

or, if one prefers the expression, to mercantile reality. This has become well known and widely understood by the public as well as by the commercial interests involved. . . . So far from thinking first of a purchase from the dealer and then separately, of obtaining finance from an outside source, the identity or even existence of the finance company or bank which is going to provide the money is a matter to [the customers] of indifference; they look to the dealer, or his representative, as the person who fixes the payment terms and makes all the necessary arrangements. . . . If this is so, a general responsibility of the finance company for the acts, receipts and omissions of the dealer in relation to the proposed transaction of hire-purchase ought to flow from this structure of relationship and expectation, built up from accepted custom and methods of dealing; a general responsibility which requires to be displaced by evidence of particular circumstances rather than to be positively established in each individual case."

Until a final choice between these views is authoritatively made by the House of Lords it is submitted that the presumption of agency favoured by Lord DENNING, Lord Justice DONOVAN and Lord WILBERFORCE is, in the latter's words more consistent with " mercantile reality " and is to be preferred.[1]

Alternatively, it may be clear that A is an agent but obscure for which of two parties he acts. Thus an agent employed by an insurance company to solicit business is undoubtedly an agent of the company for some purposes but it was held in *Newsholme Brothers* v. *Road Transport and General Insurance Co., Ltd.*[2] that where he helped the insured to complete the proposal form, he acted as agent for the insured. This means that the insured will be liable for misrepresentation or non-disclosure where he tells the agent the truth but the agent records his statement inaccurately on the form. Granted that the insured will normally regard communication to the agent as communication to the insurer and that the agent's commission is dependent on the proposal being acceptable to the insurer this has the makings of an unsatisfactory rule in practice. It is not surprising therefore that it has been rejected in Ghana,[3] reversed by legislation in Jamaica[4] and restrictively distinguished in England.[5]

Scope of the present inquiry

Of the two aspects of agency, only the second concerns a book purporting to deal with the general principles of contract law. We shall, therefore, consider the formation and termination of agency and also the position of third parties with whom the agent contracts, but shall omit all reference to the rights and liabilities of the principal and agent *inter se*.

---

1. Cf. Hughes, 27 M.L.R. 395.
2. [1929] 2 K.B. 356. This conclusion is often reinforced by clauses in the proposal form.
3. *Mohamed Hijazi* v. *New India Assurance Co., Ltd.* 1969 (1) African L.R. Comm. 7.
4. Insurance Act 1971, s. 74 (1).
5. *Stone* v. *Reliance Mutual Insurance Society, Ltd.,* [1972] 1 Lloyds Rep. 469; Reynolds, 88 L.Q.R. 462; followed with approval by Supreme Court of Canada in *Blanchette* v. *C.I.S., Ltd.* (1973), 36 D.L.R. (3d) 561.

SECTION II.   FORMATION OF AGENCY

The relationship of principal and agent may arise in any one of five ways: by express appointment, by virtue of the doctrine of estoppel, by the subsequent ratification by the principal of a contract made on his behalf without any authorization from him, by implication of law in cases where it is urgently necessary that one man should act on behalf of another, and by presumption of law in the case of cohabitation.

A.   EXPRESS APPOINTMENT

Except in one case no formality, such as writing, is required for the valid appointment of an agent. An oral appointment is effective. This is so even though the contract which the agent is authorized to make is one that is required by law to be evidenced by writing, such as a contract to buy or to take a lease of land. Thus if an agent appointed orally signs a contract in his own name for the purchase of land, the principal can give parol evidence to show the existence of the agency, and can then enforce the contract against either the agent or the vendor.[1]

Informal appointment sufficient

The one exception is where the authority of the agent is to execute a deed on behalf of the principal, in which case the agency itself must be created by deed. The agent, in other words, must be given a power of attorney. Instances of transactions for which a deed is necessary are conveyances of land, leases exceeding three years, and the transfer of a share in a British ship. So if an agent is authorized to execute a conveyance of land to a purchaser, he must be appointed by deed, but this is not necessary if his authority is merely to enter into a contract for the sale of the land.

Authority to execute a deed must be given by deed

B.   AGENCY BY ESTOPPEL

The subject of agency by estoppel may be introduced by a quotation from Lord CRANWORTH:

> " No one can become the agent of another person except by the will of that person. His will may be manifested in writing, or orally or simply by placing another in a situation in which according to the ordinary rules of law, or perhaps it would be more correct to say, according to the ordinary usages of mankind, that other is understood to represent and act for the person who has so placed him. . . . This proposition, however, is not at variance with the doctrine that where one has so acted as from his conduct to lead another to believe that he has appointed someone to act as his agent, and knows that that other person is about to act on that belief, then, unless he interposes, he will in general be estopped from disputing the agency, though in fact no agency really existed . . . Another proposition to be kept constantly in view is, that the burden of proof is on the person dealing with anyone as an agent, through whom he seeks to charge another as principal. He must

---

1. *Heard* v. *Pilley* (1869), 4 Ch. App. 548.

show that the agency did exist, and that the agent had the authority he assumed to exercise, or otherwise that the principal is estopped from disputing it."[1]

Apparent agency as effective as agency expressly created

While, therefore, a person cannot be bound as principal by a contract made without his authority, yet if the proved result of his conduct is that A appears to be his agent and makes a contract with a third person who relies on that appearance, he may be estopped from denying the existence of the authority. An apparent or ostensible agency is as effective as an agency deliberately created. Appearance and reality are one.

Examples of agency by estoppel

If, for instance, a member of a partnership retires without notifying the public, he will be bound by contracts made by the remaining partners with persons who had previously had dealings with the firm or who were aware of his membership, provided, of course, that they had no notice of his retirement.[2] A retiring member must give reasonable public notice of his retirement, or he will be guilty of conduct calculated to induce others to rely on his credit. Again, if P has been accustomed to accept and to pay for goods bought on his behalf by A from X, he may be liable for a purchase made in the customary manner, even though it is made by A fraudulently after he has left his employment.[3] In such a case A would appear to X to retain his former authority. Or suppose that a husband has for several years paid for articles of luxury bought by his wife at X's shop and then forbids her to pledge his credit any further in this manner; it cannot be doubted that, failing an express warning to X, he will be liable as principal if she makes similar contracts in the future.[4]

In all these cases a person who has no authority whatever to represent another is nevertheless regarded as an apparent agent. But, as we shall see later, the doctrine of estoppel, employed here to create the relationship of principal and agent, plays an even more important part where a regularly constituted agent exceeds his actual authority.[5]

C.   RATIFICATION

Statement of the rule

If A, without any precedent authority whatsoever, purports to contract with X for and on behalf of P, and later P ratifies and adopts the contract, the relationship of principal and agent arises between P and A.

" In that case the principal is bound by the act whether it be for his detriment or advantage, and whether it is founded on a tort or a contract, and with all the consequences which follow from the same act done by his authority."[6]

---

1. *Pole* v. *Leask* (1863), 33 L.J. Ch. 155, at pp. 161–2. See also *Spiro* v. *Lintern,* [1973] 3 All E.R. 319; [1973] 1 W.L.R. 1002.
2. *Scarf* v. *Jardine* (1882), 7 App. Cas. 345, *per* Lord SELBORNE, at p. 349.
3. *Summers* v. *Solomon* (1857), 26 L.J.Q.B. 301. This case was distinguished in *Hambro* v. *Burnand,* [1903] 2 K.B. 399.
4. *Debenham* v. *Mellon* (1880), 5 Q.B.D. 394, at p. 403.
5. *Infra,* pp. 478 *et seq.*
6. *Wilson* v. *Tumman* (1843), 6 Man. & G. 236, at p. 242.

If a principal ratifies part of a contract he is taken to have ratified it *in toto*. He cannot select such of its provision as may operate to his advantage.[1] The ratification relates back to the contract made by A, and both X and P are in exactly the same position as if P had been the original contracting party. *Omnis ratihabitio retrotrahitur ac priori mandato aequiparatur.*

Ratification relates back to the contract of the agent

> Suppose that on May 1st, X offers to buy land from A who in fact is manager and agent of the property on behalf of P. On May 2nd, A accepts this offer on P's behalf though he has no actual or apparent authority to do so. On May 4th, X purports to revoke the offer; on May 10th, P ratifies the acceptance of A.

Here the ratification relates back to acceptance, *i.e.* to the moment when there was a finally concluded contract between X and A. It follows, therefore, that X's attempted revocation is inoperative as being too late, and that P is entitled to claim specific performance.[2] There can, however, be no ratification unless the offer has been unconditionally accepted, for, unless and until this is proved, no contract exists to be ratified. If A's acceptance on May 2nd was not absolute, but was expressly made subject to ratification by P, there would be no complete contract until P ratified, and a revocation by X before that date would be effective.[3]

The pre-requisites of ratification are as follows:

First, the person who makes the contract must profess at the time of making it to be acting on behalf of, and intending to bind, the person who subsequently ratifies the contract.[4] Ordinarily, the person making the contract will be required to name his professed principal, but it has been said to be sufficient if the principal, though not named, is " capable of being ascertained " at the time of the contract,[5] an expression which is presumably employed here to mean " identifiable." So understood, it would cover, for instance, the case of a person contracting " on behalf of my brother."[6] It is not, however, sufficient that

(i) Contract must be professedly made on behalf of the principal

---

1. *Cornwal* v. *Wilson* (1750), 1 Ves. Sen. 509; *Re Mawcon, Ltd.,* [1969] 1 W.L.R. 78, at p. 83, *per* PENNYCUICK, J.
2. *Bolton Partners* v. *Lambert* (1889), 41 Ch.D. 295. This case, though approved in *Lawson (Inspector of Taxes)* v. *Hosemaster, Ltd.,* [1966] 2 All E.R. 944; [1966] 1 W.L.R. 1300, was severely criticized by Fry in his *Specific Performance*, note A. He regards the contract between X and P as being one made without consensus. The court said that it was made when A accepted, but at that moment P had not consented to such a contract being made on his behalf. It was a contract made at the will of a stranger and without the will of one of the contracting parties. There is force in this criticism, though it is coloured by contemporary pre-occupation with the idea of consensus. It is true that the effect of the decision is to impose a liability upon X if P so wishes, while leaving P a free choice in the matter. The decision was also doubted by the Privy Council in *Fleming* v. *Bank of New Zealand,* [1900] A.C. 577, at p. 587.
3. *Watson* v. *Davies,* [1931] 1 Ch. 455; *Warehousing & Forwarding Co. of East Africa, Ltd.* v. *Jafferali & Sons, Ltd.,* [1964] A.C. 1; [1963] 3 All E.R. 571, P.C.
4. *Keighley, Maxsted & Co.* v. *Durant,* [1901] A.C. 240; *Imperial Bank of Canada* v. *Begley,* [1936] 2 All E.R. 367.
5. *Watson* v. *Swann* (1862), 11 C.B.N.S. 756, at p. 771, *per* WILLES, J.; *Keighley, Maxted & Co.* v. *Durant,* [1901] A.C. 240, at p. 255; *Eastern Construction Co., Ltd.* v. *National Trust Co., Ltd., and Schmidt,* [1914] A.C. 197, at p. 213.
6. " It is not necessary that he should be named but there must be such a description of him as shall amount to a reasonable designation of the person intended to be bound by the contract," *Watson,* v. *Swann, supra,* at p. 771, *per* WILLES, J.

the person contracting should merely indicate that he is acting as agent without more. He must name, or otherwise sufficiently identify, the person for whom he professes to act. *A fortiori*, if he makes no allusion to agency, but gives the appearance of contracting in his own right, the contract cannot later be adopted by another for whom in truth he intended to act. This primary requirement, that an agent should be obliged to advertise his intention, though now well established, is scarcely consistent with the earlier and equally well established doctrine of the undisclosed principal, under which a principal can enforce a contract made by an agent *with his authority* even though the existence of the agency was not disclosed to the other contracting party.[1] The doctrine of ratification may be anomalous, but it is difficult to appreciate why it should not apply to an agency which is not only unauthorized, but also undisclosed, if an undisclosed principal can avail himself of an authorized act. In *Keighley, Maxsted & Co.* v. *Durant*,[2] Lord JAMES, in repudiating this suggestion, said:

> " To establish that a man's thoughts unexpressed and unrecorded can form the basis of a contract so as to bind other persons and make them liable on a contract they never made with persons they never heard of seems a somewhat difficult task."

It is, however, a difficulty that has been readily surmounted by the law in its evolution of the doctrine of the undisclosed principal. In the *Keighley, Maxsted* case:

> A was authorized by P to buy wheat at 44s. 3d. a quarter on a joint account for himself and P. Wheat was unobtainable at this price, and therefore in excess of his authority he agreed to buy from X at 44s. 6d. a quarter. Though he intended to purchase on the joint account, A contracted in his own name and did not disclose the agency to X. The next day P ratified the purchase at the unauthorized price, but ultimately he and A failed to take delivery.

An action brought by X against P for breach of contract failed on the ground that the purchase had not been professedly made on his behalf. Apparently ignoring the doctrine of the undisclosed principal, Lord MACNAGHTEN remarked that " obligations are not to be created by, or founded upon, undisclosed intentions."

(ii) Must be competent principal at time of contract

The second condition of ratification is that at the time when the contract was made the agent must have had a competent principal.[3] This condition is not satisfied, for instance, if he purported to act on behalf of an alien enemy.[4] Nor is it satisfied if he purported to contract on behalf of a principal who at the time of the contract lacked legal personality, for rights and obligations cannot attach to a non-existent person. This is important in the case of contracts made on behalf of a company projected but not yet formed. ●

1. *Infra*, pp. 472–5.
2. [1901] A.C. 240.
3. *Kelner* v. *Baxter* (1866), L.R. 2 C.P. 174; *Scott* v. *Lord Ebury* (1867), L.R. 2 C.P. 255.
4. *Boston Deep Sea Fishing & Ice Co., Ltd.* v. *Farnham,* [1957] 3 All E.R. 204; [1957] 1 W.L.R. 1051.

If, for instance, it is proposed to form a motor garage company provided that a certain plot of land can be obtained, and A., purporting to act on behalf of the projected company, makes a contract for the purchase of the land, the contract cannot be ratified by the company upon its formation.

As ERLE, C.J., said in the leading case of *Kelner* v. *Baxter*:[1]

" When the company came afterwards into existence it was a totally new creature, having rights and obligations from that time, but no rights or obligations by reason of anything which might have been done before."

The proper course to adopt in the case of such a potential company is to provide that if the company is not registered by a certain date the contract shall be null and void, but that if it is so registered there shall be a transfer to it of the contractual rights and liabilities.

Whether a person who contracts on behalf of a non-existent principal is himself liable depends upon the circumstances. The fact that the principal when he comes into existence is not liable does not necessarily mean that the agent is in all cases an effective party to the contract. As was said in an Australian case:

" The fundamental question *in every case* must be what the parties intended or must be fairly understood to have intended."[2]

The agent may so conduct himself as to become a party, and if this is the common intention and if it does not contradict any written instrument, then, as in *Kelner* v. *Baxter*,[3] the contract is enforceable by and against him. But if there is nothing in the circumstances to show that he contracted personally, there is no rule which converts him automatically into a principal merely because at the time of the contract there was nobody else capable of being bound.[4] Thus in one case, a memorandum of a contract for the sale of goods by a company was signed by the sellers:

" Yours faithfully, Leopold Newborne (London), Ltd.,"

after which was written the name Leopold Newborne. On it appearing that the company was incapable of being a contracting party since it had not been registered when the memorandum was completed, it was held that Leopold Newborne himself could not sue the buyers for non-acceptance of the goods, since there was nothing to show that he intended himself to be the seller. The only contracting party was the company, and all that Newborne intended to do by the addition of his own name was to authenticate the signature of the company.[5] The position has been somewhat altered, though to an extent

---

1. (1866), L.R. 2 C.P., at p. 183.
2. *Summergreene* v. *Parker* (1950), 80 C.L.R. 304, at p. 323, *per* FULLAGER, J. See also *Black* v. *Smallwood* (1965–6), 39 A.L.J.R. 405. For a general discussion, see Baxt, 30 M.L.R. 328.
3. (1866), L.R. 2 C.P. 174.
4. *Hollman* v. *Pullin* (1884), 1 Cab. & El. 254; *Newborne* v. *Sensolid* (*Great Britain*), *Ltd.*, [1954] 1 Q.B. 45; [1953] 1 All E.R. 708.
5. *Newborne* v. *Sensolid* (*Great Britain*), *Ltd.*, *supra*, criticized by Gross, 87 L.Q.R. 367, at pp. 382–5.

that is not wholly clear, by s. 9 (2) of the European Communities Act 1972 which provides :[1]

> " Where a contract purports to be made by a company or by a person as agent for a company, at a time when the company has not been formed, then subject to any agreement to the contrary the contract shall have effect as a contract entered into by the person purporting to act for the company or as agent for it and he shall be personally liable on the contract accordingly."

It will be seen that this provision makes no change in the position of the company, which still cannot ratify the contract. It is clearly intended however to increase the number of cases where the agent is personally liable. How far it in fact does so will depend on the meaning given to the words " subject to any agreement to the contrary " since it could be argued that words showing that A signs as agent express an agreement that he is not to be personally liable. If this were correct *Newborne* v. *Sensolid (Great Britain), Ltd.* would still be decided the same way. But it may be suspected that the courts will try to give more content to the subsection.

(iii) Void contracts cannot be ratified

The third essential is that there should be an act capable of ratification. Any contract made by A professing to act on behalf of P is capable of ratification, even though A acted fraudulently and with intent to benefit himself alone,[2] provided, however, that it is a contract which P could validly have made. A contract that is void in its inception cannot be ratified. Thus, as we have seen in the case of corporations, the shareholders of a company cannot ratify an *ultra vires* contract made by the directors.[3] It would seem on principle that a forgery is incapable of ratification not because it is a legal nullity, as indeed it is, but because a forger does not profess to act as an agent. The question arose in *Brook* v. *Hook* :[4]

> P's name was forged by A to a joint and several promissory note for £20 purporting to be made by P and A in favour of X. In order to save A, P later signed the following memorandum:
>
> " I hold myself responsible for a bill dated November 7th for £20 bearing my signature and that of A."

What A had written in effect was: " Here is P's signature written by himself." He did not say or imply, " I make this note as agent of P." The majority of the court, therefore, repudiated the suggestion that P was liable as having ratified the contract of November 7th, for as KELLY, C.B., observed in an interlocutory remark: " The defendant could not ratify an act which did not profess to be done for him or on his account."[5]

---

1. See Prentice 89 L.Q.R. 518, at pp. 530–533; Farrar, and Powles, 36 M.L.R. 270 at p. 277.
2. *Re Tiedemann and Ledermann Frères,* [1899] 2 Q.B. 66.
3. *Supra,* p. 425.
4. (1871), L.R. 6 Exch. 89.
5. See also *per* Lord BLACKBURN in *M'Kenzie* v. *British Linen Co.* (1881), 6 App. Cas. 82, at p. 99.

D. AGENCY OF NECESSITY

There is a limited class of case in which, on the ground of urgent necessity, one person may be bound by a contract made by another on his behalf but without his authority. This doctrine, which the courts are reluctant to extend,[1] probably applies only where there is already some existing contractual relationship between the principal and the person who acts on his behalf, as there is for instance between the owner and the master of a ship. It is extremely doubtful whether a person can be bound by the act of a complete stranger.[2] It is well settled, however, that the master of a ship is entitled, in cases of accident and emergency, to enter into a contract which will bind the owners of the cargo, notwithstanding that it transcends his express authority, if it is *bona fide* made in the best interests of the owners concerned.[3] The same power is possessed by a land carrier in respect of perishable goods.[4]

Authority of masters of ships

A person who seeks to bind a principal on these grounds bears the onus of proving that the course adopted by the carrier was reasonably necessary in the circumstances, and also that it was practically impossible to communicate with the cargo owners.

E. PRESUMED AGENCY IN THE CASE OF COHABITATION

Marriage does not give the wife any innate power to bind her husband by contracts with third persons, but where she is living with him there is a presumption, though no more, that she is entitled to pledge his credit for necessaries which are suitable to his style of living and which fall within the domestic department usually confided to the care of the wife.[5]

Presumptive right of wife to pledge husband's credit for household necessaries

> " There is a presumption that she has such authority in the sense that a tradesman, supplying her with necessaries upon her husband's credit and suing him, makes out a *prima facie* case against him, upon proof of that fact and of the cohabitation. But this is a mere presumption of fact founded upon the supposition that wives cohabiting with their husbands ordinarily have authority to manage in their own way certain departments of the household expenditure, and to pledge their husband's credit in respect of matters coming within those departments."[6]

The presumption applies equally in the case of a woman living with a man as his mistress.[7]

---

1. *Munro* v. *Willmott*, [1949] 2 K.B. 295; [1948] 2 All E.R. 983.
2. *Jebara* v. *Ottoman Bank*, [1927] 2 K.B. 254, at p. 271, *per* SCRUTTON, L.J.
3. *The Argos* (1873), L.R. 5 P.C. 134; *Notara* v. *Henderson* (1872), L.R. 7 Q.B. 225.
4. *Sims* v. *Midland Rail. Co.*, [1913] 1 K.B. 103, at p. 112; *Sachs* v. *Miklos*, [1948] 2 K.B. 23, at p. 35; [1948] 1 All E.R. 67. The wife's agency of necessity was abolished by Matrimonial Proceedings and Property Act 1970, s. 41.
5. *Debenham* v. *Mellon* (1880), 6 App. Cas. 24, at p. 36; *Miss Gray, Ltd.* v. *Earl of Cathcart* (1922), 38 T.L.R. 562.
6. *Debenham* v. *Mellon* (1880), 5 Q.B.D. 394, at p. 402, *per* THESIGER, L.J.
7. *Ryan* v. *Sams* (1848), 12 Q.B. 460.

Meaning of
" neces-
saries "

Necessaries for this purpose have been authoritatively defined
as " things that are really necessary and suitable to the style in
which the husband chooses to live, in so far as the articles fall
fairly within the domestic department which is ordinarily confided
to the management of the wife."[1] It is the ostensible not the
justifiable mode of living that sets the standard, and if a husband
chooses to live beyond his means his liability may be correspondingly increased.[2] Necessaries include clothing, both for the wife
and her children, articles of household equipment, food, medicines
and medical attendance, and the hiring of servants. The liability
of the husband, however, is always subject to the proviso that
the goods are suitable and reasonable not only in kind but also
in quantity. An action cannot be maintained against him in
respect of extravagant orders.[3]

Onus of
proof lies
on the
tradesman

The tradesman bears the burden of proving affirmatively to
the satisfaction of the court that the goods supplied to the wife
are necessaries.[4] If he is unable to do this, as for instance where
the goods consist of jewels[5] or articles of luxury such as a gold
pencil case or a guitar,[6] his only action lies against the wife, unless
he can show an express or implied assent by the husband to the
contract.

> " If a tradesman is about to trust a married woman for what are
> not necessaries, and to an extent beyond what her station in life
> requires, he ought in common prudence to enquire of the husband
> is she has his consent for the order she is giving."[7]

It was held in 1870 that a judge may withdraw a case from a jury
if he considers that there is no reasonable evidence upon which
they could classify the goods as necessaries.[8]

How the
presumption
may be
rebutted

Even where the goods, however, are undoubtedly necessaries
the husband is only presumptively liable, and he may rebut the
presumption and so escape liability. The presumption is rebutted
if he proves that he expressly warned the tradesman not to supply
goods on credit; that his wife was already supplied with sufficient
articles of that kind[9] or with a sufficient allowance with which to
purchase them;[10] or that he had expressly forbidden her to pledge
his credit.[11] The reason why an express prohibition not communicated to the tradesman is a sufficient rebuttal is that the
right of a wife to bind her husband rests solely upon the law of
agency and, as we have seen, no one can occupy the position of a
principal against his will. At the same time it is important to
observe that if the husband has held his wife out in the past to
the plaintiff so as to invest her with apparent authority under the

---

1. *Phillipson v. Hayter* (1870), L.R. 6 C.P. 38, *per* WILLES, J., at p. 42.
2. *Waithman v. Wakefield* (1807), 1 Camp. 120.
3. *Lane v. Ironmonger* (1844), 13 M. & W. 368.
4. *Phillipson v. Hayter* (1870), L.R. 6 C.P. 38, at p. 42.
5. *Montague v. Benedict* (1825), 3 B. & C. 631.
6. *Phillipson v. Hayter, supra*, footnote 4.
7. *Montague v. Benedict*, (1825), 3 B. & C. 631, at p. 636, *per* BAYLEY, J.
8. *Phillipson v. Hayter* (1870), L.R. 6 C.P. at p. 40.
9. *Seaton v. Benedict* (1828), 5 Bing. 28.
10. *Morel Brothers & Co., Ltd. v. Earl of Westmorland*, [1904] A.C. 11.
11. *Jolly v. Rees* (1863), 15 C.B.N.S. 628.

doctrine of estoppel, a mere private prohibition addressed solely to her will not relieve him from liability in respect of her future purchases of a similar nature. In such a case it is his duty to convey an express warning to the tradesman.

SECTION III. POSITION OF PRINCIPAL AND AGENT WITH REGARD TO THIRD PARTIES

The question to be considered here is whether the principal or the agent is capable of suing, or of being sued, by the third party with whom the agent has completed the contract. The position of the agent with regard to such a third party varies according to the circumstances. Presuming that the agent is authorized to make the contract, there are three possible cases.

Three cases to be considered

First, the agent may not only disclose to the third party the fact that he is a mere agent, but may also name his principal.

Secondly, he may disclose the fact of the agency but withhold the name of the principal.

(i) Agency and name of principal disclosed

Thirdly, he may conceal both facts, in which case the third party will believe, contrary to the truth, that the agent is himself the principal and that nobody else is interested in the contract.

(ii) Agency alone disclosed

(iii) Agency not disclosed

In considering the question whether the principal or the agent is a competent party to litigation the courts have gradually evolved certain general rules which vary with each of these three cases. The *prima facie* rule is, for instance, that if the contract is made for a named principal, then the principal *alone* can sue or be sued. It is important, however, to recognize at once that these rules are of a purely general character—mere rebuttable presumptions that are capable of being displaced by proof that the parties intended otherwise. Too much force must not be attributed to them, for at bottom the question whether the agent or the principal is competent to sue or to be sued is one of construction dependent *inter alia* upon the form of the contract between the agent and the third party. In short, the intention of the parties, so far as it appears from the circumstances, is decisive, but if no clear intention is evident then the question is determined by certain general principles that have been laid down to meet the three different cases.

Whether the contract is that of the principal or agent is a matter of intention

Our discussion of the matter is based upon the following classification:

A. The agent has authority and is known to be an agent, and his principal is (1) named; (2) not named.

B. The agent has authority in fact but he does not disclose the existence of the agency.

A. THE AGENT HAS AUTHORITY AND IS KNOWN TO BE AN AGENT

1. HIS PRINCIPAL IS NAMED

As a general rule principal alone can sue and be sued

The general rule in this case is traditionally stated as follows:

> " The contract is the contract of the principal, not that of the agent, and *prima facie* at common law the only person who can sue is the principal and the only person who can be sued is the principal."[1]

Normally the agent possesses neither rights[2] nor liabilities[3] with regard to third parties. This general rule, however, though constantly repeated, is, as we have said, far from inflexible. It

Rule may be expressly excluded

may be excluded by the express intention of the parties. In the words of WRIGHT, J.:

> " Also, and this is very important, in all cases the parties can by their express contract provide that the agent shall be the person liable either concurrently with or to the exclusion of the principal, or that the agent shall be the party to sue either concurrently with or to the exclusion of the principal."[4]

Thus, an agent may sue or be sued upon a written contract in which he states: " I for my own self contract," though, of course, the principal also remains liable and entitled.[5]

So too cases have arisen where a seller, when asked by an agent to supply goods to a named principal, refuses to do so unless the agent assumes sole liability for payment. In such a case, of course, the agent makes himself liable if he accepts the condition, and the seller cannot afterwards charge the principal. The judges have sometimes explained the position by saying that the seller is held to an election made at a time when he was free to choose between the one party and the other.[6]

Rule may be implicitly excluded

Further, the intention to make the agent a party may be inferred as well as expressed, and it is purely a question of construction in each case, dependent upon the form and terms of the particular contract and upon the surrounding circumstances, whether such an intention is disclosed.

> " The intention for which the court looks is an objective intention of both parties, based on what two businessmen making a contract of that nature, in those terms and those surrounding circumstances must be taken to have intended."[7]

---

1. *Montgomerie* v. *United Kingdom Steamship Association*, [1891] 1 Q.B. 370, at p. 371, *per* WRIGHT, J.
2. *Fairlie* v. *Fenton* (1870), L.R. 5 Exch. 169.
3. *Paquin* v. *Beauclerk*, [1906] A.C. 148.
4. *Montgomerie* v. *United Kingdom Steamship Association*, [1891] 1 Q.B. 370, at p. 372.
5. *Fisher* v. *Marsh* (1865), 6 B. & S. 411, at p. 415, *per* BLACKBURN, J.
6. *Calder* v. *Dobell* (1871), L.R. 6 C.P. 486, at p. 494, citing *Addison* v. *Gandasequi* (1812), 4 Taunt. 574; *Paterson* v. *Gandasequi* (1812), 15 East 62.
7. *The Swan*, [1968] 1 Lloyd's Rep. 5, at p. 12, *per* BRANDON, J.

The tenor of the decisions is that if a man signs a contract in his own name without any qualification, something very strong indeed on the face of the contract is needed to exclude his personal liability[1]; but if his signature is qualified by such expressions as " on account of," " for and on behalf of " or " as agent," his personal liability is certainly negatived.[2]

To infer the intention of parties is seldom a simple matter, but in this particular context the chief sources of enlightenment are, first, the description of the parties in the body of the contract and, secondly, the signature of the agent.

Guides to the intention of the parties

If in *both* places the agent is referred to as agent, it is almost impossible to regard him as a contracting party; but if in neither place is there any mention of the agency, it is almost impossible to deny that he is a contracting party.

If he is described as agent in one part of the contract only, whether in the body or in the signature, it is presumed that he is not a contracting party, but the presumption may be rebutted from the context.

2. HIS PRINCIPAL IS NOT NAMED

Does the mere non-disclosure of the name of the principal vary the position of the parties? Once more the general rule is that the agent drops out, but once more whether he does so or not depends essentially upon the intention of the parties. It is still a question of construction, dependent *inter alia* upon the form of the contract or the nature of the agent's business, whether they intended that the agent should possess rights and liabilities. Where, however, the name of the principal has not been disclosed an intention that the agent shall be a contracting party will more readily be inferred. Obviously, where there has been no such disclosure, greater significance is to be attached to the rule already cited that, if a man signs a contract in his own name, there must be something very strong on the face of the contract to deprive him of rights and liabilities. But the contract is construed according to its natural meaning and, if it clearly shows that the agent must have been understood to have contracted merely as an agent, then, despite the fact that the principal for whom he acted has not been named, effect is given to the natural meaning of the words, and he drops out of the transaction.

Position of the parties depends upon intention

The position may be illustrated by the case of *Southwell* v. *Bowditch*:[3]

Position illustrated by *Southwell* v. *Bowditch*

A broker issued a contract note couched in these terms:

" Messrs. Southwell. I have this day sold by your order to my principals, etc. 1 per cent. brokerage.

(Signed) W. A. Bowditch."

---

1. *Cooke* v. *Wilson* (1856), 1 C.B.N.S. 153, at p. 162, *per* CRESSWELL, J. *Gadd* v. *Houghton* (1876), 1 Ex. D. 357, at p. 360.
2. *Gadd* v. *Houghton, supra*; *Universal Steam Navigation Co., Ltd.* v. *James McKelvie & Co.*, [1923] A.C. 492; *Lester* v. *Balfour Williamson Merchant Shippers, Ltd.*, [1953] 2 Q.B. 168; [1953] 1 All E.R. 1146. It is a little difficult to reconcile *The Swan*, [1968] 1 Lloyd's Rep. 5, with these authorities; see Legh-Jones, 32 M.L.R. 327; *contra*, Reynolds, 85 L.Q.R. 92.
3. (1876), 1 C.P.D. 374.

It will be observed that the defendant, though referring to principals, signed this contract in his own name without any additional words to show that he signed in the capacity of agent, but nevertheless it was held that he was not personally liable for the price of the goods sold. In the course of his judgment Jessel, M.R., said:

> " There is nothing whatever on the contract to show that the defendant intended to act otherwise than as broker. No doubt it does not absolutely follow from the defendant appearing on the contract to be a broker that he is not liable as principal. There are two ways in which he might so be made liable: first, intention on the face of the contract making the agent liable as well as the principal; secondly, usage."

Special cases

Exceptional cases where agent is a contracting party

Whether the principal has been named or not, there are three exceptional cases in each of which the position of the agent is determined by special rules. These are where the agent executes a deed in his own name; where he puts his name to a negotiable instrument; and where there is some relevant trade usage. We will take these cases separately.[1]

(i) Contracts under seal

(i) If agent contracts under seal, he alone liable and entitled

If an agent makes a contract *under seal* on behalf of another it has long been established that he is personally liable and entitled under it, and that the principal has neither rights nor obligations.[2] This is what is called a " technical rule," *i.e.*, to quote the words of Martin, B., a rule " which is established by authority and precedent, which does not depend upon reasoning or argument, but is a fixed established rule to be acted upon, and only discussed as regards its application."[3]

Power of attorney is an exception

It formerly produced this inconvenient result, that a man who gave a power of attorney to another in order, for instance, that his affairs might be administered during his absence or illness, could neither sue nor be sued upon contracts made under its authority if they were made by deed. This particular inconvenience has, however, been removed by legislation.[4]

Principal can sue if agent is his trustee

The technical rule, however, is subject to this limitation, that if the agent enters into a sealed contract as *trustee* for the principal, whether the trust is disclosed on the face of the contract or not, and he refuses to enforce it against the other party, then the principal, *qua* beneficiary, may himself enforce any proprietary right to which he is entitled by bringing an action against the

---

1. Some of these cases may occur when the agent is acting for an undisclosed principal, but as this is not likely to happen in practice, it seems more convenient to deal with them here. It was formerly thought that a fourth exceptional case is where an agent contracts on behalf of a foreign principal; *infra*, pp. 470–1.
2. *Re International Contract Co., Pickering's Claim* (1871), 6 Ch. App. 525; *Schack* v. *Anthony* (1813), 1 M. & S. 573.
3. *Chesterfield Colliery Co.* v. *Hawkins* (1865), 3 H. & C. 677, at pp. 691–2.
4. Law of Property Act 1925, s. 123.

third party and the agent.[1] It would seem to follow that in such a case the principal is equally liable to be sued by the third party.

(ii) Negotiable instruments

An agent contracts no personal liability under a negotiable instrument in the issue of which he is implicated unless he adds his name as a party to it; but if he does appear as a party then his liability depends upon whether he signs as acceptor or in some other capacity such as drawer or endorser.

Where he appears as acceptor the crucial question is whether the bill is drawn on him or not. If it is drawn on him in his own name, his acceptance renders him personally liable even though he adds words to his signature describing himself as agent. To escape liability he must add words indicating that he is acting in a purely ministerial capacity.[2] In one case, for instance, Charles, the agent of a company, wrote the following across the face of a bill which had been drawn on him, not on the company:

"Accepted for the company. W. Charles. Purser."

It was held that he was personally liable.[3]

If, however, the bill is not drawn on the agent, his acceptance, even though unqualified, does not render him liable.[4] Thus, for instance, if a bill is drawn on a company, the directors incur no personal liability if they write the following on the instrument:

"Accepted. X and Y, directors of the company."

Where an agent draws or endorses a negotiable instrument the position is as follows. If he signs his name without any qualification he is personally liable.[5] If he adds a qualification there are two classes of cases. A qualification which clearly indicates that he is contracting as agent for another, as, for example, where he writes: "For and on behalf of Jones, as agent," relieves him of personal liability;[6] but an ambiguous qualification, which leaves it doubtful whether he is acting in a purely representative capacity or not, renders him liable. The endorsement, for instance, "X and Y, Directors," will render X and Y liable, for the word "Directors" does not necessarily show that they were acting as agents, but may equally well have been used to explain why their names appeared on the bill at all.[7]

(iii) Trade usage

The position of an agent as a contracting party may be determined by a trade usage. In one case, for instance, X and Y,

Margin notes:

(ii) Where agent is a party to a negotiable instrument

Bill accepted by agent

Bill drawn or endorsed by agent

(iii) Trade usage

---

1. *Harmer* v. *Armstrong*, [1934] 1 Ch. 65; [1933] All E.R. Rep. 778. In such a case the rights and liabilities of the parties are governed by the doctrine discussed, *supra*, pp. 439 *et seq.*
2. Bills of Exchange Act 1882, s. 26.
3. *Mare* v. *Charles* (1856), 5 E. & B. 978.
4. *Stacey & Co., Ltd.* v. *Wallis* (1912), 106 L.T. 544.
5. *The Elmville*, [1904] P. 319.
6. *Elliott* v. *Bax-Ironside*, [1925] 2 K.B. 301, at p. 307, *per* SCRUTTON, L.J.
7. *Rew* v. *Pettet* (1834), 1 Ad. & El. 196; *Elliott* v. *Bax-Ironside, supra.*

who were brokers in the Colonial fruit trade, signed the following contract:

> " We have this day sold for your account to our principal, etc.
>
> (Signed) X and Y, Brokers."

The principal, whose name was disclosed before delivery, refused to accept the whole of the goods, and an action for non-acceptance succeeded against the agent on proof of a custom in the fruit trade that a broker was personally liable if the name of the principal was not inserted in the written contract.[1] A custom, however, is disregarded if it is inconsistent with the contract.[2]

Foreign principal

Contract by agent on behalf of foreign principal

One of the trade usages established by the law merchant was that a person who contracted as agent for a foreign principal was to be regarded as having contracted as principal to the exclusion of the foreigner. In 1873, BLACKBURN, J., said:

> " Where a foreigner has instructed English merchants to act for him, I take it that the usage of trade established for many years has been that it is understood that the foreign constituent has not authorized the merchants to establish privity between him and the home supplier. On the other hand, the home supplier, knowing that to be the usage, unless there is something in the bargain showing the intention to be otherwise, does not trust the foreigner, and so does not make the foreigner responsible to him and does not make himself responsible to the foreigner."[3]

Modern effect of foreign nationality of principal

The law merchant, however, is not immutable, and with the vast increase in international trade this particular usage has steadily waned in importance and has now disappeared. As long ago as 1917, its continued existence was doubted by such an experienced judge as BRAY, J.,[4] and its final extinction has now been confirmed.[5] In every case, foreign element or no foreign element, the question whether the agent becomes a party to the contract or whether privity of contract has been created between his principal and the third party must be determined in the light of the intention of the parties as disclosed by the terms of the contract and the surrounding circumstances. The nationality or domicil of the principal is merely one of those circumstances, and even so it is only of minimal importance. The statement of Lord BLACKBURN no longer represents the law.[6] A case in which the intention of the parties was disclosed by the terms of the contract itself was *Miller, Gibb &*

---

1. *Fleet* v. *Murton* (1871), L.R. 7 Q.B. 126.
2. *Barrow and Brothers* v. *Dyster, Nalder & Co.* (1884), 13 Q.B.D. 635.
3. *Elbinger Act. Für Fabrication von Eisenbahn Materiel* v. *Claye* (1873), L.R. 8 Q.B. 313, at p. 317. See authorities there cited.
4. *Miller, Gibb & Co.* v. *Smith and Tyrer, Ltd.*, [1917] 2 K.B. 141; see also *H. O. Brandt* v. *H. N. Morris & Co.*, [1917] 2 K.B. 784, at p. 797.
5. *Teheran-Europe Co., Ltd.* v. *S. T. Belton (Tractors), Ltd.*, [1968] 2 Q.B. 53; affirmed, [1968] 2 Q.B. 545; [1968] 2 All E.R. 886. See Hudson, 29 M.L.R. 353.
6. *Holt and Moseley (London), Ltd.* v. *Cunningham Partners* (1949), 83 Ll. L. Rep. 141, at p. 145; *Rusholme, Bolton and Roberts, Hadfield, Ltd.* v. *S. G. Read & Co. (London), Ltd.*, [1955] 1 All E.R. 180; [1955] 1 W.L.R. 146, 150, where the foreign principal was undisclosed; *Teheran-Europe Co., Ltd.*, v. *S. T. Belton (Tractors), Ltd.*, *supra*.

Co. v. *Smith and Tyrer, Ltd.*,[1] where the facts were these: A firm called Smith & Tyrer, Ltd., executed the following instrument on behalf of a foreign principal:

> Contract by which our principals sell through the agency of Smith & Tyrer, Ltd., wood brokers, Liverpool, and Messrs. Miller, Gibb & Co., of Liverpool, buy, etc.
>
> (Signed) By authority of our principals
>
> SMITH & TYRER, LTD.,
>
> CHAS. H. TYRER, managing director,
> as agents.

The Court of Appeal had no difficulty in holding that the intention was to exclude the personal liability of the agents.

> " It seems to me difficult for the parties to have used clearer words to show that the principals were to be liable and the agents were not to be liable. . . . The agents were not professing to contract at all, the principals were; and the agents state expressly that they have authority from their principals to sign the contract."[2]

Indeed, to have denied that the agents had acted in a purely representative capacity would have flatly contradicted the tenor of the instrument.

Where agent is in fact principal

It remains to consider a peculiar situation that may arise where a man, though purporting to be an agent, is in fact himself the principal. Here there is no doubt that he is personally liable.[3] This seems to be commonsense. As SCRUTTON, L.J., once remarked " I am sure it is justice. It is probably the law for that reason."[4]

If the supposed agent is in fact the principal he may be sued

Moreover the agent in such a case can himself enforce the contract, provided that the supposed principal has not been named and also that the terms of the contract show that the identity of the party is not material. This was decided in *Schmaltz* v. *Avery*,[5] where the facts were these:

If supposed principal not named agent may sue

> A charterparty was executed between X, the owner of the ship, and A, which expressly stated that A was acting as agent of the freighters. It contained these words: " This charterparty, being concluded on behalf of another party, it is agreed that all responsibility on the part of A shall cease as soon as the cargo is shipped." Actually A was himself the freighter, and he later brought an action against X.

It was argued that the action would not lie, since X had relied for the fulfilment of the contract upon the undisclosed freighters with whom he believed himself to be dealing. This argument failed and the action was allowed. It was obvious, in accordance with the doctrine of the undisclosed principal, that the freighters, if they had actually existed, could have enforced the contract. The only question was whether one person can fill the characters both of principal and agent, or rather, whether he can repudiate

1. [1917] 2 K.B. 141.
2. [1917] 2 K.B., at p. 163, *per* BRAY, J.
3. *Jenkins* v. *Hutchinson* (1849), 13 Q.B. 744, at p. 752, *per* Lord DENMAN.
4. *Gardiner* v. *Heading,* [1928] 2 K.B. 284.
5. (1851), 16 Q.B. 655; followed in *Harper* v. *Vigers,* [1909] 2 K.B. 549.

that of agent and assume that of principal. It is no doubt true that the identity of the other party is often a matter of vital importance, but in this case the court was of opinion that as the name of the freighter had never been demanded it was impossible to presume that X would not have made the contract had he known A to be the principal.

If supposed principal named agent cannot sue

A person who has contracted as agent cannot, however, assume the character of principal if the name of his supposed principal has been given.[1]

B. THE AGENT HAS AUTHORITY IN FACT BUT HE DOES NOT DISCLOSE THE EXISTENCE OF THE AGENCY

Doctrine of the undisclosed principal

Where an agent, having authority to contract on behalf of another, makes the contract in his own name, concealing the fact that he is a mere representative, the doctrine of the undisclosed principal comes into play. By this doctrine either the agent, or the principal when discovered, may be sued; and either the agent or the principal may sue the other party to the contract.

There is nothing remarkable in this doctrine so far as it concerns the agent. The existence of an enforceable contract between him and the third party is scarcely deniable, for he purports to act on his own behalf and the other party is content with this apparent state of affairs. At any rate it is well settled that the contract is enforceable either by[2] or against[3] the agent. The primary liability that rests upon him as being a party to the contract is not destroyed by the fact that the principal also may be added as a party.[4] Parol evidence is admissible to introduce a new party, i.e., the principal, but is never admissible for the purpose of discharging an apparent party, i.e., the agent.

Principal may sue

What is more curious about the doctrine is that the principal should be allowed to intervene, for at first sight it seems inconsistent with elementary principles that a person should be allowed to enforce a contract that he has not in fact made. On the other hand this right of intervention is in many cases both just and convenient. If, for instance, the agent of an undisclosed seller were to go bankrupt after delivery of the goods but before payment of the price, the money, unless it were demandable by the seller direct from the buyer, would go to swell the assets divisible among the general creditors of the agent. Considerations of this nature ultimately produced the rule, though without any manifest enthusiasm on the part of the business community, that a principal may disclose his existence and may himself maintain an action against the person with whom his agent contracted.[5] Thus, for example, if two or more arrange that one of themselves shall buy goods in his own name on their joint behalf, they may

1. *Fairlie* v. *Fenton* (1870), L.R. 5 Exch. 169.
2. *Sims* v. *Bond* (1833), 5 B. & Ad. 369.
3. *Saxon* v. *Blake* (1861), 29 Beav. 438.
4. *Higgins* v. *Senior* (1841), 8 M. & W. 834.
5. *Schrimshire* v. *Alderton* (1743), 2 Stra. 1182.

jointly or severally sue the vendor in the event of a breach of the contract.[1]

These rights possessed by the agent and by the principal against the third party are independent rights, except that the rights of the agent are subordinate to those of the principal.[2] If, for example, an action for breach of contract brought by the agent against the third party is dismissed, this does not preclude a similar action by the principal. It cannot be said that the agent sued on behalf of his principal and that therefore the latter is estopped from taking further proceedings.

The right of action possessed by the undisclosed principal is, however, subject to two limitations:

First, the authority of the agent to act for the principal must have existed at the time of the contract.[3] *Two limitations upon right of principal to sue*

Secondly, if the contract, expressly or by implication, shows that it is to be confined in its operation to the parties themselves, the possibility of agency is negatived and no one else can intervene as principal.[4] Whether this is the intention of the parties is a matter of construction. Thus it has been held that for an agent to describe himself as " owner "[5] or " proprietor "[6] of the subject matter of the contract precludes the principal, whether disclosed or not, from suing or being sued. In such a case the other party contracts upon the basis that the person with whom he is dealing is sole owner of the subject-matter, and as Lord HALDANE once said:

> " Where it is a term of the contract that he should contract as owner of that property, you cannot show that another person is the real owner."[7]

On the other hand, the description of a person as " charterer "[8] or " tenant "[9] or " landlord "[10] no more negatives the existence of agency than would the description " contracting party."

As a corollary to the right of intervention by an undisclosed principal it is well established that when discovered he may be sued upon the contract made by his agent.[11] Nevertheless the third party must elect which of these two inconsistent rights he will enforce, for the contract cannot be enforced against both the principal and the agent. *Third party may sue either principal or agent*

Doctrine of election

> " If a man is entitled to one of two inconsistent rights it is fitting that where with full knowledge he has done an unequivocal act

---

1. *Skinner* v. *Stocks* (1821), 4 B. & Ald. 437.
2. *Pople* v. *Evans,* [1969] 2 Ch. 255; [1968] 2 All E.R. 743.
3. *Keighley, Maxsted & Co.* v. *Durant,* [1901] A.C. 240, at p. 251, *per* Lord JAMES OF HEREFORD. See the remarks of DIPLOCK, L.J. in *Garnac Grain Co. Inc.* v. *H. M. F. Faure and Fairclough, Ltd., and Bunge Corporation,* [1966] 1 Q.B. 650, at p. 666; [1965] 3 All E.R. 273. See *supra,* pp. 458–462.
4. See two notes by P.A.L. in 61 L.Q.R. 130–3; 62 L.Q.R. 20–2. See also Goodhart and Hamson, 4 C.L.J. 320, at p. 352–3.
5. *Humble* v. *Hunter* (1848), 12 Q.B. 310, at p. 317.
6. *Formby Brothers* v. *Formby* (1910), 102 L.T. 116.
7. *Fred Drughorn, Ltd.* v. *Rederiaktiebolaget Transatlantic,* [1919] A.C. 203, at p. 207.
8. *Ibid.*
9. *Danziger* v. *Thompson,* [1944] K.B. 654; [1944] 2 All E.R. 151.
10. *Epps* v. *Rothnie,* [1945] K.B. 562; [1946] 1 All E.R. 146.
11. *Thomson* v. *Davenport* (1829), 9 B. & C. 78.

showing that he has chosen the one he cannot afterwards pursue the other, which after the first choice is by reason of the inconsistency no longer his to choose."[1]

Whether the conduct of the third party shows an unequivocal election to resort to the agent alone or to the principal alone is a question of fact that must be decided in the light of all the relevant circumstances. For instance, the initiation by him of proceedings against one of the two parties is strong evidence of a final election. Yet it is not necessarily conclusive, for further evidence may show that the right of action against the other party had not been abandoned.[2] This was the decision reached by the Court of Appeal in *Clarkson Booker, Ltd.* v. *Andjel.*[3]

> The plaintiffs supplied air tickets to the value of £728 7s. 6d. to the defendant, a travel agent, with whom, on several occasions in the past, they had dealt as principal. Later, P & Co., also operating as travel agents, disclosed that the defendant had in fact acted solely as their agent.

The plaintiffs wrote separate letters to the defendant and to P & Co. threatening proceedings if payment were not made. After waiting for some five weeks they issued a writ against P & Co., but on learning two months later that the company was insolvent they proceeded no further with the action. They then issued a writ against the defendant and judgment was given in their favour in the court of first instance. The defendant appealed on the ground that the plaintiffs, by serving the earlier writ on P & Co. had elected to exonerate him personally from liability.

It was held that no such election had been made. The threat to proceed against the defendant had never been withdrawn; his position had not been prejudiced by the action against P & Co.; and above all it was to him alone that in the past the plaintiffs had always looked for payment.

Had the plaintiffs obtained judgment against P & Co. they would, indeed, have been precluded from suing the defendant, not because they had made a final election, but because the law does not countenance the co-existence of two judgments in respect of the same debt or cause of action.[4] " There shall not be more than one judgment on one entire debt."[5] If, for instance, the third party obtains judgment against a defendant who is in fact an agent, he cannot sue the principal, even though at the time of the action against the defendant he was ignorant of the principal's existence and even though the judgment remains unsatisfied.[6] He must first get that judgment set aside and then sue the principal.[7]

Juridical basis of the doctrine of the undisclosed principal

The juridical basis of the doctrine of the undisclosed principal has aroused considerable controversy.[8] The anomalous feature of

---

1. *United Australia, Ltd.* v. *Barclays Bank, Ltd.,* [1914] A.C. 1, *per* Lord ATKIN, at p. 30.
2. *Clarkson Booker, Ltd.* v. *Andjel,* [1964] 2 Q.B. 775; [1964] 3 All E.R. 260. For a critique of the doctrine of election, see Reynolds, 86 L.Q.R. 318.
3. *Supra,* footnote 2.
4. *Kendall* v. *Hamilton* (1879), 4 App. Cas. 504, at p. 515, *per* Lord CAIRNS.
5. *Hammond* v. *Schofield,* [1891] 1 Q.B. 453, at p. 457, *per* VAUGHAN WILLIAMS, J.; *Moore* v. *Flanagan,* [1920] 1 K.B. 919, at pp. 925–6.
6. *Kendall* v. *Hamilton* (1879), 4 App. Cas. 504, at p. 514.
7. *Partington* v. *Hawthorne* (1888), 52 J.P. 807.
8. 3 L.Q.R. 359; Ames, *Lectures on Legal History,* pp. 453–63: Goodhart and Hamson 4 C.L.J. 320; Higgins, 28 M.L.R. 167.

the doctrine is that it allows " one person to sue another on a contract not really made with the person suing."[1] This patently ignores the common law requirement of privity of contract, and the view of Lord LINDLEY, that " the contract is in truth, although not in form, that of the undisclosed principal himself," has found few supporters.[2]

If, therefore, we look no further than the common law, the rule that the undisclosed principal can sue or be sued must find its justification in business convenience, though this will not warrant the conclusion that privity of contract exists between him and the third party. However, it has been suggested by high authority that the doctrine can be rationalized as avoiding circuity of action if the aid of equity is invoked. " for the principal could in equity compel the agent to lend his name in an action to enforce the contract against the contractor, and would at common law be liable to indemnify the agent in respect of the performance of the obligations assumed by the agent under the contract."[3]

C. THE EFFECT OF A PAYMENT TO THE AGENT

It may happen that either the principal or the third party settles with the agent, who, however, by reason of bankruptcy or fraud, fails to pass the money on to the creditor. The question then arises whether the payer is liable to pay over again. There are two separate cases. *(margin: Effect where principal or third party settles with agent)*

First, the principal, having instructed his agent to buy goods, pays the purchase price to the agent, who fails to pay the seller. *(margin: Two cases)*

Secondly, the principal instructs his agent to sell goods; the agent sells to a buyer and receives payment from him, but does not pay the principal.

In the first case, the general rule is that the principal remains liable to the seller, provided at least that the agent was known by the seller to be acting as an agent.[4] The seller, however, may be estopped by his conduct from taking advantage of this rule. If his conduct unequivocally showed that he looked to the agent alone for payment and thereby induced the principal, after the debt became due, to settle with the agent, resort cannot afterwards be had to the principal.[5] To gain this immunity the principal must show that he was reasonably misled by the seller's conduct into settling with the agent. If, for instance, the seller takes security from the agent and gives him a receipt for the purchase price, the principal will be discharged if he settles with the agent *(margin: (i) Agent for purchase is paid by principal but does not pay seller)*

---

1. Pollock, 3 L.Q.R. 359.
2. *Keighley Maxsted & Co.* v. *Durant,* [1901] A.C. 240, at p. 261. The fallacy of the view has been exposed by Goodhart and Hamson, *op. cit.*
3. *Freeman and Lockyer* v. *Buckhurst Park Properties (Magnal), Ltd.,* [1964] 2 Q.B. 480, at p. 503, *per* DIPLOCK, L.J.
4. *Irvine* v. *Watson* (1879), 5 Q.B.D. 102; affirmed (1880), 5 Q.B.D. 414.
5. *Macfarlane* v. *Giannacopula* (1858), 3 H. & N. 860.

on the faith of the receipt.[1] The whole subject was reviewed in
Irvine v. *Watson*,[2] where the facts were these:

> P employed A, a broker, to buy oil for him. A bought from S,
> telling him that he was buying for a principal but not disclosing
> the name. The terms of the sale were that payment should be
> made " by cash on or before delivery," but, despite this, S delivered
> the oil without receiving payment. P, unaware that S had not
> been paid, in good faith paid A. A became insolvent, whereupon
> S sued P. It was proved that it was not the invariable custom in
> the oil trade to insist upon pre-payment even where the terms were
> cash on or before delivery.

It was argued on behalf of P that, since he knew that the contract
provided for payment in cash on or before delivery, he was
justified in presuming that S would not have made delivery
without receipt of the money. This argument did not prevail.
The clause in the contract providing for cash on or before delivery
was not sufficient to raise an estoppel, since S had a perfect right
to deliver without requiring pre-payment. Had the invariable
custom been to exact pre-payment, the conclusion might well have
been different.

Agent not
known to
be an agent The question remains whether the rule is different if the seller
is unaware of the agency and deals with the agent as sole principal.
If the person who is in fact principal *bona fide* settles with the
agent, does he remain liable for the price? It was decided in
Heald v. *Kenworthy*[3] that even here the general rule applies
and that failing estoppel the principal may be compelled to make
a second payment. In that case:

> An undisclosed principal, who had authorized an agent to buy
> goods on his behalf, was sued for the price by the seller. He
> pleaded that within a reasonable time after the sale and not unduly
> early he had *bona fide* paid his agent in full.

It was held on demurrer that this plea was bad. The general rule
was stated as follows in the head note:

> " Where a principal authorizes his agent to pledge his credit, and
> the latter makes a purchase on his behalf and thereby creates a
> debt, the principal is not discharged by payment to the agent if
> the money is not paid over to the seller, unless the latter by his
> conduct makes it unjust that the principal should be sued, *e.g.*,
> where the seller by his words or conduct induces the principal to
> believe that a settlement has been come to between the seller and
> the agent, in consequence of which the principal pays the amount
> of the debt to the agent."

This rule, however, was somewhat rudely disturbed sixteen
years later by the decision in *Armstrong* v. *Stokes*.[4] In that case:

> P & Co. employed A & Co., commission merchants, who acted
> sometimes for themselves and sometimes as agents, to buy goods
> on their behalf. A & Co. bought from S, with whom they had
> often had dealings in the past. S did not inquire whether A & Co.
> were on this occasion acting for principals. P & Co. in accordance
> with their usual custom paid A & Co. in full on the next settling
> day, but the money did not reach S.

---

1. *Wyatt* v. *Marquis of Hertford* (1802), 2 East. 147.
2. (1879), 5 Q.B.D. 102; affirmed (1880), 5 Q.B.D. 414.
3. (1855), 10 Exch. 739.
4. (1872), L.R. 7 Q.B. 598.

An action brought by S against P & Co. failed. The court considered that, as P & Co. had paid A & Co. at a time when S still gave exclusive credit to A & Co., S could not afterwards claim from P & Co. On the surface, therefore, *Armstrong* v. *Stokes* is a flat reversal of *Heald* v. *Kenworthy*. Which decision represents the modern law? Was the later distinguished from the earlier decision by some form of estoppel? On the whole it is safer to follow *Heald* v. *Kenworthy*. *Armstrong* v. *Stokes* was severely criticized by the Court of Appeal in *Irvine* v. *Watson*, where its reconsideration at some later date was foreshadowed,[3] and the better opinion is that it turned in some measure upon the fact that A & Co. were not normal agents but commission merchants.

The second case in which the effect of a settlement with an agent requires consideration is where the agent, having sold his principal's goods, receives payment from the buyer but does not pay the money over to his principal. Whether the buyer is in these circumstances liable to pay over again depends entirely upon whether the agent is authorized to receive the purchase money. If he possesses this authority, the buyer is discharged from further liability; if not the liability remains. The general rule is that an agent authorized to sell is not authorized to receive payment.[1] The buyer, therefore, who seeks to avoid a double payment, must prove that the authority existed in fact. If the principal has expressly authorized the agent to accept payment, the matter is of course clear; but failing this the buyer must prove either that what he did was the usual and well recognized practice in that particular type of agency, or that the agent had ostensible authority to receive the money.[2] (ii) Agent for sale is paid by buyer, but does not pay principal

The right to set-off one debt against another raises a similar problem. If an agent authorized to sell goods owes a personal debt to the buyer, can the latter set this off against the purchase price that is due to the principal? The answer is that he enjoys this right only if he has been led to believe by the conduct of the principal that the agent is himself the owner of the goods sold. The law has been summarized by MARTIN, B., in the following words: Set-off

> " Where a principal permits an agent to sell as apparent principal and afterwards intervenes, the buyer is entitled to be placed in the same situation at the time of disclosure of the real principal as if the agent had been the real contracting party, and is entitled to the same defence, whether it be by common law or by statute, payment or set-off, as he was entitled to at that time against the agent, the apparent principal."[3]

The question generally arises where the principal has entrusted the agent with possession of the goods.[4] In this case the buyer is entitled to a set-off if he proves that the agent sold the goods in his own name as if they were his own, that he himself *bona fide* believed the agent to be the principal in the transaction, and

---

1. (1879), 5 Q.B.D. 414, at p. 421. For a re-appraisal of the decision, see Higgins, 28 M.L.R. 167, at pp. 175–8.
2. *Drakeford* v. *Piercy* (1866), 7 B. & S. 515; *Butwick* v. *Grant,* [1924] 2 K.B. 483.
3. *Butwick* v. *Grant, supra.*
4. *Isberg* v. *Bowden* (1853), 8 Exch. 852, at p. 859.
5. *George* v. *Clagett* (1797), 7 Term Rep. 359.

that before he was undeceived in this respect the set-off had accrued.[1]

It is clear, therefore, that no right of set-off exists if the buyer knows the agent to be an agent though ignorant of the principal's identity, or if he knows that the agent sometimes deals as agent, sometimes on his own account, but does not trouble to ascertain the capacity in which he is acting in the present transaction.[2]

SECTION IV. UNAUTHORIZED ACTS OF THE AGENT

A. THE POSITION OF THE PRINCIPAL

Principal liable only for authorized acts

It is obvious that the principal is bound by every contract or disposition of property made by the agent with his authority. The reverse is equally obvious. If a man acts as agent without any authority whatsoever, or if an agent exceeds his authority, the principal (apart from ratification), is not liable at all in the first case and in the second is not liable for the excess. Thus, if the managing committee of a club has no authority to buy goods on credit, an order given for wine by one of the members does not bind his colleagues. The same rule applies where an agent is adjudicated bankrupt after having disposed of his principal's goods contrary to instructions. In this case the principal is not reduced to proving in the bankruptcy equally with the other creditors, but can recover the whole price if the agent has wrongfully sold goods, and can recover in full money or property which may have passed to the trustee in bankruptcy.[3] A similar rule applied at common law to a wrongful disposition by an agent of goods which had been entrusted to him by a principal.[4] This rule, however, and the maxim upon which it was based—*nemo dat quod non habet*—has been largely modified by subsequent legislation.[5]

Different kinds of authority

Nevertheless, to say that a principal is liable only for what has been done within the authority of his agent leaves open the critical question: What is the meaning of " authority " in the eyes of the law? The meaning is not self-evident, for what has not in fact been authorized may none the less be regarded by the law as authorized. The position with regard to this matter has been re-stated and clarified by two modern decisions of the Court of

---

1. *Montagu* v. *Forwood*, [1893] 2 Q.B. 350; applied, *Lloyds and Scottish Finance, Ltd.* v. *Williamson*, [1965] 1 All E.R. 641; [1965] 1 W.L.R. 404.
2. *Cooke* v. *Eshelby* (1887), 12 App. Cas. 271.
3. *Taylor* v. *Plumer* (1815), 3 M. & S. 562; *Re Strachan, Ex parte Cooke* (1876), 4 Ch.D. 123.
4. *Cole* v. *North Western Bank* (1875), L.R. 10 C.P. 354, at p. 362, *per* BLACKBURN, J.
5. *Infra*, pp. 481 *et seq.*

Appeal.[1] These show that a distinction must be drawn between the agent's *actual* authority on the one hand, and his *apparent or ostensible* authority on the other.

> " An actual authority is a legal relationship between principal and agent created by a consensual agreement to which they alone are parties. Its scope is to be ascertained by applying ordinary principles of construction of contracts, including any proper implications from the express words used, the usages of trade or the course of business between the parties."[2]

Thus actual authority may be express or implied.

> " It is *express* when it is given by express words, such as where a board of directors pass a resolution which authorizes two of their number to sign cheques. It is *implied* when it is inferred from the conduct of the parties and the circumstances of the case, such as where the board of directors appoint one of their number to be managing director. They thereby impliedly authorize him to do all such things as fall within the usual scope of that office."[3]

If the agent enters into a contract with a third party within the scope of his actual authority the result is to create contractual obligations between the principal and the third party. It is irrelevant that the latter was unaware of the existence of the authority, and irrelevant even that the agent acted with improper motives with a desire solely to promote his own interests.[4]

On the other hand, " ostensible or apparent authority is the authority of the agent as it *appears* to others."[5] Its operation has been described as follows by DIPLOCK, L.J.

> " An apparent or ostensible authority is a legal relationship between the principal and the contractor created by a representation, made by the principal to the contractor, intended to be and in fact acted upon by the contractor, that the agent has authority to enter on behalf of the principal into a contract of a kind within the scope of the " apparent " authority, so as to render the principal liable to perform any obligations imposed upon him by such contract. . . . The representation, where acted upon by the contractor by entering into a contract with the agent, operates as an estoppel, preventing the principal from asserting that he is not bound by the contract. It is irrelevant whether the agent had actual authority to enter into the contract."[6]

Implied and apparent authority are not mutually exclusive. " Generally they co-exist and coincide, but either may exist without the other and their respective scopes may be different."[7] But normally the third party will rely upon the apparent authority of the agent, since all that he will know of the actual authority,

---

1. *Freeman and Lockyer* v. *Buckhurst Park Properties (Magnal), Ltd.,* [1964] 2 Q.B. 480; [1964] 1 All E.R. 630, especially the judgment of DIPLOCK, L.J.; *Hely-Hutchinson* v. *Brayhead, Ltd.,* [1968] 1 Q.B. 549; [1967] 3 All E.R. 98.
2. *Freeman and Lockyer* v. *Buckhurst Park Properties (Magnal), Ltd.,* [1964] 2 Q.B., at p. 502; [1964] 1 All E.R., at p. 644, *per* DIPLOCK, L.J.
3. *Hely-Hutchinson* v. *Brayhead, Ltd.,* [1968] 1 Q.B., at p. 583; [1967] 3 All E.R., at p. 102.
4. *Hambro* v. *Burnand,* [1904] 2 K.B. 10.
5. *Hely-Hutchinson* v. *Brayhead, Ltd.,* [1968] 1 Q.B. 549, *per* Lord DENNING, at p. 583.
6. *Freeman and Lockyer* v. *Buckhurst Park Properties (Magnal), Ltd.,* [1964] 2 Q.B., at p. 503; [1964] 2 All E.R., at p. 644.
7. *Ibid.*

whether express or implied, will be what he hears from the principal or agent, and that may or may not be true.

Meaning of
" represen-
tation "

The " representation " that creates an apparent authority generally arises from some conduct on the part of the principal, as for instance where he holds the agent out as entitled to act for him in a business capacity.[1]

> " By so doing the principal represents to anyone who becomes aware that the agent is so acting that the agent has authority to enter on behalf of the principal into contracts with other persons of the kind which an agent so acting in the conduct of the principal's business has usually ' actual ' authority to enter into."[2]

Examples
of apparent
authority

It is impossible to classify precisely and exhaustively the circumstances in which a principal is thus liable on the basis of apparent authority, but the position may be clarified by examples.[3]

Authority
to do what
is usual in a
particular
trade

Thus, an agent who is employed to conduct a certain business transaction is deemed to possess authority to do everything usually incidental to a business transaction of that type.[4] In *Dingle* v. *Hare*,[5] for instance, an agent with authority to sell artificial manure warranted to the buyer that it contained 30 per cent. phosphate of lime. Upon proof that it was usual to give a warranty of this nature in the artificial manure trade, it was held that the principal was liable for its breach, although he had not authorized the agent to enter into such an undertaking.

> " But when the jury "—said BYLES, J.—" found that it was usual to sell these artificial manures with a warranty, the nice distinction as to the extent of the agent's authority became quite immaterial. An agent to sell has a general authority to do all that is usual and necessary in the course of such employment."

Again, an agent employed as manager of a certain class of business, to the conduct of which the drawing of bills of exchange is normally incidental, is implicitly authorized to draw upon his principal.[6] If it is the usual practice of hotel managers to purchase cigars, then purchases of this nature made by a manager will bind his principal.[7]

A question that has led to recent litigation is whether an estate agent, employed to sell property, has implied authority to accept a deposit from a prospective purchaser. If, for example, the agent receives a deposit before a binding contract has been completed, and then either misappropriates it or becomes insolvent, the problem is to decide which of two innocent parties is to suffer. Must the depositor lose his money or is the principal liable for its return? According to the prevalent judicial view,

---

1. For the wide scope of the ostensible authority possessed by the secretary of a company, see *Panorama Developments (Guildford), Ltd.* v. *Fidelis Furnishing Fabrics, Ltd.,* [1971] 2 Q.B. 711; [1971] 3 All E.R. 16.
2. [1971] 2 Q.B., at pp. 503–4; [1971] 3 All E.R., at p. 644. The usage with regard to the epithets appropriate to qualify " authority " is not completely consistent either among judges or commentators; e.g. " implied " is sometimes used to mean " apparent."
3. For an illuminating account of which free use has been made in these pages, see Ewart, *Estoppel*, pp. 488 *et seq.*
4. *Sutton* v. *Tatham* (1839), 10 A. & E. 27, at p. 30, *per* LITTLEDALE, J.
5. (1859), 7 C.B.N.S. 145.
6. *Edmunds* v. *Bushell and Jones* (1865), L.R. 1 Q.B. 97.
7. *Watteau* v. *Fenwick*, [1893] 1 Q.B. 346. See Hornby, [1961] C.L.J. 239.

natural justice supports the claim of the prospective purchaser, in the absence of special circumstances.

> " It is the prospective vendor who has chosen the estate agent; who has clothed him with the capacity of agent; and who has enabled him to ask for and receive a deposit in connection with the business to which the agency relates."[1]

This view now represents the law.[2] The Court of Appeal has held that the taking of a deposit is " reasonably incidental to the functions of an estate agent "[3] and, therefore that throughout the pre-contract period he holds it by virtue of his agency. The principal is responsible for what results from the exercise by the agent of his implied authority.

Again, an agent employed to act at a definite place, such as a market, has apparent authority to do what persons transacting business at that place usually do. In the words of ALDERSON, B.:

Authority to contract according to local usage

> " A person who deals in a particular market must be taken to deal according to the custom of that market, and he who directs another to make a contract at a particular place must be taken as intending that the contract may be made according to the usage of that place."[4]

The Factors Act 1889, which repealed a series of Acts passed in 1823, 1842 and 1877, amplified further the doctrine of apparent authority. The object of these statutes was to determine the effect of unauthorized dispositions of goods made by factors and other similar agents in favour of third persons acting *bona fide*. A principal, for instance, delivers goods to a factor with instructions that they are not to be disposed of but are to be retained pending further directions. The factor, however, in breach of his authority, sells or pledges the goods to a third party who acts *bona fide* and for value. Is the principal to be allowed to rely upon the maxim *nemo dat quod non habet*, and to succeed in an action of trover against the third party? The common law doctrine of ostensible ownership, analogous to the doctrine of ostensible agency, could indeed have settled this problem without any aid from the legislature, for it was designed to meet just such a case as that proposed above.

Factors had apparent authority to sell at common law

> The doctrine is that if the owner of goods acts in such a way as to induce the belief in a third party that the ownership is vested in X, and if in *bona fide* reliance upon this belief the third party enters into some transaction with X under which he acquires the goods for value, the owner is estopped from disputing the validity of the transaction.

In such circumstances the apparent ownership is in the eye of the law equivalent to real ownership. Since a factor is a mercantile agent whose ordinary course of business is to dispose of the

---

1. *Burt v. Claude Cousins & Co., Ltd.,* [1971] 2 Q.B. 426, at p. 452, *per* MEGAW, L.J. SACHS, L.J., agreed; Lord DENNING, M.R., disagreed.
2. *Ryan v. Pilkington,* [1959] 1 All E.R. 689; [1959] 1 W.L.R. 403; *Burt v. Claude Cousins & Co., Ltd., supra,* distinguished, *Barrington v. Lee,* [1972] 1 Q.B. 326; [1971] 3 All E.R. 1231. In *Goding v. Frazer,* [1967] 3 All E.R. 234; [1967] 1 W.L.R. 286, SACHS, J., held that on the failure of the contract the deposit was recoverable from the vendor as being money had and received to the use of the purchaser.
3. *Burt v. Claude Cousins & Co., Ltd.,* [1971] 2 Q.B., at p. 445, *per* SACHS, L.J.
4. *Bayliffe v. Butterworth* (1847), 1 Exch. 425, at p. 429.

goods of which he is in possession, it is obvious that to put him in possession must induce the belief in the business community that he enjoys the powers of disposition usually exercised by this type of agent. The courts, indeed, recognized this fact to a large extent, for they held that if a factor *sold* the goods of which he was in possession his principal was estopped from denying his authority to sell. They refused, however, to make other forms of disposition equally binding upon the principal. Although the well-established custom was for factors who had received goods for disposal to advance money to the owner and then to pledge the goods in order to keep themselves in funds, the courts persistently held that a pledge, as distinct from a sale, did not raise an estoppel against the owner so as to confer a good title on an innocent pledgee.

Factors had no apparent authority to pledge at common law

> " It was a hard doctrine "—said Lord ELLENBOROUGH—" when the pawnee was told that the pledger of goods had no authority to pledge them, being a mere factor for sale; and yet since the case of *Paterson* v. *Tash*[1] that doctrine has never been overturned."[2]

Authority of factors extended by statute

The Factors Act, however, now affords adequate protection to persons who *bona fide* enter into transactions with mercantile agents as defined by the Act.[3] Section 2 (1) provides as follows:

> Where a mercantile agent is, with the consent of the owner, in possession of goods or of the documents of title to goods, any sale, pledge or other disposition of the goods, made by him when acting in the ordinary course of business of a mercantile agent, shall, subject to the provisions of this Act, be as valid as if he were expressly authorized by the owner of the goods to make the same; provided that the person taking under the disposition acts in good faith, and has not at the time of the disposition notice that the person making the disposition has not authority to make the same.

This provision is extended by a later section to the case where a buyer, having obtained goods with the consent of the seller, later transfers their possession to a person who receives them in good faith under a sale, pledge or other disposition. In this event, the buyer in making the disposition is placed in the same position by the Act as if he were a mercantile agent in possession of the goods with the consent of the owner. It is irrelevant that such is not his true description.[4]

Limitations placed upon apparent authority ineffective unless known to third party

Finally, it must be stressed that once " an agent is clothed with ostensible authority, no private instructions prevent his acts within the scope of that authority from binding his principal."[5] Limitations in fact imposed upon the powers of the agent and ignored by him will not exonerate the principal from liability, unless, of course, their existence is known to the third party to the transaction.[6]

---

1. (1743), 2 Stra. 1178.
2. *Pickering* v. *Busk* (1812), 15 East. 38, at p. 44.
3. The statutory definition is: " A mercantile agent having in the customary course of his business as such agent authority either to sell goods, or to consign goods for the purpose of sale, or to buy goods, or to raise money on the security of goods."   See Factors Act 1889, s. 1 (1).
4. Factors Act 1889, s. 9; substantially reproduced in s. 25 (2) of the Sale of Goods Act 1893; *Newtons of Wembley, Ltd.* v. *Williams*, [1965] 1 Q.B. 560; [1964] 3 All E.R. 532.
5. *National Bolivian Navigation Co.* v. *Wilson* (1880), 5 App. Cas. 176, *per* Lord BLACKBURN, at p. 209.
6. *Watteau* v. *Fenwick*, [1893] 1 Q.B. 346.

B. THE POSITION OF THE AGENT

If a man contracts as agent without any authority in that behalf, the question arises whether he acquires either benefits or liabilities under the transaction.

With regard to benefits, the rule is that if a man contracts as agent for a *named* principal who has given no authority and who does not later ratify the contract, the self-styled agent acquires no rights whatsoever, since the solvency of the supposed principal may have induced the third party to enter into the transaction.[1] Thus, a purchaser at an auction sale signed a memorandum as agent for a named principal, and later sued in his own name to recover the deposit. He attempted to give evidence proving that he was the principal in the transaction, but the evidence was held to be inadmissible.[2]

A acquires no rights if without authority he contracts for named principal

On the other hand, if a man without any precedent authority contracts as agent but does not disclose the name of his supposed principal, it has been held in *Schmaltz* v. *Avery*[3] that he is entitled to maintain an action in his own name on the contract.

Aliter if principal un-named

The position with regard to the liability of an unauthorized agent is clear. It varies according to the state of his belief.

Liability of unauthorised agent

If he knows that he possesses no authority to act as agent, but nevertheless makes a representation to the contrary and in consequence causes loss to the party with whom he contracts, he may be sued in tort for the deceit.[4]

(i) Where he knows that he has no authority

If, on the other hand, he mistakenly though innocently believes that he possesses authority, he cannot be liable in tort for deceit. Nor can he be made liable upon the contract which he purported to make on behalf of the principal, since this was not his contract, nor was it regarded as such by the third party. Thus in *Smout* v. *Ilbery*:[5]

(ii) Where he believes that he has authority

> A wife, acting as the authorized agent of her husband, continually bought goods from the plaintiff, an English tradesman. The plaintiff knew that the husband was in China. The husband died without the knowledge of the parties, and the plaintiff sued the wife to recover the price of goods supplied to her after her authority had been revoked by the death of the principal.

The plaintiff sued on the contract of sale but failed, for it was clear that both in fact and in intention it was the husband, not the wife, who was the buyer.

A contractual basis upon which the agent himself can be held liable was, however, ultimately established in *Collen* v. *Wright*.[6]

---

1. *Bickerton* v. *Burrell* (1816), 5 M. & S. 383; *Fairlie* v. *Fenton* (1870), L.R. 5 Ex. 169.
2. *Bickerton* v. *Burrell, supra.*
3. (1851), 20 L.J.Q.B. 228, followed in *Harper & Co.* v. *Vigers Brothers,* [1909] 2 K.B. 549.
4. *Polhill* v. *Walter* (1832), 3 B. & Ad. 114.
5. (1842), 10 M. & W. 1.
6. (1857), 8 E. & B. 647. See Fifoot, *English Law and its Background,* pp. 174-7.

In that case:

> A, describing himself as the agent of P, agreed in writing to
> lease to the plaintiff a farm which belonged to P. Both the plaintiff
> and A believed that A had the authority of P to make the lease,
> but this in fact was not the case. The plaintiff, having failed in a
> suit for specific performance against P, later sued to recover as
> damages from A's executors the costs that he had incurred in the
> suit.

The action succeeded. The court inferred from the circumstances
a separate and independent contract by which A promised that
he possessed the authority of P and in consideration of this
promise the plaintiff agreed to take a lease of the farm. WILLES,
J., in delivering the judgment of the majority of the Exchequer
Chamber, said:

> " The obligation arising in such a case is well expressed by saying
> that a person professing to contract as agent for another, impliedly,
> if not expressly, undertakes to, or promises, the person who enters
> into such contract upon the faith of the professed agent being duly
> authorized, that the authority which he professes to have does in
> point of fact exist. The fact of entering into the transaction with
> the professed agent, as such, is good consideration for the promise."

The decision, in other words, is an early example—perhaps the
forerunner—of the so-called " collateral contract "[1] which has
been discussed in an earlier chapter,[2] though it has frequently
been regarded as having established a particular doctrine called
" implied warranty of authority." This is a misleading description of the reasoning in the case. The court did not imply a
term or warranty in an already existing contract. It constructed
a new and independent contract based upon the exchange of
promises; on the one side that the authority existed and on the
other that a lease would be taken.

Doctrine of
Collen v.
Wright
extends to
all transac-
tions

The doctrine thus propounded in *Collen* v. *Wright* was at
once accepted by the profession and it has since been given wide
currency. It is not confined to contracts, but extends to every
business transaction into which a third party is induced to enter by
a representation that the person with whom he is dealing has
authority from some other person.[3] As BRAMWELL, L.J., put it
in a later case: " If a person requests and, by asserting that he
is clothed with the necessary authority induces another to enter
into a negotiation with himself and into a transaction with the
person whose authority he represents that he has, in that case
there is a contract by him that he has the authority of the person
with whom he requests the other to enter into the transaction."[4]

Agent liable
if he acts in
ignorance
that his
authority
has ter-
minated

The result is the same if an authority that has been expressly
conferred is ended by some event, such as the death or the
lunacy of the principal, which supervenes without the knowledge

---

1. See Wedderburn, [1959] C.L.J. 68.
2. *Supra*, pp. 57 *et seq.*
3. *Firbank's Executors* v. *Humphreys* (1886), 18 Q.B.D. 54; *Starkey* v. *Bank of
   England*, [1903] A.C. 114; *V/O Rasnoimport*, v. *Guthrie & Co., Ltd.*, [1966]
   1 Lloyd's Rep. 1.
4. *Dickson* v. *Reuter's Telegram Co.* (1877), 3 C.P.D. 1, at p. 5.

of the agent. This occurred, for instance, in *Yonge* v. *Toynbee*,[1] where the facts were these:

> P instructed A, a solicitor, to defend an action on his behalf, but he became insane before the action was begun. In ignorance of P's insanity A entered an appearance, delivered a defence and took other steps in connection with the litigation. When the plaintiff learned of P's condition he got the proceedings struck out and then sued to recover his costs from A, who, he contended, had defended the action without authority.

This contention was upheld. Although the solicitor's authority had automatically terminated with the insanity of the principal, his conduct tacitly guaranteed its continued existence. " I can see no difference of principle," said BUCKLEY, L.J., " between the case where the authority never existed at all and the case in which the authority has once existed and has ceased to exist."[2]

SECTION V.   TERMINATION OF AGENCY

Agency is determinable either by act of the parties or by operation of law. It is determined by act of the parties if there is a mutual agreement to that effect; or if the authority of the agent is renounced by him or revoked by the principal. Determination by operation of law occurs by the happening of some event which renders the agency unlawful and also by the death, insanity or bankruptcy of one of the parties. We will consider these methods *seriatim*.

Summary of the law

A.   TERMINATION BY ACT OF THE PARTIES

An agent who renounces his authority or a principal who revokes the authority may find that he has rendered himself liable for breach of contract. In deciding whether a breach has been committed, much will depend upon whether or not the actual relationship between the parties is akin to that which exists between an employer and an employee.

Effect of renunciation or revocation of authority

If the result of their agreement is to create an immediate and continuing *nexus* between them, as for example where the agent has promised to devote his time and energy on behalf of the principal in return for reward, their relationship bears a close analogy to that between an employer and employee. The agent has agreed to serve the principal; the principal has agreed to accept and to pay for that service. It is clear, therefore, that any unilateral termination of the relationship by either party will be wrongful unless it is in accordance with the contract. If there is an express term dealing with the matter, *cadit quaestio*. If not, all depends upon the construction of the contract. In the case of every contract, whether it be one of agency or not, the common intention of the

(i) Where principal and agent under continuing binding obligations

---

1. [1910] 1 K.B. 215.
2. *Ibid.*, at p. 226.

parties with regard to the power of termination must be ascertained
in the light of all the admissible evidence.

> " An agreement which is silent about determination will not be
> determinable unless the facts of the case, such as the subject matter
> of the agreement, the nature of the contract or the circumstances in
> which the agreement was made support a finding that the parties
> intended that it should be determinable.[1]

Thus in *Martin-Baker Aircraft Co.* v. *Canadian Flight Equipment*:[2]

> A was appointed sole selling agent on the North American Con-
> tinent of all the products of P & Co. He agreed to use his best en-
> deavours to promote sales in that territory, to act as general marketing
> consultant for P & Co. and not to become interested in the sale of
> competitive products. His remuneration was to be a commission
> at the rate of 17½ per cent. on orders obtained by him.

P & Co. desired to determine the relationship, but A contended
that it was terminable only by mutual consent. There could
be no doubt that the mutual promises constituted a contract
binding upon both parties. There was express provision for
the summary termination of the relationship in two particular
events, but no similar provision to meet other circumstances.
McNair, J., construed the contract as being closely analogous to
one between master and servant and therefore as one that could
not rationally be regarded as establishing a permanent bond
between the parties. One party alone could not, indeed, terminate it summarily, but he could terminate it by serving reasonable notice on the other, that is to say in the instant case, twelve
months' notice.

The presence or absence of a power of termination is a
question which raises formidable difficulties throughout the
law of contract—difficulties endemic in the application of rules
of construction. Such rules are not docile servants and are the
more intractable where unaccompanied by some initial presumption. Buckley, J., in *Re Spenborough Urban District
Council's Agreement*[3] denied the existence of any presumption
either in favour of or against terminability. He was, indeed,
confronted with inconsistent *dicta* in two House of Lords cases[4]
and he may well have felt reluctant to choose between them.
Neither of them was in fact concerned with problems of agency or
employment, and in these two types of contract at least the
possibility of termination is tolerably well settled.[5]

(ii) Where
principal
and agent not
contractually
bound to do
anything

In many cases of agency, the relationship between the parties,
unlike that between employer and servant, imposes no binding
obligation upon either party. This is so, for instance, where
an owner puts the sale of his property into the hands of an estate

---

1. *Re Spenborough Urban District Council's Agreement*, [1968] Ch. 139, at
   p. 147, *per* Buckley, J.; [1967] 1 All E.R. 959, at p. 962.
2. [1955] 2 Q.B. 556.
3. [1968] Ch. 139, at p. 147.
4. *Llanelly Railway and Dock Co.* v. *London and North Western Rail. Co.*,
   (1875) L.R. 7 H.L. 550; *Winter Garden Theatre (London), Ltd.* v. *Millenium
   Productions, Ltd.*, [1948] A.C. 173; [1947] 2 All E.R. 331.
5. The question of terminability in the law of contract as a whole is discussed
   by Carnegie, 85 L.Q.R. 392. He argues cogently in favour of a general
   presumption of terminability in all contracts of unspecified duration.

agent on commission terms. Here, the agent is not bound to do anything. Nor, at the outset, is the principal bound to do anything, for his only promise is to pay commission if and when the agent has brought about the intended result.[1] Only then does a contractual *nexus* arise between the parties. This is another example of a promise that ripens into a contract upon the performance of a specified act, as in the case where a reward is offered for the supply of information. We have seen that the revocability of such offers is the subject of debate but it is clear that the property owner may revoke his mandate before his obligation to pay matures, *i.e.*, at any time before the authorized act is performed by the agent.[2] Thus, a commission agreement is a speculative contract under which the agent must take the risk that the prospective purchaser whom he has introduced may not be accepted as such by his principal.[3]

The general principles that govern the contract between the principal and agent in such a case were stated by Lord RUSSELL OF KILLOWEN in *Luxor (Eastbourne), Ltd.* v. *Cooper.*[4]

Commission agreements

> " (1) Commission contracts are subject to no peculiar rules or principles of their own; the law which governs them is the law which governs all contracts and all questions of agency. (2) No general rule can be laid down by which the rights of the agent or the liability of the principal under commission contracts are to be determined. In each case these must depend upon the exact terms of the contract in question, and upon the true construction of those terms. And (3) contracts by which owners of property, desiring to dispose of it, put it in the hands of agents on commission terms, are not (in default of specific provisions) contracts of employment in the ordinary meaning of those words. No obligation is imposed on the agent to do anything."

The second and, in the present context, the most important observation of Lord RUSSELL is in effect that the principal's liability for the payment of commission depends on whether, on the proper interpretation of the contract between him and the agent, the event has happened upon which the commission is to be paid.[5] The agent is not entitled to claim payment for work as such, but only for an event, i.e. the event required by his contract with the principal. Moreover, there is no implied condition that the principal will do nothing to prevent the agent from earning his commission. The effect, therefore, of this ruling is that the principal may terminate the contract at any time before the agent has accomplished what he undertook to do. This was decided in the *Luxor* case[6] itself, where the facts were these:

> P authorized A to negotiate for the sale of certain properties and promised to pay him a commission of £10,000 " on completion of the sale " if a price of £175,000 were procured. A obtained an offer to purchase at this price and the offer was accepted by P.

Luxor (Eastbourne), Ltd. v. *Cooper*

1. *Luxor (Eastbourne), Ltd.* v. *Cooper,* [1941] A.C. 108, at pp. 124, 141, 153; [1941] 1 All E.R. 33, at pp. 45, 55, 63. Murdoch, 91 L.Q.R. 357.
2. *Motion* v. *Michaud* (1892), 8 T.L.R. 253; affirmed (1892), 8 T.L.R., at p. 447. See *supra*, pp. 51-4.
3. See Ash, *Willing to Purchase*, p. 3.
4. [1941] A.C. 108, at p. 124; [1941] 1 All E.R. 33, at p. 43.
5. *Ackroyd & Sons* v. *Hasan*, [1960] 2 Q.B. 144, at p. 154, *per* UPJOHN, L.J.
6. [1941] A.C. 108; [1941] 1 All E.R. 33.

Both the offer and acceptance, however, were made "subject to contract," a formula which, as we have seen, postpones the creation of a binding contract.[1] P availed himself of this rule and refused to proceed further with the transaction.

A was unable to recover £10,000 by way of commission, since there had been no *completion of the sale*, the stipulated event that was to convert P's promise into an obligation. The action was brought, therefore, to recover damages for breach of an implied term alleged to be contained in the agency contract. It was argued that P had implicitly promised that he "would do nothing to prevent the satisfactory completion of the transaction so as to deprive the [agent] of the agreed commission."

This attempt to invoke the doctrine of *The Moorcock*[2] failed. The contract did not lack business efficacy merely because it left P free to ignore or disown what A had done. The chances are that an agent of this type will reap substantial profit for comparatively little effort, and the possibility that he may lose the fruits of his labour at the caprice of the principal is a business risk that in practice is recognized and accepted. Moreover, it would be almost impossible to frame an implied term that would fairly and reasonably provide for the varying contingencies that may complicate such an agency, as for example the habit of entrusting the sale of a house to several agents each acting on a commission basis.

Whether commission payable is a question of construction

Thus the guiding rule in every case is " that before you find the commission payable you must be satisfied that the condition on which it is payable has been satisfied."[3] The intention of the parties as to the exact meaning of the condition must be ascertained by construing the actual words by which it is defined in the contract. Broadly speaking the intention which as a matter of probability the court should impute to the parties is that if no sale in fact results from the agent's efforts no commission shall be payable. This is the normal expectation of the vendor. Where the condition is described in general or ambiguous terms, such is the intention that the courts have usually attributed to the parties.[4] Examples of descriptive words that have led to this construction are where the agent has agreed to introduce " a purchaser ";[5] " a person willing and able to purchase ";[6] " a person ready, able and willing to purchase ";[7] " a person prepared to enter into a contract to purchase."[8]

---

1. *Supra*, p. 35.
2. *Supra*, pp. 132-5.
3. *A. L. Wilkinson, Ltd.* v. *Brown*, [1966] 1 All E.R. 509; [1966] 1 W.L.R. 194, at p. 197, *per* HARMAN, L.J.; *Jaques* v. *Lloyd D. George & Partners, Ltd.*, [1968] 1 W.L.R. 625, at p. 630, *per* Lord DENNING, M.R.
4. *Midgley Estates, Ltd.* v. *Hand*, [1952] 2 Q.B. 432, at pp. 435-6; [1952] 1 All E.R. 1394, *per* JENKINS, L.J.
5. *Jones* v. *Lowe*, [1945] K.B. 73; [1945] 1 All E.R. 194.
6. *Dellafiora* v. *Lester*, [1962] 3 All E.R. 393; [1962] 1 W.L.R. 1208.
7. *Dennis Reed, Ltd.* v. *Goody*, [1950] 2 K.B. 277; [1950] 1 All E.R. 919. But cf. *Christie Owen and Davies, Ltd.* v. *Rapacioli*, [1974] Q.B. 781; [1974] 2 All E.R. 311.
8. *Ackroyd & Sons* v. *Hasan*, [1960] 2 Q.B. 144; [1960] 2 All E.R. 254; *A. L. Wilkinson, Ltd.* v. *Brown*, [1966] 1 All E.R. 509; [1966] 1 W.L.R. 194. In the former of these cases, WINN, J., in the court of first instance, [1959] 1 W.L.R. 706, at p. 711, insisted that any such phrase as " introduce a person who is prepared to enter into a contract " must always be construed as " a person who *does* enter into a contract." This view was not favoured by the Court of Appeal, but it has been vigorously defended by Peter Ash in *Willing to Purchase*, pp. 91 *et seq.*

Nevertheless, if the condition upon which commission is payable is defined in clear and unambiguous terms, effect will be given to it even though for some reason or other the sale turns out to be abortive.[1] Thus in *Midgley Estates, Ltd.* v. *Hand,*[2] the bargain was that commission should be payable as soon as a purchaser introduced by the agent " shall have signed a legally binding contract within a period of three months from this date." The agents satisfied this condition and were held to be entitled to their commission notwithstanding the ultimate failure of the sale owing to the financial collapse of the purchaser.

Where a sale fails owing to the default of the principal, commission is payable if the default is wilful, but not if it is due merely to his inability to prove his title to the *res vendita.*[3]

One clear case in which an authority cannot be unilaterally revoked by the principal is where it is coupled with an interest held by the agent. If, for instance, a borrower, in consideration of a loan, authorizes the lender to receive the rents of Blackacre by way of security, the authority remains irrevocable until repayment of the loan in full has been effected.

Authority coupled with an interest is irrevocable

> " Where an agreement is entered into on a sufficient consideration [or by deed] whereby an authority is given for the purpose of securing some benefit to the donee of the authority, such an authority is irrevocable. This is what is usually meant by an authority coupled with an interest and which is commonly said to be irrevocable."[4]

This doctrine applies, however, only where the authority is created in order to protect the interest of the agent; it does not extend to a case where the authority has been given for some other reason and the interest of the agent arises later. This was the issue in *Smart* v. *Sanders,*[5] where the facts were as follows:

> Goods were consigned by the principal to a factor for the purpose of being sold. The factor later advanced £3,000 to the principal. The principal then countermanded his instructions to sell the goods, but nevertheless they were sold by the factor.

In the action that was subsequently brought against him, the factor argued that the authority to sell which he had undoubtedly been given had become irrevocable, since in his capacity as lender he had acquired an interest in the proceeds of sale. This argument did not prevail. The authority arose prior to and independently of the creation of the interest, and therefore it was not irrevocable under the general doctrine, but could become so only if an express agreement to that effect were made. Had a contract of loan been concluded between the parties by which the factor had been put into possession of the goods with authority to sell them and to repay himself out of the proceeds, the authority would have been irrevocable.

---

1. *Midgley Estates, Ltd.* v. *Hand,* [1952] 2 Q.B. 432, at p. 436.
2. *Supra*; applied in *Sheggia* v. *Gradwell,* [1963] 3 All E.R. 114; [1963] 1 W.L.R. 1049, Lord DENNING dissenting. This surprising decision was criticized by SALMON, L.J., in *Wilkinson, Ltd.* v. *Brown, supra,* at pp. 202–3.
3. *Blake & Co.* v. *Sohn,* [1969] 3 All E.R. 123; [1969] 1 W.L.R. 1412.
4. *Smart* v. *Sanders* (1848), 5 C.B. 895, at p. 917, *per* WILDE, C.J.
5. (1848), 5 C.B. 895.

Such, then, is the position where the principal revokes the authority of the agent. The fact that similar rules apply in the reverse case where the agent renounces his employment scarcely needs elaboration. If the revocation is in breach of contract, the principal may successfully institute an action for damages.[1]

B. TERMINATION BY OPERATION OF LAW

A contract of agency is automatically determined by the occurrence of some event which renders the continuance of the relationship unlawful, as, for example, where the principal becomes an alien enemy owing to the outbreak of war.[2]

The death of the principal determines the agency and relieves his estate from liability upon contracts made by the agent after his death, even though made in the honest belief that he was still alive.[3] On the other hand the agent is liable in such a case under the doctrine of the independent or " collateral " contract.[4] In the case of a power of attorney, however, it has been enacted that if the attorney makes any payment or does any act in good faith in pursuance of the power, he shall not thereby incur liability by reason that without his knowledge the principal has died, or become bankrupt or has revoked the power.[5]

The death of the agent likewise determines the agency.[6]

A difficult question arises where an agent makes a contract with a third party after his principal has become insane. There are only two relevant authorities: *Drew* v. *Nunn*[7] and *Yonge* v. *Toynbee*.[8] In *Drew* v. *Nunn*:

> The defendant, when sane, gave his wife authority to act for him and held her out to the plaintiff, a tradesman, as clothed with that authority. He became insane and was confined in an asylum. During this period, his wife bought goods on credit from the plaintiff who was unaware that the defendant had become mentally deranged. The defendant recovered his reason and resisted an action to recover the price of the goods supplied to his wife.

Two questions required an answer.

First, does insanity terminate the authority of the agent? This received an affirmative answer from BRETT, L.J., and BRAMWELL, L.J., though COTTON, L.J., felt some doubt. Since the husband could no longer act for himself, his wife could no longer act for him. The effect of this ruling is that the insanity of the principal renders the contract *between the principal and agent* void, so that for instance no commission is payable on transactions later effected by the agent.

The second question then arose: What is the effect where the principal, having held out another as his agent, becomes insane and

---

1. *Hochster* v. *De La Tour* (1853), 2 E. & B. 678.
2. *Stevenson* v. *Aktiengesellschaft für Cartonnagen-Industrie*, [1918] A.C. 239.
3. *Blades* v. *Free* (1829), 9 B. & C. 167.
4. *Yonge* v. *Toynbee*, [1910] 1 K.B. 215; *supra*, pp. 483-5.
5. Law of Property Act 1925, s. 124 (1).
6. *Friend* v. *Young*, [1897] 2 Ch. 421.
7. (1879), 4 Q.B.D. 661.
8. [1910] 1 K.B. 215.

a third person deals with the agent without notice of the insanity? The court held that the principal remains liable for what the agent has done in his capacity as agent. Having held him out in that capacity, he has made a representation upon which third parties are entitled to act and to continue to act if they have no notice of the insanity. In the words of BRAMWELL, L.J.:

> " Insanity is not a privilege—it is a misfortune which must not be allowed to injure innocent persons. It would be productive of mischievous consequences if insanity annulled every representation made by a person afflicted with it without any notice being given of his malady."[1]

It is submitted that the decision accords with commonsense and with the view that a distinction must be drawn between the *authority* and the *power* of the agents, i.e. between his authority to act for the principal and his power to put his principal in a contractual relationship with third parties. The latter may continue after the former has ceased.[2]

But though the rule laid down in *Drew* v. *Nunn* may be regarded as satisfactory, it has been confused by the decision of the Court of Appeal in *Yonge* v. *Toynbee*.[3] The facts in this case, which have already been given,[4] were broadly similar to those in *Drew* v. *Nunn*, except that the agent was ignorant of his principal's insanity when he contracted with the third party. The court applied the rule in *Collen* v. *Wright*[5] and held that the agent was personally liable as having impliedly warranted the existence of his authority. The application of this rule would seem to be in conflict with the decision in *Drew* v. *Nunn* that in similar circumstances the agent is still empowered to create a contractual relationship between his principal and a third party. If an agent has indeed this power, the principal should in logic be exclusively liable. It is possible, however, that *Yonge* v. *Toynbee* may be distinguished on the facts. First, in the action as framed, the principal could not possibly have been held liable, since a person under a disability may not defend any proceedings except by his guardian *ad litem*.[6] Secondly, and this carried great weight with SWINFEN EADY, J., the agent was a solicitor, an officer of the court upon whom the judiciary and other parties to litigation place great reliance. Much confusion would ensue " if a solicitor were not to be under any liability to the opposite party for continuing to act without authority in cases where he originally possessed one."[7]

An agency is terminated by an act of bankruptcy committed by the principal, if he is later adjudicated bankrupt upon a petition presented within three months after the commission of the act. In other words the adjudication relates back to the

Yonge v. *Toynbee*

Bankruptcy of principal

---

1. *Drew* v. *Nunn* (1879), 4 Q.B.D., at p. 668.
2. Powell, *The Law of Agency*, 2nd Edn., pp. 5–6 and 389–391. See Higgins, 1 *Tasmanian Law Review* 569, where the distinction is examined in a most helpful article.
3. [1910] 1 K.B. 215.
4. *Supra*, p. 485.
5. *Supra*, p. 483.
6. R.S.C. Ord. 80, r. 2 (1); replacing Ord. 16B, r. 2 (1).
7. *Yonge* v. *Toynbee*, [1910] 1 K.B. 215, at p. 233, *per* SWINFEN EADY, J. This reasoning did not impress BUCKLEY, L.J., *ibid.*, at pp. 228–9.

act of bankruptcy, provided that it is followed within three months by a successful petition. Despite this general rule, however, every act done or contract made by the agent before the receiving order is valid in favour of a third person dealing with him for value and without notice of an act of bankruptcy,[1] and is also valid in favour of the agent in the sense that he is freed from personal liability if, at the time of acting, he had no notice of an available act of bankruptcy.[2]

---

1. Bankruptcy Act 1914, s. 45.   *Re Douglas Ex parte Snowball*, (1872), 7 Ch. App. 534.
2. *Elliott* v. *Turquand* (1881), 7 App. Cas. 79.

CHAPTER THREE

The Voluntary Assignment of Contractual Rights and Liabilities

SECTION I. THE ASSIGNMENT OF CONTRACTUAL RIGHTS[1]

WE have seen that by the general rule of the common law a contract between A and B cannot confer rights or liabilities upon C. It remains to consider whether the right created by a contract can be expressly assigned by its owner to a third party. If A has sold goods of the value of £10 to B, can he assign to C the right to receive the £10? It is important to appreciate at the outset the significance of the word " assignment." What we have to ascertain is whether C, by virtue merely of the assignment, without the collaboration of the assignor and without the consent of the debtor, can enforce payment of the debt to himself. In short, can an assignee bring an action on his own initiative against a recalcitrant debtor? Does an assignment bind the debtor as well as the assignor?

> Meaning of " assignment "

This topic is generally described as the assignment of choses in action.

> Meaning of " chose in action "

> " Chose in action is a known legal expression used to describe all personal rights of property which can only be claimed or enforced by action, and not by taking physical possession."[2]

---

1. See Bailey, 47 L.Q.R. 516; 48 L.Q.R. 248 and 547.
2. *Torkington* v. *Magee,* [1902] 2 K.B. 427, at p. 430, *per* CHANNELL, J.

It is a term that comprises a large number of proprietary rights, such as debts, shares, negotiable instruments, rights under a trust, legacies, policies of insurance, bills of lading, patents, copyrights and rights of action arising out of tort or breach of contract. Many of these have been made assignable by statute, as, for instance, policies of life or marine insurance,[1] negotiable instruments,[2] copyrights,[3] bills of lading[4] and shares in companies.[5] Our concern, however, is to show that apart from such statutory provisions a chose in action is also assignable in equity. We shall deal principally with ordinary contractual rights.

A. THE ASSIGNABILITY OF CONTRACTUAL RIGHTS

Assignment not recognized at common law

At common law a chose in action, such as a right arising under a contract, cannot be assigned so as to entitle the assignee to sue for its recovery in his own name. The assignment gives the assignee a right against the assignor personally, but not an independent right of action against the debtor. An action for recovery must be brought by or in the name of the assignor, and this depends upon the willingness of the assignor to lend his name to the proceedings. The assignee can, of course, enforce payment by taking a power of attorney authorizing him to sue on behalf of the assignor, but in this case he recovers the debt not as assignee, but as directly representing the person of the assignor.[6] The common law rule is subject to two exceptions, for from the earliest times it was recognized that the Crown might make or take an assignment of choses in action; and with the growth of the doctrine of negotiability rights under bills of exchange and promissory notes became freely assignable.[7]

Assignment permitted in equity

The notion that a contractual right is incapable of transfer represents an archaic and inconvenient view, and it is therefore not remarkable that it was soon repudiated by equity. As early as the beginning of the seventeenth century the court of chancery recognized and enforced the assignment of choses in action generally.

" At common law a debt was looked upon as a strictly personal obligation, and an assignment of it was regarded as a mere assignment of a right to bring an action at law against the debtor. . . .   But the courts of equity took a different view. They admitted the title of an assignee of a debt, regarding it as a piece of property, an asset capable of being dealt with like any other asset, and treating the necessity of an action at law to get it in as a mere incident."[8]

---

1. Policies of Assurance Act 1867, s. 1: Marine Insurance Act 1906, s. 50 (2).
2. Bills of Exchange Act 1882; *infra,* pp. 509 *et seq.*
3. Copyright Act 1956, s. 36 (1) (3).   Assignment must be written.
4. Bills of Lading Act 1855, s. 1.
5. Companies Act 1948, s. 73.   Assignment must be made in the manner prescribed by the articles of the particular company.
6. *Master* v. *Miller* (1791), 4 Term. Rep. 320, at p. 340.
7. Holden, *The History of Negotiable Instruments in English Law.*
8. *Fitzroy* v. *Cave,* [1905] 2 K.B. 364, at p. 372, *per* COZENS-HARDY, L.J.

An equitable assignment cannot of course transfer the right of action at law, but it confers upon the assignee the right to invoke the aid of equity. Equity considers that as done which ought to be done, and, since the parties have agreed that the common law right under the contract is the property of the assignee, the assignor must allow an action at law to be brought in his own name so as to make the transaction effectual.

> " An assignment . . . operates in equity by way of agreement, binding the conscience of the assignor, and so binding the property from the moment when the contract becomes capable of being performed."[1]

No particular form is required to constitute a valid equitable assignment. The transaction upon which the assignee relies need not even purport to be an assignment nor use the language of an assignment. If the intention of the assignor clearly is that the contractual right shall become the property of the assignee, then equity requires him to do all that is necessary to implement his intention. The only essential and the only difficulty is to ascertain that such is the intention. Lord MacNaghten, speaking of an equitable assignment, said:

> *No formalities required for equitable assignment*

> " It may be addressed to the debtor. It may be couched in the language of command. It may be a courteous request. It may assume the form of mere permission. The language is immaterial if the meaning is plain."[2]

Where there is a contract between the owner of a chose in action and another person which shows a clear intention that such person is to have the benefit of the chose, there is without more a sufficient assignment in the eye of equity. It follows, therefore, that to perfect the title *as between assignor and assignee* no notice to the debtor is necessary.[3] The object of notice, as we shall see later, is to prevent the debtor from paying the assignor, and also to give the assignee priority over other assignees.[4]

Notice to debtor not necessary to perfect the assignment

Our next inquiry is to ascertain the exact effect of an equitable assignment as regards the assignee's right of action against the debtor. Can an equitable assignee always sue the debtor by bringing an action in his own name? The answer to this question depends, first, upon the nature of the right assigned, *i.e.* whether it is a legal or an equitable chose in action; secondly, upon the nature of the assignment, *i.e.* whether it is absolute or non-absolute.

Effect of assignment depends upon two factors

A legal chose in action is a right that can be enforced by an action at law, as, for example, a debt due under a contract. An equitable chose in action is a right that was enforceable before

(i) Whether the chose in action is legal or equitable

---

1. *Tailby* v. *Official Receiver* (1888), 13 App. Cas. 523, at p. 546, *per* Lord MacNaghten.
2. *Brandt's Sons & Co.* v. *Dunlop Rubber Co.,* [1905] A.C. 454, at p. 462. *Re Wale,* [1956] 3 All E.R. 280, at p. 283; [1956] 1 W.L.R. 1346, at p. 1350; *Letts* v. *Inland Revenue Commissioners,* [1956] 3 All E.R. 588, at p. 592; [1957] 1 W.L.R. 201, at pp. 212–14. In principle, it would seem that the assignor need not inform the assignee of what he has done. The decisive factor is the assignor's intention, see *Comptroller of Stamps (Victoria)* v. *Howard-Smith* (1936), 54 C.L.R. 614, at p. 622.
3. *Gorringe* v. *Irwell India Rubber Works* (1886), 34 Ch.D. 128.
4. *Infra*, p. 503.

the Judicature Act 1873 only by a suit in equity.   It is a right connected with some form of property, such as trust property, over which Chancery formerly had exclusive jurisdiction, and it is exemplified by a legacy or by an interest in a trust fund.

(ii) Whether the assignment is absolute or not

An absolute assignment is one by which the entire interest of the assignor in the chose in action is for the time being transferred unconditionally to the assignee and placed completely under his control.   To be absolute it is not necessary, however, that the assignment should take the form of an out and out transfer which deprives the assignor for ever of all further interest in the subject-matter.   Thus, it is now well settled that a mortgage in the ordinary form, *i.e.* an assignment of a chose in action as security for advances, with a proviso for redemption and reassignment upon repayment of the loan, is an absolute assignment.[1] In such a case the whole right of the mortgagor in the subject-matter passes for the time being to the mortgagee, and the fact that there is an express or implied right to re-assignment upon redemption does not destroy the absolute character of the transfer. In *Hughes* v. *Pump House Hotel Co.*:[2]

> A building contractor executed a written instrument by which, in consideration of his bankers allowing him an overdraft, and by way of security to them for all money due or falling due in the future under his account, he assigned to them all moneys due or to become due to him under his building contracts.   He also empowered the bankers to settle all accounts in connection with the buildings and to give receipts for money paid for work done by him.

It was held that the written instrument, since it unconditionally assigned for the time being all moneys due or to become due under the building contracts, constituted an absolute assignment.

From absolute assignments must be distinguished, firstly, conditional assignments; secondly, assignments by way of charge; and thirdly, assignments of part of a debt.

Conditional assignment distinguished

A conditional assignment is one which is to become operative or to cease to be operative upon the happening of an uncertain event.   An example of this occurred in *Durham Brothers* v. *Robertson*,[3] where:

> A firm of builders executed the following document in favour of the plaintiffs: " Re Building Contract, South Lambeth Road.   In consideration of money advanced from time to time we hereby charge the sum of £1,080, which will become due to us from John Robertson on the completion of the above buildings, as security for the advances, and we hereby assign our interest in the above-mentioned sum *until the money with added interest be repaid to you.*"

It was held that this was merely a conditional assignment.   At first sight, perhaps, it appears difficult to reconcile this decision with that given in *Hughes* v. *Pump House Hotel Co.*,[4] but if the position of the respective debtors is considered, the difference between the two cases becomes apparent.   In the present case

---

1. *Tancred* v. *Delagoa Bay and East Africa Rail. Co.* (1889), 23 Q.B.D. 239; *Hughes* v. *Pump House Hotel Co.,* [1902] 2 K.B. 190.
2. [1902] 2 K.B. 190.
3. [1898] 1 Q.B. 765.
4. *Supra* footnote 1.

the whole sum due from Robertson was not assigned to the plaintiffs, but only so much of it as would suffice to repay the money actually advanced together with interest.   The document stated in effect that when that amount was paid, which was an uncertain event, the interest of the assignee was automatically to cease.   Thus the debtor, Robertson, became directly concerned with the state of accounts between the assignor and assignee, for he would not be justified under the document in making a payment to the latter after the money actually lent with interest had been repaid.   In *Hughes* v. *Pump House Hotel*, on the other hand, the debt was in terms transferred completely to the assignee. There was no limitation of the amount for which the assignment should be effective, there was to be no automatic reverter to the assignor upon repayment of the loan, and therefore the debtors, until they received notice of redemption and actual re-assignment, would be entitled to make payments to the assignee without reference to the state of accounts between him and the assignor.

The distinction, then, is this: Where a re-assignment is necessary, as it is in the case of an assignment by way of mortgage, " notice of the re-assignment will be given to the original debtor, and he will thus know with certainty in whom the legal right to sue him is vested.   On the other hand, where the assignment is conditional, the original debtor is left uncertain as to the person to whom the legal right is transferred."[1]

An assignment by way of charge is one which merely entitles the assignee to payment out of a particular fund and which, unlike the case of a mortgage, does not transfer the fund to him.[2]   Thus in *Jones* v. *Humphreys*:[3]

A schoolmaster assigned to a money-lender so much of his salary as should be necessary to repay a sum of £22 10s. which he had already borrowed and any further sums which he might borrow.

Assignment by way of charge distinguished

It was held that this was not an absolute assignment of the salary, but a mere security which entitled the money-lender to have recourse to the salary according to the state of the school-master's indebtedness.

After considerable conflict of judicial opinion it is now settled that the assignment of a definite part of a debt is not an absolute assignment.[4]   To be absolute an assignment must transfer the chose in action in its entirety.

Assignment of part of a fund distinguished

We are now in a position to state the effect of an equitable assignment upon the right of recovery vested in the assignee. The effect may be stated in three rules.

Effect of equitable assignment

---

1. Ashburner, *Principles of Equity*, 2nd Edn., p. 238.
2. *Tancred* v. *Delagoa Bay and East Africa Rail. Co.* (1889), 23 Q.B.D. 239, at p. 242, *per* DENMAN, J.; *Burlinson* v. *Hall* (1884), 12 Q.B.D. 347, at p. 350.
3. [1902] 1 K.B. 10.   Where there is no intention to assign a debt to X, he may in certain circumstances be able to maintain an action for money had and received against the debtor; *Shamia* v. *Joory*, [1958] 1 Q.B. 448; [1958] 1 All E.R. 111, *infra*, pp. 653–5.
4. *Re Steel Wing Co., Ltd.*, [1921] 1 Ch. 349; *Williams* v. *Atlantic Assurance Co.*, [1933] 1 K.B. 81; [1932] All E.R. Rep. 32; *Walter and Sullivan, Ltd.* v. *J. Murphy & Sons, Ltd.*, [1955] 2 Q.B. 584; [1955] 1 All E.R: 843.   The title to the part assigned, however, passes to the assignee in equity.

(a) Absolute assignment of equitable chose: assignee may sue in his own name

(a) An absolute assignment of an *equitable* chose in action entitles the assignee to bring an action in his own name against the debtor.[1] If, for instance, A assigns to B the whole of his beneficial interest in a legacy, B can sue the executor in his own name. The common law prohibition of assignments has, of course, never applied to a chose that was within the exclusive jurisdiction of equity, and since the absolute character of the transfer makes it unnecessary to examine the state of accounts between the parties, there is no reason why the assignor should be a party to the action.

(b) Non-absolute assignment of equitable chose: assignor must be a party to an action

(b) The non-absolute assignment of an *equitable* chose in action does not entitle the assignee to sue in his own name, but requires him to join the assignor as a party. This joinder of the assignor is necessary on practical grounds, for in every case where an assignment is not absolute, as, for instance, where it is conditional or by way of charge, the state of accounts between the parties is the critical factor. The debtor occupies the position of a stakeholder who is willing to pay the person rightfully entitled, but as neither he nor the court knows what the exact rights of the parties are it is essential that the assignor should be a party to the action in order that his interest may be bound. Again, if an assignment affects part only of the assignor's interest, the court cannot adjudicate finally without the presence of both parties.

> " The absence of such parties might result in the debtor being subjected to future actions in respect of the same debt, and moreover might result in conflicting decisions being arrived at concerning such debt."[2]

By the same reasoning the assignor cannot recover the amount remaining due to him from the debtor without joining the assignee as a party to the action.[3]

(c) Assignment of legal chose: assignor must be a party to an action

(c) An assignment, whether absolute or not, of a *legal* chose in action does not entitle the assignee to sue in his own name, but requires him to join the assignor as a party to any action he may bring for the recovery of the right assigned. The reason for this is due to the different views taken by common law and equity. A legal chose is one that would be recoverable only in a common law court, and since the rule at law was that a contractual right was incapable of assignment, it followed that the court could not allow an assignee to sue in his own name. The solution was for the assignor to sue personally or to join in the action brought by the assignee, and the court of chancery would compel him to collaborate in this fashion in order to complete the equitable title that he had transferred. This would necessitate the institution of a suit in chancery as a preliminary to the common law action.[4] Such, however, is no longer the case, and the practice has long been for the assignee to join a contumacious assignor as co-defendant with the debtor.[5]

---

1. *Cator v. Croydon Canal Co.* (1841), 4 Y. & C. Ex. 593, at pp. 593–4.
2. *Re Steel Wing Co.*, [1921] 1 Ch. 349, at p. 357, *per* P. O. LAWRENCE, J.
3. *Walter and Sullivan, Ltd.* v. *J. Murphy & Sons, Ltd.*, [1955] 2 Q.B. 584; [1955] 1 All E.R. 843.
4. *Wood v. Griffith* (1818), 1 Swan. 44, at pp. 55–6, *per* Lord ELDON.
5. *Bowden's Patents Syndicate, Ltd.* v. *Herbert Smith & Co.*, [1904] 2 Ch. 86, at p. 91, *per* WARRINGTON, J.

These equitable rules with regard to the assignment of choses in action were adequate except in one respect. Where the assignment related to a legal chose in action the machinery of recovery was unnecessarily complicated, since the assignee might be compelled to initiate chancery proceedings before he was qualified to sue at law. There is no reason in nature why the assignee of an ordinary debt should, as regards his right of recovery, be in any different position from the assignee of a purely equitable right such as a share in a trust fund; yet owing solely to a conflict between law and equity he was compelled in the former case to sue in collaboration with the assignor, while in the latter he could sue alone. This was an anachronism which called for abolition when the Judicature Act 1873 amalgamated the superior courts of law and equity into the Supreme Court of Judicature. The main purpose of this legislation " was to enable a suitor to obtain by one proceeding in one court the same ultimate result as he would previously have obtained either by having selected the right court, as to which there frequently was a difficulty, or after having been to two courts in succession, which in some cases he had to do under the old system."[1] In pursuance of this policy, section 25 (6) of the Act introduced a statutory form of assignment which enabled the assignee of a legal chose in action to sue in his own name, subject to certain conditions. This provision has now been replaced by the Law of Property Act 1925,[2] in a section which runs as follows:

Statutory assignee of legal chose may now sue in his own name

Judicature Act 1873

> Any absolute assignment by writing under the hand of the assignor (not purporting to be by way of charge only) of any debt or other legal thing in action, of which express notice in writing has been given to the debtor, trustee, or other person from whom the assignor would have been entitled to claim such debt or thing in action, is effectual in law (subject to equities having priority over the right of the assignee) to pass and transfer from the date of such notice:
>
> (a) the legal right to such debt or thing in action;
> (b) all legal and other remedies for the same; and
> (c) the power to give a good discharge for the same without the concurrence of the assignor.

Law of Property Act 1925

The phrase in the statute " debt or other legal thing in action " is misleading. It might be supposed that it bore the same meaning as before the Judicature Act 1873, and that it was confined to such *choses in action* as were recoverable only in a common law court. It has, however, been interpreted judicially to mean " all rights the assignment of which a court of law or equity would before the Act have considered *lawful*," and it therefore includes equitable as well as legal *choses in action*.[3]

There are three conditions that must be satisfied if an assignment is to derive validity from the statute:

Essentials of statutory assignment

it must be absolute;

it must be written; and

written notice must be given to the debtor.

---

1. *Torkington* v. *Magee*, [1902] 2 K.B. 427, at p. 430, *per* CHANNELL, J.
2. Section 136.
3. *King* v. *Victoria Insurance Co., Ltd.*, [1896] A.C. 250, at p. 254; *Re Pain, Gustavson* v. *Haviland*, [1919] 1 Ch. 38, at pp. 44–5.

If void as
a statutory
assignment
may be valid
in equity

If there is a failure to comply with either of the last two conditions, or if compliance with the first is impossible, as, for instance, where the assignment is conditional or by way of charge, the transaction is not void. It is void as a statutory assignment but it still stands as a perfectly good equitable assignment. This means that the assignee of the legal chose in action cannot take advantage of the new machinery set up by the Act and bring an action in his own name, but must fall back upon the rules governing equitable assignments and join the assignor as a party. It is still the law that an assignee of a legal chose in action, who for some reason or other cannot prove a good statutory assignment, must make the assignor either a co-plaintiff or a co-defendant to any action that he brings.[1]

The statute
has only
affected
procedure

The statute has not altered the law in substance. It is merely machinery. It does not confer a right of action which did not exist before, but enables the right of action that has always existed to be pursued in a less roundabout fashion.[2] It " has not made contracts assignable which were not assignable in equity before, but it has enabled assigns of assignable contracts to sue upon them in their own names without joining the assignor."[3] Again it " does not forbid or destroy equitable assignments or impair their efficacy in the slightest degree."[4]

Is con-
sideration
necessary
for equitable
assignment?

An assignment, whether of a legal or an equitable chose in action, which satisfies the requirements of the statute, transfers the title by virtue of the statute itself and requires no consideration.[5] A question, however, that has been much canvassed is whether a non-statutory, *i.e.* an equitable assignment, is effective as between assignor and assignee if made for no consideration.[6] Is a gift of the chose in action valid and irrevocable? The answer depends upon a distinction, fundamental throughout equity, between a completed and an incomplete assignment.

Not necessary
for completed
assignment

The equitable assignment of a chose, *if completed*, even though it is unsupported by consideration, is just as effective and just as irrevocable as the gift of personal chattels perfected by delivery of possession.[7] It is, indeed, almost superfluous to say that " a person *sui juris*, acting freely, fairly and with sufficient knowledge, has it in his power to make, in a binding and effectual

1. *Performing Right Society, Ltd.* v. *London Theatre of Varieties, Ltd.*, [1924] A.C. 1, at pp. 14, 20, 30–31.
2. *Re Westerton, Public Trustee* v. *Gray*, [1919] 2 Ch. 104, at pp. 112–13. In Australia it has been held that since the introduction of a statutory form of assignment, all assignments must follow the statutory form. Thus the statutory rules displace the equitable rules though an inperfect assignment may in some cases take effect as a contract to assign. *Olsson* v. *Dyson* (1969), 120 C.L.R. 365. This is not an illogical view but it clearly does not represent English law, which treats the statutory rules as supplementing and not supplanting those of equity.
3. *Tolhurst* v. *Associated Portland Cement Manufacturers* (1900), *Ltd.*, [1903] A.C. 414, at p. 424, *per* Lord LINDLEY.
4. *Brandt's Sons & Co.* v. *Dunlop Rubber Co.*, [1905] A.C. 454, at p. 461, *per* Lord MACNAGHTEN.
5. *Re Westerton, Public Trustee* v. *Gray*, [1919] 2 Ch. 104, at pp. 112–13.
6. Marshall, *The Assignment of Choses in Action*, Chap. IV; Megarry, 59 L.Q.R. 58, 208, Holland, 59 L.Q.R. 129, Hall, [1959] C.L.J. 99.
7. *Spellman* v. *Spellman*, [1961] 2 All E.R. 498, at p. 501, [1961] 1 W.L.R. 921, at p. 925, *per* DANCKWERTS, J.; Diamond, 24 M.L.R. 789.

manner, a voluntary gift of any part of his property, whether capable or incapable of manual delivery, whether in possession or reversion."[1]

On the other hand it is equally clear that a gratuitous agreement to assign a chose in action, like a gratuitous promise to give any form of property, is *nudum pactum* unless made under seal, and creates no obligation either legal or equitable.

Necessary for agreement to assign

> " The rule in equity comes to this : that so long as a transaction rests in expression of intention only, and something remains to be done by the donor to give complete effect to his intention, it remains uncompleted, and a court of equity will not enforce what the donor is under no obligation to fulfil. But when the transaction is completed, and the donor has created a trust in the object of his bounty, equity will interfere to enforce it."[2]

Thus the question in each case is whether the transaction upon which the voluntary assignee relies constitutes a perfect and complete assignment or not, and this in turn depends upon the meaning of a completed assignment. The general principle of law is that a gift is complete as soon as everything has been done by the donor that, according to the nature of the subject-matter, is necessary to pass a good title to the donee. A good title is vested in the donee if he has been placed in such a position that he is free to pursue the appropriate proprietary remedy on his own initiative, without the necessity of seeking the further collaboration of the donor. Whether the donee has been put in this position depends upon the nature of the *res donata*. If, for instance, A delivers a chattel to B with the intention of passing the ownership, he has done all that the law requires for the transfer of the property in the chattel, and it is clear that B has obtained a title which he can protect by an action of trover. But if the donative intention has not been fulfilled by delivery of the chattel or alternatively by the creation of a trust in favour of the donee, the gift remains incomplete and the intended donee is remediless. He cannot compel the donor to fulfil the promise to give. The promise is *nudum pactum* at common law for want of consideration, and it is a well established principle of equity that the court will not perfect an imperfect gift—will not constrain a donor to take the requisite steps for the transfer of ownership.[3]

What constitutes a completed assignment

(1) In general

Applying these principles to the gift by way of equitable assignment of an existing *chose in action*, all that is necessary is to ascertain whether the donee is in a position to pursue the appropriate remedy against the debtor without the necessity of any further act on the part of the assignor. If so, the gift is complete and its efficacy remains undisturbed by the absence of consideration.[4] Whether the donee is in this position depends upon the nature of the equitable assignment.

(2) In the case of an existing chose in action

1. *Kekewich* v. *Manning* (1851), 1 De G.M. & G. 176, at p. 188, *per* KNIGHT BRUCE, L.J.   *Re McArdle,* [1951] Ch. 669, at p. 674; [1951] 1 All E.R. 905, at p. 908.
2. *Harding* v. *Harding* (1886), 17 Q.B.D. 442, at p. 444, *per* WILLS, J.
3. *Ellison* v. *Ellison* (1802), 6 Ves. 656.   *Milroy* v. *Lord* (1862), 4 De G.F. & J. 264, at p. 274, *per* TURNER, L.J.
4. *Re McArdle,* [1951] Ch. 669, at p. 677; [1951] 1 All E.R. 905, at pp. 909–10.

An equitable assignment is one that does not satisfy the requirements of the Law of Property Act.[1]   It may fail in this respect for two different reasons.

First, it may be defective in form because not made in writing.[2] Secondly, it may not be absolute.

(a) Absolute
asignment
not in the
statutory
form

To take the first defect, it is now clear that a mere failure to observe the statutory form is immaterial in the present context. It does not prevent the assignment from being perfect and complete in the eyes of equity.   An absolute assignment of an existing *chose in action*, whether legal or equitable, is complete as soon as the assignor has finally and unequivocally indicated that it is henceforth to belong to the assignee.   Nothing more is necessary.

This has always been true of the equitable *chose in action*, since this was a species of property formerly within the exclusive jurisdiction of Chancery and therefore free from the restrictions of the common law.   It was not, however, formerly true of the legal *chose in action*.   This was recoverable only by an action at law and, since common law did not recognize the assignment of contractual rights, the assignee, though admitted by equity to have acquired a good title, was inevitably obliged to sue in the name of the assignor.   To this extent, the collaboration of the assignor was necessary to perfect the transaction.   But when the existing practice was admitted of allowing the assignee to satisfy the requirement of joinder of parties by merely adding the assignor as a defendant,[3] nothing remained to be done by the assignor to complete the transaction.   At the present day, therefore, the absolute assignment of a legal or equitable *chose in action*, though not in the statutory form, is effective despite the want of consideration.[4]

---

1. *Supra,* p. 499.
2. The statutory requirement of written notice to the debtor is irrelevant in the present context, for notice is not necessary to perfect the assignment between the assignor and assignee: *Holt* v. *Heatherfield Trust, Ltd.,* [1942] 2 K.B. 1, at pp. 4–5; [1942] 1 All E.R. 404, at p. 407, though it is necessary for other reasons, *infra,* p. 503.
3. *E. M. Bowden's Patents Syndicate, Ltd.* v. *Herbert Smith & Co.,* [1904] 2 Ch. 86, at p. 91.
4. *Harding* v. *Harding* (1886), 17 Q.B.D. 442; *Re Patrick, Bills* v. *Tatham,* [1891] 1 Ch. 82; *Re Griffin, Griffin* v. *Griffin,* [1899] 1 Ch. 408; *Holt* v. *Heatherfield Trust, Ltd.,* [1942] 2 K.B. 1; [1942] 1 All E.R. 404; *Re McArdle,* [1951] Ch. 669; [1951] 1 All E.R. 905.   The *dictum* of PARKER, J., in *Glegg* v. *Bromley,* [1912] 3 K.B. 474, at p. 491, that: " If there be no consideration there can be no equitable assignment," must be confined to the assignment of a *future* debt, with which alone the case was concerned, see *per* LUSH, L.J., in *German* v. *Yates* (1915), 32 T.L.R. 52.   *Re McArdle,* the facts of which have been given, *supra,* p. 61, is in one respect a difficult case. The so-called assignment was written and therefore it satisfied the statute as regards form.   On the assumption, however, that the document was what it purported to be, i.e., an agreement to transfer a specific sum of £488 in consideration of the promisee carrying out certain future improvements, the Court of Appeal was apparently prepared to treat it as a valid equitable assignment of the £488 (at pp. 677, 910 respectively).   This seems a curious approach to what would have been a normal and valid contract.   Why should the promisee do more than sue for breach?   If the document had in terms assigned the £488 in consideration of improvements already executed, it would indeed have been necessary to plead an assignment, for the past nature of the consideration would have prevented any claim in contract. But it would have been a statutory assignment.

The second class of equitable assignment is one which is not of an absolute character, though it may be in writing as required by the statute.   In this case the assignment is not yet complete, for something still remains to be done to complete the title of the assignee.   If it is conditional, as when its efficacy depends upon the consent of a third party, it remains incomplete until the condition is satisfied;[1] if it is by way of charge, as in *Jones* v. *Humphreys*,[2] nothing definite is due until the state of accounts between the assignor and assignee has been finally settled and divulged to the debtor.   Since the assignment is unsupported by consideration and since the assignee is not yet entitled to demand payment from the debtor, there is no escape from the rule that equity will not perfect an imperfect gift.

(b) Assignment in the statutory form, but not absolute

Another possible defect, distinct in nature, is that the assignment may relate to future property, such as a share of money that may fall in on the death intestate of a person now living, or the damages that may be recovered in a pending action.   In such a case what purports to be an assignment is nothing more than an agreement to assign, under which even in equity nothing is capable of passing until the subject-matter comes into present existence.   The agreement binds the conscience of the assignor, and, if supported by consideration, it binds the subject-matter when it comes into existence.[3]   Until this event occurs, however, the agreement cannot be converted into a completed assignment, for there is nothing definite capable of forming the subject-matter of a transfer.[4]   It follows, therefore, that the donee of a future chose in action is remediless.   He cannot allege a completed assignment, and he cannot enforce a gratuitous promise.

(c) Assignment of future chose in action

B. RULES THAT GOVERN ASSIGNMENTS, WHETHER STATUTORY OR EQUITABLE

I. NOTICE

Written notice to the debtor or other person from whom the right assigned is due is necessary to complete the title of one who claims to be a statutory assignee under the Law of Property Act. It becomes effective at the date on which it is received by or on behalf of the debtor.[5]   The written notice is an essential part of the statutory transfer of the title to the debt and therefore it is ineffective unless strictly accurate—accurate, for instance, as regards the date of the assignment and *semble* as regards the amount due from the debtor.[6]

Statutory assignment

---

1. *Re Fry, Chase National Executors and Trustees Corporation* v. *Fry*, [1946] Ch. 312; [1946] 2 All E.R. 106.
2. *Supra*, p. 497.
3. *Re Trytel, Ex parte the Trustee of the property of the Bankrupt* v. *Performing Right Society, Ltd. and Soundtrac Film Co., Ltd.*, [1952] 2 T.L.R. 32.
4. *Tailby* v. *Official Receiver* (1888), 13 App. Cas. 523, at p. 546, *per* Lord MacNaughten;   *Glegg* v. *Bromley*, [1912] 3 K.B. 474, at p. 489.
5. *Holt* v. *Heatherfield Trust, Ltd.*, [1942] 2 K.B. 1, at pp. 5–6; [1942] 1 All E.R. 404, at pp. 407–8.
6. *W. F. Harrison & Co., Ltd.* v. *Burke*, [1956] 2 All E.R. 169; [1956] 1 W.L.R. 419.

Equitable assignment. Notice not essential but desirable for two reasons

On the other hand, notice is not necessary to perfect an equitable assignment. Even without notice to the debtor the title of the assignee is complete, not only against the assignor personally,[1] but also against persons who stand in the same position as the assignor, as, for instance, his trustee in bankruptcy, a judgment creditor or a person claiming under a later assignment made without consideration.[2]

Nevertheless, there are at least two reasons why failure to give notice may seriously prejudice the title of an equitable assignee.

(i) To bind debtor

Firstly, an assignee is bound by any payments which the debtor may make to the assignor in ignorance of the assignment.[3]

(ii) To gain priority

Secondly, it is established by the rule in *Dearle* v. *Hall*[4] that an assignee must give notice to the debtor in order to secure his title against other assignees. An assignee who, at the time when he completes the transaction, has no notice of an earlier assignment and who himself gives notice of the transaction to the debtor, gains priority over an earlier assignee who has failed to give a like notice. The fact that he has discovered the existence of the prior assignment at the time when he gives notice is immaterial, provided that he had no actual or constructive knowledge of it when his own assignment was completed.[5]

Form of notice

The form of the notice depends upon the nature of the right assigned. If what is assigned is an equitable interest in land or in personalty then notice is required by statute to be in writing,[6] but in other cases no formality is required. The one essential in all cases is that the notice should be clear and unambiguous. It must expressly or implicitly record the fact of assignment, and must plainly indicate to the debtor that by virtue of the assignment the assignee is entitled to receive the money.[7] If it merely indicates that on grounds of convenience payment should be made to a third party as agent of the creditor, the debtor is not liable if he pays the creditor direct.[8]

2. AN ASSIGNEE TAKES SUBJECT TO EQUITIES

Assignee subject to defences available against assignor

An assignee, whether statutory or not, takes subject to all equities that have matured at the time of notice to the debtor. This means that the debtor may plead against the assignee all defences that he could have pleaded against the assignor at the time when he received notice of the assignment.

---

1. *Gorringe* v. *Irwell India Rubber Works* (1886), 34 Ch.D. 128.
2. *Re Trytel, Ex parte the Trustee of the property of the Bankrupt* v. *Performing Right Society, Ltd. and Soundtrac Film Co., Ltd.,* [1952] 2 T.L.R. 32.
3. *Stocks* v. *Dobson* (1853), 4 De G.M. & G. 11. See also *Warner Brothers Records, Inc.* v. *Rollgreen, Ltd.,* [1975] 2 All E.R. 105; [1975] 2 W.L.R. 816.
4. (1828), 3 Russ. 1.
5. *Mutual Life Assurance Society* v. *Langley* (1886), 32 Ch.D. 460.
6. Law of Property Act 1925, s. 137 (3). See *Van Lynn Developments, Ltd.* v. *Pelias Construction Co., Ltd.,* [1969] 1 Q.B. 607; [1968] 3 All E.R. 824.
7. *James Talcott, Ltd.* v. *John Lewis & Co., Ltd., and North American Dress Co., Ltd.,* [1940] 3 All E.R. 592.
8. *Ibid.,* at p. 596.

" The authorities upon this subject, as to liabilities, show that if a man does take an assignment of a chose in action he must take his chance as to the exact position in which the party giving it stands."[1]

A simple illustration is afforded by *Roxburghe v. Cox*:[2]

Lord Charles Ker, an army officer, assigned to the Duke of Roxburghe the money that would accrue to him from the sale of his commission. This money, amounting to £3,000, was paid on December 6th to the credit of his account with his bankers, Messrs. Cox. On that date his account was overdrawn to the extent of £647. On December 19th the Duke gave notice of the assignment to Messrs. Cox.

It was held that Messrs. Cox could set off the debt of £647 against the right of the Duke to the sum of £3,000. In the course of his judgment, JAMES, L.J., said:

" Now an assignee of a chose in action . . . takes subject to all rights of set-off and other defences which were available against the assignor, subject only to this exception, that after notice of an assignment of a chose in action the debtor cannot by payment or otherwise do anything to take away or diminish the rights of the assignee as they stood at the time of the notice. That is the sole exception. Therefore the question is, was this right of set-off existing at the time when the notice was given by the Duke of Roxburghe? Under the old law the proper course for the Duke to take would have been, not to come into a court of equity, but to use the name of Lord Charles Ker at law. . . In that case set-off could have been pleaded as against the assignor, and in the present mode of procedure that defence is equally available."[3]

Even unliquidated damages may by way of counter-claim be set off by the debtor against the assignee, provided that they flow out of and are inseparably connected with the contract which has created the subject-matter of the assignment.[4] Thus if a builder assigns to the plaintiff money that will be due from the defendant upon completion of a building, the defendant may set-off against the claim of the plaintiff any damage caused to him by the delay or by the defective work of the builder.[5] But nothing in the nature of a personal claim against the assignor can be used to defeat the assignee. Thus in *Stoddart v. Union Trust, Ltd.*:[6]

Assignee not subject to personal claims against assignor

A fraudulently induced B to buy a paper from him for £800. The right to the £800 was assigned by A to C, who was ignorant of the fraud. When sued by C for the debt of £800, B pleaded that by reason of the fraud of A he had sustained damage in excess of £800 and that no money was due from him.

It was held that this claim to damages could not succeed against the assignee, C. It is, of course, true that if a contract is voidable against the assignor by reason of his fraud or other misconduct, it is equally voidable against the assignee, but in this case the debtor, B, did not seek to rescind the contract. He recognized

---

1. *Mangles* v. *Dixon* (1852), 3 H.L. Cas. 702, at p. 735, *per* Lord ST. LEONARDS.
2. (1881), 17 Ch.D. 520.
3. *Ibid.*, at p. 526.
4. *Newfoundland Government* v. *Newfoundland Rail. Co.* (1888), 13 App. Cas. 199, at p. 213.
5. *Young* v. *Kitchin* (1878), 3 Ex. D. 127.
6. [1912] 1 K.B. 181.

the existence of the contract but claimed damages for the deceit of the assignor. This, however, was nothing more than to claim damages against C for a fraud of which he was innocent. " The claim for damages is a personal claim against the wrongdoer; it is something *dehors* the contract."[1]

3. RIGHTS INCAPABLE OF ASSIGNMENT

The rights that are incapable of assignment include pensions and salaries payable out of national funds to public officers, and alimony granted to a wife, but the most important examples are a bare right of litigation and rights under contracts that involve personal skill or confidence.

Bare right of action not assignable

Any assignment is void if it savours of maintenance, i.e. if it amounts to assistance given to one of the parties to an action by a person who has no legitimate interest in that action. This is the basis of the rule that a " bare right of action " is unassignable.[2] What this means is that if all that is assigned is the right to recover unliquidated damages for a breach of contract or for a tort, or for waste,[3] or to set aside a transaction for fraud,[4] the assignment is void. It seeks to transfer nothing more than " a hostile right to bring parties into court."[5]

Nevertheless, a right of action may be validly assigned if it is a subsidiary but an essential part of the main subject-matter of the assignment. If, for example, A sells his interest in property or his benefit of a contract to B he may also assign to B any right of action that is necessary to render the proprietary or contractual right effective. The question always is whether the right of action is one of the incidents attached to the property or contract while in the hands of the assignor.[6] PARKER, J., summed up the authorities in these words:

> " The question was whether the subject-matter of the assignment was, in the view of the court, property with an incidental remedy for its recovery, or was a bare right to bring an action either at law or in equity."[7]

As the Court of Appeal had said in an earlier case:

> " An assignment of a mere right of litigation is bad; but an assignment of property is valid, although that property may be incapable of being recovered without litigation."[8]

Thus, an agreement by a vendor of the fee simple in land that the purchaser shall be entitled to recover by action rents already due from the tenant in possession, and also to sue in respect of injuries and dilapidations committed previously to the purchase,

---

1. [1912] 1 K.B., at p. 194, *per* KENNEDY, L.J.
2. Marshall, *The Assignment of Choses in Action*, pp. 49–65.
3. *Defries* v. *Milne*, [1913] 1 Ch. 98.
4. *Prosser* v. *Edmonds* (1835), 1 Y. & C. Ex. 481.
5. *Ibid.*, at p. 496, *per* Lord ABINGER. Cf. *Di Guilo* v. *Boland* (1958), 13 D.L.R. 2(d) 510.
6. *Dawson* v. *Great Northern and City Rail. Co.*, [1905] 1 K.B. 260, at p. 271, *per* STIRLING, L.J.
7. *Glegg* v. *Bromley*, [1912] 3 K.B. 474, at p. 490.
8. *Dawson* v. *Great Northern and City Rail. Co.*, [1905] 1 K.B. 260, at p. 270, *per curiam*.

constitutes a valid assignment of a cause of action.[1]   Again, if
goods shipped on the defendant's vessel are delivered in a damaged
condition, the consignee, after being indemnified for his loss by the
insurers, may assign to the latter his right to recover damages from
the defendants.   He assigns the benefit of his contract with the
shipowners to the insurers together with the attached right to
recover damages for breach.[2]

It may be added that there is nothing objectionable in the
assignment of the fruits of litigation, which for this purpose are on
all fours with other forms of property.   In *Glegg* v. *Bromley*[3] for
instance, a wife mortgaged to her husband whatever damages she
might recover in her pending action against X.   This was an
assignment of future property under which nothing would pass to
the husband unless and until the property came into existence
upon the successful conclusion of the action.   Therefore, no
question of maintenance could ever arise.

If A purports to assign the benefit of a contract which he
has made with B, it is essential to consider whether the position
of B, the person liable, will be prejudicially affected.   No man
can be compelled to perform something different from that which
he stipulated for, and any assignment that will put him in this
position is void.[4]   If, for instance, the contract between A and
B involves personal skill or confidence, each party can insist
upon personal performance by the other, for otherwise he would
not receive that to which he is entitled.   Thus an agreement by
an author to write a book for a publisher is a personal contract,
the benefit of which cannot be assigned by the publisher without
the consent of the author.[5]   In fact, the rule would seem to be
that assignment "is confined to those cases where it can make no
difference to the person on whom the obligation lies to which of
two persons he is to discharge it."[6]   In *Kemp* v. *Baerselman*[7] for
instance:

> The defendant, a provision merchant, agreed to supply the
> plaintiff, a cake manufacturer, with all the eggs that he should
> require for manufacturing purposes for one year, there being a
> stipulation that if supplies were maintained the plaintiff would not
> buy eggs elsewhere.   At the time of the contract the plaintiff had
> three places of business, but four months later he transferred his
> business to the National Bakery Company, to which he purported
> to assign the benefit of his contract with the defendant.

It was held that the contract was intended to be a personal one,
and that it could not be assigned against the will of the defendant.
The eggs were to be supplied as the plaintiff, whose needs
throughout the year could be estimated at the time of the contract,

Marginal notes: Assignment of fruits of litigation · Assignment must not prejudice debtor

---

1. *Williams* v. *Protheroe* (1829), 2 Moo. & P. 779; *Ellis* v. *Torrington*, [1920] 1
   K.B. 399.
2. *Compania Colombiana de Seguros* v. *Pacific Steam Navigation Co.*, [1965]
   1 Q.B. 101; [1964] 1 All E.R. 216.
3. *Supra.*
4. *Tolhurst* v. *Associated Portland Cement Manufacturers* (1900), *Ltd.*, [1902]
   2 K.B. 660, at p. 670.
5. *Stevens* v. *Benning* (1854), 1 K. & J. 168; affirmed (1855), 6 De G.M. & G,
   223; *Reade* v. *Bentley* (1857), 3 K. & J. 271; *Griffith* v. *Tower Publishing Co.*.
   [1897] 1 Ch. 21.
6. *Tolhurst* v. *Associated Portland Cement Manufacturers* (1900), *Ltd.*, [1902]
   2 K.B. 660, at p. 668, *per* COLLINS, M.R.
7. [1906] 2 K.B. 604.

should require; and again, the plaintiff was not to purchase eggs elsewhere. This last provision would cease to benefit the defendant, and would, indeed, become meaningless, if the contract were assigned to another person.[1]

What is the position if the contract sought to be assigned itself prohibits assignment? Such prohibitions are common, for example, in contracts of hire-purchase. Much must depend on the precise wording of the prohibition but it is thought that only very clear words will make the assignment ineffective between assignor and assignee though the assignment will probably be ineffective against the debtor.[2]

C. NOVATION DISTINGUISHED FROM ASSIGNMENT

Novation distinguished from assignment

The assignment of a debt as described in the preceding pages, which operates as an effective transfer without the consent or the collaboration of the debtor, is distinguishable from novation, a transaction to which the debtor must be a party.

Meaning of novation

Novation is a transaction by which, with the consent of all the parties concerned, a new contract is substituted for one that has already been made. The new contract may be between the original parties, *e.g.*, where a written agreement is later incorporated in a deed; or between different parties, *e.g.*, where a new person is substituted for the original debtor or creditor.[3] It is this last form, the substitution of one creditor for another, that concerns us at the moment. The effectiveness of such a substitution was concisely illustrated by BULLER, J.

" Suppose A owes B £100, and B owes C £100, and the three meet, and it is agreed between them that A shall pay C the £100; B's debt is extinguished, and C may recover the sum against A."[4]

In this case a contract is made between A, B and C, by which the original liability of A to B is discharged in consideration of his promise to perform the same obligation in favour of C, the other party to the new contract. A transaction of this nature, however, is not effective as a novation unless an intention is clearly shown that the debt due from A to B is to be extinguished. Otherwise the novation fails for want of consideration.[5]

Thus novation, unlike assignment, does not involve the transfer of any property at all, for it comprises, (a) the annulment of

---

1. *Tolhurst* v. *Associated Portland Cement Manufacturers (1900), Ltd.*, [1902] K.B. 660, which at first sight seems difficult to reconcile with the general rule, was decided on the ground that the terms of the contract, when properly construed, provided for assignment; see *Nokes* v. *Doncaster Amalgamated Collieries, Ltd.*, [1940] A.C. 1014, at p. 1020, *per* Lord SIMON, [1940] 3 All E.R. 549, at p. 552.
2. See Guest, *The Law of Hire Purchase*, para. 700; Atiyah, 5 Business L.R. 24; *Re Turcan* (1888), 40 Ch.D. 5; *United Dominions Trust* v. *Parkway Motors, Ltd.*, [1955] 2 All E.R. 557; [1955] 1 W.L.R. 719; *Spellman* v. *Spellman*, [1961] 2 All E.R. 498; [1961] 1 W.L.R. 921 (Diamond, 24 M.L.R. 789); *Wickham Holdings, Ltd.* v. *Brooke House Motors, Ltd.*, [1967] 1 All E.R. 117, [1967] 1 W.L.R. 295 (Diamond, 30 M.L.R. 322).
3. *Scarf* v. *Jardine* (1882), 7 App. Cas. 345, at p. 351, *per* Lord SELBORNE.
4. *Tatlock* v. *Harris* (1789), 3 T.R. 174, at p. 180.
5. *Liversidge* v. *Broadbent* (1859), 4 H. & N. 603.

one debt and then (b) the creation of a substituted debt in its place.[1]

D. NEGOTIABILITY DISTINGUISHED FROM ASSIGNABILITY

A negotiable instrument is like cash in the sense that the property in it is acquired by one who takes it *bona fide* and for value.   Just as the true owner cannot recover stolen money once it has been honestly taken by a tradesman in return for goods, so also the *bona fide* holder for value obtains a good title to a negotiable instrument even though the title of the previous holder is defective. This is one of the cases in which the maxim *nemo dat quod non habet* has no application.   One who delivers either cash or a negotiable instrument can pass a better title than he himself possesses.   The law on negotiability has passed through three historical stages.   It began as a body of custom among merchants; it was later incorporated by the courts into the common law; it was then consolidated by the Bills of Exchange Act 1882.

Negotiable instrument is similar to cash

For an instrument to be negotiable, two things must concur:

Essential elements

Firstly, it must be one which is transferable by delivery by virtue either of statute or of the law merchant.

Secondly, it must be in such a state that nothing more than its delivery is required to transfer the right which it contains to a transferee.

We may illustrate these attributes from the case of a cheque. According to the usage of bankers as recognized by the courts, it has long been established that the mere delivery of a cheque is capable of transferring to the deliveree the right to demand the amount for which it is drawn.   Whether delivery, without more, will transfer this right depends, however, upon the state of the cheque.   If a cheque for £100 is made payable to " Edward Coke *or bearer* " it is negotiable in the fullest sense of the term, for by its very terms its mere delivery to William Blackstone entitles the latter to demand £100 from the bank.   The position, however, is different if the cheque is made payable to " Edward Coke *or order*."   The words " Edward Coke *or order* " mean that the bank will pay any person to whom Coke, by a declaration of his intention on the back of the instrument, orders payment to be made.   Before this intention has been declared, however, the cheque is not a negotiable instrument, for delivery alone does not entitle the deliveree to demand payment.   An order, called an *endorsement*, must be added by the payee Coke.   If he merely signs his own name on the back, he is said to endorse the cheque *in blank*, and the result is that the bank will pay any person who tenders the instrument and demands payment.   In other words, the effect of an endorsement in blank is to render the cheque payable to bearer and thus to confer upon the holder for the time being a good title.[2]   Coke, however, may *specially endorse*

Must be in such a state that property in it passes by delivery

---

1. *Re United Railways of Havana and Regla Warehouses, Ltd.,* [1960] Ch. 52, at pp. 84, 86, affirmed, [1961] A.C. 1007; [1960] 2 All E.R. 332, H.L.
2. Section 2 of the Cheques Act 1957, however, has now removed the necessity for an endorsement in blank where a cheque payable to order is cashed at the payee's own bank or credited to his account there.

the cheque, *i.e.*, in addition to signing his own name he may write
on the back " Thomas Littleton *or order*." The effect of this is
that the bank will pay Littleton or any person designated by him,
so that if he merely signs his own name the cheque once more
becomes negotiable. The law has been summed up by BLACK-
BURN, J., in the following words:[1]

> " It may therefore be laid down as a safe rule that where an
> instrument is by the custom of trade transferable, like cash, by
> delivery, and is also capable of being sued upon by the person
> holding it *pro tempore,* then it is entitled to the name of a negotiable
> instrument. . . . The person who, by a genuine indorsement, or,
> where it is payable to bearer, by a delivery, becomes a holder, may
> sue in his own name on the contract, and if he is a *bona fide* holder
> for value, he has a good title notwithstanding any defect of title in the
> party (whether indorser or deliverer) from whom he took it."

A cheque remains freely transferable notwithstanding that it is
crossed " not negotiable." The effect of the crossing merely is
that a later holder can acquire no better title than the person from
whom he took it. Again, the transferability of a cheque is
unaffected even if crossed " account payee " or " account payee
only." The significance of these words is that if the cheque is
paid into the account of some person other than the payee the
bank is put on enquiry.[2]

No instrument is negotiable unless recognized as such by statute or mercantile usage An instrument does not possess the benefit of negotiability
merely because it contains an undertaking by one of the parties
to pay a definite sum of money to any holder for the time being.
To rank as negotiable it must be recognized as such either by
statute or by the law merchant. Cheques, bills of exchange and
promissory notes are now negotiable by virtue of the Bills of
Exchange Act 1882, but there are certain other instruments
which still derive their negotiability from the law merchant.
This part of the law is of comparatively recent origin.

> " It is neither more nor less than the usages of merchants and
> traders in the different departments of trade, ratified by the decisions
> of courts of law, which, upon such usages being proved before
> them, have adopted them as settled law with a view to the interests
> of trade and the public convenience; the court proceeding herein
> on the well-known principle of law that, with reference to trans-
> actions in the different departments of trade, courts of law, in
> giving effect to the contracts and dealings of the parties, will assume
> that the latter have dealt with one another on the footing of any
> custom or usage prevailing generally in the particular department.
> By this process, what before was usage only, unsanctioned by legal
> decision, has become engrafted upon, or incorporated into, the
> common law, and may thus be said to form part of it."[3]

Mercantile usage sanctioned by the courts A custom of the mercantile world by which a certain document
is treated as negotiable, if proved to be of a sufficiently general
nature, may be adopted by the courts, and it is by this process
that the list of negotiable instruments has gradually been increased.
In determining whether a custom has become so well established

---

1. *Crouch* v. *Credit Foncier of England* (1873), L.R. 8 Q.B. 374, at pp. 381–2,
   adopting a passage in *Smith's Leading Cases,* 13th Edn., pp. 533–4.
2. *Universal Guarantee Pty., Ltd.* v. *National Bank of Australasia, Ltd.,* [1965]
   2 All E.R. 98; [1965] 1 W.L.R. 691, P.C.
3. *Goodwin* v. *Robarts* (1875), L.R. 10 Exch. 337, at p. 346, *per* COCKBURN, C.J.

as to be recognizable by the courts, the length of time for which it has prevailed is of great importance; but in the modern world a still more important factor is the number of transactions of which it has formed the basis, and, if its adoption by merchants is frequent and widespread, the fact that it is of very recent origin does not prevent its judicial recognition.[1]   Among the instruments which owe their negotiability to the usage of merchants are Exchequer Bills, certain bonds issued by foreign Governments or by English or foreign companies, and debentures payable to bearer.

The transfer of a negotiable instrument differs from the assignment of a contractual right in three important respects.

Negotiability distinguished from assignability

Firstly, since one of the characteristics of a negotiable instrument is that the person liable for payment, as for instance, the acceptor of a bill of exchange or the banker in the case of a cheque, is under a duty to pay the holder for the time being, it follows that upon a transfer of the instrument there is no necessity that he should be notified by the new holder of the change of ownership.

No notice required in case of transfer

Secondly, unlike the assignee of a contractual right, the transferee of a negotiable instrument does not take subject to equities.   A holder for value who takes an instrument without notice of any defect in the title of the person who negotiated it to him acquires a perfect title.   Thus in *Miller* v. *Race*:[2]

Transferee does not take subject to equities

> On December 11th, 1756, the mail coach from London to Chipping Norton was robbed and a bank note that had been posted by a London debtor to his creditor in the country was stolen.   The next day the note was cashed by the plaintiff, who took it in the usual course of his business and without any notice that it had been stolen. It was held that the plaintiff was entitled to recover payment from the Bank of England.

Thirdly, the rule that consideration must move from the promisee, which as we have seen applies to contracts in general,[3] does not apply to a negotiable instrument, for the holder can sue for payment without proof that he himself gave value.   The only essential is that consideration should have been given at some time in the history of the instrument.   The Bills of Exchange Act provides that:

Extent to which consideration is necessary

> Where value has *at any time* been given for a bill the holder is deemed to be a holder for value as regards the acceptor and all parties to the bill who became parties prior to such time, *i.e.* prior to the time at which value was given.[4]

If, for instance, A accepts what is called an *accommodation bill* in favour of B, *i.e.* makes himself liable to pay (say) £100 to B or to B's order without receiving consideration, he is not liable without more to pay this amount to B; but if B negotiates the bill to C in payment for goods received, C acquires a right of action against A and B; and further, if C makes a gift of the bill to D the latter has a similar right of action against A and B.

Accommodation bill

---

1. *Edelstein* v. *Schuler*, [1902] 2 K.B. 144, at p. 154, *per* BIGHAM, J.
2. (1758), 1 Burr. 452.
3. *Supra*, pp. 69–72.
4. Section 27 (2).

Presumption that consideration has been given

As regards consideration, there is another respect in which negotiable instruments are free from a general principle of contract law. The general rule requires proof by a plaintiff to an action for breach of contract that he has given consideration, but in the case of a negotiable instrument the consideration is presumed to have been given. The burden is on the defendant to prove that none has been given.[1]

Presumption that holder took in good faith

Moreover, the holder is presumed to have taken the instrument in good faith and without notice of any illegality or other defect in the title of the person who negotiated it to him. There is this difference, however, between a plea of no consideration and a plea of illegality, that, once it has been shown that the instrument is vitiated by illegality as between previous parties, the burden of proving that he himself took in good faith passes to the holder.[2]

SECTION II. THE ASSIGNMENT OF CONTRACTUAL LIABILITIES

Burden of contract cannot be assigned without consent of creditor

The question that arises here is whether B can assign the obligation that rests upon him by virtue of his contract with A to a third person, C, so that the contractual liability is effectively transferred from him to C. Can he substitute somebody else for himself as obligor? English law has unhesitatingly answered this question in the negative. In the words of COLLINS, M.R.:

> " It is, I think, quite clear that neither at law nor in equity could the burden of a contract be shifted off the shoulders of a contractor on to those of another without the consent of the contractee. A debtor cannot relieve himself of his liability to his creditor by assigning the burden of the obligation to somebody else; this can only be brought about by the consent of all three, and involves the release of the original debtor."[3]

Burden assignable by a novation to which creditor is a party

Novation, therefore, is the only method by which the original obligor can be effectively replaced by another. A, B and C must make a new contract by which in consideration of A releasing B from his obligation, C agrees that he will assume responsibility for its performance. This transaction is frequently required upon the retirement of one of the partners of a firm. B, the retiring partner, remains liable at law for partnership debts contracted while he was a member of the firm; but if a particular creditor, A, expressly agrees with him and with the remaining members to accept the sole liability of the latter for past debts in place of the liability of the firm as previously constituted, the right of action against B is extinguished. As is said in the head-note to *Lyth* v. *Ault and Wood*:[4]

---

1. *Mills* v. *Barber* (1836), 1 M. & W. 425.
2. See *supra*, pp. 307–9, where the subject is illustrated by reference to wagering contracts.
3. *Tolhurst* v. *Associated Portland Cement Manufacturers (1900), Ltd.,* [1902] 2 K.B. 660, at p. 668.
4. (1852), 7 Exch. 669.

" The acceptance by a creditor of the sole and separate liability of one of two or more joint debtors is a good consideration for an agreement to discharge all the other debtors from liability."

An agreement by a creditor, A, to accept the liability of C in substitution for that of his former debtor, B, need not be express. Acceptance may be inferred from his conduct. Whether this inference is justifiable depends, of course, upon the circumstances. Thus, if a trader knows that a certain partner has retired, but nevertheless continues to deal with the newly constituted firm, the inference, in the absence of further rebutting circumstances, is that he regards the existing partners as solely liable.[1]

Implied novation

Except by novation, then, it is impossible for a debtor, B, to make a contract with C, by which he extinguishes his existing obligation to A and assigns it to C. The assignment may well be binding between himself and C, but it cannot *per se* deprive A of his right to proceed against B as being the contracting party. On the other hand, there are many cases in which vicarious performance is permissible in the sense that the promisee, A, cannot object that the work has been done by a third person, provided always, of course, that it has been done in accordance with the terms of the contract.

Vicarious performance is as a rule sufficient

" Much work is contracted for, which it is known can only be executed by means of sub-contracts; much is contracted for as to which it is indifferent to the party for whom it is to be done, whether it is done by the immediate party to the contract, or by someone on his behalf."[2]

If, for instance, B, who has contracted to deliver goods to A or to do work for A, arranges that C shall perform this obligation, then A is bound to accept C's act as complete performance, if in fact it fulfils all that B has agreed to do.[3] A cannot disregard the performance merely because it is not the act of B personally. *Qui facit per alium facit per se.*

The essential fact to appreciate, however, in this case of delegated performance is that the debtor, B, who has assigned his liability to C, is not relieved from his obligation to ensure due performance of his contract with A. B still remains liable to A, and C cannot be sued by A for non-performance or for defective performance.[4] The legal effect of the delegation is that A cannot repudiate a performance which satisfies the terms of the contract merely because it has not been completed by the original contracting party, B. In other words, the so-called assignment of an obligation is not an assignment in the true sense of the term, since it does not result in the substitution of one debtor for another. In the case of rights one creditor may be substituted for another, but the principle with regard to obligations is that they cannot be

Vicarious performance does not release contracting party

---

1. *Hart* v. *Alexander* (1837), 2 M. & W. 484; *Bilborough* v. *Holmes* (1876), 5 Ch.D. 255.
2. *British Waggon Co.* v. *Lea* (1880), 5 Q.B.D. 149, at p. 154, *per curiam.*
3. *British Waggon Co.* v. *Lea* (1880), 5 Q.B.D. 149; *Tolhurst* v. *Associated Portland Cement Manufacturers* (1900), Ltd., [1903] A.C. 414, at p. 417, *per* Lord MacNaghten.
4. *Schmaling* v. *Thomlinson* (1815), 6 Taunt. 147.

"shifted off the shoulders of a contractor on to those of another without the consent of the contractee."[1]

Vicarious
performance
of personal
contract is
no perform-
ance
It is not, however, permissible in all cases to delegate the task of performance to another person. Each case depends upon its own particular circumstances. In the words of Lord GREENE:

> "Whether or not in any given contract performance can properly be carried out by the employment of a sub-contractor, must depend on the proper inference to be drawn from the contract itself, the subject-matter of it and other material surrounding circumstances."[2]

For instance, a contract of carriage may normally be sub-contracted by the carrier, but this will not avail the contractor if the subject matter of the load is an easy and a frequent target for lorry thieves.[3]

Moreover, it is clear that delegation is not permissible if personal performance by B, the promisor, is the essence of the contract. If it can be proved that A relied upon performance by B and by B only, the inability or unwillingness of B to perform his obligation discharges A from all liability, even though performance has been completed by a third person in exact accordance with the agreed terms.[4] Vicarious performance of a personal contract is not performance in the eye of the law. It neither discharges the debtor nor binds the creditor. If it can be shown that A has contracted with B because he reposes confidence in him, as for example where he relies upon his individual skill, competency, judgment, taste or other personal qualifications,[5] or if it is clear that he has some private reason for contracting with B and with B only,[6] then the inference is that the contract is one of a personal nature which does not admit of vicarious performance. Thus, it has been held that the personal skill and care of the warehouseman is of the essence of a contract for the storage of furniture, and that if he employs a sub-contractor he does so at his own risk.[7] A case which goes perhaps to the verge of the law is *Robson and Sharpe v. Drummond*,[8] where the facts were these:

> B agreed to build a carriage and to hire it out to A for five years for a yearly payment of 75 guineas. B was to keep the carriage in repair, to paint it once within the five years and to supply new wheels when required. More than two years later B retired from business and he purported to assign to his successor, C, all his interest in the contract with A.

It was held that the contract was personal and that A was entitled to reject the performance offered by C. Although PARKE, J. expressed his unhesitating opinion that A was entitled to the benefit of the judgment and taste of B himself throughout the five years, it might perhaps have been objected that, as the carriage

---

1. Per COLLINS, M.R., cited, *supra*, p. 508.
2. *Davies v. Collins*, [1945] 1 All E.R. 247, at p. 250.
3. *Garnham, Harris and Elton, Ltd.* v. *Alfred W. Ellis (Transport), Ltd.*, [1967] 2 All E.R. 940; [1967] 1 W.L.R. 940 (copper wire).
4. *British Waggon Co.* v. *Lea* (1880), 5 Q.B.D. 149, at p. 153.
5. *Robson and Sharpe* v. *Drummond* (1831), 2 B. & Ad. 303.
6. *Boulton* v. *Jones* (1857), 2 H. & N. 564, *supra*, p. 229.
7. *Edwards* v. *Newland & Co.* (*E. Burchett, Ltd., Third Party*), [1950] 2 K.B. 534; [1950] 1 All E.R. 1072.
8. (1831), 2 B & Ad. 303.

had been designed and built by B to the satisfaction of A, the only detail which in any sense depended upon these personal qualifications was the painting. In a later case the Court of Appeal refused to apply the principle of this decision to a contract by which B had agreed to hire out railway wagons to A and to keep them in repair for seven years.[1]

---

1. *British Waggon Co.* v. *Lea* (1880), 5 Q.D. 149.

CHAPTER FOUR

The Involuntary Assignment of Contractual Rights and Liabilities

THE automatic assignment by operation of law of contractual rights and liabilities may occur upon the death or bankruptcy of one of the contracting parties.

Death

The general rule of common law, that the maxim *actio personalis moritur cum persona* does not apply to an action for breach of contract, has been confirmed by statute. This provides that on the death of a contracting party " all causes of action subsisting against or vested in him shall survive against or, as the case may be, for the benefit of, his estate."[1] If the deceased made a contract with X, his personal representatives, whether executors or administrators, may recover damages for its breach, or may themselves perform what remains to be done and then recover the contract price.[2] Conversely, they may be sued by X in their representative capacity for a breach of the contract, whether committed before or after the death of the deceased, though they are liable only to the extent of the assets in their hands.[3]

This rule that the right of action survives does not apply where personal considerations are the foundation of the contract. This is the position, for instance, where the contracting parties are master and servant,[4] or racehorse owner and jockey.[5] Thus, if a servant dies his executors are not faced with the alternative of performing the services or of paying damages; if the master dies, the servant is discharged of his obligation to serve.[6]

Bankruptcy

The object of bankruptcy proceedings is to collect all the property of the bankrupt and to divide it rateably among his creditors. The rule, therefore, is that any right of action for breach of contract possessed by him which relates to his property and which, if enforced, will swell his assets, passes to his trustee

---

1. Law Reform (Miscellaneous Provisions) Act 1934, s. 1 (1). For a discussion of the effect of death, see North, 116 N.L.J. 1364.
2. *Marshall* v. *Broadhurst* (1831), 1 Cr. & J. 403.
3. *Wentworth* v. *Cock* (1839), 10 Ad. & El. 42; *Cooper* v. *Jarman* (1866), L.R. 3 Eq. 98; *Ahmed Angullia bin Hadjee Mohamed Salleh Angullia* v. *Estate and Trust Agencies* (1927), *Ltd.,* [1938] A.C. 624; [1938] 3 All E.R. 106.
4. *Farrow* v. *Wilson* (1869), L.R. 4 C.P. 744.
5. *Graves* v. *Cohen* (1929), 46 T.L.R. 121.
6. *Farrow* v. *Wilson, supra.*

in bankruptcy.[1] Instances are a contract by a third person to deliver goods or to pay money to the bankrupt. On the other. hand, the right to sue for an injury to the character, feelings or reputation of a bankrupt, though arising from a breach of contract, does not vest in the trustee.[2]

> " The right of action does not pass where the damages are to be estimated by immediate reference to pain felt by the bankrupt in respect to his body, mind or character, and without immediate reference to his rights of property."[3]

For instance, in *Wilson* v. *United Counties Bank*,[4] a trader entrusted the financial side of his business to a bank during his absence on military duty in the European war of 1914. He was subsequently adjudicated bankrupt owing to the negl:gent manner in which this contractual duty was performed, and, in an action which he and the trustee brought against the bank, damages of £45,000 were awarded for the loss to his estate and of £7,500 for the injury to his credit and reputation. It was held that of these two sums the £7,500 belonged personally to the bankrupt as representing compensation for damage to his reputation, while the £45,000 went to the trustee for the benefit of the creditors.

If a bankrupt has made a contract for personal services, the question whether his right to sue for its breach remains with him or passes to his trustee depends upon the date of breach. If the breach occurs before the commencement of the bankruptcy, the right of action passes to the trustee; if it occurs after this date the right of action remains with the bankrupt, subject to the power of the trustee to intervene and to retain out of the sum recovered what is not required for the maintenance of the bankrupt and his family. Thus the person entitled to recover damages against an employer for the wrongful dismissal of the bankrupt varies according as the dismissal occurs before or after the bankruptcy.[5]

Contracts for personal services

---

1. *Beckham* v. *Drake* (1849), 2 H.L. Cas. 579, at p. 627; *Jenning's Trustee* v. *King*, [1952] Ch. 899; [1952] 2 All E.R. 608.
2. *Rose* v. *Buckett*, [1901] 2 K.B. 449.
3. *Beckham* v. *Drake*, *supra*, at p. 604, *per* ERLE, J.
4. [1920] A.C. 102.
5. *Drake* v. *Beckham* (1843), 11 M. & W. 315 (before bankruptcy); *Bailey* v. *Thurston*, [1903] 1 K.B. 137 (after bankruptcy).

PART VII
DISCHARGE OF CONTRACT

SUMMARY

DISCHARGE OF CONTRACT

THE discharge of a contract means in general that the parties are freed from their mutual obligations. The extent of their freedom depends, however, upon the mode of discharge.

A contract is discharged in four ways:

(1) *By performance*

If both parties perform their promises the contract is completely terminated. If only one party performs, he alone is discharged and he acquires a right of action against the other. This right of action may itself be discharged by what is called an accord and satisfaction, i.e., by a new agreement under which the party in default is relieved from his liability in consideration of a promise by him to give or do something other than that which he was bound to do by the original contract.

(2) *By express agreement*

The parties may agree that their contract shall be terminated, and in this case whether their respective obligations are to be totally or only partially discharged depends of course upon the terms of the agreement. If the original contract is wholly or partially executory, the consideration for the discharging agreement is the mutual release of liability; but if it has been completely performed by one party, his discharge of the other must be under seal or must take the form of an accord and satisfaction supported by a fresh consideration.

(3) *Under the doctrine of frustration*

Under this doctrine a contract is sometimes discharged if a later event renders its performance impossible or sterile. In this case, the parties are discharged at common law from all obligations that became exigible after the occurrence of the frustrating event, and by statute from certain obligations maturing even before the event.

(4) *By breach*

It is only in certain circumstances that a breach operates as a discharge of the contract, but when it has this effect it relieves the innocent party from all liability, past or future. Moreover the party in default becomes liable to an action for damages from which he cannot effectually be released except by accord and satisfaction.

CHAPTER ONE

Discharge by Performance

SECTION I. THE GENERAL DOCTRINE THAT PERFORMANCE MUST BE PRECISE AND EXACT

Discharge by
performance
distinguished
from breach

The normal method of discharge is where both parties perform their obligations. In this event, of course, the contract is completely extinguished in the sense that both parties are freed from further liability. A second possibility is that one of the parties fails to perform his obligations and thus commits a breach of the contract. Here the other party, if he has performed or is ready and willing to perform his side of the contract, is alone discharged. The party in default remains liable. This situation, discharge by breach, is discussed in a later chapter,[1] and we are now concerned only with the effect of performance by both parties.

Performance
must be
precise and
exact

At first sight there seems little to be said about this. Nevertheless the topic is not so simple as it might seem, since it requires an answer to the question: What is meant by " performance "? The answer is that as a general rule the law does not regard a promisor as discharged unless he has completely and precisely performed the exact thing that he agreed to do. The strictness of the law in this respect is well illustrated by the duty of the seller to make delivery of the goods in exact accordance with the terms of the contract. Thus, if he delivers more goods than have been ordered, the buyer may reject the whole consignment

---

1. *Infra*, p. 568 *et seq.*

and cannot be required to select the correct quantity out of the bulk delivered.[1]   Again, if less than the correct quantity is delivered, the buyer may reject the goods.[2]   If the seller delivers the goods ordered accompanied by goods of a different description not ordered, the buyer may accept those which are in accordance with the contract and reject the rest, or he may reject the whole consignment.[3]   In one case, for instance:

> A agreed to sell to B tinned fruits and to deliver them in cases each containing thirty tins.   He tendered the correct quantity ordered, but about half the cases contained only twenty-four tins.

It was held that the buyer was entitled to reject the whole consignment.[4]

One result of this strict rule is that a party who has only partially performed his obligations cannot recover anything for the work that he has done.   A shipowner who fails to reach the agreed port of destination receives no freight for the distance that he has carried the goods; a builder who has agreed to construct a house for a lump sum and who abandons the work after erecting the greater part of the building is entitled to no remuneration. No remedy is open to the partial performer.

Partial performance gives no right to payment

In the first place, he cannot recover the whole contract price less the damages that he may be adjudged to pay in respect of his own breach of contract, for he has not satisfied the condition precedent to his right of recovery.   The consideration for his right to demand payment, namely, his promise to complete the work, is entire and indivisible, and by failing partially it fails altogether.[5]

Secondly, he cannot sue upon a *quantum meruit* to recover the value of the work that he has done.   The reason is that such an action is founded upon an implied promise by the other party to pay a reasonable sum for the work actually done, and it was laid down in *Britain* v. *Rossiter*[6] that such an implication is impossible so long as the express contract to pay the full amount remains in existence.   Nothing can be implied which is inconsistent with the express contract.   As one writer has put it:

> " Where the parties have provided that certain work shall be done for a lump sum, no judge can assert that it was their intention that a reasonable sum should be paid for each part of the work as it was performed."[7]

The effect of the general doctrine is unjustly to enrich the party to whose advantage a partial performance has operated.   The unhappy results that follow when the doctrine is pressed to its

Injustice of the rule

---

1. Sale of Goods Act 1893, s. 30 (2); *Cunliffe* v. *Harrison* (1851), 6 Exch. 903.
2. Sale of Goods Act 1893, s. 30 (1).
3. *Ibid.*, s. 30 (3); *Levy* v. *Green* (1857), 8 E. & B. 575
4. *Re Moore & Co. and Landauer & Co.*, [1921] 2 K.B. 519.
5. Notes to *Pordage* v. *Cole* (1669), 1 Wm. Saund. 319: Williams, 57 L.Q.R. 373, 490.
6. (1879), 11 Q.B.D. 123.
7. Williams, *The Law Reform (Frustrated Contracts) Act*, p. 3.

logical conclusion are vividly illustrated by the old case of *Cutter*
v. *Powell*.[1]

> The defendant agreed to pay Cutter thirty guineas provided that
> he proceeded, continued and did his duty as second mate in a
> vessel sailing from Jamaica to Liverpool. The voyage began on
> August 2nd and Cutter died on September 20th when the ship was
> nineteen days short of Liverpool.

An action by Cutter's widow to recover a proportion of the
agreed sum failed, for by the terms of the contract the deceased
was obliged to perform a given duty before he could demand
payment. Such a result is manifestly unjust, and the injustice
becomes even more apparent when the failure to perform is due
to the occurrence of some event beyond the volition of the parties
which makes further performance either impossible or meaningless. This is a particular aspect of the subject that is discussed in
a later chapter under the heading of discharge by frustration; but
it is pertinent to remark here that if, for instance, A agrees to erect
machinery on B's premises for a fixed sum of money, and his work,
when nearly complete, is totally destroyed by an accidental fire,
he cannot at common law recover one penny for what he has done.[2]

Necessity for
exceptions to
the rule Such, then, is the basic doctrine and such are some of its
results. For purely practical reasons, however, the common law
has been driven in some circumstances to adopt a lower standard
than that of precise and exact performance, and to engraft
exceptions upon the general rule that the partial fulfilment by a
promisor of his obligation does not entitle him to payment. The
necessity for this less rigid attitude can be illustrated by a hypothetical case. Suppose that A agrees to erect in B's house an
oil-burning furnace of a given dimension, and guarantees that it
will consume not more than a stated amount of oil and that it will
be noiseless. The furnace corresponds with the description and
its consumption of oil does not exceed what was promised, but it
is not completely noiseless. Is it to be said that B can return the
furnace, since A has not performed his obligations *in toto*? To
allow him to do so would be to introduce uncertainty and confusion
into everyday commercial dealings. There has been substantial
though not precise performance, and B is sufficiently protected if
he is allowed to recover damages for breach of warranty. This is
in fact, as we shall see, the limit of his rights in such a case. He
is not allowed to rescind the contract for so slight a divergence
from the path of strict performance.

Effect
of the
exceptions The law, then, recognizes that performance short of precise
and exact performance will in certain circumstances preclude the
promisee from treating the contract as discharged by breach.
Between discharge by performance and discharge by breach it
acknowledges an intermediate situation in which the promisor is
protected even though he has not fulfilled his obligations to the
letter. These exceptions to the general rule may now be discussed.

---

1. (1795), 6 Term. Rep. 320; see also *Sinclair* v. *Bowles* (1829), 9 B. & C. 92;
    Vigers v. *Cook*, [1919] 2 K.B. 475; Stoljar, 34 Can. Bar Rev. 288.
2. *Appleby* v. *Myers* (1867), L.R. 2 C.P. 651; *infra*, p. 563.

SECTION II. EXCEPTIONS TO THE GENERAL DOCTRINE

The question that requires an answer may be formulated thus:

> In what circumstances and within what limits may a party, who has not himself completely performed his obligations, maintain an action for damages?

Omitting the case of frustration for separate and later treatment, there are five situations in which a party is protected against his own failure to observe the requirement of strict performance. Between them they cover a wide field and represent a considerable inroad upon the general doctrine. Their common feature is that the party at fault is allowed recovery only to the extent of his performance. When he sues upon a *quantum meruit*,[1] this is obvious; but equally, when he sues for the contract price, the loss caused by his own partial failure of performance is set off in the defendant's favour. Thus the seller of goods who has committed a breach of warranty may recover the price, less the amount of loss suffered by the buyer by reason of the breach.

The following are the five exceptions to the general doctrine.

I. DIVISIBLE CONTRACTS

The common law rule, that a party who has not completely fulfilled his obligations cannot recover anything for the work that he has done, applies when the contract is entire, not when it is divisible. An entire contract is one in which it has been expressly or implicitly agreed that neither party shall be entitled to demand performance, either in whole or in part, until he himself has completely fulfilled, or is ready and willing to fulfil, his own promise. To put this in other language, a contract is entire if the promises are interdependent and concurrent. Thus there is always a presumption in favour of entirety, since in the normal case A undertakes his obligation subject to the implied condition that performance will not be due from him unless B completes or tenders performance on his side. If B fails in this respect, A can rescind the contract. Thus a promise in restraint of trade made by a servant is dependent upon the obligation of the master to employ and pay him in accordance with the contract, and therefore if he is wrongfully dismissed he is discharged from the obligation of the restraint.[2] A divisible contract is one which is so framed that it permits one party to demand performance without tendering performance himself. Here the promises are independent of each other. In the case, for instance, of a sale on credit, the seller's obligation to deliver the goods is independent of the buyer's obligation to pay the price. The latter does not become payable

---

1. *Infra*, p. 657 *et seq.*
2. *General Billposting Co., Ltd.* v. *Atkinson*, [1909] A.C. 118.

before the expiration of the credit period merely because the seller has already fulfilled his promise to deliver the goods.   Again, it has long been the rule that a tenant's covenant to pay rent is independent of the landlord's covenant to repair the premises, and that therefore he is not discharged from his obligation to pay merely because the landlord is not ready and willing to fulfil his obligation.[1]

Whether contract is divisible depends upon intention

The question whether a contract is entire or divisible, which at times is one of considerable difficulty, depends upon the inference to be drawn from the circumstances.   Normally, as we have seen, there is a presumption in favour of entirety, but in the case, for instance, of a contract to work materials into the property of another the *prima facie* rule, failing an express agreement to the contrary, is that payment can be demanded for what has already been done.   In the words of BLACKBURN, J.[2]:

> " Bricks built into a wall become part of the house; thread stitched into a coat which is under repair, or planks and nails and pitch worked into a ship under repair, become part of the coat or the ship; and therefore, generally and in the absence of something to show a contrary intention, the bricklayer, or tailor or shipwright is to be paid for the work and materials he has done and provided, although the whole work is not complete.   It is not material whether in such a case the non-completion is because the shipwright did not choose to go on with the work, as was the case in *Roberts* v *Havelock*,[3] or because in consequence of a fire he could not go on with it, as in *Menetone* v. *Athawes*."[4]

In divisible contract payment due for partial performance

Roberts v. *Havelock* is a strong case, for the contract there held to be divisible was one by which a shipwright had agreed to put a ship " into thorough repair."

The essential fact to observe, however, is that if the contract is construed as divisible, as frequently occurs where a seller agrees to deliver goods by instalments, the right to payment is not conditional on complete performance.   Payment keeps pace with performance and is " recoverable *toties quoties* by action on a *quantum meruit*."[5]   Thus in *Roberts* v. *Havelock* the shipwright was allowed to recover part payment before he had completed the work.

2. PREVENTION OF PERFORMANCE BY THE PROMISEE

Payment due if complete performance obstructed

If a party to an entire contract performs part of the work that he has undertaken and is then prevented by the fault of the other party from proceeding further, the law does not allow him to be deprived of the fruits of his labour.[6]   He is entitled, of course, to recover damages for breach of contract, but alternatively he can recover reasonable remuneration on a *quantum meruit* for what he

---

1. *Taylor* v. *Webb*, [1937] 2 K.B. 283; [1937] 1 All E.R. 590.
2. *Appleby* v. *Myers* (1867), L.R. 2 C.P. 651, at pp. 660–1.   The court held that the plaintiff had in fact agreed that no payment should be due until the whole work had been completed.   See *infra*, p. 563.
3. (1832), 3 B. & Ad. 404.
4. (1764), 3 Burr. 1592.
5. 2 *Smith's Leading Cases*, p. 1; notes to *Cutter* v. *Powell*.
6. *Appleby* v. *Myers* (1867), L.R. 2 C.P. 651, at p. 661.

has done.   The leading authority for this obvious rule is *Planché* v. *Colburn*,[1] which is discussed later.[2]

3. ACCEPTANCE OF PARTIAL PERFORMANCE BY THE PROMISEE

Although a promisor has only partially fulfilled his obligations under the contract, it may be possible to infer from the circumstances a fresh agreement by the parties that payment shall be made for the work already done or for the goods in fact supplied. Where this inference is justifiable the plaintiff sues on a *quantum meruit* to recover remuneration proportionate to the benefit conferred upon the defendant, but an essential of success is an implicit promise of payment by the defendant.

Implied contract to pay for partial performance

> Thus it has been held that if a ship freighted to Hamburg is prevented by restraints of princes from arriving, and the consignees accept the cargo at another port to which they have directed it to be delivered, they are liable upon an implied contract to pay freight *pro rata itineris*.[3]

An implicit promise to pay connotes a benefit received by the promisor, but the receipt of the benefit is not in itself enough to raise the implication.   No promise can be inferred unless it is open to the beneficiary either to accept or to reject the benefit of the work.[4]   This option exists where partial performance takes the form of short delivery under a contract for the sale of goods. If less than the agreed quantity of goods is delivered, and the buyer, instead of exercising his right of rejection, elects to accept them, he must pay for them at the contract rate.[5]   The position where there is no option and therefore no right to sue on a *quantum meruit* is well illustrated by *Sumpter* v. *Hedges*.[6]   In that case the plaintiff, who had agreed to erect upon the defendant's land two houses and stables for £565, did part of the work to the value of about £333 and then abandoned the contract.   The defendant himself completed the buildings.   It was held that the plaintiff could not recover the value of the work done.   COLLINS, L.J., said:

> "There are cases in which, though the plaintiff has abandoned the performance of a contract, it is possible for him to raise the inference of a new contract to pay for the work on a *quantum meruit* from the defendant's having taken the benefit of that work, but, in order that that may be done, the circumstances must be such as to give an option to the defendant to take or not to take the benefit of the work done . . . Where, as in the case of work done on land, the circumstances are such as to give the defendant no option whether he will take the benefit of the work or not, then one must look to other facts than the mere taking the benefit in order to ground the

---

1. (1831), 8 Bing. 14.
2. *Infra*, pp. 658-9.
3. *Christy* v. *Row* (1808), 1 Taunt. 300.   But the acceptance must be such as to raise the fair inference that the further carriage of the cargo is dispensed with; *St. Enoch Shipping Co., Ltd.* v. *Phosphate Mining Co.*, [1916] 2 K.B. 624, at p. 628.
4. *Munro* v. *Butt* (1858), 8 E. & B. 738.
5. Sale of Goods Act 1893, s. 30 (1).
6. [1898] 1 Q.B. 673.

inference of a new contract.   In this case I see no other facts on
which such an inference can be founded.   The mere fact that a
defendant is in possession of what he cannot help keeping, or even
has done work upon it, affords no ground for such an inference.
He is not bound to keep unfinished a building which in an incomplete
state would be a nuisance on his land."

4. THE DOCTRINE OF SUBSTANTIAL PERFORMANCE

The courts, in their desire to do justice between contracting
parties, have developed what is called the doctrine of substantial
performance, which in effect has somewhat relaxed the requirement of exact and precise performance of entire contracts.[1]
According to this doctrine, which dates back to Lord MANSFIELD's
judgment in *Boone* v. *Eyre* in 1779,[2] if there has been a substantial
though not perhaps an exact and literal performance by the
promisor, the promisee cannot treat himself as discharged.
Despite a minute and trifling variation from the exact terms by
which he is bound, the promisor is permitted to sue on the
contract, though he is of course liable in damages for his partial
non-performance.   According to this doctrine, the question
whether entire performance is a condition precedent to any
payment is always a question of construction.[3]   Thus in *Cutter*
v. *Powell*[4] the court construed the contract to mean that the sailor
was to get nothing unless he served as mate during the whole
voyage.   Again, in a contract to erect buildings or to do work on
another's land for a lump sum, the contractor can recover nothing
if he abandons operations when only part of the work is completed,
since his breach has gone to the root of the contract.   But if,
for example, the contractor has completed the erection of the
buildings, there has been substantial performance and the other
party cannot refuse all payment merely because the work is not
in exact accordance with the contract,[5] any more than the
employer in *Cutter* v. *Powell* could have repudiated all liability if
on one or two occasions the sailor had failed in his duty as mate.[6]
In such circumstances the present rule is that " so long as there is
substantial performance the contractor is entitled to the stipulated
price, subject only to a cross-action or counter-claim for the
omissions or defects in execution."[7]   If this were not the case
and if exact performance in the literal sense were always required,
a tradesman who had contracted to decorate a house according
to certain specifications for a lump sum might find himself in an
intolerable position.   If, for instance, he had put two coats of
paint in one room instead of three as agreed, the owner would

1. See Williams, 57 L.Q.R. 373, 490; Corbin, 28 Yale L.J. 739; Morison, 28
   L.Q.R. 398; 29 L.Q.R. 61; Ballantine, 5 Minnesota L.R. 329.
2. (1779), 1 Hy. Bl. 273, n.
3. *Hoenig* v. *Isaacs*, [1952] 2 All E.R. 176.
4. *Supra*, p. 524.
5. *H. Dakin & Co., Ltd.* v. *Lee*, [1916] 1 K.B. 566, approved and followed in
   Hoenig v. *Isaacs*, [1952] 2 All E.R. 176, despite the *dicta* in *Eshelby* v. *Federated
   European Bank, Ltd.*, [1932] 1 K.B. 423.
6. *Hoenig* v. *Isaacs, supra, per* SOMERVELL, L.J.
7. 2 Smith, L. C. 13th Edn., at p. 19, approved in *Hoenig* v. *Isaacs, supra.*   See
   also *Broom* v. *Davis* (1794), cited 7 East, 480 n, *Bolton* v. *Mahadeva*, [1972]
   2 All E.R. 1322; [1972] 1 W.L.R. 1009.   Cf. Beck 38 M.L.R. 413.

be entitled to take the benefit of all that had been done throughout the house without paying one penny for the work.[1]

5. BREACH OF WARRANTY

There is little that need be said about this at the present juncture. It is only necessary to recall what we have already seen, that the law distinguishes between conditions and warranties—between major and minor obligations.[2] Although a promisor who fails to implement a warranty cannot show precise and exact performance, this is not a sufficient reason for withholding from him recompense for what he may have done in fulfilment of his obligations. If the promisee unjustifiably elects to repudiate his obligation because of the failure, the promisor may sustain an action for breach of contract, but must submit to a diminution of damages in respect of his own breach of warranty. This rule represents in effect an application of the doctrine of substantial performance. A party must pay if he has received substantially the whole of what he was promised. The same principle is implicit in that section of the Sale of Goods Act which provides that even the breach of a condition by the seller does not always discharge the contract, and that if the buyer has accepted the goods it must be treated as a breach of warranty giving ground for a right only to damages.[3]

Breach of warranty does not discharge the contract

SECTION III. TENDER OF PERFORMANCE

If A, one party to a contract, cannot complete performance without the concurrence of the other party, B, it is obvious that an offer by him to perform and a rejection of that offer by B entitles him to a discharge from further liability. His readiness to perform has been nullified solely by the conduct of the other party. The rule, therefore, is that a tender of performance is equivalent to performance. In *Startup* v. *Macdonald*[4]:

Tender of performance is equivalent to actual performance

> The plaintiffs agreed to sell ten tons of oil to the defendant and to deliver it to him " within the last fourteen days of March," payment in cash to be made at the expiration of that time. Delivery was tendered at 8.30 p.m. on March 31st, a Saturday, but the defendant refused to accept or to pay for the goods owing to the lateness of the hour.

It was held that the tender of the oil was in the circumstances equivalent to performance and that the plaintiffs were entitled to recover damages for non-acceptance. The law is stated with such lucidity by ROLFE, B., that the following passage from his judgment deserves emphasis:

> " In every contract by which a party binds himself to deliver goods or pay money to another, he in fact engages to do an act

---

1. *Mondel* v. *Steel* (1841), 8 M. & W. 858, at p. 870, *per* PARKE, B.; *H. Dakin & Co., Ltd.* v. *Lee*, [1916] 1 K.B. 566, at p. 579, *per* COZENS HARDY, M.R.
2. *Supra,* pp. 135–144.
3. Section 11 (1) (c), as amended by the Misrepresentation Act 1967, s. 4.
4. (1843), 6 Man. & G. 593.

which he cannot completely perform without the concurrence of the party to whom the delivery or the payment is to be made. Without acceptance on the part of him who is to receive, the act of him who is to deliver or to pay can amount only to a tender.   But the law considers a party, who has entered into a contract to deliver goods or pay money to another, as having substantially performed it if he has tendered the goods or the money . . . provided only that the tender has been made under such circumstances that the party to whom it has been made has had a reasonable opportunity of examining the goods or the money tendered, in order to ascertain that the thing tendered really was what it purported to be.   Indeed without such an opportunity an offer to deliver or pay does not amount to a tender.   Now to apply this principle to the present case. The contract was to deliver the oil before the end of March.   The plaintiffs did tender the oil to the defendant at a time which, according to the express finding of the jury, left him full opportunity to examine, weigh and receive it, before the end of March.   If he had then accepted it . . . the contract would have been literally performed, and the neglect of the defendant to perform his part of the contract . . . cannot in my opinion in any manner affect the rights of the plaintiffs . . . They had fulfilled all they had contracted to do "[1]

The effect, however, of a tender varies according as the subject-matter is goods or money.

Effect of a tender of goods

If A actually produces goods of the correct quantity and quality to B, the rejection of his offer entirely discharges him from further liability and entitles him to recover damages for breach of contract.[2]

Effect of a tender of payment

If A produces to B the exact amount of money that he is contractually bound to pay, it is true that he need make no further tender, but nevertheless his obligation to pay the debt remains. If he is sued for breach he merely pays the money into court, whereupon the costs of the action must be borne by B.[3]

Requisites of valid tender

In order to constitute a valid tender of money, " there must be an actual production of the money, or a dispensation of such production "[4]; and also payment must be offered in what is called " legal tender," i.e., in the current coin of the realm or in Bank of England notes according to the rules established by law.   These rules prescribe that Bank of England notes are good tender for any amount;[5] gold coins for any amount; coins of cupro-nickel or silver exceeding ten new pence in value for any amount up to ten pounds; coins of cupro-nickel or silver of not mote than ten new pence in value up to five pounds only; coins of bronze for any amount up to twenty new pence only.[6]   The debtor must not ask for change but must tender the precise amount due, unless he is content to leave the surplus with the creditor.[7]

Time fixed for performance, essential at common law

If the parties fix a definite time for the completion of performance, the question arises whether it must be precisely observed.   Is time of the essence of the contract?[8]

The principle at common law is that, in the absence of a

---

1. At pp. 610–11.
2. *Startup* v. *Macdonald, supra.*
3. *Griffiths* v. *School Board of Ystradyfodwg* (1890), 24 Q.B.D. 307.
4. *Finch* v. *Brook* (1834), 1 Bing. N.C. 253, at p. 256, *per* TINDAL, C.J.; *Farquharson* v. *Pearl Assurance Co.,* [1937] 3 All E.R. 124.
5. Currency and Bank Notes Act 1954, s. 1.
6. Coinage Act 1971, s. 2.
7. *Robinson* v. *Cook* (1815), 6 Taunt. 336.
8. Stoljar, 71 L.Q.R. 527.

contrary intention, time is essential, even though it has not been expressly made so by the parties. Performance, therefore, must be completed upon the precise date specified, otherwise an action lies for breach.[1] A good illustration is afforded by the rule that, unless a contrary intention is clearly shown, a time fixed for delivery in a contract for the sale of goods must be exactly observed.[2]

On the other hand courts of equity, which have had to consider the matter in connection with suits for specific performance, have always taken a less rigid view.[3] Their view is that time is not necessarily essential, and if they can do so without injustice they will decree specific performance notwithstanding the failure of the plaintiff to observe the time fixed for completion.[4] This is especially so in the case of contracts for the sale of land. But the maxim that in equity the time fixed for completion is not of the essence of the contract does not mean that stipulations as to time may always be disregarded. Lord PARKER has made this clear in a well-known passage:

Not necessarily essential at equity

> " But this maxim never had any application to cases in which the stipulation as to time could not be disregarded without injustice to the parties, when, for example, the parties, for reasons best known to themselves, had stipulated that the time fixed should be essential, or where there was something in the nature of the property or the surrounding circumstances which would render it inequitable to treat it as a non-essential term of the contract. It should be observed, too, that it was only for the purposes of granting specific performance that equity in this class of case interfered with the remedy at law. A vendor who . . . had by his conduct lost the right to specific performance had no equity to restrain proceedings at law based on the non-observance of the stipulation as to time."[5]

In short, time is of the essence of the contract even in equity if such is the real intention of the parties. Moreover an intention to this effect may be expressly stated or may be inferred from the nature of the contract or from its attendant circumstances. By way of summary it may be said that time is essential in equity, firstly, if the parties expressly stipulate in the contract that it shall be so;[6] secondly, if, in a case where one party has been guilty of undue delay, he is notified by the other that unless performance is completed within a reasonable time the contract will be regarded as broken;[7] and lastly, if the nature of the surrounding circumstances or of the subject-matter makes it imperative that the agreed date should be precisely observed. Under this last head it has been held that a date fixed for completion is essential if contained in a contract for the sale of property which fluctuates

When time essential at equity

---

1. *Parkin* v. *Thorold* (1852), 16 Beav. 59.
2. *Bowes* v. *Shand* (1877), 2 App. Cas. 455 (sale of rice); *Reuter* v. *Sala* (1879), 4 C.P.D. 239 (sale of pepper); *Sharp* v. *Christmas* (1892), 8 T.L.R. 687 (sale of potatoes); *Hartley* v. *Hymans*, [1920] 3 K.B. 475, at p. 484.
3. 71 L.Q.R. 556.
4. *Stickney* v. *Keeble*, [1915] A.C. 386, at p. 415, *per* Lord PARKER; *Williams* v. *Greatrex*, [1956] 3 All E.R. 705; [1957] 1 W.L.R. 31.
5. *Stickney* v. *Keeble*, [1915] A.C. 386, at p. 416.
6. *Hudson* v. *Temple* (1860), 29 Beav. 536.
7. *Stickney* v. *Keeble*, [1915] A.C. 386; *Parkin* v. *Thorold* (1852), 16 Beav. 59; *Hartley* v. *Hymans*, [1920] 3 K.B. 475, at pp. 595–6; *Charles Rickards, Ltd.* v. *Oppenheim*, [1950] 1 K.B. 616; [1950] 1 All E.R. 420; *Ajit* v. *Sammy*, [1967] 1 A.C. 259.

in value with the passage of time, such as a public house,[1] business premises,[2] a reversionary interest[3] or shares of a speculative nature liable to considerable fluctuation in value.[4]

Equitable rule now prevails

The Law of Property Act 1925,[5] re-enacting section 25 of the Judicature Act 1873, provides as follows:

> Stipulations in a contract, as to time or otherwise, which according to rules of equity are not deemed to be or to have become of the essence of the contract, are also construed and have effect at law in accordance with the same rules.

The effect of this enactment is that, where the case is one in which equity would in a suit for specific performance have regarded a stipulation as to time as non-essential, then every court, even in an action for damages, must adopt the same attitude; but if the contract is one not capable of specific enforcement in equity, if for instance it is a mercantile contract, the equitable doctrine does not apply, and the common law view that time is essential prevails.[6] In the case, however, of the sale of goods, it is enacted that stipulations as to time of *payment* are not deemed to be of the essence of the contract unless a different intention appears from the terms of the contract. Whether any other stipulation as to time is essential or not depends on the terms of the contract.[7]

1. *Lock* v. *Bell*, [1931] 1 Ch. 35; [1930] All E.R. Rep. 635.
2. *Harold Wood Brick Co.* v. *Ferris*, [1935] 2 K.B. 198; [1935] All E.R. Rep. 603.
3. *Newman* v. *Rogers* (1793), 4 Bro. C.C. 391.
4. *Hare* v. *Nicoll*, [1966] 2 Q.B. 130; [1966] 1 All E.R. 285.
5. Section 41.
6. *Reuter* v. *Sala* (1879), 4 C.P.D. 239, at p. 249, *per* COTTON, L.J.
7. Sale of Goods Act 1893, s. 10 (1).

CHAPTER TWO

Discharge by Express Agreement

Eodem modo quo oritur, eodem modo dissolvitur. What has been created by agreement may be extinguished by agreement. An agreement by the parties to an existing contract to extinguish the rights and obligations that have been created is itself a binding contract, provided that it is either made under seal or supported by consideration.

> A contract may be discharged by a later contract

Consideration raises no difficulty if the contract to be extinguished is still executory, for in such a case each party agrees to release his rights under the contract in consideration of a similar release by the other. The discharge in such a case is bilateral, for each party surrenders something of value. The position is different where the contract to be extinguished, which we will call in future the original contract, is wholly executed on one side, as for instance where a seller has delivered the goods but the buyer has not paid the price. Here the seller has performed his part, and if he were merely to agree that the original contract should be discharged, i.e., that the buyer should be released from his obligation of payment, he would receive nothing of value in exchange. The buyer would have neither suffered a detriment himself nor have conferred an advantage upon the seller, but would be in the position of a donee. This, in other words, is a unilateral discharge, and it is ineffective unless it is made under seal or unless some valuable consideration is given by the buyer. Unilateral discharge in return for consideration is generally called accord and satisfaction. The accord is the agreement for the discharge of the original contract; the satisfaction is the consideration conferred upon the party who has performed his obligations.

> Bilateral discharge

> Unilateral discharge

Discharge by deed, which is equally effective in both cases, requires no discussion, but we will now deal separately with bilateral and unilateral discharge effected by a simple contract.

SECTION I. BILATERAL DISCHARGE

Contract, whether under seal or not, dischargeable if wholly or partially executory

This form of discharge is available to the parties whether their contract is either wholly or partially executory.   In the case of a contract for the sale of goods, for instance, it is available not only where there has been no payment and no delivery, but also where there has been partial though not complete delivery of the goods. It is immaterial that the contract is contained in a deed.   There was, indeed, a technical rule at common law that a contract under seal could not be dissolved, either wholly or partially, except by another contract under seal;[1] but courts of equity took an opposite view and held that a simple contract which extinguished or varied the deed was a good defence to an action on the deed.   This has become the rule in all courts since 1873, for the Judicature Act of that year provided that " in all matters in which there is any conflict or variance between the rules of equity and the rules of the common law with reference to the same matter, the rules of equity shall prevail."[2]   Thus in *Berry* v. *Berry*[3] :

> A husband covenanted in a deed of separation to pay his wife £18 a month.   Eight years later, by a written contract not under seal, he agreed to pay her £9 a month and 30 per cent. of his earnings if they exceeded £350 a year.

It was held that this simple contract was a good defence to an action brought by the wife to recover the sum fixed by the deed of separation.

Form of discharge where executory contract unenforceable unless evidenced in writing

A problem, however, that requires discussion arises where the executory contract is one which is rendered unenforceable by action unless supported by adequate written evidence as prescribed by statute.[4]   In such a case the question is whether the discharging contract must also conform to the statutory requirement. If, for example, a contract for the sale of land contains the written evidence required by the Law of Property Act 1925,[5] must an agreement to discharge it also comply with the Act? It was laid down by the House of Lords in the leading case of *Morris* v. *Baron & Co.*[6] that the solution of this problem depends upon the extent to which the parties intended to alter their existing contractual relations.   Their intention in this respect must be collected from the terms of the discharging contract. There are three possibilities.[7]

(i) Partial discharge

Firstly, the intention revealed by the second agreement may be merely to vary or modify the terms of the prior contract without altering them in substance.   It has long been established that

---

1. *West* v. *Blakeway* (1841), 2 Man. & G. 729.
2. Re-enacted in the Judicature Act 1925, s. 44.
3. [1929] 2 K.B. 316; [1929] All E.R. Rep. 281.
4. Examples of such statutes are the Statute of Frauds, s. 40 (contract of guarantee), *supra*, p. 178; Law of Property Act 1925, s. 40 (1) (contract for the sale or other disposition of land), *supra*, p. 184; see *United Dominions Corporation (Jamaica), Ltd.* v. *Shoucair*, [1969] 1 A.C. 340; [1968] 2 All E.R. 904, P.C.
5. Section 40 (1).
6. [1918] A.C. 1.
7. Stoljar, 35 Can. Bar Rev. 485.

such a partial discharge is ineffective unless it is contained in a contract that also provides the written evidence required by the relevant statute. An oral variation leaves the written contract intact and enforceable. What the parties are taken to intend is not that the first contract shall be extinguished, but that it shall continue as varied. Yet effect cannot be given to their intention, since there is no written evidence of the contract as now varied. A statute such as the Statute of Frauds or the Law of Property Act 1925 requires that the whole, not part, of the contract, shall be evidenced by writing.[1]

Secondly, the parties may intend to extinguish the original contract in its entirety and to put an end to their contractual relations. In this case the original contract is rescinded even though the discharging contract is not evidenced as required in the case of the original contract. Thus, an oral agreement to abrogate a written contract for the sale of land is effective.[2] The requirements of the Law of Property Act are directed to the creation of an enforceable contract, not to its extinction.

(ii) Discharge simpliciter

Thirdly, the intention of the parties may be to extinguish the former written contract, but to substitute for it a new and self-contained agreement. The result of such a bargain is that the prior written contract is rescinded, but the substituted agreement, if made orally, is unenforceable for want of written evidence.[3]

(iii) Original contract extinguished but replaced by fresh agreement

A difficult question of construction that may arise in this context is to discover what the parties intended to accomplish by their later oral agreement. Did they intend to extinguish the original contract altogether and to substitute a new contract in its place, or did they intend merely to vary the original contract? If the first of these hypotheses is correct, then the later contract effectively extinguishes the original contract but is itself unenforceable. If, on the other hand, the object of the parties was to modify their existing rights and obligations, the later contract is entirely destitute of effect. In order to decide this question the terms of the oral agreement must be examined; and if it is found that they are so far inconsistent with the original contract as to destroy its substance, though perhaps the shadow remains, the inference is that the parties intended to abrogate their former contract by the substitution of a new and self-contained agreement.

> " A written contract may be rescinded by parol either expressly or by the parties entering into a parol contract entirely inconsistent with the written one, or, if not entirely inconsistent with it, inconsistent with it to an extent that goes to the very root of it."[4]

To justify the conclusion in favour of abrogation, however, the inconsistency must relate to something fundamental.

---

1. *Morris* v. *Baron & Co.,* [1918] A.C. 1, at p. 31; *British and Beningtons, Ltd.* v. *N. W. Cachar Tea Co.,* [1923] A.C. 48, at p. 62, in both cases *per* Lord ATKINSON.
2. *Goman* v. *Salisbury* (1684), 1 Vern. 240; *Morris* v. *Baron & Co., supra,* at p. 18, *per* Lord HALDANE; at p. 26, *per* Lord DUNEDIN.
3. *Morris* v. *Baron & Co.,* [1918] A.C. 1; *infra,* p. 536.
4. *British and Beningtons, Ltd.* v. *N. W. Cachar Tea Co.,* [1923] A.C. 48, at p. 62, *per* Lord ATKINSON.

> " What is of course essential is that there should have been made manifest the intention in any event of a complete extinction of the first and formal contract, and not merely the desire of an alteration, however sweeping, in terms which still leave it subsisting."[1]

The manner in which the courts deal with this problem may be illustrated by two contrasting cases.

In *Morris* v. *Baron & Co.*,[2] the facts were as follows:

> Morris agreed to sell goods to Baron & Co. He delivered only part of the goods, valued at £888 4s., and six months later began proceedings to recover this sum. The company counter-claimed for £934 17s. 3d. as damages for non-delivery of the whole of the goods. Before this action came to trial, the parties compromised the dispute. They made an oral contract under which the action was to be withdrawn; the company was to have another three months within which to pay the sum due under the contract; it was to have the option either to accept or to refuse the undelivered goods; it was to be allowed £30 to meet the expenses incurred owing to the failure of Morris to make complete delivery.

Ten months later, the £888 4s. was still unpaid and Morris brought a second action to recover this sum. The company admitted liability, but again counter-claimed for damages in respect of the undelivered goods. The action failed for two reasons.

Firstly, Morris could not claim under the original contract. It had been extinguished. Its terms were so fundamentally inconsistent with the provisions of the compromise as to justify the inference that the parties intended to replace it by an entirely new contract.[3]

Secondly, neither Morris nor Baron & Co. could base any claim on the compromise, which itself amounted to a contract for the sale of goods.[4] Since it was made orally, it was unenforceable under section 4 of the Sale of Goods Act 1893, which still applied to such a contract at the time when *Morris* v. *Baron & Co.* was decided.[5] It operated to extinguish the original contract, but it could not be actively enforced.

On the other hand, *United Dominions Corporation (Jamaica), Ltd.* v. *Shoucair*[6] was a case in which the facts disclosed an intention to retain, not to abrogate, the original contract:

> A loan, secured by a mortgage and carrying interest at 9 per cent., was made in Jamaica by the appellants to the respondent. Owing to a rise in the local bank rate, the respondent at the request of the appellants agreed in writing to alter the rate of interest to 11 per cent. This written agreement was unenforceable since it did not comply with the Jamaican Moneylenders Act which corresponds to section 6 of the English Act of 1927. The Jamaican Act does not apply to loans bearing interest at 9 per cent. or less and therefore it did not affect the mortgage. The appellants, realising that they could not enforce the agreement of variation, sued for the recovery of interest at 9 per cent. due under the mortgage.

---

1. *Ibid.*, at p. 19, *per* Lord HALDANE.
2. [1918] A.C. 1.
3. See especially Lord ATKINSON, at p. 33.
4. See [1918] A.C., at p. 10, *per* Lord FINLAY; at p. 29, *per* Lord DUNEDIN; at p. 34, *per* Lord ATKINSON; at p. 36, *per* Lord PARMOOR.
5. *Supra*, p. 177. The repeal of this section of the Sale of Goods Act has greatly reduced the area of this question of construction.
6. [1969] 1 A.C. 340; [1968] 2 All E.R. 904.

The Privy Council gave judgment for the appellants. The parties intended by their written agreement to keep the mortgage alive, but to amend its provision relating to the rate of interest. But the mortgage remained intact, since it could not be affected by an amendment that infringed the statute. " If the new agreement reveals an intention to rescind the old, the old goes; and if it does not, the old remains in force and unamended."[1]

Such, then, is the law where the variation is made for the mutual advantage of both parties. A different and a slightly more complex situation may arise where the alteration of the contractual terms is designed to suit the convenience of one only of the parties. One party may accede, perhaps reluctantly, to the request of the other, and promise that he will not insist upon performance according to the strict letter of the contract. This is an indulgence that is a common feature of commercial life. In the case of a contract for the sale of goods, for instance, approval may be given to the request either of the seller or the buyer that the date of delivery be postponed for a short time. An arrangement of this kind for a substituted mode of performance is generally described as either a waiver or a forbearance by the party who grants the indulgence.[2]

Waiver of a contractual term by one party at the request of the other

The efficacy of such a waiver is open to the technical objection that it is unsupported by consideration. If, for instance, the seller agrees at the request of the buyer to postpone delivery until July 1st, but ultimately refuses to deliver on the latter date, it is arguable that according to strict doctrine he has a complete answer to an action for breach of contract. The buyer is theoretically in a difficult position. He was not ready and willing to accept delivery at the contract date, so that he himself is guilty of a breach; and he gave no consideration for the promise by the seller to extend the time for delivery. If a similar concession is made orally in the case of a guarantee or a contract for the sale of land, there is the further difficulty that the requirements of the Statute of Frauds or the Law of Property Act have not been satisfied.

Doctrinal difficulties affecting waiver

The natural instinct of judges, however, is to uphold reasonable arrangements for the relaxation of contractual terms and to refuse to be unduly distracted by strict doctrine. Even at common law they have been at pains to implement the intention of the parties; but in the efforts to do this they have not only ignored the question of consideration, but have propounded a supposed distinction between variation and waiver which has no substance and which has merely served to confuse matters. There is support for two common law propositions.

Effect of waiver at common law

Firstly, a waiver cannot be repudiated by the party for whose benefit it has been granted, so that if A abstains at B's request from insisting upon performance according to the exact terms of the contract, B is compelled to treat this indulgence as effective.

(i) Waiver binding upon the party at whose instance it was granted

---

1. [1969] 1 A.C., at p. 348.
2. For a fuller discussion of this subject, see Cheshire and Fifoot, 63 L.Q.R. 283, at pp. 289–301.

Thus, if in the case of a written contract for the sale of goods to be delivered on June 1st the seller at the request of the buyer extends the time for acceptance until July 1st, the buyer, if he defaults on the latter date, cannot escape liability by averring that the seller did not deliver according to the original contract and that the parol variation is ineffective.[1]

(ii) Waiver generally binds the party who grants it

Secondly, there is considerable authority for the rule that even the party who grants the indulgence cannot go back on his agreement.[2] Thus, in the example just given, the seller is not allowed to withhold delivery on July 1st on the ground that the buyer himself committed a breach by his failure to accept the goods at the contract date.

Unsatisfactory state of the common law

These common law decisions, though dictated by a laudable desire to sustain reasonable arrangements between business men, are disfigured by at least two blemishes.

(i) Baseless distinction between variation and waiver

The first and more serious is that they affect to make everything turn upon a supposed distinction between the variation and the waiver of a contractual term. If the subject-matter of the arrangement is a written contract falling under the Statute of Frauds or the Law of Property Act, it is said that a variation must be evidenced by writing, but that a waiver may be parol. Yet the enigma is to formulate some test by which to distinguish the one from the other. The search will be in vain. When we are told, for instance, that an agreed alteration of the date at which delivery is due constitutes a variation, but that a forbearance by one party at the request of the other to call for delivery until a month later than the contract date is a waiver,[3] it becomes apparent that the dichotomy is visionary and one from which reason recoils. The truth is that every alteration of the kind with which we are concerned is a variation of the contract, but that it is called a waiver when the court is willing to give effect to the intention of the parties. The unfortunate result is the virtual impossibility of anticipating what view the court will take.

(ii) Uncertainty of principle upon which validity of waiver rests

The second respect in which the common law attitude is unsatisfactory is the uncertainty of the legal principle upon which the validity of a waiver rests. There is little doubt that at bottom it is estoppel. A seller of goods, for instance, who promises the buyer that he will not insist upon acceptance of delivery at the exact contractual date, ought not to be allowed to go back on his word. Yet waiver cannot technically be justified on this ground, for according to established doctrine only a statement of existing fact, not a promise *de futuro*, can raise an estoppel at common law.[4]

Treatment of waiver by equity

In this state of confusion it is not unnatural that recourse should be had to the more intelligible principle adopted by equity. The equitable doctrine, which must prevail in all courts,

1. *Hickman* v. *Haynes* (1875), L.R. 10 C.P. 598; *Ogle* v. *Earl of Vane* (1868), L.R. 3 Q.B. 272; *Levey & Co.* v. *Goldberg*, [1922] 1 K.B. 688.
2. *Leather Cloth Co.* v. *Hieronimus* (1875), L.R. 10 Q.B. 140; *Tyers* v. *Rosedale and Ferryhill Iron Co.* (1875), L.R. 10 Exch. 195; *Panoutsos* v. *Raymond. Hadley Corporation of New York*, [1917] 2 K.B. 473; *Hartley* v. *Hymans*, [1920] 3 K.B. 475.
3. See, for example, *Besseler, Waechter, Glover & Co.* v. *South Derwent Coal Co., Ltd.*, [1938] 1 K.B. 408, at p. 416; [1937] 4 All E.R. 552, at p. 556.
4. *Jorden* v. *Money* (1854), 5 H.L. Cas. 185; *supra*, p. 89.

carries in the present connexion the principle of estoppel to its logical conclusion. It has been stated in these words by BOWEN, L.J.:

> " If persons who have contractual rights against others induce by their conduct those against whom they have such rights to believe that such rights will either not be enforced or will be kept in suspense or abeyance for some particular time, those persons will not be allowed by a court of equity to enforce the rights until such time has elapsed, without at all events placing the parties in the same position as they were in before."[1]

In short, a voluntary concession granted by one party, upon the faith of which the other may have shaped his conduct, remains effective until it is made clear by notice or otherwise that it is to be withdrawn and the strict position under the contract restored. The concession raises an equity against the party who consented to it. If, for instance, in the case of a written contract for the sale of goods the buyer at the request of the sellers orally consents to the postponement of delivery, he cannot peremptorily hold the sellers to the original contract. No repudiation of his waiver will be effective except a clear intimation to them that he proposes to resume his strict rights. Normally he will do this by giving express notice of his intention, but this method is not essential and anything will suffice which makes it abundantly clear that the concession is withdrawn. Within a reasonable time thereafter the original position will be restored. The rights of the seller under such a waiver have been stated by DENNING, L.J. *Attitude of equity more satisfactory*

> " If the defendant, as he did, led the plaintiffs to believe that he would not insist on the stipulation as to time and that if they carried out the work he would accept it, and they did it, he could not after-wards set up the stipulation as to time against them. Whether it be called waiver or forbearance on his part, or an agreed variation or substituted performance, does not matter. It is a kind of estoppel. By his conduct he evinced an intention to affect their legal relations. He made, in effect, a promise not to insist on his strict legal rights. That promise was intended to be acted on, and was in fact acted on. He cannot afterwards go back on it."[2]

The former theoretical difficulties that there is no consideration or nothing in writing to support the variation no longer nullify the effect of this quasi-estoppel.[3]

The operation of this doctrine of waiver is well illustrated by *Charles Rickards, Ltd.* v. *Oppenheim*[4] where the facts were as follows:

> Early in 1947 the defendant ordered from the plaintiffs a Rolls Royce chassis, and in July the plaintiffs agreed that a body should be built for it within " six or at most seven months." The body was not completed seven months later, but the defendant agreed to wait another three months. At the end of this extended period the body was still not built. The defendant then gave a final notice that if the work were not finished within a further period of four weeks he would cancel the order. The body was not

---

1. *Birmingham and District Land Co.* v. *London and North Western Rail. Co.* (1888), 40 Ch.D. 268, at p. 286.
2. *Charles Rickards, Ltd.* v. *Oppenheim*, [1950] 1 K.B. 616, at p. 623; [1950] 1 All E.R. 420, at p. 423.
3. *Ibid.*, at pp. 622-3 and 422-3 respectively.
4. [1950] 1 K.B. 616; [1950] 1 All E.R. 420.

finished within this period and the defendant cancelled the order. The completed body was tendered to the defendant three months later, but he refused to accept it.

This was a case where the time of delivery was of the essence of the contract.   The defendant's agreement, however, that delivery should be postponed for three months constituted a waiver of his right in this respect, and if the body had been completed within the extended time he would have been estopped from denying that the contract had been performed.   But by granting a further and final indulgence of four weeks' delay he had given reasonable notice that time was once more to be of the essence of the matter, and, since the car was not ready within this final period, the plaintiffs were in breach of their contract.   The Court of Appeal, therefore, gave judgment for the defendant.

Again, if the rent book relating to premises, let originally on a weekly tenancy, contains the words " one month's notice each party," but this is later crossed out and replaced by a statement, initialled by the landlord, which runs " one month's notice from tenant; two years' notice from landlord," the new promise made by the landlord is without consideration.   But if the tenant acts on the faith of the promise by remaining in possession and continuing to pay rent he is entitled to receive two years' notice.[1]

Thus equity ignores any fancied distinction between variation and waiver, and in this particular context it refuses to obscure the underlying theory of estoppel by distinguishing a statement of fact from a promise *de futuro*.   This is an application of the doctrine of promissory estoppel which we have discussed more fully elsewhere.[2]

SECTION II. UNILATERAL DISCHARGE

Meaning of unilateral discharge

A contract, which has been performed by A but has not been performed by the other party B, may be the subject of unilateral discharge.   In the majority of cases B has committed a breach of the contract in the sense that he is not ready and willing to perform his obligation, as for instance where he is unable to pay for goods that have been delivered to him under a contract of sale. In such a case A may agree to release B from his obligation.   A release given by deed is effective.   A release expressed in an agreement not under seal, however, as we have already seen, is *nudum pactum* unless A receives some valuable consideration in return for the right that he abandons.[3]   Since B has received all that he is entitled to receive under the contract, he cannot aver, as he can in the case of bilateral discharge, that by the mere acceptance of the release he furnishes consideration to A.

1. *Wallis* v. *Semark,* [1951] 2 T.L.R. 222.   For an earlier authority to the same effect, see *Bruner* v. *Moore,* [1904] 1 Ch. 305.
2. *Supra,* pp. 89–97.
3. *Supra,* p. 533.

The agreement, if supported by the necessary consideration, is called accord and satisfaction.   This has been judicially defined as follows:

Accord and satisfaction defined

> " Accord and satisfaction is the purchase of a release from an obligation, whether arising under contract or tort, by means of any valuable consideration, not being the actual performance of the obligation itself.   The accord is the agreement by which the obligation is discharged.   The satisfaction is the consideration which makes the agreement operative."[1]

If, for instance, £50 is due for goods sold and delivered, a promise by the seller to accept a cash payment of £45 in discharge of the buyer's obligation is not a good accord and satisfaction, since the buyer is relieved of a liability to pay £5 without giving or promising anything in return.[2]   A promise by the buyer, however, to confer upon the seller some independent benefit, actual or contingent, may constitute sufficient consideration for the acceptance of the smaller sum.[3]   Thus in 1602 it was said that " the gift of a horse, a hawk or a robe " would suffice, since it would not have been accepted by the creditor had it not been more beneficial to him than the money.[4]   This reasoning even persuaded the divisional court in *Goddard* v. *O'Brien*[5] to hold that the payment of a smaller sum by cheque instead of in cash was an independent benefit sufficient to rank as consideration; but the Court of Appeal has now refused to follow this decision.[6]   Yet, the general rule remains that the acceptance by a creditor of something different from that to which he is entitled may discharge the debtor from liability.

Examples of accord and satisfaction

Thus a promise by the debtor to pay a smaller sum at a date earlier than that on which it is contractually due,[7] or to pay a larger sum at a later date, is a good accord and satisfaction if accepted by the creditor.   Again, if A claims from B a sum that is not finally determined, as for example where he demands £50 on a *quantum meruit* for services rendered or demands £50 by way of damages for libel, his promise to release B in consideration of the payment of a lesser sum than that claimed is a good accord and satisfaction.   In other words the payment of a lesser sum is satisfaction if the sum claimed is unliquidated, but not if it is liquidated.[8]

The essential fact is, then, that an accord without satisfaction is ineffective.   This statement, however, is ambiguous.   Is the discharge effective as soon as the debtor has promised to give the satisfaction, or only when the promise has been implemented?

Satisfaction may be executory

---

1. *British Russian Gazette, Ltd.* v. *Associated Newspapers, Ltd.*, [1933] 2 K.B. 616, at pp. 643–4; [1933] All E.R. Rep. 320, at p. 327; the definition was adopted from *Salmond and Winfield on Contracts*, p. 328.
2. *Foakes* v. *Beer* (1884), 9 App. Cas. 605; *supra*, p. 86.
3. *Foakes* v. *Beer* (1884), 9 App. Cas. 605, at p. 613, *per* Lord SELBORNE.
4. *Pinnel's Case* (1602), 5 Co. Rep. 117a.
5. (1882), 9 Q.B.D. 37.
6. *D. and C. Builders, Ltd.* v. *Rees*, [1966] 2 Q.B. 617; [1965] 3 All E.R. 837, *supra*, p. 88.
7. Co. Litt. 212b.
8. *Wilkinson* v. *Byers* (1834), 1 Ad. & El. 106.

In other words, is it sufficient if the consideration is executory? The correct answer is given by SCRUTTON, L.J., in these words:

> "Formerly it was necessary that the consideration should be executed: 'I release you from your obligation in consideration of £50 now paid by you to me.' Later it was conceded that the consideration might be executory: 'I release you from your obligation in consideration of your promise to pay me £50 and give me a letter of withdrawal.' The consideration on each side might be an executory promise, the two mutual promises making an agreement enforceable in law, a contract. Comyns put it in his Digest, and the passage was approved by PARKE, B., in *Good* v. *Cheesman*[1] and by the Court of King's Bench in *Cartwright* v. *Cooke*:[2] 'An accord, with mutual promises to perform, is good, though the thing be not performed at the time of action; for the party has a remedy to compel the performance,' that is to say, a cross-action on the contract of accord."[3]

Question of intention whether satisfaction is executory

The modern rule is, then, that if what the creditor has accepted in satisfaction is merely his debtor's promise to give consideration, and not the performance of that promise, the original cause of action is discharged from the date when the agreement is made.[4]

This, however, raises a question of construction in each case, for it has to be decided as a fact whether it was the making of the promise itself or the performance of the promise that the creditor consented to take by way of satisfaction.

> Suppose for instance, that a buyer is unable to pay £50 which is due for goods delivered and that the seller agrees to discharge him from his obligation of immediate payment in consideration of receiving a bill of exchange from a third party, X, for £55 payable four months hence.

If the seller were to sue for the £50 before receipt of the bill of exchange, the question would arise whether he had committed a breach of the agreement. This would depend upon whether the agreement constituted a good accord and satisfaction, and this in turn would depend upon the true bargain between the parties. Did they mean that the discharge should be complete when X promised to give the bill or only when he actually gave it?

The question of construction that arises in such a case is well illustrated by *British Russian Gazette, Ltd.* v. *Associated Newspapers, Ltd.*,[5] where the facts relevant to the present matter were as follows:

Question illustrated by *British Russian Gazette* v. *Associated Newspapers*

> Mr. Talbot agreed to compromise two actions of libel, which had been commenced by him and by the *British Russian Gazette,* in respect of certain articles in the *Daily Mail.* His promise was expressed in a letter couched in these terms: "I accept the sum of one thousand guineas on account of costs and expenses in full discharge and settlement of my claims . . . and I will forthwith instruct my solicitors to serve notice of discontinuance; or to take other steps . . . to end the proceedings now pending." Before payment of the thousand guineas had been made, Talbot disregarded this compromise and proceeded with the action.

1. (1831), 2 B. & Ad. 328, at p. 335.
2. (1832), 3 B. & Ad. 701, at p. 703.
3. *British Russian Gazette, Ltd.* v. *Associated Newspapers, Ltd.*, [1933] 2 K.B. 616, at p. 644; [1933] All E.R. Rep. 320, at p. 327.
4. *Morris* v. *Baron*, [1918] A.C. 1, at p. 35, *per* Lord ATKINSON; *Elton Cop Dyeing Co.* v. *Broadbent & Son, Ltd.* (1919), 89 L.J.K.B. 186; *British Russian Gazette, Ltd.* v. *Associated Newspapers, Ltd.*, [1933] 2 K.B. 616; [1933] All E.R. Rep. 320.
5. [1933] 2 K.B. 616; [1933] All E.R. Rep. 320.

If this letter meant that Talbot agreed to discharge the defendants from their obligation in consideration of their promise to make the payment, his continuance of the libel action constituted a breach of a good accord and satisfaction. His argument, of course, was that there was no binding discharge until actual payment, but this did not prevail with the Court of Appeal. It was held that the letter recorded an agreement in which the consideration was a promise for a promise: " In consideration of your promise to pay me a thousand guineas, I promise to discontinue proceedings." The defendants were, therefore, entitled to enforce the accord by way of counterclaim.

There is one exception to the rule that a unilateral discharge requires consideration. It is enacted that if the holder of a bill of exchange or of a promissory note either unconditionally renounces his rights in writing or delivers the instrument to the person liable, the effect is to discharge the obligation of the acceptor or promisor even though no consideration is received.[1]

---

1. Bills of Exchange Act 1882, ss. 62 and 89.

CHAPTER THREE

Discharge under the Doctrine of Frustration

SECTION I. NATURE AND RATIONALE OF THE DOCTRINE

Stultification of contract by subsequent event

AFTER the parties have made their agreement, unforeseen contingencies may occur which prevent the attainment of the purpose that they had in mind. The question is whether this discharges them from further liability.

Basic rule as to absolute contracts

In the seventeenth century the judges in *Paradine* v. *Jane*[1] laid down what is sometimes called the rule as to absolute contracts. It amounts to this: When *the law* casts a duty upon a man which, through no fault of his, he is unable to perform, he is excused for non-performance; but if he binds himself *by contract* absolutely to do a thing, he cannot escape liability for damages by proof that as events turned out performance is futile or even impossible. The alleged justification for this somewhat harsh principle is that a party to a contract can always guard against unforeseen contingencies by express stipulation; but if he voluntarily undertakes an absolute and unconditional obligation he cannot complain merely because events turn out to his disadvantage. It has accordingly been held, for instance, that if a builder agrees to construct a house by a certain date and fails to do so because a strike occurs[2] or because the soil contains a latent defect which suspends operations[3] he is none the less liable. Again, if a shipowner agrees that he will load his ship with guano at a certain place in West Africa, he is liable in damages notwithstanding that no guano is obtainable.[4]

---

1. (1947), Aleyn, 26. Simpson 91 L.Q.R. 247 at 269–273.
2. *Budgett & Co.* v. *Binnington & Co.,* [1891] 1 Q.B. 35.
3. *Bottoms* v. *York Corporation* (1892), 2 Hudson's B. C., 4th Edn., 208.
4. *Hills* v. *Sughrue* (1846), 15 M. & W. 253.

Nevertheless, starting with the case of *Taylor* v. *Caldwell*[1] in 1863, a substantive and particular doctrine has gradually been evolved by the courts which mitigates the rigour of the rule in *Paradine* v. *Jane* by providing that if the further fulfilment of the contract is brought to an abrupt stop by some irresistible and extraneous cause for which neither party is responsible, the contract shall terminate forthwith and the parties be discharged.[2]

Mitigation of rule as to absolute contracts

The most obvious cause which brings this doctrine into operation, and the one which provided the issue in the parent case of *Taylor* v. *Caldwell*, is the physical destruction of the subject-matter of the contract before performance falls due. Another, equally obvious, is a subsequent change in the law which renders performance illegal. A less obvious cause, but nevertheless one that has occasioned a multitude of decisions in the last seventy years and which has brought about a rapid development in this branch of the law, is what is called the " frustration of the common venture." Owing to an event that has supervened since the making of the contract, the parties are frustrated in the sense that the substantial object that they had in view is no longer attainable. Literal performance may still be possible, but nevertheless it will not fulfil the original and common design of the parties. What the courts have held in such a case is that, if some catastrophic event occurs for which neither party is responsible and if the result of that event is to destroy the very basis of the contract, so that the venture to which the parties now find themselves committed is radically different from that originally contemplated, then the contract is forthwith discharged.[3] Mere hardship or inconvenience to one of the parties is not sufficient to justify discharge. " There must be as well such a change in the significance of the obligation that the thing undertaken would, if performed, be a different thing from that contracted for."[4] Two simple illustrations may be given of circumstances which have been held sufficiently catastrophic to change the significance of the obligation.

The doctrine of frustration

> In *Krell* v. *Henry*,[5] the plaintiff agreed to let a room to the defendant for the day upon which Edward VII was to be crowned. Both parties understood that the purpose of the letting was to view the coronation procession, but this did not appear in the agreement itself. The procession was cancelled owing to the illness of the king.

The Court of Appeal took the view that the procession was the foundation of the contract and that the effect of its cancellation

---

1. (1863), 3 B. & S. 826.
2. *Denny, Mott and Dickson, Ltd.* v. *James B. Fraser & Co., Ltd.*, [1944] A.C. 265, at pp. 272, 274; [1944] 1 All E.R. 678, at pp. 681, 683.
3. *Sir Lindsay Parkinson & Co.* v. *Works & Public Buildings Commissioners*, [1949] 2 K.B. 632, at p. 665; [1950] 1 All E.R. 208, at p. 227, *per* ASQUITH, L.J.; *Cricklewood Property and Investment Trust, Ltd.* v. *Leighton's Investment Trust, Ltd.*, [1945] A.C. 221, at p. 228; [1945] 1 All E.R. 252, at p. 255, *per* Lord SIMON; *Davis Contractors, Ltd.* v. *Fareham U.D.C.*, [1956] A.C. 696, at pp. 728–9, *per* Lord RADCLIFFE.
4. *Davis Contractors, Ltd.* v. *Fareham U.D.C.*, *supra*, at pp. 728–9, *per* Lord RADCLIFFE. But Parliament can by statute give the courts power to vary agreements because of changed circumstances as it has done in the case of maintenance agreements, Matrimonial Causes Act 1973, s. 35.
5. [1903] 2 K.B. 740. The decision has not escaped judicial criticism; see *Larrinaga & Co.* v. *Société Franco-Americaine des Phosphates de Medulla* (1922), 28 Com. Cas. 1, at p. 7, *per* Lord FINLAY; *Maritime National Fish, Ltd.* v. *Ocean Trawlers, Ltd.*, [1938] A.C. 524, at p. 529, *per* Lord WRIGHT.

was to discharge the parties from the further performance of their obligations. It was no longer possible to achieve the substantial purpose of the contract. A similar result was reached in *Tatem, Ltd.* v. *Gamboa.*[1] In that case:

> In June, 1937, at the height of the Spanish Civil War, a ship was chartered by the plaintiffs to the Republican Government for a period of thirty days from July 1st, for the express purpose of evacuating civilians from the North Spanish ports to French Bay ports. The hire was at the rate of £250 a day until actual redelivery of the ship. This rate was about three times that prevailing in the market for equivalent ships not trading with Spanish ports. After one successful voyage, the ship was seized by the Nationalists on July 14th and detained in Bilbao until September 7th, when she was released and ultimately redelivered to the plaintiffs on September 11th. The hire had been paid in advance up to July 31st, but the Republican Government refused to pay for the period from August 1st to September 11th, on the ground that the common venture of the parties had been frustrated by the seizure of the ship.

GODDARD, J., held that the seizure had destroyed the foundation of the contract and that the Republican Government was not liable. He said:

> " If the foundation of the contract goes, either by the destruction of the subject-matter or by reason of such long interruption or delay that the performance is really in effect that of a different contract, and the parties have not provided what in that event is to happen, the performance of the contract is to be regarded as frustrated."[2]

Theories
as to the
basis of
the doctrine

The precise legal theory upon which this doctrine of frustration is based has aroused much controversy. No fewer than five theories have been advanced at one time or another;[3] but the essential question is whether the courts strive to give effect to the supposed intention of the parties or whether they act independently and impose the solution that seems reasonable and just.

The former method was preferred by BLACKBURN, J., in *Taylor* v. *Caldwell*[4] in 1863, when he made the first breach in the long established rule as to absolute contracts. In that case, A had agreed to give B the use of a music hall on certain specified days for the purpose of holding concerts. The hall was accidentally destroyed by fire six days before the contract date, and B claimed damages for breach of the agreement. BLACKBURN, J., held the contract to be discharged, but he found it necessary to walk with circumspection in order to reconcile reason and justice with the established rule as to absolute contracts. His reasoning was that a contract is not to be construed as absolute if the parties must from the beginning have known that its fulfilment depended upon the continued existence of some particular thing, and therefore must have realized that this continuing existence was the foundation of the bargain. In such a case, he said, the contract " is subject to an implied condition that the parties shall be excused in case, before breach, performance becomes impossible from the perishing of the thing without default of the contractor."[5] In short,

1. [1939] 1 K.B. 132; [1938] 3 All E.R. 135.
2. [1939] 1 K.B. 132, at p. 139; [1938] 3 All E.R. 134, at p. 144.
3. McNair, *Legal Effects of War*, 4th Edn., pp. 156 *et seq.*; and see his articles in 35 L.Q.R. 84, 56 L.Q.R. 173.
4. (1863), 3 B. & S. 826.
5. At pp. 883–4.

he attributed a conventional character to an obviously reasonable, if not inevitable, solution. Thus arose the theory of the implied term. No express term for the discharge of the contract was made by the parties, but had they anticipated and considered the catastrophic event that in fact happened, they would have said, " if that happens it is all over between us."[1] In implying such a term it has been said that " the law is only doing what the parties really (though subconsciously) meant to do themselves."[2]

This theory, though it still has its unrepentant adherents,[3] has been heavily attacked in recent years and has substantially been replaced by the more realistic view that the court imposes upon the parties the just and reasonable solution that the new situation demands. Perhaps the most careful analysis of this theory has been made by Lord WRIGHT, and the following two passages from his speech in a leading case illustrate his view that the doctrine of frustration has been invented by the courts in order to supplement the defects of the actual contract. In the first passage he said:

> " Where, as generally happens, and actually happened in the present case, one party claims that there has been frustration and the other party contests it, the court decides the issue and decides it *ex post facto* on the actual circumstances of the case. The data for decision are, on the one hand the terms and construction of the contract, read in the light of the then existing circumstances, and on the other hand the events which have occurred. It is the court which has to decide what is the true position between the parties."[4]

The second passage is as follows:

> " The event is something which happens in the world of fact, and has to be found as a fact by the judge. Its effect on the contract depends on the meaning of the contract, which is matter of law. Whether there is frustration or not in any case depends on the view taken of the event and of its relation to the express contract by ' informed and experienced minds '."[5]

It is perhaps fair to say that this is now the more generally accepted view. To attempt to guess the arrangements that the parties would have made at the time of the contract, had they contemplated the event that has now unexpectedly happened, is to attempt the impossible. Instead, the courts refuse to apply the doctrine of frustration unless they consider that to hold the parties to further performance would, in the light of the changed

---

1. *F. A. Tamplin S.S. Co., Ltd.* v. *Anglo-Mexican Petroleum Products Co., Ltd.*, [1916] 2 A.C. 397, at p. 404, *per* Lord LOREBURN.
2. *Hirji Mulji* v. *Cheong Yue Steamship Co., Ltd.*, [1926] A.C. 497, at p. 504, P.C.
3. *Port Line, Ltd.* v. *Ben Line Steamers, Ltd.*, [1958] 2 Q.B. 146, at p. 162 (DIPLOCK, J.); and see *British Movietonews, Ltd.* v. *London and District Cinemas, Ltd.*, [1952] A.C. 166, at pp. 183 (Lord SIMON) and 187 (Lord SIMONDS); *Joseph Constantine Steamship Line, Ltd.* v. *Imperial Smelting Corporation, Ltd.*, [1942] A.C. 154, at p. 163 (Lord SIMON).
4. *Denny, Mott and Dickson, Ltd.* v. *James Fraser & Co., Ltd.*, [1944] A.C. 265, at pp. 274–5; [1944] 1 All E.R. 678, at p. 683. In an extra-judicial utterance Lord WRIGHT was more out-spoken. " The truth is," he said, " that the court or jury as a judge of fact decides the question in accordance with what seems to be just and reasonable in its eyes. The judge finds in himself the criterion of what is reasonable. The court is in this sense making a contract for the parties, though it is almost blasphemy to say so "; *Legal Essays and Addresses*, p. 259.
5. *Ibid.*, at pp. 276 and 684, respectively.

circumstances, alter the fundamental nature of the contract.[1] In an illuminating passage, Lord RADCLIFFE has said:

> " By this time it might seem that the parties themselves have become so far disembodied spirits that their actual persons should be allowed to rest in peace. In their place there rises the figure of the fair and reasonable man. And the spokesman of the fair and reasonable man, who represents after all no more than the anthropomorphic conception of justice, is and must be the court itself. So perhaps it would be simpler to say at the outset that frustration occurs whenever the law recognizes that without default of either party a contractual obligation has become incapable of being performed because the circumstances in which performance is called for would render it a thing radically different from that which was undertaken by the contract. *Non haec in foedera veni.* It was not this that I promised to do."[2]

SECTION II. OPERATION OF THE DOCTRINE

The doctrine of frustration illustrated

It is not possible to tabulate or to classify the circumstances to which the doctrine of frustration applies, but we will illustrate its operation by a reference to a few of the cases in which it has been invoked.[3]

Contract of personal services discharged by supervening incapacity

Upon proof that the continuing availability of a physical thing or a given person is essential to the attainment of the fundamental object which the parties had in view, the contract is discharged if, owing to some extraneous cause, such thing or person is no longer available. *Taylor* v. *Caldwell*[4] sufficiently illustrates the case of a physical thing, but the rule laid down in that decision applies with equal force if it is a fundamental requirement that a person should remain available. Thus, a contract to perform services which can be rendered only by the promisor personally necessarily contemplates that his state of health, which at present is sufficiently good for the fulfilment of his obligations, will continue substantially unchanged, and if this ceases to be so owing to his death or illness, the court decrees that both parties shall be discharged from further liability.[5] A similar decree may be made if in time of war one of the parties is interned[6] or is called-up for military

---

1. *Tsakiroglou & Co., Ltd.* v. *Noblee and Thorl G.m.b.H.,* [1962] A.C. 93, at p. 115, *per* LORD SIMONDS.
2. *Davis Contractors, Ltd.* v. *Fareham U.D.C.,* [1956] A.C. 696, at pp. 728-9; see also Lord REID, at pp. 719-20. *Ocean Tramp Tankers Corporation* v. *V/O Sovfracht, The Eugenia,* [1964] 2 Q.B. 226, at pp. 238-9; [1964] 1 All E.R. 161, *per* Lord DENNING.
3. For a more detailed statement, see McNair, *Legal Effects of War,* 4th Edn., pp. 177 *et seq.*; Webber, *Effect of War on Contracts,* 2nd Edn., pp. 394 *et seq.*
4. *Supra,* p. 546. Compare *Baily* v. *De Crespigny* (1869), L.R. 4 Q.B. 180; a covenant by a lessor not to allow the erection of any building upon a paddock fronting the demised premises was discharged when a railway company compulsorily acquired and built a station on the paddock.
5. *Boast* v. *Firth* (1868), L.R. 4 C.P. 1. *Condor* v. *The Barron Knights, Ltd.,* [1966] 1 W.L.R. 87. Obviously not every illness will bring the contract to an end. To draw the line it will be necessary to consider the extent of the illness and the nature and terms of the contract: *Marshall* v. *Harland and Wolff Ltd.,* [1972] 2 All E.R. 715; [1972] 1 W.L,R. 899; *Hebden* v. *Forsey & Son,* [1973] I.C.R. 607.
6. *Unger* v. *Preston Corporation,* [1942] 1 All E.R. 200.

service,[1] provided that the interruption in performance is likely to be so long as to defeat the purpose of the contract. Contracts liable to discharge on this ground include an agreement to act as the agent of a music hall artiste,[2] to perform at a concert,[3] not to remove a child from school without a term's notice,[4] and a contract of apprenticeship.[5]

Another cause of frustration is the non-occurrence of some event which must reasonably be regarded as the basis of the contract. This is well illustrated by the coronation cases, especially by *Krell* v. *Henry*,[6] but it is not necessary to expand the account already given of that decision.[7] It should be observed, however, that discharge will not be decreed if the event cannot reasonably be regarded as the real basis of the contract. The same judges who decided *Krell* v. *Henry* had already refused in *Herne Bay Steamboat Co.* v. *Hutton*[8] to regard a somewhat similar contract as frustrated. In that case an agreement was made that the plaintiffs' ship should be " at the disposal of " the defendant on June 28th to take passengers from Herne Bay " for the purpose of viewing the naval review and for a day's cruise round the fleet." The review was later cancelled, but the fleet remained at Spithead on June 28th. It was held that the contract was not discharged. The case is not easy to distinguish from *Krell* v. *Henry*, but perhaps the explanation is that the holding of the review was not the sole adventure contemplated. The cruise round the fleet, which formed an equally basic object of the contract, was still capable of attainment.

Discharge owing to non-occurrence of an event

So fine a distinction reflects a difficulty that frequently occurs when the doctrine of frustration falls to be applied to a contract that is not in fact incapable of performance. The doctrine is certainly applicable if the object which is the foundation of the contract becomes unobtainable, but the judges are equally insistent that the motive of the parties is not a proper subject of inquiry. That the distinction, however, between motive and object is not always clear is apparent from the *Herne Bay* case.

Distinction between object and motive

> Suppose, for example, that a car is hired in Oxford to go to Epsom on a future date which in fact is known by both parties to be Derby day. If the Derby is subsequently abandoned, the question whether the contract is discharged or not depends upon whether the court regards the race as the foundation of the contract, or merely as the motive which induced the contract. Must the case be equated with *Krell* v. *Henry* or with *Herne Bay Steamboat Co.* v. *Hutton*?

A common cause of frustration, especially in time of war, is interference by the Government in the activities of one or both of the parties. For example, the acts contemplated by the

Discharge owing to interference by the Government

---

1. *Morgan* v. *Manser*, [1948] 1 K.B. 184; [1947] 2 All E.R. 666; *Marshall* v. *Glanvill*, [1917] 2 K.B. 87. Similarly if one of the parties is imprisoned; *Hare* v. *Murphy Brothers*, [1974] 3 All E.R. 940, [1974] I.C.R. 603.
2. *Morgan* v. *Manser, supra.*
3. *Robinson* v. *Davison* (1871), L.R. 6 Exch. 269; *Poussard* v. *Spiers and Pond* (1876), 1 Q.B.D. 410.
4. *Simeon* v, *Watson* (1877), 46 L.J.Q.B. 679.
5. *Boast* v. *Firth, supra.* Cf. *Mount* v. *Oldham Corporation*, [1973] 1 Q.B. 309; [1973] 1 All E.R. 26.
6. [1903] 2 K.B. 740.
7. *Supra,* p. 545.
8. [1903] 2 K.B. 683.

contract may be prohibited for an indefinite duration, the labour
or materials necessary for performance may be requisitioned, or
premises upon which work is to be done may be temporarily
seized for public use. In such cases the contract is discharged if
to maintain it would be to impose upon the parties a contract
fundamentally different from that which they made. A well-
known example is *Metropolitan Water Board* v. *Dick, Kerr & Co.*[1]
In that case:

> By a contract made in July, 1914, the respondents agreed with the
> appellants to construct a reservoir within six years, subject to a
> proviso that the time should be extended if delay were caused by
> difficulties, impediments or obstructions howsoever occasioned.
> In February, 1916, the Minister of Munitions ordered the res-
> pondents to cease work and to disperse and sell the plant.

It was held that the provision for extension of time did not cover
such a substantial interference with the performance of the work
as this, and that the contract was completely discharged. The
interruption was likely to be so long that the contract, if resumed,
would be radically different from that originally made.

Whether the outbreak of war or an interference by the
Government discharges a contract depends upon the actual
circumstances of each case. The principle itself is constant,
but the difficulty of its application remains. Discharge must be
decreed only if the result of what has happened is that, if the
contract were to be resumed after the return of peace or the
removal of the interference, the parties would find themselves
dealing with each other under conditions completely different
from those that obtained when they made their agreement. The
contract must be regarded as a whole and the question answered
whether its purpose as gathered from its terms has been defeated.[2]
The answer often turns upon the probable duration of the interference. Business men must not be left in indefinite suspense
and as Lord WRIGHT has said:

> " If there is a reasonable probability from the nature of the
> interruption that it will be of indefinite duration, they ought to be
> free to turn their assets, their plant and equipment and their business
> operations into activities which are open to them, and to be free
> from commitments which are struck with sterility for an uncertain
> future period."[3]

The question whether the interruption will be of indefinite
duration, rendering further performance of the contract impracticable, must be considered by the court in the light of the
circumstances existing at the moment when it occurred. What
view would a reasonable man have formed at that moment,
without regard to the fuller information available to the court
at the time of the trial? Would the reasonable inference have
been that the interruption was indefinite in duration or merely
transient?[4]

1. [1918] A.C. 119.
2. *Denny, Mott and Dickson, Ltd.* v. *James B. Fraser & Co., Ltd.*, [1944]
    A.C. 265, at p. 273, *per* Lord MACMILLAN; [1944] 1 All E.R. 678, at p. 682.
3. [1944] A.C. 265, at p. 278, *per* Lord WRIGHT; [1944] 1 All E.R. 678, at
    p. 685.
4. *Atlantic Maritime Co., Inc.* v. *Gibbon*, [1954] 1 Q.B. 88; [1953] 2 All E.R.
    1086.

That individual views may vary as to whether an interference is calculated to defeat the purpose of a contract is well illustrated by two cases. In *F. A. Tamplin Steamship Co., Ltd.* v. *Anglo-Mexican Petroleum Products Co., Ltd.*[1] there was a sharp conflict of judicial opinion in the House of Lords. The facts were these:

> A tanker was chartered for five years from December, 1912, to December, 1917, to be used by the charterers for the carriage of oil. In February, 1915, she was requisitioned by the Government and used as a troopship. The charterers were willing to pay the agreed freight to the owners, but the latter, desirous of receiving the much larger sum paid by the Government, contended that the requisition had frustrated the commercial object of the venture and had therefore put an end to the contract.

The House of Lords by a bare majority rejected this contention. Of the majority Lord PARKER took the view that there was nothing concrete capable of frustration, since the parties never contemplated a definite adventure. The owners were not concerned in the charterers doing any specific thing except paying freight as it fell due. Lord LOREBURN, though admitting that the parties contemplated a continuing state of peace and did not envisage loss of control over the ship, denied that the interruption was of such a character as to make it unreasonable to keep the contract alive. Judging the situation as at the date of the requisition, there might be many months during which the ship would be available for commercial purposes before the five years expired in December, 1917.[2] On the other hand, Lords HALDANE and ATKINSON took the opposite view. Lord HALDANE was of opinion that the entire basis of the contract so far as concerned its performance at any calculable date in the future was swept away. Lord ATKINSON regarded the requisition as constituting such a substantial invasion of the freedom of both parties that the foundation of the contract had disappeared.

In the second case—*Tsakiroglou & Co., Ltd.* v. *Noblee and Thorl G.m.b.H.*[3]—the House of Lords had to consider the effect of the closing of the Suez Canal in 1956, an event which had already provoked a diversity of judicial opinion.

> On the 4th October, 1956, sellers agreed to sell to buyers Sudanese groundnuts for shipment c.i.f. Hamburg, and to ship them during November/December, 1956.[4] On the 7th October, they booked space in one of four vessels scheduled to call at Port Sudan in these two months. On 2nd November, the Suez Canal was closed to traffic. The seller failed to make the shipment and, when sued for damages, claimed that the contract had been frustrated.

The nature and extent of the contractual obligations were clear. The seller under a c.i.f. contract must prepare an invoice of the goods, ship goods of the right description at the port of shipment, procure a contract of affreightment providing for delivery at the

F. A. Tamplin S.S. Co., Ltd. v. *Anglo-Mexican Petroleum Products Co., Ltd.*

Tsakiroglou v. *Noblee and Thorl G.m.b.H.*

---

1. [1916] 2 A.C. 397.
2. [1916] A.C., at p. 405.
3. [1962] A.C. 93; [1961] 2 All E.R. 179.
4. A c.i.f. contract is one under which the agreed price covers the cost of the goods, the premium for their insurance and the freight for their carriage. The buyer's obligation is to pay the price upon the delivery of the shipping documents, not upon the delivery of the goods.

agreed destination, effect an adequate insurance of the cargo and send the shipping documents, i.e. the invoice, bill of lading and insurance policy, to the buyers.

So much being clear, the sole question to be decided was whether shipment via the Cape of Good Hope would constitute a fundamental alteration in the contractual obligations of the sellers. Would such a mode of performance be radically different from what they had agreed to perform?

The House of Lords unanimously repudiated the suggestion. The freight and perhaps the insurance would be more expensive, but extra expense does not *per se* justify a finding of frustration; the voyage to Hamburg would take four weeks longer than by the canal, but no delivery date was fixed by the contract. Since no particular route had been agreed to, the sellers were bound to choose one that was practicable in the circumstances. The argument, that every c.i.f. contract contains an implied term requiring the sellers to send the goods by the usual and customary route, found no favour with their Lordships, for even if such be the rule, what is usual must be estimated at the time when the obligation is performed, not when the contract is made.[1]

Discharge owing to supervening illegality

In many cases of Government interference the discharge of the contract may equally be justified on the ground that further performance has been made illegal. " It is plain," said Lord MACMILLAN, " that a contract to do what it has become illegal to do cannot be legally enforceable. There cannot be default in not doing what the law forbids to be done."[2] Thus, a contract for the sale of goods to be shipped from abroad to an English port is terminated as to the future if supervening legislation prohibits the importation of goods of that description.[3] The result is the same if the goods are to be shipped to a foreign port, and while the contract is still executory war breaks out with the country of destination.[4] To continue the contract would involve trading with the enemy.

Effect when parties expressly provide for the frustrating event

Two further factors which affect the operation of the doctrine of frustration require particular notice.

The first is relevant where a contingency for which the parties have expressly provided occurs in fact, but assumes a more fundamental and serious form than perhaps they contemplated. The question of construction that arises here is whether the express provision is intended to be a complete and exclusive solution of the matter in the sense that its object is to govern any form,

---

1. As to the effect of closure of the Suez Canal on voyage charter parties, see the differing views in *Société Franco-Tunisienne D'Armement* v. *Sidermar S.P.A.* [1961] 2 Q.B. 278; [1960] 2 All E.R. 529; *Ocean Tramp Tankers Corporation* v. *V/O Soufracht, The Eugenia,* [1964] 2 Q.B. 226; [1964] 1 All E.R. 161; *Palmco Shipping Inc.* v. *Continental Ore Corporation,* [1970] 2 Lloyd's Rep. 21. Charter-parties usually now contain a " Suez Canal clause " which purports to determine the rights of the parties if the ship proceeds *via* the Cape instead of through the canal. The obscurity of the clause, however, has raised difficulties; see, for example, *Achille Lauro Fugioacchino & Co.* v. *Total Societa Italiana per Azioni,* [1969] 2 Lloyd's Rep. 65.
2. *Denny, Mott and Dickson, Ltd.* v. *James B. Fraser & Co., Ltd.,* [1944] A.C. 265, at p. 272; [1944] 1 All E.R. 678, at p. 681.
3. *Denny Mott and Dickson, Ltd.* v. *James B. Fraser and Co., Ltd., supra.*
4. *Zinc Corporation, Ltd.* v. *Hirsch,* [1916] 1 K.B. 541.

fundamental or not, that the contingency may take. Unless it is intended to be of this all embracing character, it will not prevent the discharge of the obligation if in the result the effect of the contingency is to frustrate the essential object of the contract. The leading case is *Jackson* v. *Union Marine Insurance Co., Ltd.*[1]

> A ship was chartered in November, 1871, to proceed with all possible despatch, *dangers and accidents of navigation excepted*, from Liverpool to Newport and there to load a cargo of iron rails for carriage to San Francisco. She sailed on January 2nd, but on the 3rd ran aground in Carnarvon Bay. She was got off by February 18th and taken to Liverpool where she was still under repair in August. On February 15th the charterers repudiated the contract.

The question was whether the charterers were liable for not loading the ship, or whether the time likely to be required for repairs was so long as to excuse their failure to do so. The question put to the jury, which they answered in the affirmative, was " whether such time was so long as to put an end in a commercial sense to the commercial speculation entered upon by the shipowner and the charterers." On this finding it was held that the adventure contemplated by the parties was frustrated and the contract discharged. A voyage to San Francisco carried out after the repair of the ship would have been a totally different adventure from that originally envisaged. The express exception, read literally, no doubt covered the accident that had happened, and it would have precluded the charterers from recovering damages in respect of the delay; but it was not intended to cover an accident causing injury of so extensive a nature.

In a later case, a contract was made in 1913 by which shipowners undertook to provide charterers with certain vessels in each of the years 1914 to 1918, and it was agreed that if war broke out shipments might at the option of either party be suspended until the end of hostilities. After the start of the war, ROWLATT, J., held that the contract was discharged, not merely suspended. The suspension clause was not intended by the parties to cover a war of such a catastrophic nature and with such dislocating effects as in fact occurred.[2]

A second relevant factor is whether one of the parties has himself been responsible for the frustrating event. " Reliance," said Lord SUMNER, " cannot be placed on a self-induced frustration."[3] The point arose in a neat form in *Maritime National Fish, Ltd.* v. *Ocean Trawlers, Ltd.*,[4] where: {.margin-note: Party cannot rely upon self-induced frustration}

> The appellants chartered from the respondents a steam trawler which was useless for fishing unless it was fitted with an otter trawl. To the knowledge of both parties it was a statutory offence to use an otter trawl except under licence from the Canadian Minister

---

1. (1874), L.R. 10 C.P. 125. And see *Bank Line, Ltd.* v. *A. Capel & Co.*, [1919] A.C. 435. See also the remarks of DIPLOCK, J., on the *Jackson* case in *Tsakiroglou & Co., Ltd.* v. *Noblee and Thorl G.m.b.H.*, [1960] 2 Q.B. 318, at pp. 330–1; [1959] 1 All E.R. 45, at p. 50. See also *Metropolitan Water Board* v. *Dick, Kerr & Co.*, [1918] A.C. 119; *supra*, p. 550.
2. *Pacific Phosphate Co., Ltd.* v. *Empire Transport Co., Ltd.* (1920), 36 T.L.R. 750.
3. *Bank Line, Ltd.* v. *A. Capel & Co.*, [1919] A.C. 435, at p. 452.
4. [1935] A.C. 524; [1935] All E.R. Rep. 86. See also *Mertens* v. *Home Freeholds Co.*, [1921] 2 K.B. 526.

of Fisheries. Later, the appellants, who had four other ships of their own, applied for five licences, but were granted only three. In naming the ships to which these licences should apply they excluded the trawler chartered from the respondents.

The appellants contended that they were not liable for the hire due under the charterparty, since performance had been frustrated by the refusal of the Minister to grant the full number of licences. The Privy Council, however, refused to regard this fact as sufficient to bring the case within the doctrine, for " the essence of frustration is that it should not be due to the act or election of the party," and here it was the appellants themselves who had chosen to defeat the common object of the adventure. On the other hand, the phrase " self-induced frustration " does not imply that every degree of fault will preclude a party from claiming to be discharged.

> " The possible varieties [of fault] are infinite, and can range from the criminality of the scuttler who opens the sea-cocks and sinks his ship, to the thoughtlessness of the prima donna who sits in a draught and loses her voice. I wish to guard against the supposition that every destruction of *corpus* for which a contractor can be said, to some extent or in some sense, to be responsible, necessarily involves that the resultant frustration is self-induced within the meaning of the phrase."[1]

Onus of proving frustration self-induced

This rule, that a party cannot claim to be discharged by a frustrating event for which he is himself responsible, does not require him to prove affirmatively that the event occurred without his fault. In accordance with the maxim—*ei incumbit probatio qui dicit non qui negat*—the onus of proving that the frustration was self-induced rests upon the party raising this allegation.[2] For instance:

> On the day before a chartered ship was due to load her cargo an explosion of such violence occurred in her auxiliary boiler that the performance of the charter-party became impossible. The cause of the explosion could not be definitely ascertained, but only one of three possible reasons would have imputed negligence to the shipowners.

It was held by the House of Lords that, since the charterers were unable to prove that the explosion was caused by the fault of the owners, the defence of frustration succeeded and the contract was discharged.[3] It should perhaps be noted that in many cases a self-induced frustrating event will be a breach of contract but this will not necessarily be so. In *Maritime National Fish, Ltd.* v. *Ocean Trawlers, Ltd.,*[4] the applicants were not contractually bound to licence the chartered trawler but could not excuse failure to pay hire by relying on the absence of a licence.

---

1. *Joseph Constantine Steamship Line, Ltd.* v. *Imperial Smelting Corporation, Ltd.,* [1942] A.C. 154, at p. 179; [1941] 2 All E.R. 165, at p. 175, *per* Lord RUSSELL OF KILLOWEN.
2. *Joseph Constantine Steamship Line, Ltd.* v. *Imperial Smelting Corporation, Ltd.,* [1942] A.C. 154, at p. 179; [1941] 2 All E.R. 165, at p. 175, *per* Lord RUSSELL OF KILLOWEN.
3. *Ibid.,* [1942] A.C. 154; [1941] 2 All E.R. 165.
4. *Supra,* p. 553. See also *Hare* v. *Murphy Brothers* [1974] 3 All E.R. 940; [1974] I.C.R. 603.

A controversial question that is still undecided by the House of Lords is whether the doctrine of frustration can be applied to a lease of land. If, for instance, land which has been let for building purposes for 99 years is, within five years from the beginning of the tenancy, completely submerged in the sea or zoned as a permanent open space, can it be said that the fundamental purpose of the contract has been frustrated and that the term itself must automatically cease?[1]

It is, indeed, well settled by a number of decisions that if, during the continuance of the lease, the premises are requisitioned by the Government[2] or destroyed by fire[3] or by enemy action,[4] the tenant remains liable on his covenants to pay rent and to repair the property. But these decisions, which assume that individual covenants by a landlord or tenant are absolute, do not preclude the possibility that an event may be regarded as frustrating the fundamental purpose of the contract and therefore as terminating the lease altogether. The view that has so far prevailed, at least in the lower courts, is that leases are outside the doctrine of frustration. This is based on the fact that a lease creates not merely a contract, but also an estate. Thus in *London and Northern Estates Co.* v. *Schlesinger*,[5] it was held that the lease of a flat was not terminated by the fact that the tenant had become an alien enemy and was therefore prohibited from residing on the premises. LUSH, J., said:

> " It is not correct to speak of this tenancy agreement as a contract and nothing more. A term of years was created by it and vested in the appellant, and I can see no reason for saying that, because this order disqualified him from personally residing in the flat, it affected the chattel interest which was vested in him by virtue of the agreement."[6]

A contract is frustrated when the venture cannot be carried out, but in the case of a lease the venture contemplated by the parties is the transfer of an estate to the tenant. The contractual obligations are but incidental to this transfer, and, even if one or more of them cease to bind the tenant because of some supervening cause, this does not affect the continuance of the estate.[7] The foundation of the agreement is the creation of the estate, and so long as the foundation exists there is no frustration.[8] This last way of stating the law has been stigmatized by Lord SIMON as coming perilously near to arguing in a circle, for why should frustration be excluded merely because the foundation happens

Controversy whether doctrine of frustration applies to a lease

Judicial views on the controversy

1. Yahuda, 21 M.L.R. 637.
2. *Whitehall Court, Ltd.* v. *Ettlinger*, [1920] 1 K.B. 680.
3. *Matthey* v. *Curling*, [1922] 2 A.C. 180. Atiyah, *Accidents, Compensation and the Law*, p. 318, points out that it normal practice for landlords to insure against such loss.
4. See *Redmond* v. *Dainton*, [1920] 2 K.B. 256.
5. [1916] 1 K.B. 20.
6. At p. 24. This statement was approved by the Court of Appeal in *Whitehall Court, Ltd.* v. *Ettlinger*, [1920] 1 K.B. 680, at pp. 686, 687, which decision was approved by Lord ATKINSON in *Matthey* v. *Curling*, [1922] 2 A.C. 180, at p. 237.
7. *Cricklewood Property and Investment Trust, Ltd.* v. *Leighton's Investment Trust, Ltd.*, [1945] A.C. 221, at pp. 233–4, *per* Lord RUSSELL OF KILLOWEN; [1945] 1 All E.R. 252, at p. 258.
8. *Ibid.*, [1945] A.C. 221, at p. 245, *per* Lord GODDARD; [1945] 1 All E.R. 252, at p. 265.

to be the transfer of an estate?[1] In his view there is no difficulty in applying the doctrine of frustration, at any rate to a building lease. The object in such a case is to erect buildings on the site for the benefit of the lessor and lessee, and if for instance the site is zoned for ever as an open space, it could reasonably be said that the fundamental purpose of the transaction had been defeated.[2] Lord WRIGHT has taken the same view: the doctrine is modern and flexible and ought not to be restricted by an arbitrary formula.[3]

The
Cricklewood
case

These opinions were expressed in *Cricklewood Property and Investment Trust, Ltd.* v. *Leighton's Investment Trust, Ltd.*[4]

> In May, 1936, a building lease was made to the lessees for a term of ninety-nine years. Before any buildings had been erected the war of 1939 broke out and restrictions imposed by the Government made it impossible for the lessees to erect the shops that they had covenanted to erect. In an action brought against them for the recovery of rent they pleaded that the lease was frustrated.

It was held unanimously by the House of Lords that the doctrine of frustration, even if it were capable of application to a lease, did not apply in the instant circumstances. The compulsory suspension of building did not strike at the root of the transaction, for when it was imposed the lease still had more then ninety years to run, and therefore the interruption in performance was likely to last only for a small fraction of the term.

Present
law as to
leases

Lord RUSSELL and Lord GODDARD, L.C.J., took a contrary view to that of Lord SIMON and Lord WRIGHT, and expressed the opinion that the doctrine of frustration cannot apply to a demise of real property. Lord PORTER expressed no opinion on the question. The result of these conflicting *dicta* is that until the House of Lords resolves the problem the decisions of the lower courts stand, and the doctrine is excluded in the case of a lease.[5]

It is submitted however that if the question should come before the House of Lords, the view that a lease is capable of being frustrated is to be preferred. It is no doubt true that in many cases the object of the parties is *in fact* to transfer an estate but it surely goes too far to say that this is so *as a matter of law*. In many cases the parties may contemplate that the risk of unforeseen disasters will pass to the Lessee on the execution of the lease just as surely as if he had taken a conveyance of the fee simple but this will not always be so. If the lease is for a specific purpose which becomes impossible of achievement, there may be a strong case for holding the lease frustrated. Similar arguments may apply if the lease is of short duration and here it is relevant to observe that a contractual licence to use land is certainly capable of frustration,[6] and that the distinction between leases and licences is notoriously hard to draw.[7] These views derive

---

1. *Ibid.,* [1945] A.C. 221, at p. 229; [1945] 1 All E.R. 252, at p. 256.
2. *Ibid.*
3. *Ibid.,* [1945] A.C. 221, at p. 241; [1945] 1 All E.R. 252, at p. 263.
4. [1945] A.C. 221; [1945] 1 All E.R. 252.
5. *Denman* v. *Brise,* [1949] 1 K.B. 22; [1948] 2 All E.R. 141. *Cusack-Smith* v. *London Corporation,* [1956] 1 W.L.R. 1368.
6. *Taylor* v. *Caldwell* (1863), 3 B & S. 826; *Krell* v. *Henry,* [1903] 2 K.B. 740.
7. Cheshire, *Modern Real Property,* 12th Edn., pp. 577 *et seq.*

considerable support from the decision of the Supreme Court of Canada in *Highway Properties, Ltd.* v. *Kelly, Douglas & Co.*,[1] that for the purpose of applying the rules about breach " it is no longer sensible to pretend that a commercial lease . . . is simply a conveyance and not also a contract."[2]

In the *Cricklewood* case the two Law Lords who were of opinion that the doctrine of frustration can never apply to a lease confined their remarks to the case of an executed lease under which a legal estate has passed to the tenant before the occurrence of the frustrating event.[3] It might be argued that, their objection that the tenant cannot invoke the doctrine, since he has obtained the estate the creation of which was the venture contemplated by the parties, applies equally to the equitable interest that vests in the tenant under an *enforceable* contract for the grant of a lease, even though he has not gone into possession and no lease has been executed.   In these circumstances, equity, applying its principle that what ought to be done is to be regarded as already done, allows either party to sue for specific performance and thus to enforce the transfer of the legal estate in accordance with the contract. Broadly speaking, the tenant is in the same position as if a lease had in fact been executed in his favour. Therefore, where the contract is still capable of fulfilment in the sense that it can be specifically performed, the tenant, though at the moment entitled only to an equitable interest, may be unable to rely upon the doctrine of frustration.

On the other hand since the transfer of the equitable interest depends on the availability of specific performance, it may perhaps more plausibly be argued that if the contract is frustrated, specific performance will no longer be available and the equitable interest will revest in the Lessor.   If this is correct the decisive question is whether the contract to grant the lease should be treated as frustrated. GOFF, J., had no doubt in *Rom Securities, Ltd.* v. *Rogers (Holdings), Ltd.*[4] that the doctrine of frustration could apply to an agreement for a lease, at least before entry into possession.

Similar reasoning may apply to a contract for the sale of land. The effect of such a contract, pending the conveyance of the legal estate, is to pass the equitable interest to the purchaser. The contract is specifically enforceable at the instance of either party. Normally, therefore, the doctrine of frustration will not apply. The sole decision on the matter is *Hillingdon Estates Co.* v. *Stone-field Estates, Ltd.*[5] where the facts were these:

> By a contract dated January 13th, 1938, the vendors agreed to sell to the purchasers certain land in Middlesex, which was to be used for building development. Ten years later, in October, 1948, the Middlesex County Council made a compulsory purchase order affecting the land. The purchasers, to whom no conveyance of the legal estate had yet been made, then brought an action claiming that the foundation of the contract was the development of the

Marginal notes:

Agreement to lease as distinguished from executed lease

Contract for the sale of land

---

1. (1971), 17 D.L.R. (3d) 710. See *infra*, p. 578.
2. (1971), 17 D.L.R. (3d) 710 at p. 721, *per* Laskin, J.
3. *Per* Lord RUSSELL OF KILLOWEN, [1945] A.C., at p. 233; *per* Lord GODDARD, at p. 244.
4. (1967), 205 Estates Gazette 427.
5. [1952] Ch. 627; [1952] 1 All E.R. 853.

land, that development had been frustrated by the compulsory order and that therefore the contract was extinguished. On the other hand, the vendors counterclaimed for specific performance of the contract.

The action of the purchasers was dismissed and the counterclaim allowed. VAISEY, J., stressed the fact that the compulsory order raised no obstacle to the conveyance of the legal estate, and he held that the contract, far from being frustrated, could and should be carried out.[1]

This decision should probably be regarded as deciding that on the facts the contract was not frustrated rather than that a contract for the sale of land cannot be frustrated. The transfer of the equitable interest will often be relevant to a decision as to whether the contract has in fact been frustrated. So on the purchase of a house, since an equitable interest passes to the purchaser on exchange of contracts, he should insure against fire from that moment and can hardly thereafter argue that destruction by fire frustrates the contract. It would appear excessively mechanical to argue that whenever an equitable interest has passed, the doctrine of frustration is excluded and so to hold would be inconsistent with a House of Lords decision treating an option to purchase land as capable of frustration.[2]

SECTION III. EFFECT OF THE DOCTRINE

Frustrating event discharges contract immediately

Presuming that a contract is frustrated by the operation of the doctrine, it is now necessary to examine the legal consequences. The first point to appreciate is the moment at which the discharge becomes operative. The rule established at common law is that the occurrence of the frustrating event " brings the contract to an end forthwith, without more and automatically."[3]

> " In my opinion," said Lord WRIGHT. " the contract is automatically terminated as to the future, because at that date its further performance becomes impossible in fact in circumstances which involve no liability for damages for the failure on either party."[4]

It is worth noting that it is not a logical necessity that impossibility of performance should operate to discharge a contract. In many Continental systems it is viewed rather as a defence[5] and English law might have accommodated it in the same way. In most cases only one party's performance is impossible—the other's obligation consisting in payment. In such a situation the party who could not perform might plead impossibility of

---

1. To a certain extent, however, he seems to have been influenced by the long delay that had occurred between the contract and the action brought by the purchasers: see [1952] Ch., at p. 635. *Quaere* whether this was relevant.
2. *Denny, Mott and Dickson, Ltd.* v. *James B. Frazer & Co., Ltd.*, [1944] A.C. 265; [1944] 1 All E.R. 678.
3. *Hirji Mulji* v. *Cheong Yue Steamship Co.*, [1926] A.C. 497, *per* Lord SUMNER, at p. 505.
4. *Fibrosa Spolka Akcyjna* v. *Fairbairn Lawson Combe Barbour, Ltd.*, [1943] A.C. 32, at p. 70; [1942] 2 All E.R. 122, at p. 140. But see the criticism of Williams, *Law Reform (Frustrated Contracts) Act* 1943, pp. 41–2.
5. See Nicholas, 48 Tulane L.R. 946, at pp. 954–966.

performance and the other total failure of consideration.[1] English
law has not taken this path in general and this has concealed the
undoubted existence of cases where impossibility does excuse
but does not discharge. Thus we have seen[2] that a prolonged
illness may frustrate a contract of personal service while a shorter
and less serious illness will not do so. The shorter illness however while not bringing the contract to an end, will usually
excuse absence from work. Similarly a statute may operate to
provide a defence for non-performance of the contract without
discharging it.[3]

The contract is terminated as to the future only. Unlike one
vitiated by mistake, it is not void *ab initio*. It starts life as a
valid contract, but comes to an abrupt and automatic end the
moment that the common adventure is frustrated. From this
premise the common law drew inferences which, though sometimes harsh, were not illogical. The rule adopted by the judges
until 1943 may thus be stated:

> Each party must fulfil his contractual obligations so far as they
> have fallen due before the frustrating event, but he is excused from
> performing those that fall due later.[4]

In *Krell* v. *Henry*,[5] for instance, it was held that the plaintiff could
not recover the agreed rent from the defendant, since it did not fall
due until the last minute of June 24th, and before this moment
had arrived the abandonment of the procession had been an-
nounced. In *Jackson* v. *Union Marine Insurance Co.*[6] the ground-
ing of the ship under charter terminated the contract, with the
result that the owners were not bound to provide an alternative
vessel, nor were the charterers bound to pay freight.

This common law principle, since it meant that any loss
arising from the termination of the contract must lie where it had
fallen, might well cause hardship to one or other of the parties, as
is shown by *Chandler* v. *Webster*.[7] In that case:

The rule in Chandler v. Webster

> X agreed to let a room in Pall Mall to Y for the purpose of
> viewing the coronation procession of 1902. The price was £141 15s.
> payable immediately. Y paid £100, but he still owed the balance
> when the contract was discharged on June 24th owing to the
> abandonment of the procession. It was held, not only that Y had
> no right to recover the sum of £100, but also that he remained
> liable for the balance of £41 15s.

If attention is confined to the contract the decision is logical
enough. The obligation to pay the £141 had matured before
the moment of frustration. The plaintiff's counsel, however,
argued that he was entitled to disregard the contract and to
recover in quasi-contract the £100 actually paid, on the ground

---

1. See Lord PORTER in *Joseph Constantine Steamship Line, Ltd.* v. *Imperial
   Smelting Corporation, Ltd.*, [1942] A.C. 154, at p. 203; Weir, [1970] C.L.J.
   189; For a similar analysis of initial impossibility, see Stoljar, *Mistake and
   Misrepresentation*, Chap. 3.
2. *Supra*, p. 548.
3. See, e.g. Remuneration, Charges and Grants Act 1975, s. 1.
4. See the *Fibrosa* case, [1943] A.C. 32, at p. 58; [1942] 2 All E.R. 122, at
   p. 134.
5. *Supra*, p. 545.
6. *Supra*, p. 553.
7. [1904] 1 K.B. 493.

of a total failure of consideration.[1] But the Court of Appeal held that, as the doctrine of frustration does not avoid a contract *ab initio* but ends it only from the moment of frustration, it was inadmissible to predicate a *total* failure of consideration. The quasi-contractual remedy was therefore inapplicable. In the words of COLLINS, M.R.:

> " If the effect were that the contract were wiped out altogether, no doubt the result would be that money paid under it would have to be repaid as on a failure of consideration. But that is not the effect of the doctrine [of frustration]; it only releases a party from further performance of the contract. Therefore the doctrine of failure of consideration does not apply."[2]

Chandler v. *Webster* overruled by the *Fibrosa* case

If, as in *Chandler* v. *Webster*, the money was due before the date of frustration, the loss lay upon the debtor; but it was borne by the creditor if, as in *Krell* v. *Henry*, the obligation to pay did not mature until after the discharge of the contract.

It is not surprising, therefore, that the decision in *Chandler* v. *Webster* should have caused general dissatisfaction. But, despite judicial criticism,[3] it was not until 1942 that the House of Lords succeeded, in the *Fibrosa* case,[4] in avoiding the consequences of the rule that the contract remained in full force up to the moment of frustration. The facts of the case were as follows:

> The respondents, an English company, agreed in July, 1939, to sell and to deliver within three or four months certain machinery to a Polish company in Gdynia. The contract price was £4,800, of which £1,600 was payable in advance. Great Britain declared war on Germany on September 3rd, and on September 23rd the Germans occupied Gdynia. The contract was therefore frustrated. On September 7th the London agent of the Polish company requested the return of £1,000 which had been paid in July to the respondents. The request was refused on the ground that " considerable work " had already been done on the machinery.

It was, of course, clear that when the money was paid it was due under an existing contract, so that it could not be recovered by an action based upon the contract. The House of Lords held, however, that it was recoverable in quasi-contract. They set themselves, with sufficient success, to defeat the assumption upon which the Court of Appeal in *Chandler* v. *Webster* had proceeded, namely, that there could be no total failure of consideration unless the contract was void *ab initio*. Lord SIMON surmounted the difficulty by distinguishing the meaning of consideration, as used in this quasi-contractual sense, from that normally given to it in contract. He said:

> " In English law, an enforceable contract may be formed by an exchange of a promise for a promise, or by the exchange of a promise for an act—I am excluding contracts under seal—and thus, in the law relating to the formation of contract, the promise to do a thing

---

1. It will be seen later (pp. 648 *et seq.*) that there are certain circumstances where the law, in its dislike of unjust enrichment, allows a person to sustain an action for money had and received, and by this quasi-contractual remedy to recover a payment for which he has received nothing.
2. [1904] 1 K.B. 493, at p. 499.
3. See the various criticisms summarized by Lord WRIGHT in the *Fibrosa* case, [1943] A.C. 32, at p. 71; [1942] 2 All E.R. 122, at p. 140.
4. *Fibrosa Spolka Akcyjna* v. *Fairbairn Lawson Combe Barbour, Ltd.*, [1943] A.C. 32; [1942] 2 All E.R. 122.

may often be the consideration. But when one is considering the law of failure of consideration and of the quasi-contractual right to recover money on that ground, it is, generally speaking, not the promise which is referred to as the consideration, but the performance of the promise. The money was paid to secure performance, and, if performance fails, the inducement which brought about the payment is not fulfilled."[1]

Others of their Lordships, such as Lord ATKIN and Lord MAC-MILLAN, were content to repudiate *Chandler* v. *Webster* as devoid of authority. The result at least was to overrule that decision and to enable the Polish company to succeed in quasi-contract.

The rule established by the *Fibrosa* case has thus diminished the injustice of the former law, but since it operates only in the event of a total failure of consideration, it does not remove every hardship. On the one hand, it does not permit the recovery of an advance payment if the consideration has only partly failed, i.e., if the payer has received some benefit, though perhaps a slender one, for his money.[2] On the other hand, the payee, in his turn, may suffer an injustice. Thus, while he may be compelled to repay the money on the ground that the payer has received no benefit, he may himself, in the partial performance of the contract, have incurred expenses for which he has no redress. In the words of Lord SIMON:

The law still unsatisfactory despite the Fibrosa case

> "He may have incurred expenses in connection with the partial carrying out of the contract which are equivalent, or more than equivalent, to the money which he prudently stipulated should be prepaid, but which he now has to return for reasons which are no fault of his. He may have to repay the money, though he has executed almost the whole of the contractual work, which will be left on his hands. These results follow from the fact that the English common law does not undertake to apportion a prepaid sum in such circumstances—contrast the provision, now contained in section 40 of the Partnership Act 1890 for apportioning a premium if a partnership is prematurely dissolved."[3]

The *Fibrosa* case, therefore, while it removed the worst consequences of the decision in *Chandler* v. *Webster*, left other difficulties untouched. A further attempt to clarify the law has, however, been made by the Law Reform (Frustrated Contracts) Act 1943, which gives general effect to the recommendations of the Law Revision Committee.[4]

The preliminary fact to observe is that the Act is confined to a case where " a contract governed by English law has *become impossible of performance or been otherwise frustrated*, and the parties thereto have for that reason been discharged from the further performance of the contract."[5] In other words, the statutory provisions do not apply where a contract is discharged by breach or for any reason other than impossibility or frustration.

Law Reform (Frustrated Contracts) Act 1943

---

1. This reasoning, which is now only of historical interest because of the Act of 1943, *infra*, has not escaped criticism: see Gow, 3 I.C.L.Q. 303, at pp. 311–12.
2. *Fibrosa Spolka Akcyjna* v. *Fairbairn Lawson Combe Barbour, Ltd.*, [1943] A.C. 32, at pp. 54–5, *per* Lord ATKIN; at p. 56, *per* Lord RUSSELL; [1942] 2 All E.R. 122, at pp. 131, 132, 133.
3. [1943] A.C. 32, at p. 49; [1942] 2 All E.R. 122, at p. 129.
4. 7th Interim Report, Cmd. 6009 (1939).
5. Section 1 (1). For a full account of the Act, see Williams, *Law Reform (Frustrated Contracts) Act*.

General
effect of
the Act

In general it may be said that the Act makes two fundamental changes in the law. First, it amplifies the decision in the *Fibrosa* case by permitting the recovery of money prepaid, even though at the date of frustration there has been no total failure of consideration. Secondly, it allows a party who has done something in performance of the contract prior to the frustrating event to claim compensation for any benefit thereby conferred upon the other. In this respect it modifies the common law rule laid down, for instance, in *Cutter* v. *Powell*.[1] We will now consider the Act under these two general headings.

Advance
payment less
expenses
recoverable

(i) The right to recover money paid

Section 1 (2) enacts as follows:

> All sums paid or payable to any party in pursuance of the contract before the time when the parties were so discharged (in this Act referred to as "the time of discharge") shall, in the case of sums so paid, be recoverable from him as money received by him for the use of the party by whom the sums were paid, and, in the case of sums so payable, cease to be so payable.

This confirms the reversal by the *Fibrosa* case of *Chandler* v. *Webster*.[2] On May 1st, A agrees to hire a room from B for the purpose of viewing a procession on June 26th, and by the terms of the contract he is required to pay the agreed price on May 7th. On June 23rd, the procession is abandoned, and therefore the contract is discharged at common law. If A has already fulfilled his obligation to pay the price, he has a statutory right of recovery; if he has not done so, he is statutorily free from liability.

The subsection then proceeds to offset this relief to the party on whom the contractual duty of payment rests by giving a limited protection to the payee in so far, but only in so far, as he has incurred expense in the course of fulfilling the contract. This protection is expressed in the following proviso:

> Provided that, if the party to whom the sums were so paid or so payable incurred expenses before the time of discharge in or for the purpose of the performance of the contract, the court may, if it considers it just to do so having regard to all the circumstances of the case, allow him to retain or, as the case may be, to recover the whole or any part of the sums so paid or payable, not being an amount in excess of the expenses so incurred.

The extent of the protection thus afforded to the payee may become clearer if the proviso is sub-divided. It then becomes apparent that:

> (a) If the party to whom the sums have been *paid* has incurred expenses before the time of discharge in, or for the purpose of, the performance of the contract, the court may in its discretion allow him to *retain* the whole or any part of such sums, not being an amount in excess of the expenses incurred.
> (b) If the party to whom the sums were *payable* has incurred expenses before the time of discharge in, or for the purpose of, the performance of the contract, the court may in its discretion allow him to *recover* the whole or any part of such sums, not being an amount in excess of the expenses incurred.[3]

---

1. *Supra,* p. 524.
2. *Supra,* pp. 559–61.
3. Section 1 (2), proviso.

It will thus be noticed that a party can receive no allowance for his expenditure unless it was incurred before the occurrence of the frustrating event.

This discretionary power of the court to make an allowance for expenses was beyond the power of the House of Lords in the *Fibrosa* case. But if the facts of that case were to recur and if, for example, machinery of a special nature, not realizable in the open market, had been substantially completed by the English company under the contract, the court would be able to order the repayment to the Polish company of a proportion only of the prepaid amount.

(ii) The right to recover compensation for partial performance

It will be recalled that, in accordance with the doctrine of strict performance established at common law in such cases as *Cutter* v. *Powell*, a man who fails to complete *in toto* his obligation under an entire contract can often recover nothing for what he may have done, even though the non-completion is due to an extraneous cause which, through no fault of his own, frustrates the common adventure or even renders further performance altogether impossible.[1] An outstanding example of the injustice that this doctrine may cause is afforded by *Appleby* v. *Myers*.[2]

> The plaintiffs, in consideration of a promise to pay £459, agreed to erect machinery on the defendant's premises, and to keep it in order for two years from the date of completion. When the erection was nearly complete an accidental fire entirely destroyed the premises together with all that they contained.

An action brought to recover £419 for work done and materials supplied failed. Under the doctrine of frustration the effect of the destruction of the subject-matter of the contract was that both parties were excused from the further performance of their obligations. The plaintiffs were not bound to erect new machinery; the defendant was not bound to pay for what had been done, since his obligation to pay had not matured at the time when the contract was discharged.

An attempt to deal with difficulties of this nature, however, has now been made by the Act. Section 1 (3) enacts that:

> " Where any party to the contract has, by reason of anything done by any other party thereto in, or for the purpose of, the performance of the contract, obtained a valuable benefit (other than a payment of money . . .) before the time of discharge, there shall be recoverable from him by the said other party such sum (if any) not exceeding the value of the said benefit to the party obtaining it as the court considers just."

In estimating the amount of the sum to be recovered, the court must consider all the circumstances of the case, especially any expenses that the benefited party may have incurred in the performance of the contract before the time of discharge, and also

Marginal notes:

Effect of the Act upon common law requirement of complete performance

Party benefited by partial performance may be required to pay

---

1. *Supra*, p. 524.
2. (1867), L.R. 2 C.P. 651.

whether the circumstances causing the frustration have affected the value of the benefit.[1]

The Act goes a long way towards removing the injustice of the common law rule. If, for instance, a builder agrees for a lump sum to erect a warehouse, and when he has completed a part of the work further construction is prohibited by the Government owing to the outbreak of war, he may in the discretion of the court be awarded a sum commensurate with the value of the benefit conferred upon the other contracting party. It is not clear, however, whether this particular subsection does full justice, for it is only where " a valuable benefit " has been " obtained " by the other party that the court is empowered to give relief. If, for instance, the facts of *Appleby* v. *Myers* were to recur, it could be argued that, since the completed work had been totally destroyed, no benefit would have been conferred on the defendant. The loss, for which neither party was to blame, would fall entirely on the builder and this view has been taken in a Newfoundland case.[2] On the other hand it has been suggested,[3] that, by a liberal interpretation of the subsection, a " valuable benefit " might be said to have been " obtained " by the owner by the mere fact that the work has been done on his land in accordance with the contract, even though it may be destroyed before it has brought him any sensible advantage.

This view can be reinforced by two further arguments, one technical, the other substantial. The technical argument is that the Act talks of obtaining a benefit " *before* the time of discharge." This suggests that the time to ask the question benefit *vel non* is the moment before the frustrating event. At this moment the position of the customer is the same whether in the next moment the contract is to be frustrated by a Government ban on building or the destruction of the premises. The substantial argument is that it is inconceivable in modern circumstances that such a contract could be undertaken without either the builder or the customer carrying insurance against fire and a just allocation of the loss must necessarily take this into account. A wide construction of " benefit " would enable the court to do this. In this respect it should be noted that the " benefit " is not an entitlement but simply a ceiling on liability.

General provisions of the Act

It should be noted that the Act binds the Crown; that it applies to contracts whenever made, provided that the time of discharge occurs on or after July 1st, 1943; and that it may be excluded by the parties in the sense that if their contract contains a provision to meet the event of frustration, the provision applies to the exclusion of the Act.[4]

Contracts excluded from the Act

The Act does not apply to the following classes of contract:[5]

(a) A contract for the carriage of goods by sea or a charterparty (except a time charterparty or a charterparty by way of demise).

---

1. Section 1 (3) (a) and (b).
2. *Parsons Brothers, Ltd.* v. *Shea* (1965), 53 D.L.R. (2d) 86.
3. Webber, *Effect of War on Contracts*, 2nd Edn., p. 687; Glanville Williams, *op. cit.*, pp. 48–51.
4. Section 2 (1), (2), and (3).
5. Section 2 (5).

Two important common law rules governing these excepted contracts therefore remain in force.

The first is that, if the contract provides that the freight shall not become payable until the conclusion of the voyage, the shipowner is entitled to no remuneration if he is prevented from reaching the stipulated port of discharge by some frustrating event. If, for example, the agreed port is Hamburg and the shipowner puts into Antwerp owing to the outbreak of war with Germany, he cannot recover freight unless the shipper voluntarily accepts delivery at Antwerp.[1] The second rule is that freight paid in advance is regarded as a payment at the risk of the shipper and is not recoverable, either in whole or in part, if, owing to the frustration of the contract or to any other cause, the goods are not delivered.[2] It is customary, however, to insure against the risks engendered by these two rules.

Charter-parties

(b) A contract of insurance.

The doctrine of frustration is not normally applicable to a contract of insurance, for the customary understanding in this type of business and indeed the rule of law, is that, once the premium is paid and the risk assumed by the insurer, " there shall be no apportionment or return of premium afterwards,"[3] even though the subject-matter of the risk may vanish before the period of cover has elapsed.[4] " If I insure against sickness on January 1st and die on February 1st, my executors cannot get back 11/12th of the premium."[5] So too, if a house which has been insured against fire is requisitioned by a Government department before expiry of the policy, the assured is not entitled to recover any part of the premium.

Contracts of insurance

(c) The Act excepts from its provisions:

> Any contract to which section 7 of the Sale of Goods Act 1893 applies, or any other contract for the sale or for the sale and delivery of specific goods, where the contract is frustrated by reason of the fact that the goods have perished.[6]

Certain contracts for the sale of goods

This subsection is clumsily drafted and is difficult to understand, but its effect appears to be as follows.[7]

It excludes two classes of contract.

(1) " Any contract to which section 7 of the Sale of Goods Act 1893 applies." Section 7 provides that:

> " Where there is an agreement to sell specific goods and subsequently the goods, without any fault on the part of the seller or buyer, perish before the risk passes to the buyer, the agreement is thereby avoided."

It will be observed that for this section to operate, four elements must be present:

---

1. *St. Enoch Shipping Co.* v. *Phosphate Mining Co.,* [1916] 2 K.B. 624.
2. *Byrne* v. *Schiller* (1871), L.R. 6 Ex. 319. Of course, if the goods are lost owing to the shipowner's default the freight already paid is included in the damages.
3. *Tyrie* v. *Fletcher* (1777), 2 Cowp. 666, at p. 668, *per* Lord MANSFIELD.
4. Webber, *op. cit.,* p. 693.
5. Speech by the Attorney-General on the Committee stage of the Bill, 1943, cited Webber, *op. cit.,* p. 679, note 4.
6. Section 2 (5) (c).
7. For a full discussion, see Williams, *op. cit.* pp. 81–90.

(i) There must be an agreement to sell, not a sale.

By section 4 of the Sale of Goods Act, the concept of " contract of sale " is sub-divided into a " sale " and an " agreement to sell." If the property in the goods is transferred to the buyer under the contract, there is a " sale "; if the property is not immediately transferred by virtue of the contract, there is an " agreement to sell."

(ii) The risk must not have passed to the buyer.

The general rule for the passing of the risk is stated in section 20 of the Sale of Goods Act.

> " Unless otherwise agreed, the goods remain at the seller's risk until the property therein is transferred to the buyer, but when the property therein is transferred to the buyer, the goods are at the buyer's risk whether delivery has been made or not."

In other words, risk *prima facie* follows the property. In the case of an agreement to sell, therefore, since the property remains with the seller, so also does the risk, and this is what normally happens. The parties, however, may " agree otherwise " and may thus arrange that while the seller remains the owner of the goods, the risk shall pass to the buyer.[1] If such is the arrangement, section 7 of the Sale of Goods Act does not apply.

(iii) The goods must be specific.

By section 62 of the Sale of Goods Act, " specific goods means goods identified and agreed upon at the time a contract of sale is made." It is clear, therefore, that a contract for the sale of unascertained or generic goods cannot satisfy this definition, as where A agrees to sell to B " a dozen bottles of 1919 port " or " 500 quarters of wheat." A will fulfil his contract by delivering any dozen of such bottles or any 500 quarters of wheat, and it is obvious that, as the subject-matter of such contract has no individuality, it cannot perish. *Genus nunquam perit*. It seems, moreover, that goods will still be unascertained even if the source from which they are to come is specifically defined, provided that the actual goods to be delivered are not yet identified.[2] If, for example, A agrees to sell " a dozen bottles of the 1919 port now in my cellar," the goods are not specific in the statutory sense. No particular dozen bottles have yet been set aside and earmarked for the contract. To this case also section 7 of the Sale of Goods Act is inapplicable.

(iv) The goods must have perished.

The word " perish " includes cases not only where the goods have been physically destroyed, but also where they are so damaged that they no longer answer to the description under

---

1. The separation of property and risk may also be the result of a trade custom. Thus in *Bevington and Morris* v. *Dale & Co., Ltd.* (1902), 7 Com. Cas. 112, A agreed to sell furs to B " on approval." The furs were delivered to B and then stolen from him. By the Sale of Goods Act, s. 18, sub-s. (4), the property had not yet passed to B and therefore by the normal operation of s. 20, the risk would still be with A. But A proved a custom of the fur trade that goods were at the risk of persons ordering them " on approval " and B was therefore held liable for the invoice price.
2. *Howell* v. *Coupland* (1876), 1 Q.B.D. 258. *Aliter* if the contract is for all the port in my cellar: *Sainsbury* v. *Street*, [1972] 3 All E.R. 1127; [1972] 1 W.L.R. 834.

which they were sold, as, for instance, where dates, carried on a ship which sinks but is later raised, are irretrievably contaminated with sewage.[1] But, unless the goods have perished within this extended meaning of the word, section 7 does not apply. If the contract is frustrated by some other event, as where the goods are requisitioned by the Government after the agreement has been made, the section is excluded.[2]

If the above four elements are all present, section 7 declares that the contract is " avoided." The result is that the seller cannot be sued by the buyer for breach of contract in failing to make delivery; though, as the risk remains with the seller, it is he who bears the loss of the goods.

(2) The second class of contract excluded from the Law Reform (Frustrated Contracts) Act 1943 is:

> Any other contract for the sale or for the sale and delivery of specific goods, where the contract is frustrated by reason of the fact that the goods have perished.

The problem here is to discover what type of contract is covered by these words and is not caught by section 7 of the Sale of Goods Act. In each case the goods must be " specific " and in each case the cause of the frustration must be their perishing. The difference must therefore lie in the absence of the first or the second of the two elements discussed above. If there is a " sale " or if, though there is only an agreement to sell, the risk, by custom or by the terms of the particular agreement, is to pass immediately to the buyer, the Act of 1943 does not apply. In these cases the risk is with the buyer and if, due to some catastrophe not due to the seller's fault, the goods perish before delivery, it is the buyer who must bear the loss.

From this summary it will be seen that, in the first type of contract of sale excluded from the Act of 1943, the risk has not passed to the buyer, while in the second type it has so passed. It thus seems that all contracts for the sale of specific goods are kept outside the operation of that Act, whether the risk has passed or not, provided only that the cause of frustration is the perishing of the goods. But if the goods are not specific or if the frustration is due to some other reason, such as requisitioning, the Act of 1943 applies.

These statutory provisions are a little bewildering, and it is difficult to see why an arbitrary distinction should have been made between different contracts for the sale of goods or, indeed, why it was thought necessary to exclude any such contract from the operation of the Act in a case where the doctrine of frustration is relevant. There seems no reason why the statutory provisions for the apportionment of loss should not have been permitted in the case of any contract for the sale of goods.

---

1. *Asfar & Co.* v. *Blundell*, [1896] 1 Q.B. 123.
2. *Re Shipton, Anderson & Co. and Harrison Brothers & Co.*, [1915] 3 K.B. 676.

CHAPTER FOUR

Discharge By Breach[1]

SECTION I.	Forms of Breach	568
SECTION II.	The Effect of Breach	573

SECTION I.   FORMS OF BREACH

The two forms of breach that may discharge a contract

A BREACH of contract, no matter what form it may take, always entitles the innocent party to maintain an action for damages, but the rule established by a long line of authorities is that the right of a party to treat a contract as discharged arises only in two types of case.

Firstly, where the party in default has repudiated the contract before performance is due or before it has been fully performed.

Secondly, where the party in default has committed what in modern judicial parlance is called a *fundamental* breach. A breach is of this nature if, having regard to the contract as a whole, the promise that has been violated is of major as distinct from minor importance.

We will deal separately with these two causes of discharge.

(1) Repudiation

Repudiation in the present sense occurs where a party intimates by words or conduct that he does not intend to honour his obligations when they fall due in the future.[2] In the words of Lord BLACKBURN:

> " Where there is a contract to be performed in the future, if one of the parties has said to the other in effect ' if you go on and perform your side of the contract I will not perform mine,' that in effect, amounts to saying ' I will not perform the contract.' In that case the other party may say, ' you have given me distinct notice that you will not perform the contract. I will not wait until you have broken it,[3] but I will treat you as having put an end to the contract, and if necessary I will sue you for damages, but at all events I will not go on with the contract.' "[4]

---

1. Devlin, [1966] C.L.J. 192; Treital, 30 M.L.R. 139.
2. This is the most usual sense in which the word is used by the judges and it is retained in the present account, though admittedly it is ambiguous and has been adopted in other contexts; see *Heyman* v. *Darwins, Ltd.,* [1942] A.C. 356, at pp. 378, 398; [1942] 1 All E.R., at pp. 350, 360.
3. Since the repudiation itself is an immediate breach of the contract, Lord BLACKBURN clearly meant that the innocent party need not wait until performance falls due.
4. *Mersey Steel and Iron Co.* v. *Naylor Benzon & Co.* (1884), 9 App. Cas. 434.

Repudiation may be either explicit or implicit. An example of the former type is afforded by *Hochster* v. *De la Tour*,[1] where the defendant agreed in April to employ the plaintiff as his courier during a foreign tour commencing on June 1st. On May 11th he wrote that he had changed his mind and therefore would not require a courier. The plaintiff sued for damages before June 1st and succeeded.

Express repudiation

A repudiation is implicit where the reasonable inference from the defendant's conduct is that he no longer intends to perform his side of the contract. Thus, " if a man contracts to sell and deliver specific goods on a future day, and before the day he sells and delivers them to another, he is immediately liable to an action at the suit of the person with whom he first contracted."[2] So also, if A conveys a house to C which he had previously agreed to devise to B, A will be taken to have repudiated the contract.[3] The leading authority on this type of case is *Frost* v. *Knight*[4] where the defendant, having agreed to marry the plaintiff upon the death of his father, broke off the engagement during the latter's lifetime. The plaintiff immediately sued for damages and was successful. This particular situation can no longer recur, since actions for breach of promise of marriage have now been abolished,[5] but the principles laid down in *Frost* v. *Knight* are still of general application.

Implicit repudiation

The result, then, of a repudiation, whether explicit or implicit, is that the innocent party acquires an immediate cause of action. But he need not enforce it. He can either stay his hand and wait until the day for performance arrives or treat the contract as discharged and take immediate proceedings.

A breach of contract caused by the repudiation of obligations not yet ripe for performance is called an *anticipatory breach*. The word anticipatory is perhaps a little misleading, for at first sight it seems illogical to admit that a contract can be capable of breach before the time for its performance has arrived. KELLY, C.B., for instance, denied this possibility when *Frost* v. *Knight* was argued before the Court of Exchequer. " If it can be called a breach at all, it is a promissory or prospective breach only; a possible breach, which may never occur, and not an actual breach."[6] This, however, is an untenable view. On appeal to the Exchequer Chamber, COCKBURN, C.J., demonstrated that the defendant, in retracting his promise to marry the plaintiff, violated not a future, but an existing obligation.

The doctrine of the anticipatory breach

" The promisee has an inchoate right to the performance of the bargain, which becomes complete when the time for performance has arrived. In the meantime he has a right to have the contract kept open as a subsisting and effective contract."[7]

1. (1853), 2 E. & B. 678.
2. *Hochster* v. *De la Tour, supra, per* Lord CAMPBELL, at p. 688.
3. *Synge* v. *Synge*, [1894] 1 Q.B. 466; *Lovelock* v. *Franklyn* (1846), 8 Q.B. 371.
4. (1872), L.R. 7 Exch. 111. See also *Short* v. *Stone* (1846), 8 Q.B. 358 (A married C having already promised to marry B).
5. Law Reform (Miscellaneous Provisions) Act 1970, s. 1 (1), which came into force on January 1st, 1971. See Cretney, 33 M.L.R. 534.
6. *Frost* v. *Knight* (1870), L.R. 5 Exch. 322, at pp. 326–7.
7. *Frost* v. *Knight* (1872), L.R. 7 Exch. 111, at p. 114.

Thus, the promisee, while awaiting performance, is entitled to assume that the promisor will himself remain ready, willing and able to perform his side of the contract at the agreed date. Any conduct by him which destroys this assumption " is a breach of a presently binding promise, not an anticipatory breach of an act to be done in the future."[1]

Proof of repudiation

Whether a breach of contract amounts to a repudiation is " a serious matter not to be lightly found or inferred."[2] What has to be established is that the defaulting party has made his intention clear beyond reasonable doubt no longer to perform his side of the bargain. Proof of such an intention requires an investigation *inter alia* of the nature of the contract, the attendant circumstances and the motives which prompted the breach. In the words of Lord SELBORNE:

> " You must look at the actual circumstances of the case in order to see whether the one party to the contract is relieved from its future performance by the conduct of the other; you must examine what that conduct is so as to see whether it amounts to a renunciation, to an absolute refusal to perform the contract . . . and whether the other party may accept it as a reason for not performing his part."[3]

A refusal to proceed with the contract must not be regarded in isolation, for it may be that the party *bona fide*, albeit erroneously, concluded that he was justified in staying his hand. " A mere honest misapprehension, especially if open to correction, will not justify a charge of repudiation."[4] If, for instance, his refusal to proceed is based upon a misconstruction of the agreement, it does not represent an absolute refusal to fulfil his obligations, provided that he shows his readiness to perform the contract according to its true tenor. He has merely put its true tenor in issue.[5]

Contract for delivery of goods by instalments

The question of repudiation often arises where, in the case of a contract for the sale of goods to be delivered by instalments which are to be separately paid for, either the seller makes short deliveries or the buyer neglects to pay for one or more of the instalments. A default of either kind does not necessarily amount to a discharge. It depends in each case, as the Sale of Goods Act 1893 provides, upon the terms of the contract and the particular circumstances whether the breach is repudiation of the whole contract or merely a ground for the recovery of damages.[6]

Mersey Steel and Iron Co. v. Naylor Benzon

There have been many decisions upon instalment contracts, several of which are difficult to reconcile; but the leading authority is *Mersey Steel and Iron Co. v. Naylor Benzon*,[7] where the facts were these:

---

1. *Bradley* v. *Newsom* [1919] A.C. 16, at pp. 53–4, *per* Lord WRENSBURY.   See Lloyd, 37 M.L.R. 121.
2. *Ross Smyth & Co., Ltd.* v. *Bailey, Son & Co.,* [1940] 3 All E.R. 60, at p. 71, *per* Lord WRIGHT.
3. *Mersey Steel and Iron Co.* v. *Naylor Benzon & Co.* (1884), 9 App. Cas. 434, at pp. 438–9; *James Shaffer, Ltd.* v. *Findlay, Durham and Brodie,* [1953] 1 W.L.R. 106; *Peter Dumenil & Co., Ltd.* v. *James Ruddin, Ltd.,* [1953] 2 All E.R. 294; [1953] 1 W.L.R. 815.
4. *Ross Smyth & Co., Ltd.* v. *Bailey, Son & Co., Ltd.,* [1940] 3 All E.R. 60, at p. 72, *per* Lord WRIGHT.
5. *Sweet and Maxwell, Ltd.* v. *Universal News Services, Ltd.,* [1964] 2 Q.B. 699, especially *per* BUCKLEY, J., at p. 737; [1964] 3 All E.R. 30, at p. 45.
6. Section 31 (2); *Decro-Wall International S.A.* v. *Practitioners in Marketing, Ltd.,* [1971] 2 All E.R. 216; [1971] 1 W.L.R. 361.
7. (1884), 9 App. Cas. 434.

The respondents sold to the appellants 5,000 tons of steel, to be delivered at the rate of 1,000 tons monthly, commencing in January, and payment to be made within three days after receipt of shipping documents. In January the sellers delivered about half the correct quantity, and in February made a further delivery, but shortly before payment for these deliveries became due, a petition was presented for winding-up their company. Thereupon the buyers, acting *bona fide* under the erroneous legal advice that pending the petition they could not safely pay the price due without the leave of the court, refused to make any payment unless this leave was obtained. The sellers then declared that they would treat this refusal to pay as discharging them from all further obligation.

It was held that it was impossible to ascribe to the conduct of the buyers the character of a repudiation of the contract.

" It is just the reverse; the purchasers were desirous of fulfilling the contract; they were advised that there was a difficulty in the way, and they expressed anxiety that that difficulty should be as soon as possible removed by means which were suggested to them, and which they pointed out to the solicitors of the company."[1]

It will often be difficult in a contract for delivery by instalments to decide whether a particular breach defeats the whole object of the contract so as to amount to a complete repudiation of his obligations by the party in default. It has been indicated, however, by the Court of Appeal that the chief considerations are " first, the ratio quantitatively which the breach bears to the contract as a whole, and secondly, the degree of probability or improbability that such a breach will be repeated."[2] It has also been recognized that the further the parties have proceeded in the performance of the contract the more difficult it is to infer that a breach represents a complete repudiation of liability.[3]

The summary dismissal of an employee, founded upon his alleged repudiation of the contract, affords a further illustration of the warning that repudiation is a serious matter not lightly to be inferred. So drastic a step by the employer will not be justified unless the conduct of the employee has disclosed a deliberate intention to disregard the essential requirements of a contract of service.[4]

Wrongful dismissal of a servant

The second class of case in which a party is entitled to treat himself as discharged from further liability is where his co-contractor, without expressly or implicitly repudiating his obligations, commits a fundamental breach of the contract. Of what nature, then, must a breach be before it is to be called " fundamental? " There are two alternative tests that may provide the answer. The court may find the decisive element either in the importance that the parties would seem to have attached to the term which has been broken or to the seriousness of the conse-

(2) Fundamental breach

1. (1884), 9 App. Cas. 434, *per* Lord SELBORNE, at p. 441.
2. *Maple Flock Co., Ltd.* v. *Universal Furniture Products (Wembley), Ltd.*, [1934] 1 K.B. 148, at p. 157.
3. *Cornwall* v. *Henson*, [1900] 2 Ch. 298, at p. 304, *per* COLLINS, L.J.
4. Contrast, for instance, *Laws* v. *London Chronicle (Indicator Newspapers)*, [1959] 2 All E.R. 285; [1959] 1 W.L.R. 698 (dismissal not justified), with *Pepper* v. *Webb*, [1969] 2 All E.R. 216; [1969] 1 W.L.R. 514 (dismissal justified); See Grime, 32 M.L.R. 575

quences that have in fact resulted from the breach. We have already discussed this question at length[1] and suggested that although the tests are often stated as alternatives, they may in fact both have a part to play.

If one applies the first test the governing principle is that everything depends upon the construction of the contract in question. The court has to decide whether, at the time when the contract was made, the parties must be taken to have regarded the promise which has been violated as of major or of minor importance. In the words of BOWEN, L.J.:

> " There is no way of deciding that question except by looking at the contract in the light of the surrounding circumstances, and then making up one's mind whether the intention of the parties, as gathered from the instrument itself, will best be carried out by treating the promise as a warranty sounding only in damages, or as a condition precedent by the failure to perform which the other party is relieved of his liability."[2]

Distinction between major and minor promises and breaches

Wherever one looks to promise or breach one of the difficulties has been to formulate with any approach to precision the degree of importance that a promise or breach must possess to warrant the discharge of the contract. A variety of phrases has been used in an endeavour to meet this need. It has been said, for instance, that no breach will discharge the innocent party from further liability unless it goes to the whole root of the contract, not merely to part of it,[3] or unless it goes so much to the root of the contract that it makes further performance impossible;[4] or unless it affects the very substance of the contract.[5] SACHS, L.J., " at the risk of being dubbed old-fashioned," has recently stated his preference for the expression " goes to the root of the contract," which has been the favourite of the judges for at least 150 years.

> " That leaves the question whether the breach does go to the root as a matter of degree for the court to decide on the facts of the particular case in the same way as it has to decide which terms are warranties and which are conditions."[6]

To speak of " the root of the contract " is, no doubt, to rely on a metaphor; and Lord SUMNER once said that " like most metaphors it is not nearly so clear as it seems."[7] It does not solve the problem, but rather re-states it in picturesque language. Yet a picture is not without value; and the phrase may help judges to crystallize the impression made on their minds by the facts of a particular case. In the Australian case of *Tramways*

---

1. *Supra,* pp. 135–144.
2. *Bentsen* v. *Taylor, Sons & Co.* (No. 2), [1893] 2 Q.B. 274, at p. 281. The use of the phrase " condition precedent " in this context is unfortunate and tends to confusion: *supra,* p. 136.
3. *Davidson* v. *Gwynne* (1810), 12 East 381, at p. 389, *per* Lord ELLENBOROUGH.
4. *Hong Kong Fir Shipping Co., Ltd.* v. *Kawasaki Kaisen Kaisha, Ltd.,* [1962] 2 Q.B. 26, at p. 64, *per* UPJOHN, L.J.; [1962] 1 All E.R. 474, at p. 484.
5. *Wallis, Son and Wells* v. *Pratt and Haynes,* [1910] 2 K.B. 1003, at p. 1012, *per* FLETCHER MOULTON, L.J.
6. *Decro-Wall International S.A.* v. *Practitioners in Marketing, Ltd.,* [1971] 2 All E.R. 216, at p. 227; [1971] 1 W.L.R. 361, at p. 374.
7. *Bank Line, Ltd.* v. *A. Capel & Co.,* [1919] A.C. 435, at p. 459.

Advertising Pty., Ltd. v. *Luna Park (N.S.W.), Ltd.*,[1] JORDAN, C.J. said:

> " The test of essentiality is whether it appears from the general nature of the contract considered as a whole, or from some particular term or terms, that the promise is of such importance to the promisee that he would not have entered into the contract unless he had been assured of a strict or substantial performance of the promise, as the case may be, and that this ought to have been apparent to the promisor."

Illustrations of cases in which the question of fundamental breach has been raised will be found at an earlier stage in this book.[2] But it may be useful to call attention to the early case of *Ellen* v. *Topp*,[3] where the facts were these:

> An infant was placed by his father as apprentice to learn the trade of a master who was described in the contract as an " auctioneer, appraiser and corn factor." After about half the contractual period had elapsed the master abandoned his trade as a corn factor, where- upon the apprentice absented himself on the ground that this abandonment relieved him from further liability.

The master sued for breach of contract and argued that his retire- ment from the actual practice of one of the three trades did not discharge the contract, since he was still able to teach the appren- tice the theory of a corn factor's business. It was held, however, that the apprentice was discharged from further liability. The object of the contract, as clearly shown by its terms, was that the infant should serve the master after the manner of an apprentice in the three trades specified; but, as the court explained, service of this nature imports that the master shall actually carry on the trade which the apprentice is to learn, for otherwise " the one is teaching and the other learning the trade, not as master and apprentice, but as instructor and pupil." In the present case, therefore, the master had wilfully made it impossible for the essential object or the substantial benefit of the contract to be attained.

SECTION II.   THE EFFECT OF BREACH

It must be observed that, even if one of the parties wrongfully repudiates all further liability or has been guilty of a fundamental breach, the contract will not automatically come to an end. Since its termination is the converse of its creation, principle demands that it should not be recognized unless this is what both parties intend. The familiar test of offer and acceptance serves to determine their common intention. Where A and B are parties to an executory contract and A indicates that he is no longer able or willing to perform his outstanding obligations, he in effect makes an offer to B that the contract shall be discharged.

Effect of repudiation or funda- mental breach

---

1. (1938), 38 S.R.N.S.W. 632, at p. 641. Though the decision of the learned Chief Justice was reversed (1938), 61 C.L.R. 286, his test of essentiality was unanimously approved by the High Court of Australia in the later case of *Associated Newspapers, Ltd.* v. *Bancks* (1951), 83 C.L.R. 332.
2. *Supra*, pp. 159 *et seq.*
3. (1851), 6 Exch. 424.

Therefore B is presented with an option.　He may either refuse
or accept the offer.[1]　More precisely, he may either affirm the
contract by treating it as still in force, or on the other hand he
may treat it as finally and conclusively discharged.　The consequences vary according to the choice that he prefers.

(i) Innocent
party may
treat the
contract as
still in force

If the innocent party chooses the first option and, with full
knowledge of the facts, makes it clear by words or acts, or even
by silence,[2] that he refuses to accept the breach as a discharge of
the contract, the effect is that the *status quo ante* is preserved
intact.　The contract " remains in being for the future on both
sides.　Each [party] has a right to sue for damages for *past or
future breaches*."[3]　Thus, for instance, a seller of goods who
refuses to treat a fundamental breach as a discharge of the contract
remains liable for delivery of possession to the defaulting buyer,
while the latter remains correspondingly liable to accept delivery
and to pay the contractual price.[4]

The significance of the rule that the contract continues in
existence is well illustrated by the case where a party has repudiated his obligations.

> " In that case he[5] keeps the contract alive for the benefit of the
> other party as well as his own; he remains subject to all his own
> obligations and liabilities under it, and enables the other party not
> only to complete the contract, if so advised, notwithstanding his
> previous repudiation of it, but also to take advantage of any super-
> vening circumstance which would justify him in declining to
> complete it."[6]

The case of *Avery* v. *Bowden* illustrates the way in which
supervening circumstances may operate to relieve the party in
default from all liability.[7]

> The defendant chartered the plaintiff's ship at a Russian port
> and agreed to load her with a cargo within forty-five days.　Before
> this period had elapsed he repeatedly advised the plaintiff to go away
> as it would be impossible to provide him with a cargo. The plaintiff,
> however, remained at the port in the hope that the defendant would
> fulfil his promise, but the refusal to load was maintained, and then,
> before the forty-five days had elapsed, the Crimean war broke out
> between England and Russia.

On the assumption that the refusal to load amounted to a complete
repudiation of liability by the defendant, the plaintiff might have
treated the contract as discharged; but his decision to ignore

---

1. *Denmark Productions, Ltd.* v. *Boscobel Productions, Ltd.,* [1969] 1 Q.B. 699
   at p. 731; [1968] 3 All E.R. 513, at p. 527, *per* WINN, L.J.
2. *Ibid.,* at pp. 732 and 527–8 respectively.
3. *Harbutt's Plasticine Co., Ltd.* v. *Wayne Tank and Pump Co., Ltd.,* [1970]
   1 Q.B. 447, at pp. 464–5; [1970] 1 All E.R. 225, at p. 233, *per* Lord DENNING,
   M.R.
4. *R. V. Ward, Ltd.* v. *Bignall,* [1967] 1 Q.B. 534; [1967] 2 All E.R. 449.
   The position that arises if, instead of merely continuing to tender performance, the innocent party fully completes his side of the contract in
   defiance of a repudiation, thereby increasing the loss flowing from the
   breach, was considered by the House of Lords in *White and Carter (Councils),
   Ltd.* v. *McGregor,* [1962] A.C. 413; [1961] 3 All E.R. 1178; discussed
   infra, p. 600.
5. I.e. the innocent party.
6. *Frost* v. *Knight* (1872), L.R. 7 Exch. 111, at p. 112, *per* COCKBURN, C.J.;
   see also *Johnstone* v. *Milling* (1886), 16 Q.B.D. 460, at p. 467, *per* Lord
   ESHER.
7. (1885), 5 E. & B. 714.

this repudiation resulted, as events turned out, in the defendant being provided with a good defence to an action for breach. He would have committed an illegal act if he had loaded a cargo at a hostile port after the declaration of war.

On the other hand, a refusal to treat a breach of contract as a discharge may operate to the disadvantage of the defendant. Suppose that, in the case of a contract for the sale of goods to be delivered in May, the seller announces in February that he will not make delivery, but the buyer refuses to accept this repudiation and ultimately sues for breach at the contractual date for performance. The measure of damages will depend upon the market price of the goods, not at the date of the repudiation but at the time appointed for performance. If, therefore, the market price of the goods is higher in May than it was in February the amount payable by the seller as damages will be correspondingly higher.[1]

It is obvious that a party who elects to disregard a repudiation by his co-contractor cannot recover damages at law for breach of contract: if the contract is still in being it has not yet been broken. As ASQUITH, L.J., remarked in one case: " An unaccepted repudiation is a thing writ in water and of no value to anybody; it affords no legal rights of any sort or kind."[2] But this is not true where the equitable remedy of specific performance is sought. If the circumstances justify it, equity is prepared to protect the innocent party even though he cannot plead the breach of contract upon which the common law remedy of damages depends. In one case, for instance: *(Specific performance may be decreed)*

> By a written contract signed on February 19th, the vendor agreed to sell a plot of land to the purchaser, completion to be on August 19th. A few minutes later the vendor repudiated the contract. The purchaser elected to affirm the contract and on August 2nd, some six weeks before the agreed date for completion, he sued for a decree of specific performance. The court granted the decree.[3]

This did not mean that the purchaser could call for the land to be conveyed to him before August 19th, but that on that date he would be at liberty, without taking out a new writ, to apply for a consequential direction requiring the vendor to execute a conveyance.

It is often said that the wrongful dismissal of a servant employed under a contract of personal services provides an exception to the rule that a party may elect to keep a repudiated contract alive and that despite the unjustifiable repudiation of his obligations by the employer, the employee, though ready and willing to serve for the agreed period, has no option but to treat the contract as discharged.[4] On the other hand it has been doubted whether this is correct.[5] It is true that as a rule specific per- *(Can servant wrongly dismissed treat contract as still in force?)*

---

1. *Roper* v. *Johnson* (1873), L.R. 8 C.P. 167; *Michael* v. *Hart*, [1902] 1 K.B. 482.
2. *Howard* v. *Pickford Tool Co.*, [1951] 1 K.B. 417, at p. 421.
3. *Hasham* v. *Zenab*, [1960] A.C. 316; R.E.M., 76, L.Q.R. 200.
4. See, e.g. *Denmark Productions, Ltd.* v. *Boscobel Productions, Ltd.*, [1969] 1 Q.B. 699; [1968] 3 All E.R. 513, at p. 726, *per* SALMON, L.J.; at p. 737 and p. 524 respectively, *per* HARMAN, L.J.; *contra*, at pp. 731–2, *per* WINN, L.J. See Freedland, 32 M.L.R. 314.
5. See, e.g. *Decro-Wall International S.A.* v. *Practitioners In Marketing, Ltd.*, [1971] 2 All E.R. 216; [1971] 1 W.L.R. 361, *per* SALMON, L.J., at pp. 223, 369–370, respectively, and *per* SACHS L.J., at pp. 229, 376, respectively.

formance will not be ordered of a contract of personal service[1] and that since a servant cannot ordinarily perform his contract of employment if his master wrongfully excludes him from the workplace, in practice he must sue either for damages for breach of contract, in which case he must do what he reasonably can to mitigate his loss by obtaining other employment,[2] or on a *quantum meruit* for the value of the work that he has already done.[3] But contracts of service are not unique in the non-availability of specific performance and in many contracts the innocent party will eventually be compelled to terminate the contract if the other party remains obdurate in his refusal to perform. Exceptionally, therefore, where damages will not afford him an adequate remedy, the servant may obtain a declaration that his contract of service still subsists.[4]

(ii) Innocent party may treat the contract as discharged

If, on the other hand, the innocent party elects to treat the contract as discharged, he must make his decision known to the party in default. Once he has done this, his election is final and cannot be retracted.[5] The effect is to terminate the contract for the future as from the moment when the acceptance is communicated to the party in default. The breach does not operate retrospectively. The previous existence of the contract is still relevant with regard to the past acts and defaults of the parties. Thus the party in default is liable in damages both for any earlier breaches and also for the breach that has led to the discharge of the contract, but he is excused from further performance.[6] But this does not mean, in the case of an anticipatory breach, that the obligations which would have matured after the election are to be completely disregarded. They may still be relevant to the assessment of damages. This is exemplified by *Moschi* v. *LEP Air Services, Ltd.*[7] on the following facts;

> The defendant company agreed to pay £40,000 to the plaintiffs in seven weekly instalments. X, the managing director of the defendants, personally guaranteed the payment of this debt. At the end of three weeks, the payments were so seriously in arrear as to amount to a repudiation of the contract by the defendants. On

---

1. See *infra*, pp. 615–6. The rule that a servant cannot obtain specific performance is deduced from the undoubtedly sensible rule that the master cannot get specific performance. This may have made excellent sense in the eighteenth century but in a modern industrial context it no longer appears inevitable. Historically the law would appear to be moving slowly but perceptibly toward a remedy by way of reinstatement. See Williams, 38 M.L.R. 292.
2. *Infra*, p. 604.
3. *Planché* v. *Colburn* (1831), 5 C. & P. 58; *infra*, pp. 658–9.
4. *Hill* v. *C. A. Parsons & Co., Ltd.*, [1971] 3 All E.R. 1345; [1972] 1 Ch. 305. Cf. *Sanders* v. *Ernest A. Nevil, Ltd.*, [1974] 3 All E.R. 327; [1974] I.C.R. 565; see Thomson, 89 L.Q.R. 331.
5. *Scarf* v. *Jardine* (1882), 7 App. Cas. 345, at p. 361, *per* Lord BLACKBURN. Such is the general principle wherever there is a choice between two remedies. The election must be made without unreasonable delay; *Allen* v. *Robles*, [1969] 3 All E.R. 154; [1969] 1 W.L.R. 1193.
6. *Mussen* v. *Van Diemen's Land Co.*, [1938] Ch. 253, at p. 260; [1938] 1 All E.R. 210, *per* FARWELL, J.; *Boston Deep Sea Fishing and Ice Co.* v. *Ansell* (1888), 39 Ch.D. 339, at p. 365, *per* BOWEN, L.J.; *Fibrosa Spolka Akcyjna* v. *Fairburn Lawson Combe Barbour, Ltd.*, [1943] A.C. 32, at p. 65, *per* Lord WRIGHT; *R. V. Ward, Ltd.* v. *Bignall,* [1967] 1 Q.B. 534, at p. 548; [1967] 2 All E.R. 449, *per* DIPLOCK, L.J.; Goff & Jones, *The Law of Restitution*, pp. 341–2.
7. [1973] A.C. 331; [1972] 2 All E.R. 393.

December 22nd, the plaintiffs accepted this repudiation and then sued the guarantor, X, for the recovery of £40,000, less what had already been paid.

One of the defences raised by the guarantor was that he was not liable in respect of instalments falling due after December 22nd.

This defence was rejected by the House of Lords.

This decision is in line with the earlier decision of the Court of Appeal in the case of *The Mihalis Angelos*.[1]

> By clause 11 of a charter-party, the owners stated that their ship was " expected ready to load at Haiphong under this charter about July 1st, 1965." Clause 11 provided that, if the ship was not ready to load on or before July 20th, 1965, the charterers should have the option of cancelling the contract. On July 17th, the charterers repudiated the contract and the owners accepted the repudiation. The majority of the Court of Appeal held that the option to cancel the contract was not exercisable before July 20th even though on the 17th it was certain that the ship would not arrive before July 20th. The charterers were thus guilty of an " anticipatory breach."[2]

One question that arose was whether the owners could recover substantial damages in respect of the wrongful repudiation on the ground that its acceptance by them had put an end to the contract, together with the right of cancellation. The arbitrators took the view that though the contract was terminated in the sense that its performance was no longer binding upon the owners, yet " it (or its ghost) " survived for the purpose of measuring the damages. The Court of Appeal accepted this view and granted the owners only nominal damages. In the case of an anticipatory breach, the innocent party is entitled to recover the true value of the contractual rights which he has lost. If these " were capable by the terms of the contract of being rendered either less valuable or valueless in certain events, and if it can be shown that those events were, at the date of acceptance of repudiation, predestined to happen, then in my view the damages which he can recover are not more than the true value, if any, of the rights which he has lost, having regard to those predestined events."[3] So, since the charterers would certainly have lawfully cancelled on July 20th, the owners has suffered no loss.

Three further points must be made on the assumption that the innocent party has elected to treat the contract as discharged.

Firstly, it has been decided by the Court of Appeal in a recent case that this right of election is not open to the innocent party if the contract is contained in a lease.[4] The facts were as follows: *(No right of election if contract contained in a lease)*

> A lease of a garage for fourteen years, granted by the plaintiffs, an oil company, to the defendants, contained a tying covenant by which the defendants agreed to sell only motor fuel supplied by the plaintiffs. Payment for each load supplied was to be cash on delivery. On two occasions, the cheques given by the defendants were not honoured, whereupon the plaintiffs refused to supply more fuel unless they first received a banker's draft for each load ordered

1. [1971] 1 Q.B. 164; [1970] 3 All E.R. 125.
2. Or, rather, they would have been if owners had not themselves been in breach of condition; see *supra*, pp. 142-3.
3. *Ibid.*, [1971] 1 Q.B., at p. 210; [1970] 3 All E.R. 125, at p. 142, *per* MEGAW, L.J.
4. *Total Oil (Great Britain), Ltd.* v. *Thompson Garages (Biggin Hill), Ltd.*, [1972] 1 Q.B. 318; [1971] 3 All E.R. 1226.

prior to its dispatch from their depôt.   This alteration of an essential
term amounted to a repudiation of the contract, and the defendants
accepted it as a discharge from liability to observe the tying covenant.

In the present action an injunction was sought restraining the
defendants from selling fuel other than that supplied by the
plaintiffs.   The Court of Appeal held that the plaintiffs were
entitled to this relief.

There was no obvious authority upon which the court could
rely.   Lord DENNING, M.R., however, stressed that the tying
covenant was inseparable from the lease.   Together, they formed
one composite legal transaction.   He then invoked the doctrine
of frustration, and recalled that in *Cricklewood Property and
Investment Trust, Ltd.* v. *Leighton's Investment Trust, Ltd.*,[1] two
of the Law Lords were of opinion that frustration does not bring
a lease to an end.[2]   He then said: " Nor, I think, does repudiation
and acceptance."[3]   EDMUND DAVIES, L.J., and STEPHENSON,
L.J., agreed with his reasoning.

Thus the lease and its contracts still stood, and so long as the
plaintiffs remained in breach of their obligations they could not
enforce the tying covenant.   But in the opinion of the court, they
had a *locus poenitentiae*, and since they had now agreed to resume
the practice of cash on delivery, they were entitled to the injunction
which they claimed.

The reasoning in this decision raises more than one difficulty.
For instance, it is by no means clear that the analogy drawn
between discharge by repudiation and discharge by frustration
can be sustained.   The two situations are quite distinct and are
governed by different rules and principles.   Moreover, even if
the analogy is conceded, the *Cricklewood* case offers slender
support for the view that the doctrine of frustration does not
apply to a lease.   The House of Lords was equally divided on
the question.   Again, according to established principle, there
was no scope for the operation of a *locus poenitentiae*, and no
authority was cited to support the possibility in the instant
context.

It is noteworthy that in this case the tenant did not purport to
terminate the lease and the decision might perhaps be supported
on the ground that he could not elect to terminate part of the
transaction but must choose between terminating the lease and
keeping the whole transaction alive.   Obviously this would be an
unattractive choice to the tenant but the distinction is important
in the converse case of repudiation by a tenant to which the Court
of Appeal's reasoning is equally applicable.

It is interesting to note that different reasoning was adopted
by the Supreme Court of Canada in *Highway Properties Ltd.* v.
Kelly, Douglas & Co.[4]

> The plaintiff was the developer of a shopping centre and let premises
> in the centre to the defendant for 15 years for use as a supermarket.
> The defendant covenanted to open for business within 30 days of
> completion " and to carry on its business on the said premises

---

1. [1945] A.C. 221; *supra*, p. 552.
2. Lord RUSSELL OF KILLOWEN and Lord GODDARD.
3. [1971] 3 All E.R., at p. 1229; [1971] 3 W.L.R., at p. 983.
4. (1971), 17 D.L.R. (3d) 710.

continuously." This covenant was of great importance to the plaintiff since the viability of such shopping centres as a whole depends on a number of major shops acting as magnets for customers. The willingness of other shopkeepers to take tenancies of the smaller units is often dependent on the presence of such major stores within the complex. The defendant opened for business but after five months abandoned the premises and removed its stock. The plaintiff elected to retake possession of the premises with a view to re-letting. Eventually the premises were re-let in a partitioned form to three new tenants at a lower rent but the value of business at the shopping centre fell off with the closing of the supermarket and many other tenants left their premises.

The defendant argued that the plaintiff's remedies were determined by the law of land rather than the law of contract and that while it would have been open to the plaintiffs to leave the premises vacant and sue the defendant for rent, they had by terminating the lease brought their right to rent to an end. The defendant further argued that the plaintiffs could not recover damages under the ordinary principles of the law of contract for consequential loss. This argument was rejected. LASKIN, J., speaking for the court said:[1]

> " It is . . . untenable to persist in denying resort to the full armoury of remedies ordinarily available to redress repudiation of covenants, merely because the covenants may be associated with an estate in land."

Secondly, a party who treats a contract as discharged is often said to *rescind* the contract. To describe the legal position in such a manner, however, must inevitably mislead and confuse the unwary. In its primary and more correct sense, as we have already seen,[2] rescission means the retrospective cancellation of a contract *ab initio*, as for instance where one of the parties has been guilty of fraudulent misrepresentation. In such a case the contract is destroyed as if it had never existed, but its discharge by breach never impinges upon rights and obligations that have already matured. It would be better therefore in this context to talk of *termination* rather than of *rescission*.[3] *Rescission distinguished from discharge*

Thirdly, the discharge of a contract, based upon a reason that is in fact inadequate, may nevertheless " be supported if there are at the time facts in existence which would have provided a good reason."[4] For instance, a seller of goods deliverable by instalments makes a short delivery, whereupon the buyer claims that the contract is discharged. This, however, may be unwarranted, since an intention on the part of the seller to repudiate his obligations is not inferable from the circumstances that led to the short delivery. If it is then discovered that the goods already delivered do not comply with their contractual description, this fundamental breach suffices to justify the discharge of the contract.[5] *Discharge based on inadequate ground effective if sound alternative ground exists*

---

1. Ibid., at p. 721.
2. *Supra,* p. 264.
3. See Albery, 91 L.Q.R. 337, discussing *Horsler* v. *Zorro* [1975] 1 All E.R. 584; [1975] 2 W.L.R. 183.
4. *Universal Cargo Carriers Corporation* v. *Citati,* [1957] 2 Q.B. 401, at p. 447; [1957] 2 All E.R. 70, at p. 89, *per* DEVLIN, J.
5. Cf. *Denmark Productions, Ltd.* v. *Boscobel, Productions, Ltd.,* [1969] 1 Q.B. 699, at p. 722, *per* SALMON, L.J.; at p. 732, *per* WINN, L.J.; *The Mihalis Angelos,* [1971] 1 Q.B., at pp. 195–6, 200, and 204.

It would seem that this principle requires some qualification in the light of the decision of the Court of Appeal in *Panchaud Fréres S.A.* v. *Etablissements General Grain Co.*[1]

> The plaintiff contracted to sell to the defendant 5,300 metric tons Brazilian yellow maize c.i.f. Antwerp, shipment to be June/July 1965. The bill of landing was dated July 31st, 1965, but amongst the other shipping documents was a certificate of quality which stated that the goods were loaded August 10th to August 12th 1965. This would have entitled the defendant to reject the shipping documents but they were received without objection; (presumably, though this is not explicitly stated in the report, because the inconsistency was not detected). When the ship arrived the defendant rejected the goods on another ground ultimately held insufficient and only three years later sought to justify rejection on the ground that the goods had been shipped out of time.

The Court of Appeal held that it was too late for the defendant to rely on this ground since in the words of WINN, L.J.:[2]

> " There may be an inchoate doctrine stemming from the manifest convenience of consistency in pragmatic affairs, negativing any liberty to blow hot and cold in commercial conduct."

---

1. [1970] 1 Lloyd's Rep. 53; see also *Carvill* v. *Irish Industrial Bank, Ltd.*, [1968] I.R. 325; *Cyril Leonards & Co.* v. *Simo Securities Trust, Ltd.*, [1971] 3 All E.R. 1313, [1972] 1 W.L.R. 80.
2. [1970] 1 Lloyd's Rep. at p. 59.

PART VIII

REMEDIES FOR BREACH OF CONTRACT

Remedies for Breach of Contract[1]

SECTION I. WHERE THE BREACH DISCHARGES THE CONTRACT

WHERE a breach is of such a nature as to justify the injured party in treating the contract as discharged, he may take one of two courses.   He may, despite so violent a breach, hold the defaulting party to his promise.   If he adopts this course, he himself remains liable on the contract, but he may recover damages for any loss sustained.[2]   His alternative course is to accept the breach as discharging the contract.

General statement of the position

If he chooses the latter course, the consequences are as follows:

Rights of party who accepts the discharge

Firstly, he is relieved from further liability to perform his obligations,[3] and he may fortify his position in this respect by taking proceedings for a declaration that the contract is terminated.

Secondly, he may sue for the recovery of damages,[4] a remedy which is considered at length in the next section.

Thirdly, instead of suing for the recovery of damages for the loss of the contract, he may claim on a *quantum meruit* for the value of the work that he has already done, a course that will be advisable if that value exceeds what would have been due to him had the contract been fully performed.[5]   If, for example, he has agreed to

---

1. Lawson, *Remedies of English Law.*
2. *Bentsen* v. *Taylor, Sons & Co.*, [1893] 2 Q.B. 274, at p. 279.
3. *General Billposting Co.* v. *Atkinson*, [1909] A.C. 118.
4. *O'Neil* v. *Armstrong*, [1895] 2 Q.B. 418.
5. *Planché* v. *Colburn* (1831), 5 C. & P. 58; *De Bernardy* v. *Harding* (1853), 8 Exch. 822 (for these two cases see *infra*, pp. 652–3; *Luxor, Ltd.* v. *Cooper*, [1941] A.C. 108, at pp. 140–1, 146; [1941] 1 All E.R. 33, at pp. 55, 58, *per* Lord WRIGHT; *Heyman* v. *Darwins, Ltd.*, [1942] A.C. 356, at p. 399; [1942] 1 All E.R. 337, at p. 360.

render personal services for a sum payable upon completion of this promise, he may recover remuneration for services already rendered up to the time when the contract is discharged. If he adopts this course his claim is quasi-contractual in nature.[1]

In principle, possibility of restitutio in integrum irrelevant

A question that requires consideration is whether the injured party is precluded from treating the contract as discharged if the *status quo ante* can no longer be restored. It is, indeed, true that a contract cannot be rescinded for misrepresentation unless such *restitutio in integrum* is possible. The reason for this is clear. Since the effect of rescission in this type of case is to terminate the contract *ab initio*,[2] the parties must be relegated to their original positions, a transition that is impossible unless each party is still able to give back the advantages and take back the obligations created by the contract. But that misrepresentation and breach should be equated in this respect is contrary to principle. As we have seen, a contract which is treated by the innocent party as no longer binding upon him is not rendered retrospectively void. The *status quo ante* remains undisturbed. In the words of an Australian judge:

> " Both parties are discharged from the further performance of the contract, but rights are not divested or discharged which have already been unconditionally acquired. Rights and obligations which arise from the partial execution of the contract and causes of action which accrue from its breach alike continue unaffected."[3]

Therefore, any suggestion that there can be no discharge for breach unless it is possible for the parties to be restored to their former position is incompatible with this liberty to sue on an existing contract.

Thorpe v. Fasey an authority to the contrary

In *Thorpe* v. *Fasey*,[4] however, WYNN-PARRY, J., held that there can be no rescission for breach unless the contract can be eliminated *in toto* and the parties put in *statu quo ante*.

> A contract for the sale of 160 acres of land provided that a parcel of 40 acres should be conveyed to the purchaser on October 3rd, 1937, against a payment of £12,600; and that three further parcels of 40 acres each should be conveyed on October 3rd, 1939, 1940 and 1941 respectively, subject in each case to a payment of £8,000. The purchaser paid £12,600, went into possession of the first 40 acres and proceeded to develop the land, but then development was hindered as a result of the international situation and he defaulted in the remaining payments.

Firstly, WYNN-PARRY, J., dismissed the seller's claim for damages, on the ground that in the circumstances the purchaser's default constituted neither the failure to perform an essential term, since the time of payment had never been made of the essence of the

---

1. *Luxor, Ltd.* v. *Cooper*, [1941] A.C. 108, at p. 141; [1941] 1 All E.R. 33, at p. 55, *per* Lord WRIGHT.
2. *Supra*, p. 264.
3. *McDonald* v. *Dennys Lascelles, Ltd.* (1933), 48 C.L.R. 457, at pp. 476-7, *per* DIXON, J.; cited McGarvie, 4 Melbourne University L.R. 254, at p. 256. See also Albery, 91 L.Q.R. 337.
4. [1949] Ch. 649; [1949] 2 All E.R. 393.

contract,[1] nor a repudiation of his future obligations. Secondly,
the alternative claim for the " rescission " of the contract, that is
for its discharge, was also rejected by the learned judge, who
adopted the principle applicable to misrepresentation and held
that in no case is a contract capable of rescission unless it is possible
to cancel it *in toto* and to restore the parties to their former position.
Such restoration was precluded in the instant case, since the
purchaser had been in possession of a quarter of the property for
two years and had spent money on its development.

The judgment was based partly upon the authorities concerned
with rescission for misrepresentation, but mainly upon statements
made by the judges in the early case of *Hunt* v. *Silk*,[2] where the
facts were as follows:

> In consideration of £10 paid by the plaintiff the defendant agreed
> to let a house to him, and further agreed that within ten days he
> would repair the premises and would execute a lease for nineteen
> years. The plaintiff went into possession, but despite frequent
> requests the defendant failed to fulfil either of these obligations
> within ten days. The plaintiff, however, retained possession for a
> few days longer before he left the house. He ultimately sued in
> quasi-contract for the return of the £10, as being money had and
> received.

No such action lies at common law unless there has been a total
failure of consideration.[3] If the plaintiff has received a partial
benefit under the contract, his only remedy is an action for
damages unless the benefit is capable of restoration and is in fact
restored.[4] It would be unwarranted, however, to tear this rule
from its context and to regard it as affecting the terms upon which
a party is entitled to terminate a contract for repudiation or
essential breach. Yet in *Hunt* v. *Silk* the judges, in dismissing the
plaintiff's action, chose to make his right to recover the money
turn upon his right of rescission, though this was no part of his
cause of action. What is even more confusing is that the judgments contain general statements which appear to make the
possibility of restoring the *status quo ante* an indispensable condition of rescission. It was these statements upon which
WYNN-PARRY, J., relied in *Thorpe* v. *Fasey*. Thus, in a much
quoted passage, Lord ELLENBOROUGH said:

> " Now where a contract is to be rescinded at all it must be
> rescinded *in toto* and the parties put in *statu quo*. But here was an
> intermediate occupation, a part execution of the agreement, which
> was incapable of being rescinded."

It seems clear, however, that the *ratio decidendi* of *Hunt* v. *Silk*
was not the impossibility of making full *restitutio in integrum*. The
true explanation of the decision appears to be that the plaintiff, by
remaining in possession after the ten days had elapsed with full
knowledge of the dependant's default, had waived his right of

---

1. See *supra*, pp. 530–2.
2. (1804), 5 East 449.
3. *Infra*, pp. 648–651.
4. Goff & Jones, *The Law of Restitution*, p. 342.

rescission.[1]   This in fact is stressed in each of the three judgments delivered.

It may be added that to preclude discharge if the plaintiff has received a benefit incapable of restoration would be incompatible with the rule that, if a contractor agrees to do work for a lump sum on the plaintiff's land and abandons the work when it is partially, but not substantially, completed, the plaintiff may treat the contract as discharged without having to make recompense for the partial benefit that he has received.[2]

It is, therefore, submitted that *Thorpe* v. *Fasey* should be regarded as merely another example of the principle that only the repudiation of a contract or the commission of a fundamental breach justifies its discharge.   According to the finding of the learned judge, neither of these conditions had been satisfied.

Is property transferred by guilty party recoverable? Since the discharge of a contract has no retrospective effect, it follows in principle that the party in default cannot recover property which, in fulfilment of his contractual obligations, he may have transferred to the innocent party prior to the discharge.

" The contract remains alive for the purpose of vindicating rights already acquired under it on either side."[3]

This conclusion, however, requires modification where the property transferred is money paid by the purchaser under a contract for the sale of land or goods.   Whether it is recoverable by the purchaser if the contract is discharged by reason of his breach depends upon the construction of the contract.   The object that the parties had in view must be ascertained.[4]

Distinction between earnest and part payment If their intention was that the money should be deposited as an earnest or guarantee for the due performance of the purchaser's obligations, the rule at common law is that it is forfeited to the seller upon the discharge of the contract for the default of the purchaser, notwithstanding that it would have gone in part payment of the price had the contract been completed.[5]   " The purchaser cannot insist on abandoning the contract and yet recover the deposit, because that would be to enable him to take advantage of his own wrong."[6]

The position according to principle would appear to be the same where the purchaser has pre-paid part of the total amount that will ultimately fall due.   What has been paid under a contractual obligation that was binding upon him at the time of its

---

1. Goff & Jones *op. cit.*, p. 343; McGarvie, 4 Melbourne University L.R. 254, 305, at pp. 309–10; Salmond and Williams, *The Law of Contracts*, pp. 547–8.   Stoljar (75 L.Q.R. 53, at p. 72) explains case on ground that the defendant's default was not substantial enough to justify rescission.
2. See, for example, *Sumpter* v. *Hedges*, [1898] 1 Q.B. 673, *supra*, p. 527. This is stressed by McGarvie, 4 Melbourne University L.R. 254, 305 at p. 312.
3. *Hirji Mulji* v. *Cheong Yue Steamship Co., Ltd.*, [1926] A.C. 497, at p. 510, *per* Lord SUMNER.
4. *Mayson* v. *Clouet*, [1924] A.C. 980, at p. 985.
5. *Howe* v. *Smith* (1884), 27 Ch.D. 89.   If, however, the full amount of the deposit has not been paid at the time of discharge, the unpaid balance cannot be recovered by the seller: *Lowe* v. *Hope*, [1970] 1 Ch. 94.
6. *Howe* v. *Smith* (1884), 27 Ch.D., at p. 98, *per* BOWEN, L.J.

payment should not be affected by a breach caused by his own wrong. Yet in *Dies* v. *British and International Mining and Finance Corporation, Ltd.*,[1] STABLE, J., held, contrary to at least one decision,[2] that if a contract for the sale of goods is discharged owing to the buyer's default, the seller must return any part of the price that has been pre-paid.

> " In my judgment there would be a manifest defect in the law if, where a buyer had paid for the goods but was unable to accept delivery, the vendor could retain the goods and the money quite irrespective of whether the money so retained bore any relation to the amount of the damage, if any, sustained as a result of the breach. The seller is already amply protected, since he can recover such damage as he has sustained."[3]

When, however, money has been paid as a deposit and also where it has been agreed that a part payment shall be forfeited in the event of the payer's default, equity is prepared within limits to grant relief against the forfeiture. Nevertheless, the circumstances in which and the extent to which the relief will be given are by no means clear.

Equity may give relief against forfeiture of deposit

> Suppose, for instance, that a buyer of goods agrees to pay the price by periodic instalments and further agrees that, if he defaults in any one payment, instalments already paid shall be forfeited to the seller and possession of the goods surrendered. If, after payment of a large percentage of the price, the contract is discharged because of the buyer's default, will relief be granted to him against the forfeiture of the instalments already paid?

It is clear at least that equity, where warranted by the circumstances, will relieve the buyer to the extent of giving him further time within which to complete the contract, even though the parties have agreed that time shall be essential. In other words, the forfeiture will be suspended, provided that the buyer expresses himself ready and willing to pay the balance of the price within the extended time fixed by the court.[4]

What is doubtful is whether equity will intervene and give relief otherwise than by extending the time allowed for payment. The question was canvassed in *Stockloser* v. *Johnson*.[5] On the facts of the case the Court of Appeal agreed that intervention was not warranted, but its members differed as to the principle upon which such relief might be granted. ROMER, L.J., concluded that " in the absence of some special circumstances such as fraud, sharp practice or other unconscionable conduct of the

Extent of relief doubtful

---

1. [1939] 1 K.B. 724; and see *Stockloser* v. *Johnson*, [1954] 1 Q.B. 476, at p. 490; [1954] 1 All E.R. 630, *per* DENNING, L.J. For a convincing criticism of the decision of STABLE, J., see Salmond & Williams, *The Law of Contracts*, p. 569, note (b).
2. *Fitt* v. *Cassanett* (1842), 4 Man. & G. 898, where the money, though described in the headnote as a " deposit," was in fact paid on account of the full price.
3. [1939] 1 K.B., at p. 744.
4. *Re Dagenham (Thames) Dock Co., Ex parte Hulse* (1873), 8 Ch. App. 1022; *Kilmer* v. *British Columbia Orchard Lands, Ltd.*, [1913] A.C. 319.
5. [1954] 1 Q.B. 476; [1954] 1 All E.R. 630. See also in the Court of Appeal *Campbell Discount Co.* v. *Bridge*, [1961] 1 Q.B. 445; [1961] 2 All E.R. 97. At the moment quite different principles apply to forfeiture of deposits and to penalties (see *infra*, pp. 609–611). As to whether this should be so, see Law Commission Working Paper 61 (1975).

vendor " no intervention by the court is permissible after the contract has been rescinded, except to allow an extension of time for payment.[1]　SOMERVELL and DENNING, L.JJ., thought that the province of equity is not so circumscribed and that it may permit more general relief whenever the forfeiture clause is of a penal nature—where, that is, the sum forfeited is wholly disproportionate to the damage suffered—provided that in the circumstances it is unconscionable for the money to be retained.

For each of these views persuasive arguments may be advanced. On the one hand, precedent would clearly seem to favour the more restricted view;[2] and it may well be thought that to upset agreements contracted freely and with open eyes save on urgent grounds would defeat reasonable expectations and obstruct the course of business.　As Lord RADCLIFFE observed in another case " ' unconscionable ' must not be taken to be a panacea for adjusting any contract between competent persons when it shows a rough edge to one side or the other."[3]　On the other hand, the inexorable maxim of Lord NOTTINGHAM, cited by ROMER, L.J.,[4] that " Chancery mends no man's bargain," does scant justice to the modern law.　The twentieth century has refused to be sterilized by the dead hand of the seventeenth.　The courts have in fact " mended bargains " through the doctrines of undue influence, of " clogs on the equity of redemption," of equitable mistake.　They have allowed contracts to be severed, at least in certain types of illegality, and have wholly discharged them on the ground of frustration. Which of the two judicial views advanced in *Stockloser* v. *Johnson* will ultimately prevail must therefore await further elucidation. In one recent decision that of ROMER, L.J., was applied by SACHS, J.[5] while another seems to lean in the other direction.[6]

SECTION II.　WHERE THE BREACH DOES NOT DISCHARGE THE CONTRACT

A.　RECOVERY OF DAMAGES[7]

I. REMOTENESS OF DAMAGE AND MEASURE OF DAMAGES

Action for
damages
raises two
questions

The extent to which a plaintiff is entitled to demand damages for breach of contract was not fully considered by the courts until *Hadley* v. *Baxendale* in 1854, and, although the principle laid

---

1. *Ibid.*, at pp. 501 and 644 respectively.
2. *Hill* v. *Barclay* (1811), 18 Ves. 56; *Bracebridge* v. *Buckley* (1816), 2 Price, 200; *Barrow* v. *Isaacs*, [1891] 1 Q.B. 417; *Sparks* v. *Liverpool Waterworks Co.* (1807), 13 Ves. 428; *Wallingford* v. *Mutual Society* (1880), 5 App. Cas. 685; *Protector Loan and Annuity Co.* v. *Grice* (1880), 5 Q.B.D. 592.　See generally, Story, *Equity Jurisdiction*, ss. 1319–26.
3. *Bridge* v. *Campbell Discount Co., Ltd.*, [1962] A.C. 600, at p. 626; [1962] 1 All E.R. 385.
4. *Stockloser* v. *Johnson*, [1954] 1 Q.B. 476, at p. 495; [1954] 1 All E.R. 630, at p. 640.
5. *Galbraith* v. *Mitchenhall Estates*, [1965] 2 Q.B. 473; [1964] 2 All E.R. 653.
6. *Starside Properties, Ltd.* v. *Mustapha*, [1974] 2 All E.R. 567; [1974] 1 W.L.R. 816.
7. *McGregor on Damages*, 13th Edn. (1972); Ogus. *The Law of Damages* (1973);　Street, *Principles of the Law of Damages* (1962).

down in that case has since been repeatedly affirmed, much confusion has been caused by the loose terminology that so often
disfigures statements upon this part of the law.   Such expressions
as " remoteness of damages," " damage too remote," " remote
consequences," " measure of damages," are used interchangeably
as if they were synonymous.   The chief difficulty arises with the
words " damage " and " damages."

It is suggested that the subject would be less obscure if it is
realised that in the ultimate analysis a claim for damages raises
two distinct questions.   These emerge from the fundamental
principle that the remoteness of the damage for which compensation is claimed must be distinguished from the monetary assessment of that compensation.[1]

The first is: for what *kind* of damage is the plaintiff entitled
to recover compensation?   Damage of the most catastrophic and
unusual nature may ensue from breach, but on practical grounds
the law takes the view that a line must be drawn somewhere and
that certain kinds or types of loss, though admittedly caused as a
direct result of the defendant's conduct, shall not qualify for
compensation.   As Lord WRIGHT said in a case of tort:

(i) Question
of remoteness
of damage

> " The law cannot take account of everything that follows a
> wrongful act; it regards some subsequent matters as outside the
> scope of its selection, because ' it were infinite for the law to judge
> the cause of causes,' or consequences of consequences.   In the
> varied web of affairs the law must abstract some consequences as
> relevant, not perhaps on grounds of pure logic, but simply for
> practical reasons."[2]

To this end *Hadley* v. *Baxendale*[3] defined the kind of damage
that is the appropriate subject of compensation, and excluded all
other kinds as being too remote.   The decision was concerned
solely with what is correctly called *remoteness of damage*, and it
will conduce to clarity of thought and treatment if this expression
is reserved for every case where the defendant denies liability
for certain of the consequences that have flowed from his breach.
Whether the damage is too remote is a question for the judge.[4]

The second question, which must be kept quite distinct from
the first and which arises only after the court has decided that a
particular kind of damage is sufficiently proximate according to
the rule in *Hadley* v. *Baxendale*, concerns the principle upon
which that damage must be evaluated or quantified in terms of
money.   This may appropriately be called the question of the
measure of damages.   The principle adopted by the courts in
many cases dating back to at least 1848 is that of *restitutio in
integrum*.   If the plaintiff has suffered damage that is not too
remote, he must, so far as money can do it, be restored to the
position he would have been in had that particular damage not

(ii) Question
of measure
of damages

---

1. *Chaplin* v. *Hicks*, [1911] 2 K.B. 786, at p. 797, *per* FARWELL, L.J.; *Boys*
   v. *Chaplin*, [1968] 1 Q.B. 1, at p. 41; [1968] 2 All E.R. 283, *per* DIPLOCK, L.J.
2. *Liesbosch Dredger* v. *Edison Steamship*, [1933] A.C. 449, at p. 460.
3. (1854), 9 Exch. 341; *infra*, p. 591.
4. *Chaplin* v. *Hicks*, [1911] 2 K.B. 786, at p. 797.

occurred.[1]   Usually this has meant that the plaintiff is put into
the position he would have achieved if the contract were performed but exceptionally he has been allowed to recover damages
on the basis of returning him to the position before the contract
was made.[2]   The amount of money adjudged to be due to him
in this respect must be assessed as at the time when the contract
was broken.   Traditionally this " breach-date " rule has meant
that any change in the value of sterling after the date when the
cause of action accrued must be ignored.[3]

But the House of Lords has now mitigated the effect of this
rule in an era of fluctuating currencies by holding that in appropriate circumstances judgments may be given in a foreign
currency.[4]   Further if the plaintiff is claiming not damages at
common law but damages in lieu of specific performance under
Chancery Amendment Act 1858 (Lord Cairns Act) damages will be
assessed as at the date of judgment.[5]

The principle according to which the amount of monetary
compensation is measured, is subordinate and ulterior in application to the rule of remoteness.

> " This rule does not come into play with regard to any claimed
> head of damage until it has been determined by the rule as to
> remoteness whether that head of damage can be brought into con-
> sideration at all."[6]

The evaluation of the damage, however, must be based solely
upon the legal obligations of the defendant.   " A defendant is not
liable in damages for not doing that which he is not bound to do."[7]
An employee, for instance, who has been wrongfully dismissed, is
admittedly entitled to recover what he would have received had his
employment run its full course; but if his contractual salary was
increasable by any bonus that the employer at his discretion might
from time to time award, the assessment of damages must ignore
undeclared bonuses, even though it is highly probable that they
would have been declared had the employment continued.[8]

---

1. *Robinson* v. *Harman* (1848), 1 Exch. 850; *Wertheim* v. *Chicoutimi Pulp
   Co.,* [1911] A.C. 301, at p. 307; *The Edison,* [1932] P. 52, at pp. 62–3, *per*
   SCRUTTON, L.J.; *B. Sunley & Co., Ltd.* v. *Cunard White Star, Ltd.,* [1940] 1
   K.B. 740, at p. 745; [1940] 2 All E.R. 97, at p. 100, *per curiam.*   The
   distinction between remoteness of damage and measure of damages was
   applied in *J. D'Almeida Araujo, Lda.* v. *Sir Frederick Becker & Co., Ltd.,*
   [1953] 2 Q.B. 329; [1953] 2 All E.R. 288.   This was an action brought in
   England for breach of a contract governed by Portuguese law.
2. See *Anglia Television, Ltd.* v. *Reed,* [1972] 1 Q.B. 60; [1971] 3 All E.R. 690,
   Criticised Ogus, 35 M.L.R. 423.   For further discussion, see Ogus, Chaps.
   8, 9, and Stoljar, 91 L.Q.R. 68.
3. *Re United Railways of Havana and Regla Warehouses, Ltd.,* [1961] 1 A.C.
   1007; [1960] 2 All E.R. 332; *The Teh Hu,* [1970] P. 106; [1969] 3 All E.R. 8.
4. *Miliangos* v. *George Frank (Textiles), Ltd.,* [1975] 3 All E.R. 801.
5. See *Wroth* v. *Tyler,* [1974] Ch. 30; [1973] 1 All E.R. 897.   It is arguable
   that on the facts of that case the breach-date rule ought not to have been
   applicable at common law either.   As to Lord Cairns Act, see Jolowicz,
   [1975] C.L.J. 224.
6. *The Argentino* (1888), L.R. 13 P.D. 191, at pp. 195–8, *per* Lord ESHER, M.R.
7. *Abrahams* v. *Herbert Reiach, Ltd.,* [1922] 1 K.B. 477, at p. 482, *per* SCRUTTON,
   L.J.
8. *Lavarack* v. *Woods of Colchester, Ltd.,* [1967] 2 Q.B. 278; [1966] 3 All
   E.R. 683.

" The law is concerned with legal obligations only, and the law of contract only with legal obligations created by mutual agreement between contractors—not with the expectations, however reasonable, of one contractor that the other will do something that he has assumed no legal obligation to do."[1]

The rule that governs remoteness of damage was stated as follows by ALDERSON, B., in delivering the judgment of the court of Exchequer in *Hadley* v. *Baxendale*:

Hadley v. *Baxendale* governs remoteness of damage

" Where two parties have made a contract which one of them has broken, the damages which the other party ought to receive in respect of such breach of contract should be such as may fairly and reasonably be considered either arising naturally, i.e., according to the usual course of things, from such breach of contract itself, or such as may reasonably be supposed to have been in the contemplation of both parties, at the time they made the contract, as the probable result of the breach of it."[2]

The facts of the case were as follows:

The mill of the plaintiffs at Gloucester was brought to a standstill by a broken crank shaft and it became necessary to send the shaft to the makers at Greenwich as a pattern for a new one. The defendant, a common carrier, promised to deliver it at Greenwich on the following day. Owing to his neglect, it was unduly delayed in transit, with the result that the mill remained idle for longer than it would have done had there been no breach of the contract of carriage. The plaintiffs, therefore, claimed to recover damages for the loss of profit caused by the delay.

The evidence of the parties was conflicting, but the Court of Exchequer considered the case on the footing that the only information given to the carrier was " that the article to be carried was the broken shaft of a mill and that the plaintiffs were the millers of that mill."[3]

It was obvious that the failure of the carrier to perform the contract punctually was the direct cause of the stoppage of the mill for an unnecessarily long time, and, if the plaintiffs were entitled to an indemnity against all the consequences of the breach, they should have been awarded damages for the loss of profit. At the trial the jury did indeed allow the claim, but on appeal the court ordered a new trial. ALDERSON, B., demonstrated that, in accordance with the principle that he had just expressed, there were only two possible grounds upon which the plaintiffs could sustain their claim. Firstly, that in the usual course of things the work of the mill would cease altogether for the want of the shaft. This, he said, would not be the normal occurrence, for, to take only one reasonable possibility, the plaintiffs might well have had a spare shaft in reserve. Secondly, that the special circumstances were so fully disclosed that the inevitable loss of profit was made apparent to the defendant. This, however, was not the case, since the only communication

---

1. *Ibid.,* at p. 292, *per* DIPLOCK, L.J.
2. (1854), 9 Exch. 341, at p. 354.
3. (1854), 9 Exch. 341, at p. 355, *per* ALDERSON, B. In *Victoria Laundry (Windsor), Ltd.* v. *Newman Industries, Ltd.,* [1949] 2 K.B. 528, at p. 537; [1949] 1 All E.R. 997, at p. 1001, the Court of Appeal pointed out that the headnote to *Hadley* v. *Baxendale* is definitely misleading in its statement that the carrier was told of the stopping of the mill and the necessity for the immediate delivery of the shaft.

proved was that the article to be carried was the shaft of a mill and that the plaintiffs were the owners of the mill.   The jury, therefore, should not have taken the loss of profit into consideration in their assessment of damages.

The two branches of the rule in *Hadley* v. *Baxendale*

The words " either," and " or," used in the formulation of the rule as explained by ALDERSON, B., shows that .it contains two branches.   The first deals with the normal damage that occurs in the usual course of things; the second with abnormal damage that arises because of special or exceptional circumstances.   The defendant is taken to have contemplated both kinds of damage, but where it is abnormal only if he knew of the special circumstances at the time of the contract.

Importance of the *Victoria Laundry* case

In *Victoria Laundry (Windsor), Ltd.* v. *Newman Industries, Ltd.*,[1] the test of remoteness of liability laid down by ALDERSON, B., was reformulated by ASQUITH, L.J., in what is generally regarded as a classic exposition of the developed law.   In the course of delivering the judgment of the court, he summarized the substance of the test in the following three propositions.

> " In cases of breach of contract, the aggrieved party is only entitled to recover such part of the loss actually resulting as was at the time of the contract reasonably foreseeable as liable to result from the breach.
>
> What was at that time reasonably so foreseeable depends upon the knowledge then possessed by the parties or, at all events, by the party who commits the breach.
>
> For this purpose knowledge ' possessed ' is of two kinds; one imputed, the other actual.   Everyone, as a reasonable person, is taken to know the ' ordinary course of things ' and consequently what loss is liable to result from a breach of contract in that ordinary course.   This is the subject-matter of the ' first rule ' in *Hadley* v. *Baxendale*.   But to this knowledge, which a contract-breaker is assumed to possess whether he actually possesses it or not, there may have to be added in a particular case knowledge which he actually possesses of special circumstances outside the ' ordinary course of things,' of such a kind that a breach in those special circumstances would be liable to cause more loss.   Such a case attracts the operation of the ' second rule ' so as to make additional loss also recoverable."[2]

The case concerned a claim made by a buyer for the recovery of the business profits that he had lost owing to the delayed delivery of a chattel essential to the furtherance of his trade, a type of question that not infrequently comes before the courts.   The facts were these:

> The plaintiffs, launderers and dyers, decided to extend their business.   For this purpose and for the purpose of obtaining certain dyeing contracts of an exceptionally profitable character, they required a larger boiler.   The defendants, an engineering firm, contracted to sell and deliver to the plaintiffs on 5th June a certain boiler of the required capacity.   This, however, was damaged in the course of removal and was not delivered until the following 8th November.   The defendants were aware of the nature of the plaintiffs' business and they were informed in more than one letter before the conclusion of the contract that the plaintiffs were " most anxious " to put the boiler into use " in the shortest possible space of time."

---

1. [1949] 2 K.B. 528; [1949] 1 All E.R. 997.
2. *Ibid.,* at p. 539.

In an action for breach of contract, the plaintiffs claimed (a) damages for the loss of profit, assessed by them at £16 a week, that they would have earned through the extension of their business but for the delay in delivery of the boiler, and (b) damages, assessed at £262 a week, for the loss of the exceptional profits that they would similarly have earned on the " highly lucrative " dyeing contracts. In the opinion of the Court of Appeal, the defendants, with their engineering experience and with the knowledge of the facts possessed by them, could not reasonably contend that the likelihood of some loss of business was beyond their prevision. They were, indeed, ignorant that the plaintiffs had in prospect the " highly lucrative " dyeing contracts and so could not be liable specifically for the " highly lucrative " profits that the plaintiffs had hoped to make. Even so, however, the plaintiffs were not precluded from recovering a general, if conjectural, sum which might represent the *normal* profit to be expected from the completion of the dyeing contracts. The case, therefore, was remitted to an Official Referee to ascertain the damage that might reasonably be expected to result from the failure to extend the business and the inability to execute normal dyeing contracts.

In *The Heron II*,[1] however, the House of Lords differed from the judgment of ASQUITH, L.J., with regard to the criterion by which to determine the remoteness of damage arising from a breach of contract. They demonstrated that the question is not, as ASQUITH, L.J., said, whether the damage should have been foreseen by the defendant, but whether the probability of its occurrence should have been within the reasonable contemplation of both parties at the time when the contract was made, having regard to their knowledge at that time. The law of contract and of tort differ in this respect. A tortfeasor is liable for any damage which is of such a kind as should have been foreseen by a reasonable man, however unlikely its occurrence might have been.[2] Of these two criteria, that of reasonable foresight is the more stringent. A tortfeasor is generally a stranger to the injured person, and it falls to the law to define both the persons to whom he owes a duty of care and also the extent of that duty. The intention of the parties is irrelevant.

> " But in contract the parties have only to consider the consequences of a breach to the other; it is fair that the assessment of damages should depend upon their assumed common knowledge and contemplation and not on a foreseeable but most unlikely consequence."[3]

It has been held, however, that if the kind of damage caused by a breach of contract is within the reasonable contemplation of the parties at the time when the contract was made and is therefore not

[marginal note:] Test of liability in contract is whether probability of loss within contemplation of both parties

---

1. [1969] 1 A.C. 350. Pickering, 31 M.L.R. 203.
2. *The Wagon Mound,* [1961] A.C. 388; [1961] 1 All E.R. 404.
3. *The Heron II,* [1969] 1 A.C. 350, at p. 422, *per* Lord UPJOHN. See also p. 413, *per* Lord PEARCE. Yet, in certain transactions, such as that of a contract of carriage, the law of tort and of contract overlap. If, e.g. in *Hadley* v. *Baxendale* the shaft had been negligently dropped and injured, would the criterion of liability have been foresight or the reasonable contemplation of the parties? See Hamson, [1969] C.L.J. 15.

too remote, it is immaterial that its results are far more serious than could have been reasonably contemplated.[1]

Same test for
both
branches of
Hadley v.
Baxendale

The criterion of reasonable contemplation, as it may shortly be described, applies to both branches of the rule in *Hadley* v. *Baxendale*.   The difference in this respect between the two is that in the case of the first branch the " horizon of contemplation " is confined to loss which arises naturally in the usual course of things and which is therefore presumed to have been within the contemplation of the parties.   The second branch, by reason of the special knowledge possessed by the defendant, extends the horizon of contemplation to loss that does not arise in the usual course of things.[2]

How to
express
the requisite
degree of
probability

A further question arises when the courts seek to apply the criterion of reasonable contemplation.   What is the degree of probability required and how is it to be defined, if indeed it is capable of exact definition?   In the *Victoria Laundry* case, ASQUITH, L.J., said:

> " In order to make the contract-breaker liable under [*Hadley* v. *Baxendale*] it is not necessary that he should have actually asked himself what loss is liable to result from a breach . . . It suffices that, if he had considered the question, he would as a reasonable man have concluded that the loss in question was liable to result . . . Nor, to make a particular loss recoverable, need it be proved that upon a given state of knowledge the defendant could, as a reasonable man, foresee that a breach must necessarily result in that loss.   It is enough if he could foresee it was likely so to result.   It is indeed enough . . . if the loss (or some factor without which it would not have occurred) is a ' serious possibility ' or a ' real danger.'   For short, we have used the word ' liable ' to result.   Possibly the colloquialism ' on the cards ' indicates the shade of meaning with some approach to accuracy."[3]

In *The Heron II*, the House of Lords indulged in a punctilious, and at times involved, analysis of these phrases used by the learned Lord Justice.   Their Lordships all deprecated the phrase " on the cards."   Thus Lord PEARCE discarded it as a useful test.   " I suspect," he said, " that it owes its attraction, like many other colloquialisms, to the fact that one may utter it without having the trouble of really thinking out with precision what one means oneself or what others understand by it, a spurious attraction which in general makes colloquialism unsuitable for definition, though it is often useful as shorthand for a collection of definable ideas."[4]   But, while their Lordships unanimously rejected the use of this phrase, they could not agree upon a suitable substitute. Lord REID distrusted the expression " liable to result."   " Liable," he said, " is a very vague word, but I think that one would usually say that when a person foresees a very improbable result he foresees that it is liable to happen."[5]   His Lordship preferred

---

1. *Vacwell Engineering Co., Ltd.* v. *B.D.H. Chemicals, Ltd.*, [1971] 1 Q.B. 111; [1970] 3 All E.R. 553.   *Wroth* v. *Tyler*, [1974] Ch. 30; [1973] 1 All E.R. 897.   But everything here turns on the classification of " kind of damage." So in the *Victoria Laundry* case profits and exceptional profits were treated as different kinds.
2. *The Heron II*, [1969] 1 A.C. 350, at pp. 415–6, *per* Lord PEARCE; [1967] 3 All E.R., at p. 712.
3. [1949] 2 K.B., at p. 540.
4. [1969] 1 A.C., at p. 415; [1967] 3 All E.R., at p. 711.
5. *Ibid.*, at pp. 389 and 694 respectively.

" not unlikely," or " quite likely " to happen. Lord HODSON, on the other hand, disapproved of " likely to result " and preferred " liable to result," the phrase which ASQUITH, L.J., had suggested. " If the word ' likelihood ' is used it may convey the impression that the chances are all in favour of the thing happening, an idea which I would reject."[1] Lord UPJOHN was content to adopt the phrases " a real danger " or " a serious possibility."[2] If, indeed, a single phrase must be chosen " liable to result " seems to have secured the most general assent.

It is questionable whether this exercise in semantics is of any great value. Lord MORRIS of Borth-y-Gest showed little enthusiasm for it,[3] and when the case was before the Court of Appeal, SELLERS, L.J., remarked that " the phrases and words of *Hadley* v. *Baxendale* have been hallowed by long user and gain little advantage from the paraphrases or substitutes. The ideas and factors conveyed by the words are clear enough."[4] As Lord UPJOHN said in the House of Lords, " the assessment of damages is not an exact science ";[5] and it may be added that the search for such an elusive quantity as a person's assumed contemplation can scarcely be governed by any particular formula.

During the twenty years that elapsed between the *Victoria Laundry* case and *The Heron II*, the judgment of ASQUITH, L.J., remained unchallenged. DEVLIN, J., considered that it had liberated judges of first instance from the bondage of the earlier authorities.[6] In a later case in the House of Lords, Lord GUEST, Lord UPJOHN and Lord PEARSON all cited it with approval.[7] Moreover it has emerged virtually unscathed from its ordeal in *The Heron II* except with regard to the test of liability.[8]

Continuing importance of Victoria Laundry case

The two branches of *Hadley* v. *Baxendale* do not represent two separate rules, and it may sometimes be difficult to identify which is applicable. Loss of profits arising from the breach of a trading contract, at least made between experienced parties, will more frequently than might be expected fall under the first branch; for each party " must be taken to understand the ordinary practices and exigencies of the other's trade or business."[9] This is well illustrated by the actual facts of *The Heron II*.[10]

> The appellant, a shipowner, agreed to carry a cargo of sugar belonging to the respondents from Constanza to Basrah. He knew that there was a sugar market at Basrah and that the respondents were sugar merchants, but did not know that they intended to sell the cargo immediately on its arrival, at the market rate, and that if the ship were nine days late, the price might have dropped during that period. Owing to the appellant's default, the voyage was delayed by at least nine days, and the sugar fetched a lower price than it would have done had it arrived on time

1. *Ibid.,* at pp. 410–11 and 708 respectively.
2. *Ibid.,* at pp. 425 and 717 respectively.
3. *Ibid.,* at pp. 399 and 699 respectively.
4. [1966] 2 Q.B. 695, at p. 722.
5. [1969] 1 A.C., at p. 425; [1967] 3 All E.R., at p. 715.
6. *Heskell* v. *Continental Express, Ltd.,* [1950] 1 All E.R. 1033, at p. 1048.
7. *East Ham Corporation* v. *Bernard Sunley & Sons, Ltd.,* [1966] A.C. 406; [1965] 3 All E.R. 619.
8. *Aruna Mills, Ltd.* v. *Dhanrajmal Gobindram,* [1968] 1 Q.B. 655, at p. 668; [1968] 1 All E.R. 113.
9. *Monarch Steamship Co., Ltd.* v. *Karlshamns Oljefabriker (A/B),* [1949] A.C. 196, at p. 224; [1949] 1 All E.R. 1, *per* Lord WRIGHT.
10. [1969] 1 A.C. 350; [1967] 3 All E.R. 686.

The consequential loss fell to be borne by the appellant under the first branch of the rule, for though he had no knowledge of special circumstances he could and should at the very least have contemplated that if the ship arrived nine days late the respondents would suffer some financial loss.

Again, if the parties are in the fruit trade between England and Spain and one of them agrees to carry a consignment of oranges to London, he is presumed to know that owing to seasonal fluctuations, the prices available at Covent Garden may largely depend upon the arrival of the goods within the stipulated time.[1]

First branch of rule in *Hadley* v. *Baxendale* illustrated

The first question, then, is—What loss arises in the usual course of things from the breach of a contract where there is nothing exceptional known to the defendant? It is impossible, of course, to answer the question in general, for just as contracts vary infinitely in character so also do the types of loss that their non-performance normally causes. The nature of the damage that ensues " in the usual course of things " from a breach obviously varies with the circumstances of each contract. It is proposed, therefore, to illustrate the nature of the subject from the particular case of the sale of goods.

(i) Failure by seller to deliver goods: remoteness of damage

What the buyer is deprived of in the usual course of things by a non-delivery is the value of the goods at the time and place of delivery, less the price payable by him under the contract. If the seller, for instance, has promised to deliver a hundred tons of coal of a specified quality at £20 a ton upon January 1st at Oxford and fails to do so, the injury to the buyer is that he lacks possession of a hundred tons of coal for which he would have paid £2000. This loss of value, if the seller has no actual or constructive knowledge of further exceptional circumstances, is the only *natural* result of the breach, the only kind of damage that ensues *in the usual course of things*. Every other kind of loss, though actually and directly suffered by the buyer, is in the eye of the law abnormal, not within the reasonable contemplation of the seller in ordinary circumstances, and therefore too remote. Thus, to take one common example, a sub-contract loss is usually too remote, i.e. a buyer, who has agreed before delivery to resell the goods to a third person at a price higher than the contract price, loses the profit that he would have made on the resale had delivery been made to him; but nevertheless the loss is too remote, since it is not the natural and normal result of a failure to deliver sold goods.[2] In order to recover for this exceptional loss he must prove that at the time of the contract the seller knew of special circumstances that signalized the probable resale of the goods.[3]

Failure by seller to deliver goods: measure of damages

To turn now to the measure of damages, we must recall that the principle here is to effect a *restitutio in integrum* so far as the actionable damage is concerned. The actionable damage, namely,

---

1. *Ardennes (Cargo Owners)* v. *Ardennes (Owners)*, [1951] 1 K.B. 55; [1950] 2 All E.R. 517.
2. *Williams Brothers* v. *Agius,* [1914] A.C. 510.
3. *Hall* v. *Pim*, [1927] All E.R. Rep. 226, as explained in *Finlay & Co.* v. *N.V. Kwik Hoo Tong,* [1929] 1 K.B. 400, at pp. 411–12, 417–18; [1928] All E.R. Rep. 110, at pp. 114–15, 118–19; *Patrick* v. *Russo-British Grain Export Co.,* [1927] 2 K.B. 535; *Brading* v. *F. McNeill & Co., Ltd.,* [1946] Ch. 145; *Household Machines, Ltd.* v. *Cosmos Exporters, Ltd.,* [1947] K.B. 217; [1946] 2 All E.R. 622.

that which occurs in the usual course of things, is, as we have seen, the loss of the value of the goods at the time and place of delivery, diminished by the price.   The buyer, therefore, must be placed in the position that he would have occupied had he received a hundred tons of coal of the specified quality in Oxford on January 1st after paying for it at the rate of £20 a ton.   All that is required to put him in this position is sufficient money to enable him to buy similar coal in the open market.

> " The market value is taken because it is presumed to be the true value of the goods to the purchaser.   In the case of non-delivery, where the purchaser does not get the goods he purchased, it is assumed that these would be worth to him, if he had them, what they would fetch in the open market; and that, if he wanted to get others in their stead, he could obtain them in that market at that price."[1]

The actual sum payable by way of damages for the actionable damage depends, therefore, upon the difference between the market and the contract prices upon the day appointed for delivery. If, for instance, the market price is higher by two pounds a ton than that fixed by the contract the buyer is entitled to two hundred pounds, but if it is less than the contract price he will receive only nominal damages.   Thus section 51 of the Sale of Goods Act 1893, in dealing with damages for non-delivery, provides as follows:

> Where there is an available market for the goods in question the measure of damages is *prima facie* to be ascertained by the difference between the contract price and the market or current price of the goods at the time or times when they ought to have been delivered, or, if no time was fixed, then at the time of refusal to deliver.[2]

A difficulty in estimating what sum suffices for the purchase of similar goods arises where there is no available market.   In this case the value of the goods must be otherwise ascertained.   If, for instance, the buyer has agreed to resell the goods, it is generally accepted that their resale price may be taken as representing their value, and the seller will be required to pay the difference between the sale and resale prices even though he had no notice of the sub-contract.[3]

A slightly different analysis is required in the reverse case where it is the buyer who breaks the contract.   The loss resulting from such a breach must inevitably vary with the particular circumstances and especially with the character of the seller and the local demand for goods of the kind in question.

(ii) Failure by buyer to accept goods

If the seller is not a dealer, if, for example, he is a householder who has agreed to sell an antique table to the defendant, his loss is the deprivation of the purchase price upon a certain date, less the value of the table that he still unwillingly possesses. He will be indemnified against this loss, therefore, if he is able to

Position where seller is not a dealer

---

1.   *Wertheim* v. *Chicoutimi Pulp Co.,* [1911] A.C. 301, at p. 307.
2.   Section 51 (3).
3.   *Stroud* v. *Austin & Co.* (1883), Cab. & El. 119; *Patrick* v. *Russo-British Grain Export Co.,* [1927] 2 K.B. 535; *France* v. *Gaudet* (1871), L.R. 6 Q.B. 199.   See also *Kwei Tek Chao* v. *British Traders and Shippers, Ltd.,* [1954] 2 Q.B. 459, at p. 489; [1954] 1 All E.R. 779, at p. 797, *per* DEVLIN, J.

sell the table to another person and if he recovers from the
defendant the difference between the price thus received and the
price fixed by the first contract should the latter be the higher.
Section 50 of the Sale of Goods Act,[1] indeed, provides that the
indemnity shall *prima facie* be measured on this basis.

> Where there is an available market for the goods in question the
> measure of damages is *prima facie* to be ascertained by the difference
> between the contract price and the market or current price at the
> time or times when the goods ought to have been accepted, or, if
> no time was fixed for acceptance, then at the time of refusal to
> accept.

**Position
where
seller is a
dealer**

Where, however, the plaintiff seller is a dealer in the particular
goods sold, the position may be different.   In such a case, what
ensues from the breach in the usual course of things is that the
plaintiff loses the profit that he would have made had the sale to
that particular buyer been completed, and he is entitled to be
recompensed for that loss.   It is no answer to say that he has sold,
or may readily sell, the goods to another person, for even if he has
been successful the fact remains that he has profited from one sale
instead of from two.   This was the position in *W. L. Thompson,
Ltd.* v. *Robinson (Gunmakers), Ltd.,*[2] where the facts were as
follows:

> The defendants refused to accept delivery of a Vanguard motor-
> car which they had agreed to buy from the plaintiffs, dealers in new
> and second-hand cars, carrying on business in the East Riding of
> Yorkshire.   The price, from which no dealer was allowed to depart,
> was that fixed by the manufacturers.   The plaintiffs mitigated their
> loss by persuading their supplier to take the car back.   The defen-
> dants, while admitting their breach of contract, invoked section 50
> of the Sale of Goods Act and contended that they were liable only
> for nominal damages, since the plaintiffs could have sold the car to
> another customer or could, as they had in fact done, return it to
> their supplier.

On this hypothesis, the plaintiffs had suffered only trivial loss.
UPJOHN, J., however, rejected the contention.   Section 50
provides only a *prima facie* rule, and it is inapplicable where the
difference between the contract and the market price does not
indemnify the plaintiff for the loss which is normally caused and
has in fact been caused to him by the breach in question.   What
the plaintiffs had lost was the profit on that particular bargain.
In the words of the learned judge:

> " Apart altogether from authority and statute it would seem to
> me on the facts which I have to consider to be quite plain that the
> plaintiffs' loss in this case is the loss of their bargain.   They have
> sold one Vanguard less than they otherwise would.   The plaintiffs,
> as the defendants must have known, are in business as dealers in
> motor-cars and make their profit in buying and selling motor-cars;
> what they have lost is their profit on the sale of this Vanguard."[3]

**Meaning of
" available
market "**

Judgment was, therefore, given for the plaintiffs for £61 1s. 9d.
The learned judge also considered the meaning of the statutory
phrase " available market," upon which there is little authority.

---

1. Section 50 (3).
2. [1955] Ch. 177; [1955] 1 All E.R. 154.   The same principle applies in the
case of a contract to hire goods: *Inter-office Telephones, Ltd.* v. *Robert
Freeman Co., Ltd.,* [1958] 1 Q.B. 190.
3. [1955] Ch. 177, at p. 183; [1955] 1 All E.R. 154, at p. 157.

Does it mean something in the nature of an established market, such as the Liverpool Cotton Exchange or the Baltic Exchange? Such had been the opinion of JAMES, L.J., in *Dunkirk Colliery Co.* v. *Lever*.[1]

Though in view of the circumstances the question was academic in the instant case, UPJOHN, J., favoured a more extended definition of the expression. In his view, an available market exists if the situation in the particular trade in the area is such that the goods can freely and readily be resold in the event of the purchaser's default.[2] If, as in the later case of *Charter* v. *Sullivan*,[3] Vanguard cars could have been sold as quickly as they came into stock, only nominal damages would have been recoverable, for in those circumstances the defendants' default would have been a matter of indifference to the plaintiffs. On the contrary, the position in the East Riding was that the supply of those particular cars exceeded the demand and thus the loss of that sale was injurious.[4] It is respectfully submitted, however, that the view of UPJOHN, J., is to be preferred where the seller is a dealer or a manufacturer, for even though he resells the article he will none the less have lost his profit on the abortive sale.[5]

It now remains to consider the case where, owing to special circumstances known at the time of the contract to the party ultimately in default, the breach causes losses outside the natural course of events. The position then is that the horizon of contemplation attributable to him is expanded. He is taken to have contemplated the kind of loss that was liable to arise in the usual course of things from a breach, having regard to the special circumstances of which he had actual or constructive knowledge. Thus the extent of his liability varies with the extent of his knowledge. In the *Victoria Laundry* case,[6] for instance, the defendants knew that the boiler was required by a laundry and dyeing firm not as a spare part, but for immediate use in the running of its business. They should have contemplated, therefore, that some loss of business profits would ensue in the normal course of events if delivery of the boiler were unduly delayed. But the loss flowing from the inability of the firm to fulfil the lucrative dyeing contracts was too remote, since the very existence of those contracts was unknown to the defendants.

Second branch of rule in Hadley v. Baxendale illustrated

---

1. (1878), 9 Ch.D. 20, at p. 24.
2. This was the view adopted in the case of a defaulting seller by the High Court of Australia fifty years earlier in *Francis* v. *Lyon*, [1907] 4 C.L.R. 1023, at p. 1036, *per* GRIFFITH, C.J.: " I understand the term ' available market ' to mean that the circumstances, including conditions of time and place, are such that a purchaser having the purchase money in his hands can, there and then, if he so desires, buy other goods of the same quality."
3. [1957] 2 Q.B. 117; [1957] 1 All E.R. 809.
4. [1955] Ch., at p. 187; [1955] 1 All E.R., at p. 159. Another view as to the meaning of " available market " was taken in *Charter* v. *Sullivan*, [1957] 2 Q.B. 117, at pp. 125–6, *per* JENKINS, L.J. See *McGregor on Damages*, 13th Edn., paras. 549–551, 633–634.
5. See *Cameron* v. *Campbell and Worthington, Ltd.*, [1930] S.A.S.R. 402. So far as the reasoning in *Thompson* v. *Robinson* turns on the dealer being bound by a price maintenance scheme, the decision may now be suspect. But the general principle that a dealer–seller may be compensated for loss of a bargain is not dependent on the existence of binding price maintenance schemes.
6. *Supra*, p. 592.

Thus the crux of the matter is whether the special circumstances were within the actual or constructive knowledge of the defaulting party at the time of the contract. This may be illustrated by two relevant cases.

In *Pilkington* v. *Wood*[1] the facts were these:

> In April, 1950, the plaintiff, desiring to live near his place of business in Surrey, bought a house in Hampshire for £6,000, having been advised by the defendant, his solicitor, that the title was good. He raised the purchase money by a bank overdraft and went into occupation.   In December, 1951, he decided to sell the house as he now wished to reside in Lancashire, where he was about to obtain employment.   A purchaser was found who was willing to pay £7,500 for the house and for certain additional land recently acquired by the plaintiff, but it was then discovered that the property was not saleable at that price, since the title was bad.

The defendant, having admitted that he had been negligent in his investigation of the title, was clearly liable to pay by way of damages the difference between the market value in April of the house with a good title and its market value at that date with the defective title, a difference which the learned judge estimated at £2,000.[2]   It was claimed, however, that additional damages were payable by reason of the following facts.

> The plaintiff gave evidence that his inability to sell the Hampshire house had precluded him from raising the money required for the purchase of a residence in Lancashire.   He had been forced, therefore, to reside in a Lancashire hotel during the week and each week-end to visit his wife who had continued to occupy the Hampshire house.   In the light of these and other exceptional circumstances, he claimed compensation in respect *inter alia* of the following heads of damage:
>
> (a) The cost of the valuation of the Hampshire house.
> (b) Interest on his bank overdraft.
> (c) Expenses resulting from the mode of living forced upon him after he had obtained work in Lancashire, namely, £175 for hotel expenses, £250 for car journeys between Hampshire and Lancashire, £50 for nightly telephone calls to his wife.

Harman, J., held that none of these items was admissible, since at the time of the contract with the solicitor none could be described as likely to result from a breach.   The first two items derived from the plaintiff's own impecuniosity, a misfortune which, though common enough, was not within the actual or constructive knowledge of the defendant.   To attribute to him foresight of the third item would imply a degree of prescience possessed by few. In the words of the learned judge:

> " The change of place of the plaintiff's employment was not one of the chances that could have been known to either of them.   It was the voluntary act of the plaintiff, not the result of any contract

---

1. [1953] Ch. 770; [1953] 2 All E.R. 810.
2. The plaintiff had not obtained what he had contracted and paid for, i.e. a house with a good title.   Distinguish *Ford* v. *White & Co.*, [1964] 2 All E.R. 775; [1964] 1 W.L.R. 885, where he obtained at the market value precisely what he had contracted for, i.e. and subject to a restriction against building upon part of it.   Therefore, although he had a right of action against his solicitor who had wrongly advised him that no restriction existed, all that he was entitled to recover was the difference between the market value of the land and the price actually paid.   Since there was no such difference, no damages were recoverable.

existing when the contract was made. The plaintiff chose a new job in Lancashire; he might as well have selected one more remote in Kamschatka or less remote in Hampshire. The defendant cannot be responsible for the expense. The plaintiff might have bought or rented accommodation suitable to his new employment, and there is no evidence that the defendant knew that his financial position might render this impracticable. Still less can the defendant be called upon to pay for the telephone calls, a luxury no doubt exemplary, yet uxorious."[1]

The second authority is *Diamond* v. *Campbell-Jones.*[2]

In July, 1956, the defendants contracted to sell leasehold premises in Mayfair to the plaintiff for £6,000. The defendants wrongfully repudiated the contract. The only question raised was that of damages.

The plaintiff claimed the profit that he would have made if he had converted the ground floor into offices and the four upper floors into maisonettes. The defendants, while they acknowledged that such a conversion was a possible use of the premises, denied that they knew or should have known that the plaintiff had bought with this intention. The plaintiff, indeed, admitted that the conversion was " only one of alternative possible methods of turning the bargain to account." BUCKLEY, J., held that he could recover only the difference between the purchase price and the market value at the date of the breach of contract.

" Special circumstances are necessary to justify imputing to a vendor of land a knowledge that the purchaser intends to use it in any particular manner. In my judgment neither the fact that [the house] was ripe for conversion, nor indeed the fact that everybody recognised this, was sufficient ground for imputing to the vendors knowledge that the purchaser was a person whose business it was to carry out such conversions or that he intended, or was even likely, to convert the house himself for profit."[3]

We have seen that in cases of frequent occurrence, such as a contract for the sale of goods, certain rules relating to the measure or assessment of damages have gradually been evolved, as for instance the rule that a defaulting seller must pay to the buyer the difference between the market and the contract price of the goods. But in general there is no specific rule upon the matter, and it is left to the good sense of the court to assess as best it can what it considers to be an adequate recompense for the loss suffered by the plaintiff. The assessment may well be a matter of great difficulty, indeed in some cases one of guesswork; but the fact that it cannot be made with mathematical accuracy is no reason for depriving the plaintiff of compensation. A case in point is *Chaplin* v. *Hicks*[4] where the facts were these:

Difficulty of assessing damages no bar to plaintiff

---

1. [1953] Ch. 770, at p. 780; [1953] 2 All E.R. 810, at p. 815.
2. [1961] Ch. 22; [1960] 1 All E.R. 583.
3. [1961] Ch. 22; [1960] 1 All E.R. 583, at pp. 36 and 591 respectively.
4. [1911] 2 K.B. 786; distinguished, *Sykes* v. *Midland Bank Executor and Trustee Co., Ltd.,* [1971] 1 Q.B. 113, at p. 129, *per* SALMON, L.J. See also *Hall* v. *Meyrick,* [1957] 2 Q.B. 455, in the lower court. Compensation is not limited to lost pecuniary benefits. So a plaintiff who books a holiday with a tour operator may recover for loss of enjoyment if the holiday is spoilt by a breach of contract. See *Jarvis* v. *Swans Tours, Ltd.,* [1973] 1 Q.B. 233; [1973] 1 All E.R. 71; *Jackson* v. *Horizon Holidays, Ltd.,* [1975] 3 All E.R. 92; [1975] 1 W.L.R. 1468.

The defendant, an actor and theatrical manager, agreed with the plaintiff that if she would attend a meeting at which he proposed to interview forty-nine other actresses, he would select twelve out of the fifty and would give remunerative employment to each of these successful candidates.   He broke his contract with the plaintiff by failing to give her a reasonable opportunity to attend the interview.

In an action for breach of contract, he contended that only nominal damages were payable, since the plaintiff would have had only a chance of one in four of being successful, a chance moreover which depended among other imponderables upon his own volition.   Nevertheless, it was held by the Court of Appeal that the award of £100, given by the jury, must stand.

"Where by contract." said FLETCHER MOULTON, L.J., " a man has a right to belong to a limited class of competitors, he is possessed of something of value, and it is the duty of the jury to estimate the pecuniary value of that advantage if it is taken from him."[1]

Effect of tax liability on damages

It is clear, therefore, that no court may avoid the task of assessing damages on the ground of its difficulty.   But, as *Chaplin* v. *Hicks* shows, the inquiry may well be speculative. The obligations thus imposed have been increased in recent years by the decision of the House of Lords in *British Transport Commission* v. *Gourley*[2] that, in the course of assessment, account may have to be taken of the plaintiff's liability for taxation.   In measuring the damages for the loss of income or profits, the court must deduct an amount equivalent to the sum that he would have paid by way of income tax had he continued to receive such yearly income.   As the object of damages is to compensate the plaintiff, not to punish the defendant, it might indeed seem logical to award the plaintiff, not a gross sum, but a net sum, reached after the deduction of his own liabilities to the Inland Revenue.   *Gourley's* case itself was a decision in the law of tort; but, as the function of damages in contract is similarly compensatory and not retributive, the principle upon which it rested is no less applicable to contract.   It has, in fact, been so applied: in *Beach* v. *Reed Corrugated Cases, Ltd.*,[3] to a claim for wrongful dismissal, and in *Re Houghton Main Colliery Co.*[4] to breach of contract in general.   The principle, however, operates only if the damages awarded to the plaintiff will not, in his hands, be liable to taxation.   Otherwise the plaintiff would in effect pay tax twice over and would not receive just compensation for the breach of contract or tort committed by the defendant.

" It is impossible to maintain that there can be derived from *Gourley's* case any principle requiring taxation to be taken into account in assessing damages where both the lost earnings or profits and the damages are taxable."[5]

---

1. *Chaplin* v. *Hicks*, [1911] 2 K.B., at p. 796.
2. [1956] A.C. 185; [1955] 3 All E.R. 796.
3. [1956] 2 All E.R. 652; [1956] 1 W.L.R. 807.   See also *Shindler* v. *Northern Raincoat Co., Ltd.,* [1960] 2 All E.R. 239, at p. 250; [1960] 1 W.L.R. 1038, at p. 1050.
4. [1956] 3 All E.R. 300; [1956] 1 W.L.R. 1219.   The authorities were reviewed by the Court of Appeal in *Parsons* v. *B.N.M. Laboratories, Ltd.,* [1964] 1 Q.B. 95; [1963] 2 All E.R. 658.
5. *Per* PEARSON, L.J., in *Parsons* v. *B.N.M. Laboratories, Ltd.,* [1964] 1 Q.B., at p. 136; [1963] 2 All E.R., at p. 679.

The logic of the principle may be impeccable, but the difficulties involved in its application are formidable. Thus in *Beach v. Reed Corrugated Cases, Ltd.*, the plaintiff, had he not been wrongly dismissed, would have received as salary over the next ten years the sum of £48,000. But he had a large private fortune which, to estimate his tax liability, had to be taken into account. In the result, and admittedly as a pure conjecture, PILCHER, J., reduced the damages to £18,000. So, too, in *Re Houghton Main Colliery Co.*: Difficulty of applying principle

> The company was under contract to pay two employees pensions at monthly rates of £160 and £75 respectively. The company went into voluntary liquidation. This was, as against the two employees, a breach of contract, since it prevented the company from continuing to pay the pensions. For the purposes of the liquidation the two pension rights were capitalized at £14,000 and £10,000 respectively.

These two sums had therefore to be treated as damages caused by the breach of contract; and, in deference to the decision of the House of Lords, WYNN-PARRY, J., ruled that they must be subject to deduction for income tax. How to assess this deduction was a more difficult question. The learned judge proposed to adjourn the case in the hope that the parties' accountants could reach an agreed figure. He offered them " guidance ": thus the damages were not to be taken as falling within a single fiscal year but were to be spread over a number of years. If unhappily the accountants were unable to agree, the case would have to come back to him, and he would then have to reach a decision as best he could. The truth is that in such cases the assessment of the amount to be deducted is a matter of guess-work rather than of calculation.[1]

Here as elsewhere, therefore, logic produces practical difficulties. Its results, moreover, may be ludicrous. In some circumstances it may well be cheaper to break a contract than to keep it; and, if an exact rather than a conjectural estimate were required of the tax liability involved, a preliminary case on this particular question might itself have to be fought up to the House of Lords. The whole question was reviewed in 1958 by the Law Reform Committee,[2] but, as its members were divided among themselves upon the solution, no recommendations were made. In the one case of wrongful dismissal, however, the Finance Act 1960 has modified the principle of *Gourley's* case by providing that any excess over £5,000 of the sum awarded to the plaintiff as damages for loss of employment shall be taxable in his hands and thus be payable without reduction by the defendant.[3] The effect of the statute is this: Effect of Finance Act 1960

> An award of £5,000 or less does not attract taxation, and therefore the damages must be reduced in accordance with the principle of *Gourley's* case.

---

1. See, for instance the remarks of Lord REID in *Taylor* v. *O'Connor*, [1971] A.C. 115, at p. 129.
2. Law Reform Committee, 7th Report (*Effect of Tax Liability on Damages*), Cmnd. 501.
3. Section 38; *Bold* v. *Brough, Nicholson and Hall, Ltd.*, [1964] 3 All E.R. 849; [1964] 1 W.L.R. 201; applying *Parsons* v. *B.N.M. Laboratories, Ltd.*, *supra*.

If the damages awarded exceed £5,000, the excess is taxable in the plaintiff's hands, but the first £5,000, since it is not taxable, must be reduced.[1]

Whatever the difficulties or indeed the absurdities which attend its application, it is clear that—subject to this statutory exception— the principle laid down in *Gourley's* case is now established in English law.   So much was assumed by the House of Lords both in *Parry* v. *Cleaver*[2] and in *Taylor* v. *O'Connor*.[3]   It is interesting to notice that the Supreme Court of Canada has rejected the reasoning of the decision,[4] and that the High Court of Australia has still to pass judgment upon it.[5]

2. MITIGATION

Duty of plaintiff to mitigate the damage

The rules given above are subject to this limitation, that the law imposes a duty upon the plaintiff to take all reasonable steps to mitigate the loss caused by the breach of contract, and debars him from claiming compensation for any part of the damage which is due to his neglect to do so.[6]   Whether the plaintiff has failed to take a reasonable opportunity of mitigation is a question of fact dependent upon the particular circumstances of each case, and the burden of proving such failure rests upon the defendant.[7] It has thus been held that the master of a ship, upon the failure of the charterer to provide a cargo in accordance with the contract, should normally accept cargo from other persons at the best freight obtainable.[8]   The wrongful dismissal of a servant has often raised this question of mitigation.   In *Brace* v. *Calder*,[9] for instance:

> The defendants, a partnership consisting of four members, agreed to employ the plaintiff as manager of a branch of the business for two years.   Five months later the partnership was dissolved by the retirement of two of the members, and the business was transferred to the other two, who offered to employ the plaintiff on the same terms as before.   He rejected the offer.

The dissolution of the partnership constituted in law a wrongful dismissal of the plaintiff, and in his action for breach of contract he sought to recover the salary that he would have received had he

---

1. Sections 37 and 38.   The primary object of these sections was to discourage what has come to be known as the " golden handshake "; *Parsons* v. *B.N.M. Laboratories, Ltd.,* [1964] 1 Q.B. 95, at p. 137, *per* HARMAN, L.J.
2. [1970] A.C. 1; [1969] 1 All E.R. 555.
3. [1971] A.C. 115; [1970] 1 All E.R. 365.
4. *Ontario* v. *Jennings* (1966), 57 D.L.R. (2d.) 644; Samuels, 30 M.L.R. 83.
5. For the position in Australia, see the Third Australian edition of Cheshire and Fifoot, *The Law of Contract,* pp. 730–732.
6. *British Westinghouse Electric and Manufacturing Co.* v. *Underground Electric Rys. Co. of London,* [1912] A.C. 673, at p. 689, *per* Lord HALDANE.
7. *Payzu, Ltd.* v. *Saunders,* [1919] 2 K.B. 581.
8. *Harries* v. *Edmonds* (1845), 1 Car. & Kir. 686, N.P.
9. [1895] 2 Q.B. 253.   See also *Shindler* v. *Northern Raincoat Co., Ltd.,* [1960] 2 All E.R. 239; [1960] 1 W.L.R. 1038; and *Yetton* v. *Eastwoods Froy, Ltd.,* [1966] 3 All E.R. 353; [1967] 1 W.L.R. 104, examples of a reasonable refusal to accept alternative employment.   The question arose in a more unusual form in *Lavarack* v. *Woods of Colchester, Ltd.,* [1967] 1 Q.B. 278; [1966] 3 All E.R. 683.

served for the whole period of two years. It was held, however, that he was entitled only to nominal damages, since it was unreasonable to have rejected the offer of continued employment.

A particularly instructive case is that of *Payzu, Ltd.* v. *Saunders*,[1] where the plaintiff had been the victim of a wrongful repudiation by the defendant.

> Under a contract to deliver goods by instalments, payment to be made within one month of each delivery, less two and a half per cent. discount, the buyers failed to make punctual payment for the first instalment. The seller treated this as sufficient to repudiate the contract, but offered to continue deliveries at the contract price if the buyers would pay cash at the time of each order. This offer was rejected. The price of the goods having risen, the buyers sued for breach of contract.

It was held in the first place that the seller was liable in damages, since the circumstances did not warrant his repudiation of the contract. On the other hand, it was held that the buyers should have mitigated their loss by accepting the seller's offer, and that the damages recoverable were not to be measured by the difference between the contract and market price, but by the loss that would have been suffered had the offer been accepted. " In commercial contracts," said SCRUTTON, L.J., " it is generally reasonable to accept an offer from the party in default."[2]

But the burden which lies on the defendant of proving that the plaintiff has failed in his duty of mitigation is by no means a light one, for this is a case where a party already in breach of contract demands positive action from one who is often innocent of blame. This may be illustrated from *Pilkington* v. *Wood*, the facts of which have already been given.[3] It was there argued by the defendant's solicitor that the plaintiff, the purchaser of the Hampshire house, should have mitigated his loss by taking proceedings against the vendor for having conveyed a defective title. The proposed action, however, would have involved complicated litigation upon a somewhat difficult provision in the Law of Property Act 1925, and it was far from clear that it would have succeeded. HARMAN, J., therefore held that the purchaser was under no duty to embark upon such a hazardous venture, merely " to protect his solicitor from the consequences of his own carelessness."

Onus on defendant to prove breach of the duty

An illustration of a different kind is afforded by *James Finlay & Co.* v. *N. V. Kwik Hoo Tong H.M.*[4]

> Sugar, which under a contract of sale ought to have been shipped in September, was not in fact shipped by the sellers until October. They nevertheless tendered a bill of lading which stated, though not fraudulently, that the shipment had been made in September. This was a breach of contract, since " it is well settled that on a sale of goods a condition as to the time of shipment is vital and is of the essence of the contract."[5] The buyers, being unaware of the late shipment, re-sold the goods to X & Co., merchants in Bombay, under a contract containing a clause that " the bill of lading shall be con-

---

1. [1919] 2 K.B. 581.
2. [1919] 2 K.B., at p. 589.
3. [1953] Ch. 770; [1953] 2 All E.R. 810, *supra*, pp. 600–1.
4. [1929] 1 K.B. 400; [1928] All E.R. Rep. 110.
5. *Ibid.*, at p. 407, *per* SCRUTTON, L.J.

clusive evidence of the date of shipment." X and Co. discovered that the sugar had not been shipped in September, and therefore refused to take delivery.

The buyers were, of course, entitled to recover damages from the original sellers, but it was contended that they should have forced the sub-contract on X & Co. by relying upon the conclusive evidence clause in the bill of lading. This contention was rejected. The Court of Appeal took the view that for the buyers to have insisted upon payment by X & Co. of the agreed price after their discovery that the goods were not in accordance with the contract, having been shipped in the wrong month, " would violate the standard of morality which should attach to an English firm of standing and would in fact ruin their credit in India."[1]

Mitigation and anticipatory breach

The problem of mitigation is presented in a special light in the case of the so-called " anticipatory breach." It has already been seen that, if a defendant repudiates in May a contract for the delivery of goods in July, the plaintiff has an option.[2] On the one hand, he may accept the repudiation and sue at once for breach of contract: he will then be under the ordinary duty to mitigate.[3] On the other hand, he may refuse the repudiation, hold the defendant to the contract and await the date of performance. If he prefers this course, the contract remains alive and no question of damages or of mitigation has yet arisen.

> " It cannot be said that there is any duty on the part of the plaintiff to mitigate his damages before there has been any breach which he has accepted as a breach."[4]

The reasoning is logical; but the result may be grotesque. In *White and Carter (Council), Ltd.* v. *McGregor* :[5]

> The business of the appellants was to supply litter bins to local councils throughout Great Britain. They were not paid by the councils, but by traders who hired advertising space on the bins. On June 26th, 1957, the respondent agreed to hire space for three years beginning on the date when the first advertisement was exhibited. Later in the same day the respondent wrote to cancel the contract. The appellants refused to accept the repudiation. Up to this moment they had taken no steps to carry out the contract. But they now prepared advertisement plates, attached them to the bins and continued to display them for the next three years. They made no attempt to minimise their loss by procuring other advertisers to take the respondent's place. In due course they sued the respondent for the full contract price.

The House of Lords, by a majority of three to two, held that they were entitled to succeed.

The implications of the decision were exposed by Lord KEITH.

---

1. *Ibid.*, at p. 410, *per* SCRUTTON, L.J.
2. See *supra*, pp. 573–7.
3. *Roth & Co.* v. *Taysen, Townsend & Co.* (1895), 1 Com. Cas. 240; affirmed, (1896), 12 T.L.R. 211.
4. *Shindler* v. *Northern Raincoat Co., Ltd.;* [1960] 1 W.L.R. 1038, at p. 1048. See *Brown* v. *Muller* (1872), L.R. 7 Exch. 319; *Tredegar Iron and Coal Co., Ltd.* v. *Hawthorn Brothers & Co.* (1902), 18 T.L.R. 716.
5. [1962] A.C. 413; [1961] 3 All E.R. 1178; distinguished, *Hounslow London Borough Council* v. *Twickenham Garden Developments, Ltd.,* [1971] 1 Ch. 233, at pp. 251–4. The decision in *White and Carter (Council), Ltd.* v. *McGregor* is criticised by Goodhart in 78 L.Q.R. 263, and defended by Nienaber in [1962] C.L.J. 213.

" If it is right it would seem that a man who has contracted to go to Hong Kong at his own expense and make a report, in return for a remuneration of £10,000, and who, before the date fixed for the start of the journey and perhaps before he has incurred any expense, is informed by the other contracting party that he has cancelled or repudiated the contract, is entitled to set off for Hong Kong and produce his report in order to claim in debt the stipulated sum."[1]

The result, as Lord KEITH described it, is " startling," and invites some method of avoiding it which will not offend accepted principle. The means may be found, it is suggested, as soon as it is realised that the mitigation rule is not a rule *sui generis*, functioning in isolation, but an example of the wider if vaguer doctrine of causation. Alike in contract and in tort a plaintiff may claim compensation only for the loss caused by the defendant's wrongful act: any loss created by his own unreasonable conduct he must bear himself. In a case in 1955, HODSON, L.J., had to consider the question

" whether the damages flow from the breach in accordance with the ordinary law of damages for breach of contract. Were they the natural and probable consequences of the breach? If not, they are too remote . . . The question is one of causation. If the master, by acting as he did, either caused the damage by acting unreasonably in the circumstances in which he was placed, or failed to mitigate the damage, the defendants would be relieved from the liability which would otherwise have fallen on them."[2]

The appellants in *White and Carter (Council), Ltd.* v. *McGregor*, as they had refused the repudiation, were entitled to remain inactive and await the date of performance. But they were not content to be passive. They embarked upon a course of conduct which cost money, served no useful purpose and was, as they knew, unwanted by the respondent. They had chosen, in other words, to inflate their loss; and, while under no duty to mitigate, they were surely bound not to aggravate the damage. In the words of HODSON, L.J., quoted above, they had " acted unreasonably in the circumstances in which they had been placed," and the respondent should have been " relieved from the liability which would otherwise have fallen on him." Their expense was self-imposed and was not caused by the breach of contract.

3. LIQUIDATED DAMAGES AND PENALTY

The parties to a contract may agree beforehand what sum shall be payable by way of damages in the event of breach, as, for example, where a builder agrees that he will pay £5 a day for every day that the building remains unfinished after the contractual date for completion. A sum fixed in this manner falls into one of two classes.

Damages fixed in anticipation of breach

---

1. [1962] A.C., at p. 442; [1961] 3 All E.R., at p. 1190. One apparent implication of the decision is that it enables a plaintiff to obtain the advantages of a decree of specific performance in circumstances that would not normally attract the remedy, a possibility anticipated in the Australian case of *Automatic Fire Sprinklers Pty., Ltd.* v. *Watson* (1946), 72 C.L.R. 435, at p. 451.
2. *Compania Naviera Maropan, S.A.* v. *Bowaters Lloyd, Pulp and Paper Mills, Ltd.*, [1955] 2 Q.B. 68, at pp. 98–9; [1955] 2 All E.R. 241, at pp. 251–2. For a parallel case in tort, see *The Pacific Concord, Owners of Georgidore* v. *Owners of Pacific Concord*, [1961] 1 All E.R. 106; [1961] 1 W.L.R. 873.

Difference
between
penalty
and liquidated
damages

Firstly, it may be a genuine pre-estimate of the loss that will be caused to one party if the contract is broken by the other.   In this case it is called liquidated damages and it constitutes the amount, no more and no less, that the plaintiff is entitled to recover in the event of breach without being required to prove actual damage.

> " Liquidated damages means that it shall be taken as the sum which the parties have by the contract assessed as the damages to be paid, whatever may be the actual damage."[1]

Secondly, it may be in the nature of a threat held over the other party *in terrorem*—a security to the promisee that the contract will be performed.[2]   A sum of this nature is called a penalty, and it has long been subject to equitable jurisdiction.   Courts of equity have taken the view that, since a penalty is designed as mere security for the performance of the contract, the promisee is sufficiently compensated by being indemnified for his actual loss, and that he acts unconscionably if he demands a sum which, though certainly fixed by agreement, may well be disproportionate to the injury.[3]   The rule, therefore, is that a plaintiff who brings an action for the enforcement of a penalty can recover compensation only for the damage that he has in fact suffered.   He is not entitled to recover the sum stated in the contract if he has not in fact suffered so much loss.

> " Beyond the penalty you shall not go; within it you are to give the party any compensation which he can prove himself entitled to."[4]

A penalty covers but does not assess the damage.[5]   Where, however, the stipulated sum does not compensate for the actual loss suffered, the plaintiff has an election.   He may either sue on the penalty clause, in which case he cannot recover more than the stipulated sum; or he may sue for breach of contract and recover damages in full.[6]   There is no such option in the case of liquidated damages.

Whether a
sum is a
penalty or
not depends
upon
intention of
parties

It is always, therefore, a question of importance whether a conventional sum is liquidated damages or a penalty.   This is a question of construction " to be decided upon the terms and inherent circumstances of each particular contract, judged of as at the time of making the contract, not as at the time of the breach."[7]   What has to be ascertained is whether it can reasonably be inferred that the parties intended to form a genuine pre-estimate of the damage likely to ensue from a breach.

---

1. *Wallis* v. *Smith* (1882), 21 Ch.D. 243, at p. 267, *per* COTTON, L.J.
2. Lord RADCLIFFE has expressed scepticism at the assumption that a penalty is based on the idea that it is a threat *in terrorem* of the other party: *Bridge* v. *Campbell Discount Co.*, [1962] A.C. 600, at p. 622; [1962] 1 All E.R. 385, at p. 395.
3. Story, *Equity Jurisprudence*, s. 1316.
4. *Wilbeam* v. *Ashton* (1807), 1 Camp. 78, *per* Lord ELLENBOROUGH.
5. *Public Works Commissioner* v. *Hills*, [1906] A.C. 368, at p. 375.
6. *Wall* v. *Rederiaktiebolaget Luggude*, [1915] 3 K.B. 66, approved *Watts, Watts & Co., Ltd.* v. *Mitsui & Co., Ltd.*, [1917] A.C. 227.   See *Cellulose Acetate Silk Co., Ltd.* v. *Widnes Foundry* (1925), *Ltd.*, [1933] A.C. 20, at p. 26.   Hudson, 90 L.Q.R. 31;   Gordon, 90 L.Q.R. 296; Hudson, 91 L.Q.R. 25.
7. *Dunlop Pneumatic Tyre Co., Ltd.* v. *New Garage and Motor Co., Ltd.*, [1915] A.C. 79, at pp. 86–7; *Lombank, Ltd.* v. *Excell*, [1963] 3 All E.R. 486.

" The distinction between penalties and liquidated damages depends on the intention of the parties to be gathered from the whole of the contract. If the intention is to secure performance of the contract by the imposition of a fine or penalty, then the sum specified is a penalty; but if, on the other hand, the intention is to assess the damages for breach of the contract, it is liquidated damages."[1]

The onus of showing that the specified sum is a penalty lies upon the party who is sued for its recovery.[2]

The fact that the parties may have used the expressions " penalty " or " liquidated damages " does not conclude the matter, and the court must still decide whether the sum fixed is a genuine forecast of the probable loss.[3] The expressions used must not, however, be disregarded, and if, for instance, the sum is made payable as a penalty the onus of disproving that this is its correct character lies on the party who claims that it was intended to be liquidated damages.[4]

Certain rules for the guidance of the judge have been laid down by the courts and these were usefully summarized by Lord DUNEDIN in *Dunlop Pneumatic Tyre Co., Ltd.* v. *New Garage and Motor Co., Ltd.*[5] They are as follows:

Rules for guidance of court

(a) The conventional sum is a penalty if it is extravagant and unconscionable in amount in comparison with the greatest loss that could possibly follow from the breach.[6]

(b) If the obligation of the promisor under the contract is to pay a certain sum of money, and it is agreed that if he fails to do so he shall pay a larger sum, this larger sum is a penalty.[7] The reason is that, since the damage arising from breach is capable of exact definition, the fixing of a larger sum cannot be a pre-estimate of the probable damage.

(c) Subject to the preceding rules, it is a canon of construction that, if there is only one event upon which the conventional sum is to be paid, the sum is liquidated damages.[8] This was held to be the case, for instance, where it was provided in a contract for the construction of sewerage works that, if the operations were not complete by April 30th, the contractor should pay £100 and £5 for every seven days during which the work was unfinished after that date.[9]

(d) If a single lump sum is made payable upon the occurrence of one or more or all of several events, some of which may occasion serious and others mere trifling damage, there is a presumption (but no more) that it is a penalty.[10] This presumption, however, is

---

1. *Law* v. *Redditch Local Board*, [1892] 1 Q.B. 127, at p. 132, *per* LOPES, J.
2. *Robophone Facilities, Ltd.* v. *Blank*, [1966] 1 W.L.R. 1428, at p. 1447.
3. *Dunlop Pneumatic Tyre Co.* v. *New Garage and Motor Co.*, [1915] A.C. 79, at p. 86, *per* Lord DUNEDIN.
4. *Willson* v. *Love*, [1896] 1 Q.B. 626, at p. 630, *per* Lord ESHER.
5. [1915] A.C. 79, at p. 86 *et seq.*
6. *Clydebank Engineering and Shipbuilding Co.* v. *Yzquierdo-y-Castaneda, Don Jose Ramos,* [1905] A.C. 6, especially at p. 10.
7. *Kemble* v. *Farren* (1829), 6 Bing. 141.
8. *Law* v. *Redditch Local Board*, [1892] 1 Q.B. 127.
9. *Ibid.*
10. *Lord Elphinstone* v. *Monkland Iron and Coal Co.* (1886), 11 App. Cas. 332, at p. 342, *per* Lord WATSON. *Inter-office Telephones, Ltd.* v. *Robert Freeman Co., Ltd.*, [1958] 1 Q.B. 190, at p. 194.

weakened if it is practically impossible to prove the exact monetary loss that will accrue from a breach of the various stipulations. The sum fixed by the parties in such a case, if reasonable in amount, will be allowed as liquidated damages.[1] Two cases will illustrate the distinction: In the *Dunlop Pneumatic Tyre Co.* case:[2]

> The Dunlop Company supplied tyres to the defendants under an agreement, headed " Price Maintenance Agreement," by which the defendants bound themselves not to tamper with the marks on the goods, not to sell below the listed prices, not to supply persons who were on a suspended list, not to exhibit or export without consent, and to pay £5 by way of liquidated damages for every tyre, tube or cover sold or offered in breach of the agreement.

It was held that the sum of £5 was liquidated damages. A fine of £5 for selling, for example, a single tube below the list price might seem disproportionate to the harm caused; but the news of the undercutting would soon spread and the resultant damage to Dunlop's selling organization would be impossible to estimate. It was, therefore, reasonable to quantify the damage at a fixed but not extravagant figure.

The Court of Appeal reached the opposite conclusion in the somewhat similar case of *Ford Motor Co.* v. *Armstrong*,[3] where the facts were these:

> The defendant, a retailer, in consideration of receiving supplies from the Ford Company, agreed not to sell any car or parts below the listed price, not to sell Ford cars to other motor dealers, and not to exhibit any car supplied by the company without their permission. He also agreed that for every breach of this agreement he would pay £250 as being " the agreed damage which the manufacturer will sustain."

In the view of the majority of the court the £250 was a penalty. It was not only substantial but was arbitrary and fixed *in terrorem*, for, since it was made payable for various breaches differing in kind, its very size prevented it from being a reasonable pre-estimate of the probable damage.[4]

The necessity of deciding between liquidated damages and penalty may clearly involve the courts in nice distinctions; and the problem has arisen in an acute form on the construction of a

Hire-
purchase
contracts

hire-purchase contract, in this as in other respects a fertile mother of actions. Some semblance of order has been imposed by the House of Lords in *Campbell Discount Co., Ltd.* v. *Bridge*.[5]

> The appellant made a hire-purchase contract with the respondents for a second-hand car. The total hire-purchase price was £482, of which £105 was due at once and the balance by 36 monthly instalments. The appellant met the initial payment and the first instalment, and then, after writing to the respondents that he would not be able to pay any more, he returned the car to the dealers. Clause 9 of the contract provided that " if the hiring be terminated for any reason before the vehicle becomes the property of the hirer, the hirer shall . . . pay to the owners . . . by way of agreed compensation

---

1. *Dunlop Pneumatic Tyre Co.* v. *New Garage and Motor Co.,* [1915] A.C. 79, at pp. 95–6, *per* Lord ATKINSON.
2. *Supra.*
3. (1915), 31 T.L.R. 267.
4. See also *Alder* v. *Moore,* [1961] 2 Q.B. 57; [1961] 1 All E.R. 1.   Goodhart, 77 L.Q.R. 300; Goff, 24 M.L.R. 637.
5. [1962] A.C. 600; [1962] 1 All E.R. 385.

for depreciation of the vehicle such further sum as may be necessary to make the rentals paid and payable hereunder equal to two-thirds of the hire-purchase price." The respondents sued on this clause for £206, being two-thirds of the price less the initial payment and the first instalment.

The county court judge held that the clause, despite its wording, imposed a penalty and dismissed the action. The Court of Appeal reversed this decision. They were of opinion that, on the true construction of the facts, the hirer had not broken his contract but had merely exercised his right to terminate it. As there had been no breach, no question of penalty arose and the hirer must pay the sum stipulated in the event of termination. The House of Lords, by a majority of four to one, restored the judgment of the county court. They held that the hirer had in fact broken his contract, that they must therefore decide whether the clause offered a genuine pre-estimate of damages or imposed a penalty, and that it was a penalty.

> " I find it impossible ", said Lord MORTON,[1] " to regard the sum stipulated in clause 9 as a genuine pre-estimate of the loss that would be suffered by the respondents in the events specified in the same clause . . . This was a second-hand car when the appellant took it over on hire-purchase. The depreciation in its value would naturally become greater the longer it remained in the appellant's hands. Yet the sum to be paid is largest when, as in the present case, the car is returned after it has been in the hirer's possession for a very short time, and gets progressively smaller as time goes on."

In Lord RADCLIFFE's words, " it is a sliding scale of compensation, but a scale that slides in the wrong direction." It was therefore unnecessary to examine the curious conclusion which would seem to follow the construction of the facts adopted by the Court of Appeal, that the person who keeps his contract is worse off than he who breaks it.[2]

In conclusion, it is well to heed the salutary warning of DIPLOCK, L.J., that: " The court should not be astute to descry a penalty clause in every provision of a contract which stipulates a sum to be payable by one party to the other in the event of a breach by the former." Such a stipulation reflects good business sense and is advantageous to both parties. It enables them to envisage the financial consequences of a breach; and if litigation proves inevitable it avoids the difficulty and the legal costs, often heavy, of proving what loss has in fact been suffered by the innocent party.[3]

---

1. *Ibid.*, at pp. 616 and 391 respectively; applied, *E. P. Finance Co., Ltd. v. Dooley*, [1964] 1 All E.R. 527; [1963] 1 W.L.R. 1313; *United Dominions Trust (Commercial) v. Ennis*, [1968] 1 Q.B. 54; [1967] 2 All E.R. 345.
2. See Wedderburn, [1961] C.L.J. 156; Fridman, 24 M.L.R. 507; 26 M.L.R. 198. See also *Financings, Ltd. v. Baldock*, [1963] 2 Q.B. 104; [1963] 1 All E.R. 443. As to the effect of *Campbell Discount Co., Ltd. v. Bridge* upon the decision of the Court of Appeal in *Phonographic Equipment (1958), Ltd. v. Muslu*, [1961] 3 All E.R. 626; [1961] 1 W.L.R. 1379, see *Lombank, Ltd. v. Excell*, [1964] 1 Q.B. 415; [1963] 3 All E.R. 486, C.A. This latter case overrules the decision of WINN, J., in *Lombank, Ltd. v. Cook*, [1962] 3 All E.R. 491; [1962] 1 W.L.R. 1133.
3. *Robophone Facilities, Ltd. v. Blank*, [1966] 1 W.L.R. 1428, at p. 1447.

B. SPECIFIC PERFORMANCE

Definition

A decree of specific performance is a decree issued by the court which constrains a contracting party to do that which he has promised to do.   It is a form of relief that is purely equitable in origin and is one of the earliest examples of the maxim that equity acts *in personam.*

Specific
performance
decreed
only where
common law
remedy
inadequate

It originated in the realization that there are many cases in which the remedy available at common law is not adequate. The normal remedy for breach of contract is the recovery of damages at common law.   In most cases this affords adequate reparation, as, for example, where the contract is for the sale of goods easily procurable elsewhere, or for the delivery of stocks or shares for which there is a free market; but in many instances, and especially where a vendor refuses to convey the land sold, a mere award of damages would defeat the just and reasonable expectations of the plaintiff.   The fundamental rule, therefore, is that specific performance will not be decreed if there is an adequate remedy at law.[1]   The purpose of such a decree is to ensure that justice is done.   " The court gives specific performance instead of damages, only when it can by that means do more perfect and complete justice."[2]   In one case, for instance, where the court refused specific performance of the defendant's promise to make good a gravel pit which he had quarried, the Master of the Rolls explained the position as follows:

> " This court does not profess to decree a specific performance of contracts of every description.   It is only where the legal remedy is inadequate or defective that it becomes necessary for courts of equity to interfere . . . In the present case complete justice can be done at law.   The matter in controversy is nothing more than the sum it will cost to put the ground in the condition in which by the covenant it ought to be."[3]

The contrary conclusion was reached in *Beswick* v. *Beswick*,[4] the facts of which have already been given.[5]   In that case the plaintiff was not only the administratrix of her late husband's estate but also the person to whom the annuity had been made payable by the contract between the husband and the defendant.   Being a stranger to that contract, her only course was to claim payment of the annuity by suing in her representative, not in her personal, capacity.   The defendant argued that *qua* administratrix her only right was to recover compensation for such loss as the estate had in fact suffered.   Therefore, so the argument ran, since the non-payment of the annuity after the husband's death caused no loss to his estate, the only remedy available either to the plaintiff or to the estate was the recovery of nominal damages.   This argument was

---

1. *Cuddee* v. *Rutter* (1720), 1 P. Wms. 570, where specific performance of an agreement to transfer £1,000 South-Sea Stock was refused.
2. *Wilson* v. *Northampton and Banbury Junction Rail. Co.* (1874), 9 Ch. App. 279, at p. 284, *per* Lord SELBORNE.
3. *Flint* v. *Brandon* (1803), 8 Ves. 159.
4. [1968] A.C. 58; [1967] 2 All E.R. 1197.   See, on the present aspect of the decision, Treitel 30 M.L.R. 690.
5. *Supra*, p. 443.

rejected by the House of Lords. To accept it would be repugnant to the concept of justice.[1] A decree of specific performance would clearly have been available to the husband had the agreement made the annuity payable in his lifetime, and it followed that this remedy was equally available to his personal representatives under the instant contract.

Where a contract contains interdependent undertakings, a plaintiff cannot obtain an order for specific performance if he is in breach of his own obligations or if he fails to show that he is ready and willing to perform his outstanding obligations in the future.[2]

Plaintiff must not be in breach of contract

The exercise of the equitable jurisdiction to grant specific performance is not a matter of right in the person seeking relief, but of discretion in the court.[3] This does not mean that the decision is left to the uncontrolled caprice of the individual judge, but that a decree which would normally be justified by the principles governing the subject may be withheld, if to grant it in the particular circumstances of the case will defeat the ends of justice.

Specific performance a discretionary remedy

"Indeed," said Lord PARKER, "the dominant principle has always been that equity will only grant specific performance if, under all the circumstances, it is just and equitable so to do."[4]

Thus the plaintiff will be left to his remedy at law if a decree of specific performance would inflict a hardship on the defendant, as for example where the enforcement of a restrictive covenant would be a burdensome futility owing to a change in the neighbourhood brought about by the plaintiff himself;[5] or where the defendant will be unable to enter the land that he has agreed to buy unless he is fortunate enough to obtain a licence from adjoining owners;[6] or where the plaintiff attempts to take advantage of an obvious mistake made by the defendant.[7]

Mutuality is often said to be a condition of specific performance. This statement really involves two assertions, which may be called positive and negative mutuality. The first is exemplified by the vendor of land who can obtain specific performance even though damages would usually be an adequate remedy because the purchaser is entitled to specific performance and it is thought unfair to deny to the vendor what is granted to the purchaser. Negative mutuality involves denial of specific performance to a plaintiff because it would not be available to the defendant. Thus, an infant cannot maintain an action for specific performance, since it is not maintainable against him.[8] Again, if the defendant agrees to form a company for the purpose of working the plaintiff's patent, and the plaintiff agrees that he

The principle of mutuality

---

1. Lord PEARCE alone thought that the damages would be substantial, but whether nominal or substantial he agreed that the agreement was specifically enforceable: [1968] A.C., at p. 88; [1967] 2 All E.R., at p. 1212.
2. See, for instance, *Australian Hardwoods Pty., Ltd.* v. *Railways Commissioners,* [1961] 1 All E.R. 737; [1961] 1 W.L.R. 425.
3. *Lamare* v. *Dixon* (1873), L.R. 6 H.L. 414, at p. 423, *per* Lord CHELMSFORD.
4. *Stickney* v. *Keeble,* [1915] A.C. 386, at p. 419.
5. *Duke of Bedford* v. *British Museum Trustees* (1822), 2 My. & K. 552.
6. *Denne* v. *Light* (1857), 8 De G. M. & G. 774.
7. *Supra,* pp. 235–7.
8. *Flight* v. *Bolland,* (1828) 4 Russ. 298; *Lumley* v. *Ravenscroft,* [1895] 1 Q.B. 683.

will devote the whole of his time to the interests of the company, there can be no specific performance at the instance of the plaintiff for, as we shall see,[1] he himself cannot be compelled to render personal services to another.[2]

It has been doubted whether mutuality amounts to a rule.[3] Certainly it is subject to several exceptions.   If, for instance, the defendant has signed the memorandum required by section 40 of the Law of Property Act 1925,[4] in order to render a contract to sell land actionable against " the party to be charged," it is specifically enforceable at the instance of the plaintiff, though he himself has signed nothing.[5]   Again, a vendor who has agreed to sell a larger interest in land than in fact he is entitled to, cannot enforce the contract; but the purchaser can compel him to convey at a reduced price such interest as he has.[6]

The analogous remedy of injunction

Another way in which the performance of a contract *in specie* may be enforced is by the grant of an injunction.   An injunction is either prohibitory or mandatory.   So far as concerns the law of contract, a prohibitory injunction is granted only in the case of a negative promise.   If, for instance, the defendant has broken his agreement not to ring the church bell at five o'clock each morning[7] or not to sell beer other than that brewed by the plaintiff,[8] the court will order him to refrain from doing what he has expressly promised not to do.   This is equivalent to " the specific performance by the court of that negative bargain which the parties have made."[9]

A mandatory injunction, on the other hand, is restorative in its effect, not merely preventive.   It directs the defendant to take positive steps to undo what he has already done in breach of the contract.   Thus he may be compelled to demolish or modify a building which he has erected[10] or to remove a road which he has constructed[11] if what he has done is not in accordance with the terms of the contract.   It has been stressed by BUCKLEY, J., however, that such a drastic remedy must not be granted unless in the circumstances it will produce a fair result.   The advantage that will accrue to the plaintiff must be balanced against the detriment likely to be suffered by the defendant.

> " A plaintiff should not, of course, be deprived of relief to which he is justly entitled merely because it will be disadvantageous to the defendant.   On the other hand he should not be permitted to insist on a form of relief which will confer no appreciable benefit on himself and will be materially detrimental to the defendant."[12]

---

1. *Infra,* p. 615.
2. *Stocker* v. *Wedderburn* (1857), 3 K. & J. 393.
3. Particularly in the United States.   See Ames, *Lectures on Legal History,* p. 370; Cardozo, *Growth of the Law,* pp. 14–16; Stone, 16 Col. L.R. 443, *Epstein* v. *Gluckin* 233 N.Y. 490 (1922). See also *O'Regan* v. *White* [1919] 2 I.R. 392.   Cf. Fry, *Specific Performances,* 6th Edn., pp. 219–228.
4. *Supra,* p. 182 *et seq.*
5. *Morgan* v. *Holford* (1852), 1 Sm. & G. 101, at p. 116.
6. *Horrocks* v. *Rigby* (1878), 9 Ch.D. 180.
7. *Martin* v. *Nutkin* (1724), 2 P. Wms. 266.
8. *Clegg* v. *Hands* (1890), 44 Ch.D. 503.
9. *Doherty* v. *Allman* (1878), 3 App. Cas. 709, at p. 720, *per* Lord CAIRNS.
10. *Lord Manners* v. *Johnson* (1875), 1 Ch.D. 673; *Jackson* v. *Normanby Brick Co.,* [1899] 1 Ch.D. 438.
11. *Charrington* v. *Simons & Co.,* [1970] 2 All E.R. 257; [1970] 1 W.L.R. 725.
12. *Charrington* v. *Simons & Co.,* [1970] 1 W.L.R., at p. 730.

In accordance with the general principle that equity does nothing in vain, there are two particular types of contract of which specific performance will not be granted. These are contracts for personal service, and those in which performance cannot be ensured without the constant superintendence of the court.

Two kinds of contract that are not specifically enforceable

Since it is undesirable, and indeed in most cases impossible, to compel an unwilling party to maintain continuous personal relations with another, it is well established that a contract for personal services is not specifically enforceable at the suit of either party.

Contract for personal services

> "The courts," said JESSEL, M.R., "have never dreamt of enforcing agreements strictly personal in their nature, whether they are agreements of hiring and service, being the common relation of master and servant, or whether they are agreements for the purpose of pleasure, or for the purpose of scientific pursuits, or for the purpose of charity or philanthropy."[1]

This denial of relief has been extended to contracts of agency,[2] of partnership,[3] and of apprenticeship.[4] In all such cases the plaintiff must pursue his remedy at law.

The only possible relief other than damages that can be granted to the plaintiff in such a case is an injunction, *i.e.* an order which forbids the defendant to perform a like personal service for other persons. If, for instance, as in *Lumley* v. *Wagner*,[5] the defendant has agreed that she will sing at the plaintiff's theatre in London for three months from April 1st and will not sing elsewhere during that period, it is obvious that an injunction prohibiting a breach of the negative part of the agreement may tempt the defendant to fulfil the positive part. The question is whether the courts will coerce the defendant in this oblique manner. They are confronted with a dilemma, for they must not decree specific performance of a contract for personal services, and they must not encourage a deliberate breach of contract by refusing an injunction in a case which is normally subject to this form of relief.

Performance of personal services may be encouraged by injunction

Since the decision of Lord ST. LEONARDS in *Lumley* v. *Wagner* it is well settled that the courts have jurisdiction to forbid the infringement of a negative stipulation, even though it is accessory to a positive covenant for the performance of personal services. The inability of the plaintiff to prove that he will suffer damage if the stipulation is broken is not a bar to the grant of an injunction.[6]

Jurisdiction to grant injunction

---

1. *Rigby* v. *Connol* (1880), 14 Ch.D. 482, at p. 487; *Francis* v. *Municipal Councillors of Kuala Lumpur*, [1962] 3 All E.R. 633; [1962] 1 W.L.R. 1411. Distinguish *Vine* v. *National Dock Labour Board*, [1957] A.C. 488; [1956] 3 All E.R. 939 where the plaintiff obtained a declaration that his name had been wrongfully removed from the register of dockers. See Ganz, 30 M.L.R. 288. This rule has often been associated with the analytically distinct rule that wrongful dismissal automatically terminates a contract of employment. Both principles may be in retreat before a trend to give servants a right of reinstatement. See *supra*, pp. 575–6. See especially *Hill* v. *C. A. Parsons & Co.*, [1972] 1 Ch. 305; [1971] 3 All E.R. 1345; Bridge, 88 L.Q.R. 391, Hall [1972A] C.L.J. 47.
2. *Chinnock* v. *Sainsbury* (1860), 30 L.J. Ch. 409.
3. *Scott* v. *Rayment* (1868), L.R. 7 Eq. 112.
4. *Webb* v. *England* (1860), 29 Beav. 44.
5. (1852), 1 De G. M. & G. 604.
6. *Marco Productions, Ltd.* v. *Pagola*, [1945] K.B. 111; [1945] 1 All E.R. 155.

Thus injunctions have been issued in the case of agreements not to sing elsewhere than at the plaintiff's theatre;[1] not, during the period of employment, to engage in any business similar to that carried on by the employer;[2] and not, during the period of employment, to act as a film artist for any motion picture company other than the employer's.[3]

No injunction possible if equivalent to specific enforcement

Nevertheless the courts invariably refuse the issue of an injunction if it will inevitably result in the enforcement *in specie* of a contract not otherwise specifically enforceable.[4]

If, for instance, A agrees to give the whole of his time to the service of B and not to serve anybody else *in any capacity whatever*, an injunction will not be granted, for its inevitable result would be to compel A to work for B or otherwise to starve. It is one thing to tempt him to perform the contract, another to subject him to irresistible compulsion. As LINDLEY, L.J., said in a leading case:

> " What injunction can be granted in this particular case which will not be, in substance and effect, a decree for specific performance of this agreement? It appears to me the difficulty of the plaintiffs is this, that they cannot suggest anything which, when examined, does not amount to this, that the man must either be idle or specifically perform the agreement into which he has entered."[5]

On the other hand, if A agrees to serve B as a film actress, and not to act for another film company, an injunction will be granted forbidding her to break the negative stipulation. In this case she is not faced with the alternative of starvation or of service with B, since there are many other ways in which she may earn a living.[6]

No injunction unless express negative contract by defendant

The distinction which the judges have drawn in these cases borders upon sophistry, and suggests that, while bound to follow *Lumley* v. *Wagner* when it forms a precise precedent, they are ready to adopt any possible argument to avoid it.[7] Thus in recent years they have insisted that in no circumstances will an injunction be granted unless the defendant has entered into an independent negative stipulation by which he expressly precludes himself from acting inconsistently with his positive contract.[8] There is no doubt, for instance, that an agreement by the defendant " to give the whole of his time " to the plaintiff's business, which is positive in form, imports the negative stipulation that he will not give any of his time to others; but the courts have so far refused to

---

1. *Lumley* v. *Wagner* (1852), 1 De G. M. & G. 604.
2. *William Robinson & Co., Ltd.* v. *Heuer*, [1898] 2 Ch. 451.
3. *Warner Brothers Pictures Incorporated* v. *Nelson*, [1937] 1 K.B. 209; [1935] 3 All E.R. 160; *Marco Productions, Ltd.* v. *Pagola*, [1945] K.B. 111; [1946] 1 All E.R. 155.
4. *Whitwood Chemical Co.* v. *Hardman*, [1891] 2 Ch. 416; *Ehrman* v. *Bartholomew*, [1898] 1 Ch. 671.
5. *Whitwood Chemical Co.* v. *Hardman*, [1891] 2 Ch. 416, at p. 427. An injunction was refused on this ground in *Page One Records, Ltd.* v. *Britton*, [1967] 3 All E.R. 822; [1968] 1 W.L.R. 157. The court, however, has a discretion and may sever a covenant which, as it stands, is too wide; *Rely-a-Bell Burglar and Fire Alarm Co.* v. *Eisler*, [1926] Ch. 609.
6. *Warner Brothers Pictures Incorporated* v. *Nelson*, [1937] 1 K.B. 209; [1936] 3 All E.R. 160.
7. See the remarks of JESSEL, M.R., in *Fothergill* v. *Rowland* (1873), L.R. 17 Eq. 132, at pp. 140–1.
8. *Mortimer* v. *Beckett*, [1920] 1 Ch. 571.

say that " because a person has agreed to do a particular thing, he is therefore to be restrained from doing everything else which is inconsistent with it."[1]

Specific performance will not be decreed if constant supervision is required to ensure obedience by the defendant. In the words of Ashburner: " The court only makes a positive order for the performance of an act which can be, as a rule, done *uno flatu*."[2] Therefore a continuing contract, to be performed from day to day by a series of acts, will not be specifically enforced. In *Ryan* v. *Mutual Tontine Westminster Chambers Association*:[3]

Acts requiring supervision not specifically enforceable

> The lessor of a flat in a block of buildings agreed that he would appoint a resident porter who should perform certain duties for the benefit of the tenants, such as the cleansing of the common passages and stairs, the delivery of letters and the acceptance of articles for safe custody. He appointed a porter who was by avocation a cook and who absented himself for several hours each day in order to act as *chef* at a neighbouring club. During his absence his duties were performed by various boys and charwomen not resident on the premises.

It was held that, though the lessor had committed a breach of contract, the only remedy was an action for damages.

Again the court will not as a rule enforce specific performance of a contract to erect or repair buildings, for not only is it unable to superintend the execution of the work, but also in most cases damages afford an adequate remedy. The one exception to this rule occurs where the defendant has purchased or taken a lease of land from the plaintiff and has agreed to erect a building upon it. In this case the plaintiff will succeed in an action for specific performance if the following conditions are satisfied:[4]

Contract to build sometimes enforced

Firstly, the particulars of the work must be so clearly specified that the court can ascertain without difficulty exactly what it is that requires performance.

Secondly, the interest of the plaintiff in the performance of the work must be of such a substantial nature that he will not be adequately compensated for breach of the contract by damages.[5]

Thirdly, the defendant must, under the contract, be in possession of the land on which the work is to be done.[6]

A plaintiff who failed in a suit in equity for specific performance was originally driven to sue for damages at common law, and it was not until 1858 that the power to award damages as an alternative form of relief was conferred upon the Court of Chancery. In that year Lord Cairns' Act[7] provided that in all cases in which the court had jurisdiction to grant an injunction or an order for specific performance it should be entitled to award damages to the party injured either in addition to or in substitution for such

Damages may be awarded instead of specific performance

1. *Whitwood Chemical Co.* v. *Hardman*, [1891] 2 Ch. 416, at p. 426, *per* LINDLEY, L.J.
2. *Equity*, p. 388.
3. [1893] 1 Ch. 116. But cf. *Beswick* v. *Beswick*, [1968] A.C. 58; [1967] 2 All E.R. 1197, discussed *supra*, p. 612.
4. *Wolverhampton Corporation* v. *Emmons*, [1901] 1 K.B. 515.
5. *Molyneux* v. *Richard*, [1906] 1 Ch. 34, at pp. 43–6.
6. *Carpenters Estates, Ltd.* v. *Davies,* [1940] Ch. 160; [1940] 1 All E.R. 13.
7. 21 and 22 Vict. c. 27.

injunction or specific performance.[1] A plaintiff, therefore, could not claim damages under this Act unless he first proved that he was entitled to specific performance.   The present Chancery Division, however, unlike its predecessor the Court of Chancery, is in better case, for the Judicature Act 1873[2] provided that the High Court of Justice and the Court of Appeal shall grant all such remedies whatsoever as the parties may appear to be entitled to in respect of any legal or equitable claim, so that, as far as possible, all matters in controversy may be finally determined.   Nowadays, therefore, a plaintiff " may come into court and say, ' if you think I am not entitled to specific performance of the whole or any part of the agreement, then give me damages.' "[3]

Specific delivery of chattels

Analogous to the specific performance of contracts is the specific delivery of goods.   At common law the delivery or restitution of an article cannot be enforced.   The remedy in tort for the wrongful withholding of a chattel is either trover for the recovery of damages, or detinue for the recovery of possession.   A plaintiff, however, who succeeds in detinue does not necessarily regain possession, for the judgment gives the defendant the option of returning the chattel or of paying its value.   Again, the remedy against a vendor for non-delivery of the goods sold is an action for damages.

Equitable jurisdiction to order delivery

Equity, however, has long possessed jurisdiction to order the delivery of specific chattels whether the cause of complaint is a breach of contract or not, but it has never been prepared to grant this relief unless the article is of such exceptional value and importance that damages would clearly be an inadequate remedy.[4] Thus specific delivery has been ordered of the famous Pusey horn,[5] an ancient altar piece,[6] and a valuable painting.[7]

Statutory jurisdiction

The common law rule, however, was modified by the Mercantile Law Amendment Act 1856, which provided that in actions for breach of contract to deliver specific goods the court at its discretion might make an order for the delivery of the goods without giving the defendant an option to pay damages.[8] This enactment has been repealed and replaced by the following section of the Sale of Goods Act 1893:[9]

> In any action for breach of contract to deliver specific or ascer-
> tained goods the court may, if it thinks fit . . . direct that the contract
> shall be performed specifically, without giving the defendant the
> option of retaining the goods on payment of damages.

---

1. The Act was repealed by the Statute Law Revision and Civil Procedure Act 1883, but its effect was preserved by a general section (s. 5) in the repealing Act.
2. Now the Judicature Act 1925, section 43.
3. *Elmore* v. *Pirrie* (1887), 57 L.T. 333, *per* KAY, J.
4. Story, *Equity*, s. 709; White and Tudor, *Leading Cases in Equity*, vol. II, pp. 404–9;
5. *Pusey* v. *Pusey* (1684), 1 Vern. 273.
6. *Duke of Somerset* v. *Cookson* (1735), 3 P. Wms. 390.
7. *Lowther* v. *Lowther* (1806), 13 Ves. 95.   In *Dougan* v. *Ley* (1946), 71 C.L.R. 142, the High Court of Australia, after concluding that this equitable principle applies to chattels of exceptional value in the business sense, ordered the specific performance of a contract to sell a vehicle which was already licensed as a taxi-cab.   The exceptional value derived by the buyer from the contract and reflected in the price lay in the fact that the number of licences issued by the local authority was strictly limited.
8. 19 and 20 Vict. c. 97, s. 2.
9. Section 52.

The power given by this section is exercisable whether the property has passed to the buyer or not,[1] always provided that the goods are specific or ascertained.[2] It is, however, a discretionary power and will not be exercised if the chattel is an ordinary article of commerce of no special value or interest, such as a piano[3] or a set of ordinary chairs,[4] where damages will be adequate compensation for the plaintiff. The power given by s. 52 is not an exhaustive statement of the law of specific performance in relation to sale of goods. The court retains an inherent jurisdiction to order specific performance of a contract for the sale of unascertained goods where damages would be an insufficient remedy.[5]

SECTION III. EXTINCTION OF REMEDIES

A right of action for breach of contract may be expressly released either by a release under seal or by accord and satisfaction, or it may be extinguished by the effluxion of time in accordance with the provisions of the Limitation Act 1939. The first two methods have already been described.[6]

The Limitation Act 1939 contains three provisions that impose a time limit within which an action for a breach of a contract must be brought.

The statutory time limits

First, an action founded on simple contract or on tort shall not be brought after the expiration of six years from the date on which the cause of action accrued.[7]

(i) Action founded on simple contract

The expression " cause of action " means the factual situation stated by the plaintiff which, if substantiated, entitles him to a remedy against the defendant.[8] If, when analysed, it discloses a breach of contract, it accrues when that breach occurs, from which moment time begins to run against the plaintiff. The fact that actual damage is not suffered by him until some date later than the breach does not extend the time within which he must sue. If, on the other hand, the factual situation discloses the commission of the tort of negligence, which is not actionable unless actual damage is proved, the cause of action does not accrue until the damage is in fact sustained. When, therefore, the defendant has

Meaning of " cause of action "

---

1. *Jones* v. *Tankerville*, [1909] 2 Ch. 440, at p. 445, *per* PARKER, J.
2. " Specific " means " goods identified and agreed upon at the time a contract of sale is made "; Sale of Goods Act, s. 62 (1). " Ascertained " probably means " identified in accordance with the agreement *after* the time a contract of sale is made ": *Re Wait*, [1927] 1 Ch. 606, at p. 630, *per* ATKIN, L.J.
3. *Whiteley* v. *Hilt*, [1918] 2 K.B. 808, at p. 819.
4. *Cohen* v. *Roche*, [1927] 1 K.B. 169. The chattels dismissed by the learned judge, McCARDIE, J., as " ordinary articles of commerce of no special value or interest " were in fact eight genuine Hepplewhite chairs which had been sold to the plaintiff in 1925 for £60.
5. *Sky Petroleum, Ltd.* v. *V.I.P. Petroleum, Ltd.*, [1974] 1 All E.R. 954; [1974] 1 W.L.R. 576; Treitel, [1966] J.B.L. 211.
6. *Supra,* pp. 533 and 540.
7. Section 2 (1) (a). The period is three years if damages are claimed for personal injuries caused by negligence, nuisance or breach of duty, whether the duty arises contractually or not: Law Reform (Limitation of Actions, etc.) Act 1954, s. 2 (1). By the Limitation Act 1975, this period may be extended if certain conditions are satisfied.
8. *Letang* v. *Cooper*, [1965] 1 Q.B. 232; [1964] 2 All E.R. 929.

acted negligently in the performance of a contract, the time at which the plaintiff's cause of action accrues will not emerge until the source of the duty has been determined.   Is it a duty imposed by the contract or is it the general duty of care required in tort by the law of negligence?   This problem arose in *Bagot* v. *Stevens Scanlan & Co.*[1] on the following facts:

> The defendants, a firm of architects, agreed to supervise the laying of a drainage system on the plaintiff's land.   The work was completed in February, 1957.   About the end of 1961, several of the drainage pipes broke with the result that much damage was caused to the land.   On April 2nd, 1963, the plaintiff sued for damages on the ground that the defendant had neglected his duty to use reasonable care and skill in the supervision of the work.

The preliminary question was whether this action was founded on contract or on tort.   If the duty of care arose *ex contractu*, the action was barred, for the last moment at which its breach occurred was at the completion of the work in February, 1957, more than six years before.   If the duty arose in tort independently of the contract, the plaintiff's claim was not barred, since his cause of action had not accrued until the end of 1961 when the land was damaged.   It was held that the relationship between the parties was essentially contractual and therefore that the duty arose *ex contractu*.

> " It was a contractual relationship, a contractual duty, and any action brought for failure to comply with that duty is, in my view, an action founded on contract.   It is also, in my view, an action founded on contract alone."[2]

(ii) Action upon a specialty

Secondly, an action upon a contract under seal cannot be brought after the expiration of twelve years after the date on which the cause of action accrued.[3]

(iii) Action for an account

Thirdly, an action for an account (*e.g.* by a principal against his agent) cannot be brought in respect of any matter which arose more than six years before the commencement of the action.[4]   This enactment refers to the equitable remedy which has long superseded the common law action for an account.

The right to an account which exists where there is a fiduciary relationship between the parties is not, however, subject to this time-limit of six years.[5]   A fiduciary is regarded as a trustee of any property that he holds on behalf of others, and the Limitation Act provides that an action by a beneficiary for the recovery of property still in the hands of a trustee shall not be subject to any statutory period of limitation.[6]

Effect of defendant's fraud

As a general rule the fact that the plaintiff fails to discover the existence of his cause of action until the expiration of the statutory period does not prevent the operation of the statute.

---

1. [1966] 1 Q.B. 197; [1964] 3 All E.R. 577.
2. *Ibid.*, at p. 204, *per* DIPLOCK, L.J.   To the same effect, see *Howell* v. *Young* (1826), 5 B. & C. 259 (solicitor and client); *Jarvis* v. *Moy, Davies, Smith, Vandervell & Co.*, [1936] 1 K.B. 399 (stockbroker and client).
3. Section 2 (3).   The period was formerly 20 years.
4. Section 2 (2).
5. *Burdick* v. *Garrick* (1870), 5 Ch. App. 233; *Soar* v. *Ashwell*, [1893] 2 Q.B. 390, especially the judgment of BOWEN, L.J.
6. Section 19 (1) (b).   The doctrine of *laches*, however, applies to such an action; *infra*, p. 626.

This rule, however, works a hardship where his ignorance has Law prior to 1940 been caused by the fraud of the defendant. The plaintiff may be the victim of fraud in two respects. Firstly, his action may be based upon the fraud of the defendant. In these circumstances an action of deceit is available to him, but he may remain ignorant of the fact until time has run against him.[1]

Secondly, his cause of action, whatever its nature, may have been fraudulently concealed by the defendant, as for example, by the deliberate destruction of evidence. Common law and equity took different views on these situations.

In both cases equity took the view that time did not begin to run against the plaintiff until he had discovered or ought to have discovered the fraud. At common law, on the other hand, the defendant's fraud did not prevent time from running. After the Judicature Act 1873, the equitable doctrine prevailed when the cause of action had been fraudulently concealed, but it remained doubtful whether it applied to a common law action of deceit when the plaintiff was ignorant of the deceit.[2]

A similar difficulty existed prior to the statute in the case of money paid or property transferred under a mistake of fact. If the plaintiff claimed purely equitable relief, as for example where a trustee claimed the repayment of money mistakenly paid to a *cestui que trust*, time did not begin to run against the plaintiff until he had discovered or ought to have discovered the mistake,[3] but in an action at common law time began to run from the date of payment or transfer.[4]

The Act of 1939, however, has removed these difficulties and Present law with regard to fraud has simplified the law by extending the equitable principles to all actions to which the statutory periods apply. Section 26 provides as follows:

> Where in the case of any action for which a period of limitation is prescribed by this Act, either—
>
> (a) the action is based upon the fraud of the defendant or his agent or of any person through whom he claims or his agent,[5] or
> (b) the right of action is concealed by the fraud of any such person as aforesaid, or
> (c) the action is for relief from the consequences of mistake,
>
> the period of limitation shall not begin to run until the plaintiff has discovered the fraud or the mistake, as the case may be, or could with reasonable diligence have discovered it:
>
> Provided that nothing in this section shall enable any action to be brought to recover, or enforce any charge against, or set aside any transaction affecting, any property which—
>
> (i) in the case of fraud, has been purchased for valuable consideration by a person who was not a party to the fraud and did not at the time of the purchase know or have reason to believe that any fraud had been committed, or

---

1. *Beaman* v. *A.R.T.S., Ltd.*, [1949] 1 K.B. 550, at p. 558; [1949] 1 All E.R. 465.
2. Preston & Newsom, *Limitation of Actions*, 2nd Edn., pp. 228–9.
3. *Brooksbank* v. *Smith* (1836), 2 Y. & C. (Ex.) 58.
4. *Baker* v. *Courage & Co.*, [1910] 1 K.B. 56.
5. As to the meaning of " any person through whom he claims or his agent," see *Eddis* v. *Chichester Constable*, [1969] 2 Ch. 345; [1969] 2 All E.R. 912.

(ii) in the case of mistake, has been purchased for valuable
consideration, subsequently to the transaction in which the
mistake was made, by a person who did not know or have
reason to believe that the mistake had been made.[1]

It has been decided that this proviso, which in terms applies only
to actions for the *recovery* of property, applies also to an action to
recover damages for conversion.[2]

For the purposes of section 26 (b), the word " fraud " is not
confined to deceit as understood by the common law, and it does
not involve any moral turpitude.   It denotes the type of conduct
that was stigmatized by the old Chancery ·Court as " equitable
fraud."[3]   This concept defies exact definition, but it comprises
inter alia " conduct which, having regard to some special relationship between the two parties concerned, is an unconscionable
thing for the one to do towards the other."[4]

The operation of this equitable doctrine is well illustrated by
Applegate v. *Moss*.[5]

> By a contract made in February, 1957, the defendant agreed to
> build two houses for the plaintiffs and to support them on a raft
> foundation reinforced with a steel network of a specified type.   He
> employed a Mr. Piper, an independent contractor, to do the work.
> The plaintiffs went into occupation of the houses when they were
> completed towards the end of 1957.   In 1965, it was observed that,
> owing to the defective manner in which the foundations had been
> constructed, the houses were irreparable and unsafe for habitation.
> There was no raft, the reinforcement was grossly inferior to that
> specified and wide cracks had appeared beneath the houses.

The plaintiffs claimed damages for breach of contract.   Despite
the fact that their action was brought more than six years after the
breach of contract, they succeeded on the ground that there had
been concealed fraud within the meaning of section 26 (b) of the
Limitation Act 1939.   " The builder put in rubbishy foundations
and then covered them up."[6]   The contention that the defendant
was not responsible for the misdeeds of Mr. Piper failed.   One
reason was the finding of the trial judge that he was aware of the
defective way in which the work was being performed.   But even
if this could not be fully substantiated, he was responsible for
what Mr. Piper had failed to do.   The normal rule, that a man is
not liable for the acts or omissions of his independent contractor,
is not to be extended to a case under the statute where the defendant
has agreed that *he* will erect a house.[7]

---

1. *Phillips-Higgins* v. *Harper*, [1954] 1 Q.B. 411; [1954] 1 All E.R. 116.
2. *Eddis* v. *Chichester Constable*, [1969] 2 Ch. 345, *per* Lord DENNING, M.R., and
FENTON ATKINSON, L.J.; WINN, L.J., expressed no opinion on the point.
In the instant case, however, the protection afforded by the proviso could not
avail the purchaser since he had notice of the fraud.   Jackson, 32 M.L.R.
692.
3. *Clark* v. *Woor*, [1965] 2 All E.R. 353; [1965] 1 W.L.R. 650 (a simple
illustration of the operation of s. 26).
4. *Kitchen* v. *Royal Air Force Association*, [1958] 1 W.L.R. 563, at p. 573, *per*
Lord EVERSHED, M.R.   *Applegate* v. *Moss, supra*, at p. 413, *per* Lord
DENNING, M.R., at p. 417, *per* MEGAW, L.J.
5. [1971] 1 Q.B. 406.   See also *King* v. *Victor Parsons & Co.*, [1973] 1 All
E.R. 206; [1973] 1 W.L.R. 29.
6. *Ibid.*, at p. 413, *per* Lord DENNING, M.R.
7. *Ibid.*, at p. 415, *per* EDMUND DAVIES, L.J.

Special provisions are made to meet the case of a plaintiff who is an infant or of unsound mind at the time when his cause of action accrues. Such a person may sue despite the disability, but is not prejudiced if he fails to do so, for it is enacted that the action may be brought at any time within six years from the removal of the disability or from his death, whichever event first occurs, notwithstanding that the period of limitation from the accrual of the cause of action has expired.[1]

Extension of time in case of disability

It must be observed that there is no extension of time unless the disability exists when the cause of action accrues. When time has once begun to run it is not stopped by the subsequent occurrence of some disability, as for example where the plaintiff becomes insane soon after the accrual of the cause of action.[2] Again, if a person under a disability is succeeded by another person in like case there is no further extension of time by reason of the disability of the second person.[3]

Supervening disability

Where the same person is affected by successive disabilities, as for example where a plaintiff who is an infant at the accrual of the cause of action later becomes insane, the question whether there is a further extension of time depends upon whether there is an interval between the disabilities. Successive disabilities, unless they are separated by an interval, exclude the operation of the statute. If, for instance, the plaintiff is an infant when his cause of action accrues but becomes insane before he reaches his majority, time does not begin to run until the insanity is determined; but if he is sane at eighteen time begins to run against him and is not stopped by his later insanity, however soon this may occur.[4]

Successive disabilities

There was one case prior to 1940 in which the disability of the defendant prevented time from running, namely, where at the time of the accrual of the cause of action he was beyond the seas. In this case a statute of Anne provided that time should not begin to run in his favour until he returned from beyond the seas.[5] This statute has now, however, been repealed.[6]

Defendant's absence beyond seas no longer a disability

In the particular case of a claim to a debt or other liquidated sum, it has long been recognized that time which has started to run against the creditor may be stopped and made to start afresh by an acknowledgment of liability, or by a part payment made by the debtor. This is so even though the acknowledgment or payment is not given until after the expiration of the full statutory period. The law on the matter, however, was far from uniform before 1940. There were express statutory provisions that determined the effect of an acknowledgment in the case of actions relating to land, but the only enactment that concerned contracts

Effect of acknowledgment or part payment

---

1. Sections 22 and 31 (2). In this context a person of unsound mind means a person who, by reason of mental disorder within the meaning of the Mental Health Act 1959, is incapable of managing and administering his affairs; *Kirby* v. *Leather*, [1965] 2 Q.B. 367; [1965] 2 All E.R. 441. The Criminal Justice Act 1948 removed as from April 18th, 1949, the former disability of a convict sentenced to death or to penal servitude.
2. Section 22 (a).
3. Section 22 (b).
4. *Borrows* v. *Ellison* (1871), L.R. 6 Exch. 128.
5. 4 & 5 Anne, c. 3, s. 19.
6. Limitation Act 1939, Schedule.

was the Civil Procedure Act 1833,[1] which applied to specialty debts alone. It provided that if a written acknowledgment was signed by the party liable upon a contract under seal or by his agent, the creditor could sustain an action at any time within the next twenty years. There was no direct statutory provision that an acknowledgment of a simple contract debt should be effective, but a doctrine on the matter was gradually evolved by the courts. This judge-made rule was that any acknowledgment which amounted to an express or to an implied promise to pay took the case out of the statute and made time begin afresh. The existence of this doctrine, once it had been judicially established, was recognized by two statutes, one of which required that the acknowledgment should be in writing and signed by the person chargeable,[2] while the other made the signature of his agent sufficient.[3] There was frequently, however, the greatest difficulty in deciding whether a particular acknowledgment amounted to a promise to pay, for if it failed to satisfy this test it was totally ineffective.[4] There is no necessity any longer to discuss the somewhat subtle distinctions that formerly obscured the subject, for simple contract debts have now been put upon the same footing as specialty debts. The Act of 1939 provides as follows:

> Where any right of action has accrued to recover any debt or other liquidated pecuniary claim . . . and the person liable or accountable therefor acknowledges the claim or makes any payment in respect thereof, the right shall be deemed to have accrued on and not before the date of the acknowledgment or the last payment.[5]

Such an acknowledgment does not create a new cause of action.

> " The subsection does not change the nature of the right: it provides that in the specific circumstances of an acknowledgment or payment the right shall be given a notional birthday and on that day, like the phoenix of fable, it rises again in renewed youth—and also like the phoenix it is still itself."[6]

The acknowledgment must be in writing and must be signed by the person making it.[7] An acknowledgment or a payment may be made by the agent of the person liable, and it must be made to the person, or to the agent of the person, who is the claimant of the debt.[8] The Privy Council has suggested that an acknowledgment is not effective unless it is an admission of a present debt subsisting at the date of signature and that it is not enough to admit that the debt existed in the past. On this basis, the entry of a debt in the annual balance sheet of a company does not operate as an acknowledgment, since it is usually completed some considerable time before it is signed at the annual general meeting.[9] More recently however this suggestion was rejected by

---

1. Section 5.
2. Statute of Frauds Amendment Act 1828 (Lord Tenterden's Act), s. 1.
3. Mercantile Law Amendment Act 1856, s. 13.
4. See for example *Spencer* v. *Hemmerde*, [1922] 2 A.C. 507.
5. Limitation Act 1939, s. 23 (4).
6. *Busch* v. *Stevens*, [1963] 1 Q.B. 1, at p. 6, *per* LAWTON, J.; [1962] 1 All E.R. 413, at p. 415.
7. Limitation Act 1939, s. 24 (1).
8. Limitation Act, s. 24 (2).
9. *Consolidated Agencies, Ltd.* v. *Bertram, Ltd.*, [1965] A.C. 470; [1964] 3 All E.R. 282.

BRIGHTMAN, J., in *Re Gee & Co. (Woolwich), Ltd.*[1] Provided that the present existence of the debt is admitted, the precise amount of what is due need not be stated. It is sufficient if this is ascertainable by extrinsic evidence.[2]

The effect of an acknowledgment or a part payment by one of a number of persons liable for a liquidated debt is determined by the statute. An acknowledgment binds the person acknowledging and his successors only, not his co-debtors; but a part payment binds all the co-debtors unless it is made after the expiration of the statutory period, *i.e.* after the expiration of six or twelve years according as the debt is due under a simple or a sealed contract.[3] A part payment operates for the benefit of all the co-debtors, and it is only fair that if they take the advantage they should also take the disadvantage; but a payment made after the statutory period has run its full course can scarcely be an advantage to those who are already free from liability.[4]

Acknowledgment or payment by co-debtors

An acknowledgment is not effective unless it relates to a debt or other liquidated sum.[5] Thus if A is entitled to recover unliquidated damages for breach of a contract by B, an acknowledgment by B of his liability does not revive the cause of action.[6]

Acknowledgment confined to liquidated debt

If the statutory period expires before action brought, the plaintiff's *right* is not extinguished. He is merely deprived of his two remedies of action and set-off. The statute is procedural not substantive.[7] A statute-barred debt is still payable despite the fact that its payment cannot be enforced by action, and if there is any other method by which the creditor can obtain satisfaction it is at his disposal. Thus if a debtor pays money on account of debts, some of which are statute-barred and some not, and does not expressly indicate that the payment is made in respect of those which are still actionable, the creditor may appropriate the money to those that are statute-barred.[8] Again if a party is entitled to a lien on goods for a general balance, and he gets possession of the goods of his debtor, he may hold them until his whole demand is satisfied notwithstanding that it is barred by the Limitation Act.[9]

Effect of the Statute is to bar the remedy, not to extinguish the right

It is expressly enacted that the statutory provisions shall not apply to any claim for specific performance of a contract or for an injunction or for other equitable relief.[10] The object of this section is to preserve those principles applicable to claims for relief that, prior to the Judicature Act 1873, could be entertained only by courts of equity. The attitude of equity with regard to Statutes of Limitation and to a failure to pursue a remedy with expedition may, so far as contracts are concerned, be summarized in two propositions.

Effect of lapse of time on equitable claims

---

1. [1975] Ch. 52; [1974] 1 All E.R. 1149.
2. *Dungate* v. *Dungate,* [1965] 3 All E.R. 818; [1965] 1 W.L.R. 1477, explaining *Good* v. *Parry,* [1963] 2 Q.B. 418; [1963] 2 All E.R. 59.
3. Limitation Act, s. 25 (5), (6).
4. Law Revision Committee 5th Interim Report, p. 28.
5. *Whitehead* v. *Howard* (1820), 2 Brod. & Bing. 372.
6. *Boydell* v. *Drummond* (1808), 2 Camp. 157, at p. 162.
7. *Rodriguez* v. *Parker,* [1967] 1 Q.B. 116; [1966] 2 All E.R. 349.
8. Law Revision Committee 5th Interim Report, p. 32; *Mills* v. *Fowkes* (1839), 5 Bing. N.C. 455.
9. *Spears* v. *Hartley* (1800), 3 Esp. 81.
10. Section 2 (7).

In some
cases equity
acts on the
analogy of
the statute

First, in the case of equitable claims that formerly fell within its concurrent jurisdiction, equity acts on the analogy of the current Limitation Act.   In the words of Lord WESTBURY:

> " Where the remedy in equity is correspondent to the remedy at law, and the latter is subject to a limit in point of time by the Statute of Limitations, a court of equity acts by analogy to the statute, and imposes on the remedy it affords the same limitation.   This is the meaning of the common phrase that a court of equity acts by analogy to the Statute of Limitations, the meaning being that, where the suit in equity corresponds with an action at law which is included in the words of the statute, a court of equity adopts the enactment of the statute as its own rule of procedure."[1]

Hence the Limitation Act 1939, after enacting that its provisions shall not apply to a claim for equitable relief, says " except in so far as any provision thereof may be applied by the court by analogy . . . "[2] Section 2 (2), for instance, provides that an action for an account shall not be brought in respect of any matter which arose more than six years before the commencement of the action.   This section does not apply to an equitable claim for an account, as for example where the executor of a deceased partner claims against the surviving partner, but nevertheless relief will be withheld if the statutory period of six years has expired.[3]   Any proceedings in equity to recover a simple contract debt are subject to this doctrine of analogy.   Thus an action brought in the Chancery Division by one *cestui que trust* against another *cestui que trust* to recover money paid by the trustee to the latter under a mistake of fact is in the nature of a common law action for money had and received, and, by analogy to the Limitation Act, the claim will be barred after the lapse of six years.[4]

The equitable
doctrine of
laches

The second proposition is that in the exercise of its exclusive jurisdiction—in the case of purely equitable claims—equity, in accordance with the maxim *vigilantibus et non dormientibus lex succurrit*, refuses to grant relief to stale claims.   A plaintiff who has been dilatory in the prosecution of his equitable claim and has acquiesced in the wrong done to him is said to be guilty of *laches* and is barred from relief, although his claim is not affected by any statute of limitation.

No exact rule can be laid down as to when laches will or will not bar a claim.   It is a question that depends in each case upon the degree of diligence that might reasonably have been expected from the plaintiff, but the two important factors to be considered are acquiescence on the part of the plaintiff and the length of the delay.

> " The doctrine of laches in courts of equity is not an arbitrary or a technical doctrine.   Where it would be *practically unjust* to give a remedy, either because the party has by his conduct done that which might fairly be regarded as an equivalent to a waiver of it, or where by his conduct and neglect he has, though perhaps not waiving that remedy, put the other party in a situation in which

---

1. *Knox* v. *Gye* (1872), L.R. 5 H.L. 656, at p. 674.
2. Section 2 (7).
3. *Knox* v. *Gye, supra.*
4. *Re Robinson, McLaren* v. *Public Trustee,* [1911] 1 Ch. 502.

it would not be reasonable to place him if the remedy were afterwards to be asserted, in either of these cases lapse of time and delay are most material "[1]

In the case of contracts the doctrine is well illustrated by an action for specific performance or for the rescission of a contract on the ground of misrepresentation. Those who seek specific performance of contracts must be unusually vigilant and active in asserting their rights, especially where the subject-matter of the contract is one that fluctuates in value from day to day. Thus, in the leading case of *Pollard* v. *Clayton*:[2]

Effect of delay on suit for specific performance

> The defendants agreed to raise and sell at a fixed price per ton to the plaintiffs all the coal contained in a particular mine. After performing this contract in part the defendants refused to deliver any more coal, but instead sold it to other persons, and when objection was taken to their default they referred the plaintiffs to their solicitors. The plaintiffs waited for eleven months after this before filing a bill for specific performance.

It was held that the delay which occurred after the plaintiffs had become aware of the breach of contract was a complete bar to their equitable claim.

The effect of lapse of time upon the right to sue for rescission of a contract has already been considered.[3]

This doctrine of laches is preserved by the Limitation Act 1939, in a section which provides that:

> " Nothing in this Act shall affect any equitable jurisdiction to refuse relief on the ground of acquiescence or otherwise."[4]

---

1. *Lindsay Petroleum Co.* v. *Hurd* (1874), L.R. 5 P.C. 221, at p. 239, *per* Lord SELBORNE.
2. (1855), 1 K. & J. 462.
3. *Supra*, p. 269.
4. Section 29.

PART IX
QUASI-CONTRACT

Quasi-Contract

SECTION I. INTRODUCTION AND RATIONALE

THE very title of this chapter will at once lead the practised reader to suspect the pedigree of the cases with which he is to deal. The prefix " quasi " is commonly used by lawyers when they wish to extenuate, if not to justify, a classification which, though convenient in practice or hallowed by tradition, is not supported by logic. The present instance is no exception to the rule. Under the general heading of quasi-contract is grouped a number of cases, which, however else they may be rationalized, have at least this element in common, that they have little or no affinity with contract. A simple illustration is afforded by the action to recover money paid by mistake. If a plaintiff, on an

The expression " quasi-contract " is a misnomer

erroneous interpretation of the facts, pays to the defendant a sum of money which he does not really owe, law, no less than justice, will require the defendant to restore it.   But his obligation is manifestly not based upon consent, even in the extended meaning borne by the word in the English law, and its description as a quasi-contractual liability serves only to emphasize its remoteness from any genuine conception of contract.   The anomaly is not peculiar to our own jurisprudence.   In all systems and in all ages the difficulty has been experienced of grouping a residuary class of case which seems to defy definition.   The Roman lawyers were content to explain them as misfits.   Justinian refers to " those obligations which do not originate, properly speaking, in contract, but which, as they do not arise from a delict, seem to be quasi-contractual."[1]   The English lawyers may pray in aid the accident of history.   The action of assumpsit, accepted in the early part of the seventeenth century as the normal remedy for breaches of contract, was extended in the latter part of that century to cases which in truth were not contractual at all.[2] It was natural for lawyers, whose juristic logic was conditioned by the forms of action, to think of these cases in terms of their remedy, and, as indebitatus assumpsit had an all-pervading odour of contract, to regard them as in some measure to be grouped with contract.   It has thus become necessary to treat of them in a book on contract, not only because of their well-established nomenclature, but also because they are, in some instances at least, involved almost inextricably with contractual language and procedure.

Attempts at rationalisa-tion

So long as English lawyers were content to enumerate the cases of quasi-contract for which they provided a remedy as so many species of indebitatus assumpsit they evaded the odious task of rationalisation.   But as soon as the urge was felt to explore their furistic basis controversy was born.   The first and most ambitious attempt to provide such a basis was made by Lord MANSFIELD in *Moses* v. *Macferlan* in 1760.[3]   He was concerned to explain, and not only to apply, the action for money had and received to the plaintiff's use.

> " The gist of this kind of action," he said, " is that the defendant, upon the circumstances of the case, is obliged by the ties of natural justice and equity to refund the money."

It should be observed that Lord MANSFIELD did not use the word " equity " to denote the jurisdiction of Chancery but as a synonym for *jus naturale*.[4]   Nor, while he based the obligations of quasi-contract upon the duty of restoring benefits unjustly obtained, did he assert that in every such case an action would lie.   As he declared in *Weston* v. *Downes*, " I am a great friend to the action for money had and received, and therefore I am not for stretching, lest I should endanger it."[5]   The principle of unjust benefit

---

1. Just. Inst. III.   Tit. xxvii, pr.
2. *Supra*, p. 10.
3. (1760) 2 Burr. 1005.
4. See FARWELL, L.J., in *Baylis* v. *Bishop of London*, [1913] 1 Ch. 127, at p. 137.
5. (1778), 1 Doug. K.B. 23, at. p. 24.

explained the cases falling within the scope of quasi-contract: it did not automatically invoke the remedy.

Subject to these qualifications the rationalization of quasi-contract upon the basis of unjust benefit was accepted for over a hundred years.[1] But when, in the course of the nineteenth century, the forms of action were replaced by the dichotomy of tort and contract, Lord MANSFIELD's views were challenged. The various actions grouped under the insidious title of quasi-contract were clearly not tortious; if the new antithesis of the common law were inevitable, they must perforce be contractual. And, as they were equally clearly not based upon any genuine consent, they must rest upon an implied or hypothetical agreement. Such, at least, was the conclusion of Lord SUMNER in *Sinclair* v. *Brougham* in 1914.[2] His major premise was the rigid and exclusive classification of common law actions into tort and contract. Into one or other category all must fall. It followed that actions for money had and received and all other quasi-contractual remedies must be classified as contractual. This view was supported by the historical fact that their origin lay in the writ of assumpsit. " All these causes of action are common species of the genus *assumpsit*. All now rest, and long have rested, upon a notional or imputed promise to pay."[3] The criterion of unjust benefit, moreover, even if, in defiance of true principle, it were to prevail, was vague and ambiguous and difficult to apply.

Lord Mansfield's views challenged by Lord Sumner

Lord SUMNER's judgment tended to sway judicial opinion against Lord MANSFIELD's doctrine. In *Holt* v. *Markham*[4] Lord Justice SCRUTTON referred to the " now discarded doctrine of Lord MANSFIELD " and lamented the development of the action for money had and received as a " history of well-meaning sloppiness of thought." In *Morgan* v. *Ashcroft*[5] Lord GREENE, in more temperate language, agreed that " Lord MANSFIELD's views upon those matters, attractive though they be, cannot now be accepted as laying the true foundation of the claim." In *Re Diplock, Diplock* v. *Wintle*, WYNN-PARRY, J., in the court of first instance, regarded the action for money had and received as " a common law action on the case founded upon an implied promise to pay," and the Court of Appeal, while reversing his judgment on other grounds, agreed with him on this.[6] But the concept of unjust benefit has not lacked its judicial supporters. Lord WRIGHT in the *Fibrosa* case confessed his sympathy with Lord MANSFIELD.[7]

Diversity of judicial opinion

---

1. See *Edwards* v. *Bates* (1844), 7 Man. & G. 590; *Freeman* v. *Jeffries* (1869), L.R. 4 Ex. 189; Bullen and Leake, *Precedents of Pleading*, 3rd Edn., p. 44.
2. [1914] A.C. 398, at p. 452. See also Lord HALDANE, at p. 415.
3. [1914] A.C., at p. 452.
4. [1923] 1 K.B. 504, at p. 513.
5. [1938] 1 K.B. 49, at p. 62.
6. [1947] Ch. 716, at p. 724; [1947] 1 All E.R. 522, at pp. 527, 528; and on appeal, [1948] Ch. 465, at pp. 480, 481; [1948] 2 All E.R. 318, at p. 326. The House of Lords, affirming the decision of the Court of Appeal, expressed no opinion upon the basis of quasi-contract at common law. The case is reported *sub nom. Ministry of Health* v. *Simpson*, [1951] A.C. 251; [1950] 2 All E.R. 1137.
7. *Fibrosa Spolka Akcyjna* v. *Fairbairn, Lawson Combe Barbour, Ltd.*, [1943] A.C. 32, at p. 61. See also his remarks in *Brooks Wharf and Bull Wharf, Ltd.* v. *Goodman Brothers*, [1937] 1 K.B. 534, at p. 545; [1936] 3 All E.R. 696, at p. 707.

" It is clear ", he said, " that any civilized system of law is
bound to provide remedies for cases of what has been called unjust
enrichment or unjust benefit, that is, to prevent a man from retaining
the money of, or some benefit derived from, another which it is
against conscience that he should keep.　Such remedies in English
law are generically different from remedies in contract or in tort, and
are now recognized to fall within a third category of the common
law which has been called quasi-contract or restitution."

Lord WRIGHT then pointed out that Lord SUMNER's observations
in *Sinclair* v. *Brougham* were *obiter dicta* and added:[1]

" Serious legal writers have seemed to say that these words of the
great judge in *Sinclair* v. *Brougham* closed the door to any theory
of unjust enrichment in English law.　I do not understand why or
how.　It would indeed be a *reductio ad absurdum* of the doctrine of
precedents.　In fact, the common law still employs the action for
money had and received as a practical and useful, if not complete or
ideally perfect, instrument to prevent unjust enrichment, aided by
the various methods of technical equity, which are also available, as
they were found to be in *Sinclair* v. *Brougham.*"

So, too, Lord ATKIN in *United Australia, Ltd.* v. *Barclays
Bank, Ltd.*, while he found it necessary to admit that the action
was based upon a fictitious contract, characterized the fiction as
" obvious," " fanciful " and " transparent."

" These fantastic resemblances of contracts invented in order to
meet requirements of the law as to forms of action which have now
disappeared should not in these days be allowed to affect actual
rights.　When these ghosts of the past stand in the path of justice
clanking their mediæval chains, the proper course for the judge is
to pass through them undeterred."[2]

Yet a third school of judges has discreetly treated the whole
problem as an open question.　In three cases, decided in 1950 and
in 1951, Lord RADCLIFFE preferred not to argue " whether the
action for money had and received does or does not depend on an
imputed promise to pay;" Lord PORTER thought that " the exact
status of the law of unjust enrichment was not yet assured;" while
Lord SIMONDS more frigidly declined to " embark on the rather
arid dispute " as to the basis of the action.[3]

Upon this prolonged judicial controversy three observations
may be allowed.　In the first place, the dichotomy of tort and
contract upon which Lord SUMNER founded his argument is an
innovation of the nineteenth century, remote from the development of the common law and scarcely to be trusted as a guide
to its decisions.[4]　To associate the writ of *indebitatus assumpsti*

---

1. [1943] A.C., at p. 64.
2. [1941] A.C. 1, at pp. 27–9; [1940] 4 All E.R. 20, at pp. 35–37.　In *Metropolitan Police District Receiver* v. *Croydon Corporation*, [1957] 2 Q.B. 154,
infra, p. 639, the Court of Appeal discussed the questions involved in the
case in the language of " unjust enrichment " and " unjust benefit."
3. See *Boissevain* v. *Weil*, [1950] A.C. 327, at p. 341; [1950] 1 All E.R. 728,
at p. 734; *Reading* v. *A.-G.*, [1951] A.C. 507, at p. 513; [1951] 1 All E.R.
617, at p. 619; *Ministry of Health* v. *Simpson*, [1951] A.C. 251, at p. 275;
[1950] 2 All E.R. 1137, at p. 1146.
4. The point was taken by Lord DUNEDIN in *Sinclair* v. *Brougham*, [1914] A.C.
398, at p. 432.　See also Lord WRIGHT in his article on the case, *Legal
Essays and Addresses*, p. 1, and in 57 L.Q.R. 200.

with the idea of agreement is to be guilty of what Lord Justice SCRUTTON might have called a " well-meaning distortion of historical perspective." In the second place, the necessity, to which Lord SUMNER was driven, of basing the action for money had and received on the implication of a contract, betrays the difficulties inherent in his solution. In the whole scheme of English law few phrases may be found more doubtful and more treacherous than that of " implied contract ". In the third place, the reproach of ambiguity with which Lord MANSFIELD's principle was visited seems scarcely less merited by Lord SUMNER's creed. The proof of unjust benefit is at least as simple and intelligible as the pursuit of a fictitious contract. Lord Justice SCRUTTON himself seems to have admitted the hazards of the latter exercise and to be content to chastise Lord MANSFIELD without the fatigue of constructing an alternative theory. " I agree with Lord SUMNER's view that it is very hard to reduce to one common formula the conditions under which the law will imply a promise to repay money received to the plaintiff's use. I do not think the time has come in this case to do it."[1]

Academic, as well as judicial, opinion has been divided upon the merits of Lord MANSFIELD's doctrine. But in the latest and most searching study of English quasi-contract, Goff and Jones have accepted as its rationale the principle of unjust benefit or or unjust enrichment. This principle " presupposes three things: first, that the defendant has been enriched by the receipt of a benefit; secondly, that he has been so enriched at the plaintiff's expense; and thirdly, that it would be unjust to allow him to retain the benefit."[2] The learned authors have also faced, and turned to profit, a contibutory difficulty in the analysis and development of quasi-contract: the fact that it transcends the traditional demarcation between law and equity. It is significant that both in *Sinclair* v. *Brougham* and in *Re Diplock* the judges were driven to examine both common law and equity; and Lord WRIGHT said of the former case that it " demonstrated a category of claims distinct from contract or tort or trust."[3] The merger of quasi-contract in a distinct and generic doctrine of restitution, which Lord WRIGHT thus envisaged, has been widely advocated in the United States. In his *Unjust Enrichment: A Comparative Analysis* Dawson has shown that the law of quasi-contract in the United States is wider in scope than in England. Lord MANSFIELD had based his rationalisation upon the common count for money had and received.[3] In this count the transfer or the receipt of money was an essential element. In the United States there are no distinctions based on the form or nature of the grain received. It is a working hypothesis that " any unexplained gain (not only money) must ordinarily be restored through quasi-contract if a money judgment will suffice."

Restitution a generic doctrine

---

1. In *Holt* v. *Markham*, [1923] 1 K.B. 504, at p. 514.
2. *The Law of Restitution* (1966), especially at p. 14.
3. Wright, *Legal Essays and Addresses*, p. 1.
4. *Supra*, pp. 632–3.

American lawyers, moreover, have developed with enthusiasm the concept of the constructive trust, with its offshoot the equitable lien. This concept " has taken a place beside quasi-contract as a general remedy, giving specific rather than money restitution."[1]

In England, Goff and Jones have accepted the need for a merger of the relevant rules, not only of common law and equity but also of admiralty law, as components of a distinct branch of jurisprudence. It will be interesting to see if either the courts or the legislature will follow this generous lead and finally free quasi-contract of its historical associations with assumpsit.

SECTION II. CLASSIFICATION OF QUASI-CONTRACTS

Difficult to classify the cases

THE intractable nature of the material comprised under the title of quasi-contract is evident not only in the competing offers of rationalisation, but also in the varied, and sometimes desperate, attempts that have been made at classification. Before the abolition of the forms of action, it was enough to use the language of pleading and to talk of actions for money had and received by the defendant to the plaintiff's use. Since their abolition a more logical analysis has been sought, if not found. In 1931 Professor Winfield defined " genuine " quasi-contract as " liability, not exclusively referable to any other head of the law, imposed upon a particular person to pay money to another particular person on the ground of unjust benefit."[2] A liability which has to be described as " not exclusively referable to any other head of the law " would seem especially difficult to disentangle from other and more orthodox types of obligation; and, indeed, the large range of doubtful country to be covered is indicated by Professor Winfield's fourfold classification into pseudo-quasi-contracts, pure quasi-contracts, quasi-contracts alternative to some other form of liability and doubtful quasi-contracts.[3] In *The Law of Restitution* Goff and Jones recognize three main classes: (1) Where the defendant has acquired a benefit from or by the act of the plaintiff, (2) Where the defendant has acquired from a third party a benefit for which he must account to the plaintiff, (3) Where the defendant has acquired a benefit through his own wrongful act. Each class has a number of sub-divisions. For the purpose of the present book, which may not anticipate the judicial or legislative adoption of restitution as a separate and comprehensive branch of English law, it is perhaps sufficient to group decided cases under two main heads, those which are generally accepted as quasi-contractual and those which remain doubtful.

Two main classes

---

1. Dawson, *Unjust Enrichment : A Comparative Analysis*, pp. 22, 25–26, 30–32, 34–35.
2. Winfield, *Province of the Law of Tort,* p. 119.
3. *Ibid.,* at p. 148.

A. GENUINE QUASI-CONTRACTS

Those cases which are generally accepted as genuine quasi-contracts may, for the sake of convenience, be considered under six separate heads.

I. MONEY PAID BY THE PLAINTIFF TO THE DEFENDANT'S USE

If the plaintiff has been compelled to pay money for which the defendant is liable, he may sue the defendant for the amount so paid. In this short and simple statement of the law two points must be stressed. To succeed in his claim the plaintiff must prove (1) that he has been constrained to pay the money and (2) that it is money for which the defendant was legally liable.

(i) The plaintiff must have been constrained to pay the money

Voluntary payment not recoverable

The distinction must be drawn at once between sums which the plaintiff has been constrained to pay by reasonable fear of some legal process brought or to be brought against him and sums which he pays voluntarily on the defendant's behalf. The Roman law, indeed, through its doctrine of *negotiorum gestio*, catered for the volunteer who incurred expense in the necessary protection of the defendant's property.[1] But the English common law knows no such doctrine. In the words of Lord BOWEN,

> "The general principle is, beyond all question, that work and labour done or money expended by one man to preserve or benefit the property of another do not, according to English law, create any lien upon the property saved or benefited, nor, even if standing alone, create any obligation to repay the expenditure. Liabilities are not to be forced upon people behind their backs any more than you can confer a benefit upon a man against his will."[2]

Thus in *Macclesfield Corporation* v. *Great Central Railway*[3] a canal company, the predecessors in title of the defendants, had, under statutory powers, made a canal by cutting through an old highway, which they carried by a new bridge over the canal. The roadway of the bridge had become dangerous through lack of repair, and the corporation, as the highway authority, called upon the defendants to repair it. When the defendants refused, the corporation did the work itself. It was held by the Court of Appeal that the legal duty to repair was cast upon the defendants and not upon the corporation. The corporation had therefore acted as a mere volunteer in the work it had done and, whatever the remedy whereby the defendants could be required to perform their duty, it could not sue the defendants in quasi-contract for the sums expended.

The generally accepted view that common law forbids the

---

1. See Buckland, *Text-book of Roman Law*, 2nd Edn., p. 537.
2. *Falcke* v. *Scottish Imperial Insurance Co.* (1886), 34 Ch.D. 234, at p. 248.
3. [1911] 2 K.B. 528.

recovery of a voluntary payment was doubted in the case of *Schneider* v. *Eisovitch*.[1]

> The plaintiff had been injured, and her husband killed, through the negligence of the defendant while all three were motoring in France.   While she was still unconscious, her brother-in-law flew out from England to help her and bring her home.   It was clear that he acted simply as a volunteer.   The plaintiff claimed to include his expenses in her damages and undertook to pay them over to him.

PAULL, J., allowed her to recover these expenses.   " Strict legal liability is not the be-all and end-all of a tortfeasor's liability." In the later case of *Gage* v. *King*, DIPLOCK, J., felt bound to differ from PAULL, J.,[2] but in two recent cases the Court of Appeal has approved the view of PAULL, J.[3]

Exceptional case of salvage at sea

One clear exception to the rule is in the case of salvage at sea. The owner of a ship or of a cargo is bound to compensate a plaintiff who rescues his property from imminent peril, and this obligation has always been regarded as quasi-contractual.

> " It is a legal liability, arising out of the fact that property has been saved, that the owner of the property who has had the benefit of it shall make remuneration to those who have conferred the benefit upon him, notwithstanding that he has not entered into any contract on the subject."[4]

The exception, however, as it depends, not on the common law, but on the maritime law administered in Admiralty jurisdiction, is of the character that proves the rule.[5]

Nature of the constraint

At common law, therefore, the mere volunteer, officious or benevolent, has no right of action.   Only if the plaintiff has paid money under constraint is he entitled to sue the defendant for restitution.   The nature of the constraint varies with the circumstances.   The most direct form is the pressure of some such legal process as distress of goods, actual or threatened.   A simple illustration is afforded by the eighteenth-century case of *Exall* v. *Partridge*:[6]

> Exall had left his carriage upon Partridge's premises, and Partridge's landlord, as permitted by the current law, distrained on all the goods on the premises, including this carriage.   To prevent the seizure of the carriage, Exall paid to the landlord the arrears of rent due by Partridge.   It was held that he could recover the sums so paid from Partridge.

A somewhat different form of legal constraint is exemplified by the case of *Brooks Wharf* v. *Goodman Brothers*:[7]

1. [1960] 2 Q.B. 430; [1960] 1 All E.R. 169.   See Goodhart, 76 L.Q.R. 187.
2. [1961] 1 Q.B. 188; [1960] 3 All E.R. 62.   See also *Allen* v, *Waters & Co.*, [1935] 1 K.B. 200; *Wilson* v. *McLean* (1961), 106 C.L.R. 523.
3. *Cunningham* v. *Harrison*, [1973] Q.B. 942, [1973] 3 All E.R. 463; *Donnelly* v. *Joyce*, [1974] Q.B. 454; [1973] 3 All E.R. 475.
4. *The Five Steel Barges* (1890), 15 P.D. 142, at p. 146.
5. On maritime salvage in general see Goff and Jones, *The Law of Restitution*, pp. 248–61.
6. (1799), 8 Term. Rep. 308.
7. [1937] 1 K.B. 534; [1936] 3 All E.R. 696.

A contract was made between the plaintiffs and the defendants whereby the plaintiffs agreed to warehouse certain goods which the defendants were importing from Russia, and the defendants agreed to pay certain wharf charges. As soon as the goods were imported, the defendants became liable for the customs duties. But, before the defendants had paid them, the goods were stolen from the wharf without negligence on the plaintiffs' part. The authorities then made a demand on the plaintiffs, as warehousemen, for the amount of the duties under the Customs Consolidation Act 1876, and the plaintiffs paid. Had they refused, they would have committed an offence against the Act. It was held that the plaintiffs could recover the amount as money paid to the use of the defendants.

In the first of these cases the plaintiff was constrained by the threatened loss of his property, and in the second by the fact that he would otherwise have committed a statutory offence. Each in its different way illustrates the nature of the constraint required by the law. To catalogue in detail the types of coercion which will create a quasi-contractual liability would be difficult and, in the context of this book, improper. One or two further instances must suffice.[1] Thus a surety who pays to the creditor the whole amount due by the principal debtor may recover it from the latter, or he may sue for a contribution from his co-sureties. In such a case, " the bottom of contribution is a fixed principle of justice, and is not founded in contract."[2] So, too, one of a number of joint tortfeasors, who has been compelled to pay the entire damages to the injured party, may recover a contribution from his associates. This right, indeed, was at one time denied at the common law;[3] but, after a gradual judicial amelioration,[4] it has now been recognized by statute as a general rule.[5]

(ii) The defendant must have been legally liable to pay the money

The circumstances must show that, although for different reasons, each party is under a legal necessity of payment. Thus in *Brooks Wharf* v. *Goodman Brothers*[6] the plaintiffs could be made to pay the duties as warehousemen and the defendants were liable as importers of the goods. It is, however, sometimes a matter of difficulty to determine whether a legal liability is cast upon the defendant; and two cases offer a neat illustration of the problems with which the Courts may be confronted. These cases, *Metropolitan Police District Receiver* v. *Croydon Corporation* and *Monmouthshire County Council* v. *Smith*, as they were based on similar facts and involved the same question of law, were conveniently considered together by the Court of Appeal.[7]

---

1. The limits of the doctrine are discussed by Winfield in 60 L.Q.R. 341.
2. *Per* EYRE, C. B., in *Deering* v. *Winchelsea* (1787), 2 B. & P. 270, at p. 272. See also *Marsack* v. *Webber* (1860), 6 H. & N. 1. But this principle does not apply where the surety intervenes voluntarily and not at the request of the debtor: *Owen* v. *Tate*, [1975] 2 All E.R. 129; [1975] 3 W.L.R. 369.
3. *Merryweather* v. *Nixan* (1799), 8 Term. Rep. 186.
4. *E.g. Adamson* v. *Jarvis* (1827), 4 Bing. 66.
5. Law Reform (Married Women and Tortfeasors) Act 1935, Part II, section 6.
6. [1937] 1 K.B. 534; [1936] 3 All E.R. 696: *supra*, p. 638.
7. [1956] 2 All E.R. 785 and 800; affirmed, [1957] 2 Q.B. 154; [1957] 1 All E.R. 78.

Two
similar
cases

In each case a policeman had been injured through the negligence of the defendants. In each case he sued the defendants in tort and recovered damages. In each case the Police Authority, as required by statute, paid him wages while he was absent from duty through illness. In neither case, therefore, could he claim from the defendants any sum representing the loss of wages, since *ex hypothesi* he had not lost any. In each case the Police Authority now sued the defendants in quasi-contract to recover the amount of the wages they had paid. This money, it was clear, they were bound themselves to pay, and the only question was whether, by some means or other, they could fasten an equal liability upon the defendants. In the *Metropolitan Police* case SLADE, J., gave judgment for the plaintiffs, and in the *Monmouthshire* case LYNSKEY, J., gave judgment for the defendants. The Court of Appeal preferred the view of LYNSKEY, J., and held that the defendants were not liable.[1]

Reliance was placed upon the conclusion drawn from the authorities by Lord WRIGHT in *Brooks Wharf* v. *Goodman Brothers* and thus summarized by LYNSKEY, J.

A common
liability
necessary

" The essence of the rule clearly is that there must be a common liability to pay money to a particular person; that the plaintiff has been compelled to pay it by law; that the defendant is liable to pay that money; and that the defendant's debt or liability has been discharged by the plaintiff's payment."[2]

The fatal flaw in the plaintiffs' argument in the two police cases was that, while they themselves were certainly under a legal duty to pay the money represented by the wages, the defendants were not. The duty of the defendants was to compensate their victims for the loss and injury caused by their negligence. This they had done; for, as already observed, the policemen had lost no wages and required on this account no compensation. Nor could the plaintiffs show that the defendants, by their negligence, had caused them any pecuniary loss or enriched themselves at the plaintiffs' expense. In the words of Lord GODDARD, " the plaintiffs' financial position has not been altered by a sixpence. Their duty is to pay wages whether the policeman is on duty or not, so long as his absence from duty is caused by an injury received in the course of his duty."[3] MORRIS, L.J., admitted that the defendants were perhaps fortunate in having injured a person who must be paid wages whether injured or not. But this was a natural hazard of the game.

" The wrongdoer does not know at the moment of the accident whether he is going to incur a large or a small liability. If he knocks down a professional man earning a large income by his own personal endeavours, the liability for loss of earnings as an item of special damage may be very high. If he knocks down somebody earning a very low wage, this liability may be low. . . . If he knocks down somebody who was going to be paid wages whether he was at work or not, then it seems to me that there is no liability for that item of the damages."[4]

---

1. [1957] 2 Q.B. 154; [1957] 1 All E.R. 78.
2. [1956] 2 All E.R., at p. 809. See [1937] 1 K.B., at p. 544.
3. [1957] 2 Q.B. 154, at p. 164.
4. [1957] 2 Q.B., at p. 165.

2. MONEY PAID UNDER A MISTAKE OF FACT

The general rule has thus been stated.

> " Where money is paid to another under the influence of a mistake, that is, upon the supposition that a specific fact is true which would entitle the other to the money, but which fact is untrue, and the money would not have been paid if it had been known to the payer that the fact was untrue, an action will lie to recover it back."[1]

The obligation thus envisaged, while it is imposed upon the defendant against his will and is independent of contract, is agreeable to commonsense; but its application is not unattended with difficulty. Four points require attention.

(i) To entitle the plaintiff to recover, the mistake upon which he has acted must be one of fact, not of law. The distinction was drawn by Lord ELLENBOROUGH in *Bilbie* v. *Lumley* in 1802 and affirmed in *Brisbane* v. *Dacres* in 1813.[2] The Judicial Committee of the Privy Council, however, held in 1960 that a plaintiff may recover money paid on a mistake of law provided that he is not *in pari delicto* with the defendant.[3] They relied especially on the observations of Lord MANSFIELD in a number of cases between 1760 and 1780.[4] But it is difficult to believe that these observations survived the decisions in *Bilbie* v. *Lumley* and *Brisbane* v. *Dacres*. In 1943, indeed, CROOM-JOHNSON, J., thought the proposition that " a voluntary payment under a mistake of law cannot be recovered " to be " beyond argument at this period in our legal history."[5] English juristic opinion is categorical. Perhaps the most impressive statement is that of Winfield in his edition of *Pollock on Contracts*: " money paid under a mistake of law cannot in any case be recovered."[6]

[margin note: Mistake must be one of fact, not of law]

But while, upon the weight and length of authority, the distinction, it is feared, must still be maintained, the exact demarcation between fact and law has never been determined. All that can be done in the present context is to indicate, by a citation of opposing instances, the considerations present to the minds of judges when they seek to make the distinction.[7] A mistake as to

[margin note: Difficulties of distinguishing law and fact]

---

1. Per PARKE, B., in *Kelly* v. *Solari* (1841), 9 M. & W. 54, at p. 58.
2. (1802), 2 East, 469, and (1813), 5 Taunt. 143, respectively. See Jackson, *History of Quasi-Contract*, pp. 59–61.
3. *Kiriri Cotton Co., Ltd.* v. *Dewani*, [1960] A.C. 192; [1960] 1 All E.R. 177. In *The Law of Restitution*, pp. 79–86 Goff and Jones support the views of the Judicial Committee in this case and argue that the crucial test is not to be found in the distinction between law and fact but in the question whether the money was paid to settle an honest claim. The argument is attractive; but the distinction drawn between mistake of law and mistake of fact, difficult as it is, is firmly if regrettably rooted in the cases.
4. See *Smith* v. *Bromley* (1760), 2 Doug. K.B. 696; *Browning* v. *Morris* (1778), 2 Cowp. 790, at p. 792; *Lowry* v. *Bourdieu* (1780), 2 Doug. K.B. 468, at p. 472.
5. *Sawyer and Vincent* v. *Windsor Brace, Ltd.*, [1943] K.B. 32; [1942] 2 All E.R. 669.
6. 13th Edn., p. 378. See also Stoljar, *The Law of Quasi-Contract*, pp. 43–49.
7. For a discussion of the difficulties attending the distinction, see Winfield, 59 L.Q.R. 327.

the particular transaction for which or as to the particular individual to whom the money is paid is clearly one of fact.   In *Admiralty Commissioners* v. *National Provincial and Union Bank of England, Ltd.*,[1] sums of money paid into the account of a customer of the bank in the belief that he was still alive, when in fact he was dead, were recovered.   In *Norwich Union Fire Insurance Society, Ltd.* v. *Price, Ltd.*:[2]

> A cargo of lemons shipped from Messina to Sydney were insured under a policy of marine insurance.   In the belief that the cargo had been damaged through a peril of the seas, the insurers paid its value to the insured.   It later appeared that the lemons had been sold *en route*, not because of sea damage, but because they were found to be ripening so fast as to prevent them reaching their destination in a merchantable state.

It was held that the insurers could recover the payment as money paid under a mistake of fact.   On the other hand, a mistake as to the existence or construction of a statute is equally clearly one of law.   Thus in *Sharp Brothers and Knight* v. *Chant*:[3]

> The landlord and tenant of a small house agreed that the rent should be increased by 6d. a week.   For some months the tenant paid and the landlord received the rent at the new rate, both parties being unaware of the passage of a Rent Restriction Act (since repealed) which made any such increase irrecoverable by the landlord.

It was held that the money had been paid under a mistake of law and that the tenant could neither sue for it nor deduct it from any future payments to his landlord.   So, too, in *National Pari-Mutuel Association, Ltd.* v. *R.*:[4]

> The suppliant company had paid betting duty to the Crown in respect of a totalisator, having formed the opinion that they were required to do so by s. 15 of the Finance Act 1926.   It was later decided by the House of Lords in another case, where the facts were similar, that the duty was not payable.

The company sought by a petition of right to recover the amount of that duty, but failed on the ground that they had acted under a mistaken apprehension of the law.   In the same way a mistaken view of regulations issued under statutory authority precludes recovery.   In *Holt* v. *Markham*:[5]

> The plaintiffs, acting as Government agents, paid the defendant on demobilization an excessive gratuity without appreciating the fact that, by virtue of a certain regulation, he was entitled only to a gratuity at a lower rate.

The mistake was held to be one of law and the plaintiffs failed to recover the excess payment.

1. (1922), 127 L.T. 452.
2. [1934] A.C. 455; [1934] All E.R. Rep. 352.
3. [1917] 1 K.B. 771.
4. (1930), 47 T.L.R. 110.
5. [1923] 1 K.B. 504.

In the cases so far cited the line between law and fact may be drawn with some degree of precision. But when the parties act on the interpretation not of a statute or of a statutory regulation but of a private document, the position is less clear. The construction of a written contract, as was observed in an earlier part of this book,[1] is a matter of law. If it is erroneous, it follows that the error also is one of law. In *Ord* v. *Ord*:[2]

> Husband and wife entered into a deed of separation whereby the husband covenanted to pay the wife an annual sum of money " free of any deduction whatever." Assuming that this prevented him from deducting income tax, he paid the annuity without such deduction. He was wrong in his assumption, since it had been ruled in earlier cases that these words did not apply to income tax.

It was held by LUSH, J., that he could not recover the amount of the tax as he had acted under a mistake not of fact but of law. In *Rogers* v. *Ingham*[3] the erroneous construction of a will was similarly regarded as involving a question of law.

While, however, payments made on an erroneous construction of a deed, a written contract or a will have thus been held to be made under a mistake of law, it has also been held that ignorance of the existence of a private right of property is a mistake of fact, even if such ignorance results from a false interpretation of the law. In *Cooper* v. *Phibbs*[4] the plaintiff agreed to rent a salmon fishery in Ireland in ignorance of the fact that it already belonged to him as tenant under a settlement. The House of Lords held that the plaintiff was entitled to have the agreement set aside and the amount of the rent repaid. Lord WESTBURY, referring to the maxim, *Ignorantia iuris haud excusat*, declared that in that phrase

> " the word *ius* is used in the sense of denoting general law, the ordinary law of the country. But when the word *ius* is used in the sense of denoting a private right, that maxim has no application. Private right of ownership is a matter of fact; it may be the result also of matter of law; but if parties contract under a mutual mistake and misapprehension as to their relative and respective rights, the result is that the agreement is liable to be set aside as having proceeded upon a common mistake. Now that was the case with these parties—the respondents believed themselves to be entitled to the property, the petitioner believed that he was a stranger to it, the mistake is discovered, and the agreement cannot stand."[5]

It is not easy to reconcile the view here expressed with the cases already cited upon the construction of deeds and wills. Sir Frederick Pollock pointed out that the House of Lords was concerned in *Cooper* v. *Phibbs* only to allow or to refuse an equitable remedy and suggested that the case has no relevance to a common law action for money had and received. Some colour has more recently been lent to this suggestion by the statement of Lord SIMONDS that, where the court is concerned exclusively with the equitable rules for the administration of assets, the distinction between mistake of law and mistake of fact is irrelevant.[6] Winfield,

---

1. *Supra*, p. 113.
2. [1923] 2 K.B. 432.
3. [1876] 3 Ch.D. 351.
4. (1867), L.R. 2 H.L. 149.
5. L.R. 2 H.L., at p. 170.
6. *Ministry of Health* v. *Simpson*, [1951] A.C. 251, at pp. 270–4; [1950] 2 All E.R. 1137, at pp. 1143–1146.

on the other hand, was of opinion that the respective areas of law and of fact are the same in common law and in equity;[1] and his view seems to be supported by the opinion of the Privy Council in *Norwich Union Fire Insurance Society, Ltd.* v. *Price*,[2] where Lord WRIGHT used *Cooper* v. *Phibbs* as an appropriate analogy to a claim in quasi-contract. If this latter view is correct, it can only be said that, while an erroneous interpretation of a written document is itself a mistake of law, an erroneous belief in the existence of a right of property founded upon such an interpretation is a mistake of fact. The distinction seems as superfluous as it is subtle.

No satis-
factory test
for dis-
tinguishing
law and fact

It must be said, in conclusion, that the whole relationship of law and fact remains incoherent and continues to embarrass many branches of English law. Its relevance to the definition of misrepresentation has already been noted.[3] In that context Sir George JESSEL attempted a solution that has often been quoted. It depended, he thought, on whether the law had been segregated from the facts or whether the legal position had been condensed into a bare statement of fact. If the facts are first stated and then the conclusion of law is drawn, the result is a statement of law; but if the legal position is stated baldly as a fact, it is still a statement of fact even though it involves a conclusion of law.[4] He gave the following illustration.[5]

> " Suppose a man is asked by a tradesman whether he can give credit to a lady, and the answer is, ' You may, she is a single woman of large fortune.' It turns out that the man who gave that answer knew that the lady had gone through a ceremony of marriage with a man who was believed to be a married man and that she had been advised that the marriage ceremony was null and void, though it had not been declared so by any court, and it afterwards turned out that they were all mistaken, that the first marriage of the man was void, so that the lady was married. He does not tell the tradesman all these facts, but states that she is single. That is a statement of fact. If he had told him the whole story and all the facts and said, ' Now, you see, the lady is single,' that would have been a misrepresentation of law."

The solution here suggested seems neither satisfactory nor conclusive. The same statement would appear to be one of fact or of law according merely to the degree of detail by which it is accompanied. The judges, in truth, whether they are dealing with misrepresentation or with mistake, have failed to find a workable differentiation between law and fact. The failure may well be due to the intractable and unrealistic nature of the problem. Its artificiality is emphasized by the case of *Solle* v. *Butcher*, already discussed in the section on common mistake.[6] In that case a flat, in existence in 1939, was damaged in the war and afterwards repaired and altered. The question was whether

---

1. Pollock, *Principles of Contract,* 13th Edn., at pp. 374–9; and Winfield, 59 L.Q.R. 327, at p. 338–342.
2. [1934] A.C. 455; [1934] All E.R. Rep. 352; *supra*, p. 636.
3. *Supra*, pp. 250–1.
4. *Eaglesfield* v. *Marquis of Londonderry* (1876), 4 Ch.D. 693.
5. *Ibid.*, at pp. 702–3.
6. [1950] 1 K.B. 671; [1949] 2 All E.R. 1107, *supra*, p. 215.

the reconstruction was so extensive as to make it in substance a new flat. If so, it was outside the scope of the Rent Restriction Acts; if not, it was within them. It was held by a majority of the Court of Appeal that this was a question of fact. The diversity of opinion in the Court reflected, not so much the choice of the test to be applied, as the form in which the question was to be put. If the judges were content to inquire whether the flat were new or old, the question was clearly one of fact; but if they proceeded to ask whether the Rent Restriction Acts applied, this was equally clearly one of law. How they will frame their inquiry in any particular situation must remain conjectural, and no sure guide can be found in the cases.

(ii) The mistake of fact upon which the plaintiff relies need not have arisen in connection with any supposed contract. In *Baylis* v. *Bishop of London*,[1] for instance, the plaintiff succeeded in recovering the amount of a tithe rent-charge which he had paid in error to a Bishop. But in the majority of the cases the mistake is in fact connected with an apparent contract; and, where this is the position, it would appear that, to justify a claim for the repayment of money in quasi-contract, the plaintiff must prove the same sort of mistake as would entitle him to treat the contract as void *ab initio*.[2] These circumstances have been considered in an earlier chapter, to which the reader is referred.[3]

Mistake not necessarily connected with contract

(iii) The person who has paid the money has no right of recovery if he knew that the payment was not due. But suppose that, though he did not realise the true position, he would have known it, had he not been careless in his investigation of the facts. Is he still entitled to rely on his mistake or is he debarred by his carelessness? The general rule is that carelessness is irrelevant. The means of knowledge are not to be regarded as synonymous with knowledge. In *Kelly* v. *Solari*:[4]

Effect where mistake due to carelessness

> The plaintiff was the director of a Life Insurance Company. The defendant's husband had been insured, but had not paid the last premium. The insurance had therefore lapsed, and the lapse had been noted in the Company's office. On her husband's death, the defendant claimed the insurance monies, and the plaintiff, forgetting the lapse, paid them to her. It was held that the money might be recovered by the plaintiff.

But one qualification of this rule must be observed. The money is not recoverable if the court draws the inference that the plaintiff has paid it at his own risk, irrespective of the true state of the facts.

---

1. [1913] 1 Ch. 127.
2. It has been contended that the legal requirements are not identical in the two sets of circumstances and that there may be a mistake which would invalidate an executory contract, but which would not create a cause of action for money paid. See Landon, 51 L.Q.R. 650, and 52 L.Q.R. 478. The arguments against this contention which, to the present authors, appear convincing, are set out by Tylor, 52 L.Q.R. 27, and by Hamson, 53 L.Q.R. 118.
3. *Supra*, pp. 205 *et seq.*
4. (1841), 9 M. & W. 54. See also *R. E. Jones, Ltd.* v. *Waring and Gillow*, [1926] A.C. 670 and *Turvey* v. *Dentons* (1923), *Ltd.*, [1953] 1 Q.B. 218; [1952] 2 All E.R. 1025.

Recklessness or indifference may estop him, where carelessness will not. In the words of PARKE, B., in the case last cited,

> " If, indeed, the money is intentionally paid without reference to the truth or falsehood of the fact, the plaintiff meaning to waive all inquiry into it, and that the person receiving shall have the money at all events, whether the fact be true or false, the latter is certainly entitled to retain it. But, if it is paid under the impression of the truth of a fact which is untrue, it may, generally speaking, be recovered back, however careless the party paying may have been in omitting to use due diligence to inquire into the fact. In such a case the receiver was not entitled to it, nor intended to have it."[1]

Can a voluntary payment be recovered?

(iv) A question that has long troubled the courts is whether the mistake must have led the plaintiff to believe that he was legally bound to pay the money or whether a purely voluntary payment is equally recoverable. On the assumption that the facts were as he erroneously supposed them to be, must he have thought himself under a legal duty to pay or is it enough that he merely wished to make a gift? If, for instance, A has given a sum of money to B in the erroneous belief that B is pursuing a particular piece of research or has no means of subsistence, can he sue in quasi-contract when he discovers his error? BRAMWELL, B., in 1856 had little doubt of the answer.

> " In order to entitle a person to recover back money paid under a mistake of fact, the mistake must be as to a fact, which, if true, would make the person paying liable to pay the money; not where, if true, it would merely make it desirable that he should pay the money."[2]

This *dictum* has sometimes been approved and sometimes criticized, but it seems probable that it no longer represents the law. The whole question was discussed in the case of *Morgan* v. *Ashcroft*.[3] A bookmaker, through the error of his clerk, overpaid a client and now sought to recover the excess as money paid under a mistake of fact. In the Court of Appeal he failed on two grounds: first, because to unravel the accounts between the parties would involve the examination of transactions declared void by the Gaming Act 1845, and, secondly, because, even if the position as supposed by the bookmaker had been the true position, he would still have been under no liability to pay, and the mistake was therefore not such as to entitle him to sue for the recovery of the money.

It is possible to use this decision, coloured though it was by preoccupation with the Gaming Act, to support the view expressed by BRAMWELL, B. But the Court of Appeal received his dictum with considerable reserve. The distinction, in their opinion, was not so much between the compulsory and voluntary nature of the payment as between the serious and trivial character of the mistake. It was certainly true that a payer who believed himself to be discharging a legal duty when he was in fact making a gift was labouring under a vital mistake and was entitled to recover

---

1. 9 M. & W., at p. 59.
2. *Aiken* v. *Short* (1856), 1 H. & N. 210, at p. 215.
3. [1938] 1 K.B. 49. See also *Kerrison* v. *Glyn, Mills, Currie & Co.* (1911), 81 L.J.K.B. 465; and, in general, Winfield, 59 L.Q.R. 327, at pp. 335–8.

the money so paid. It was also true that to confuse one species of voluntary payment with another could not normally be regarded as such a mistake. In the words of Lord GREENE:

> " If a father, believing that his son has suffered a financial loss, gives him a sum of money, he surely could not claim repayment if he afterwards discovered that no such loss had occurred."[1]

But it was possible to imagine cases where, despite the voluntary character of the transaction, the mistake was still vital. SCOTT, L.J., was prepared to recognize

> " the possibility that there may be cases of charitable payments or other gifts made under a definite mistake of person to be benefited or of the substantial nature of the transaction,"[2]

where an action for money had and received would lie.

The doubts here expressed have now been repeated and, it would seem, confirmed by the subsequent case of *Larner* v. *London County Council*.[3]

> The plaintiff, an employee of the defendants, was called up for service in the Royal Air Force, and the defendants, in pursuance of their general policy, made up the difference between his service pay and his civil wages. The plaintiff undertook to notify all changes in his service pay, but this he failed to do and the defendants over-paid him. When he returned to their service, they began to deduct from his wages the amount of the over-payment. Before this process had been completed, the plaintiff sued to recover the sums already deducted, and the defendants counter-claimed for the balance of the over-payment.

The Court of Appeal gave judgment for the defendants. The plaintiff admitted that the money had been paid under a mistake of fact but argued that it was a purely voluntary payment and therefore, in the words of BRAMWELL, B., money which it was " merely desirable " and not necessary that the defendants should pay. The Court of Appeal admitted that, as the plaintiff was under a legal duty to do military service, there was no consideration for the defendants' promise to supplement his pay and that this promise could not have been enforced by action in the courts. But they also felt that, as the defendants were " bound in honour " to keep their promise, it should not be regarded as wholly gratuitous and must be considered as " a matter of duty." This attempt to introduce a hybrid obligation, half-way between law and morality, is not convincing;[4] if the promise was not legally binding, it was surely voluntary. It is better to assume that, as a result of the decision, the *dictum* of BRAMWELL, B., is no longer to be accepted as the decisive test of an action brought to recover money paid under a mistake of fact, and that, as suggested in *Morgan* v. *Ashcroft*, a purely voluntary payment may be recovered if only it has been induced by a mistake regarded by the court as sufficiently serious in character.

---

1. [1938] 1 K.B., at p. 66.
2. [1938] 1 K.B., at p. 74.
3. [1949] 2 K.B. 683; [1949] 1 All E.R. 964.
4. It is countenanced, however, by the *dicta* of the House of Lords in *National Association of Local Government Officers* v. *Bolton Corporation,* [1943] A.C. 166, at pp. 180, 187; [1942] 2 All E.R. 425, at pp. 430, 434.

3. MONEY PAID IN PURSUANCE OF AN INEFFECTIVE CONTRACT

Meaning of "ineffective"

The word " ineffective " is not a term of art.   It is here chosen as a comprehensive expression, free from technical associations, to include a variety of cases where the plaintiff has paid money to the defendant in pursuance of a transaction which he believes to be a contract, but which turns out in fact to be nugatory.   The transaction may indeed have begun as a valid contract, but have been rendered ineffective by the default of the defendant or through the operation of the doctrine of frustration; or, while originally assumed to be a contract, it may have been invalidated *ab initio* as a result of mistake or illegality.   In either event the plaintiff now seeks the return of his money.   The cases may be grouped into three classes.

(i) Total failure of consideration

Plaintiff's option where contract discharged by breach

If the plaintiff has paid money to the defendant in pursuance of a valid contract and the defendant then fails completely to carry out his part of it, the plaintiff is offered an option.   He may either rest his claim on the basis of contract and seek damages for its breach, or he may treat the contract as at an end and sue in quasi-contract for the return of the money.   It may seem anomalous to allow the plaintiff to alternate between two inconsistent remedies, the one contractual and the other quasi-contractual.   But the position may, perhaps, be justified.   The defendant's failure is certainly a breach of contract for which an action will lie; but, if it is of a vital character, it may, with equal propriety, be regarded as a discharge of the contract.   If, then, the plaintiff seeks the repayment of his money, his claim may have to be based on quasi-contract, as the contract itself has ceased to exist.   Whatever the merits of this justification, the option has been open to the plaintiff since the eighteenth century,[1] and its exercise is simply a matter of tactics.   Thus in *Wilkinson v. Lloyd*:[2]

> The plaintiff agreed to buy from the defendant certain shares in a private company operating under a deed of settlement.   It was necessary, under the terms of this deed, for each shareholder to be approved by the directors of the company.   The plaintiff received a transfer of the shares from the defendant and paid for them.   Meanwhile, before this payment and without the plaintiff's knowledge, the directors had passed a resolution refusing to allow any transfer of shares by the defendant, as he had instituted certain legal proceedings against the company.   The transfer to the plaintiff was therefore not approved by the directors.   The shares depreciated in value.

The plaintiff could doubtless have claimed damages for this depreciation in an action of contract against the defendant.   He

1. See Jackson, *History of Quasi-Contract,* pp. 84–6, for cases and arguments.
2. (1845), 7 Q.B. 27.

preferred, however, to treat the contract as discharged by the defendant's failure to secure an effective transfer of the shares, and to sue in quasi-contract for the return of the money. It was held that the defendant was bound to procure the assent of the directors and to take all necessary steps to invest the plaintiff with the property in the shares, that his failure to do so went to the root of the contract and that the plaintiff could recover.

For the plaintiff thus to succeed in quasi-contract it is clear that there must be a *total* failure of consideration. If the plaintiff receives some part of the expected benefit, the contract remains in being and any action brought can only be in contract for damages. In *Whincup* v. *Hughes*:[1]

Distinction between total and partial failure of consideration

> The plaintiff apprenticed his son to a watchmaker and jeweller for the term of six years, paying a premium of £25. The master instructed the apprentice for a year and then died. The plaintiff now sued the master's executrix to recover the whole, or some part, of the premium on the ground of failure of consideration.

It was held that, as the consideration had not wholly failed, the action could not be maintained. In the words of BRETT, J.,

> " Where a sum of money has been paid for an entire consideration, and there is only a partial failure of consideration, neither the whole nor any part of such sum can be recovered."

While the principle is clear, it is not always easy to distinguish a total from a partial failure of consideration. An interesting illustration of the problem is afforded by the case of *Rowland* v. *Divall*.[2]

> The plaintiff bought a motor car from the defendant and used it for several months. He then discovered that the defendant had never had any title to the car, and the plaintiff was compelled to restore it to the true owner.

The plaintiff sued the defendant to recover the amount of the purchase money as on a total failure of consideration. The defendant argued, *inter alia*, that, as the plaintiff had enjoyed the use of the car for several months, there was no such total failure, and that the plaintiff should be limited to his remedy in damages for breach of contract. The Court of Appeal rejected this argument. It was the duty of the defendant, as seller, to pass the property in the car to the buyer, and, if he failed to do so, there was a fundamental breach which entitled the plaintiff to treat it as discharged. The latter, after all, had contracted, not to hire, but to buy the car. As ATKIN, L.J., said:[3]

> " It seems to me that in this case there has been a total failure of consideration, that is to say that the buyer has not got any part of

---

1. (1871), L.R. 6 C.P. 78. If the plaintiff can, and does, restore to the defendant such benefit as he has received, he may be able to sue in quasi-contract. Moreover, the facts may be such as to relieve the plaintiff of his obligation to restore: *Rowland* v. *Divall*, [1923] 2 K.B. 500. See Goff and Jones, *The Law of Restitution*, p. 342.
2. [1923] 2 K.B. 500. See also *Valentini* v. *Canali* (1889), 24 Q.B.D. 166: *supra*, p. 415.
3. [1923] 2 K.B., at p. 506.

that for which he paid the purchase money. He paid the money in order that he might get the property and he has not got it."

Application to hire-purchase

The reasoning in this case has been applied by analogy to a contract of hire-purchase. In *Warman* v. *Southern Counties Car Finance Corporation, Ltd.*,[1]

> the plaintiff made a hire-purchase contract with the defendants for a motor-car of which the defendants were described as owners. The plaintiff paid 4 of the 12 monthly instalments and then learnt that X claimed to be the owner of the car. He nevertheless paid the balance of the instalments and exercised his option of purchase. X then demanded the car and the plaintiff gave it up to him.

The plaintiff now sued the defendants for breach of the condition of title (treated as a breach of warranty *ex post facto*) and won. The defendants counter-claimed for a reasonable sum as rent for the hire of the car during the period in which it was in the plaintiff's possession, and lost. There had been a total failure of consideration for which, had he been so minded, the plaintiff could have sued in quasi-contract and which prevented the defendants from recovering any sum of money whether under the hire-purchase contract or by way of *quantum meruit*. FINNEMORE, J., thus explained the position.[2]

> " A hire-purchase agreement is in law an agreement in two parts. It is an agreement to rent a particular chattel for a certain length of time. If during the period or at the end of the period the hirer does not wish to buy the chattel, he is not bound to do so. On the other hand, the essential part of the agreement is that the hirer has the option of purchase, and it is common knowledge—and I suppose common sense—that, when people enter into a hire-purchase agreement, they enter into it, not so much for the purpose of hiring, but for the purpose of purchasing by a certain method, by what is, in effect, deferred payments . . . Now I think it might well be right to say that, if at any stage the option to purchase goes, the whole value of the agreement to the hirer has gone with it. If he wanted an agreement merely to hire a car he would make it, but he enters into a hire-purchase agreement because he wants to have the right to purchase the car; that is the whole basis of the agreement, the very foundation of it. I should have thought . . . that, if the defendants break the contract or are unable to carry it out, they are not entitled to claim on a sort of *quantum meruit* and say: ' Anyhow, although I could not carry out the agreement and could not give you the title to this car, you had the use of it for six or seven months and you must pay the hiring charges for those months '."

Ultra Vires contract

Special difficulties arise where a company has purported to make a contract which is *ultra vires*. The purported contract does not in truth exist and the company may not be sued upon it.[3] But if a person has paid money to the company in pursuance of the supposed contract, may he bring an action in quasi-contract? There has been a total failure of consideration, and the action would seem to be available. This assumption is supported

---

1. [1949] 2 K.B. 576; [1949] 1 All E.R. 711.
2. *Ibid.*, at pp. 582 and 714 respectively. The reasoning in *Rowland* v. *Divall*, and presumably its application in *Warman* v. *Southern Counties Car Finance Corporation, Ltd.*, was criticised by the Law Reform Committee (12th Report: Cmnd. 2958, 1966).
3. *Supra*, pp. 423–7.

by *Re Phoenix Life Assurance Co., Burgess and Stock's Case*.[1]
A company, whose powers were confined to the business of life
assurance, issued policies of marine insurance. The company was
wound up. It was held that at common law persons who had paid
premiums on such policies could recover them as money had and
received to their use, and that they could prove for their amount
in the winding-up of the company. In *Sinclair v. Brougham* the
validity of this decision was left open;[2] and the courts may well
follow and apply it in the future. In principle the result should be
the same if the company itself sues to recover money paid to
another party under an *ultra vires* contract. In *Brougham* v.
Dwyer in 1913 the liquidator of the Birkbeck Building Society was
held entitled to recover money paid to a customer in the course of
an *ultra vires* banking business. But this decision is not easy to
reconcile with *Sinclair* v. *Brougham*, which arose out of the same
liquidation; and the courts may be reluctant to accept it.[3]

(ii) Money paid in pursuance of a void contract

The plaintiff may have paid money to the defendant in pursuance of a transaction which he thought to be a valid contract,
but which in truth, through the operation of some rule of law, is
null and void. As a matter of logic such money should be recoverable in quasi-contract. The hypothesis upon which its payment
rested is erroneous, and, as the event shows, it was in fact paid
for nothing at all. This logical conclusion is, as a general rule,
accepted by the common law. Thus, as has already been seen,
money paid on a fundamental mistake of fact may be recovered.[4]

*Contract
void at
common law*

Where, however, the transaction is avoided, not by the common law but by statute, the position is more complicated. The
context of the statute, its purpose or the ambiguities of its language, may exclude the logical consequences and prevent the
recovery of the money. Difficulties have arisen in particular
upon the interpretation of the Gaming Acts and of the Infants'
Relief Act 1874. These statutes have been dealt with at length
in earlier parts of this book,[5] and it is not desired to repeat the
arguments and conclusions there set forth. The reader is
reminded only that the transactions caught by these Acts are
rendered, not illegal, but only void; and the refusal of the courts
to allow a quasi-contractual claim for the return of money paid
by the plaintiff to the defendant must therefore be based either
upon the peculiar construction of the statutes or upon the assumed
dictates of public policy.

*Contract
void by
statute*

(iii) Money paid in pursuance of an illegal contract

When, by the provisions of a statute, or indeed under the
common law concept of public policy, a contract is rendered void,

---

1. (1862), 2 J. & H. 441.
2. [1914] A.C. 398, at pp. 414 and 440.
3. *Brougham* v. *Dwyer* (1913), 108 L.T. 504. In *Bell Houses, Ltd.* v. *City Wall Properties, Ltd.*, MOCATTA, J., left the question open: [1965] 3 All E.R. 427, at p. 434; [1966] 1 Q.B. 207, at p. 226. See Goff and Jones, *The Law of Restitution*, 321–4, and Polack, [1966] C.L.J. 28.
4. *Supra*, pp. 641 *et seq.*
5. *Supra*, Part IV, Chap. 3, and Part V, Chap. 1.

money paid may—as stated above—be recovered unless a particular statute provides otherwise. But when a contract is made illegal, whether by statute or as offending public policy, the general rule is that a party may not sue to recover his money if, to sustain his claim, he must rely on the illegality and disclose his guilt. *In pari delicto potior est condicio defendentis.* The moral reprobation, expressed by Chief Justice WILMOT in 1767, still reverberates in the courts.

> " Whoever is a party to an unlawful contract, if he hath once paid the money stipulated to be paid in pursuance thereof, he shall not have the help of the court to fetch it back again. You shall not have a right of action when you come into a court of justice in this unclean manner to recover it back."[1]

A striking instance of this principle is to be found in the case of *Parkinson* v. *College of Ambulance, Ltd., and Harrison.*[2]

> The secretary of the defendant charity fraudulently represented to the plaintiff that the charity was in a position to divert the fountain of honour in his direction and to procure him at least a knighthood, if he would make an adequate donation. After a certain amount of bargaining, the plaintiff paid £3,000 to the charity and undertook to do more when the knighthood was forthcoming. The plaintiff, however, did not receive the knighthood and sought the return of the money as had and received to his use.

It was held by LUSH, J., that the action must fail. The transaction was manifestly illegal and the plaintiff no less clearly a willing party to it.

Exceptions   There are two exceptions to this general rule. In the first place, the parties may not be *in pari delicto*: advantage may have been taken of the plaintiff's comparative innocence or defenceless condition. In the second place, there may be a *locus pœnitentiæ*: the contract may still be executory and nothing may have been done to implement the unlawful design. Each of these exceptions seems consonant with commonsense, and their implications have already been discussed.[3]

4. MONEY HAD AND RECEIVED FROM A THIRD PARTY TO THE PLAINTIFF'S USE

In the preceding species of quasi-contract the plaintiff and the defendant had been in close relationship to each other. The plaintiff had paid money to the defendant's use, or he had paid it to him under a mistake of fact, or he had paid it to him in pursuance of a transaction which he believed to be a binding contract but which, in the event, had proved to be nugatory. This close relationship, however, may be lacking.

Suppose that X pays money to B and instructs B to pay it to A; or that B has in his hands a fund belonging to X and that X directs B to pay A out of this fund. If B fails to carry out his instructions, may A sue B? It is clear that no contract exists between A and B, and it is equally clear that the mere fact

---

1. *Collins* v. *Blantern* (1767), 2 Wilson, 341.
2. [1925] 2 K.B. 1. See also *Boissevain* v. *Weil*, [1950] A.C. 327; [1950] 1 All E.R. 728.
3. *Supra,* pp. 349–356.

that B may be under a contractual liability to X and that X wishes to benefit A will not enable A to sue B; for A will be met, at least at common law, by the doctrine of privity. It has nevertheless been held in a number of cases that, once B has notified A that he is ready and willing to pay the money, A may sue B in quasi-contract if B fails to do so.[1]

This branch of the law has a long if tenuous history. It was held in the fourteenth century that the plaintiff could bring the writ of account to recover money which the defendant had received from a third party " to his use."[2] In 1625 debt was allowed as an alternative to account, provided that a definite sum of money was involved; and later in the same century debt was in practice superseded, here as elsewhere, by *indebitatus assumpsit*.[3] A few scattered cases are reported in the eighteenth and early nineteenth centuries. Perhaps the most instructive is the case of *Stevens* v. *Hill* in 1805.[4]

History of the doctrine

> The defendant was a " navy agent ": he received moneys payable to naval officers. Admiral Smith wrote the following order " Out of my half-pay, which will become due the 1st of January, pay to Stevens £15." He sent the order to the plaintiff. The plaintiff brought it to the defendant, who said that " he had then no money of Admiral Smith's in his hands, but that he would pay it out of the Admiral's money when he received it." The defendant later received £40 on the Admiral's account, but did not pay the plaintiff.

The plaintiff sued the defendant in quasi-contract and obtained judgment. In the words of Lord ELLENBOROUGH, " it was an appropriation of so much to the use of the holder of the draft and made him liable on the receipt of any money upon the credit of which it was drawn."

In the course of the nineteenth century some confusion was caused by the emphasis placed upon privity of contract, which was allowed at times to obstruct the plaintiff's claim. The objection was patently improper, and the fallacy was exposed by BLACKBURN, J., in *Griffin* v. *Weatherby*.[5] The plaintiff relied, not on the original contract between the defendant and the third party, but on a distinct and quasi-contractual claim.

The dearth of modern authority makes the more interesting the case of *Shamia* v. *Joory*.[6]

Shamia v. Joory

---

1. On this branch of quasi-contract, see Jackson, *History of Quasi-Contract*, pp. 30–4, 93–103, and Goff and Jones, *The Law of Restitution*, pp. 369–73.
2. (1368), Y.B. Pasch. 41 Ed. III, fo. 10, pl. 5; Fifoot, *History and Sources of the Common Law*, pp. 272 and 285.
3. *Harris* v. *de Bervoir* (1625), Cro. Jac. 687; *Brown* v. *London* (1670), 1 Vent. 152.
4. (1805), 5 Esp. 247.
5. (1868), L.R. 3 Q.B. 753.
6. [1958] 1 Q.B. 448; [1958] 1 All E.R. 111. See Davies, 75 L.Q.R. 220. The case is criticised by Goff and Jones in *The Law of Restitution*, at p. 372. Cf. Stoljar, *The Law of Quasi-Contract*, pp. 84–6.

The plaintiff was a citizen of Iraq, studying in England to be a dentist. The defendant was another citizen of Iraq, also living in England. The plaintiff's brother, X, lived in Iraq. As a result of business dealings between X and the defendant, the defendant owed X £1,300. X wished to make a present of £500 to his brother, the plaintiff, and asked the defendant to give the plaintiff this sum out of the money due by the defendant to X. The plaintiff, when he had been told by his brother of this arrangement, wrote to the defendant and asked for the £500. The defendant, in reply, sent the plaintiff a letter in Arabic, the translation of which appeared to be: " Enclosed you will find a cheque for £500, which belongs to you." The plaintiff presented the cheque to his bank, but it was not paid.

The plaintiff now sued the defendant for money had and received to his use. Defendant's counsel admitted that, where X had transferred to B a sum of money or a " fund," and directed B to pay it to A, B became liable in quasi-contract to A as soon as he had notified A that he accepted this liability. But he argued that in the present case there was no money or fund to which this principle could attach: there was only a debt due by the defendant to X.

BARRY, J., rejected this contention. It was not necessary that a definite sum of money should have been entrusted to one man in order to be transferred to another. Nor was there any magic in the word " fund."

> " All that the law requires is that there must be in the hands of or accruing to [the defendant] either a sum of money or a monetary liability over which the transferor has a right of disposal. It matters not from what source the liability arises, and I see no reason why it should not include a debt for money lent or goods sold or services rendered or a debt of any other kind."[1]

Summary of existing law

He therefore gave judgment for the plaintiff.

A may therefore sue B for money had and received to his use provided:

(1) that B has in his hands money belonging to X or is under a monetary liability of any kind to X;

(2) that X directs B to pay the whole or part of the sum involved to A; and

(3) that B notifies A that he is ready and willing to pay him.

Implications of doctrine

In the case of *Shamia* v. *Joory*, it may be allowed, the invocation of quasi-contract served the ends of justice, and the extension of the doctrine from a specific sum or a particular fund to a general " monetary liability " seems inherently a natural and almost inevitable development.[2] It has, nevertheless, some interesting implications. The " monetary liability " in *Shamia* v. *Joory* was neither more nor less than a debt due upon a contract, and it is perhaps worth while to set the result of the case against established contractual principles. Three hypothetical situations may be envisaged.

---

1. [1958] 1 All E.R., at p. 114.
2. The medieval and seventeenth-century requirement that a definite sum of money should be involved was a facet of the old writ of debt.

(1) X makes a contract with B whereby X agrees to write a book for B and B agrees to pay A £100. A is a stranger to the contract and may not sue upon it.

(2) X makes a contract with B whereby X agrees to write a book for B and B agrees to pay X £100. X writes the book and assigns to A his right to receive the £100. A may sue B if the rules for the assignment of choses in action are satisfied.[1]

(3) X makes a contract with B whereby X agrees to write a book for B and B agrees to pay X £100. X writes the book and then asks B to pay the money to A. B is liable to A in quasi-contract provided that he has notified A that he is ready and willing to pay him.

The third situation may easily be distinguished from the first. The parties are not attempting from the outset to make a stranger the beneficiary of the contract. It is not, at first sight, so easy to distinguish it from the second. In each case it is sought to transfer a contractual right, and it would almost seem that, by exploiting the action for money had and received, the parties may avoid the rules governing the assignment of choses in action. If this were indeed the position, the essentials of a statutory assignment could be ignored and the controversial question evaded as to the function, if any, of consideration in an equitable assignment.[2] But there is at least one clear distinction between the claim in quasi-contract and the assignment of a chose in action. Whereas in an assignment the debtor's consent is irrelevant, in quasi-contract it is all important. Unless he has acknowledged to the third party his readiness to pay him, he cannot be sued by him.

5. CLAIMS AGAINST WRONGDOERS

A plaintiff, who has suffered loss through a wrongful act committed against him by the defendant, may in certain circumstances be entitled to sue the defendant in quasi-contract for money had and received to his use. He may for instance have been compelled by the improper pressure of the defendant to pay money which could not lawfully have been demanded from him. In *Maskell* v. *Horner*:[3]

Where the wrong is not a tort

> The plaintiff in 1900 started business as a dealer near Spitalfields Market. The defendant, who owned the market, demanded tolls from him and threatened to seize his goods if he would not pay. The plaintiff refused, and the goods were seized. The plaintiff then sought legal advice, and, learning that other dealers paid the tolls, himself paid under protest. From 1900 to 1912 the tolls were demanded each year under threat of seizure and paid under protest. In 1912 the Chancery Division of the High Court held that such demands were unwarranted, and the plaintiff then sought to recover the sums paid as money had and received to his use. His action was successful.

---

1. *Supra*, pp. 483–575.
2. *Supra*, pp. 500–503.
3. [1915] 3 K.B. 106. See also *Parker* v. *Bristol and Exeter Rail. Co.* (1851), 6. Exch. 702.

Where the
wrong is
a tort

In such a case as this the defendant's conduct would not seem to come within the definition of a tort, and the action in quasi-contract affords the only remedy.   In the majority of cases, however, the defendant will have been guilty of a tort, and the plaintiff, if he is allowed to sue in quasi-contract, is offered an alternative remedy.   Before the abolition of the forms of action many circumstances combined to recommend *indebitatus assumpsit* over its competitors in trespass or in case.   The plaintiff could escape the dangerous verbosity inherent in the science of special pleading, he enjoyed a longer period of time in which to bring his action, he could proceed even if the original wrongdoer had died.[1] Most of these advantages are now common to both forms of procedure; but the alternative of quasi-contract still offers sufficient advantages over an action in tort to lend colour to the famous couplet,

> " Thoughts much too deep for tears subdue the court,
>   When I *assumpsit* bring, and god-like waive a tort."[2]

Examples
where the
claim is
sustainable

It is not profitable to attempt a precise enumeration of the types of tort to which the claim in quasi-contract is alternative. It is clear, indeed, that such a claim is out of place where, as in defamation, the plaintiff cannot offer a quantitative estimate of his loss.   But within the limits thus circumscribed the most usual cases are those of conversion, trespass and deceit.   It was to avoid the necessity of proving the exact value of the goods lost that a plaintiff first sought to replace conversion by *indebitatus assumpsit*, and the earliest reported instance is that of *Lamine* v. *Dorrell* in 1705.[3]

Conversion

> The defendant had acted as administrator and had sold debentures forming part of the deceased's estate.   The grant of administration was subsequently revoked, and the plaintiff, as rightful executor, recovered in quasi-contract the proceeds of the sale.

POWELL, J., said:

> " The plaintiff may dispense with the wrong and suppose the sale made by his consent, and bring an action for the money they were sold for as money received to his use."

Trespass

In trespass a good example is offered by the case of *Neate* v. *Harding*.[4]

> The plaintiff had for some time been in receipt of poor relief. The defendants, who were parish officers, suspecting that she had been concealing financial resources, entered her house, found a sum of money therein and took it away.   The entry and the removal of the money were trespasses.   But it was held that the plaintiff might waive the torts and sue for the value of the money in *indebitatus assumpsit*.

Deceit

A final illustration may be drawn from deceit.   In *Refuge Assurance Co.* v. *Kettlewell*:[5]

---

1. See Winfield, *Province of the Law of Tort*, pp. 143–6.
2. From *The Circuiteers*, an eclogue by Adolphus, in 1 L.Q.R. 233.   See Winfield, *Province of the Law of Tort*, p. 145, and Goff and Jones, *The Law of Restitution*, pp. 436–7.
3. 2 Ld. Rayn, 1216.
4. (1851) 6 Exch. 349.
5. [1909] A.C. 243.

The plaintiff held a policy of assurance on her brother's life. She was disinclined to pay any more premiums, but was persuaded to continue by the Company's agent, who said that, if she paid for five more years, she would get a free policy. This statement was false to the agent's knowledge, but was made without the authority of the Company. After making payments for the five years, the plaintiff discovered that she was not to have a free policy.

It was held that, as the Company had benefited during this period by the amount of the premiums, they could be compelled to restore their value to the plaintiff in quasi-contract.

Since, in all such cases as these, the remedies in tort and in quasi-contract are alternative, the plaintiff may not enforce both; he must choose between them. But his choice will not finally be determined until he has recovered judgment upon one or the other. He is not to get satisfaction twice, but he may try both ways of getting it once. The whole question was discussed by the House of Lords in *United Australia, Ltd.* v. *Barclays Bank, Ltd.*[1]

Choice of remedies

A cheque had been drawn in favour of the plaintiffs. Their secretary dishonestly indorsed it to the X Company of which he was a director. The defendants collected the cheque and credited the proceeds to the X Company. The plaintiffs sued the X Company in quasi-contract, but before they obtained judgment the company went into liquidation and the action was discontinued. The plaintiffs lodged a proof in the winding-up proceedings, but this was not admitted and no money was received. There were in fact no assets. The plaintiffs now sued the defendants in conversion.

The defendants contended that, as the plaintiffs had pursued their remedy in quasi-contract against the company, they had waived their claim in tort and had lost their option. But the House of Lords gave judgment for the plaintiffs. Lord SIMON explained the nature of the choice open to them.[2]

" The substance of the matter is that [a plaintiff] is claiming redress either in the form of compensation—that is, as damages for a tort—or in the form of restitution of money to which he is entitled but which the defendant has wrongfully received. The same set of facts entitles the plaintiff to claim either form of redress. At some stage of the proceedings the plaintiff must elect which remedy he will have. There is, however, no reason of principle or convenience why that stage should be deemed to be reached until the plaintiff applies for judgment."

6. CLAIMS ON A *QUANTUM MERUIT*

The common law has long provided a convenient remedy when the plaintiff seeks, not a precise sum alleged to be due to him, but a reasonable remuneration for services rendered. He is then said to sue on a *quantum meruit*. Confusion has been caused in classifying the cases to which this remedy applies through the dual character with which it is invested. Sometimes

Claim on a quantum meruit may be contractual or quasi-contractual

---

1. [1941] A.C. 1; [1940] 4 All E.R. 20. See Wright, 57 L.Q.R. 184.
2. [1941] A.C., at p. 29; [1940] 4 All E.R., at p. 37.

it operates as a legitimate remedy in contract, and sometimes as a quasi-contractual remedy.   Its incidence thus cuts across the logical distinction between contract and quasi-contract.[1]

Instances of contractual claims

Examples of its application as a purely contractual action have already been given.[2]   It is sufficient here to recall the two main instances.   It may be used to recover a reasonable price or reasonable remuneration where a contract has been made for the supply of goods or services, and no precise sum has been fixed by the agreement;[3]   or it may serve the plaintiff where an original contract to which he was a party has been replaced by a new one, and he now seeks payment for work done or goods supplied under this substituted agreement.   In the words of Lord ATKIN,[4]

> " If I order from a wine merchant twelve bottles of whisky at so much a bottle, and he sends me ten bottles of whisky and two of brandy, and I accept them, I must pay a reasonable price for the brandy."

But if a plaintiff has made an agreement to do work for the defendant in return for a specified fee and now sues on a *quantum meruit* for extra work done, he must satisfy the court that the original agreement has been discharged.   He must be off with the old contract before he can be on with the new.[5]

Quasi-contractual claims

Work done under contract that is discharged by defendant's breach

The place of *quantum meruit* in quasi-contract may similarly be illustrated by two types of cases.

In the first place, the plaintiff may seek to recover reasonable remuneration for work done in pursuance of a contract, which has been discharged by the default of the defendant.   In such a case *quantum meruit* may be alternative to a claim in damages for breach of contract.   Thus in *De Bernardy* v. *Harding*:[6]

> The defendant proposed to erect and let seats to view the funeral of the Duke of Wellington.   He agreed that the plaintiff should advertise the seats outside England and sell tickets, and that he should receive a commission on all the tickets thus sold.   The plaintiff prepared advertisements and paid printers, but, before he had sold any tickets, the defendant wrongfully revoked his authority.

It was held that the plaintiff could sue in *quantum meruit* for the work already done.   ALDERSON, B., said:

> " Where one party has absolutely refused to perform, or has rendered himself incapable of performing, his part of the contract, he puts it in the power of the other party either to sue for a breach of it or to rescind the contract and sue on a *quantum meruit* for the work actually done."

The point had previously arisen in 1831 in the difficult case of *Planché* v. *Colburn*.[7]

---

1. On the somewhat delicate character of this distinction, see Winfield, *Province of the Law of Tort*, pp. 157–60, and Denning, 55 L.Q.R. 54.
2. *Supra*, pp. 526–8.
3. See now Sale of Goods Act 1893, s. 8 (2).   For a simple example of *quantum meruit* in its purely contractual form, see *Powell* v. *Braun*, [1954] 1 All E.R. 484.
4. In *Steven* v. *Bromley & Son*, [1919] 2 K.B. 722, at p. 728.
5. *Gilbert & Partners* v. *Knight*, [1968] 2 All E.R. 248.
6. (1853), 3 Exch. 822.
7. The pleadings, facts and judgments in this case must be gathered from the following reports: 5 C. & P. 58; 8 Bing. 14; 1 Moore & Scott 51.

The plaintiff had agreed to write for " The Juvenile Library," a series published by the defendants, a book on Costume and Ancient Armour. He was to receive £100 on the completion of the book. He collected material and wrote part of the book, and then the defendants abandoned the series. There were negotiations for the publication of the book as a separate work, but these fell through, apparently as the plaintiff felt that he had written especially for children and that to publish his work as a *magnum opus* would injure his reputation. He claimed alternatively on the original contract and on a *quantum meruit*.

The claim on the original contract seems to have disappeared in the course of the argument, perhaps because, as pleaded by the plaintiff, it necessitated the completion and delivery of the work before the payment was due, and the plaintiff had done neither of these things. But, on the alternative submission, it was held:

> (1) that the original contract had been discharged by the defendants' breach,
> (2) that no new contract had been substituted,
> (3) that the plaintiff could obtain 50 guineas as reasonable remuneration on a *quantum meruit*. This claim was independent of the original contract and was based on quasi-contract.

TINDAL, C.J., said:[1]

> " I agree that, when a special contract is in existence and open, the plaintiff cannot sue on a *quantum meruit*, and part of the question here, therefore, was whether the contract did exist or not. It distinctly appeared that the work was finally abandoned; and the jury found that no new contract had been entered into. Under these circumstances, the plaintiff ought not to lose the fruit of his labour."

Whether or not the claim in *quantum meruit* is, in any particular case, alternative to an action for breach of contract, it is clear that it is itself independent of the original contract between the parties and is sustained, not because it represents an agreement reached between the parties, but because the law will compel the defendant not to disappoint the plaintiff of the " fruit of his labour."

The second instance of the use of *quantum meruit* as a quasi-contractual remedy is to be found where the plaintiff has rendered services in pursuance of a transaction, supposed by him to be a contract, but which, in truth, is without legal validity. The rationale here is similar to that employed to support an action for money paid in respect of an " ineffective " contract,[2] and differs from it only in the circumstance that the plaintiff sues, not for the return of a precise sum, but for a reasonable remuneration. A convenient illustration is afforded by the case of *Craven-Ellis* v. *Canons, Ltd.*[3]

Work done under void contract

> The plaintiff was appointed managing director of a company by an agreement under the company's seal which provided for his remuneration. By the articles of association each director was

---

1. 8 Bing., at p. 16.
2. *Supra*, pp. 648 *et seq*.
3. [1936] 2 K.B. 403; [1936] 3 All E.R. 1066. See Denning, 55 L.Q.R. 54.

required to obtain certain qualification shares within two months of his appointment.   Neither the plaintiff nor the other directors ever obtained these shares.   The plaintiff nevertheless, purporting to act under the agreement, rendered services for the company and sued for the sums specified in the agreement, or, alternatively, for a reasonable remuneration on a *quantum meruit.*

The Court of Appeal held that the agreement was void, since the persons purporting to act as directors had no authority and could not bind the company.   The claim in contract must therefore fail.   But, as services had in fact been rendered whereby the company had benefited, the alternative claim on the *quantum meruit* could succeed.   GREER, L.J., was careful to emphasize the quasi-contractual nature of this claim.

> " The obligation to pay reasonable remuneration for the work done when there is no binding contract between the parties is imposed by a rule of law, and not by an inference of fact arising from the acceptance of services or goods.   It is one of the cases referred to in books on contracts as obligations arising *quasi ex contractu.*"[1]

B. DOUBTFUL QUASI-CONTRACTS

In a number of cases where the law affords a remedy, it is difficult to determine whether this is founded upon a genuine, if tacit, consent and is contractual, or whether it is independent of consent and is quasi-contractual.   The following are the most important of these cases.

I. ACCOUNTS STATED

Two kinds of accounts stated

The plaintiff who sues upon an account stated proceeds upon the assumption that the defendant has admitted a debt to be due to him.   In the course of its long history, however, this remedy has become applicable to two separate sets of circumstances.[2] On the one hand it is applicable where the parties, after a series of mutual dealings, have agreed to make up their accounts, to set off one item against another, and to be answerable only for the balance.   If the result of this accounting process is to disclose a balance in the plaintiff's favour, for which he now sues, the action is clearly based upon a genuine consent and is contractual in character.   On the other hand, in the absence of any such mutual arrangement, the plaintiff may be suing upon an I.O.U. or other

---

1. [1936] 2 K.B., at p. 412.   Whether a company, which has purported to make an *ultra vires* contract, may itself sue on a *quantum meruit* was treated as an open question by MOCATTA, J., in *Bell Houses, Ltd.* v. *City Wall Properties, Ltd.*, [1966] 1 Q.B. 207, at p. 226; [1965] 3 All E.R. 427, at p. 436.   Doubts have been expressed by Polack in [1966] C.L.J. 29.   The cognate question of a possible action for money had and received has been discussed *supra*, pp. 650–1.
2. See Jackson, *History of Quasi-Contract*, pp. 105–111.

acknowledgment by the defendant that a certain sum is due to him. If the law attached a liability to this acknowledgment, irrespective of its origin or merits, the liability might well be described as quasi-contractual. In the modern law, however, it is regarded as no more than prima facie evidence of a debt, which may be rebutted by further evidence. It seems better, therefore, to treat this type of account stated as a rule of evidence rather than of substantive law, and to keep the whole subject outside the realm of quasi-contract.[1]

2. JUDGMENT DEBTS

The liability to pay a sum adjudged to be due by a court of competent jurisdiction, whether it be an English, or, in certain cases, a foreign tribunal, has sometimes been classified under the head of quasi-contract.[2] It is, of course, clear that, despite its traditional title of " Contract of Record," such a liability is independent of consent. It is also clear that its historical place in the forms of action, supported at first by an action of debt and later by *indebitatus assumpsit*, has induced a superficial analogy to quasi-contract. But it would seem absurd, in the modern jurisprudence, to admit its affinity to private law at all. It is an overriding obligation of public law and outside the field of the present work.[3]

Contract of record

3. MONEY DUE UNDER STATUTE, BYE-LAW OR CUSTOM

The language of tradition has sometimes encouraged the inclusion within the category of quasi-contract of claims for money due under statute or bye-law, or by the force of custom. There are, indeed, several *dicta* in early cases, where *indebitatus assumpsit* was employed to recover such money, which support this classification.[4] But, as in the cognate case of judgment debts, there is nothing save the associations of obsolete procedure to justify its survival in the modern law, and the force of the legislation or custom behind the claim surely suffices to explain the ground of liability without recourse to the already overburdened rationale of quasi-contract.

Not a case of quasi-contract

---

1. See the judgments of the House of Lords in *Camillo Tank Steamship Co.* v. *Alexandria Engineering Works* (1921), 38 T.L.R. 134, and of the Privy Council in *Siqueira* v. *Noronha*, [1934] A.C. 332. Cf. Winfield, *Province of the Law of Tort*, pp. 167–168.
2. See 8 Halsbury's, *Laws of England*, 3rd Edn., s. 447. Jenks, *Digest of English Civil Law*, 4th Edn., para. 697.
3. See Jackson, *History of Quasi-Contract*, pp. 28, 125; Winfield, *Province of the Law of Tort*, pp. 149–150; *supra*, pp. 10–11. For a modern example of this class of liability, see *H.M. Treasury* v. *Harris*, [1957] 2 All E.R. 455; [1957] 2 Q.B. 516.
4. For a review of these cases, see Winfield, *Province of the Law of Tort*, pp. 178–181; *supra*, p. 11.

4. CLAIMS FOR NECESSARY GOODS SUPPLIED TO PERSONS UNDER INCAPACITY

Claim for
necessary
goods
is probably
quasi-
contractual

A more controversial question arises where money is claimed for necessary goods supplied to a person labouring under an incapacity which affects his power to contract, such as lunacy, drunkenness or infancy.   There is ground for the view that, as a matter of history, the early tendency was to regard such claims as based upon pure contract, and some jurists are of the opinion that they retain this character in the current law.[1]   The balance of judicial opinion, however, is inclined to classify them as quasi-contractual.   A general statement to this effect was made by COTTON, L.J., in *Re Rhodes, Rhodes v. Rhodes.*[2]

> " Whenever necessaries are supplied to a person, who, by reason of disability, cannot himself contract, the law implies an obligation on the part of such person to pay for such necessaries out of his own property."

The case from which this citation is taken concerned the liability of a lunatic, and Lord LINDLEY supported Lord Justice COTTON in his classification.[3]   A similar view had been expressed by POLLOCK, C.B., in the case of necessaries supplied to a person in a state of intoxication.[4]   Judicial opinion is less unanimous in the case of infants.   In *Nash* v. *Inman*[5] divergent views were expressed by BUCKLEY, L.J., and by FLETCHER MOULTON, L.J.   Lord Justice BUCKLEY based the infant's liability upon contract; but Lord Justice FLETCHER MOULTON had no doubt that the liability was quasi-contractual.

> " An infant, like a lunatic, is incapable of making a contract of purchase in the strict sense of the words; but if a man satisfies the needs of the infant or lunatic by supplying to him necessaries, the law will imply an obligation to repay him for the services so rendered, and will enforce that obligation against the estate of the infant or lunatic.   The consequence is that the basis of the action is hardly contract.   Its real foundation is an obligation which the law imposes on the infant to make a fair payment in respect of needs satisfied. In other words the obligation arises *re* and not *consensu*."

The position is now governed by statute.   By section 2 of the Sale of Goods Act 1893, it is enacted that

> Where necessaries are sold and delivered to an infant or minor, or to a person who by reason of mental incapacity or drunkenness is incompetent to contract, he must pay a reasonable price therefor.

---

1. See Holdsworth, 55 L.Q.R. 37, at p. 47;   Goff and Jones, *The Law of Restitution*, pp. 309–11.
2. (1890), 44 Ch.D. 94, at p. 105.
3. (1890), 44 Ch.D. 94, at p. 107.
4. *Gore* v. *Gibson* (1845), 13 M. & W. 623, at p. 626.
5. [1908] 2 K.B. 1, at pp. 8 and 12.

The emphasis on the actual delivery of the goods, the hypothesis of contractual incompetence, the allowance only of a reasonable price, all tend to discourage the possibility of basing the action upon contract. While, therefore, the question must still be treated as open to argument, it would seem better to-day to regard all these claims as quasi-contractual.[1]

---

1. This view was taken by Lord WRIGHT in his article on *Sinclair* v. *Brougham*, 6 C.L.J. 305, at p. 318. It was been objected that, if this view is accepted, the supply of necessary goods to an infant must be treated separately from the supply of services: Goff and Jones, *The Law of Restitution*, pp. 309–11. Such a divorce, however, may be justified if the latter type of case is brought within the category of beneficial contracts of service: see *supra*, pp. 404–6.

INDEX

A

ABSOLUTE CONTRACT,
basic rule as to, 544
mitigation of rule, 545

ACCEPTANCE,
assent, inference from conduct, 33
communication of—
generally, 41 *et seq.*
mode described by offeror, 43
no mode prescribed, 43, 44
offeror may prescribe method, 43
post, communications through, 44 *et seq.*
See also POST
silence, effect of, 41
waiver, 41
conditional assent is not, 34, 35
counter-offer distinguished from, 33, 34
fact of, establishing, 33 *et seq.*
history of offer and acceptance, 13
inchoate agreement does not give rise to, 37, 38
incomplete until received by offeror, 43, 44
postal exception, 44
invalid where posted after offeree's death, 57
knowledge of offer, whether acceptor must have, 47–49
meaningless words no bar to, 38, 39
mistake, effect of, 223, 224
"offer and acceptance", generally, 32
provisional agreement, effect of, 35
recall before reaching offeror, 47
retrospective, may be, 39
standing offer, amounting to, 40
"subject to contract", 35
tender, of, 39–41
written document, parties acting upon faith of, 36

ACCOMMODATION BILL,
negotiation of, 511

ACCORD AND SATISFACTION,
definition, 84n, 521, 533, 541
discharge of contract, for, 521
examples of, 541
satisfaction—
may be executory, 541, 542
question of intention whether executory, 542

ACCOUNT,
action for, period of limitation, 620, 626
form of action, 653

ACCOUNT STATED,
infant and, 402, 413, 414
meaning, 414, 660, 661
quasi-contract, doubtful case of, 660, 661

ACTION,
covenant, 2
debt, 2, 3, 4
detinue, 3, 4
forms of, history of, 2 *et seq.*
on the case, 4–6, 9
assumpsit, 4–6
See also ASSUMPSIT
misfeasance, for, 5
nonfeasance, for, 5

ADEQUACY,
consideration, of, 74
See also CONSIDERATION

ADHESION,
contracts of, 24

ADMINISTRATION OF JUSTICE,
contracts prejudicial to, illegal, 338–341

ADVERTISEMENT,
auction, of, not offer to hold it, 27
legal liability arising from, 107, 108
offer or invitation to treat, whether, 29

AFFIRMATION,
contract, of—
breach of contract, where, 574–576
misrepresentation, where—
express or implicit, 268
generally, 264
lapse of time is evidence of, 269
rescission, right of, lost by, 268

AGENCY. *See also* AGENT
act of parties, termination by, 485–490
apparent, as effective as where expressly created, 458
aspects of, 454
authority coupled with interest is irrevocable, 489
bankruptcy of principal, 491, 492
cohabitation, presumed in case of, 463–465
commission agreements, 487–489
contracts under seal, 468
death of principal, effect of, 484, 490
estoppel, by, 457, 458
examples of, 458
evidence, parol, to show existence of, 457
exception to rule that only parties to bargain can be bound, as, 433, 434, 454
express appointment, creation by, 457
foreign principal, 470, 471
formation of, generally, 457–465
intention of parties, guides to, 466, 467
meaning, 454
mental disability of principal, 490, 491
necessity, of—
married woman, abolition of, 463n
ship's master, 463
negotiable instruments, 469

OMNIBUS,
free pass, driver not protected by conditions attached to, 157
offer of carriage by running, 31

ONUS OF PROOF,
damages—
mitigate, failure to, 605
specified sum a penalty, whether, 609
frustration, whether self-induced, 554
fundamental breach, 161
misrepresentation—
knowledge of untruth, 255
Misrepresentation Act 1967, s. 2 (1),
117, 261
negligent, damages for, 117, 261
mutual or unilateral mistake, 225
necessaries, whether articles are, 403,
464
negotiable instrument—
consideration given for, 512
illegality, 512
rectification of written agreement, 222,
223
restraint of trade, 378
security given in respect of wagering
contract, 308, 309
undue influence, 291

OPINION,
statement of, may constitute statement
of fact, 249, 250

ORAL CONTRACT,
contents, evidence of, 113
partly written, 114, 115

P

PARENT,
agreement with child, whether contractual, 105, 106

PART PAYMENT,
co-debtors, by, 625
composition with creditors, 97, 98
deposit distinguished, 586–588
effect of, on limitation of action, 623–625
promise to pay less than amount due,
84–87, 88
stranger, by, 97, 98

PART PERFORMANCE,
doctrine of—
acts required by, nature of, 196–199
application to contracts concerning
land, 195, 196
explained, 194
modern justifications of, 195
scope of, 196
underlying basis of, 194, 195
specific performance, decree of, 194, 196

PARTNERSHIP,
infant may repudiate on coming of age,
409
member retiring without notice to
public, 458
novation on retirement of partner, 512
specific performance of contract of, not
available, 615

PASSENGER,
road or rail, by, restriction on limiting
liability to, 145, 156, 157, 167

PAST CONSIDERATION. *See* Consideration

PATENT,
licence granted by proprietors of, 93, 94

PAYMENT,
agent, to, effect of, 475–478
frustration, recovery of sums paid before,
562, 563
lesser sum, as accord and satisfaction,
541
money, of, recovery of—
defendant's use, paid to, 637–640
illegal contract, under, 651, 652
improper pressure, paid under, 655
in pursuance of ineffective contract,
648–651
infant, by, 411, 412
mistake of fact, paid under, 641
carelessness, mistake due to, 645,
646
ignorance of private rights, 643
mistake of law distinguished, 641,
642, 644, 645
not necessarily connected with contract, 645
tort, defendant guilty of, 656
void contract, under, 651
voluntary, whether recoverable, 637,
638, 646, 647
tender of, effect, 530

PENALTY,
covers but does not assess damage, 608
intention of parties as test, 608, 609
liquidated damages distinguished, 607–
611
option to sue on, or to sue for damages,
608
rules for guidance of court as to whether,
609, 610
threat *in terrorem*, as, 608

PERFORMANCE,
discharge by—
distinguished from breach, 522
generally, 521, 522 *et seq.*
divisible contract—
effect of intention, 526
entire contract distinguished, 525, 526
payment due for partial performance,
526
doctrine of, 522–524
exceptions, 525 *et seq.*
entire contract, of, 522, 525, 526, 528
illegal executory contract, of, repentance before, 354, 355
illegal, of lawful contract, 360, 361
injunction, enforced by, 614
lawful, separate promise, 362
manner prohibited by statute, 360
meaning, 522
must be precise and exact, 522
part, doctrine of, 194–199
partial—
acceptance of, by promisee, 527, 528
frustration, before, compensation for,
563, 564

Printed in Great Britain by Chapel River Press, Andover, Hants.